Handbooks in American Art, No. 2

This publication has been made possible by grants from the National Endowment for the Arts, in Washington, D.C., a Federal agency, and the Women's Committee of the Philadelphia Museum of Art

The Pennsylvania German Collection

Beatrice B. Garvan

Philadelphia Museum of Art

Editor	Jane Iandola Watkins
Assistant Editor	Sherry Babbitt
Project Assistant	Stephanie Toothman
Translations	Frederick Weiser, Alan Keyser
Consultant for Glass Section	Miriam E. Mucha
Conservation	Tom Robinson
Special Photography	Will Brown

Reprinted 1999

Printed in Canada

Library of Congress Cataloging in Publication Data

Philadelphia Museum of Art.
  The Pennsylvania German collection.

  (Handbooks in American art; no. 2)
  Bibliography: p.
  Includes index.
  1. Art industries and trade, Pennsylvania Dutch—
Catalogs. 2. Art industries and trade—Pennsylvania—
Philadelphia—Catalogs. 3. Philadelphia Museum of Art—
Catalogs. I. Garvan, Beatrice B. II. Title.
III. Series
NK835.P4P5 1982 745'.089310748'074014811 79-93027
ISBN 0-87633-035-9   AACR1

CONTENTS

FOREWORD

In 1891 when the Philadelphia Museum of Art was still called the
Pennsylvania Museum and School of Industrial Art, Edwin Atlee
Barber, an adviser who was to become the Museum's Honorary
Curator of the Department of American Pottery and Porcelain
(1892–1901), its Curator (1901–6), and eventually the Museum's
Director (1907–16), found a plate that was to lead the Museum toward
the acquisition of Pennsylvania German art. Of characteristic
redware, the sgraffito-decorated plate has a charming inscription
incised through the creamy glaze, which translated reads: "If loving
were injurious to health, the doctor would avoid it; and if it would
hurt the maidens, then they would not endure it," and, on the
reverse, the name of the potter Samuel Troxel and the date May the
16th 1826. Edwin A. Barber responded to the plate's aesthetic and
regional appeal and, conscious of the early goal of the Museum to
educate and to promote good design in industry, he persuaded John
T. Morris, a member of the Board, to support the purchases of this
ware. The next year, 1892, the Museum was able to fill a case with
slip- and sgraffito-decorated pottery, the first public collection of
Pennsylvania German art. Mr. Morris presented his own collection
between 1892 and 1908. In 1918 a benefactor of the Museum,
Margaret L. Baugh, gave a fund in memory of Barber for the
continuing purchase of Pennsylvania German redware; as a result,
the redware collection now numbers nearly 250 pieces.

Edwin A. Barber was enthusiastic about other aspects of
Pennsylvania German art. In 1897 he discovered a piece of fraktur
work, a writing sample, which was then a curiosity in the museum
world. He described it that year, "I have a very interesting old paper

'sampler' made by a Pennsylvania Dutchman, illuminated in several colors and decorated with the conventional tulip, bird, etc. This is dated 1804 and measures 13 by 8 inches. The designs are exactly similar to those on the old pottery, and I have secured this for the Museum, as I thought it would be of considerable interest to frame it and place it in the case with the old pottery." Since then the Museum has acquired over 100 frakturs.

When Mrs. William D. Frishmuth revealed an interest in the technology of the Pennsylvania Germans, and began to collect tools, implements, books, and textiles, Barber encouraged her. She set up an exhibition of this material herself in a case in Memorial Hall, until 1928 the home of the Museum. Before Barber died in 1916, Mrs. Frishmuth gave the Museum her entire collection.

By 1920 there were several collectors of Pennsylvania German art who enjoyed it and competed for it. One was J. Stogdell Stokes, a trustee and future President of the Board (1933–47), who passionately collected furniture. In 1926 he persuaded his friends Mr. Pierre S. du Pont and Mr. and Mrs. Lammot du Pont to buy and install the great kitchen and bedroom from the miller's house at Millbach; he then furnished it from his own collection.

Since the Museum's interest in Pennsylvania German art was so established, it was natural for Titus C. Geesey to give the Museum his great collection of Pennsylvania German art between 1953 and 1969. The extraordinary range, depth, and quality of his collection are a tribute to his own eye and the prodigious energy of his weekly rounds of dealers' shops across several counties.

The Museum on its own has made purchases like the important Huber wardrobe in 1957. And there have been further major gifts like the bequest of a fraktur collection by Mr. and Mrs. William M. Elkins in 1950 and the gift of three dower chests from Mr. and Mrs. Robert L. Raley in 1978.

This Handbook, which records in detail the pieces that make up the Museum's large collection of Pennsylvania German art, is the work of Beatrice B. Garvan, Associate Curator of American Art. With an enthusiasm and energy I believe Edwin A. Barber and Titus Geesey would have admired, she has indefatigably explored archives for information about objects in the collection and made discoveries. Jane Iandola Watkins has worked closely with Mrs. Garvan, painstakingly editing the text and overseeing the layout, which makes this a visual reference tool documenting and providing access to the collection. This is the second in the Museum's series of Handbooks in American Art. The first, *The Thomas Eakins Collection*, by Theodor Siegl, with an introduction by Evan H. Turner, was published in 1978. The National Endowment for the Arts, with characteristic generosity and perception, gave a grant toward the realization of this Handbook.

Jean Sutherland Boggs
The George D. Widener Director
June 1982

PREFACE

This book has been created and produced as a guide to the
Philadelphia Museum's interesting and important collections of
objects made by Germanic peoples who settled in Pennsylvania.
Within the Museum the objects are held by several curatorial depart-
ments, primarily American Art, and also by medium, in the depart-
ments of Prints, Drawings and Photographs, and Costume and
Textiles. Within the collections of each department this material
is but a small proportion, and within the holdings of the whole
Museum, these Pennsylvania German collections, given by collectors in units, or acquired one by one, number about 1,115 objects out
of an estimated total of 400,000.

The objects that are light- or temperature-sensitive, such as
fraktur and textiles, nestle snugly in acid-free boxes in climate-
controlled storerooms, and are exhibited on a limited basis for
relatively short periods of time. Furniture, monitored for humidity
and protected by glass from the inevitable dust created by daily
gallery traffic, although labeled, is sometimes too remote for close
scrutiny of specialists. As the Museum's business is preservation
and conservation, as well as exhibition, objects are not always
on view, and some pieces are on extended loan at historic sites
throughout the state. Since the collections are thus spread out, the
depths of the primary and study collections are hardly known to
researching scholars, European colleagues intrigued by American
versions of their rural arts, collectors, and the casual or local visitor
whose ancestors may have made or owned these objects. Recog-
nizing the Museum's commitment to preservation, and given the
limited spaces for exhibition of any collection as a whole, this

Handbook has been designed to broaden the scope of the Museum's ability to provide access to collections. Every object in the collection is included. Each short description provides information not visible in a photograph, such as construction, signatures, watermarks, or inscriptions. Color eludes words. However, naming colors is vitally important for attribution or study of textiles and fraktur, and the color words in the descriptions, although inherently imprecise, are intended to provide guidance and suggest materials and techniques. The accession number at the end of each text is the key to locating and identifying that object within the Museum.

The Pennsylvania Germans applied artistry to the objects of daily life—utensils, tools, and house furnishings—and decorated most elaborately documents recording church membership and family celebrations. Traditions of form and decoration came with the European settlers from various areas of Germanic Europe—the Palatinate, Switzerland, Alsace, Silesia, and Moravia. The objects in the Philadelphia Museum's Pennsylvania German collections reflect the strong artistic traditions of the immigrants who settled in Pennsylvania before 1840. Later objects reflect the changing attitudes and customs of European craftsmen who immigrated after the mid-19th century. Names and dates inscribed on objects may be correlated with genealogical materials and art historical methods to provide reasonable attributions. If an object is totally anonymous as to maker, and the majority of this material is, the tentative attributions based on provenance or on technological analysis of the object itself lean toward inclusion rather than exclusion in this Handbook. Curators, collectors, and computer wizards with years of experience in each medium probably will eventually solve some of the questions posed by anonymous objects. My research in the regional museums of the British Isles deleted many of the generic objects previously included in our Pennsylvania German category. The same visual research in regional museums in France, at Colmar, Strasbourg, Lunéville, Mulhouse, and Nancy, at Munich, and in Switzerland between Basel and Bern, resulted in deletions from our American department to the European Decorative Arts department and probably there will be more candidates for reattribution.

The majority of the objects were collected in Southeastern Pennsylvania, many of them at the turn of the century, when Edwin Atlee Barber and John T. Morris corresponded regularly with regional dealers and visited rural homesteads to make purchases for the Museum. Today, stories about collecting in the countryside of Pennsylvania are enticing and full of nostalgia, as they must have been for the zealous collectors like Titus C. Geesey and J. Stogdell Stokes, who made regular rounds to regional dealers on Monday mornings, after the weekend house sales. Unfortunately, the anecdotes are usually too general to establish provenance for an object, although a few have been corroborated by generous dealers who consulted with me during this cataloguing process, and that information has been included in regional attributions. Dealing and trading have dislodged objects from their original locales and increased

the difficulty of positive attribution to the place of manufacture
as Pennsylvania, or to the craftsman as Germanic. For example,
included here are redware animals—poodles that resemble lions,
smooth cats, mutts of all shapes and sizes—which have been attributed previously to Germans working in North Carolina or Virginia,
or to the English potteries run by the Vickers and Abraham James
in Chester County, Pennsylvania. Various human factors moved
objects from their place of origin. The travels of journeymen, who
plied their skills wherever the market would support them, the
migrations of families, who carried their most treasured and portable
possessions with them as they crossed the mountain ranges to
Western Pennsylvania, establishing another branch of the family
name, the deliberate marketing and distribution of printed books and
fraktur, illuminated by schoolteachers and ministers, who served
several regional parishes as they moved about, caused the fields of
academic research to be crossed so many times that some great
objects will probably remain forever anonymous, unattached to
region, owner, or maker.

As a body of material, the Pennsylvania German collections
are a rich resource for study for art historians, cultural and social
historians, authors, genealogists and collectors. They should be
a source of pride for descendants of early Pennsylvania settlers,
German or English, as national groups were working side by side,
exchanging services and often names. William Penn's "holy experi-
ment" became a prosperous joint enterprise. The pragmatism
and piety of objects made by and for the Pennsylvania German
community shine through their overlay of color and wit, setting them
apart from the objects produced by and for their Anglo-American
neighbors in rural Pennsylvania. Thomas Jefferson wrote from
Frankfurt about his trip through the Rhine Valley in 1788: "The
neighborhood of this place is that which has been to us a second
mother country. It is from the palatinate on this part of the Rhine that
those swarms of Germans have gone, who, next to the descendants
of the English, form the greatest body of our people. I have been
continually amused by seeing here the origin of whatever is not
English among us. I have fancied myself often in the upper parts of
Maryland and Pennsylvania."

These Germanic American collections at the Museum are
appropriately imbedded in an institution committed to a world view.
The collections are an inspiration and a resource; the photographs
and physical descriptions provided here serve as an index to their
enjoyment and use.

Beatrice B. Garvan
Associate Curator of American Art

ACKNOWLEDGMENTS

Stephanie Toothman handled the day-to-day organization and the logistics of moving, cleaning, scheduling photography, and recording the procedures necessary to catalogue this entire collection. She managed this massive task with rare sensitivity and meticulous organization. Many people have gladly assisted in the gathering of information that has led to the completion of this handbook. Among those who have offered their invaluable help are Edith Buxbaum, Merle Chamberlain, Laurence Channing, the late Bertram Coleman, Claire Conway, Wendy Cooper, Anthony J. Evangelista, Nonnie Frelinghuysen, Anthony N. B. Garvan, Vernon Gunnion, Howell Heaney, Mary Jane Hershey, Constantine Iandola, Patricia Kane, Peter Kemble, Alan Keyser, Joe Kindig III, John Kraft, Cathryn McElroy, Terry McNeeley, Dennis Moyer, Susan Meyers, Larry Neff, Vernon Nelson, Arlene Palmer, John Platt, Lynn Poirier, Brad Rauschenberg, Dr. and Mrs. Donald Shelley, Bruce Shoemaker, Mr. and Mrs. Richard F. Smith, John Snyder, John Strawbridge, Susan Weinstein, Frederick Weiser, Eric Wunsch, and Don Yoder.

NOTES FOR THE USE OF THE HANDBOOK

This Handbook is arranged in eight sections according to medium:
wood, metal, ceramics, glass, horn/eggshell, basketry, textiles, and
paper. Mediums are divided into categories and sub-categories of
similar objects, which are indicated by running heads to assist in
locating objects. To locate objects by known makers or artists, consult
the Biographical Index.

English translations of inscriptions on family records and
illuminated texts in the paper section follow entries for that section.

In listing dimensions, height precedes width precedes depth. In
listing materials, primary materials precede secondary materials.

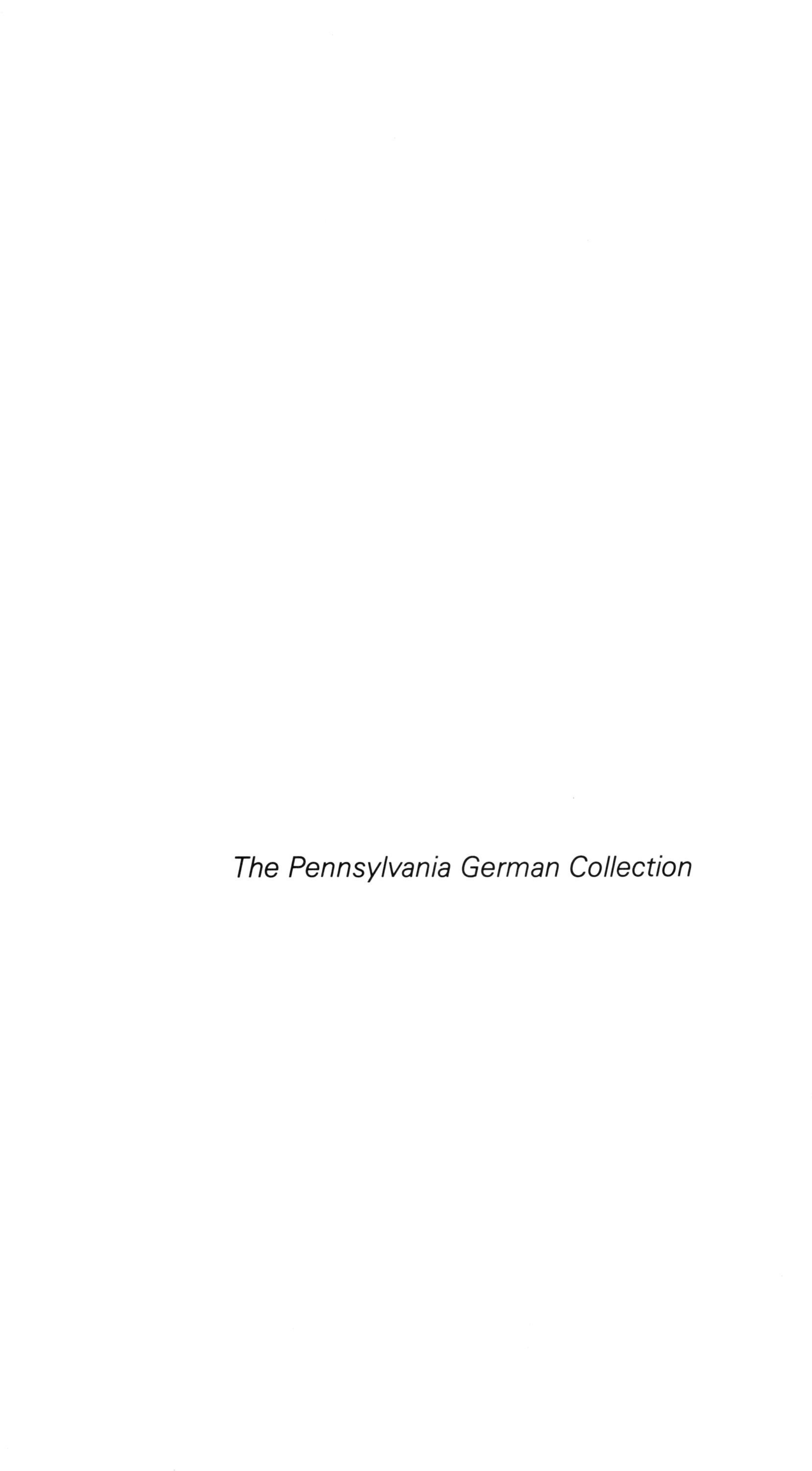

The Pennsylvania German Collection

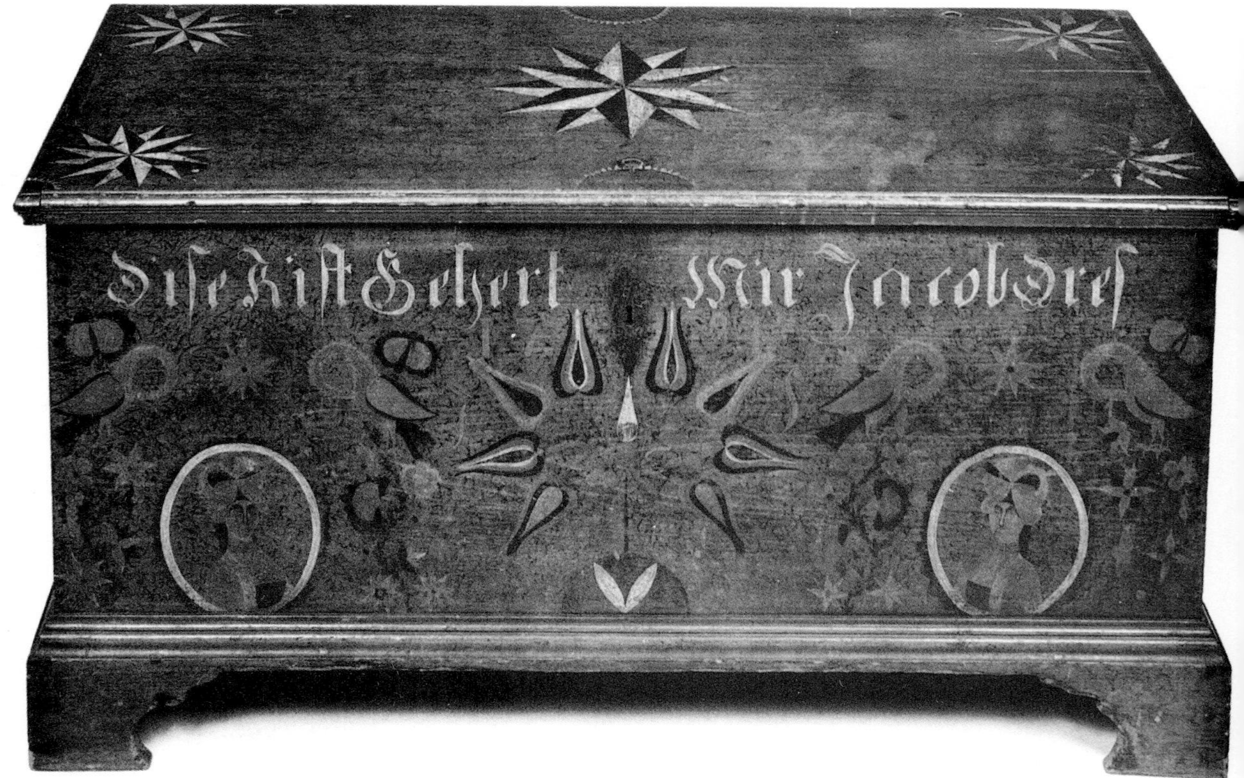

Wood

INTRODUCTION

Luxuriant forests of oak, poplar, beech, walnut, and pine covered the major portion of the territory known as Pennsylvania in the 17th century. Most diarists, European and American, who traveled through commented on the wealth of timber, but by the end of the 18th century observers were noting the depletion of these forests. Maximilian, prince of Wied, visiting Montgomery and Lehigh counties in 1832, wrote that "country people must be checked in their love of destruction of forests." While in Philadelphia, Benjamin Davis lamented in 1794 that the price of firewood was increasing yearly and that "to lessen the expense of this item in housekeeping, many of the inhabitants have introduced the use of stoves, a custom borrowed from the Germans, a frugal and industrious people, who compose a numerous class of citizens in Philadelphia." Each of these observations of prodigious as well as prudent use of wood was valid.

Wood was the essential raw material in Pennsylvania's rural counties. First-settlement buildings, for domestic, farm, or industrial use, as well as furnishings and tools, wagons and riverboats, were fashioned from it. Wood had been the primary building material in the regions of the Old World—rural Germany, Moravia, Alsace, and Switzerland—from whence settlers now known as Pennsylvania German came. Their craftsmen were familiar with its properties and tolerances and owned, or could make, the tools necessary to shape and build with wood.

CHEST
1791
See page 23, no. 12

The earliest Pennsylvania German houses and barns were of solid log construction. Mature timbers were harvested and used full girth and length for barns. The enormous size of later barns, with wood frame over a full story of stone, measuring from 15 m to 30 m long was astonishing to Pennsylvania's English citizenry. In 1810 Margaret Dwight described "Klutztown" [Kutztown] . . . "I imagine the Dutch pride themselves on building good barns, for a great many of them are very elegant—they are three and four stories high, have windows and one or two I saw with blinds—they are larger and handsomer than most of the houses."

Although the urban centers of Philadelphia, Lancaster, and Reading began early to build with brick, more and more milled lumber was used for framing or finishing, and lumber became an important commodity to rural communities, further depleting forests. It was rural industrial growth coupled with the omniverous iron industry, which fed on charcoal, that depleted the seemingly endless supply of trees by 1780. This had a cumulative and circular effect on the environment as mill-supporting streams lost their secure banks through erosion and dried up. Losses to village economies culminated about 1800, and a number of Pennsylvania German groups migrated to Canada, western Pennsylvania, and Ohio. Families who remained on the old homesteads guarded their forest resources through deed restrictions and instructions at time of inheritance. Generally the Germans were praised for their thrift and, by keeping control through land ownership, maintained a precarious balance between woodworkers and raw materials.

The specialized craftsman knew which varieties of wood to use for what, in practice a kind of pragmatic conservation. Oak was the traditional European framing timber for buildings and at first was used as such in Pennsylvania. But black oak made good charcoal, and one iron furnace could burn twenty cords per day, one acre's worth, to produce two tons of pig iron. Thus poplar, recognized for its lightweight strength, replaced oak as Pennsylvania's structural wood and was used for summer beams, as in the Millbach House (p. 7, no. 2), and as framing or secondary wood in furniture. Hickory made flexible and strong tool handles; chestnut made good fences because it was slow to rot; walnut turned well without splintering and its fine close grain polished handsomely for furniture. Soft pines, the fastest growing trees, cured quickly, were lightweight, and easily planed, shaped, or carved. Pine was rarely used whole as a structural timber. Plentiful pine leftovers were fashioned into ornamented household furnishings from inlaid table chests, chip-carved or lathe-turned boxes, and butter prints, to all sorts of toys from jumping jacks to carved birds.

County tax accounts show that carpentering was a taxable trade, although wheelwrights, turners, and joiners were considered woodworking specialists with more precise skills. Wills, inventories, estate sales, and craftsmen's accounts record a flourishing market in house furnishings made of wood. Inventories like Andrew Feree's (died 1735) distinguish between carpenter's and joiner's tools—the felling ax, broad ax, the joiner's ax, and adze—and tax lists and wills confirm the distinction. Turners, who worked with chisels and lathes, were specialists who produced ball feet, finials, spinning wheels, and table legs. The cabinetmaker, frequently listed in urban records, was rarely specified in rural records; there were only two who were so designated in Bucks and Montgomery County tax records before 1800. The most obviously Germanic forms in Pennsylvania were produced by joiners, in contrast to the conspicuous design role played by turners in English settlements. The sculpted stair newels and shaped and carved balusters in the Millbach House (p. 6, no. 1) are typical of their best work. In furniture, Pennsylvania German joiners used traditional middle European construction details such as the splined dovetail and wedged tenon, as well as the pegged mortise and tenon joint common to most joinery traditions.

A chronological arrangement of known rural Pennsylvania furniture reveals that the earliest was unpainted and was framed and finished in solid walnut. As the big walnut trees became scarce after 1770, most case furniture was made of pine or poplar and painted. Observations about raw materials are possibly coincidental with what is known about traditional materials and design in the European regions where the settlers came from: unpainted furniture with carved decoration was usual in northern Germany while colorfully painted pieces were more usual in southern Germany, Alsace, and Switzerland. Style changes in Europe also affected the look of American objects. Painted furniture was popular in most rural areas in Europe in the late 18th and early 19th centuries and became so in America with successive emigrations.

Some regional styles or schools of furniture-making developed in Pennsylvania, often in an extended family enterprise. The distinctive joinery practices such as the foot bracing on the Berks County chest (p. 24, no. 15) or the applied pilaster and arch decoration on two Lancaster County chests (p. 18, no. 1 and p. 21, no. 9), may eventually identify specific makers. Rarely were products inscribed with makers' names; it was the name of the owner and the commemorative date that was more important.

Expressions of individuality in woodworking were not limited to the professional joiner. Whittling and carving small furnishings occupied Pennsylvania Germans of all ages. Some objects were humorous, some were colorful, and many were tokens of affection and esteem, calling the "fairing," which took many forms: a butter print, a mantel ornament, a bodice busk, a ribbon box, a looking glass—courting favors presented to a woman by a man. It was a ritual that enriched the Pennsylvania German arts, and the objects made and exchanged were sentimental treasures lasting into our own time.

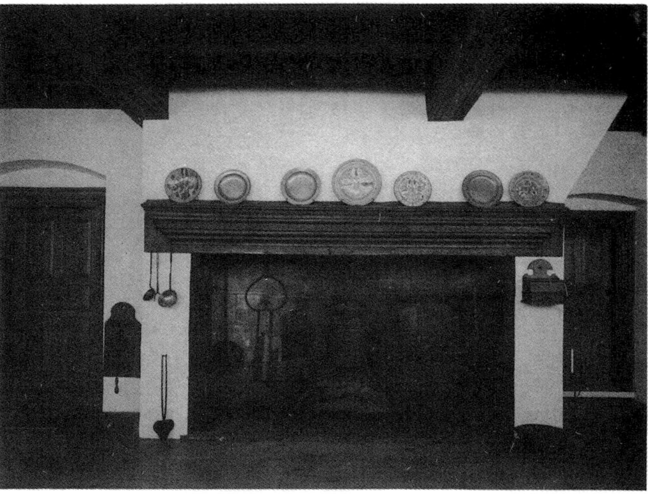

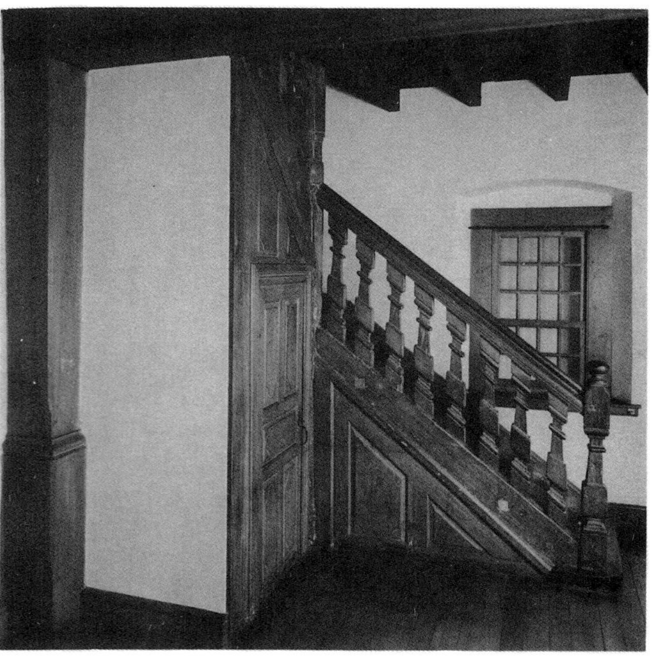

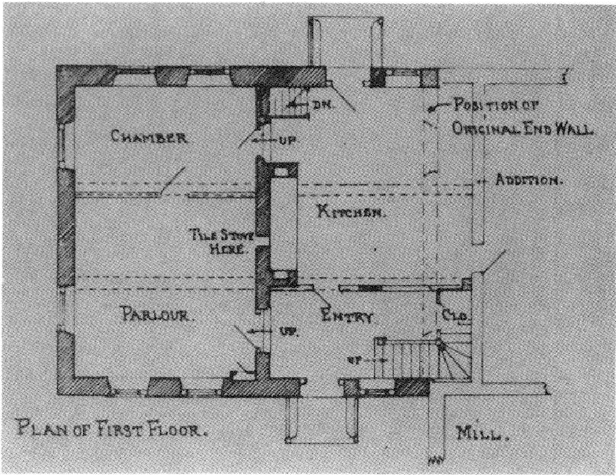

1   ARCHITECTURAL WOODWORK
Great Hall/Kitchen from
Millbach House
Millbach, Lebanon County
c. 1752

Oak, chestnut, pine, poplar, iron, granite. The Millbach house was built by George Muller (Jerg Muler), a miller at Millbach, and his wife Maria Caterina about 1752 and inherited by their son Michael (died 1814) and M. Elizabeth Muller in 1784. The kitchen, the largest room in the Millbach house when built, occupied the entire east end in the 17th-century style of the "great hall." About 1784 the east end was extended 1.2 m, the stairs moved into the southeast corner, the small windows added, and the space divided into entrance-stairhall and kitchen. The room is installed in the museum as the great hall/kitchen but also includes the addition accommodating the stairs.

Solid oak mantel lintel (382 x 49 cm), set into masonry, is hewn into flaring mantel shelf with plate groove. Stone-faced fireplace. Hearth is single slab of granite. Two warming shelves built into each side. Back opening for hot air supply for tile stove that had been set in parlor behind. Two step-up interior doors of unequal sizes flanking fireplace have raised and carved decorative panels set into frames in tongue and groove joints. Door jambs of bolection molding have raised lozenge panels at bottoms. Wrought iron hardware, staghorn pintle and socket hinges, perforated cusp latch door handles. Main entrance door is built in two units (Dutch door) with eight raised fielded panels on the interior and raised panels with carved lozenges in double relief on the exterior. Four wrought iron pintle and socket hinges, two horizontal, one vertical, bar and staple fastenings.

Corner staircase has paneled casing with set-in closet. Square hewn and carved newel post (height 124 cm) is set on first step. Corner post is rough-hewn at bottom with turned section between upper and lower handrails. Carved balusters are square in profile and tenon into solid handrails. Rails have molded sides and prominent, raised, rounded handgrip and are tenoned and pegged into newel posts. Stairs have broad treads (91 cm) and shallow risers (17 cm). At the turn, dog-leg pivot with carving like stone treads. Plain skirting board has molded edge and beaded string molding. Double-hung windows, ceiling joists, interior fireplace stonework, room plasterwork, and floor reproduced from originals at the Millbach house.

Room 5.5 m (18′) (east-west), 8.8 m (29′) (north-south)

Gift of Mr. Pierre S. du Pont and Mr. and Mrs. Lammot du Pont. 26-74-1

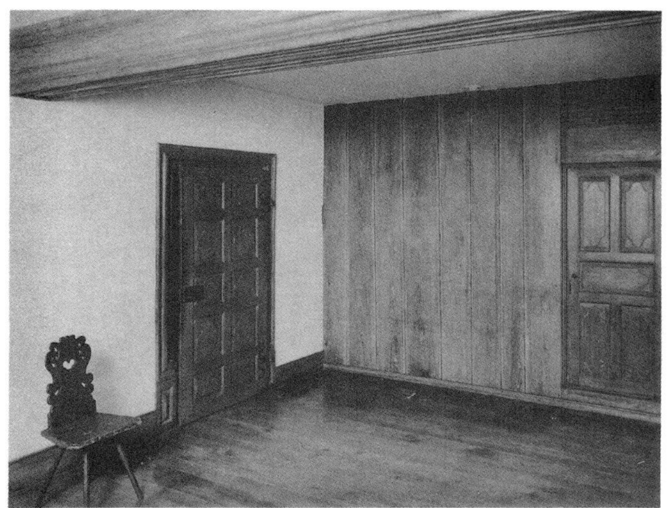

ARCHITECTURAL WOODWORK
Great Chamber from
Millbach House
Millbach, Lebanon County
c. 1752

Chestnut, poplar, pine, iron. The great
chamber was the largest bedroom in the
Millbach house and was located on the second
story over the parlor on the southwest corner.
Solid poplar summer beam running the width
of the room is 38 cm deep, 32 cm wide, and is
prominently molded with chamfered stops.
The north wall is sheathed with vertical pine
planks (height 265 cm) of random width, with
molded edges, in tongue and groove joints.
Sheathing is fitted horizontally over door. Door
sill is raised 20 cm above floor. Door is set into
casing in partition and has five raised fielded
panels with carved raised lozenge decoration.
Wrought iron pintle and socket hinges,
perforated cusp latch. Plain baseboard with
quirked bead. Entrance door to the great
chamber (130 cm wide including frame)
has been installed on the west wall to
accommodate museum traffic. Door trim
carved from solid in bolection frame with
intaglio panels at bottom matching jambs in the
great hall. Door has ten raised fielded panels
with carved and raised lozenge designs set into
pegged mortise and tenoned frame. Two
wrought iron pintle and socket hinges.

The walnut cupboard installed in the
southeast corner of the great chamber was
originally built into the parlor. The door has a
raised fielded panel with bevel-edge carved
lozenge. Two interior shelves. Wrought iron
pintle and socket hinges have extended props,
escutcheon, and lock.

Room 5.9 m (19′2″) (east-west), 5.4 m
(17′8″) (north-south)
Cupboard 111.4 x 79 x 29.8 cm
(43⅞ x 31⅛ x 11¾″)

Gift of Mr. Pierre S. du Pont and Mr. and
Mrs. Lammot du Pont. 26-74-1

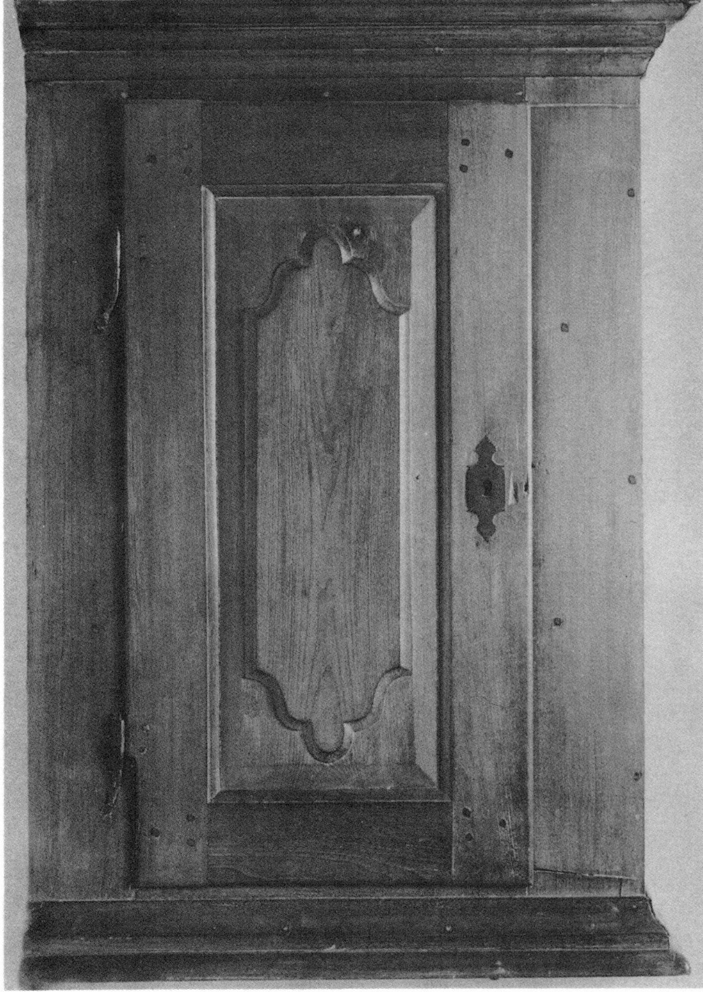

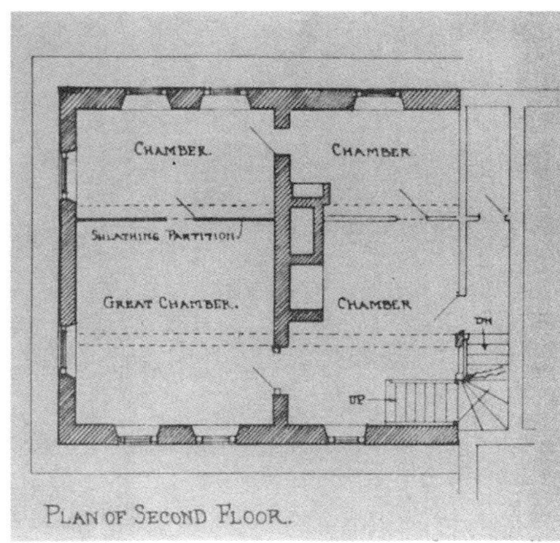

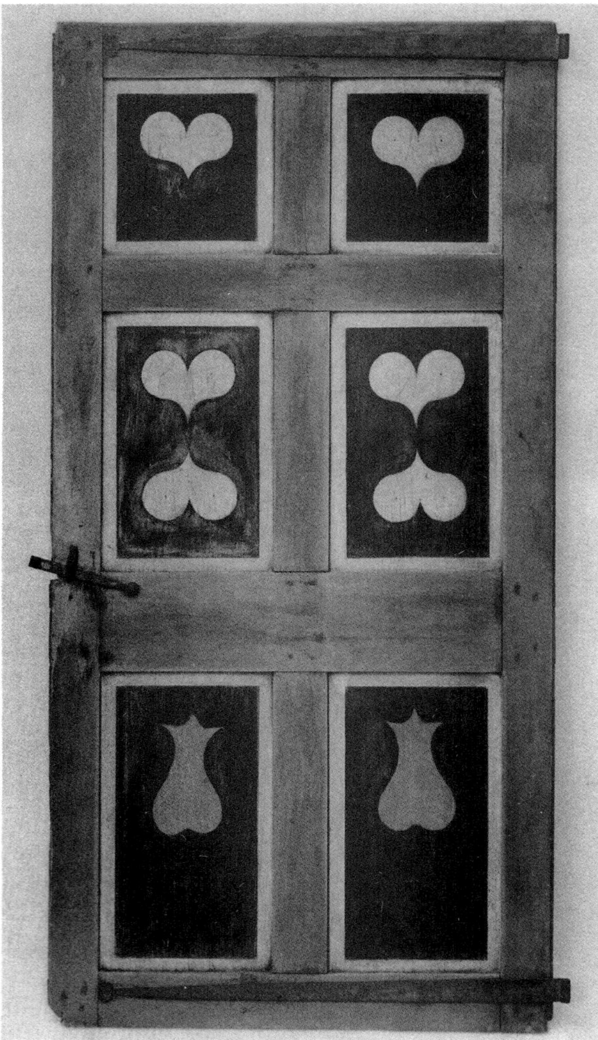

4

3 CLOSET
Lebanon County
c. 1770

Poplar; pine, iron. Panel and frame construction. Pegged mortise and tenon joints. Carved panels on front and one side. Applied cornice and base moldings, no feet. Top dovetailed to sides. Wrought iron lock and spike and pintle hinges with extended props. Escutcheon missing. Three interior shelves. Remnants of yellow paint and wood graining. Originally built into a corner.

167 x 89 x 55 cm (65¾ x 35 x 21⅝″)

Purchased: Thomas Skelton Harrison Fund. 27-41-1

4 DOOR
Berks County
1780–1800

Painted pine, iron. Panel and frame construction with pegged mortise and tenon joints and pegged tongue in groove joints. Six raised fielded panels inset into painted frame. Panels decorated with designs of white hearts and red tulips on black ground; reverse unpainted. Wrought iron strap hinges; latch replaced.

175.2 x 91.4 cm (69 x 36″)

Titus C. Geesey Collection. 53-125-18

5 DOOR
Lancaster County
1780–1800

Painted pine, iron. Panel and frame construction with pegged mortise and tenon joints. Raised molded panels painted blue green over red. Scroll hinges; cock's head wrought iron latch.

112.7 x 82.6 cm (44⅜ x 32½″)

Titus C. Geesey Collection. 54-85-30

5

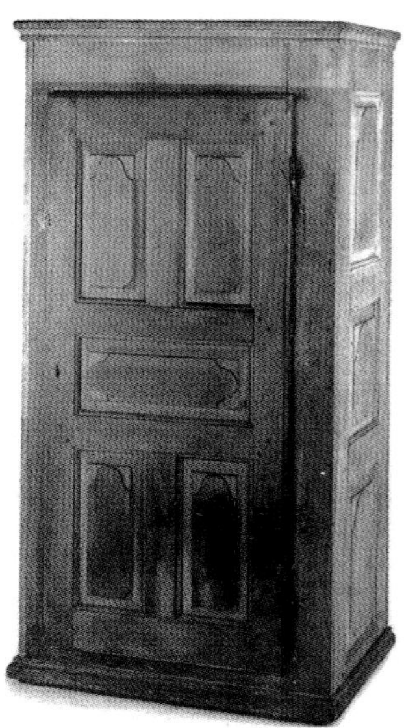

3

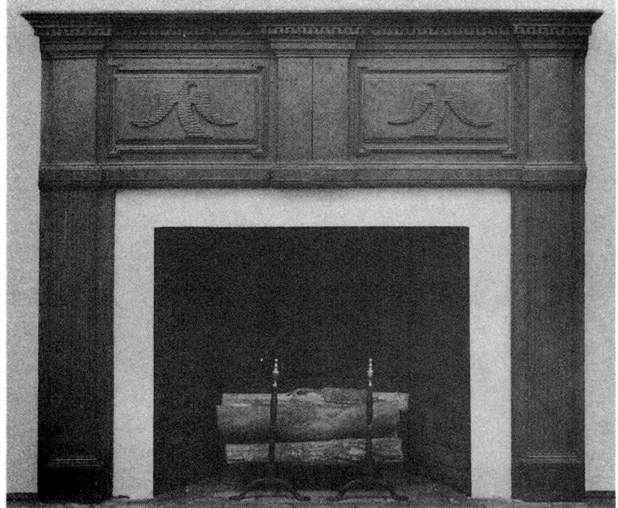

6

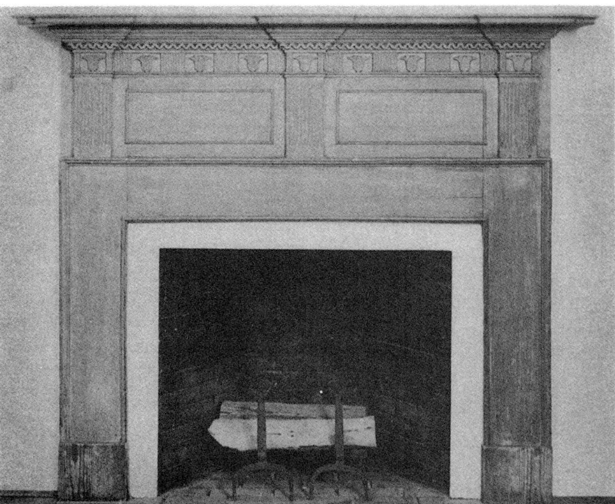

7

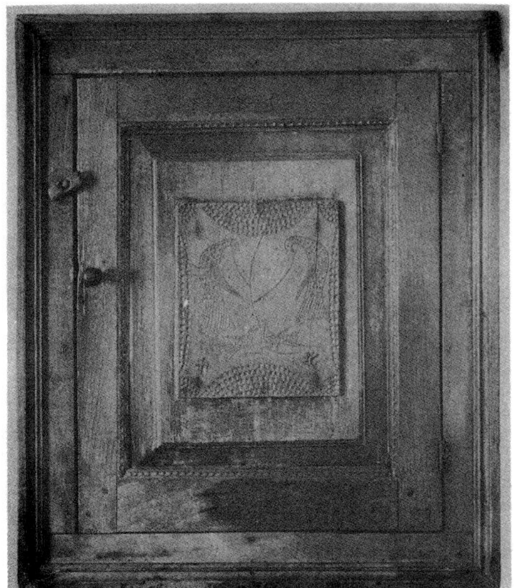

9

6 MANTEL
Indiantown, Lebanon County
1780–1800

Painted pine. Plank construction with applied decorative details: fluted pilasters, reed-carved banding in vertical and diagonal patterns, dentil fret band under mantel shelf, two eagles delineated with gouge-carving on raised panels surrounded by raised molding with crossetted corners. Painted dull red over bright red, black pilaster bases.

165.1 x 190.5 x 15.2 cm (65 x 75 x 6″)

Titus C. Geesey Collection. 54-85-72

7 MANTEL
1780–1800

Painted pine. Panel and frame construction, mortise and tenon joints. Bead and ovolo moldings, gouge-work fluting, applied carvings. Painted blue over red undercoating. Tulips painted red.

161.3 x 188 x 25.4 cm (63½ x 74 x 10″)

Titus C. Geesey Collection. 54-85-24

8 MANTEL SHELF
1780–1800

Pine. Mantel shelf set on compound molding pegged into board. Line of nail holes indicates probable use of cloth "smoke" valance. Narrow molding tacked on bottom of board. Traces of whitewash.

32.7 x 277.5 x 17.8 cm (12⅞ x 109¼ x 7″)

Titus C. Geesey Collection. 58-110-4

9 WALL CUPBOARD
c. 1800

Marked inside door: *Albert B. Jacob   1880*

Painted pine, poplar; maple, iron. Frame and panel construction with pegged mortise and tenon joints. Moldings nailed. Raised paneled door with quirked ovolo moldings. Center panel has gouge- and punch-carved decoration. Painted blue green. Cupboard was built into the wall.

73 x 63.5 x 24.2 cm (28¾ x 25 x 9½″)

Titus C. Geesey Collection. 54-85-25

8

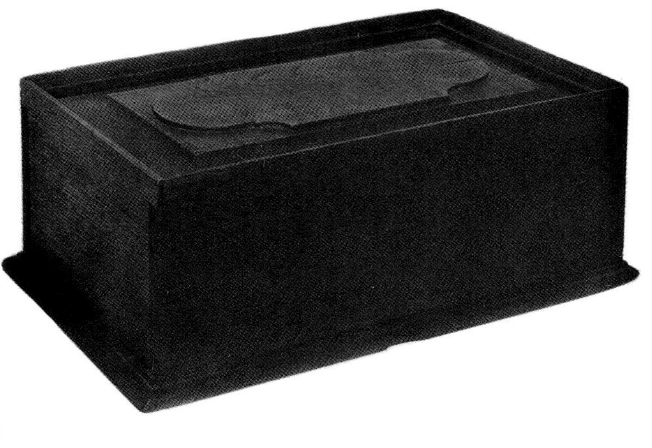

1

1

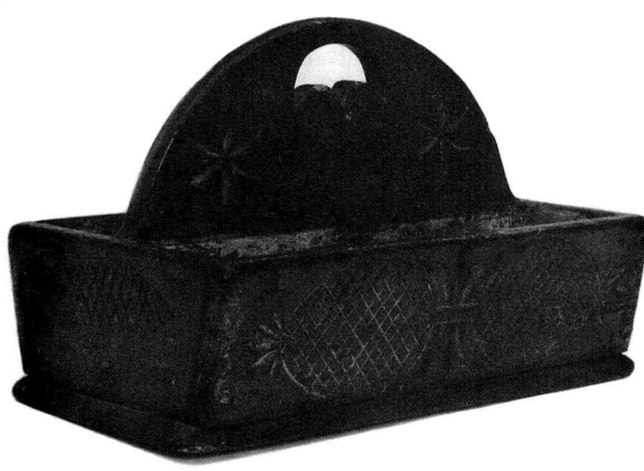

2

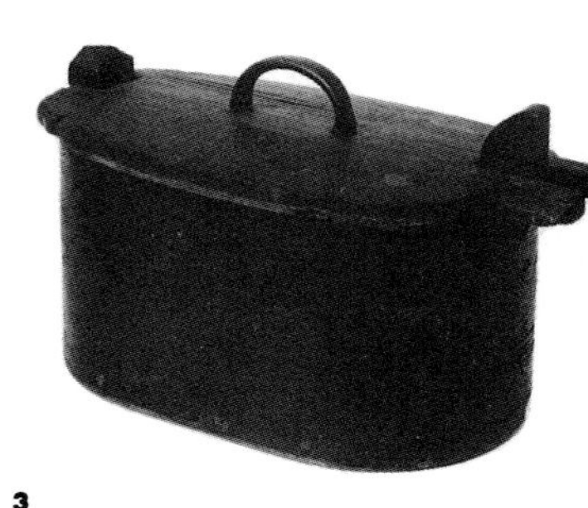

3

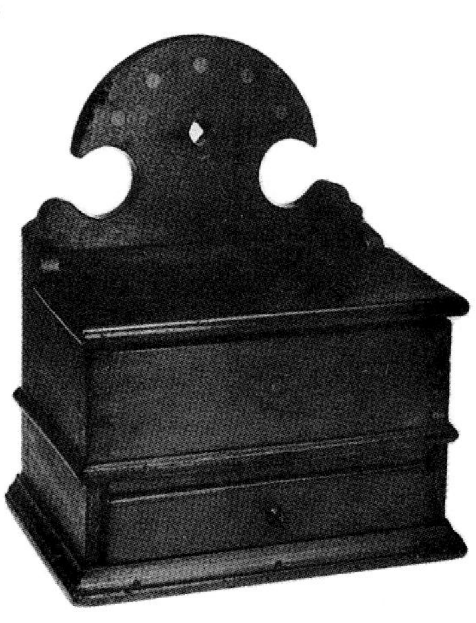

4

1 DOCUMENT BOX
1750–80

Walnut, poplar, leather. Panel and plank construction with dovetail and nailed joints. Closed end dovetailed to side pieces, bottom has extended molded edges nailed to side pieces. Removable end lifts in groove revealing dovetail drawer with leather pull. Raised panel top slides in grooves. Two interior compartments.

14 x 38.1 x 20.3 cm (5½ x 15 x 8″)

Titus C. Geesey Collection. 53-125-16a,b

2 CUTLERY BOX
1750–1800

Painted poplar. Plank construction with nailed lap joints. Carved handle gained into end pieces. Sides canted in toward bottom, which is nailed. Incised carvings (pineapples, fish, stars) on four sides and handle. Painted blue green, interior white.

22.9 x 32.4 x 22.9 cm (9 x 12¾ x 9″)

Titus C. Geesey Collection. 55-45-2

3 WORKBOX
1750–1800

Painted pine; cedar, hickory, leather. Oval box in bentwood construction. Sides meet in lapped joint sewn with leather thong. Bottom set in and tacked. Bentwood handle tenoned through bevel-edged lid. Lid cut to fit carved end posts that are pegged to sides. One post notched to lock lid for carrying. Geometric punchwork decoration. Painted blue black.

15.6 x 26 cm (6⅛ x 10¼″)

Gift of Mrs. C. Righter. 15-250

4 HANGING BOX
c. 1760

Walnut, maple and pine inlay; pine. Shaped plank construction with dovetail corners. Lid pivots on carved dowel extensions. One interior partition in till. Midband applied astragal molding. Drawer has molded edge overlapping case; three dovetails front and back, bottom nailed, four interior sections, turned knob handle. Shaped hanging board inlaid with five circles, till inlaid with geometric flower, drawer with four circles. Cyma reversa molding at base.

40.9 x 34.3 x 19.7 cm (16⅛ x 13½ x 7¾″)

Gift of J. Stogdell Stokes. 28-10-59

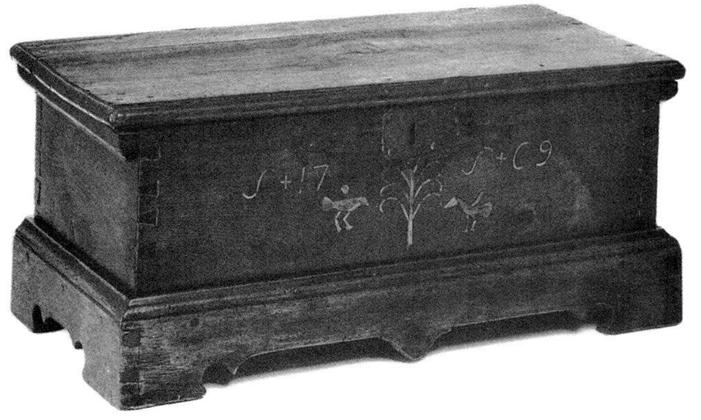

5

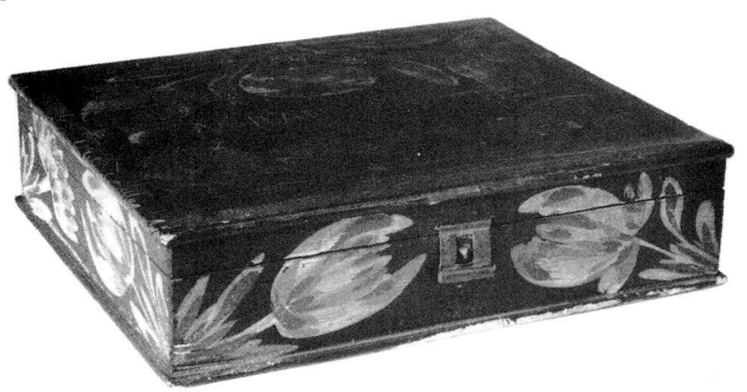

6

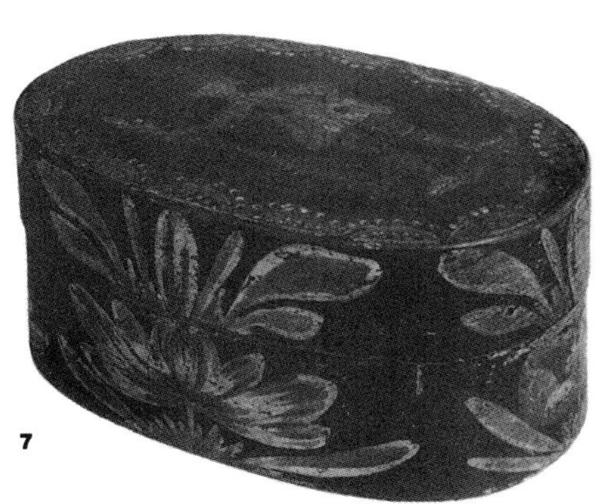

7

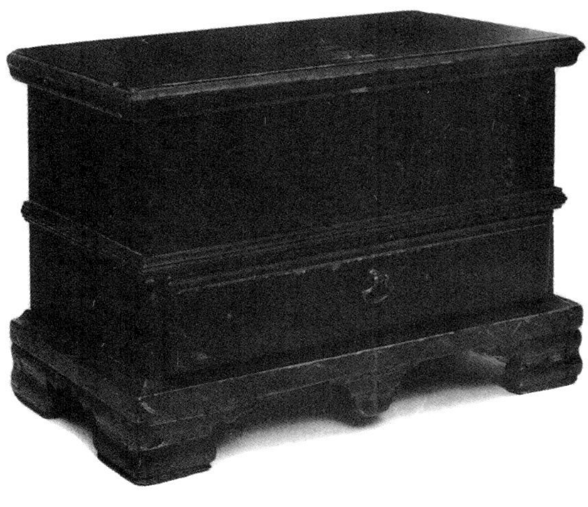

8

5 TABLE CHEST
Schuylkill County
1769

Inscribed on front in inlay: *S + 17 S + 69*

Black walnut, poplar, maple inlay. Plank construction with dovetail corners. Interior till on left has two compartments, no lid. Lid has molded edges; end battens pegged and nailed. Chest pegged into base. Straight bracket feet, shaped apron sides and front. Wrought iron hinges and escutcheon; lock missing.

27.9 x 67.3 x 31.7 cm (11 x 26½ x 12½″)

Titus C. Geesey Collection. 53-125-4

6 BOX
Reading, Berks County
1770–80

Attributed to **Heinrich Bucher**

Inscribed on lid: *M. Roudenbush's*

Painted cedar. Plank construction. Joints lapped and glued. Overhanging lid fastened to frame with brads. Wrapped and stapled steel hinges and clasp. Black ground, red and blue flowers and foliage, white outlines and inscription.

5.5 x 23.7 x 21 cm (2⅛ x 9⅜ x 8¼″)

Gift of J. Stogdell Stokes. 28-10-113

7 RIBBON BOX
Reading, Berks County
1770–80

Attributed to **Heinrich Bucher**

Painted pine. Bentwood construction; joint spliced and glued. Oval bottom and top are tacked. Flowers, foliage, and male figure in blue and red, outlined with white, painted on black ground.

16.2 x 38.5 x 24.2 cm (6⅜ x 15⅛ x 9½″)

Gift of Mrs. William D. Frishmuth. 10-296

8 TABLE CHEST
1770–1800

Painted poplar, pine. Plank construction with dovetail joints. Interior till on left has false bottom and secret compartment. Molded edge of lid butted and pegged. Scotia and astragal molding nailed above drawer. Drawer dovetailed and nailed at rear; molded edge overlaps case. Wrought iron pull and strap hinges. Painted dark red with freehand flowers springing from basket in blue and white. Cartouche on lid; zigzag and dot design on base molding, center drop, and ogee bracket feet.

26.7 x 40 x 20.3 cm (10½ x 15¾ x 8″)

Titus C. Geesey Collection. 54-85-70

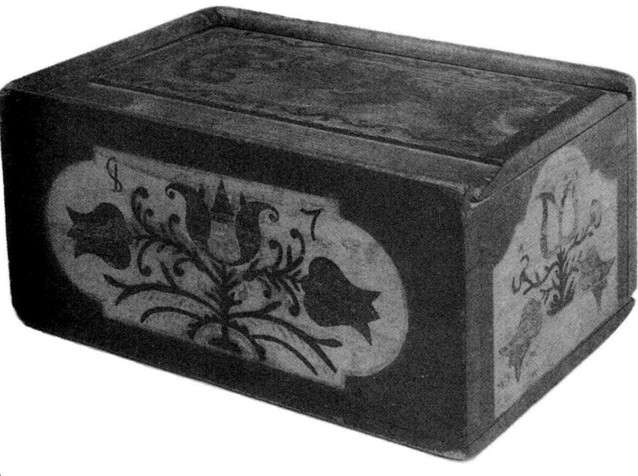

9

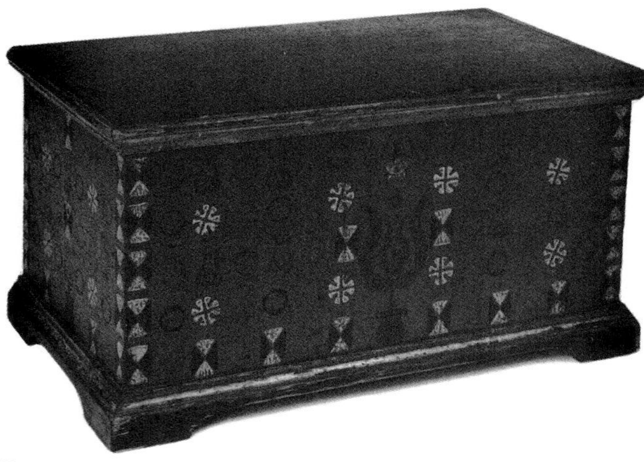

10

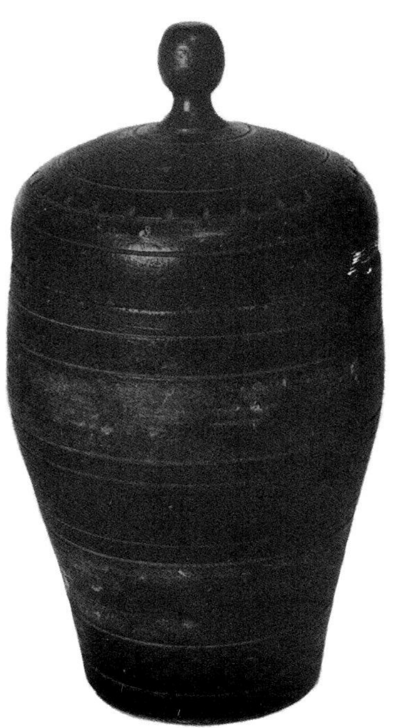

11

9 BOX
Lebanon County
1776

Inscribed on long sides: *17   76*

Painted pine, poplar. Plank construction with dovetail corners. Flush bottom nailed to sides. Raised paneled lid slides in carved groove. Carved indentation for thumb pull at center of painted sunburst. Painted gray blue with white panels, designs in blue, red, and black.

17.8 x 36.9 x 22.9 cm (7 x 14½ x 9″)

Titus C. Geesey Collection. 53-125-5a,b

10 TABLE CHEST
Schuylkill County
c. 1780

Painted yellow pine. Molded plank construction with dovetail joints. Case set into base molding with bracket feet. Lid molding applied with brads; overlaps case. Interior till on left has secret compartment under false bottom. Wrought iron pin and ring hinges replaced with brass hinges. Geometric designs stamped, blocked and/or stenciled in blue, black, and white on top, front, and sides on red brown ground.

25 x 47.5 x 27.5 cm (9⅞ x 18¾ x 10⅞″)

Gift of J. Stogdell Stokes. 28-10-108

11 TOBACCO BOX
1780–1800

Painted poplar. Turned construction. Interior hollowed out; incised lines on exterior define black and red painted bands. Lid fits over set in rim, turned knob one piece with lid.

Height 28 cm (11″), diameter 16 cm (6¼″)

Gift of John Story Jenks. 13-113

12 CUTLERY BOX
1780–1800

Black walnut, butternut inlay. Molded-edge plank construction with dovetail joints. Base with extended edge screwed to sides. Carved and pierced handle is extension of interior divider. Brass hinges. Hinged lids inlaid with daisy design.

25.4 x 38 x 26.6 cm (10 x 15 x 10½″)

Titus C. Geesey Collection. 55-94-74

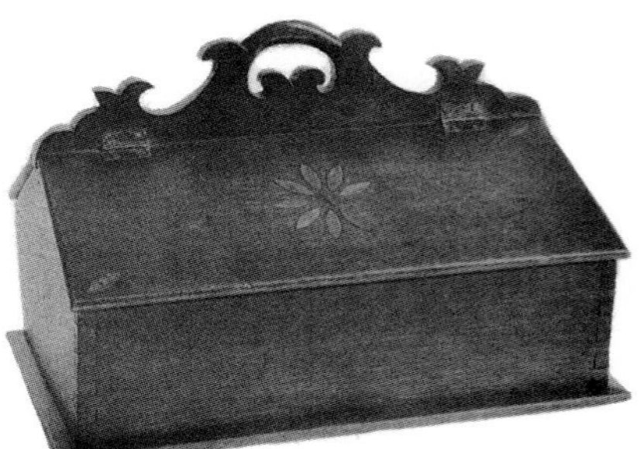

12

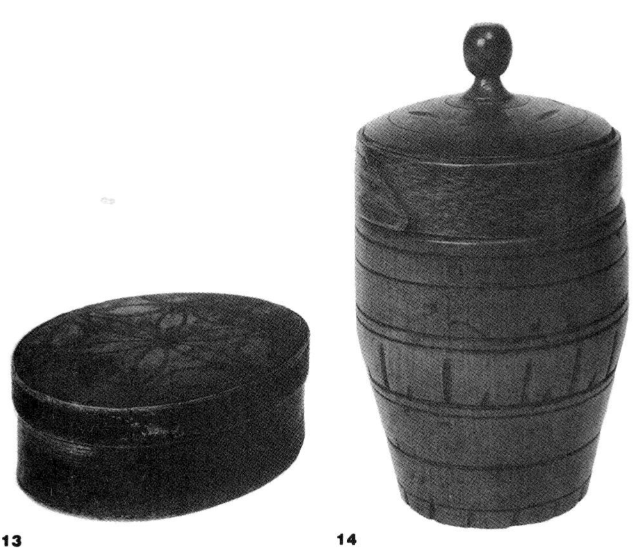

13   **14**

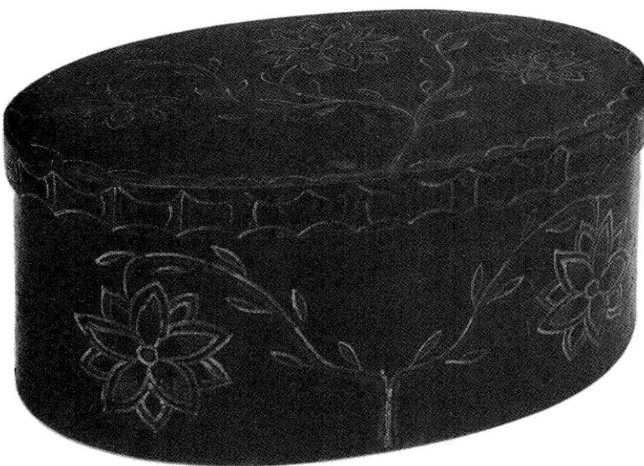

15

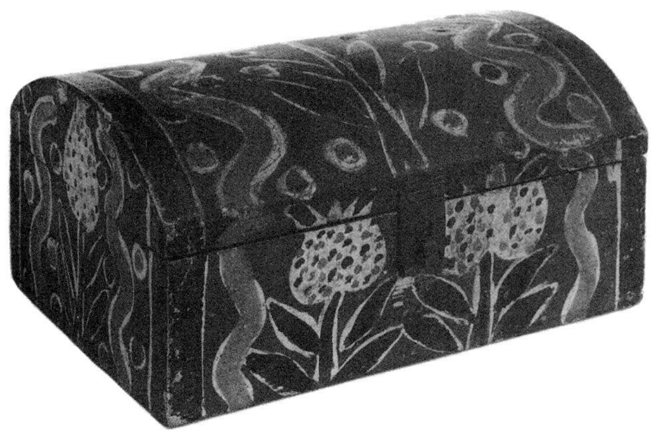

16

13   TRINKET BOX
1780–1800

Painted cedar, hickory. Sides of overlapping bentwood construction secured with nails. Lid and bottom pegged. Compass-inscribed patterns in narrow bands are chip-carved or stamped. Painted dark blue green.

8.9 x 25.4 x 19 cm (3½ x 10 x 7½")

Titus C. Geesey Collection. 54-85-134a,b

14   TOBACCO BOX
Montgomery County
1780–1810

Birch. Body of box turned. Incised decoration. Lid and knob turned. Bentwood strip tacked to edge of lid is overlapped and tacked.

Height 23 cm (9"), diameter 13.5 cm (5¼")

Gift of J. Stogdell Stokes. 39-2-4a,b

15   RIBBON BOX
c. 1800

Painted yellow pine, poplar. Bentwood construction. Sides and edge of lid overlapped and feathered, glued and stapled. Top and bottom inset and tacked. Painted dark brown with red and white designs.

18.4 x 46.3 x 30.5 cm (7¼ x 18¼ x 12")

Titus C. Geesey Collection. 54-85-66a,b

16   TRINKET CHEST
Lancaster County
c. 1800

Painted cedar. Plank construction with bentwood top, butt joints, glued and pegged. Sides lap-joined. Painted red brown with freehand designs in dark red, green, white, and yellow. Green banding on edges. Tin hasp and pin hinges.

11.4 x 22.9 x 15.9 cm (4½ x 9 x 6¼")

Titus C. Geesey Collection. 54-85-132

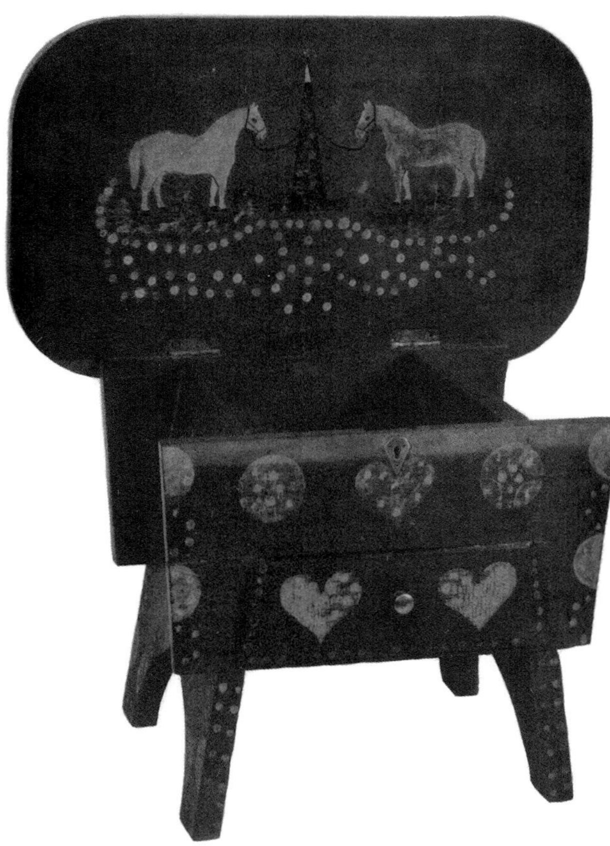

17

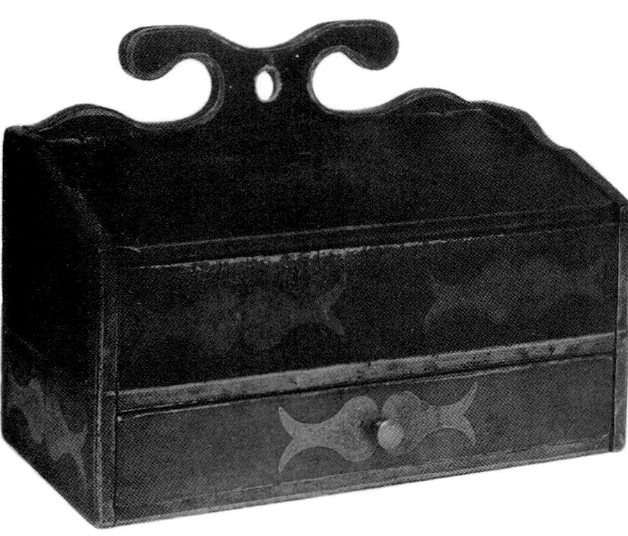

18

17 SHOE POLISH BOX
Probably Schuylkill County
1800–1830

Cherry, cedar, sugar pine. Plank construction with pegged joints. Front and backboards gained and pegged into raked side boards that extend into feet. Trapezoidal drawer has overlapping molded edge, nailed butt joint construction. Inset butt hinges. Natural wood ground with designs on four sides in red, yellow, and dark green. Ten-pointed star in a circle, two birds, and four hearts on lid.

28 x 43.2 x 25.4 cm (11 x 17 x 10″)

Titus C. Geesey Collection. 55-94-77

18 HANGING BOX
Schuylkill County
1800–1830

Painted poplar. Plank construction, butt joints, nailed. Drawer has nailed lap joints. Back extends into shaped hanging support. Blue green ground; red drawer with yellow, red, and black stenciled tulips; light blue banding. Brass pull. Looped steel wire hinges. Two interior compartments in till, three in drawer.

24.1 x 33.6 x 14.6 cm (9½ x 13¼ x 5¾″)

Titus C. Geesey Collection. 54-85-69

19 BUTTER BOX
Oley, Berks County
1800–1840

Incised on lid: *1   11   111*
Stamped, twice, on front: *G · REIFF*

Pine. Plank construction with dovetail corner joints. Bottom butted and nailed to sides. Top has three sliding sections with feathered edges fitting into grooves in sides. Fingerhold gouges. Sides grooved on interior for adjustable shelves. Wrought iron handle. Top corners bound with iron straps and nailed.

14.1 x 41.9 x 38.7 cm (5½ x 16½ x 15¼″)

Gift of Mrs. William D. Frishmuth. 02-158

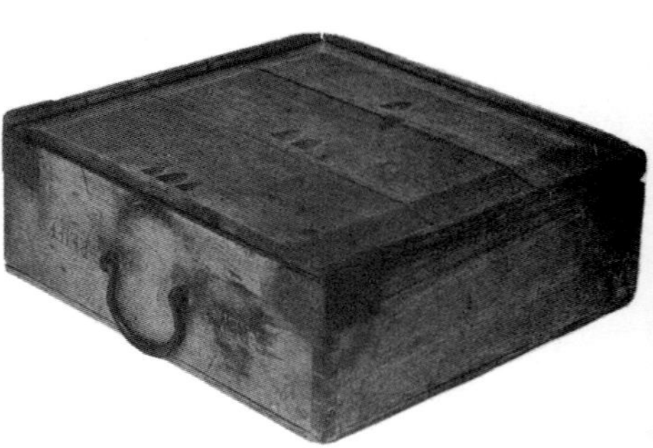

19

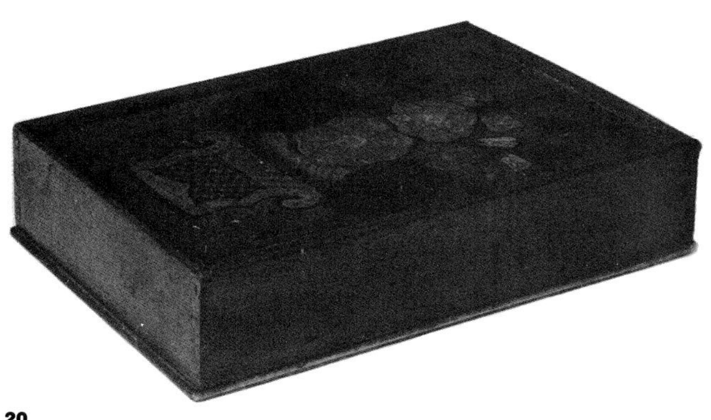

20

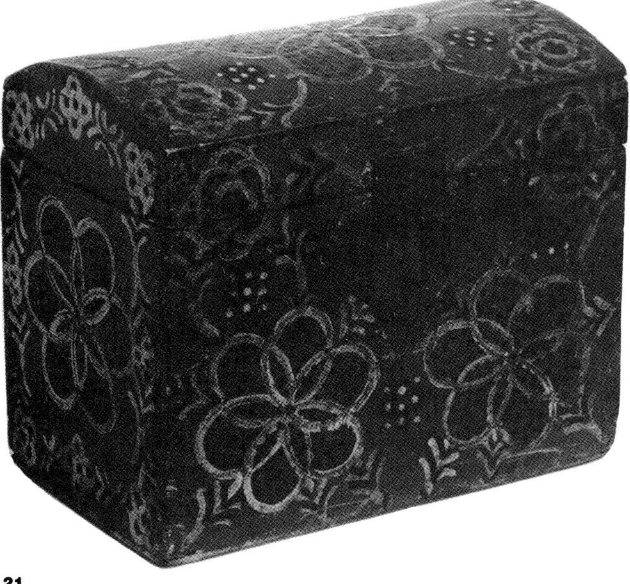

21

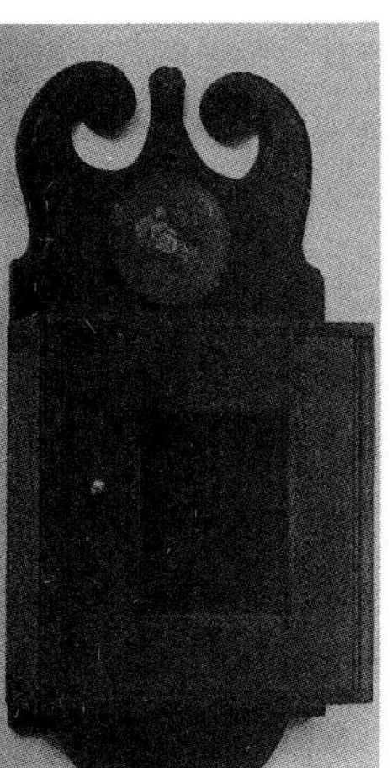

22

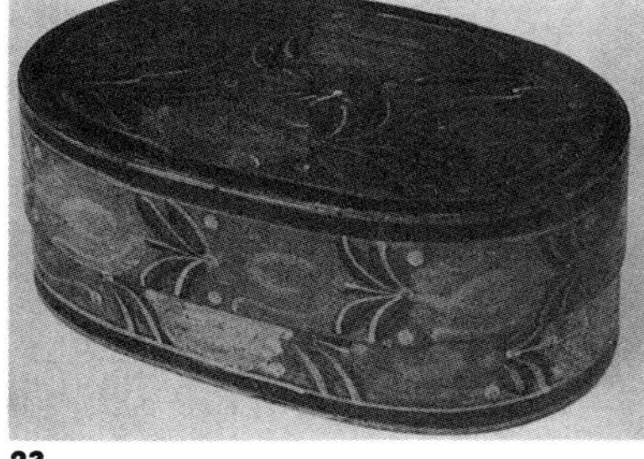

23

20 BOX
1800–1840

Painted basswood. Plank construction with dovetail corners. Bevel-edged lid slides to reveal six interior compartments. Bottom extended. Design in red, yellow, green, purple, and black on natural wood ground.

6.3 x 25.4 x 17.8 cm (2½ x 10 x 7″)

Titus C. Geesey Collection. 54-85-133a,b

21 TRINKET TRUNK
Lancaster County
1800–1840

Painted poplar, pine, tin over sheet iron. Plank construction with dovetail corners. Bottom pegged to sides. Bent lid pegged to frame. Tinned heart-shaped hasp plate bordered with punchwork. Hasp broken. Painted brown red with compass-inscribed flowers and freehand stylized foliage in black and white.

15.2 x 17.8 x 10.8 cm (6 x 7 x 4¼″)

Titus C. Geesey Collection. 54-85-136

22 WATCH HOLDER
1800–1840

Walnut. Shaped, molded plank construction with dovetail joints in box frame, mortise and tenon joints in glass doorframe with bead on vertical edges. Back hanging board has carved edge, scrolled volutes, gouge-carved rosettes and central finial. Inset floral circular plaque painted red with yellow and blue.

33 x 15.2 x 7.6 cm (13 x 6 x 3″)

Titus C. Geesey Collection. 54-85-121

23 RIBBON BOX
c. 1830

Painted pine, willow reed. Bentwood construction; joint lapped and sewn with willow reed. Oval top and bottom tacked. Red orange, yellow, and white tulips, green and white leaves, dark blue bands outlined with white on natural wood ground. Similar to European examples.

15.4 x 33.7 x 21.1 cm (6⅛ x 13¼ x 8¼″)

Gift of Mrs. William D. Frishmuth. 02-380

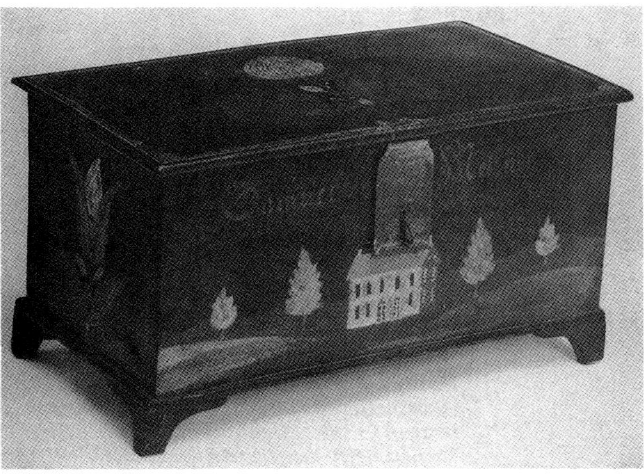

24

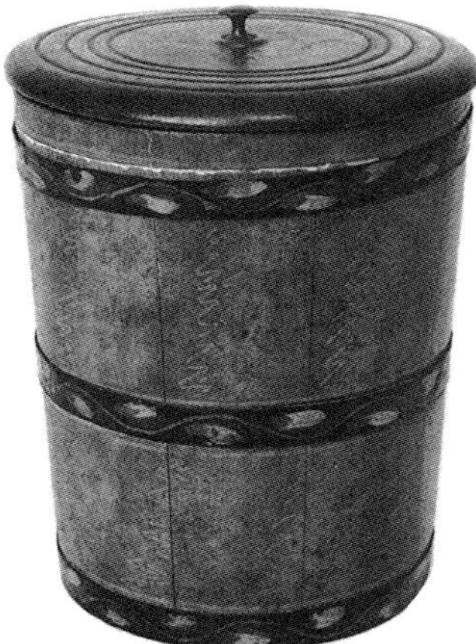

25

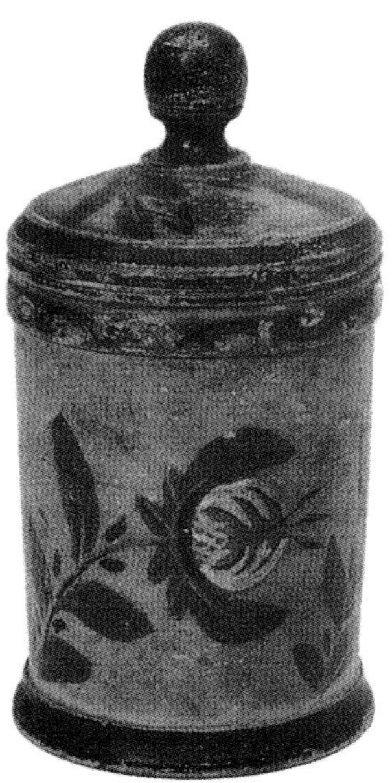

26

24 TRINKET CHEST
Fivepointsville, Lancaster County
1850–60

Jacob Weber

Inscribed on front: *Samuel Messner*

Painted pine, poplar. Lightweight plank construction with glued lap joints. Shaped bracket feet carved from solid block, fitted flush with molded extension of bottom, secured with pegs. Quirked bead molding on edge of lid. Interior till on left with lid hinging on dowels tenoned into back and front boards. Wire loop hinges, tin hasp. Painted black with green landscape, red and white house, tulip in yellow and white on each end and lid.

14.3 x 26.2 x 15.2 cm (5⅝ x 10¼ x 6″)

Titus C. Geesey Collection. 54-85-135

25 BOX
Elizabethtown Township, Lancaster County
1860–80

Joseph Long Lehn

Painted pine. Barrel construction. Vertical shaped staves meet in butt joints held with three bentwood bands. Lid with incised concentric circles and turned knob (probably a replacement) has batten tacked underside. Bottom inset and nailed. Graining visible through red wash. Black bands with yellow, green, and red running vine design. Lid reverse painted pink, box interior unpainted.

Height 23.1 cm (9⅛″), diameter 19 cm (7½″)

Gift of J. Stogdell Stokes. 28-10-78a,b

26 SPICE BOX
Elizabethtown Township, Lancaster County
1860–80

Joseph Long Lehn

Painted maple. Lathe-turned, sanded, and painted. Top inset to hold lid. Designs in red, green, yellow, white, and dark blue on pink ground: strawberries on lid; pomegranatelike form on body; white pussy willow forms on border below lid.

Height 11.4 cm (4½″), diameter 6.3 cm (2½″)

Titus C. Geesey Collection. 54-85-115a,b

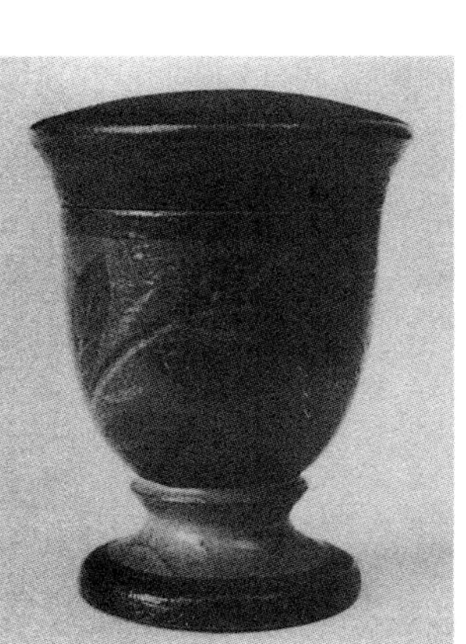

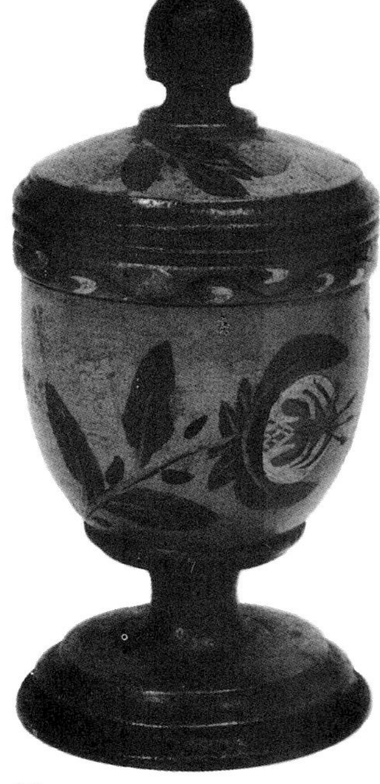

27

28

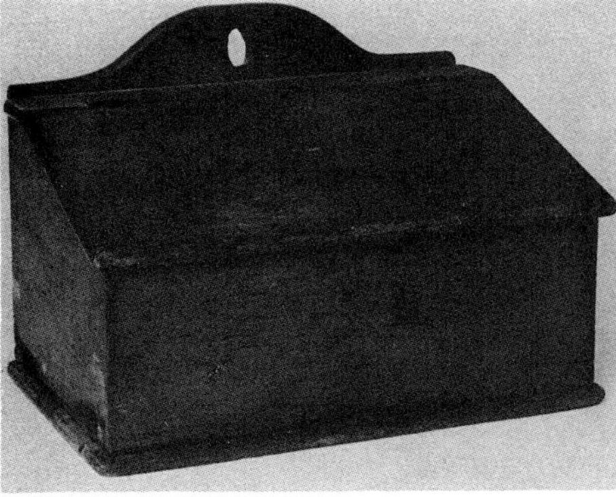

29

27 SPICE BOX
Elizabethtown Township, Lancaster County
1860–80

Joseph Long Lehn

Painted maple. Lathe-turned, sanded, and painted. Dark gray ground with strawberry design on lid and body in red, yellow, white, and black. Base red and black.

Height 5.1 cm (2″), diameter 3.8 cm (1½″)

Titus C. Geesey Collection. 54-85-117a,b

28 SPICE BOX
Elizabethtown Township, Lancaster County
1860–80

Joseph Long Lehn

Painted maple. Lathe-turned, sanded, and painted. Designs in red, green, yellow, white, dark blue on pink ground: strawberries on lid; pomegranatelike form on body; pussy willows on border below lid.

Height 12.7 cm (5″), diameter 6.3 cm (2½″)

Titus C. Geesey Collection. 54-85-114a,b

29 HANGING BOX
Lancaster County
c. 1870

Painted pine. Plank construction, dovetail corners. Bin set into bottom plank with molded front edge. Two keyed dovetails inside sloping lid. Brass butt hinges. Painted red.

26.7 x 37.2 x 22.8 cm (10½ x 14⅝ x 9″)

Gift of Miss Marie E. Bucher, in memory of Mrs. William Hipple and Mrs. David H. Bucher. 39-35-14

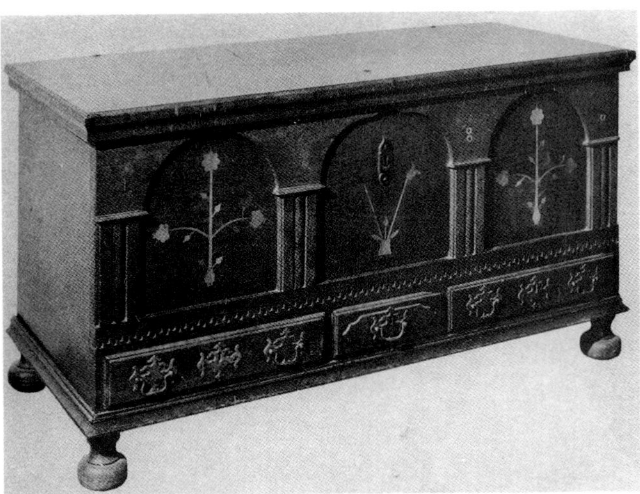

1

1 CHEST OVER DRAWERS
Lancaster County
1780

Black walnut, maple inlay. Frame, panel, and plank construction, dovetailed with pegged moldings. Architectural pilasters, arches, and dentil fret carved and secured with pegs to recessed front plank. Three drawers have molded edges overlapping case. Brass pulls, wrought iron escutcheon and strap hinges. Scotia molding at base. Turned legs and ball feet.

68.5 x 129.5 x 53.3 cm (27 x 51 x 21″)

Titus C. Geesey Collection. 53-125-8

2 CHEST OVER DRAWERS
Berks County
1780–90

Painted pine. Plank and frame construction with dovetail joints. Backboard stepped out at base to meet drawer case in dovetail joint. Bottom of chest secured with pegs through back and through skirting between shaped bracket feet. Lid molding overlaps case on sides and is flush in front; secured to lid in pegged butt joint. Drawer edges overlap case; dovetailed at four corners, bottom let into front, butted to sides and pegged. Till has molded edge on lid and bottom. Wrought iron strap hinges on back and interior of lid, crab spring lock. Brass bail handles. Painted dark green. Compass and rule lines incised. Four arch-top painted panels with yellow and black checkered arch over tan balusters framing red, black, and yellow tulips in baskets on cream color ground. Yellow banding on moldings and drawer edges. Lid undecorated.

74 x 122 x 61 cm (29⅛ x 48 x 24″)

Bequest of Mr. and Mrs. J. Stogdell Stokes. 64-113-2

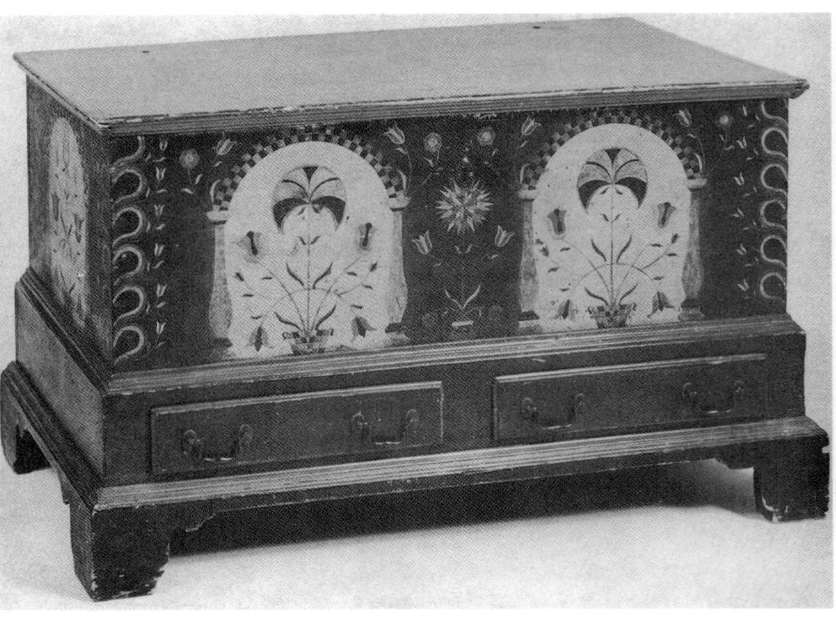

2

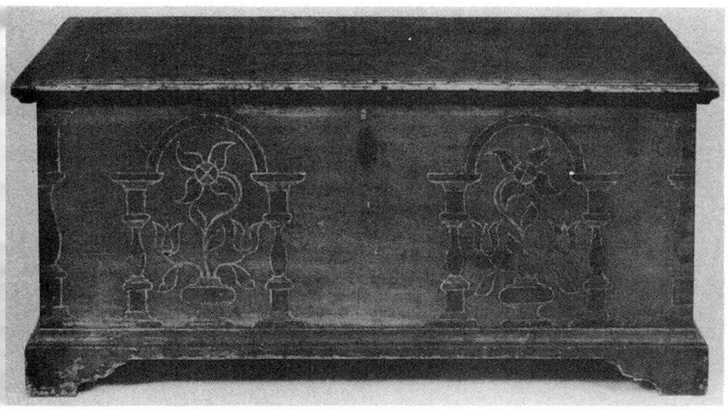

3

3   CHEST
Berks County
1780–90

Inscribed on painted arches: *Margret Schumacherin*

Painted pine, poplar. Six-plank dovetail construction. Overhung molding joins lid in pegged rabbet. Shaped bracket feet dovetailed, no support blocks. Till on left interior. Wrought iron crab lock, interior strap hinges. Natural wood ground with red and green painted balusters at four corners. Two painted baluster-supported arches frame red and green flowers in vases. Designs outlined in white. Lid undecorated.

59.7 x 130 x 56.8 cm (23½ x 51⅛ x 22⅜″)

Purchased: Baugh-Barber Fund, from the Clarence W. Brazer Collection. 25-93-2

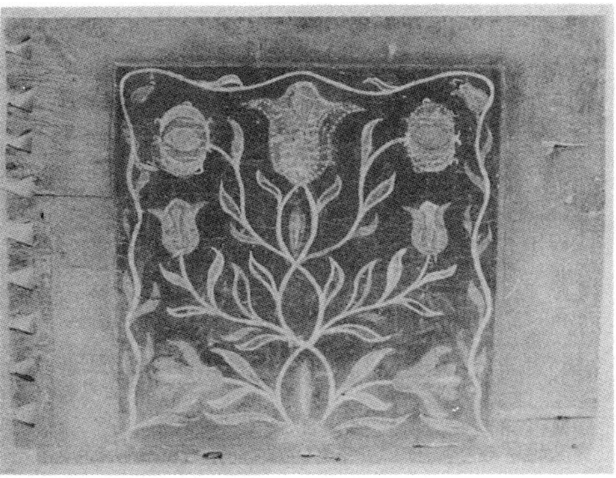

4

4   CHEST PANEL
Probably Bucks County
1780–1800

Painted pine. One-half of two-panel chest, dovetail joints. Painted design in red, yellow, and white on dark blue ground, red border.

47 x 58.4 cm (18½ x 23″)

Gift of Miss Frances Lichten. 60-91-1

5   CHEST
Bern Township, Berks County
1781

Inscribed: *JACOB JUTZAE   ANNO 1781   A H*

Painted pine. Plank construction with dovetailed corners. Lid moldings joined in dado joint with two tenons from lid through each end molding. Glue outlines probably from two frakturs fastened to inside of lid. Interior till with molded lid. Bottom of chest is extended and edge molded. Skirting at each end dovetailed to bracket feet and nailed to bottom of chest. Chest painted green black, feet red, with designs in red, cream, and black. Wrought iron strap hinges, crab spring lock.

58.4 x 128.9 x 57.2 cm (23 x 50¾ x 22½″)

Gift of Mr. and Mrs. Robert L. Raley. 1978-101-2

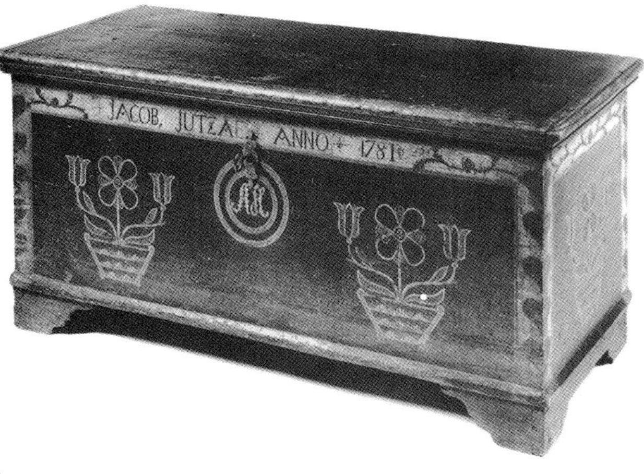

5

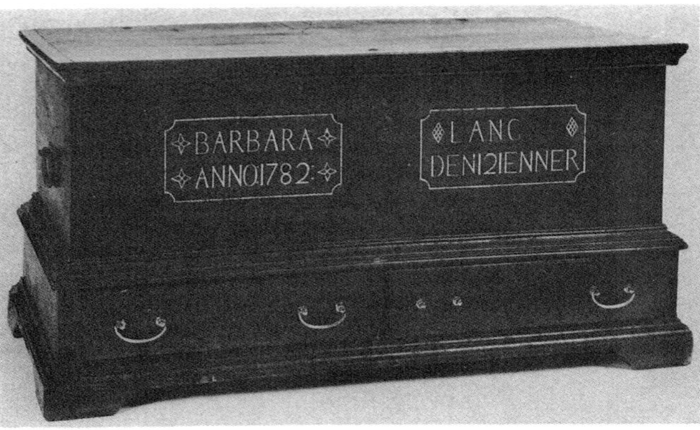

6

6   **CHEST OVER DRAWERS**
Lancaster County
1782

Inscribed: *BARBARA   ANNO:1782:
LANG   DENI2IENNER* ("the 12th January")

Walnut, sulphur inlay; pine, poplar. Panel and frame, and plank construction with mortise and tenon joints. Edge moldings join lid in dado with three open tenons through end moldings. Dovetail construction at four corners. Addition of plank on each side capped with scotia and torus molding gives stepped casing effect. Bottom plank extends under side planks and is nailed. Left-hand interior till. Drawers have molded edges that overlap case, constructed with five dovetails front and back, two bottom boards lap joined, bottom has butt joints sides and back. Bracket feet in one piece with base molding. Brass handles old replacements. Wrought iron escutcheon, strap hinges, carrying handles; lock missing.

67.6 x 132.1 x 67.3 cm (26⅝ x 52 x 26½")

Gift of Mr. and Mrs. Robert L. Raley.
1978-101-1

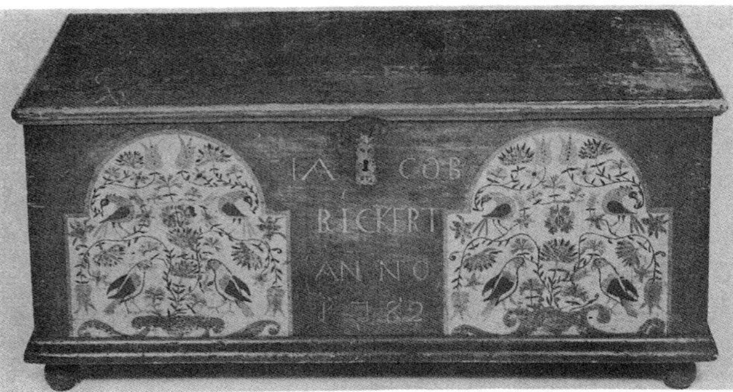

7

7   **CHEST**
Mount Joy, Lancaster County
1782

Inscribed on front: *IACOB RICKERT
ANNO 1782*

Painted poplar; pine. Six-board plank construction with dovetail corners. Cyma reversa molding on lid secured in pegged butt joint, mitered front corners. Two battens under chest bottom. Molded base. Till on left interior. Turned ball feet are replacements. Wrought iron strap hinges inside, wrought iron escutcheon. Lock is an old replacement. Painted blue green. Front panels decorated with symmetrical, freehand pattern in red, blue, yellow, green, and black on white ground. Panels outlined in orange. On lid remnants of three painted arch-topped panels that enclose pinwheels with flower designs.

58.5 x 136 x 55 cm (23 x 53½ x 21⅝")

Gift of George H. Lorimer. 25-95-1

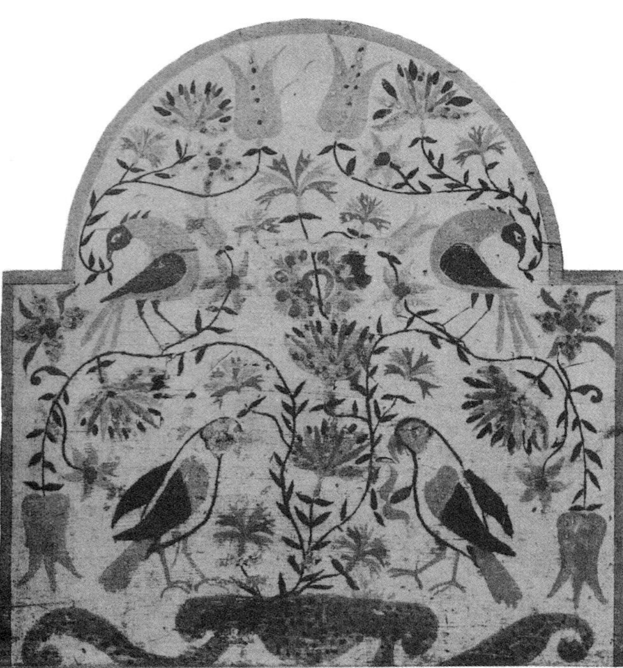

7 detail

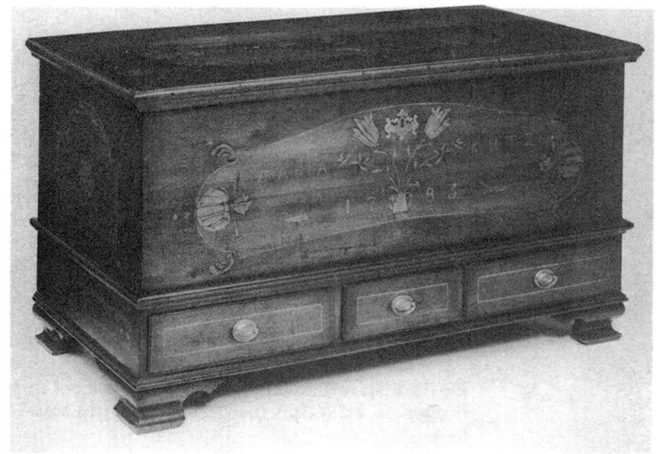

8

8 CHEST OVER DRAWERS
Maxatawny Township, Berks County
1783

Inscribed on front: *MARIA KUTZ   1783*

Black walnut, scorched and toned maple inlay; pine. Shaped and molded plank construction, dovetail corners. Overhung molding joins lid in pegged rabbet. Interior till on left. Drawer fronts overlap frame, dovetailed front and back, butted and pegged bottom. Crown molding applied above drawers. Ogee bracket feet are old replacements. Wrought iron strap hinges on back and interior on lid, crab spring lock with incised decoration of interlocking C's and crosshatching. Inlaid decoration on top and three sides. Chest found on the John Sell farm, between Kutztown and Bowers.

74 x 137 x 62 cm (29⅛ x 53⅞ x 24⅜")

Purchased: Annual Membership Fund. 14-267

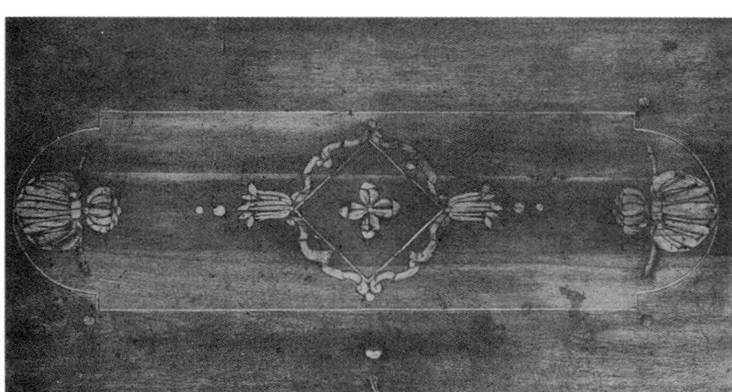

8 detail

9 CHEST
Lancaster County
1787

Inscribed on front: *1787   ANNA MARIA LESCHERIN*

Painted pine, poplar; ash or oak. Six-plank construction with dovetail corners. Fluted pilasters and arches carved and superimposed on front and pegged. Overhanging molded edge joins lid in pegged rabbet. Straight bracket feet with round holes cut through brackets (typical of Octorara, Lancaster County), with support blocks. Wrought iron hasp and lock. Strap hinges on back and inside lid. Painted dark blue green with white mottling. Red mottling on white flutes of pilasters, flowers red and blue, twining vines red and white, inscription red, and stars red, blue, and black. Compass lines incised.

58.8 x 129 x 59.6 cm (23⅛ x 50¾ x 23½")

Purchased: Baugh-Barber Fund, from the Clarence W. Brazer Collection. 25-93-4

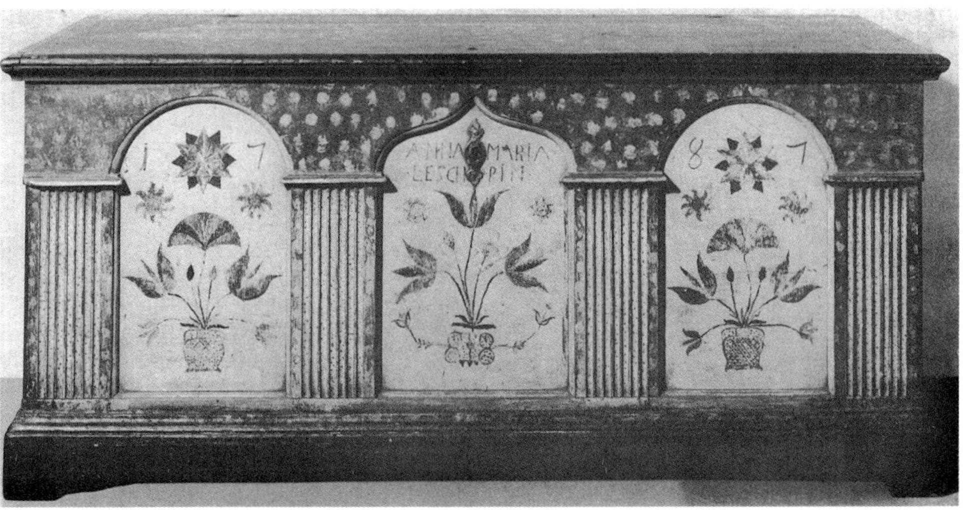

9

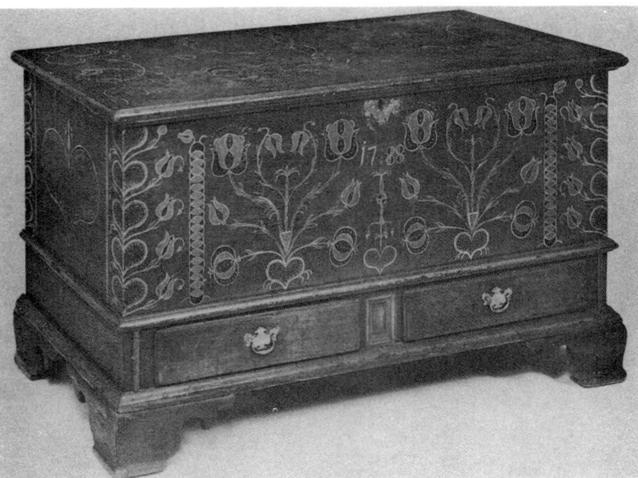

10

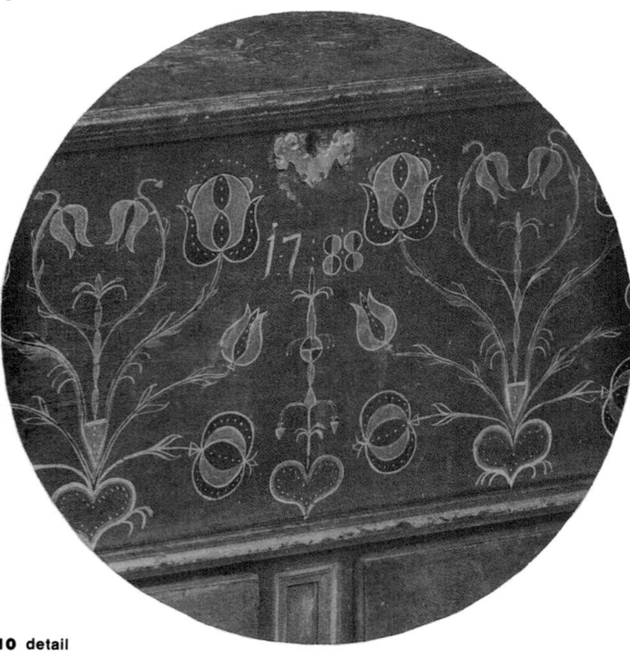

10 detail

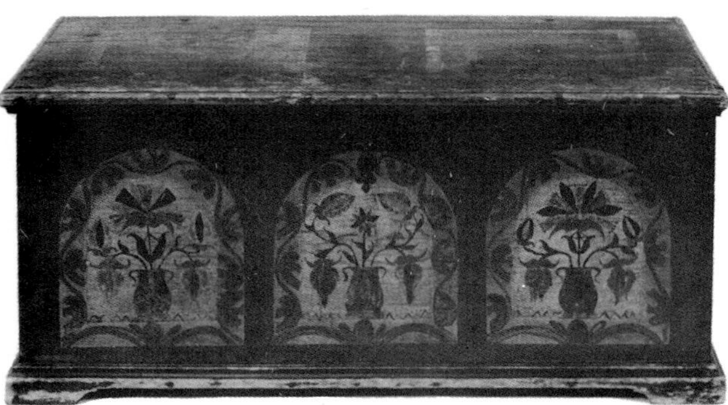

11

10 CHEST OVER DRAWERS
Berks County
1788

Inscribed on front: *1788*

Painted pine; white cedar. Six-plank construction with dovetail joints. Overhung molding joins lid in pegged rabbet with mitered front corners. Astragal molding above drawers, cyma base molding mitered and pegged. Drawers have overlapping front edges, molded top edges, pegged butt joint at front, dovetailed at back; bottom butted at sides, nailed at back. Interior till on left. Feet replaced. Brass pulls and escutcheon replaced. Painted with blue green wash, red moldings. Designs in red, black, and white. Wrought iron hinges on back and inside lid, wrought iron lock.

77.5 x 127.6 x 90.2 cm (30½ x 50¼ x 35½")

Titus C. Geesey Collection. 58-110-2

11 CHEST
Jonestown, Lebanon County
c. 1790

Painted pine; cedar. Six-plank dovetail construction. Overhanging molded edge pegged to lid boards. Base molding and bracket feet. Wrought iron strap hinges inside, escutcheon. Till on left has molded lid. On blue ground, three arched front panels bordered in gold yellow with dark red brown and green running vine. Red and blue flowers, green and brown leaves, black two-handled vases with crosshatching. Indented compass dot at center of each panel. Rectangular top panels have gold yellow borders, but design is obliterated.

56 x 128 x 57 cm (22 x 50⅜ x 22½")

Gift of J. Stogdell Stokes. 28-10-96

12

12 CHEST

Rapho Township, Lancaster County
1791

Attributed to John Flory

Inscribed on front: *Dise Kist Gehert Mir Jacob Dres 1791 JF* ("This chest belongs to me. Jacob Dres")

Painted poplar; pine. Six-plank construction with dovetail joints. Overhung molding joins lid in pegged rabbet. Base molding and feet in one piece. Interior till on left. Baluster-shaped wrought iron strap hinges on back and inside lid. Escutcheon, crab spring lock with wrigglework decoration, and bail handles each end with clenched posts. Lid has brown mottling or graining over natural wood; front has mottling over tan paint. Designs and inscription in red, black, and ivory. Five black and white compass-inscribed stars, two sunbursts on lid. Base molding red. Found in Elizabethtown.

63.5 x 127 x 61 cm (25 x 50 x 24")

Titus C. Geesey Collection. 58-110-1

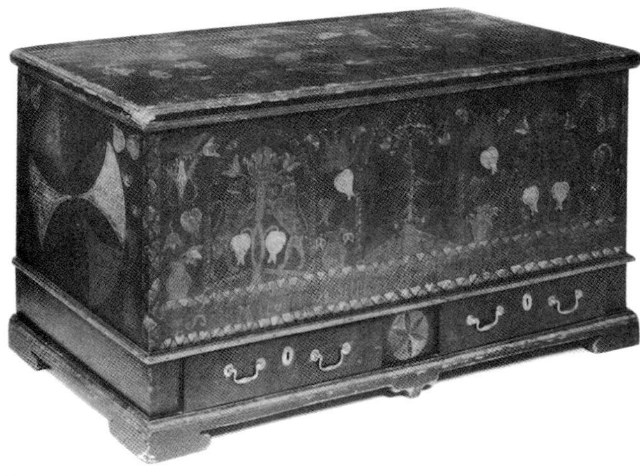

13

13 CHEST OVER DRAWERS

Bern Township, Berks County
1796

Inscribed on front: *Mar ·ri ·chen ·Grim ·in · Jahr ·CRST* [?]*·1796 den 10 ·MO ·LH* ("Marie Catherine Grim. In the year of Christ 1796 8th 10th month")

Painted poplar. Plank construction with dovetail joints. Lid and center moldings mitered and pegged. Drawers of dovetail construction have molded edges overlapping case; bottom in pegged butt joint. Bracket feet and base molding are replacements; originals were tenoned through bottom plank. Wrought iron strap hinges on back and interior lid, iron lock, escutcheon. One brass bail handle; three bails replaced. Drawers and base painted black, moldings red. Varnish altered original blue green ground to dark green. Design and geometric patterns in red, black, ivory, and yellow.

65 x 129 x 59 cm (25⅝ x 50¾ x 23¼")

Purchased: Baugh-Barber Fund, from the Clarence W. Brazer Collection. 25-93-1

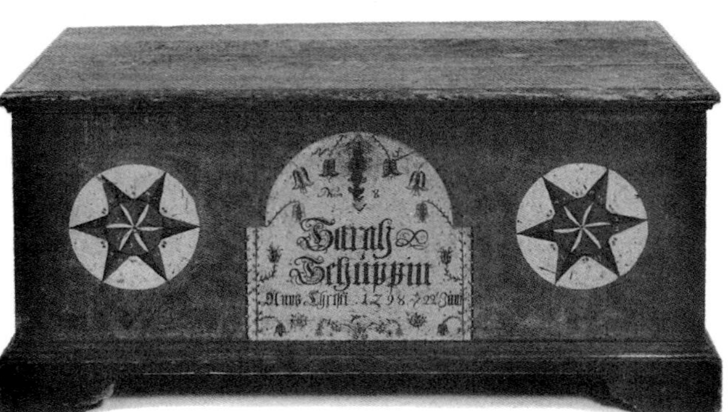

14

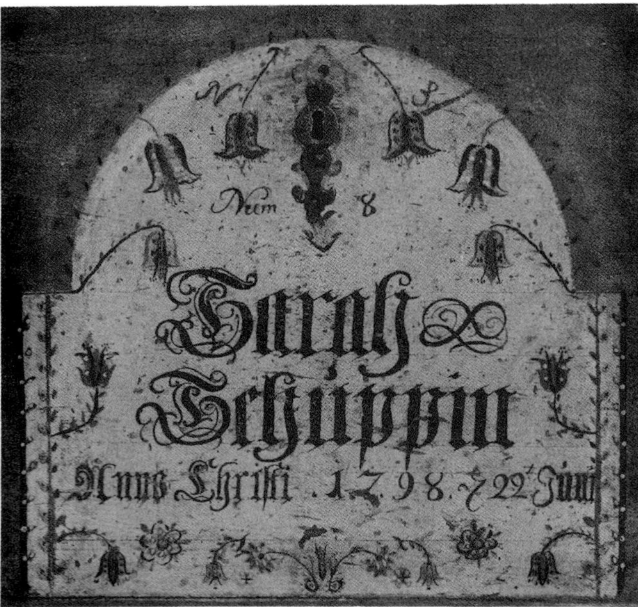

14 detail

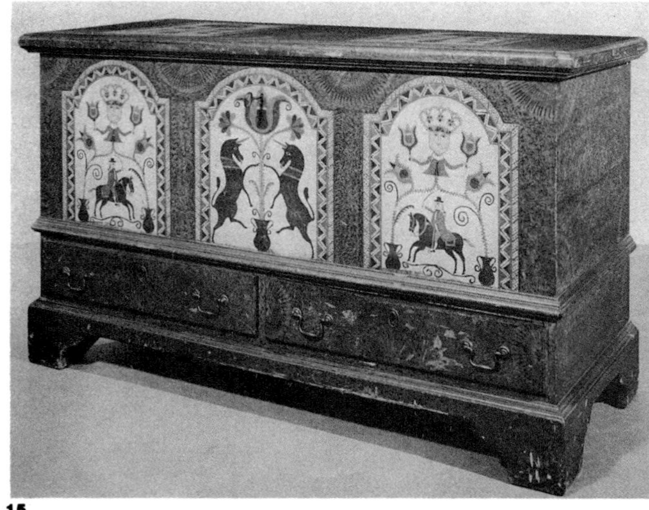

15

14 CHEST
1798

Inscribed on front: *NS Num 8 Sarah Schuppin Anno Christi 1798 y 22 Juni*
Marked on bottom in script: *NS*

Painted poplar; pine. Plank construction with dovetail joints. Bottom lapped and pegged to sides. Lid molding mitered at front corners, pegged rabbet joint. Bracket feet without support blocks. Interior till on left. Crab spring lock. Hinges replaced. Blue green mottled "sponge" painting over wood graining. Dark blue green feet and base molding. Front panel has white ground with flowers and inscription in blue green and mustard yellow flanked by compass-inscribed stars on white ground. Lid undecorated.

57.2 x 119.3 x 57.2 cm (22½ x 47 x 22½")

Gift of Thomas Skelton Harrison. 13-111

15 CHEST OVER DRAWERS
Berks County
1803

Inscribed on lid: *1803   Margreth Bladten*

Painted pine; poplar. Plank construction with dovetail joints. Lid has three open tenons through overhung edge molding at each end joined in rabbet at front and pegged. Interior till on left has molded edge on lid and bottom. Straight bracket feet braced with carved and fitted tapering diagonal pieces nailed to bottom board. Drawers have molded edges overlapping case, dovetails at four corners individually wedged with a fine cut of poplar. Wrought iron strap hinges on back with spiky tulip terminals inside on lid. Brass handles and escutcheon. Red orange ground faded to tan. Brown mottling or graining, and fans made with putty roll. Three front panels: two on lid have white ground with symmetrical flower design in black, red, yellow, and green.

77.5 x 137.5 x 57 cm (30½ x 54⅛ x 22½")

Gift of Arthur Sussel. 45-12-1

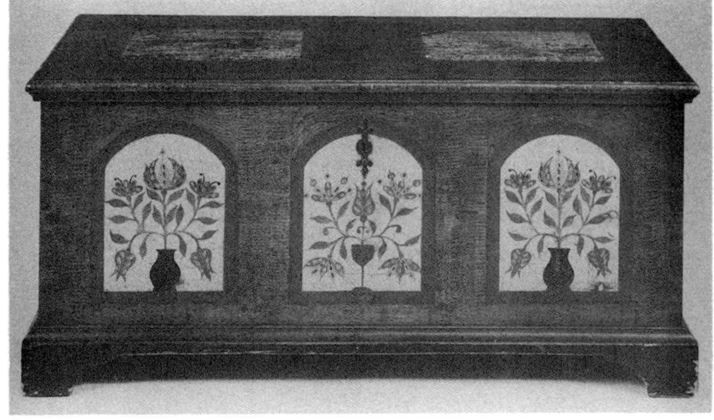

16

16 CHEST

Jonestown, Lebanon County
1804

John Selzer

Inscribed on center vase: *John Selzer 1804*

Painted pine; poplar. Six-plank dovetail construction. Overhung molding joins lid in pegged rabbet, mitered front corners. Plain bracket feet, no blocks. Interior till with lid. Wrought iron escutcheon and interior strap hinges. Painted wood graining on lid, front, and ends made by rolling putty over wet surface of vinegar wash over brown paint. Compass and rule lines incised. Front panels have white backgrounds, red borders with red and yellow lilies and tulips, green foliage, black vases and green center vase. Base molding and feet painted black.

62.4 x 132 x 57.8 cm (24½ x 52 x 22¾")

Purchased: Baugh-Barber Fund, from the Clarence W. Brazer Collection. 25-93-3

---

17 CHEST

York or Lancaster County
1829

Marked inside lid in pencil: *Elizabeth Himes March 1829   In the state of Pennsylvania The County of York*

Painted pine; poplar. Plank construction. Dovetail joints at four corners. Lid has keyed batten inside at center, moldings with mitered front corners nailed to lid in butt joint. Interior left-hand till. Turned feet set into bottom board on dowels. Butt hinges, lock replaced. Painted brown with three medallions on front and lid, flowers in red, green, and yellow on mottled white ground, red heart on each end.

55.9 x 88.3 x 52.7 cm (22 x 34¾ x 20¾")

Gift of Mr. and Mrs. Robert L. Raley. 1978-101-3

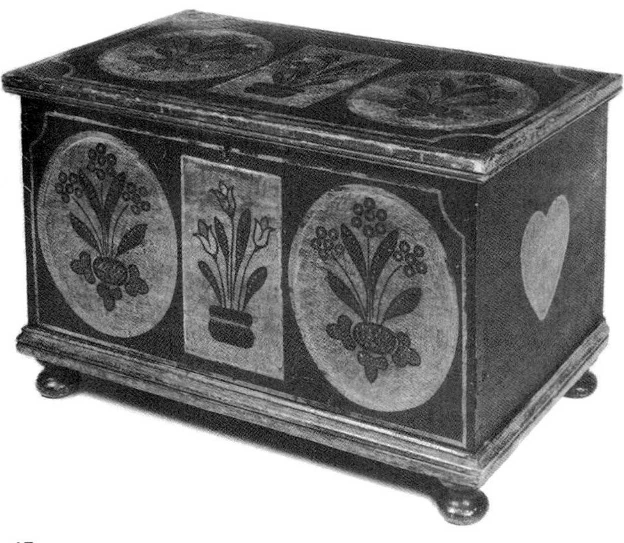

17

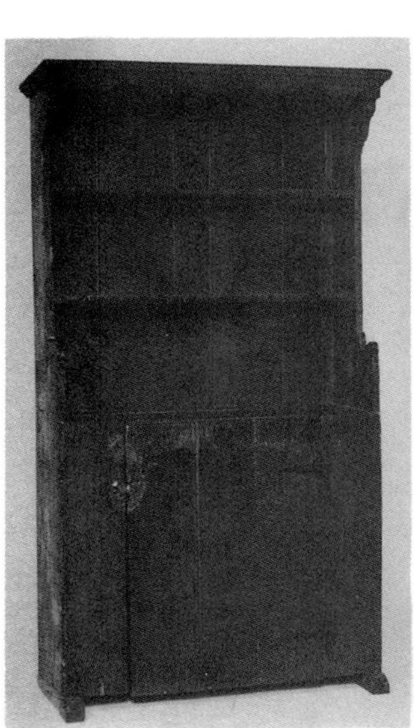

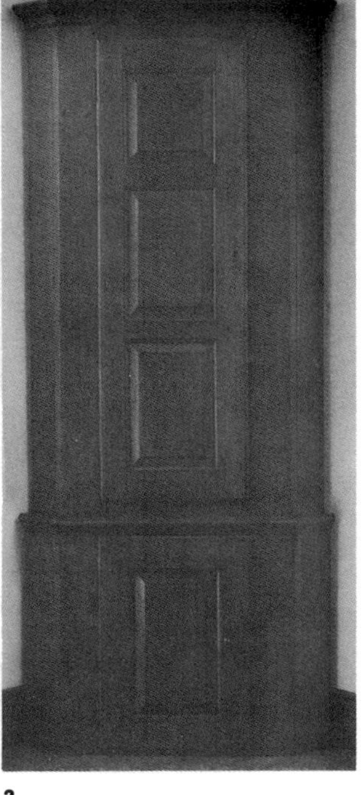

1   **CUPBOARD**
Lancaster County
c. 1750

Painted pine, oak. Shaped and molded plank construction. Cavetto cornice molding; carved, scalloped valance. Four backboards are beaded and joined in tongue in groove. One shelf pierced for hanging cutlery; plate grooves, lowest has applied wood strip. Closed base; door of beaded tongue in groove vertical planks has wood twist latch and wrought iron spike hinges. Molded trestle feet. Painted dark blue green on front, right side, and back.

195.8 x 107.7 x 38.5 cm (77⅛ x 42⅜ x 15⅛″)

Gift of J. Stogdell Stokes. 28-10-75

2   **CORNER CUPBOARD**
c. 1750

Black walnut; poplar. Cupboard in one unit, canted corners. Frame and panel construction with pegged mortise and tenon joints. Raised ovolo-framed panels on upper and lower doors. Applied compound moldings at cornice and waist. Wrought iron pintle and socket hinges with extended props. Brass escutcheon on upper door; wood knob with latch, lower door. Five shelves.

235 x 113 x 54 cm (92½ x 44½ x 21¼″)

Gift of J. Stogdell Stokes. 28-10-109

3   **HANGING CUPBOARD**
Lebanon County
1750–70

Walnut, yellow pine; poplar. Plank, panel and frame construction. Front butted and pegged to sides which are extended and scroll-carved to support shelf with pegged molded edge. Door has raised panel in ovolo-molded frame joined in open mortise and tenon with single pegs. One interior shelf. Drawer edge overlaps case; dovetailed at four corners, bottom feathered and let into sides and front, nailed at back. Wrought iron clenched spike and pintle hinges with extended props. Brass handles, wood knob.

129.5 x 83.8 x 49.4 cm (51 x 33 x 19½″)

Titus C. Geesey Collection. 69-284-24

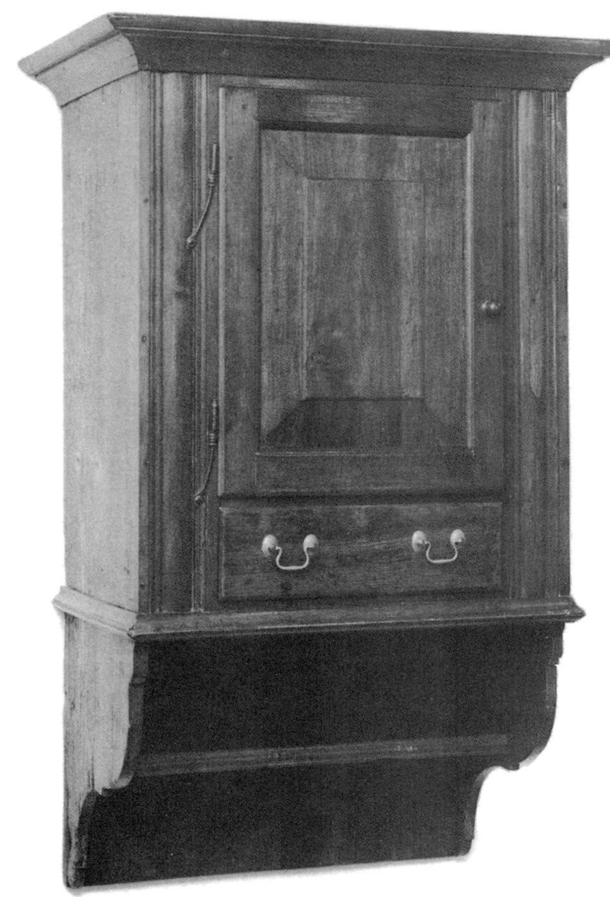

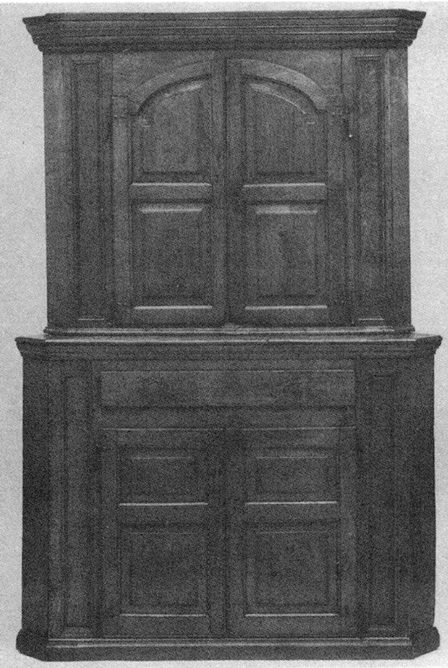

4

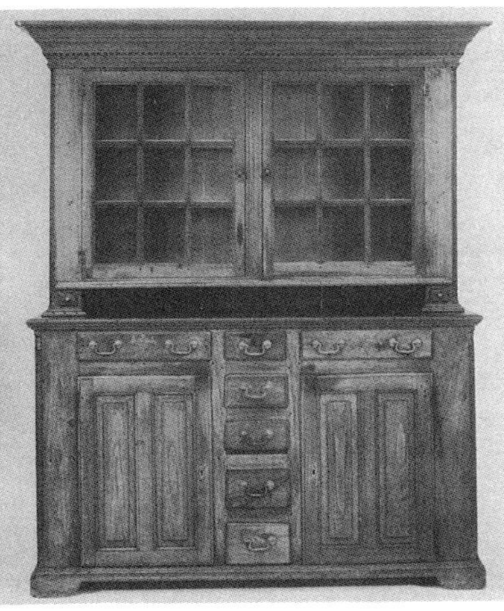

5

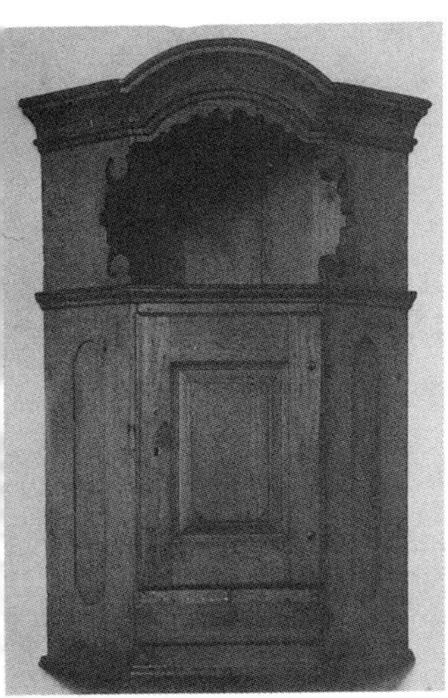

6

4 CORNER CUPBOARD
Lancaster County
1750–70

Black walnut; pine, poplar. Plank, panel and frame construction with pegged mortise and tenon joints. Built in two units. Canted corners. Vertical panels inset in quirked ovolo frames flank doors with raised panels. Drawer edges overlap frame; drawer pulls and escutcheon missing. One shelf each in upper and lower units. Eight wrought iron rivet and pintle hinges with extended props, escutcheon. Interior painted white. Compass-inscribed flower on lower panels of upper doors probably not original.

218.4 x 139.7 x 71.1 cm (86 x 55 x 28″)

Bequest of Mr. and Mrs. William M. Elkins. 50-92-82a,b

5 CUPBOARD
Montgomery County
1750–80

Black walnut; poplar; glass. Panel and frame construction with pegged mortise and tenon joints. Carved dentil molding, fluted center post, quarter columns with capping bands, chamfered cupboard and base sections. Molded edges of drawers overlap frame. Upper backboards beaded and joined in tongue in groove, painted red orange. Two shelves upper, one slotted for cutlery. Base unit has one shelf behind raised panel doors. Moldings have mitered corners and are fastened to frame with square wood pegs. Plain bracket feet have dovetailed corners. Wrought iron spike and pintle hinges with extended props. Brass pulls.

210.2 x 182.9 x 48.9 cm (82¾ x 72 x 19¼″)

Titus C. Geesey Collection. 53-125-1

6 HANGING CORNER CUPBOARD
Lebanon County
c. 1750–1800

Pine. Shaped, molded plank construction, mortise and tenon joints. Arched top has deep scotia molding with applied half-round bead. Quirked ogee molding below shelf. Door has inset raised fielded panel framed with cyma recta and scotia moldings. Oval panel inset in each canted side. Drawer edges overlap case, dovetailed front and back at top and bottom edges; bottom boards, front, and sides pegged. Iron pintle and socket hinges with concealed plates riveted. Evidence of red paint on interior.

122 x 91.4 x 46 cm (48 x 36 x 18⅛″)

Gift of J. Stogdell Stokes. 28-10-1

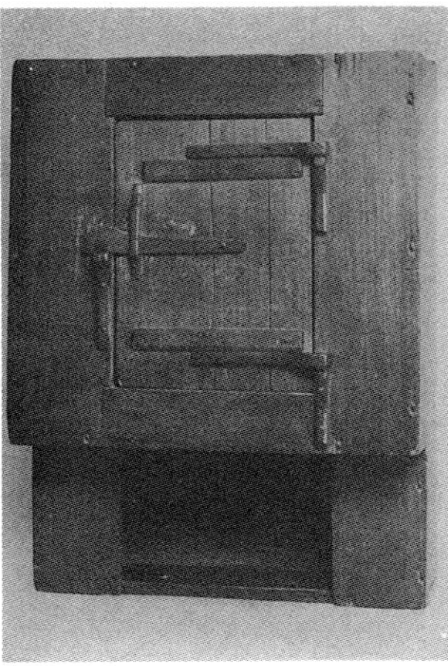

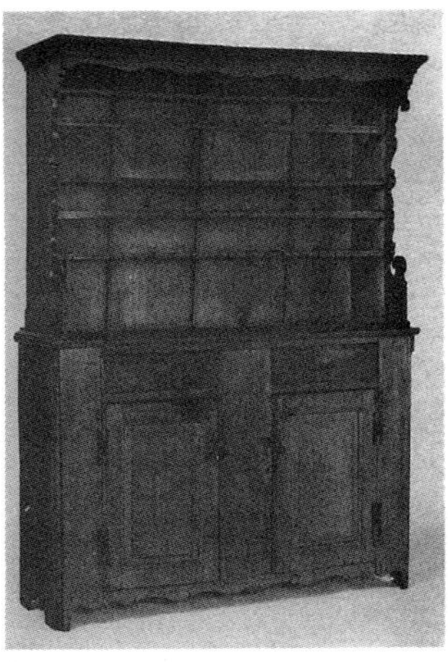

7   8

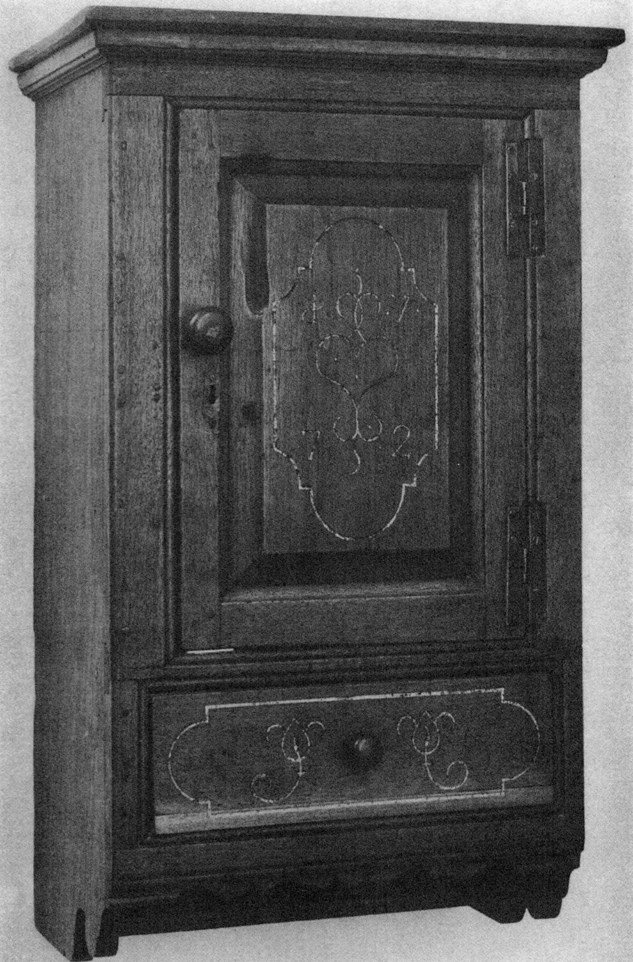

9

7   HANGING CUPBOARD
Ephrata, Lancaster County
c. 1760

Pine, poplar; cedar. Frame construction. Butt and lap joints secured with wrought nails. Batten door. One interior shelf. Carved cedar lift latch and post hinges.

64 x 48.4 x 22.8 cm (25¼ x 19 x 9″)

Gift of J. Stogdell Stokes. 28-10-97

---

8   CUPBOARD
Lancaster County
1770–90

Inscribed on drawers: *P.D.R.   1790   E.D.F.*

Black walnut; pine. Upper unit set inside edge moldings on cupboard unit. Upper unit has molded cornice, scalloped valance, scroll-carved recessed sides. Back is bead-edged tongue in groove vertical planking. Three shelves upper unit, one pierced for hanging cutlery, guard rails inset into side planks. Cupboard unit has raised panels in ovolo-molded frames. One interior shelf. Inset quarter round with abacus at front corners. Scalloped skirting nailed to bottom. Feet are shaped extensions of side and front framing. Hinges and drawer handles replaced.

203 x 152 x 43.5 cm (79⅞ x 59⅞ x 17⅛″)

Gift of J. Stogdell Stokes. 28-10-76

---

9   HANGING CUPBOARD
Lancaster County
1772

Inscribed on front in inlay: *17   72*

Walnut, sulphur inlay; pine, cedar. Frame and panel construction with pegged open mortise and tenon joints. Horizontal pieces have T-shaped tenons. Backboards tongue in groove. Door has raised panel in ovolo-molded frame. Knob on wood dowel an old addition. Drawer front joined to sides in three dovetails, four in back; bottom feathered into sides and front, nailed at back. Drawer has wood spring lock released through finger hole in framing. Bottom front of drawer repaired. Side boards extended with carved scrolled edges to support shelf with molded edge. Two interior shelves have rounded edges. Wrought iron escutcheon. H hinges not original.

83.7 x 45.7 x 30 cm (33 x 18 x 11⅞″)

Titus C. Geesey Collection. 53-125-9

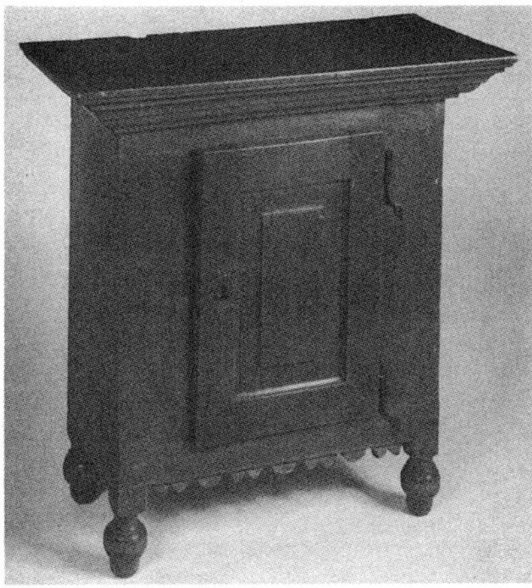

10

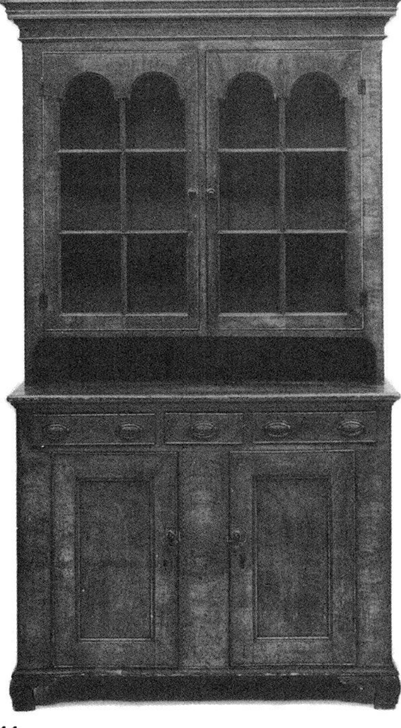

11

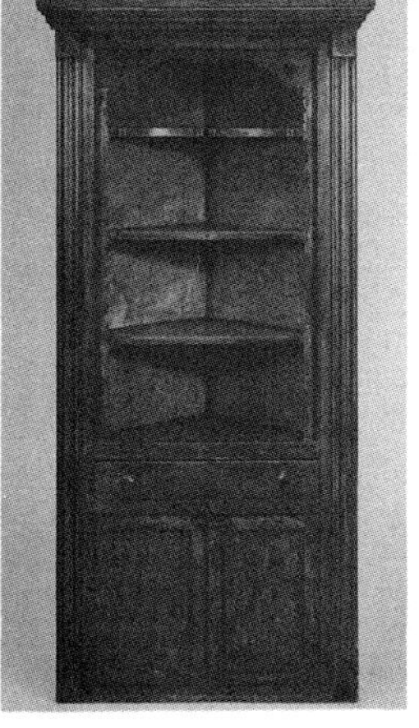

12

10 CUPBOARD
1780–1800

Marked on bottom: *AA*

Painted pine; oak. Plank construction. Sides and back butted and nailed tongue in groove. Sides joined to top in open dovetail. Bead-edged backboards splined together. Bottom let into grooves in sides. Door has pegged mortise and tenon frame with raised panel. Wrought iron clenched spike and pintle hinges with extended props. Escutcheon replaced; original was a wood knob and swivel. Turned oak feet nailed from inside through bottom, probably not original. Originally wall-mounted cupboard with shelf below. Painted red.

76.2 x 70.8 x 35.3 cm (30 x 27⅞ x 13⅞")

Titus C. Geesey Collection. 69-284-17

11 CUPBOARD
Montgomery County
1780–1815

Marked inside right glass door: *1815 Jones*

Painted poplar; pine; glass. Shaped, molded plank construction, pegged joints. Diagonal reed molding under cornice. Glass panes set in molded muntins. Doors and three drawers have beaded edges. Lower doors inset with panels in ovolo-molded and pegged mortise and tenon frame. One interior shelf. Chamfered corners upper and lower units. Flat surfaces painted: lower unit in brick red on tan to simulate wood graining; upper unit in red on yellow. Feet and base molding green. Brass drawer pulls, butt hinges. Top base lock, escutcheon, and plate rails missing.

213 x 121 x 52.3 cm (83⅞ x 47⅝ x 20⅝")

Purchased: Annual Membership Fund. 16-274

12 CORNER CUPBOARD
Probably Bucks County
1790–1800

Pine; poplar. One unit. Plank, frame and panel construction, pegged and nailed. Overlapping butt joint center back. Rope-carved gadroon under molded cornice; pilasters terminate in rosette-carved blocks; plain base. Inset bead-edged shelves, top shelf is replacement. Scalloped facing and heart valance probably not original. Door panels inset into quirked ovolo-molded frame with beaded edge. Looped wire hinges, turned wood pulls. Traces of red paint remain.

202.5 x 98.4 x 70.5 cm (79¾ x 38¾ x 27¾")

Titus C. Geesey Collection. 54-85-75

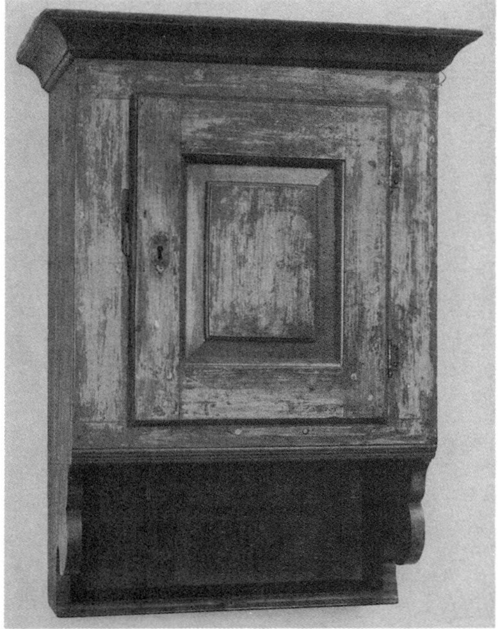

13

13 HANGING CUPBOARD
1792

Inscribed on backboard: *17 • 92*

Painted pine. Plank, panel and frame construction, butt, mortise and tenon joints. Front boards meet sides in pegged butt joint. Sides extended into scroll-carved support for recessed shelf with molded edge. Door panel set into ovolo-molded frame in pegged mortise and tenon construction. Wrought iron butt hinges, shaped escutcheon. One interior shelf. Remnants of red paint.

45 x 57.1 x 31 cm (17½ x 22½ x 12″)

Titus C. Geesey Collection. 54-85-120

14 CUPBOARD
Mount Joy, Lancaster County
1800–1830

Painted poplar, pine; glass. Two units. Plank, panel and frame construction. Bottom of base unit dovetailed to sides. Vertical backboards have beaded tongue in groove joints. Framing of base, top, and doors is pegged mortise and tenon. Diagonal reeding carved under molded cornice. Edge and loop-carved moldings applied on base, incised on upper unit. Pinwheel carving on center stiles. Splayed bracket feet. Upper shelves have plate grooves and slots for cutlery. One shelf in base unit. Underpainted in orange, then green yellow, and partially overpainted with red. Interior painted orange. Wrought iron butt hinges, brass pulls.

216.5 x 152.4 x 52.1 cm (85¼ x 60 x 20½″)

Titus C. Geesey Collection. 55-45-8a,b

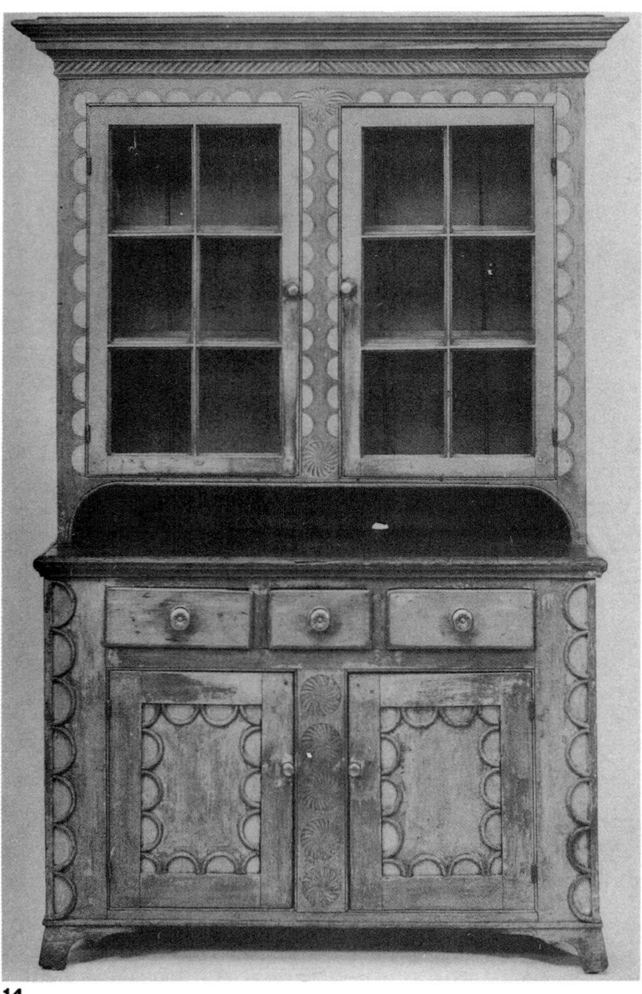

14

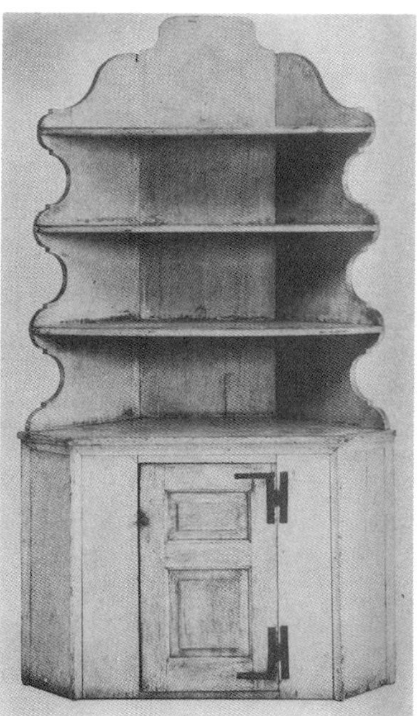

15

15 CORNER CUPBOARD
c. 1820

Painted yellow pine, poplar. Shaped and molded heavy plank construction joined with wood pegs and nails. Lock replaced with wood knob and swivel catch. Moldings pegged and nailed. One interior shelf. Gray paint over painted oak graining.

208 x 190 x 48.9 cm (81¾ x 74¾ x 19¼")

Purchased: Subscription and Museum Funds. 23-23-66

16 CUPBOARD
Zimmerman's Town (Pittman),
Mahantango Valley, Schuylkill County
1830

Michael Brown

Inscribed on front of lower unit:
1830 CONCORTIA CONCORTIA

Painted poplar, pine; pine. Two units in frame, plank and panel construction, pegged blind mortise and tenon joints. Compound cornice of quirked ovolo and scotia moldings. Fluted quarter columns with Doric capitals, bases, and lamb's tongue chamfers. Upper backboards tongue in groove, center board split. Two interior shelves upper, one lower. Raised bead on drawer edges. Mitered compound molding top edge of base unit. Inset panels, wrought iron hinges, replaced pulls on lower doors. Base molding and scrolled ogee bracket feet. Painted yellow pink under wheel-patterned mottling in red. Upper doors cream with red stars, blue green at center. White interior has been repainted. Base drawer and door panels painted cream with designs in red, blue green, and yellow, borders blue green. Inscription stenciled and bordered in yellow on blue green.

211.5 x 167.6 x 85.1 cm (83¼ x 66 x 33½")

Titus C. Geesey Collection. 54-85-32a,b

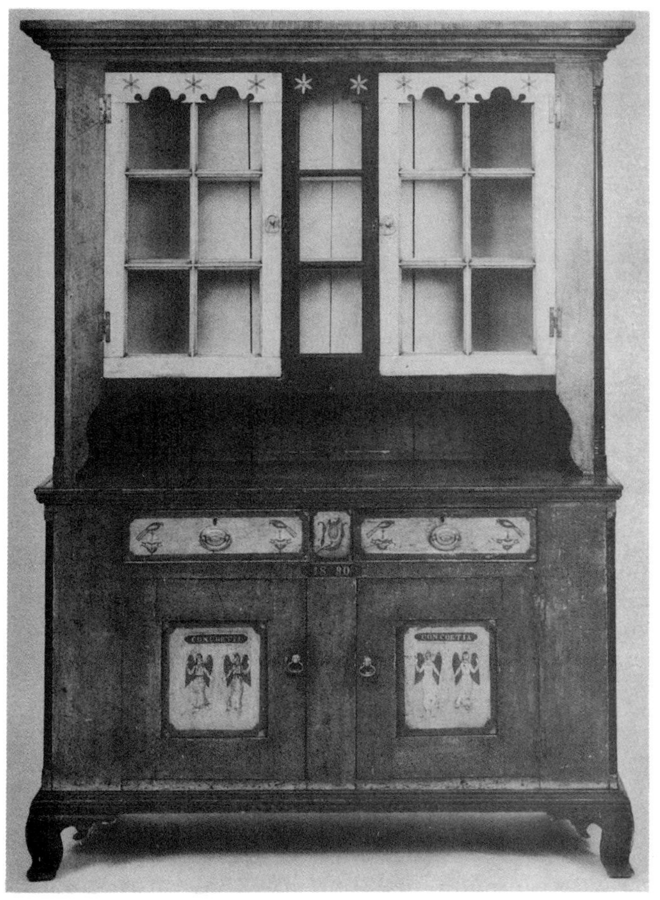

16

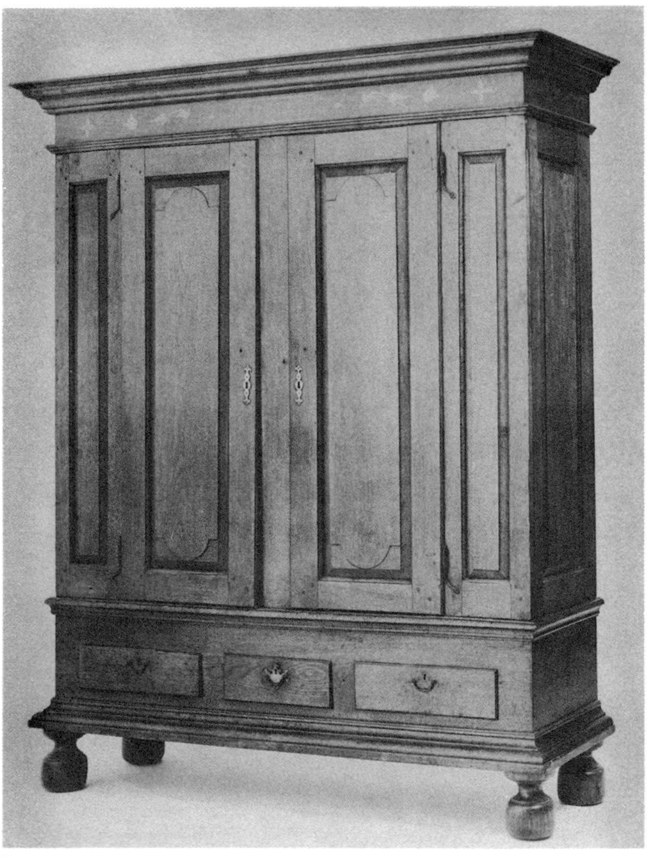

1

1 WARDROBE
Lancaster County
1775

Inscribed on front in inlay: *17 •PT •BR •75*

Walnut, maple inlay. Three demountable units of cornice, cupboard, drawers. Frame and panel construction with pegged butt and mortise and tenon joints. Two doors with single raised carved arch panels, top and bottom, are suspended from end units with single vertical raised panels. Doors swing from spike hinges with extended props. Backboards in tongue in groove joints. Base unit has three drawers in dovetail construction. Replaced brass handles. Restored feet.

194.3 x 180.3 x 55.9 cm (76½ x 71 x 22″)

Purchased: Special Museum Fund. 16-332

2 WARDROBE
Manheim and Warwick townships, Lancaster County
1779

Attributed to **Peter Holl** and **Christian Huber**

Inscribed on front in inlay: *GEORG HUBER ANNO 1779*

Black walnut, sulphur inlay; poplar, pine, oak, iron. Three demountable units of cornice, cupboard, and drawers tenoned and pegged together. Four sides in frame and panel construction with mortise and tenon joints. Sides join front in pegged butt joints, stepped out drawer unit is dovetailed. Extended cornice with Doric soffit in rectangular units of eighteen mutules (three by six) alternating with rectangular sunken molded panels. Carved dentil meander fret over cyma and bolection molded frieze. Front frame has intaglio-carved vertical panels and relief-carved fleurs-de-lis in four corners of four front door panels. Side panels are relief-carved with fleurs-de-lis and centered six-pointed star. Cupboard unit is set into deep scotia molding of base unit. Drawers have overlapping molded edges, dovetail construction at four corners. Drawer bottoms tenoned into front boards meeting overlapping sides in butt joint. Feet are old replacements. Vertical interior divider with hanging hooks and pegs. Wrought iron spike and pintle hinges with

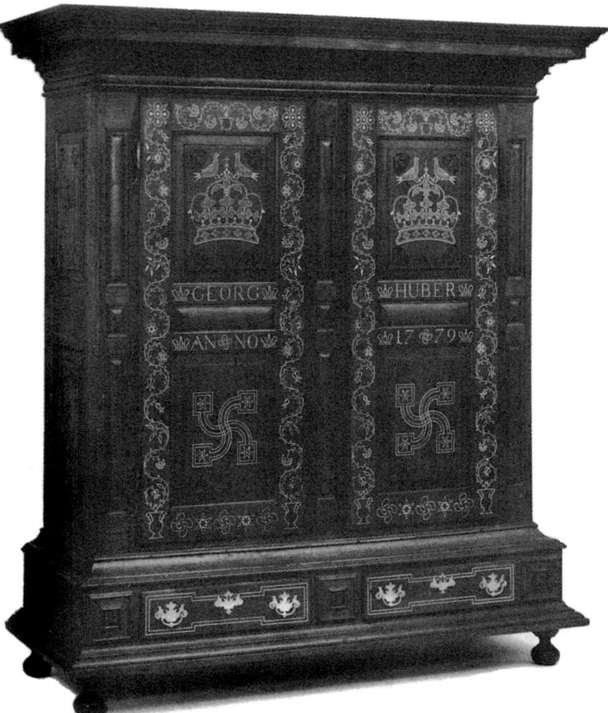

2

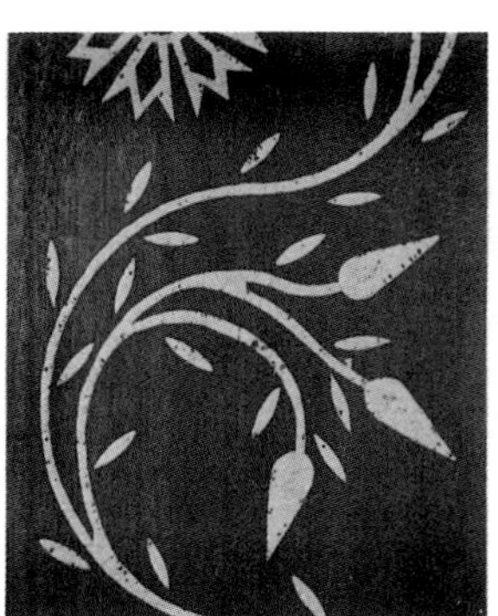

2 detail

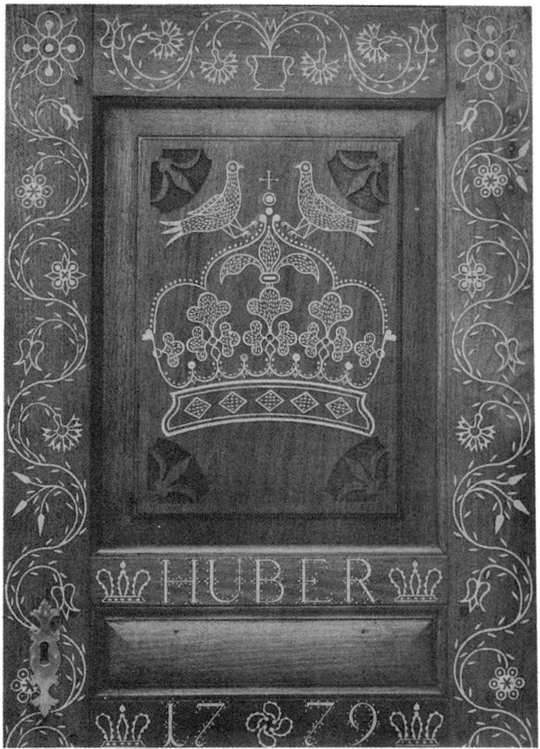

2 detail

extended props, escutcheons. Brass drawer hardware old replacements. The carved dentil molding, elaborate cornice, and carved fleurs-de-lis against a stippled background were adapted from a plate from an architectural design book, possibly Giacomo Barozzi Vignola's *Cinque ordini d'architettura*, published in a German edition as the *Civil-Baukunst*, in Augsburg in 1759, illustrated with French plates, which shows the exact details found on this wardrobe. The motifs, inlaid with sulphur on the wardrobe, were adapted from patterns used extensively by linen-damask weavers working in Switzerland and Strasbourg in Alsace and were probably brought to Lancaster County.

Purchased near Neffsville by Lydia Davis Garber Hunsecker (Mrs. Peter; 1813–1903) to Mary Rebecca Hunsecker Hostetter (Mrs. Jacob Henry; 1851–1922) to Adele Hostetter Hershey (Mrs. Hiram F.) to Ruth Hershey Irion (Mrs. Louis A.).

211 x 198.2 x 69.8 cm (83⅛ x 78 x 27½")

Purchased. 57-30-1

---

3 CABINET
Lancaster County
1780–1800

Marked on bottom of center drawer in pencil: *zin*[?]

Cherry, maple inlay; pine, sugar pine; glass. Cabinet over drawers built in two units. Plank and frame construction with pegged blind mortise and tenon joints. Muntins molded and curved in arched doors. Pediment has applied, carved daisy volutes; striated, carved tulip finials; applied, carved shell center top. Feet carved from solid. Inset, chamfered corners with lamb's tongue top and bottom of both units. Drawer edges overlap case and have three dovetails front and back, molded top edges, bottoms feathered and let into sides and front; drawers run on extensions of sides. Inlay of tulips in a pot on skirt.

248.2 x 100.3 x 54.6 cm (97¾ x 39½ x 21½")

Titus C. Geesey Collection. 54-85-26a,b

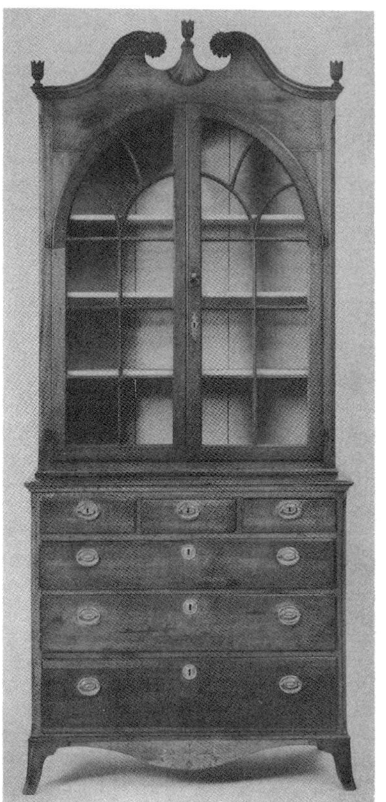

3

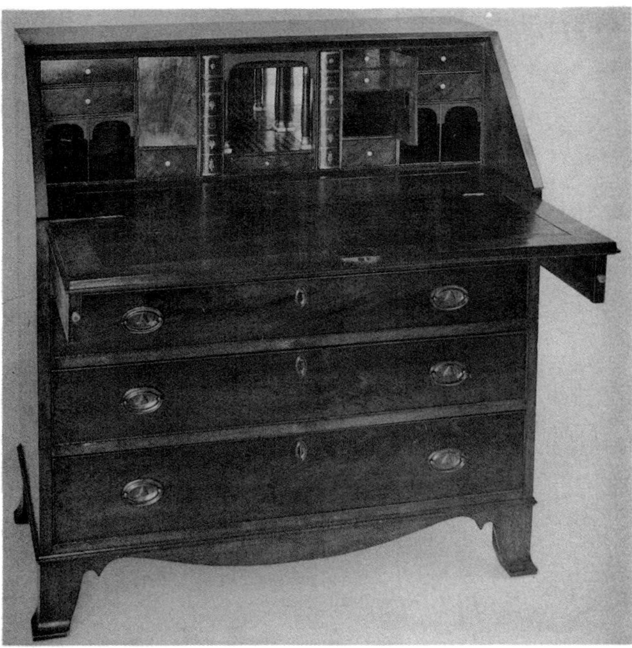

4

4 DESK

Northampton County
c. 1790

Jacob Bachman

Inscribed on bottom: *Jacob Bachman*
Marked: *Waschingtons Leben 1 Waschingtons
Leben 11*

Cherry, cherry and mahogany veneer; walnut,
poplar, leather, ivory; mirror glass. Plank and
tenon construction. Sides dovetailed to bottom.
Top joins sides in mitered rabbet. Drawer rails
and runners tenoned into sides and glued.
Backboards joined in tongue in groove and
nailed in a rabbet. Bracket feet have glued
blocks. Drawers of cherry, dovetail
construction, veneered fronts with molded
bead strip nailed. Edges of lid joined in tongue
in groove, front veneered with oval. Interior
drawer pulls ivory; brass drawer pulls
replaced. Lid, drawer fronts, and feet
mahogany veneer. Interior doors cherry
veneer. Faux-livre drawers have gold tooling
on red leather and flank mirrored compartment
with floor painted blue green and white; black
columns have gilded bases. Tambour door
pulls down over compartment and drawers.

114.5 x 106.5 x 56 cm (45 x 41⅞ x 22″)

Gift of Mrs. Walter J. Kohler. 63-103-1

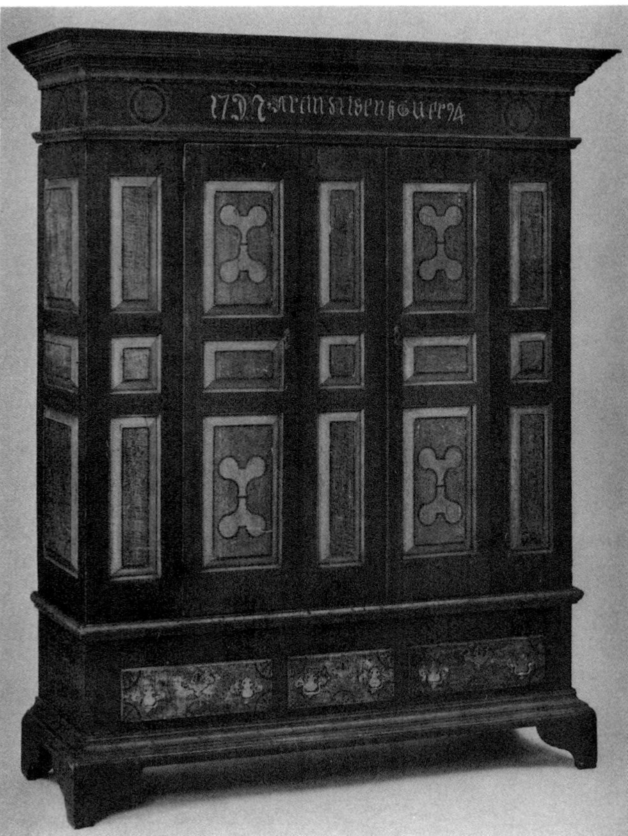

5

5 WARDROBE

Greenwich Township, Berks County
1794

Inscribed below cornice: *17 Martin
Eisenhauer 94*

Painted pine; poplar. Built in three
demountable units. Pegged panel and frame
construction. Four backboards have beaded
edge, tongue in groove joints. Cornice section
receives tenons of back, sides, and front frame.
Cupboard section set into molding on base unit
which has three drawers over straight bracket
feet braced with corner blocks. Dovetail
corners in cornice and base, and in drawer
construction three front and back. Cupboard
has pegged mortise and tenon joints sides and
front and is in six pieces secured with wedge
pegs. Painted gray blue ground. Cornice and
drawer designs compass-inscribed in black.
End and front panels painted ivory with
stippling and outlining in ground color, panel
bevels and hearts stippled in red. Moldings
red, inscription white. Wrought iron hinges,
locks; brass pulls, escutcheons (one replaced).

204.5 x 159.7 x 50.2 cm (80½ x 62⅞ x 19¾″)

Purchased: Annual Membership Fund. 16-413

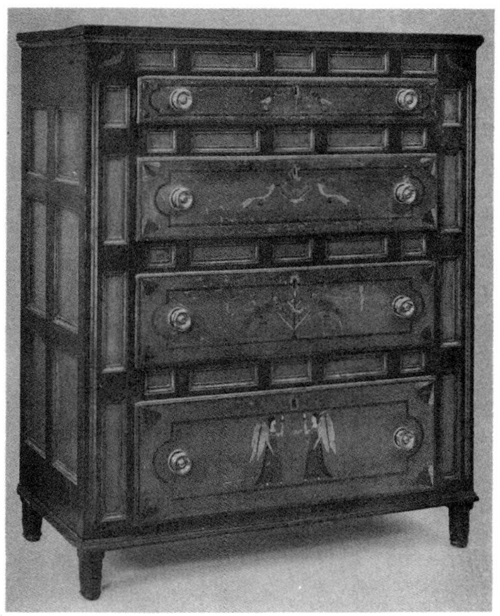

6

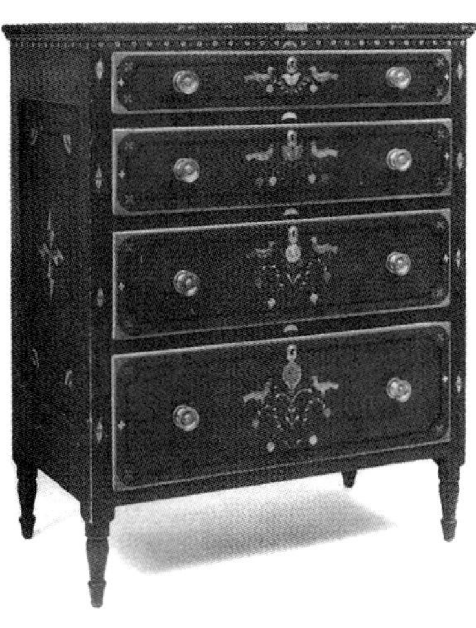

7

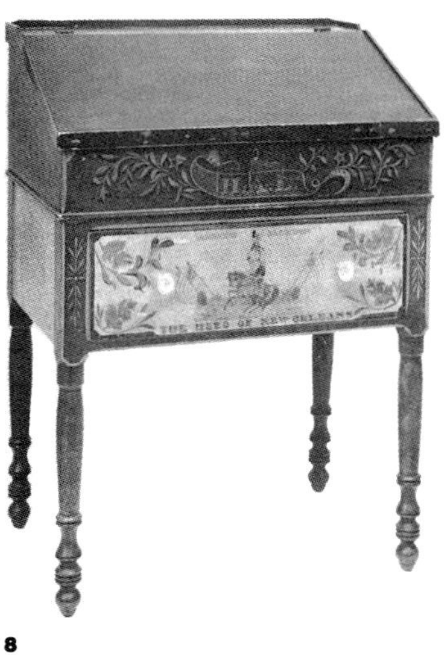

8

6   CHEST OF DRAWERS
Zimmerman's Town (Pittman),
Mahantango Valley, Schuylkill County
c. 1820

Painted poplar; pine, cedar. Solid frame and panel construction with pegged mortise and tenon joints. Side and front vertical panels inset. Horizontal panels between drawers carved from solid. Drawers overlap frame. Cavetto molding at top, scotia molding with bead around base. Turned legs tenon into corner posts. Plain brass pulls; escutcheons missing. Frame painted dark green, panels and drawers red. Designs and figures green and yellow.

130 x 111 x 50.3 cm (51⅛ x 43¾ x 19¾")

From the Clarence W. Brazer Collection.
25-96-1

7   CHEST OF DRAWERS
Zimmerman's Town (Pittman),
Mahantango Valley, Schuylkill County
1820–40
Jacob Maser

Painted pine, poplar. Frame and panel construction, pegged mortise and tenon joints. Corner posts extended into turned legs. Drawers overlap frame. Applied cyma reversa molding at top. Frame painted blue green with yellow green end panels and drawers. Florets at top stenciled or stamped. Black banding, yellow and red designs with ivory half moons between drawers. Stippling and dotting on birds and stems.

132.1 x 110.5 x 58.4 cm (52 x 43½ x 23")

From the A. H. Rice Collection. 25-68-1

8   DESK
c. 1827

Inscribed on front: *H.A.L. E. Pluribus Unum   Andrew Jackson   The Hero of New Orleans*

Painted pine, poplar, cherry. Frame and plank construction with dovetail joints in desk section, mortise and tenon in drawer section. Box has brown graining over red; painted with freehand yellow and black foliage and inscription. Sloped lid has nailed raised edge; painted black. Unpainted interior has three compartments over center drawer. Desk drawer has four dovetails front, three back, bottom let into sides and front; painted tan with figure in black and red, horse brown and red, flags red, white, and blue, floral sprays green, frame black, stenciled gold designs and lettering. Legs turned in vase and ring design, painted red.

104.2 x 76.2 x 52.1 cm (41 x 30 x 20½")

Titus C. Geesey Collection. 54-85-98

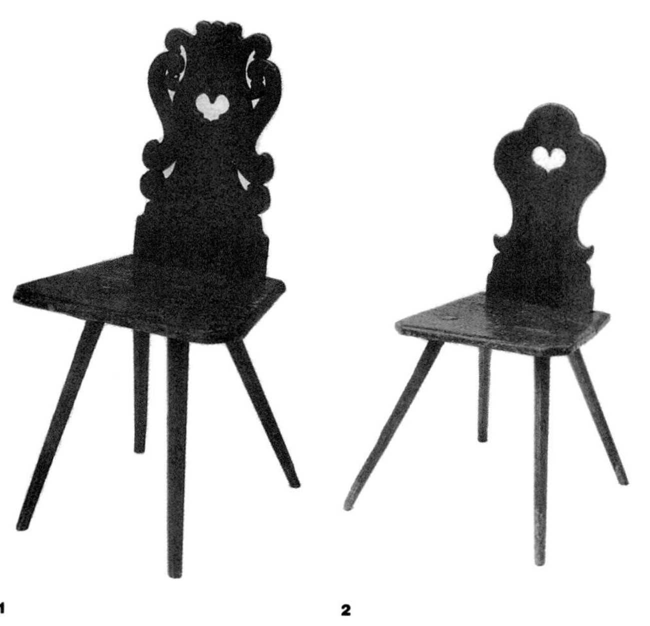

1   2

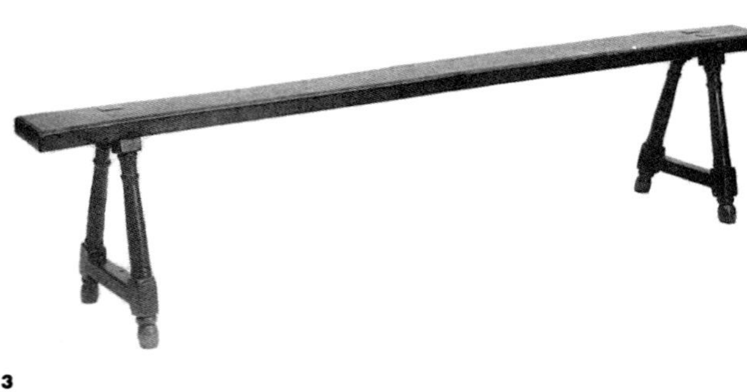

3

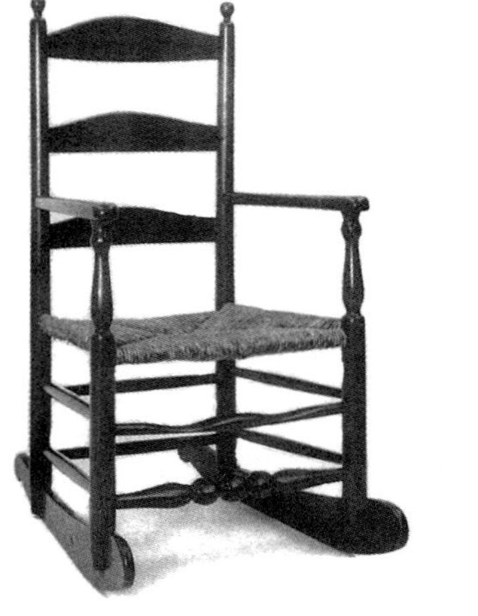

4

1 BACK STOOL
Lebanon County
c. 1750

Pine, poplar, oak; maple. Plank construction with pegged tenon joints. Faceted, tapered, splayed legs tenoned and wedged through maple battens that join seat in keyed dovetail. Scrolled and pierced back, slightly raked, tenoned through seat and battens and cleated.

90.5 x 48 x 36.5 cm (35⅝ x 18⅞ x 14⅜")

Gift of J. Stogdell Stokes. 28-10-65

2 BACK STOOL
Lehigh County
c. 1750

Oak. Plank construction with pegged tenon joints. Shaped and pierced back plank tenoned through seat and pegged. Keyed dovetail battens under seat. Four faceted, tapering, splayed legs tenoned through battens and seat plank and wedged.

88 x 45.5 x 35.5 cm (34⅝ x 17⅞ x 14")

Gift of J. Stogdell Stokes. 28-10-66

3 PAIR OF BENCHES (LONG FORMS)
c. 1750

Black walnut. Shaped and molded seat plank. Turned, splayed legs tenoned through seat. Stretchers secured with pegged mortise and tenon joints.

53 x 233 x 16.1 cm (20⅞ x 91¾ x 6⅜")

Gift of J. Stogdell Stokes. 35-36-1a,b

4 ROCKING ARMCHAIR
1750–60

Walnut. Tenon construction. Turned front posts and back stiles. Shaped arms tenoned and pegged into stiles. Arch top and bent back slats are tenoned and pegged into stiles. Eight turned stretchers; lower front has three ball turnings and tapered terminals. Legs pegged to rockers shaped with upward curve at front, downward scroll at back. Woven flag seat.

102.7 x 57.4 x 76 cm (40⅜ x 22⅝ x 29⅞")

Titus C. Geesey Collection. 69-284-16

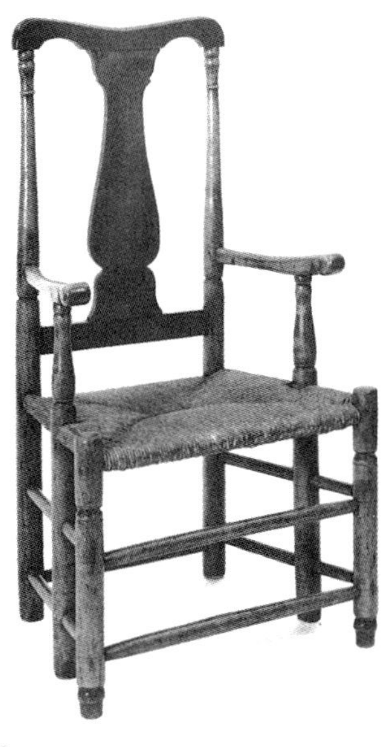

5

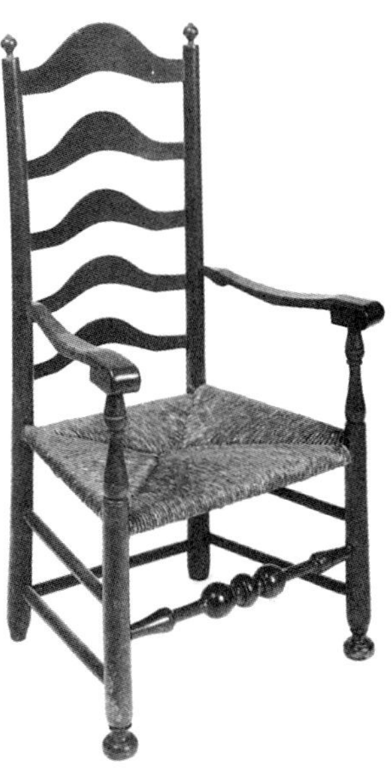

6

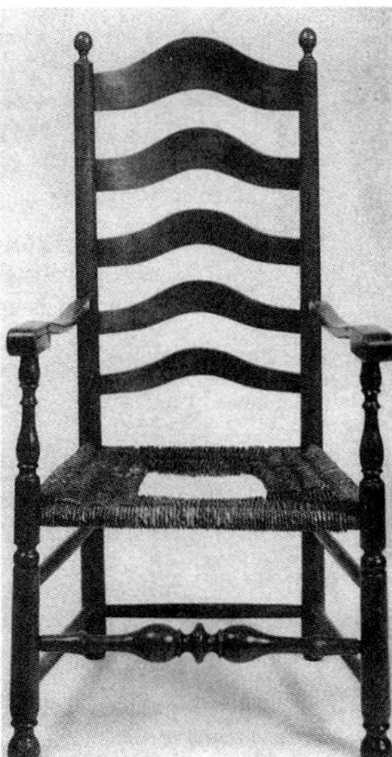

7

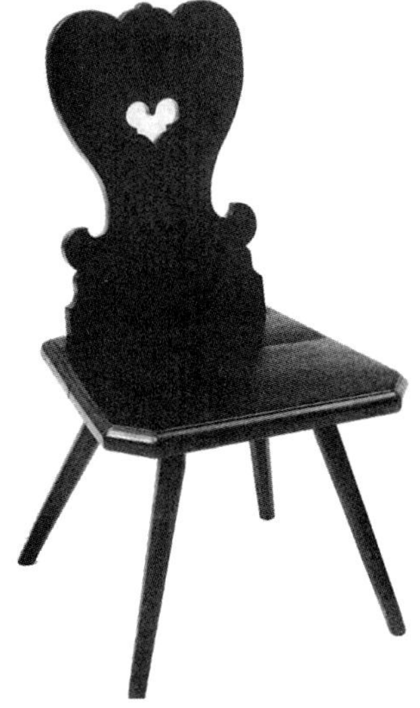

8

5 ARMCHAIR
Berks County
1750–70

Maple, poplar, cherry. Pegged tenon construction. Six turned maple legs; middle legs extend to support carved arms in pegged tenon joint. Side seat rails and side stretchers tenoned through middle leg and into front leg and back stile. Vase-shaped poplar splat tenoned into crossbar and cherry crest rail. Turned stiles tenoned into crest rail and pegged. Front feet added. Evidence of rockers. Woven flag seat.

106.7 x 58.4 x 44.5 cm (42 x 23 x 17½")

Titus C. Geesey Collection. 69-284-23

6 ARMCHAIR
1750–80

Painted maple, hickory. Tenon construction. Front legs, feet, and arm posts turned from single piece. Six stretchers; front has carrot terminals, ball turnings. Carved armrests tenoned into stiles and pegged. Back slats bent and arched top and bottom, tenoned into stiles, top rung pegged from back. Tapered back feet. Red brown paint. Flag seat on hickory rails.

114.2 x 59.6 x 48.2 cm (45 x 23½ x 19")

Titus C. Geesey Collection. 69-284-14

7 ARMCHAIR
1750–80

Cherry. Tenon construction. Front legs, feet, and arm posts in one piece, with ball and vase turnings. Six stretchers; front has carrot terminals, double vase and disk turning. Carved arm supports tenoned and pegged into stiles. Five back slats arched and bent, tenoned into stiles, top slat pegged through back. Tapered back feet and egg-shaped finials on back stiles. Woven flag seat supported commode pot.

113.3 x 61.5 x 42 cm (44⅝ x 24¼ x 16½")

Titus C. Geesey Collection. 69-284-15

8 BACK STOOL
Bethlehem, Lehigh County
1750–80

Inscribed on back: *K   MB*
Marked under seat: *K   MB*

Walnut; oak. Plank construction. Plank seat has molded edge, keyed oak battens underneath. Back tenoned through seat and cleated. Octagonal tapered legs tenoned through batten and seat and wedged.

79.7 x 45.1 x 45.1 cm (31⅜ x 17¾ x 17¾")

Gift of Miss May Audubon Post. 30-44-2

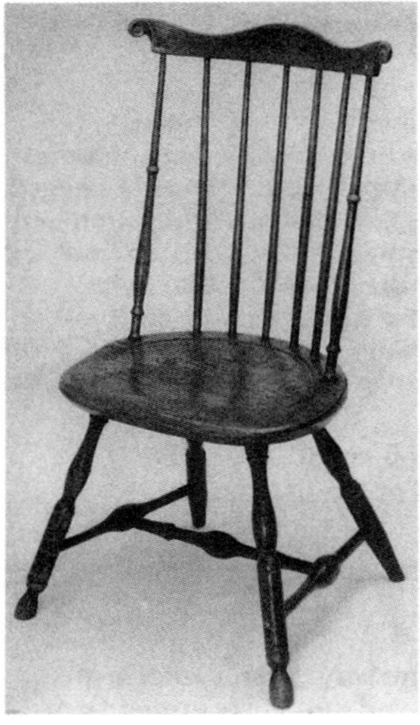

9

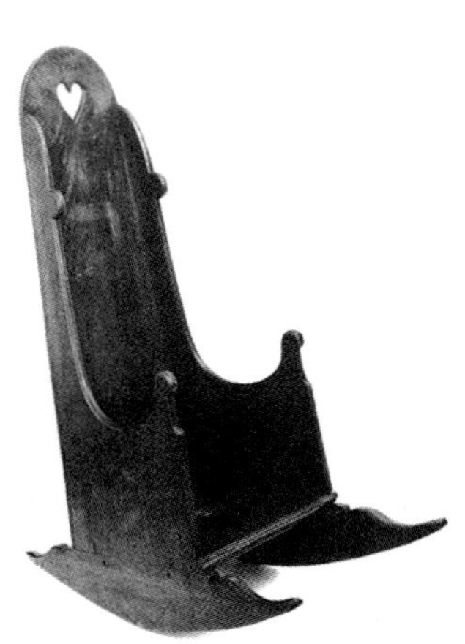

10

9 SIDE CHAIR
Lancaster County
1760–80

Painted maple, poplar, hickory. Wedged tenon construction. Carved oval seat. Turned, splayed legs tenoned through seat and wedged. Front legs have turned feet, back legs tapered. Side and cross stretchers tenoned and pegged. Five turned hickory spindles tenoned into seat and into bent, shaped crest rail and pegged. Turned, raked side posts tenoned through seat and wedged. Painted blue green over gray over red brown.

88.9 x 53.3 x 43.2 cm (35 x 21 x 17")

Titus C. Geesey Collection. 54-85-29

---

10 CHILD'S COMMODE CHAIR
1760–1800

Black walnut. Plank construction, pegged and nailed joints. Shaped side planks tenoned and pegged into rockers. Pot probably suspended from wide rim.

78.7 x 36.8 x 59.7 cm (31 x 14½ x 23½")

Titus C. Geesey Collection. 55-45-10

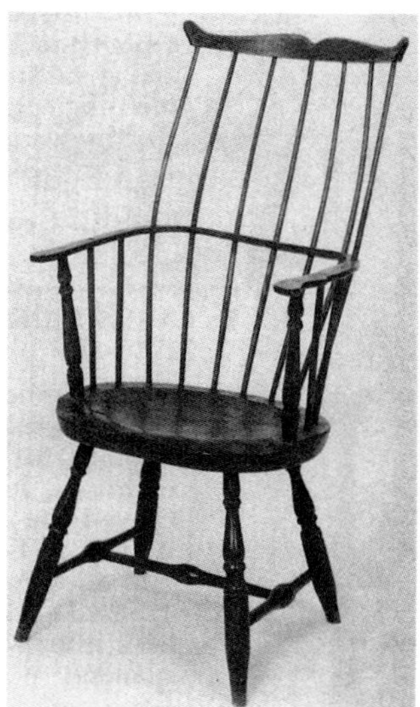

11

11 ARMCHAIR
Lancaster County
1770–80

Painted pine, maple, hickory. Tenon and wedge construction. Carved pine seat. Turned, splayed legs and arm posts tenoned through seat and wedged. Carved and bent crest rail; carved armrests spliced into back support. Back spindles tenoned into seat, through back support, and into crest rail and pegged. Side spindles tenoned into seat, through arm supports and wedged. Painted dark blue green.

109.2 x 55.9 x 43.2 cm (43 x 22 x 17")

Titus C. Geesey Collection. 54-85-28

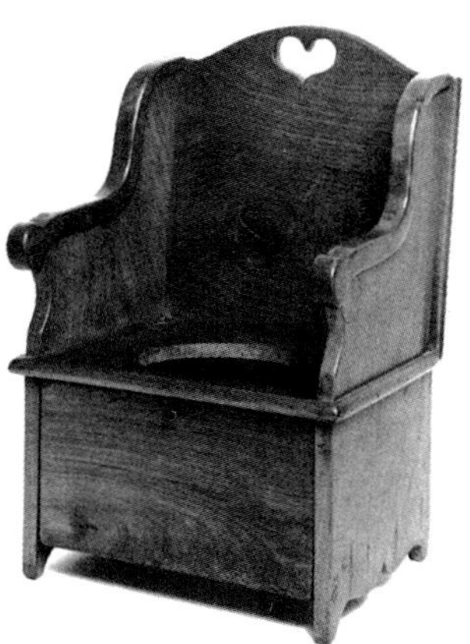

12

12 CHILD'S COMMODE CHAIR
1770–1800

Black walnut. Carved and shaped plank construction. Lap joints nailed and screwed. Lower front panel pivots on dowels set into sides. Pot missing.

53 x 33 x 28.5 cm (20⅞ x 13 x 11¼")

Gift of J. Stogdell Stokes. 37-42-1

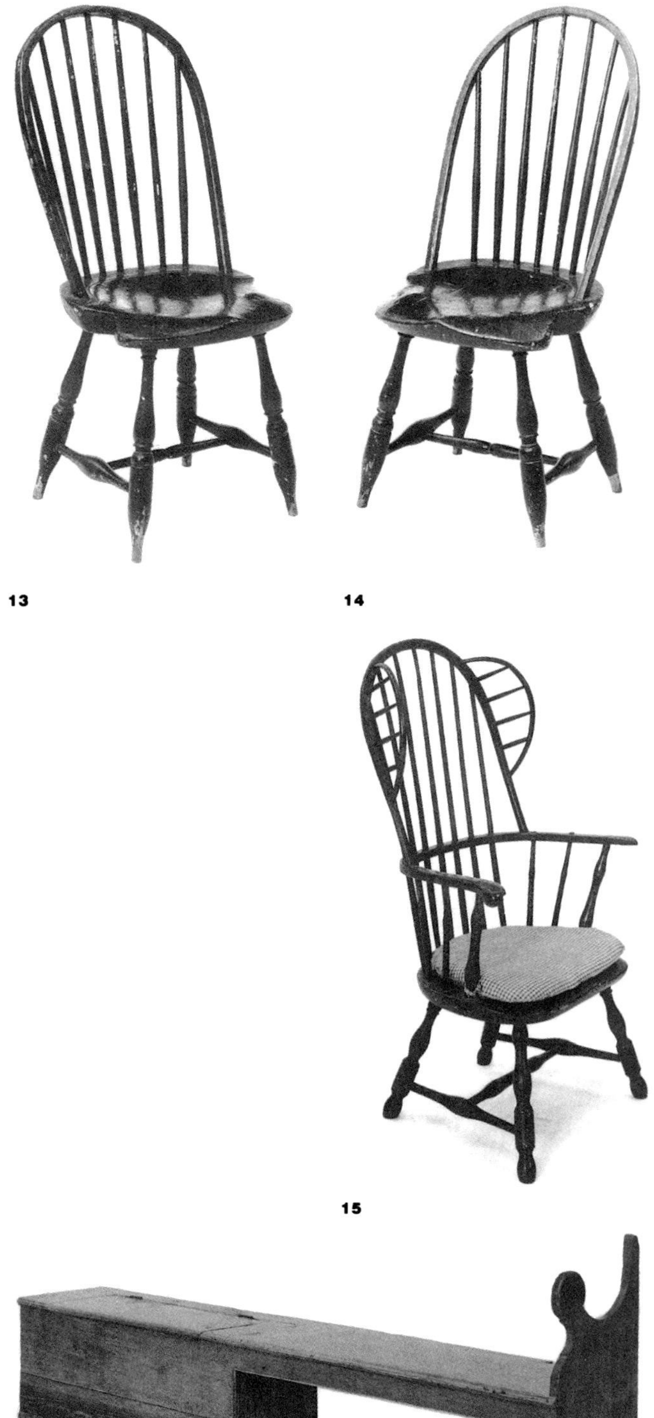

13

14

15

16

13 SIDE CHAIR
Lancaster County
1770–1800

Painted poplar, maple, oak. Bentwood, wedged
and pegged tenon construction. Splayed,
turned legs, with three stretchers, are tenoned
through carved seat and wedged. Ends of
hooped back tenoned through seat and
wedged. Turned spindles tenoned into seat
and into bow of the back and pegged. Painted
dark red brown and varnished.

91.4 x 40.6 x 38.1 cm (36 x 16 x 15")

Titus C. Geesey Collection. 54-85-96

14 SIDE CHAIR
Lancaster County
1770–1800

See chair no. 13.

90.2 x 41.3 x 31.8 cm (35½ x 16¼ x 12½")

Titus C. Geesey Collection. 54-85-97

15 ARMCHAIR
1770–1800

Painted poplar, maple, oak, hickory. Wedged
and pegged tenon construction. Turned legs
and arm posts tenoned through shaped seat
and wedged. Back spindles tenoned into seat,
through curved back support, into bowed
cresting, and nailed from back. Wing spindles
and frame tenoned through bow back and
wedged. Seat had been fitted for a chamber
pot. Painted brown.

107.8 x 58.8 x 46.9 cm (42½ x 23⅛ x 18½")

Titus C. Geesey Collection. 58-110-15

16 BENCH WITH BIN
1770–1800

Painted pine. Plank construction with wedged
tenon joints. Shaped end plank receives
molded-edge seat plank in two wedged tenons,
front board gained into top and nailed.
Woodbin at end has nailed butt joints. Base
molding mitered. Blue over red paint.

78.7 x 243.8 x 39.3 cm (31 x 96 x 15½")

Titus C. Geesey Collection. 55-45-5

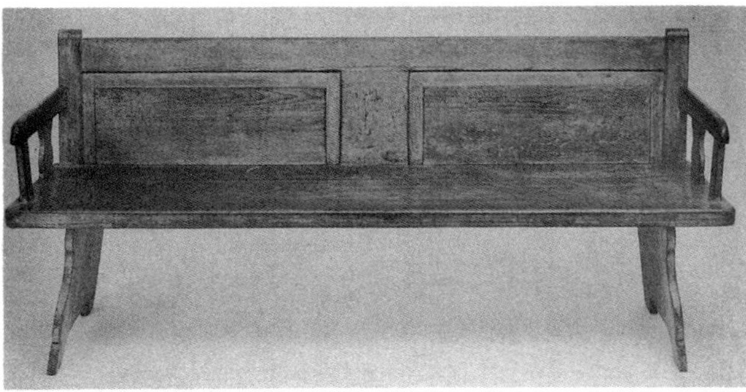

17

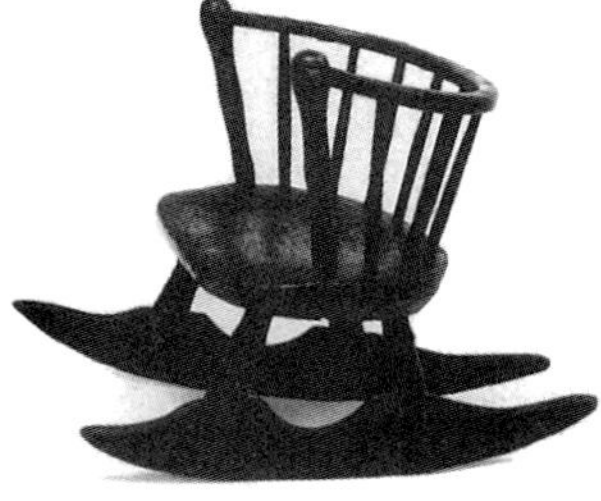

18

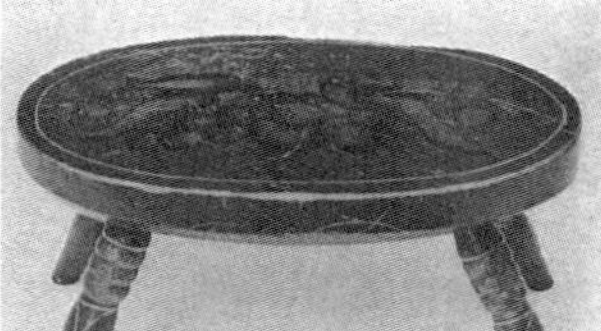

21

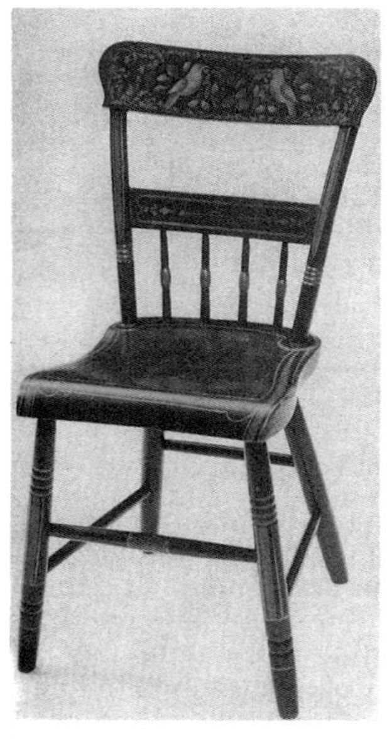

19

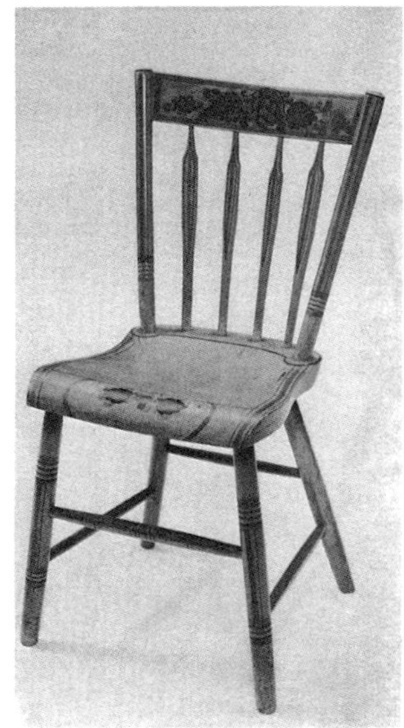

20

17 **SETTEE**
Cocalico Township, Lancaster County
1780–1800

Pine. Frame and panel construction with pegged mortise and tenon joints. Shaped plank legs tenoned through seat and wedged. Shaped arm supports tenoned through seat and into armrests; front supports pegged. Raised panel back. Found in Slackwater area.

82.5 x 183 x 55.2 cm (32½ x 72 x 21¾")

Titus C. Geesey Collection. 55-45-6

18 **CHILD'S ROCKING CHAIR**
c. 1800

Poplar, maple, hickory. Spindle back, carved seat. Curved back rail tenoned into front posts. Splayed legs tenoned into seat, cut for rockers, and pegged.

41 x 37.1 x 57.7 cm (16 x 14⅝ x 22¾")

Gift of Mrs. William D. Frishmuth. 09-103

19 **SIDE CHAIR**
Bucks County
1800–1840

Painted maple, poplar. Wedged tenon, pegged and glued joints. Legs, back spindles, and stiles tenoned into shaped seat. Back rail tenoned into stiles and pegged; shaped crest rail. Ring turnings on legs and stiles. Painted brown with designs in green and red over gold, touches of copper bronze.

69.2 x 45.1 x 38.1 cm (27¼ x 17¾ x 15")

Titus C. Geesey Collection. 58-110-17

20 **SIDE CHAIR**
Lancaster County
1810–40

Marked under seat: *MIXX*

Painted poplar, maple. Wedged tenon and glued joints. Arrow spindles tenoned into shaped seat and curved crest rail. Stiles tenoned through seat and wedged. Legs tenoned into seat. Ring-turned legs and stiles. Painted green yellow. Stenciled silver grapes, bronze leaves, green fillips with gray banding.

84.5 x 45.8 x 38.7 cm (33¼ x 18 x 15¼")

Titus C. Geesey Collection. 58-110-16

21 **FOOTSTOOL**
1820–40

Painted poplar, maple. Tenon construction. Shaped plank top, ring-turned legs tenoned and glued into top. Painted dark green. Stenciled designs in red, blue, silver, and gold; gray striping.

17.8 x 34.3 x 19 cm (7 x 13½ x 7½")

Titus C. Geesey Collection. 54-85-95

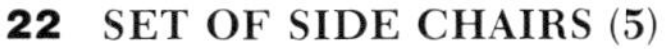

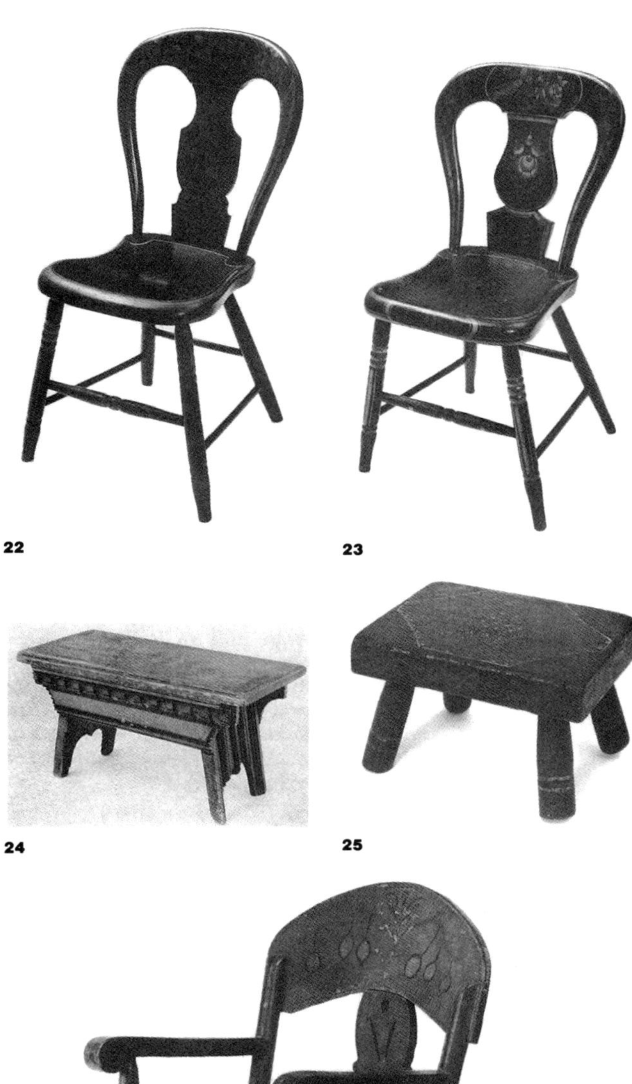

22

23

24

25

26

22 SET OF SIDE CHAIRS (5)
1830–40

Painted maple, poplar. Shaped plank, mortise and tenon construction. Hoop back and legs tenoned through carved seat. Flat vase-shaped back splat tenoned into seat and crest rail. Painted brown, stenciled flowers and fruit in red, green, silver, and bronze.

84.5 x 46.3 x 38.1 cm (33¼ x 18¼ x 15″)

Gift of R. Wistar Harvey. 40-16-78—82

23 SIDE CHAIR
c. 1840

Painted maple, poplar. Turned legs tenoned into shaped plank seat. Four stretchers tenoned and glued into legs, turned stiles tenoned through seat. Curved crest rail and flat lyre-shaped splat. Painted dark brown. Bird and floral motifs stenciled in red, green, and silver. Freehand striping.

84.5 x 46.3 x 38.1 cm (33¼ x 18¼ x 15″)

Gift of Mrs. Hampton L. Carson. 25-71-1

24 FOOTSTOOL
c. 1840

Inscribed on top: *A.B.G.*

Painted pine, cedar. Plank construction with butt joints. Edges molded and chip-carved, flat surfaces decorated with dentils and moldings. Painted yellow; black and red banding, red inscription.

24.1 x 44.5 x 22.2 cm (9½ x 17½ x 8¾″)

Titus C. Geesey Collection. 55-45-1

25 FOOTSTOOL
1840–80

Painted oak. Turned legs let into plank top. Painted dark green, red, yellow, and black.

18.5 x 22.8 x 17.1 cm (7¼ x 9 x 6¾″)

Gift of Mrs. Hampton L. Carson. 16-291

26 CHILD'S ROCKING CHAIR
1850–80

Painted pine, maple, ash. Shaped plank construction. Turned legs, back posts, and arm posts are tenoned, nailed, and screwed. Rockers nailed. Painted brown with freehand designs in black and green.

48.9 x 29.2 x 47 cm (19¼ x 11½ x 18½″)

Titus C. Geesey Collection. 58-110-43

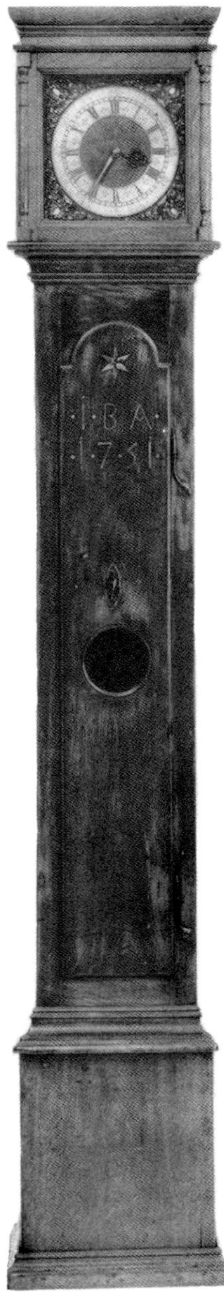

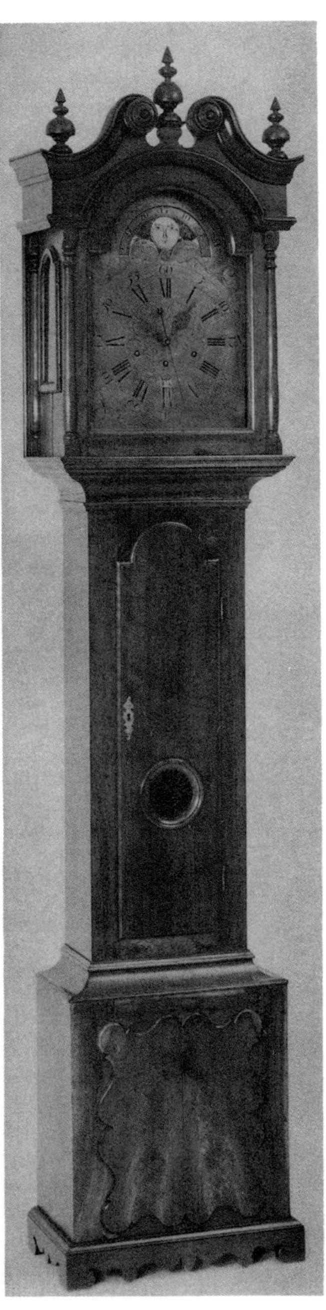

1 **TALL CASE CLOCK**
Lancaster County
1751

Inscribed on door in inlay: *·I ·B ·A ·*
·1 ·7 ·5 ·1 ·

Black walnut; holly, glass, brass, pewter, iron.
Case: Shaped and molded plank construction,
pegged and nailed. Square top with cornice
molding, three-quarter colonnettes in front,
one-quarter in back, rectangular side windows.
Wrought iron spike and pintle hinge with
extended prop, pointed elliptical escutcheon.
Dial: Square, painted iron dial with attached
pewter chapter ring and spandrels. Iron
minute and hour hands. Movement: Thirty-
hour brass-bushed iron-plate movement.
Plates separated by three squared, iron pillars
with extended, turned, and tapped ends
passing through front plate to carry the dial.
Two iron brackets and two iron spikes permit
movement to be suspended from two hooks on
the case backboard. Open-ended wire pinions.
Anchor recoil escapement with open-ended
crutch fork. Two-piece iron pendulum
suspension cock, with thread loop, riveted to
back plate. Two-rope pull up. Pulleys with
ratchet wheels have tailless ratchet clicks.
Rack-and-snail striking with rack hook locking
and separate repeat-on-demand lever. Similar
to movements made by Friedrich Mollinger of
Mannheim, Germany, and George Hoff, Sr., of
Lancaster, Pennsylvania.

203 x 42 x 27.3 cm (80 x 16½ x 10¾")

Gift of J. Stogdell Stokes. 35-36-3

2 **TALL CASE CLOCK**
Cocalico Township, Lancaster County
1763–70

Jacob Gorgas

Inscribed on dial: *Jacob Gorgas Near Ephrata*

Cherry; pine, walnut, brass, iron. Case: Frame
and plank construction. Molded scrolled
bonnet with turned walnut finials. Engaged
three-quarter colonnettes at front, one-quarter
at back. Pendulum door overlaps case.
Scalloped edge decorative panel at base in two
pieces (mirror) of crotch-grained cherry is
glued to case. Mahogany feet and base molding
old restorations. Dial: Painted moon wheel
shows moon and sun with view of Ephrata
cloister. Square calendar aperture. Iron hour,
minute, and sweep-second hands. Movement:
Eight-day, sweep-second; three-train, musical,
brass movement with plates separated by
tapped and turned brass pillars extending
through front plate to carry the dial.

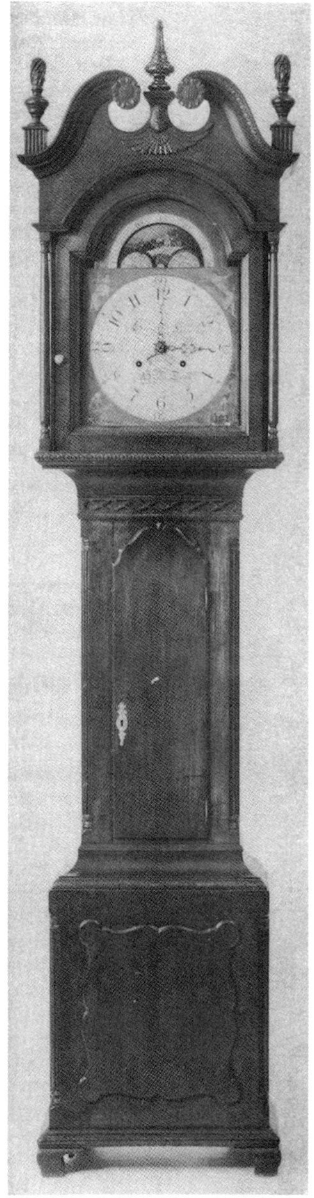

3

Common (single) train hour and quarter-hour strike. Rack-and-snail striking with rack hook locking. Quarter-hour strike indexed by four graduated lifting pins and stepped first through third rack teeth. Double-toothed gathering pallet. Five-tune brass musical pin barrel automatically shifted by a triskelion mounted on the second arbor which engages three pins of a combined pin wheel and contrate, five-step snail wheel. Hoop wheel locking. Selections: "God Save the King"; "Now Thank We All Our God"; "The Doxology"; and two unidentified tunes. Sequence: Hour struck by iron hammer on larger of two vertically nested bells; musical selection played by brass hammers on eleven horizontally nested bells; first-, second-, and third-quarter hours struck on vertically nested bells; then striking of next hour. Second of two iron hammers used in striking quarter-hours is engaged and disengaged by a cam and rocking lever. "Silence" lever for musical train missing. Anchor recoil escapement with closed crutch fork. English bridge pendulum suspension. Smooth cable drums with tailed ratchet wheel clicks on time and strike trains, tailless click on musical train.

241.3 x 57.1 x 29.8 cm (95 x 22½ x 11¾")

Titus C. Geesey Collection. 54-85-1a,b

---

3 TALL CASE CLOCK
Sumneytown, Montgomery County
1770–1800

George Faber

Cherry; poplar, brass. Case: Frame construction, molded, scrolled bonnet top. Carved egg and dart on scroll and bottom edge of works case. Stylized daisy rosettes applied. Turned finials. Carved winged head applied. Freestanding colonnettes at four corners. Carved tulip set over glass and into molded arch-topped frame of sidelights. Fluted quarter columns on pendulum case and base. Blind fret front and sides. Raised scallop-edged panel applied to base. Ogee bracket feet worn. Case stained plum red mahogany. Brass strap hinges. Escutcheon replaced. Dial: Painted allegorical spandrels depict four seasons. Two painted scenes on moon wheel: a ship flying the Union Jack flag and a landscape. Possibly painted by Benjamin Whitman (Berks County). Calendar aperture.

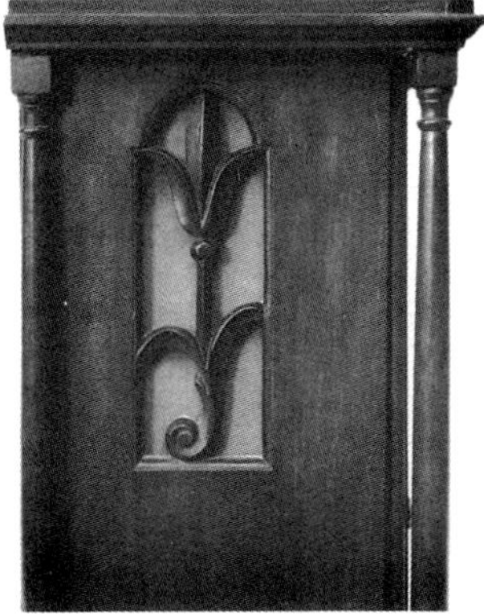

3 detail

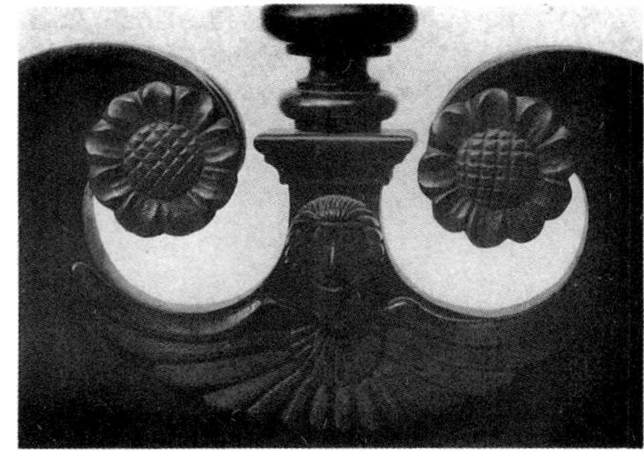

3 detail

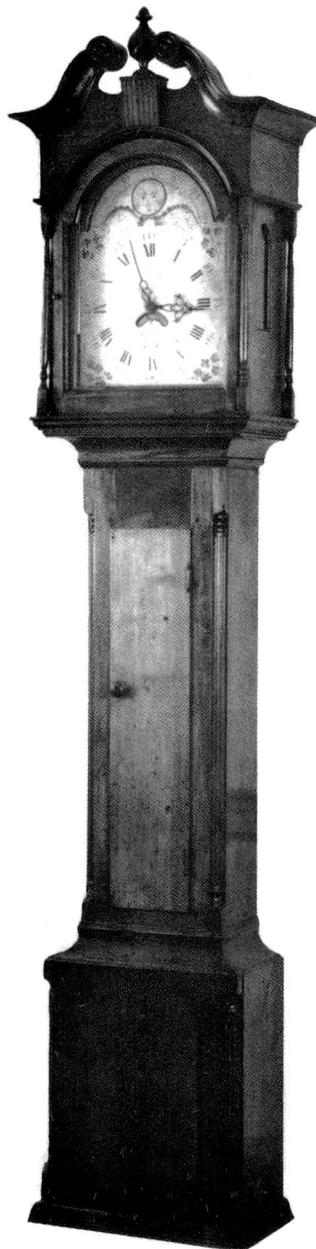

Dial attached directly to movement by squared, iron, dial feet. Movement: Eight-day, bell-strike, sweep-second, brass movement. Plates separated by four turned brass pillars. Ogee arch removed from bottom edge of each plate to provide "feet." Anchor recoil escapement. Open-ended crutch fork. Smooth cable drums with tailless ratchet wheel clicks. English bridge pendulum suspension with wood pendulum rod and brass-sheathed bob. Repeat-on-demand rack-and-snail striking with gathering pallet and rack pin (dial side) locking. Movement fastened to seat board by two J-head bolts. Note: Style of case dates about 1770, and painted dial, about 1780. Uneven oxidation and size of dial in relation to its frame indicate that this clock was probably assembled about 1800.

219 x 53 x 28.6 cm (86¼ x 20⅞ x 11¼")

Gift of Mrs. Frederick Thurston Mason, in memory of her sister Miss Anna P. Stevenson. 14-18

4　**TALL CASE CLOCK**
Bedminster Township, Bucks County
1782–85

Jacob Saleda

Marked inside case: *John Pittnam*
April 3, 1821　cleaned

Black walnut; poplar, iron, brass, glass. Case: Plank construction with pegged mortise and tenon joints. Applied arched molding around glass face. Four engaged colonnettes at corners. Fluted quarter columns with turned concave capitals and base ending in slight chamfer top and bottom. Plain rectangular pendulum door overlaps case. Deep scotia molding between waist and base. Base has fluted quarter columns. Raised decorative panel applied to base. Base molding, horizontal reeding, probably not original. Scroll of bonnet and finial restored. Butt hinges. Dial: Painted white with spandrels of flowers. Calendar in curved slit below hand post. Hours in roman numerals, minutes and seconds in arabic numbers.

225 x 41.2 x 35 cm (88⅝ x 16¼ x 13¾")

Gift of Mrs. C. E. Warner. 13-484

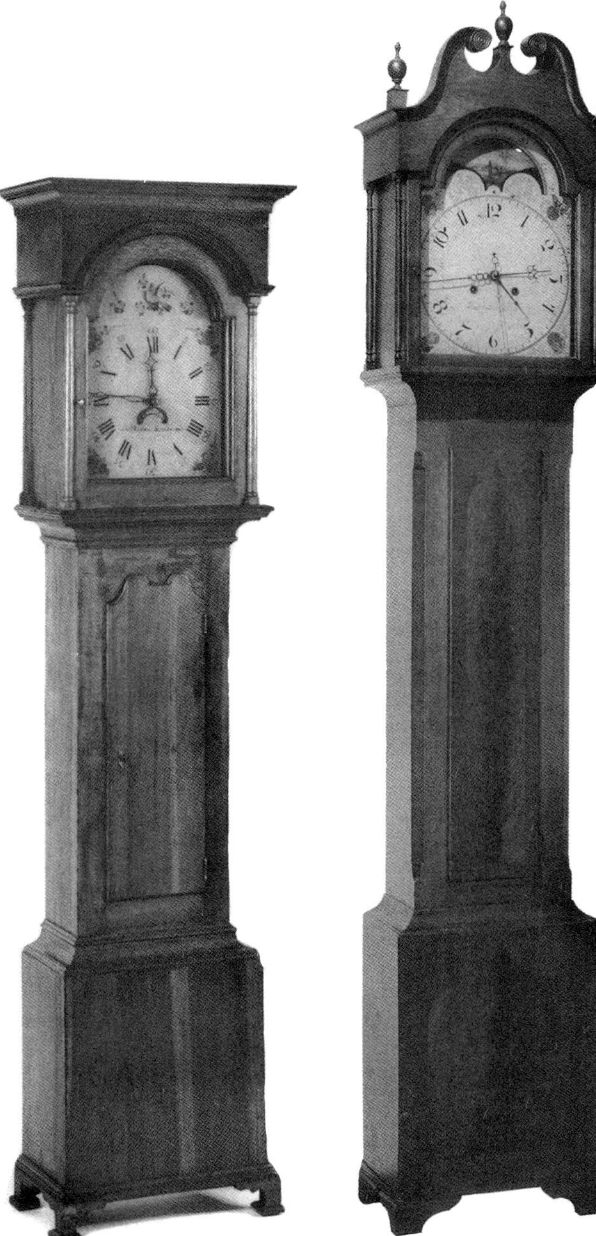

5 **TALL CASE CLOCK**
Nockamixon Township, Bucks County
1795–1800

Michael Striepy

Inscribed on face: *Michael Striepy*

Poplar; oak, glass, brass, iron. Case: Plank construction with lapped, dovetailed upper bonnet. Flat top hood with arched face, applied cyma recta and scotia cornice molding, two engaged colonnettes. Shaped pendulum door, brass strap hinges, escutcheon, ogee bracket feet. Fragments of red paint or old mahogany stain remain. Dial: Probably English, painted white background, flowers in spandrels, bird at top, roman numerals, calendar inset below dial post. Movement: Pennsylvania thirty-hour brass movement. Plates separated by four turned brass pillars. Ogee arches cut from bottom edge of both plates to provide "feet." Anchor recoil escapement. Closed crutch fork. Huygens endless chain. Pulley ratchet wheel with tailless ratchet click. Repeat-on-demand rack-and-snail striking with rack hook locking. English bridge pendulum suspension.

203 x 52.1 x 27.3 cm (79⅞ x 20½ x 10¾")

Gift of the estate of Dr. Charles Koder. 27-59-1

---

6 **TALL CASE CLOCK**
Hanover, York County
1800–1820

Jacob Hostetter

Inscribed: *Jacob Hostetter*
Trade card inside top: *D. Wolff   Watchmaker and Jeweler   1903 Vine Street Philadelphia watch and clock repairing a specialty. Clocks wound and attended to by the year.*

Walnut, poplar; iron, brass, steel, glass. Case: Frame and panel construction with blind mortise and tenon joints. Solid wood scroll top bonnet with turned ball finials, three-quarter colonnettes. Lower case has chamfered corners terminating in carved lamb's tongue motifs top and bottom. Veneered door and base section have crotch-grained pointed arch panels framed with wide banding with mitered corners. Plain bracket feet. Dial: Enameled face with hour, minute and sweep calendar hand, sun and moon dial with fisherman and square-rigged ship flying tricolor (horizontal stripes of blue, white, and red). Movement: Eight-day brass works, rack-and-snail strike, dead beat escapement.

260.3 x 50.8 x 27 cm (102½ x 20 x 10⅝")

Gift of Pendleton G. Watnough. 60-88-1

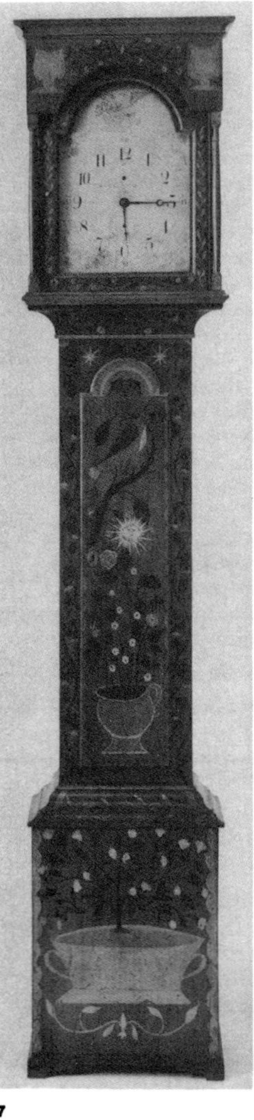

7

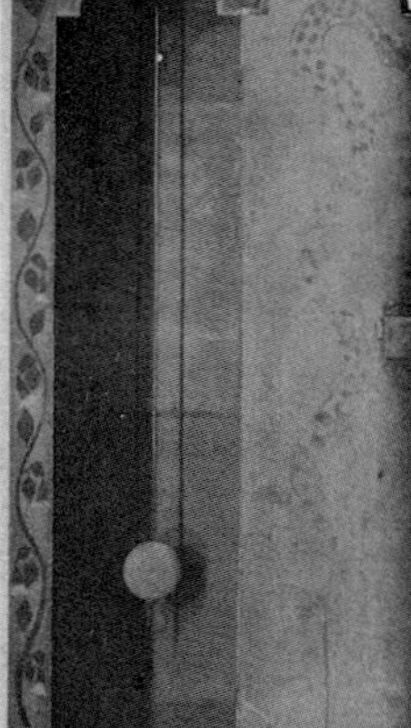

7 detail

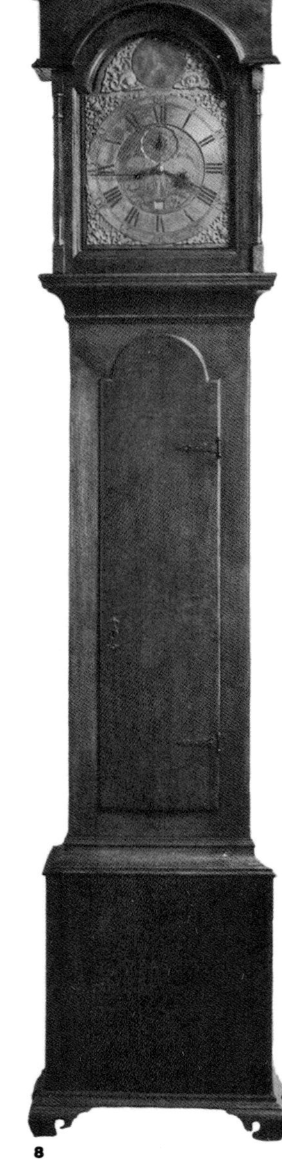

8

7   TALL CASE CLOCK
Zimmerman's Town (Pittman),
Mahantango Valley, Schuylkill County
1800–1830

Painted poplar, pine, walnut; brass, iron, glass.
Case: Frame and plank construction, pegged
and glued. Flat top bonnet capped with scotia
molding. Four freestanding turned walnut
colonnettes at corners. Arch-topped side
windows. Arch-topped pendulum door, brass
butt hinges, and escutcheon. Pull is
replacement. Front and sides of waist joined in
rabbet with glued support blocks. Compound
ogee moldings at top of base section, shaped
bracket feet. Painted orange red ground, green
foliage, white flowers, yellow vases and urns.
Interior door painted in orange red ground,
with freehand yellow spotted snake. Dial:
Solid arch wooden dial with seconds and
calendar circles, painted white with eagle
bearing shield at top, spandrels in floral sprays.
Movement: Five pillar thirty-hour, two-weight,
pull up wood movement. Wood plates. Count
wheel striking. Anchor recoil escapement.
Works similar to those made in Connecticut.

230.5 x 49.5 x 10.9 cm (90¾ x 19½ x 4¼″)

Titus C. Geesey Collection. 54-85-67a,b

8   TALL CASE CLOCK
Norriton Township, Montgomery County
1770

David Rittenhouse

Inscribed: *David Rittenhouse   Norriton
1770*
Marked on back in chalk: *John Pittman Oct 2
1823   Sept. 8 1826.*

Black walnut, poplar; brass, iron, glass. Case:
Dovetailed plank, pegged mortise and tenon
construction, nailed. Scrolled pediment has
applied carved sunflower rosettes, center finial
missing. Bonnet joined in four open dovetails
at front corners. Small arch-topped side lights,
engaged half colonnettes at back, three-quarter
colonnettes in front. Pendulum case and base
unit have chamfered corners with lamb's
tongue detail top and bottom. Front of case has
mitered corners and joins sides in nailed butt
joint. Ogee bracket feet, partially cut off, have
fitted, carved reinforcements nailed to bottom.
Dial: Arched, engraved dial with inscribed
disk. Hours in roman numerals, minutes and
seconds in arabic numbers. Calendar aperture.
Dial attached directly to movement. Movement: Eight-day, bell-strike, brass movement. Two winding holes. Rack-and-snail
striking.

233.1 x 47 x 29.2 cm (92 x 18½ x 11½″)

Gift of John D. McIlhenny. 43-40-1

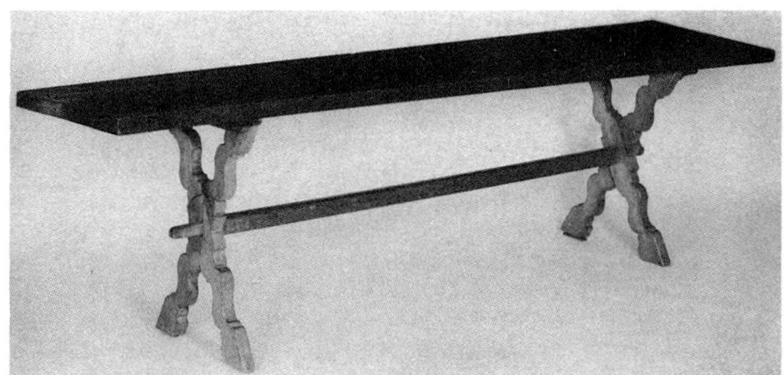

1 **TABLE**
Lebanon County
c. 1730

Walnut, pine, cedar. Plank construction with pegged and wedged tenons. Plank top with shaped battens in keyed dovetail joint through which carved pegs dowel through top of legs. Additional support battens added. Shaped legs cross in lap joint secured by wedged tenon extensions of single stretcher. From the Gingrich Mennonite meetinghouse.

80.6 x 289.5 x 57 cm (31¾ x 114 x 22½")

Titus C. Geesey Collection. 69-284-21

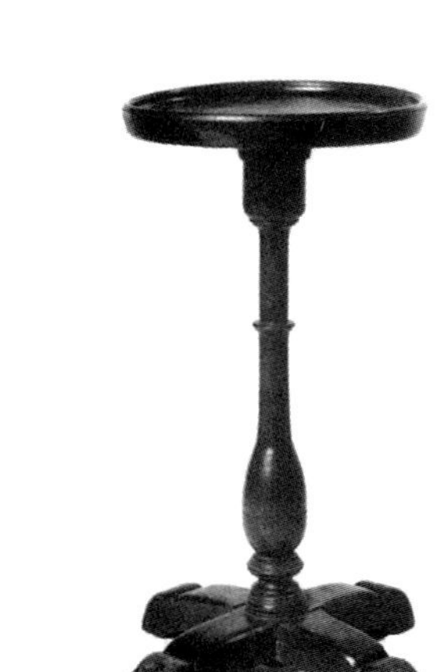

2 **TABLE**
1740–70

Walnut, maple. Turned walnut shaft is tenoned through the lap-joined base. Maple top is turned in one piece with the socket, which fits over the shaft.

Height 71.1 cm (28"), diameter 57.2 cm (22½")

Gift of the heirs of J. Stogdell Stokes. 52-7-4

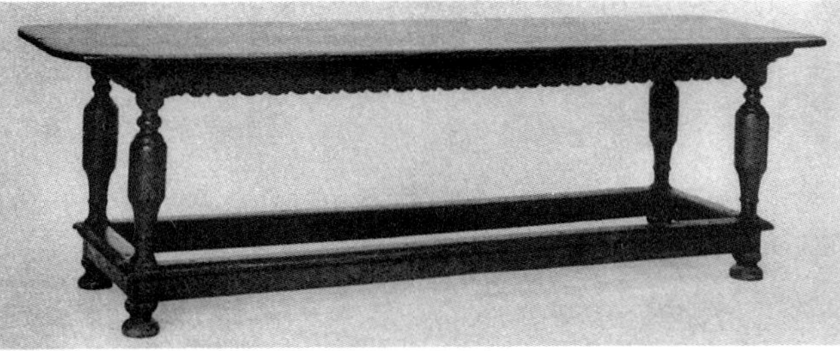

3 **TABLE**
c. 1750

Oak. Plank and frame construction with pegged mortise and tenon joints. Removable top made of two planks with rounded corners pegged to two battens secured to frame through holes drilled to receive carved dowel pins. Bottom edge of top frame carved on four sides. Baluster-turned legs tenoned through horizontal molded-edge footrest stretchers. Bracing frame under footrest with beaded bottom edge, tenoned into leg block and pegged. Turned feet tenoned into leg block and pegged.

71 x 239 x 74.5 cm (28 x 94⅛ x 29⅜")

Gift of J. Stogdell Stokes. 35-36-2

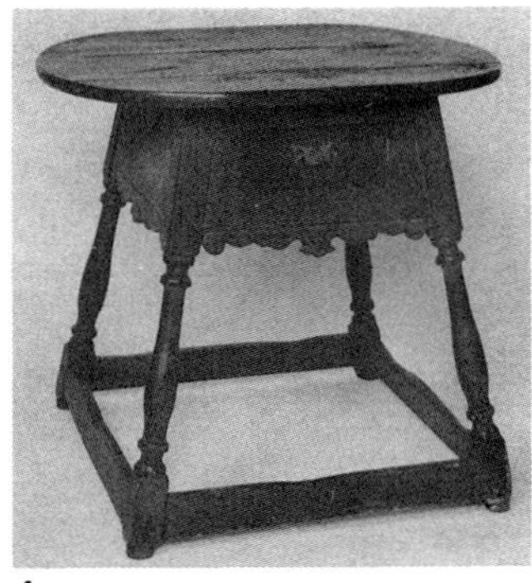

4

4 TABLE
c. 1750

Painted pine, poplar; cedar, walnut. Frame and panel construction, pegged mortise and tenon joints. Turned, splayed legs, molded stretchers. Oval top of three planks pegged to frame. Carved skirting on four sides. Drawer nailed in butt joints at four corners, bottom feathered and let into front and sides. Lock missing from center drawer, bail handle added. Painted brown.

72.5 x 84 x 69 cm (28½ x 33⅛ x 27⅛")

Gift of J. Stogdell Stokes. 28-10-110

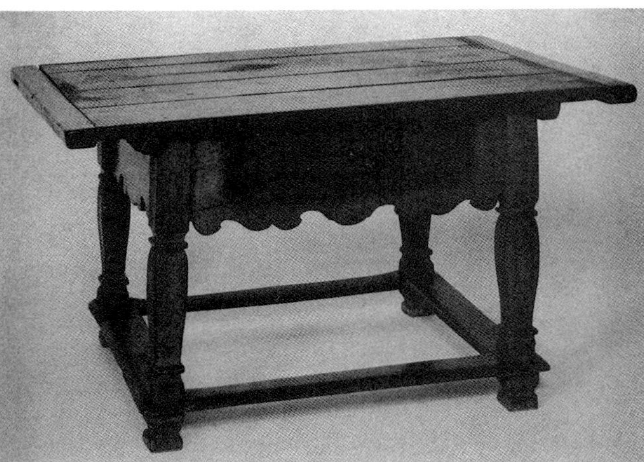

5

5 TABLE
Lebanon County
c. 1750

Black walnut; poplar. Pegged mortise and tenon frame construction. Four-plank removable top has keyed batten ends and support battens let into underside. Carved legs (square in profile) and skirting. Flat footrest stretchers. Drawer possibly restored.

68 x 135 x 90 cm (26¾ x 53⅛ x 35⅜")

Gift of J. Stogdell Stokes. 24-64-1

6 TABLE
Lancaster County
c. 1750

Oak. Trestle construction. Shaped legs crossed in lap joint. Stretcher tenoned through legs at cross and wedged. Footrest stretchers let into feet and nailed. Three-plank top with two battens in keyed dovetails grooved to receive drawer runner. Suspended drawer missing.

73 x 138 x 84 cm (28¾ x 54⅜ x 33⅛")

Gift of J. Stogdell Stokes. 24-23-1

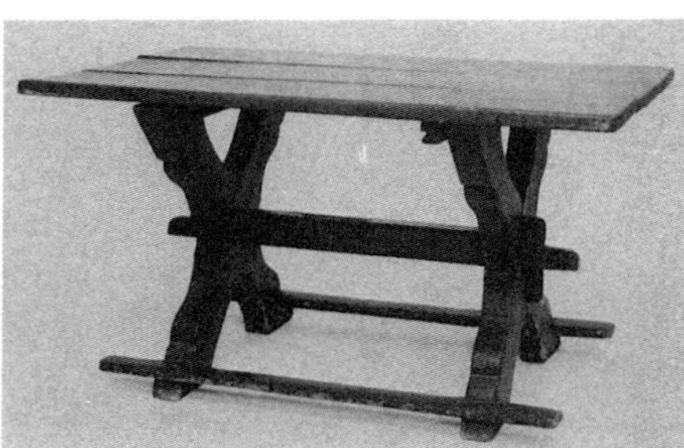

6

7 TABLE
c. 1750

Black walnut; pine. Frame and plank construction with mortise and tenon joints. Removable three-plank top secured with carved hand pegs through two battens. Drawers ride on extension of sides; have molded overlapping edges; four dovetails each corner, bottom feathered and let into sides and front; turned wood pulls. Carved apron applied to front frame. Disk turnings on four legs. Stretchers molded top and bottom, tenoned into legs.

74.9 x 137.7 x 79.4 cm (29½ x 54¼ x 31¼")

Titus C. Geesey Collection. 53-125-3

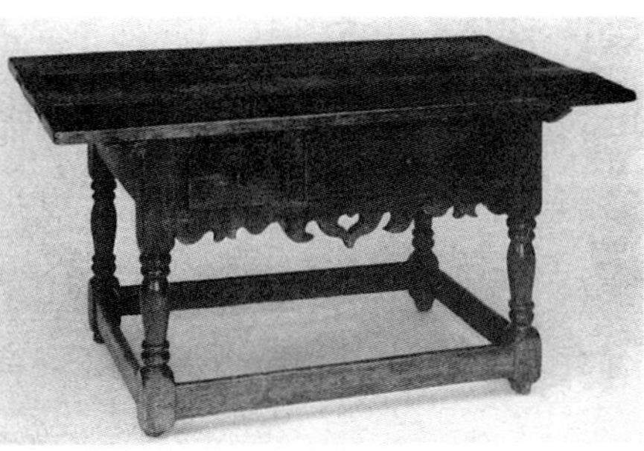

7

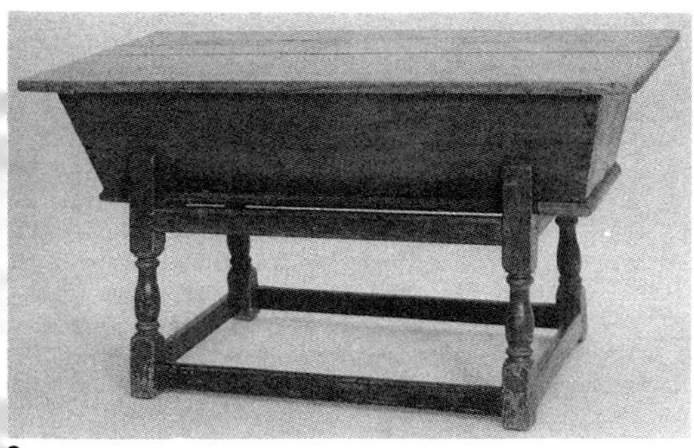

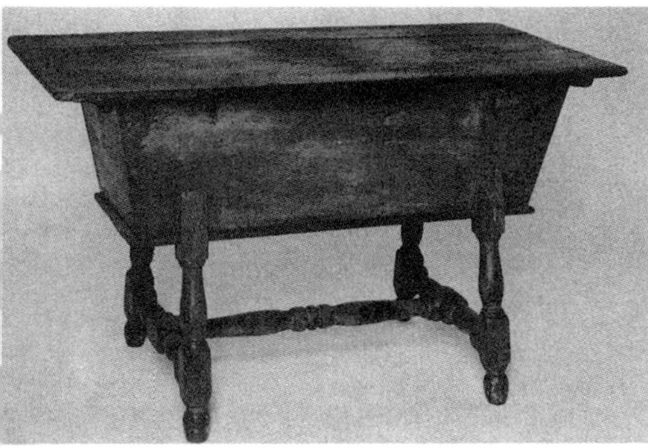

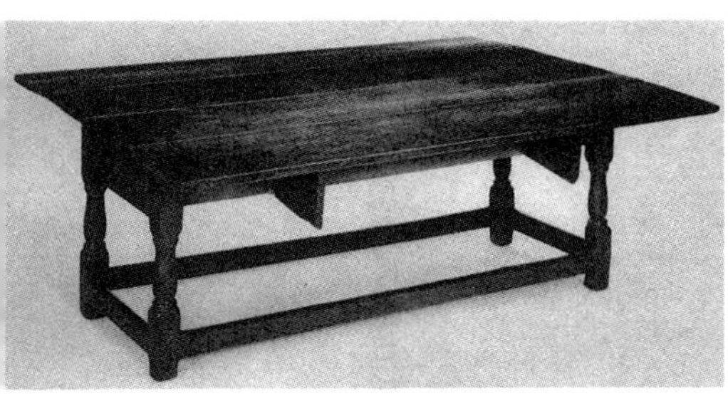

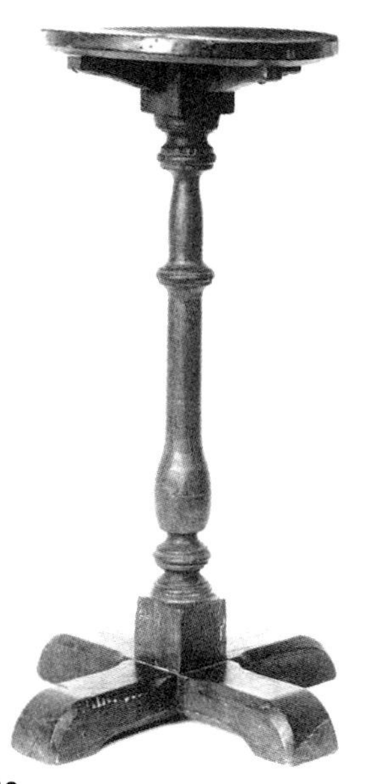

8 DOUGH TABLE
1750–80

Painted pine, oak. Frame and plank construction with dovetail, mortise and tenon joints. Two-plank removable lid has keyed dovetail battens. Bottom butted to sides and ends and nailed, edge covered with molding and pegged. Frame has turned, splayed legs, joined by eight molded stretchers in pegged mortise and tenon joints. Feet worn off. Remnants of red paint.

72.4 x 134.6 x 68.7 cm (28½ x 53 x 27″)

Titus C. Geesey Collection. 69-284-25a,b

9 DOUGH TABLE
1750–1800

Poplar. Plank construction with dovetail corners. Sides let into bottom. Two battens under two-plank removable top. Turned, raked legs nailed to sides. Turned stretchers meet legs in mortise and tenon joints.

70 x 122 x 63 cm (27½ x 48 x 24¾″)

Gift of J. Stogdell Stokes. 28-10-84

10 CANDLESTAND
1750–1800

Painted pine. Turned shaft has square block at bottom which tenons through lap-joined carved base, secured with metal plate. Rimless circular top supported by four carved supports which tenon into hewn square top of shaft. Painted dark red.

Height 73.6 cm (29″), diameter 32.1 cm (12⅝″)

Titus C. Geesey Collection. 55-45-3

11 TABLE
Southern Lancaster County
1760–70

Marked on drop leaf: *J. Sorman*

Painted pine; poplar, walnut. Frame and plank construction, pegged joints. Drop-leaf table with four-plank top in rule joints. Two swing supports for each drop leaf. Drawers at each end with molded edges overlapping frame; dovetail construction, walnut pulls. Turned legs with stretchers. Feet worn off. Remnants of dark green paint.

71.1 x 183 x 71.1 cm (28 x 72 x 28″)

Titus C. Geesey Collection. 55-45-7

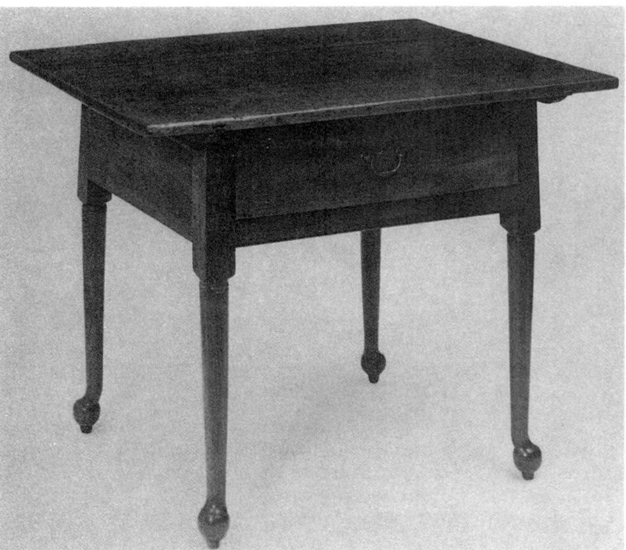

12

12 TABLE
1760–80

Black walnut; poplar. Frame and plank constuction with pegged mortise and tenon joints. Removable top has keyed battens with molded edges through which four carved pins are doweled through frame. Drawer with brass pull has molded overlapping edge; dovetail construction at four corners; bottom let into front and sides, nailed at back; two compartments. Straight, turned legs with pad feet on raised points.

74.6 x 91.5 x 64.7 cm (29⅜ x 36 x 25½")

Titus C. Geesey Collection. 69-284-18

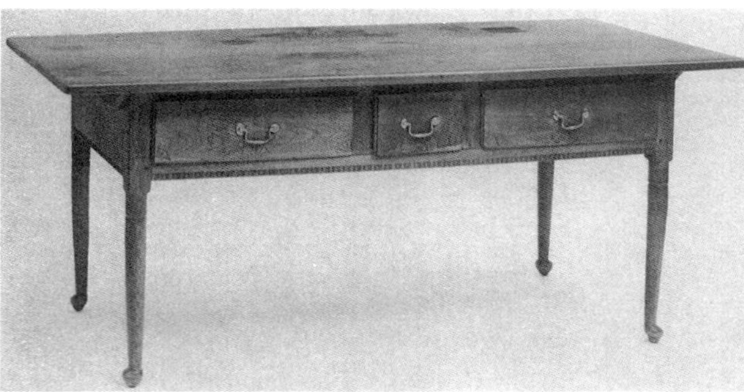

13

13 TABLE
1760–1800

Black walnut; pine. Frame construction with mortise and tenon joints. Removable plank top supported by two battens on underside joined to frame with carved dowels. Three drawers have molded overlapping edges; four corners dovetailed, bottoms feathered and let into front and sides. Semicircular and quarter-carved fans on lower edges of drawer fronts. Lower edge of frame is carved in linen-fold banding. Turned tapering legs, raised pad feet. Brass bail handles.

77.5 x 179.1 x 79.4 cm (30½ x 70½ x 31¼")

Titus C. Geesey Collection. 53-125-2

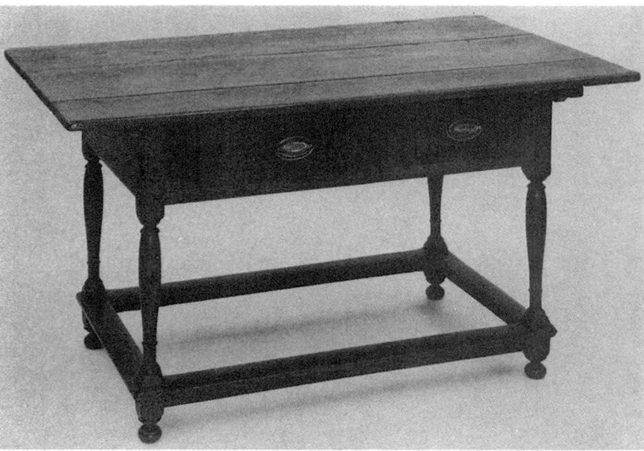

14

14 TABLE
c. 1770

Black walnut; poplar, pine. Frame and panel construction with pegged mortise and tenon joints. Battens in keyed dovetail on underside of splined three-board top. Two unequal drawers have molded edges overlapping frame. Oval bail brasses cover single hole of original pull. Flat footrest stretchers mitered and lapped. Ball feet probably replacements.

77.2 x 142.2 x 81.2 cm (30⅜ x 56 x 32")

Bequest of Mr. and Mrs. William M. Elkins. 50-92-80

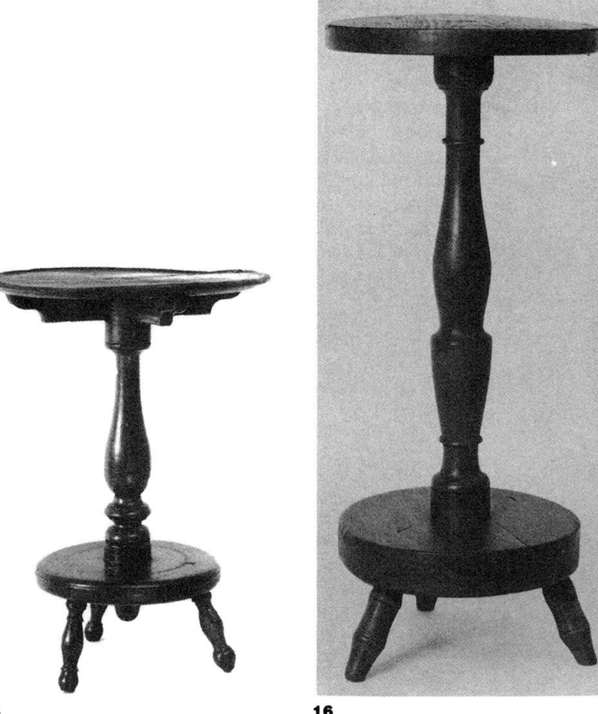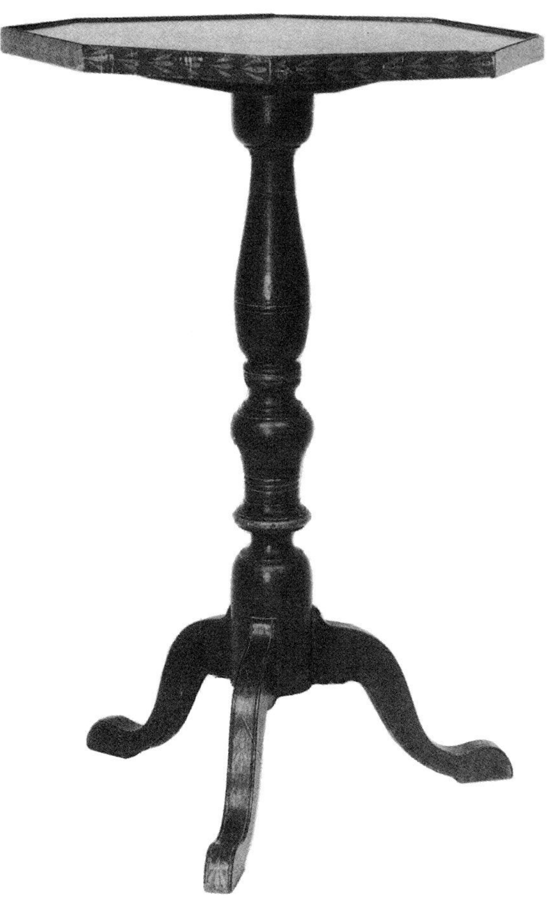

15 TABLE
1770–1800

Poplar, maple. Turned shaft tenoned through round base and pegged. Three splayed, turned legs tenoned into base. At top of shaft, four carved brackets tenoned into pillar to support round top with raised, molded edge.

Height 62.2 cm (24½″), diameter 43.9 cm (17¼″)

Titus C. Geesey Collection. 55-45-4

16 CANDLESTAND
1780–1800

Painted pine, poplar, oak, maple. Turned shaft tenoned through top and wedged; at base wedged with encircling chips. Three turned, shaped, splayed feet tenoned into base. Top has shrunk across grain. Painted red.

Height 71.1 cm (28″), approximate diameter 31.4 cm (12⅜″)

Titus C. Geesey Collection. 58-110-48

17 TABLE
1800–1830

Painted poplar, maple. Turned shaft tenoned and pegged into shaped batten supporting octagonal top with applied edge molding. Three flat cabriole legs tenoned into base of shaft and secured with three-armed iron plate. Painted brown with leaf design and banding stenciled in yellow. Shaft painted red, green, and yellow. Varnished.

77.5 x 49.5 cm (30½ x 19½″)

Titus C. Geesey Collection. 62-203-2

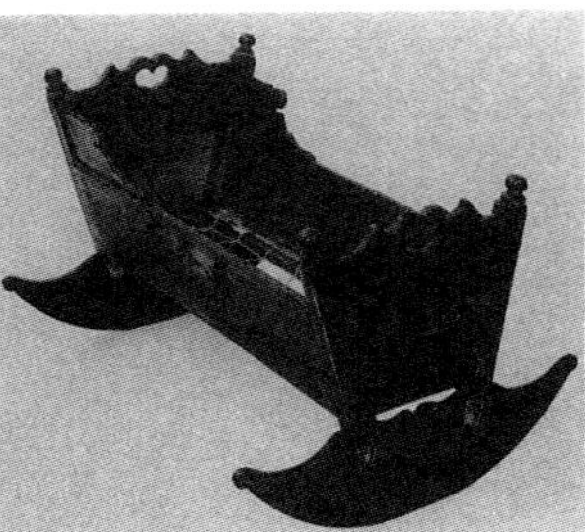

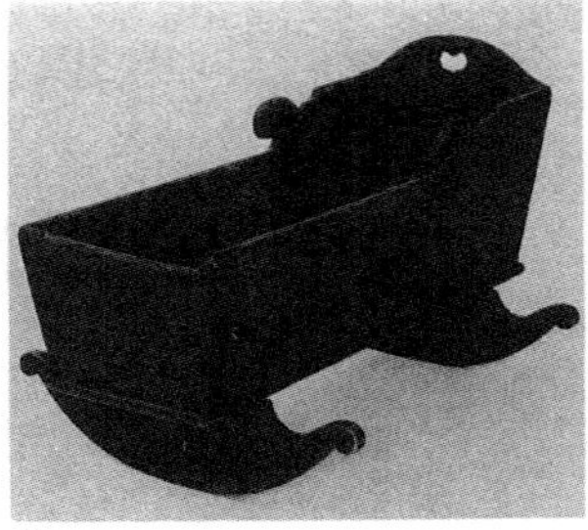

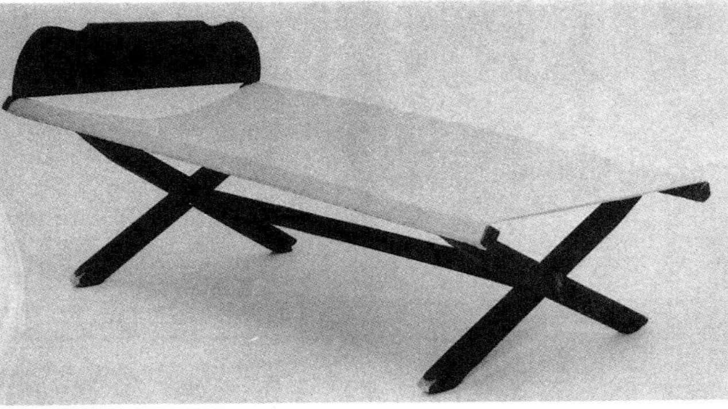

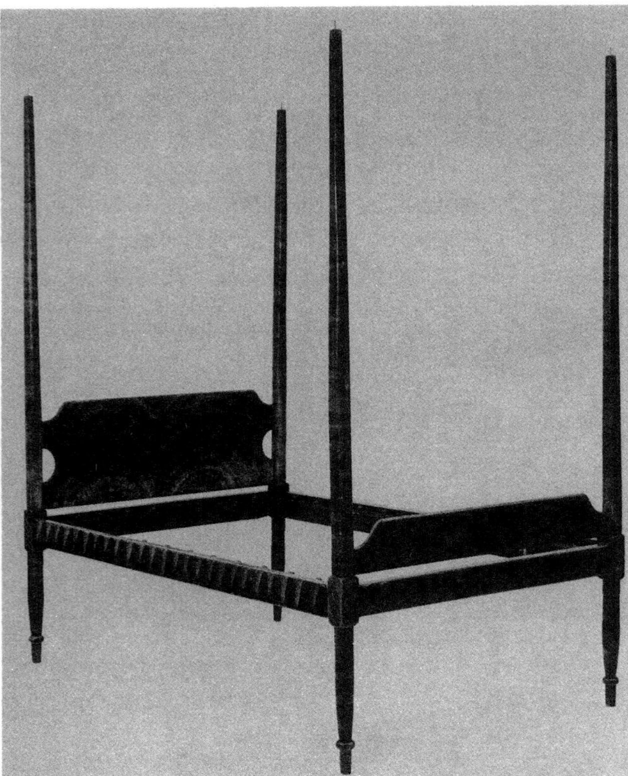

1 CRADLE
Lebanon or Dauphin County
c. 1750

Poplar, pine; walnut. Frame and panel construction with pegged mortise and tenon joints. Post tops have turned knobs to hold mosquito netting and rocking ribbons. Bottoms cut out to receive rockers (replacements), which are pegged. Three knobs each side for securing restraining ribbons or strings. Bottom frame drilled for rope or sacking (canvas) bottom. Evidence of red orange paint.

62 x 99 x 72.4 cm (24⅜ x 39 x 28½")

Gift of J. Stogdell Stokes. 30-18-1

2 CRADLE
1750–1800

Painted poplar; pine, maple. Plank construction, dovetail joints. Canted sides meet post and headboard in dovetail joints. Plank bottom meets sides in butt joint. Sides pierced with four holes for security ribbons or strings. Scrolled maple rockers pegged to bottom. Painted brown.

59.5 x 97.8 x 66.2 cm (23⅜ x 38½ x 26⅛")

Gift of Mrs. William D. Frishmuth. 02-180

3 COT
Bucks County
1780–1830

Painted poplar, oak. Shaped plank headboard tenoned into top rails and pegged. Dowel extension of square stretcher tenoned through crossed legs and pinned. Painted blue green. Canvas "spring." Known as a workman's portable sacking-bottom cot.

79.5 x 199 x 95 cm (31¼ x 78⅜ x 37⅜")

Gift of J. Stogdell Stokes. 28-10-7

4 BED
1790–1810

Painted poplar. Frame construction, mortise and tenon joints at head- and footboard and rails. Iron bolts secure tenoned side rails. Turned roping pegs. Tester frame meets in lap joints, pinned with wood dowels set into tops of posts. Painted red orange with sponge graining in dark brown.

215.9 x 189.9 x 125.7 cm (85 x 74¾ x 49½")

Titus C. Geesey Collection. 58-110-3

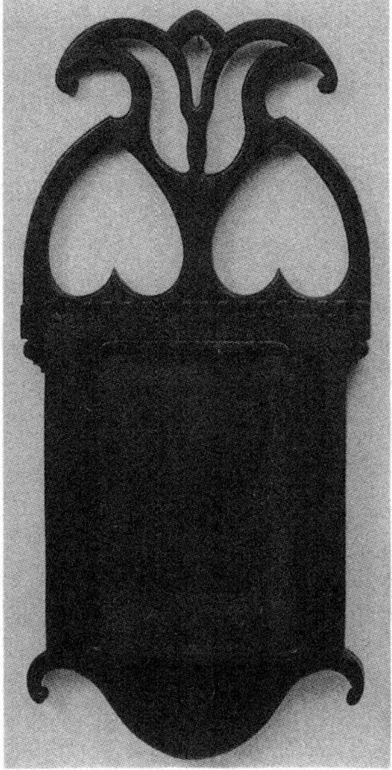

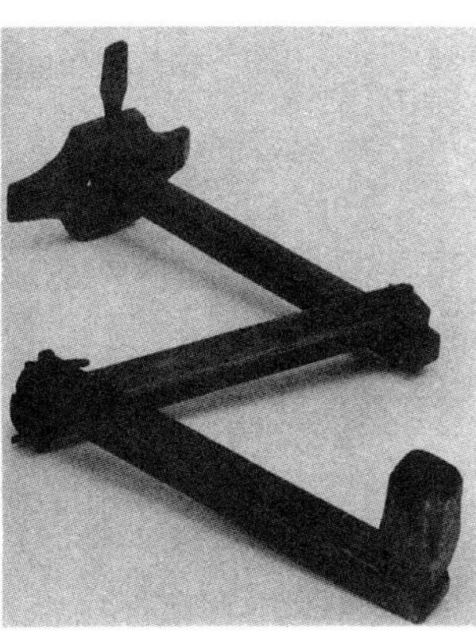

2

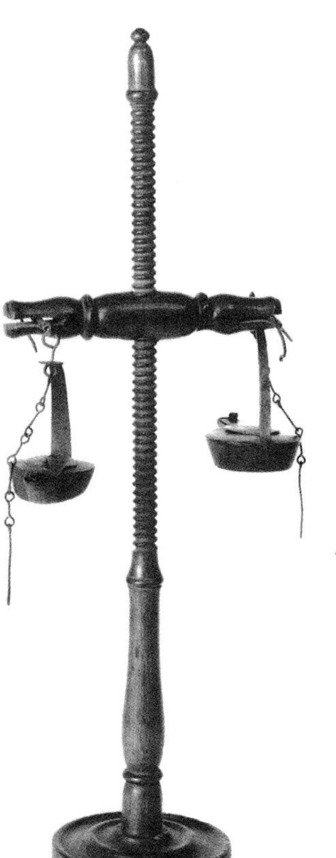

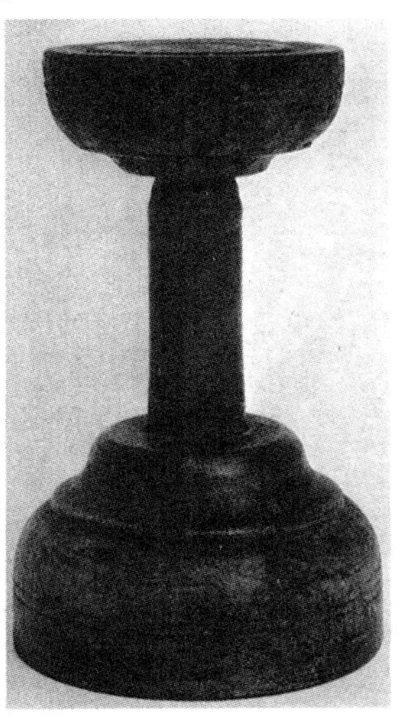

4

1 LOOKING GLASS
Bucks County
1750–80

Black walnut. Frame cut and carved from single piece; pierced upper section in one piece with carved dentil fret. Channel molding around mirrored glass. Walnut backboard held with wrought nails.

59.5 x 28.5 cm (23½ x 11¼")

Titus C. Geesey Collection. 55-45-9

---

2 CANDLEHOLDER
1750–80

Pine, poplar. Tenon construction for accordion action. Carved, molded-edge wall plate with two screw holes receives arm of holder that is pinned with carved peg. Arms meet in overlapping swivel joint, pegged and secured with wood cotter pins top and bottom. Carved candleholder at end.

75.4 x 15.9 cm (29⅝ x 6¼")

Gift of Mrs. William D. Frishmuth. 02-90

---

3 LAMPSTAND
1750–1800

Hickory, ash, oak. Turned shaft tenoned through turned base and wedged. Upper shaft with acorn finial has carved threads on which support arm rotates for height adjustment. Shown with two oil lamps.

66.6 x 21.6 cm (26¼ x 8½"), diameter 14 cm (5½")

Titus C. Geesey Collection. 28-10-79

---

4 LAMPSTAND
1750–1800

Maple. Turned base and top receive turned shaft in tenon joints.

Height 17.8 cm (7"), diameter 11.5 cm (4½")

Titus C. Geesey Collection. 54-85-4b

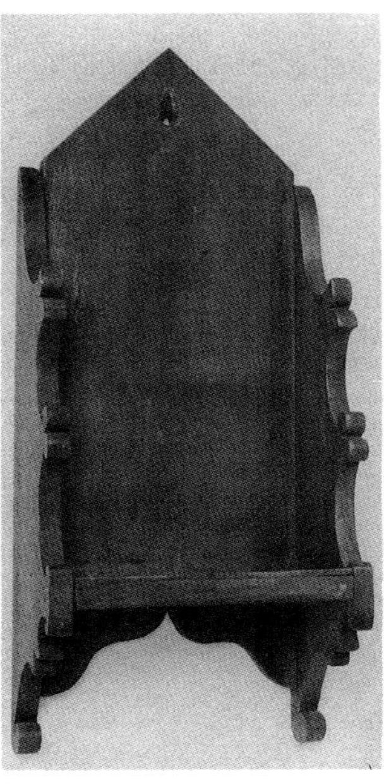

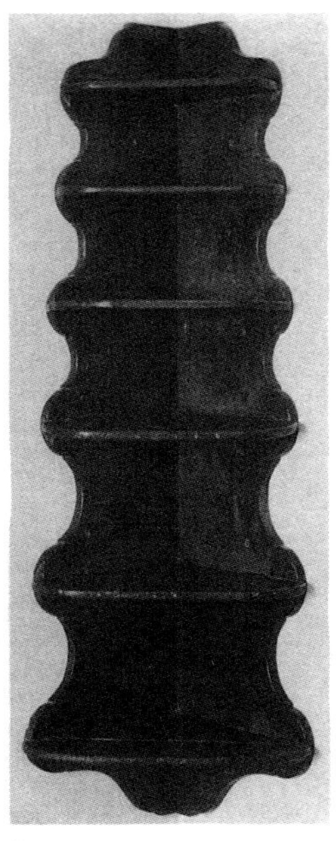

5

6

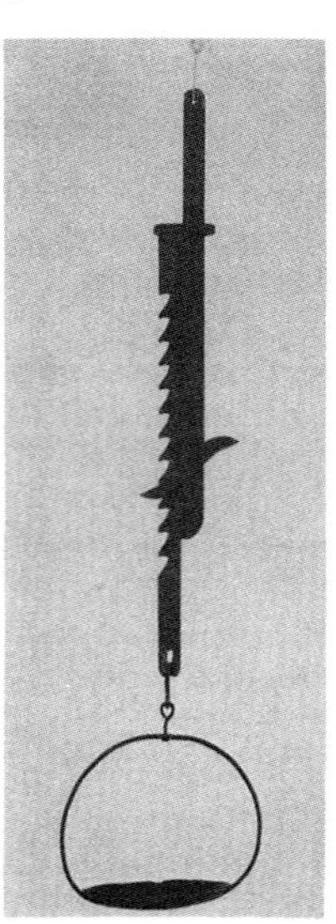

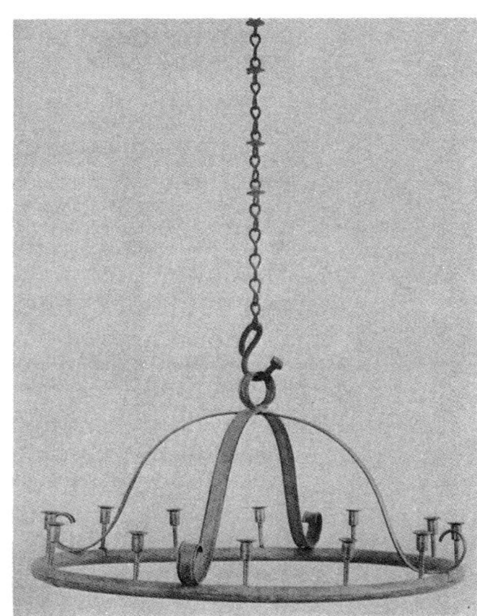

7

8

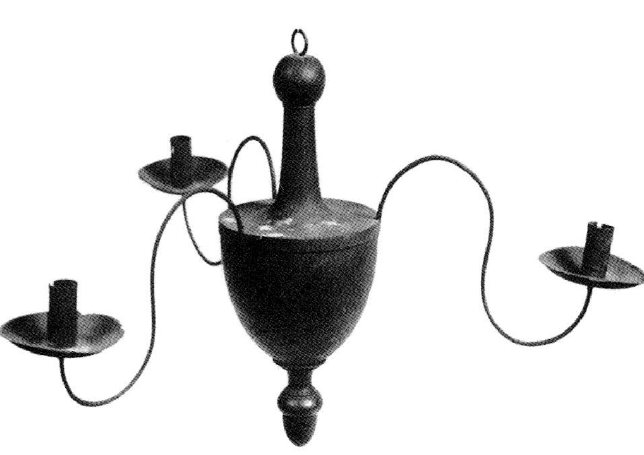

9

5 **HANGING SHELF**
1750–1800

Walnut. Plank construction. Shelf set into sides
and pegged. Hole cut through shelf. Probably
for a clock.

55.9 x 25.4 x 12.7 cm (22 x 10 x 5″)

Titus C. Geesey Collection. 54-85-3

6 **HANGING CORNER SHELF**
1770–1800

Walnut. Plank construction, nailed joints.
Shelves set into sides and nailed. Top shelf
probably a replacement. Top may have been
cut off.

143.5 x 49.5 cm (56½ x 19½″)

Titus C. Geesey Collection. 53-125-17

7 **TRAMMEL**
1780–1800

Painted pine. Tenon and peg construction.
Straight, wood arm fits through collar of ratchet
arm. Curved catch pivots on wood peg. Hole at
top and bottom for hooks or wires. Painted red.
Shown with an iron lamp.

53.3 x 14 cm (23 x 5½″)

Titus C. Geesey Collection. 55-45-13a

8 **CHANDELIER**
1800–1820

Painted hickory, tin, pewter. Bentwood
construction. Oval ring made in two units;
bottom oval is one bent piece, top is pieced
and shaped. Pewter candleholders screw into
ring. Flaring, scrolled tin supports have
molded edges fastened with screws. Painted
green gray.

40.6 x 84.5 x 61.9 cm (16 x 33¼ x 24⅜″)

Titus C. Geesey Collection. 55-45-11

9 **CHANDELIER**
1800–1820

Painted poplar, maple, iron. Central core
turned in lidded urn-shape with ball finial
inset with iron hanging loop. Acorn finial and
spool turning at base attached. Three iron arms
in S curves support iron candleholders set in
shallow bobeche. Wood painted brown red.

60 x 104 cm (23⅝ x 40⅞″)

Purchased: Joseph E. Temple Fund, from the
Clarence W. Brazer Collection. 26-24-4

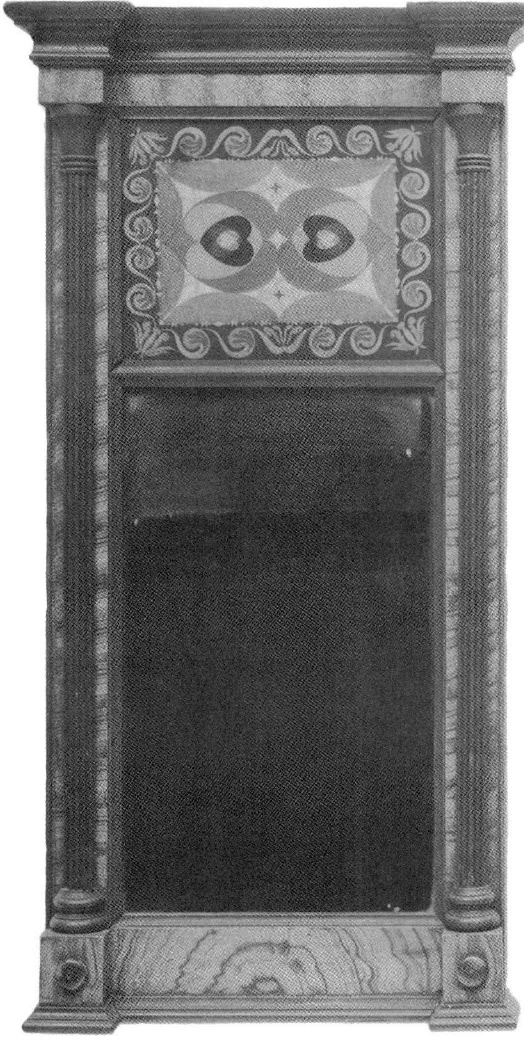

10

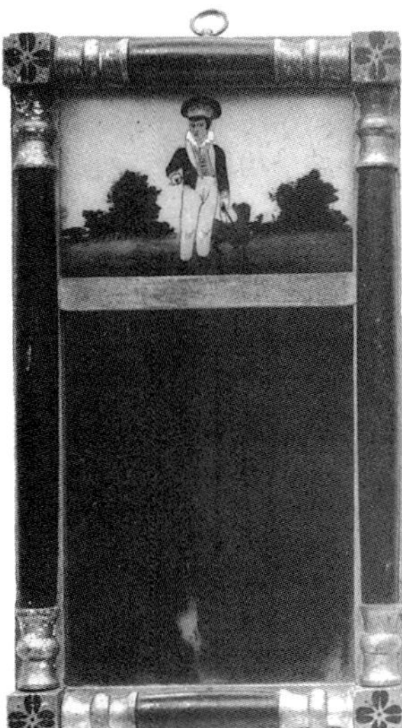

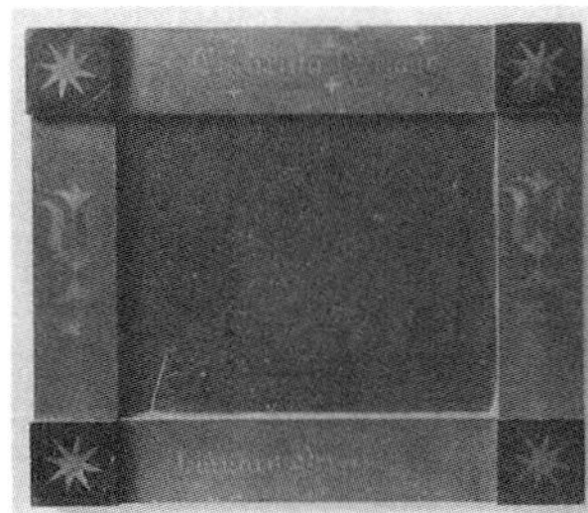

10 LOOKING GLASS
Bucks County
1800–1830

Painted pine, poplar; glass. Frame construction, glued and nailed. Backboards inset and secured with brads. Compound cornice molding of quirked ovolo, scotia, and astragal, breaks forward at corners to receive half-round, reeded colonnettes with Doric bases, Corinthian capitals. Scotia and ovolo moldings at base. Panels of the looking glass and reverse painting on glass set into frame of scotia molding. Glass is painted red, green, yellow; border red. Marbelized frame red brown on yellow.

80 x 38.1 cm (31½ x 15″)

Titus C. Geesey Collection. 54-85-65

11 LOOKING GLASS
1830–40

Painted pine, poplar; mirrored glass. Frame constructon. Turned, split balusters and square corners applied to flat frame surface. Reverse-painted glass and mirror inset into frame and separated by horizontal frame mitered into side pieces. Painted black with yellow gold. Reverse-painted glass has figure with black dots in green, yellow, tan, and white against green landscape, blue sky.

47.9 x 27.9 cm (18⅞ x 11″)

Titus C. Geesey Collection. 62-203-1

12 LOOKING GLASS
Tulpehocken Township, Berks County
1846

Inscribed: *Catarina German February Den 12, 1846*

Painted poplar. Plank construction with finger joints. Decorative corner blocks applied. Mirror inset behind frame, backboard inset with brads. Painted red with black corners, stenciled gold stars and tulips.

30 x 35.1 cm (11¾ x 13⅞″)

Gift of Miss Frances Lichten. 58-89-1

13 SPITTOON
c. 1850

Pine. Plank construction. Turned feet and finials terminate square corner posts. Top edge has carved spool molding. Split sausage molding applied to bottom, nailed. Bottom let into side pieces. Held sawdust.

17.5 x 29 cm (6⅞ x 11⅜″)

Gift of J. Stogdell Stokes. 28-10-58

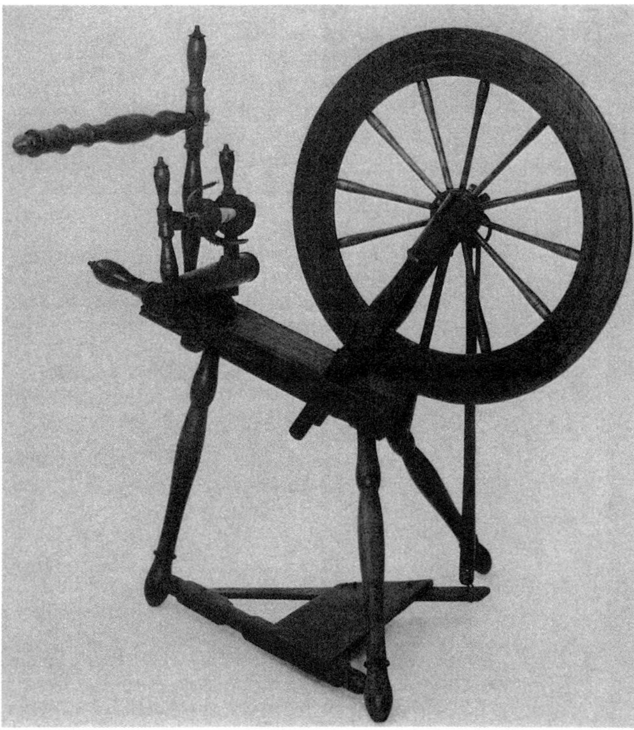

1

1   SINGLE FLAX SPINNING WHEEL
c. 1750

Maple, oak, leather, iron. Turned, splayed legs
tenoned into rectangular block. Turned
wheel-supports tenoned through block. Foot
treadle pivots on tenons fitted into turned
stretcher and pegged to board wired to drive
mechanism. Free-moving bobbin. Distaff not
shown.

128 x 84 cm (50⅜ x 33⅛″)

Gift of Mrs. William D. Frishmuth. 02-262

2   TONGS
1750–1800

Hickory. Two planks with shaped handles
taper sharply to fit through cut in rectangular
collar. Loosely pegged to pivot. Used to lift wet
flax or squeeze wool.

60.8 x 21.1 cm (23⅞ x 8¼″)

Gift of Mrs. William D. Frishmuth. 10-153

3   HATCHEL
1750–1800

Oak, iron. Shaped board has inset iron spikes
(33) in offset rows. Sheath box has nailed
butt joints.

10.5 x 38.5 x 12 cm (4⅛ x 15⅛ x 4¾″)

Gift of Mrs. William D. Frishmuth. 02-211b

4   HATCHEL
1750–1800

Maple, pine, iron. Board has chip-carved ends,
shaped molded edge. Offset rows of iron spikes
set into iron sleeve nailed to center of board.
Spike sheath has nailed butt joints.

11.9 x 49.9 x 10.5 cm (4⅝ x 19⅝ x 4⅛″)

Gift of Mrs. William D. Frishmuth. 02-211c

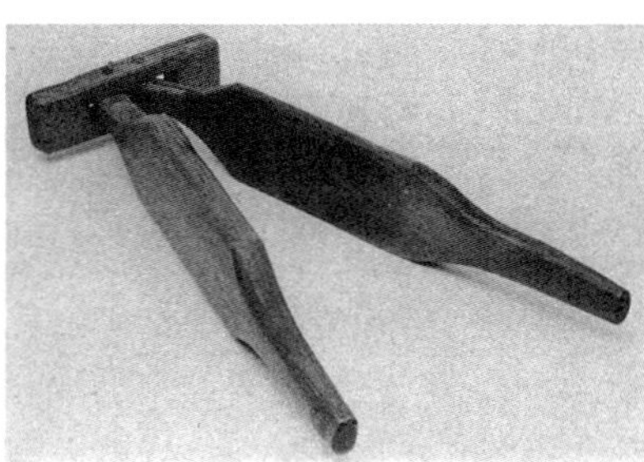

2

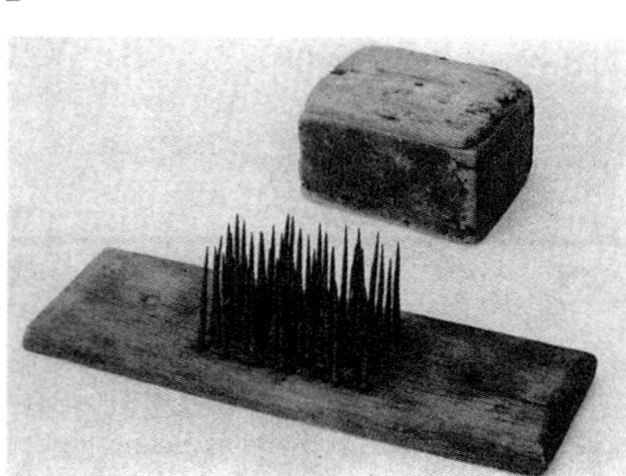

3

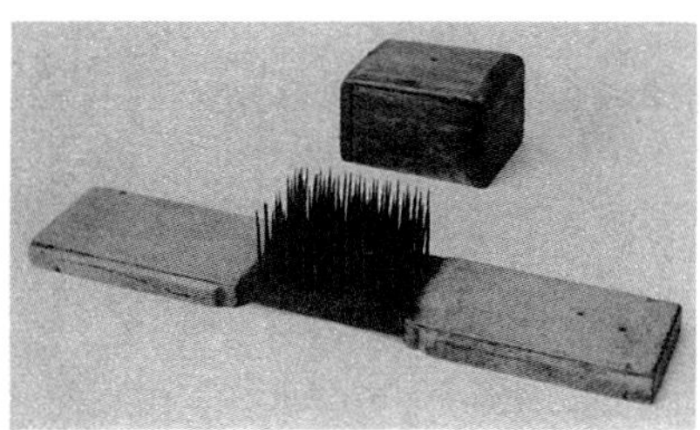

4

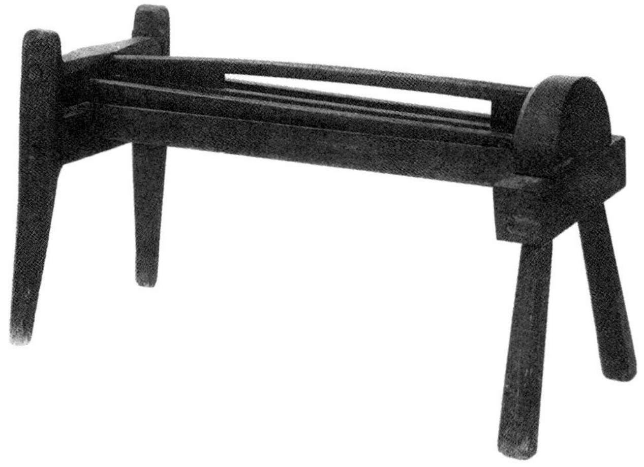

5

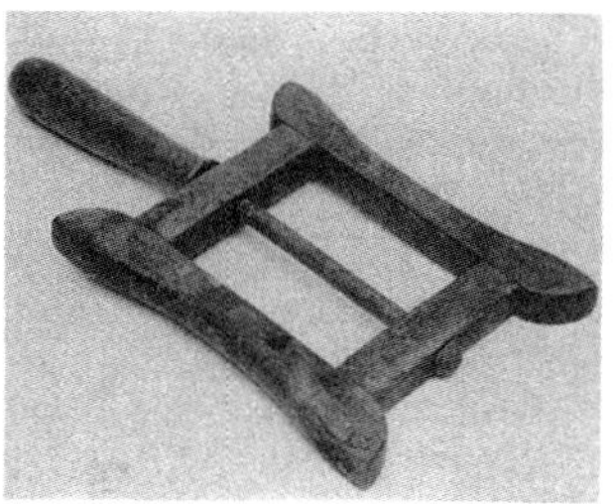

6

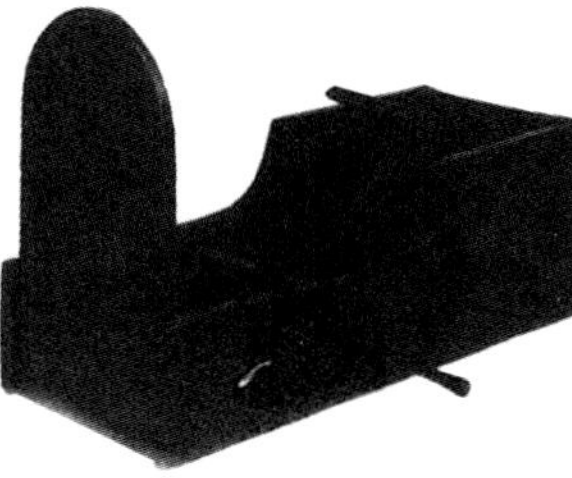

7

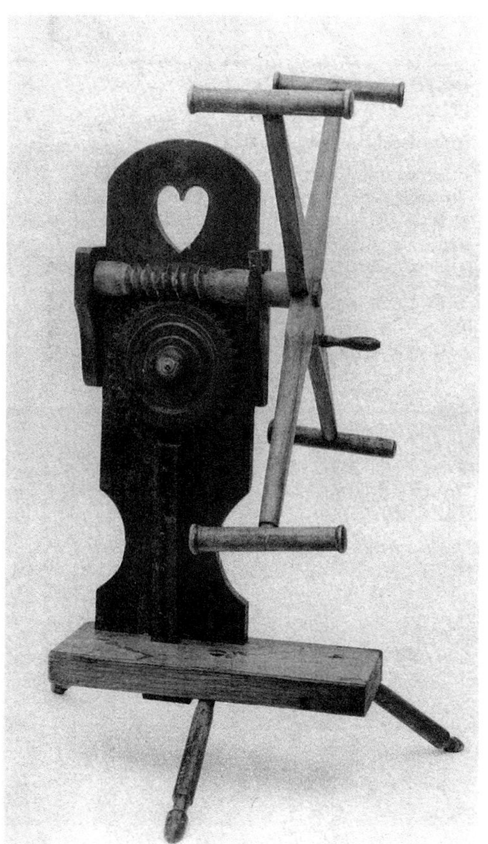

8

5 FLAX BRAKE
1750–1800

Red oak, cherry, walnut. Frame construction with pegged open mortise and tenon joints. Splayed legs set and wedged in hewn frame. Pivoting on hewn dowels, the shaft fits between two dull "knives," to break and separate woody boon (casing) of flax from fibers. Solid, shaped head block straightens the fibers.

68.6 x 121.9 x 45.7 cm (27 x 48 x 18")

Gift of Mrs. William D. Frishmuth. 02-289

6 HAND REEL
1750–1800

Walnut. Pegged mortise and tenon construction. Shaped frame rotates on dowel extension of turned handle. Hole drilled through one side for tying end of yarn.

24.7 x 12.2 cm (9¾ x 4¾")

Gift of Mrs. William D. Frishmuth. 02-188

7 TAPE LOOM
1750–1800

Pine. Butt construction with pegged joints. Shed board is let into sides and slotted and drilled for warp threads. The two hand cranks tenoned and pegged into sides turn the armed reel and the shed stick for warp and are locked with ratchets and pins.

45 x 67.3 cm (17¾ x 26½")

Gift of Mrs. William D. Frishmuth. 02-246

8 MEASURING REEL
1750–1800

Walnut, ash, maple, oak. Plank construction with nailed and tenoned joints. Four-spoked wheel with arms lap-joined, rounded T-shaped ends, receives tenon of horizontal wooden worm which turns a carved wood gear mounted on side of shaped, vertical plank. Pointer is tenoned to gear, through plank, and moves over an inscribed circle divided into twenty units. Two revolutions of wheel move counter one unit.

93.3 x 57.5 cm (36¾ x 22⅝"), radius 34.6 cm (13⅝")

Titus C. Geesey Collection. 69-284-22

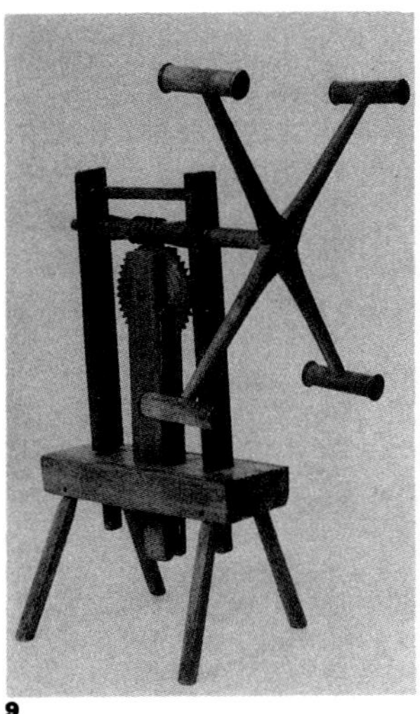

9

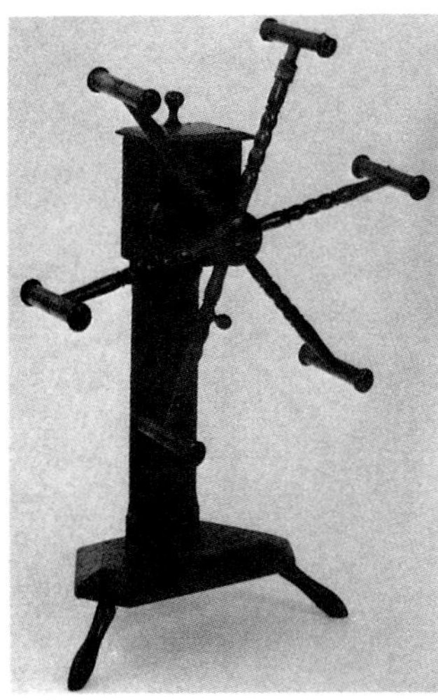

10

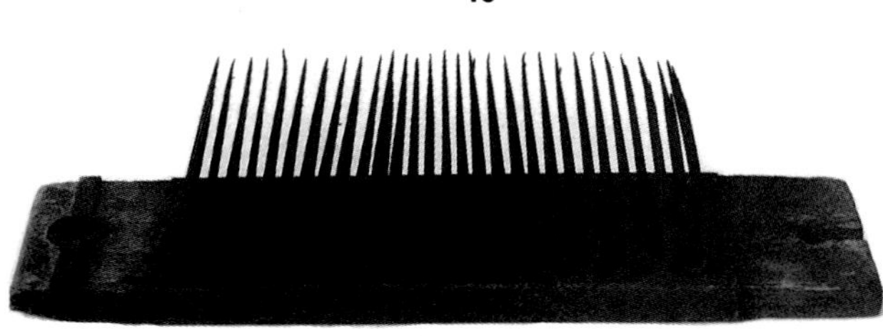

11

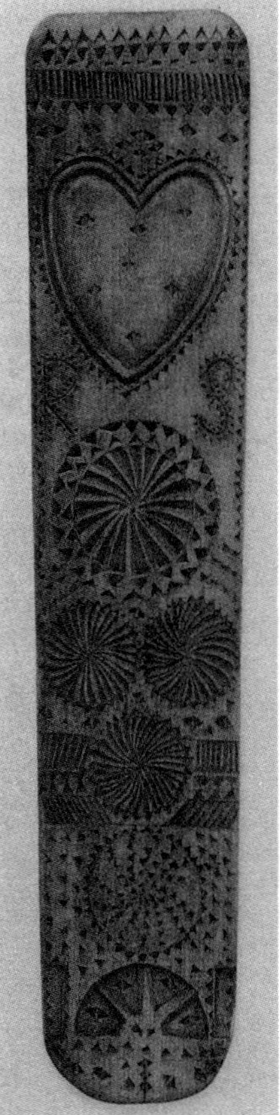

12

9 MEASURING REEL
1750–1800

Oak, maple. Four shaped, splayed legs tenoned and pinned into base with chip-carved ends. Wheel tenoned and pinned through two vertical boards narrowing into tenons through base and pegged. Carved gear wheel pegged between two boards narrowing into tenons through base and pegged. Wheel fitted with peg that clicks, for measuring. Rotating arms meet in lap joint secured with peg through tenon of turning shaft.

96.4 x 49.4 cm (38 x 19½"), radius 33 cm (13")

Gift of Mrs. Samuel D. Biddle. 34-23-3

10 MEASURING REEL
1750–1800

Oak, cherry, iron. Plank and tenon construction with pegged butt joints. Three turned, splayed legs tenoned into base. Vertical board supporting reel mechanism, tenoned through base and pegged, has chamfered corners with lamb's tongue detail. Box containing spring measuring device has pegged butt joints. Rounded face plate incised with dial divided into 15 units numbered clockwise 10 to 150. Metal tulip-shaped meter is set to click after desired number of revolutions of rotating arms. Tulip painted in black above dial.

88.9 x 85.1 cm (35 x 33½"), radius 31 cm (12¼")

Gift of Mrs. William D. Frishmuth. 02-276

11 HATCHEL
1772

Inscribed on side: *H W 1772*

Pine, iron. Plank fitted with iron sleeve through which iron spikes (84) protrude. Sleeve nailed and decorated with punchwork. Fitted with nailed iron band with center hole; one band missing. Hatchel fitted with sheath box.

9.5 x 37.7 x 9.7 cm (3¾ x 14⅞ x 3⅞")

Gift of Mrs. William D. Frishmuth. 02-211a

12 BUSK
1777

Inscribed obverse: *R.S.;* reverse: *1777 RS PLAC 22*

Hickory. Shaped, carved piece for stiffening bodice of dress. Front is chip-carved with heart and wheel designs and initials.

31.7 x 6.7 cm (12½ x 2⅝")

Gift of Mrs. William D. Frishmuth. 12-34

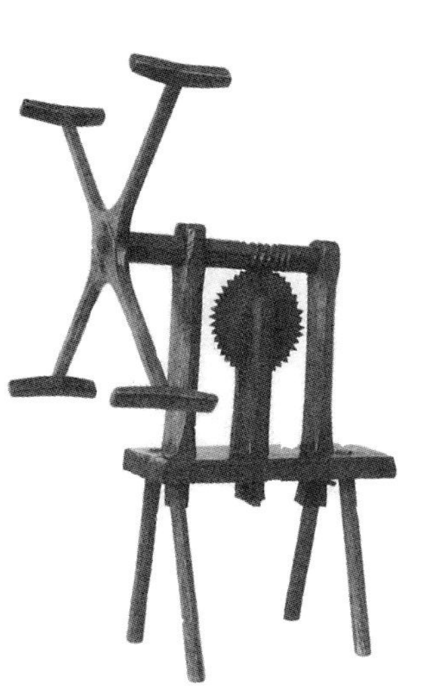

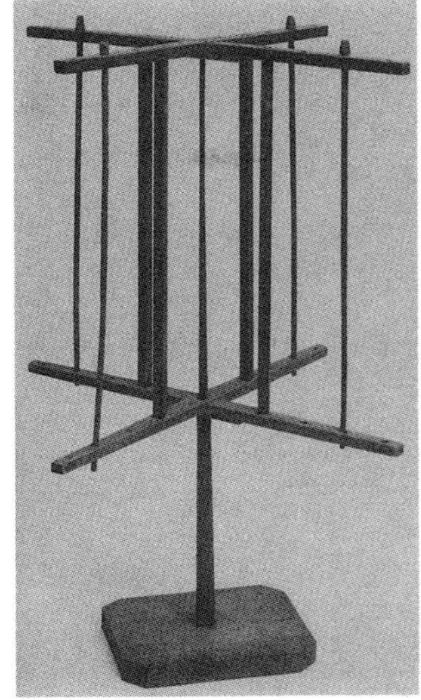

13

15

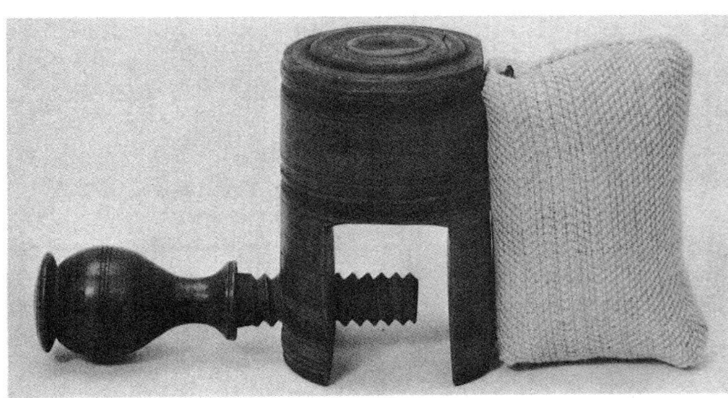

14

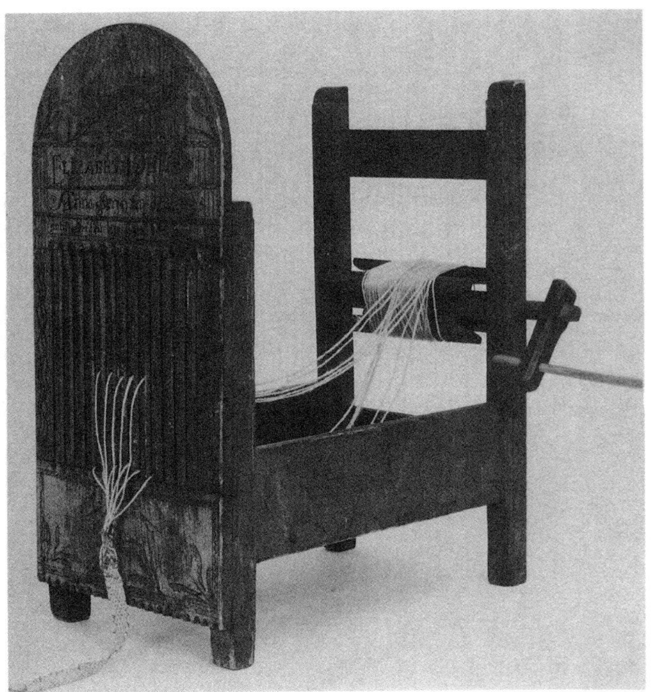

16

13 MEASURING REEL
1780–1800

Oak, hickory. Carved and shaped plank construction with pegged and wedged joints. Four shaped legs tenoned through base and wedged. Boards supporting rotating arms and gear wheel tenoned through base and pegged. Arms meet in nailed lap joint. Forty revolutions of arms complete one rotation of gear.

100 x 61 cm (39⅜ x 24″), radius 33 cm (13″)

Gift of Albert C. Barnes. 38-6-1

---

14 PINCUSHION
1780–1800

Painted maple. Pincushion tacked to turned cylindrical form cut out to fit over table edge. Carved fastening screw has turned vase-shaped handle. Cover replaced. Painted red, yellow, and green.

15.5 x 9 cm (6⅛ x 3½″)

Gift of J. Stogdell Stokes. 28-10-111

---

15 SWIFT
1790–1840

Pine, poplar, maple, chestnut. Tenon construction. Crossed arms in ship lap joint with tapering center support tenoned through bottom and into top. Adjustable winding pins have arrowlike carved knobs and tenon through upper and lower crossed arms. Chestnut base probably replaced.

70 x 75 cm (27½ x 29½″)

Gift of Mrs. Samuel D. Biddle. 34-23-4

---

16 TABLE LOOM
Lower Milford Township, Bucks County
1795

John Drissell

Inscribed: *Elizabeth Drissell   Anno den 9 ten October, 1795   John Drissell his hand Anno 1795*

Painted pine. Plank construction with mortise and tenon joints. Heddle end painted yellow with green vines; inscription black.

53.3 x 43.2 x 22.9 cm (21 x 17 x 9″)

Purchased: Annual Membership Fund. 16-272

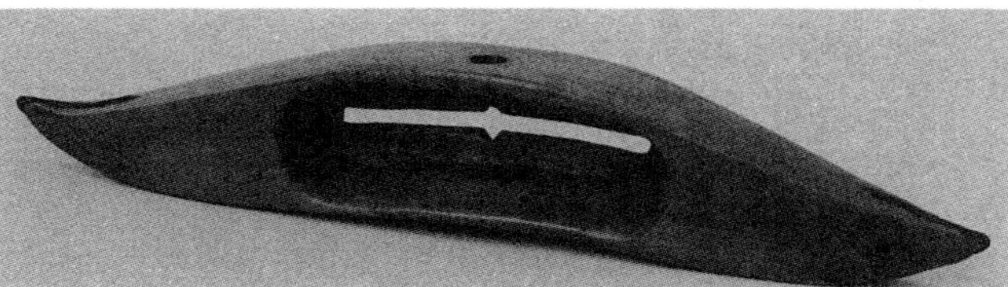

17

17 SHUTTLE
1800–1820

Cherry, iron. Carved and shaped with iron set into ends. Center cavity for bobbin with slit for thread. Used weaving wool coverlets.

27.9 x 4.1 cm (11 x 1⅝")

Gift of Mrs. William D. Frishmuth. 02-699

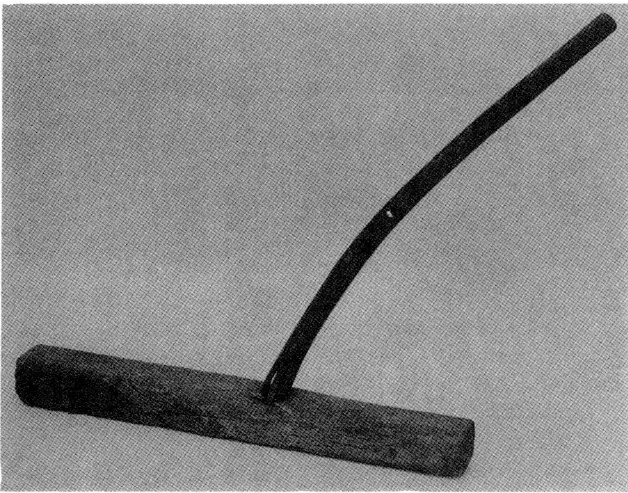

18

18 FLAX FLAIL
1800–1830

Pine, hickory. Shaped, solid club with flat bottom, tenoned crooked handle. Used for crushing flax seed-bolls to release seeds.

67.3 x 70.5 x 8.3 cm (26½ x 27¾ x 3¼")

Gift of Mrs. William D. Frishmuth. 02-291

19 SWINGLING KNIFE
1800–1830

Hickory. Single piece of shaped wood. Handle carved in slight angle to double-edged tapering blade. Used with shaped board ("swinglestock") to separate flax stems from fibers.

48.3 x 8.3 cm (19 x 3¼")

Gift of Mrs. William D. Frishmuth. 02-241

19

20 SWINGLING KNIFE
1800–1830

Cherry. Single piece of shaped wood. Carved rounded handle projects from double-edged blade with rounded end.

55.5 x 9.3 cm (21⅞ x 3⅝")

Gift of Mrs. William D. Frishmuth. 02-242

20

21 TAPE LOOM
1800–1830

Cherry. Shaped plank, heddle reed of sawed slots and drilled holes allowed alternate warp sheds. Used resting on a hard surface, held between the legs, and secured to wall or fixed object with strings through two drilled holes.

64.2 x 19.5 cm (25¼ x 7⅝")

Gift of Mrs. William D. Frishmuth. 02-248

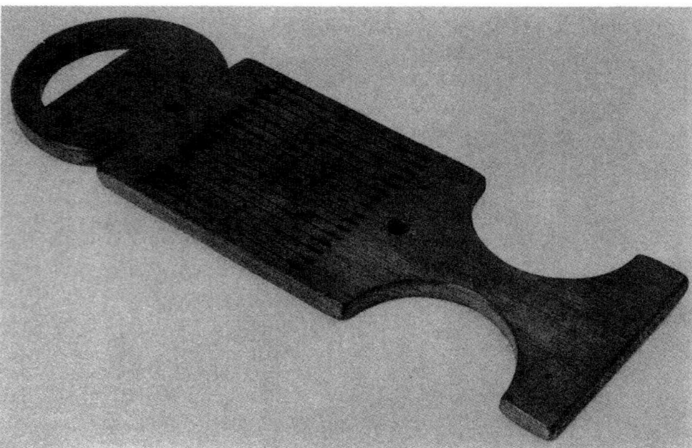

21

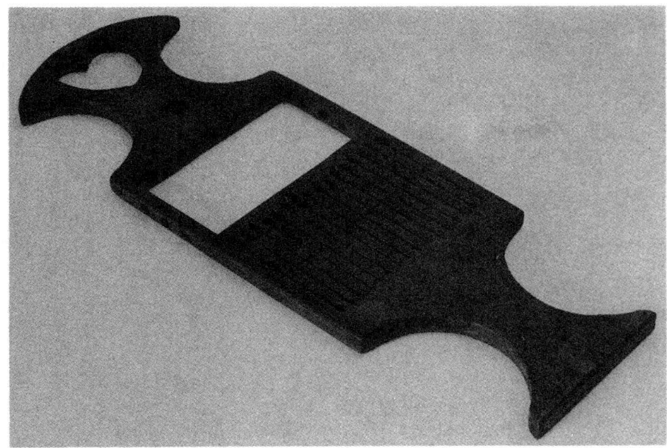

22

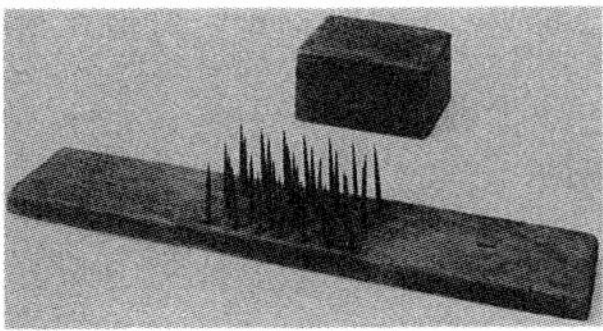

23

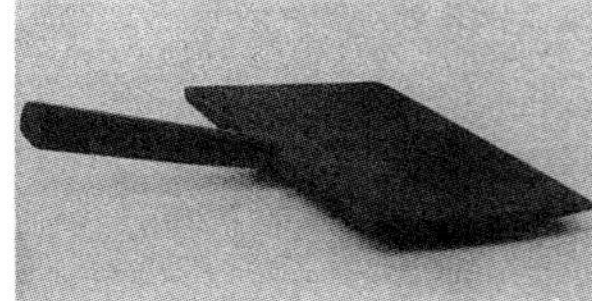

24

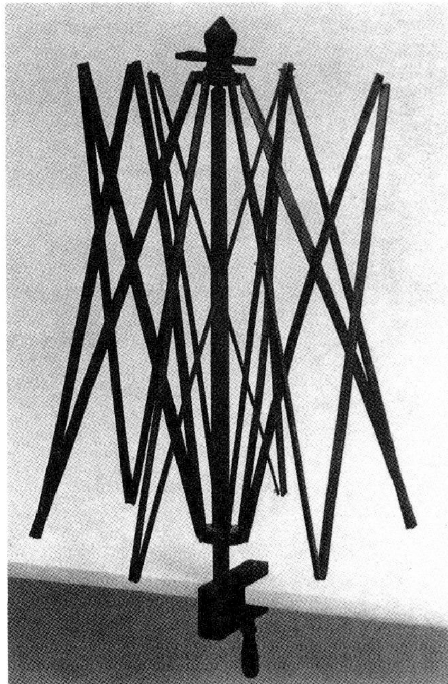

25

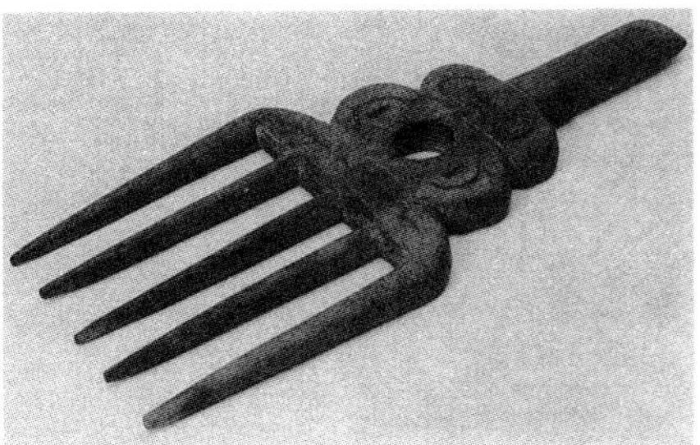

26

22 TAPE LOOM
1800–1830

Cherry. Shaped plank, heddle reed of sawed slots and drilled holes for alternate warp sheds. Three holes drilled in sides for roller bars (missing). Rested on hard surface, held between the legs, secured to fixed object or wall with string through center hole.

64 x 20.5 cm (25¼ x 8⅛")

Gift of Mrs. William D. Frishmuth. 02-249

23 HATCHEL
1800–1850

Inscribed flanking spikes: *L C*

Maple, iron. Flat board has small hole each end. Iron spikes (33) in offset rows at crossings of grid incised on board. Spike sheath has nailed butt joints.

12.8 x 61.5 x 12.8 cm (5 x 24¼ x 5")

Gift of Mrs. William D. Frishmuth. 02-211d

24 WOOL CARDER
1800–1850

Maple, pine, wire. Shaped handle meets flat board in lap joint secured with nails. Wire bristles worked through leather tacked to board. One of a pair.

25.3 x 24.7 cm (9⅞ x 9¾")

Gift of Mrs. William D. Frishmuth. 02-236a

25 SWIFT
1800–1850

Stamped on vise: *H. Kauffman*

Walnut, ash. Vise with wood tightening screw is drilled to receive turned shaft of swift. Arms wired at ends to permit umbrella action. Base socket raises to open. For drying and winding yarn.

79 x 12.5 cm (31⅛ x 4⅞")

Gift of Mrs. William D. Frishmuth. 02-240

26 WEAVING FORK
1800–1850

Incised reverse: *R. L.*

Walnut. Shaped and carved with five equal tines, scalloped neck, tapering handle. Incised line decoration. Used for straightening warps on loom.

18 x 8 cm (7⅛ x 3⅛")

Gift of Mrs. William D. Frishmuth. 07-373

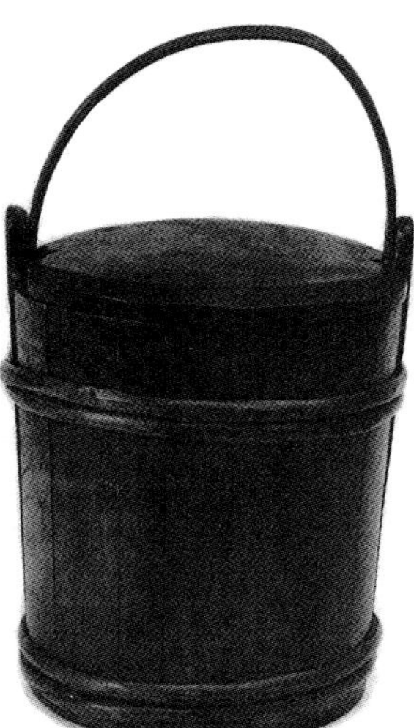

1

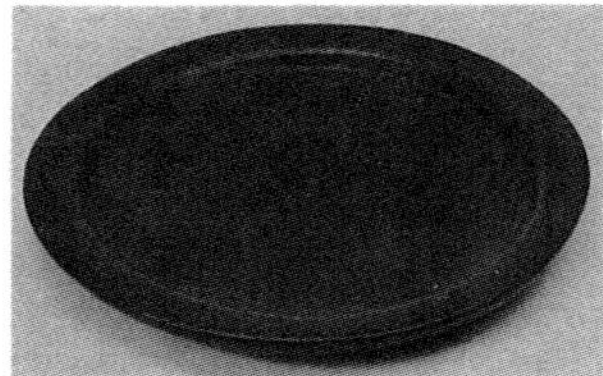

2

1 PAIL
1750–80

Pine, willow. Vertical staves meet in butt joints. Bent willow thongs encircle top and bottom and are screwed. Bottom set in and nailed through staves. Bentwood handle meets extensions of two staves and is pegged. Solid, shaped lid cut out to fit handle.

Height 42.8 cm (16⅞″), diameter 21.2 cm (8⅜″)

Gift of Mrs. William D. Frishmuth. 02-159

2 TRENCHER
1750–1800

Maple. Shaped and turned from single plank. Raised, flat rim on obverse.

Diameter 27 cm (10⅝″)

Gift of Mrs. William D. Frishmuth. 02-484

3 APPLE PARER
1750–1800

Walnut, pine, iron. Pegged mortise and tenon construction. Device secured with screwed vise. Iron crank arm with turned handle turns notched wheel which gears into arm supporting three-pronged iron spit. Movable arm fitted with peeling blade missing.

54 x 21.7 cm (21¼ x 8½″)

Gift of Mrs. William D. Frishmuth. 02-195

4 PIE CRIMPER
1753

Inscribed obverse: *H · R;* reverse: *1753*

Boxwood, copper. Shaped and carved shaft with fluted crimping wheel rotating on peg. Chip-carved designs on handle; concentric hearts on reverse, tulip on top. Ridges of bead molding on shaft. Fluted wheel made from coin of George I, about 1714.

14.1 x 4.2 cm (5½ x 1⅝″)

Gift of Mrs. William D. Frishmuth. 10-304

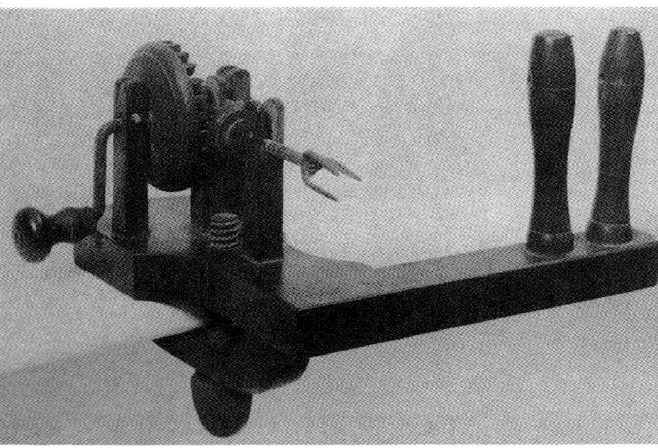

3

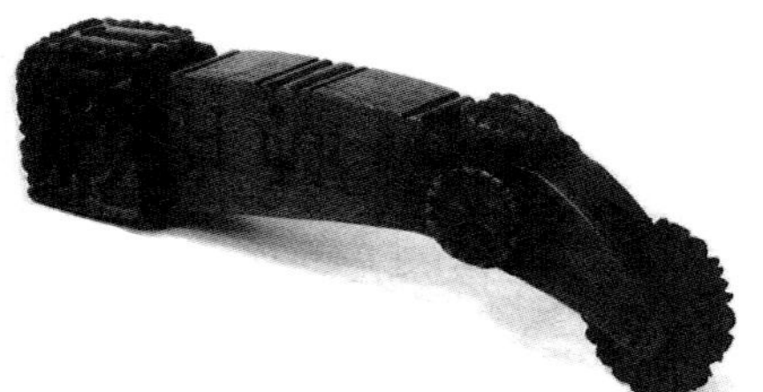

4 obverse

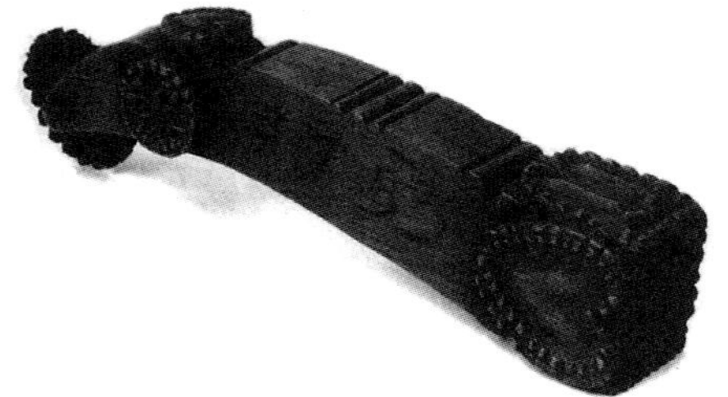

4 reverse

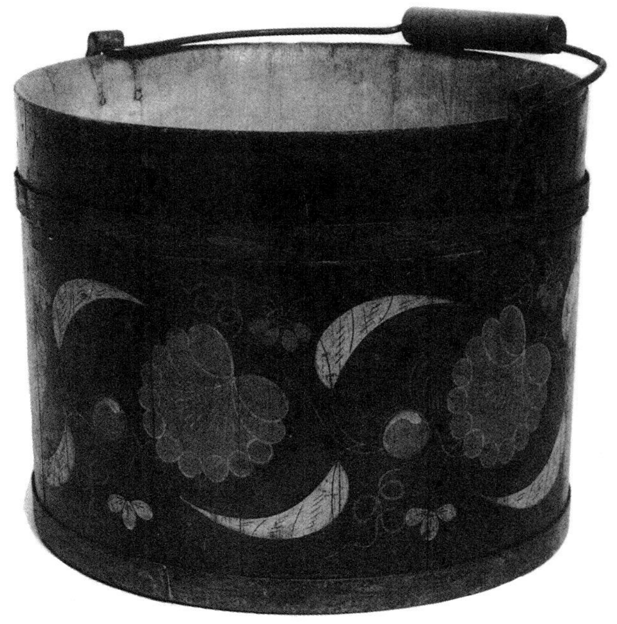

5

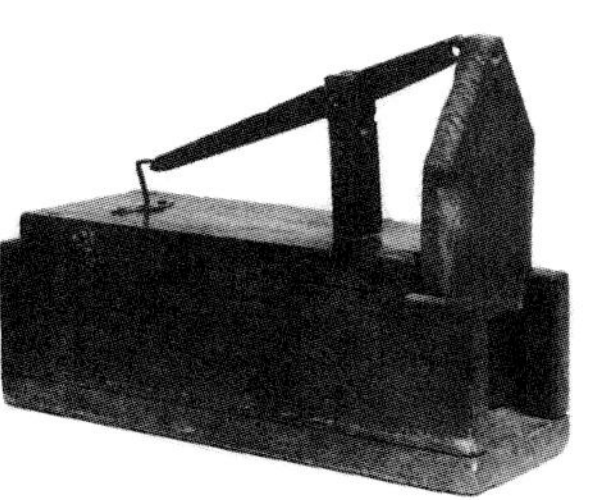

6

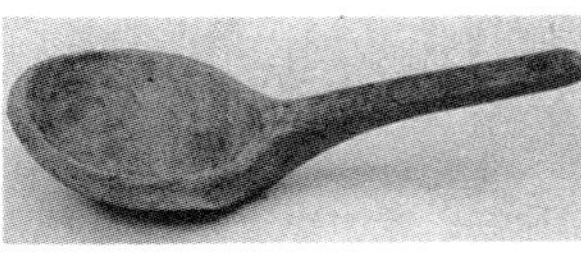

7

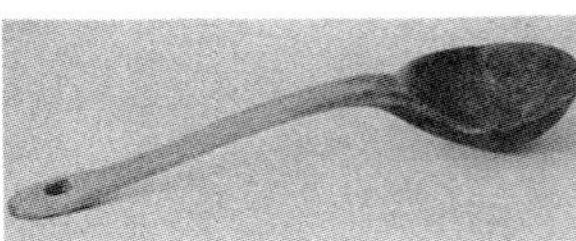

8

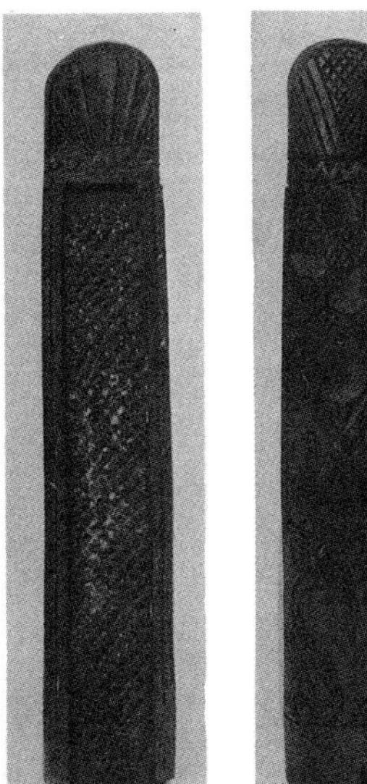

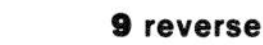

9 obverse   **9 reverse**

5 PAIL
1780–1800

Painted pine; maple, tin, iron. Shaped staves with notched sides bound with iron hoops at top and bottom. Looped iron handle grommets nailed to staves. Bent iron wire handle has turned maple grip. Painted dark green with red, yellow, and green floral designs.

Height 25.4 cm (10″), diameter 29.8 cm (11¾″)

Titus C. Geesey Collection. 54-85-71

6 TRAP
1780–1800

Oak, brass, iron. Plank construction with nailed butt joints. Sliding door drops when metal spring inside is released from baited hook. Back is perforated tin.

20 x 10.5 x 32.7 cm (7⅝ x 4⅛ x 12⅞″)

Gift of Francis T. Chambers, Jr. 30-61-1

7 LADLE
1780–1800

Pine. Shaped, straight handle, carved and scooped bowl. Hanging hole in handle.

32.7 x 13.7 cm (12⅞ x 5⅜″)

Gift of Mrs. William D. Frishmuth. 02-667

8 LADLE
1780–1800

Maple burl. Shaped, arched handle in one piece with carved burl bowl. Hanging hole in handle.

43.6 x 14.1 cm (17⅛ x 5½″)

Gift of Mrs. William D. Frishmuth. 02-666

9 NUTMEG GRATER
1780–1800

Walnut, tin. Carved and gouged wood shaft with grooved molded edges that hold sliding perforated tin grater.

16.5 x 3.1 cm (6½ x 1¼″)

Gift of Mrs. William D. Frishmuth. 10-303

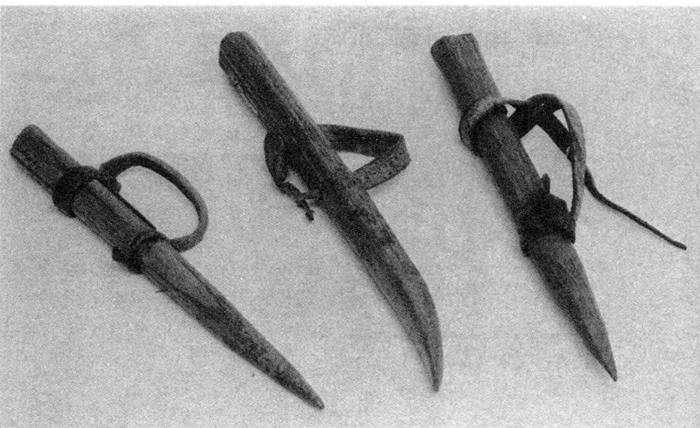

10

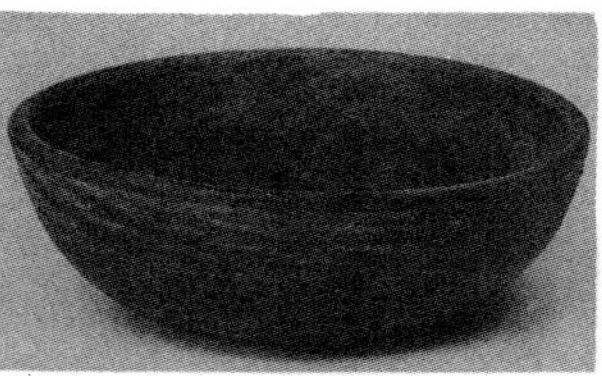

11

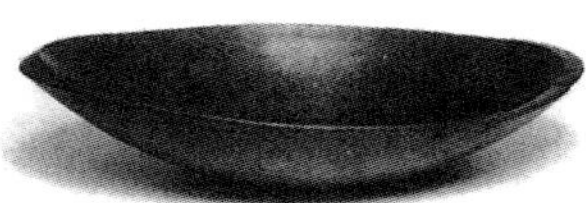

12

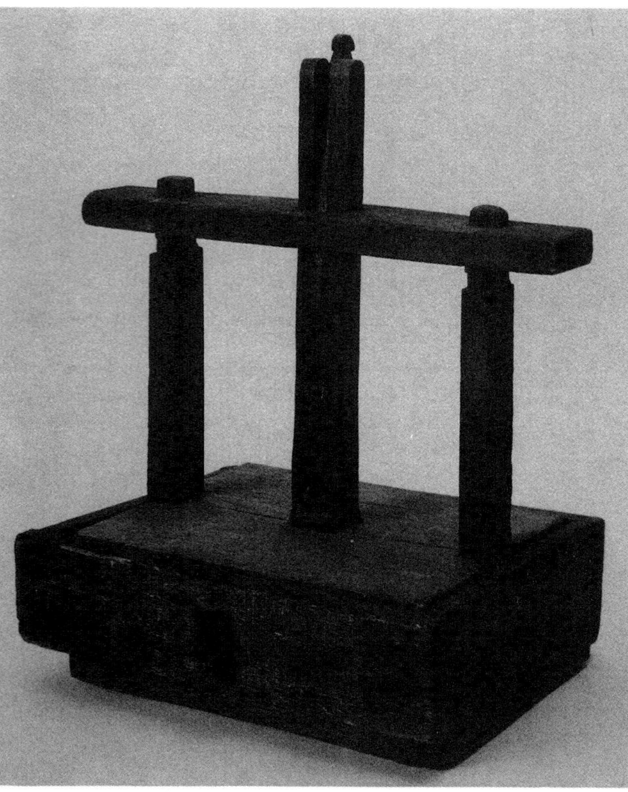

13

10 CORN SHELLERS (3)
1780–1800

Oak, maple, leather. Shaped spikes with thong finger grips. Leathers secured through holes or around incised groove. Spikes worn on fingers of one hand and raked over cob to remove kernels.

Length (a) 11.6 cm (4½″), (b) 12.4 cm (4⅞″), (c) 11.8 cm (4⅝″)

Gift of Mrs. William D. Frishmuth. 05-139a,b,c

11 BOWL
1780–1800

Maple. Smooth, flat bottom and rounded edges. Turned from single block.

Height 6.8 cm (2⅝″), diameter 20 cm (7⅞″)

Gift of Mrs. William D. Frishmuth. 07-363

12 BOWL
1780–1800

Maple. Gouged and carved from single block into elliptical shape.

11 x 61 x 34.2 cm (4¼ x 24 x 13½″)

Gift of J. Stogdell Stokes. 37-13-4

13 DEAD-FALL TRAP
1780–1800

Oak, poplar, pine. Butt construction with nailed joints, inset bottom. Wood lever at entrance hole trips notched ratchet out of its slot to release heavy block that kills rodent in box.

47 x 41.2 cm (18½ x 16¼″)

Gift of Mrs. William D. Frishmuth. 02-214

14 PIE CRIMPER
c. 1800

Incised on handle: *M H*

Pine, copper. Shaped, turned handle cut to receive fluted copper wheel that rotates on rivet.

Height 13.6 cm (5⅜″), diameter wheel 4.8 cm (1⅞″)

Gift of Mrs. William D. Frishmuth. 07-374

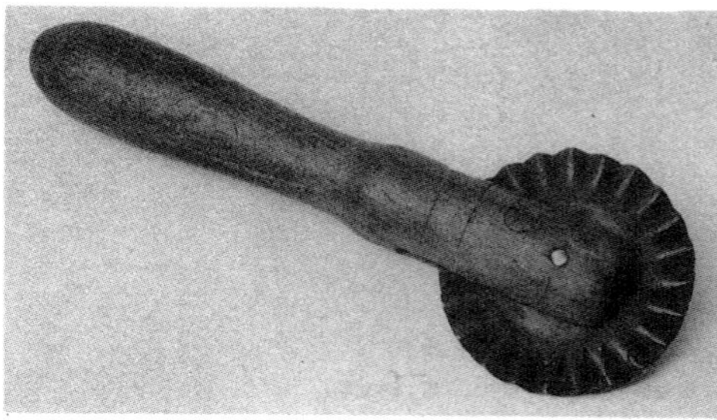

14

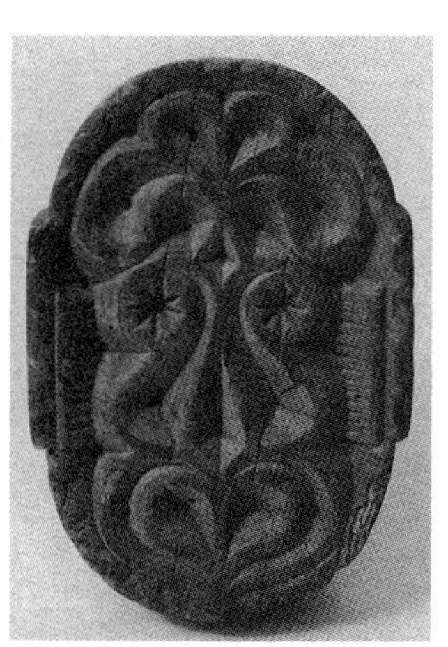
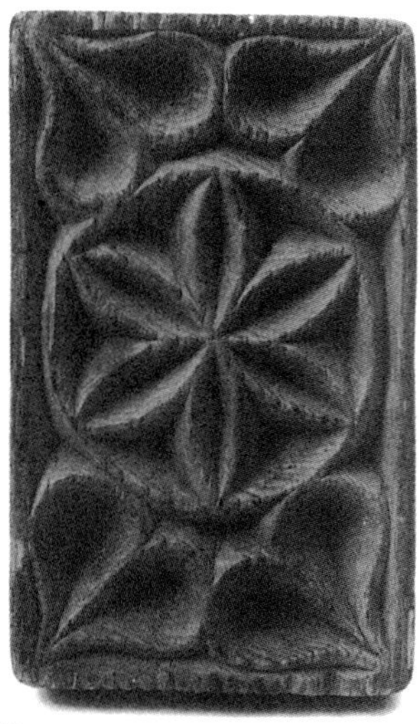

15   16

15 **SMOOTHING BLOCK**
c. 1800

Cedar. Hand-cut ellipse with fingerholds. Relief and intaglio carving bordered with zigzag notching, punctuated with countersunk holes. Smooth surface on reverse for pressing.

12.8 x 8.8 x 3.3 cm (5 x 3½ x 1¼")

Titus C. Geesey Collection. 55-94-34

16 **SMOOTHING BLOCK**
1800–1820

Incised reverse: *EF*

Pine. Hand-cut block with canted sides for grasping. Obverse has relief-carved design; reverse has incised initials and swirling swastika.

12.1 x 7 x 2.5 cm (4¾ x 2¾ x 1")

Titus C. Geesey Collection. 55-94-33

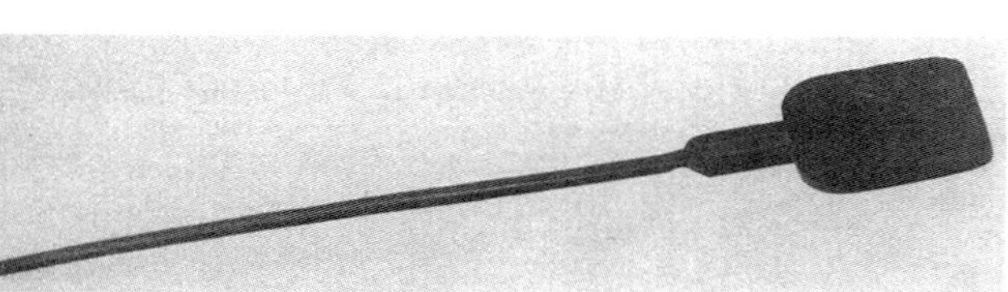

17

17 **PEEL**
1800–1830

Marked on paddle: ⅛ x ⅛

Oak. Handle has square profile with rounded edges; joins neck of shovel in pegged finger joint; one peg wedged.

189.2 x 29.3 cm (74½ x 11½")

Gift of Mrs. William D. Frishmuth. 02-559

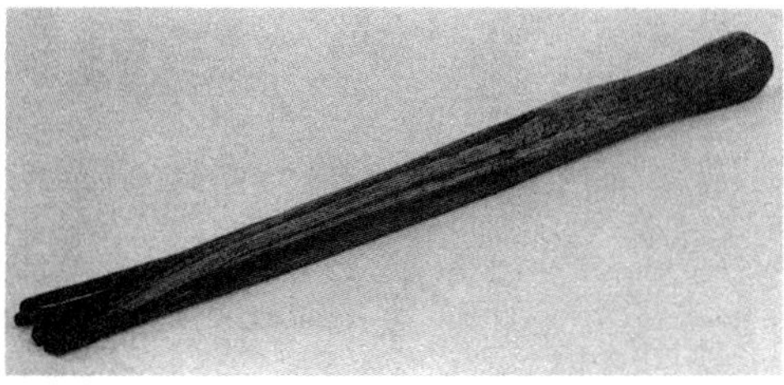

18

18 **EGG WHIP**
1800–1850

Hickory. Shaped stick, handle at one end, two-thirds of length split into eight parts.

Height 32.6 cm (12⅞"), diameter 2.5 cm (1")

Gift of Mrs. William D. Frishmuth. 02-532

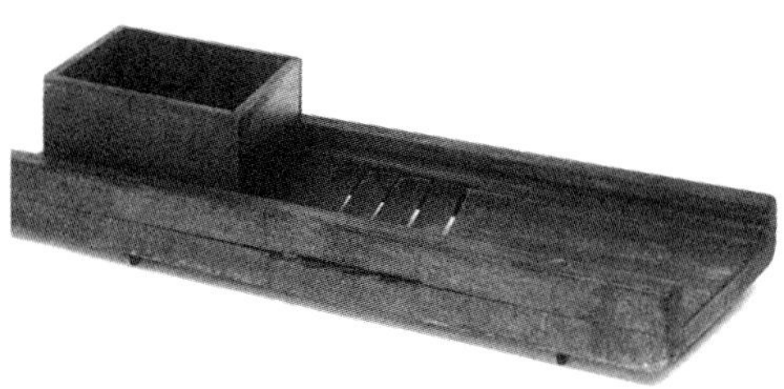

19

19 **CABBAGE SHREDDER**
1800–1850

Oak, pine, iron. Plank construction, nailed and bolted. Cabbage box has butt joints, nailed; sides have projecting molding that slides in grooves in sides of cutting trough. Slanted cutting knives set in frame are secured by bolts.

19 x 90.5 x 31.7 cm (7½ x 35⅝ x 12½")

Gift of Mrs. William D. Frishmuth. 02-204

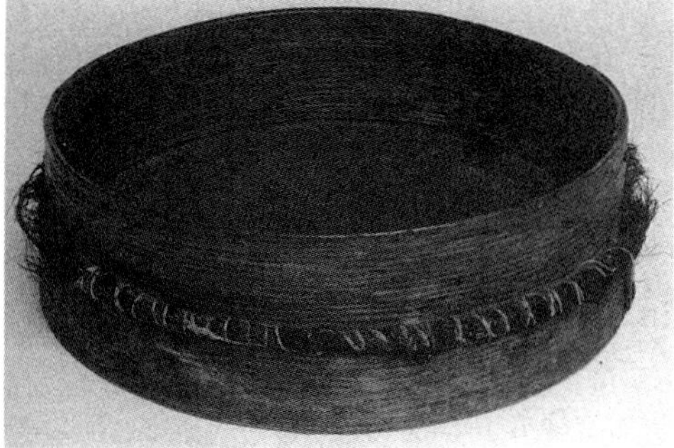

20

20 **SIEVE**
1800–1850

Red oak, horsehair. Bentwood construction with clinch-nailed overlapping joint. Woven horsehair mesh held by bentwood splints, finished with wrapping of tow linen.

Height 8.9 cm (3½"), diameter 28 cm (11")

Gift of J. Stogdell Stokes. 36-19-4

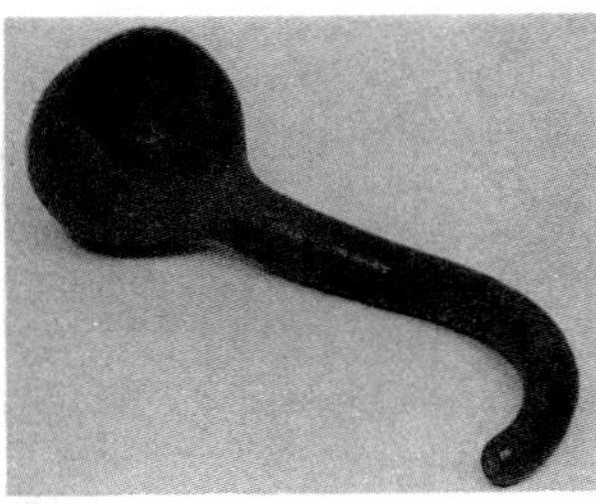

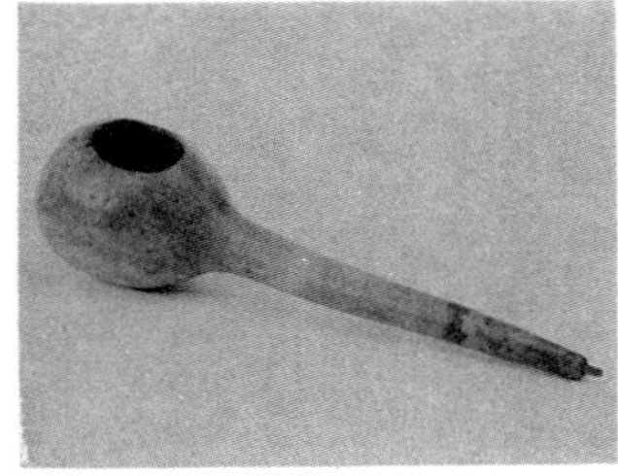

21

22

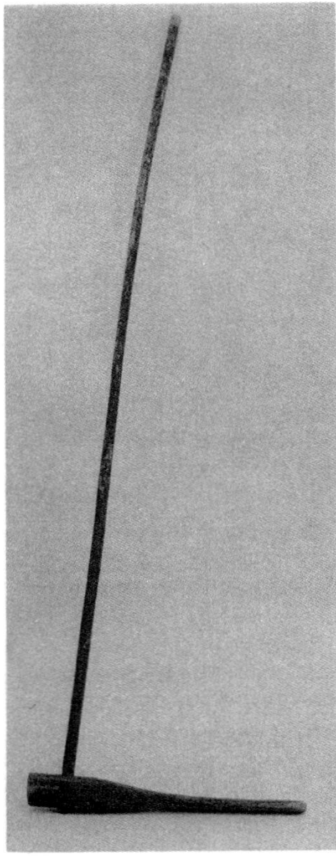

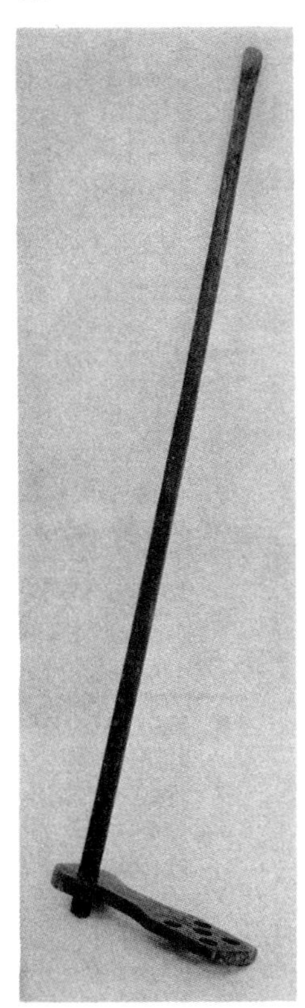

23

24

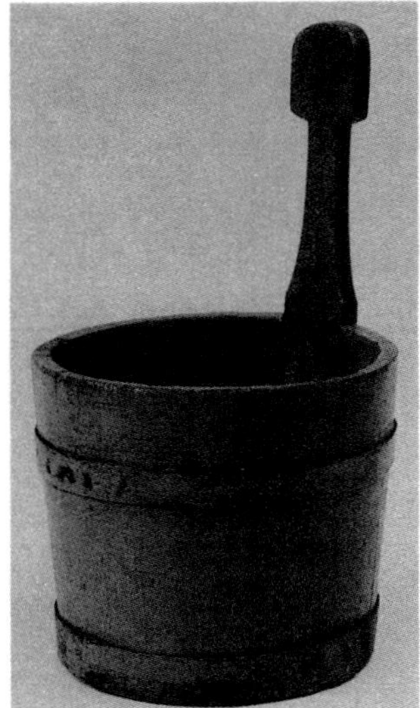

25

21 LADLE
1800–1850
Gourd. Natural twist to neck of gourd forms handle. Bowl hollowed out.
22.1 x 7.8 cm (8¾ x 3″)
Gift of Mrs. William D. Frishmuth. 02-546

22 LADLE
1800–1850
Gourd. Bowl hollowed out. Stem remains on handle.
46.4 x 13 cm (18¼ x 5⅛″)
Gift of Mrs. William D. Frishmuth. 02-537

23 APPLE-BUTTER STIRRER
1800–1850
Oak, maple. Long arm tenoned through head and wedged.
149.8 x 50.8 cm (59 x 20″)
Gift of Mrs. William D. Frishmuth. 02-192

24 APPLE-BUTTER STIRRER
1800–1850
Maple, oak. Pole handle tenoned through end of shaped stirrer and pegged. Paddle end of stirrer has five round holes.
119.2 x 33.6 cm (46⅞ x 13¼″)
Gift of Mrs. William D. Frishmuth. 02-193

25 PIGGIN
1800–1850
Painted pine, iron. Shaped staves in butt joints encircled with two iron bands, nailed. One stave elongated into shaped handle. Painted pink brown, varnished.
Height 39.4 cm (15½″), diameter 22.9 cm (9″)
Gift of Mrs. William D. Frishmuth. 02-196

26 DRY MEASURE
1840–1900
Pine. Bentwood construction, ends feathered and tacked. Circular bottom tacked. Interior painted red.
Height 9.4 cm (3¾″), diameter 14 cm (5½″)
Gift of Mrs. William D. Frishmuth. 02-376

26

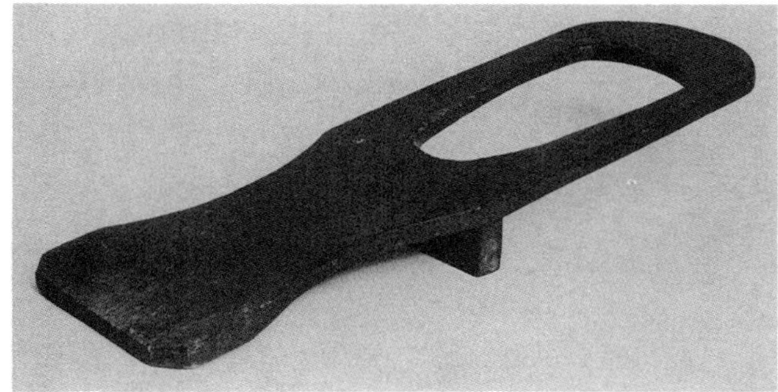

27

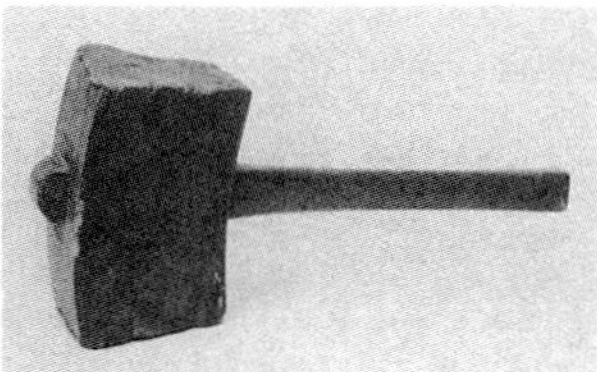

28

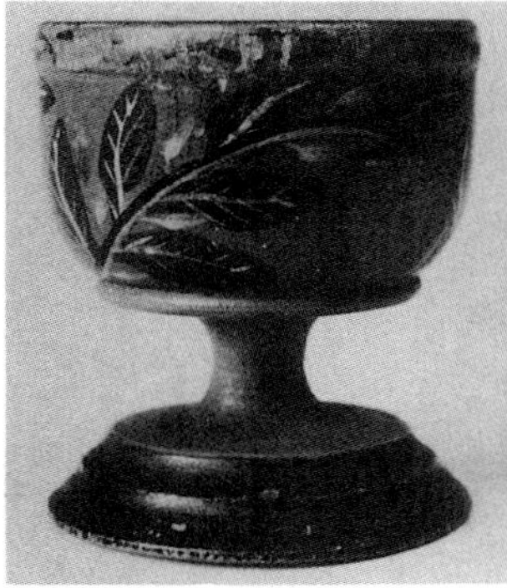

29

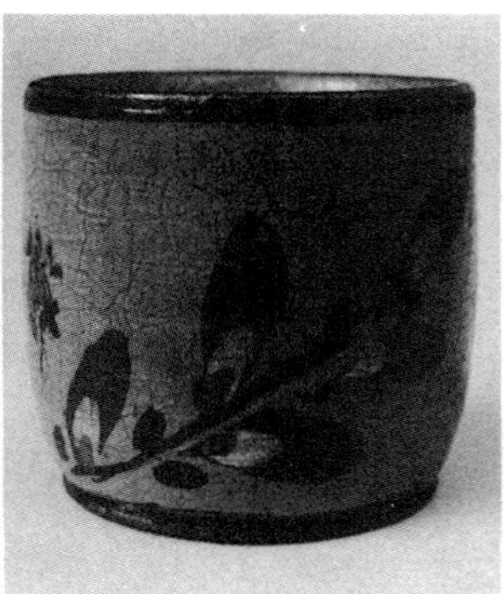

30

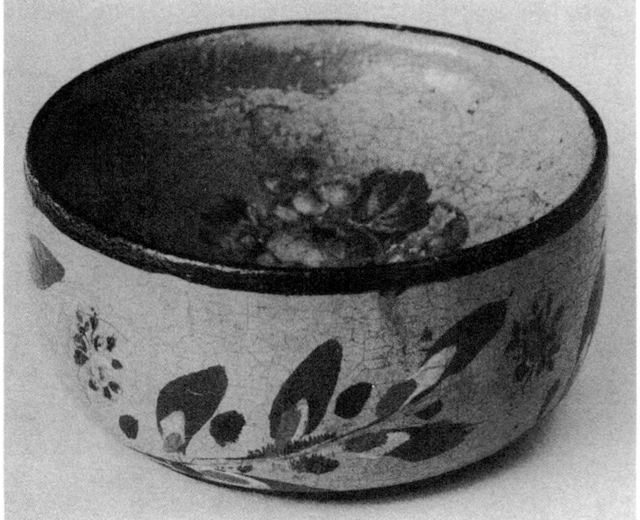

31

27 BOOTJACK
c. 1850

Painted pine. Flat, shaped board cut out to
receive heel of a boot; raised on wood block
secured with screws. Painted green.

61 x 17.3 cm (24 x 6¾″)

Gift of J. Stogdell Stokes. 28-10-103

28 MALLET
Chester County
1850–60

Stamped on head, top, and bottom:
I. GARTSIDE

Beech burl, hickory. Shaped head. Rounded
handle flattens into wedged tenon joint.

37.8 x 17.4 cm (14⅞ x 6⅞″)

Gift of Mrs. William D. Frishmuth. 02-191

29 SALT
Elizabethtown Township, Lancaster County
c. 1860–80

Joseph Long Lehn

Painted maple. Lathe-turned, sanded, painted.
Gray blue body, yellow interior. Strawberry
design is red, green, white, black, and yellow;
stem is scarlet with green and black border.

Height 4.1 cm (1⅝″), diameter 3.5 cm (1⅜″)

Titus C. Geesey Collection. 54-85-118

30 CUP
Elizabethtown Township, Lancaster County
1880–92

Joseph Long Lehn

Painted maple. Lathe-turned. Pink ground
with freehand painting of pussy willows in red,
green, white, black, and yellow. Interior has
decalcomania of flower cluster.

Height 6.3 cm (2½″), diameter 3.5 cm (1⅜″)

Titus C. Geesey Collection. 54-85-119a

31 BOWL
Elizabethtown Township, Lancaster County
1890

Joseph Long Lehn

Marked on label pasted to bottom: *Made by
Joseph Lehn in his 93rd year, January 20, 1890.*

Painted maple. Lathe-turned. Pink ground
with pussy willows in red, green, white, black,
and yellow. Interior floral decalcomania.

Height 3.8 cm (1½″), diameter 7.3 cm (2⅞″)

Titus C. Geesey Collection. 54-85-119b

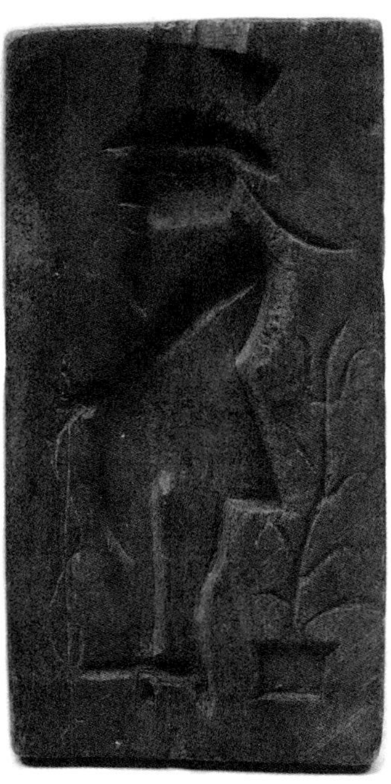

1

1

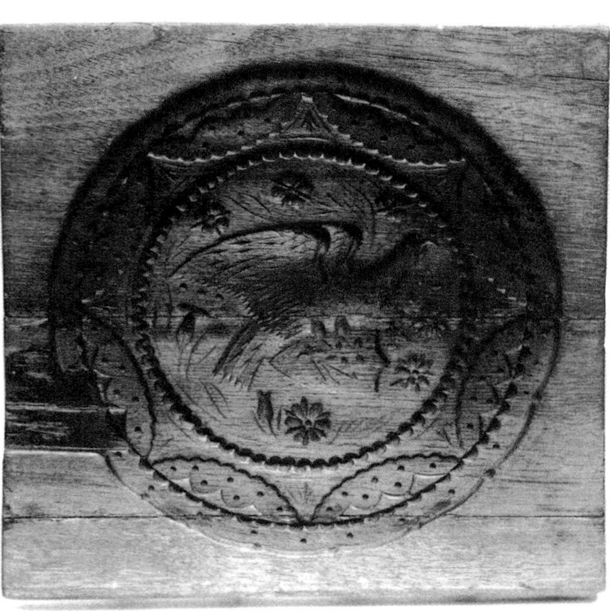

2

1 PASTRY MOLD
1800–1820

Maple. Hand-carved intaglio design. Used for springerle.

12.1 x 6.2 x 1.2 cm (4¾ x 2⅜ x ½″)

Titus C. Geesey Collection. 55-94-38

2 PASTRY MOLD
1800–1820

Walnut. Carved intaglio design encircled with gouged and punched decorations of bands and swags. Used for springerle.

30.5 x 29.2 x 2.2 cm (12 x 11½ x ⅞″)

Titus C. Geesey Collection. 55-94-13

3 PASTRY MOLD
1800–1850

Maple. Obverse of block has two designs, gouged and punch-carved. Reverse has gouged fingerholds and incised flower and foliage motif.

14.5 x 6.8 x 1.3 cm (5¾ x 2⅝ x ½″)

Gift of Mrs. Jones Wister. 13-564

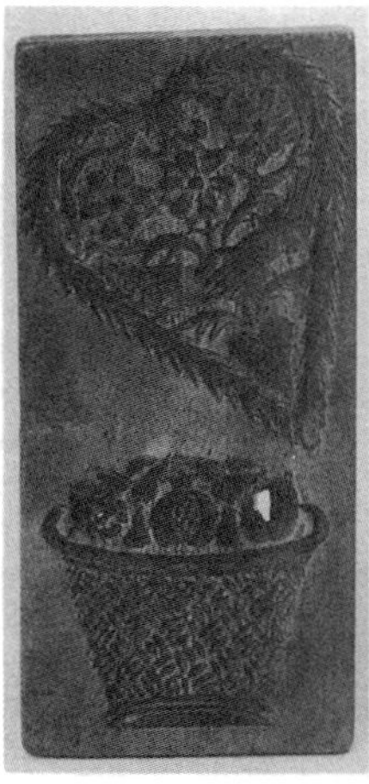

3 obverse   **3 reverse**

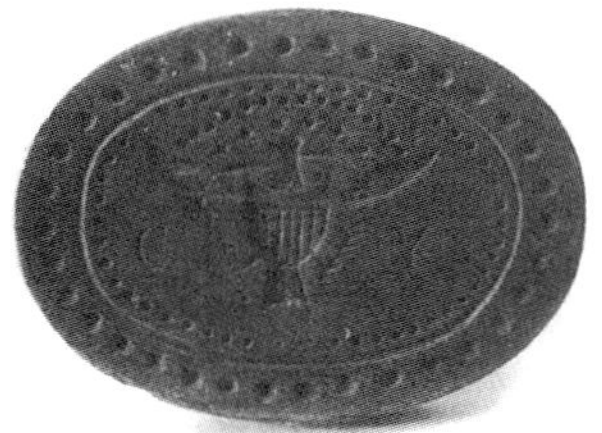

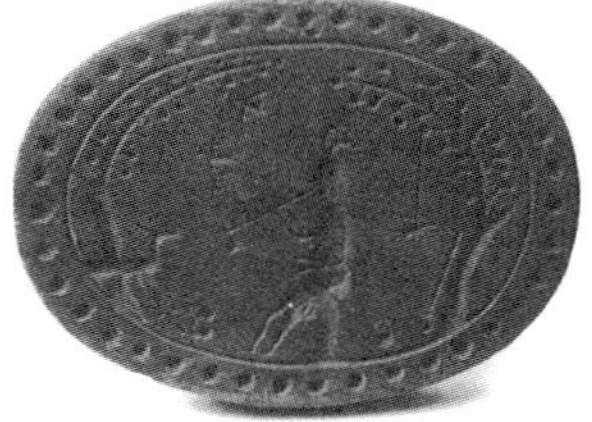

4 obverse   **4 reverse**

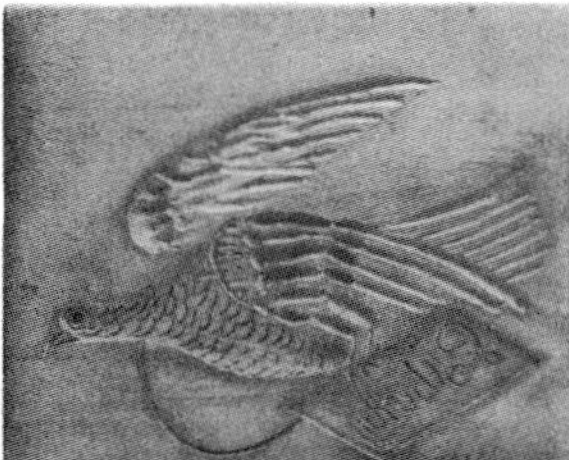

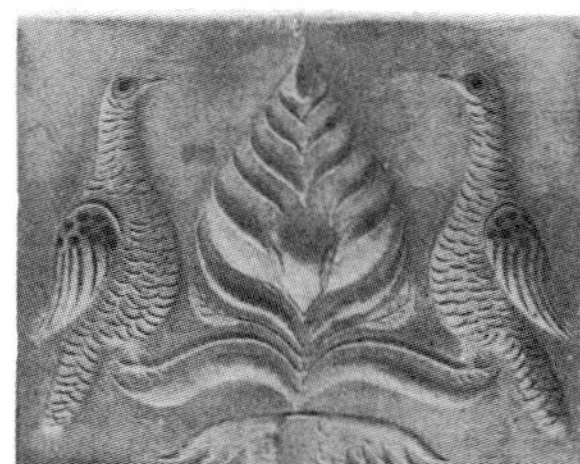

5 obverse   **5 reverse**

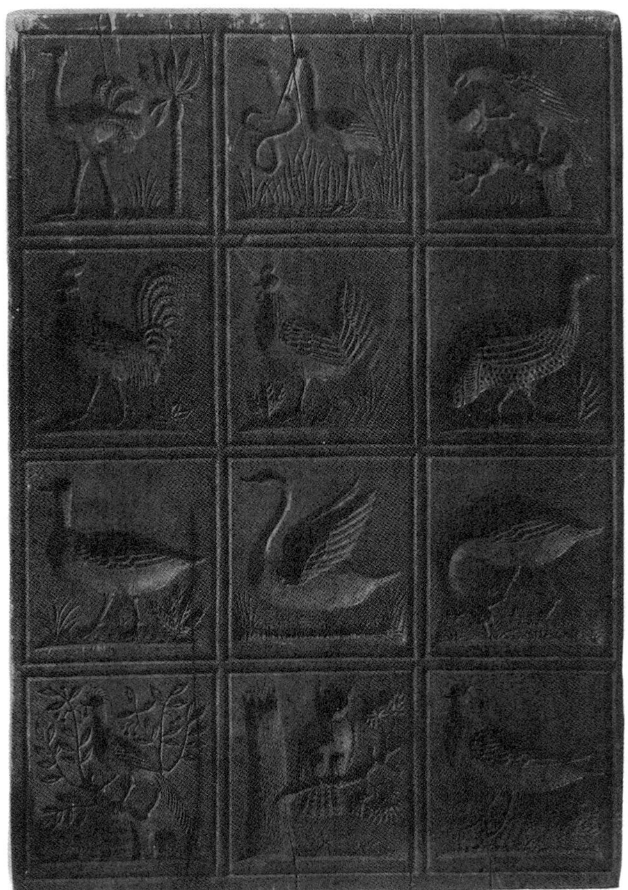

6

4   PASTRY MOLD
1818

Incised obverse: *C Y 1818*

Poplar. Hand-cut block with intaglio carving on obverse and reverse. Each design enclosed by double border of incised line and dots.

16.2 x 12.1 x 2.5 cm (6⅜ x 4¾ x 1")

Titus C. Geesey Collection. 55-94-36

5   PASTRY MOLD
Berks County
1825–30

Incised on side: *E L No 8;* reverse: *Liberty*

Boxwood. Hand-cut block with intaglio carving on obverse and reverse. Used for springerle.

7.6 x 9.8 x 1.9 cm (3 x 3⅞ x ¾")

Titus C. Geesey Collection. 55-94-37

6   PASTRY MOLD
Lancaster, Lancaster County
1843

Incised reverse: *C. G. Weiss. 1843   C.G.W.*

Maple. Hand-shaped board with intaglio carving. Obverse divided into twelve squares with carved designs of birds in native habitats. Probably used for springerle.

20.3 x 14 x 2.5 cm (8 x 5½ x 1")

Titus C. Geesey Collection. 55-94-35

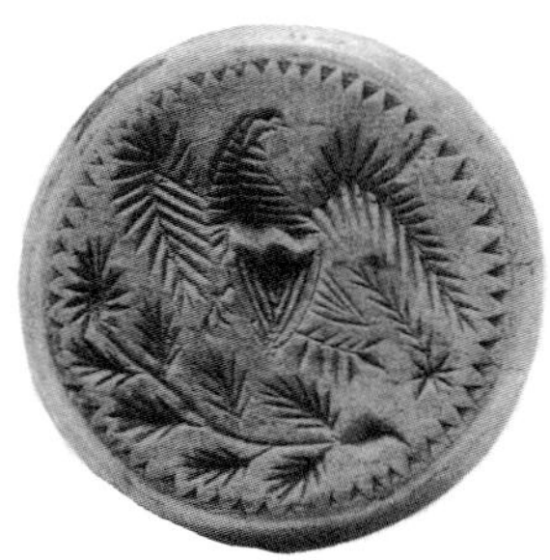

1 obverse

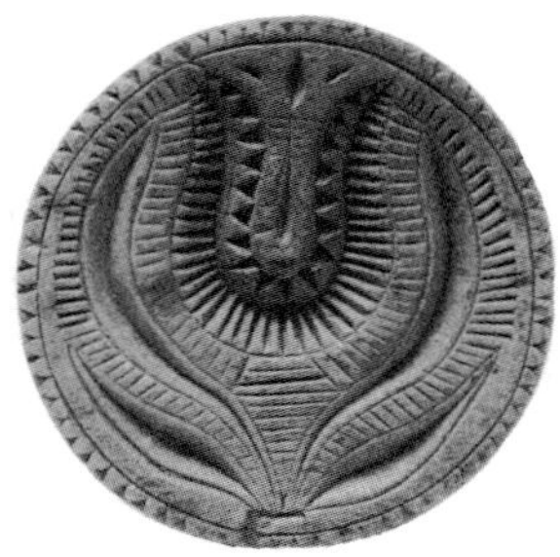

1 reverse

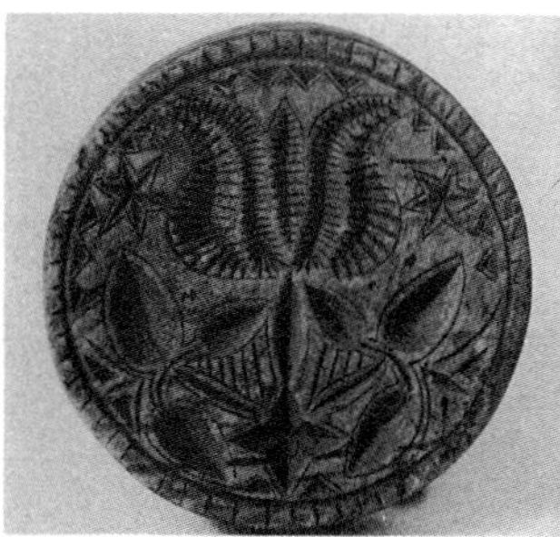

2 obverse

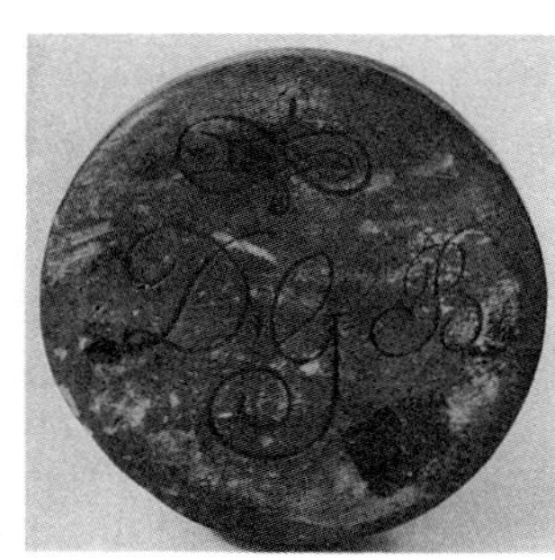

2 reverse

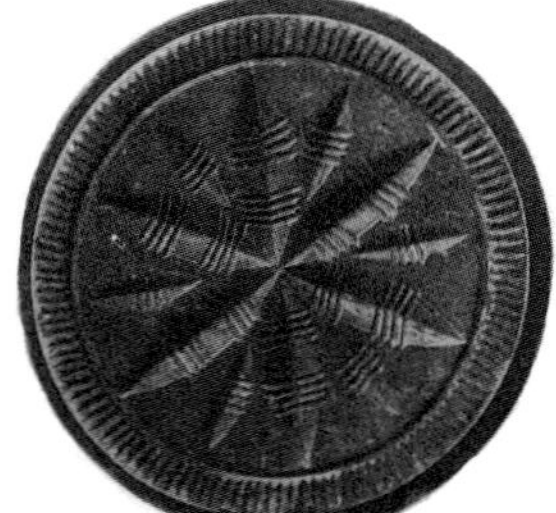

3 reverse

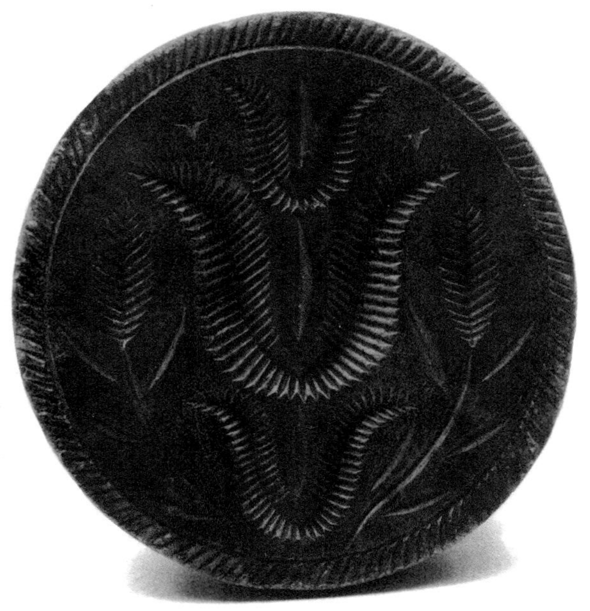

3 obverse

1 DOUBLE BUTTER PRINT
1800–1820

Poplar. Chip- and gouge-carved disk with carved intaglio designs on obverse and reverse. Each design encircled with border of chip-carved triangles. Oval aperture possibly a handle.

Height 2.8 cm (1⅛″); diameter obverse 10.1 cm (4″), reverse 8.5 cm (3⅜″)

Titus C. Geesey Collection. 55-94-28

2 DOUBLE BUTTER PRINT
1800–1820

Incised reverse: *D. G B*

Maple. Hand-cut block with carved and incised intaglio design with fluted border on obverse and decorative calligraphic design incised on reverse. Rim decorated with incised star motifs.

Height 2.5 cm (1″), diameter 11.1 cm (4⅜″)

Titus C. Geesey Collection. 55-94-30

3 DOUBLE BUTTER PRINT
1800–1820

Maple. Double print has connecting stem lathe-turned from single piece of wood. Carved intaglio designs on obverse and reverse have striated borders.

Height 6.3 cm (2½″); diameter obverse 9.5 cm (3¾″), reverse 8.2 cm (3¼″)

Titus C. Geesey Collection. 55-94-31

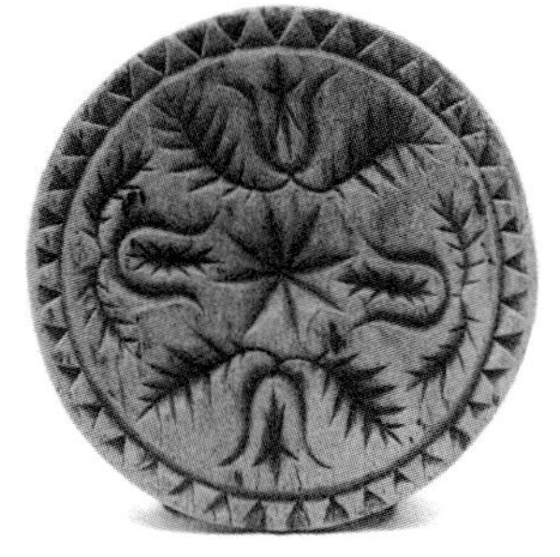

4 obverse

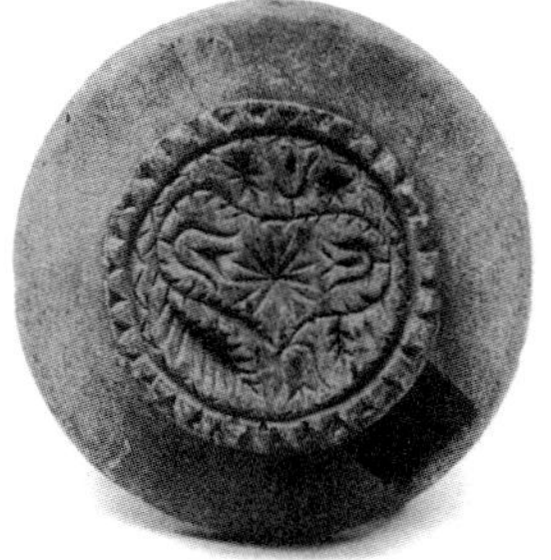

4 reverse

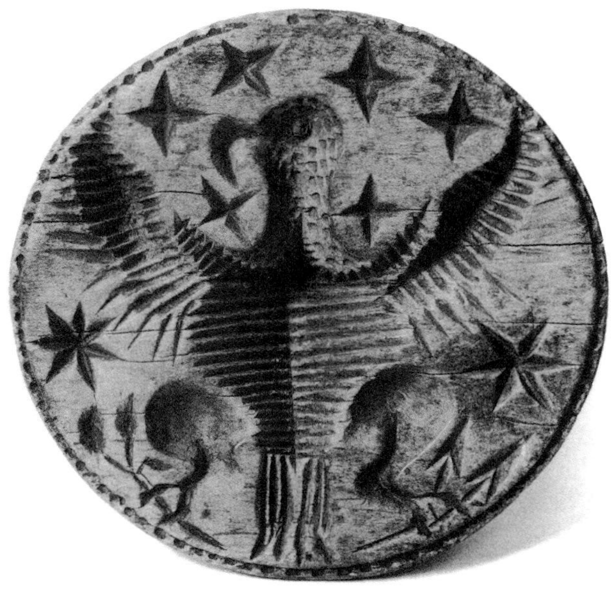

5

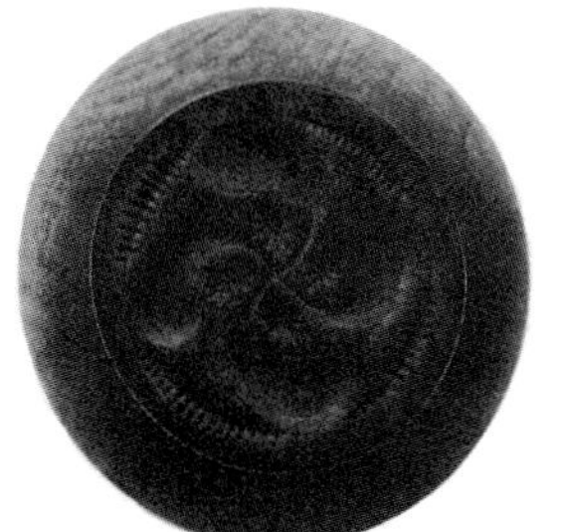

6 obverse

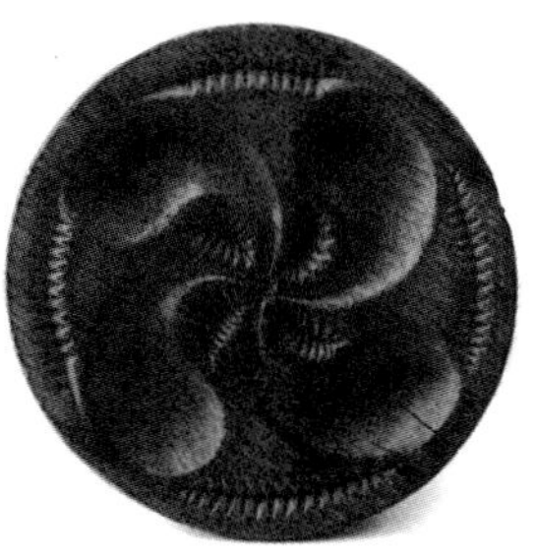

6 reverse

4 DOUBLE BUTTER PRINT
1800–1820

Poplar. Hand-cut from one piece. Chip- and gouge-carved intaglio designs on obverse and reverse, bordered with radiating triangles.

Height 2.8 cm (1⅛″); diameter obverse 10.8 cm (4¼″), reverse 7 cm (2¾″)

Titus C. Geesey Collection. 55-94-29

5 BUTTER PRINT
1800–1840

Maple. Chip- and gouge-carved circular block has shrunk to an oval. Obverse has carved intaglio design with punched border. Reverse has handle socket, handle missing.

2.5 x 13 cm (1 x 5⅛″)

Titus C. Geesey Collection. 55-94-24

6 DOUBLE BUTTER PRINT
1800–1850

Pine. Turned from one piece. Carved and gouged intaglio design on obverse and reverse.

Height 6.1 cm (2⅝″); diameter obverse 10.8 cm (4¼″), reverse 7 cm (2¾″)

Titus C. Geesey Collection. 55-94-26

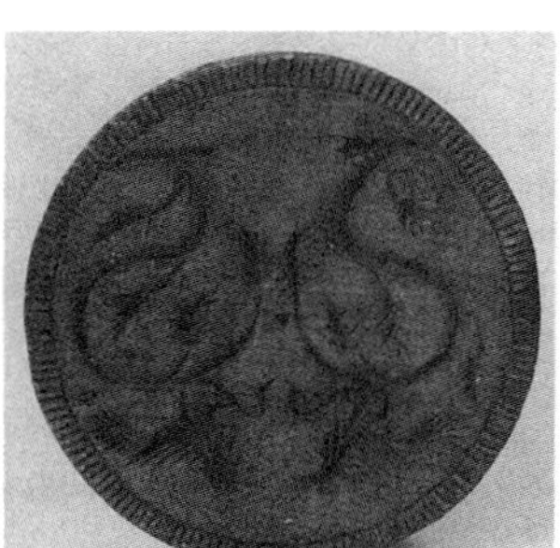

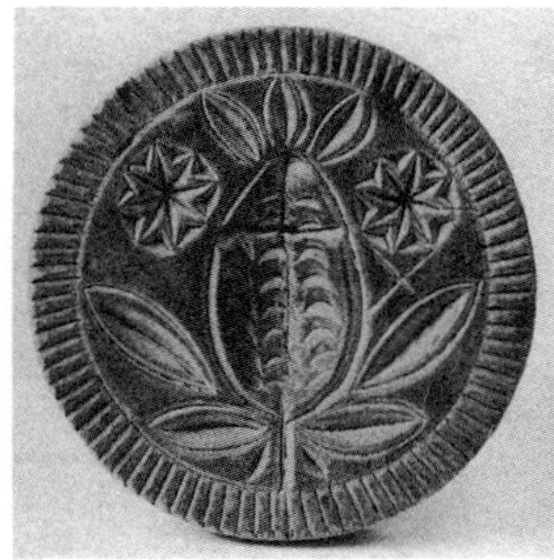

7

8

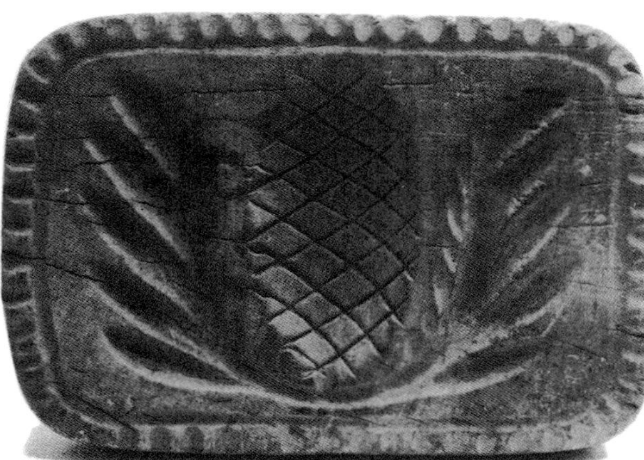

9

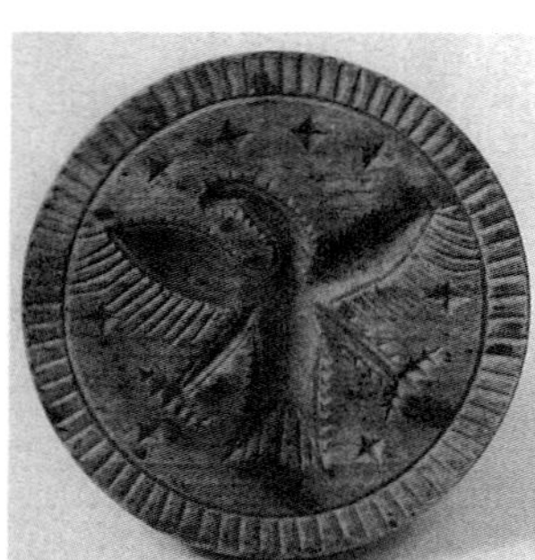

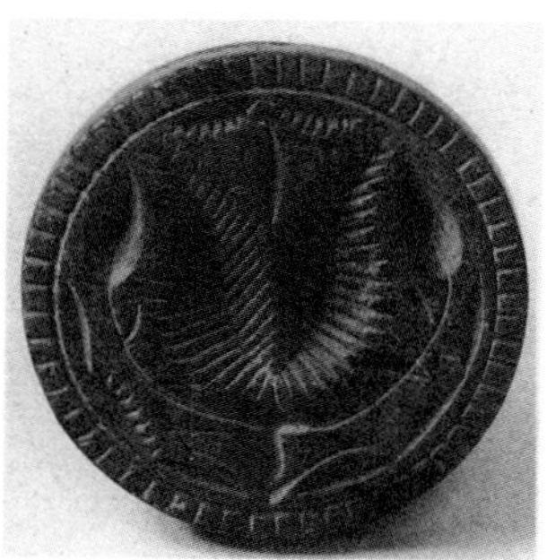

10

11

7 BUTTER PRINT
1800–1850

Pine. Chip- and gouge-carved design on hand-cut circle. Obverse has carved intaglio design with fluted border. Groove carved in reverse for fingerhold.

Height 2.2 cm (⅞″), diameter 11.4 cm (4½″)

Titus C. Geesey Collection. 55-94-27

8 BUTTER PRINT
1820–50

Maple. Disk and handle turned from one piece. Carved design encircled with striated border of chip and gouge carving.

Height 7 cm (2¾″), diameter 10.8 cm (4¼″)

Titus C. Geesey Collection. 55-94-20

9 BUTTER PRINT
1820–60

Maple. Block and handle cut from single piece. Carved intaglio design on face with border of incised line and cuts made with gouge chisel.

9.5 x 12.1 cm (3¾ x 4¾″)

Titus C. Geesey Collection. 55-94-22

10 DOUBLE BUTTER PRINT
c. 1850

Pine. Print and handle lathe-turned from single piece. Chip- and gouge-carved designs on obverse and reverse (tulip).

Height 3.7 cm (1½″); diameter obverse 11.4 cm (4½″), reverse 6.3 cm (2½″)

Titus C. Geesey Collection. 55-94-25

11 BUTTER PRINT
c. 1850

Maple. Print and handle lathe-turned from one piece with chip-carved design encircled by fluted border.

Height 7.6 cm (3″), diameter 8.9 cm (3½″)

Gift of Miss Frances Lichten. 60-91-4

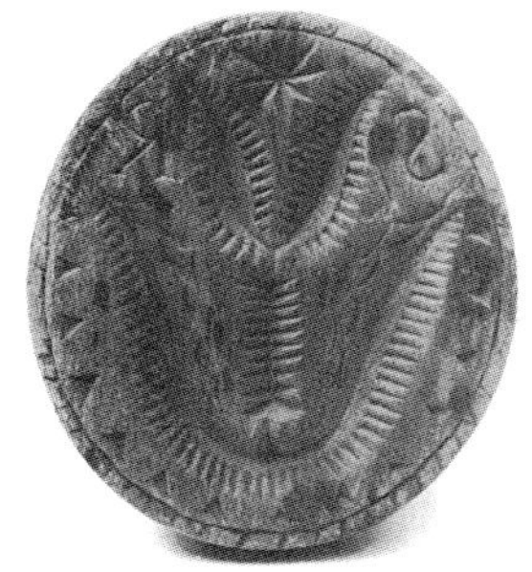

12

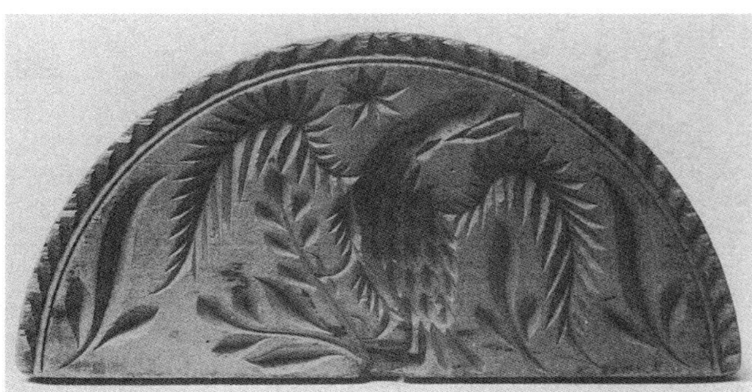

13

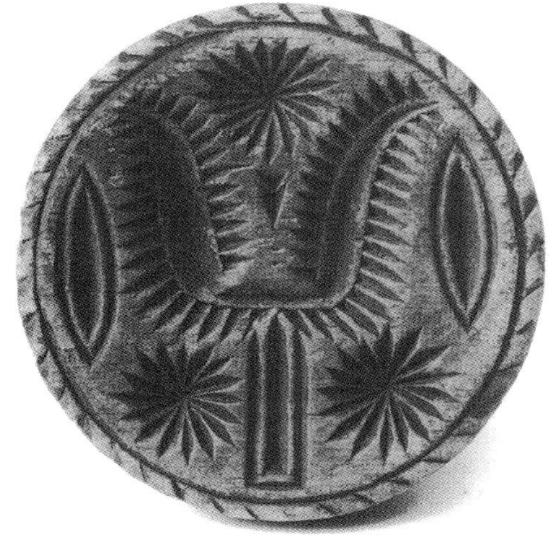

14

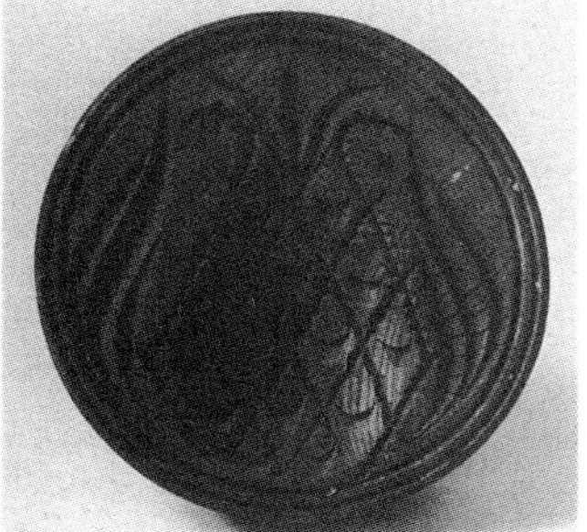

15

12 BUTTER PRINT
c. 1850

Incised obverse: *SR*

Poplar. Handle and print hand cut from one piece, with chip-carved design bordered by striated lines and triangles.

31.1 x 27.9 x 6.6 cm (12¼ x 11 x 2⅝″)

Gift of Miss Frances Lichten. 60-91-3

13 BUTTER PRINT
c. 1850

Poplar, maple. Semicircular block with carved intaglio design and border of braid design in chip carving. Turned maple handle tenoned into block and pinned with nail. Probably mass-produced.

8.6 x 17.8 x 12.1 cm (3⅜ x 7 x 4¾″)

Titus C. Geesey Collection. 55-94-23

14 BUTTER PRINT
c. 1850

Poplar. Lathe-turned with chip- and gouge-carved design with border of diagonally striated lines.

Height 4.2 cm (1⅝″), diameter 7 cm (2¾″)

Titus C. Geesey Collection. 55-94-32

15 BUTTER PRINT
c. 1870

Oak. Lathe-turned disk with inserted handle. Carved intaglio design on face with double-bead border.

Height 8.9 cm (3½″), diameter 9.2 cm (3⅝″)

Titus C. Geesey Collection. 55-94-21

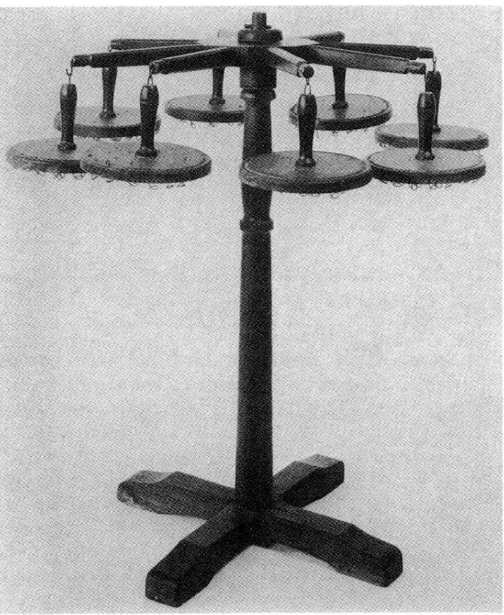

1

1

1 CANDLE DIP
1750–1800

Oak, pine, black walnut, poplar, maple. Lap and tenon construction. Shaped crosspieces of oak and pine base meet in lap joint. Turned central shaft tenoned through base and wedged. Eight arms radiate from octagonal block that revolves on tenon terminal of central shaft and is secured with wedge and removable pin. Wire hooks at end of spokes suspend handles of disks fitted with wires to hold candlewicks.

Height 97.6 cm (38⅜″), diameter 96 cm (37¾″)

Gift of Mrs. William D. Frishmuth. 02-116

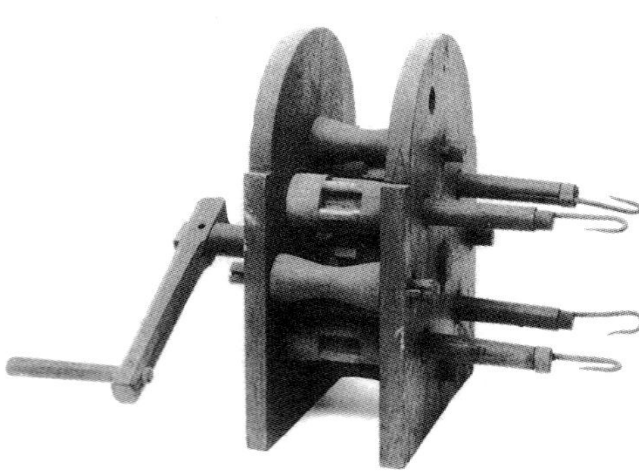

2

2 ROPE TWISTER
1780–1810

Oak. Two shaped planks are connected by four hourglass-shaped cylinders, tenoned and pegged. Pegged crank handle tenons through and turns carved gear, which turns notched cylinders, which rotate on extended dowels with iron hooks. Hemp strands are fastened to iron hooks and twisted into rope.

38.4 x 23.2 x 56.2 cm (15⅛ x 9⅛ x 22⅛″)

Gift of Mrs. William D. Frishmuth. 02-177

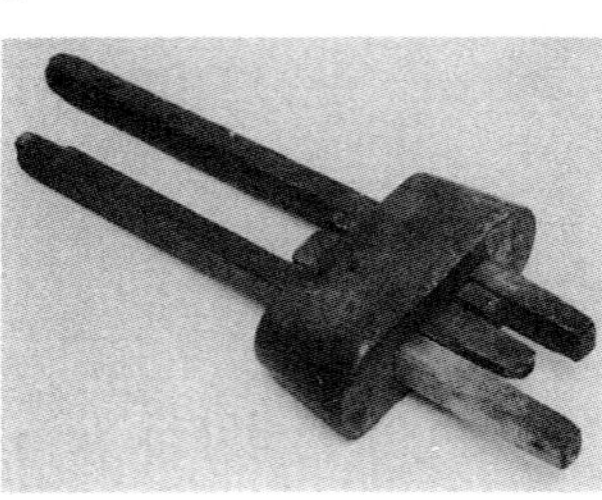

3

3 MORTISING GAUGE
c. 1800

Maple. Long bars tenoned through stem are held in marking position by shaped wedges. Nails or marking pins missing from bars.

22.5 x 9.9 cm (8⅞ x 3⅞″)

Gift of Mrs. William D. Frishmuth. 03-76

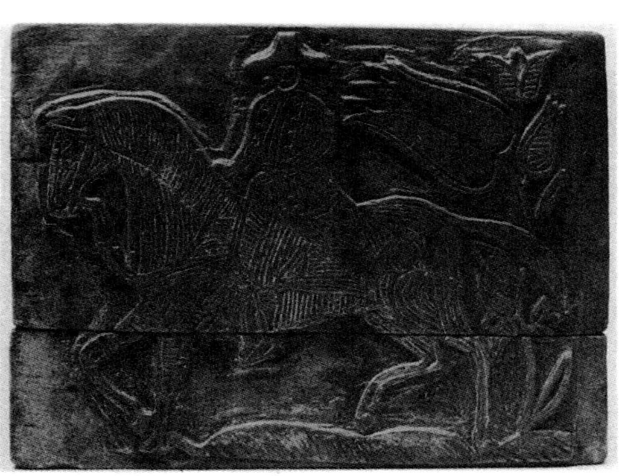

4

4 PRINTING BLOCK
1800–1820

Poplar. Two planks joined with two iron dowels. Relief-carved figure of mounted Continental soldier, probably George Washington. Traces of red, green, blue, and yellow pigments.

24.5 x 33 x 1.9 cm (9⅝ x 13 x ¾″)

Titus C. Geesey Collection. 62-203-4

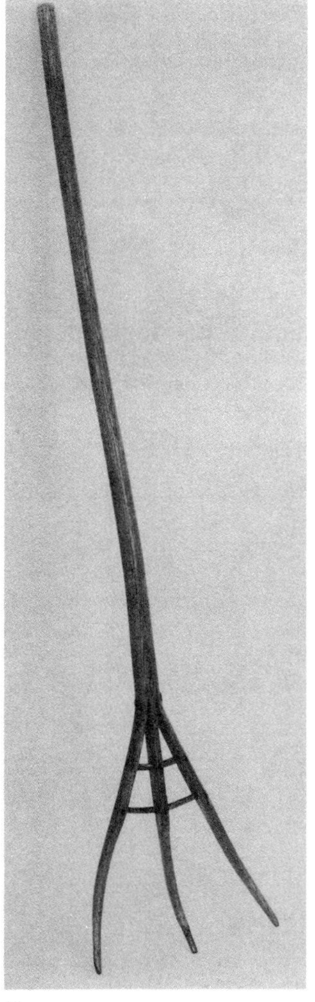

5 **HAY FORK**
1800–1850

Stamped on handle: *H* [?] *HAW*

Hickory. Bent construction with pinned dowels. Three shaped prongs formed by saw cuts in solid length. Nailed hickory dowels spread and secure each prong. Crotch riveted to prevent splitting.

135.5 x 28.6 cm (53⅜ x 11¼″)

Gift of Mrs. William D. Frishmuth. 02-217

---

6 **WING COMPASS**
1800–1850

Black cherry, iron. Two arms with chamfered edges toward foot. Movable arm tenoned into stabile arm and held with iron rivet. Curved measuring arc (wing) tenoned and pegged at end (part of wing missing). Iron shoes and spikes. No calibrations inscribed. Used by a cooper or wheelwright.

42.5 x 22 cm (16¾ x 8⅝″)

Gift of Mrs. William D. Frishmuth. 02-185

---

7 **TAR BUCKET**
1800–1850

Pine, iron, leather. Butted staves bound by two encircling iron bands and nailed. Leather carrying handles knotted through holes drilled at top, each side. Probably hung on axle of Conestoga wagon.

Height 25.3 cm (10″), diameter 14 cm (5½″)

Gift of Mrs. William D. Frishmuth. 02-205

---

8 **PESTLE**
1800–1850

Oak. Turned, shaped shaft with flared turnings at each end.

Length 21.9 cm (8⅝″)

Anonymous gift. 39-27-1

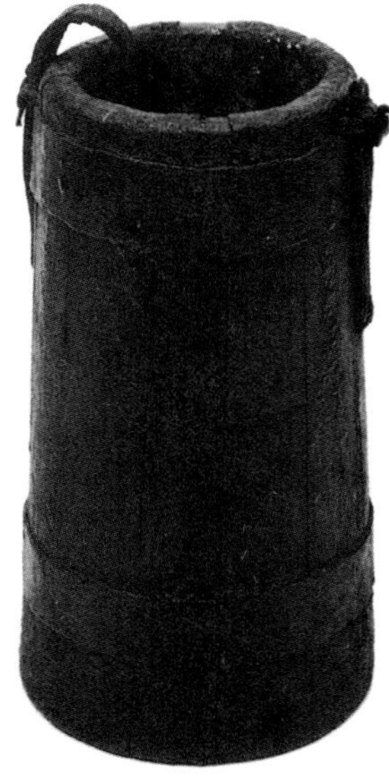

5

7

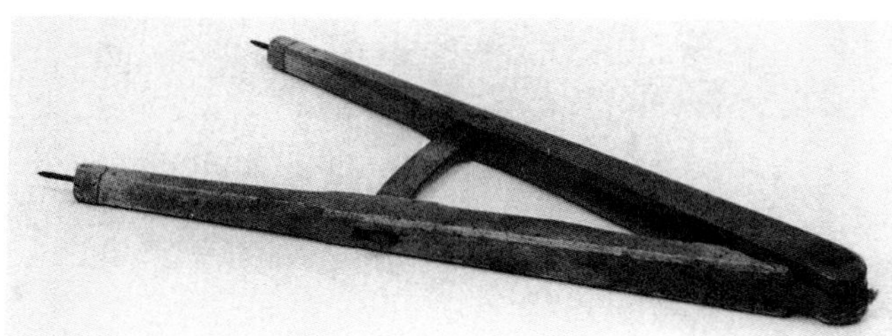

6

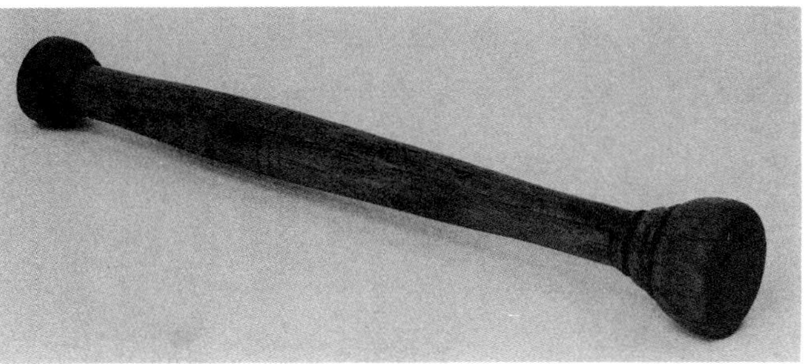

8

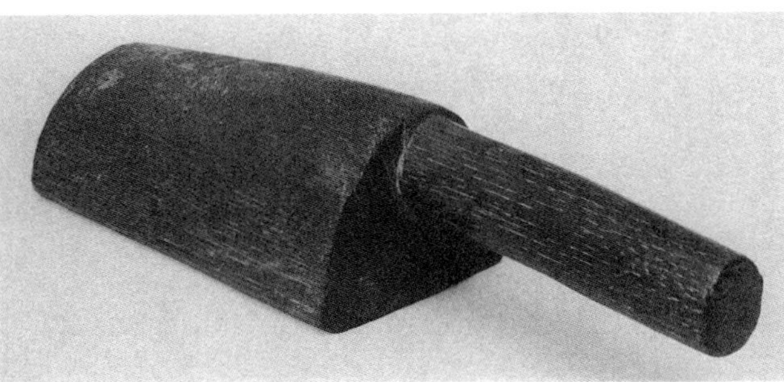

1 BAT
1800–1820
Oak. Carved from solid including handle.
28.5 x 9 cm (11¼ x 3½")
Gift of the heirs of Mrs. Sarah Louisa
Oberholtzer. 41-39-4

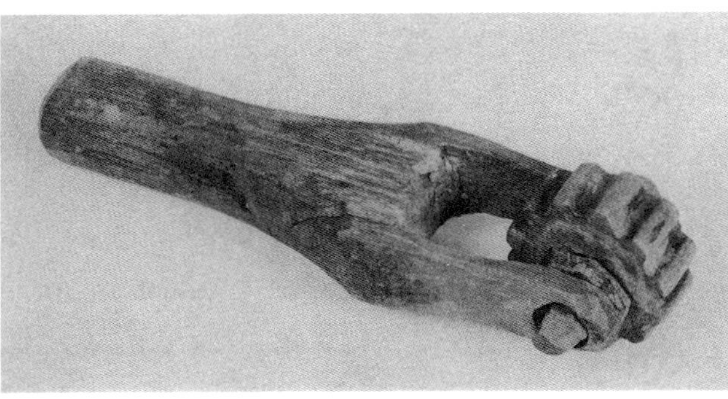

2 COGGLE
Montgomery County
1800–1850
Peter Headman
Poplar. Coggle drum carved in straight flutes
with one wood washer that rotates on wedged
wood peg on arms carved from handle.
9.5 x 2.9 cm (3¾ x 1⅛")
Gift of Edwin A. Barber. 96-242

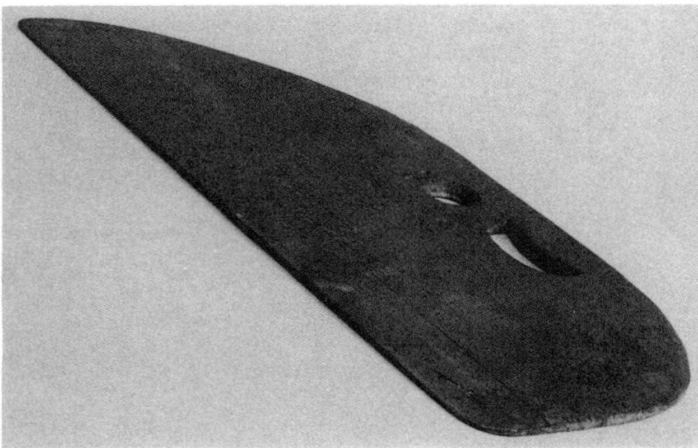

3 PALETTE
West Whiteland Township, Chester County
1806–22
Poplar. Flat board with one straight edge.
Thumb and fingerholds cut out.
Length 42 cm (16½")
Gift of the heirs of Mrs. Sarah Louisa
Oberholtzer. 41-39-1

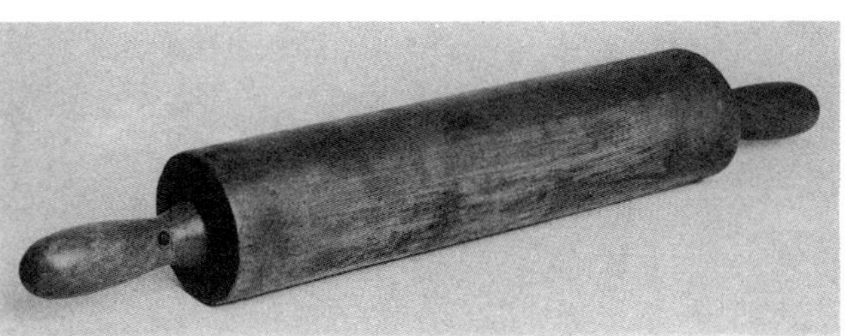

4 ROLLER
Nockamixon Township, Bucks County
1825–30
David Haring
Maple. Dowel through roller tenoned into
turned, shaped handles secured with pegs.
Length 58.4 cm (23")
Gift of Abel Brinton Haring. 01-66j

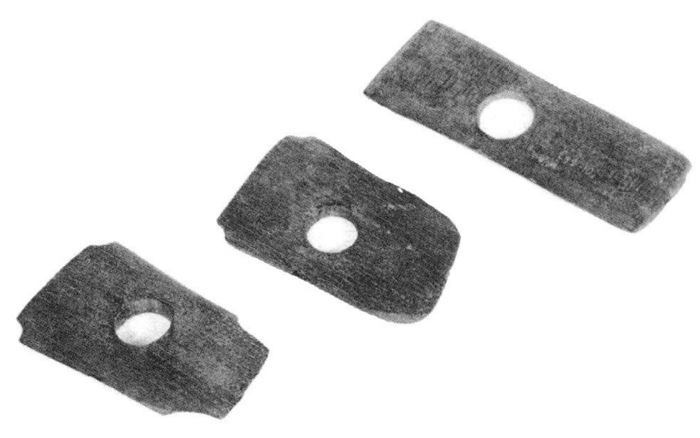

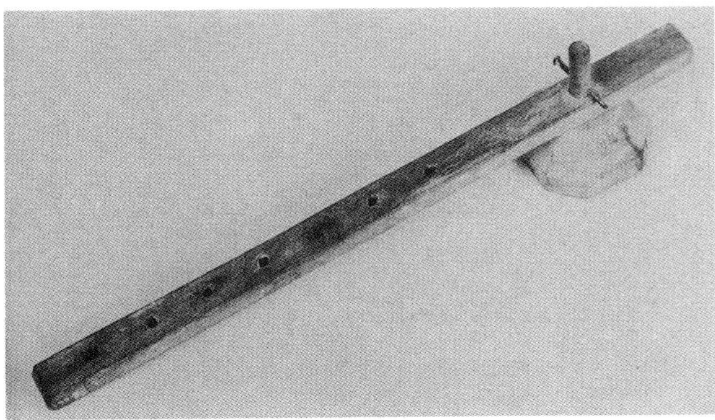

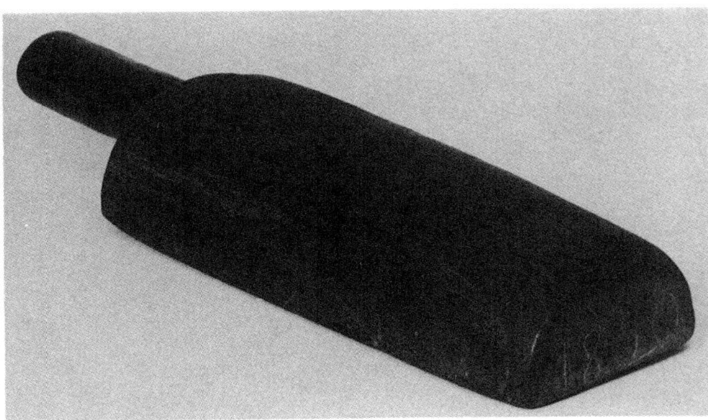

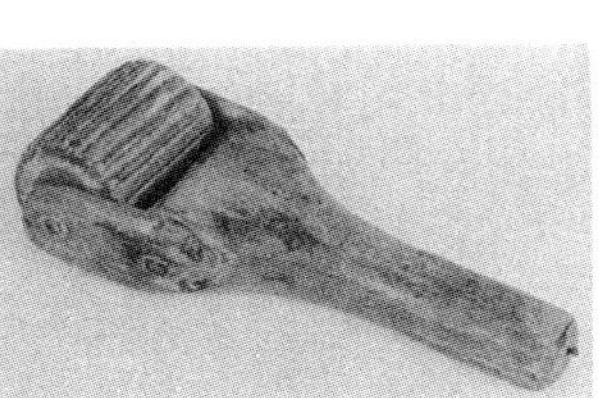

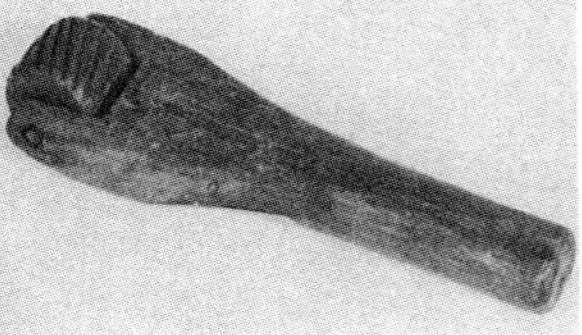

5

5 RIBS (3)
Nockamixon Township, Bucks County
1825–50

David Haring

Beech, ash. Used to smooth pottery on the wheel.

Length (g) 8.3 cm (3¼″), (h) 11.7 cm (4⅝″), (i) 8.3 cm (3¼″)

Gift of Abel Brinton Haring. 01-66g,h,i

6 DISK CUTTER
Nockamixon Township, Bucks County
1825–50

David Haring

Walnut. Carved disk doweled through arm and nailed. Arm calibrated for radii 7.6 to 22.9 cm, holes for scoring stylus.

30.5 x 5.4 cm (12 x 2⅛″)

Gift of Abel Brinton Haring. 01-66b

7 BAT
Nockamixon Township, Bucks County
1850

Jared R. Haring

Inscribed: *1850*

Walnut. Carved from solid including handle.

34 x 9.2 cm (13⅜ x 3⅝″)

Gift of Abel Brinton Haring. 01-66k

8 COGGLE
Nockamixon Township, Bucks County
1850–80

Maple, iron. Arms nailed to carved handle. Fluted drum rotates on two wood pegs.

17.8 x 7 cm (7 x 2¾″)

Gift of Abel Brinton Haring. 01-66f

9 COGGLE
Nockamixon Township, Bucks County
1861

Jared R. Haring

Walnut, iron. Fluted drum rotates on iron dowel supported by arms carved from extended handle.

18.4 x 4.9 cm (7¼ x 1⅞″)

Gift of Abel Brinton Haring. 01-66e

6

7

8   **9**

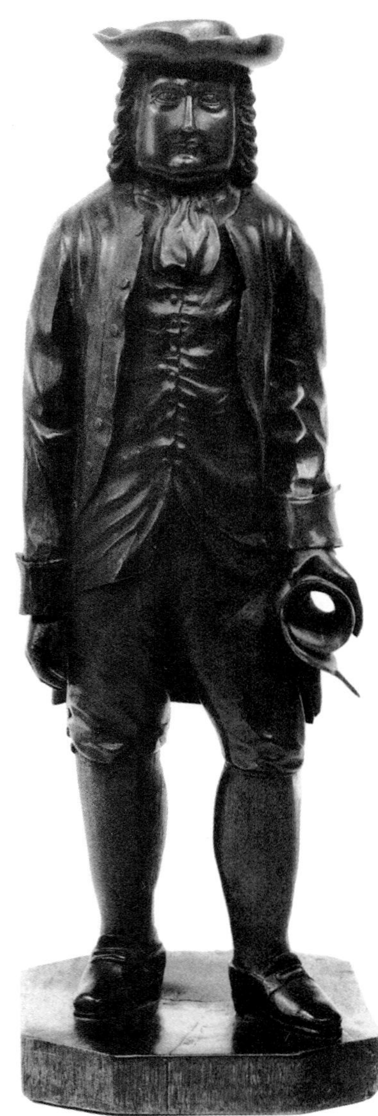

1   **WILLIAM PENN**
Berks County
1770–1800

Black walnut. Full-length figure and base shaped and carved from single block.

51 x 18.4 cm (20 x 7¼″)

Gift of J. Stogdell Stokes. 38-1-1

2   **BUCK DEER**
Tulpehocken Township, Berks County

Attributed to **John Reber**

Painted pine, iron wire. Body carved from the solid; legs and neck tenoned into body. Gessoed and painted mottled light gray, brown, black, and white. Antlers are painted gesso over wire.

29.3 x 19.9 cm (11½ x 7⅞″)

Titus C. Geesey Collection. 55-94-5

3   **ELK**
Tulpehocken Township, Berks County

Attributed to **John Reber**

Painted pine, iron wire. Body carved from the solid; legs and neck tenoned into body. Gessoed and painted on all surfaces in brown, tan, and gray with black. Antlers are painted gesso over wire.

27 x 27.3 cm (10⅝ x 10¾″)

Titus C. Geesey Collection. 55-94-4

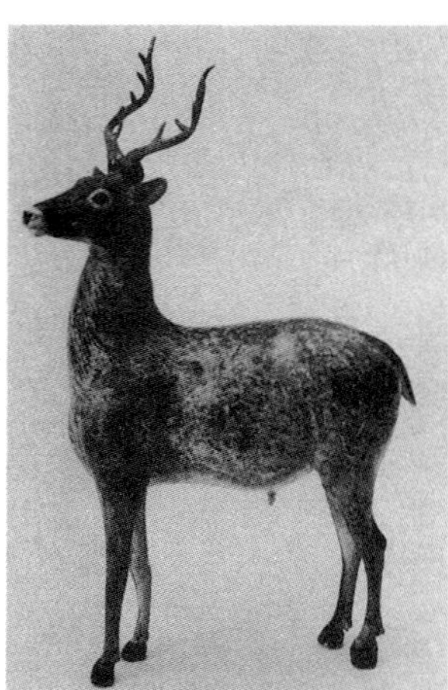

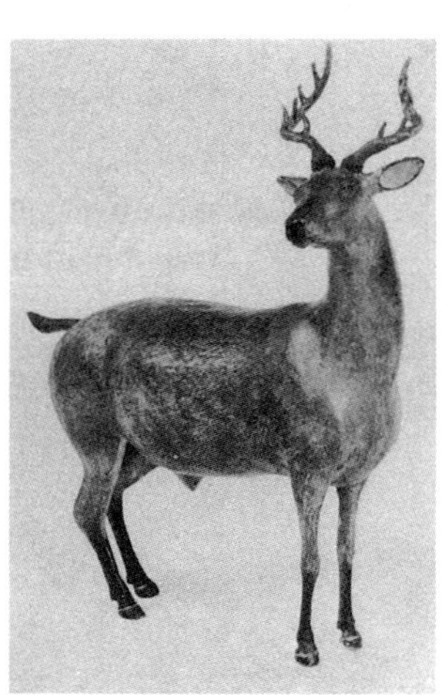

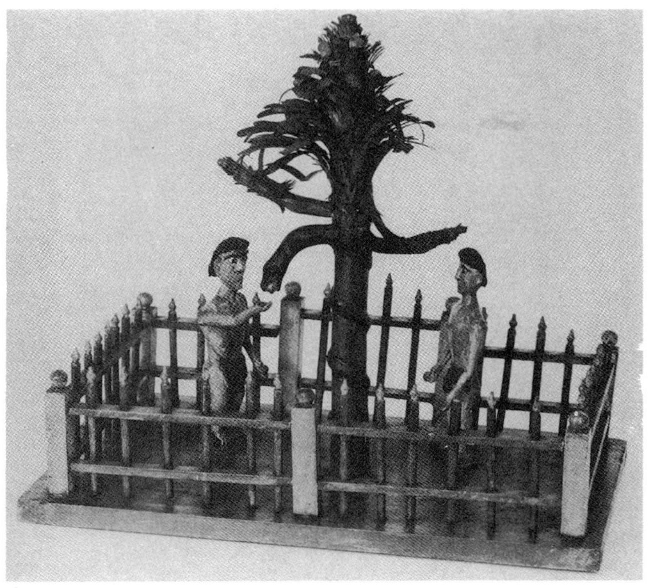

4

4 GARDEN OF EDEN
Cumberland County
1860–90

Attributed to **Wilhelm Schimmel**

Painted pine, hickory. Carved forms of Adam, Eve, and tree with wrapped snake. Adam and Eve stand on bases which are tacked. Eve's extended arm carved separately and pinned to shoulder. Spiked-finial picket fence has rectangular corner posts with ball finials. Tree shaved at top depicting foliage. Gessoed and painted white, green, brown, red, and black, and varnished.

50.8 x 57.8 x 38.7 cm (20 x 22¾ x 15¼")

Titus C. Geesey Collection. 55-94-2

---

5 SHEPHERD AND HIS FLOCK
Cumberland County
1860–90

Attributed to **Wilhelm Schimmel**

Painted pine, cotton. Carved shepherd figure gessoed and painted green, brown, and black. Cotton tufts affixed to sheep.

20 x 40.7 x 19.7 cm (7⅞ x 16 x 7¾")

Titus C. Geesey Collection. 55-94-3

---

6 SQUIRREL
Cumberland County
1860–90

Attributed to **Wilhelm Schimmel**

Painted pine. Carved from single block. Gessoed and painted brown with black markings, yellow and white tail and stripe on nose, yellow and red nut, and green base.

14 x 4.8 x 8.2 cm (5½ x 1⅞ x 3¼")

Bequest of Mr. and Mrs. William M. Elkins. 50-92-216

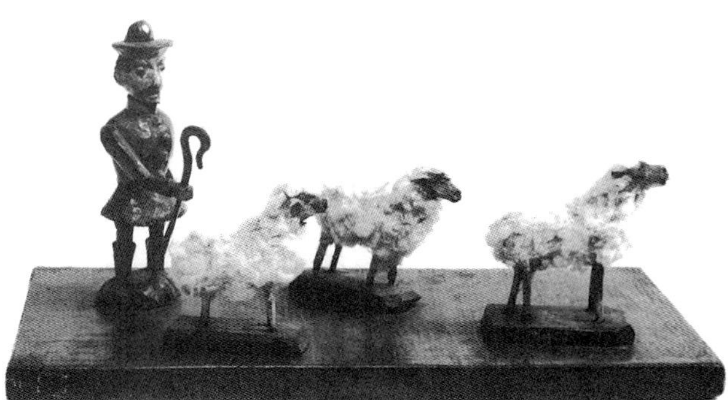

5

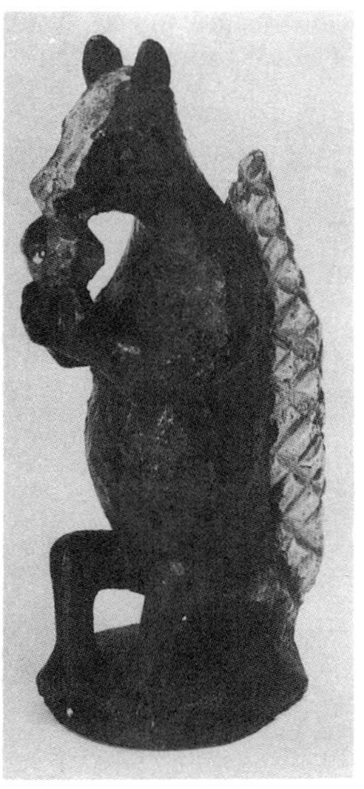

6

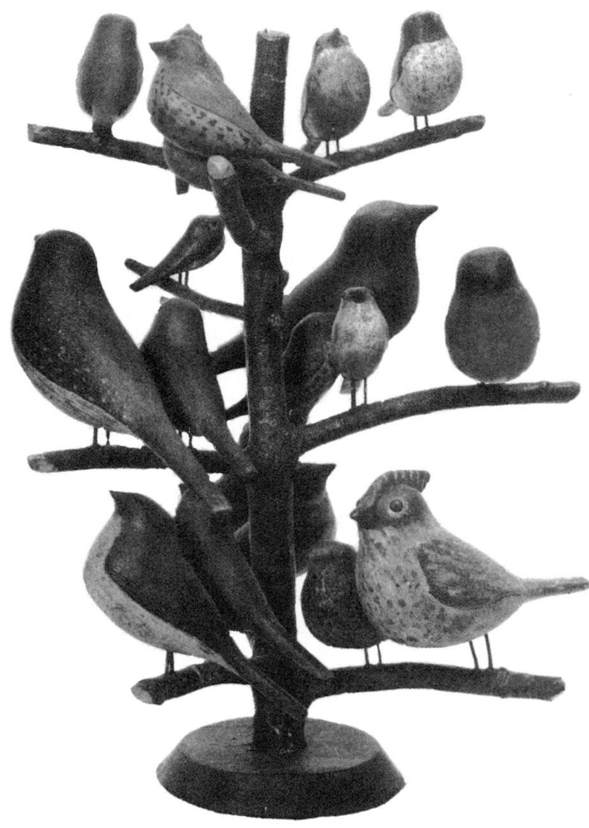

1

1 BIRD TREE
1800–1820

Pine, painted pine, wire, iron. Three turned, graduated disks form base. Natural branch tenoned into base and glued. Nineteen birds perch on wire legs driven into branches. Eyes are iron brads. Birds multicolored.

44 x 32 cm (17⅜ x 12⅝")

Bequest of Mr. and Mrs. William M. Elkins. 50-92-201

2 PEACOCK
Tulpehocken Township, Berks County

Attributed to **John Reber**

Painted pine, cedar. Carved in three pieces: head and neck, body, tail. Tail gouged with chisel. Legs and claws of gesso built up on wire armature. Painted dark green, yellow, gray black, blue, and red, with mottling.

21.6 x 38.1 cm (8½ x 15")

Titus C. Geesey Collection. 55-94-6

3 BIRD
1800–1850

Painted pine, wire, glass. Carved form on twisted wire legs with one claw of each foot imbedded in base. Bead eyes. Painted tan with brown streaks.

Height 9.2 cm (3⅝")

Bequest of Mr. and Mrs. William M. Elkins. 50-92-204a

4 BIRD
1800–1850

Painted pine, wire, glass. Carved form on twisted wire legs with one claw of each foot imbedded in base. Painted green with yellow breast. Bead eyes.

Height 9.8 cm (3⅞")

Bequest of Mr. and Mrs. William M. Elkins. 50-92-204b

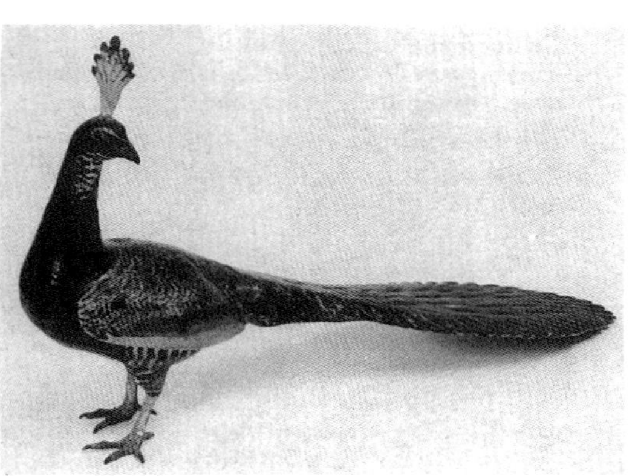

2

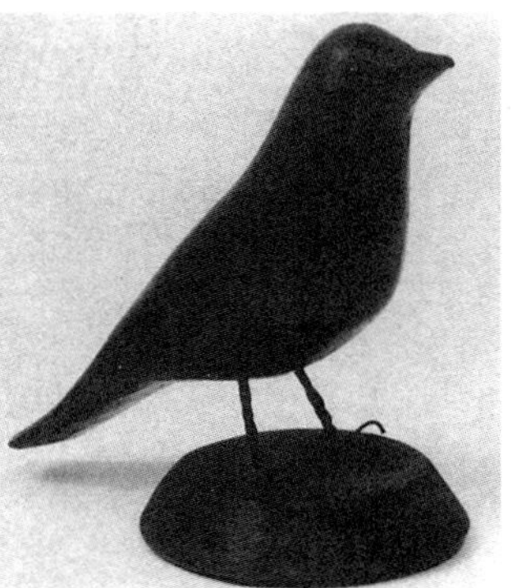

3

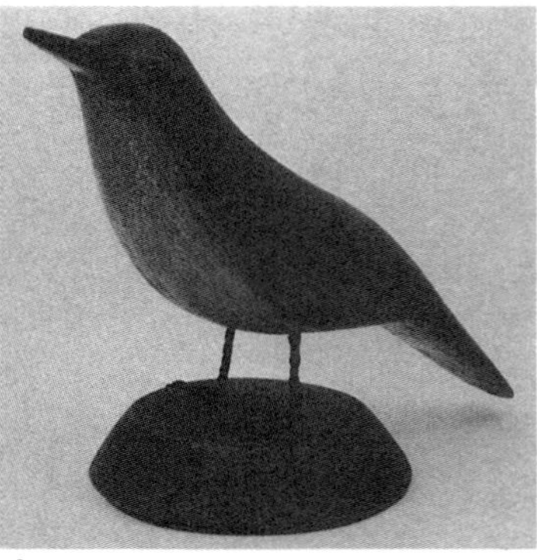

4

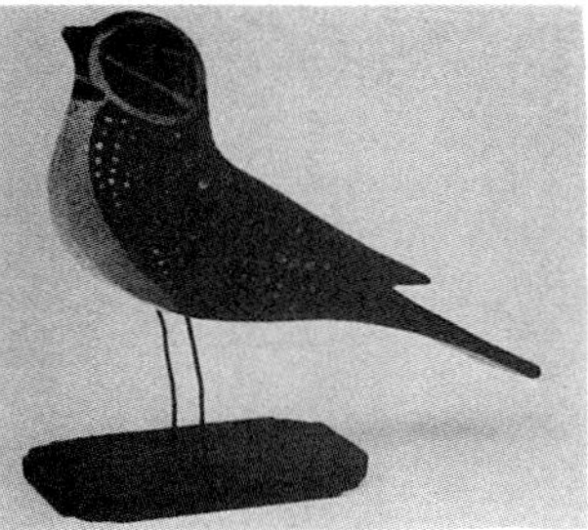
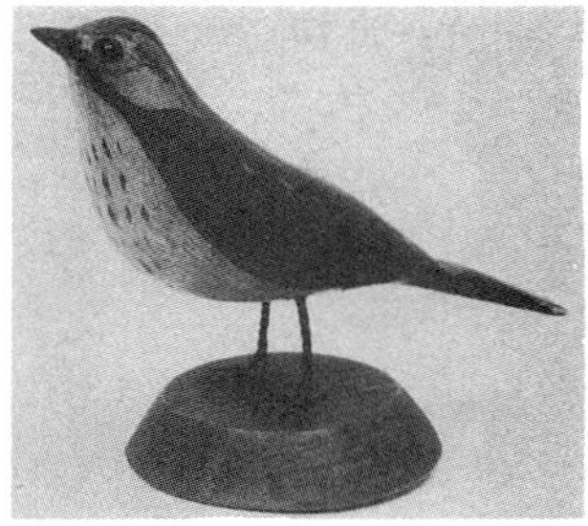

5   **6**

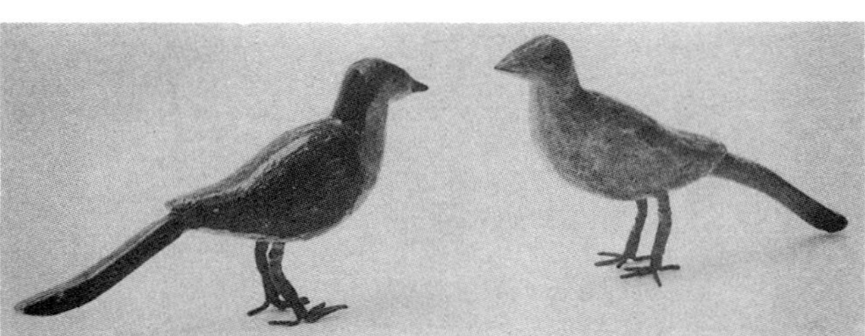

7

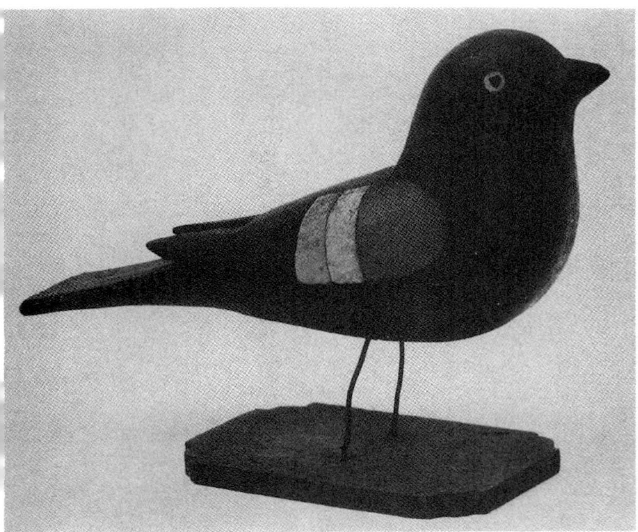

8

5   BIRD
1800–1850

Painted pine, wire. Carved form on straight wire legs implanted in rectangular base with shaped corners. Painted black with white breast and markings, red crest.

Height 11.3 cm (4⅜″)

Bequest of Mr. and Mrs. William M. Elkins. 50-92-205

6   BIRD
1800–1850

Painted pine, wire, glass. Carved form on twisted wire legs with extended claws. Painted black with spotted white breast, yellow around beaded eye.

Height 8.9 cm (3½″)

Bequest of Mr. and Mrs. William M. Elkins. 50-92-206

7   TWO BIRDS
1800–1850

Painted pine, wire, cloth. Carved forms on wire legs wrapped with cloth, freestanding on four splayed, wire claws. Painted yellow and brown.

Height (a) 6.3 cm (2½″), (b) 6.8 cm (2⅝″)

Bequest of Mr. and Mrs. William M. Elkins. 50-92-210a,b

8   BIRD
1800–1850

Painted pine, wire. Carved form on wire legs set into base with contoured corners. Painted black with red, white, and yellow markings.

Height 9.7 cm (3¾″)

Bequest of Mr. and Mrs. William M. Elkins. 50-92-211

9   CHICKEN
1800–1850

Painted pine, wire. Carved form on painted wire legs set into rectangular block. Painted black and white.

Height 9.4 cm (3¾″)

Bequest of Mr. and Mrs. William M. Elkins. 50-92-217

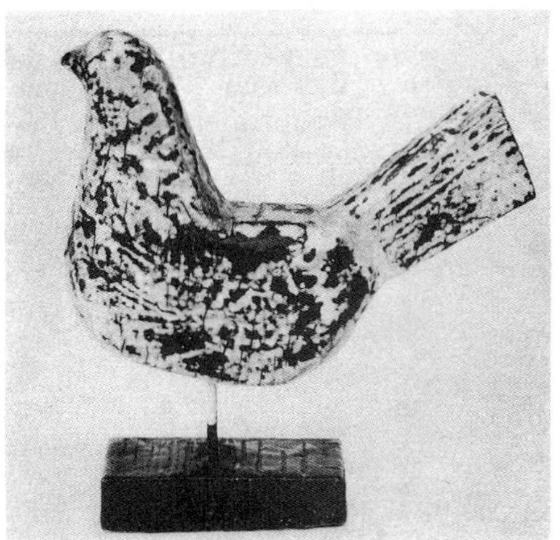

9

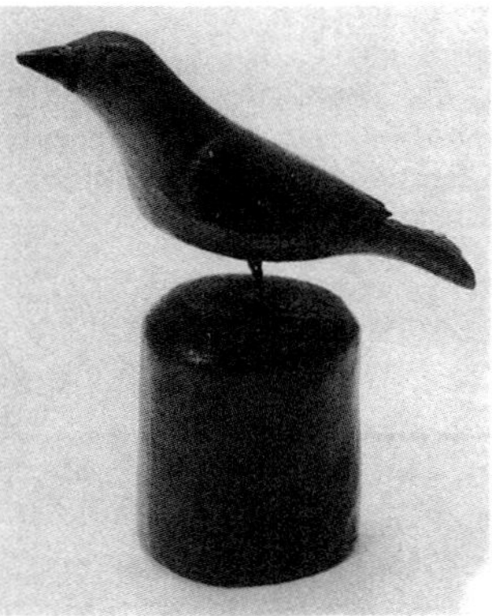

10

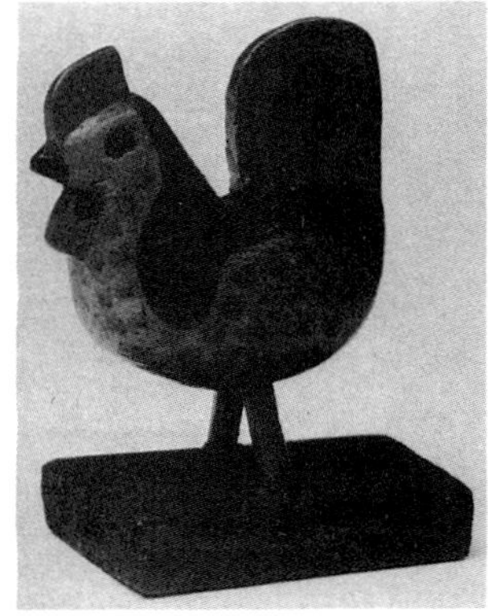

11

10 BIRD
1820–50

Painted pine, wire. Carved form stands on twisted wire legs inserted into separate base. Bird painted red with black markings; base, red with green top.

Height 12.7 cm (5"), diameter base 4.4 cm (1¾")

Bequest of Mr. and Mrs. William M. Elkins. 50-92-213

---

11 ROOSTER
1820–60

Painted pine. Carved form. Splayed legs tenoned into body and base. Body painted yellow; comb, sack, and markings orange brown; base green.

15.9 x 6.3 cm (6¼ x 2½")

Bequest of Mr. and Mrs. William M. Elkins. 50-92-218

---

12 OWL
1820–70

Painted pine. Carved from single block. Painted brown with yellow beak and eyes, white tuft, black pupils and markings.

18.4 x 8.5 cm (7¼ x 3⅜")

Titus C. Geesey Collection. 62-203-9

---

13 BIRD
1825–75

Painted pine. Bird sits on rectangular pedestal on carved base block; all carved from single block. Relief-carved leaf and heart motifs on sides of base; edges of base and wings notched; plumage simulated by incised lines. Bird painted green with red breast, yellow head, black eyes, beak, and markings. Brown leaves and heart on base.

9.5 x 12.7 cm (3¾ x 5")

Bequest of Mr. and Mrs. William M. Elkins. 62-203-7

---

14 BIRD AT TROUGH
1825–75

Painted pine, wire. Individually carved bird, trough, pedestal, and base; nailed. Bird's legs are dowels set into body and rim of trough; beak formed from split wire. Painted brown with sponged yellow markings.

18.4 x 16.5 cm (7¼ x 6½")

Bequest of Mr. and Mrs. William M. Elkins. 50-92-226

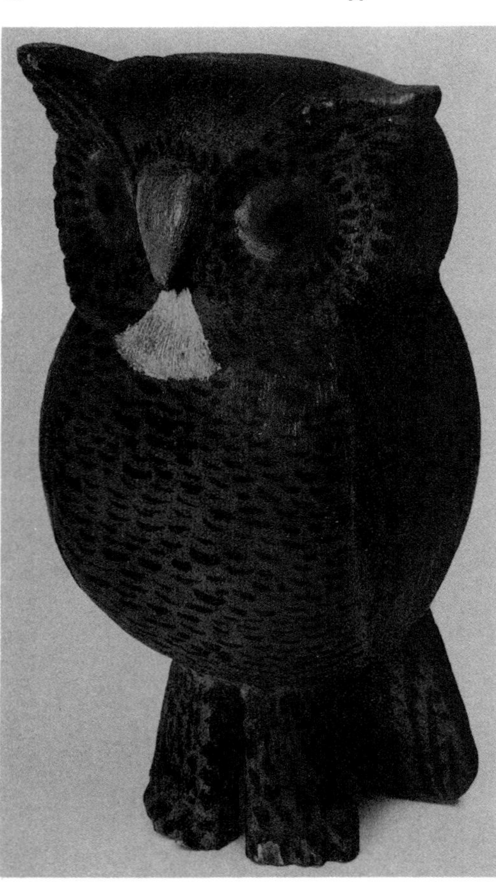

12

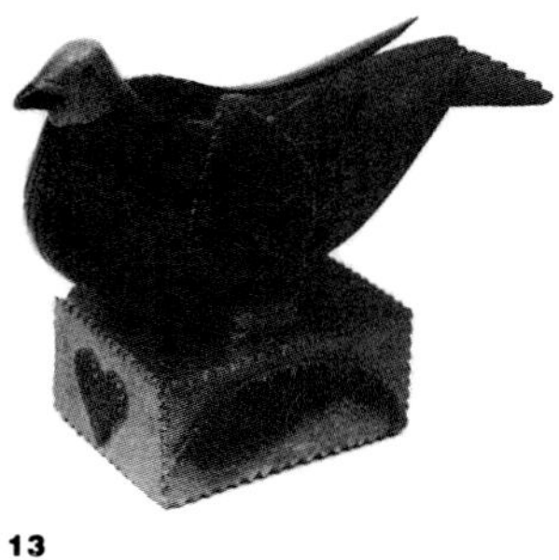

13

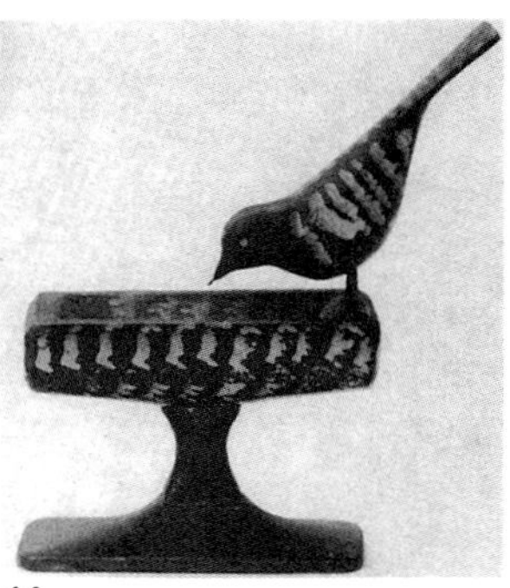

14

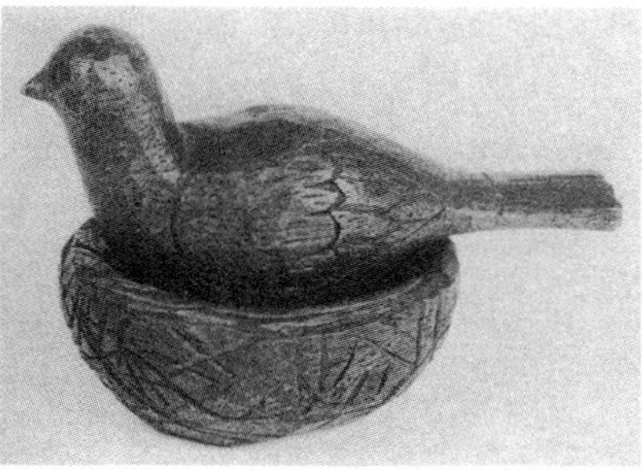

15

16

15 BIRD IN NEST
1850–70

Walnut. Carved forms with scratch-carved tail feathers and woven nest. Hole drilled through nest into bird indicates possible use as a finial.

3.6 x 5.1 cm (1⅜ x 2″)

Bequest of Mr. and Mrs. William M. Elkins. 50-92-212a,b

16 TWO EAGLETS
Cumberland County
1850–90

Attributed to **Wilhelm Schimmel**

Painted pine. Carved from single blocks. Gessoed and painted yellow with yellow, black, and red markings and green bases.

14 x 10.8 cm (5½ x 4¼″)

Bequest of Mr. and Mrs. William M. Elkins. 50-92-207a,b

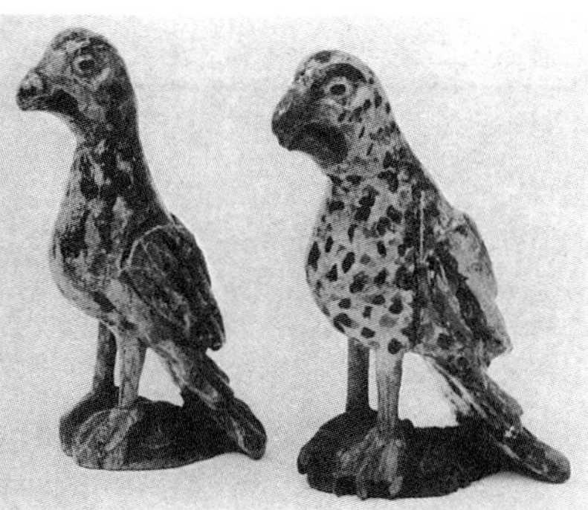

17 EAGLE
Cumberland County
1860–90

Wilhelm Schimmel

Painted pine. Carved form; wings dovetailed into main body. Gessoed and painted red, yellow, black, and dark green.

30.5 x 42.3 cm (12 x 16⅝″)

Titus C. Geesey Collection. 62-203-5

18 BIRDS ON PEDESTAL
Cumberland County
1860–90

Attributed to **Wilhelm Schimmel**

Painted pine. Birds and base carved from single block; foliage carved individually with pegged ends, stuck into holes in base. Gessoed and painted; yellow birds with red and green markings; green and red foliage; green base.

12.1 x 12.1 cm (4¾ x 4¾″)

Bequest of Mr. and Mrs. William M. Elkins. 50-92-208

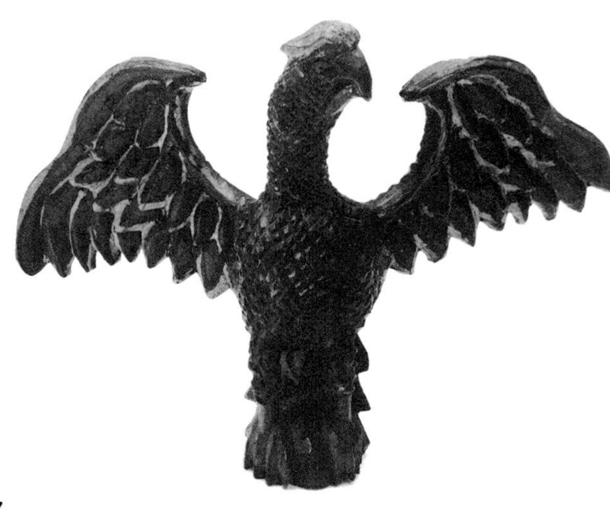

17

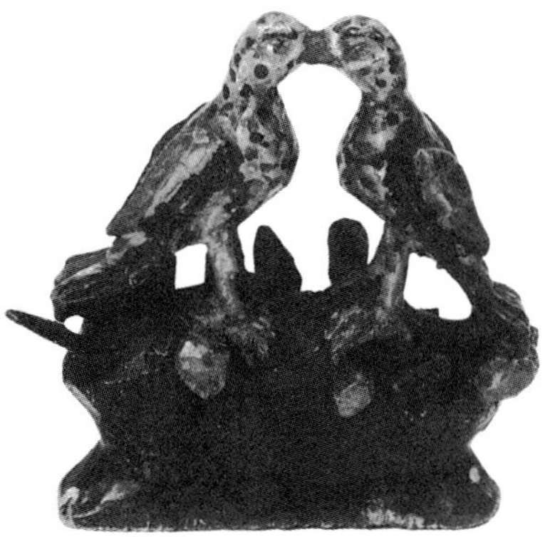

18

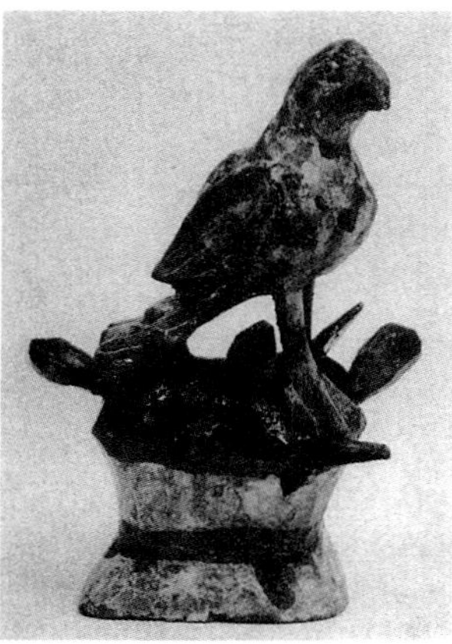

19

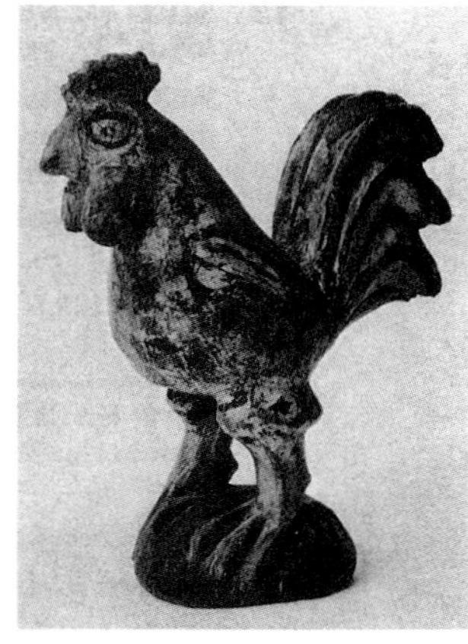

20

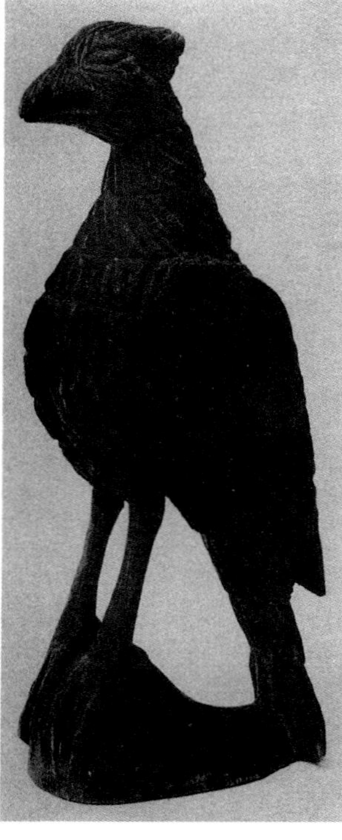

21

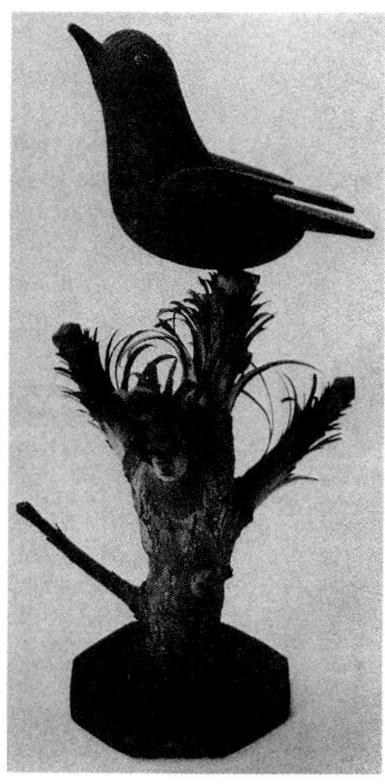

22

19 BIRD ON PEDESTAL
Cumberland County
1860–90

Attributed to **Wilhelm Schimmel**

Painted pine. Bird and base carved from single block. Leaves and flowers carved individually with pegged ends, stuck into holes in base. Gessoed and painted; body yellow with green and yellow markings; base yellow with red stripes; foliage green, red, and yellow.

13 x 6 cm (5⅛ x 2⅜")

Bequest of Mr. and Mrs. William M. Elkins. 50-92-209

---

20 ROOSTER
Cumberland County
1865–90

Attributed to **Wilhelm Schimmel**

Painted pine. Carved form. Gessoed and painted red, yellow, black, and dark green.

21.6 x 17.8 cm (8½ x 7")

Titus C. Geesey Collection. 62-203-6

---

21 EAGLE
Cumberland County
1890–1920

Attributed to **Aaron Mountz**

Pine. Carved from one piece. Unpainted.

22.6 x 9.8 cm (8⅞ x 3⅞")

Bequest of Mr. and Mrs. William M. Elkins. 50-92-215

---

22 BIRD ON TREE
Cumberland County
c. 1900

Possibly by **Aaron Mountz**

Painted pine, natural pine, tacks. Carved bird with incised markings; metal tacks for eyes. Four branches shaved to resemble foliage. Branch nailed to octagonal base.

Height 19.1 cm (7½")

Bequest of Mr. and Mrs. William M. Elkins. 50-92-214

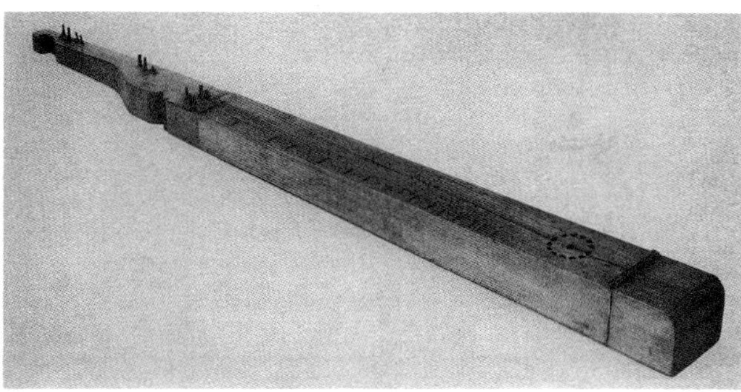

1

1　ZITHER
Bucks County
1780–1850

Pine, iron, wire. Top and sides mitered and glued. Shaped end piece set into sides has four pairs of metal pins to attach strings. Low wire bridge tacked. Higher bridge of strip iron fastened below sound holes in circle cut into soundboard. Fourteen frets incised on finger board. Low wire bridge at end of sounding box. Three units of five, three, and four wrest pins. Shaped, scrolled neck.

101.6 x 3.8 cm (40 x 3½")

Purchased. 13-442

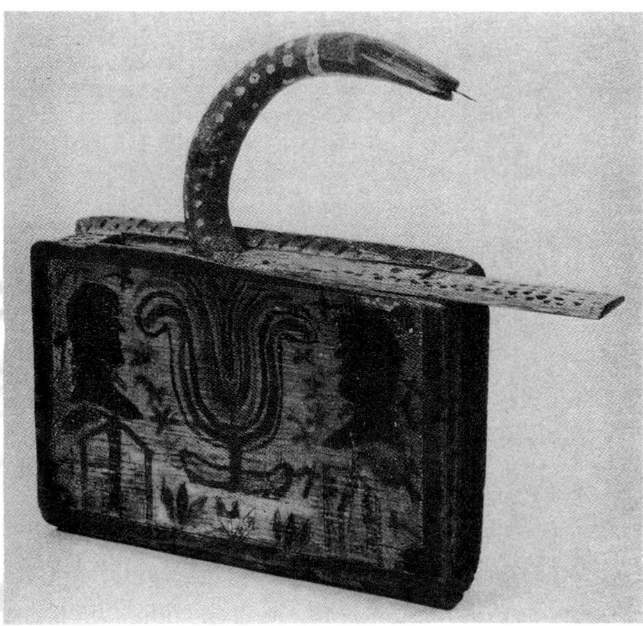

2

2　TRICK BOX
1800–1850

Painted pine, steel, wire. Box carved from solid block. Snake carved in three pieces and glued. Long edge of box slides in grooves and connects with wire to base of snake, which pops up as strip slides out. Fang made of steel spike strikes precisely at finger pull. Box painted to resemble a book with profiles and tulips. Edges white, spotted in black. Spine red and black with white striping. Snake red with white spots.

16.2 x 11.1 cm (6⅜ x 4⅜")

Titus C. Geesey Collection. 55-94-8

3　GROUNDHOG
1800–1850

Painted pine, leather, resin. Body carved from single block, coated with brown-stained gesso dappled with black. Leather tail attached with glue; resin eyes.

15.4 x 45.2 cm (6 x 17¾")

Titus C. Geesey Collection. 55-45-12

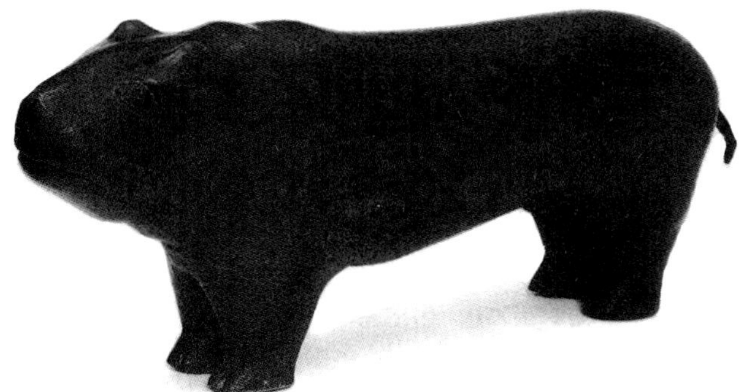

3

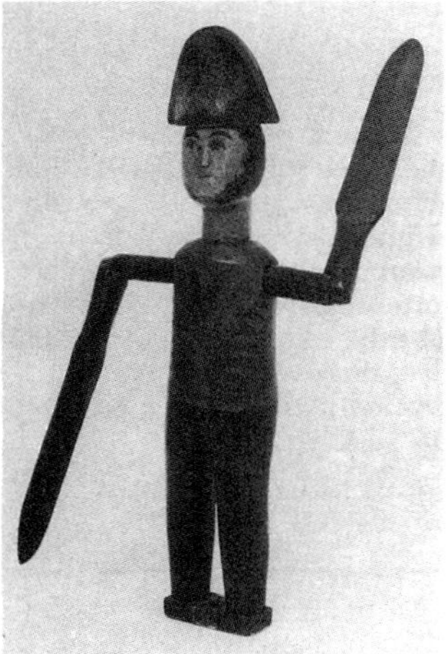

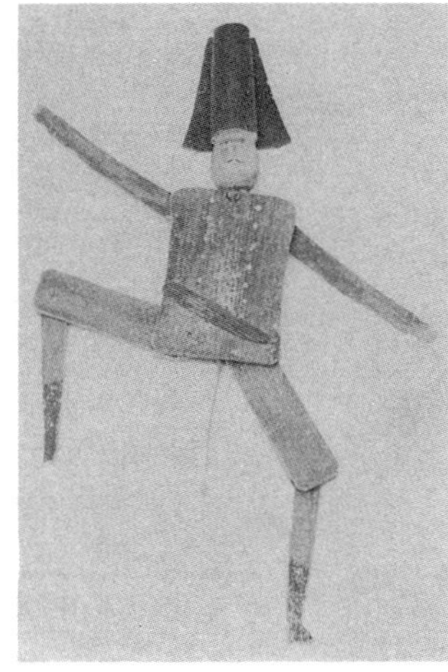

4

5

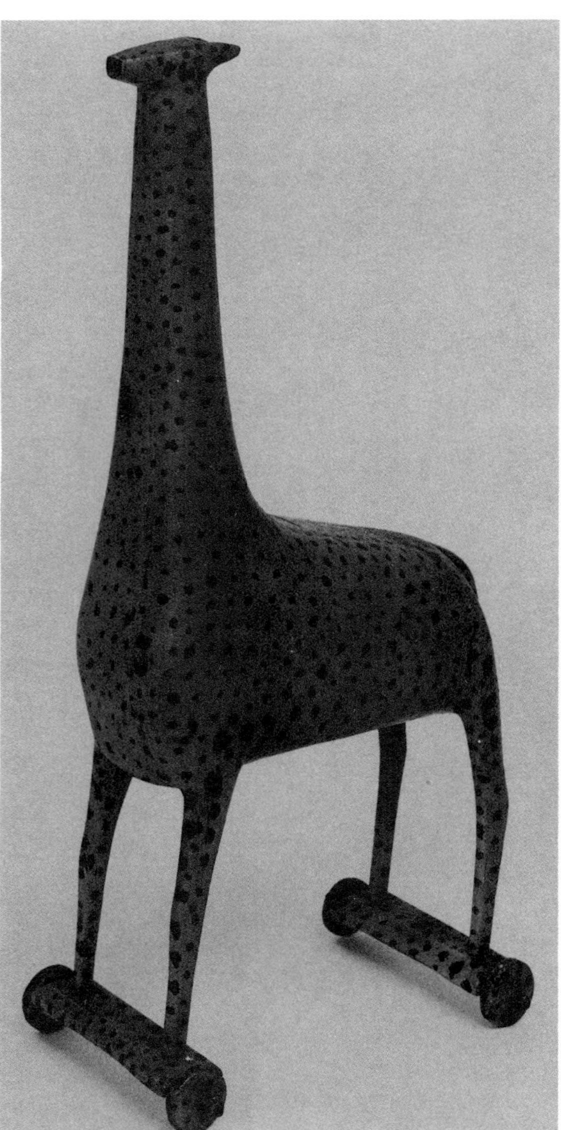

6

4   WHIRLIGIG
1812–40

Painted pine, wire. Carved figure. Head and neck unit tenoned into body. Separate hat fastened with wire pin. Wire axle runs through shoulders into arms and is hinged to wind paddles. Legs painted black, body and arms red and yellow, face pink with black detail.

28.6 x 14 cm (11¼ x 5½")

Titus C. Geesey Collection. 55-94-7

5   JUMPING JACK
1820–50

Painted pine, iron, string. Soldier figure hinged with iron rivets at joints of arms, legs, knees. Pulling string moves arms and legs. Painted soldier costume on front, repetitive dotted pattern on back.

35.6 x 7.6 cm (14 x 3")

Purchased: Annual Membership Fund. 16-295

6   GIRAFFE
1840–60

Painted pine, oak. Carved form of body in three pieces. Legs tenoned into bases which are glued to oak axles pegged through rotating wheels. Gessoed and painted yellow with brown dots.

38.2 x 17.2 cm (15 x 6¾")

Titus C. Geesey Collection. 62-203-8

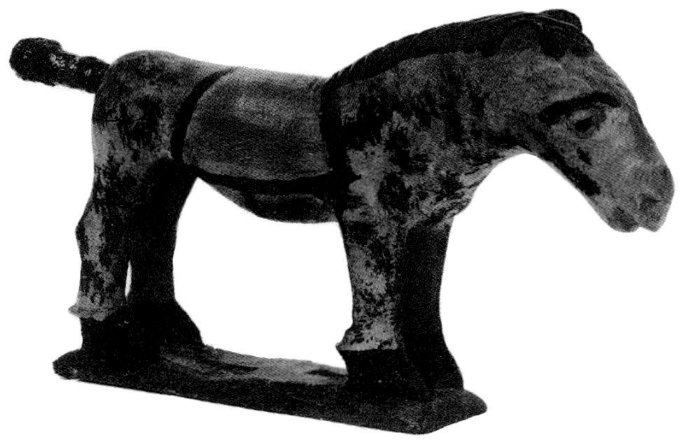

7

7 HORSE
Cumberland County
1850–90

Attributed to **Wilhelm Schimmel**

Painted poplar. Horse and base carved from
one block. Carved details of eyes, mane,
mouth, nostrils, ground. Evidence of horsehair
used with, or instead of, attached wood tail.
Gessoed and painted light brown with black
details. Red and yellow saddle, green ground.

15.9 x 29.2 cm (6¼ x 11½")

Titus C. Geesey Collection. 54-85-137

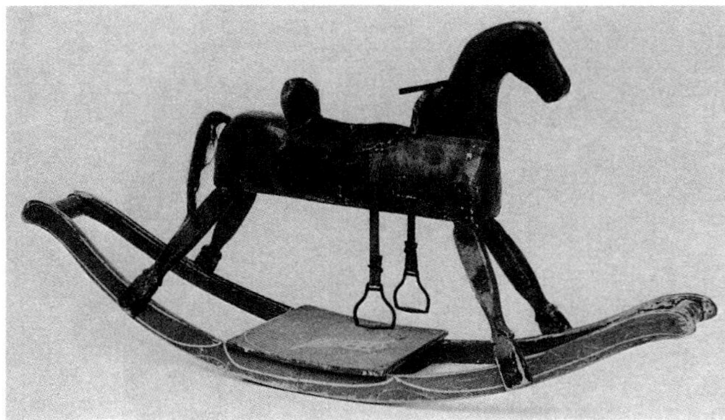

8

8 ROCKING HORSE
c. 1860

Painted pine, leather, horsehair, oilcloth, iron.
Carved head and body are solid. Shaped, flat
legs tenoned into body and half-lapped over
rockers and screwed. Saddle, leathers, and
bridle fastened with nails. Shaped rockers
connected by tenoned and pegged stretchers;
central overlapping platform pegged. Painted
red with black, rockers and platform blue
green with red and white striping and flower
design.

61.5 x 124.5 cm (24¼ x 49")

Titus C. Geesey Collection. 58-110-42

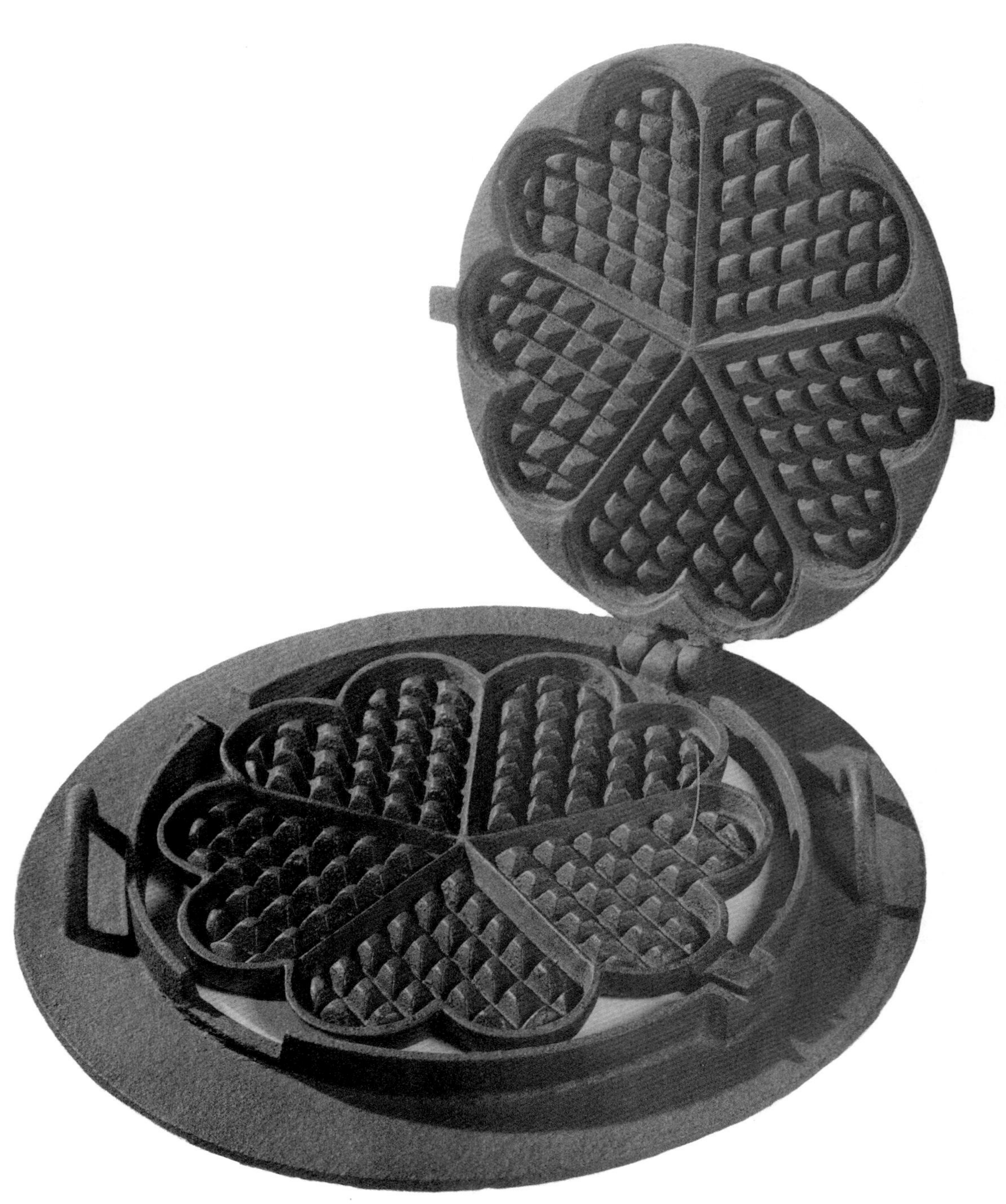

Metal

INTRODUCTION

Pennsylvania Germans were masterworkers in metals. Specialists, like coppersmiths, whose chef d'oeuvre was the bulbous form of the still, pewterers like William Will, clockmakers like David Rittenhouse, and gunsmiths like Jacob Kuntz, who depended upon the English community as well as upon their German brethren for their markets, frequently settled in or around the urban centers of Reading, Lancaster, or Philadelphia. Self-sufficient religious settlements like Ephrata or the Moravian community of Bethlehem had their own metal specialists. Rural communities had blacksmiths, usually a clockmaker, and occasionally a whitesmith, who did finishing work and also made locks.

By far the most numerous metalworkers were blacksmiths and their iron objects were end products of a process involving a team of skilled workmen. Unlike the carpenter or the joiner, who could fell his own tree to shape his barn or table, the blacksmith was dependent upon a complicated and expensive manufacturing process for his raw material. Just as the great forests assured economic security for woodworkers, the chunks of magnetite ores staining soil and roads with streaks of rust provided investors with visual evidence of the mineral wealth of Pennsylvania. Black sand on the banks of the Delaware indicated the presence of iron oxides and exploration of surface strata uncovered plentiful veins of ore

WAFFLE IRON
1800–1850
See page 133, no. 67

feasible for mining in Berks, Lebanon, and Lancaster counties. A deep strata of limestone for flux, grand forests for fuel and charcoal, and plentiful water power for forge hammers placed the raw materials of iron manufacturing in hand.

Pennsylvania Germans were involved more or less in every aspect of mining and manufacturing of iron in Pennsylvania. Although most of the venture capital was from London or Philadelphia and many ironmasters like Peter Grubb and Thomas Rutter were Cornish or Welsh with English mining experience, a few Germans like Henry William Stiegel, John Jacob Huber, and Dietrich Welker managed their own furnaces. A hierarchy of workers was required for iron manufacturing: the founder made sand molds and casts from them; the gutterman controlled the flow of the hot metal into the channels of the molds; the keeper maintained the furnace temperature; and several laborers, called fillers, fed the furnace stack with layers of charcoal, limestone, and ore. Tax and furnace records reveal that most of these workers were German or Swiss.

The main production of ore furnaces was cast iron, shaped in elongated lumps called pigs. These were carted to various forges or directly to blacksmiths. Forges, smaller operations than furnaces, were usually located near a mill, on a fast-falling stream. Water powered the enormous forge hammers, which beat the pigs into thick bars. These were heated, beaten and reheated, and beaten again, in a process that gradually converted the brittle structure of cast iron into the tensile strength of wrought iron.

Furnaces also cast plate stoves. Distinctly a middle European contribution to American comfort, iron stoves are listed in most 18th-century inventories of Pennsylvania German houses of more than three rooms and were also used in English households. Smaller items were also cast, such as griddle slabs and kettles of various sizes, which hung from trammels.

The blacksmith was essential to agrarian life in all Pennsylvania counties. Nails and hooks, chains and tools, were made and repaired in the daily routine of the blacksmith. The Pennsylvania German blacksmith rarely marked his work, and if he did, he simply stamped initials. Sets of cooking implements were sometimes decorated (p. 125 nos. 27, 28) and occasionally marked for owners (p. 132, no. 62).

Other metalworkers such as tinsmiths, who flourished in Philadelphia and surrounding counties, offered all kinds of tin-plated utensils from lanterns and coffeepots to candle molds and sausage guns, although the cookie cutter was their most popular product. Pennsylvania German tinsmiths used two distinctive European decorative techniques: punchwork, a raised pattern created by punching with a round-ended chisel from the inside before assembling the piece; and wrigglework, a design or wide line produced by pivoting a chisel in a zigzag pattern. Cut or slit work was often used in conjunction with the other techniques. The most popular forms of English painted tinware were copied by Pennsylvania tinsmiths. Pennsylvania painted tinware tends to have blurred edges and overlapping transparent layers of color, featuring more painterly effects than the stenciled appearance of painted tin from other regions.

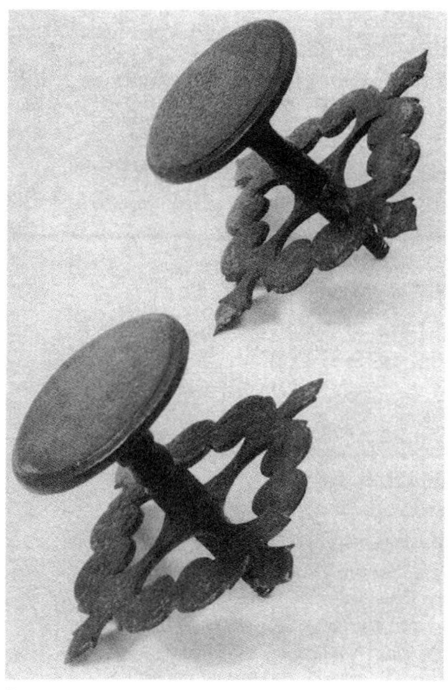

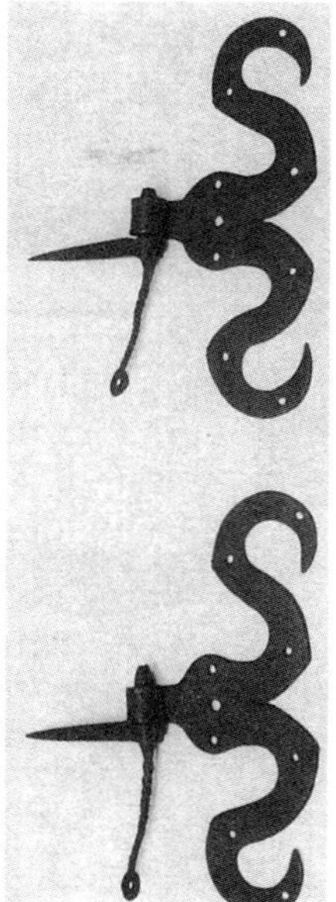

1 PULLS (2)
Chester County
1700–1800

Wrought iron. Handles welded to shafts decorated with different swage blocks. Shafts have hand-threaded ends.

Top 8.5 x 11.7 cm (3⅜ x 4⅝″)
Bottom 8.2 x 11.1 cm (3¼ x 4⅜″)

Titus C. Geesey Collection. 53-125-11i

2 PAIR OF RAM'S HORN HINGES
Lancaster County
1710–50

Wrought iron. Pintle and spike hinges with twisted, extended props. Heavy plates have beveled edges. Tool marks evident on reverse. Made for house in Lancaster County built about 1710.

Top 33.5 x 16 cm (13⅛ x 6¼″)
Bottom 34.5 x 16.5 cm (13⅝ x 6½″)

Purchased: Joseph E. Temple Fund. 24-61-1a,b,2a,b

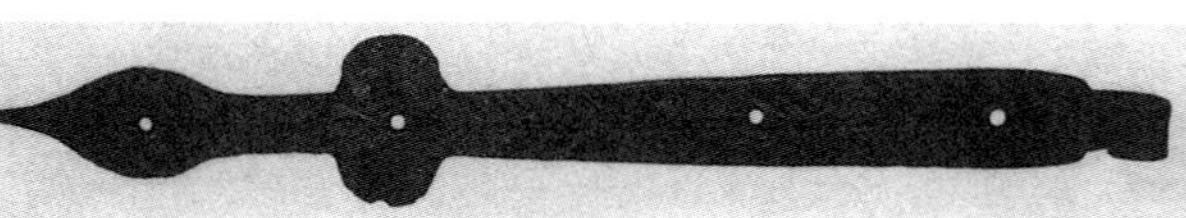

3 HINGE
Lebanon County
1720–50

Wrought iron. Obverse decorated in feather pattern. Tooling marks evident on reverse. Pintle missing.

67.6 x 10.2 cm (26⅝ x 4″)

Titus C. Geesey Collection. 53-125-11n

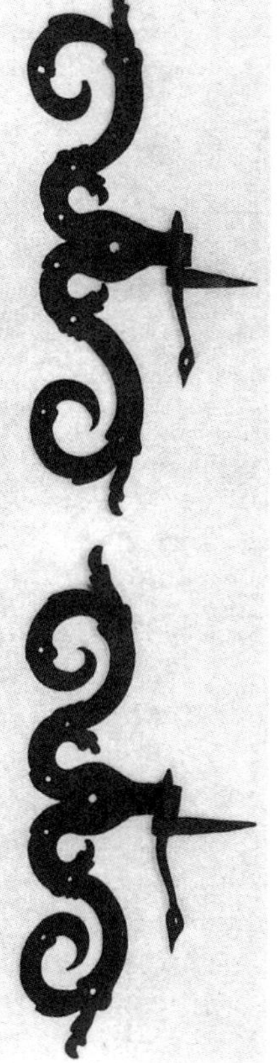

4 PAIR OF STAGHORN HINGES
1720–1800

Wrought iron. Pintle and spike hinges with extended props. Tooling marks evident.

Top 50.5 x 23.5 cm (19⅞ x 9¼″)
Bottom 50.2 x 26.1 cm (19¾ x 10¼″)

Titus C. Geesey Collection. 53-125-11k

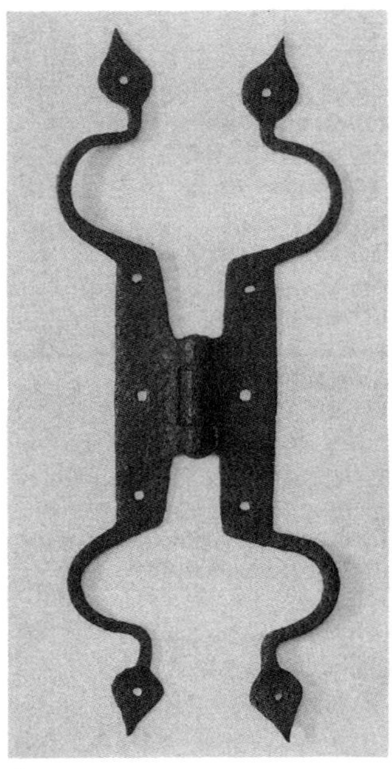

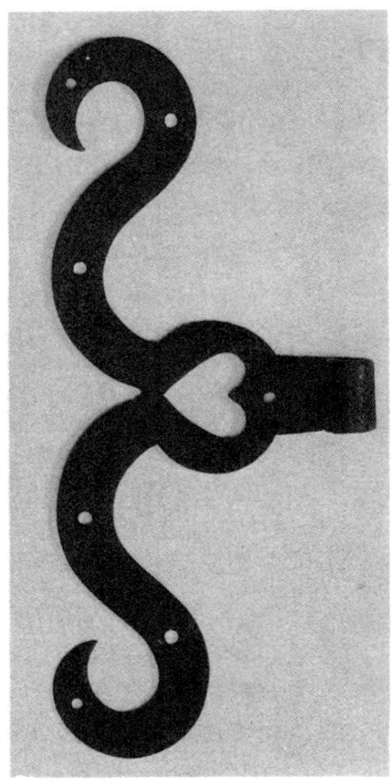

5

6

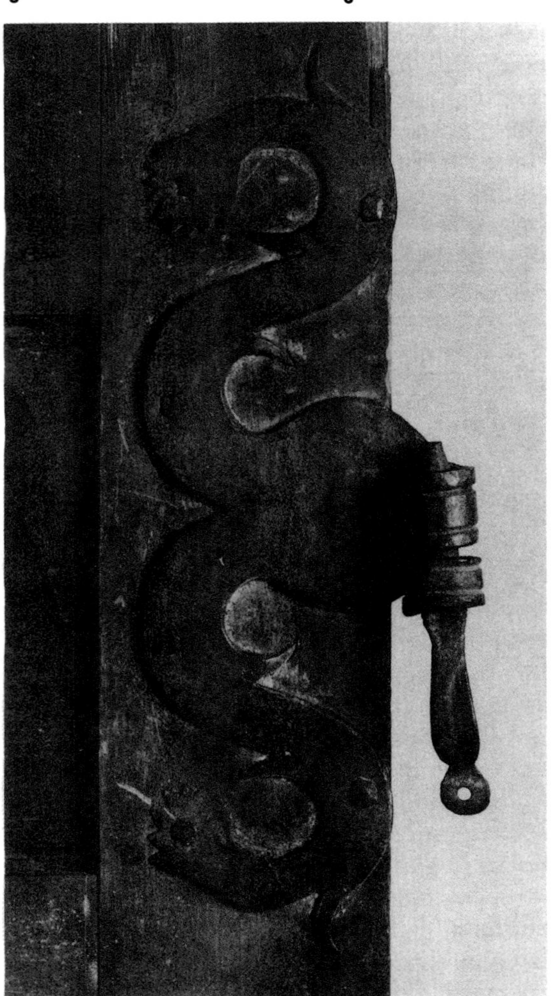

7

5 HINGE
1730–80

Wrought iron. Evidence of yellow ocher paint.
Wrought nails.

34.3 x 14.3 cm (13½ x 5⅝")

Titus C. Geesey Collection. 53-125-10h

6 HINGE
1750–1800

Wrought iron. Pintle missing. Wrought nails.

33.5 x 15.2 cm (13¼ x 6")

Titus C. Geesey Collection. 53-125-10g

7 PAIR OF HINGES
1750–1800

Wrought iron. Shaped plate in coiled-dragon
design. Pintle and socket hinge with extended
prop. Pair mounted on door (*See* Wood,
Architecture no. 5).

33 x 11.4 cm (13 x 4½")
29.2 x 13.3 cm (11½ x 5¼") (not shown)

Titus C. Geesey Collection. 54-85-30a

8 PAIR OF COCK'S HEAD HINGES
1750–1800

Wrought iron. Beveled edges. Vertical file
marks on obverse. Wrought nails.

Left 20 x 10.5 cm (7⅞ x 4⅛")
Right 22.2 x 11 cm (8¾ x 4⅜")

Titus C. Geesey Collection. 53-125-11e

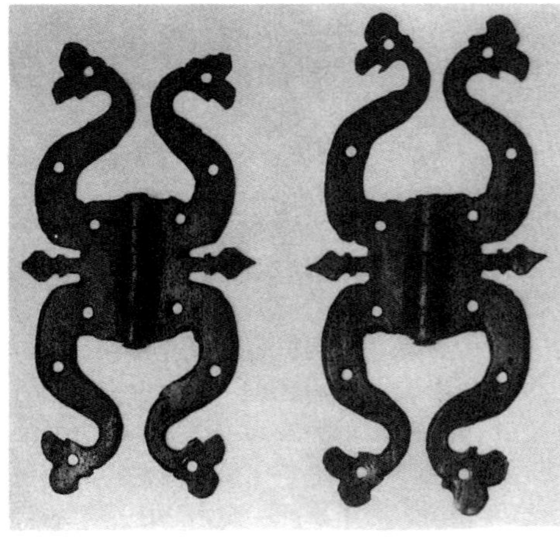

8

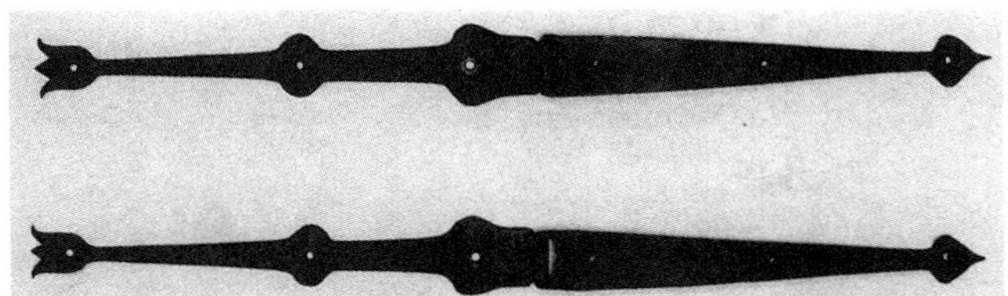

9

9 PAIR OF STRAP HINGES
1750–1800

Wrought iron. Beveled edges. Straps join in wicket-type hinges. Tooling marks on reverse. For chest or interior door.

71.7 x 5.8 cm (28¼ x 2¼")

Titus C. Geesey Collection. 53-125-11l

---

10 PAIR OF STRAP HINGES
1750–1800

Wrought iron. Beveled edges. Decorative edge cuts at spike holes. Hammer marks on reverse. Wrought nails.

46 x 23.5 cm (18⅛ x 9¼")

Titus C. Geesey Collection. 53-125-10i

---

11 STRAP HINGE
1750–1800

Wrought iron. Beveled edges. Tooling marks on reverse.

54 x 27.9 cm (21¾ x 11")

Titus C. Geesey Collection. 53-125-11m

---

12 PAIR OF STRAP HINGES
1750–1800

Wrought iron. Circular terminals hammered thinner than shafts. Tooling marks and evidence of red paint on reverse. Wrought nails.

Top 60 x 31.1 cm (23⅝ x 12¼")
Bottom 61 x 29.2 cm (24 x 11½")

Titus C. Geesey Collection. 53-125-10j

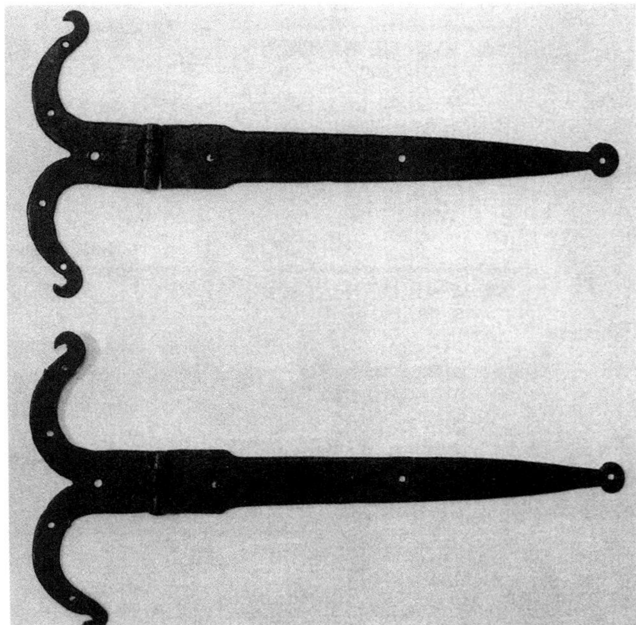

10

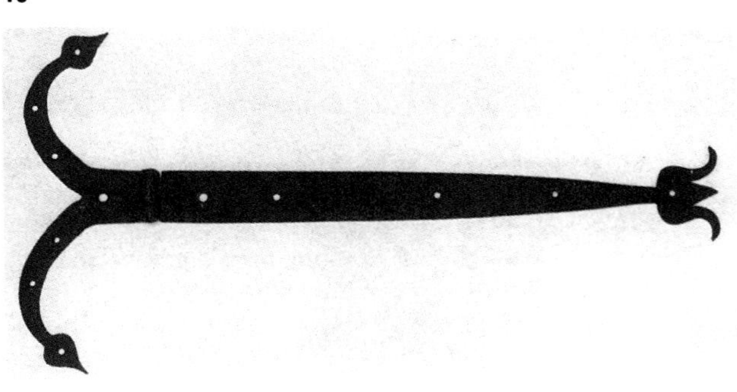

11

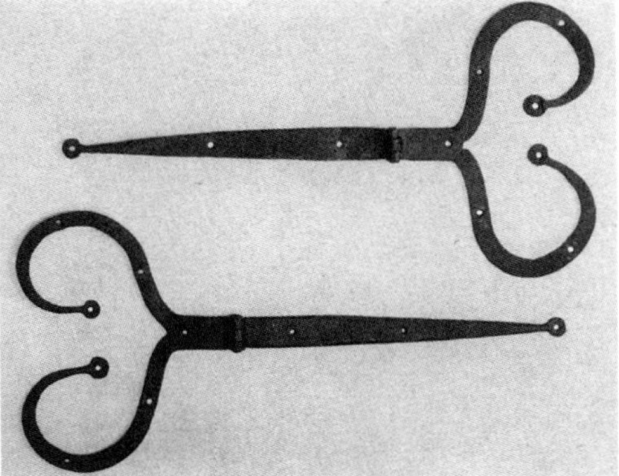

12

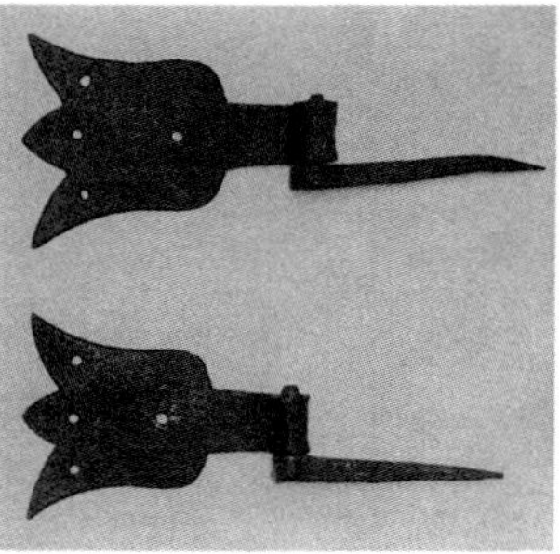

13

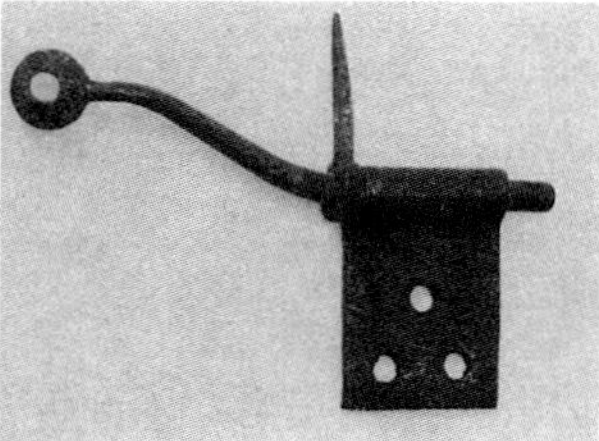

14 left

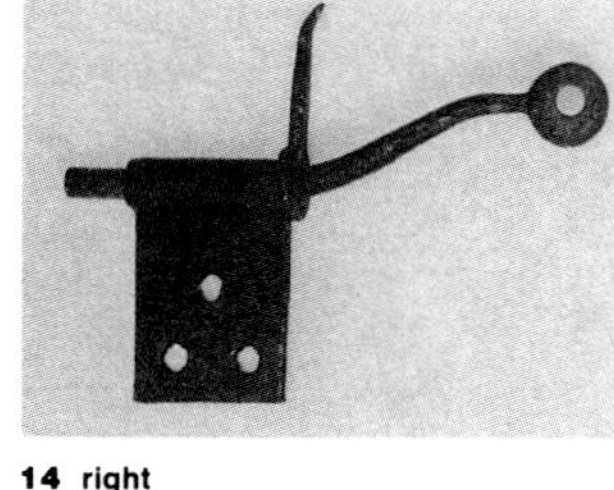

14 right

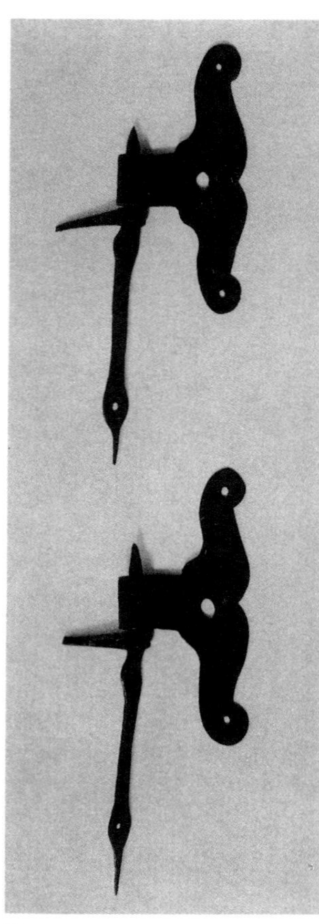

15

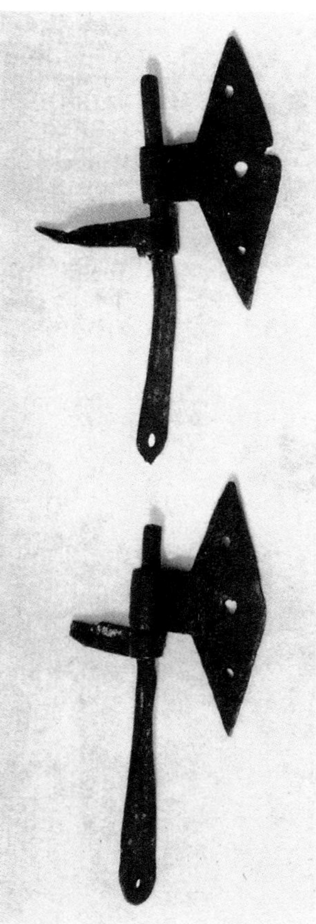

16

13 PAIR OF HINGES
1750–1800

Wrought iron. Tooling marks on heavy plate sockets. Pintles and solid spikes. Beveled edges. Pitted surfaces. Wrought nails.

Top 31 x 12.7 cm (12¼ x 5″)
Bottom 28.3 x 12.6 cm (11⅛ x 5″)

Titus C. Geesey Collection. 53-125-11h

14 PAIR OF HINGES
1750–1800

Wrought iron. Rectangular plates with solid spikes and pintles with extended props. Wrought nails.

8.9 x 3.7 cm (3½ x 1½″)

Titus C. Geesey Collection. 53-125-10e

15 PAIR OF HINGES
1750–1800

Wrought iron. Bat-wing plates with clenching spikes and pintles with extended props. Wrought nails.

Top 12.5 x 4.5 cm (4⅞ x 1¾″)
Bottom 13 x 4.5 cm (5⅛ x 1¾″)

Titus C. Geesey Collection. 53-125-11f

16 PAIR OF HINGES
1750–1800

Wrought iron. Ax-shaped plates with clenching spikes and pintles with extended props. Traces of white paint. Wrought nails.

Top 12.1 x 9.3 cm (4¾ x 3⅝″)
Bottom 12.4 x 7.3 cm (4⅞ x 2⅞″)

Titus C. Geesey Collection. 53-125-11j

17 PAIR OF HINGES
1750–1800

Wrought iron. Tooling marks on reverse. Beveled edges. Wrought nails.

Left 17.8 x 8.5 cm (7 x 3⅜″)
Right 18.4 x 8.1 cm (7¼ x 3⅛″)

Titus C. Geesey Collection. 53-125-11g

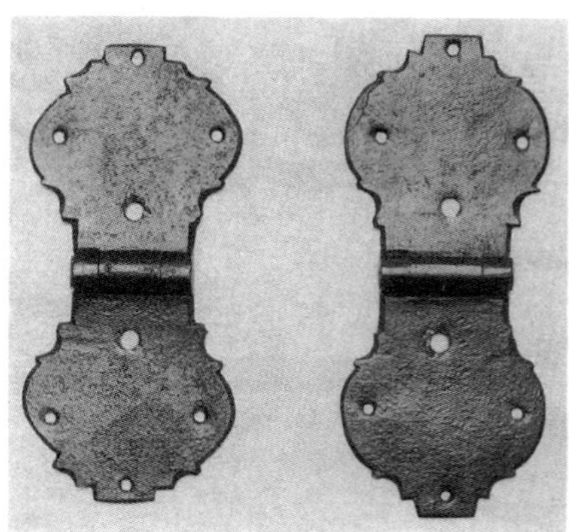

17

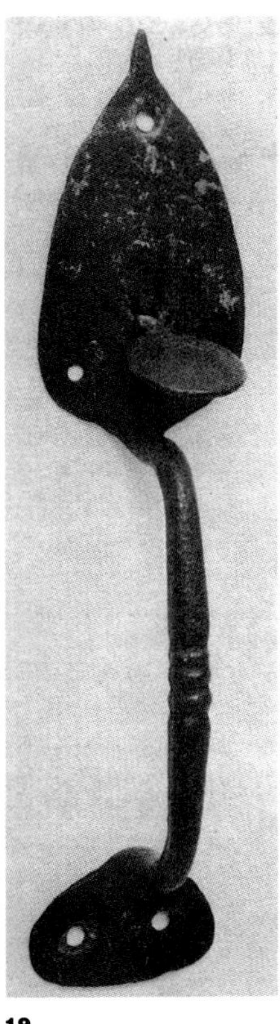

18

19

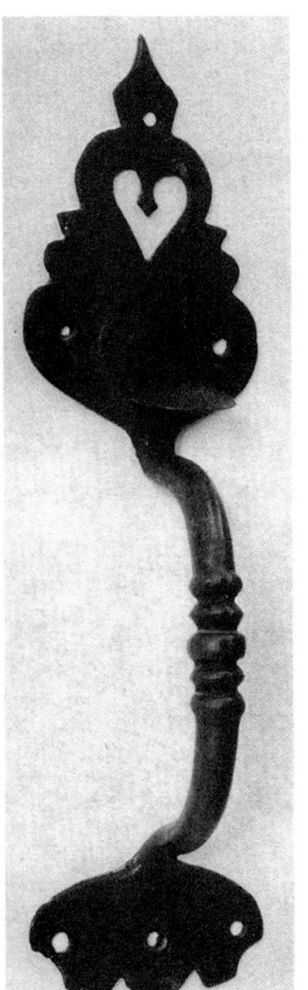

20

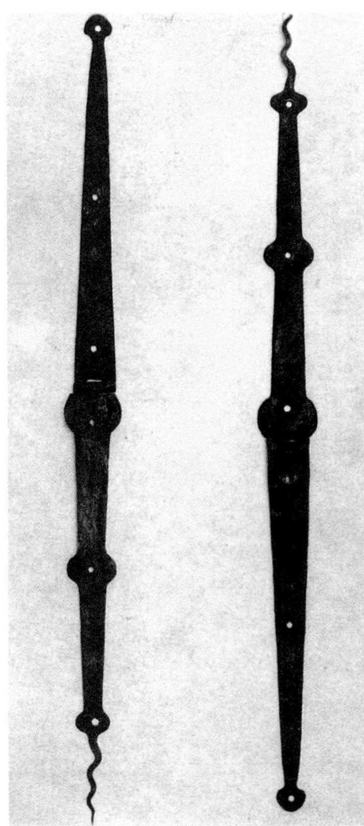

21

18 THUMB LATCH
1750–1800

Wrought iron. Perforated cusp latch. Flat thumbpiece pivots on notched, straight lift. Round handle has disk-and-ball design made with swage block. Traces of dark green paint on obverse.

29.5 x 6.5 cm (11⅝ x 2½")

Titus C. Geesey Collection. 53-125-11c

---

19 THUMB LATCH
1750–1800

Wrought iron. Perforated cusp latch. Flat thumbpiece pivots on notched, straight lift. Round handle with swage-block decoration. Wrought nails.

28.5 x 6.5 cm (11¼ x 2½")

Titus C. Geesey Collection. 53-125-11b

---

20 THUMB LATCH
1750–1800

Wrought iron. Perforated cusp latch. Convex thumbpiece pivots on notched, straight lift. Heavy handle with swage-block decoration.

33 x 9.3 cm (13 x 3⅝")

Titus C. Geesey Collection. 53-125-11a

---

21 PAIR OF STRAP HINGES
1750–1850

Wrought iron. Tooling and red paint on reverse.

Left 88 x 7 cm (34⅝ x 2¾")
Right 90.2 x 6.7 cm (35½ x 2⅝")

Titus C. Geesey Collection. 53-125-10k

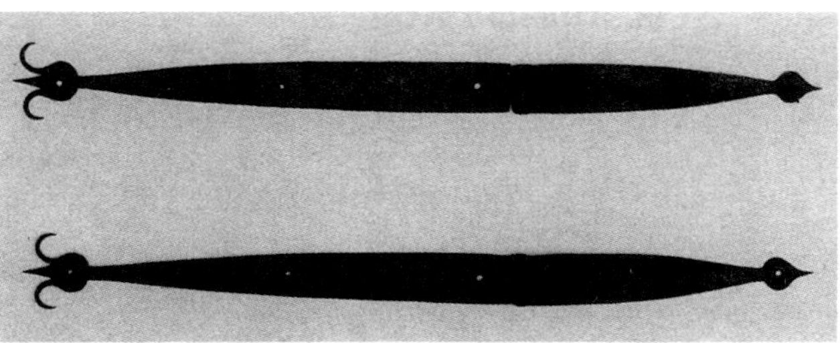

22

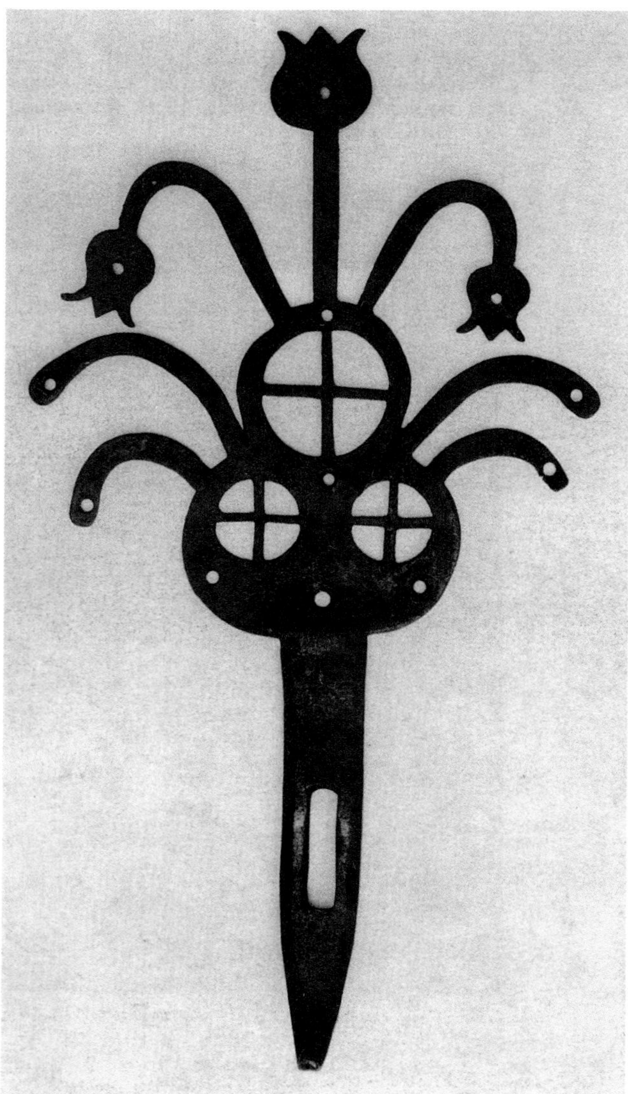

24

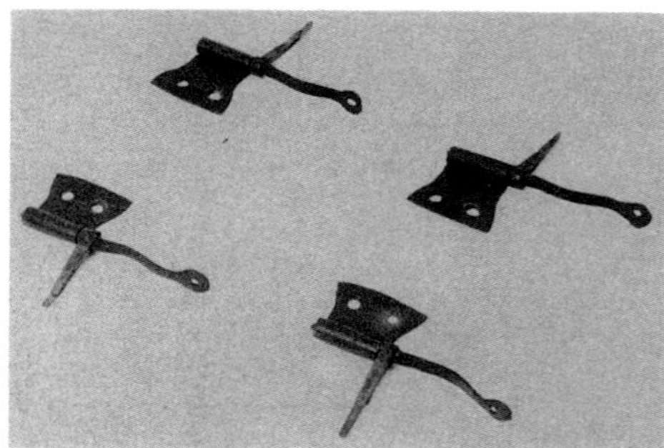

23

22 PAIR OF STRAP HINGES
1770–1800

Wrought iron. Straps terminate in pointed leaf and spiky tulip designs. Wicket-type hinges. Wrought nails. Probably for a dower chest.

76 x 3.2 cm (29⅞ x 1¼")

Gift of Mrs. William D. Frishmuth. 10-310,a

23 HINGES (4)
1770–1800

Wrought iron. Ax-shaped plates and pintles with extended props. Clenching spikes. Wrought nails.

10.1 to 10.5 x 8.2 to 9.8 cm (4 to 4⅛ x 3¼ to 3⅞")

Titus C. Geesey Collection. 53-125-10f

24 HASP
Lancaster County
1770–1800

Painted wrought iron. Flat escutcheon with slot for locking loop. Symmetrical nail holes. Painted red. For a Conestoga wagon toolbox.

38.1 x 22.2 cm (15 x 8¾")

Titus C. Geesey Collection. 53-125-12

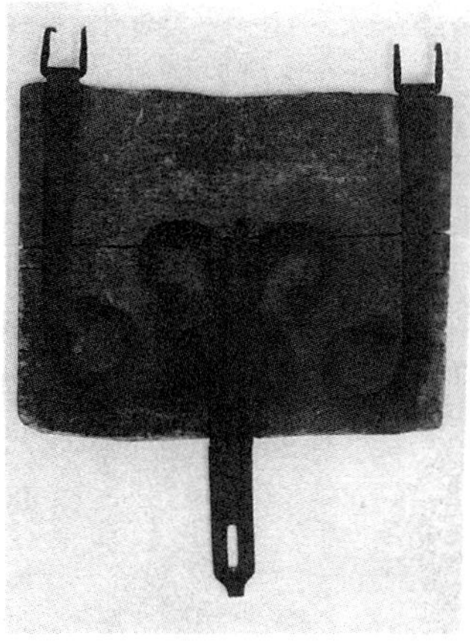

25

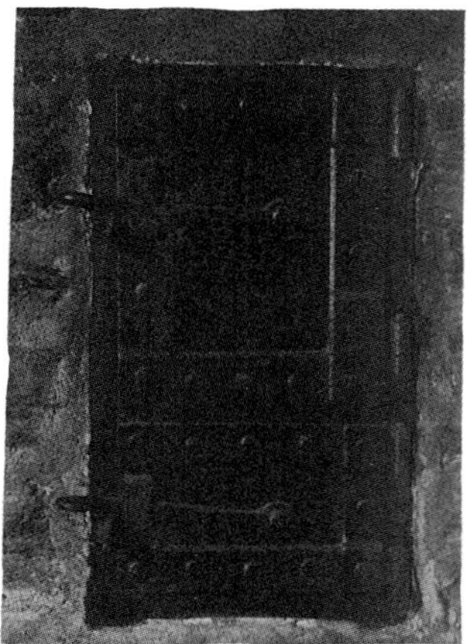

26

25 HASP AND HINGES
Lancaster County
1770–1800

Wrought iron. Scrolled strap hinges and hasp plate. Hasp is hinged and pierced to receive locking loop. From a Conestoga wagon box.

Lid 41 x 35.8 cm (16⅛ x 14⅛")

Purchased: Joseph E. Temple Fund. 24-61-8

26 DOUBLE-OVEN DOOR
1770–1800

Wrought iron. Two doors set in iron frame built into chimney stonework. Each door bound at edges with riveted iron straps. Plain pintles and socket hinges. Lift latch has spiral-twist handle.

Upper door 26.7 x 22.9 cm (10½ x 9")
Lower door 14 x 22.9 cm (5½ x 9")

Titus C. Geesey Collection. 58-110-5

27 THUMB LATCH
1770–1800

Wrought iron. Perforated cusp latch. Heavy, flat thumbpiece pivots on notched, straight lift. Wrought nails.

18.7 x 7 cm (7⅜ x 2¾")

Titus C. Geesey Collection. 53-125-10c

28 THUMB LATCH
1770–1800

Wrought iron. Perforated cusp latch. Flat thumbpiece pivots on notched, straight lift. Curved, rounded handle ends in barbed spike which jams into door. Decorative cusp in the form of a female (the breasts formed from heads of wrought nails) in a wide skirt, with incised features, standing on a heart-shaped form.

29.2 x 4 cm (11½ x 1⅝")

Titus C. Geesey Collection. 53-125-10a

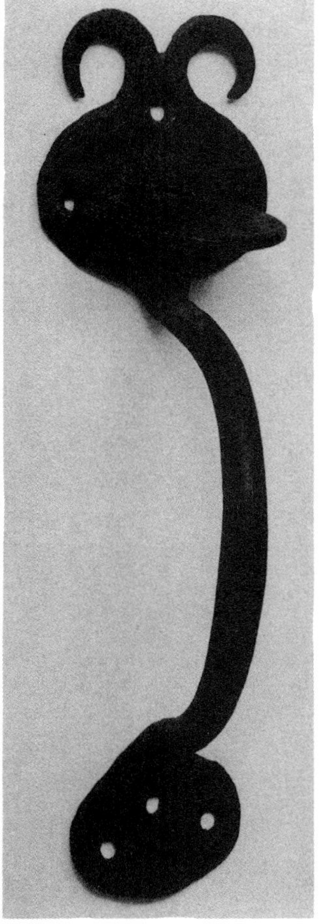

27

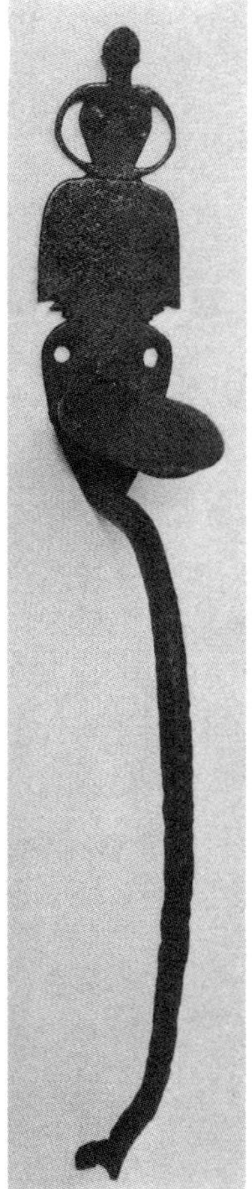

28

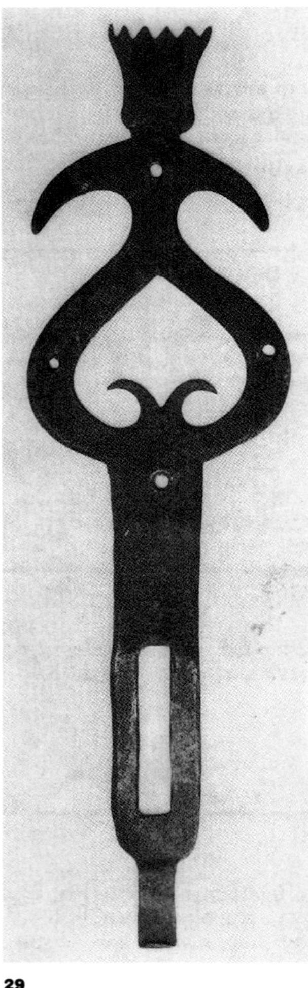

29

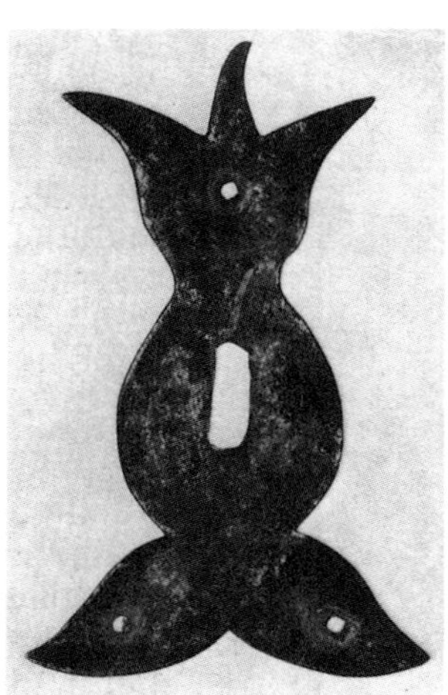

30

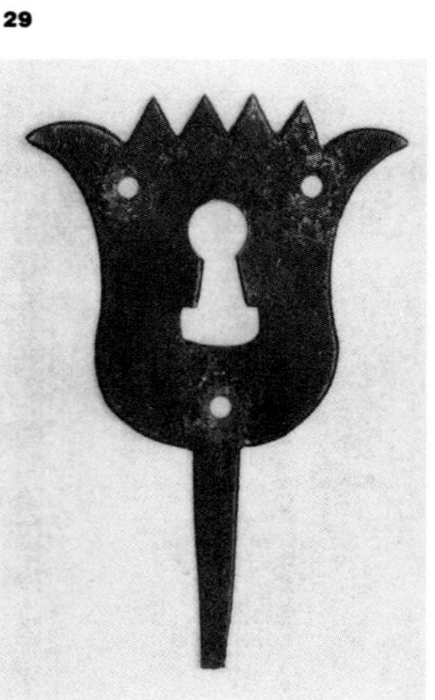

31

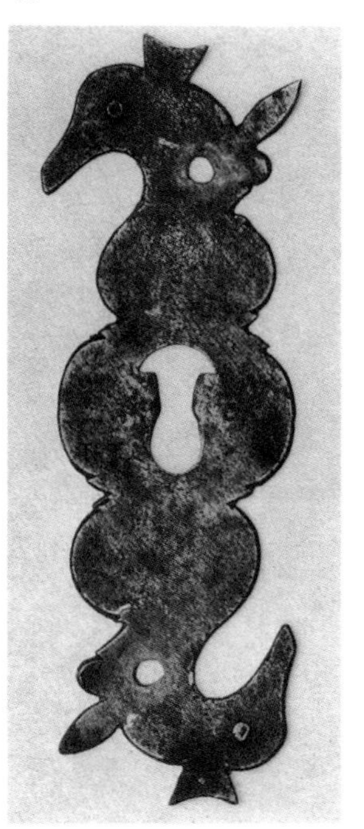

32

29 HASP
Lancaster County
1770–1850

Wrought iron. Hasp with slot for locking loop. Shaft had been straightened for display. For a Conestoga wagon toolbox.

35.6 x 10.2 cm (14 x 4″)

Titus C. Geesey Collection. 53-125-13

---

30 ESCUTCHEON
1780–1820

Sheet iron. Thin. Tulip shape. Traces of orange paint on reverse. Wrought nails.

10.5 x 7 cm (4⅛ x 2¾″)

Titus C. Geesey Collection. 53-125-10m

---

31 ESCUTCHEON
1800–1850

Sheet iron. Thin. Tulip shape. Straight edges. Wrought nails.

14 x 8.9 cm (5½ x 3½″)

Titus C. Geesey Collection. 53-125-10n

---

32 ESCUTCHEON
1800–1850

Sheet iron. Thin. Cock's head design. Raised eyes punched from back. Wrought nails.

12.7 x 4 cm (5 x 1⅝″)

Titus C. Geesey Collection. 53-125-10l

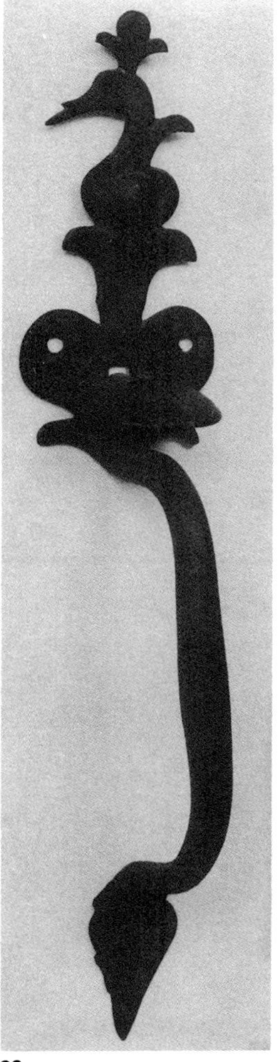

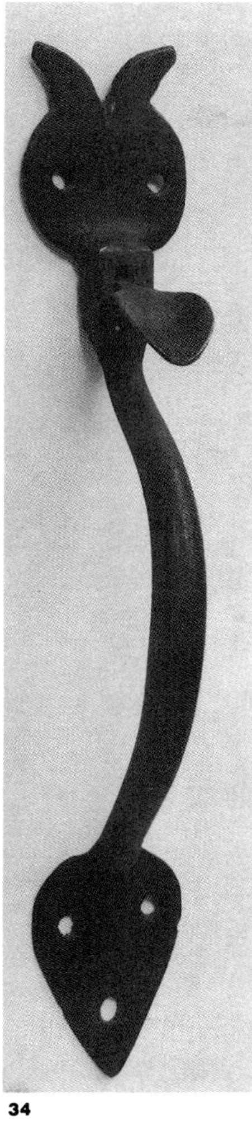

33

35

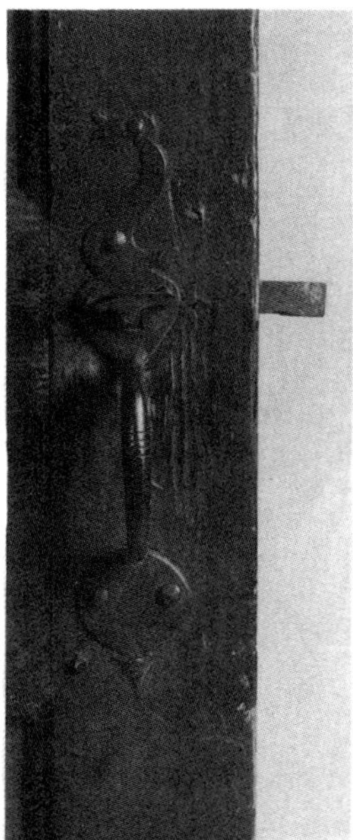

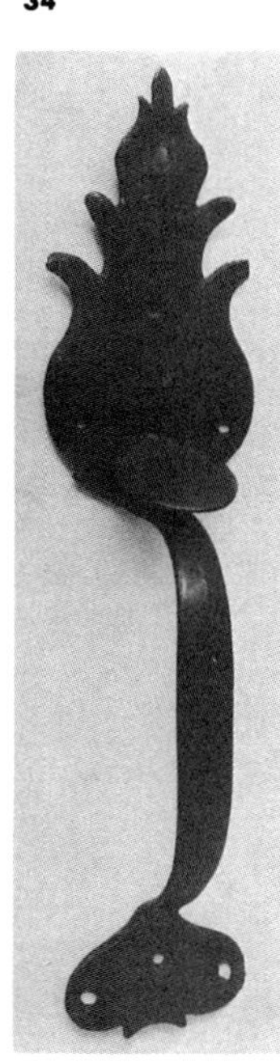

36

33 THUMB LATCH
1825–50

Wrought iron. Perforated cusp latch. Convex thumbpiece pivots on notched, straight lift that ends in downward hook. Rounded handle. Wrought nails with finished heads.

19.7 x 5.1 cm (7¾ x 2″)

Titus C. Geesey Collection. 53-125-10d

34 THUMB LATCH
1840–60

Wrought iron. Swivel lift latch. Concave thumbpiece pivots on rivet in slot. Lift ends in downward curve.

30.5 x 5.7 cm (12 x 2¼″)

Titus C. Geesey Collection. 53-125-10b

35 THUMB LATCH AND HARDWARE
1840–60

Wrought iron. Perforated cusp latch. Flat thumbpiece pivots on notched lift with downward-curved end. Handle decorated with incised lines. Mounted on door (*See* Wood, Architecture no. 5).

26.7 x 5.1 cm (10½ x 2″)

Titus C. Geesey Collection. 54-85-30b

36 THUMB LATCH
1840–60

Wrought iron. Perforated cusp latch. Flat thumbpiece pivots on notch in shaft that ends in downward hook. Flat handle.

27.5 x 6.5 cm (10⅞ x 2½″)

Titus C. Geesey Collection. 53-125-11d

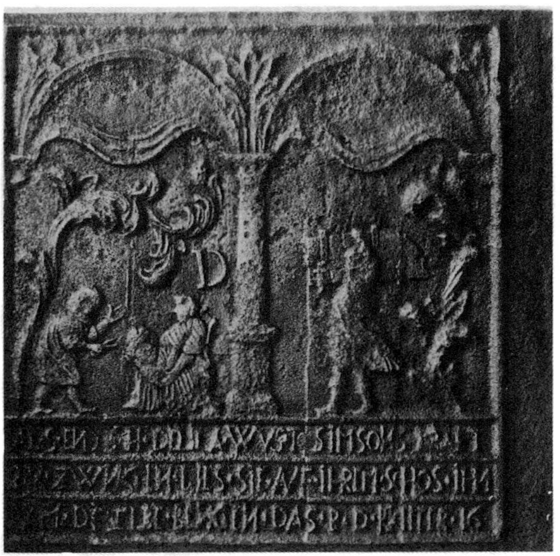

1

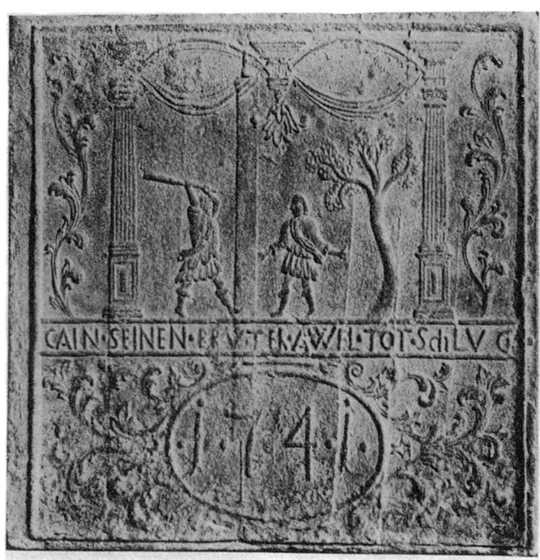

2

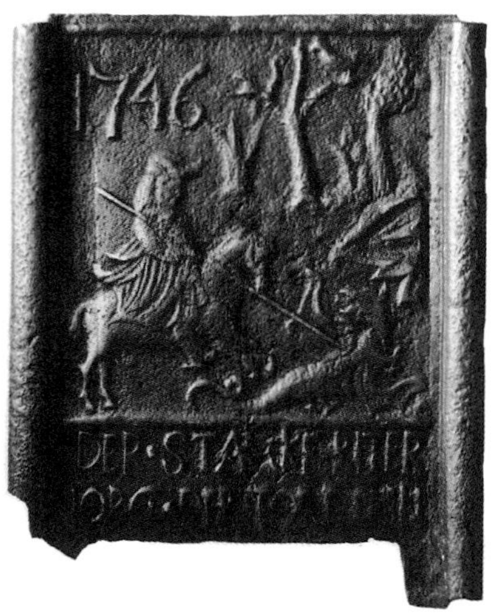

3

1   **STOVE PLATE**
1740–60

Inscribed: *D   ALS · ENDLICH · DELIA · WVST · SIMSONS · KRAFT   ZV · ZWINGEN · LIES · SIE · AVF · IHREM · SCHOS · IHN   VM · DESELBE · BRINGEN · DAS · B · D · RICHTER · 16* ("When at last Delilah learned how to overcome Samson's strength, she brought him to it on her lap. The Book of Judges, 16")

Cast iron. Right side plate of five-plate jamb stove. Open-sand cast. Central pilaster supports double arches with festoons. On the right is Samson carrying an arch-topped door from the gate of Gaza. On the left is Samson reclining on Delilah's lap and an old man holding scissors.

61.6 x 62.9 cm (24¼ x 24¾")

Gift of John T. Morris. 14-276

2   **STOVE PLATE**
Durham Township, Bucks County
1741

Durham Furnace

Inscribed: *CAIN · SEINEN, BRVTER · AWEL · TOT · SCHLVG   · i · 74 · i.* ("Cain killed his brother Abel. 1741")

Cast iron. Left side plate of five-plate jamb stove. Open-sand cast. Figure of Cain swinging club at Abel, who stands under a tree next to draped arches supported by fluted columns. Floral scrolling on sides and around cartouche. Vertical marks from unevenly joined mold boards. From the Henry C. Mercer collection.

66 x 66 cm (26 x 26")

Purchased. 99-1142

3   **STOVE PLATE**
1746

Inscribed: *1746   DER · STARCKE · RITER IORG · DEN · TODTEN* ("1746   The sturdy knight George, the slain")

Cast iron. Front plate of five-plate jamb stove. Open-sand cast. Design of St. George on horseback slaying the dragon with his lance. Piece missing at bottom.

59.7 x 51.4 cm (23½ x 20¼")

Gift of John T. Morris. 14-277

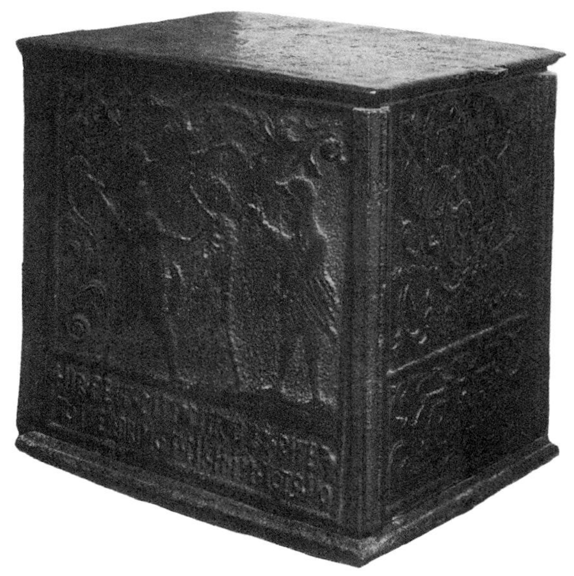

4

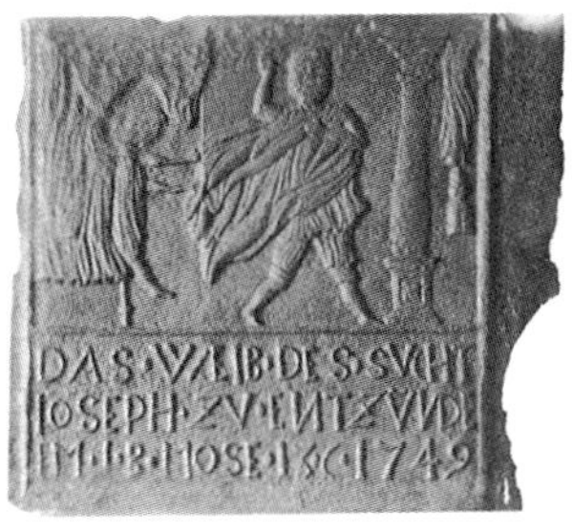

5

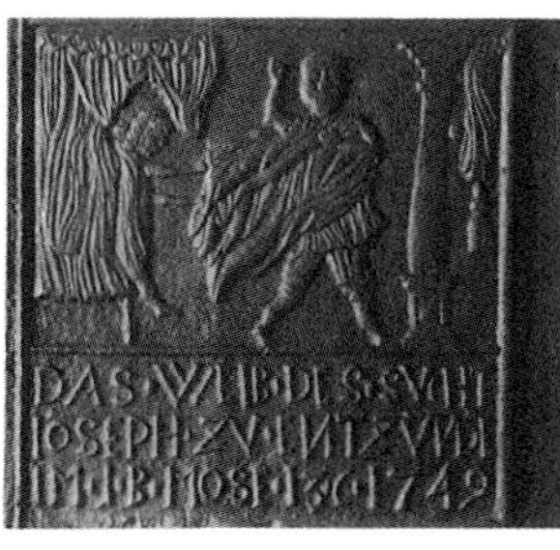

6

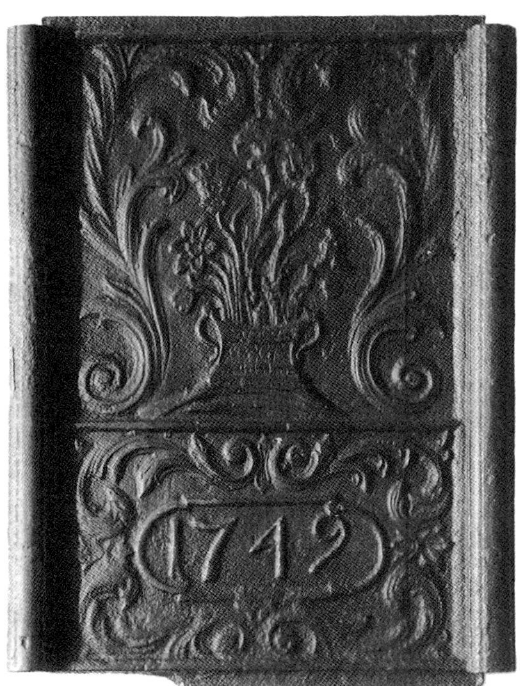

7

4 STOVE
1749

Inscribed on side plates: *HIR · FEIT · MIT · MIR · DER · BITTER · TOT · ER · BRINGT · MICH · IN · TOTS · NO.* [Here fights with me the bitter death/And brings me in death's stress.]; on front plate: *1749*

Cast iron. Five-plate jamb stove. Plates open-sand cast. Side panels show "Dance of Death" pattern: two combative noblemen are impeded by a skeleton holding a bone as a club. Front plate divided into two panels. Upper panel has ruffled aureole surrounded with winged C scrolls. Shell and foliage in spandrels and date in cartouche surrounded with leafy scrolls in lower panel.

55.9 x 58.4 x 49.5 cm (22 x 23 x 19½")

Purchased: Joseph E. Temple Fund. 14-216

5 STOVE PLATE
1749

Inscribed: *DAS · WEIB · DES · SVCHT JOSEPH · ZV · ENTZVNDE IM · I · B · MOSE · 13C · 1749.* ("The woman who seeks to corrupt Joseph. In the First Book Moses, 13 Chapter. 1749") [Genesis 39:13]

Cast iron. Right side plate of five-plate jamb stove. Open-sand cast. Scene of Potiphar's wife under bed canopy clutching the cloak of the fleeing Joseph.

61.3 x 65.4 cm (24⅛ x 25¾")

Gift of John T. Morris. 14-275

6 STOVE PLATE
1749

Inscribed: *DAS · WEIB · DES · SVCHT · JOSEPH · ZV · ENTZVNDE IM · I · B · MOSE · 13C · 1749.* ("The woman who seeks to corrupt Joseph. In the First Book Moses, 13 Chapter. 1749") [Genesis 39:13]

Cast iron. Right side plate of five-plate jamb stove. Open-sand cast. Identical to preceding (no. 5), except size. From the Henry C. Mercer collection.

66 x 63.2 cm (26 x 24⅞")

Purchased. 99-1143

7 STOVE PLATE
1749–60

Inscribed: *1749*

Cast iron. Front plate of five-plate jamb stove. Open-sand cast. Design of naturalistic flowers in basket. Date in cartouche surrounded with foliage scrolls. Damaged lower left.

62.9 x 47.6 cm (24¾ x 18¾")

Purchased: Joseph E. Temple Fund. 13-62

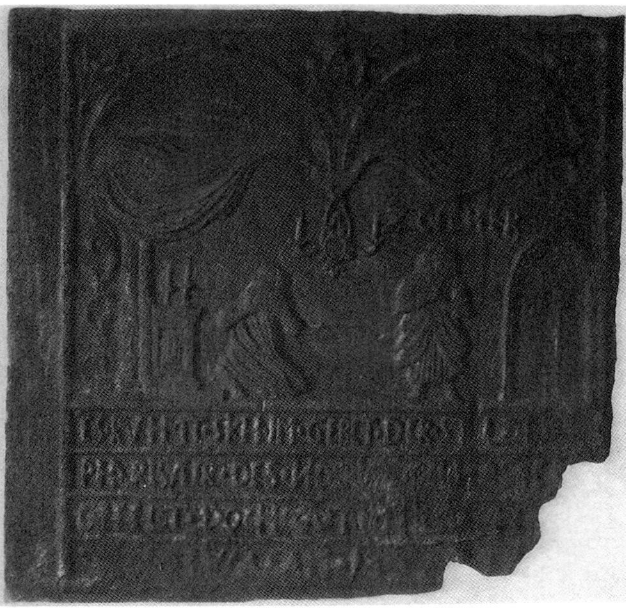

8

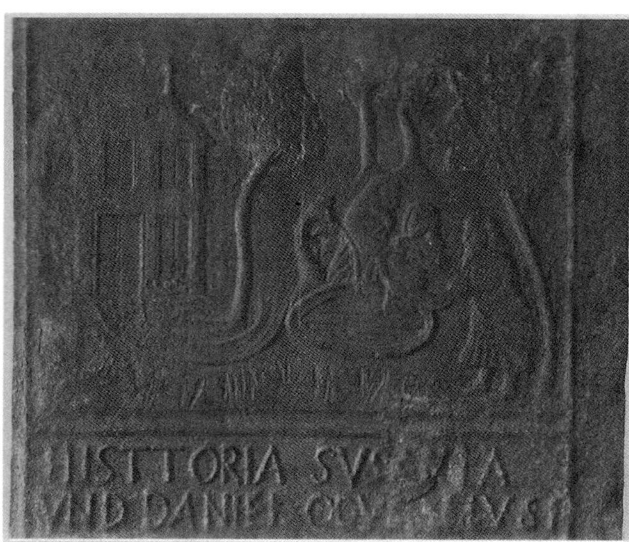

9

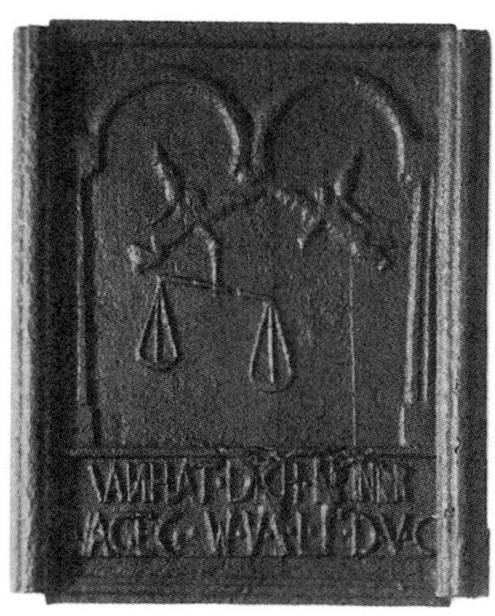

10

8   STOVE PLATE
1750–60

Inscribed: *ZOELNER   ES · RVEHMT · SICH · IM · GEBET · DER · STOLZER · PHARISAER · DES · NIDERN · ZOELNERS · HERZ · GEFELT · DOCH · GOTT · FHL · MEHR.   LVCA · AM · 18 · CAP · 1742* ("Publican   The proud Pharisee glorifies himself in prayer, but the heart of the humble Publican pleases God much better. Luke in 18 Chapter. 1742")

Cast iron. Left side plate of five-plate jamb stove. Open-sand cast. Kneeling Pharisee on left and standing Publican on right, dressed in togas, are framed under double arch with two-branched chandelier at center. Uneven boards of mold show vertical line on right between Publican and door. Damaged lower right corner.

62.2 x 64.3 cm (24½ x 25⅜")

Gift of John T. Morris. 14-268

9   STOVE PLATE
1750–60

Inscribed: *HIST · TORIA · SVSANNA   VND DANIEL, O DV. BESE LVST.* ("Story of Susanna and Daniel, O thou evil lust.")

Cast iron. Right plate of five-plate jamb stove. Open-sand cast. Susanna and the elders at pool on right, two-story mansion with winding path on left.

67 x 73.7 cm (26⅜ x 29")

Purchased: F.T.S. Darley Fund. 16-414

10   STOVE PLATE
1750–60

Inscribed: *MANHAT · DICH · N · INER WAGEG · W · V · Z · L · F · D · V · C* ("Thou art weighed in the balances and art found wanting.")

Cast iron. Front plate of six-plate stove. Open-sand cast. Two putti, one holding an unbalanced scale, on flat background within double arch and pilasters.

60.9 x 50.8 cm (24 x 20")

Purchased: Special Museum Fund. 08-693

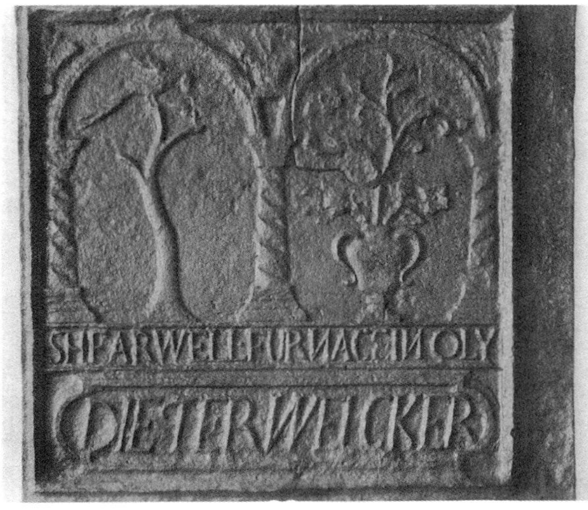

11

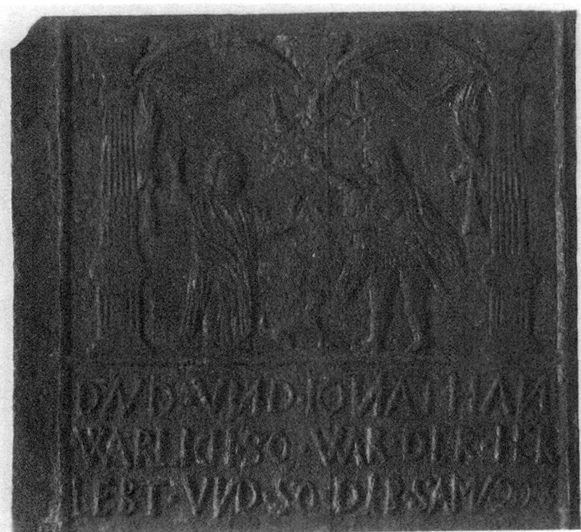

12

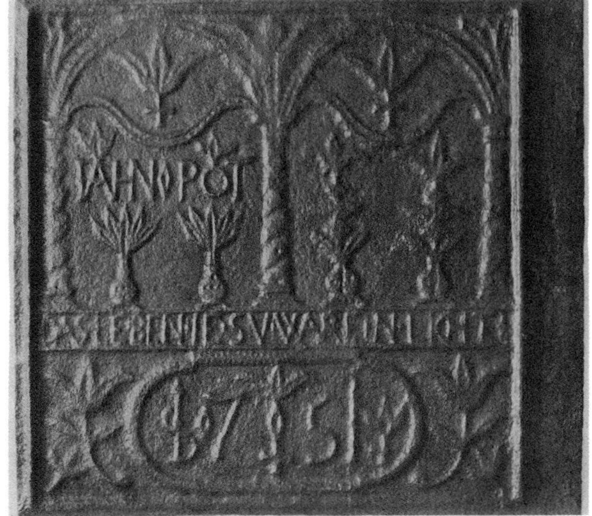

13

11 STOVE PLATE
Friedensburg, Berks County
1750–60

Shearwell Furnace
Dietrich Welker, master

Inscribed: *SHFARWELL · FURNACE · IN
OLY   DIETER · WEIKER*

Cast iron. Right side plate of five-plate jamb
stove. Open-sand cast. Design of serpentine
tree with large bird at top and curvaceous urn
with handles containing naturalistic flowers
and foliage. Design framed by plain arches
supported by twisted columns. Cracked at top.

58.4 x 61 cm (23 x 24″)

Gift of John T. Morris. 14-269

12 STOVE PLATE
1750–70

Inscribed: *DAVD · VND · JONATHAN
WARLICH · SO · WAR · DER · HER · LEBT ·
VND · SO · D · I · B · SAMV · 20 · 3.* ("David and
Jonathan, but truly as the Lord liveth, and as
the First Book Samuel 20–3") [1 Samuel 20:3]

Cast iron. Left side plate of five-plate jamb
stove. Open-sand cast. David, with cloak and
sword, meets Jonathan, in long robe. Barking
dog stands between the two figures under
tassel-festooned keyed double arches with
two-armed chandelier suspended from center.
Impression eroded.

67.3 x 69.9 cm (26½ x 27½″)

Purchased: Joseph E. Temple Fund. 13-63

13 STOVE PLATE
Warwick Township, Chester County
1751

Warwick Furnace
John Potts, master

Inscribed: *JAHN · POT   DAS LEBEN · JESV
· WAR · EIN · LICHT   1·7 51* ("John Potts   The
life of Jesus was a light   1751")

Cast iron. Right side plate of five-plate jamb
stove. Open-sand cast. Foliage and spiky tulips
in vases under two arches supported on
twisted columns. One tulip springing from a
cross at top of each arch. Curving stemmed
tulips flank cartouche with date.

61 x 65.4 cm (24 x 25¾″)

Gift of John T. Morris. 14-274

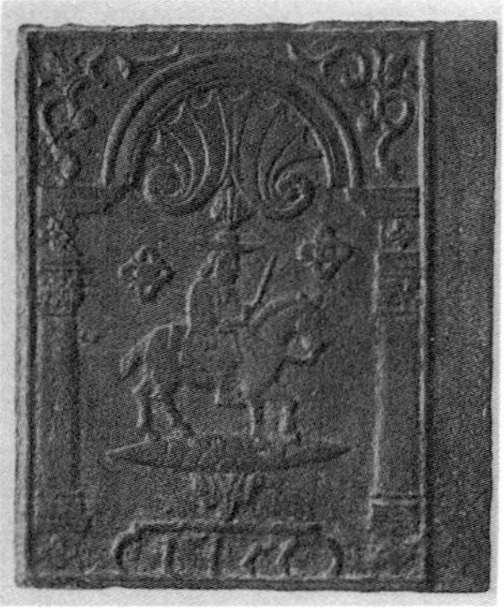

14

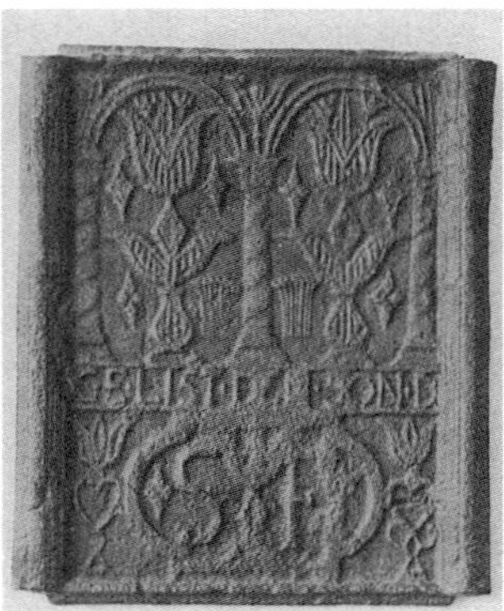

15 front

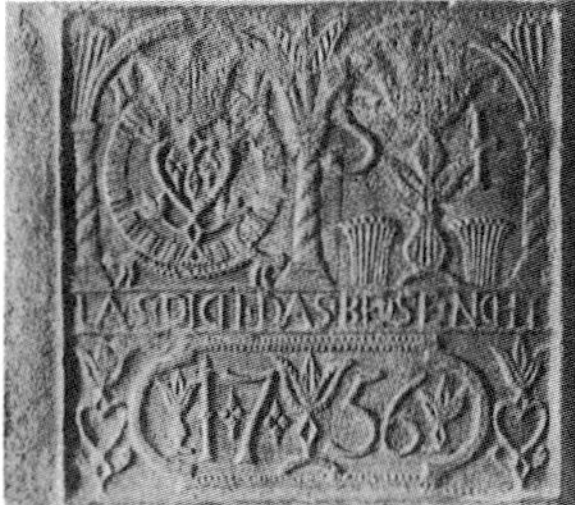

15 left

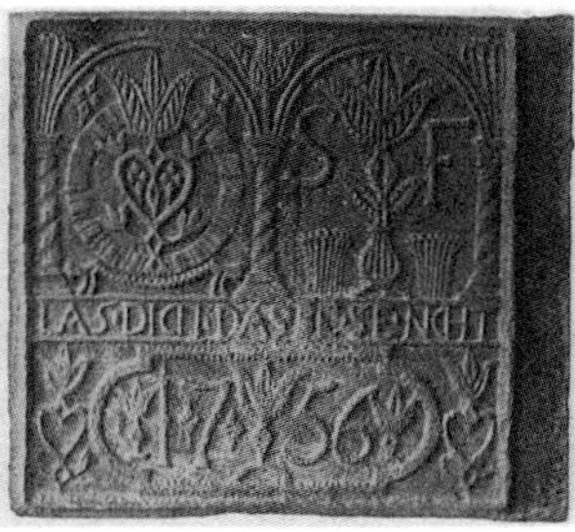

15 right

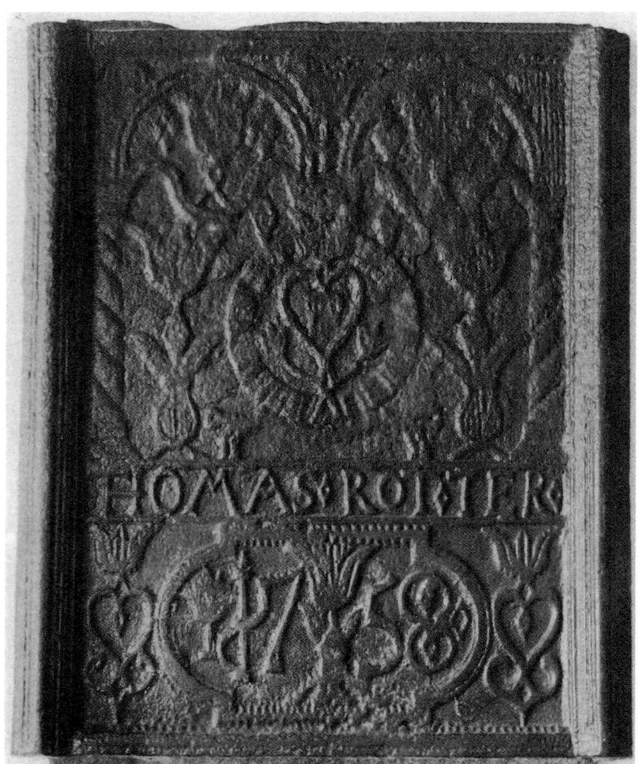

16

14 STOVE PLATE
Berks County
1756

Berkshire or **Redding Furnace**
William Bird or **William Branson**, masters

Inscribed: *1756*

Cast iron. Right side plate of five-plate jamb stove. Open-sand cast. Figure of man in broad-brimmed hat carrying upright stick or sword, on horseback. Shell is enclosed by molded arch on Corinthian pilasters. Date in cartouche.

59.7 x 52.1 cm (23½ x 20½")

Gift of John T. Morris. 14-278

15 STOVE
Durham Township, Bucks County
1756–60

Durham Furnace
Samuel Flower, master

Inscribed on sides: *S · F   LAS · DICH · DAS · BESE · NICHT   1 · 7 · 56*; on front: *GE · LIST · DEN · SON · D   S · F* ("Do not yearn for evil but") [overcome evil with good; Romans 12:21]

Cast iron. Five-plate jamb stove. Open-sand cast. Side plates have design of tulip in aureole on sheep's feet motif under double arch with spiral twist columns. Date in cartouche flanked by tulips over hearts. Front plate has tulips with fluted vases, lozenges, and wheat sheaves in double arch with twisted columns over initials in cartouche flanked with tulips over hearts. Top and bottom plates undecorated.

56.8 x 47.8 x 53 cm (22⅜ x 18⅞ x 20⅞")

Purchased: Annual Membership Fund. 16-333a–d

16 STOVE PLATE
Berks County
1758

Colebrookdale Furnace
Thomas Rutter, master

Inscribed: *THOMAS · ROT · TER   17 · 58*

Cast iron. Front plate of jamb stove. Open-sand cast. Tulips in vases flank heart in aureole under double arch with twisted pilasters. Date in cartouche with tulips over hearts.

61 x 50.8 cm (24 x 20")

Purchased: Joseph E. Temple Fund. 13-61

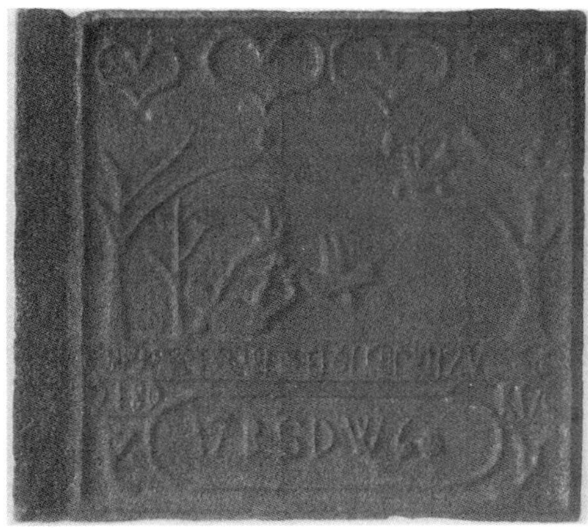

17

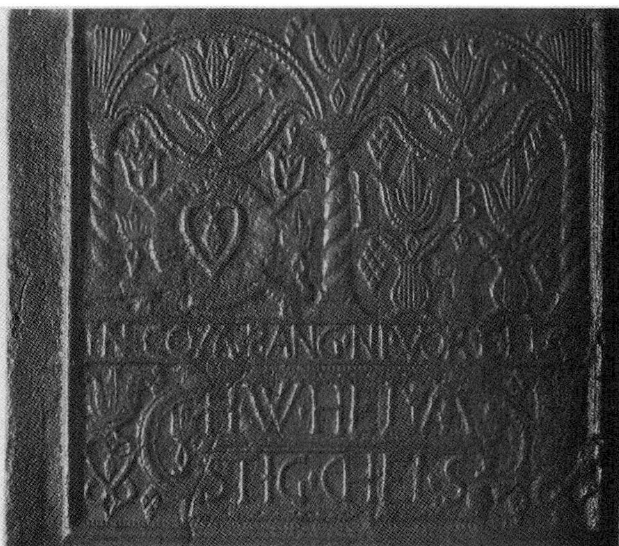

18

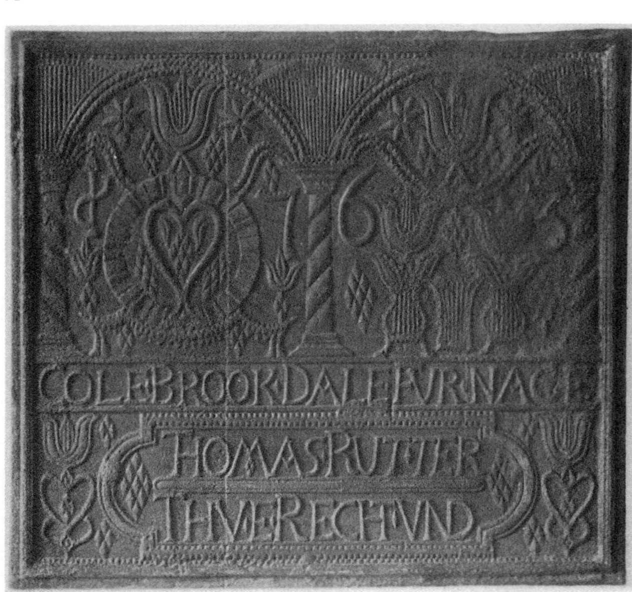

19

17 STOVE PLATE
Oley, Berks County
1760

Shearwell Furnace
Benedict Swope and **Dietrich Welker,** masters

Inscribed: *ICH, HABE. DEN. RABEN. BEFOHLEN. DICH. ZV. VERS I · B · D · K · 17 · C 17 BSDW 60* ("And I have commanded the ravens to feed thee there. Taken from the First Book of Kings, 17 Chapter") [1 Kings 17:4]

Cast iron. Left side plate of five-plate jamb stove. Open-sand cast. Design in raised relief: four hearts, center ones with drops, over three leafless trees. Two ravens feeding Elijah, two birds perching in trees.

60.3 x 66.7 cm (23¾ x 26¼")

Purchased: Special Museum Fund. 08-694

18 STOVE PLATE
Lancaster County
1760–63

Elizabeth Furnace
Henry William Stiegel, master

Inscribed: *I · B IN · COMBANGNI · VOR · ELISA H · W · HELM STIG · GHEL · S I · B* [John Barr] ("In company for Elisa H. Wilhelm Stiegel")

Cast iron. Left side plate of five-plate jamb stove. Open-sand cast. Design of tulips in fluted vases, heart in aureole with central lozenge, tulips and six-pointed stars above, under double arch supported by twisted columns. Name in cartouche flanked by tulips over hearts.

53.2 x 63.5 cm (21 x 25")

Purchased: Special Museum Fund. 12-178

19 STOVE PLATE
Berks County
1763

Colebrookdale Furnace
Thomas Rutter, master

Inscribed: *1.7.6.3 COLE · BROOK · DALE · FURNACE THOMAS · RUT · TER THV · E · RECH · VND* ("1763 Colebrookdale Furnace, Thomas Rutter. Do right and")

Cast iron. Side plate of six-plate stove. Open-sand cast. Design of tulips in fluted urns on raised legs with swag above and tulip flanked by two eight-pointed stars. Heart in aureole on raised stand with swag, tulip and stars under double arch supported on twisted columns. Cartouche flanked by tulips over hearts and lozenge motifs.

61 x 68.6 cm (24 x 27")

Purchased: F.T.S. Darley Fund. 16-416

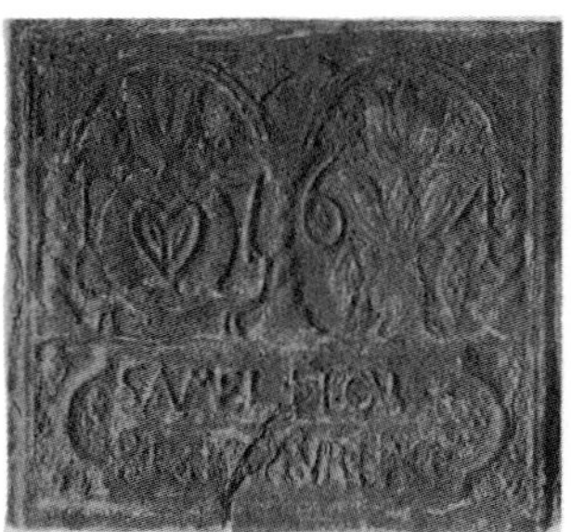

20

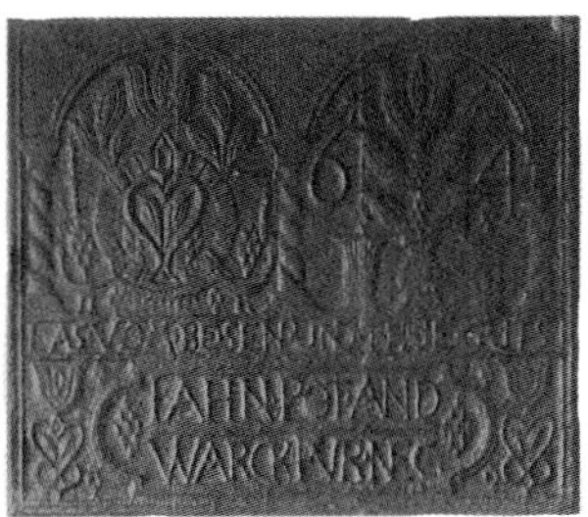

21

20 STOVE PLATE
Warwick Township, Chester County
1764

Redding Furnace
Samuel Flower, master

Inscribed: *1 · 7 · 6 · 4   SAMEL · FLOWER RETING · FURNACE*

Cast iron. Side plate of six-plate stove. Open-sand cast. Tulip in vase and heart in aureole with two eight-pointed stars. Surfaces eroded and plate cracked at bottom.

50.8 x 55.9 cm (20 x 22″)

Purchased: Special Museum Fund. 15-246

21 STOVE PLATE
Warwick Township, Chester County
1764

Warwick Furnace
John Potts, master

Inscribed: *LAS · VOM · BESEN · UND · THUE GUTES   JAHN POT · AND · WARCK · FVRNEC* ("Depart from evil and do good. John Potts and Warwick Furnace")

Cast iron. Side plate of six-plate stove. Open-sand cast. Design of tulip in vase, heart in aureole, and wheat sheaves, under double arch. From the Henry C. Mercer collection.

59.7 x 67.3 cm (23½ x 26½″)

Purchased. 99-1141

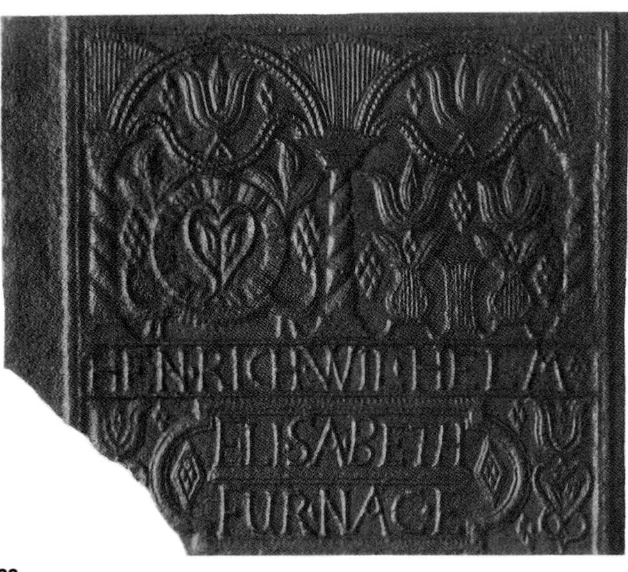

22

22 STOVE PLATE
Lancaster County
1764–66

Elizabeth Furnace
Henry William Stiegel, master

Inscribed: *HEN · RICH · WIL · HELM   ELI SA · BETH   FUR · NAC · E*

Cast iron. Left plate of five-plate stove. Open-sand cast. Pattern of two arches enclosing pair of tulips in fluted vases and heart in aureole topped with tulip on a triangle. Left corner of plate broken.

59.7 x 64.8 cm (23½ x 25½″)

Gift of John T. Morris. 14-270

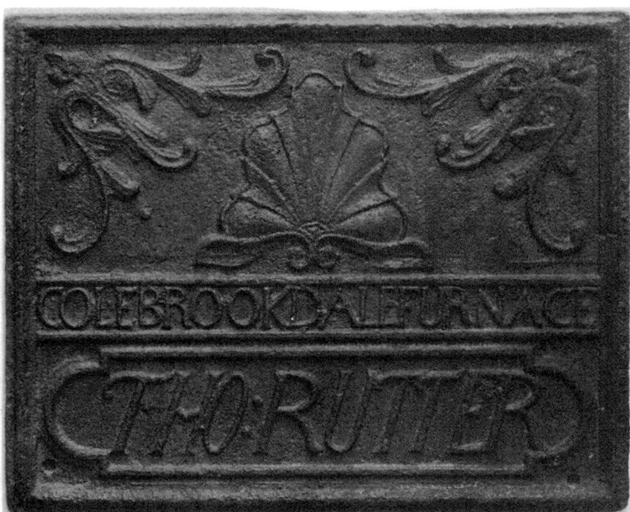

23

23 STOVE PLATE
Berks County
1770–80

Colebrookdale Furnace
Thomas Rutter, master

Inscribed: *COLEBROOKDALEFURNACE THO: RUTTER*

Cast iron. Side plate of six-plate stove. Open-sand cast.

45.3 x 57.5 cm (17⅞ x 22⅝″)

Gift of Mrs. Anna P. R. Mauser. 08-691

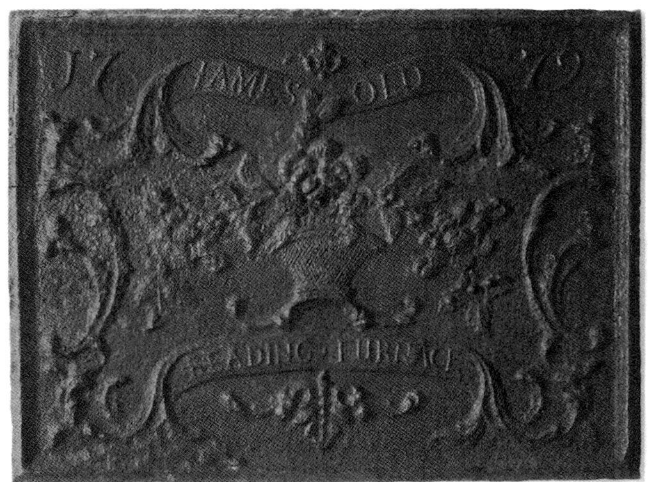

24

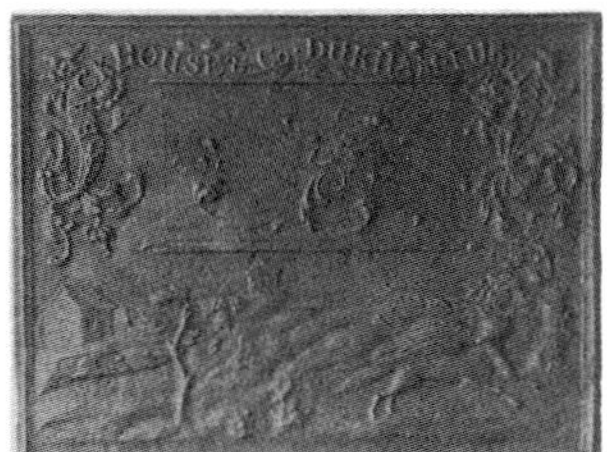

25

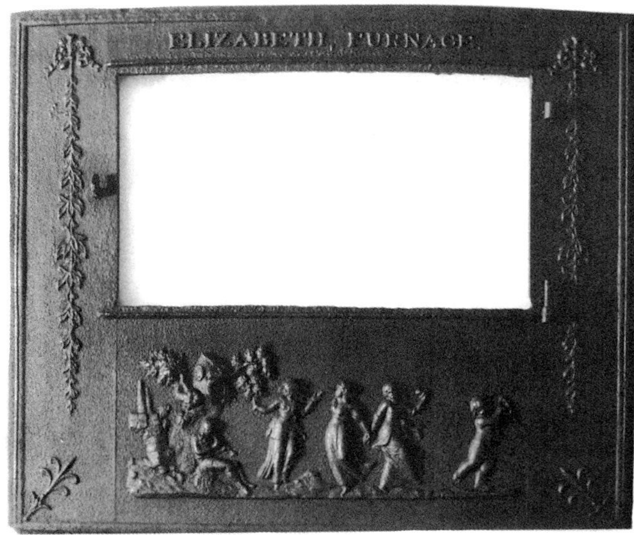

26

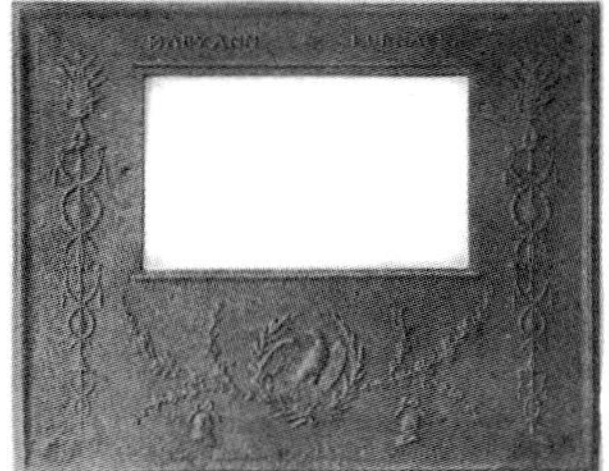

27

24 STOVE PLATE
Berks County
1772–78

Redding Furnace
James Old, master

Inscribed: *17 JAMES OLD 72   READING FURNACE*

Cast iron. Side plate of six-plate stove. Open-sand cast. Design of a wicker basket with roses. Inscription on ribbons ending in floral sprays.

45.2 x 60.3 cm (17¾ x 23¾")

Purchased: Annual Membership Fund. 12-96

---

25 STOVE PLATE
Durham Township, Bucks County
1780–90

Durham Furnace
Richard Backhouse, master

Inscribed: *BACKHOUSE & CO · DURHAM · FURNACE*

Cast iron. Side plate of ten-plate stove. Open-sand cast. Design of a running fox grasping a fowl by the neck. Landscape with one-story house on the left. Mold lines show that same mold was used for plate with oven-door opening.

63.5 x 80.6 cm (25 x 31¾")

Purchased: Annual Membership Fund. 16-334

---

26 STOVE PLATE
Lancaster County
1780–94

Elizabeth Furnace
Robert Coleman, master

Inscribed: *ELIZABETH FURNACE*

Cast iron. Side plate with door opening from a ten-plate stove. Open-sand cast. Three female figures, a putti playing a triangle, and a piper leaning against a tree in high relief and foliage in low relief with spandrels at bottom. Board joints of mold are clear. Door missing.

60.4 x 71.7 cm (23¾ x 28¼")

Purchased: Special Museum Fund. 12-151

---

27 STOVE PLATE
West Manheim Township, York County
1780–1800

Mary Ann Furnace
John Steinmetz and **John Brinton,** masters

Inscribed: *MARY ANN · FURNACE*

Cast iron. Side plate of ten-plate stove. Open-sand cast. Design of eagle within garlanded wreath, over memorial portrait busts (Franklin on left, Washington on right) centered under oven door (missing).

64.8 x 80.7 cm (25½ x 31¾")

Purchased: Special Museum Fund. 15-248

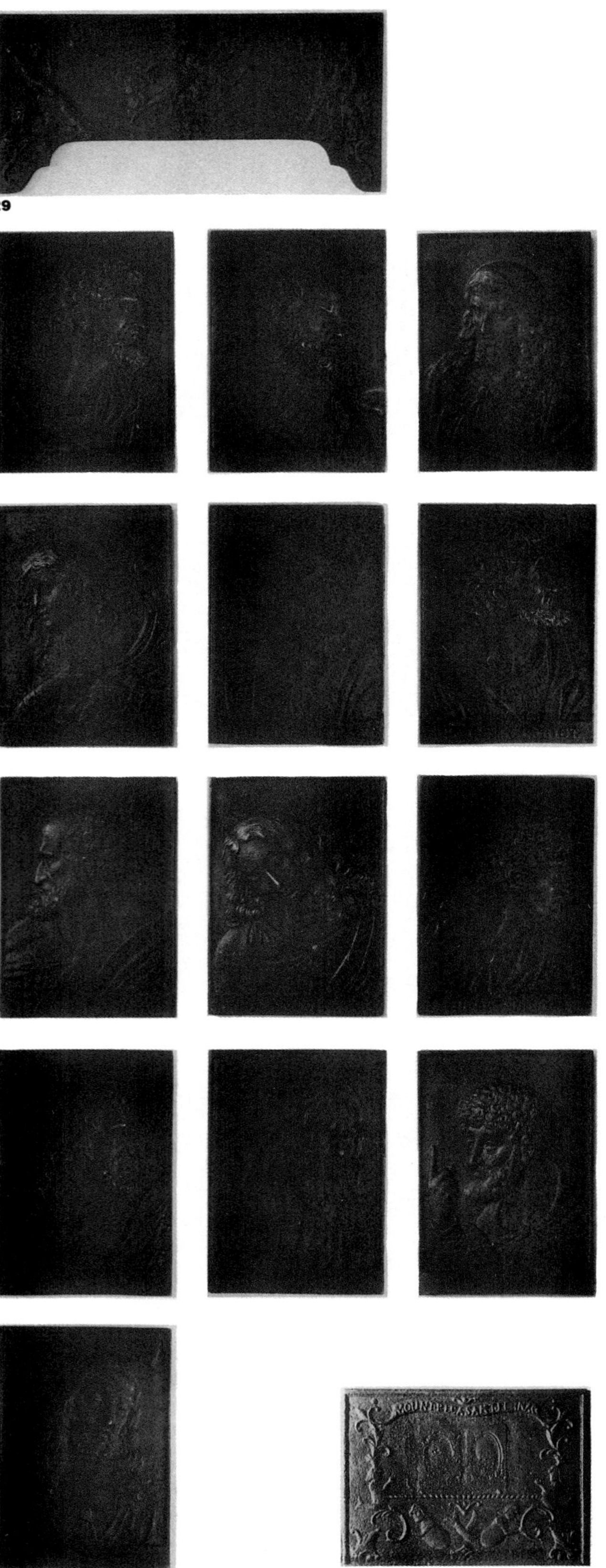

28 STOVE PLATE
Franklin County
1783

Mount Pleasant Furnace
William Benjamin and **George Chambers,**
masters

Inscribed top and bottom:
MOUNT · PLEASANT · FURNACE

Cast iron. Side plate of a ten-plate stove. Flask
cast. Inscription in banner at top. Design of
mermen with interlocking tails, holding
scrolls, and foliage spandrels at bottom.

58.5 x 80.7 cm (23 x 31¾")

Purchased: Special Museum Fund. 15-247

**29 FRONT PLATE OF A
FRANKLIN FIREPLACE**
Lancaster County
1786–1800

Mount Hope Furnace
Peter Grubb, Jr. and **George Ege,** masters

Inscribed: *PETER GRUBB · GEORGE EGE*

Cast iron. Open-sand cast. Trumpeting angel
amid swirling clouds centered under
inscription in banner and flanked by two
seated figures: a pensive Liberty with furled
flag and oval shield and an Indian holding a
tomahawk in right hand and fondling a dog
with left hand.

36.2 x 77.5 cm (14¼ x 30½")

Purchased: Special Museum Fund. 13-450

30 PORTRAIT PLAQUES (14)
Berks County
1820–30

Windsor Furnace
Jones, Keim & Company

Inscribed obverse: *SANCT JACOBUS, SANCT
MATHEUS, SANCT PHILIPPUS, SANCT
JACOBUS THE LESS, SANCT ANDREAS,
JUDAS ISCHARIOT, JUDAS, JESUS
CHRISTUS, SANCT PETRUS, S. JOHAN
EVANGELIST, ST. JUDAS THADDAUS,
SANCT SIMON, SANCT THOMAS, ST.
BARTHOLEMUS* [duplicate]; reverse: *SH*

Cast iron. Flask-cast plates. Portraits from late
eighteenth-century engravings after *Last
Supper* by Leonardo da Vinci. SH on reverse
may be mold-maker's mark. Probably used as
mantel ornaments.

10.5 x 8.2 cm (4⅛ x 3¼")

Gift of George H. Lorimer. 26-96-1a—n

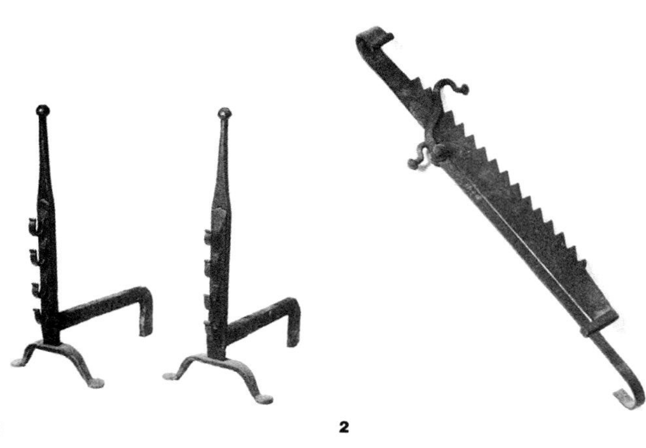

1

2

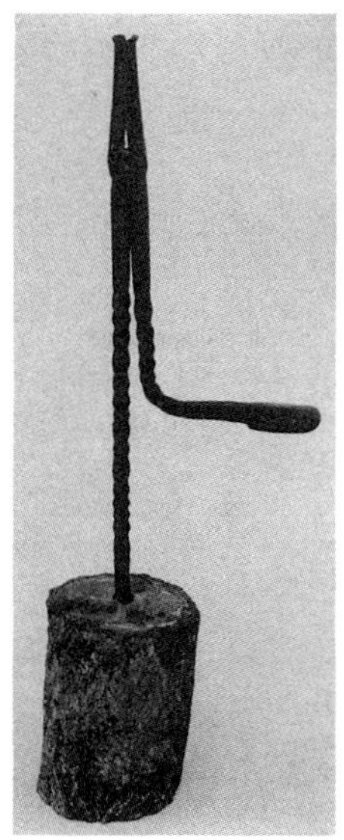

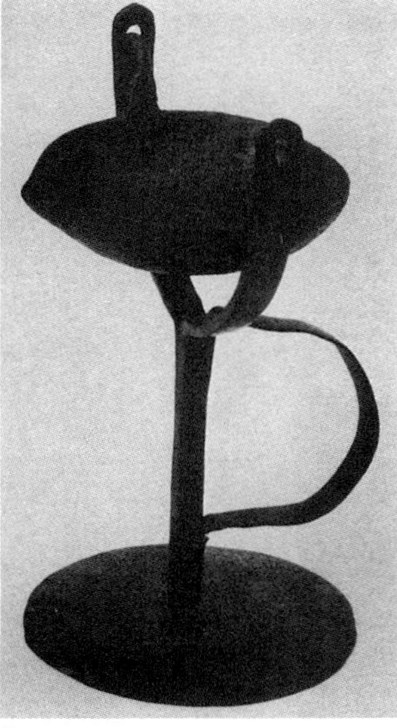

3

5

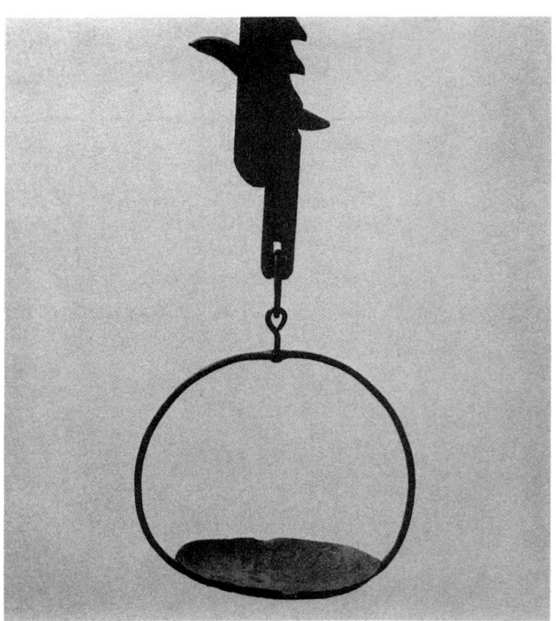

4

1 ANDIRONS
1720–1800

Wrought iron. Shaped shaft with ball finial tenoned through splayed legs and riveted. Four spit hooks on independent flat bar attached to shaft with rivet at top. Log carrier tenoned through shaft and riveted.

(a) 73.7 x 33.6 x 54.6 cm (29 x 13¼ x 21½")
(b) 73.3 x 34.3 x 52.1 cm (28⅞ x 13½ x 20½")

Gift of J. Stogdell Stokes. 28-10-6a,b

2 TRAMMEL
1720–1800

Wrought iron. Ratchet mechanism. Knobbed handles front and back control pivoting action on rivet, which locks and releases teeth for height adjustments.

90.2 x 21 cm (35½ x 8¼") (closed)

Gift of J. Stogdell Stokes. 28-10-18

3 ROPE LIGHT-HOLDER
1750–1800

Wrought iron, hemlock. Two twisted shafts hinged on a rivet have concave flare at top edge to conform to fat-soaked rope. Handle has weighted end to assure clamping. Stand set into wood base.

Height 62.8 cm (24¾")

Gift of Mrs. William D. Frishmuth. 03-341

4 OPEN-FLAME GREASE LAMP
1750–1800

Wrought iron. Oval bowl has slight dip at edge of each side to hold floating wicks. Rigid bail handle attached to underside of bowl with rivets and pierced for suspending hook. Shown with a wood trammel.

23.9 x 26 cm (9⅜ x 10¼")

Titus C. Geesey Collection. 55-45-13b

5 FAT LAMP
1750–1800

Wrought iron. Round oil pan has protruding spout to hold burning end of floating wick. Pan swings on iron hooks in frame with handle and base.

22.3 x 12.7 cm (8¾ x 5")

Gift of Mrs. William D. Frishmuth. 03-338

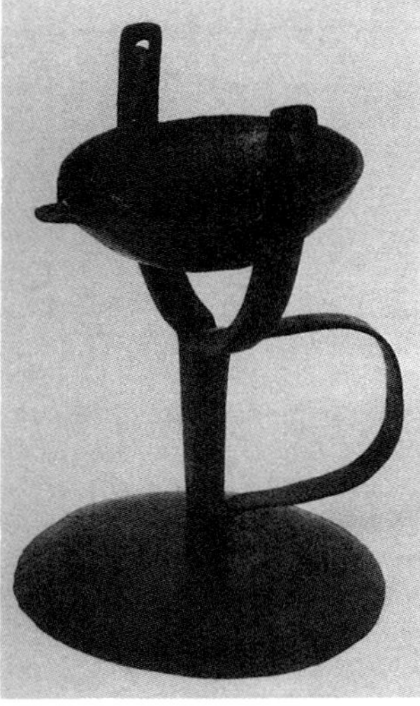

6

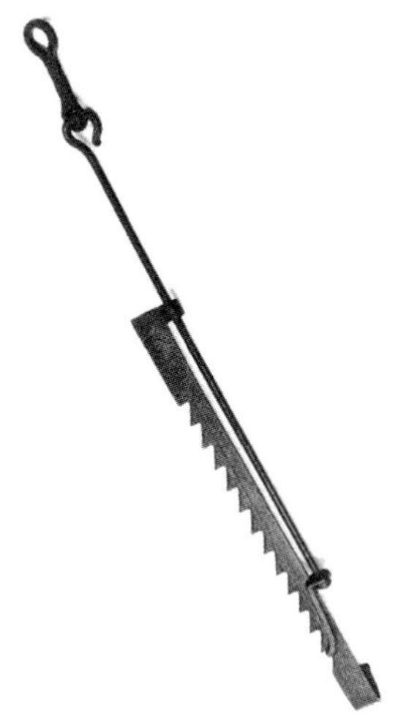

7

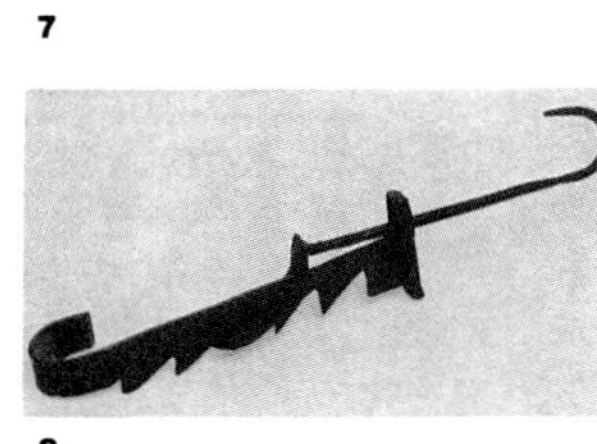

8

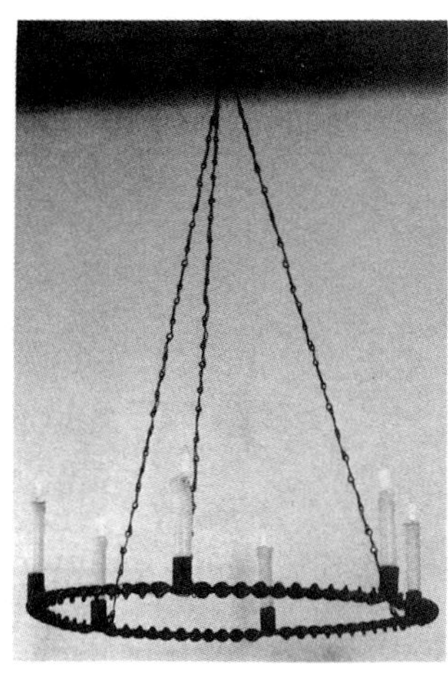

10

9

6 FAT LAMP
1750–1800

Wrought iron. Round oil pan has projecting spout to support burning end of floating wick. Pan suspended from U-shaped frame with handle and round base; pan swings to prevent spillage when carried.

22 x 11.3 cm (8⅝ x 4½")

Gift of Mrs. William D. Frishmuth. 02-112

---

7 TRAMMEL
1750–1800

Wrought iron. Ratchet mechanism adjusts on round rod which has looped end fitted with double-looped hanging piece.

73 x 6 cm (28¾ x 2⅜") (closed)

Gift of J. Stogdell Stokes. 28-10-25

---

8 SAWTOOTH TRAMMEL
1750–1800

Wrought iron. Hook hangs over wood lug pole, goes through collar of ratchet, and is riveted through an iron buckle. Height adjustments made by moving hook piece within restraining collar to release buckle from notches.

34.5 x 12 cm (13⅝ x 4¾")

Gift of J. Stogdell Stokes. 28-10-22

---

9 DOUBLE TRAMMEL
1750–1800

Wrought iron. Double-scroll hanging bars meet at top in a hook that secures in a loop for crane or lug pole. Bars of two ratchets are hooked at top. Adjusting loops have decorative scrolled levers. Zigzag and crossed-line incised decoration. One ratchet finial broken.

105.6 x 40.4 cm (41⅝ x 15⅞")

Purchased: Thomas Skelton Harrison Fund. 37-24-1

---

10 CHANDELIER
1750–1800

Wrought iron. Twisted ring with six candle sockets suspended on three chains made of wires with looped and hooked ends.

Diameter 63 cm (24¾")

Gift of J. Stogdell Stokes. 28-10-3

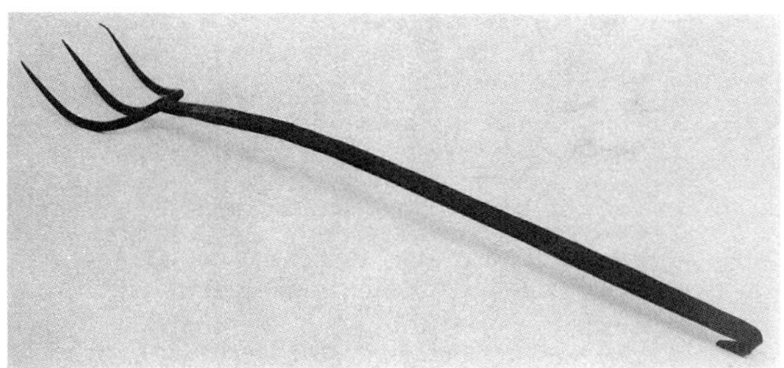

11

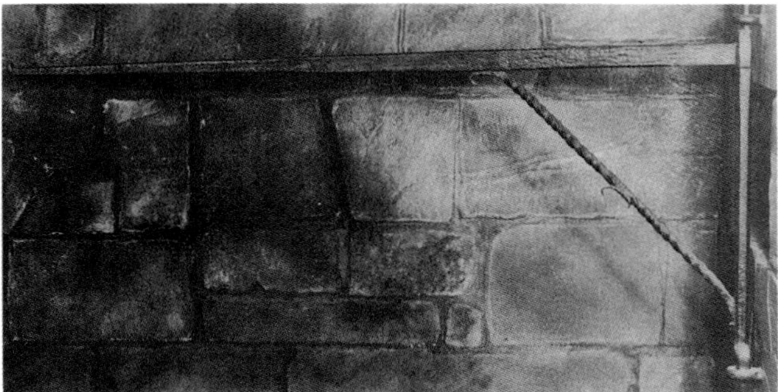

14

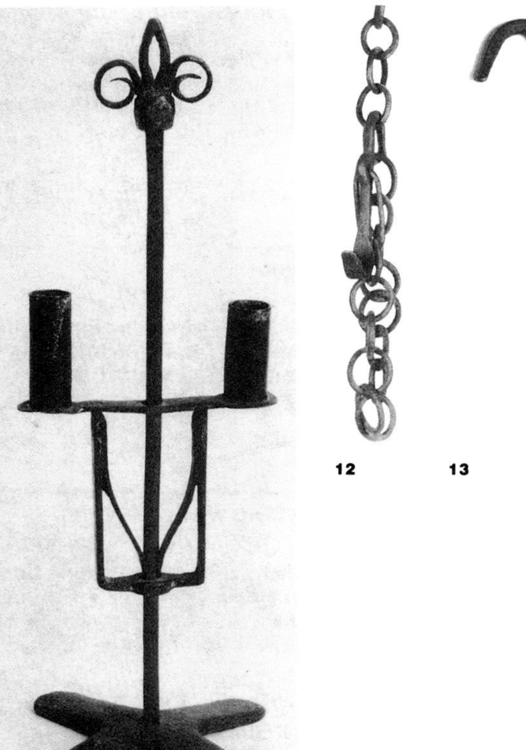

12   **13**

15

11   LOG FORK
1750–1800

Wrought iron. Long handle with hooked end joins arm of three-pronged curved fork in riveted finger joint. For moving wood in fires.

Length 67.9 cm (26¾")

Gift of J. Stogdell Stokes. 28-10-14

12   CHAIN AND POTHOOK
1750–1800

Wrought iron. Chain suspended on turnbuckle on large iron ring designed to fit over lug pole. S-shaped pothook secured to chain with elongated link. Positioning hook on chain allows height adjustments.

Length chain and turnbuckle 131.5 cm (51¾"), pothook 31.1 cm (12¼")

Gift of J. Stogdell Stokes. 28-10-4

13   POTHOOK
1750–1800

Wrought iron. S-shaped with hanging and holding hooks. Rectangular profile with twist mid-shaft.

29.8 x 5.6 cm (11¾ x 2¼")

Gift of J. Stogdell Stokes. 28-10-20

14   CRANE
1750–1800

Wrought iron. Heavy vertical post with chamfered edges has offset extension at bottom and round shaft at top fitting into eye hooks secured into fireplace wall. Crane arm is tenoned through post and tapers to hook. Decorative, twisted diagonal support is welded to crane and fitted with two scrolls serving as hooks. Crane swings out into room for loading.

91.5 x 185.4 cm (36 x 73")

Gift of J. Stogdell Stokes. 28-10-5

15   CANDLEHOLDER
1750–1800

Wrought iron. Round shaft fits into cross-shaped base. Finial fits on block with raised diamond shape on four sides. Two candle sockets on short arms. Height adjustable by spring action.

36.4 x 13.3 cm (14⅜ x 5¼")

Gift of the heirs of J. Stogdell Stokes. 52-7-5

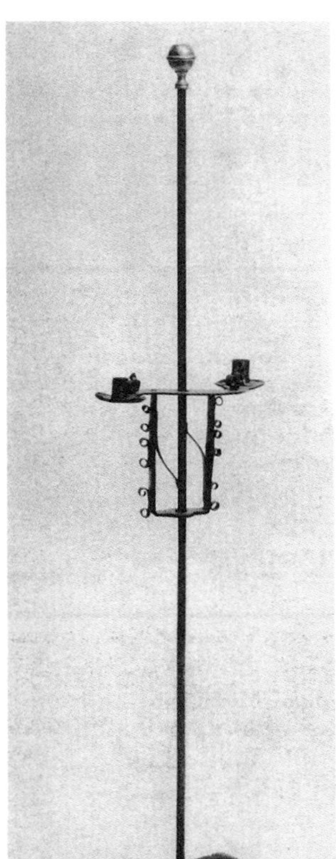

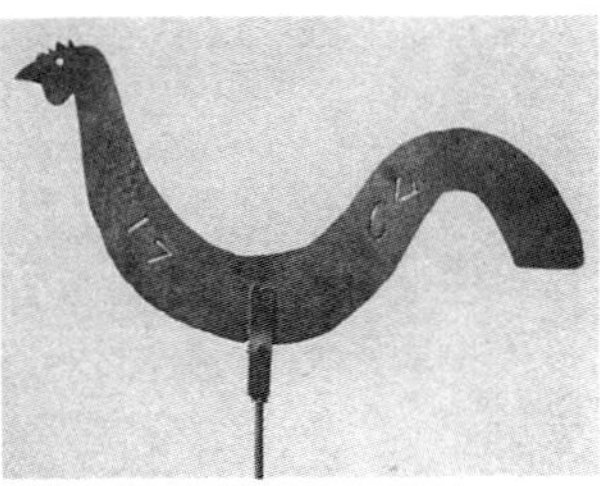

17

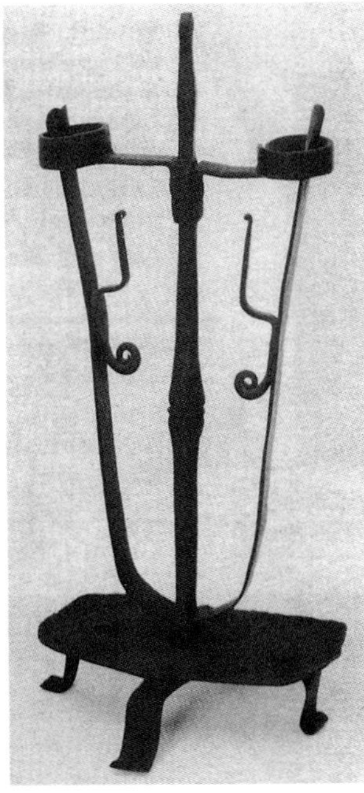

16   **18**

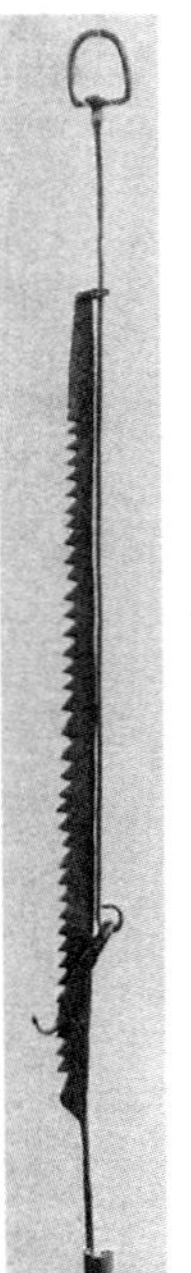

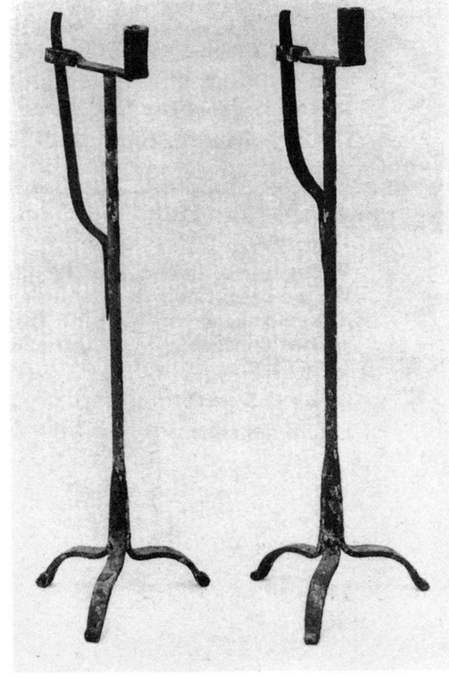

19   **20**

16 CANDLESTAND
Tulpehocken Township, Berks County
c. 1760–1800

Henry Kiplinger

Stamped on each foot of base: *HK*

Wrought iron, brass. Flaring, arched legs with
disk feet hold round rod with brass ball finial.
Candle sockets at ends of S-shaped arms on
spring-adjustable cage decorated with six
wrought loops.

151.2 x 42.6 cm (59½ x 16¾")

Titus C. Geesey Collection. 53-125-14

17 WEATHER VANE
1764

Pierced: *1764*

Wrought iron. Flat shape riveted between two
straps that clamp over squared fitting to rotate
on rod.

24.1 x 39.4 cm (9½ x 15½")

Titus C. Geesey Collection. 58-110-46

18 CANDLEHOLDER
1700–1800

Wrought iron. Central shaft shaped in middle
with swage block. Shaft fitted at top with two
arms with round collars and at bottom with two
spring bars, which are pinched to insert
candles and released to secure them. Bent legs
with rolled feet riveted into flat base.

31.5 x 14.6 cm (12⅜ x 5¾")

Gift of Mrs. Frank Thorne Patterson. 31-87-1

19 CANDLEHOLDER
1770–1800

Wrought iron. Rod with looped end for hanging
from ceiling beam has oblong catch for
adjustable ratchet; candle socket at end.

103 x 10 cm (40⅝ x 3⅞")

Gift of J. Stogdell Stokes. 29-65-1

20 PAIR OF LIGHTING STANDS
1770–1800

Wrought iron. Shafts split at bottom into three
curved legs bent at foot. Shaft riveted through
crosspiece fitted with candle socket at one end,
rush light-holder with spring action at other
end.

60.4 x 13.9 cm (23¾ x 5½")

Gift of J. Stogdell Stokes. 28-79-3a,b

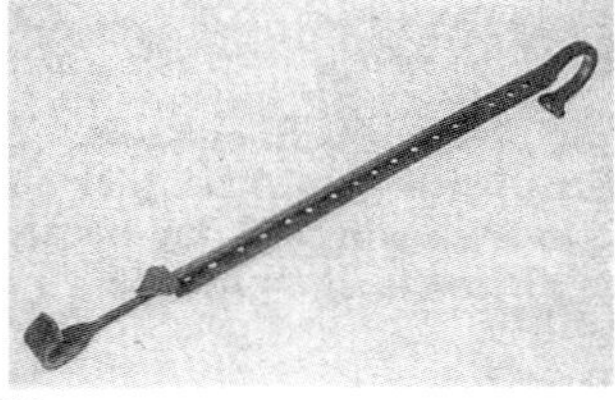

21

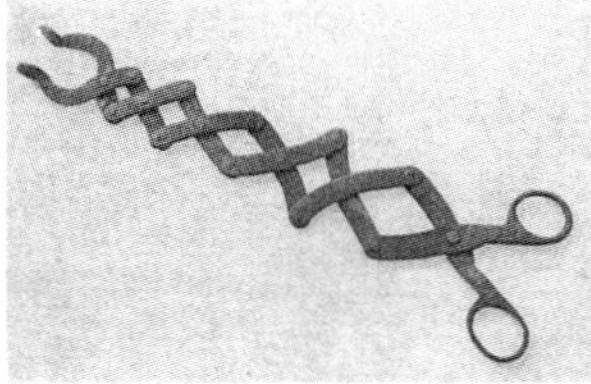

22

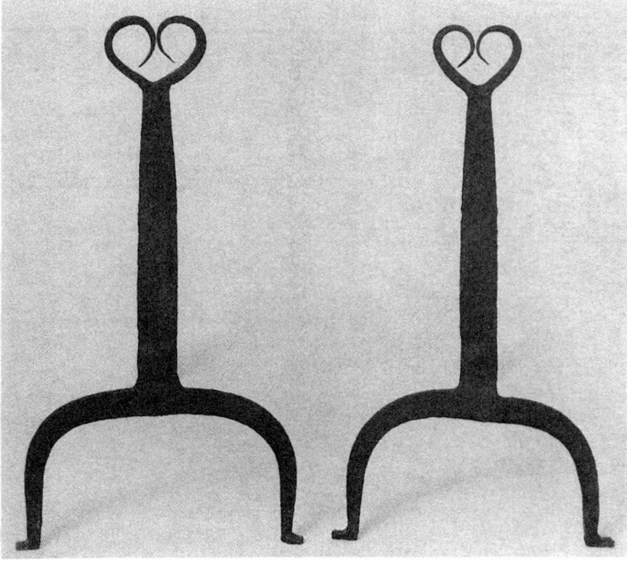

23

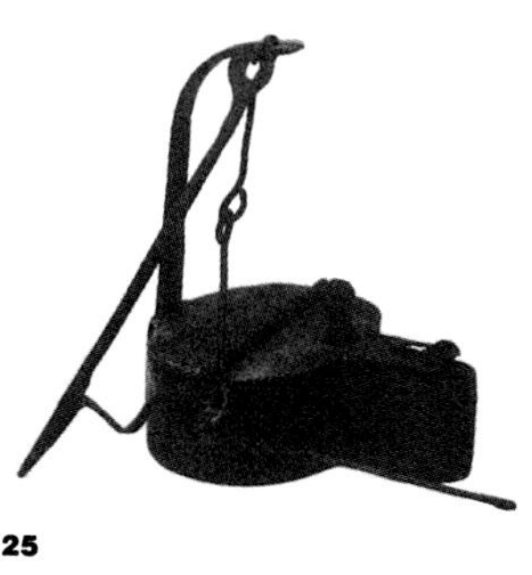

25

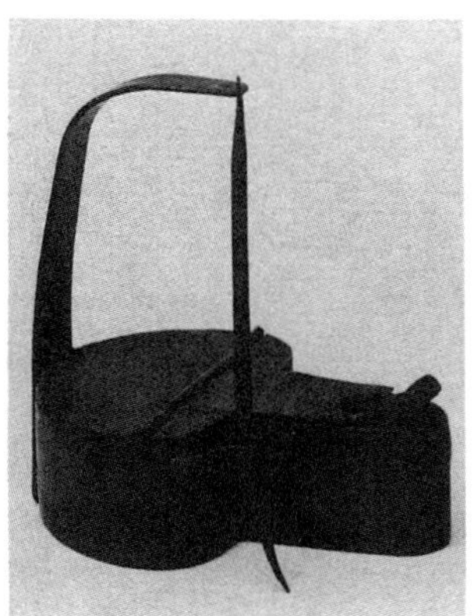

24

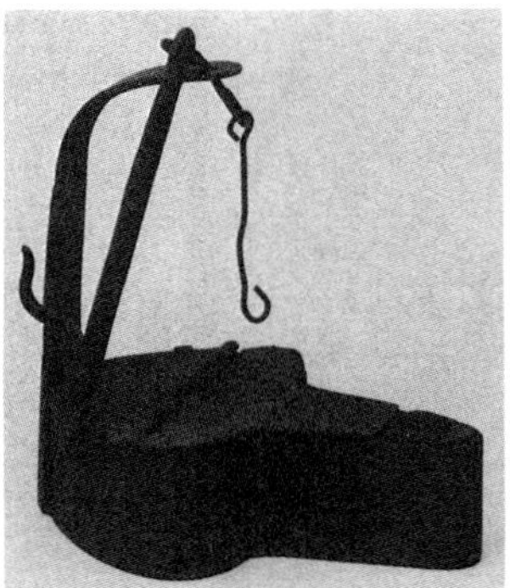

26

21 TRAMMEL
1770–1800

Wrought iron. Flat trammel bar with hooked end is pierced with holes for adjustment of rod. Flange decorated with chased flowers and scalloped border.

96.5 x 5.4 cm (38 x 2⅛")

Titus C. Geesey Collection. 58-110-11

22 COAL TONGS
1770–1800

Wrought iron. Shaped bars pivot on rivets in scissor-accordion action. For taking coals from fire.

Length 20.3 cm (8")

Gift of Mrs. William D. Frishmuth. 08-658

23 ANDIRONS
1770–1800

Wrought iron. Flat shafts split at top into facing scrolls forming heart design. Arched, flat legs with crooked feet.

40 x 21.6 x 8.9 cm (15¾ x 8½ x 3½")

Titus C. Geesey Collection. 58-110-6a,b

24 HANGING OIL LAMP
1770–1800

Wrought iron. Top is hinged to lift at front and riveted to the well at the back. Handle fitted with hanging and jamb hooks. "Betty" lamp.

8.5 x 8.9 cm (3⅜ x 3½")

Gift of Mrs. William D. Frishmuth. 02-105

25 HANGING OIL LAMP
1770–1800

Wrought iron. Hinged lid, wick spout, linked wick pick, hanging spike. "Betty" lamp.

11.2 x 8.7 cm (4⅜ x 3⅜")

Gift of Mrs. William D. Frishmuth. 02-82

26 HANGING OIL LAMP
1770–1800

Wrought iron. Hanging arm and top riveted to sides. Hinged lid, wick channel, and spike hook. Wick pick missing. "Betty" lamp.

11.3 x 6.3 cm (4½ x 2½")

Gift of Mrs. William D. Frishmuth. 02-107

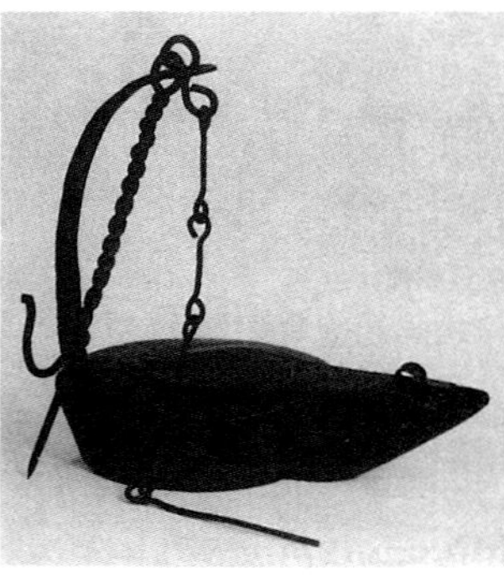

27

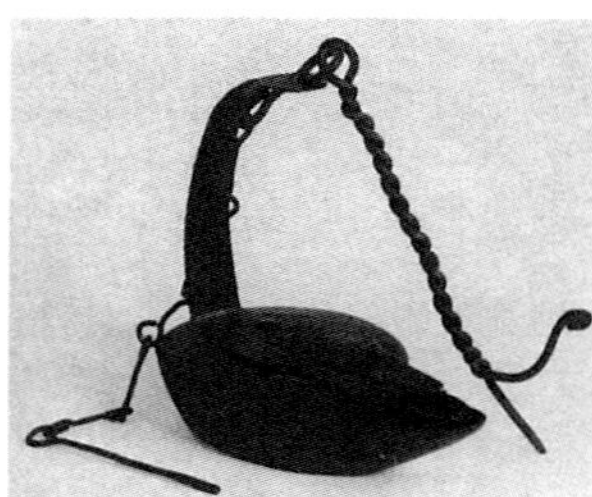
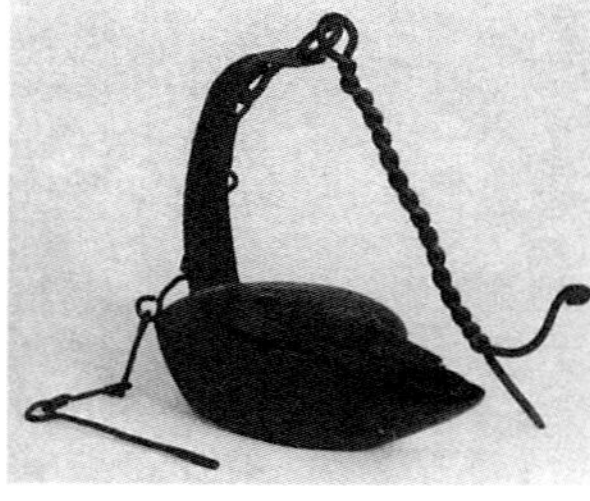

28

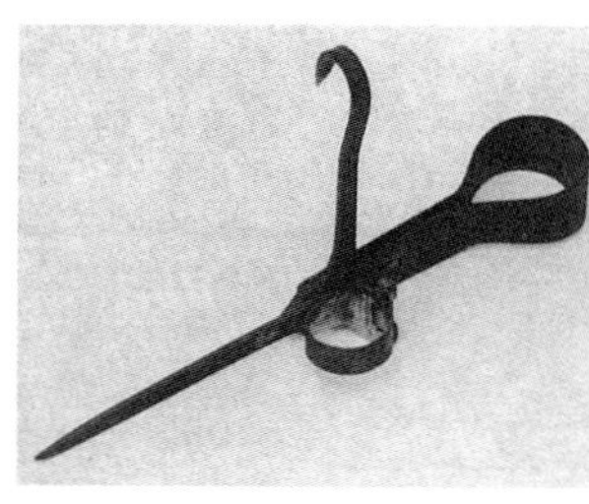

31 open

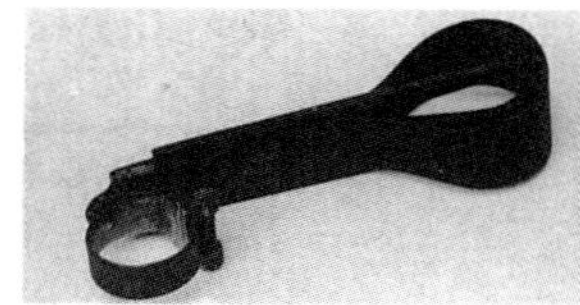

31 closed

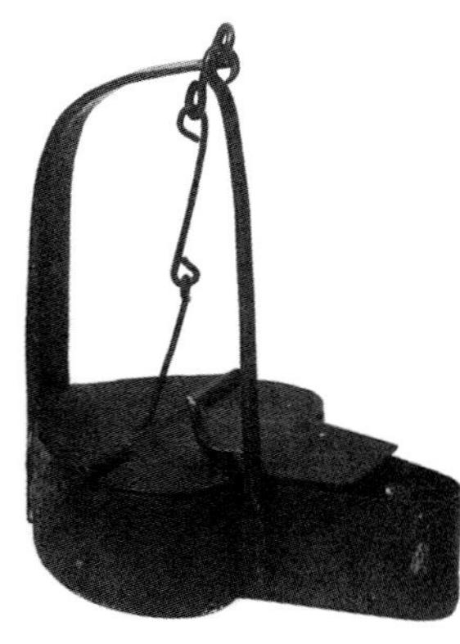

29

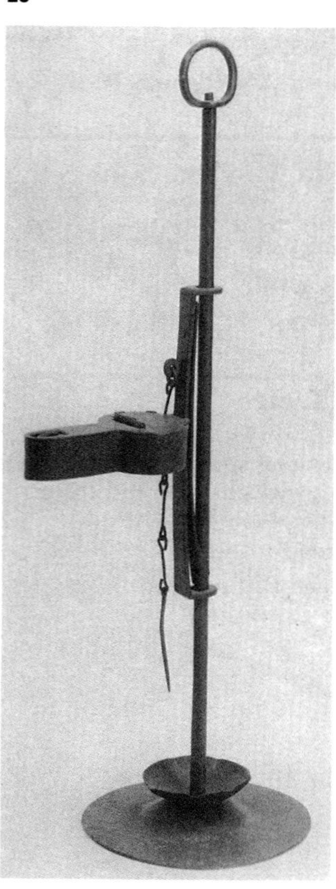

30

27 HANGING OIL LAMP
1770–1800

Wrought iron. Well is wrought in one unit. Shaped cover swivels sideways. Wick pick on hooked wire and twisted-wire hanging hook are attached through grommet on handle. "Betty" lamp.

24.1 x 6.4 cm (9½ x 2½")

Gift of J. Stogdell Stokes. 28-10-80

28 HANGING OIL LAMP
1770–1800

Wrought iron. Well is wrought in one unit. Shaped cover swivels sideways. Wick pick on hooked wire and twisted-wire hanging hook are attached through grommet on handle. "Betty" lamp.

25.4 x 7.6 cm (10 x 3")

Gift of J. Stogdell Stokes. 28-10-81

29 HANGING OIL LAMP
1770–1810

Wrought iron. Hanging arm and lid riveted to sides. Hinged lid, hanging spike, and chained wick pick. "Betty" lamp.

11.7 x 10.5 cm (4⅝ x 4⅛")

Gift of Mrs. William D. Frishmuth. 02-108

30 OIL LAMP AND STAND
1770–1820

Wrought iron. Shaft is threaded at top for ring handle and is bolted under flaring base. Iron bracket on shaft has spring device for height adjustment. Lamp has hinged lid, wick spout, and linked wick pick.

Height overall 50.2 cm (19¾"), diameter base 15.2 cm (6")

Titus C. Geesey Collection. 58-110-50

31 CANDLEHOLDER
1770–1870

Wrought iron. Handle formed from looped strip of iron. Finger joint of handle holds hanging hook and jamb spike. Hook and spike can be folded inside handle. Adjustable loop of candle socket riveted.

16.3 x 7.8 cm (6⅜ x 3")

Gift of Mrs. William D. Frishmuth. 10-372

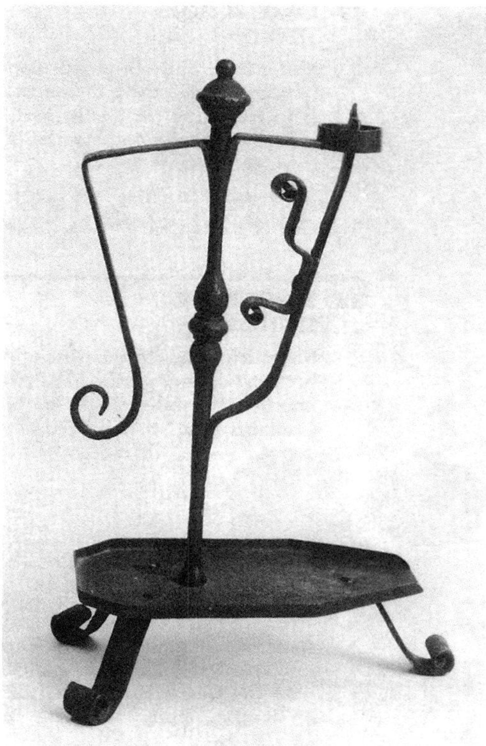

32

32 CANDLEHOLDER
1780–1800

Wrought iron. Three splayed legs with rolled feet riveted through flat pan with raised edge to catch wax or fat drippings. Shaft with swage-block decoration topped with finial and fitted with handle and candleholder with spring-action bar to secure tapering candle. Similar to European and English types.

23.8 x 18.8 cm (9⅜ x 7⅜″)

Purchased: Subscription Fund and Museum Fund. 23-23-212

33 COAL TONGS
1780–1800

Wrought iron. Three pieces of iron on each side riveted together to pivot in scissor-accordion action. Used to pluck coals from open fire.

Length 33 cm (13″) (extended)

Purchased: Subscription Fund and Museum Fund. 23-23-213

34 POTHOOK
1780–1800

Wrought iron. Flat bar divided into three graduated hooks for pots at one end. Hanging hook for use on lug pole on the other end.

49.5 x 3.2 cm (19½ x 1¼″)

Titus C. Geesey Collection. 58-110-12

35 SAWTOOTH TRAMMEL
1780–1800

Wrought iron. Hanging rod goes through collar of ratchet and is fitted with S-looped hook at top and curved ratchet lock with hook at bottom. Long sawtooth ratchet has wide hook at bottom. Lightweight construction; probably intended for chandeliers or lights suspended from ceiling beams. Shown with a chandelier.

Length 99 cm (39″)

Titus C. Geesey Collection. 58-110-13

36 CHARCOAL BASKET
1780–1810

Wrought iron. Long handles pivot in scissor action on rivet lifting lid of box. Extended flanges of handles are riveted to lid and to perforated bottom of box.

76.1 x 21 cm (30 x 8¼″)

Gift of J. Stogdell Stokes. 39-2-1

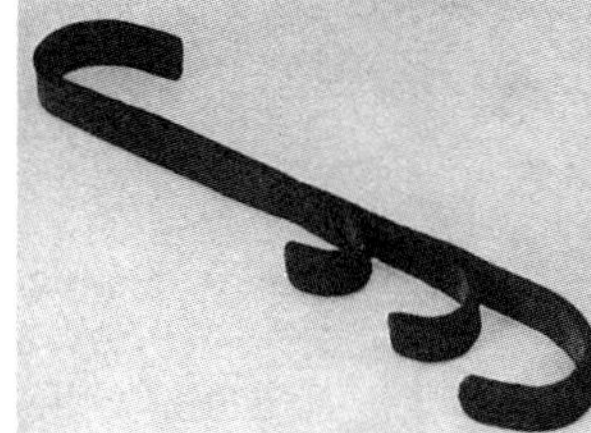

33

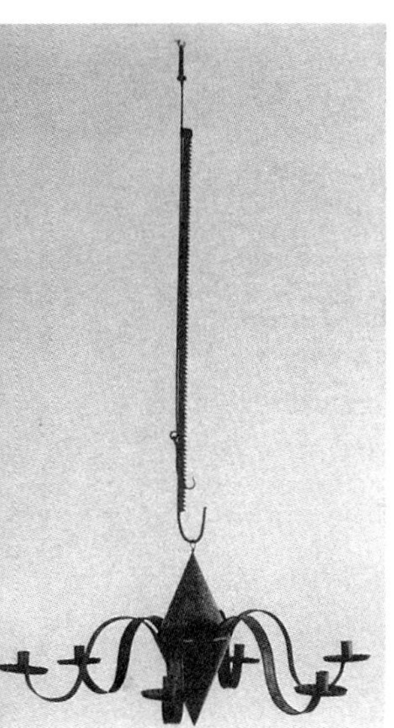

35

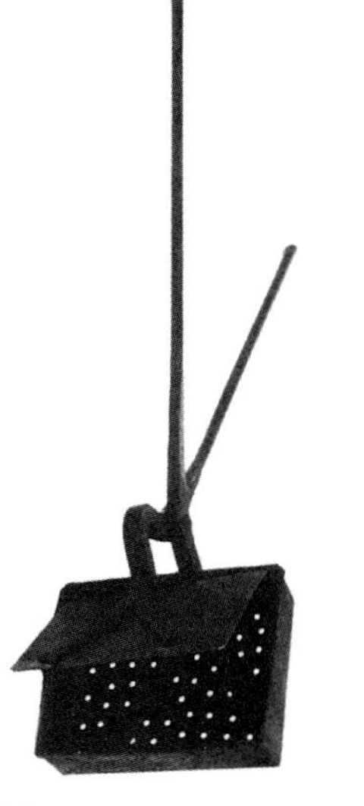

36

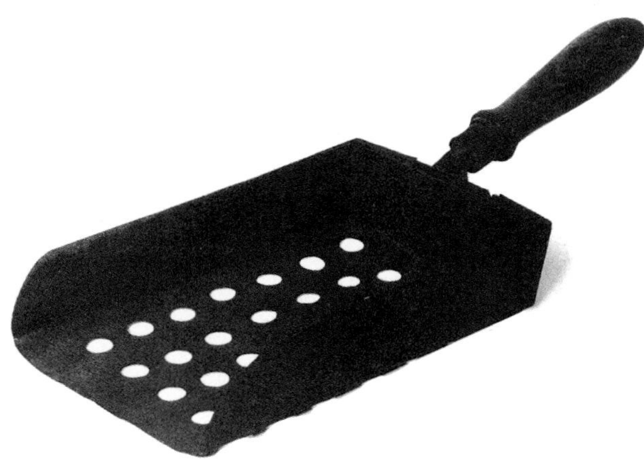

37

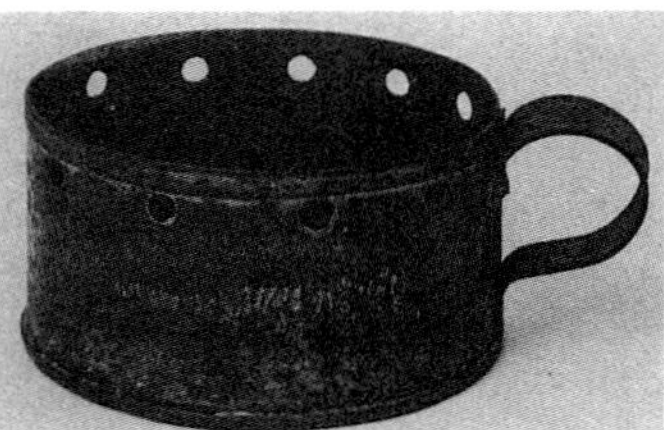

38

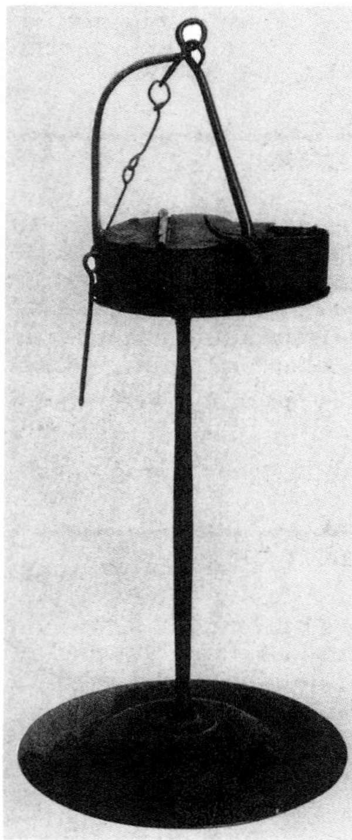

39

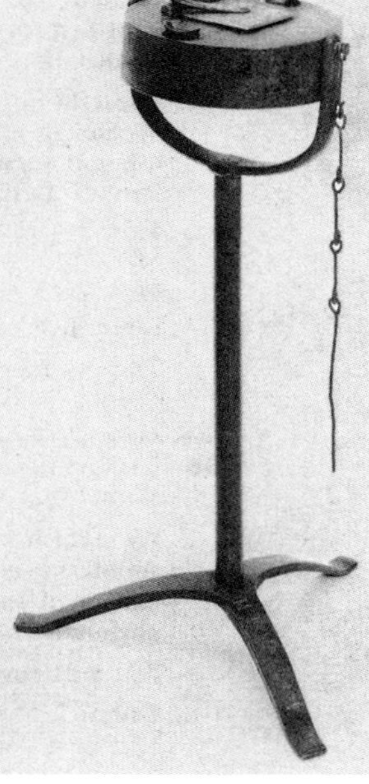

41

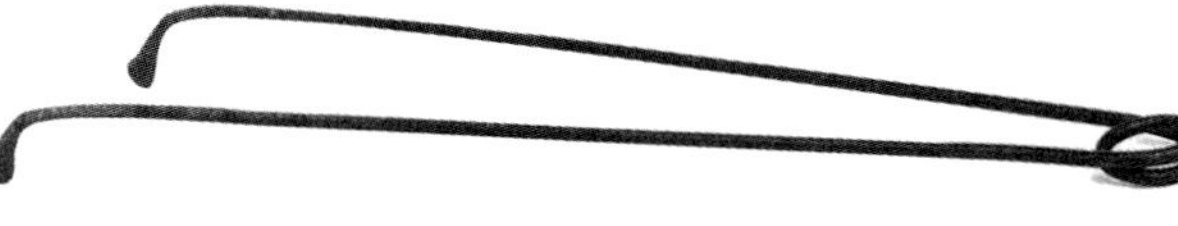

40

37 COAL SCOOP
1780–1810

Sheet iron, pine. Bent sides and perforated bottom in one piece. One end reinforced with strip riveted to inside. Turned handle fitted with iron flange (collar missing) and riveted through reinforced end.

9.5 x 36.3 x 14 cm (3¾ x 14¼ x 5½″)

Gift of J. Stogdell Stokes. 39-2-2

38 TINDERBOX
1780–1820

Sheet iron. Raised banding applied to top and bottom edges of perforated strip for sides. Bent handle with rolled edges soldered to side. Contains flint, steel, and tinder.

Height 6.7 cm (2⅝″), diameter 12.4 cm (4⅞″)

Gift of Mrs. William D. Frishmuth. 02-113

39 OIL LAMP AND STAND
1780–1820

Wrought iron. Two units. Stand has shaped shaft and flat lamp platform. Top of well riveted to sides. Hinged lid; wick pick on wire chain with hanging hook attached through grommet on handle. "Betty" lamp.

36.4 x 11.8 cm (14⅜ x 4⅝″)

Gift of J. Stogdell Stokes. 28-10-114

40 TONGS
1780–1840

Wrought iron. Round bars with flattened ends twisted at center for spring action. For lifting embers from open fires.

Length 55 cm (21⅝″)

Gift of J. Stogdell Stokes. 28-10-26

41 OIL LAMP AND STAND
Lancaster County
1790–1820

Possibly by **Michael Kline**

Marked on top of leg: *MK*

Wrought iron. Tripod stand with lamp suspended between arms on wrought pins. Two wick spouts, hinged well opening, and wick pick on hooked chain.

25.2 x 14.7 cm (9⅞ x 5¾″)

Gift of J. Stogdell Stokes. 28-10-82

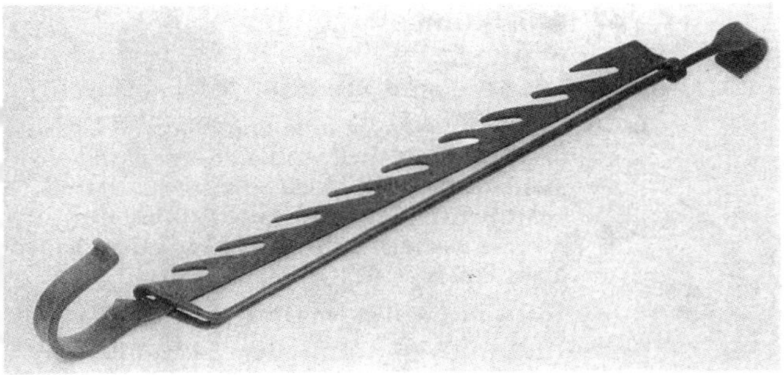

42

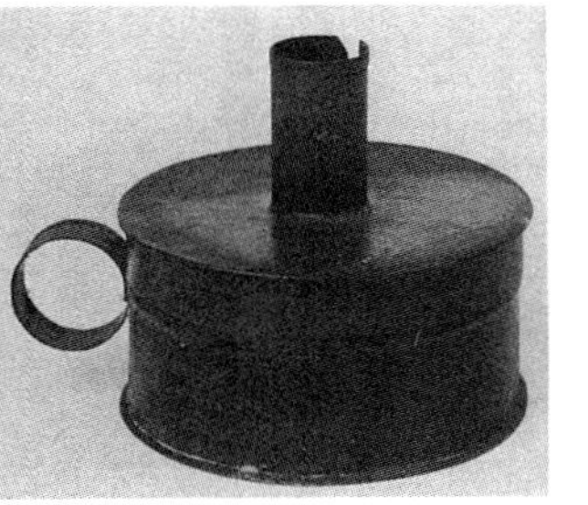

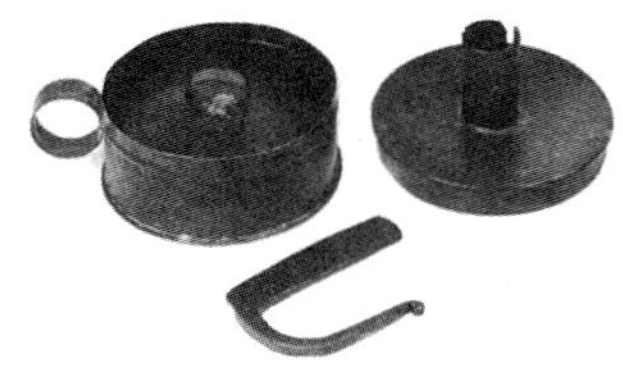

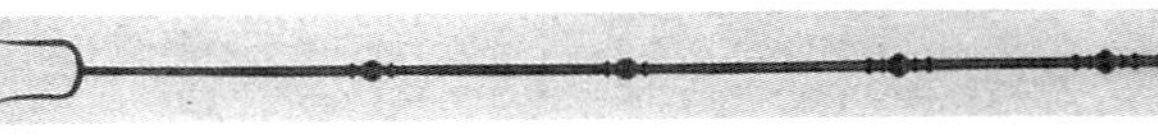

44

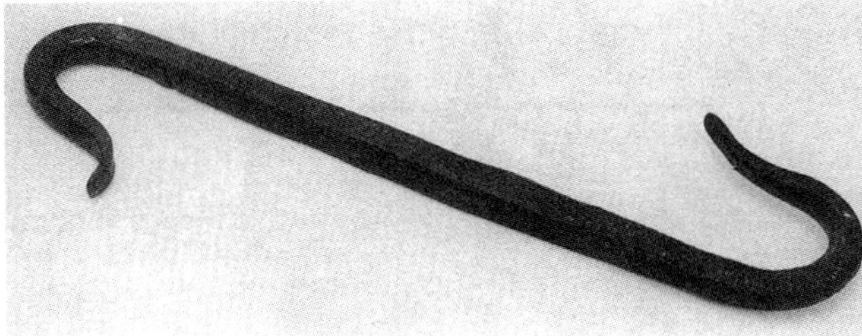

45

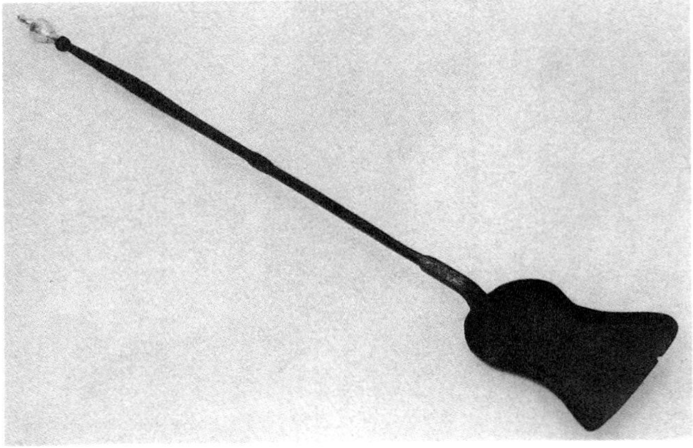

46

42 TRAMMEL
1800–1840

Wrought iron. Small hooked end fits over crane, larger open hook holds iron pots. Swinging the ratchet releases the hanging rod for height adjustments.

Length 91 cm (35⅞") (closed)

Gift of Mrs. William D. Frishmuth. 02-563

43 TINDERBOX
1800–1850

Sheet iron. Circular box with loop handle. Fitted lid with candleholder has inner flat cover and holds flint and horseshoe-shaped steel.

Height 9 cm (3½"), diameter 10.2 cm (4")

Gift of Mrs. William D. Frishmuth. 02-611

44 LOG FORK
1800–1850

Wrought iron. Long, round shaft with ball and disk swage-block decoration at intervals. Knobbed handle at one end, two-tined fork at other. For roasting meat or poking logs.

Length 105.5 cm (41½")

Gift of J. Stogdell Stokes. 33-70-4

45 POTHOOK
1800–1900

Wrought iron. Double hook for use on crane or chain.

19.5 x 8.9 cm (7⅝ x 3½")

Gift of Mrs. William D. Frishmuth. 02-570

46 SHOVEL
1805

Inscribed on handle: *R · S   1805*

Wrought iron, brass. Flat, tassel-shaped shovel with raised edges is in one piece with shaped, round shaft and fitted with urn-shaped brass finial.

Length 89 cm (35")

Titus C. Geesey Collection. 54-85-74c

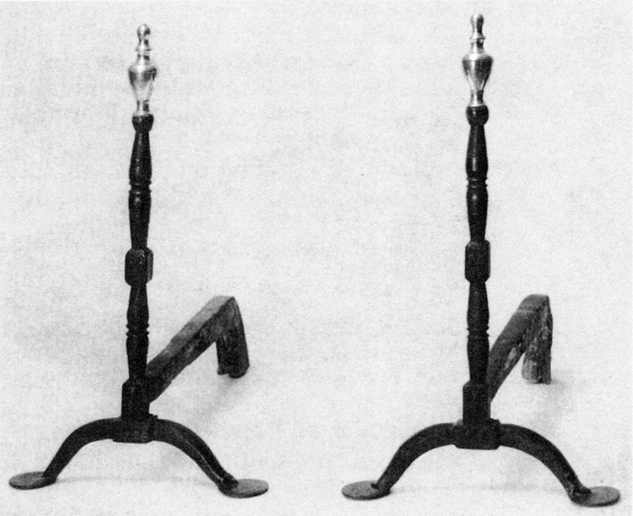

47

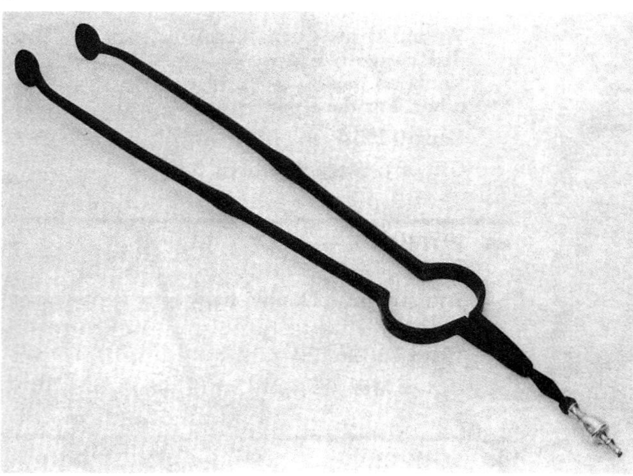

48

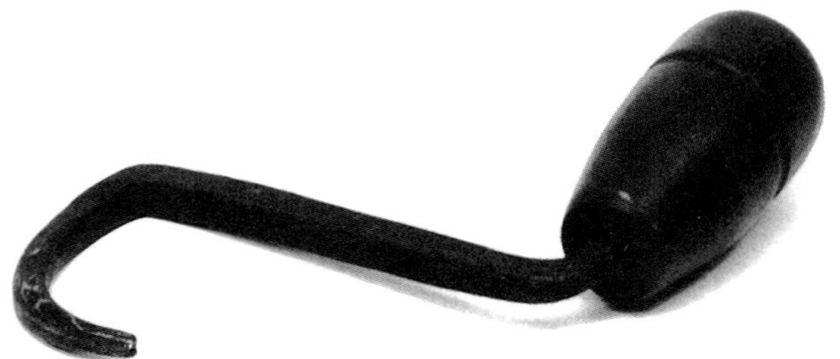

49

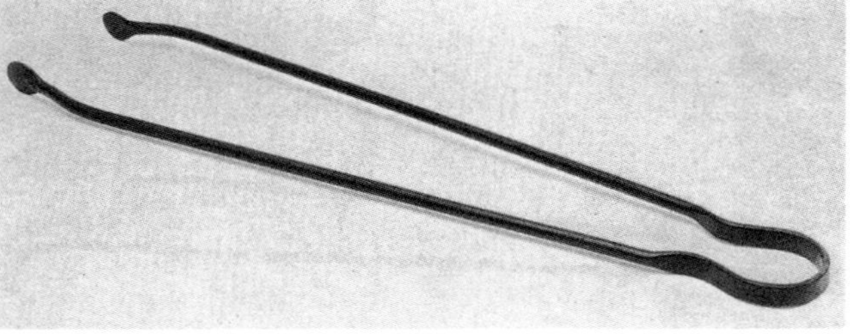

50

47 ANDIRONS
1805

Inscribed on shafts: *1805　R S*

Cast iron, wrought iron, brass. Arched legs and disk feet. Cast shaft molded from turned-wood mold. Obverse of block on shaft has raised heart between incised date and initials; reverse has raised inverted heart. Urn-shaped brass finials.

46.9 x 27.4 x 40.6 cm (18½ x 10¾ x 16″)

Titus C. Geesey Collection. 54-85-74a,b

48 TONGS
1805–20

Wrought iron, brass. Round, shaped shafts with circular pincers. Top is hinged and has urn-shaped brass finial. Probably made to match no. 47.

Length 91.3 cm (36″)

Titus C. Geesey Collection. 54-85-74d

49 POTHOOK
1820–50

Wrought iron, walnut. Turned handle fitted with wrought iron hook. Used to lift iron-handled pots from trivet or trammel.

14 x 15 cm (5½ x 5⅞″)

Gift of Mrs. William D. Frishmuth. 02-142

50 TONGS
1820–70

Wrought iron. Round shafts, flattened spring loop. Pinching ends are flattened disks. For lifting coals and embers.

Length 59.7 cm (23½″)

Gift of Mrs. William D. Frishmuth. 02-581

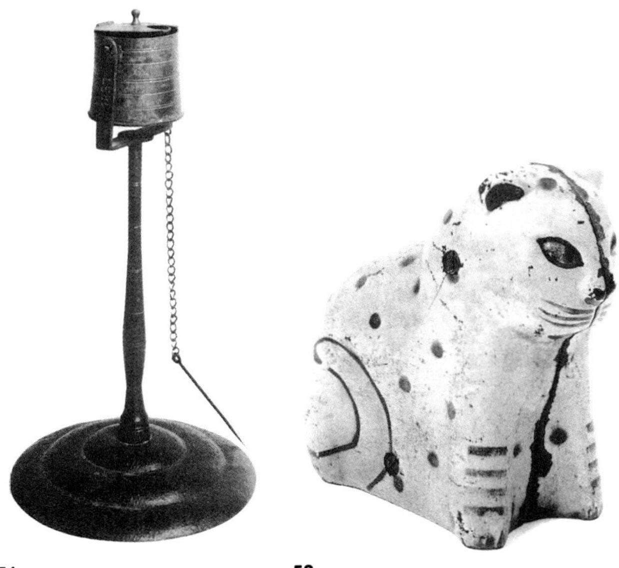

51 FAT LAMP AND STAND
Tulpehocken Township, Berks County
1837

Peter Derr

Stamped on brackets: *P. Derr   1837*

Wrought iron, brass. Swinging, lidded brass bowl with spout for wick. Wick pick on chain. Decorated with incised rings on shaft, bowl, and lid.

26.7 x 14 cm (10½ x 5½")

Titus C. Geesey Collection. 54-85-122

52 DOORSTOP
1840–60

Painted cast iron. Two pieces screwed together. Painted cream color with brown spots, whiskers, paws, and tail detail. Eyes and bow on tail painted green.

21.1 x 23.7 cm (8¼ x 9⅜")

Titus C. Geesey Collection. 58-110-49

53 OIL LAMP AND CANDLESTICK
Rapho Township, Lancaster County
1846

Jacob Long

Inscribed on well lid: *Nancy Musser   made by me J. Long   1846*

Wrought iron, brass, tin over sheet iron. Lamp top riveted to sides. Handle with linked wick pick and hanging spike is fastened with screw through flange of brass collar. Brass swivel plate with cock finial pivots sideways to open well. Tin stand is in two units that separate below lamp tray leaving candle socket in crimped bobeche. Conical base is weighted with sand.

Height overall 24 cm (9½"), diameter base 19.6 cm (7¾")

Titus C. Geesey Collection. 58-110-52a,b

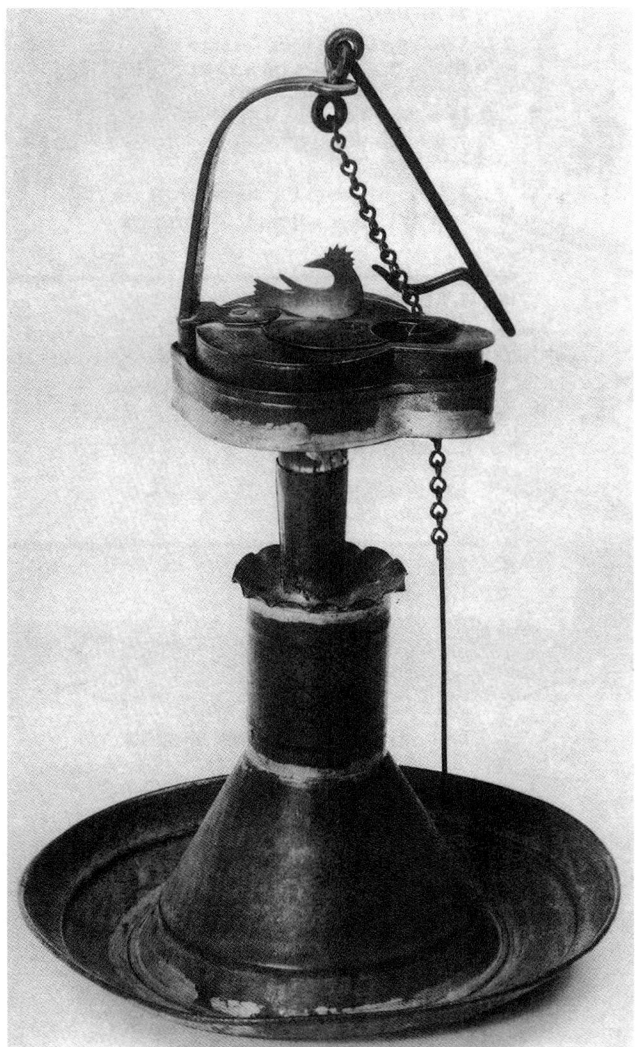

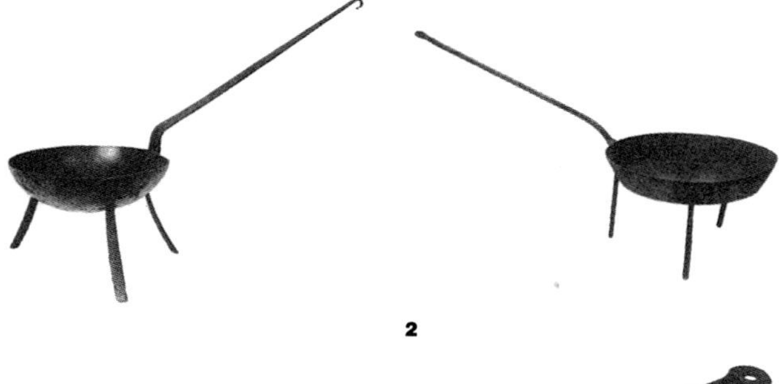

1

1   SKILLET
1750–1800

Wrought iron. Round pan with dished bottom on three splayed legs, each fastened with two rivets through flanges. Handle is attached in finger joint and tapers to hooked end.

92 x 43.2 cm (36¼ x 17")

Gift of J. Stogdell Stokes. 28-10-31

2   SKILLET
1750–1800

Wrought iron. Flat pan with flared sides riveted through heart-shaped flanges at tops of straight legs. Long handle with looped end for hanging riveted into pan through top of back leg.

79.4 x 32.6 cm (31¼ x 12⅞")

Gift of J. Stogdell Stokes. 28-10-8

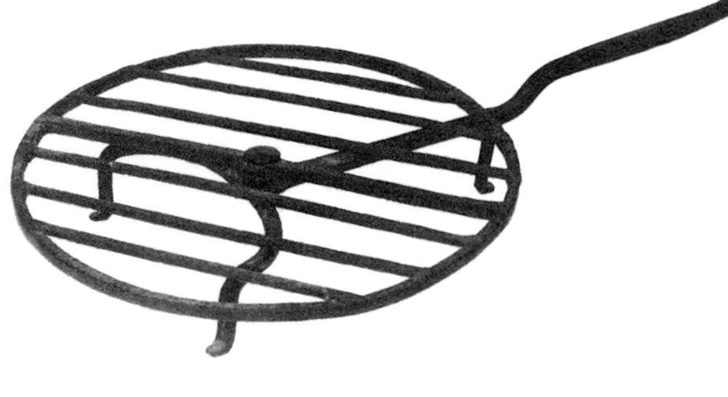

3

3   GRIDIRON
1750–1800

Wrought iron. Grids set into top edge of round frame that rotates on a rivet fitted through center grid, washer, and shaft. Shaft extends into raised handle with hanging hole. Two front legs are curved; back leg straight, with bent feet.

Length 61 cm (24"), diameter 34 cm (13⅜")

Gift of J. Stogdell Stokes. 28-10-29

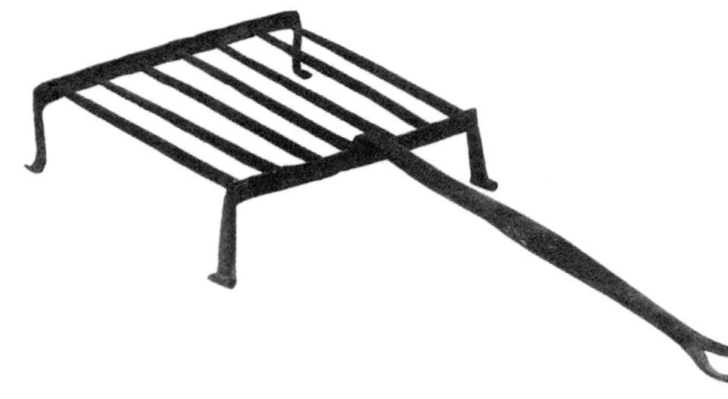

4

4   GRIDIRON
1750–1800

Wrought iron. Flat grids riveted to framing bars that extend into legs with rolled feet. Handle with heart-shaped hanging loop is riveted to frame.

65.8 x 29.8 cm (25⅞ x 11¾")

Gift of J. Stogdell Stokes. 28-10-10

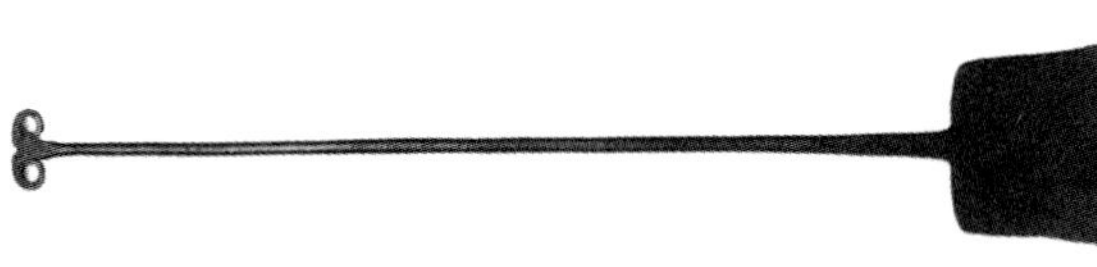

5

5   PEEL
1750–1800

Wrought iron. Flaring paddle in one piece with round shaft that divides into double-looped decorative terminal.

103.2 x 16.5 cm (40⅝ x 6½")

Gift of J. Stogdell Stokes. 28-10-13

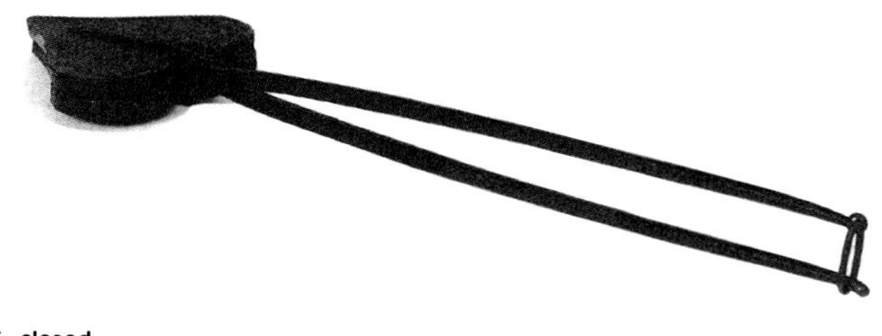

6 closed

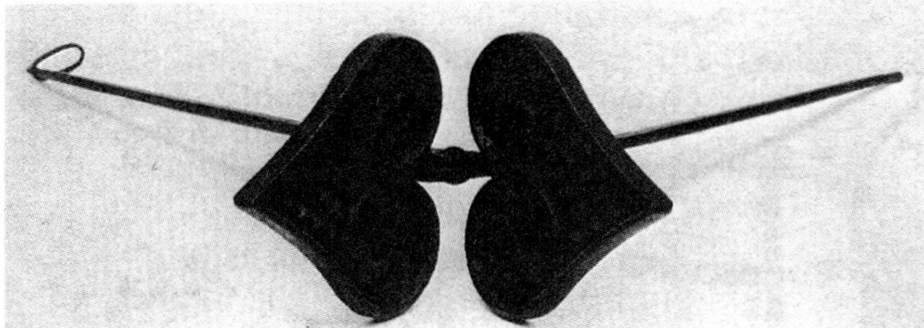

6 open

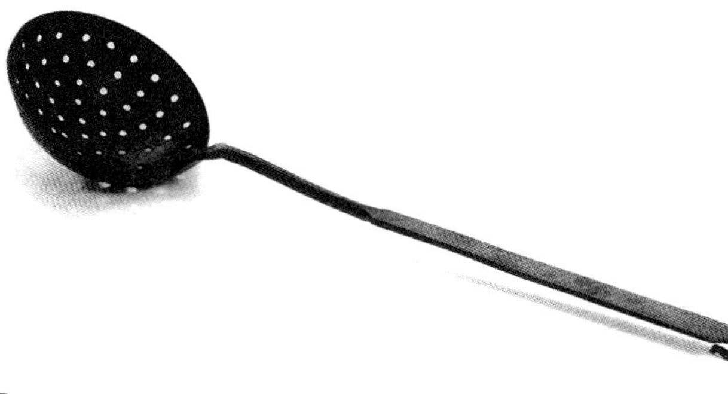

7

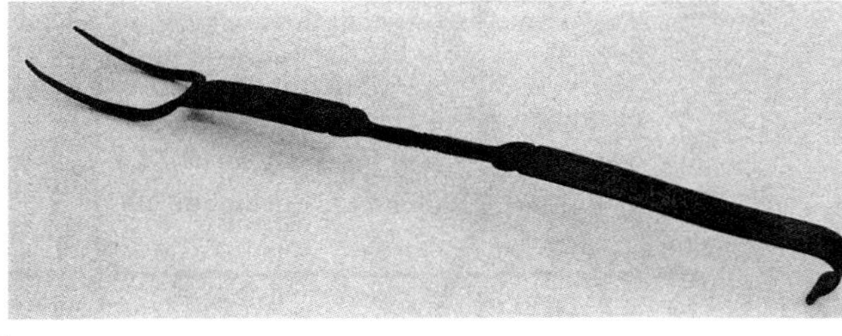

8

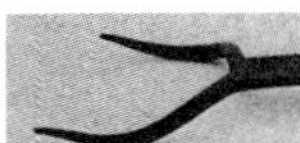

9

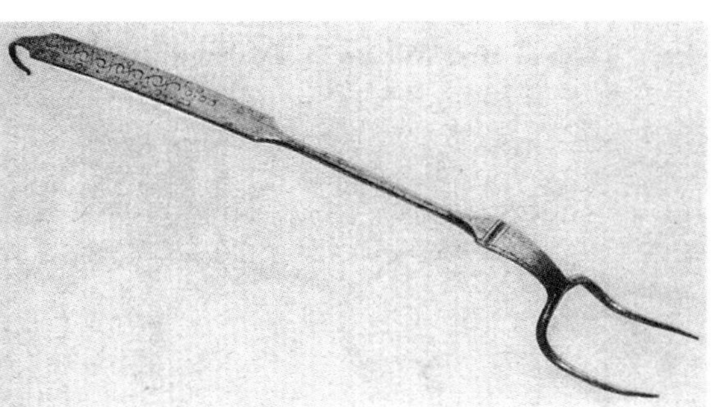

10

6 **WAFFLE IRON**
1750–1800

Cast and wrought iron. Handles close with loop at end. Handles cross to pivot on rivet and hold heart-shaped iron. Inside each iron is a pattern of two circles with swirling swastikas over diamond design.

77.4 x 20.4 cm (30½ x 8″)

Gift of J. Stogdell Stokes. 28-10-35

7 **SIEVE**
1750–1800

Wrought iron. Deep perforated bowl in one piece with shaped handle ending in hanging hook.

47.5 x 13.5 cm (18¾ x 5¼″)

Gift of J. Stogdell Stokes. 28-10-32

8 **ROASTING FORK**
1750–1800

Wrought iron. Two-tined fork with long decorative handle and hooked end for hanging. Flat section has incised border of double semicircles and dots. Handgrip in middle with swage-block decoration and flat heart at each end. Flat shaft near tines has border pattern with centered vine.

Length 46 cm (18⅛″)

Gift of J. Stogdell Stokes. 28-10-23

9 **ROASTING FORK**
1750–1800

Wrought iron. Flat handle is forged in two layers and terminates in scrolled heart. Middle of shaft is shaped for handgrip. Lower shaft flattens and splits into two round tines.

Length 50 cm (19⅝″)

Gift of J. Stogdell Stokes. 28-10-43

10 **ROASTING FORK**
Rockland Township, Berks County
1750–1800

Attributed to **John Ketterer**

Stamped on handle: *IK*

Wrought iron. Handle decorated with tangential C shapes forming running design, edged with alternating circles and dots. Handle tapers into hanging hook at top. Two-tined fork reinforced at joint with shaft.

Length 42 cm (16½″)

Gift of the Haas Foundation. 68-118-33f

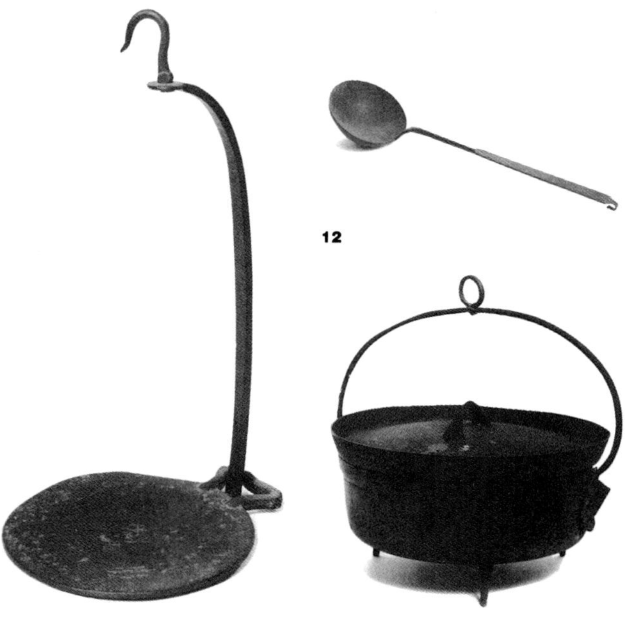

11

12

14

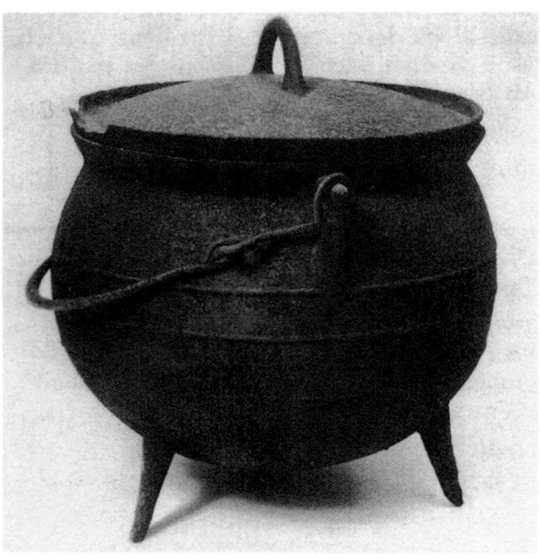

13

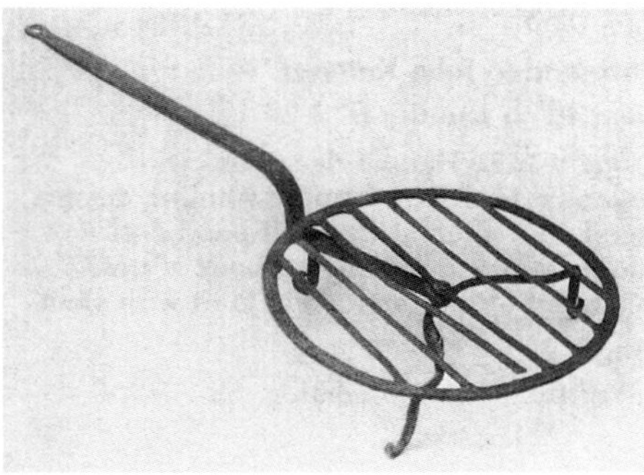

15

11 HANGING GRIDDLE
1750–1800

Wrought iron. Circular grid frame suspended from hook that is riveted through loop in top of curved shaft. Removable flat griddle plate has handle for hanging and securing over shaft for use.

Height 65.4 cm (25¾″), diameter 30.5 cm (12″)

Gift of J. Stogdell Stokes. 28-48-5a,b

12 LADLE
1750–1850

Wrought iron. Large bowl with tooling marks on reverse is in one piece with shaft that has rounded handgrip and hook at end.

49.2 x 13.3 cm (19⅜ x 5¼″)

Gift of J. Stogdell Stokes. 28-10-33

13 COVERED KETTLE
1770–1800

Cast iron. Round cast body with three raised molded rings sits on three attached tapering legs. Triangular handle-holds attached to wrought linked handle. Lid with looped handle fits inside flaring rim of pot and has raised edge to hold coals. Edge of lid is damaged.

Height 39.4 cm (15½″), diameter 39.4 cm (15½″)

Titus C. Geesey Collection. 58-110-7a,b

14 COVERED KETTLE
1770–1800

Cast iron. Deep pot on three attached splayed legs. Removable handle and hanging loop. High raised rim on fitted lid to hold coals for baking.

Height 34.7 cm (13⅝″), diameter 37.7 cm (14⅞″)

Gift of Mrs. William D. Frishmuth. 10-142

15 GRIDIRON
1770–1800

Wrought iron. Circular frame with seven grids pivots on rivet through center grid and frame. Two curved front legs and one straight back leg welded to shaft. Raised handle with hanging hole.

Length 68.7 cm (27″), diameter 31.7 cm (12½″)

Gift of Mrs. William D. Frishmuth. 02-486

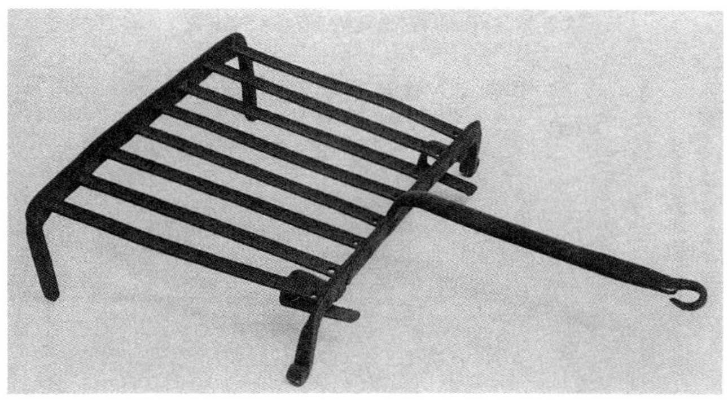

16

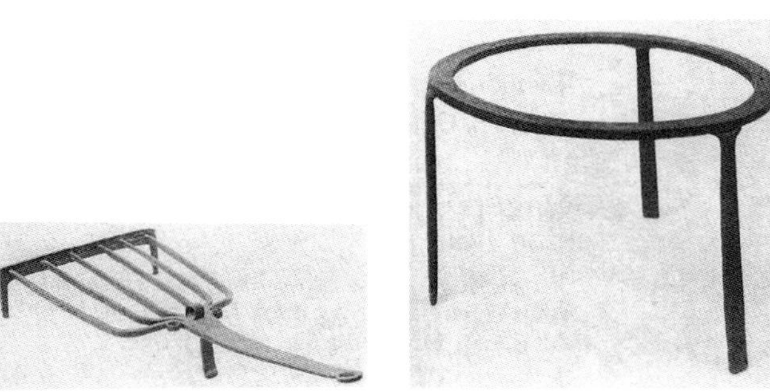

17

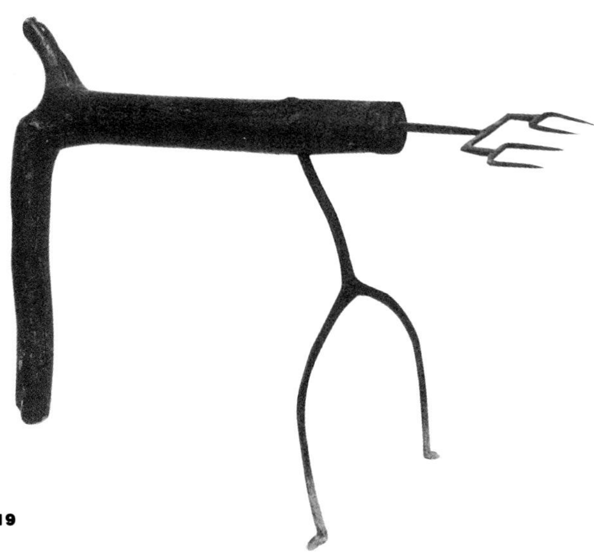

18

19

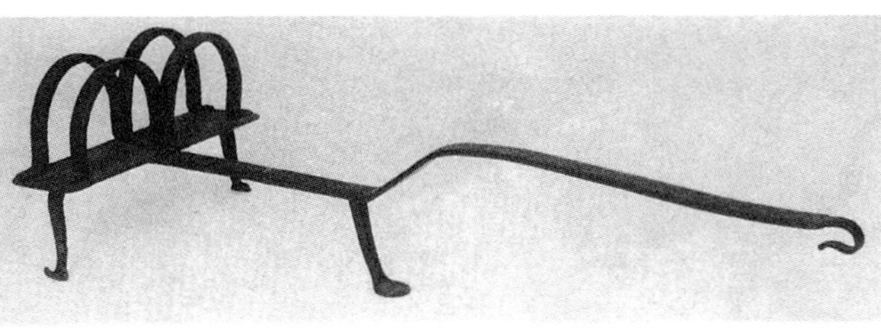

20

16 GRIDIRON
1770–1800

Wrought iron. Eight slightly channeled grids have holes at handle end for fat to run off into drip pan held on hooks riveted to back legs. Back feet are rolled. Handle has hanging hook.

38.2 x 24.3 cm (15 x 9⅝")

Gift of Mrs. William D. Frishmuth. 02-476

17 GRIDIRON
1770–1800

Wrought iron. Flat handle with hanging loop splits into six grids and three decorative scrolls. Straight leg riveted into handle at juncture. Grids supported at ends by horizontal frame on legs.

58.4 x 26.7 cm (23 x 10½")

Titus C. Geesey Collection. 58-110-10

18 TRIVET
1770–1800

Wrought iron. Flat ring welded to bent tops of three flat legs.

Height 18.3 cm (7¼"), diameter 28.4 cm (11⅛")

Gift of Mrs. William D. Frishmuth. 02-551

19 ROASTING FORK
1770–1800

Wrought iron, painted hardwood. Freestanding form made of found branch. Wrought iron front legs with disk feet on iron shaft that pierces the branch and is clenched. Four-pronged wrought iron fork has square shaft fitted into branch and is secured with iron collar.

36.2 x 55.9 x 21.3 cm (14¼ x 22 x 8⅜")

Purchased: J. Stogdell Stokes Fund. 1979-18-1

20 TOASTER
1770–1800

Wrought iron. T-shaped frame. Two pairs of arched supports welded to frame. Frame riveted to flat shaft with hooked end and support leg with disk foot. Toaster possibly a replacement for a rotating circular grid.

49.3 x 21 cm (19⅜ x 8¼")

Gift of J. Stogdell Stokes. 28-10-11

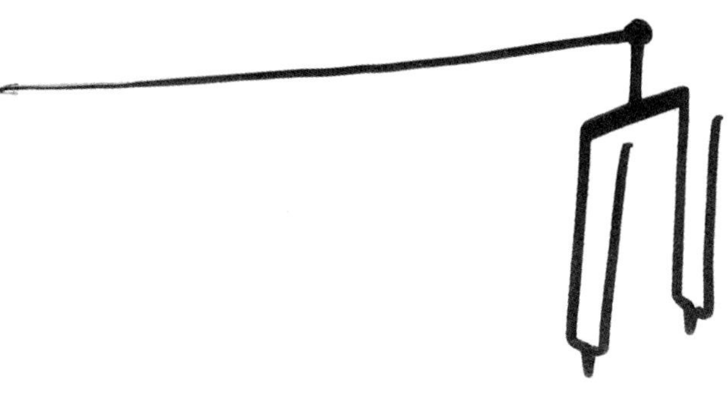

21

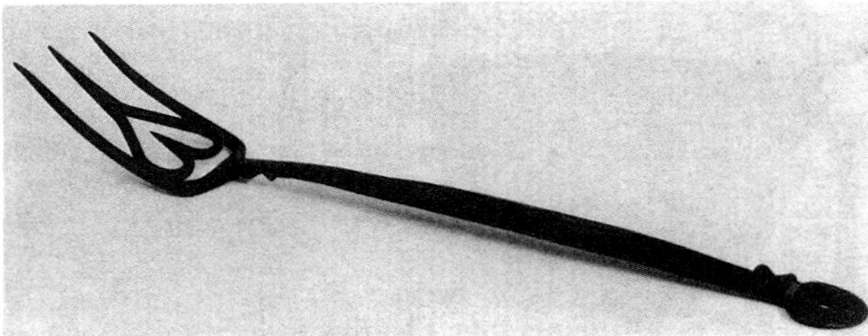

22

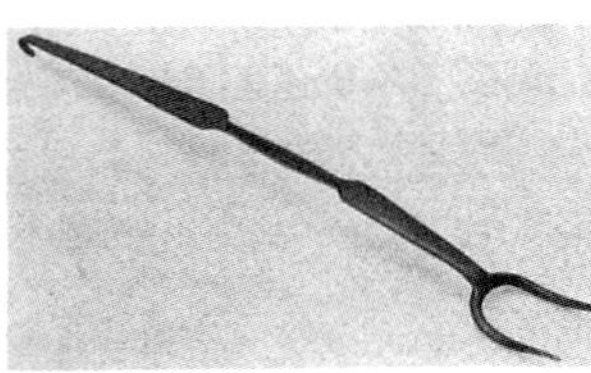

23

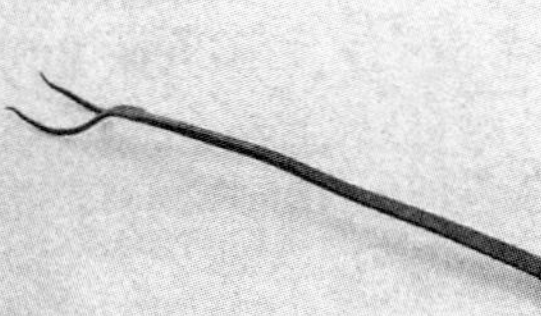

24

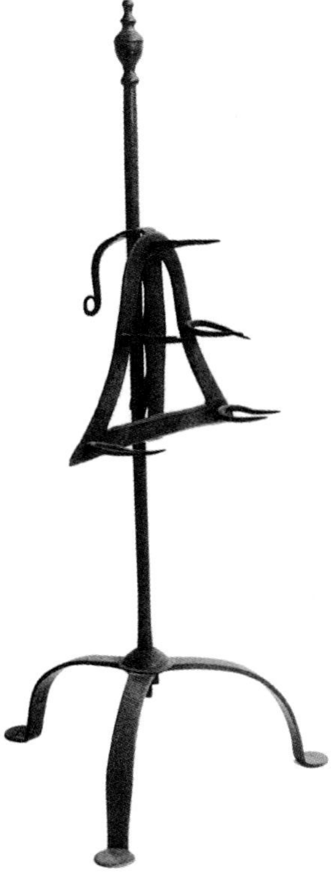

25

21 DOWN-HEARTH TOASTER
1770–1800

Wrought iron. Toaster frame with extended feet for resting on hearth pivots on a rivet which also secures the toaster to the long arm with hanging loop at end.

Length 96.5 cm (38″)

Gift of J. Stogdell Stokes. 33-70-6

22 ROASTING FORK
1770–1800

Wrought iron. Three-tined fork with center tine the point of a heart. Flat, shaped handle with molded collar on top and bottom and loop for hanging.

Length 40 cm (15¾″)

Titus C. Geesey Collection. 54-85-22

23 ROASTING FORK
1770–1800

Wrought iron. Two-tined fork with shaped handle and hanging hook has indented handgrip for firm grasp when jabbing.

Length 44.4 cm (17½″)

Gift of Mrs. William D. Frishmuth. 02-489

24 ROASTING FORK
1770–1800

Wrought iron. Two-tined fork with flat handle that turns back into hook.

Length 46.8 cm (18⅜″)

Gift of Mrs. William D. Frishmuth. 02-488

25 ROASTING STAND AND DRIP PAN
1770–1800

Wrought iron. Stand with urn finial at top is threaded and bolted under tripod base. Five two-pronged fork heads are riveted through bell-shaped frame, which moves on strap fitted with spring-action release on stand. Strap extended into carrying handle. Drip pan made of one iron sheet with sides bent up and corners flared in open pleat for pouring off fat; loop handles riveted at each end.

Height stand 68.8 cm (27⅛″)

Gift of Mr. and Mrs. J. Stogdell Stokes. 33-70-10a,b

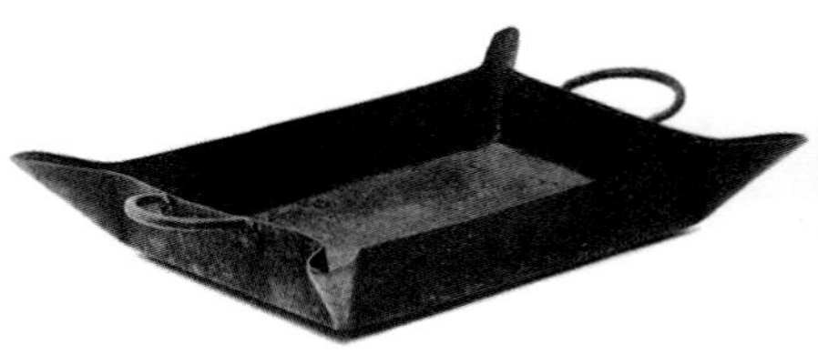

25

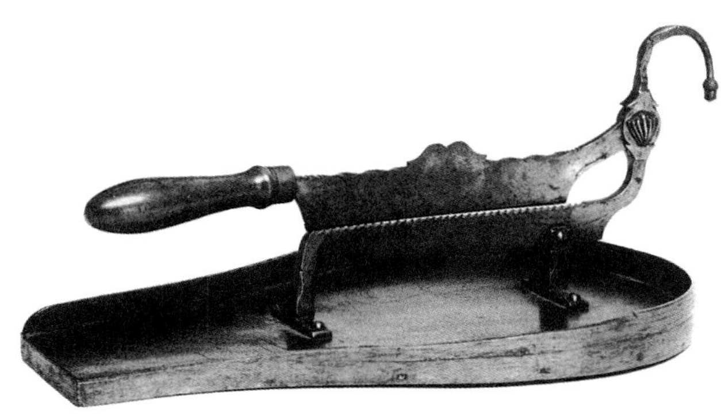

26

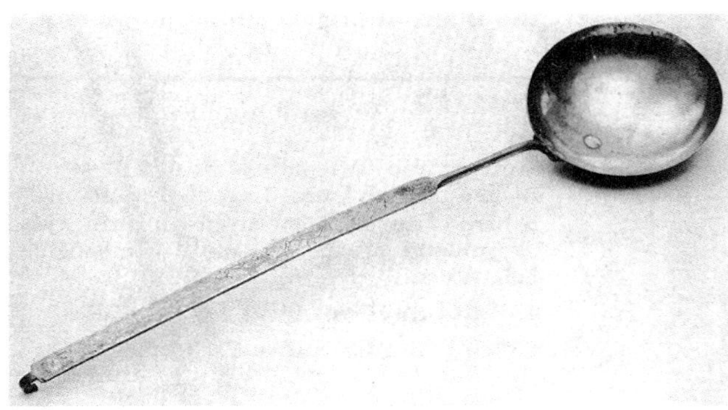

27

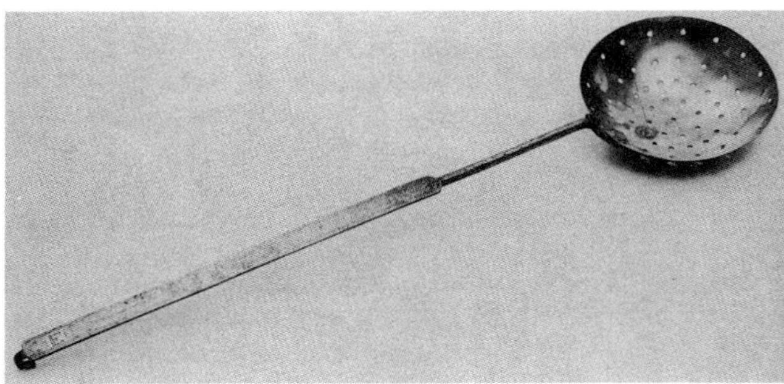

28

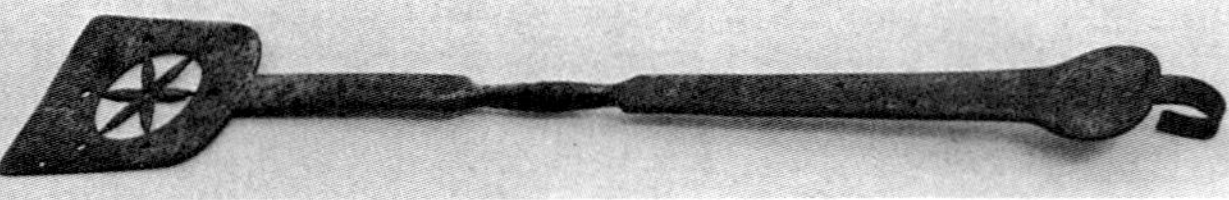

29

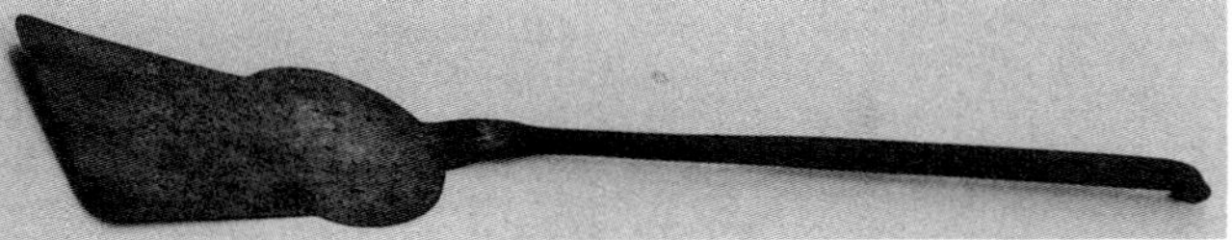

30

26 LOAF SUGAR CUTTER
1770–1800

Wrought iron, black walnut, maple. Base is shaped plank nailed to bent banding. Section of edging is missing. Iron trestle with legs bolted into base supports blade and stand. Shaped cutting blade has raised scrolls in center for finger grip. Blade pivots on rivet with decorative fluted heads. Acorn finial on stand. Turned wood handle on blade.

15.8 x 38.6 x 21.1 cm (6¼ x 15¼ x 8¼")

Gift of J. Stogdell Stokes. 39-2-3

27 LADLE
1780–1800

Marked on handle in wrigglework: *C · E*

Wrought iron, brass. Shallow brass bowl riveted to flange of iron handle. Upper handle flattened and decorated with wrigglework borders and figures of two geese catching fish. Matches no. 28.

53.3 x 13.4 cm (21 x 5¼")

Gift of the Haas Foundation. 68-118-33e

28 SIEVE
1780–1800

Marked on handle in wrigglework: *C· E*

Wrought iron, brass. Shallow perforated brass bowl riveted to flange of iron shaft. File marks on round section of handle. Upper handle flattened and decorated with wrigglework borders and fish. Matches no. 27.

56 x 14 cm (22 x 5½")

Gift of the Haas Foundation. 68-118-33g

29 SPATULA
1780–1800

Wrought iron. Flat blade in one piece with flat handle that has rounded mid-section for handgrip, terminating in flat knob and hanging hook. Blade has design of circle cut away from six-pointed star with a hole at the tip of each point. Handle edged with punched dots.

Length 45.6 cm (18")

Titus C. Geesey Collection. 54-85-13

30 SPATULA
1780–1800

Wrought iron. Flat blade is tassel-shaped and in one piece with flat handle with hooked end for hanging.

Length 37.7 cm (14⅞")

Gift of J. Stogdell Stokes. 28-10-39

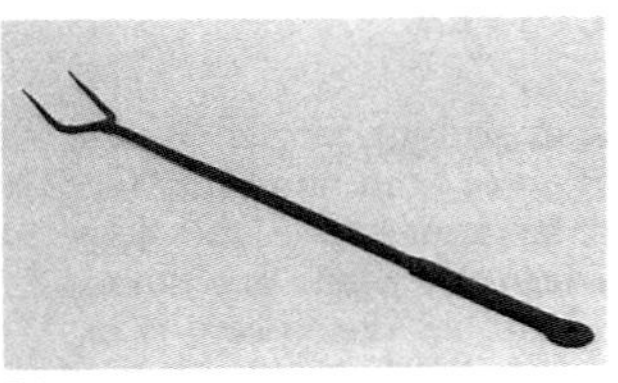

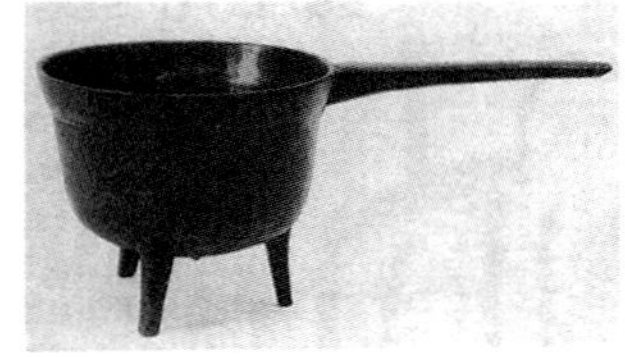

31

32

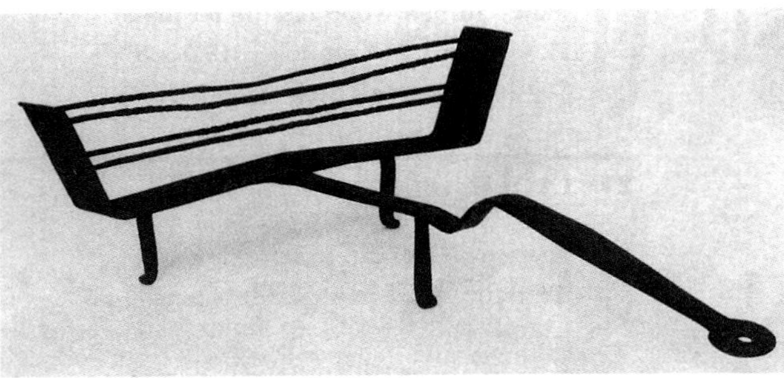

33

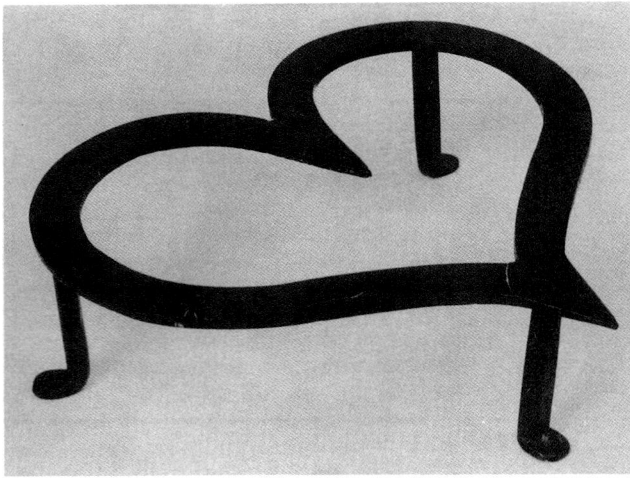

34

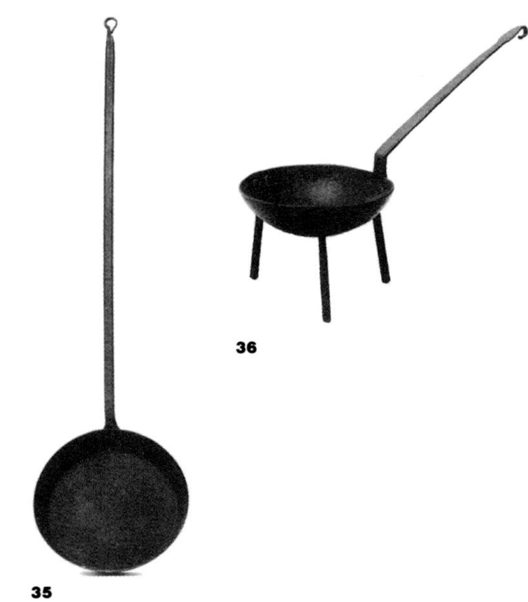

36

35

31 ROASTING FORK
1780–1800

Wrought iron. Two-tined fork on round shaft that flattens at end and terminates in hanging loop.

Length 81.3 cm (32″)

Gift of J. Stogdell Stokes. 33-70-5

32 SKILLET
1780–1800

Marked on side: *01*

Cast iron. Pot with flaring top band has three slightly splayed tapering legs and attached handle.

39.4 x 17.3 cm (15½ x 6¾″)

Gift of Mrs. William D. Frishmuth. 02-462

33 TOASTER
1780–1800

Wrought iron. Two pairs of twisted wires riveted through frame. Legs riveted through bottom of frame. Frame riveted to shaft with one support leg. Raised handle with hanging hole at end.

47 x 40.4 cm (18½ x 15⅞″)

Gift of J. Stogdell Stokes. 28-10-12

34 TRIVET
1780–1800

Wrought iron. Flat strip of iron bent into heart shape. Three legs with pad feet attached.

Height 5.2 cm (2″), length 16 cm (6¼″)

Gift of Mrs. William D. Frishmuth. 02-472

35 SKILLET
1780–1800

Wrought iron. Deep flat pan with flaring edges has long straight handle with hanging loop riveted to side.

127.5 x 35 cm (50¼ x 13¾″)

Gift of J. Stogdell Stokes. 28-48-4

36 SKILLET
1780–1800

Stamped on handle: *D · R*

Wrought iron. Shallow bowl riveted to three rectangular legs. Handle tapers into leaf form with hooked end for hanging.

52.7 x 21.6 cm (20¾ x 8½″)

Titus C. Geesey Collection. 58-110-8

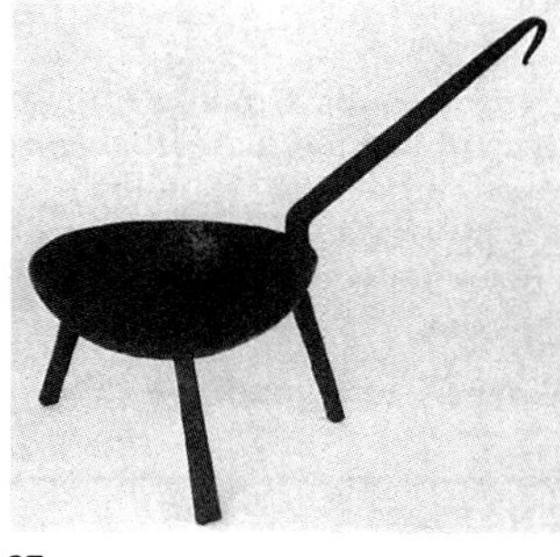

37

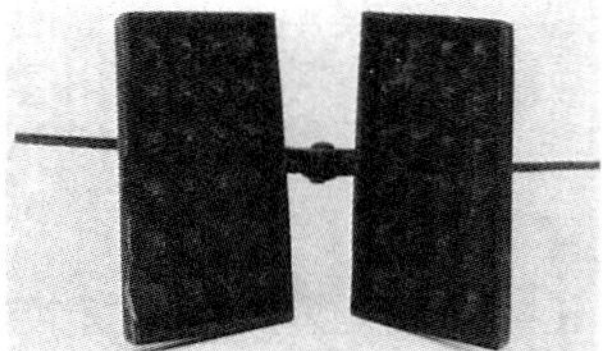

38

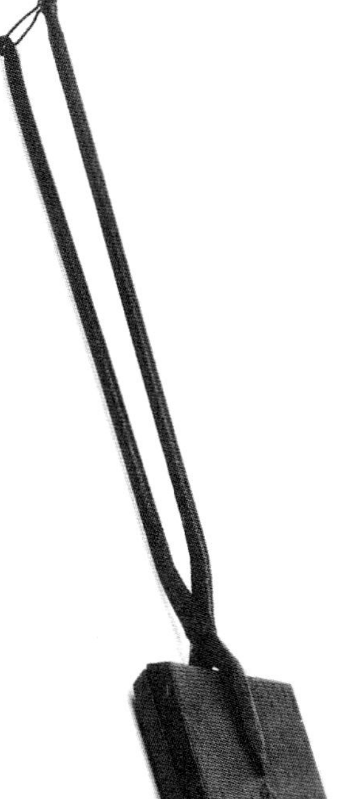

39

40

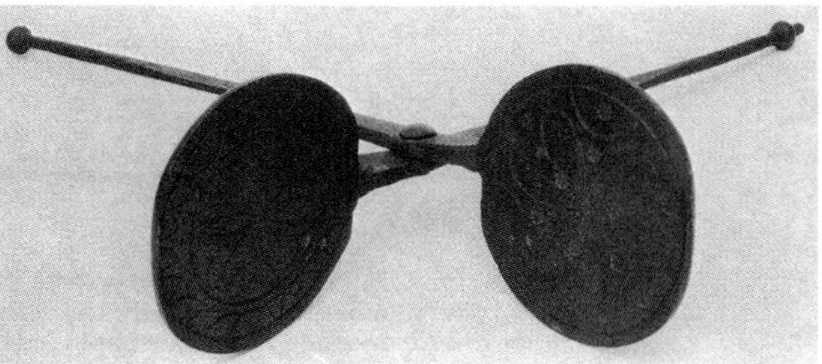

41

37 SKILLET
1780–1800

Wrought iron. Round pan with dished bottom. Three splayed legs with flat oval flanges at top riveted into pan. Long handle with hooked end for hanging has two rivets through top of back leg.

40 x 23.7 cm (15¾ x 9¼")

Gift of J. Stogdell Stokes. 28-10-9

38 WAFFLE IRON
1780–1800

Cast and wrought iron. Rectangular molds with pyramidal squares on inner surfaces. Flat hinge is riveted. One wrought handle has ring to loop over other handle.

67.2 x 15.7 cm (26½ x 6¼")

Gift of Mrs. William D. Frishmuth. 02-466

39 WAFFLE IRON
1780–1800

Marked on reverse of mold with raised form of a spruce tree

Cast and wrought iron. Rectangular molds with pyramidal squares on inner surfaces. Flat hinge is riveted. Wrought handles riveted to molds. Iron ring at end of one handle loops over other handle.

61.6 x 15.3 cm (24½ x 6")

Gift of Mrs. William D. Frishmuth. 02-467

40 HANGING GRIDDLE
1780–1800

Wrought iron. Flat griddle has raised rim which is indented in one place to pour off grease. Wrought suspension arm riveted to griddle; eye bolt at hanging end.

Height 52.1 cm (20½"), diameter 24.7 cm (9¾")

Titus C. Geesey Collection. 58-110-9

41 WAFER IRON
1780–1800

Wrought iron. Two arms are round at ends of handles, square at pivot, and flare into two disks incised with compass designs: one side has a flower in a circle with interlocking semicircles for a border; the other side has three hearts meeting at their points in a circle with stamped designs of stars in semicircles.

Length 53.5 cm (21"), diameter 15.2 cm (6")

Gift of Mrs. William D. Frishmuth. 02-465

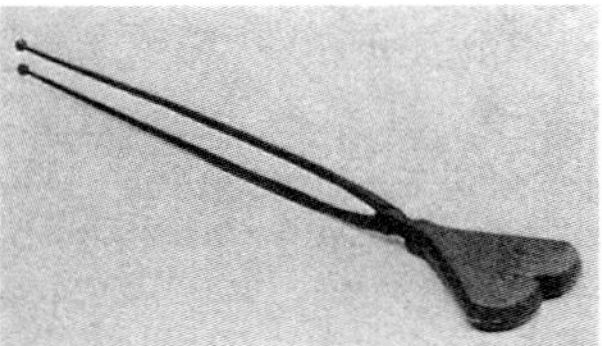

42 closed

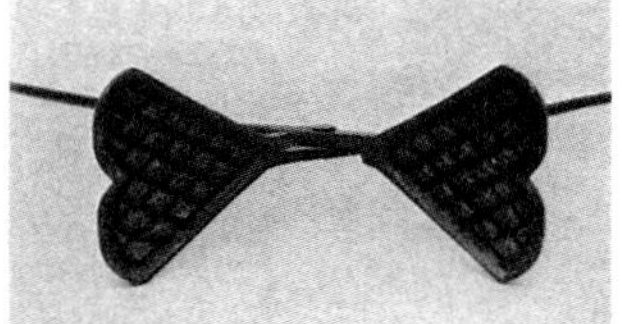

42 open

42 WAFFLE IRON
1780–1800

Cast and wrought iron. Long wrought iron arms with ball tips are welded to heart-shaped cast irons with diamond design. Handles flatten and cross with slight offset and are riveted to pivot open and shut.

76.2 x 16.8 cm (30 x 6⅝")

Gift of Mrs. William D. Frishmuth. 14-232

43 DOWN-HEARTH TOASTER
1780–1810

Wrought iron. Six hooks are riveted through support arm. Arched feet welded to bottom of hooks at each end for resting on hearth. Long handle with looped end is wrapped around support arm and welded. For toasting bread or roasting meat.

51.4 x 49.2 cm (20¼ x 19⅜")

Gift of Mrs. William D. Frishmuth. 02-674

44 ROASTING FORK
1780–1810

Wrought iron. Two curved tines at end of flat shaft that has a rounded mid-section for handgrip. Flat upper section decorated with stamped circles clustered in fours. End is hooked for hanging. Made to match nos. 45–48.

Length 38.5 cm (15⅛")

Gift of Miss Marie E. Bucher, in memory of Mrs. William Hipple and Mrs. David H. Bucher. 39-35-8

45 LADLE
1780–1810

Wrought iron. Small shallow bowl in one piece with flat handle that has rounded mid-section for handgrip. Upper handle decorated with stamped circles clustered in fours. End is hooked for hanging. Made to match nos. 44–48.

38.3 x 5.7 cm (15⅛ x 2¼")

Gift of Miss Marie E. Bucher, in memory of Mrs. William Hipple and Mrs. David H. Bucher. 39-35-12

46 LADLE
1780–1810

Wrought iron. Deep bowl in one piece with flat handle with rounded mid-section for handgrip. Upper handle decorated with stamped circles clustered in fours. End is hooked for hanging. Made to match nos. 44–48.

48.6 x 13.5 cm (19⅛ x 5¼")

Gift of Miss Marie E. Bucher, in memory of Mrs. William Hipple and Mrs. David H. Bucher. 39-35-11

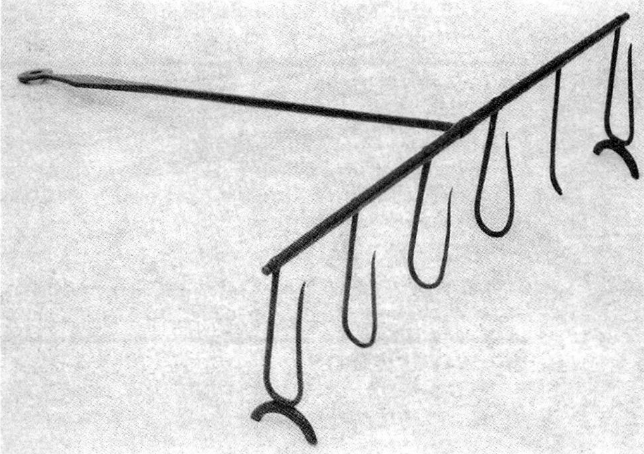

43

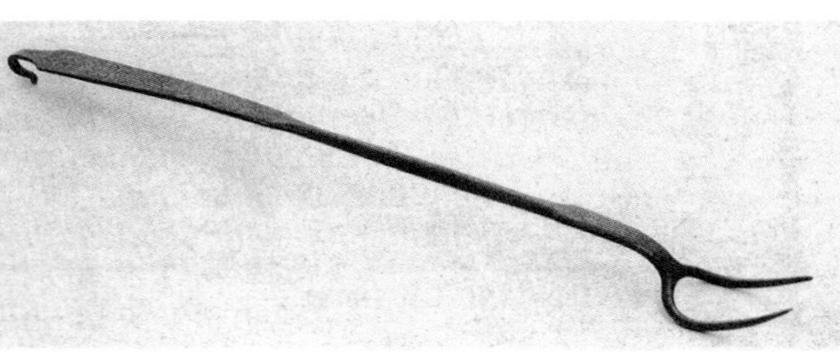

44

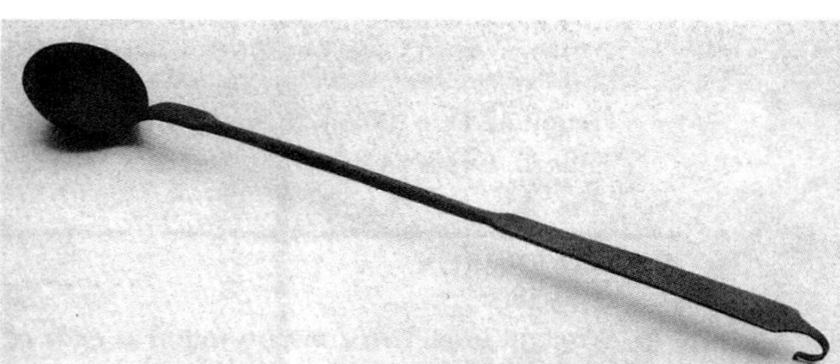

45

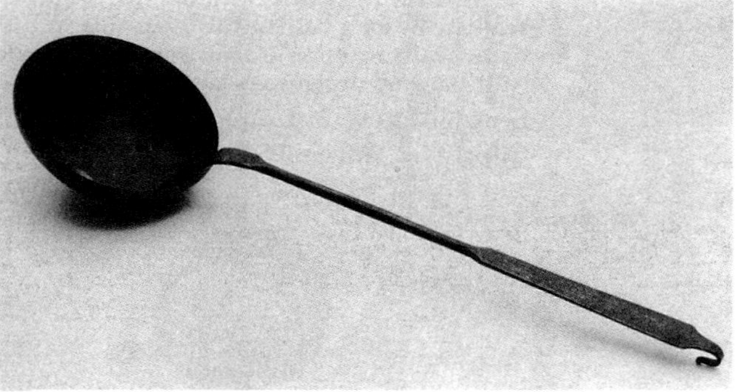

46

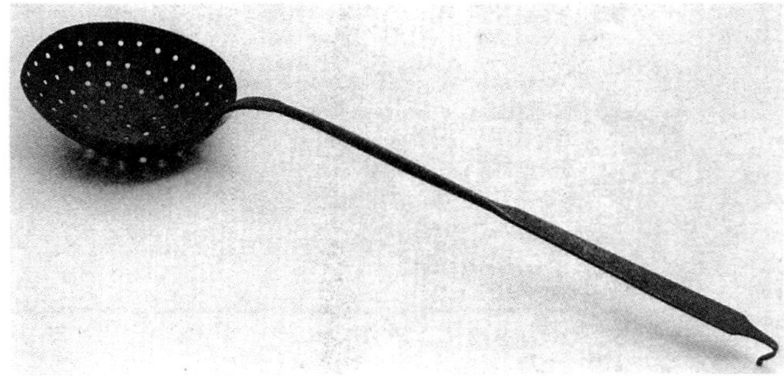

47

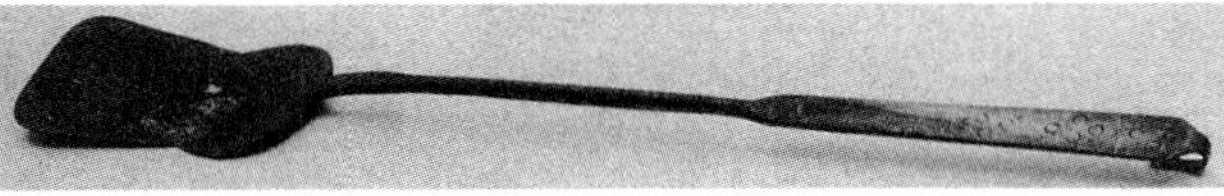

48

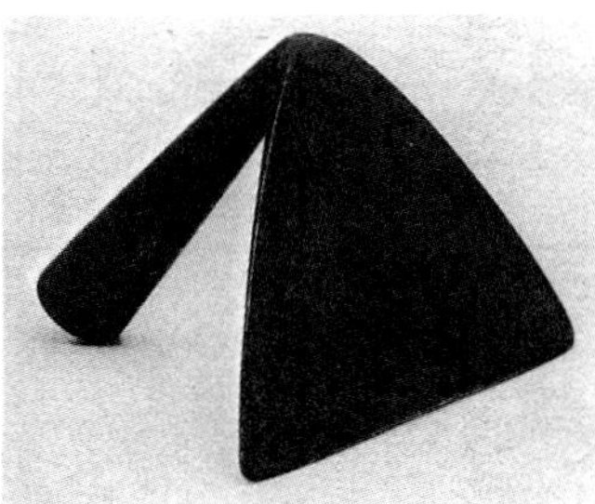

49

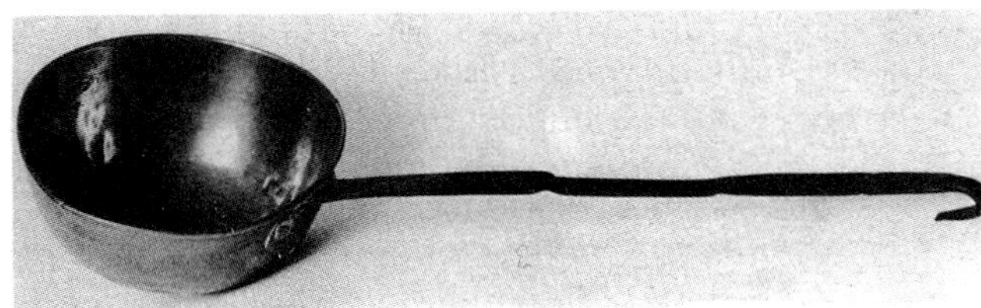

50

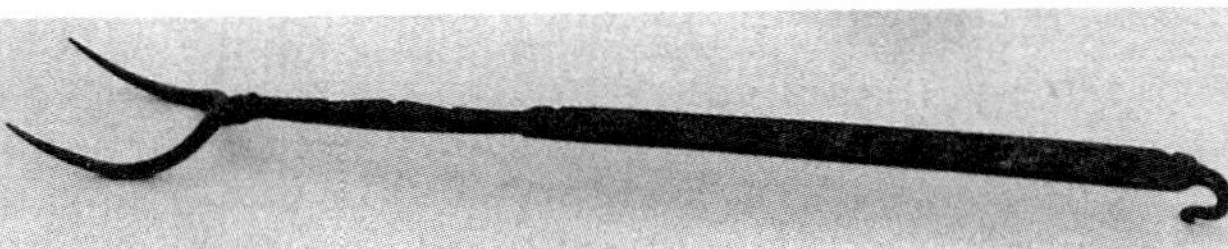

51

47 SIEVE
1780–1810

Wrought iron. Deep perforated bowl in one piece with flat handle that has rounded mid-section for handgrip. Upper handle decorated with stamped circles clustered in fours. End is hooked for hanging. Made to match nos. 44–48.

49 x 12.6 cm (19¼ x 5″)

Gift of Miss Marie E. Bucher, in memory of Mrs. William Hipple and Mrs. David H. Bucher. 39-35-9

48 SPATULA
1780–1810

Wrought iron. Tassel-shaped blade in one piece with flat handle with rounded mid-section for handgrip. Upper handle decorated with stamped circles clustered in fours. End is hooked for hanging. Made to match nos. 44–47.

44.1 x 4.7 cm (17⅜ x 1⅞″)

Gift of Miss Marie E. Bucher, in memory of Mrs. William Hipple and Mrs. David H. Bucher. 39-35-10

49 DOUGH SCRAPER
Berks or Lancaster County
1780–1810

Wrought iron. One piece of forged iron. Handle tapers to receive wooden handle; triangular blade with sharp edge.

8.1 x 11.3 cm (3⅛ x 4⅜″)

Gift of Miss Marie E. Bucher, in memory of Mrs. William Hipple and Mrs. David H. Bucher. 39-35-7

50 LADLE
1780–1810

Wrought iron, brass. Deep brass bowl with rolled edge. Flat handle has heart-shaped flange riveted to bowl, round grip midway, shaped upper section with hooked end for hanging.

55.5 x 19 cm (21⅞ x 7½″)

Gift of J. Stogdell Stokes. 28-10-17

51 ROASTING FORK
1780–1810

Wrought iron. Two-tined fork with swage-block decoration on shaft. Flat upper handle decorated with stamped patterns of flowers with eight, six, and four petals in graduated sizes.

Length 46.3 cm (18¼″)

Titus C. Geesey Collection. 54-85-21

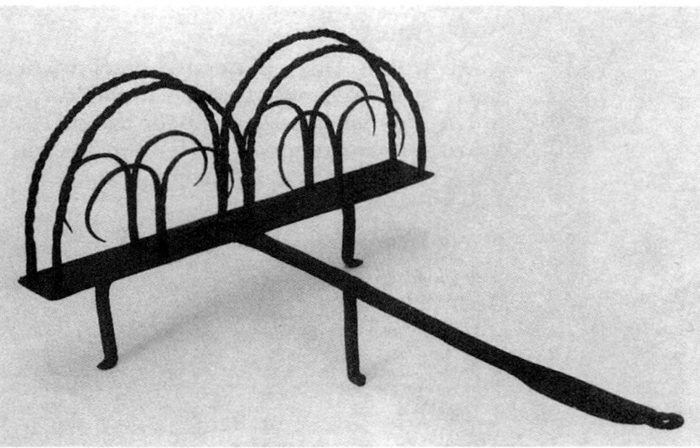

52

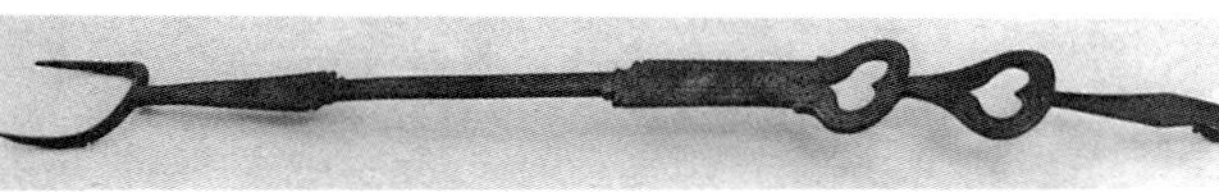

53

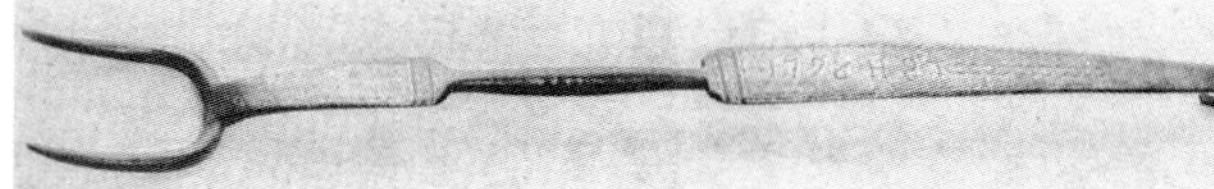

54

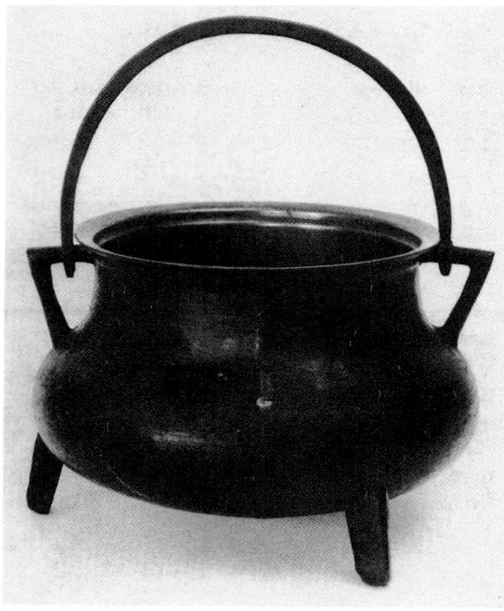

56

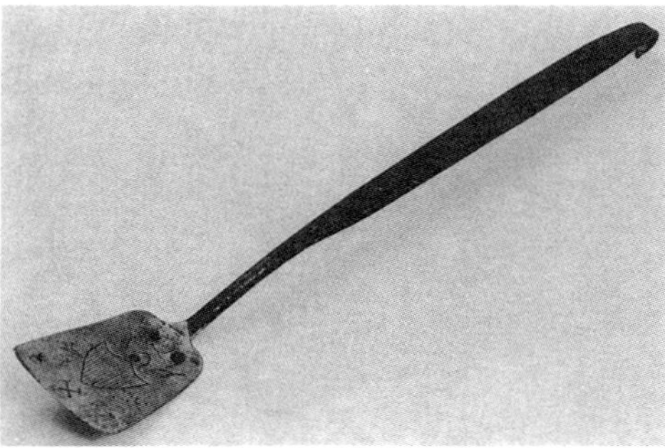

55

52 TOASTER
1780–1810

Wrought iron. T-shaped frame on three wrought legs; one leg riveted through handle. Twisted arches riveted through frame. Partial rotation on rivet.

44.4 x 33.8 cm (17½ x 13¼″)

Gift of Mrs. William D. Frishmuth. 02-583

53 ROASTING FORK
1792

Inscribed on handle: *1792   ML*

Wrought iron. Two-tined fork in one unit with flat handle, mid-section narrowed for handgrip, upper section perforated in heart-over-heart design. Hooked end for hanging. Decorated with borders of semicircles inside single line with clustered, punched stars flanking inscription.

Length 57.1 cm (22½″)

Titus C. Geesey Collection. 54-85-19

54 ROASTING FORK
Berks County
1796

Inscribed on handle: *1796 HST*

Wrought iron. Handle tapers to hanging hook at top, rounded handgrip decorated on top with swage block. Handle joined to double-pronged fork. Inscription incised with dots terminating lines. Straight and curved line bandings.

Length 46.3 cm (18¼″)

Purchased: Annual Membership Fund. 16-271

55 SPATULA
1800–1810

Wrought iron, brass. Shovel-shaped brass blade decorated with shield-bearing eagle, clouds, stars, crossed hammers, and sprig motif in corners in incised lines. Wrought flat handle riveted to blade and hooked at end for hanging.

32.4 x 5.1 cm (12¾ x 2″)

Titus C. Geesey Collection. 54-85-15

56 KETTLE
Lancaster County
1800–1820

Possibly by **Henry Wolf**

Marked below rim: *HW*

Cast iron. Deep pot on three splayed legs with carrying handle. Lid with deep edge to hold hot coals for even interior heat.

Height 24.7 (9¾″), diameter 38.3 cm (15⅛″)

Gift of Mrs. William D. Frishmuth. 02-673

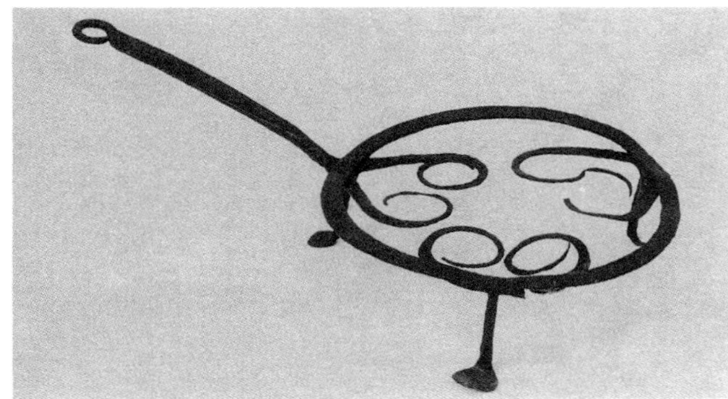

57

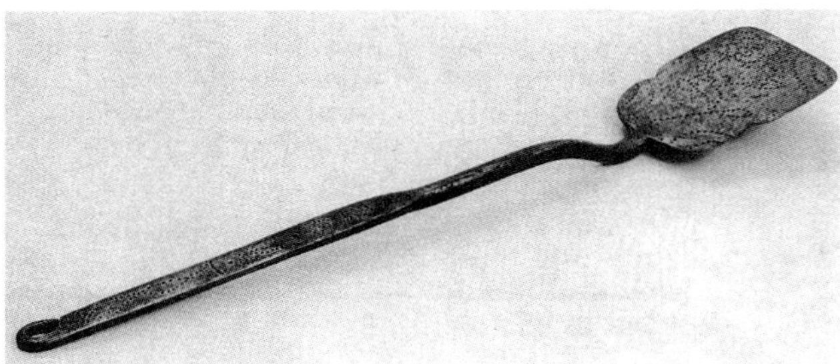

59

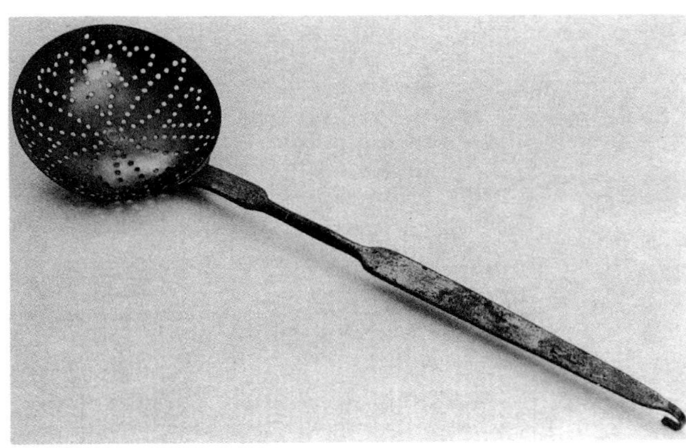

60

57 TRIVET
1800–1820

Wrought iron. Round flat ring on three straight legs with flattened feet. Three pairs of iron scrolls form heart patterns. Looped handle attached to frame.

Length 35 cm (13¾″), diameter 18.3 cm (7¼″)

Gift of Mrs. William D. Frishmuth. 02-590

58 GRIDDLE
1800–1840

Cast and wrought iron. Griddle cast with three tapered feet. Wrought hanging handle with turnbuckle loop is fitted and riveted through flanges in rim of griddle.

Height 48.9 cm (19¼″), diameter 40.6 cm (16″)

Gift of J. Stogdell Stokes. 28-10-27

59 SPATULA
1800–1840

Marked on handle in script: *JC* [or JL]

Wrought iron. Flat, shaped blade decorated with flower design in punchwork. Blade in one piece with handle that is punched with initials and crossed ellipses. Hanging loop at end.

35.6 x 6.4 cm (14 x 2½″)

Titus C. Geesey Collection. 54-85-12

60 SIEVE
1800–1840

Wrought iron, brass, copper. Shallow bowl perforated in design of six hearts between six radiating petals and fastened to flat handle with copper rivets. Handle rounded for handgrip and hooked at end for hanging.

48.2 x 14 cm (19 x 5½″)

Titus C. Geesey Collection. 54-85-16

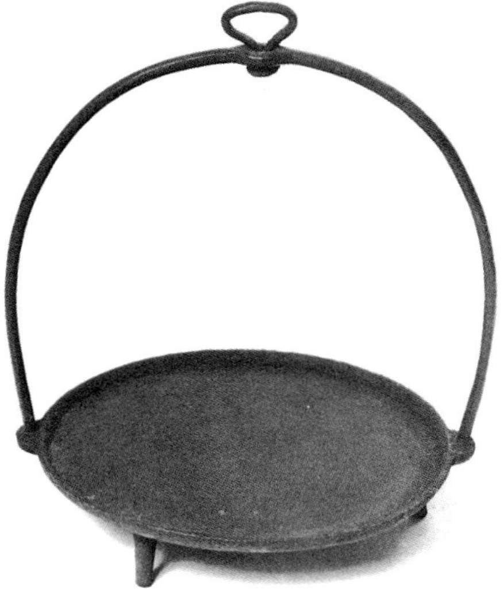

58

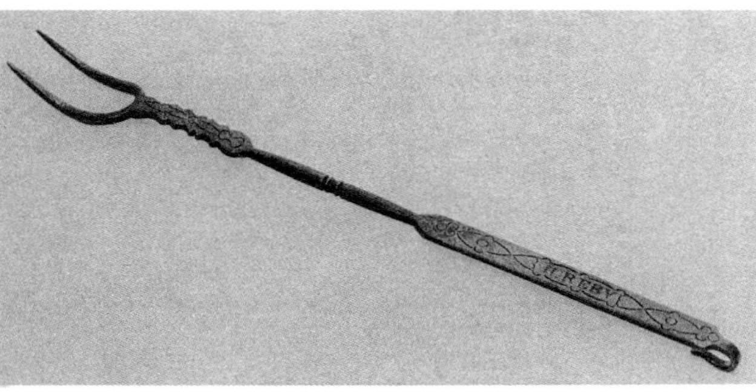

61

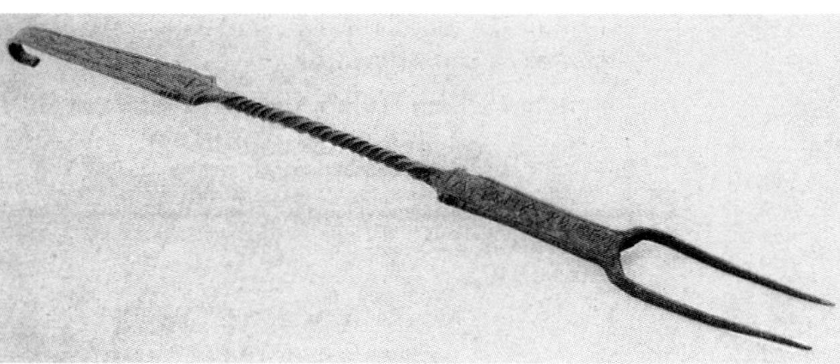

62

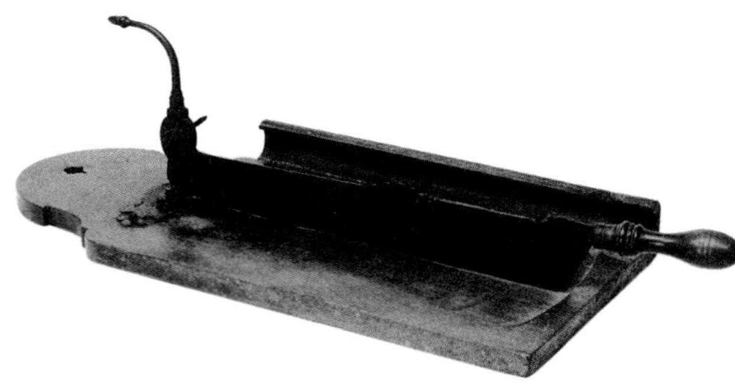

63

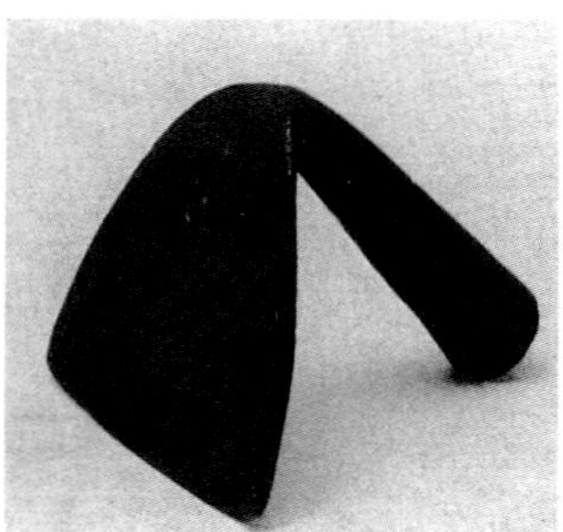

64

61 ROASTING FORK
Lancaster County
1800–1840

Inscribed on Handle: *H. R.   EBY*

Wrought iron. Two-tined fork in one piece with handle. Round mid-section has swage-block decoration. Incised lines forming hearts and ovals on handle. Hook for hanging.

Length 26.7 cm (10½″)

Titus C. Geesey Collection. 54-85-18

62 ROASTING FORK
1800–1850

Inscribed on handle: *AMTHA KNISEN*

Wrought iron. Shaft of flat handle tapers into hanging hook. Middle section is twisted. Shaft divided into two round tines. Stippled banding, inscription, and zigzag designs.

Length 42.9 cm (16⅞″)

Gift of Mrs. William D. Frishmuth. 07-162

63 CHOPPER
1800–1850

Wrought iron, walnut. Shaped board with hanging hole has carved gutter on the right side into which chopped vegetables, usually cabbage, were pushed by the blade and routed into a bowl. Long blade has scrolled center for left-hand finger grip and pivots on a pin with a wing nut. Turned wood handle. Pivoting post is centered on decorative escutcheon and fastens under board with countersunk iron nut.

7 x 74 x 36 cm (2¾ x 29⅛ x 14¼″)

Gift of J. Stogdell Stokes. 37-13-3

64 DOUGH SCRAPER
1800–1850

Wrought iron. Tapered cylindrical shaft was fitted with wood handle.

8.9 x 8.9 cm (3½ x 3½″)

Gift of Mrs. William D. Frishmuth. 02-542

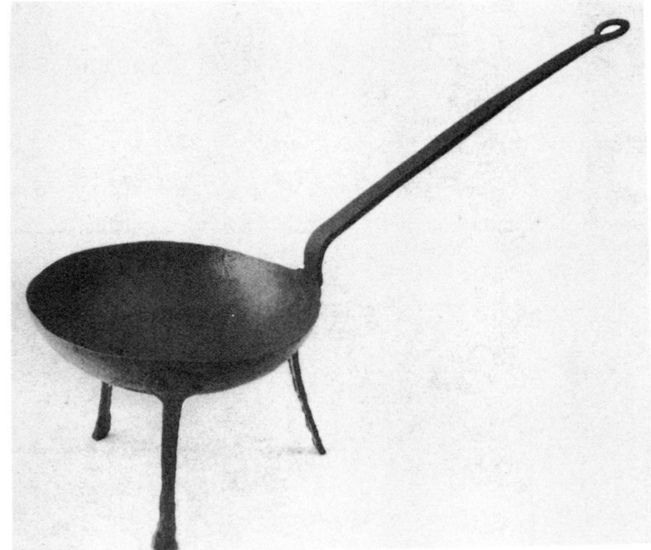

65

65 SKILLET
1800–1850

Wrought iron. Round pan attached to three wrought legs, each with two rivets. Handle has looped end.

Length 47.9 cm (18⅞"), diameter 20.3 cm (8")

Gift of Mrs. William D. Frishmuth. 02-552

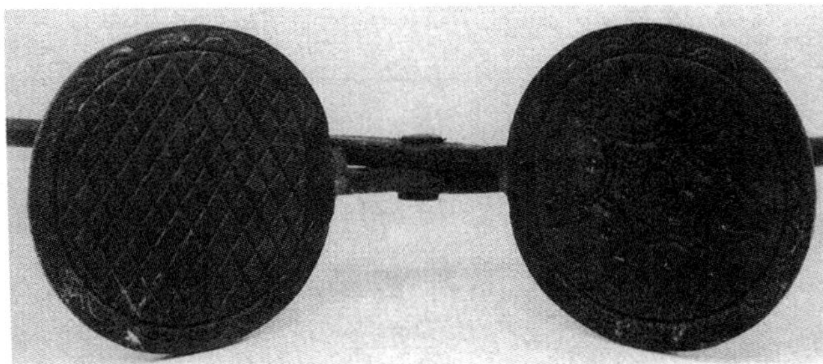

66

66 WAFER IRON
1800–1850

Marked on disk in reverse lettering: *MAHL* [Meal, or A blessing on this meal]

Cast and wrought iron. Long wrought handles with ball ends are flattened and riveted to pivot. Round cast disks incised with border pattern of semicircular scallops: one disk has diamond design; the other disk has snowflake design with eagles, roosters, and stars. Exterior not patterned.

Length 71.6 cm (28⅛"), diameter 11.7 cm (4⅝")

Gift of Mrs. William D. Frishmuth. 14-233

67 WAFFLE IRON
1800–1850

Inscribed on top: *2 Pf Mahl*
3 Schoppen Milch
6–8 Eier ¾ Pf Butter
1 [?] Selt

("2 pounds meal
3 pints milk
6–8 eggs ¾ pound butter
1 [?] salt")

Cast iron. Round frame with flanges at edge. Top hinged to frame. Design of radiating hearts with diamond design. Top has raised scallop-edged pattern and worn inscription.

Height 4.2 cm (1⅝"), diameter 37.5 cm (14¾")

Gift of J. Stogdell Stokes. 44-4-1

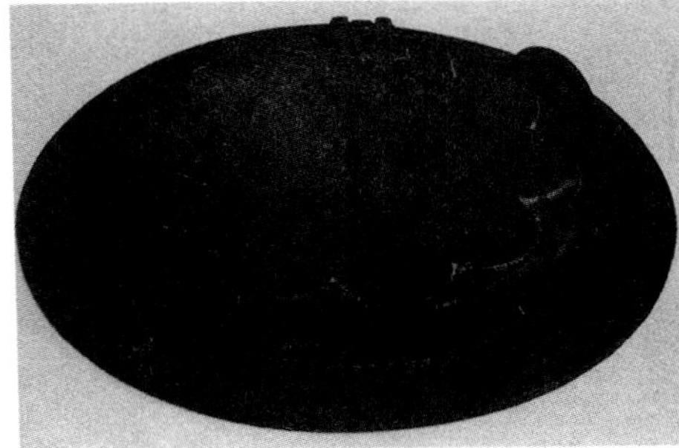

67 closed

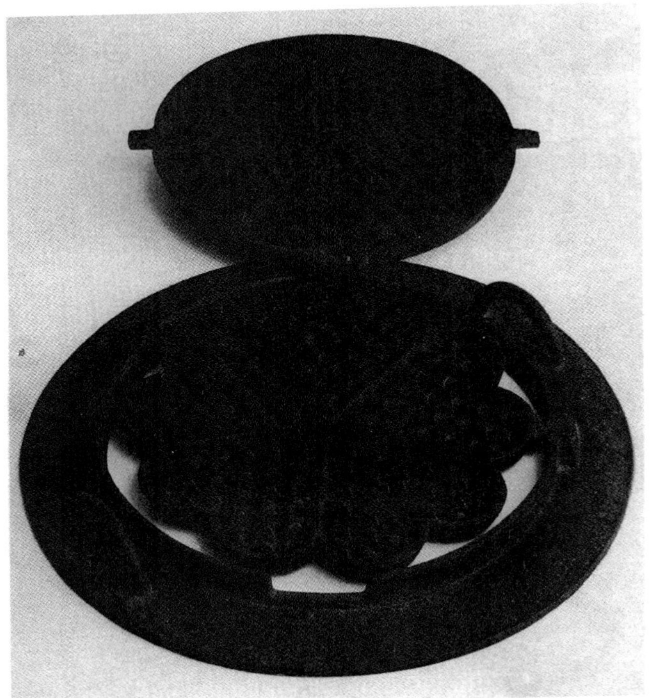

67 open

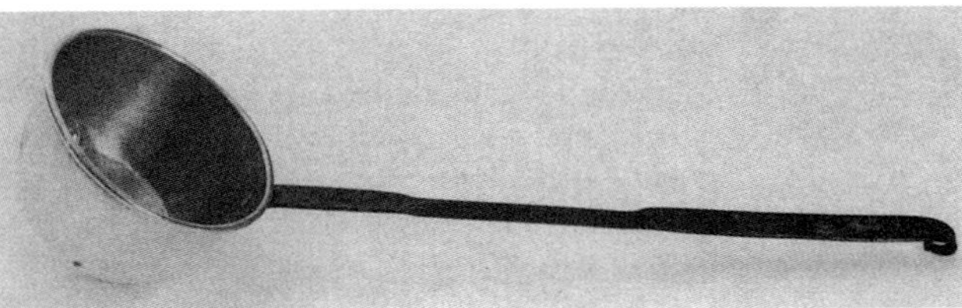

68

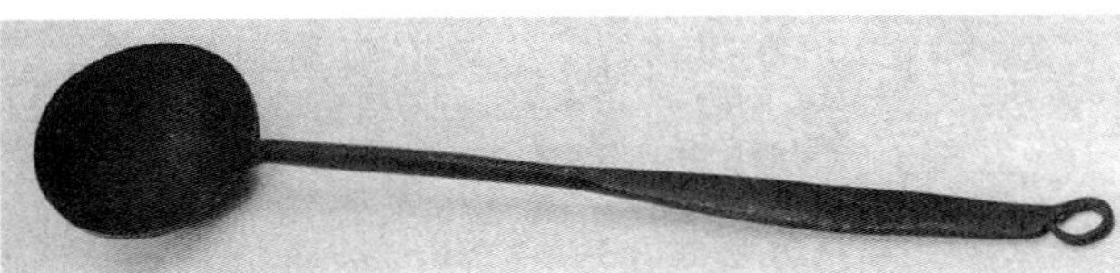

69

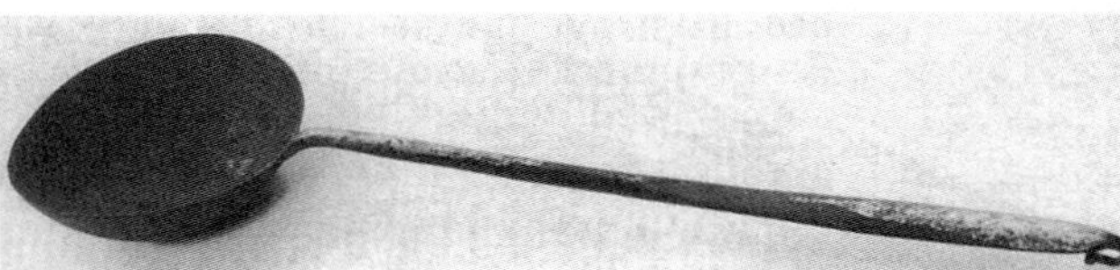

70

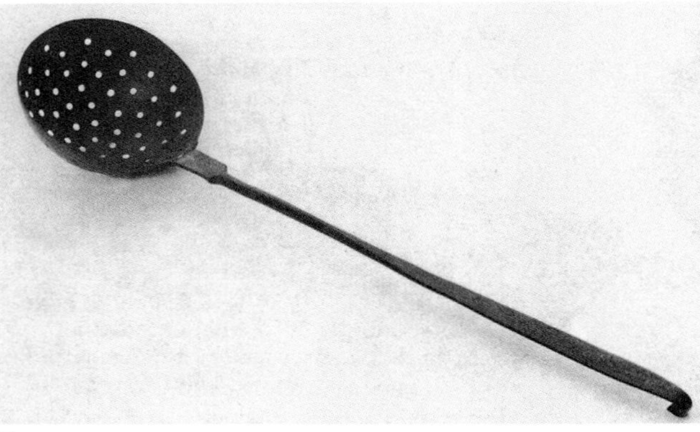

71

68 LADLE
1800–1850

Wrought iron, brass. Handle with stamped stars and hanging hook is riveted to deep cup-shaped brass ladle.

53.4 x 15 cm (21 x 5⅞″)

Gift of Mrs. William D. Frishmuth. 02-677

69 LADLE
1800–1850

Wrought iron. Deep round bowl in one piece with handle that has hanging loop.

31.2 x 6.3 cm (12¼ x 2½″)

Gift of Mrs. William D. Frishmuth. 11-67

70 LADLE
1800–1850

Wrought iron. Deep round bowl in one piece with handle; end looped for hanging.

46.5 x 12.6 cm (18¼ x 5″)

Gift of H. K. Deisher. 14-294

71 SIEVE
1800–1850

Wrought iron. Deep perforated bowl with handle riveted and looped at end for hanging. Incised vine design on handle.

48.2 x 12.5 cm (19 x 4⅞″)

Gift of H. K. Deisher. 14-293

72 SIEVE
Lancaster County
1800–1850

Stamped on handle: *W. WERNTZ*

Wrought iron, brass. Shallow perforated bowl in one piece with flat handle that has rounded mid-section and hook for hanging. Punched decoration of tulip and ellipses around inscription. Brass collar with chased decoration possibly 20th-century addition.

Length 48.9 cm (19¼″)

Titus C. Geesey Collection. 58-110-45

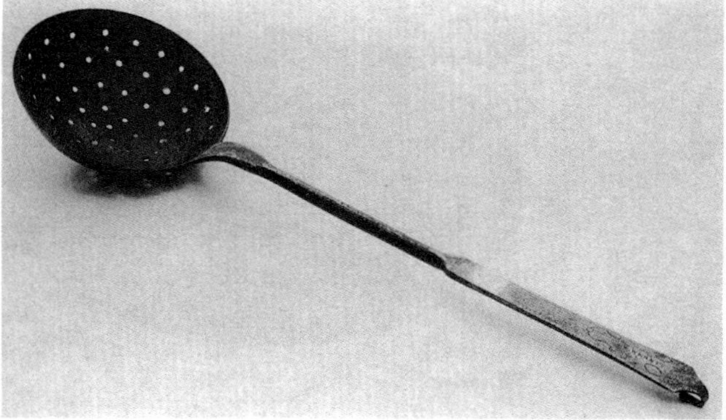

72

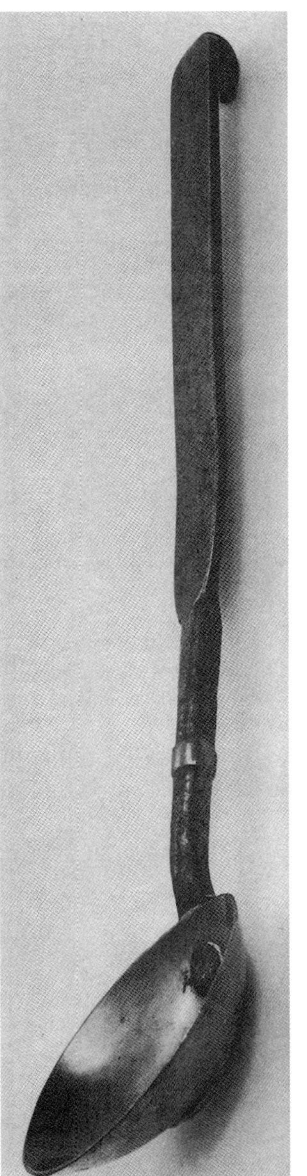

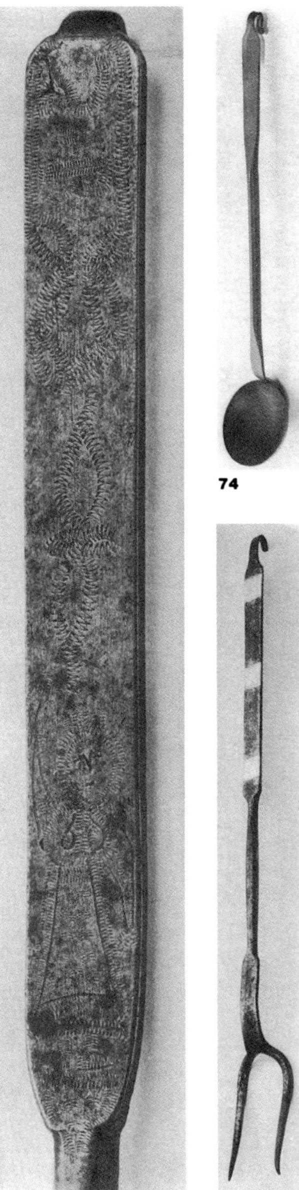

73 **73** detail

76

73 LADLE
1800–1850

Marked on handle: *SR*

Wrought iron, brass. Shallow brass bowl attached to handle with two rivets. Handle rounded near bowl and encircled by brass ring. Flattened upper handle decorated in wrigglework with figure of a woman. End of handle hooked for hanging.

24.7 x 5.7 cm (9¾ x 2¼″)

Titus C. Geesey Collection. 54-85-17

74 LADLE
1800–1850

Wrought iron. Deep bowl fastened to tapered extension of handle with two rivets. Shaped handle with hanging hook.

36.8 x 7.3 cm (14½ x 2⅞″)

Gift of Mrs. William D. Frishmuth. 02-492

74

75 SUGAR CUTTERS
1800–1850

Wrought iron. Shaped handles and blades. Spring-action handle with closure lock at top.

19.6 x 9.2 cm (7¾ x 3⅝″)

Gift of Mrs. William D. Frishmuth. 02-370

76 ROASTING FORK
1820–40

Marked in inlay in script: *L S   1827*

Wrought iron, brass. Two-tined fork with flat handle, round handgrip, and hooked end for hanging. Brass inlay possibly 20th-century addition.

Length 49 cm (19¼″)

Titus C. Geesey Collection. 58-110-44

77 SKILLET
1820–60

Wrought iron. Pan with flat bottom has flaring sides. Handle has looped end. Three wrought legs, each attached with two rivets.

Length 77 cm (30¼″), diameter 39.6 cm (15⅝″)

Gift of Mrs. William D. Frishmuth. 02-554

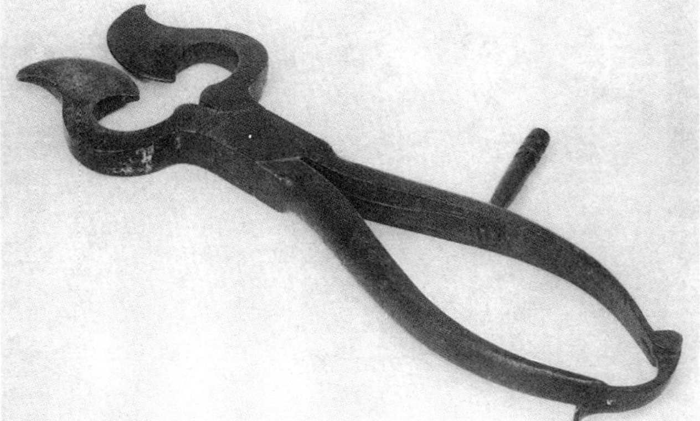

75

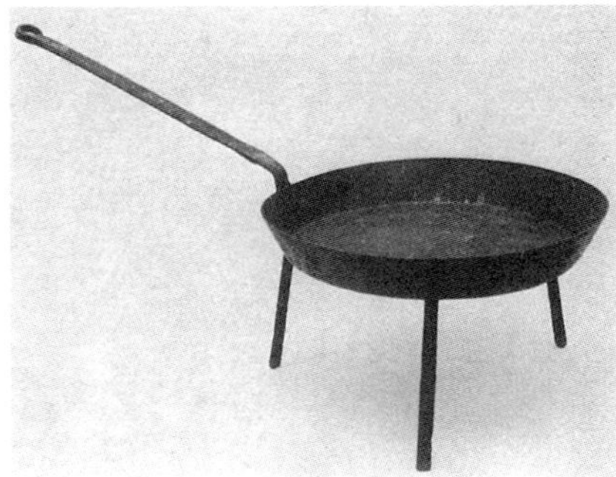

77

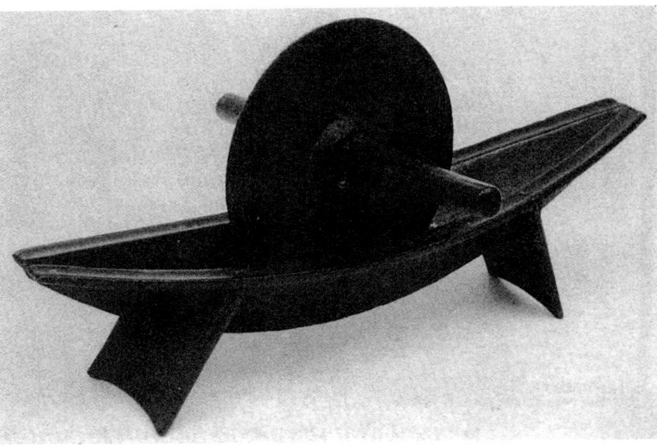

78

78 CHOPPER
1820–60

Cast iron, oak. Boat-shaped container tapers at bottom to groove. Iron disk with sharp edge has wood bar through center. Disk is rolled to and fro in groove to chop spices, nuts, or sugar.

Length 45.1 cm (17¾"), diameter disk 16.8 cm (6⅝")

Gift of Mrs. William D. Frishmuth. 02-500

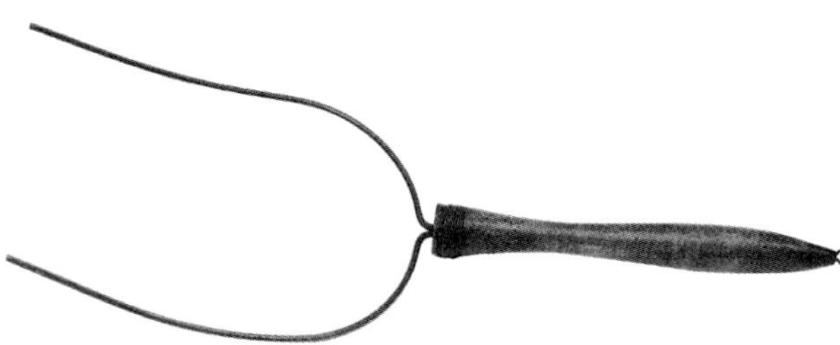

79

79 PIE FORK
1820–70

Iron, maple, wire. Turned wood handle has wire hanging loop and two widespread iron tines fitted into handle. Used to take pies from oven.

Length 45.7 cm (18")

Gift of Mrs. William D. Frishmuth. 02-475

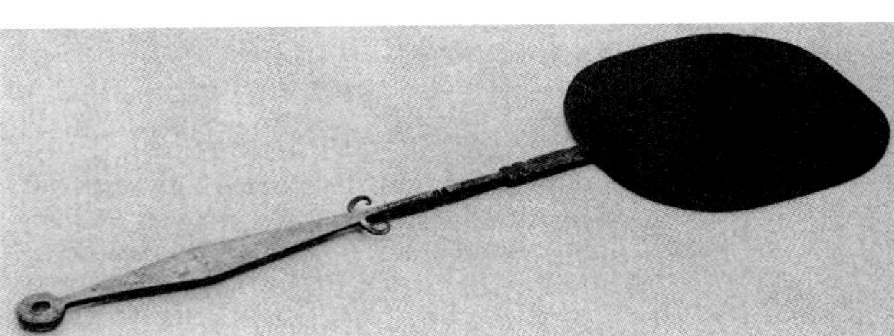

80

80 SPATULA
1825

Marked on handle in inlay: *W. Garrett 1825*

Wrought iron, brass. Flat blade in one piece with shaped handle with hanging hole at end. Shaft rounded for handgrip. Brass inscription inlaid.

48.2 x 16.5 cm (19 x 6½")

Titus C. Geesey Collection. 54-85-14

81 TRIVET
1830–50

Wrought iron. Flat bar bent into heart shape outlined with punched dots. Round legs with swage-block decoration have pad feet; front foot reticulated like a paw.

Height 5.8 cm (2¼"), length 18 cm (7⅛")

Titus C. Geesey Collection. 58-110-51

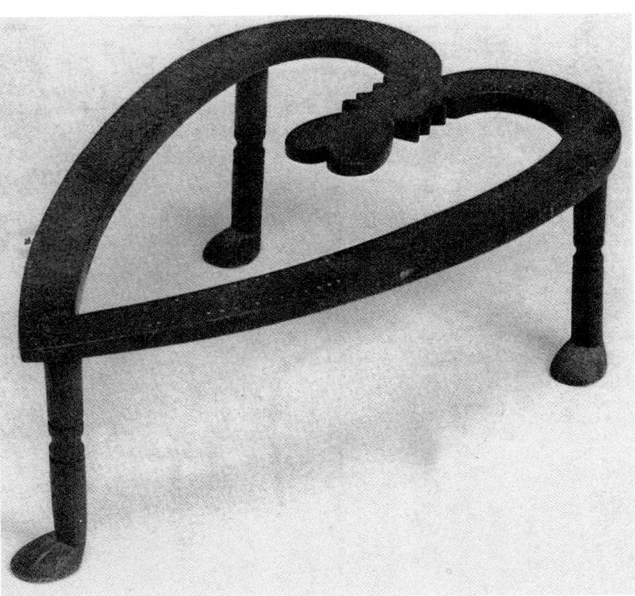

81

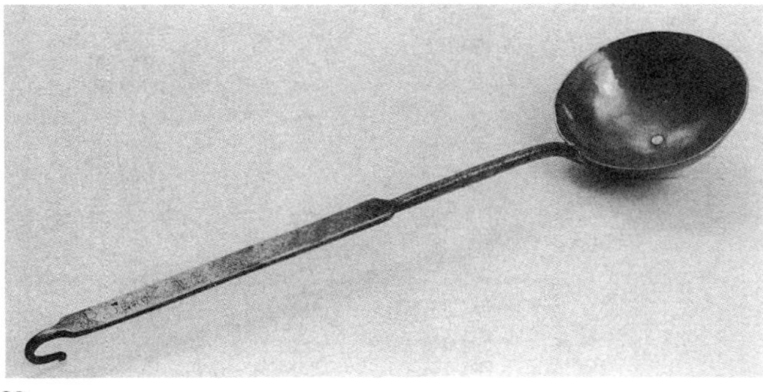

82

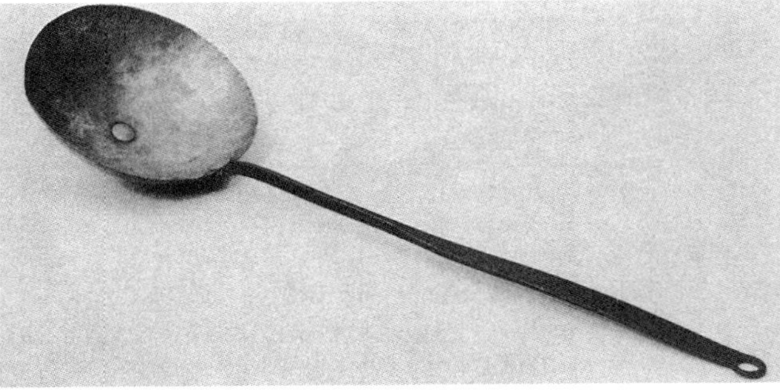

83

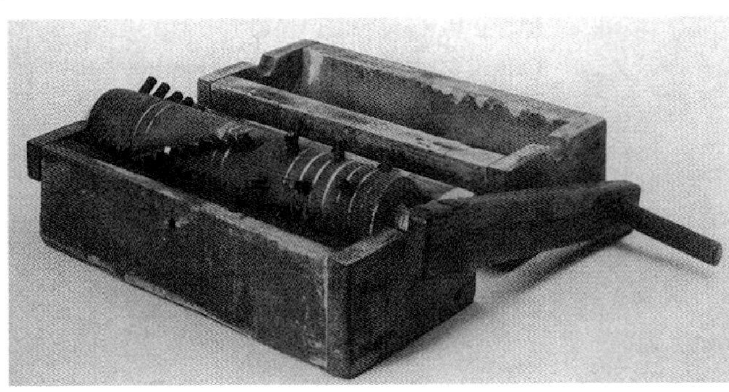

84

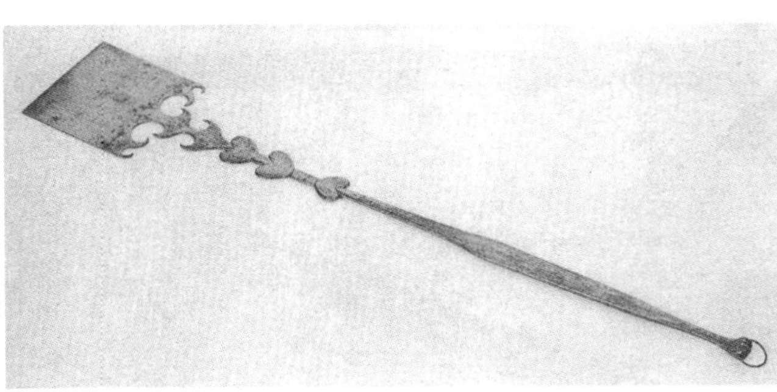

85

82 LADLE
1834

Peter Derr

Inscribed on handle: *P. DERR 1834*

Wrought iron, brass. Deep brass bowl attached to handle with three rivets. Handle flattened with hooked end for hanging.

35.6 x 8.9 cm (14 x 3½″)

Titus C. Geesey Collection. 54-85-20

83 SKIMMER
1840–60

Wrought iron, brass. Shallow brass bowl has incised lines across face and crimped edge. Bowl is riveted to iron handle with hanging loop.

52.1 x 16.6 cm (20½ x 6½″)

Gift of Mrs. William D. Frishmuth. 02-478

84 SAUSAGE CUTTER
1840–60

Sheet iron, painted pine, poplar. Plank construction, butt joints screwed. Wood tenons into crank handle. Roller inset with square iron pegs. Box fitted with stationary triangular blades alternating with iron pegs. Used in conjunction with a sausage gun.

42.5 x 19.1 cm (16¾ x 7½″) (including handle)

Gift of Mrs. William D. Frishmuth. 02-170

85 SPATULA
1856

Inscribed on obverse in script: *To Maria Lynch, Nov. 10th;* on reverse: *In remembrance of John Mullin 1856*

Wrought iron. Flat handle in one piece with blade. Blade has wavelike cut edge forming an arrow that pierces heart design on shaft. Tapered end has sculpted fist grasping wire hanging loop.

49.5 x 8.2 cm (19½ x 3¼″)

Gift of R. Wistar Harvey. 40-16-738

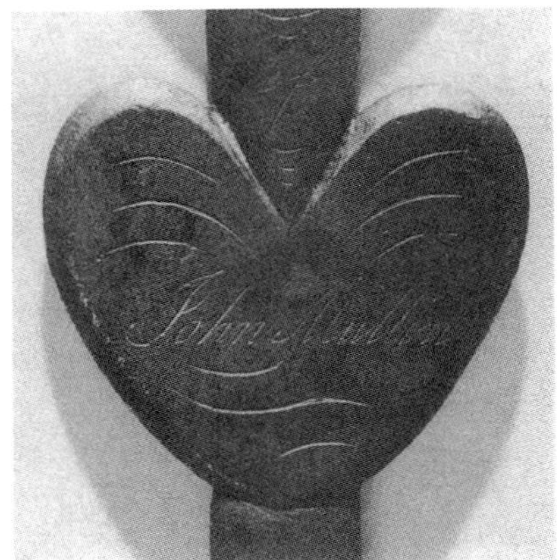

85 detail

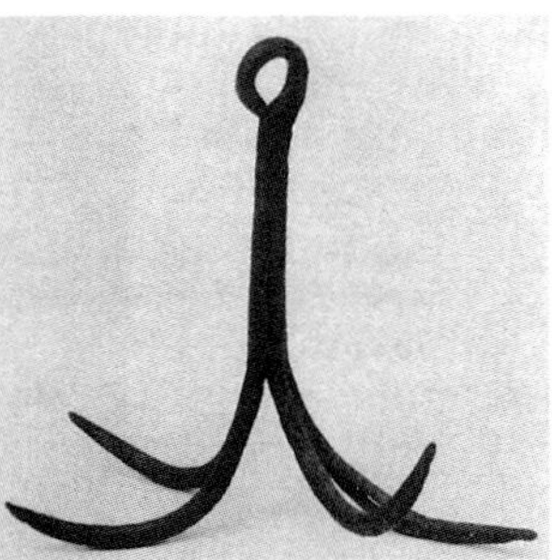

1

1 HOOK
1770–1800

Wrought iron. Single piece with ring at top. Lower stem divided into four tapering hooks. Used as a spit, well hook, or barnyard lift.

17.1 x 18.4 cm (6¾ x 7¼")

Gift of Mrs. William D. Frishmuth. 02-164

2 WOOL COMB
1770–1870

Wrought iron, maple. Fifteen tapering prongs set into iron bar that meets handle at right angle. Turned wood handle (probably a replacement) has metal collar.

13.6 x 14.3 x 18.6 cm (5⅜ x 5⅝ x 7⅜")

Gift of Mrs. William D. Frishmuth. 02-237

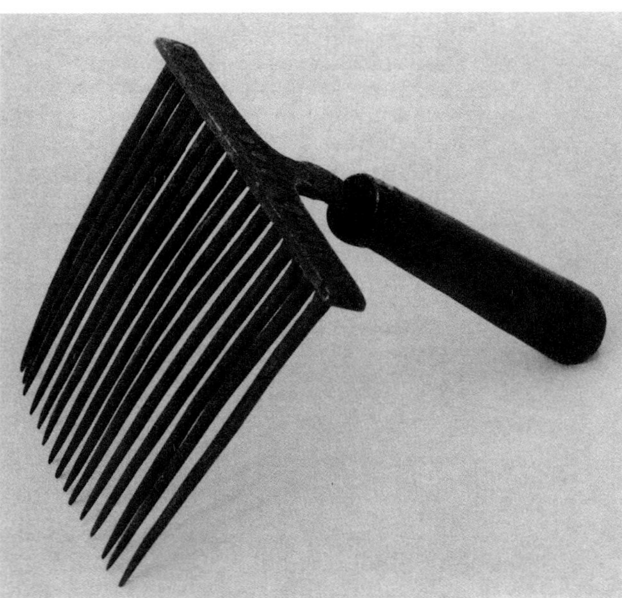

2

3 GOOSEWINGED BROADAX
Lancaster County
1800–1850

Marked on blade: *I. Scholt   IZH*

Wrought iron, oak. Broad blade with long flat poll. Hollow neck fitted with wood handle shaped to angle slightly with blade in order to protect the fingers.

65.7 x 19.8 cm (25⅞ x 7¾")

Gift of Mrs. William D. Frishmuth. 02-184

4 CLEAVER
Upper Hanover Township, Montgomery County
1800–1850

Incised on handle: *GROB*

Wrought iron, hickory. Broad blade tapers to sharp edge. Broad spine for hitting with wooden mallet.

46.1 x 10.5 cm (18⅛ x 4⅛")

Gift of Mrs. William D. Frishmuth. 02-473

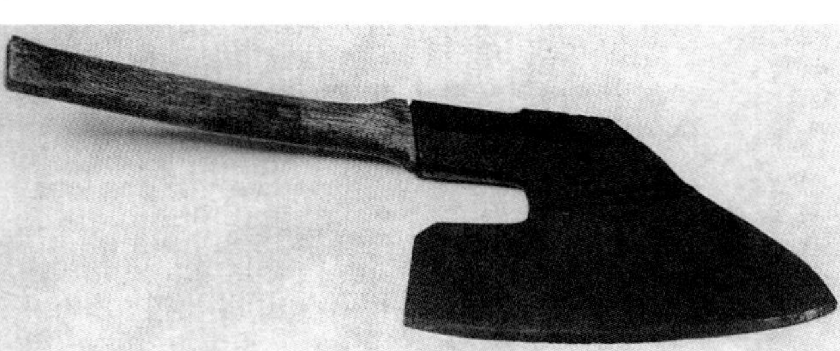

3

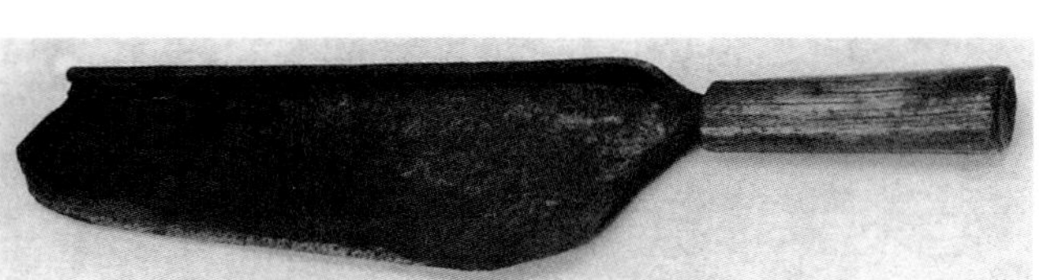

4

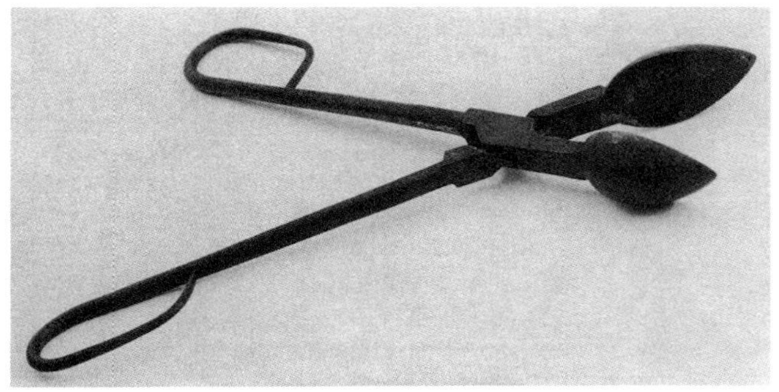

5

5 TONGS
1800–1850

Wrought iron. Scissor action. Looped handles; solid elliptical pincers.

Length 23 cm (9")

Gift of Mr. and Mrs. J. Stogdell Stokes. 33-70-7

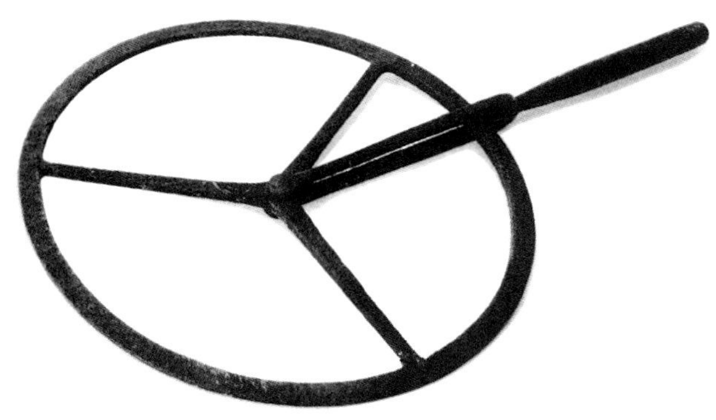

6

6 WHEELWRIGHT'S ROTARY GAUGE
1800–1850

Wrought iron. Wheel with three spokes rotates on pin fitted at end of forked handle. Wood cover for iron handle missing.

Length 31.8 cm (12½"), diameter 19.7 cm (7¾")

Gift of Mrs. William D. Frishmuth. 02-186

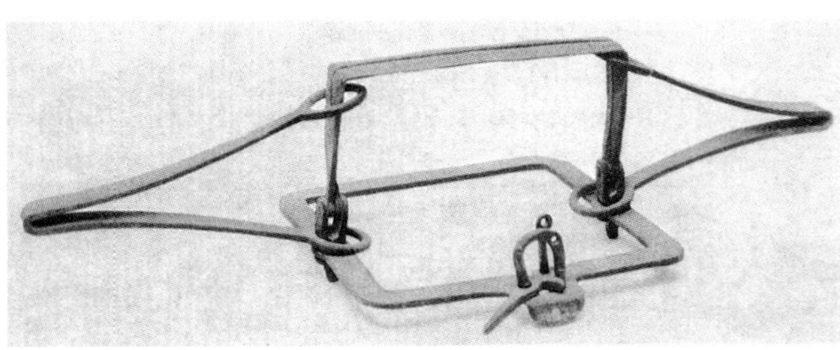

7

7 BEAR TRAP
1800–1850

Wrought iron. Square jaws without teeth held open by tong-shaped springs. Shown closed.

99 x 38.1 cm (39 x 15")

Gift of Mrs. William D. Frishmuth. 02-160

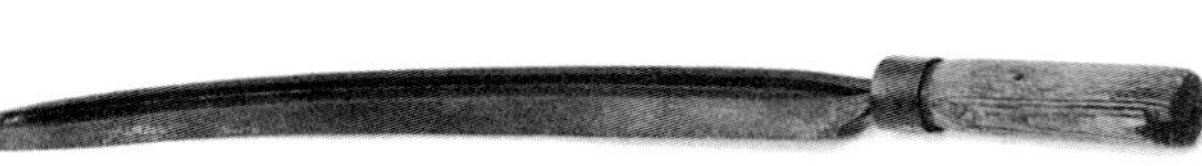

8

8 CORN KNIFE
1820–40

Wrought iron, hickory. Long blade, slightly curved with sharp cutting edge and raised spine.

68.2 x 3.8 cm (26⅞ x 1½")

Gift of Mrs. William D. Frishmuth. 02-202

9 FROE
1820–50

Wrought iron, hickory. Heavy blade tapers toward pointed end. Round handle wedged into eye. Used with a maul or froe club for splitting wood into splints, clapboards, or shingles.

Length handle 49.5 cm (19½"), blade 35.9 cm (14⅛")

Gift of Mrs. William D. Frishmuth. 02-199

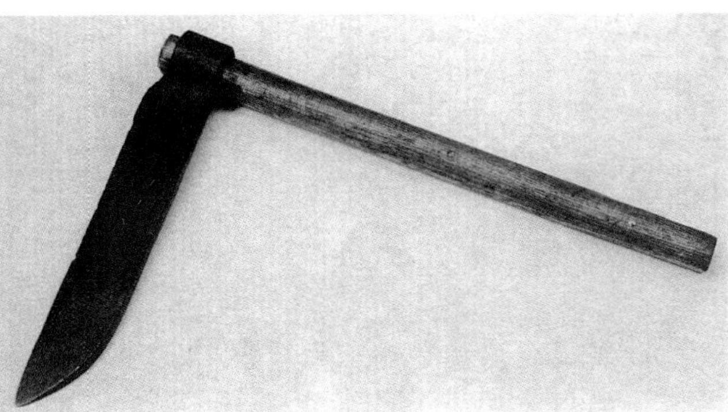

9

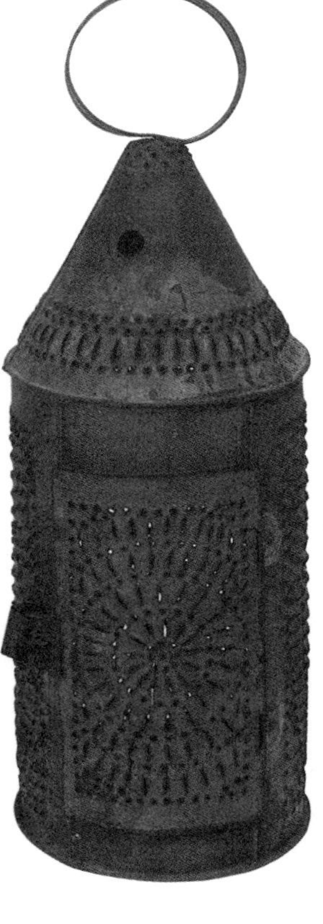

1

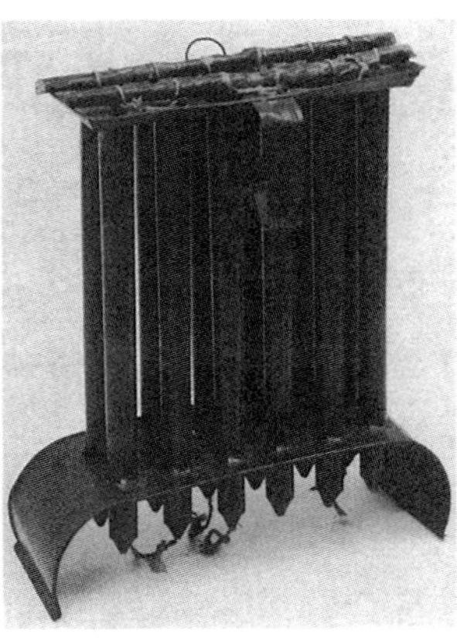

2

1 LANTERN
1770–1800

Tin over sheet iron. Lapped and soldered joints. Conical top with rolled edge, looped handle, hinged door, and hasp. Decorated in punchwork and piercing. Border around top and two holes for smoke.

Height 39.2 cm (15⅜″), diameter 15.4 cm (6″)

Gift of Mrs. William D. Frishmuth. 02-84

2 CANDLE MOLD
1770–1810

Tin over sheet iron, wood. Soldered joints. Twelve molds, raised base. Wood wick holders.

29.2 x 26.7 cm (11½ x 10½″)

Gift of R. Wistar Harvey. 40-16-726

3 BOX
1780–1800

Tin over sheet iron, wire. Made of ten panels joined in folded seams. Top edge reinforced with molded strip which is rolled with edge of box, soldered, and pinched smooth. Lid has applied flange with wired edge. Hinges and hasp pivot on wire. Loop wire handles each end. Eight panels decorated with punched heart-diamond and petals in circle designs. Used for storing bread or cheese. Similar types made in New England.

28 x 56.5 x 30.2 cm (11 x 22¼ x 11⅞″)

Purchased: J. Stogdell Stokes Fund. 1979-18-3

4 TINDERBOX
1780–1800

Tin over sheet iron. Soldered joints. Two raised midbands. Outer lid holds candle; inner lid has looped handle. Contains piece of flint, steel, and old wool for fuel.

Height 8.3 cm (3¼″), diameter 13.3 cm (5¼″)

Gift of J. Stogdell Stokes. 28-10-37

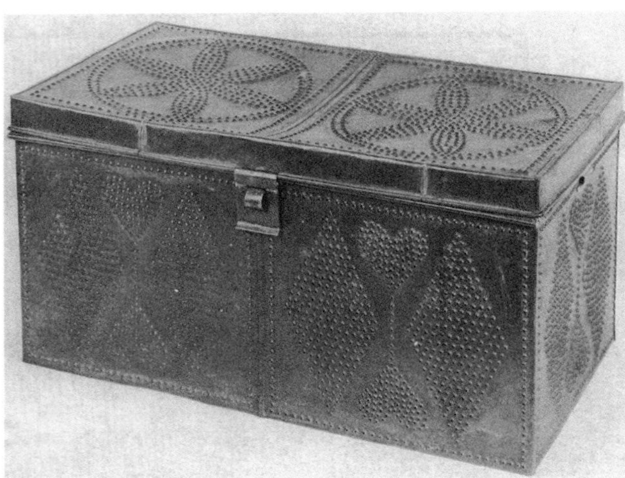

3

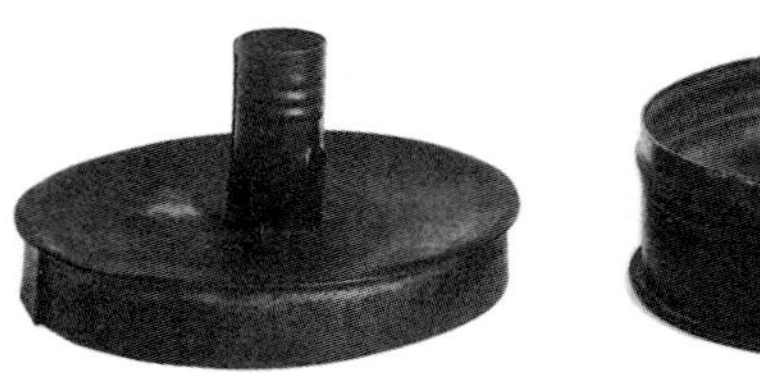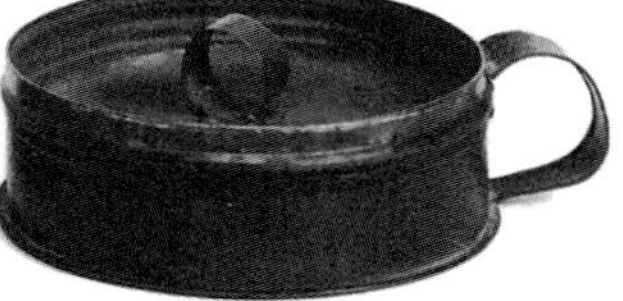

4

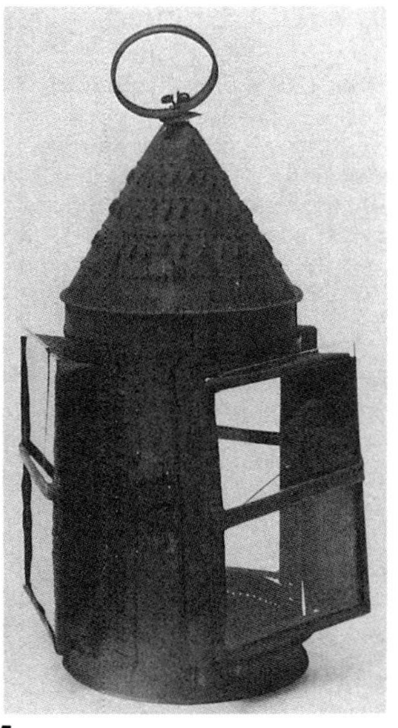

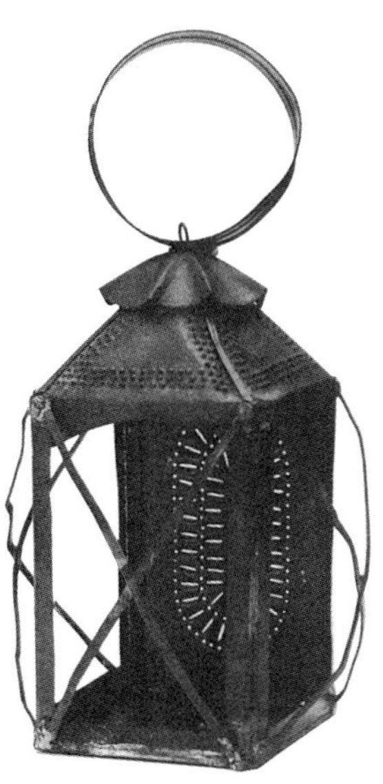

5   **7**

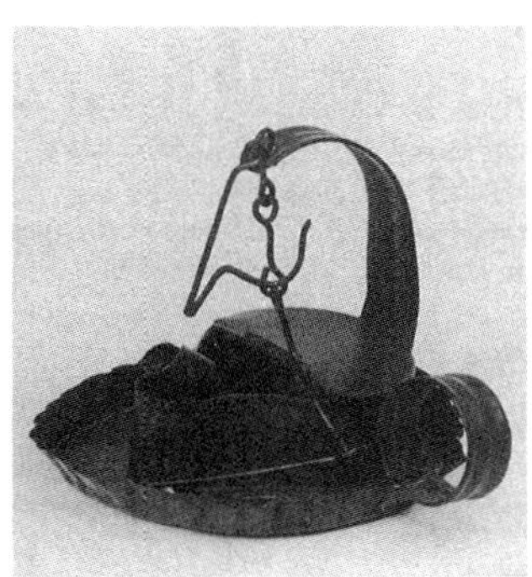

6

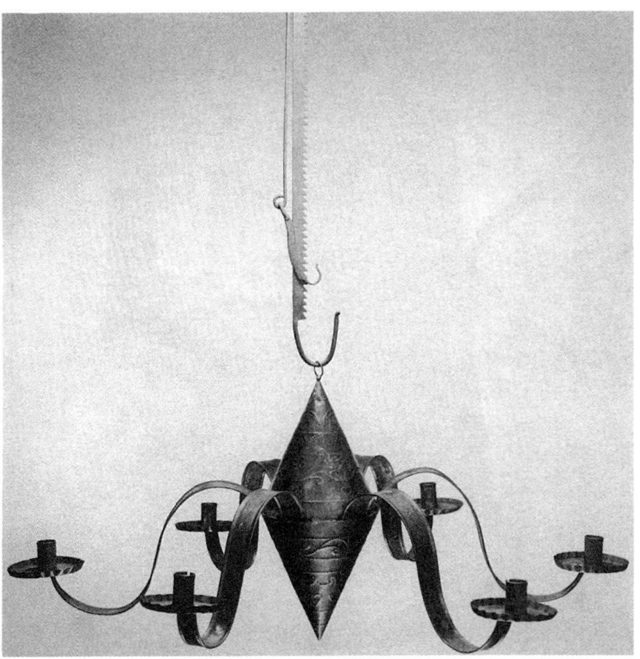

8

5   **LANTERN**
1780–1800

Tin over sheet iron, glass. Lapped and soldered joints. Conical top with looped handle attached with two twisted wires on a heart-shaped washer. Three projecting bays of tin-framed glass panels set into cylinder. Slit and punchwork border decorations.

31.3 x 20.4 cm (12⅜ x 8")

Gift of Mrs. William D. Frishmuth. 02-85

6   **HANGING OIL LAMP**
1780–1810

Tin over sheet iron. Lapped and soldered joints. Lamp soldered to fluted tray with looped handle. Fitted with wire hanging hook and chained wick pick. "Betty lamp."

10.8 x 13.2 cm (4¼ x 5¼")

Gift of Mrs. William D. Frishmuth. 02-111

7   **LANTERN**
1780–1810

Tin over sheet iron. Lapped and soldered joints. Looped handle attached with wire loop on crimped heat deflector. One side slitted and punched; three open sides with crossed tin strips to hold glass.

36 x 20.9 cm (14⅛ x 8¼")

Gift of Mrs. William D. Frishmuth. 02-87

8   **CHANDELIER**
1780–1810

Tin over sheet iron. Lapped and soldered joints. Body made of two conical units with six curved arms extending from the central joint; flattened ends support candle sockets in crimp-edged bobeches. Punched designs of running vines, birds, lyres, and hearts. Ring hook at top. Shown with an iron trammel.

34.3 x 71.1 cm (13½ x 28")

Titus C. Geesey Collection. 58-110-13,14

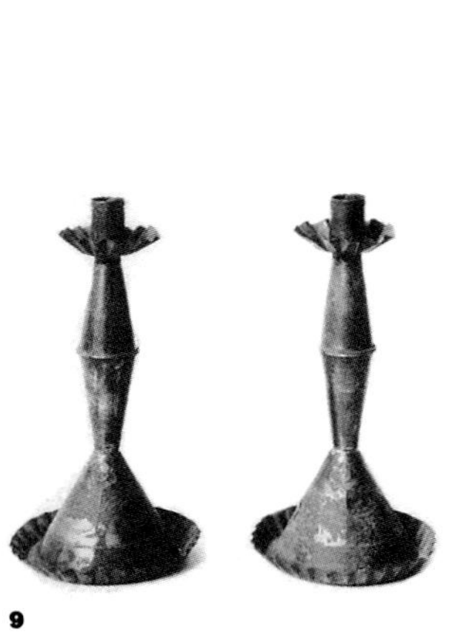

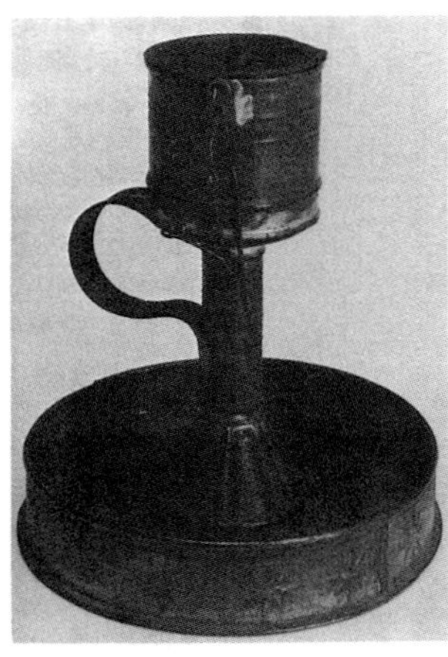

9   10

9   PAIR OF CANDLESTICKS
1780–1810

Tin over sheet iron. Lapped and soldered joints. Conical bases with crimped rim are decorated with Tudor rose and foliage in punchwork. Shafts in two units joined in raised and folded seam. Candle sockets and crimped bobeches soldered to shaft.

Height 27.8 cm (11″)

Titus C. Geesey Collection. 58-110-47a,b

10   LAMP
1780–1820

Tin over sheet iron. Soldered joints. Removable oil container with central tube for wick fits into cylinder mounted on candlestick stem. Wick pick on chain. Embossed stars on base with wire rim.

16.5 x 14.6 cm (6½ x 5¾″)

Titus C. Geesey Collection. 54-85-124

11   HANGING BOX
1780–1820

Tin over sheet iron. Folded and soldered joints. Cylindrical box has hinged lid with rolled wire edge and two hanging straps. Scrolled hasp. Decorated with embossed lines on body and lid. Probably used to store candles.

22.2 x 33.7 cm (8¾ x 13¼″)

Gift of Mrs. William D. Frishmuth. 02-98

12   PAIR OF WALL SCONCES
1780–1820

Painted tin over sheet iron. Soldered joints. Inverted heart-shaped reflector plate with crimped edges decorated with punched tulips and foliage. Candle sockets in crimp-edged bobeche soldered to curved arm. Painted blue green.

Left 28.2 x 20.5 cm (11⅛ x 8⅛″)
Right 27.3 x 19.7 cm (10¾ x 7¾″)

Titus C. Geesey Collection. 58-110-37a,b

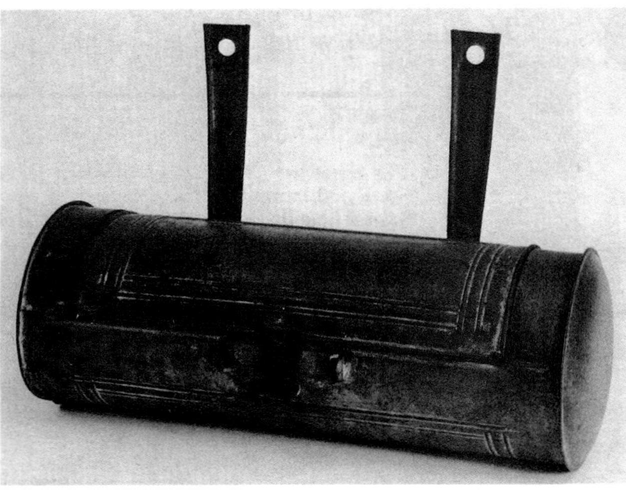

11

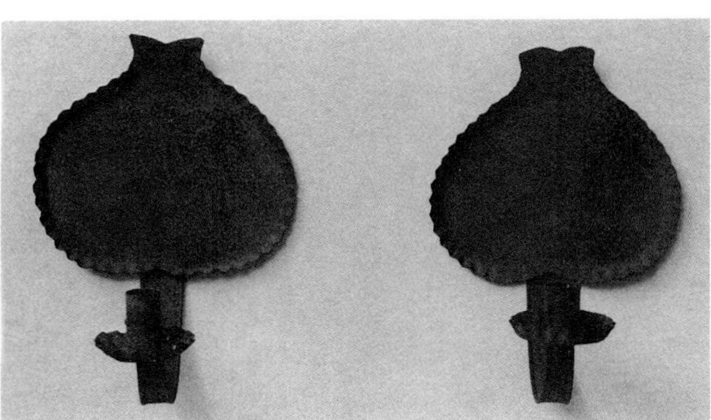

12

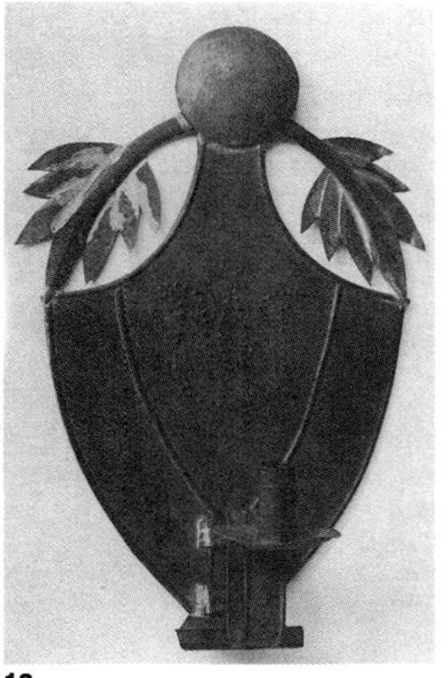
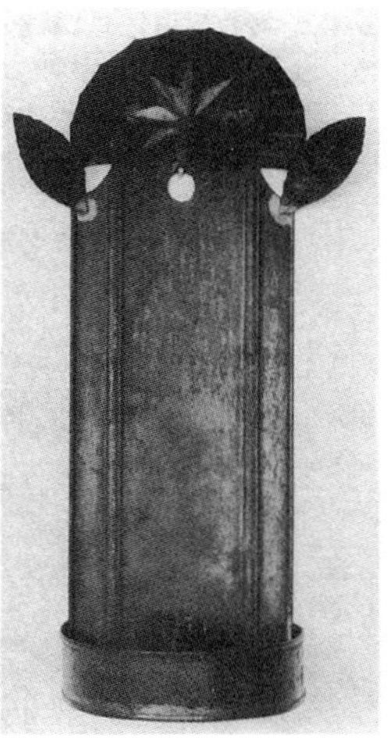

13

15

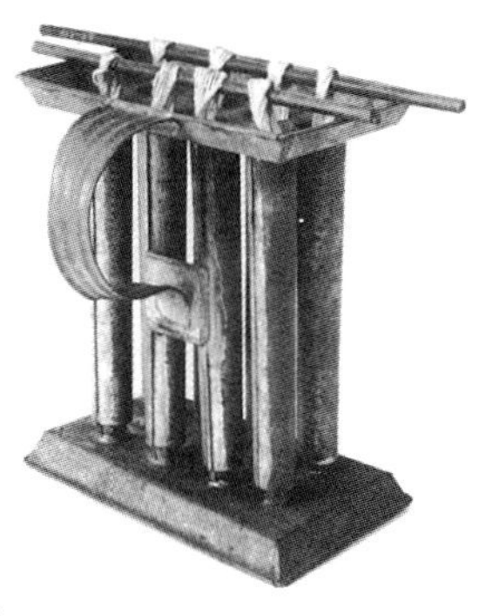

14

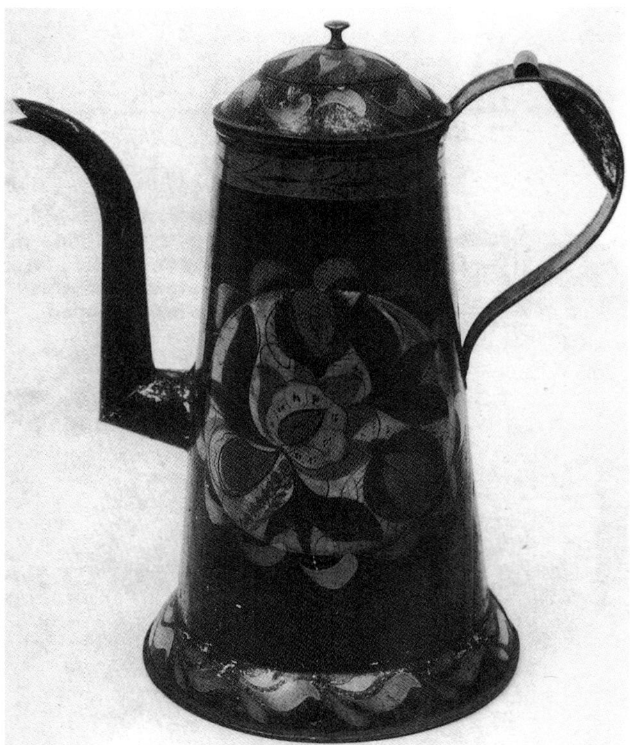

16

13 WALL SCONCE
1780–1820

Tin over sheet iron, copper. Lapped and soldered joints. Shield-shaped wall plate has wire edge; embossed decoration and punchwork tulip. Flattened ball finial in copper is soldered to top. S-curved arm of candleholder slips into two tin brackets on wall plate. Probably a church sconce.

40.6 x 24.6 cm (16 x 9⅝″)

Gift of Mrs. William D. Frishmuth. 02-91

14 CANDLE MOLD
1780–1820

Tin over sheet iron, wood. Folded, lapped, and soldered construction. Eight molds with wood wick holders at top and standing base.

19.6 x 19.2 cm (7¾ x 7½″)

Gift of Mrs. William D. Frishmuth. 02-79

15 WALL SCONCE
1780–1820

Tin over sheet iron. Soldered joints. Applied-tin ornamentation of leaves and eight-pointed star. Embossed vertical lines. Crimped edge on smoke deflector, hanging hole.

34.1 x 12.5 cm (13⅜ x 4⅞″)

Titus C. Geesey Collection. 54-85-125

16 COFFEEPOT
1780–1840

Painted tin over sheet iron, brass. Soldered joints. Hinged lid with brass finial; reinforced handle with lid guard; crooked spout; flanged base. Painted dark brown with decoration of red, green, yellow, and black fruits and flowers on white circle. Yellow band below lid and yellow fillips. Similar to imported English wares.

26.7 x 25.4 cm (10½ x 10″)

Titus C. Geesey Collection. 54-85-102

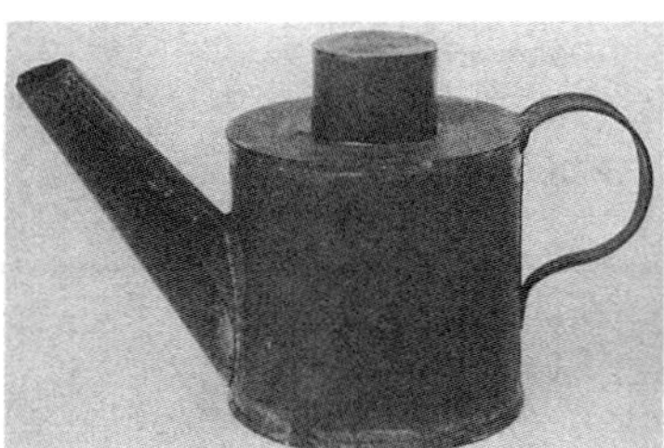

17

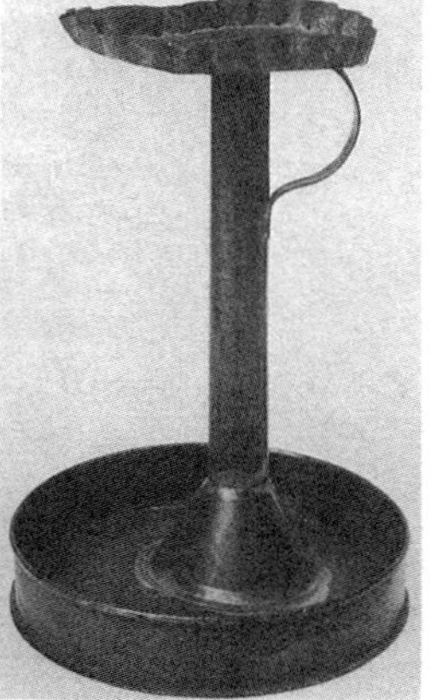

18

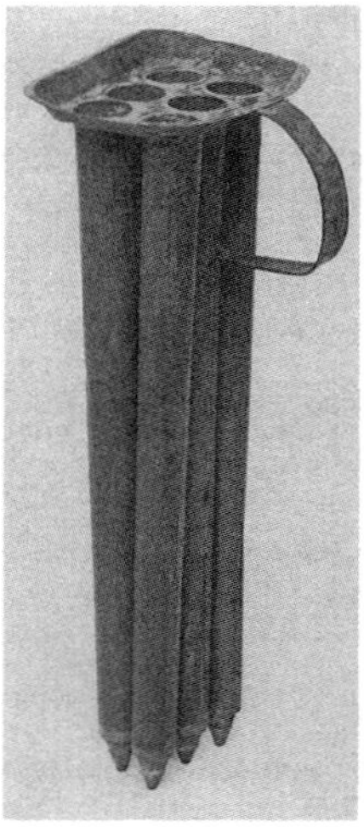

17 OIL LAMP
1780–1840

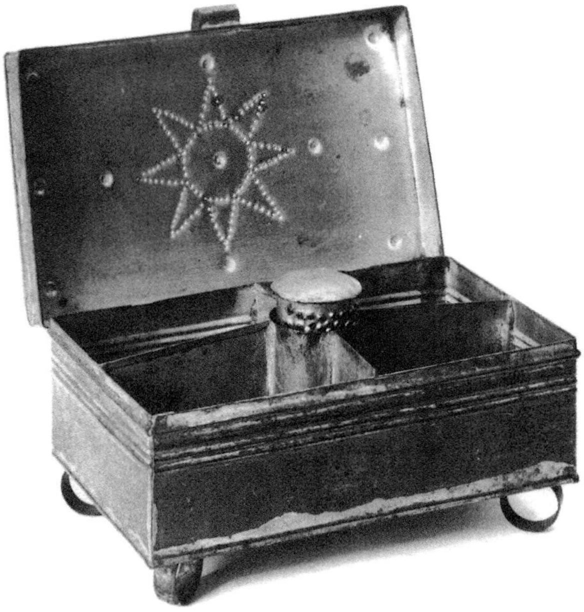

Tin over sheet iron. Lapped and soldered joints. Looped handle, straight spout, and fitted cap. Spout held wick, can held oil.

11.8 x 20 cm (4⅝ x 7⅞")

Gift of Mrs. William D. Frishmuth. 02-86

18 LAMP STAND
1780–1850

Tin over sheet iron. Soldered joints. Base has wire edge, looped handle is soldered, holder has crimped edge.

Height 21.4 cm (8⅜"), diameter 15 cm (5⅞")

Gift of Mrs. William D. Frishmuth. 02-123

19 CANDLE MOLD
1800–1820

Tin over sheet iron. Soldered joints. Six molds suspended from raised collar. Designed to be plunged into cold water to set wax.

26.4 x 10.5 cm (10⅜ x 4⅛")

Gift of Mrs. William D. Frishmuth. 02-80

20 DOUBLE WALL SCONCE
1800–1820

Tin over sheet iron. Lapped and soldered joint. Rectangular back has crimped smoke protector with hanging hole. Embossed decoration of vertical and zigzag lines. Drip pan with crimped edge holds candle sockets.

33.1 x 17.4 cm (13 x 6⅞")

Titus C. Geesey Collection. 53-125-15

19   **20**

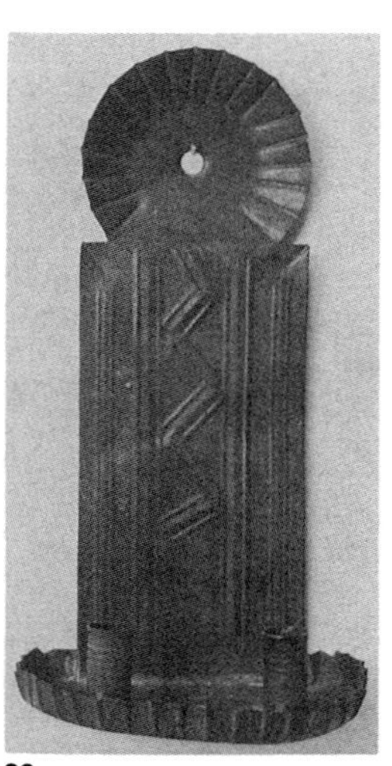

21

21 SPICE BOX
Berks or Lancaster County
1800–1820

Tin over sheet iron. Soldered joints. Raised, molded banding around top edge; looped feet. Cylindrical compartment holds punched-tin grater. Lid decorated with eight-pointed star and ten dots in raised punchwork; looped handle on front.

8.2 x 14.7 x 9.4 cm (3¼ x 5¾ x 3¾")

Gift of Miss Marie E. Bucher, in memory of Mrs. William Hipple and Mrs. David H. Bucher. 39-35-6

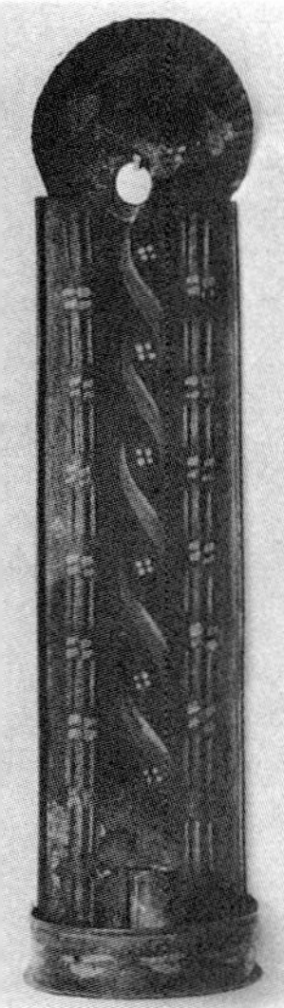 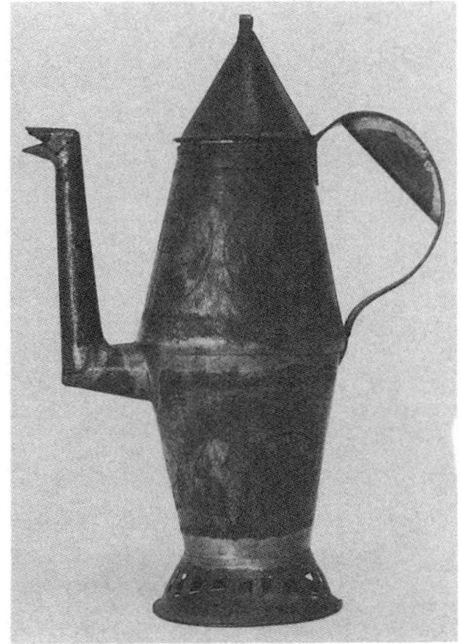

22   23

22 WALL SCONCE
1800–1840

Painted tin over sheet iron. Soldered joints. Crimped edge on smoke deflector with hanging hole. Painted black with dashes in red on base rim and between embossed lines; guilloche in green and yellow.

33.1 x 7 cm (13 x 2¾")

Titus C. Geesey Collection. 54-85-31

23 COFFEEPOT
1800–1840

Tin over sheet iron. Lapped and soldered joints. Body in two units. Reinforced handle; conical, hinged lid with double-looped finial; spout with double crook; pierced, flanged base. Wrigglework design of stemmed tulips and foliage. By same hand as no. 24.

24.7 x 16.5 cm (9¾ x 6½")

Titus C. Geesey Collection. 54-85-127

24 CREAM JUG
1800–1840

Tin over sheet iron. Lapped and soldered joints. Body in two units. Looped handle, crimped spout, flanged base. Wrigglework decoration of tasseled festoons on flange, tulips and leaves on lower body (partly obliterated by repair and burnishing); tulips, daisy, and hen on upper body. By same hand as no. 23.

12.1 x 12.7 cm (4¾ x 5")

Titus C. Geesey Collection. 54-85-128

25 ASH PROTECTOR
1800–1850

Tin over sheet iron. Soldered joints, rolled edges. Looped handle with rolled edge riveted to side. Wrigglework designs of bird, chickens, and ducks; pierced diamond shapes. Controlled draft on coals or held coals overnight.

8.9 x 35 x 19 cm (3½ x 13¾ x 7½")

Gift of Mrs. Donald Hobart. 52-94-1

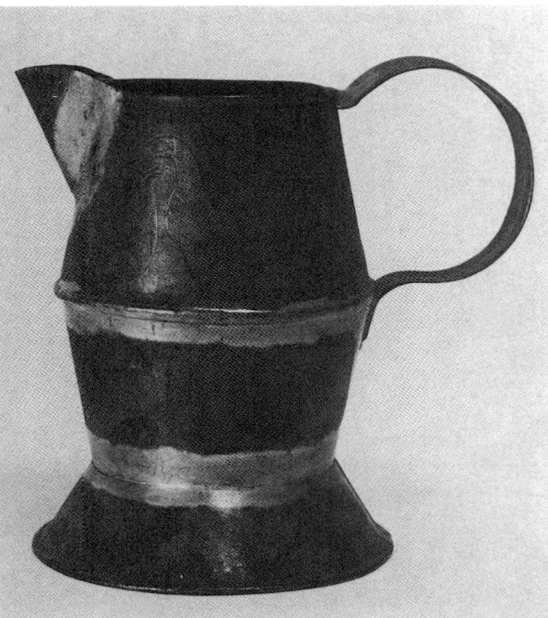

24

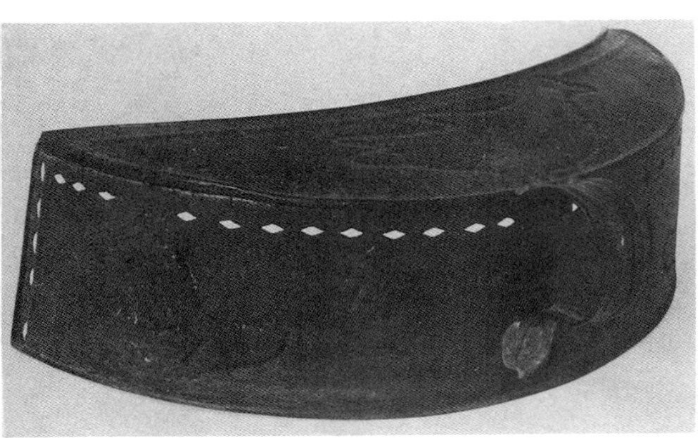

25

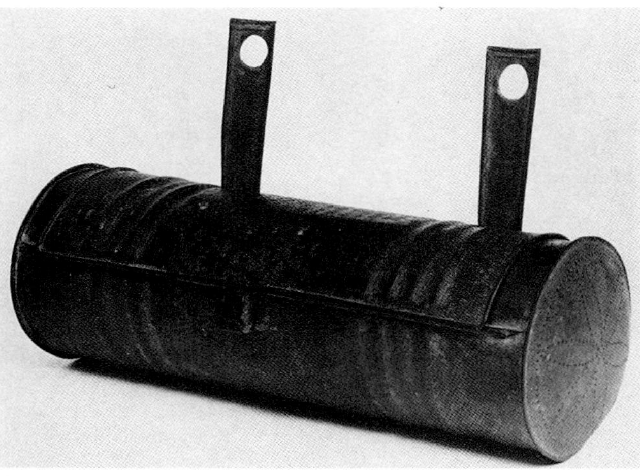

26

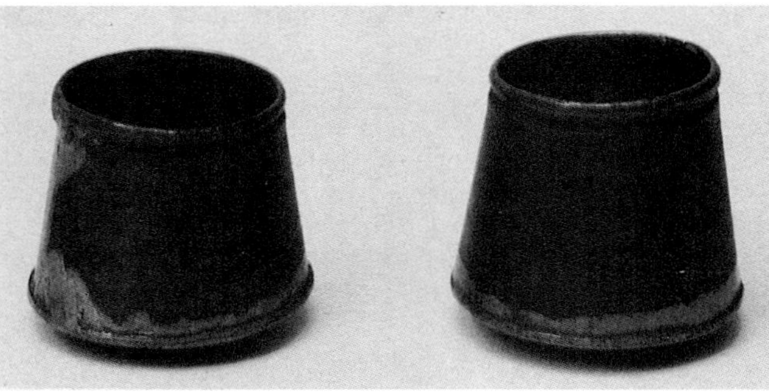

27

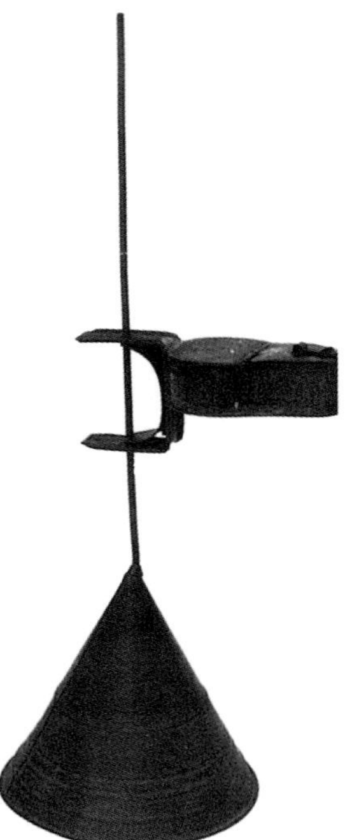

28

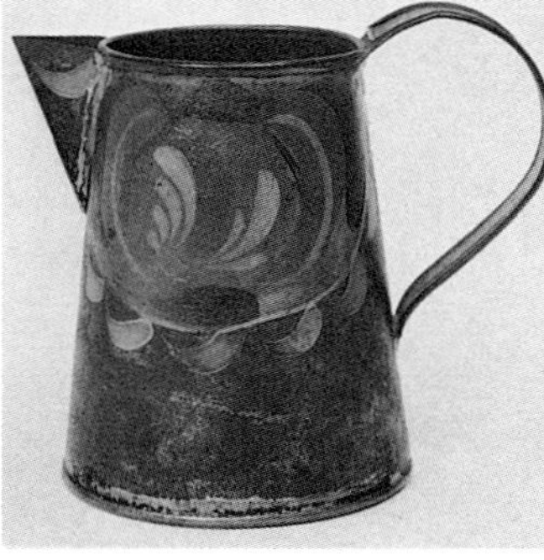

29

26 HANGING BOX
1800–1850

Tin over sheet iron. Soldered joints. Cylindrical box has hinged lid with edge rolled over wire. Scrolled hasp and two hanging straps. Slightly convex ends decorated with punchwork design of six-petaled star in circle Probably used to store candles.

22.2 x 33.7 cm (8¾ x 13¼")

Gift of J. Stogdell Stokes. 37-13-5

27 CUPS (2)
1800–1850

Tin over sheet iron. Folded and soldered joints. Possibly for medicinal use or cupping.

Height 4.2 cm (1⅝"), diameter 4.5 cm (1¾")

Gift of H. K. Deisher. 14-296,a

28 LAMP AND STAND
1800–1850

Tin over sheet iron, iron. Lapped and soldered joints. Conical base weighted with sand has embossed line decoration. Lamp has hinged lid and wick channel. Well is soldered to two arms that slide on iron shaft when spring is released.

58.6 x 16 cm (23⅛ x 6¼")

Gift of Mrs. William D. Frishmuth. 02-104

29 CREAM JUG
1810–40

Painted tin over sheet iron. Soldered joints. Handle has wire edges. Painted black with red yellow, and green decoration.

9.2 x 12.1 cm (3⅝ x 4¾")

Purchased: Special Museum Fund. 16-314

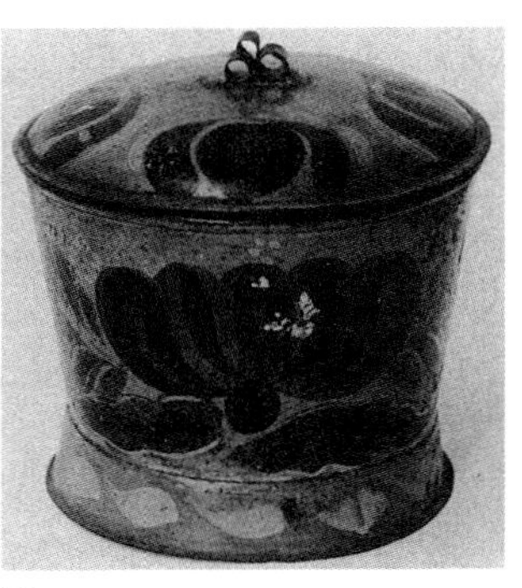

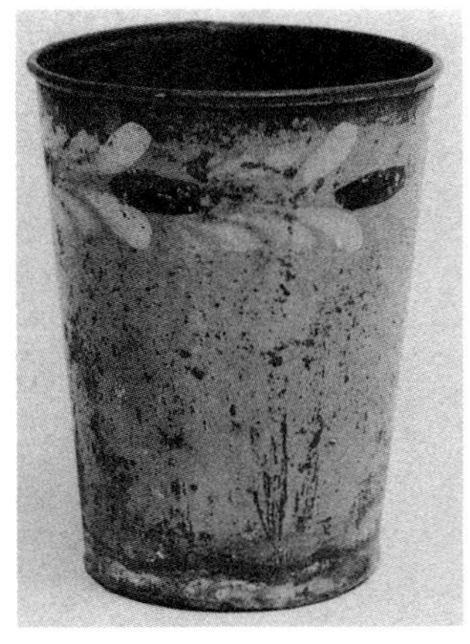

30

31

30 SUGAR BOX
1810–40

Painted tin over sheet iron. Soldered joints, folded edges. Fitted lid has looped, ribbonlike finial; attached flanged base. Painted red with black, gray, and yellow flower on one side. Yellow fillips on base.

10.1 x 10.5 cm (4 x 4⅛")

Titus C. Geesey Collection. 54-85-103a,b

31 TUMBLER
1810–40

Painted tin over sheet iron. Soldered bottom, wire rim. Painted red with yellow and black border.

Height 9.2 cm (3⅝"), diameter 7.6 cm (3")

Titus C. Geesey Collection. 54-85-106

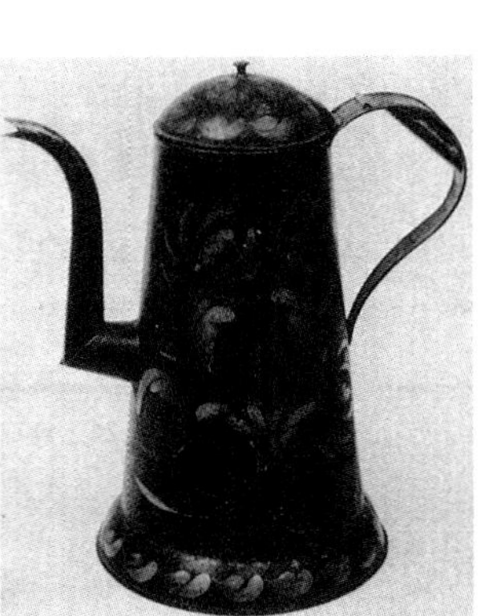

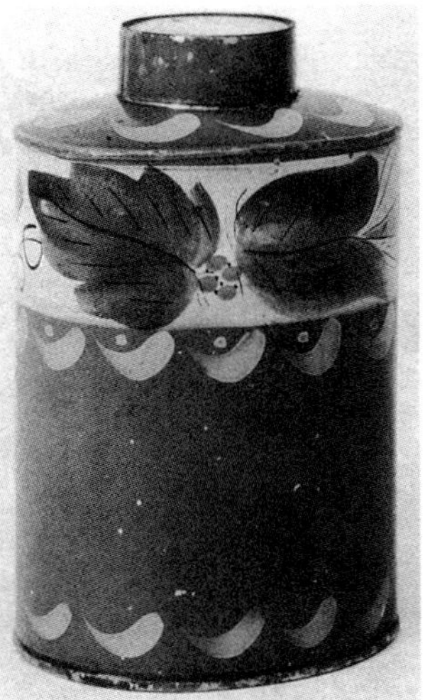

32

33

32 COFFEEPOT
1810–40

Painted tin over sheet iron. Soldered joints. Hinged lid with finial; reinforced handle with lid guard; crooked spout; flanged base. Painted black with asphaltum, decorated with red flowers and vines.

27.3 x 24.1 cm (10¾ x 9½")

Purchased: Special Museum Fund. 16-238

33 TEA CADDY
Probably Berks County
1810–40

Painted tin over sheet iron. Soldered joints. Cap fitted over short neck. Painted red with band of green leaves on yellow ground, yellow fillips.

13.2 x 8.7 cm (5¼ x 3⅜")

Purchased: Annual Membership Fund. 16-269

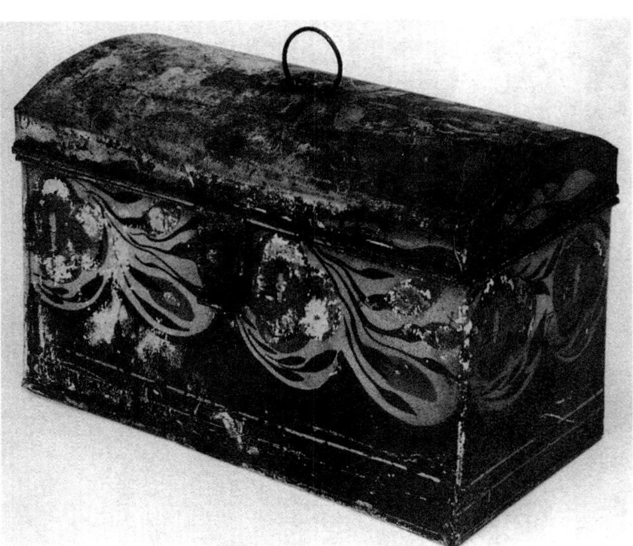

34

34 BOX
Probably Bucks County
1810–40

Painted tin over sheet iron. Soldered joints. Raised, curved lid with wire edges and pull. Painted brown with yellow lines. Roses, buds, and foliage in red and green on cream ground on three sides.

14.7 x 23.1 x 10.8 cm (5¾ x 9⅛ x 4¼")

Purchased: Special Museum Fund. 16-301

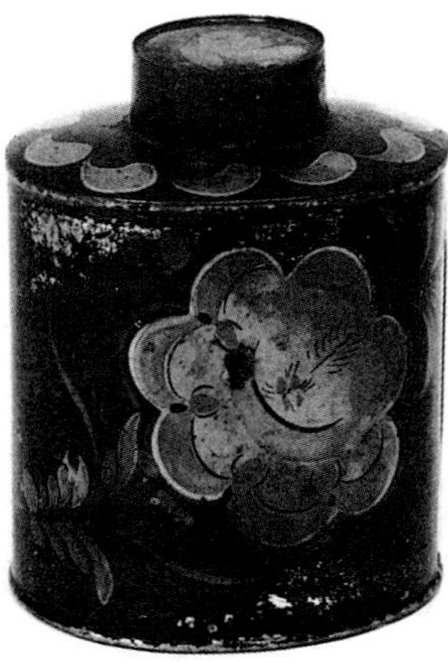

35

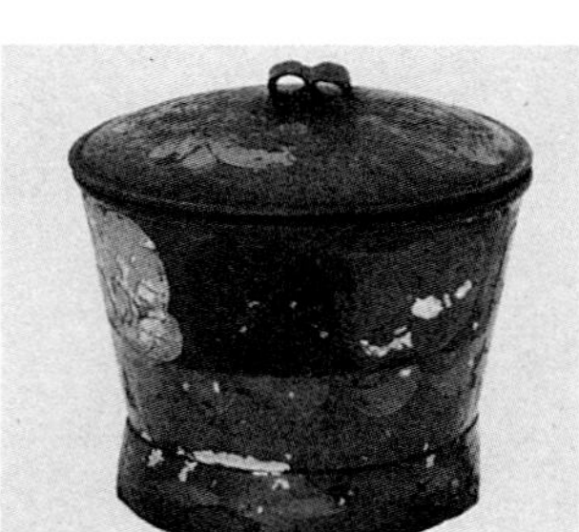

36

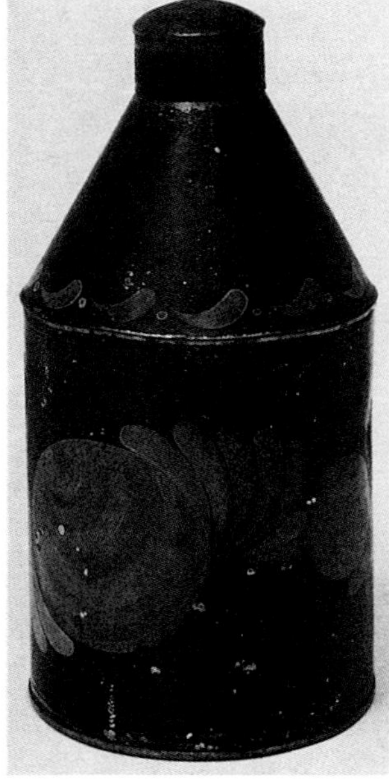

37

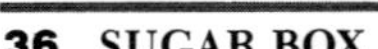

35　TEA CADDY
1810–40

Painted tin over sheet iron. Soldered joints. Cap fitted over short neck. Painted black with red, green, and yellow floral decoration.

11.5 x 8.4 cm (4½ x 3¼")

Purchased: Special Museum Fund. 16-313

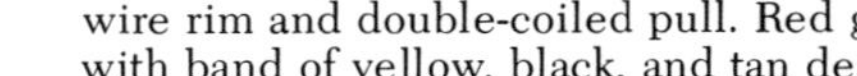

36　SUGAR BOX
Probably Bucks County
1810–40

Painted tin over sheet iron. Soldered joints. Bottom flange soldered to container. Lid has wire rim and double-coiled pull. Red ground with band of yellow, black, and tan designs. Yellow fillips and whorl.

Height 9.5 cm (3¾"), diameter base 8.5 cm (3⅜")

Purchased: Annual Membership Fund. 16-268

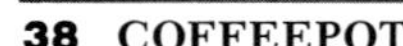

37　CANNISTER
1810–40

Painted tin over sheet iron. Soldered joints. Body in two pieces. Fitted lid with domed cover. Painted dark brown with yellow fillips and designs in red, yellow, and green.

Height 21.6 cm (8½"), diameter 10.1 cm (4")

Titus C. Geesey Collection. 54-85-105a,b

38　COFFEEPOT
1810–40

Painted tin over sheet iron. Soldered joints. Domed, hinged lid with finial; reinforced handle with lid guard; crooked spout; flanged base. Painted red with layered stenciling of white, blue, and yellow flowers and green foliage. Translucent banding over decoration at neck and base.

Height 27.3 cm (10¾"), diameter 15.9 cm (6¼")

Gift of R. Wistar Harvey. 40-16-737

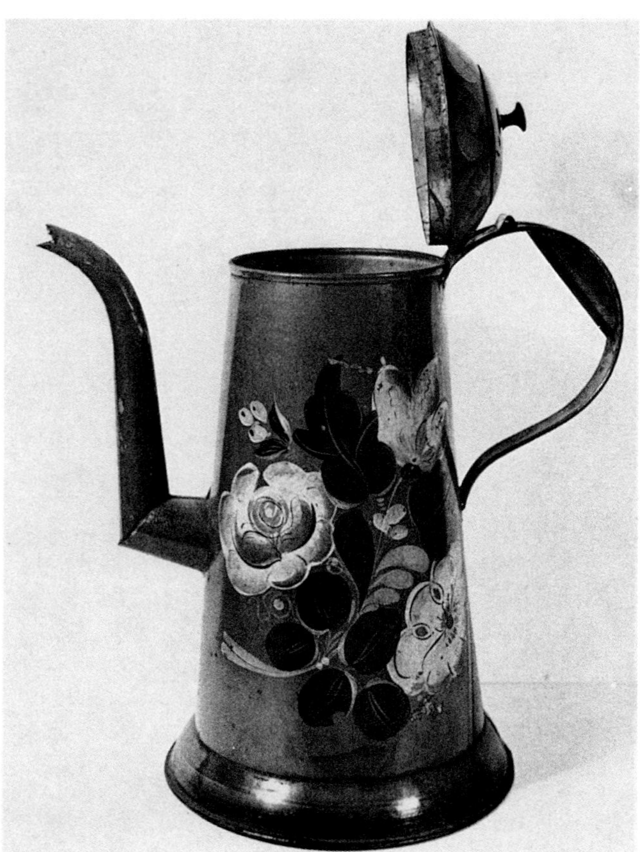

38

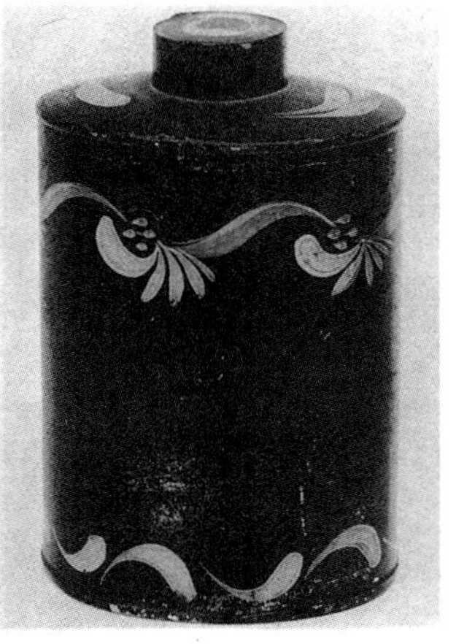
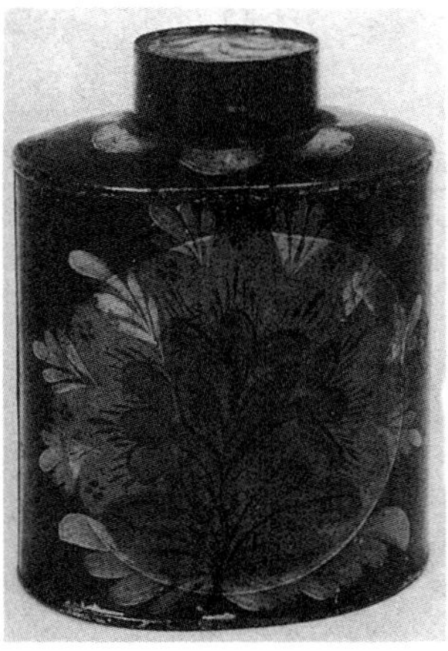

42   40

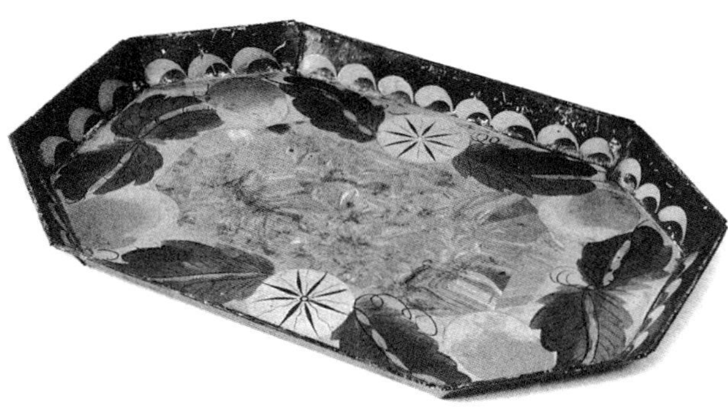

41

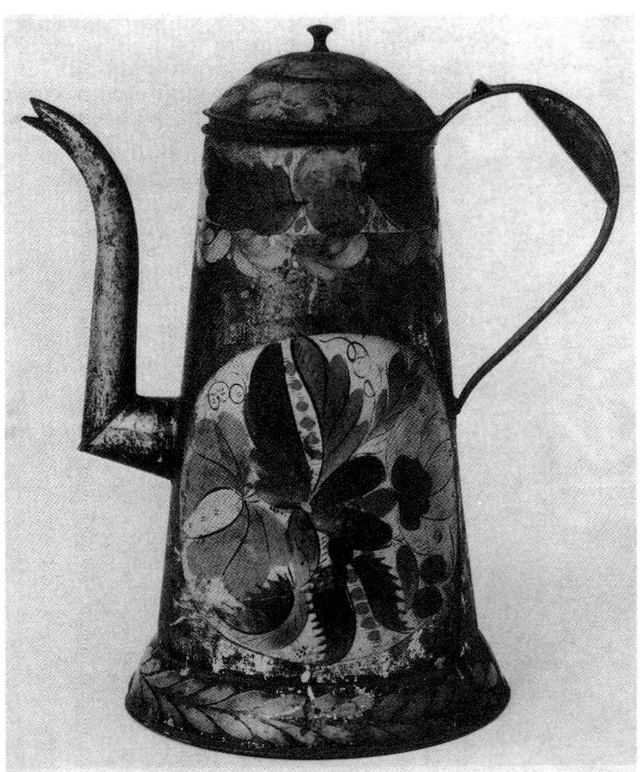

39

39 COFFEEPOT
1810–40

Painted tin over sheet iron. Soldered joints. Hinged lid with finial; crooked spout; flanged base; reinforced handle with lid guard. Painted brown with green, yellow, and red foliage on white circle. Banding of flowers around rim and lid; stenciled leaf border around base.

29.5 x 23.9 cm (11⅝ x 9⅜″)

Gift of Mrs. William D. Frishmuth. 02-481

40 TEA CADDY
1810–40

Painted tin over sheet iron. Soldered joints. Cap fitted over short neck. Painted dark brown with red and green foliage with black details on gray and white design.

Height 10.8 cm (4¼″), diameter 8.9 cm (3½″)

Titus C. Geesey Collection. 54-85-108a,b

41 TRAY
1820–40

Painted tin over sheet iron. Raised, flaring rim with wire edge. Painted dark brown in crystalized technique on octagonal center panel; border of fruit, leaves, and stars in red, yellow, brown, and green blue on ivory with black detailing. Yellow fillips on rim.

30.1 x 21.6 cm (11⅞ x 8½″)

Titus C. Geesey Collection. 54-85-100

42 TEA CADDY
1820–40

Painted tin over sheet iron. Soldered joints. Cap fitted over short neck. Painted black with scrolls in yellow, green, and red.

13 x 8.6 cm (5⅛ x 3⅜″)

Purchased. 14-203

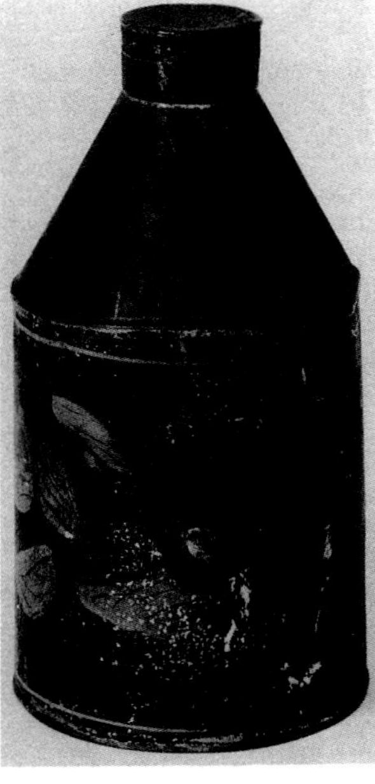

43

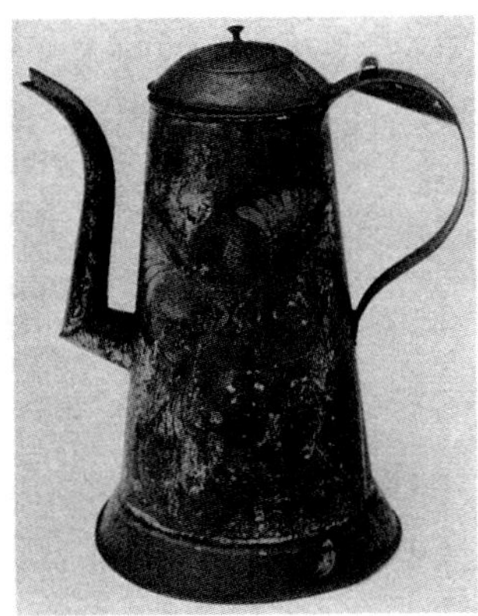

44

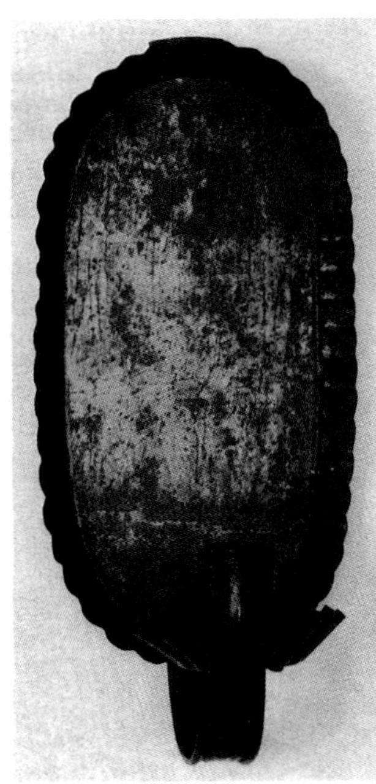

45

46

43 TEA CADDY
1820–40

Painted tin over sheet iron. Lapped and soldered joints. Cap fitted over short neck. Body in two parts. Painted black with stenciled decoration of fruit and leaves in red, green, grey, and pink.

Height 19.1 cm (7½"), diameter 10.6 cm (4⅛")

Purchased: Special Museum Fund. 16-303

44 COFFEEPOT
1820–40

Painted tin over sheet iron. Soldered joints. Domed lid with finial; crooked spout; reinforced handle with lid guard; flanged base. Painted metallic brown with design of apples and leaf forms in red and yellow.

25.4 x 25.4 cm (10 x 10")

Purchased: Special Museum Fund. 16-312

45 COFFEEPOT
1820–50

Painted tin over sheet iron. Soldered joints. Hinged lid with finial; reinforced handle with lid guard; crooked spout; flanged base. Painted red with banding of flowers and fruits in red, yellow, and green on white.

26.5 x 25.3 cm (10⅜ x 10")

Purchased: Special Museum Fund. 14-25

46 WALL SCONCE
1820–50

Tin over sheet iron. Soldered joints. Candleholder in fluted bobeche on curved arm soldered to back of wall plate with fluted rim.

27.9 x 14.1 cm (11 x 5½")

Gift of Mrs. William D. Frishmuth. 02-89

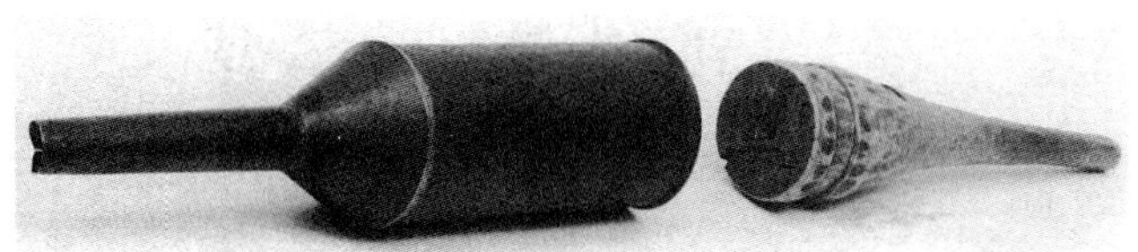

47

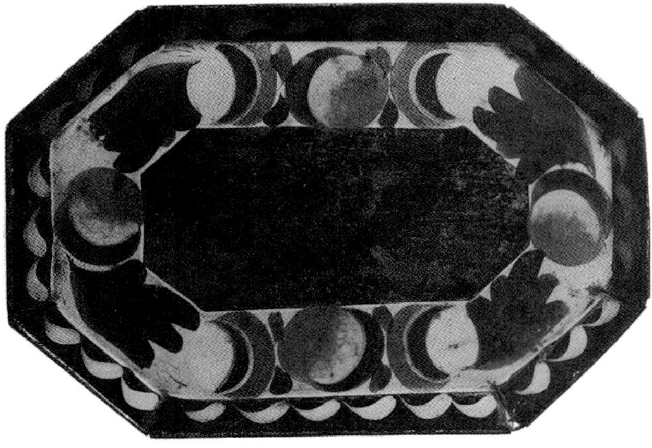

49

47 SAUSAGE GUN
1820–70

Tin over sheet iron, oak. Soldered joints. Cylinder soldered to funnel-shaped snout. Turned wood plunger has tapering handle. Sausage meat forced through long snout into packaging skins.

Length gun 32.5 cm (12¾″), plunger 28.7 cm (11¼″)

Gift of Mrs. William D. Frishmuth. 02-171a,b

48 SQUIRREL CAGE
1827

Inscribed on downspouts: *1827*

Painted tin over sheet iron. Lapped and soldered joints. House has round entrance to spoked, rotating cage. Air holes and slot for food and water at side of house opposite wheel. Front and sides painted red to simulate brick, door painted green and white; end of wheel painted red with six-pointed black star. Marbelized base.

30 x 49.5 x 18 cm (11⅞ x 19½ x 7⅛″)

Titus C. Geesey Collection. 54-85-68

49 TRAY
1830–50

Painted tin over sheet iron. Raised, flaring rim with wire edge. Painted black with dark brown rim with yellow fillips. Fruit painted red and yellow with green foliage on white band.

15.2 x 22.2 cm (6 x 8¾″)

Titus C. Geesey Collection. 54-85-101

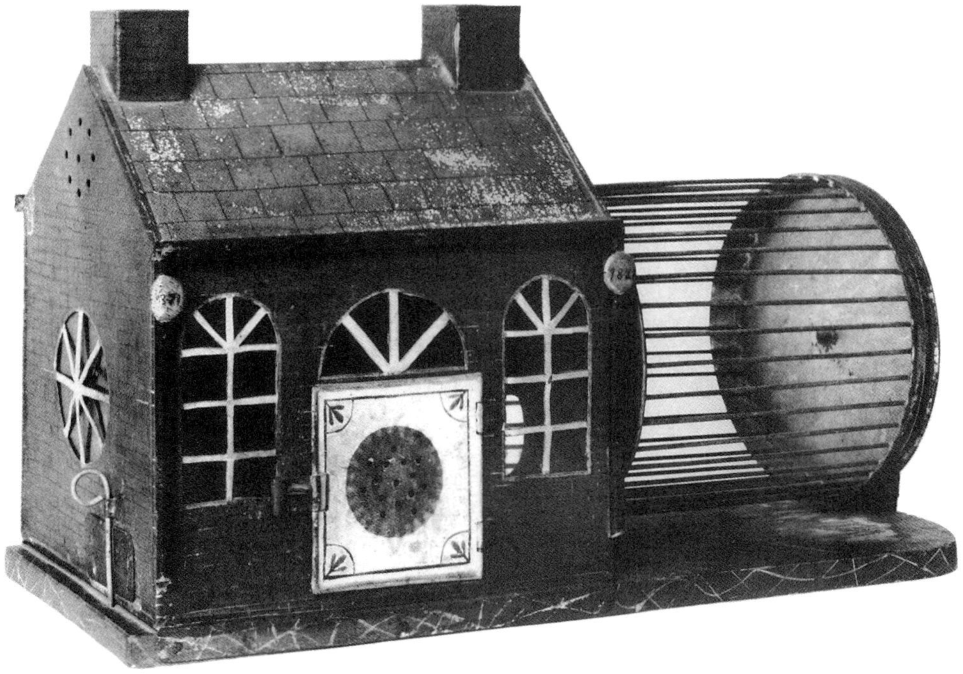

48

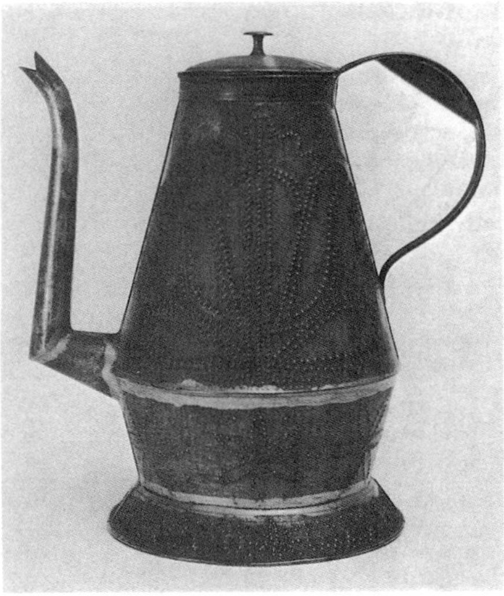

50

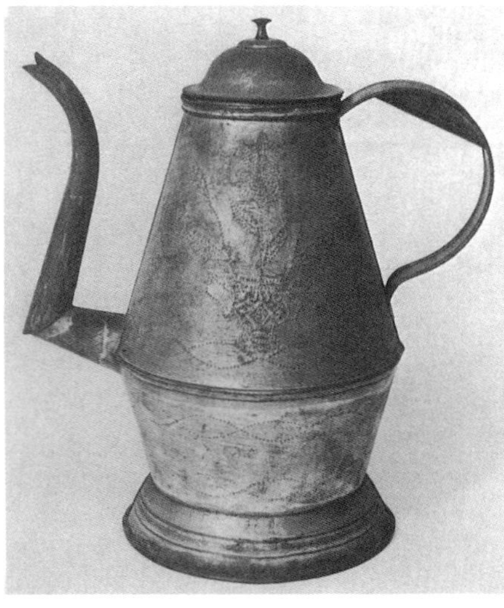

51

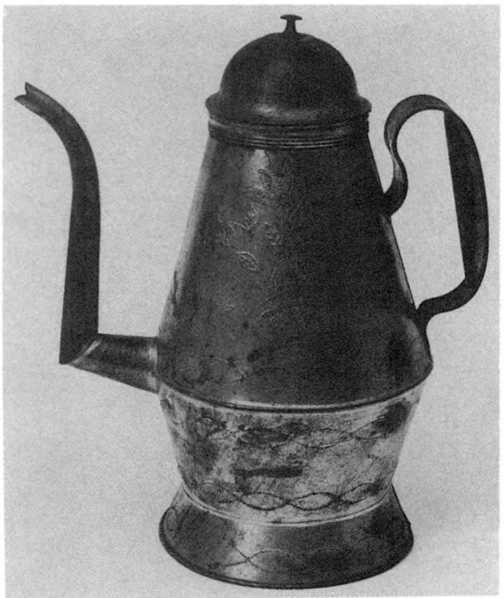

52

50 COFFEEPOT
Berks County
c. 1840

Attributed to **P. Shade**

Marked at top: *2R 1821*

Tin over sheet iron, brass. Soldered joints.
Body in two pieces. Lid with brass finial
hinged on wire of top rim; reinforced handle;
crooked spout; flanged base. Punchwork
design of stars, tulip and flowers, and circles.

29.2 x 28 cm (11½ x 11″)

Titus C. Geesey Collection. 54-85-126

---

51 COFFEEPOT
Berks County
c. 1840

Stamped on handle: *M. Uebele*

Tin over sheet iron, brass. Soldered joints.
Body in two parts. Lid with brass finial;
crooked spout; reinforced handle; flanged
base. Applied strip molding at upper rim.
Wrigglework decoration of tulip and flowers in
vase and three bands.

27.3 x 25.2 cm (10¾ x 9⅞″)

Purchased: Special Museum Fund. 16-280

---

52 COFFEEPOT
Berks County
c. 1840

J. Ketterer

Marked above spout: *S.B.   B.B.*
Impressed on handle: *J. Ketterer*

Tin over sheet iron, brass. Folded and soldered
joints. Body in two units. Crooked spout;
hinged lid with brass finial; reinforced handle;
flanged base. Reed banding applied at top.
Punchwork decoration of tulip and flowers in
vase and four bands.

28.8 x 25.9 cm (11⅜ x 10¼″)

Purchased: Special Museum Fund. 16-283

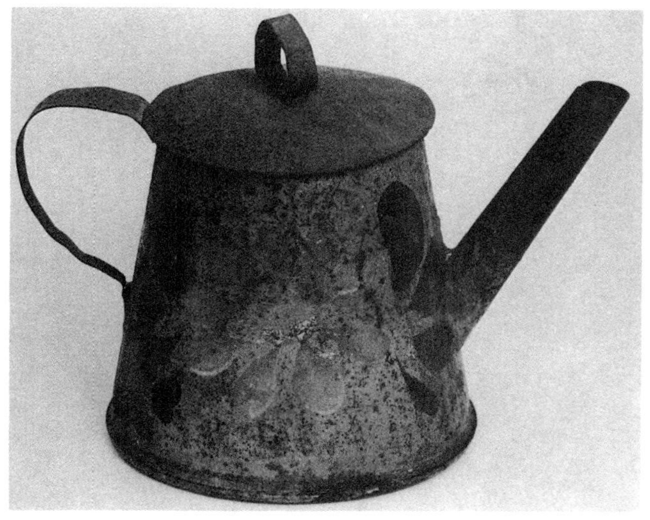

53

54

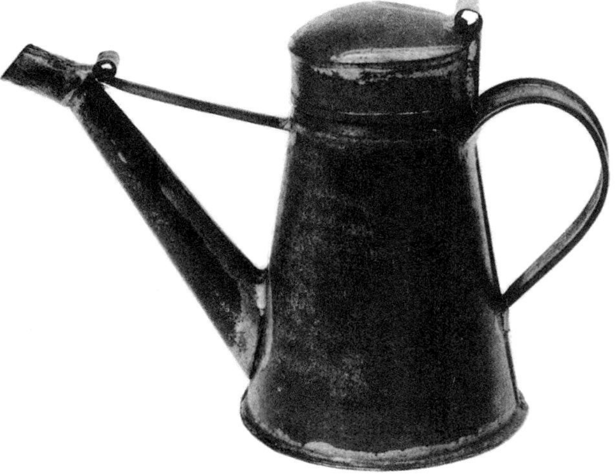

55

53 TEAPOT
1840–50

Painted tin over sheet iron. Soldered joints. Overlapping lid with loop finial, strap handle, straight spout. Painted red with pink, yellow, and green flowers. For child's use.

6.3 x 8.6 cm (2½ x 3⅜")

Purchased: Annual Membership Fund. 16-296

54 TRAY
Probably Berks County
1840–60

Painted tin over sheet iron. Raised, flaring rim with wire edge. Painted black with band of red cherries and green leaves on yellow ground.

21.8 x 31.7 cm (8⅝ x 12½")

Purchased: Special Museum Fund. 16-300

55 OILCAN
1840–70

Tin over sheet iron. Soldered joints. Hinged lid. Probably held melted lard or oil for grease lamps.

12.5 x 18.1 cm (4⅞ x 7⅛")

Gift of Mrs. William D. Frishmuth. 02-102

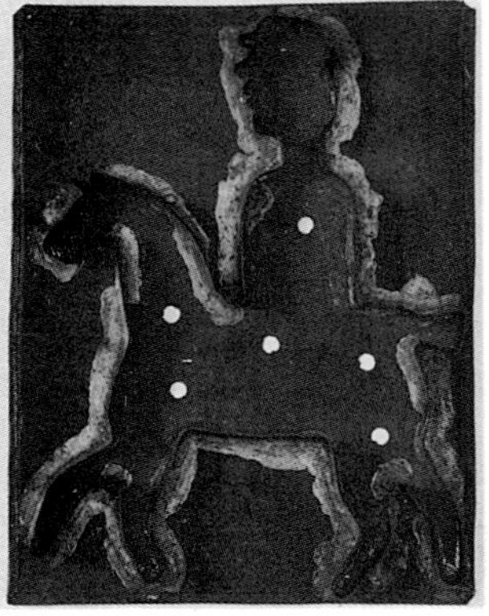

1

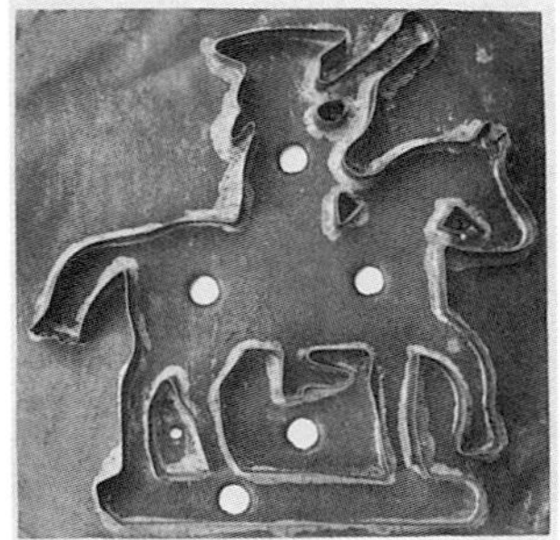

2

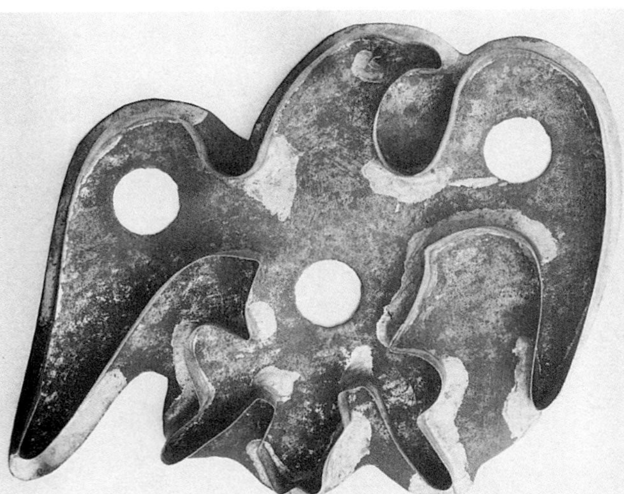

3

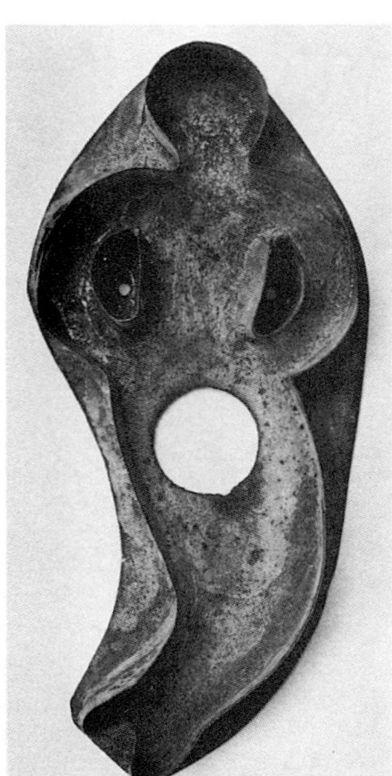

4

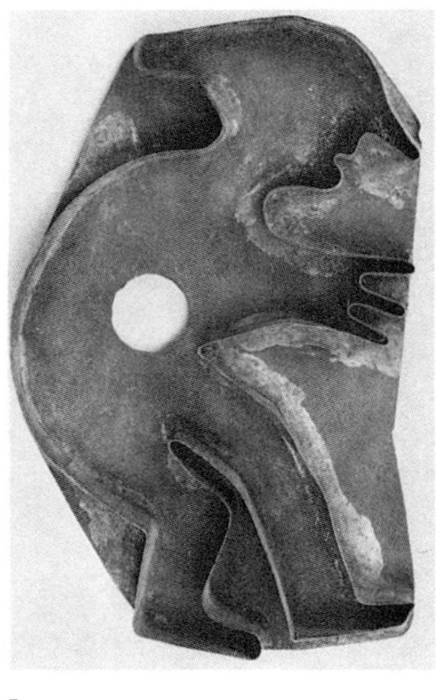

5

1 COOKIE CUTTER
1780–1810

Tinned sheet iron. Design outlined in strip
(1.6 cm wide) soldered to perforated
foundation. Folded edge. Man riding horse
with docked tail.

30.8 x 24.3 cm (12⅛ x 9½")

Gift of Mr. and Mrs. J. Stogdell Stokes. 33-70-9

2 COOKIE CUTTER
1790–1820

Tinned sheet iron. Design outlined in strip
(1.9 cm wide) soldered to perforated
foundation. Folded edge. Mounted man
blowing horn.

21.6 x 21.6 cm (8½ x 8½")

Titus C. Geesey Collection. 55-94-39

3 COOKIE CUTTER
1790–1840

Tinned sheet iron. Design outlined in strip
(1.6 cm wide) soldered to perforated
foundation. Folded edge. Mermaid.

14.6 x 7 cm (5¾ x 2¾")

Titus C. Geesey Collection. 55-94-46

4 COOKIE CUTTER
1800–1820

Tinned sheet iron. Design outlined in strip
(2.2 cm wide) soldered to perforated
foundation. Folded edge. Eagle.

14.3 x 18.4 cm (5⅝ x 7¼")

Titus C. Geesey Collection. 55-94-44

5 COOKIE CUTTER
1800–1840

Tinned sheet iron. Design outlined in strip
(1.6 cm wide) soldered to perforated
foundation. Folded edge. Belznickel.

17.5 x 11.8 cm (6⅞ x 4⅝")

Titus C. Geesey Collection. 55-94-45

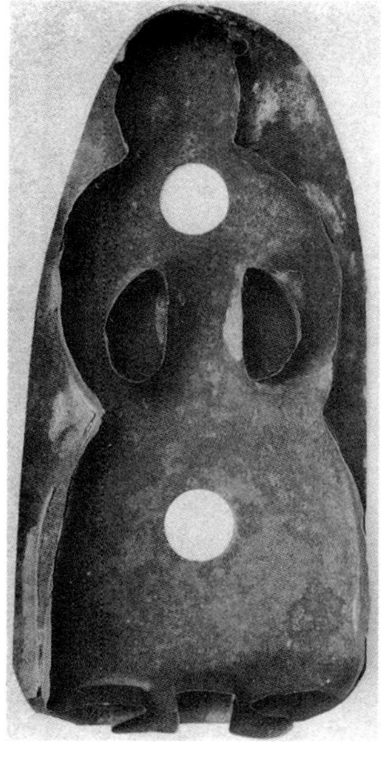

6

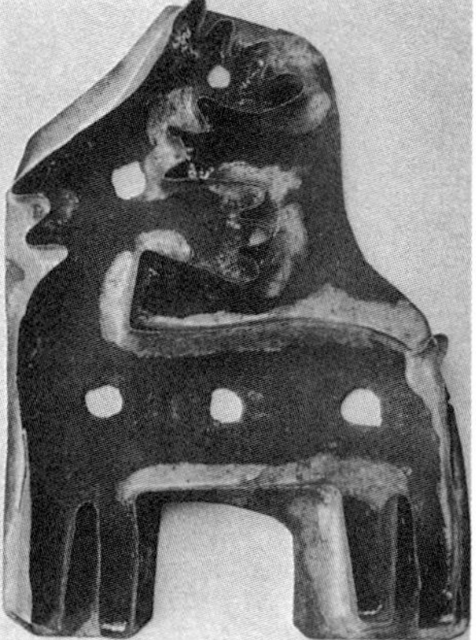

7

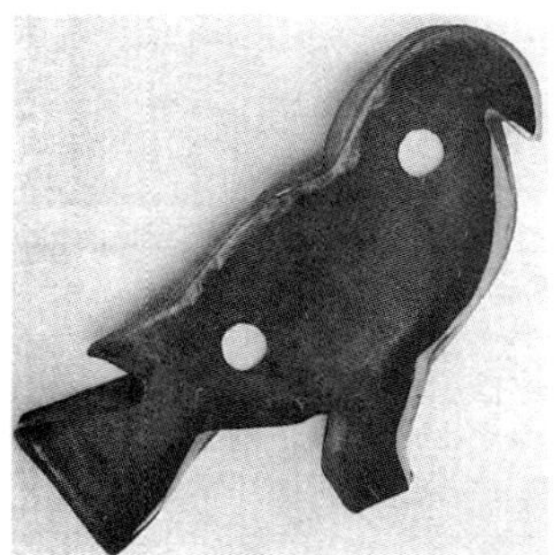

8

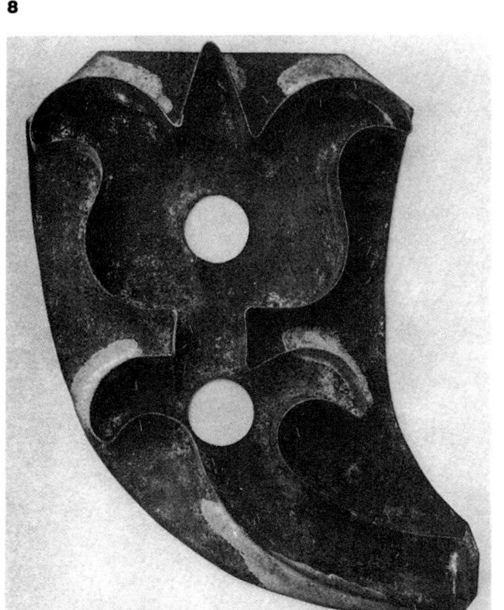

9

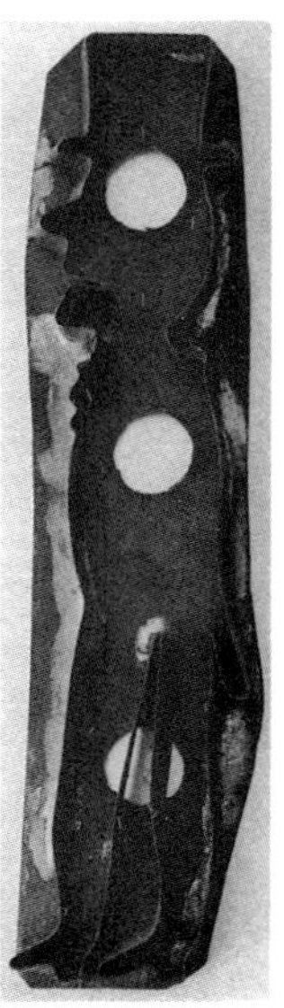

10

6 COOKIE CUTTER
1800–1840

Tinned sheet iron. Design outlined in strip (2.5 cm wide) soldered to perforated foundation. Cut edge. Coachman in bowler hat.

32.7 x 15.9 cm (12⅞ x 6¼″)

Titus C. Geesey Collection. 55-94-52

7 COOKIE CUTTER
1800–1840

Tinned sheet iron. Design outlined in strip (1.9 cm wide) soldered to perforated foundation. Cut edge. Reindeer or stag.

14.1 x 10.4 cm (5½ x 4⅛″)

Titus C. Geesey Collection. 55-94-48

8 COOKIE CUTTER
1800–1840

Tinned sheet iron. Design outlined in strip (1.6 cm wide) soldered to perforated foundation cut to shape. Cut edge. Parrot.

11.8 x 18.4 cm (4⅝ x 7¼″)

Titus C. Geesey Collection. 55-94-47

9 COOKIE CUTTER
1800–1840

Tinned sheet iron. Design outlined in strip (1.9 cm wide) soldered to perforated foundation. Cut edge. Tulip.

14.6 x 10.8 cm (5¾ x 4¼″)

Titus C. Geesey Collection. 55-94-42

10 COOKIE CUTTER
1820–50

Tinned sheet iron. Design outlined in strip (1.9 cm wide) soldered to perforated foundation. Folded edge. Man in top hat and formal attire.

19.7 x 4.8 cm (7¾ x 1⅞″)

Titus C. Geesey Collection. 55-94-41

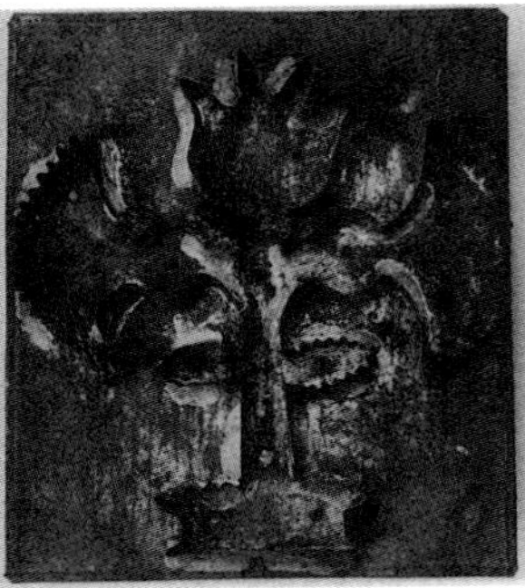

11

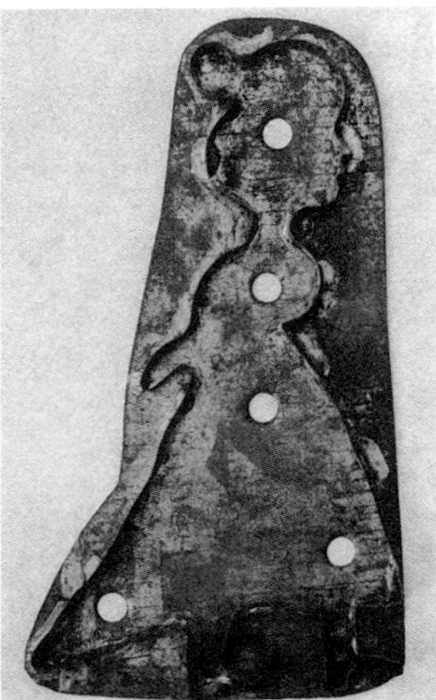

14   **12**

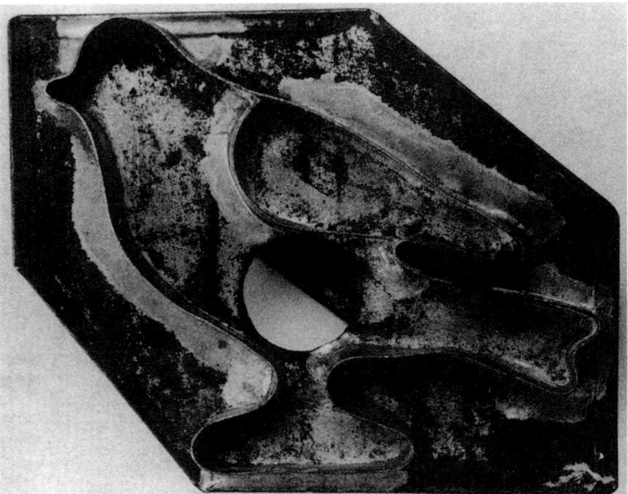

13

11 COOKIE CUTTER
1820–50

Tinned sheet iron. Design outlined in strip
(1.7 cm wide) soldered to perforated
foundation. Handle soldered to back. Folded
edge. Tulip and thistles in pot.

21.6 x 19.1 cm (8½ x 7½")

Titus C. Geesey Collection. 55-94-40

12 COOKIE CUTTER
1820–50

Tinned sheet iron. Design outlined in strip
(1.3 cm wide) soldered to perforated
foundation. Folded edge. Male figure,
possibly a trainman.

34.9 x 12.1 cm (13¾ x 4¾")

Titus C. Geesey Collection. 55-94-51

13 COOKIE CUTTER
1840–60

Tinned sheet iron. Design outlined in strip
(1.6 cm wide) soldered to perforated
foundation. Handle soldered to back.
Folded edge. Roosting bird.

7.3 x 9.5 cm (2⅞ x 3¾")

Titus C. Geesey Collection. 55-94-43

14 COOKIE CUTTER
1840–60

Tinned sheet iron. Design outlined in strip
(1.3 cm wide) soldered to perforated
foundation. Folded edge. Woman with hair
done up in a bun.

30.8 x 17.5 cm (12⅛ x 6⅞")

Titus C. Geesey Collection. 55-94-50

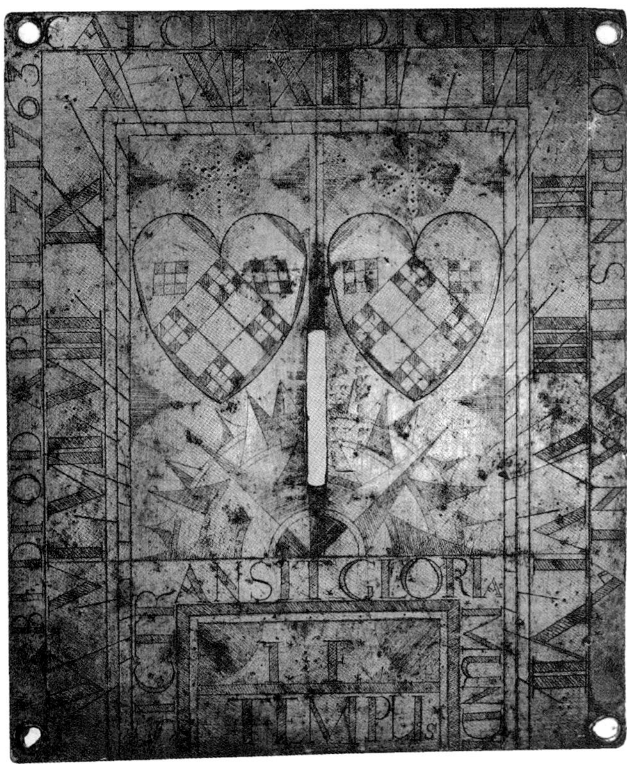

2

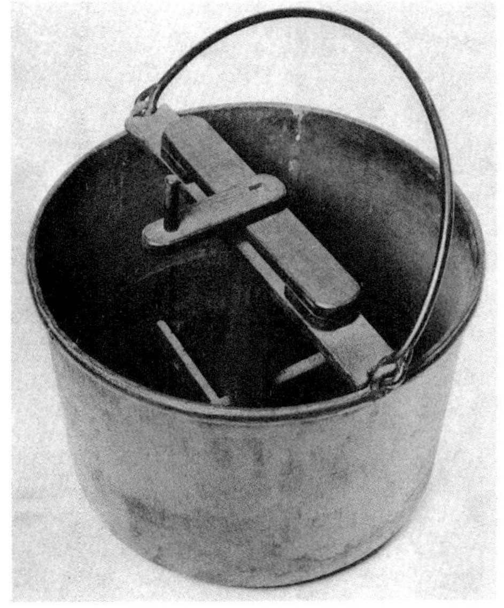

1

1   APPLE-BUTTER KETTLE
1750–1850

Copper, iron, wood. Copper kettle with deep sides. Circular iron rod at top secured with rivets. Iron handle secured to top rim. Crossed, perforated paddles rotate on round shaft suspended from wood frame fitted across kettle. Crank handle was pushed with long wood arm as kettle was suspended from lug pole over outside fire.

Height overall 73 cm (28¾"), height kettle 42.5 cm (16¾"), diameter 58.4 cm (23")

Gift of J. Stogdell Stokes. 28-10-15

2   SUNDIAL
Bedford, Bedford County
1763

Inscribed: *BEDFORD. APRIL 7. 1763. CALCULATED. FOR. LAT. 40. PENSILVANIA. V . . . XII, I . . . VII SIC. TRANSIT. GLORIA. MUNDI. I. F. TEMPUS*

Pewter. Wall-mounted dial, four corner holes for hanging, gnomon missing. Inscription and calibration engraved around edge with center pattern of two hearts and half of a compass rose.

26 x 21.6 cm (10¼ x 8½")

Titus C. Geesey Collection. 54-85-2

3   MUG
Philadelphia
1764–76

William Will

Marked inside bottom in serrated rectangle: *Wm WILL*

Molded pewter. Mug made in two pieces and assembled. Hollow handle soldered to body. Concentric skimming lines on bottom. Double incised circle around mark inside bottom.

11.5 x 13.8 cm (4½ x 5⅜")

Purchased: Annual Membership Fund. 15-222

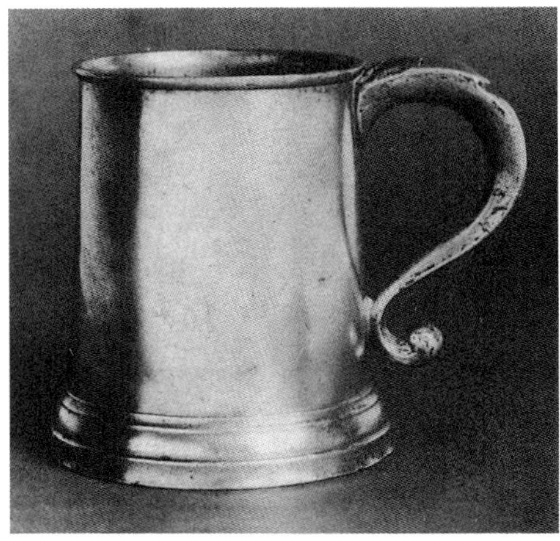

3

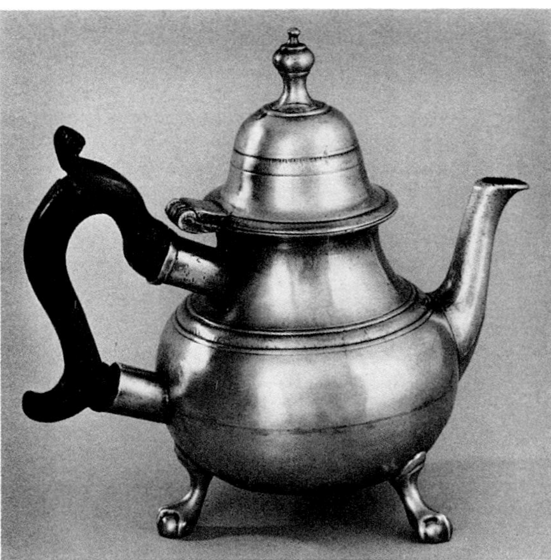

4

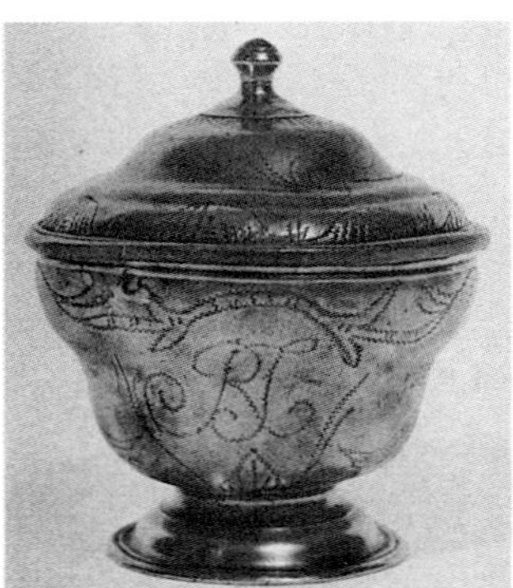

5

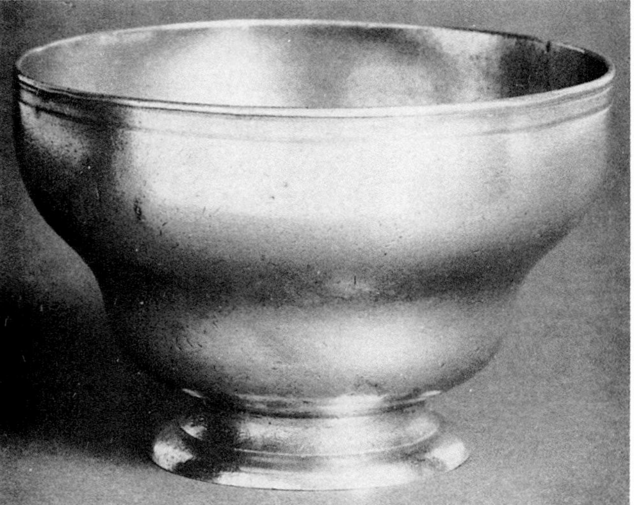

6

4   TEAPOT
Philadelphia
1764–76

William Will

Marked inside bottom in serrated rectangle:
X   Wm WILL

Molded pewter. Made of nine pieces
assembled and soldered. Wood handle an old
replacement. Feet restored.

16.7 x 17.2 cm (6½ x 6¾″) (without handle)

Gift of Lessing J. Rosenwald. 29-49-1

---

5   COVERED SUGAR BOWL
Philadelphia
1764–76

Attributed to **William Will**

Inscribed on sides: *RJ NJ*
Scratched on bottom: *RI*

Molded pewter. Body assembled from four
molded pieces. Lid knop and pedestal base
soldered. Wrigglework decoration of
serpentine stems and wavy banding on lid.
Bowl has bird with wings spread (eagle?)
and swan with wavy motif below molded
bands at top.

Height 12.1 cm (4¾″), diameter 11.4 cm (4½″)

Gift of Miss R. Annie Reeder. 96-244

---

6   SUGAR BOWL
Philadelphia
1764–80

Attributed to **William Will**

Inscribed on bottom: *ER*

Molded pewter. Bowl and foot made in two
molds and assembled. Pitted inside bowl; foot
possibly cut off at edge.

Height 7.2 cm (2⅞″), diameter 11 cm (4⅜″)

Gift of Mrs. Alfred Percival Smith. 28-95-411

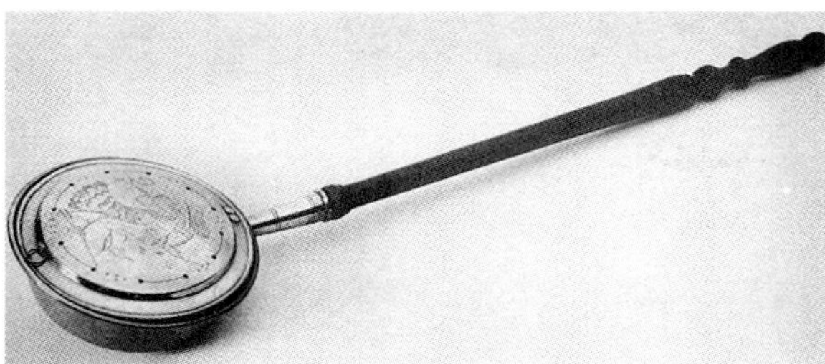

7

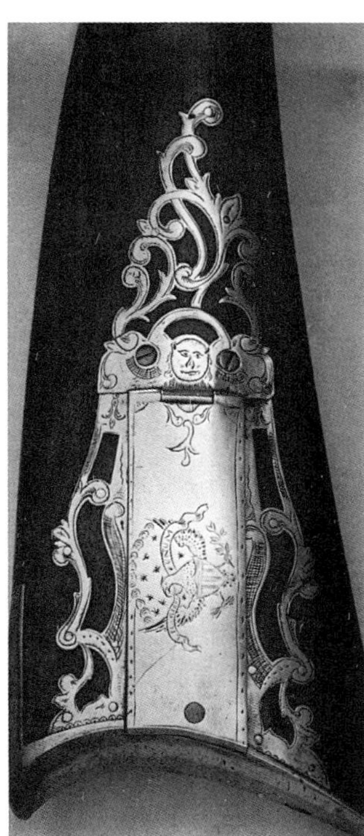

8 detail

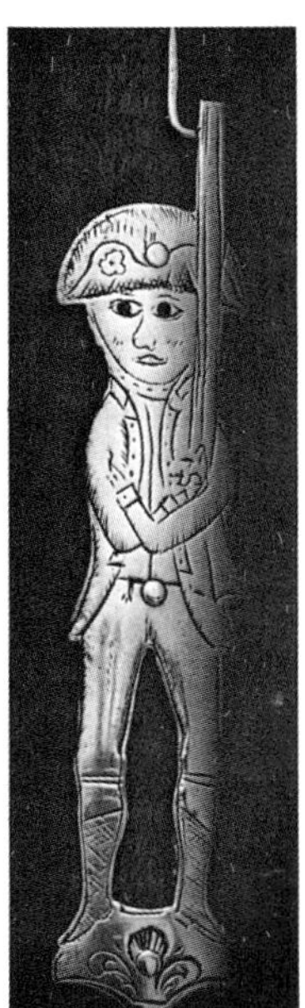

8 detail

8

8 detail

7 WARMING PAN
1770–1800

Brass, wood. Brass pan has rolled edge and attached collar. Hinged lid with wire pull decorated with engraved design of peacock, tulip, and foliage. Circling border designs of stamped squares over dots and quatrefoils alternate with pierced holes. Possibly of English manufacture for Pennsylvania market.

Length 108.6 cm (42¾″) (including handle), diameter 26.6 cm (10½″)

Titus C. Geesey Collection. 54-85-73

8 RIFLE
Germantown
c. 1780

Jacob Kuntz

Inscribed on barrel: *Jacob Kuntz;* on lock plate: *Parker and Co.;* on patchbox lid: *E Pluribus Unum*

Curly maple, brass, steel, silver, horn. Shaped maple stock inset with silver front sight and steel rear sight. Engraved on top of barrel between tang and rear sight is a hand holding a banner inscribed with maker's name. Engraved on sloping facets of barrel are eyes with scrolled cartouches. Scroll engraving on hammer. Trigger guard, butt plate, toe plate, lock-bolt plate and patchbox of brass. Patchbox engraved with shield-breasted eagle under nine stars with scrolled frame and lion's head. Inlaid each side of stock are engraved brass figures of Revolutionary soldiers holding muskets. Inlaid on cheekpiece is silver oval and eight-pointed star with engraved scrolls and borders. On each side of stock are three pairs of silver elliptical escutcheons for securing barrel wedges: two front pairs engraved, plain rear pair (probably replaced). Set into stock below cheekpiece is brass sleeve holding brass pin. Wooden ramrod (probably replaced) is carried under stock in brass piper.

Length 149 cm (58⅝″)

Titus C. Geesey Collection. 53-125-19

8 detail

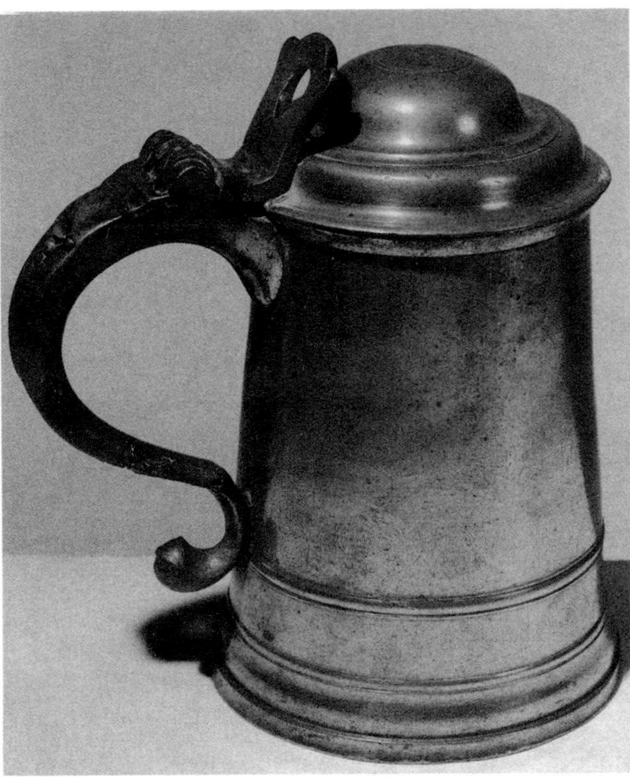

9

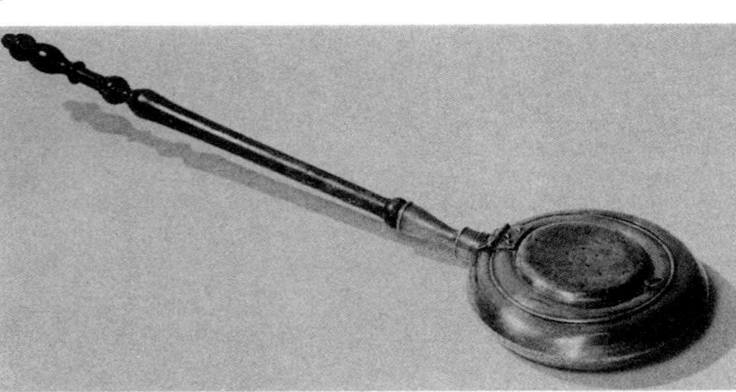

10

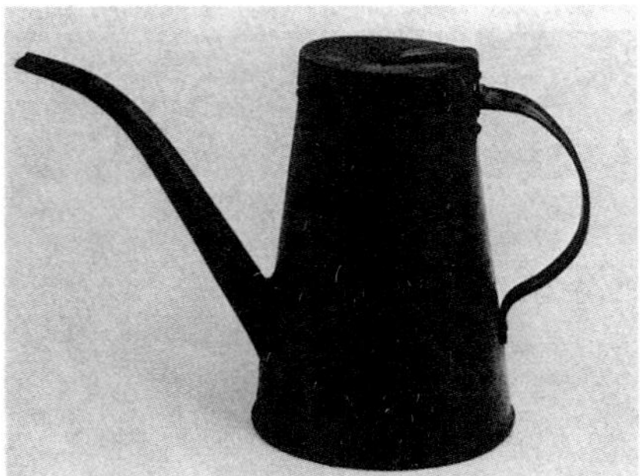

11

9 TANKARD
Philadelphia
1780–85

William Will

Inscribed outside bottom: *C·C*
Marked inside bottom: *W^m. WILL
PHILADEL   PHIA*

Molded pewter. Tankard assembled from four
parts. Hollow handle soldered to body, heavy
solid pierced purchase soldered to lid, and
hinge fitting soldered to handle. Concentric
skimming lines on domed lid and flat bottom.
Some pitting on body.

Height 20 cm (7⅞″), diameter base 12 cm (4¾″)

Gift of Mrs. William D. Frishmuth. 02-511

10 WARMING PAN
Philadelphia
1780–90

William Will

Inscribed under edge of lid: *MBG*
Stamped on bottom: *Wm WILL
PHILADELPHIA*

Molded pewter, walnut. Made from six molded
pieces. Pan joint at center has linen impression
on inside. Handle socket threaded for screwed
attachment to pan. Two-piece hinge riveted
to lid and pan. Lid made from plate mold;
decorated with wrigglework and chisel
engraving in symmetrical floral pattern;
perforated to allow heat to escape. Lid ring
held in riveted loop. Concentric spinning lines
evident on sides of pan, inside bottom, and
obverse lid. Hinge pin is brass; probably an old
replacement. The same pan mold was used by
Will for bedpans.

Length 115.6 cm (45½″) (including handle),
diameter 29.2 cm (11½″)

Gift of Mrs. J. Stogdell Stokes. 59-71-1a,b

11 OILCAN
1780–1850

Copper. Soldered joints. Hinged, fitted lid.
Loop handle with rolled edges riveted to body.
Curved spout. Used to fill oil lamps.

Height 15.6 cm (6⅛″), diameter 10.4 cm (4⅛″)

Gift of J. Stogdell Stokes. 28-10-36

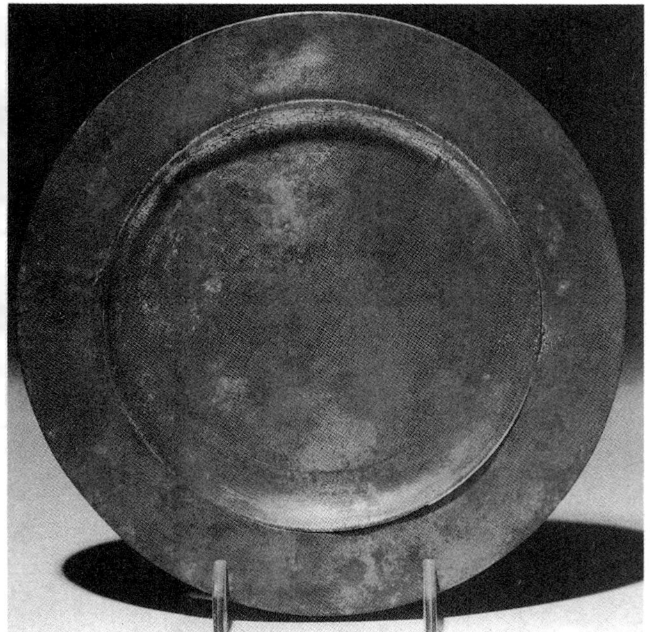

12

12 PLATE

Philadelphia
1784

William Will

Inscribed on underside of marly: *M + S 1784*
Stamped on bottom in a square: *IC*
Stamped on bottom in a square with floral
device
Marked, twice, on bottom with dove and lamb
encircled by: *WILLIAM WILL
PHILADELPHIA*

Molded pewter. Made in single mold. Thin
with raised molded edge on reverse. Marly
partially split from plate. Pitted obverse and
reverse.

Diameter 23.8 cm (9⅜")

Gift of Mrs. Fiske Boyd. 66-18-1

---

13 CANDLESTICK

Tulpehocken Township, Berks County
1820–50

Peter Derr

Stamped on thumb plate: *P.D.*

Brass, iron. Molded middle ring and base
soldered to shaft of sheet brass. Iron post in
lower section raises candle.

Height 20.9 cm (8¼")

Titus C. Geesey Collection. 54-85-123

---

14 LAMP

Tulpehocken Township, Berks County
1832

Attributed to **Peter Derr**

Stamped on handle: *PD 1832 +*

Brass, iron. Brass well with solid top, hinged
lid with knob finial, wick spout. Iron handle
with chain-linked wick pick and hanging spike
attached through grommet. "Betty" lamp.

23.5 x 8 x 9.8 cm (9¼ x 3⅛ x 3⅞")

Titus C. Geesey Collection. 55-94-78

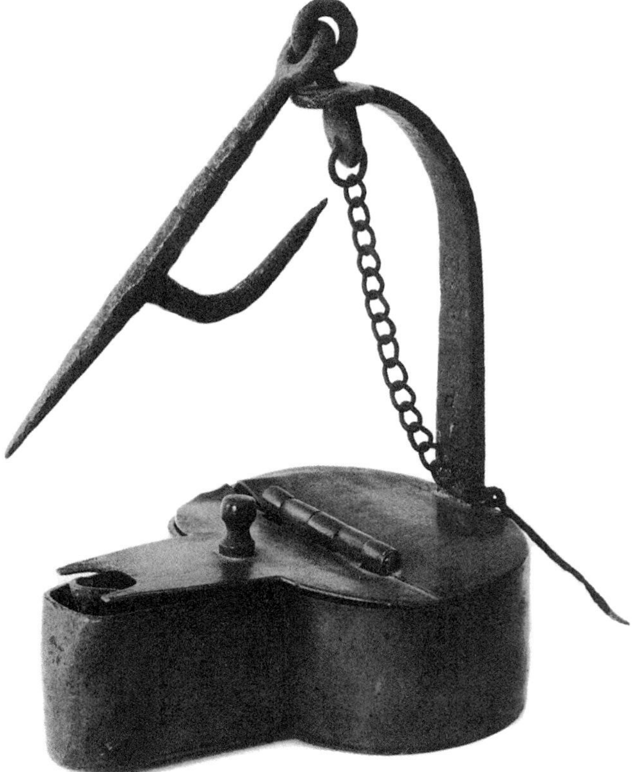

14

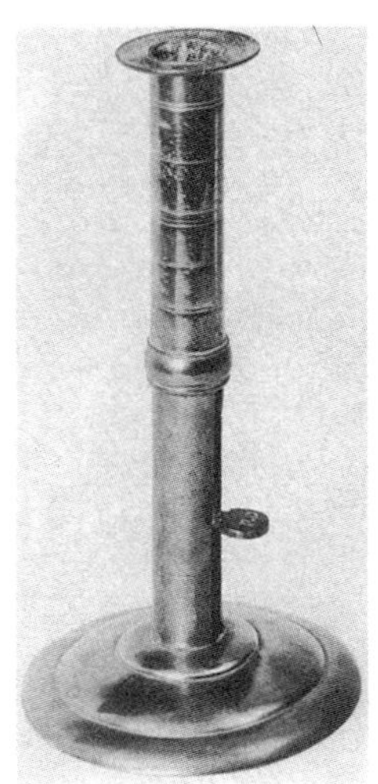

13

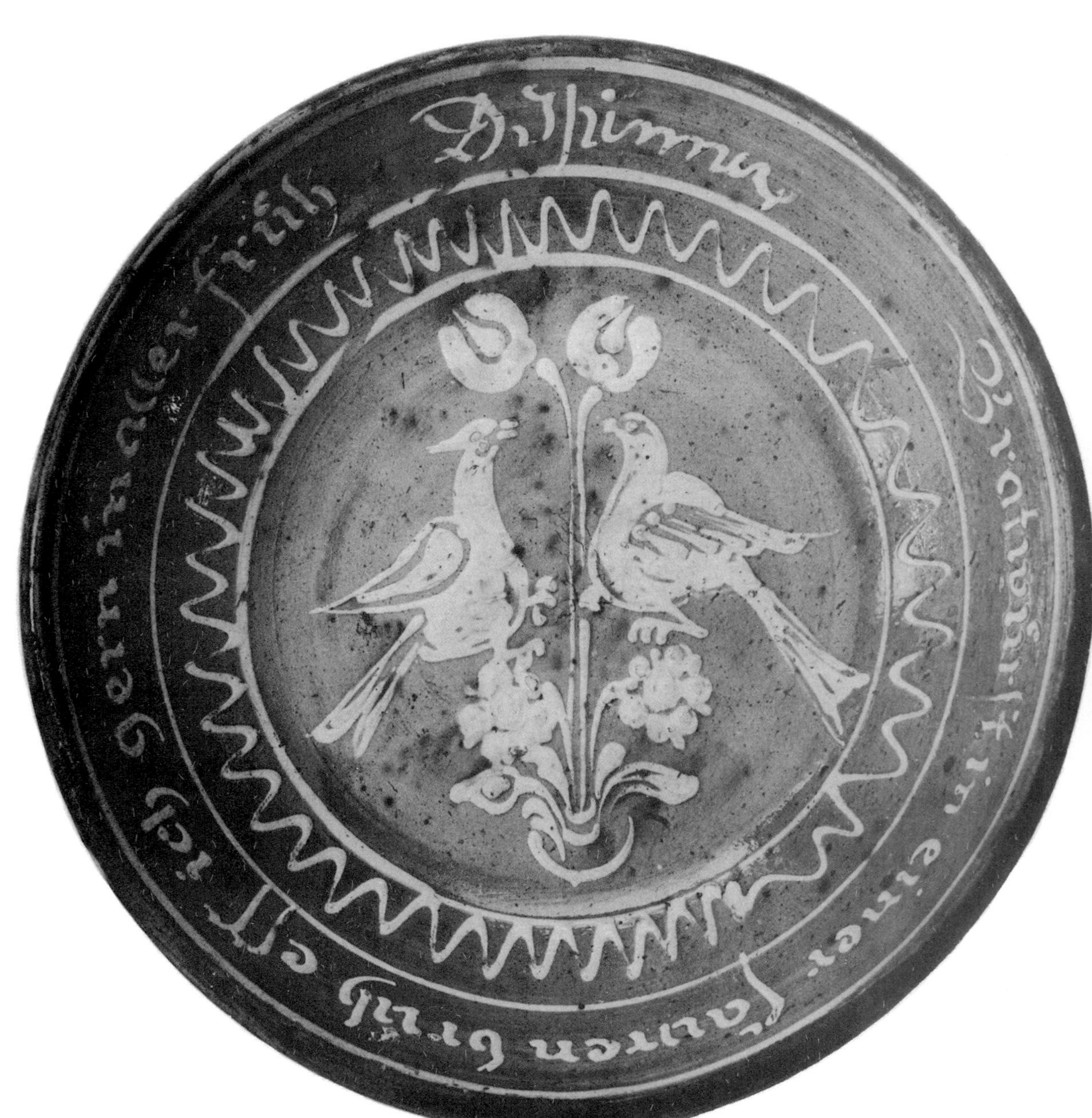

Ceramics

INTRODUCTION

Skilled European potters were active in Philadelphia and environs from the outset of settlement, making domestic vessels, tile stoves, and roof tiles. Under the wet topsoils of Pennsylvania's low-lying ground, at the edges of streams and rivers, they found slate-colored crumbly earth, mottled with yellow and lumpy with iron oxides. It was high-quality ceramic clay. Because the rich terrain could support farms on the topsoil and potteries on the subsoil, Southeastern Pennsylvania was dotted with successful full and part-time potteries. Bucks and Montgomery counties, with plentiful supplies of clay, had potteries in almost every township by 1810. Fewer potteries were active in Berks, Lehigh, and Northampton counties, since more hauling was necessary to retrieve the clay from distant swamps, or to transport finished ware to markets.

Like other income-producing seasonal work, the work of the potter was fitted into the agricultural calendar. The clay was dug in the fall: topsoil was cleared and a foot-deep layer of clay was sliced and shoveled into a wagon, hauled to the pottery and stacked. Before freezing weather, the clay was carried in baskets and dumped into a mill—a round tub with a revolving post set with knives. A horse harnessed to a sweep walked slowly around the tub, turning the blades. Water was flushed through to clean the clay and the result-ing mass of plastic earth turned from gray to yellow. The clay was

DISH
1809–11
See page 201, no. 131

163

then shaped into one hundred pound blocks and stored in a cellar
where it was kept moist but would not freeze. The finicky cleaning,
picking out pebbles, grass, and roots, was done by the potter or
his helper at the bench during the kneading process, which also
expelled air pockets. Foreign matter or air pockets left in the clay
could cause rupture during the firing. To turn a piece of pottery, a
flattened ball of clay was centered on the potter's round table, or
head, which was rotated at variable speeds by the potter pushing
a foot wheel, which in turn was connected to a balance wheel,
allowing smooth and continuous rotation. Besides turning pottery
on the wheel, Pennsylvania German potters adopted the English
method of forming a shallow pie plate by draping a rolled slab of
damp clay over a convex mold. The shaped pottery greenware
was left in a shed to firm up but not to dry out before glazing.

Earthenware the world over was waterproofed with a lead
glaze. Red lead, flint, water, and slip clay—the fine siltlike clay
scraped from fingers and pots during the smoothing process—were
mixed together and run through a glazing mill, which ground any
lumps into particles. The viscosity of the mix was important—too
thin a mixture would not cover in one coat, and too thick a mixture
would pool or pop off when cooling. The addition of iron oxide gave
the glaze a yellowish cast; manganese produced an opaque blackish
brown glaze. Copper oxide, daubed or sprinkled on designs before
glazing, produced rich green accents, and cobalt turned blue. Colors
became runny if the glaze was thin and swirled on, more precise if
the potter applied the glaze with a brush. Slip decoration, usually
trailed from a slip cup, was applied when the ware was damp. Iron
and copper oxides were sometimes added to white slip made from
very fine New Jersey sand for especially lively decoration. The
sgraffito technique was highly developed by Pennsylvania potters.
Outlines and solid areas were scratched through a coating of slip,
usually white, to reveal the red underbody, which then shone red
through the glaze.

A potter worked several weeks to prepare enough ware to fill an
up-draft kiln. The kilns were built of brick and stone, which were
chinked, then plastered over with clay to make them airtight for
firing. Since more heat was generated at the kiln bottom, heavier
wares, such as jugs, bowls, and pots, were put there, and plates, at
the top. Kiln stilts separated pieces to allow heat circulation and to
prevent glazed surfaces from touching and fusing in the firing. Two
wood fires were built on opposite sides of the kiln, connected by two
semicircular tunnels distributing the heat evenly. The heat was built
up very slowly to prevent remaining moisture in the pottery from
heating too quickly and cracking the pottery. The kiln became hot as
a furnace in twenty-four hours. Neighborhood boys, who had done
the unskilled work at the pottery, grinding lead, picking clay clean,
and hauling pots, looked forward to the all-night excitement of firing
the kiln. The kiln was stoked into dramatic full burn—the plume of
white roaring flames bursting through the vents—and kept burning
for about thirty-six hours, until all the wood was burned to coal. The
kiln was sealed tightly for about a week to allow slow cooling.

Colorful slip and sgraffito-decorated objects, the presentation pieces of the rural potter, have survived because they were special. Many were inscribed with such Old World maxims as: "Sing, pray, and go on God's way," or with such bitingly witty inscriptions as: "Love a littel and love longe for hot love is sun cold & gone," or "Virgins and rose petals disappear like rainy weather." The "Liberty for Gackson" plate is encircled with the inscription: "If loving were injurious to health, the doctor would avoid it; and if it would hurt the maidens, they would not endure it," and some were inscribed for family or friends. That most techniques, inscriptions, and designs reflect European prototypes is understandable with first-settlement potters like Jacob Stout. But generations of potters continued to make pieces that followed European forms and designs, although how those forms and designs were transmitted is still conjecture. For example, Charles Headman was the descendant of a master potter from Strasbourg in Alsace, who had settled in Philadelphia by 1771. Did Headman model his five-fingered vase of 1849 (p. 174, no. 35), which is distinctly Alsatian in form and in applied slip decoration, after a treasured European family possession or as a result of what he learned in his American apprenticeship? There was also an international mix evident in the products of the rural potteries. Jacob Scholl, of Swiss descent, used the sgraffito technique highly developed by the Pennsylvania Germans, and rouletting, with cobalt (blue) coloring on his rounded pots, possibly inspired by the popular English "scratch-blue" earthenware.

While the isolation of rural potteries and markets blurred the outlines of Old World designs and techniques, the personality of the wares produced was intensified. Some decorated pieces have a group identity. A few plates by David Spinner, John Neis, and John Leman have in common an unusual mat glaze achieved by adding more clay to the glaze formula. Such similarity could have resulted from shared expertise, skills transmitted by a traveling journeyman, or from common apprenticeships. When combined with evidence in tax, census, and genealogical records, common characteristics allow attributions to potteries as units, if not to single artisians.

The horseman designs of plates by John Neis and David Spinner closely resemble those made in Germany by Jan Murmans in about 1718 in Kamperbruck, although the leaping stags and wavy-line borders, and the inscriptions within concentric bandings in sgraffito are distinctly Swiss. The theme of the galloping horseman belonged to several European regional traditions; he was Saint Martin or Frederick the Great, for example. In Pennsylvania he may have been the "Schimmelreiter," or rider of the white horse, but was more likely George Washington or simply the local fellow dressed in his plumed helmet who opened the festivities on Battalion Day by dashing across the village green on a horse (*see* p. 199, no. 125). The rural potter with artistic skills was the cartoonist, the limner, the engraver of his local scene, who sometimes inscribed on his own wares: "From the earth with sense, the potter makes everything."

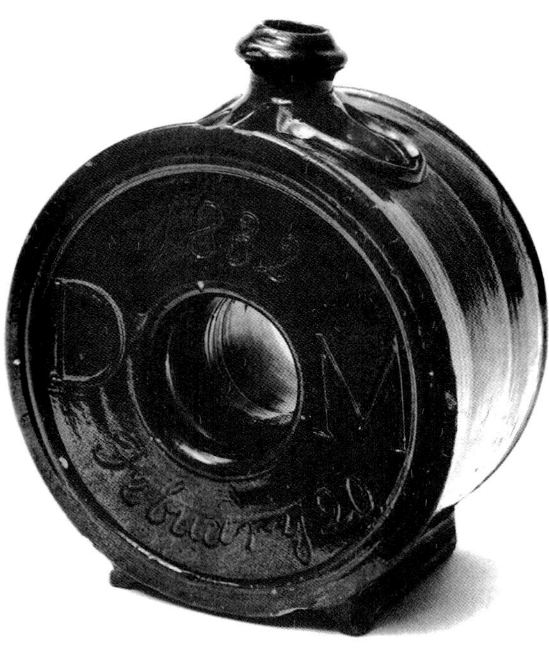

1

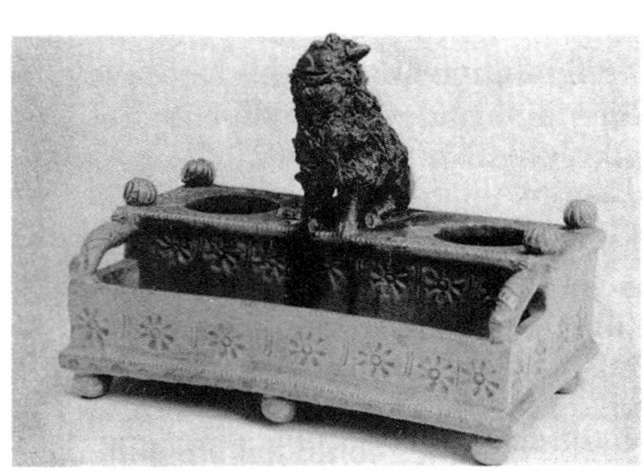

2

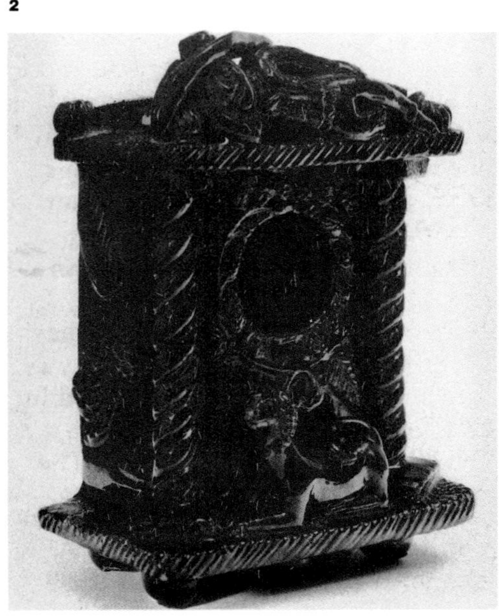

3

1　BOTTLE

1832

IAB

Inscribed obverse: *1832　DM　Febuary 20;*
reverse: *1832　DM*
Stamped, twice, on bottom: *IAB*

Wheel-thrown and modeled redware.
Extruded strips for feet and modeled neck
applied. Thick semiopaque manganese
(brown) glaze on all surfaces.

19.7 x 16.8 x 9.8 cm (7¾ x 6⅝ x 3⅞")

Titus C. Geesey Collection. 55-94-14

2　INKSTAND

1862

Ernest Bacher

Marked on bottom in script: *Ernest Bacher
Falker* [sage] *The 13/3　month 1862*

Slab and modeled redware. Rectangular
opening center back. Stamped decoration on
top, sides, and front. Coggled gadroon on base
and top. Six plain ball feet. Poodle modeled
and built up with fine ribbons of clay and
daubed with opaque manganese (brown) lead
glaze. Stand covered with semiopaque
greenish yellow lead glaze.

15 x 19.7 x 11.4 cm (5⅞ x 7¾ x 4½")

Gift of Joseph H. Himes, in memory of his wife
Eilleen C. Himes. 54-62-61

3　WATCH HOLDER

Mount Pleasant Township, Adams County
1850

Anthony Baecher

Incised on reverse: *Anthony　Baecher　1850
Lagelohner lopfer　geboren und Bayern*
("Anthony Baecher 1850, journeyman potter,
born in Bavaria")

Slab and modeled redware with applied
press-molded decoration. Five thick slabs
joined together in the form of a wardrobe with
six ball feet, four turk's head finials, and
three-quarter colonnettes with bases and
capitals. Modeled figure of Father Time on top
and figure of a dog, in the round, on base.
Press-molded flowers and foliage on sides.
Hanging hole in back. Thick opaque brown
(manganese) glaze on interior and exterior,
except back.

23.5 x 17.2 x 9.5 cm (9¼ x 6¾ x 3¾")

Gift of Joseph H. Himes, in memory of his wife
Eilleen C. Himes. 54-62-39

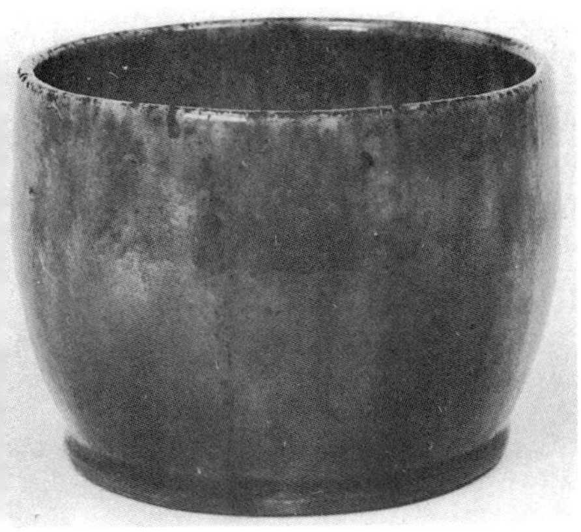

4

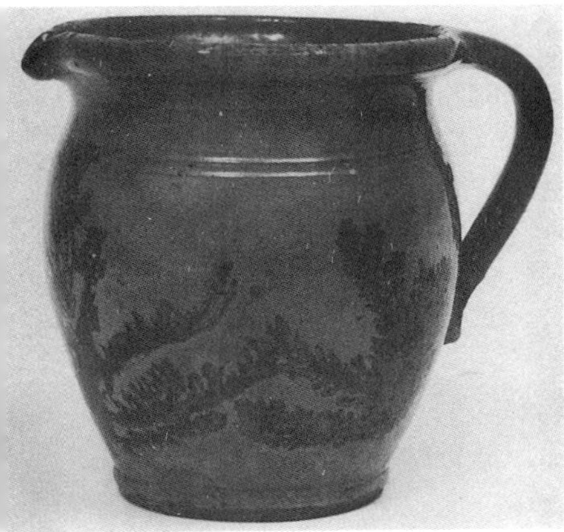

5

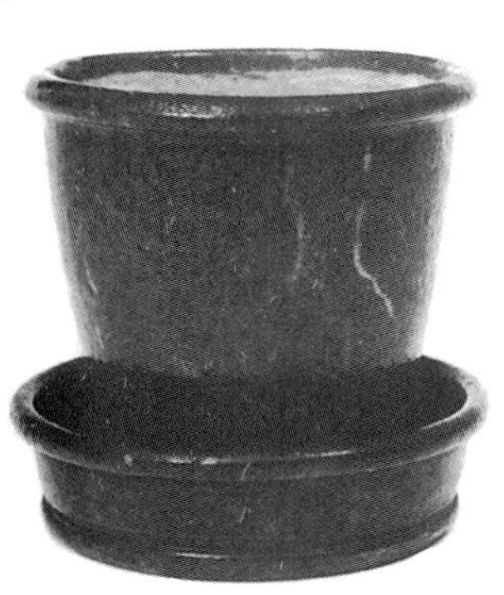

6

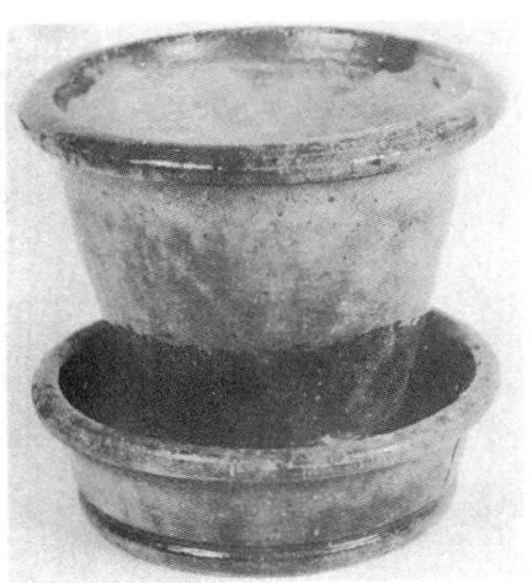

7

4 BOWL
Waynesboro, Franklin County
1835–50

John Bell

Incised on bottom: *E y*
Impressed on bottom: *John Bell*

Wheel-thrown redware. Sides striated with manganese (brown). Yellowish lead glaze on entire surface, including bottom.

Height 8.2 cm (3¼″), diameter 11.7 cm (4⅝″)

Gift of J. Stogdell Stokes. 36-19-1

---

5 PITCHER
Waynesboro, Franklin County
1840–50

Possibly by **John Bell**

Wheel-thrown buff-colored clay. Applied handle. Sponge impressions on bottom. Three dendritic motifs in manganese (brownish black). Tan-colored clear lead glaze.

11.7 x 13.8 cm (4⅝ x 5⅜″)

Purchased: Baugh-Barber Fund. 11-195

---

6 FLOWERPOT
Waynesboro, Franklin County
1860–70

John Bell

Stamped on bottom: *JOHN BELL WAYNESBORO*

Wheel-thrown redware. Straight sides with everted edge. Drainage holes in pot. Mottled green lead glaze. Pot interior unglazed.

Height 14.2 cm (5⅝″), diameter 16.2 cm (6⅜″)

Gift of J. Stogdell Stokes. 28-10-106

---

7 FLOWERPOT
Waynesboro, Franklin County
1860–70

John Bell

Stamped on bottom: *JOHN BELL WAYNESBORO*

Wheel-thrown redware. Flaring pot with everted edge is joined to deep saucer. Drainage holes in pot. Thick opaque green lead glaze. Pot interior unglazed.

Height 12.4 cm (4⅞″), diameter 13.6 cm (5⅜″)

Gift of J. Stogdell Stokes. 28-10-107

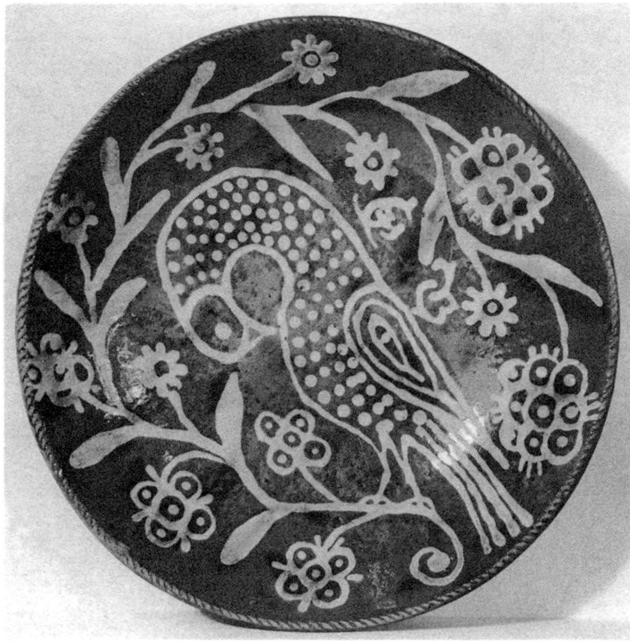

8

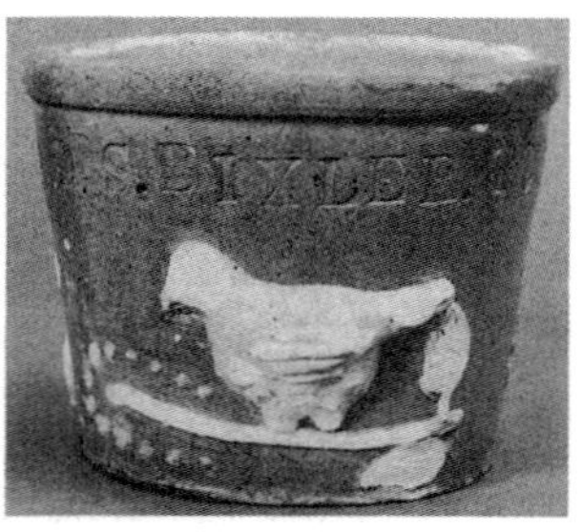

9

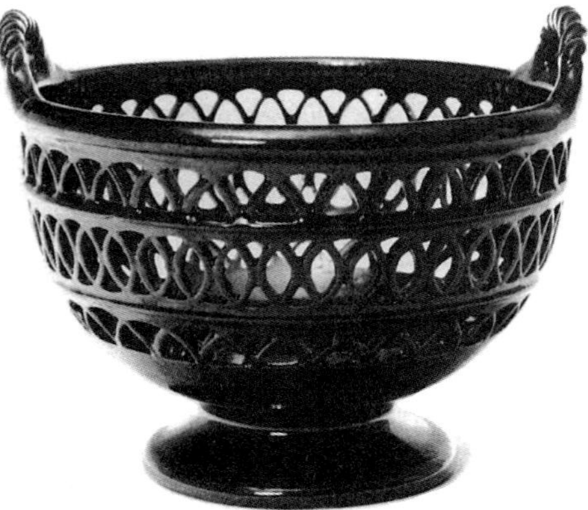

10

8 PLATE
Rockhill Township, Bucks County
1820–40

Attributed to **Benjamin Bergey**

Inscribed: *EB*

Molded redware, coggled edge. Thick white slip decoration on red body, daubed with copper oxide (green). Clear yellowish lead glaze.

Height 6.3 cm (2½"), diameter 33.6 cm (13¼")

Purchased. 93-218

9 FLOWERPOT
Earl Township, Lancaster County
1824

Absalom Bixler

Inscribed: *ABS. BIXLER. TO HIS WIFE. SARAH. 1824*

Wheel-thrown redware. Sprig-molded decoration in plaster of paris with touches of copper oxide (green). Clear lead glaze on exterior with losses on decoration.

Height 14.5 cm (5¾"), diameter 19 cm (7½")

Titus C. Geesey Collection. 55-94-15

10 PLATE
Robesonia, Berks County
1974

Lester Breininger, Jr.

Incised on bottom: *L. Breininger   Robesonia Pa   April 1974*

Molded redware, coggled edge. Surface striped with white slip patterned with five-toothed comb. Banded in copper oxide (green). Majolica gloss glaze.

Height 3.8 cm (1½"), diameter 26 cm (10¼")

Purchased: Baugh-Barber Fund. 74-107-4

11 COMPOTE
Bern Township, Berks County
1845–50

Attributed to **John George Buehler**

Wheel-thrown redware. Rope-twist handles applied. Pierced sides. Opaque manganese (brown) lead glaze.

Height 13 cm (5⅛"), diameter 16.5 cm (6½")

Purchased: Baugh-Barber Fund. 40-26-1

11

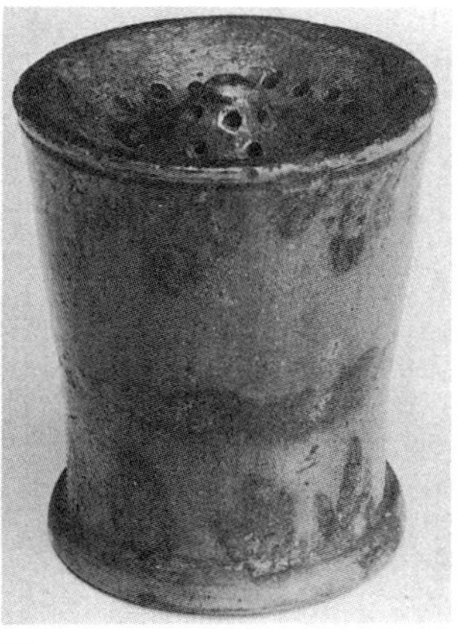

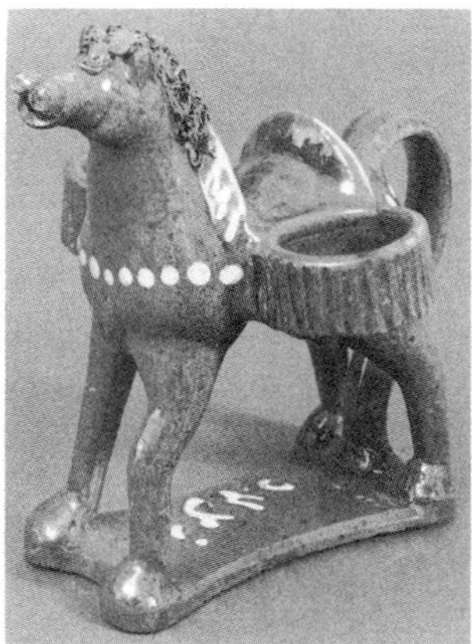

12   **13**

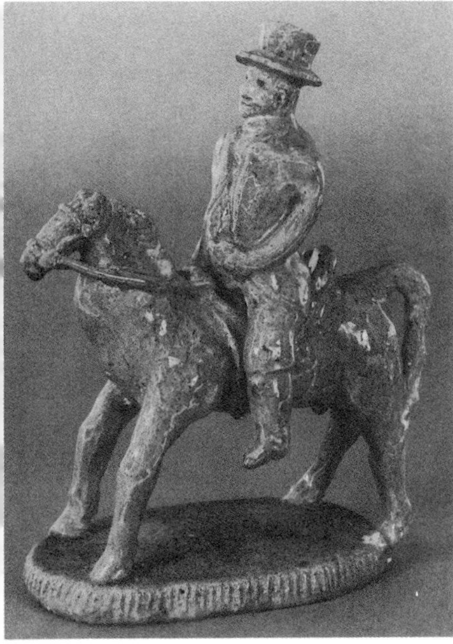

14

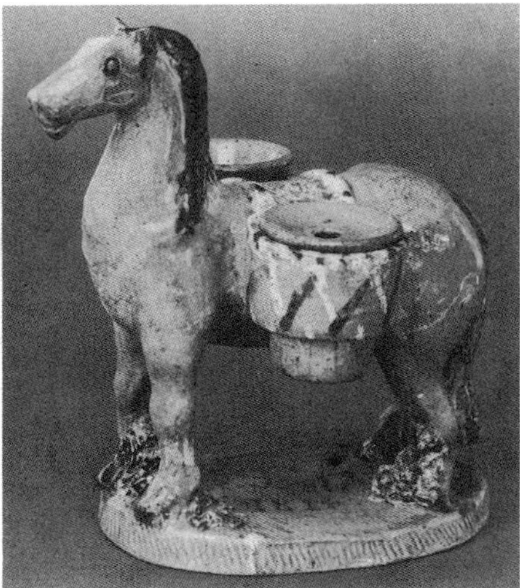

15

---

12   **SANDER**
1780–1800

JC

Incised on bottom: *JC*

Wheel-thrown redware, molded foot. Perforations are funnel-shaped for sand to pour in quickly and out slowly. White slip borders of leaves and band of foliage. Thick clear lead glaze.

Height 10.2 cm (4″), diameter 8.8 cm (3½″)

Gift of Joseph H. Himes, in memory of his wife Eilleen C. Himes. 54-62-58

---

13   **CASTOR STAND**
Bucks County
1840

Possibly by **Michael Dirstein**

Inscribed on base: *1840*

Slab and modeled redware. Clay rolled into sheet and cut for base; folded and pinched into hollow forms for torso. Wire-thin clay strips applied to neck as tangled mane. Clay strip for tail serves as handle. White slip decoration. Clear brownish lead glaze.

15 x 15.5 x 12.4 cm (5⅞ x 6⅛ x 4⅞″)

Purchased: Baugh-Barber Fund. 29-81-4

---

14   **HORSE AND RIDER**
Hilltown Township, Bucks County
1809

Jacob Fretz

Incised on base: *Jacob Fretz   1809*

Modeled and slab redware. Two units. Figure of rider is secured with shaft that fits into hole in back of horse. Thick clear brownish lead glaze over red body.

23.5 x 19 cm (9¼ x 7½″)

Titus C. Geesey Collection. 55-94-17a,b

---

15   **INKSTAND**
Hilltown Township, Bucks County
1814

Jacob Fretz

Inscribed: *J. Fretz   1814*

Modeled, wheel-thrown, and slab redware. Ink and sand-shaker pots fit into holders. Base is cut from slab. Solid horse is secured to base with modeled clay daubed with copper oxide (green) to resemble plants. Mane, tail, feet, and design on carriers in manganese (brown). White slip on legs, carriers, and blaze. Dots of copper oxide (green) on carrier. Kiln stilt marks on pot units. Clear thick orangish lead glaze.

19.6 x 20.3 cm (7¾ x 8″)

Purchased: Baugh-Barber Fund. 43-64-1a,b,c

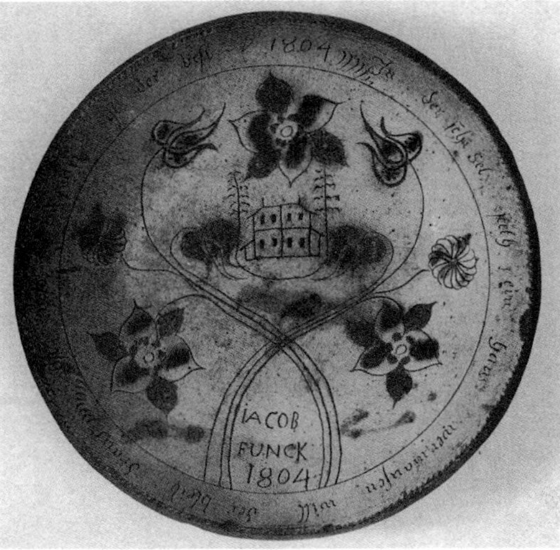

16

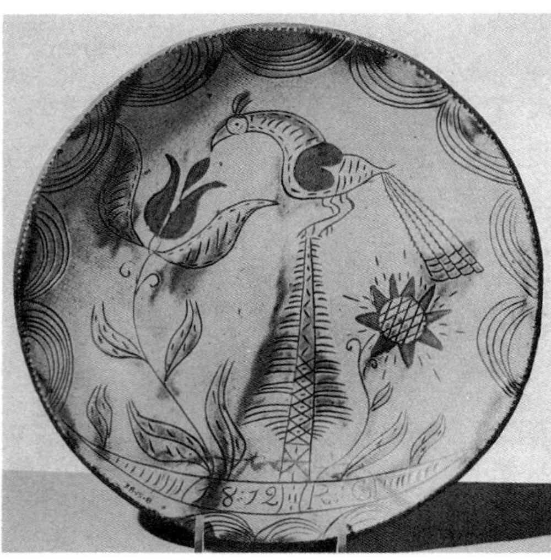

18

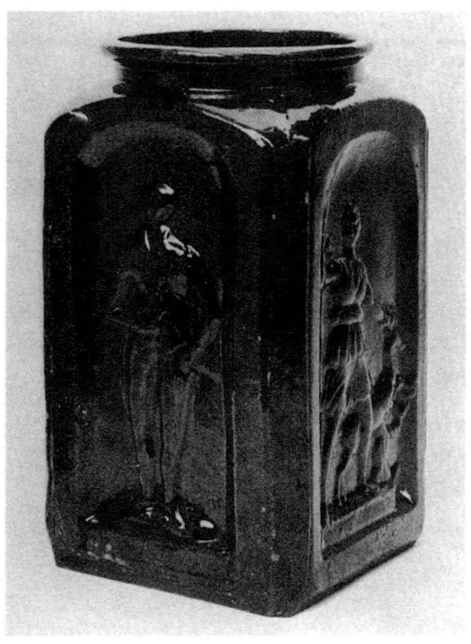

17

16 PLATE
Haycock Township, Bucks County
1804

Jacob Funck

Inscribed: *In der schisel steth ein haus wer mausen will der bleib draus. ost west mein frau ist der best   N   1804   IACOB FUNCK 1804* ("In the dish stands a house. He who would pilfer—keep out. East, west, my wife is the best. [in the year] 1804   Jacob Funck 1804")

Molded redware, coggled edge. Surface covered with white slip. Sgraffito decoration. Design daubed with copper oxide (green). Clear reddish brown lead glaze.

Height 5.4 cm (2⅛"), diameter 28 cm (11")

Purchased: John T. Morris Fund. 21-46-66

17 JAR
Lancaster County
1850–80

Henry Gast

Inscribed on front and back: *Washington*
Mark impressed on bottom: *H. GAST LA*

Molded redware. Arch-topped recessed panel with figure of Washington and inscription beneath on front and back. Diana the Huntress on sides. Clear speckled manganese (brown) lead glaze on interior, exterior, and bottom. Identical mold of Washington figure used by F.B. Norton Co., Worcester, Mass., about 1868.

23.8 x 13.3 cm (9⅜ x 5¼")

Purchased: Baugh-Barber Fund. 07-86

18 PLATE
1812

Attributed to **R. Gerber**

Inscribed: *1812   R·G*

Molded redware, coggled edge. Surface covered with white slip daubed with copper oxide (green). Sgraffito decoration. Clear yellowish lead glaze.

Height 4.8 cm (1⅞"), diameter 31 cm (12⅛")

Purchased: Baugh-Barber Fund. 38-15-8

19 STILTS
Manheim, Lancaster County
1850–56

John Gibble

Slab and modeled redware. Used to support pieces during firing in kiln. Unglazed.

1.8 x 7 cm (¾ x 2¾")

Gift of John T. Morris. 92-119—121

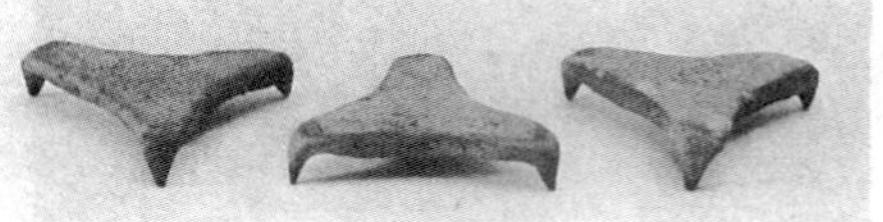

19

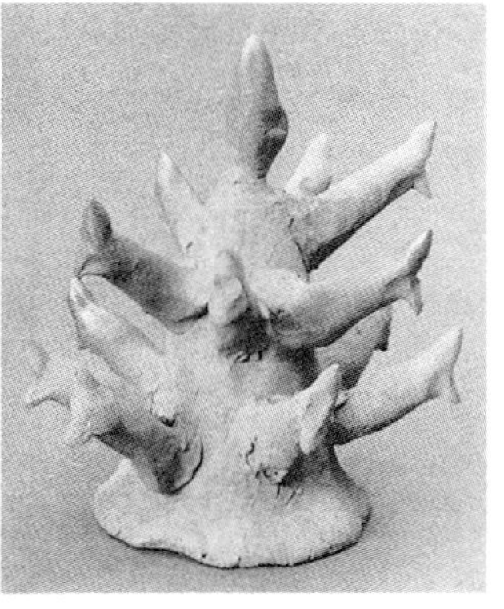

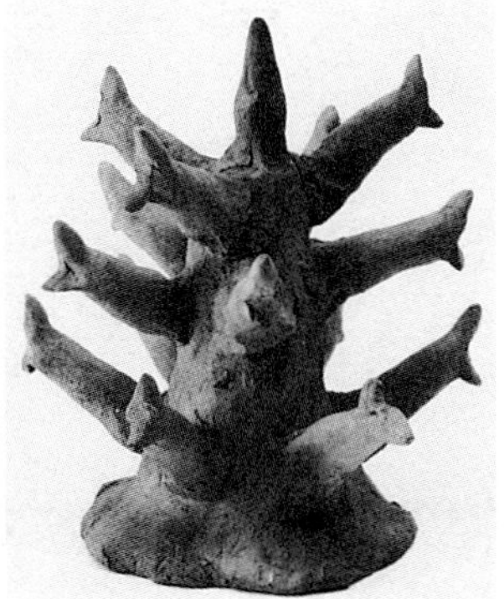

20   **21**

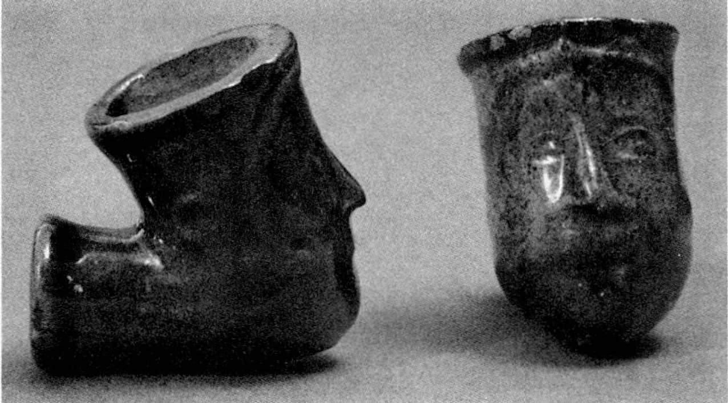

22

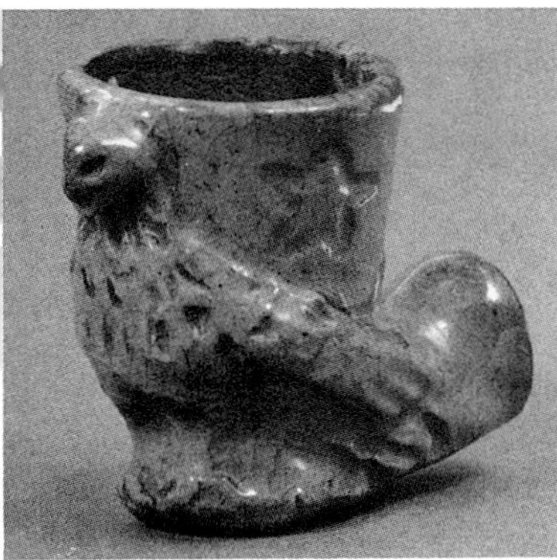

23

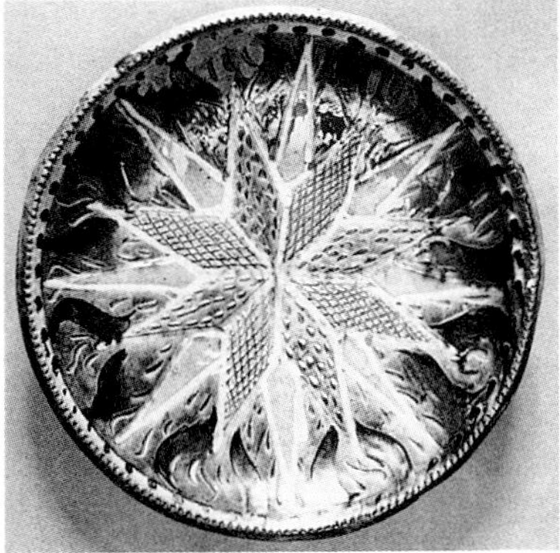

24

20 PIPE RACK
Manheim, Lancaster County
1850–56

John Gibble

Modeled redware. Hollow core with applied arms used to support pipe bowls for drying or firing in kiln. Unglazed.

11.3 x 10 cm (4⅜ x 3⅞″)

Gift of John T. Morris. 92-110

21 PIPE RACK
Manheim, Lancaster County
1850–56

John Gibble

Modeled redware. Hollow core with fifteen arms to support ceramic pipe bowls for drying or firing in kiln. Unglazed.

12 x 10.5 cm (4¾ x 4⅛″)

Gift of John T. Morris. 92-111

22 PIPE BOWLS (2)
Manheim, Lancaster County
1850–56

John Gibble

Modeled redware. Face mask on front. Daubed with manganese (brown). Clear reddish lead glaze.

3.9 x 4.1 cm (1½ x 1⅝″)

Gift of John T. Morris. 92-114, 92-118

23 PIPE BOWL
Manheim, Lancaster County
1856

John Gibble

Inscribed on back: *JG* [?] *1856*

Modeled redware. Raised form of spread eagle on front. Clear brownish lead glaze.

4 x 4 cm (1½ x 1½″)

Gift of John T. Morris. 92-113

24 PLATE
Rockland Township, Berks County
1815–25

Attributed to **Solomon Grimm**

Marked on reverse: *Grimm*

Molded redware, coggled edge. Thick, heavy body. Star design deeply incised. Plate covered with white slip, filling in outlining and banding. Decorated with copper oxide (green) and manganese (black). Sgraffito decoration of crosshatching, jabs, and broad strokes. Clear yellowish lead glaze.

Height 3.8 cm (1½″), diameter 25 cm (9⅞″)

Purchased: Baugh-Barber Fund. 1979-100-1

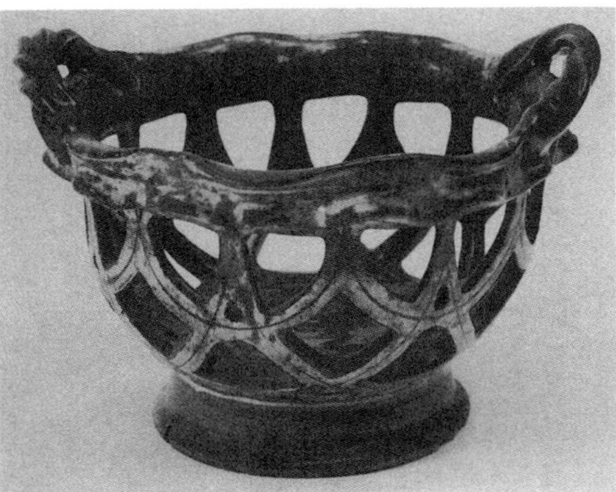

25

25 COMPOTE

Nockamixon Township, Bucks County
1830–40

David Haring

Inscribed inside rim: *DAVID HARING BUCKS COUNTY PENNSYLVAN*

Wheel-thrown and modeled redware. Raised foot, pierced sides. Upper edge folded over and modeled into ruffle. Rope-twist handles applied. White slip applied to ruffle and pierced work. Sgraffito compass line decoration. Clear yellowish lead glaze on interior and exterior.

13.6 x 20.3 cm (5⅜ x 8″)

Gift of Joseph H. Himes, in memory of his wife Eilleen C. Himes. 60-54-1

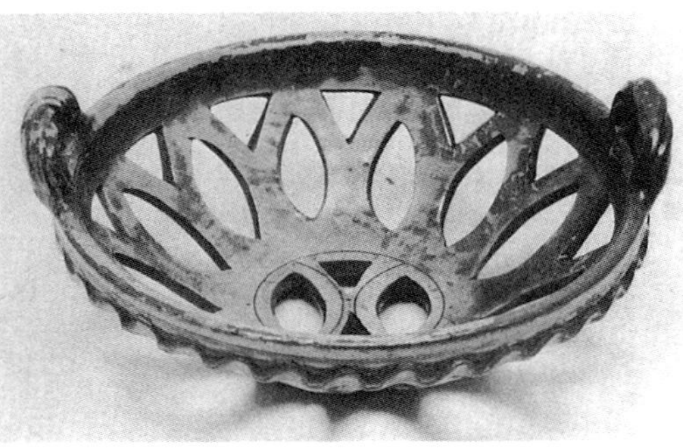

26

26 FRUIT BOWL

Nockamixon Township, Bucks County
1830–40

Attributed to **David Haring**

Wheel-thrown redware. Raised foot. Rope-twist handles applied. Top edge folded over to outside and finger-pressed into ruffle. Pierced bottom and sides. White slip applied to all surfaces. Exterior daubed with copper oxide (green). Sgraffito compass line decoration. Clear brownish yellow lead glaze on all surfaces.

11.5 x 26.4 cm (4½ x 10⅜″)

Purchased: Baugh-Barber Fund. 42-77-1

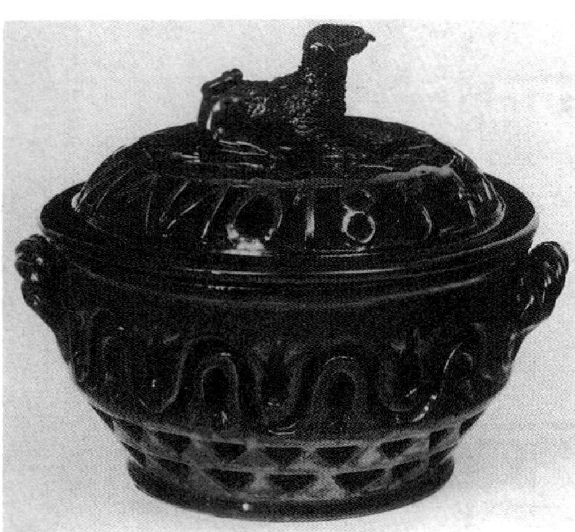

27

27 COVERED BOWL

Nockamixon Township, Bucks County
1857

Jared R. Haring

Inscribed: *ZUMAN DENKEN ANO 1857* ("A souvenir of the year 1857")

Wheel-thrown and modeled redware. Bowl inside pierced casing, joined at top edge. Bottom of outer bowl pierced with six-pointed star within compass-inscribed circle. Rope-twist handles and finial in the figure of a dog applied. Thick opaque manganese (brown) lead glaze on exterior and interior, except bottom and inside lid.

15.2 x 19 cm (6 x 7½″)

Gift of John T. Morris. 12-73

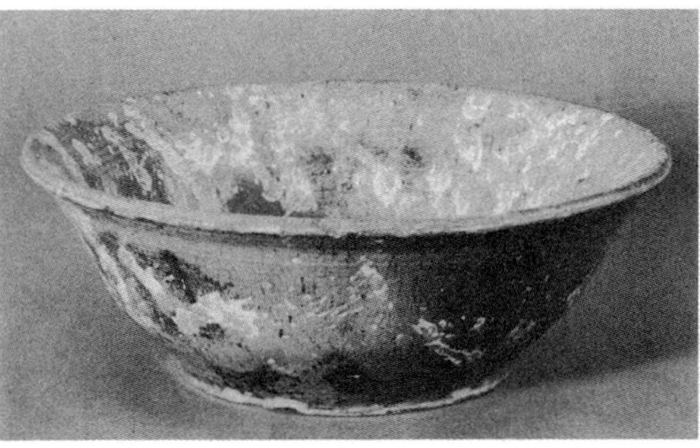

28

28 BOWL

Nockamixon Township, Bucks County
1861–80

Jared R. Haring

Wheel-thrown redware. Surfaces splashed with white slip. Clear yellowish lead glaze.

Height 10.8 cm (4¼″), diameter 31 cm (12¼″)

Gift of Jared R. Haring. 96-5

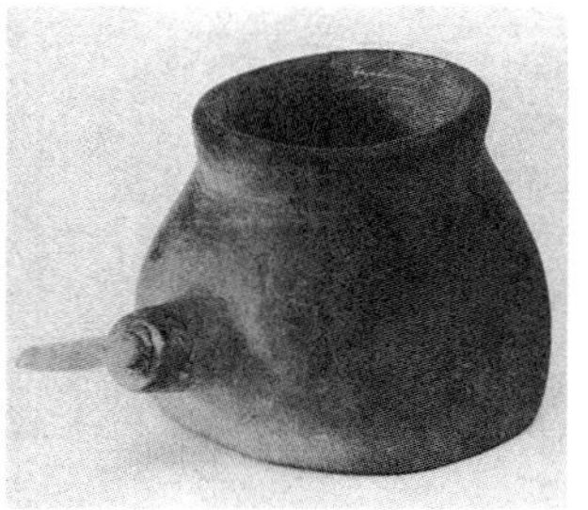
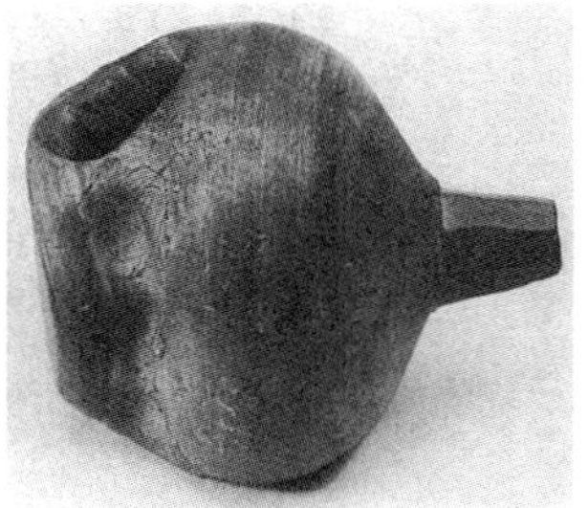

29   30

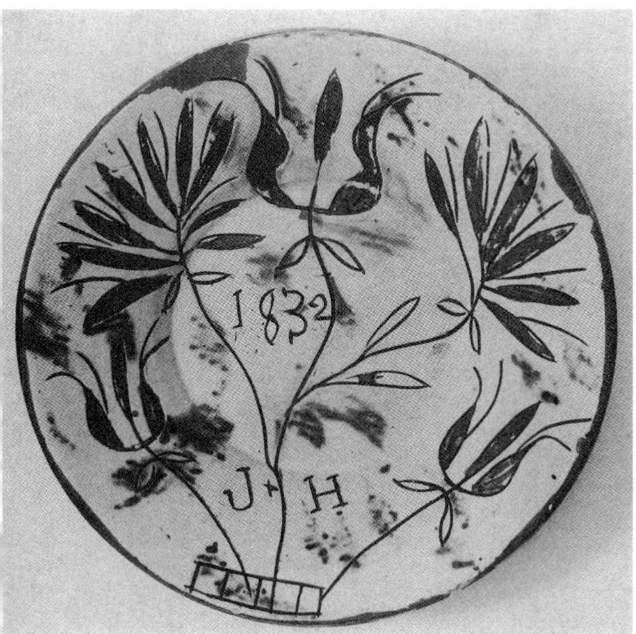

31

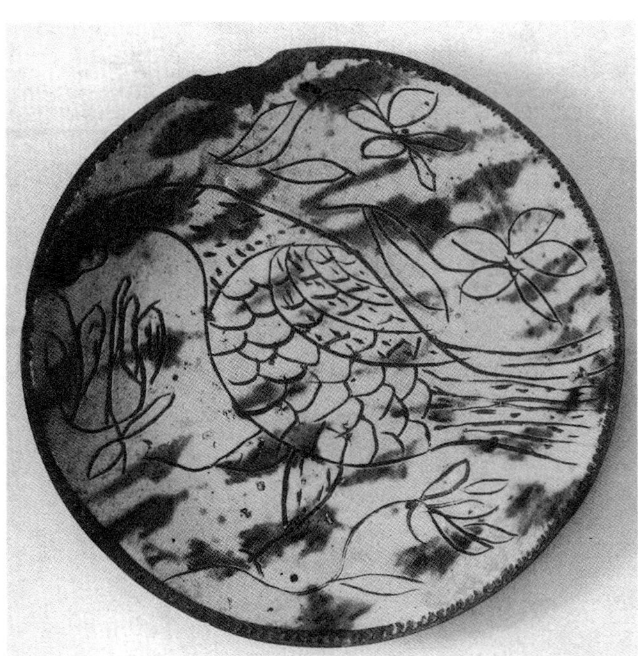

32

29 SLIP CUP
Nockamixon Township, Bucks County
1840–50

Haring Pottery

Wheel-thrown and modeled redware. Pinched
on two sides for fingerhold. Pouring spout
fitted with goose quill. Unglazed. Residue of
white slip inside.

6.5 x 7.3 x 11.7 cm (2½ x 2⅞ x 4⅝")

Gift of Abel Brinton Haring. 01-66d

---

30 SLIP CUP
Nockamixon Township, Bucks County
1850

Haring Pottery

Wheel-thrown and modeled redware.
Indented for thumb and three fingers of right
hand. Shaped spout inserted; quill missing. Air
hole for flow control. Unglazed.

8.3 x 8.3 x 10.2 cm (3¼ x 3¼ x 4")

Gift of Abel Brinton Haring. 96-65

---

31 DISH
Haycock Township, Bucks County
1832

Attributed to **Joseph Harwick**

Inscribed: *1832   J & H*

Wheel-thrown redware. Concave flaring sides,
everted edge. Surface covered with thick layer
of white slip daubed with copper oxide
(green). Sgraffito decoration. Clear yellowish
lead glaze. Surface losses.

Height 4.7 cm (1⅞"), diameter 28.6 cm (11¼")

Purchased: Baugh-Barber Fund. 38-15-10

---

32 PLATE
Haycock Township, Bucks County
1830–40

Attributed to **Joseph** or **Samuel Harwick**

Molded redware, coggled edge. Surface
covered with white slip. Sgraffito decoration
mottled with copper oxide (green). Lead glaze.
Surface losses and edge chips.

Height 3.8 cm (1½"), diameter 23.5 cm (9¼")

Purchased: Baugh-Barber Fund. 13-468

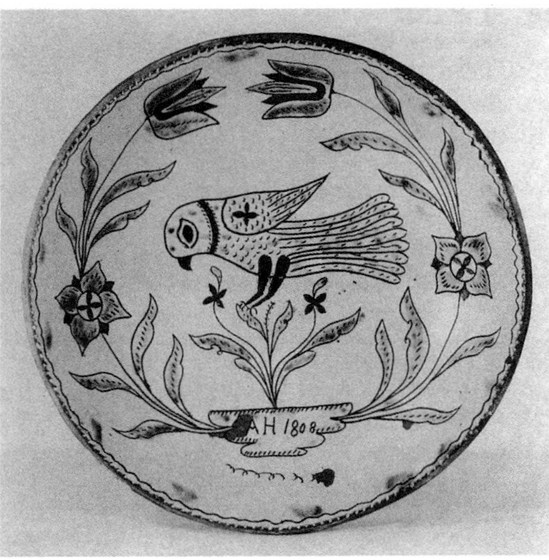

33

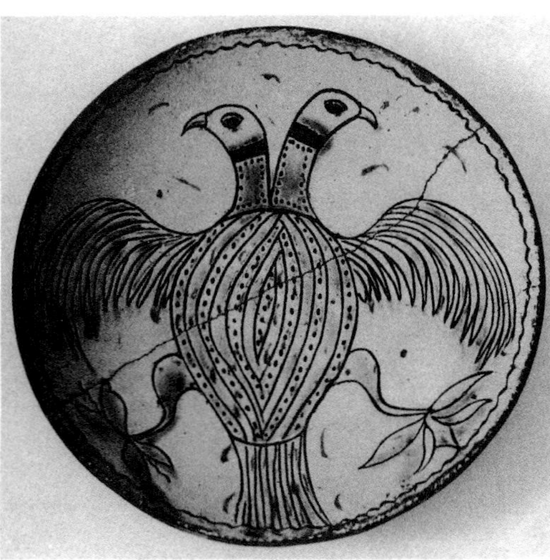

34

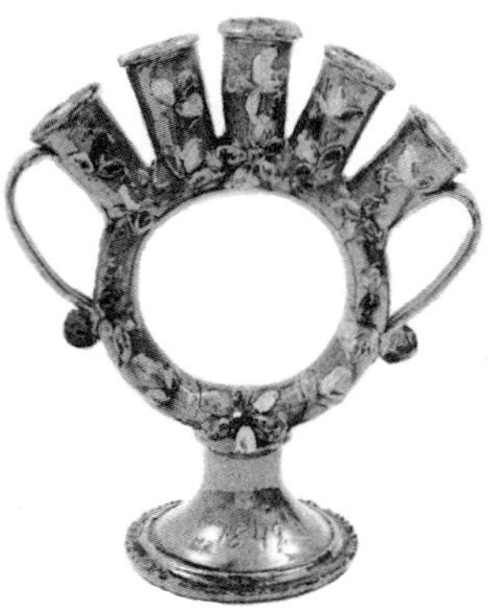

35

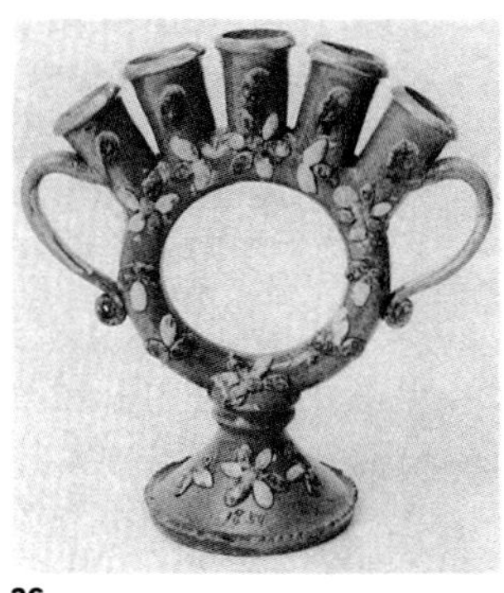

36

33 PLATE
Rockhill Township, Bucks County
1808

Attributed to **Andrew Headman**

Inscribed: *AH 1808*

Molded redware, coggled edge. Surface covered with white slip. Sgraffito decoration. Controlled copper oxide (green) daubing in design and around edge. Clear yellowish lead glaze.

Height 5.8 cm (2¼″), diameter 29.5 cm (11⅝″)

Gift of John T. Morris. 01-116

34 PLATE
Rockhill Township, Bucks County
1810–20

Attributed to **Andrew Headman**

Molded redware, coggled edge. White slip surface with sgraffito decoration. Design daubed with copper oxide (green). Clear yellowish lead glaze. Sgraffito lines unglazed.

Height 5.4 cm (2⅛″), diameter 26.3 cm (10⅜″)

Gift of John T. Morris. 03-373

35 VASE
Rockhill Township, Bucks County
1849

Attributed to **Charles Headman**

Inscribed: *1849*

Wheel-thrown and modeled redware. Applied handles. Rolled rims of "fingers," crimped edge of base, and handle touched with thin white slip colored with copper oxide (green). Bits of clay applied as flowers, daubed with thick white slip and copper oxide (green). Thick clear brownish lead glaze.

27.6 x 25 cm (10⅞ x 9⅞″)

Gift of John T. Morris. 92-88

36 VASE
Rockhill Township, Bucks County
1850

Attributed to **Charles Headman**

Incised, twice: *1850*

Wheel-thrown and modeled redware. Applied handles. Applied bits of clay form floral decoration daubed with white slip partially colored with copper oxide (green). Handles and rolled rims of "fingers" dashed with white slip. Clear yellowish lead glaze.

26.4 x 25.7 cm (10⅜ x 10⅛″)

Purchased: Baugh-Barber Fund. 45-42-7

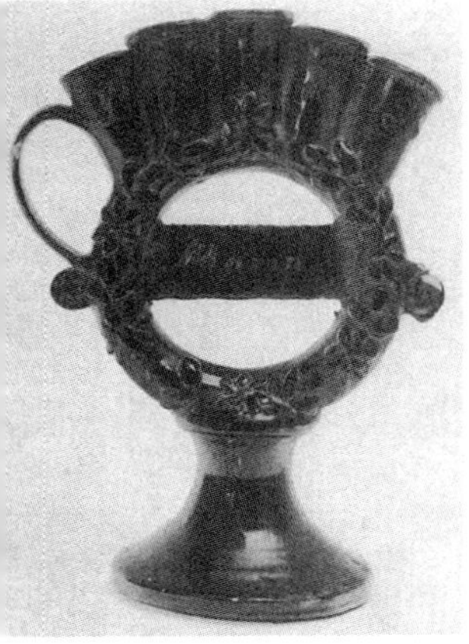

37

38

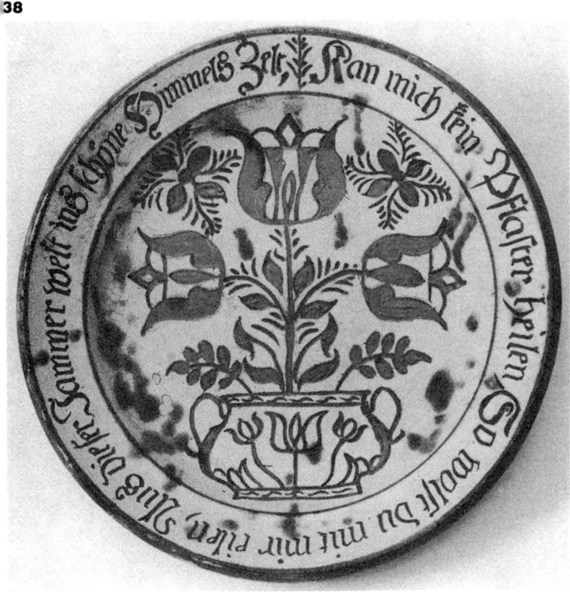

39

37 VASE

Rockhill Township, Bucks County
1848

Attributed to **John Headman**

Incised: *Maria*
Stamped: *1848*

Wheel-thrown and modeled redware. Floral wreath made of cut clay applied piecemeal. Opaque manganese (black brown) lead glaze. One handle missing.

30.5 x 21 cm (12 x 8¼″)

Purchased: Special Museum Fund. 07-189

38 DISH

Bethlehem, Northampton County
1778

Possibly by **Abraham Hubener**

Inscribed: *dass seind drei blummen auff einem sie an und nim si nicht. 1778* ("There are three flowers on one [stem] and do not take them. 1778")

Wheel-thrown redware. Straight sides, flaring rim, everted edge. Surface covered with manganese (brown) in slip. Sgraffito decoration of tulip petals, two encircling bands, and vase colored with iron (orange) in slip. Inscription and banding in thick white slip. Clear lead glaze.

Height 4.4 cm (1¾″), diameter 30.8 cm (12⅛″)

Gift of John T. Morris. 03-355

39 DISH

Upper Hanover Township, Montgomery County
1785–86

Attributed to **George Hubener**

Inscribed: *Kan mich kein Pflaster heilen, So wolst du mit mir eilen, Aus dieser Jammer welt ins schoene Himmels Zelt* ("No plaster can heal me, so you will want to hurry with me from this world into the canopy of heaven.")

Wheel-thrown redware. Rounded sides, flaring rim, rolled, everted edge. Surface covered with white slip daubed with copper oxide (green). Banding and sgraffito decoration partially colored with iron oxide (red) in slip. Clear yellowish lead glaze.

Height 5.7 cm (2¼″), diameter 34.2 cm (13½″)

Purchased: Baugh-Barber Fund. 58-124-2

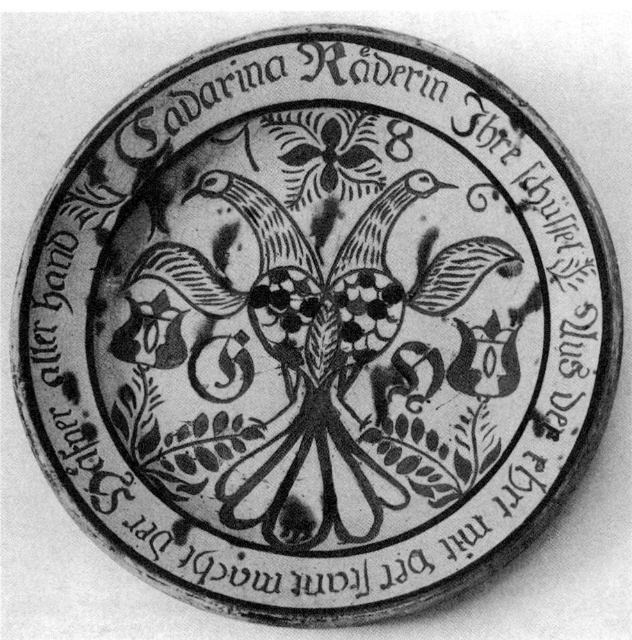

40

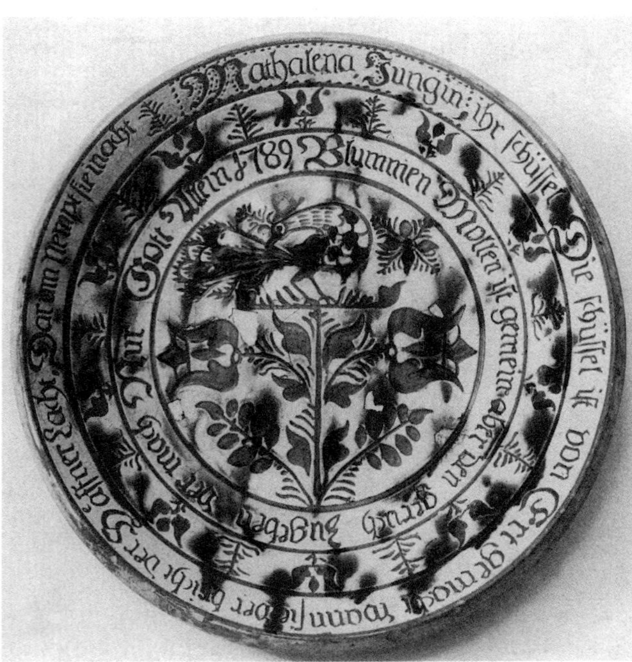

41

40 DISH

Upper Hanover Township, Montgomery
County
1786

George Hubener

Inscribed: *1786 GH Aus der ehrt mit verstant
macht der Haefner aller hand   Cadarina
Raederin Ihre schüssel* ("1786 G. H. From the
earth with sense the potter makes everything.
Cadarina Raeder, her dish.")

Wheel-thrown redware. Rounded sides, flaring
rim, rolled everted edge. Sponge marks
visible. Surface covered with white slip
daubed with copper oxide (green). Banding
and dots on birds' breasts in manganese (black
brown). Sgraffito decoration. Clear yellowish
lead glaze.

Height 5.4 cm (2⅛"), diameter 32 cm (12½")

Gift of John T. Morris. 00-21

41 DISH

Upper Hanover Township, Montgomery
County
1789

Attributed to **George Hubener**

Inscribed: *Die Schüssel ist von Ert gemacht
wann sie ver bricht der Haeffner Lacht,
Darum nempt sie in acht   Mathalena Jungin,
ihr schüssel   Blummen Mollen ist gemein
aber den geruch zugeben ver mach Nur Gott
Allein. 1789* ("The dish is made of earth, when
it breaks the potter laughs. Therefore take care
of it. Mathalena Jung, her dish. Painting
flowers is common, but giving it an odor is
given to God alone. 1789")

Wheel-thrown redware. Rounded base flares
into wide rim with deeply everted edge. White
slip-covered surface mottled with copper oxide
(green). Sgraffito decoration. Clear yellowish
lead glaze.

Height 5.7 cm (2¼"), diameter 32 cm (12½")

Gift of John T. Morris. 96-55

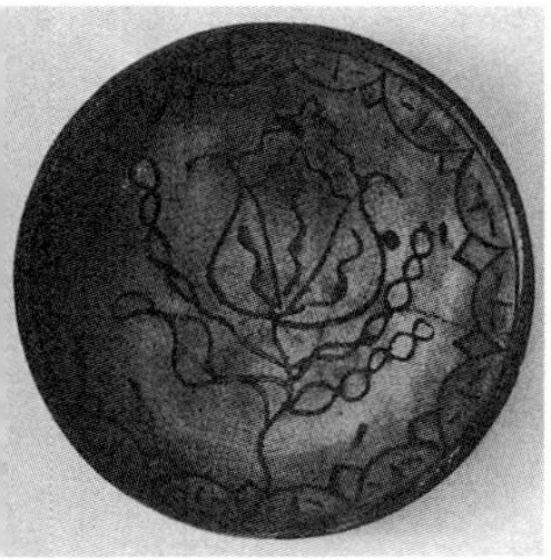

42

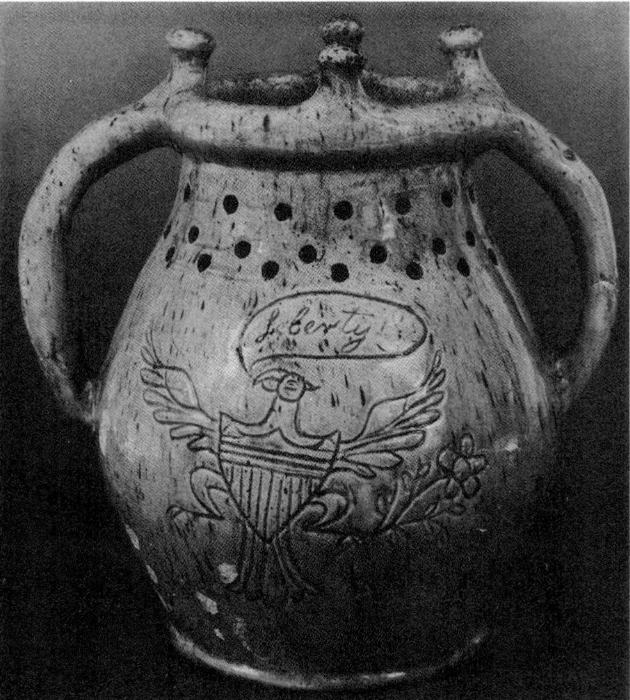

43

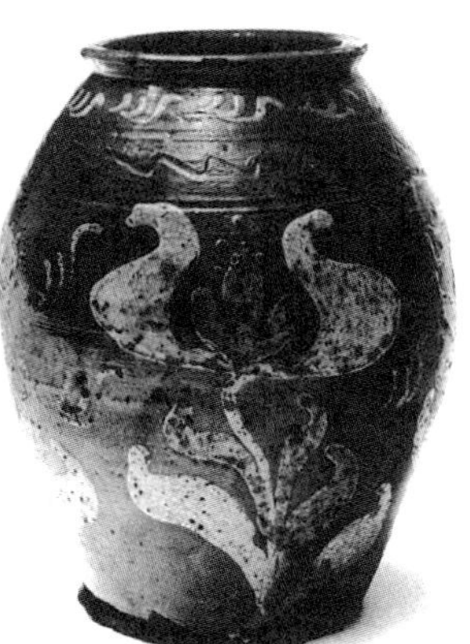

44

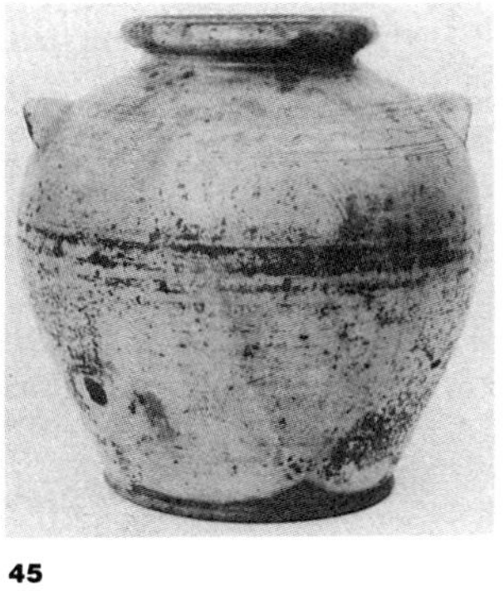

45

42 PLATE
Haycock Township, Bucks County
1814–30

Attributed to **Samuel Keller**

Marked on reverse: *SK*

Molded redware, coggled edge. Surface covered with white slip. Sgraffito decoration. Clear yellowish tan lead glaze.

Height 3.2 cm (1¼″), diameter 15.2 cm (6″)

Purchased: Baugh-Barber Fund. 38-15-3

43 PUZZLE JUG
Nockamixon Township, Bucks County
1809

Phillip Kline

Inscribed obverse: *Liberty;* reverse:
P x K   May the 5 1809
Incised on bottom: *Phillip Kline   His Muge May the 5 1809*

Wheel-thrown redware. Rolled rim, four spouts, and one handle are hollow to direct fluid past pierced neck. Clear reddish yellow lead glaze sprinkled with manganese (brown).

23 x 24 cm (9 x 9⅜″)

Gift of John T. Morris. 92-59

44 JAR
Nockamixon Township, Bucks County
1773

Attributed to **Christian Klinker**

Incised on bottom: *CK 1773*

Wheel-thrown redware. Curved sides and everted collar. Incised banding at shoulder. White slip decoration partially colored with copper oxide (green) on red body. Impurities in slip. Clear lead glaze on interior and exterior has turned grayish green.

Height 24 cm (9⅜″), diameter 19.5 cm (7⅝″)

Gift of John T. Morris. 94-21

45 JAR
Nockamixon Township, Bucks County
1787

Attributed to **Christian Klinker**

Incised on bottom: *CK 1787*

Wheel-thrown redware. Applied handles. Exterior and interior surfaces, except foot and bottom, covered with white slip and mottled with copper oxide (green). Thin clear yellowish mat lead glaze.

Height 26.1 cm (10¼″), diameter 28 cm (11″)

Purchased: Baugh-Barber Fund. 73-212-1

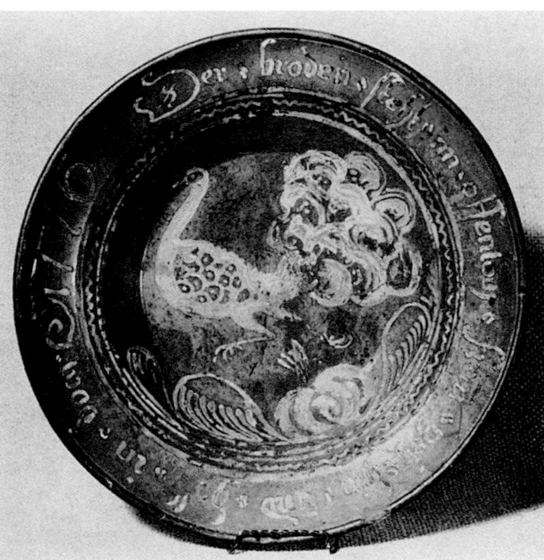

46

46 DISH

Hilltown Township, Bucks County
1776

Possibly by **John Leidy I**

Inscribed: *Der broden steht im offenloch. frau geh hin und holl in doch. 1776* ("The bread stands in the oven mouth. Woman go and get it out. 1776.")
Incised on bottom: *VIII*

Wheel-thrown redware. Slightly footed base, straight sides flaring into curved rim, raised and everted edge. White slip decoration. Clear yellowish lead glaze. Glaze losses on slip decoration.

Height 8.8 cm (3½"), diameter 39.3 cm (15½")

Purchased: Baugh-Barber Fund. 38-15-7

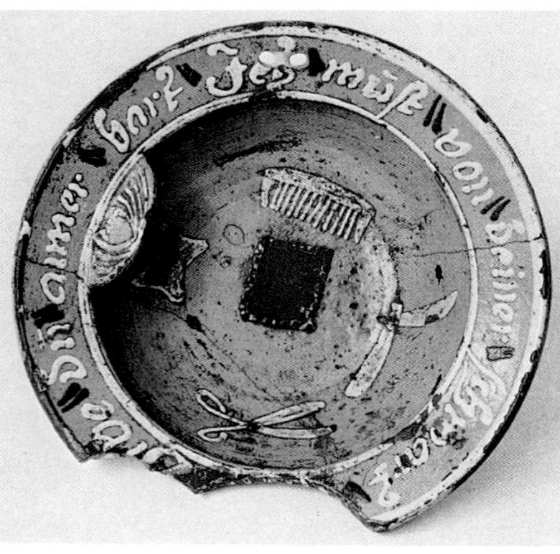

47

47 SHAVING BOWL

Hilltown Township, Bucks County
1780–1800

Probably by **John Leidy I**

Inscribed: *[?]ive du armer bart Ich muss von deiner schwart.* ("[?]You poor beard. I must leave your hide.")

Wheel-thrown redware. Raised, rounded sides, flat rim, slightly raised and everted edge. Barber's thumb rest, cut-out for chin, and two holes in rim for hanging thong. Surface covered with iron oxide (orange) in slip. Decoration in thick white slip and slip colored with copper oxide (green). Manganese (brown) daubs on rim. Clear lead glaze. Loss at edge.

Height 6 cm (2⅜"), diameter 20.5 cm (8⅛")

Gift of John T. Morris. 03-368

48 DISH

Hilltown Township, Bucks County
1790–1800

Attributed to **John Leidy I**

Wheel-thrown redware. Straight sides, flared rim, rolled everted edge. White slip surface with iron oxide (red) in decoration. Designs filled in with copper oxide (green). Clear lead glaze.

Height 4.4 cm (1¾"), diameter 25 cm (9⅞")

Purchased: Baugh-Barber Fund. 13-472

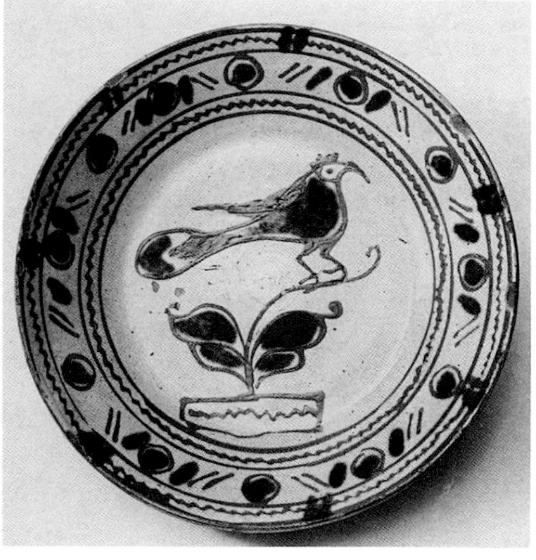

48

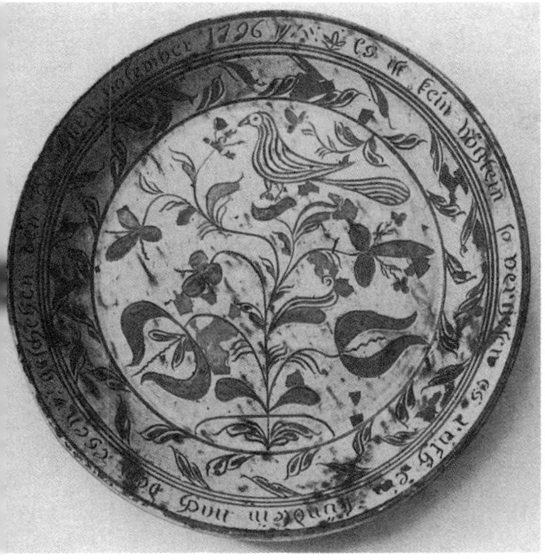

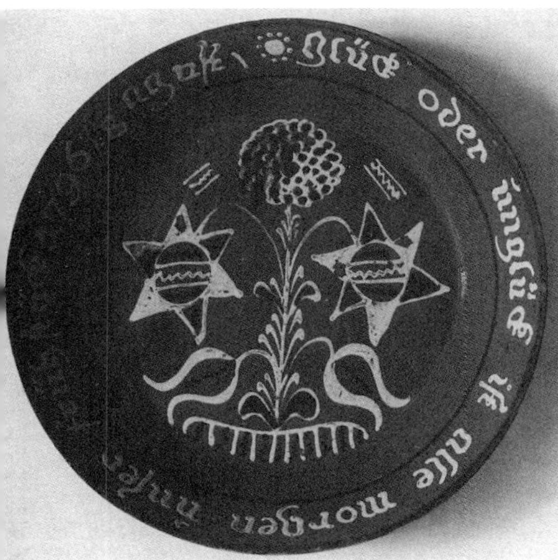

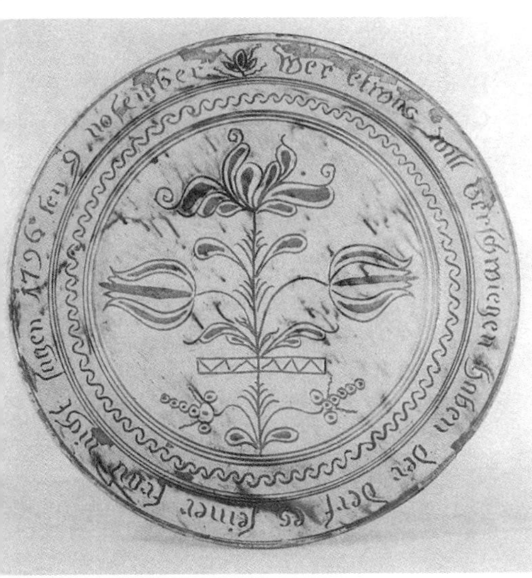

49 DISH

Hilltown Township, Bucks County
1796

Attributed to **John Leidy I**

Inscribed: *es ist kein vöglein so vergesen es ruth ein stündlein nach dem esen geschehen den 20 ichsten Nofember 1796* ("No bird is so entirely forgetful that it does not rest a short while after eating. Happened the 20th of November 1796.")

Wheel-thrown redware. Rounded sides, narrow rim, slightly everted edge. Surface covered with white slip daubed with copper oxide (green). Sgraffito banding and decoration. Thick clear yellowish lead glaze. Surface losses.

Height 6.3 cm (2½"), diameter 35 cm (13¾")

Gift of John T. Morris. 00-70

50 DISH

Hilltown Township, Bucks County
1796

Attributed to **John Leidy I**

Inscribed: *Glück oder unglück ist alle morgen unser frühstück. 1796 8 agust* ("Fortune or misfortune is our breakfast every morning. August 8, 1796")

Wheel-thrown redware. Rounded sides, flaring rim, slightly everted edge. Lightweight body. Copper oxide (green) in slip banding. Design in thick white slip colored with copper oxide (green) and manganese (brown). Clear reddish yellow lead glaze.

Height 6.7 cm (2⅝"), diameter 34 cm (13⅜")

Gift of John T. Morris. 00-69

51 DISH

Hilltown Township, Bucks County
1796

Attributed to **John Leidy I**

Inscribed: *Wer etwas will verschwiegen haben der derf es seiner frau nicht sagen. 1796 ten 9 Nofember* ("If one wishes to keep a secret, he may not tell his wife. November 9, 1796")

Wheel-thrown redware. Curved sides, narrow rim, slightly everted edge. Surface covered with white slip daubed with copper oxide (green). Sgraffito decoration and banding. Thick clear yellowish lead glaze.

Height 6.7 cm (2⅝"), diameter 35.6 cm (14")

Gift of John T. Morris. 92-43

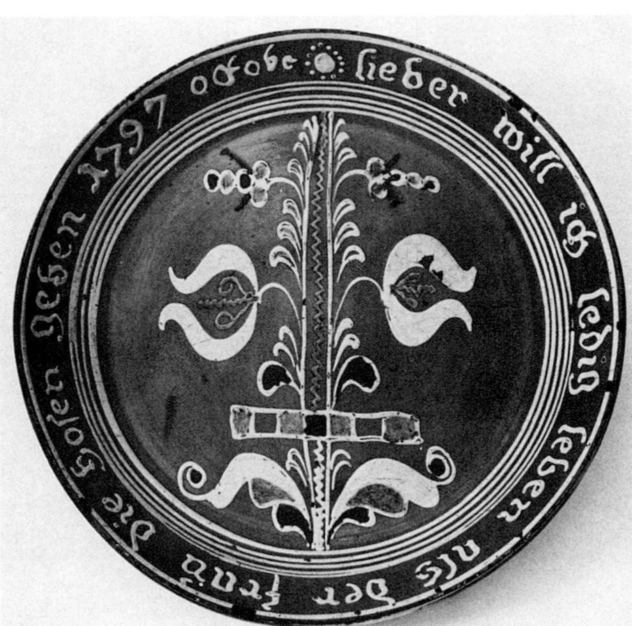

52

52 DISH
Hilltown Township, Bucks County
1797

Attributed to **John Leidy I**

Inscribed: *lieber will ich ledig leben als der frau die hosen geben. 1797 octobr* ("Rather would I single live than the wife the breeche give. October 1797")

Wheel-thrown redware. Curved sides, flaring rim, slightly everted edge. Thick white slip decoration partially colored with copper oxide (green) in slip and manganese (black brown). Thick clear reddish yellow lead glaze.

Height 5.4 cm (2⅛"), diameter 35.6 cm (14")

Gift of A. C. Harrison. 95-78

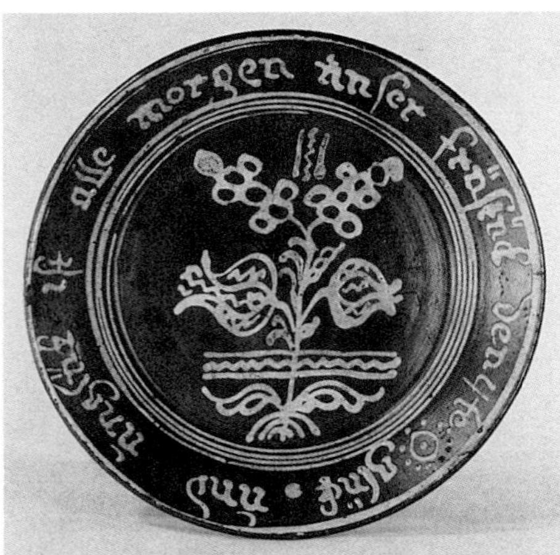

53

53 DISH
Hilltown Township, Bucks County
1797–1800

Attributed to **John Leidy I**

Inscribed: *glück und unglück ist alle morgen unser früstück. den 4 te* ("Fortune and misfortune is our breakfast every morning. The 4 [September]")

Wheel-thrown redware. Rounded sides, flaring rim, rolled everted edge. Thick white slip decoration on red body. Clear yellowish lead glaze.

Height 6 cm (2⅜"), diameter 34 cm (13⅜")

Purchased: Baugh-Barber Fund. 45-42-1

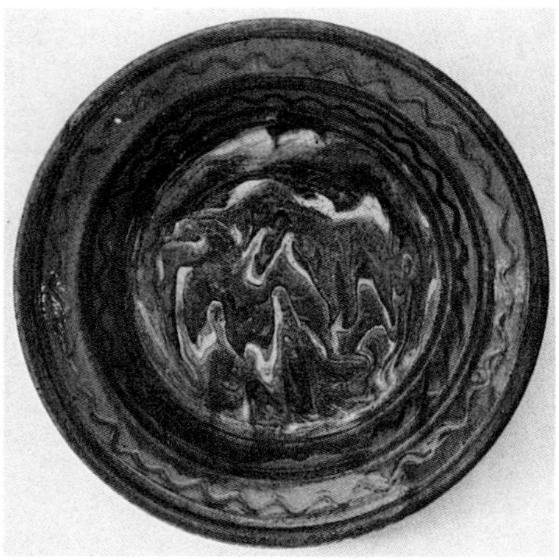

54

54 DISH
Hilltown Township, Bucks County
1797–1800

Possibly by **John Leidy I**

Incised on bottom: *VI*

Wheel-thrown redware. Straight sides, flaring rim, rolled everted edge. Copper oxide (green) in thick white slip in concentric bandings. Marbelized design in white slip colored with copper oxide (green) and manganese (brown black). Thick clear reddish lead glaze.

Height 4.8 cm (1⅞"), diameter 28.9 cm (11⅜")

Gift of Joseph H. Himes, in memory of his wife Eilleen C. Himes. 54-62-70

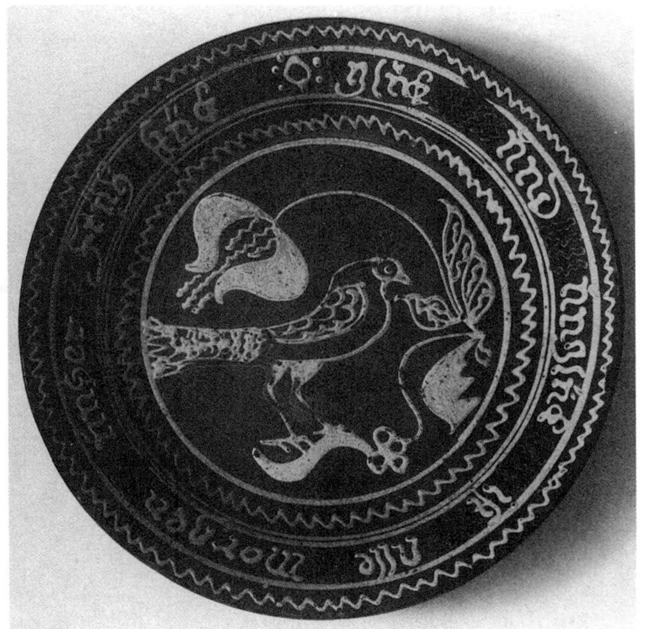

55

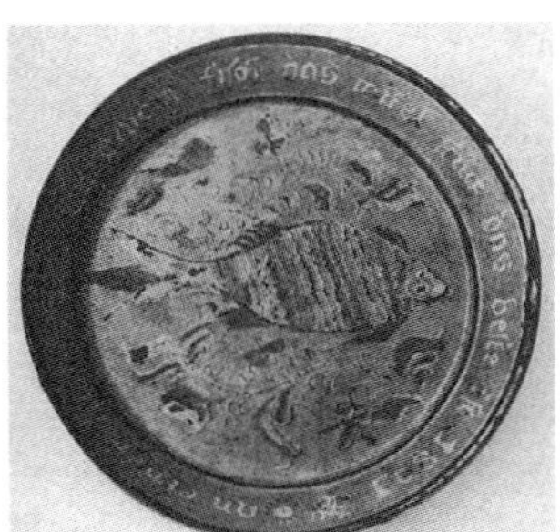

56

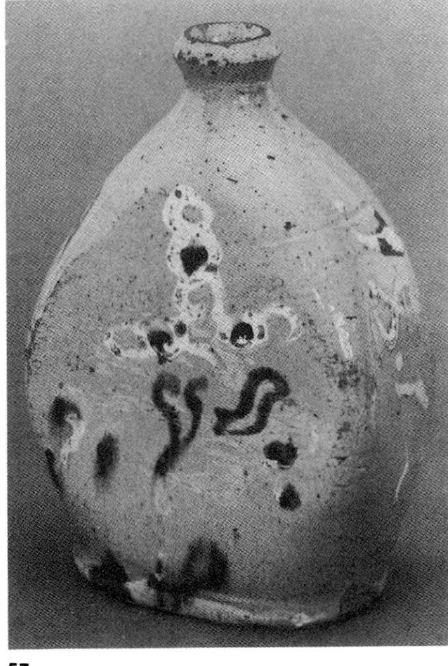

57

55 DISH
Hilltown Township, Bucks County
1798–1800

Attributed to **John Leidy I**

Inscribed: *glück und unglück ist alle morgen unser früh stück.* ("Fortune and misfortune are our breakfast every morning.")

Wheel-thrown redware. Raised bowl with straight sides and flared rim with everted edge. Decorated with thick white slip and slip colored with copper oxide (green). Clear yellowish lead glaze. Sponge marks visible on edges and reverse.

Height 5.7 cm (2¼"), diameter 35.5 cm (14")

Purchased. 93-217

56 DISH
Hilltown Township, Bucks County
1801

Attributed to **John Leidy I**

Inscribed: *an einer laufer und an einem fisch das mitel stück das beste ist. 1801* ("In a current and a fish the middle place is the best. 1801")

Wheel-thrown redware. Rounded sides, flaring rim, everted edge. Fish and foliage decoration in white slip and in slip colored with copper oxide (green). Banding in manganese (dark brown). Clear yellowish lead glaze.

Height 5.1 cm (2"), diameter 37.2 cm (14⅝")

Gift of John T. Morris. 02-13

57 BOTTLE
Hilltown Township, Bucks County
1812

Attributed to **John Leidy I**

Inscribed: *June the 19, 1812*
Incised on bottom: *4*

Wheel-thrown redware. Sides flattened, ends pinched for handgrasp. Incised banding at shoulder. Decorated with tulip (obverse) and flower (reverse) in white slip and manganese (black brown). Thick clear orange-tinged lead glaze.

15.5 x 11 cm (6⅛ x 4⅜")

Titus C. Geesey Collection. 55-94-10

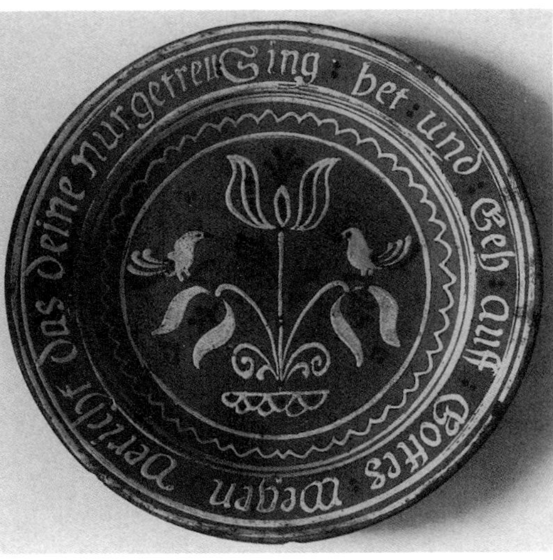

58

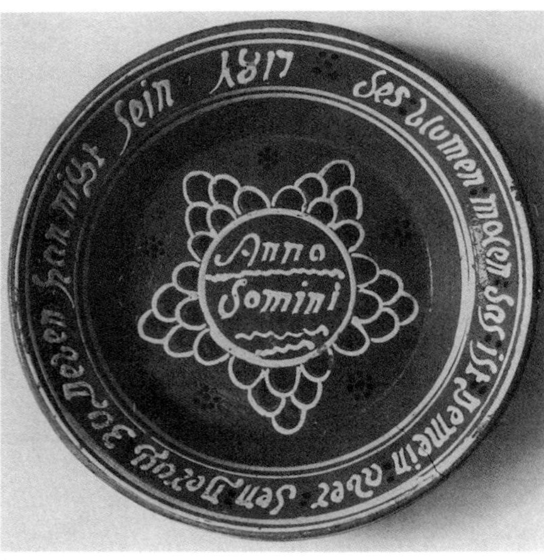

59

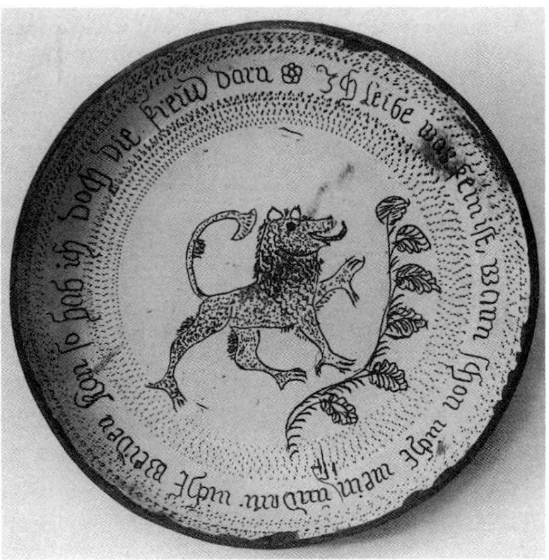

60

58 DISH
Franconia Township, Montgomery County
1800–1820

Attributed to **John Leidy II**

Inscribed: *Sing bet und Geh auff Gottes wegen Vericht das deine nur getreu* ("Sing, pray, and go on God's way. Perform what thou has to do faithfully.")

Wheel-thrown redware. Rounded sides, flaring rim, everted edge. Heavy body. Thick white slip decoration with brushed daubs of copper oxide (green) and manganese (brown). Clear orange lead glaze.

Height 6.3 cm (2½"), diameter 35.8 cm (14⅛")

Gift of John T. Morris. 00-9

59 DISH
Franconia Township, Montgomery County
1817

Attributed to **John Leidy II**

Inscribed: *Anno domini   des blumen molen das ist gemein aber den geruch zu geben kan nicht sein. 1817* ("In the year of Our Lord. Painting a flower is common, but giving it an odor cannot be done. 1817")
Incised on bottom: *VI*

Wheel-thrown redware. Concave side profile, wide rim, rolled everted edge. White slip decoration with copper oxide (green) in slip and manganese (black) in slip dots on red body. Clear lead glaze.

Height 4.5 cm (1¾"), diameter 25.4 cm (10")

Gift of John T. Morris. 03-354

60 PLATE
Upper Salford Township, Montgomery County
1820–30

John Leman

Inscribed: *Ich liebe was fein ist wann schon nicht mein ist und nur nicht werden kan so hab ich doch die freud darn* ("I love what is fine, although not mine, and never will own it yet I have the joy of it.")

Incised on reverse: *J°hanes Leman*

Molded redware, cut edge. White slip surface sgraffito decoration. Mat lead glaze; incising unglazed.

Height 3.8 cm (1½"), diameter 22 cm (8⅝")

Gift of John T. Morris. 21-46-41

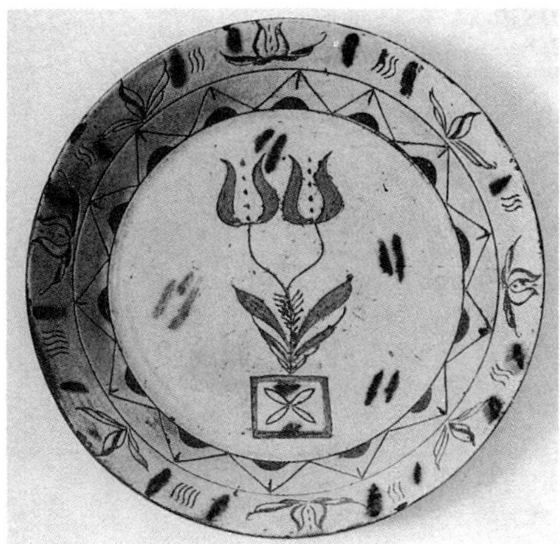

61

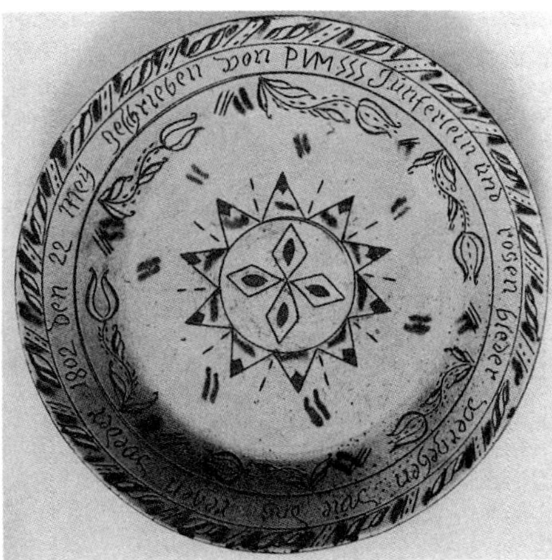

62

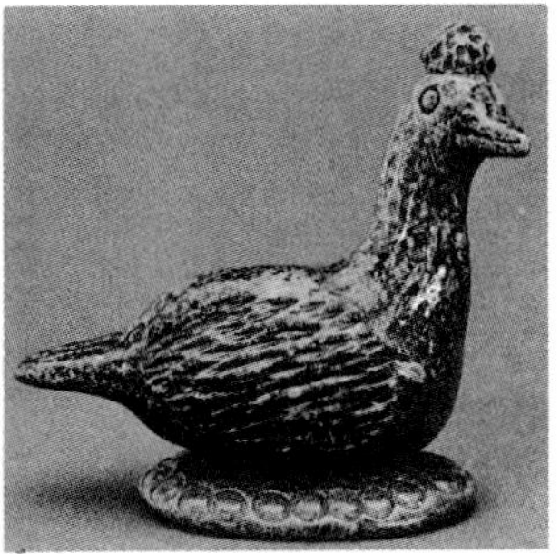

63

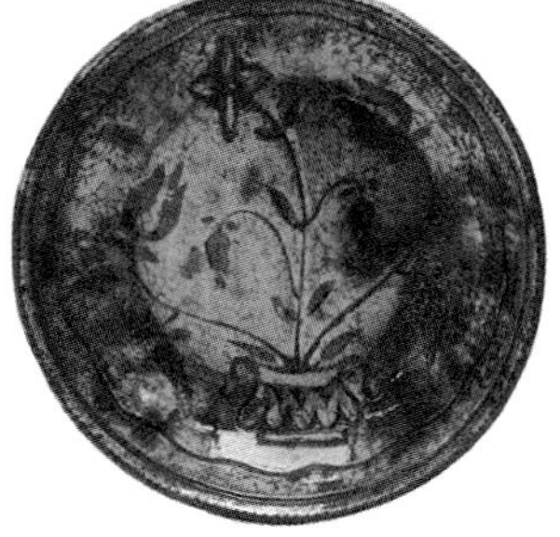

64

61 DISH
Bucks County
1800–1820

PNM

Wheel-thrown redware. Straight sides, everted edge. White slip surface with sgraffito decoration daubed with copper oxide (green). Clear lead glaze.

Height 4.7 cm (1⅞"), diameter 30.2 cm (11⅞")

Gift of John T. Morris. 00-8

62 DISH
Bucks County
1802

PNM

Inscribed: *Junferlein und rosen bleder vergehen wie das regen weder 1802 den 22 Meÿ geschrieben von PNM* ("Virgins and rose petals disappear like rainy weather. May 22, 1802, written by PNM")

Wheel-thrown redware. Rounded sides, flaring rim, square everted edge. Surface covered with white slip with parallel daubs of copper oxide (green). Sgraffito inscription and decoration. Clear yellowish lead glaze. Some pitting in glaze.

Height 5.1 cm (2"), diameter 34.9 cm (13¾")

Gift of John T. Morris. 00-7

63 BIRD RATTLE
New Berlin, Union County
1860–70

Attributed to **William Maize**

Modeled redware. Pieces of loose clay rattle inside hollow body. Mottled with manganese (brown). Clear lead glaze.

7 x 7.3 cm (2¾ x 2⅞")

Purchased: Baugh-Barber Fund. 30-59-11

64 PLATE
Montgomery County
1850–1920

Attributed to **Jacob Medinger**

Molded redware, coggled edge. White slip surface daubed with copper oxide (green). Sgraffito decoration. Thick yellowish tan lead glaze, pooled at bottom. Reverse blackened and discolored.

Height 4.1 cm (1⅝"), diameter 19.6 cm (7¾")

Purchased: Baugh-Barber Fund. 32-29-1a

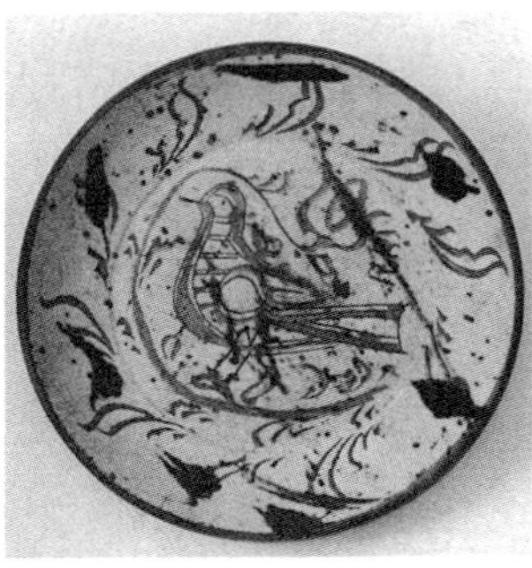

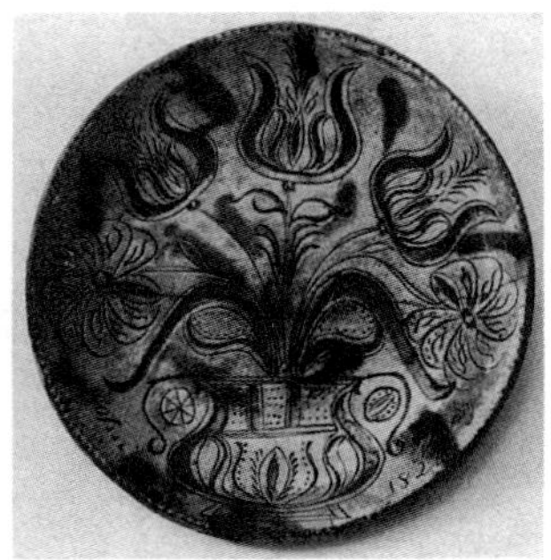

65   66

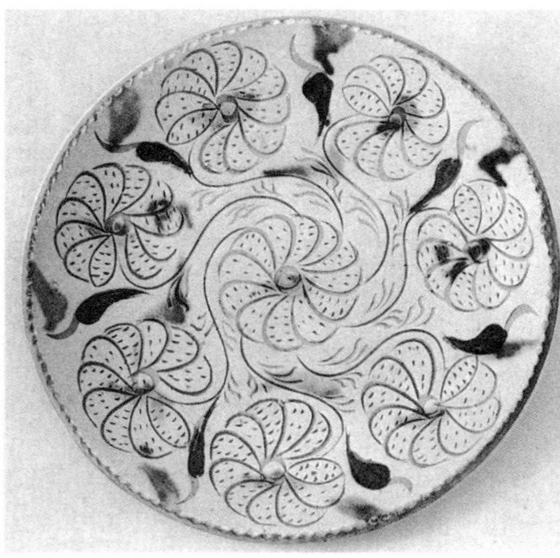

67

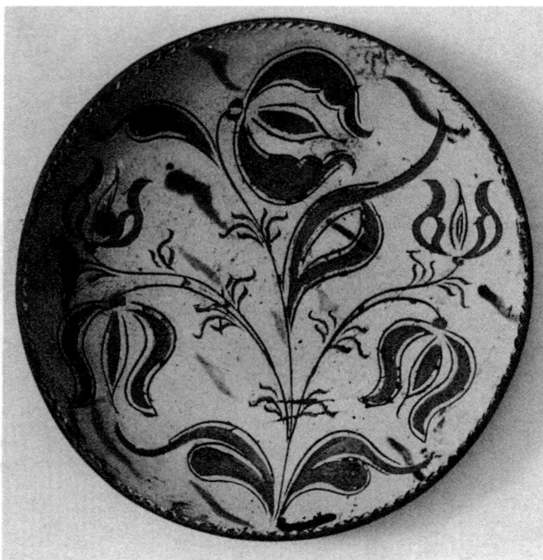

68

65   DISH
Haycock Township, Bucks County
1821

Attributed to **William Mills**

Inscribed: *1821*
Incised on reverse: 8

Wheel-thrown redware. Rounded sides, everted edge. Surface covered with white slip daubed with copper oxide (green). Sgraffito decoration. Thick clear yellowish lead glaze.

Height 4.5 cm (1¾″), diameter 27 cm (10⅝″)

Purchased: Baugh-Barber Fund. 58-160-1

66   PLATE
Haycock Township, Bucks County
1828

John Monday

Inscribed: *John   Monday   1828*

Molded redware, coggled edge. Surface covered with white slip daubed with copper oxide (green). Sgraffito decoration. Thick clear yellowish lead glaze.

Height 3.8 cm (1½″), diameter 25.7 cm (10⅛″)

Gift of John T. Morris. 00-12

67   PLATE
Haycock Township, Bucks County
1794–1844

Possibly by **Conrad Mumbouer**

Molded redware, coggled edge. Surface covered with white slip daubed with copper oxide (green). Sgraffito decoration. Foliage daubed with manganese (dark brown). Clear yellowish lead glaze.

Height 4.5 cm (1¾″), diameter 30.3 cm (11⅞″)

Purchased: Baugh-Barber Fund. 22-4-3

68   PLATE
Haycock Township, Bucks County
1794–1844

Possibly by **Conrad Mumbouer**

Molded redware, coggled edge. Heavy body. White slip surface with sgraffito decoration daubed with copper oxide (green). Clear lead glaze.

Height 4.1 cm (1⅝″), diameter 29.2 cm (11½″)

Gift of John T. Morris. 21-46-56

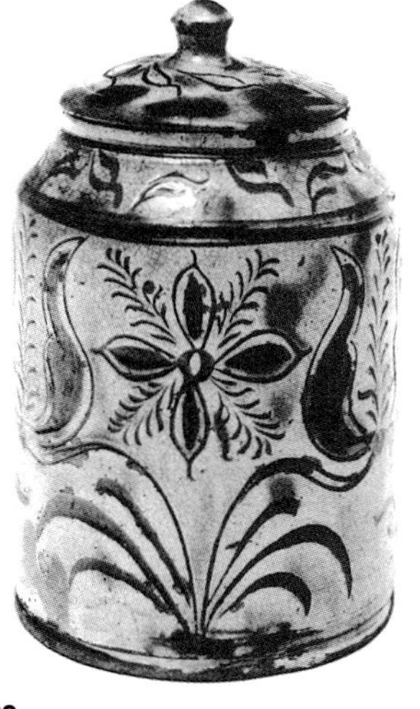

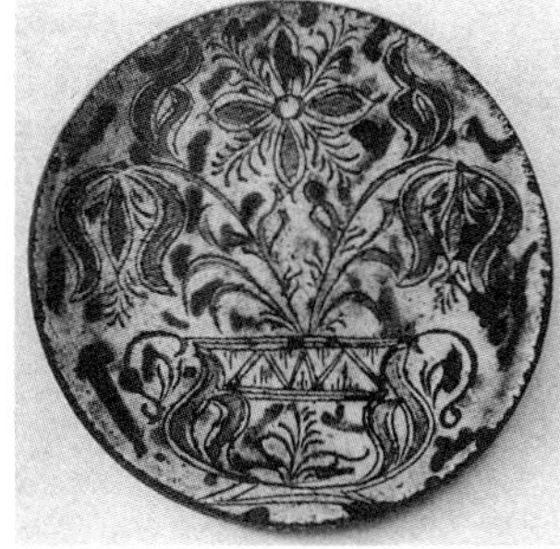

69   **70**

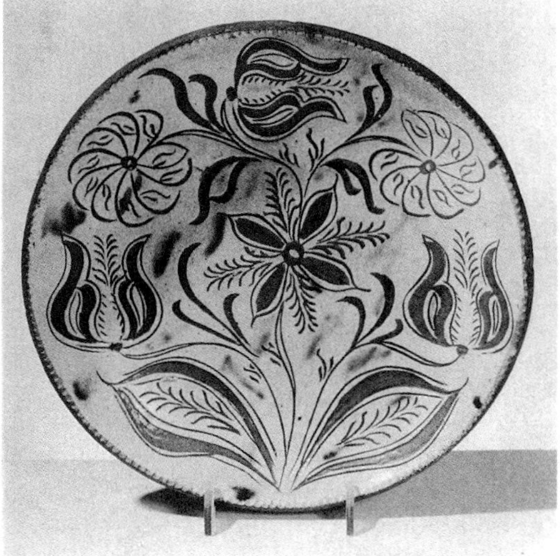

71

72

---

69 COVERED JAR

Haycock Township, Bucks County
1794–1844

Possibly by **Conrad Mumbouer**

Wheel-thrown redware. Edge of lid rests on neck and flange of lid fits inside neck of jar. Outside surfaces covered with white slip daubed with copper oxide (green). Sgraffito decoration. Clear yellowish lead glaze.

Height 20.3 cm (8″), diameter 13 cm (5⅛″)

Purchased: Baugh-Barber Fund. 38-15-14a,b

---

70 PLATE

Haycock Township, Bucks County
1794–1844

Possibly by **Conrad Mumbouer**

Molded redware, coggled edge. Surface covered with white slip. Sgraffito decoration partially colored with iron oxide (red) in lead glaze and mottled with copper oxide (green). Mat lead glaze. Reverse blackened from use.

Height 3.5 cm (1⅜″), diameter 29.9 cm (11¾″)

Purchased: Baugh-Barber Fund. 45-42-5

---

71 PLATE

Haycock Township, Bucks County
1794–1844

Possibly by **Conrad Mumbouer**

Molded redware, coggled edge. Surface covered with white slip daubed with copper oxide (green). Sgraffito decoration daubed with manganese (dark brown). Decoration highlighted with thick clear lead glaze; body has yellowish mat glaze.

Height 4.5 cm (1¾″), diameter 30.3 cm (11⅞″)

Purchased: Baugh-Barber Fund. 22-4-2

---

72 PLATE

Haycock Township, Bucks County
1794–1844

Possibly by **Conrad Mumbouer**

Molded redware, coggled edge. Surface covered with white slip daubed with copper oxide (green). Sgraffito decoration. Clear yellowish lead glaze.

Height 4.8 cm (1⅞″), diameter 29.2 cm (11½″)

Gift of Joseph H. Himes, in memory of his wife Eilleen C. Himes. 54-62-73

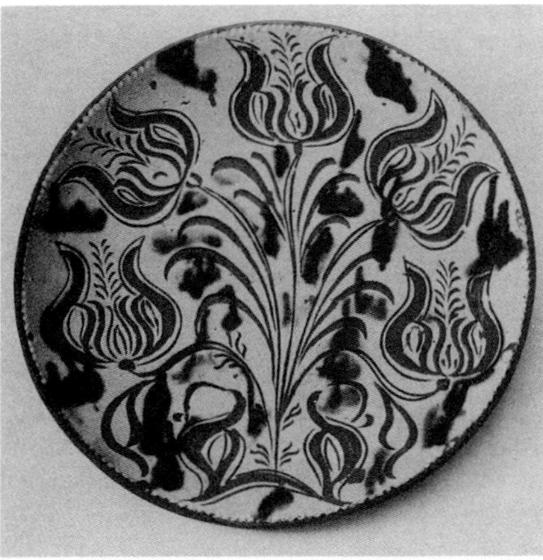

73

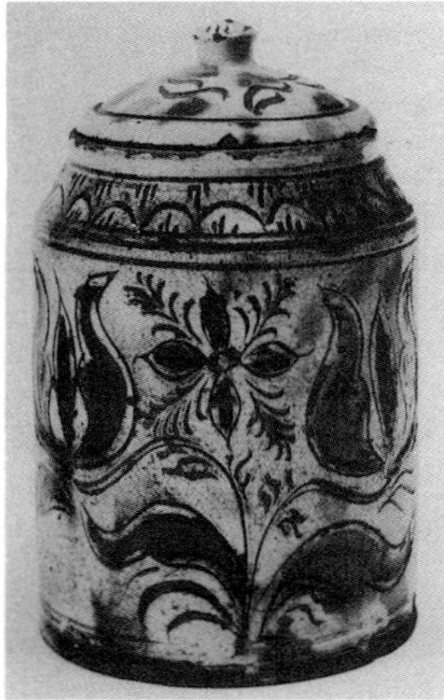

74

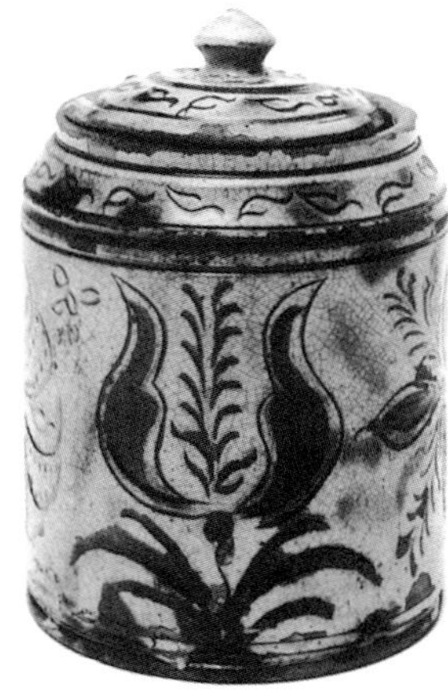

75

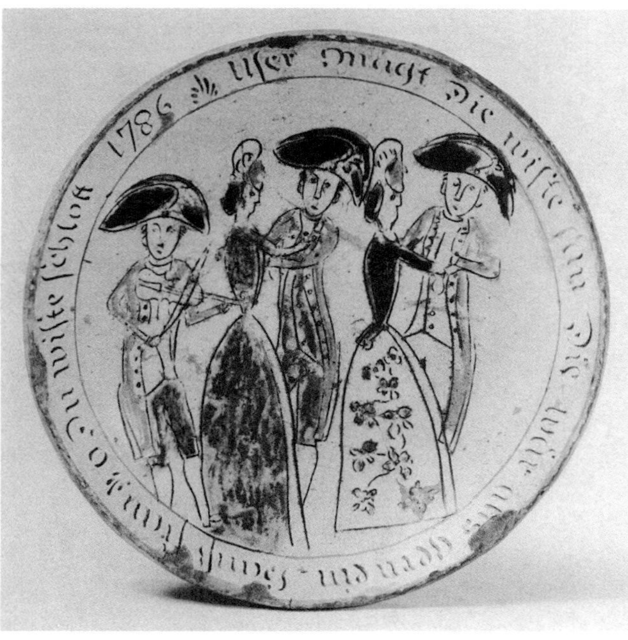

76

73 PLATE
Haycock Township, Bucks County
1794–1844

Possibly by **Conrad Mumbouer**

Molded redware, coggled edge. White slip surface daubed with copper oxide (green). Sgraffito design. Clear yellowish lead glaze. Random bits of red clay not cleaned off surface before glazing.

Height 4.5 cm (1¾″), diameter 30.3 cm (11⅞″)

Purchased: Baugh-Barber Fund. 38-15-6

---

74 COVERED JAR
Haycock Township, Bucks County
1794–1844

Possibly by **Conrad Mumbouer**

Wheel-thrown redware. Edge of lid overlaps neck and flange fits into neck of jar. Outside surfaces covered with white slip daubed with copper oxide (green). Sgraffito decoration. Clear yellowish lead glaze on all surfaces, except bottom.

Height 20.3 cm (8″), diameter 12.7 cm (5″)

Purchased: Baugh-Barber Fund. 13-478,a

---

75 COVERED JAR
Haycock Township, Bucks County
1794–1844

Possibly by **Conrad Mumbouer**

Wheel-thrown redware. Edge of lid rests on neck and flange fits into neck of jar. Surface covered with white slip daubed with copper oxide (green). Sgraffito decoration. Thick clear yellowish lead glaze.

Height 17.8 cm (7″), diameter 12.4 cm (4⅞″)

Purchased: Baugh-Barber Fund. 38-15-15a,b

---

76 PLATE
Upper Salford Township, Montgomery County
1786

Attributed to **Johannes Neis**

Inscribed: *Unser Magt Die wiste sau Die war alls gern ein Hauss frau O, Du wiste schlott 1786.* ("Our maid, the ugly pig, always wanted to be a housewife. O, you ugly slut. 1786")

Molded redware, coggled edge. Heavy body. Surface covered with white slip. Sgraffito inscription and banding. Men's coats in broad areas of sgraffito. Hats and one bodice colored with manganese (dark brown). Dress and knee breeches in copper oxide (green). Thick clear yellowish lead glaze.

Height 5.1 cm (2″), diameter 29.8 cm (11¾″)

Gift of John T. Morris. 00-20

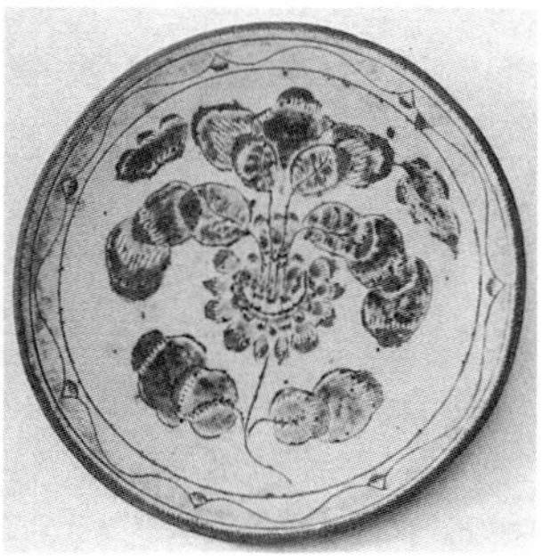

77 PLATE

Upper Salford Township, Montgomery County
1800–1810

Attributed to **John Neis**

Molded redware, coggled edge. Surface
covered with white slip. Sgraffito decoration
and pattern of punched dots in petals.
Controlled copper oxide (green) in design.
Clear reddish yellow mat lead glaze.

Height 4.2 cm (1⅝″), diameter 32.1 cm (12⅝″)

Purchased: Baugh-Barber Fund. 45-42-3

78 PLATE

Upper Salford Township, Montgomery County
1800–1810

Attributed to **John Neis**

Molded redware, coggled edge. Surface
covered with thin layer of white slip. Sgraffito
decoration with broad flat areas for horse, tips
of flowers, blanket, foliage, and border.
Designs colored with copper oxide (green).
Daubs of cobalt (blue) on flower and one leaf.
Thick clear yellowish lead glaze.

Height 4.7 cm (1⅞″), diameter 27.3 cm (10¾″)

Purchased. 93-219

79 PLATE

Upper Salford Township, Montgomery County
1800–1810

Attributed to **John Neis**

Inscribed: *Ich bin ein reitknecht als wie ein
ber ach wan ich nur im himmel wer* ("I am a
horse groom like a bear. I wish I were in
heaven.")
Incised on bottom: *JN*

Molded redware, coggled edge. Surface
covered with thin layer of white slip. Sgraffito
decoration with broad flat areas for flowers,
leaves, and vest. Punched dots at base of
flowers. Hat, vest, and boots colored with
manganese (brown). Jacket, breeches, and
foliage colored with copper oxide (green).
Large tulip, leaf, and buds colored with cobalt
oxide (blue). Thick clear yellowish lead glaze.

Height 3.8 cm (1½″), diameter 32.4 (12¾″)

Gift of John T. Morris. 92-54

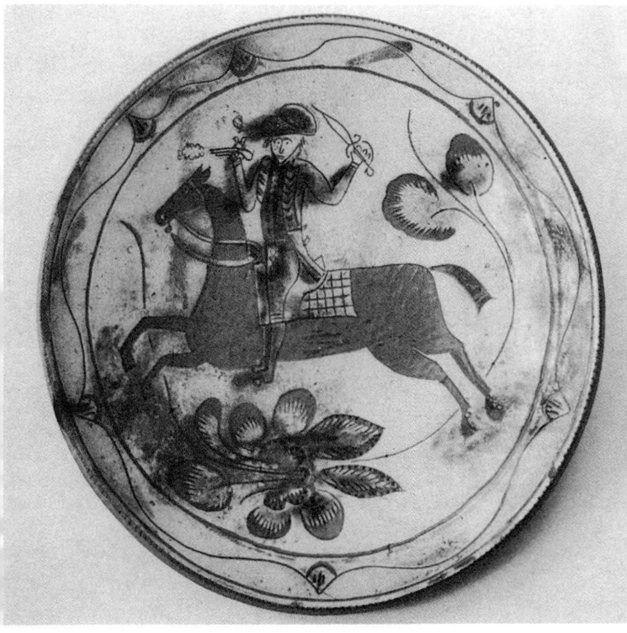

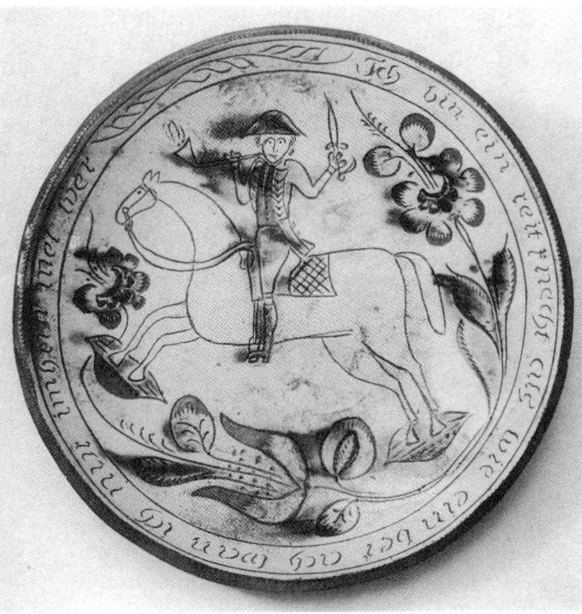

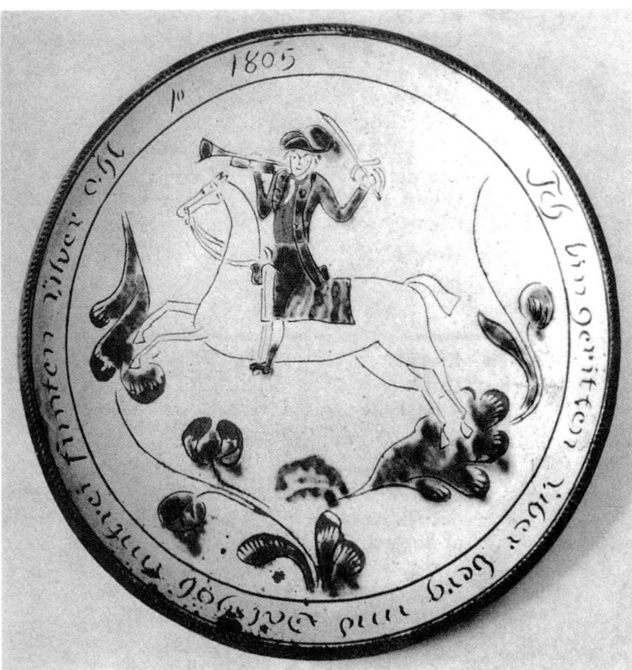

80

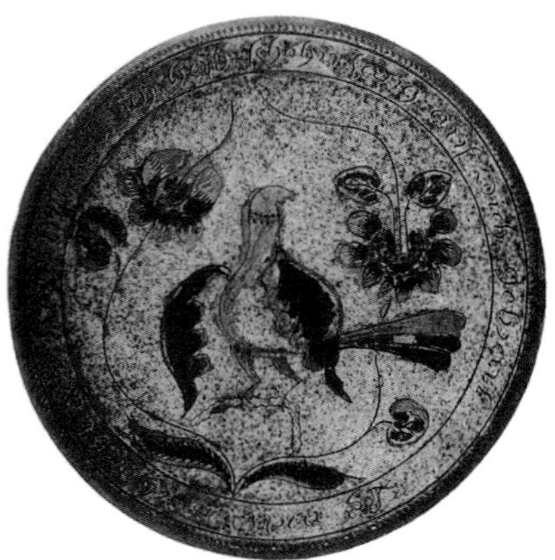

81

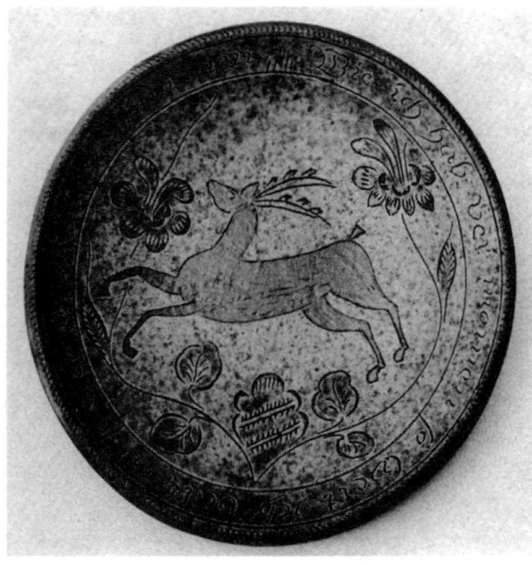

82

80 PLATE
Upper Salford Township, Montgomery County
1805

Attributed to **John Neis**

Inscribed: *Ich bin geritten uber berg und Dal hob untrei funten uwer ahl Ao 1805* ("I have ridden over hill and dale and have found disloyalty everywhere. In the year 1805")

Molded redware, coggled edge. Surface covered with white slip. Sgraffito decoration with broad flat areas for rider's vest and tips of leaves. Rider's coat and foliage colored with copper oxide (green). Manganese (brown) on hat and saddle. Saddle blanket striped green and brown. Thick clear lead glaze on colored areas and mat glaze overall.

Height 4.7 cm (1⅞″), diameter 31.7 cm (12½″)

Purchased: John T. Morris Fund. 21-46-53

81 PLATE
Upper Salford Township, Montgomery County
1810–12

Attributed to **John Neis**

Inscribed: *Es nacht mich ietzt der wohl lust art ich hab schohn lang auf dich gewart* ("Lust is still gnawing at me. I have waited for you for a long time")
Incised on reverse: *I Neis*

Molded redware, coggled edge. Heavy body. Surface pounced with copper oxide (green) while clay was damp. Sgraffito decoration with broad areas partially colored with manganese (black) in thick glaze. Punched dots on flower. Mat lead glaze.

Height 3.5 cm (1⅜″), diameter 25.4 cm (10″)

Gift of John T. Morris. 92-55

82 PLATE
Upper Salford Township, Montgomery County
1810–12

Attributed to **John Neis**

Inscribed: *Wie ich hab ver momen so wert ich balt auf Deine hochtzeit kommen* ("As I have gathered I will soon be coming to your wedding.")
Incised on reverse: *Neiss   JN*

Molded redware, coggled edge. Heavy body. Surface pounced with copper oxide (green) while clay was damp. Sgraffito decoration. Flowers and foliage highlighted with manganese (brown) in clear lead glaze. Mat lead glaze on surface.

Height 3.8 cm (1½″), diameter 25.1 cm (9⅞″)

Purchased: Baugh-Barber Fund. 38-15-9

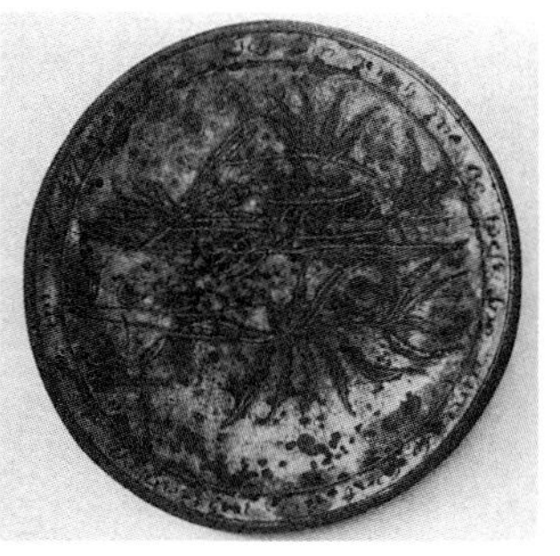
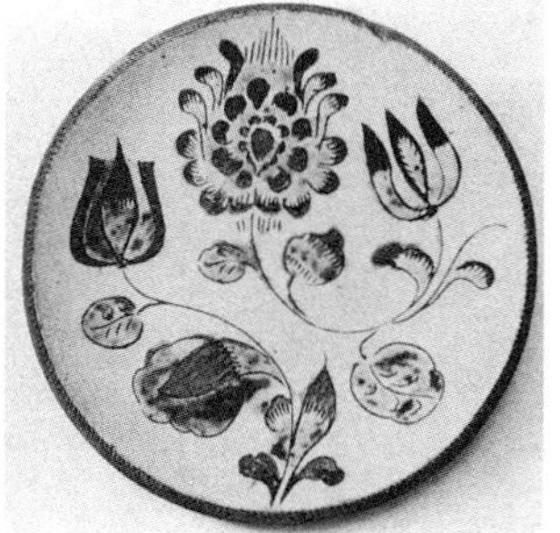

83   86

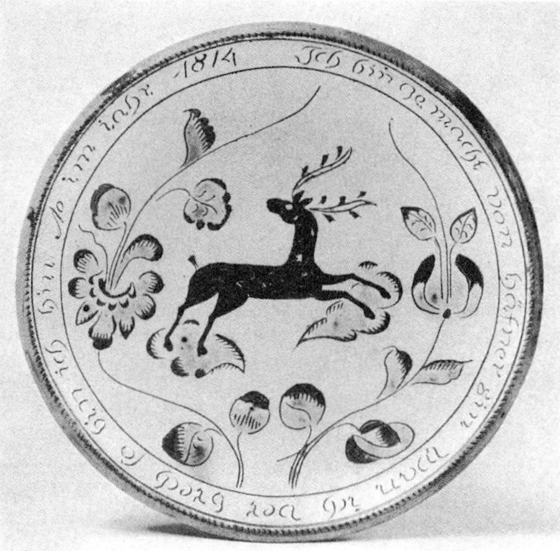

84

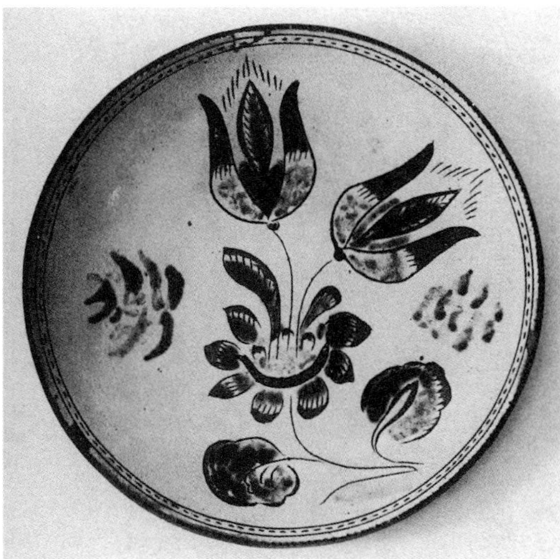

85

83 PLATE

Upper Salford Township, Montgomery County
1812

Attributed to **John Neis**

Inscribed: *Ich bin noch nie gewest wo man so
spat zu mittag est Ao im iahr 1812* ("I have
never been any place where people eat their
dinner so late. In the year 1812")

Molded redware, coggled edge. White slip
surface with random copper oxide (green).
Sgraffito decoration of rabbit and spiky foliage.
Clear yellowish lead glaze. Surface losses.

Height 4.2 cm (1⅝"), diameter 31.4 cm (12⅜")

Gift of John T. Morris. 94-24

84 PLATE

Upper Salford Township, Montgomery County
1814

Attributed to **John Neis**

Inscribed: *Ich bin gemacht von häfner zin wan
ich ver brech so bin ich hin Ao im iahr 1814*
("I am made of potters' pewter. When I break
then I am gone. In the year 1814")

Molded redware, coggled edge. Surface
covered with white slip. Sgraffito decoration.
Foliage daubed with copper oxide (green) in
thick glaze over yellowish mat lead glaze.

Height 3.5 cm (1⅜"), diameter 24.8 cm (9¾")

Purchased. 93-212

85 PLATE

Upper Salford Township, Montgomery County
1815–30

Attributed to **John Neis**

Molded redware, coggled edge. White slip
surface. Sgraffito decoration colored with
copper oxide (green), manganese (red brown),
and oxide of cobalt (blue) in thick lead glaze.
Mat lead glaze.

Height 3.2 cm (1¼"), diameter 22.5 cm (8⅞")

Gift of John T. Morris. 92-52

86 PLATE

Upper Salford Township, Montgomery County
1820–30

Attributed to **John Neis**

Molded redware, coggled edge. Surface
covered with white slip. Sgraffito decoration
dappled with copper oxide (green) and
touched with thick clear glaze. Mat lead glaze.

Height 3.2 cm (1¼"), diameter 25.1 cm (9⅞")

Purchased: John T. Morris Fund. 21-46-29

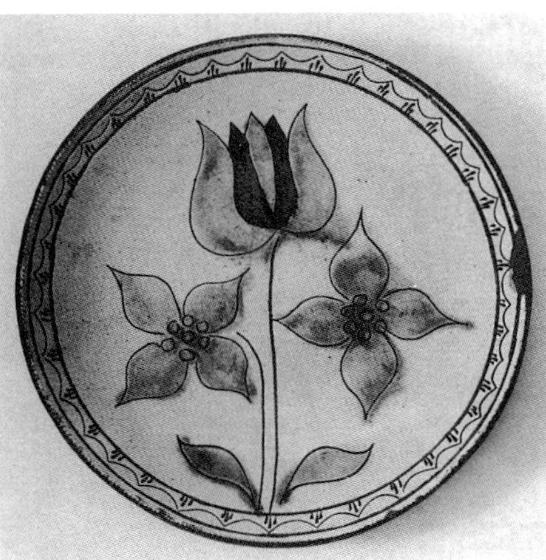

87

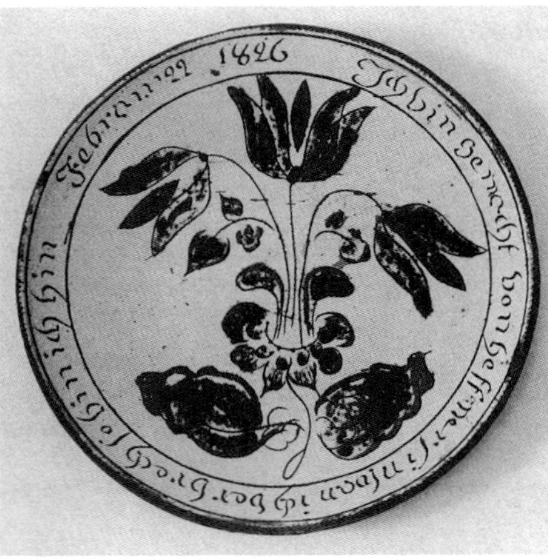

88

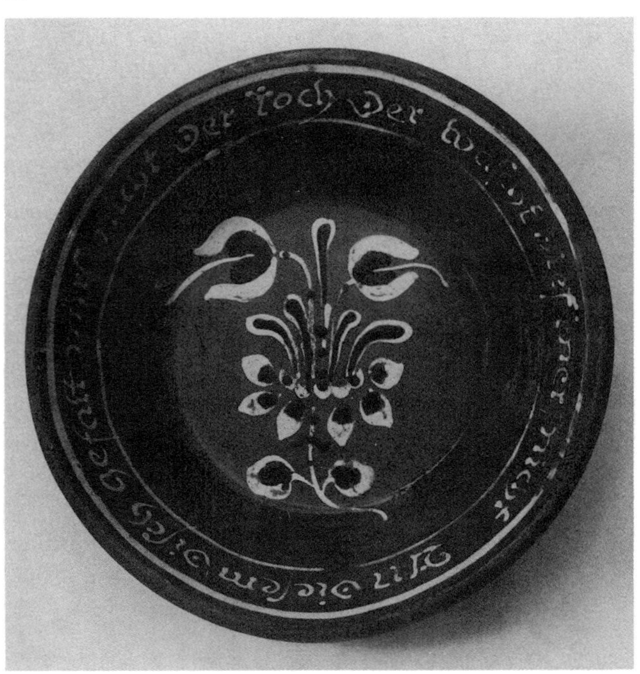

89

87 PLATE
Upper Salford Township, Montgomery County
1820–30

Attributed to **John Neis**

Molded redware, coggled edge. Surface
covered with white slip. Sgraffito decoration.
Flowers and foliage daubed with copper oxide
(green). Clear yellowish lead glaze.

Height 4 cm (1½″), diameter 23.5 cm (9¼″)

Gift of John T. Morris. 00-11

88 PLATE
Upper Salford Township, Montgomery County
1826

Attributed to **John Neis**

Inscribed: *Ich bin gemacht von heffner sin
wan ich ver brech so bin ich hin Februar 22,
1826* ("I am made of potter's thoughts. When I
break, I will be gone. February 22, 1826")

Molded redware, coggled edge. Center
slightly raised. Surface covered with white
slip. Sgraffito decoration with deep dots in
center petals and foliage. Controlled copper
oxide (dark green) on flowers and foliage. Clear
reddish yellow mat lead glaze.

Height 3.5 cm (1⅜″), diameter 25.4 cm (10″)

Purchased: John T. Morris Fund. 21-46-27

89 DISH
Upper Salford Township, Montgomery County
1845–47

Attributed to **John Neis**

Inscribed: *An diesen disch gefalt mirs nicht
Der Koch Der wascht die finer nicht.* ("This
table meets not my demands. The cook here
doesn't wash her hands.")
Incised on bottom: *8*

Wheel-thrown redware. Straight sides, everted
rolled edge. Lightweight body. Thick white
slip decoration highlighted with additional
manganese-colored (brownish black) slip.
Clear brownish lead glaze.

Height 7.3 cm (2⅞″), diameter 31.1 cm (12¼″)

Purchased: Baugh-Barber Fund. 45-42-4

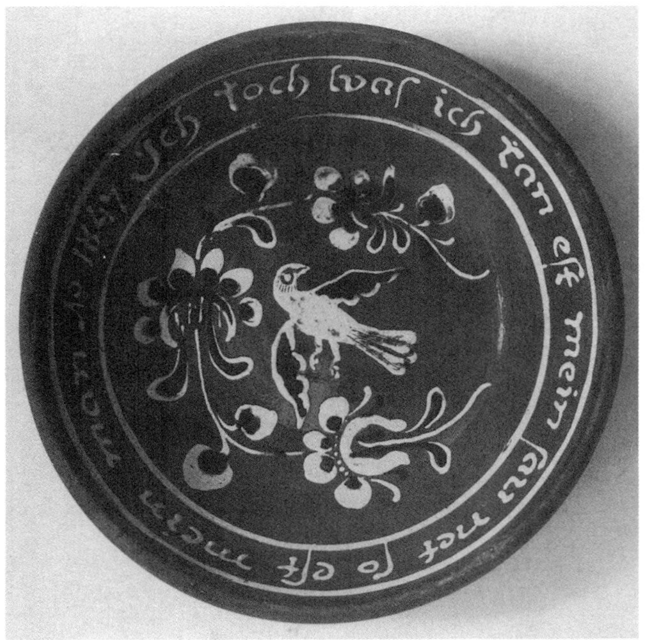

90

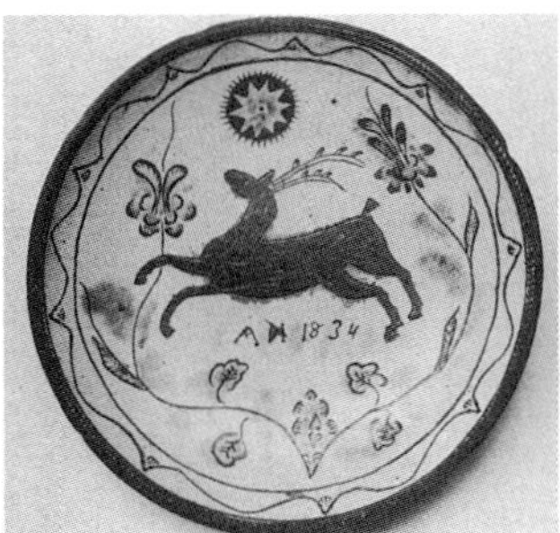

91

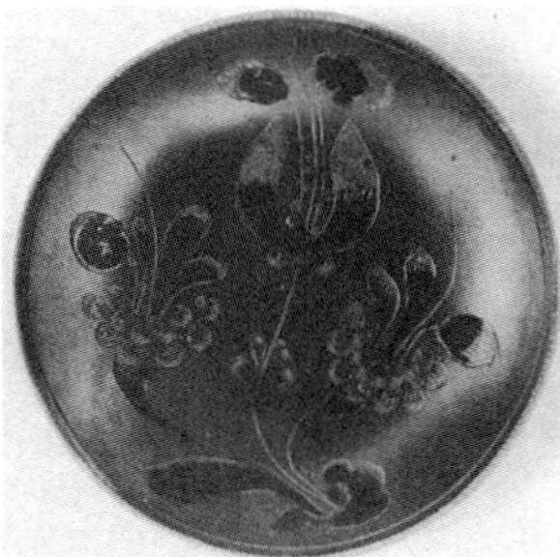

93

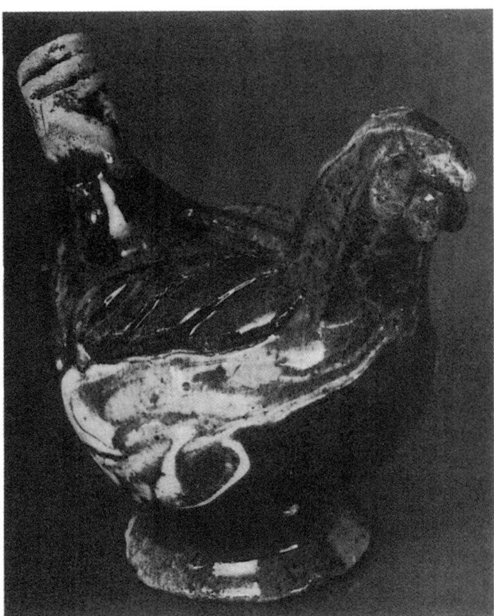

92

90 DISH
Upper Salford Township, Montgomery County
1847

Attributed to **John Neis**

Inscribed: *Ich koch was ich kan est mein sau net so est mein man Ao 1847.* ("I cook what I can. If my pig will not eat it my husband will. In the year 1847")
Incised on bottom: 8

Wheel-thrown redware. Rounded sides, everted rolled edge. Lightweight body. Thick white slip decoration highlighted with additional manganese-colored (brownish black) slip. Sgraffito detail of bird's tail and eye. Clear brownish lead glaze.

Height 6.6 cm (2⅝"), diameter 31.1 cm (12¼")

Gift of John T. Morris. 92-50

91 PLATE
Upper Salford Township, Montgomery County
1834

Attributed to **Abraham Nice**

Inscribed: *An 1834*

Molded redware, coggled edge. White slip surface. Sgraffito decoration colored with red slip and daubed with copper oxide (green) and cobalt oxide (blue). Clear lead glaze.

Height 3.8 cm (1½"), diameter 25.1 cm (9⅞")

Purchased: Baugh-Barber Fund. 06-376

92 BIRD WHISTLE AND BANK
Upper Salford Township, Montgomery County
1820–40

Attributed to **John Nice**

Wheel-thrown and modeled redware. Wings applied and incised with feather pattern. Cock's comb is missing. Daubed with white slip. Thick clear brownish glaze.

8.2 x 8.9 x 5.4 cm (3¼ x 3½ x 2⅛")

Gift of John T. Morris. 00-189

93 PLATE
Upper Salford Township, Montgomery County
1830–40

Attributed to **John Nice**

Inscribed on reverse in pencil:
Gotleib MOSER

Molded redware, coggled edge. Surface covered with manganese (black). Sgraffito decoration highlighted with manganese in thick lead glaze. Mat lead glaze. Cloth texture impressed into reverse.

Height 3.5 cm (1⅜"), diameter 22.5 cm (8⅞")

Gift of John T. Morris. 92-51

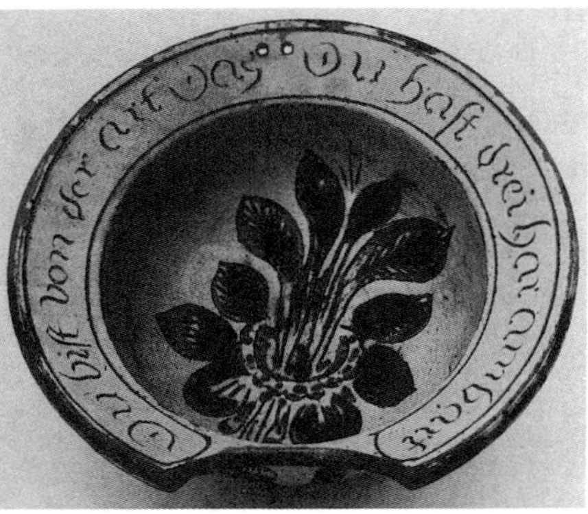

94

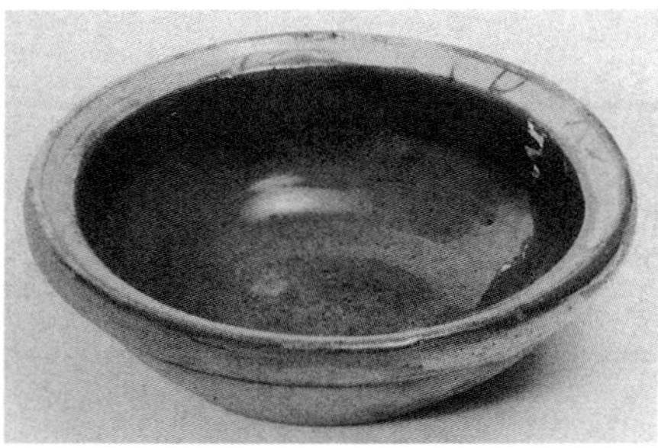

95

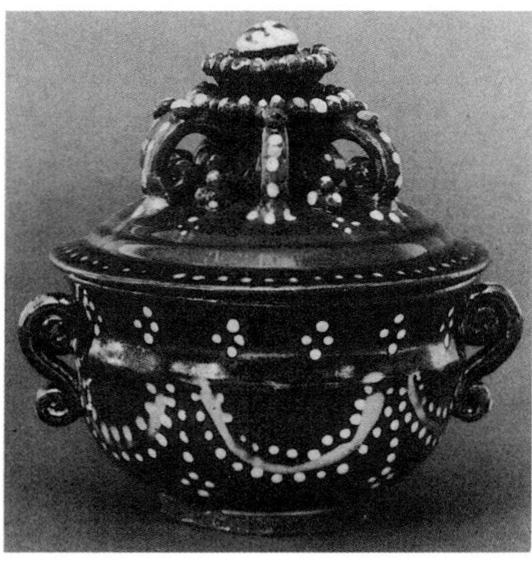

96

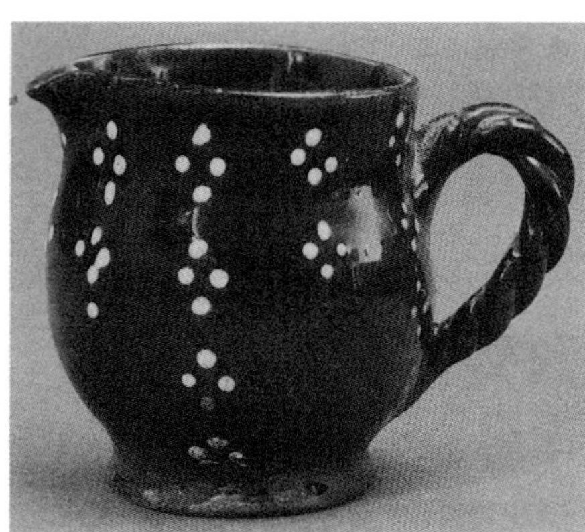

97

94 SHAVING BASIN
Upper Salford Township, Montgomery County
1830–40

Attributed to **John Nice**

Inscribed: *Du bist von der art Das du hast drei har am bart* ("You are of the type that has three hairs on the chin.")

Wheel-thrown redware. Raised foot, rounded sides, flaring edge with everted rim. Two hanging holes and section cut out for chin. Surfaces, except foot, covered with white slip. Sgraffito decoration on bottom and sides of exterior and on edge and interior of basin. Punched dots around center of flower. Designs partially colored with manganese (black) in lead glaze. Thin reddish yellow mat glaze.

Height 6.4 cm (2½"), diameter 17.5 cm (6⅞")

Purchased: Baugh-Barber Fund. 93-248

95 BOWL
Upper Salford Township, Montgomery County
1830–40

Attributed to **John Nice**

Wheel-thrown redware. Narrow rim, square everted edge. Edge banding in white slip and manganese (brownish black). Clear lead glaze.

Height 2.8 cm (1⅛"), diameter 9.4 cm (3¾")

Gift of Edwin Atlee Barber. 95-75

96 COVERED BOWL
Upper Salford Township, Montgomery County
1830–40

Attributed to **John Nice**

Wheel-thrown and modeled redware. Overhanging lid flanged to fit inside flaring neck of bowl. Knop with two flaring collars turned in one piece with lid. Beads, scrolled ornament, and bowl handles applied. Surface covered with manganese (brown) in slip. Dotted with white slip. Swag lines on bowl in tan slip. Thick brownish lead glaze on interior and exterior, except bottom.

15.2 x 15.9 cm (6 x 6¼")

Purchased. 93-215

97 PITCHER
Upper Salford Township, Montgomery County
1830–40

Attributed to **John Nice**

Wheel-thrown redware. Twisted handle applied. Manganese (brown) in slip over surfaces dotted with white slip. Thick brownish lead glaze; foot unglazed.

7.5 x 9.7 cm (2⅞ x 3¾")

Purchased. 93-216

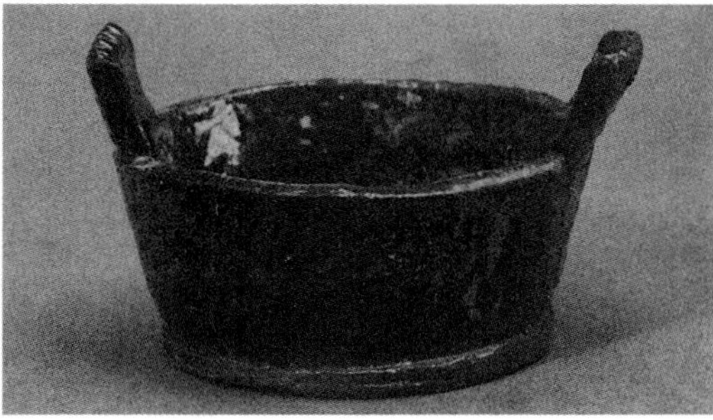

98

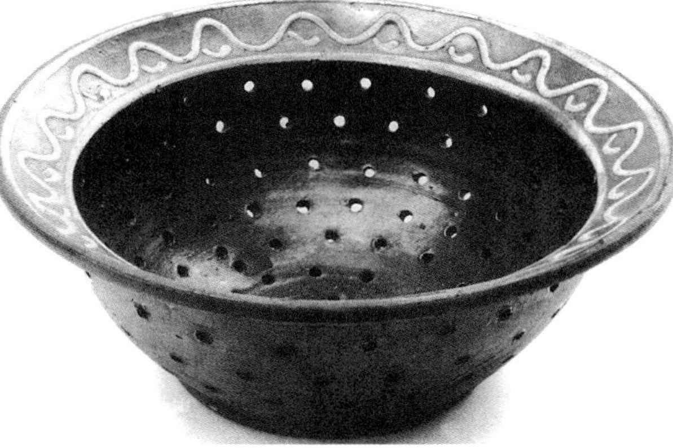

99

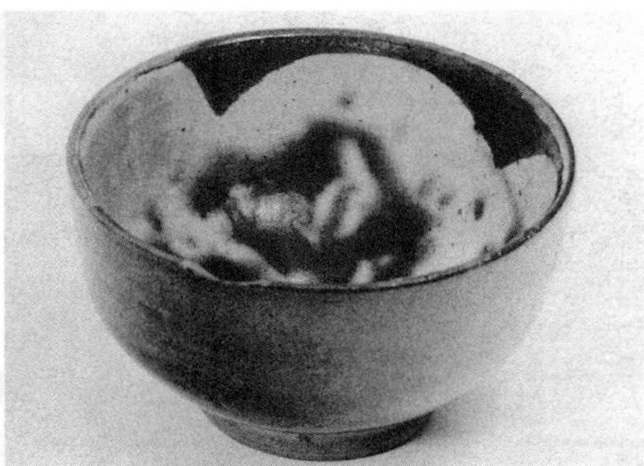

100

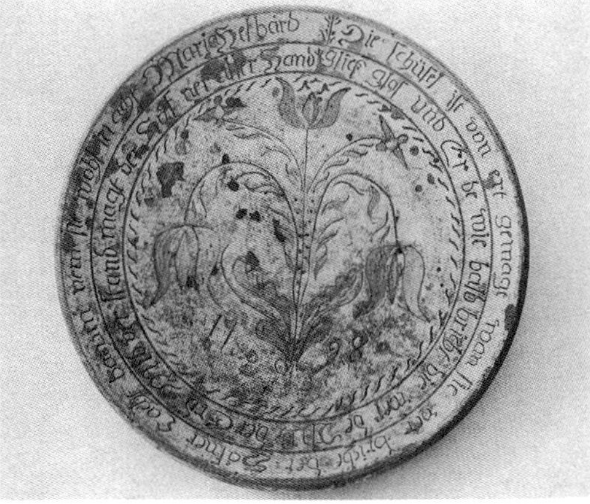

101

98 TOY TUB

Upper Salford Township, Montgomery County

1830–40

Attributed to **John Nice**

Wheel-thrown redware. Sides cut away leaving handles with coggled edges. Hole through each handle. Manganese (brownish black) in lead glaze.

4.7 x 8.1 cm (1⅞ x 3⅛″)

Purchased. 93-180

99 COLANDER

Upper Salford Township, Montgomery County

1830–50

Attributed to **John Nice**

Wheel-thrown redware. Curved sides, flaring rim, everted edge. Perforations through sides and bottom. White slip decoration. Clear brown lead glaze.

Height 13.4 cm (5¼″), diameter 34 cm (13⅜″)

Purchased: Baugh-Barber Fund. 95-89

100 BOWL

Upper Salford Township, Montgomery County

1830–50

Attributed to **John Nice**

Wheel-thrown redware. Interior decoration of white slip in petal-like pattern daubed with copper oxide (green). Thick clear lead glaze; foot unglazed.

Height 5.1 cm (2″), diameter 9.5 cm (3¾″)

Gift of Edwin Atlee Barber. 95-74

101 DISH

Limerick Township, Montgomery County

1798

Attributed to **Samuel Paul**

Inscribed: *Die schüsel ist von ert gemacht Wan sie ver bricht der Häfner lacht Darum nem sie whol in acht Maria Helbard Glick glas und Erde wie bald bricht die werde Aus der erd mit verstand macht der Häfner aller Hand 1798.* ("The dish is made of earth. When it breaks the potter laughs. Therefore take good care of it. Maria Helbard. Luck, glass, and earth, how soon the value is broken. From the earth with sense the potter makes everything. 1798")

Wheel-thrown redware. Rounded sides, everted edge. Surface covered with white slip. Sgraffito decoration. Clear yellowish lead glaze. Made for Maria Helbert Kulp.

Height 5.1 cm (2″), diameter 33 cm (13″)

Gift of John T. Morris. 00-71

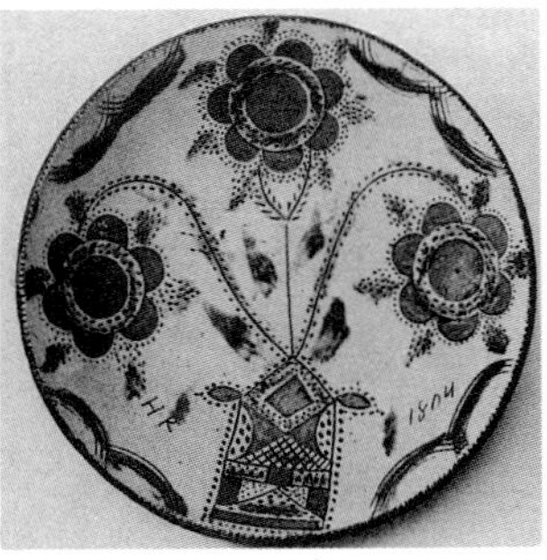

102

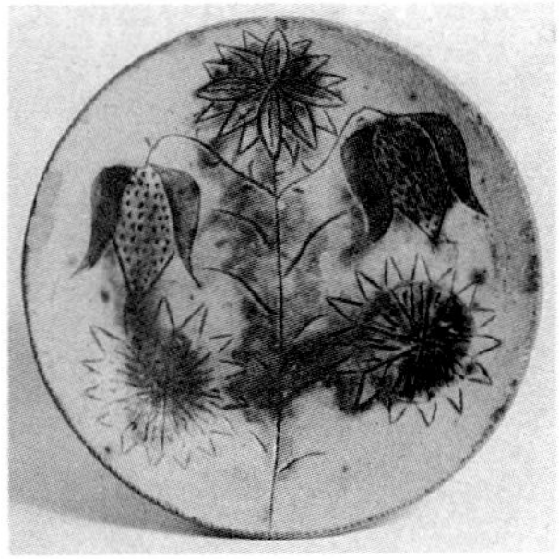

103

102 PLATE
1804

Attributed to **Heinrich Roth**
Inscribed: *HR 1804*

Molded redware, coggled edge. Raised circular band near center from mold. White slip surface with copper oxide (green) and sgraffito decoration. Clear yellowish lead glaze.

Height 5.1 cm (2″), diameter 30.5 cm (12″)

Purchased: Baugh-Barber Fund. 58-124-3

103 PLATE
Upper Hanover Township, Montgomery County
1804–20

Probably by **Henry Roudebush**

Molded redware, coggled edge. Heavy body. White slip surface with copper oxide (green) and sgraffito decoration. Clear tan lead glaze.

Height 5.2 cm (2″), diameter 30.2 cm (11⅞″)

Purchased: Baugh-Barber Fund. 74-107-1

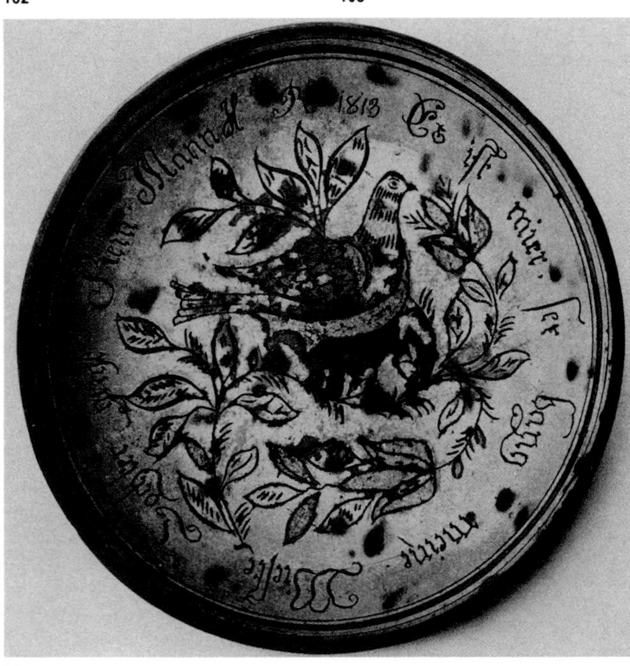

104

104 PLATE
Upper Hanover Township, Montgomery County
1813

Attributed to **Henry Roudebush**

Inscribed: *Es ist mier ser bang meine Wieste Tochter grigt Kein Mann H R 1813* ("I am afraid that my ugly daughter will get no husband. H R 1813")

Molded redware, plain edge. Slightly raised in center. Heavy body. White slip surface with copper oxide (green) and sgraffito decoration. Compass-incised lettering guide. Clear yellowish lead glaze.

Height 4.5 cm (1¾″), diameter 25.7 cm (10⅛″)

Gift of John T. Morris. 03-370

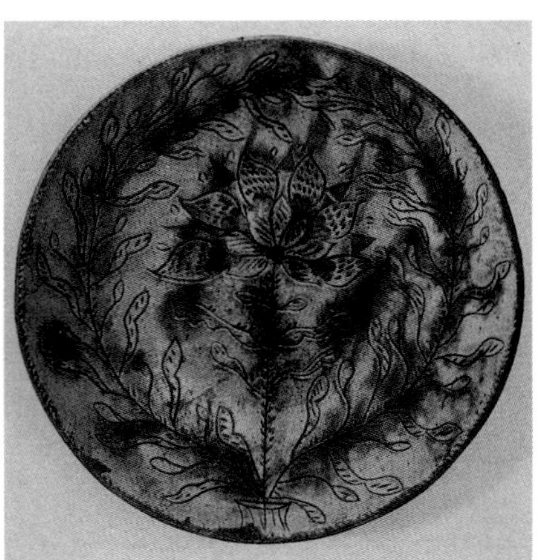

105

105 PLATE
Upper Hanover Township, Montgomery County
1815–20

Attributed to **Henry Roudebush**

Molded redware, coggled edge. White slip surface with sgraffito decoration colored with red slip and copper oxide (green). Clear lead glaze.

Height 4.8 cm (1⅞″), diameter 27.3 cm (10¾″)

Gift of John T. Morris. 08-220

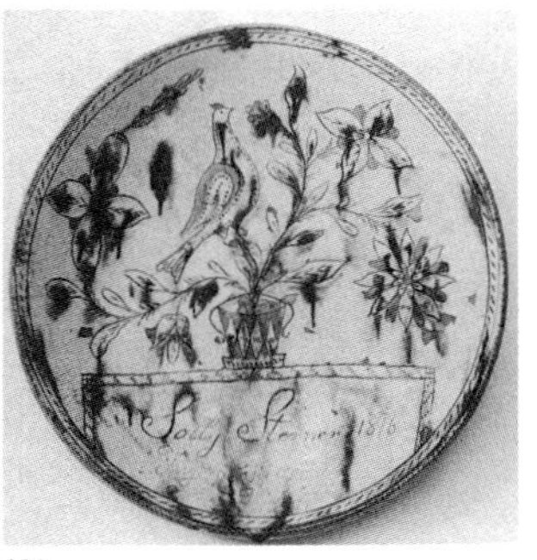
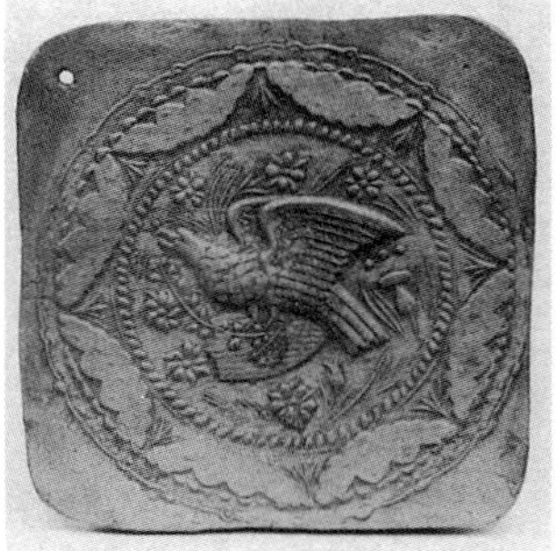

106   109

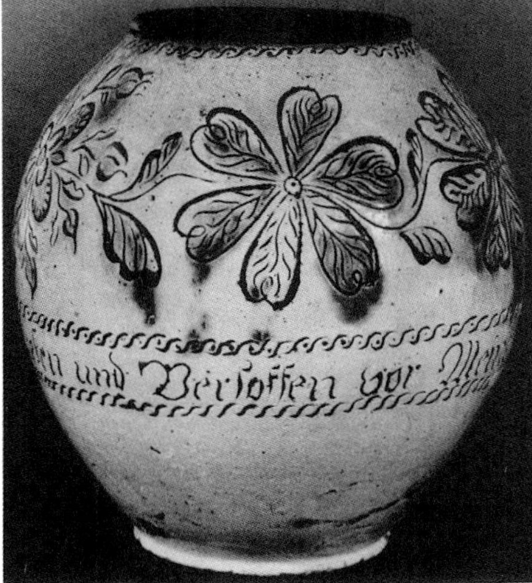

107

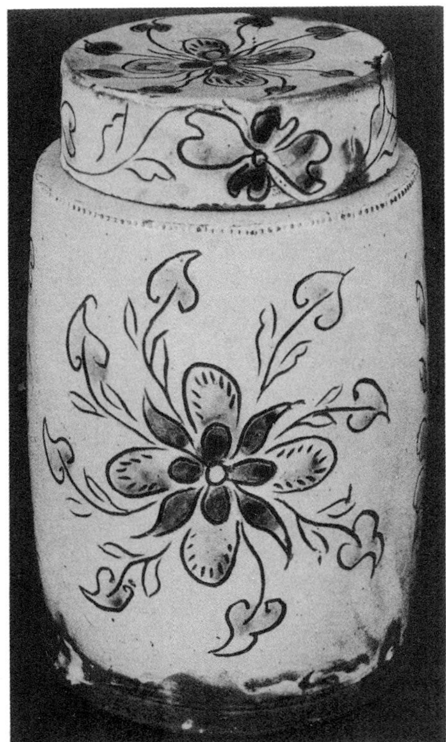

108

106 PLATE

Upper Hanover Township, Montgomery
County
1816

Henry Roudebush and **John Kichline**

Inscribed: *Sally Steiner 1816 Henry Roudebush John Kichline*

Molded redware, coggled edge. White slip surface with copper oxide (green) and sgraffito decoration. Yellowish lead glaze.

Height 5.4 cm (2⅛″), diameter 30.1 cm (11⅞″)

Gift of John T. Morris. 01-5

107 JAR

Upper Salford Township, Montgomery
County
1810–40

Attributed to **Jacob Scholl**

Inscribed: *Ulles Befressen und Berhoffen vor Meinem end macht ein ridsdig Testament.* ("To gorge and guzzle till I am spent makes a proper testament.")

Wheel-thrown redware. Surface covered with thick cream-colored slip. Sgraffito decoration daubed with copper oxide (green). Clear lead glaze. Black paint on top rim not original.

Height 19.7 cm (7¾″), diameter 20 cm (7⅞″)

Purchased. 93-210

108 COVERED JAR

Upper Salford Township, Montgomery
County
1810–40

Jacob Scholl

Marked on bottom with four-petal flower device

Wheel-thrown redware. Lid fits over deep neck of jar. Surface covered with cream-colored slip. Rouletting at shoulder. Sgraffito flowers colored with copper oxide (green) and cobalt (blue). Clear lead glaze.

Height 21 cm (8¼″), diameter 13.7 cm (5⅜″)

Gift of John T. Morris. 92-45,a

109 MOLD

Upper Salford Township, Montgomery
County
1810–40

Jacob Scholl

Marked on reverse with four-petal flower device

Slab redware. Positive impression from wood mold. Unglazed.

24.6 x 24.6 cm (9⅝ x 9⅝″)

Titus C. Geesey Collection. 55-94-12

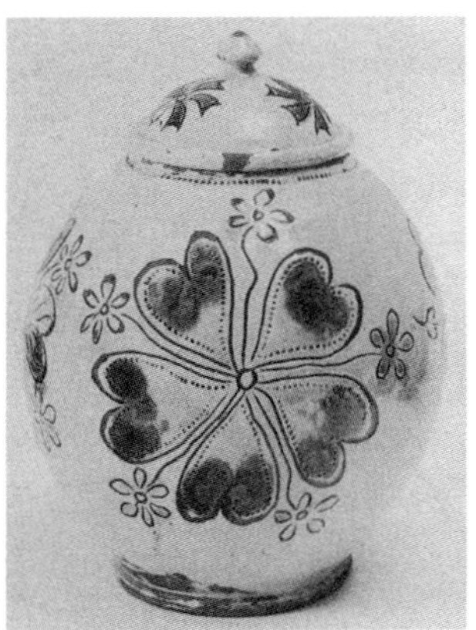

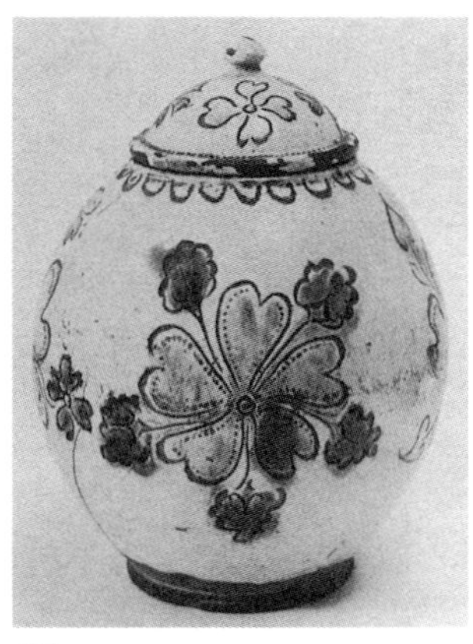

110

111

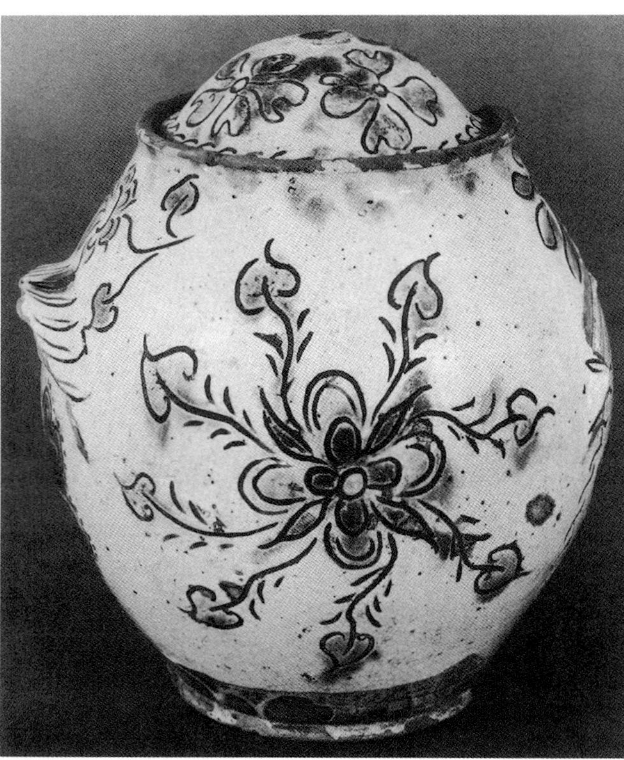

112

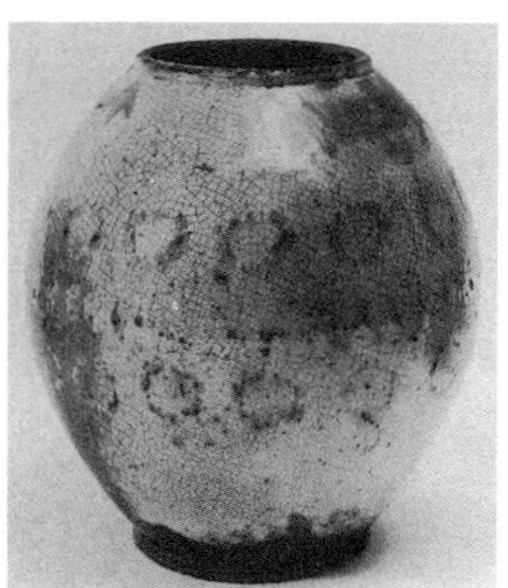

113

110 COVERED JAR
Upper Salford Township, Montgomery County
1810–40

Attributed to **Jacob Scholl**

Marked on bottom with four-petal flower device

Wheel-thrown redware. Flange on lid fits into neck of jar. Surface covered with white slip. Sgraffito designs partially colored with cobalt (blue) and copper oxide (green). Thick clear yellowish lead glaze on interior and exterior, except bottom.

Height 23.2 cm (9⅛″), diameter 18.1 cm (7⅛″)

Purchased: Baugh-Barber Fund. 22-4-7a,b

111 COVERED JAR
Upper Salford Township, Montgomery County
1810–40

Attributed to **Jacob Scholl**

Marked on bottom with four-petal flower device

Wheel-thrown redware. Surface covered with white slip daubed with copper oxide (green) and oxide of cobalt (blue) in sgraffito designs. Clear yellowish lead glaze on interior and exterior, except bottom.

Height 23.1 cm (9⅛″), diameter 17.6 cm (6⅞″)

Purchased. 93-246,a

112 COVERED JAR
Upper Salford Township, Montgomery County
1810–50

Attributed to **Jacob Scholl**

Wheel-thrown redware. Lid rests on flange within everted neck of jar. One applied handle and knop missing. Surface covered with white slip. Sgraffito decoration partially colored with cobalt (blue) and copper oxide (green). Clear lead glaze on interior and exterior is speckled with impurities.

25.1 x 18.1 cm (9⅞ x 7⅛″)

Purchased. 93-185,a

113 JAR
Upper Salford Township, Montgomery County
1810–50

Attributed to **Jacob Scholl**

Wheel-thrown redware. Two raised bands at foot. Body partially covered with cream-colored slip decorated with three cobalt (blue) bands of circles and dots. Thick clear yellowish lead glaze.

Height 20.3 cm (8″), diameter 19 cm (7½″)

Purchased. 93-186

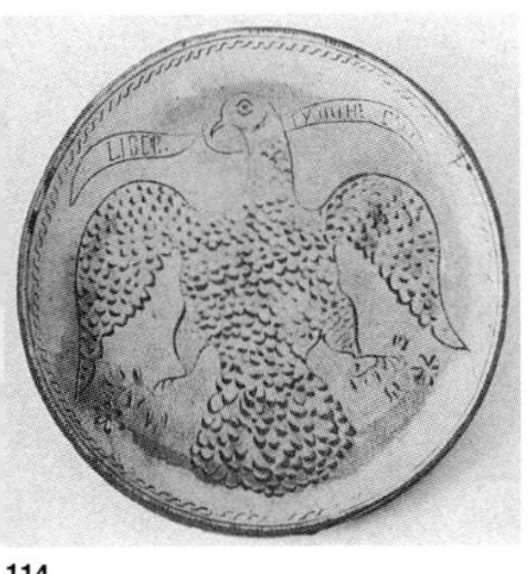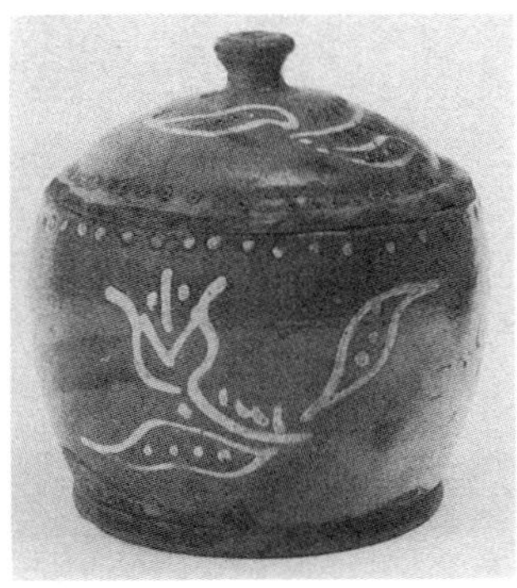

114 115

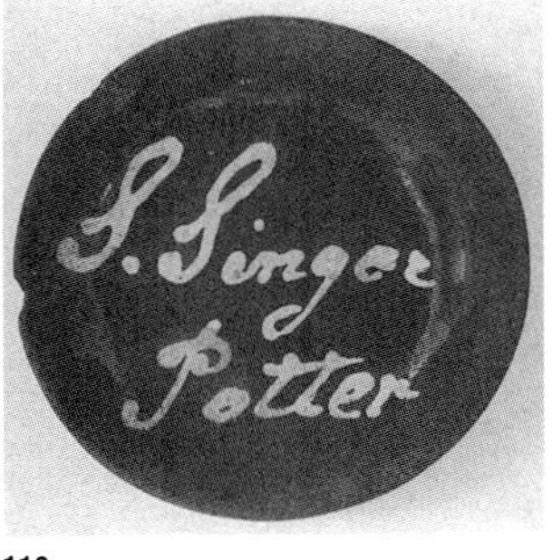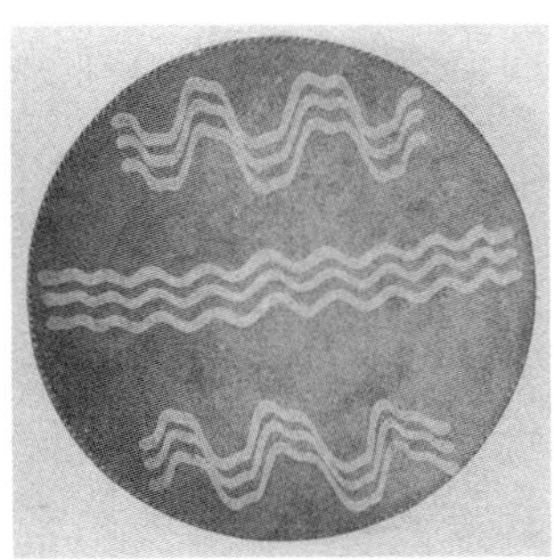

116 118

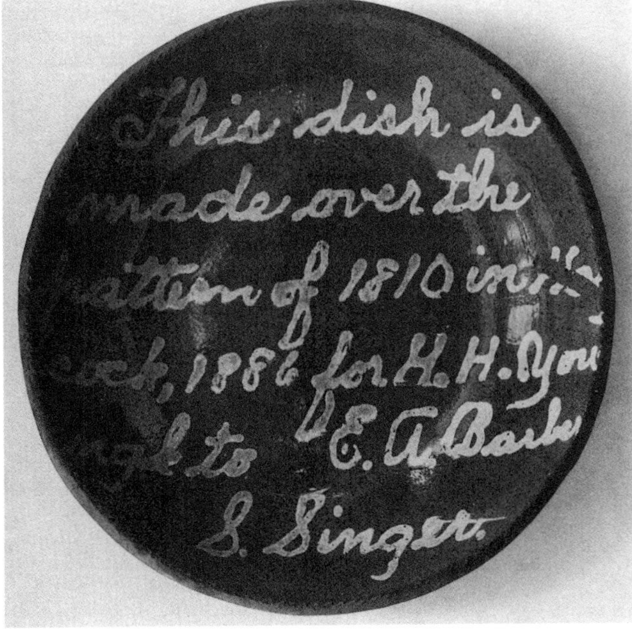

117

114 PLATE
Upper Salford Township, Montgomery
County
1832

Attributed to **Jacob Scholl**

Inscribed: *LIBER TY IN THE YEAR 1832*

Molded redware, coggled edge. Surface
covered with thick white slip lightly daubed
with copper oxide (green). Sgraffito
decoration. Clear greenish yellow lead glaze.

Height 5.1 cm (2″), diameter 28.9 cm (11⅜″)

Purchased. 93-213

115 COVERED BOWL
Berks County
1850–60

Possibly made at **Christian Schutter Pottery**

Wheel-thrown redware. Decorated with
white slip partially colored with copper oxide
(green). Clear yellowish lead glaze.

Height 13.3 cm (5¼″), diameter 13.6 cm (5⅜″)

Gift of John T. Morris. 96-258

116 PLATE
Haycock Township, Bucks County
1850–80

Simon Singer

Inscribed: *S. Singer   Potter*

Molded redware, coggled edge. White slip
flattened in molding process. Manganese
(brown) sprinklings. Clear lead glaze.

Height 5.1 cm (2″), diameter 28 cm (11⅛″)

Purchased: Baugh-Barber Fund. 39-45-1

117 PLATE
Haycock Township, Bucks County
1886

Simon Singer

Inscribed: *This dish is made over the pattern
of 1810 in Haycock, 1886 for H. H. Youngk to
E. A. Barber   S. Singer*
Incised on reverse: *Applebachville,
Bucks County. Pa.*

Molded redware, coggled edge. White slip
inscription on red body. Clear lead glaze.

Height 6.4 cm (2½″), diameter 32.7 cm (12⅞″)

Gift of Edwin Atlee Barber. 94-270

118 PLATE
Haycock Township, Bucks County
1895

Probably by **Simon Singer**

Molded redware, coggled edge. White slip
decoration on red body. Unglazed.

Height 5.1 cm (2″), diameter 31.1 cm (12¼″)

Gift of Edwin Atlee Barber. 96-64

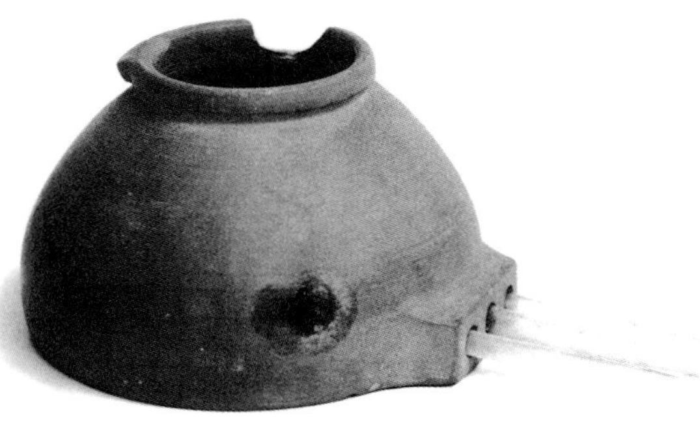

119

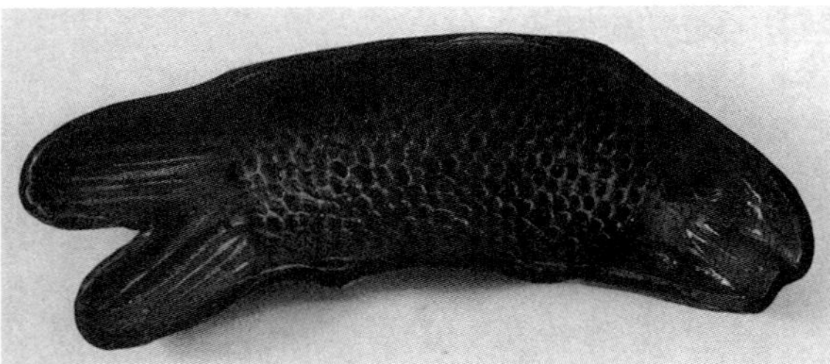

120

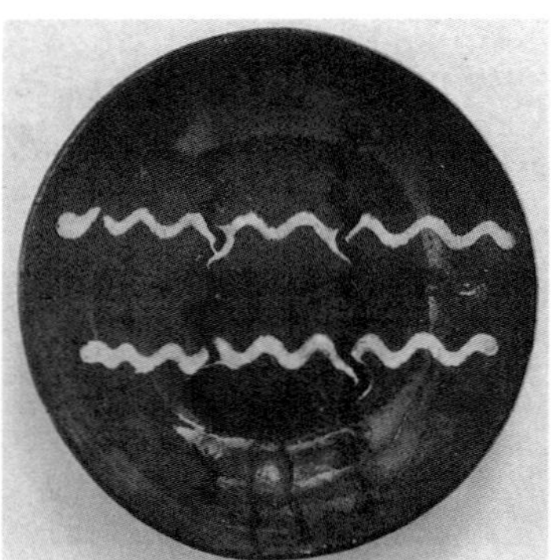

121

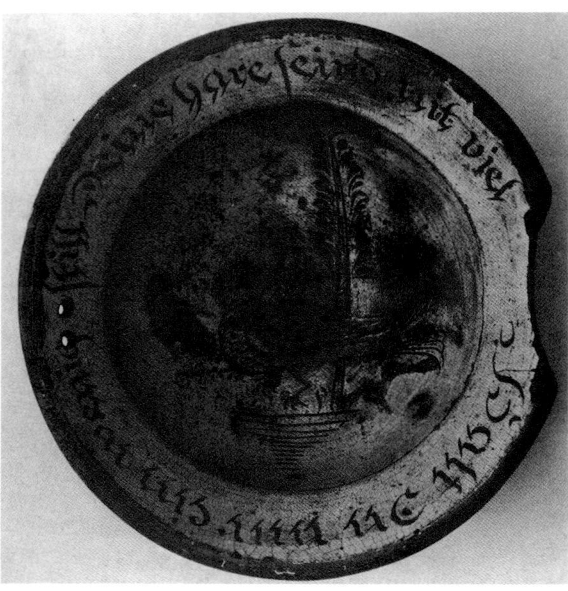

122

119 SLIP CUP
Haycock Township, Bucks County
1895

Probably from **Singer Pottery**

Wheel-thrown and modeled redware. Three holes fitted with three quills for slip trailing on redware. Top rim chipped. Unglazed.

6.6 x 11.1 cm (2⅝ x 4⅜")

Gift of Edwin Atlee Barber. 96-63

120 JELLY MOLD
Womelsdorf, Berks County
1865–80

Possibly by **Willoughby Smith**

Molded redware. Two anvil-shaped feet applied. Reddish brown lead glaze on interior; exterior unglazed.

6.4 x 31.7 x 9.9 cm (2½ x 12½ x 3⅞")

Purchased: Baugh-Barber Fund. 13-476

121 PLATE
Womelsdorf, Berks County
1865–80

Willoughby Smith

Stamped on reverse: *W. Smith WOMELSDOR*

Molded redware, cut edge. Trailed white and manganese-colored (brown) slip decoration flattened in molding process. Clear lead glaze; reverse blackened from use.

Height 3.8 cm (1½"), diameter 19 cm (7½")

Gift of David Stockwell. 49-32-1

122 SHAVING BOWL
Milford Township, Bucks County
1786–1800

Possibly by **David Spinner**

Inscribed: *Halt du nur ein wenig still Deine hare seind nit viel.* ("Keep still a short while. You do not have much hair.")

Wheel-thrown redware. Footed bowl, rounded sides, everted rolled edge. Rim and edge cut out for chin; two holes for hanging on thong. Surfaces, including bottom, covered with white slip and sgraffito decoration colored with copper oxide (green). Exterior design of spray of flowers and foliage flanking a three-story tile-roofed building. Clear yellowish lead glaze over all surfaces, except bottom rim. Design similar to products of Soufflenheim, Alsace.

Height 7.9 cm (3⅛"), diameter 18 cm (7")

Purchased: Baugh-Barber Fund. 16-321

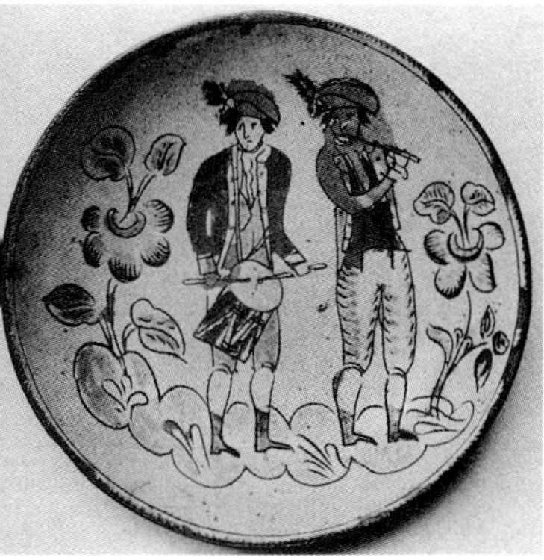

23

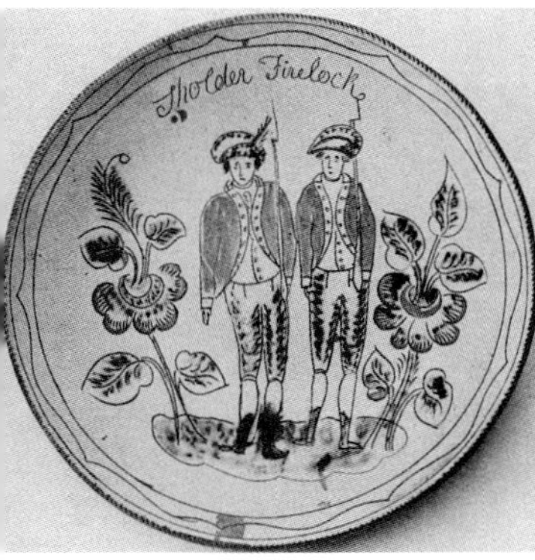

24

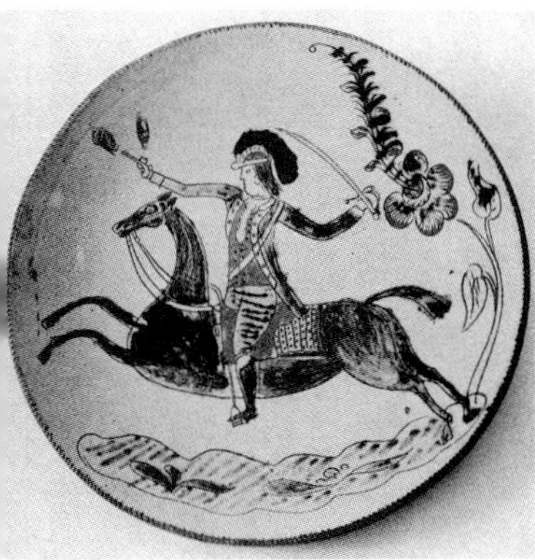

25

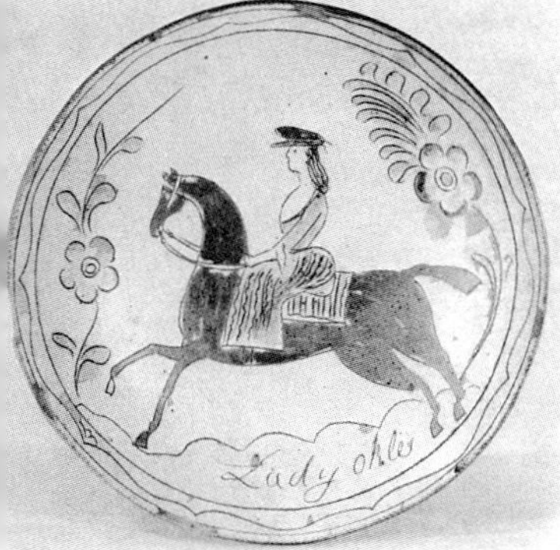

26

123 PLATE
Milford Township, Bucks County
1790–1800

Attributed to **David Spinner**

Molded redware, coggled edge. Surface
covered with white slip. Sgraffito decoration
partially colored with manganese (brown) and
copper oxide (green). Mat lead glaze.

Height 3.8 cm (1½″), diameter 24.1 cm (9½″)

Gift of John T. Morris. 00-72

124 PLATE
Milford Township, Bucks County
1790–1800

Attributed to **David Spinner**

Inscribed: *Shoulder Firelock*
Marked on reverse in pencil: *1780*

Molded redware, coggled edge. Surface
covered with white slip. Sgraffito decoration
with broad areas for jackets and flowers.
Details colored with copper oxide (green) and
manganese (brown). Oxides highlighted with
clear lead glaze. Mat lead glaze.

Height 5.1 cm (2″), diameter 29.5 cm (11⅝″)

Gift of John T. Morris. 00-199

125 PLATE
Milford Township, Bucks County
1790–1800

Attributed to **David Spinner**

Molded redware, coggled edge. Surface
covered with white slip. Sgraffito decoration
with broad flat areas for vest, saddle, tips of
flowers, and foliage. Manganese (brown) and
copper oxide (green) on details. Oxides
highlighted with thick clear lead glaze. Mat
lead glaze.

Height 5.4 cm (2⅛″), diameter 29.2 cm (11½″)

Purchased: John T. Morris Fund. 21-46-28

126 PLATE
Milford Township, Bucks County
1790–1800

Attributed to **David Spinner**

Inscribed: *Lady Okle*

Molded redware, coggled edge. Surface
covered with white slip. Sgraffito decoration
with broad areas for horse and tips of petals.
Copper oxide (green) and manganese (brown)
on details. Clear greenish yellow mat lead
glaze.

Height 5.7 cm (2¼″), diameter 29.5 cm (11⅝″)

Gift of John T. Morris. 00-73

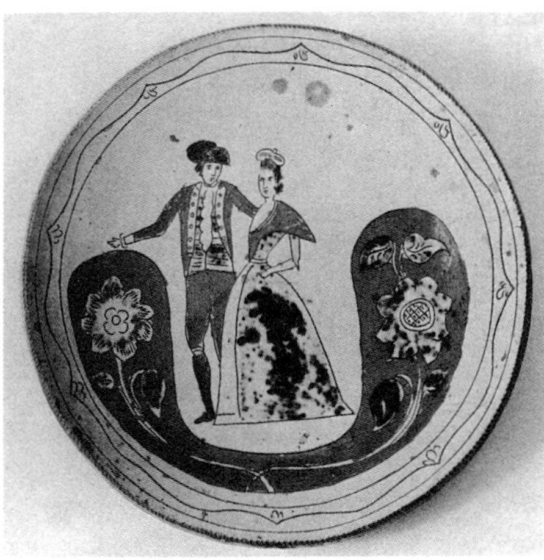

127

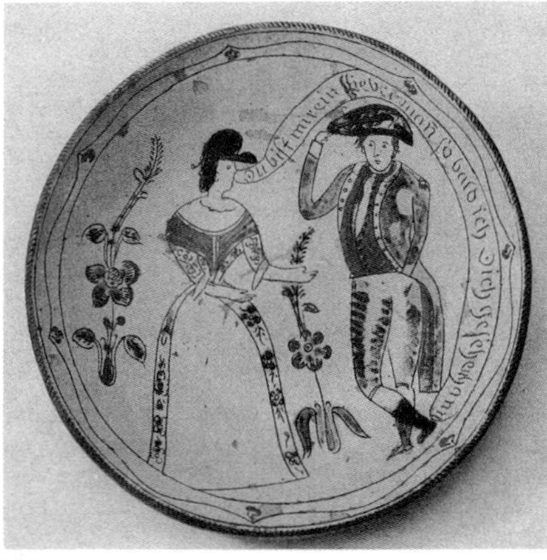

128

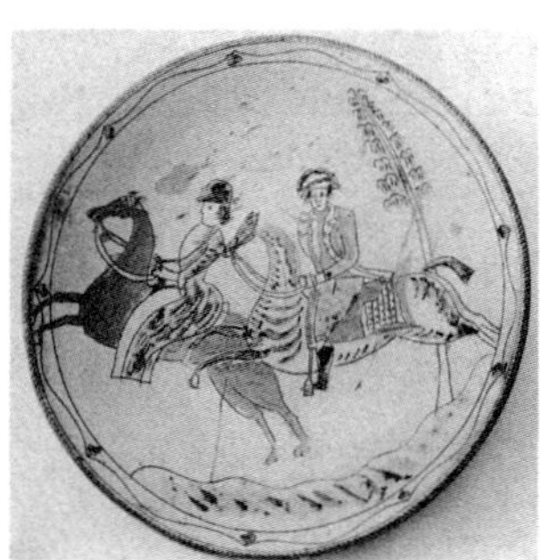

129

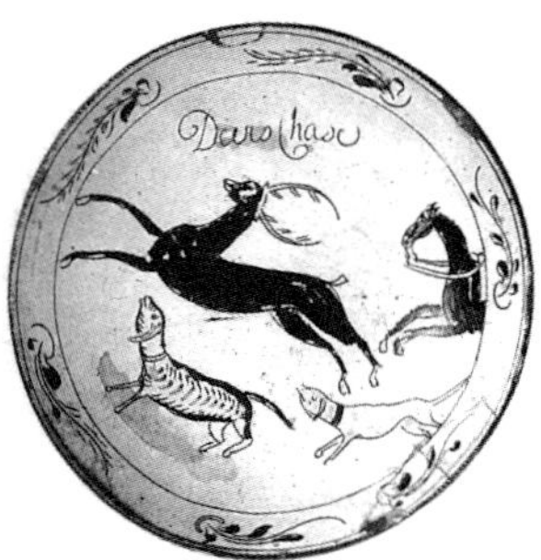

130

127 PLATE

Milford Township, Bucks County
1790–1810

Attributed to **David Spinner**

Molded redware, coggled edge. Surface
covered with white slip touched with copper
oxide (green). Broad flat areas of sgraffito
decoration. Thin clear yellowish lead glaze.

Height 5.7 cm (2¼″), diameter 29.8 cm (11¾″)

Gift of John T. Morris. 01-169

128 PLATE

Milford Township, Bucks County
1790–1810

Attributed to **David Spinner**

Inscribed: *Du bist mir ein Lieber man so bald
ich Dich gesehen hann.* ("Thou hast been a
dear man to me since first I ever looked at
thee.")

Molded redware, coggled edge. White slip
surface. Sgraffito decoration with broad areas
for woman's bodice, man's vest and coattail,
flowers and hearts. Copper oxide (green) and
manganese (brown) on figures. Clear lead
glaze.

5.7 cm (2¼″), diameter 29.5 cm (11⅝″)

Gift of John T. Morris. 00-75

129 PLATE

Milford Township, Bucks County
1790–1810

Attributed to **David Spinner**

Molded redware, coggled edge. White slip
surface. Sgraffito decoration with broad areas
for horse, vest, saddle, and blanket. Copper
oxide (green) and manganese (brown) on
details. Clear tannish lead glaze. Companion
for no. 130.

Height 5.7 cm (2¼″), diameter 29.5 cm (11⅝″)

Gift of John T. Morris. 00-76

130 PLATE

Milford Township, Bucks County
1790–1810

Attributed to **David Spinner**

Inscribed: *Deers Chase*

Molded redware, coggled edge. White slip
surface. Sgraffito decoration with broad areas
for deer, horse, and foliage. Copper oxide
(green) on details. Clear reddish tan lead
glaze. Companion for no. 129.

Height 5.7 cm (2¼″), diameter 29.5 cm (11⅝″)

Gift of John T. Morris. 00-74

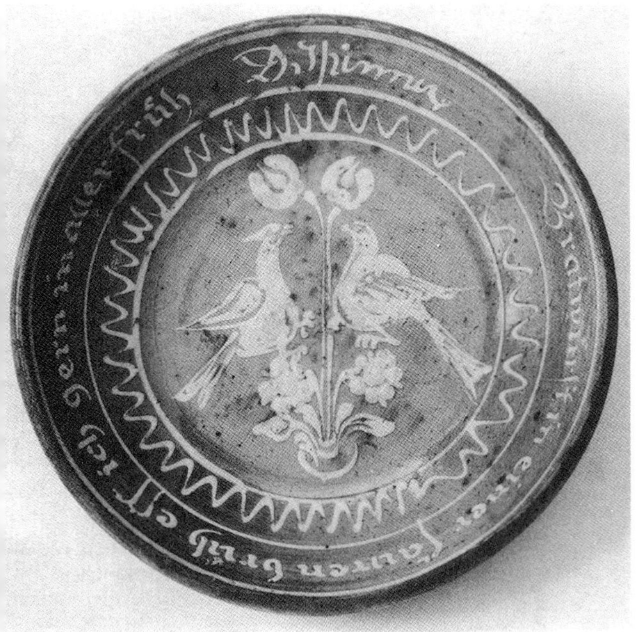

131

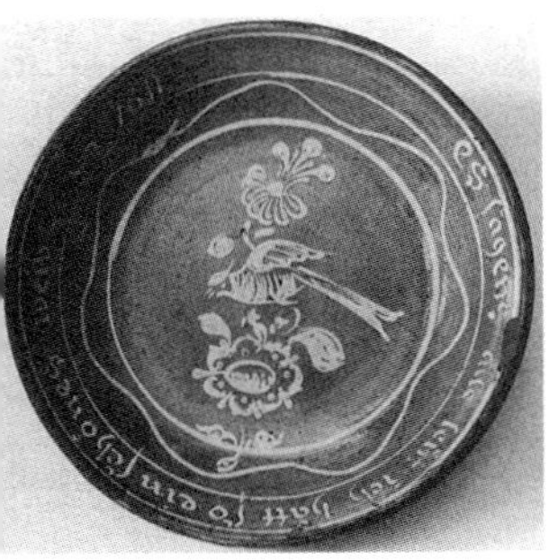

132

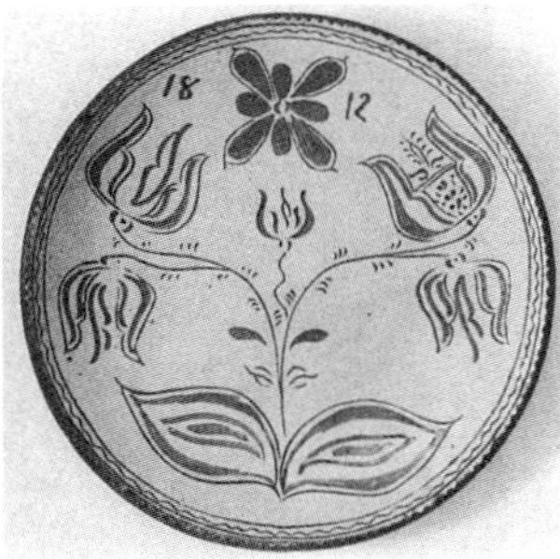

133

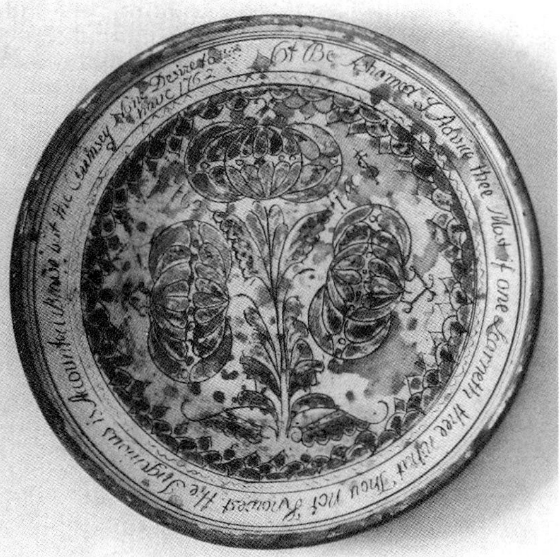

134

131 DISH
Milford Township, Bucks County
1809–11

David Spinner

Inscribed: *Bratwurst in einer sauren brüh ess ich gern in aller früh   D. Spinner* ("Every morning I like to eat fried sausage in a sour broth. D. Spinner")

Wheel-thrown redware. Rounded sides, everted rim. White slip tinted with copper oxide (green). Yellowish lead glaze.

Height 6.7 cm (2⅝"), diameter 32.1 cm (12⅝")

Gift of John T. Morris. 06-297

132 DISH
Milford Township, Bucks County
1811

David Spinner

Inscribed: *es sagens alle leit ich hatt so ein schönes weib   1811.* ("Everyone says that I have such a pretty wife. 1811")

Wheel-thrown redware. Rounded sides, everted edge. Decorated with thick white slip tinted with copper oxide (green). Clear yellowish lead glaze.

Height 6.7 cm (2⅝"), diameter 31.1 cm (12¼")

Gift of John T. Morris. 06-298

133 PLATE
Ruscomb Manor Township, Berks County
1812

Attributed to **Heinrich Stofflet**

Inscribed: *1812*

Molded redware, coggled edge. Surface covered with white slip. Sgraffito decoration with touches of copper oxide (green). Clear lead glaze.

Height 4.2 cm (1⅝"), diameter 28.9 cm (11⅜")

Gift of John T. Morris. 21-46-54

134 DISH
Rockhill Township, Bucks County
1762

Attributed to **Jacob Stout** and **John Lacy**

Inscribed: *Not Be Ashamed I Advise thee Most if one Learneth thee what Thou not Knowest the Ingenious is Accounted Brave but the Clumsey None Desire to have 1762   1762 IAC JS*

Wheel-thrown redware. Curved sides, flaring rim, everted reinforced edge. Lightweight body. White slip surface. Sgraffito decoration with copper oxide (green) and slip (orange). Clear yellowish lead glaze.

Height 7.3 cm (2⅞"), diameter 38.7 cm (15¼")

Purchased: Baugh-Barber Fund. 58-124-1

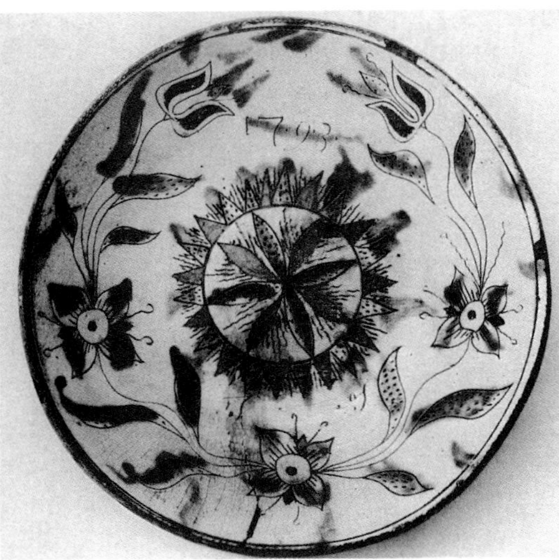

135

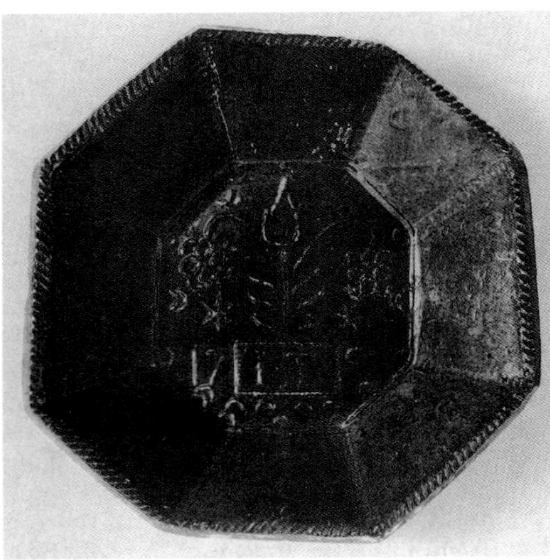

136

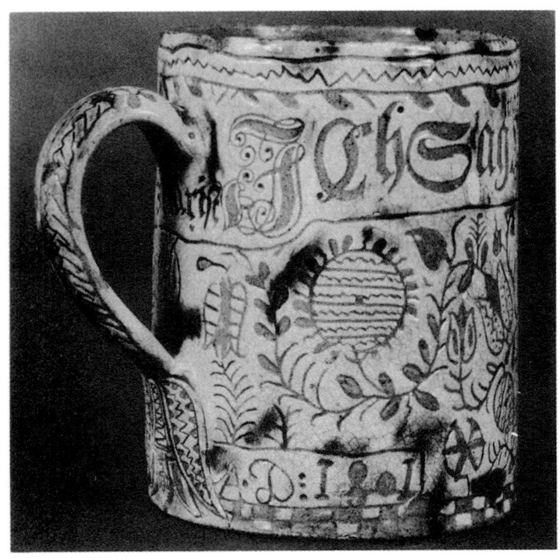

137

135 PLATE
Haycock Township, Bucks County
1793

Attributed to **Thomas Strawhen**

Inscribed: *1793   T S*

Molded redware, coggled edge. Surface
covered with white slip daubed with copper
oxide (green). Sgraffito decoration partially
colored with iron (red) in slip. Thick clear
yellowish lead glaze. Unglazed reverse has
imprint of potter's sponge.

Height 6.1 cm (2⅜″), diameter 34 cm (13⅜″)

Purchased. 93-189

---

136 DISH
Nockamixon Township, Bucks County
1794

Possibly by **Jacob Taney**

Inscribed: *17   IT   94*

Molded redware, coggled edge. Heavy body.
Octagonal form with raised symmetrical
pattern of tulip, stars, and grapes in center.
Thick clear reddish lead glaze sprinkled
with iron.

Height 4.1 cm (1⅝″), length 22.2 cm (8¾″)

Gift of John T. Morris. 01-7

---

137 MUG
Upper Hanover Township, Montgomery
County
1801

Attributed to **Henry Troxel**

Inscribed: *Ich sag was wahr ist und trinck
was klar ist. 1801.* ("I speak what is true and
drink what is clear. 1801")
Incised on bottom: *Den 8ten frbui   ani
1801.* ("The 18th [8th?] February 1801")

Wheel-thrown redware. Applied handle with
tulip shape applied over base of handle.
Surface covered with white slip daubed with
copper oxide (green). Sgraffito decoration.
Thick clear yellowish lead glaze.

14.2 x 16.5 cm (5⅝ x 6½″)

Purchased: Baugh-Barber Fund. 44-68-1

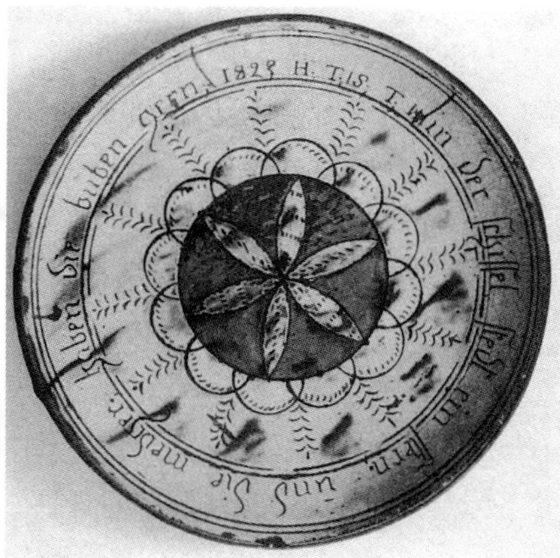

138

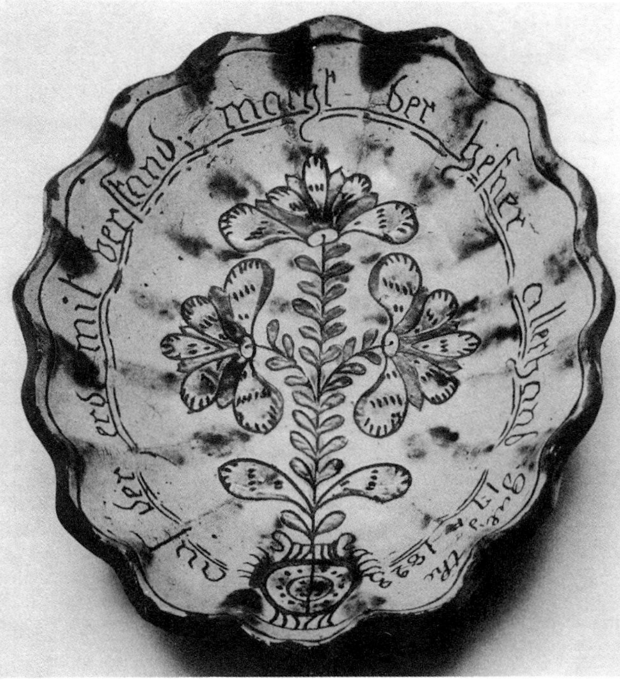

139

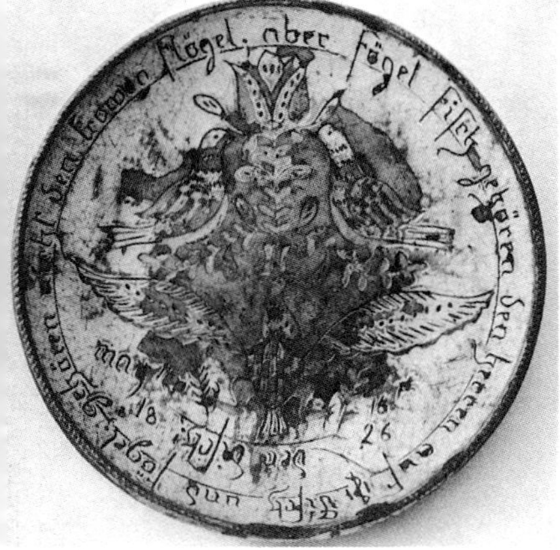

140

138 PLATE

Upper Hanover Township, Montgomery County
1823

Attributed to **Henry Troxel**

Inscribed: *in der schissel stedt ein stern und die medger haben die buben gern   1823 H. T. is T. M.* ("In the dish stands a star and the maidens are fond of the boys. 1823 H. T. is T. M.")

Molded redware, cut edge. Heavy body. Surface covered with white slip daubed with copper oxide (green). Sgraffito decoration. Compass-inscribed circles with impressed dots from compass pivot. Thick clear yellowish lead glaze.

Height 4.5 cm (1¾"), diameter 26 cm (10¼")

Purchased: Baugh-Barber Fund. 13-477

---

139 PLATE

Upper Hanover Township, Montgomery County
1823

Attributed to **Samuel Troxel**

Inscribed: *aus der erde mit verstand macht der hefner allerhand July the 17n 1823* ("From earth with sense the potter makes everything. July the 17th, 1823")

Molded redware, cut edge. Surface covered with white slip daubed with copper oxide (green). Sgraffito decoration. Clear lead glaze.

Height 5.1 cm (2"), length 24.1 cm (9½")

Gift of John T. Morris. 03-14

---

140 PLATE

Upper Hanover Township, Montgomery County
1826

Attributed to **Samuel Troxel**

Inscribed: *Fish und fögel gehören nicht den krowen flögel, aber fögel fisch gehören den herren auf den disch. May 16, 1826* ("Fish and fowl do not belong to rough fellows, but should be served only to gentlemen. May 16, 1826")

Molded redware, coggled edge. Surface covered with white slip mottled with copper oxide (green). Sgraffito decoration colored in with iron oxide (orange). Clear lead glaze. Surface losses.

Height 4.8 cm (1⅞"), diameter 28 cm (11")

Gift of John T. Morris. 92-44

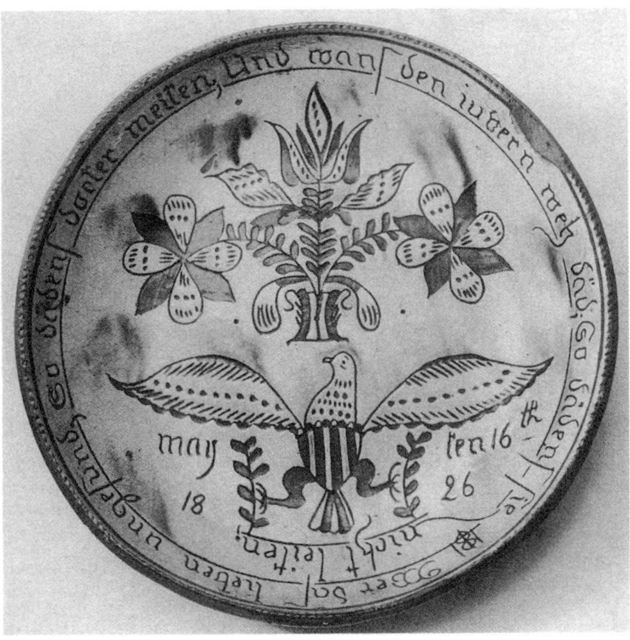

141

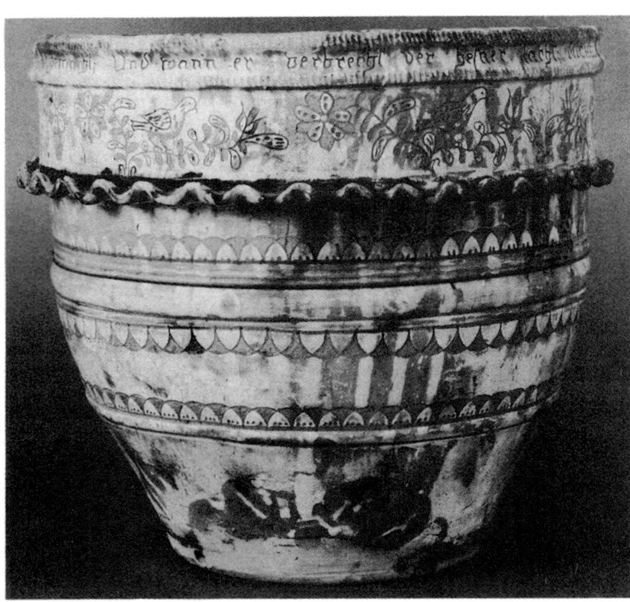

142

141 PLATE
Upper Hanover Township, Montgomery County
1826

Samuel Troxel

Inscribed: *Wer das lieben ungesund, So dädens docter meiten, Und wans den iuvern weh däd, So dädens sie nicht leiten. May ten 16th 1826* ("If loving were injurious to health, the doctor would avoid it; and if it would hurt the maidens, then they would not endure it. May the 16th 1826")
Incised on reverse in script: *Samuel Troxel Potter May the 16th 1826*

Molded redware, coggled edge. Slightly raised center. Surface covered with white slip daubed with copper oxide (green). Sgraffito decoration. Clear yellowish lead glaze with iron oxide (red) streaking from sgraffito petals and leaves.

Height 5.1 cm (2″), diameter 28.6 cm (11¼″)

Purchased. 93-211

142 FLOWERPOT
Upper Hanover Township, Montgomery County
1828

Samuel Troxel

Inscribed: *Dieser haffen [?] von erd gemacht; Und wann er verbrecht der hefner lacht. MICHEL COPE BOUGHT OF SAMUEL TROXEL · THEM FLOUER POTT. M:LxC:=1828* ("This pot is made of earth and when it breaks the potter laughs. Michel Cope bought of Samuel Troxel this flowerpot MLC 1828")
Incised on bottom: *Samuel Troxel 1828*

Wheel-thrown and modeled redware. Heavy body. Five drainage holes in bottom. Raised and incised banding, fluted ruffle, and coggled decoration. Outer surface covered with white slip mottled with copper oxide (green). Sgraffito decoration. Clear yellowish lead glaze.

Height 29.5 cm (11⅝″), diameter 35 cm (13¾″)

Gift of John T. Morris. 00-22

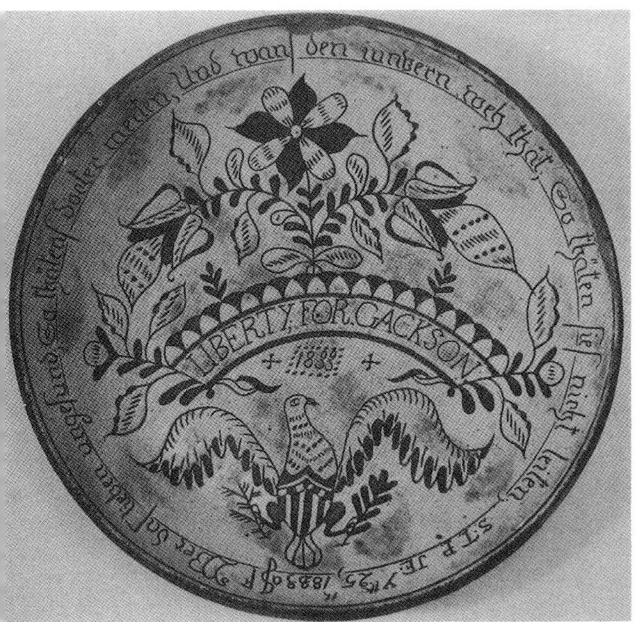

43

143 PLATE
Upper Hanover Township, Montgomery
County
1833

Samuel Troxel

Inscribed: *LIBERTY FOR GACKSON 1833
Wer das lieben ungesund So thätens docter
meiten Und wans den iunvern weh thät; So
thäten sie nicht leiten; S. T. P. JE ye 25th 1833
a[?]F* ("Liberty for Jackson. 1833. If loving
were injurious to health, the doctor would
avoid it; and if it would hurt the maidens, they
would not endure it. S[amuel] T[roxel]
P[otter] January 25, 1833 F[ecit]")

Molded redware, coggled edge. White
slip surface with copper oxide (green).
Compass-inscribed designs and sgraffito
decoration. Clear yellowish lead glaze.

Height 5.1 cm (2″), diameter 30.3 cm (11⅞″)

Purchased: Baugh-Barber Fund. 60-120-1

---

144 PLATE
1810

Attributed to **Andrew Uhler**

Inscribed: *AU March 2 1810*

Molded redware, coggled edge. Raised
circular band in center from mold. White slip
surface with copper oxide (green). Sgraffito
incising with broad flat areas. Clear lead
glaze.

Height 4.2 cm (1⅝″), diameter 27 cm (10⅝″)

Purchased: Baugh-Barber Fund. 38-15-5

---

145 PLATE
1810

Attributed to **Andrew Uhler**

Inscribed: *A. U. March 19 1810*

Molded redware, coggled edge. Raised
circular band in center from mold. Surface
covered with white slip daubed with copper
oxide (green). Sgraffito incising with broad
flat areas. Clear yellowish lead glaze.

Height 5.1 cm (2″), diameter 30.7 cm (12⅛″)

Purchased: John T. Morris Fund. 21-46-55

---

146 PLATE
Bucks County
1791

CW

Inscribed: *C W 1791*

Molded redware, coggled edge. White slip
surface with random copper oxide (green).
Sgraffito decoration. Lead glaze.

Height 5.4 cm (2⅛″), diameter 33.7 cm (13¼″)

Gift of John T. Morris. 01-4

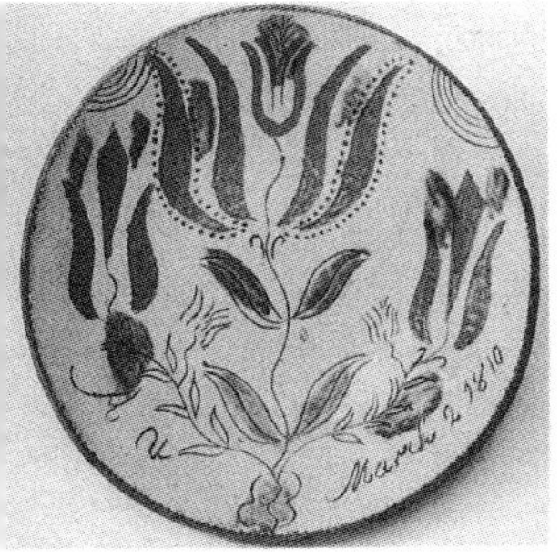

44

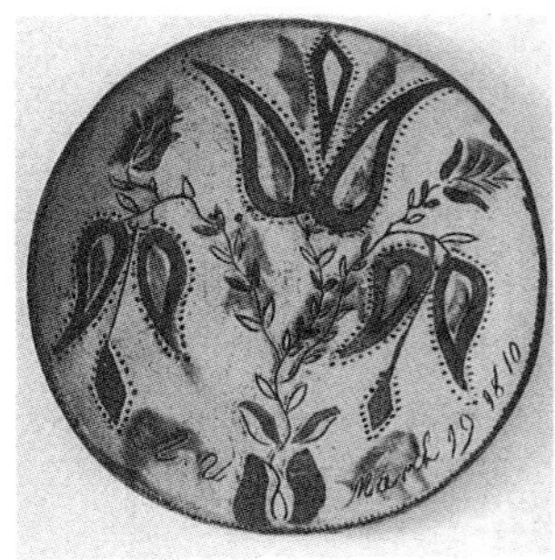

145

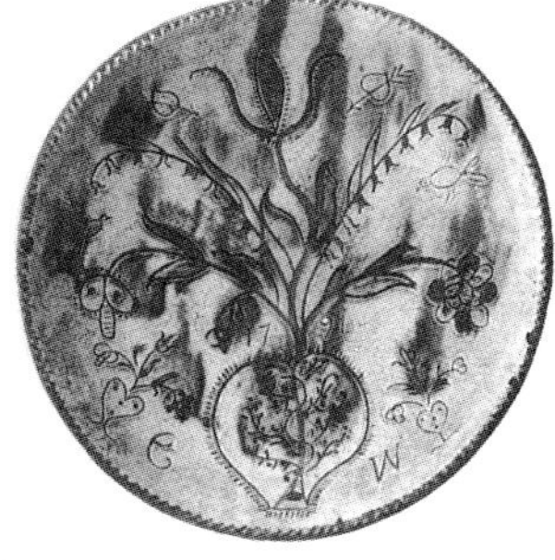

146

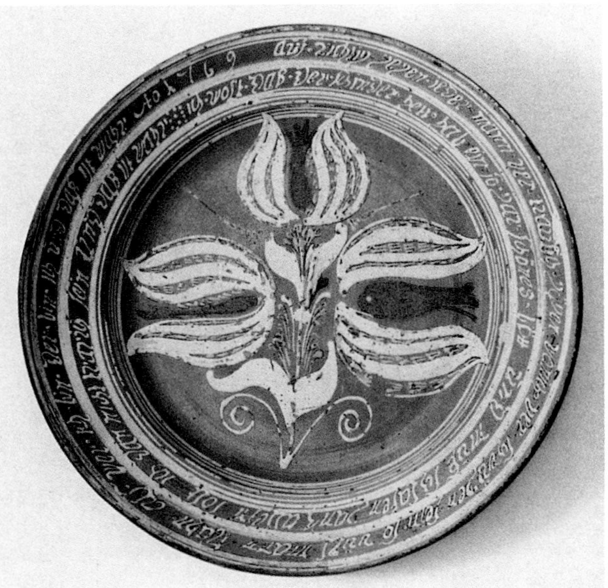

1

1

1 DISH
1769

Inscribed: *Auf richtig gegen ieder mann vertraulich gögen wönich ver schwügen sein so vüls mann kahn als wer ich bin der bin ich und dass ist wahr Ao 1769   Ich wolt dass der schinder hett hab ein so gar schones bött und muss schlafen ganz allein solt ich dan nicht trarich sein und dass ist wahr.* ("Sincere to every man, intimate to few, as quiet as possible. Thus, who I am, he I am. And that is true. In the year 1769. Wish the devil had it. I have a very beautiful bed and must sleep alone. Then should I not be sad? And this is true.")

Wheel-thrown redware. Rounded sides, flaring rim, rolled everted edge. Lightweight body. Surface decorated with white slip and copper oxide (green) in slip. Clear lead glaze. Similar to ware produced at Hesse.

Height 7 cm (2¾"), diameter 44.7 cm (17⅝")

Purchased. 93-190

2 PLATE
Bucks or Northampton County
1770–1800

Molded redware, plain rim. Heavy body. White slip banding and manganese (brownish black) in slip decoration. Slightly orange lead glaze.

Height 5.1 cm (2"), diameter 26.7 cm (10½")

Purchased: Baugh-Barber Fund. 74-107-2

3 SERVING BOWL
Bucks County
1770–1850

Molded redware, coggled edge. Heavy body. White slip decoration made with four-quill slip cup on red body. Clear lead glaze.

8.9 x 46.4 x 30 cm (3½ x 18¼ x 11¾")

Gift of Mrs. William D. Frishmuth. 12-220

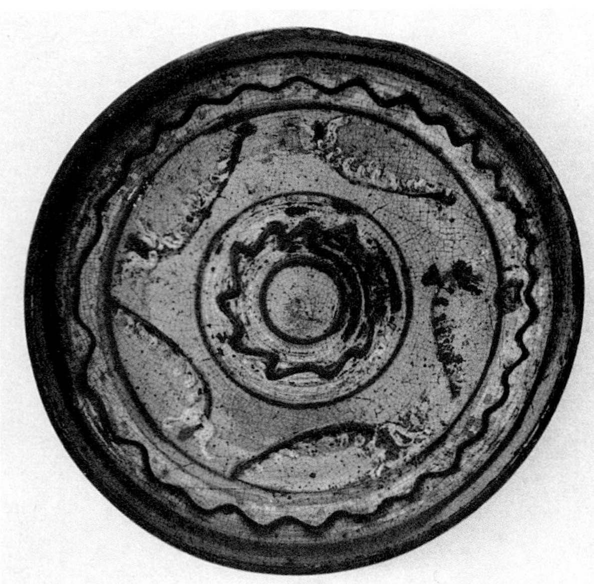

2

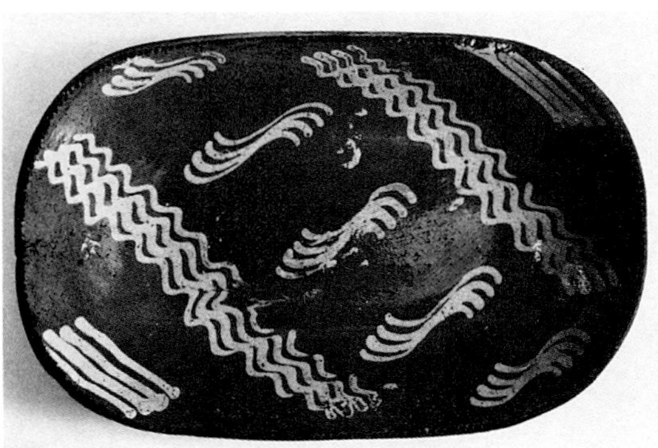

3

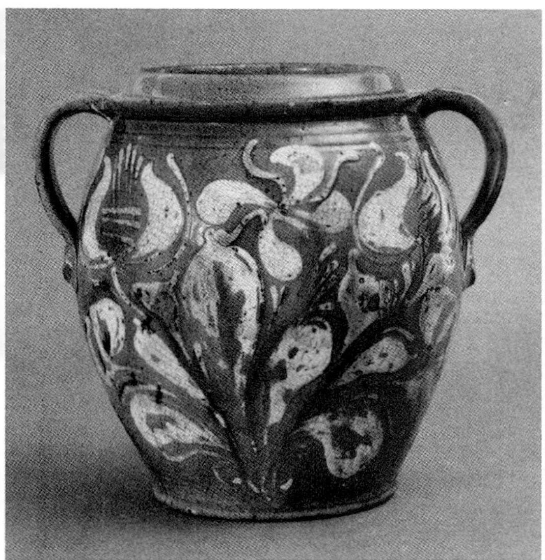

4

4 JAR
Bucks County
1773–90

Wheel-thrown redware. Applied handles.
Heavy body. Thick white slip decoration
daubed with copper oxide (green). Touches of
manganese (black brown). Thick lead glaze on
exterior and interior. Lid missing.

22.2 x 24.7 cm (8¾ x 9¾")

Purchased: Baugh-Barber Fund. 61-189-1

5 JAR
Bucks County
1780–1800

Wheel-thrown redware. Everted top edge.
Concentric bandings and white slip decoration
with manganese (brown). Clear brownish lead
glaze.

Height 28 cm (11"), diameter 27.3 cm (10¾")

Gift of J. Stogdell Stokes. 36-19-5

6 PLATE
Montgomery County
1780–1810

Molded redware, coggled edge. Heavy body.
White slip decoration on red body. Clear
yellowish lead glaze.

Height 5.4 cm (2⅛"), diameter 28.9 cm (11⅜")

Gift of John T. Morris. 11-181

7 JAR
Bucks County
1780–1820

Wheel-thrown redware. Applied handles.
Decorated with white slip touched with
copper oxide (green) and manganese (brown).
Slightly orange lead glaze on interior and
exterior, except bottom. Losses to slip
decoration. Shape similar to products of
Soufflenheim, Alsace.

13.6 x 17.7 cm (5⅜ x 7")

Gift of Joseph H. Himes, in memory of his wife
Eilleen C. Himes. 54-62-24

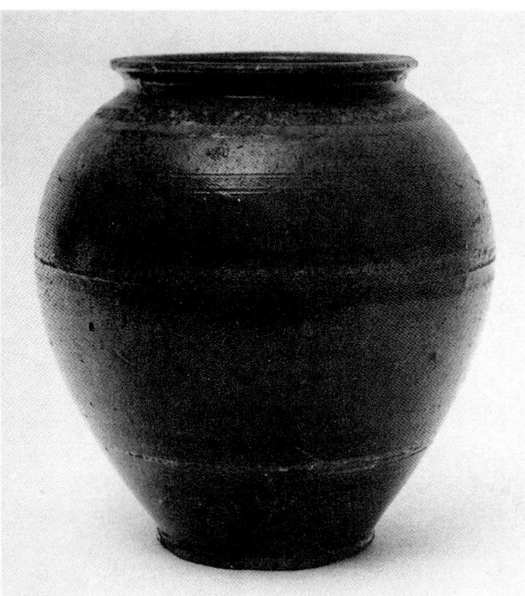

5

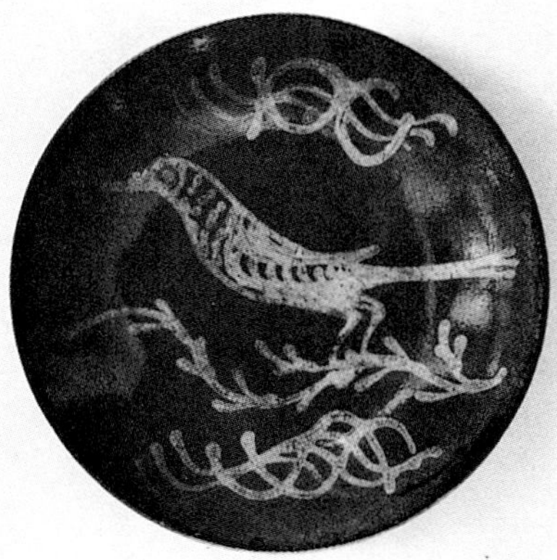

6

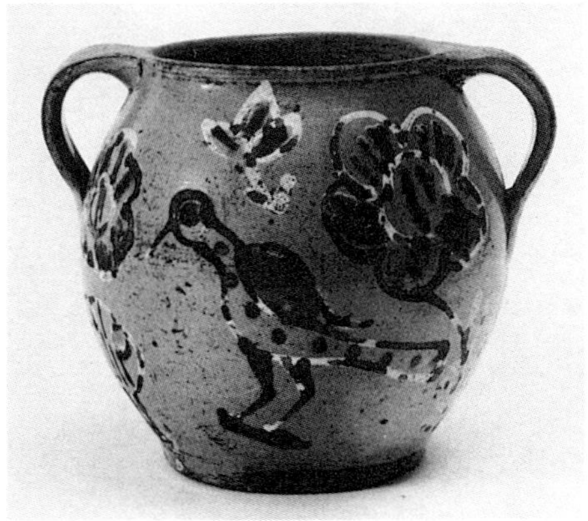

7

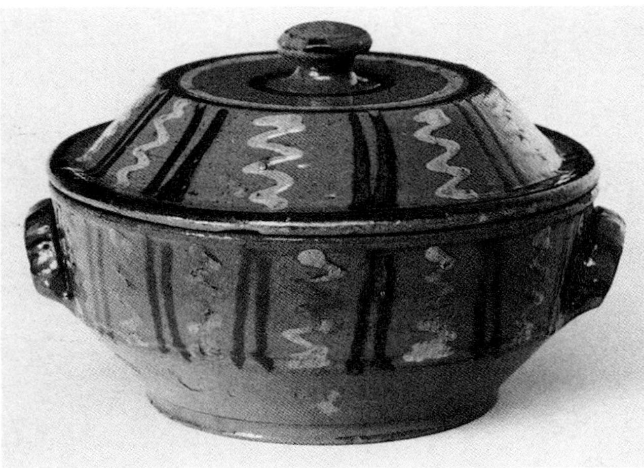

8

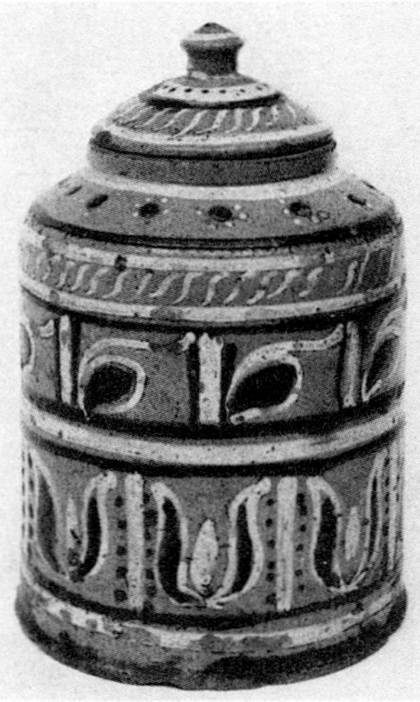

9

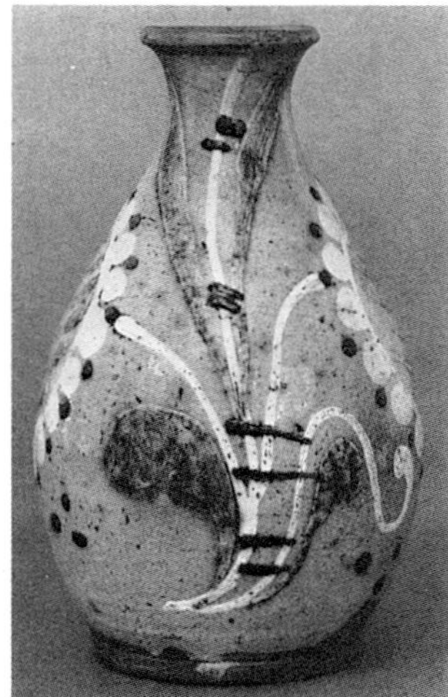

10

11

8   COVERED BOWL
Bucks County
1780–1820

Incised on bottom: *12*

Wheel-thrown redware. Applied handles and turned knop on lid. Decorated with thick white slip dashed with copper oxide (green) and manganese (brown). Thick clear yellowish lead glaze.

15 x 22.9 cm (5⅞ x 9″)

Gift of Joseph H. Himes, in memory of his wife Eilleen C. Himes. 54-62-7a,b

9   TOBACCO JAR
Montgomery County
1780–1840

Wheel-thrown redware. Heavy body. Lid has flange which fits inside neck of jar. Banding and designs in white slip and manganese (brown). Slightly orange lead glaze.

Height 22.8 cm (9″), diameter 15.7 cm (6¼″)

Purchased: Baugh-Barber Fund. 17-184,a

10   BULB VASE
Montgomery County
1790–1800

Wheel-thrown, modeled, and slab redware. Tail cut from slab; base turned and attached to hollow body. Neck and head are solid clay. Surface daubed with white slip and manganese. Beak is repaired or added after glaze. Clear lead glaze. Similar to ware produced near Strasbourg, Alsace.

17.7 x 17.7 x 10.5 cm (7 x 7 x 4⅛″)

Purchased: Baugh-Barber Fund. 22-4-4

11   BOTTLE
Lancaster County
1790–1830

Wheel-thrown redware. Decoration of white slip, copper oxide (green), and manganese (brown) in slip. Clear reddish tan lead glaze.

Height 15.9 cm (6¼″), diameter 10.2 cm (4″)

Titus C. Geesey Collection. 55-94-11

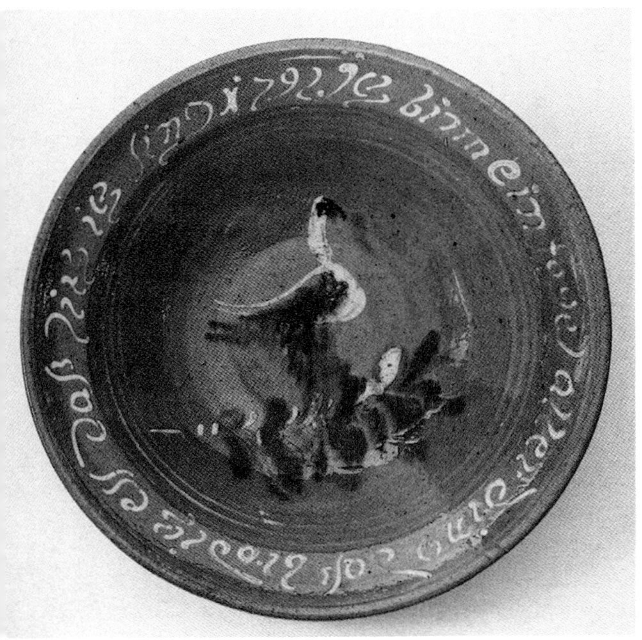

12

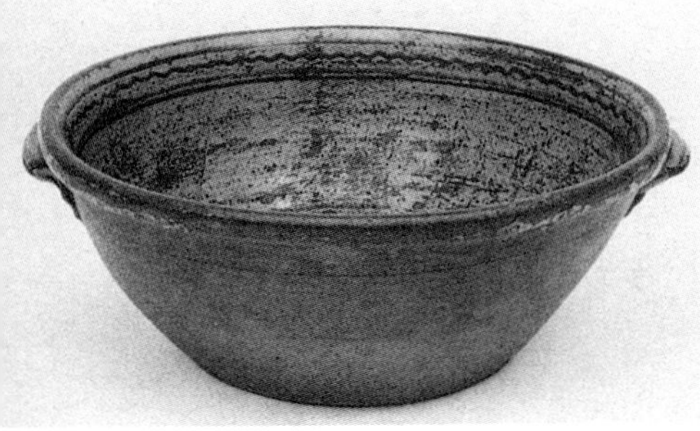

13

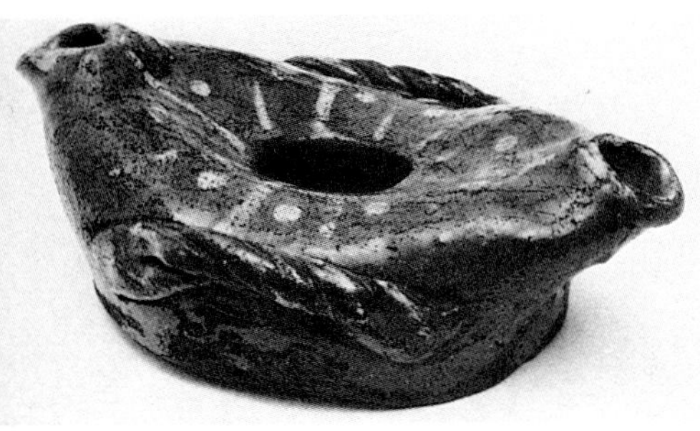

14

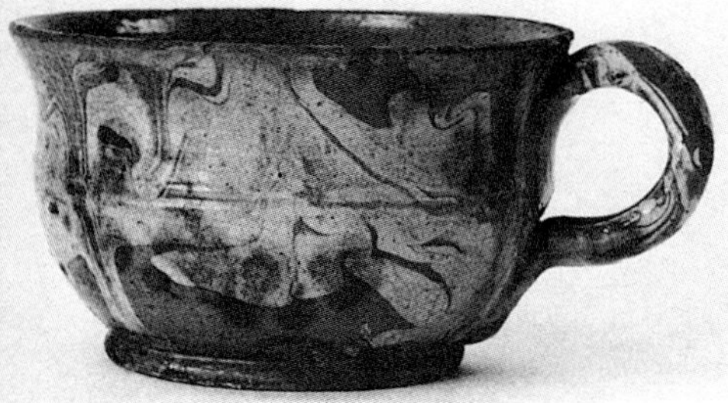

15

12 DISH
Bucks County
1792

Inscribed: *Ich binn ein fogel aller ding dass brod ich ess dass lith ich sing. 1792* ("I am a bird at all times whose bread I eat his song I sing. 1792")
Incised on bottom: *VI*

Wheel-thrown redware. Footed dish, flared rim, square everted edge. Heavy body. Incised bandings. Inscription, bird, and leaves in white slip touched with manganese (brown) and copper oxide (green). Clear orange yellow lead glaze speckled with iron.

Height 6.7 cm (2⅝"), diameter 35 cm (13¾")

Gift of John T. Morris. 00-18

13 BOWL
Bucks County
1800–1840

Wheel-thrown redware. Rounded sides, everted edge, applied handles. Heavy body. Interior covered with white slip. Thick orange lead glaze with manganese (dark brown) banding. Exterior unglazed.

16.5 x 44.5 cm (6½ x 17½")

Gift of J. Stogdell Stokes. 28-48-1

14 DOUBLE-WICK GREASE LAMP
Montgomery County
1800–1840

Modeled redware. Twist handles applied. Shaped from flat pieces and folded into boat shape. Openings at each end for wicks. Bottom incised deeply to prevent slipping off a stand. White slip decoration. Clear brownish lead glaze.

3.8 x 12.1 x 8.9 cm (1½ x 4¾ x 3½")

Titus C. Geesey Collection. 54-85-4

15 CUP
1800–1840

Wheel-thrown redware. Applied handle. Decorated with joggled white slip design and daubed with copper oxide (green) and manganese (brown). Clear lead glaze inside and out, except bottom.

5.7 x 11.5 cm (2¼ x 4½")

Gift of John T. Morris. 00-13

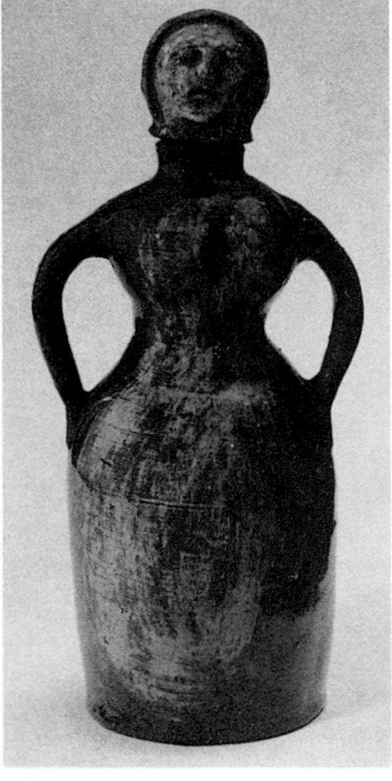

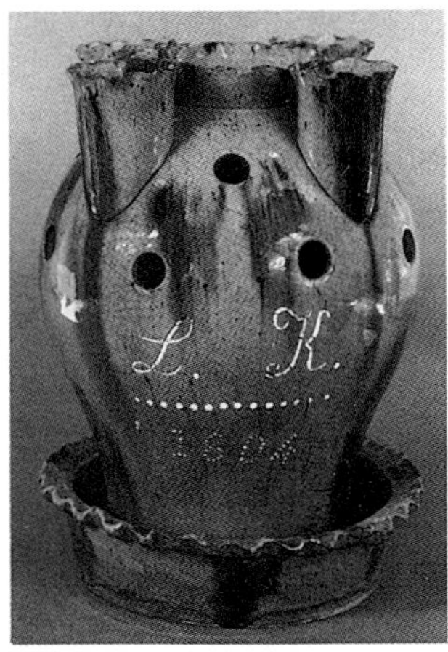

16   **17**

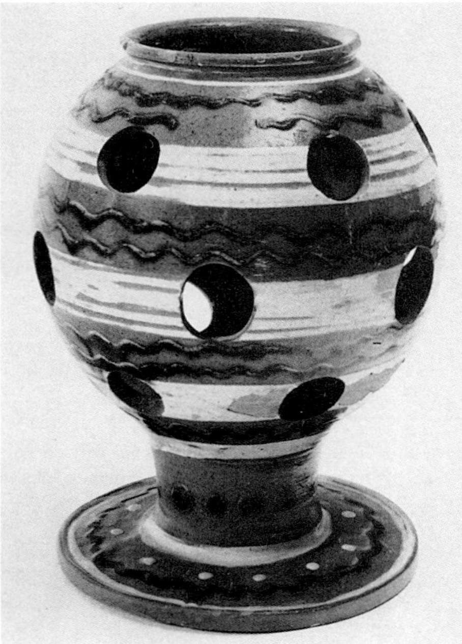

18

16 BOTTLE
1800–1850

Wheel-thrown and modeled redware. Applie‹
arms. Modeled head fitted with deep stopper
Face and apron painted with white slip. Thic‹
lead glaze. Similar in form to products of
Soufflenheim, Alsace.

24.2 x 11.7 cm (9½ x 4⅝")

Titus C. Geesey Collection. 69-284-28a,b

17 BULB PLANTER
Bucks County
1804

Inscribed: *L.K.   1804*
Incised on bottom of pot: *May 27   1804*

Wheel-thrown and modeled redware. Saucer
and pot separate. Lightweight body. Drainage
hole in pot. Fluted bulb funnels applied.
Inscription of white slip inlaid into red body.
Brilliant clear lead glaze colored with iron
oxide (red) and dappled with manganese
(black brown).

Height 27.6 cm (10⅞"), diameter 20.6 cm (8⅛")

Gift of John T. Morris. 12-92,a

18 ONION PLANTER
Montgomery County
1820–40

Wheel-thrown redware. Base and pot in one
unit; drainage holes in base. White slip
banding and dots on base. Wriggles colored
with copper oxide (green). Clear lead glaze.
Base repaired and partially resurfaced.

Height 22 cm (8⅝"), diameter 17.4 cm (6⅞")

Purchased: Baugh-Barber Fund. 93-247

19 HANGING FLOWERPOT
Chester or Franklin County
1820–50

Wheel-thrown redware. Applied finial. Three
hanging holes at top; drainage hole at side.
Surface covered with white slip and splashed
with manganese. Clear yellowish lead glaze on
surfaces, except interior.

Height 13.2 cm (5¼"), diameter 20.9 cm (8¼")

Gift of Joseph H. Himes, in memory of his wife
Eilleen C. Himes. 54-62-80

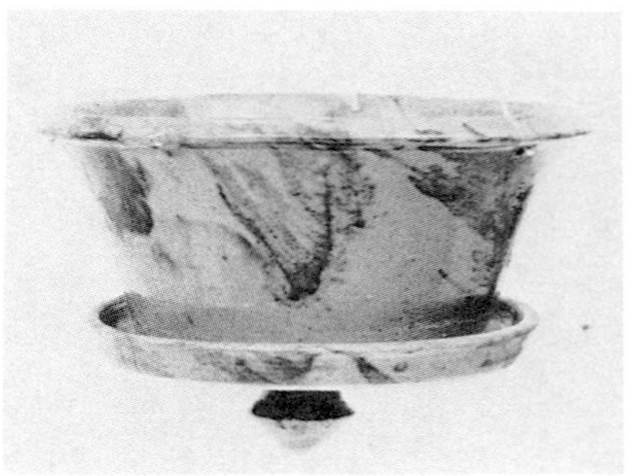

19

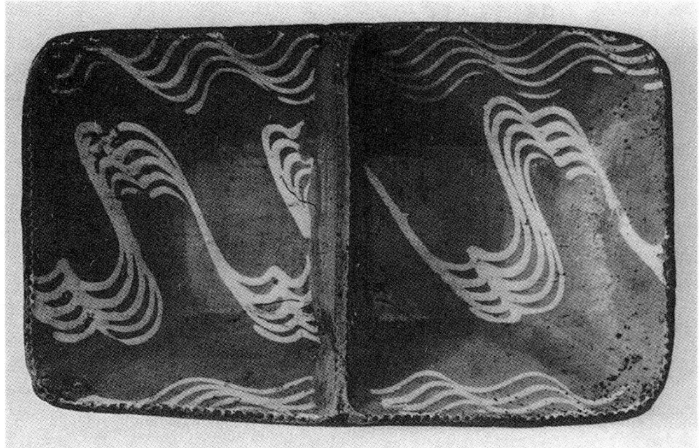

20

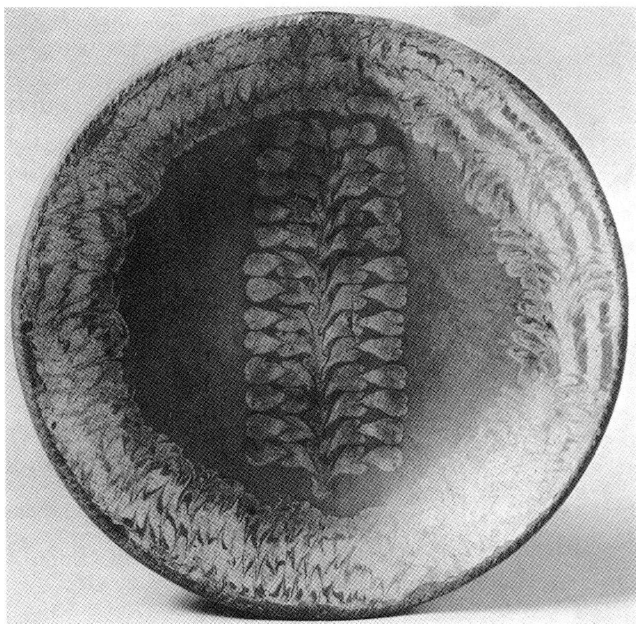

21

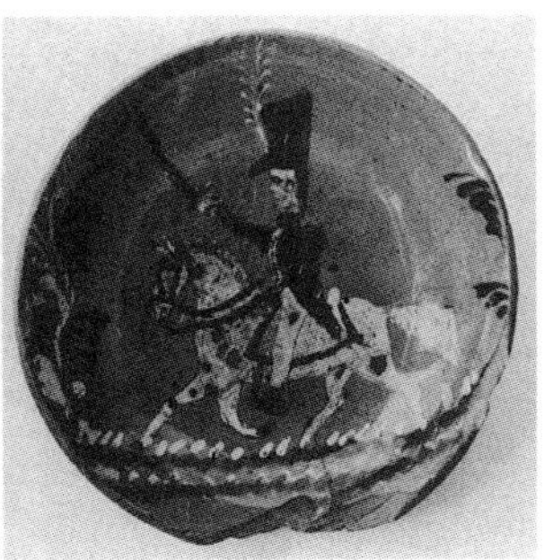

22

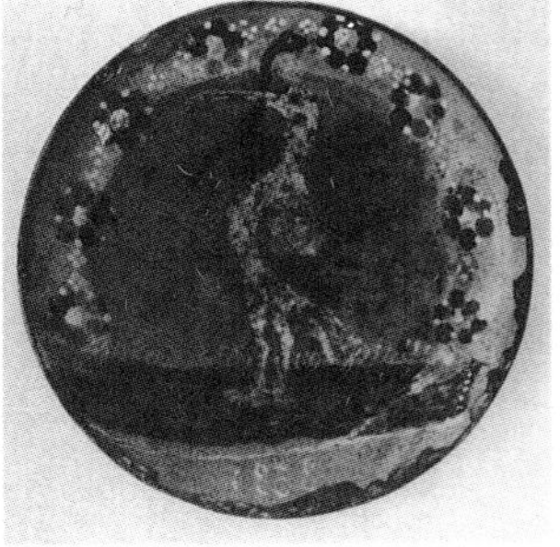

23

20 VEGETABLE DISH
Bucks County
1820–50

Molded redware, coggled edge. Divider added after trailed slip decoration. Thick clear yellowish lead glaze.

8.9 x 47 x 28.6 cm (3½ x 18½ x 11¼")

Titus C. Geesey Collection. 55-94-76

21 PLATE
1820–60

Molded redware, coggled edge. Rim decorated with white slip applied in four bands and marbelized. Center pattern applied with single-quill slip cup. Surface sprinkled with copper oxide (green). Clear yellowish lead glaze.

Height 6.2 cm (2½"), diameter 34.3 cm (13½")

Gift of Joseph H. Himes, in memory of his wife Eilleen C. Himes. 54-62-74

22 PLATE
Rockhill Township, Bucks County
Probably 1838

Inscribed: *18*[?]*8*

Molded redware, cut edge. Band of rouletting on rim. Manganese (brown), copper oxide (green), and thin white slip decoration. Sgraffito figure probably represents Andrew Jackson. Clear lead glaze. Surface losses.

Height 6.3 cm (2½"), diameter 30.2 cm (11⅞")

Gift of John T. Morris. 94-23

23 PLATE
Rockhill Township, Bucks County
1838

Inscribed: *1838*

Molded redware, cut edge. Thin white slip and manganese (brown) with sgraffito and crosshatch detail on bird (crane or heron) holding snake. Clear lead glaze. Surface losses.

Height 4.4 cm (1¾"), diameter 31.3 cm (12¼")

Gift of John T. Morris. 03-371

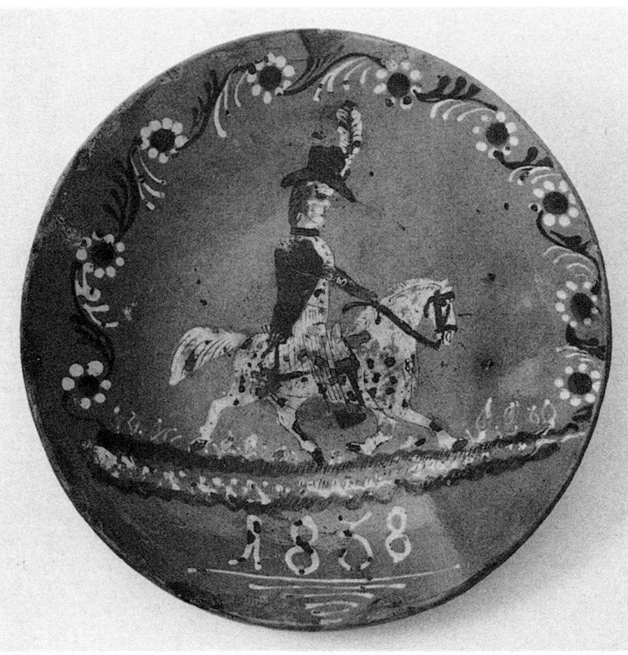

24

24 PLATE
Rockhill Township, Bucks County
1838

Inscribed: *1838*

Molded redware, cut edge. Slightly raised in center. Concentric bands of rouletting inside rim. Decoration of white slip and manganese (brown). Outlining and sgraffito on horse and rider. Clear yellowish lead glaze. By same hand as nos. 22 and 23.

Height 7.3 cm (2⅞"), diameter 38.7 cm (15¼")

Gift of John T. Morris. 02-14

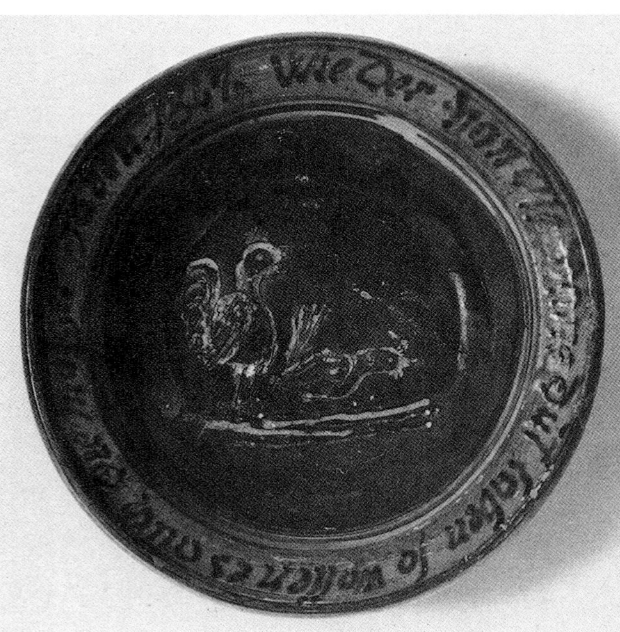

25

25 DISH
Montgomery County
1847

Inscribed: *Wie Der Han Die Häne DUT LABEN So Wollen Es auch die matger haben 1847* ("Just as the cock feeds the hen so too the young women want to have. 1847")

Wheel-thrown redware. Straight sides, flaring rim, square everted edge. Heavy body. Manganese (brown) inscription on clay body and manganese (brown) ground with white slip banding and design of cock and hen. Lead glaze. Similar to ware produced in Alsace.

Height 5.4 cm (2⅛"), diameter 22.9 cm (9")

Gift of John T. Morris. 00-78

26 PITCHER
Franklin County
1850–80

Wheel-thrown redware. Attached handle. Uneven coat of white slip on surface with encircling band of foliage applied in slips colored with copper oxide (green), manganese (dark brown), and iron oxide (rust). Joint of handle and body encircled with manganese (dark brown). Clear yellowish lead glaze.

22.5 x 20 cm (8⅞ x 7⅞")

Gift of J. Stogdell Stokes. 28-10-86

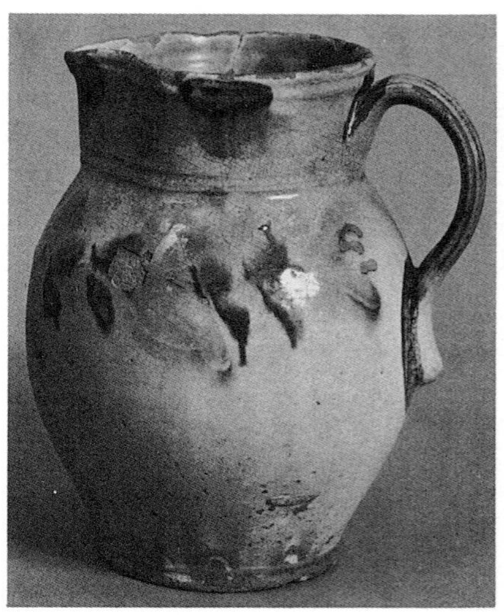

26

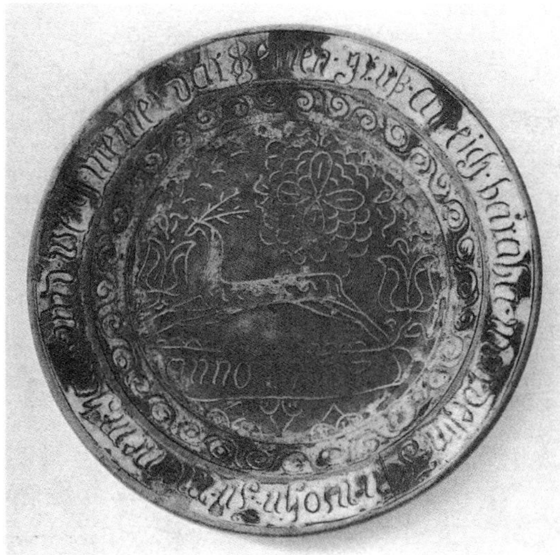

1

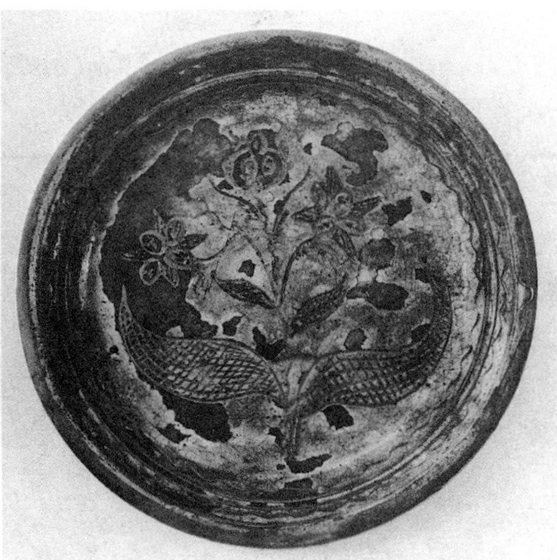

2

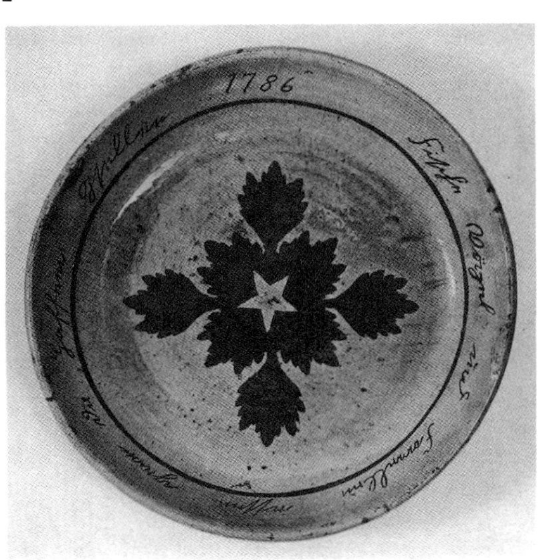

3

1   DISH
1773

Inscribed: *Jesu wohn In meinem haus und weich niemer dar einen gruss an eich Baraber Mardesin anno 1773* ("Jesus dwell in my house and never leave it. A greeting to you. Barbara Mardes. In the year 1773")

Wheel-thrown redware. Rounded sides, flaring rim, rolled everted edge. White slip surface mottled with manganese (brown). Sgraffito decoration. Clear bright yellow lead glaze.

Height 4.8 cm (1⅞"), diameter 31.7 cm (12½")

Gift of John T. Morris. 03-356

2   DISH
Montgomery County
1780–1800

Wheel-thrown redware. Curved sides, flaring narrow rim, square everted edge. Heavy body. White slip surface daubed with copper oxide (green). Sgraffito decoration. Clear yellowish lead glaze.

Height 4.1 cm (1⅝"), diameter 28.6 cm (11¼")

Gift of Miss Katherine Milhouse, in memory of Frances Lichten. 61-95-2

3   DISH
Upper Hanover Township, Montgomery County
1786

Inscribed: *Fische Vögel und Forellen essen gern die Heffner gsellen 1786* ("Fish, fowl, and trout too are relished by the potter's crew. 1786")

Wheel-thrown redware. Straight sides, rolled everted edge. White slip surface. Sgraffito inscription and banding. Design from cut paper pattern placed on body before applying slip and removed before glazing. Clear brownish lead glaze. By same hand as no. 17.

Height 5.4 cm (2⅛"), diameter 29.5 cm (11⅝")

John T. Morris Collection. 21-46-31

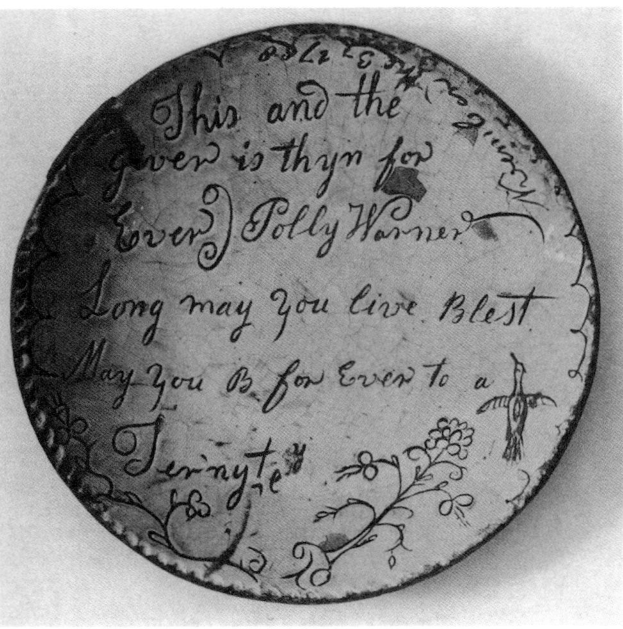

4

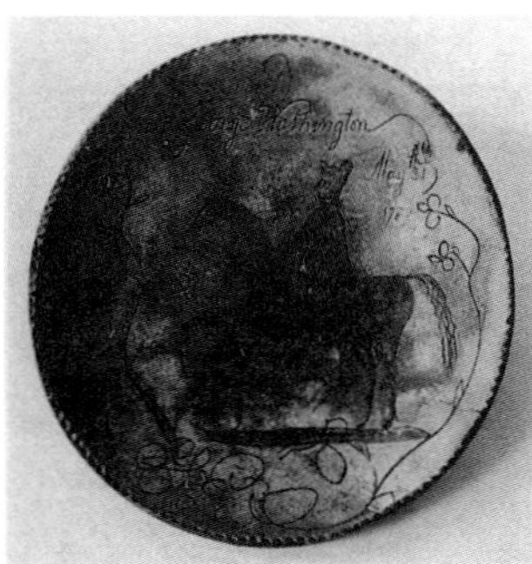

5

4 PLATE
Bucks County
1788

Inscribed: *This and the giver is thyn for Ever Polly Warner   Long may you live Blest May you B for ever to a Ternyte*ᵘ *November the 31 1788*

Molded redware, coggled edge. Surface covered with white slip. Sgraffito decoration. Clear yellow lead glaze. Surface losses.

Height 3.5 cm (1⅜″), diameter 20.3 cm (8″)

Purchased: Baugh-Barber Fund. 74-107-3

---

5 PLATE
Bucks County
1789

Inscribed: *George Washington   May 31th 1789*
Marked in slip: *BB* [BR?]

Molded redware, coggled edge. Surface covered with white slip. Sgraffito decoration colored with red slip. Clear yellowish lead glaze.

Height 5.3 cm (2⅛″), diameter 29.5 cm (11⅝″)

Purchased: Baugh-Barber Fund. 60-111-1

---

6 SHAVING BOWL
Bucks County
1793

Inscribed: *Wann ich mich thu rasieren, so thut es der bart spühren 1793* ("When I shave myself my chin feels it. 1793")

Wheel-thrown redware. Applied hanging loop on reverse. Footed bowl, curved sides, flaring rim, rolled everted edge cut out for chin. Heavy body. Surface covered with thick white slip. Sgraffito banding and decoration. Clear brownish lead glaze.

Height 7.3 cm (2⅞″), diameter 20.6 cm (8⅛″)

Purchased: Joseph E. Temple Fund. 16-111

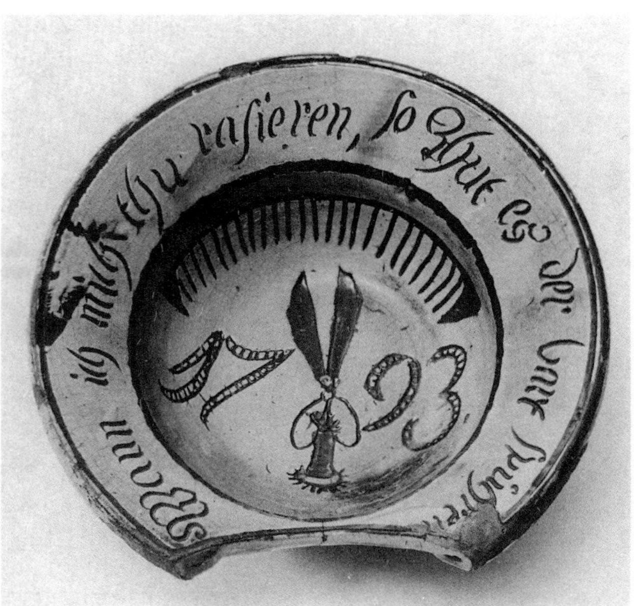

6

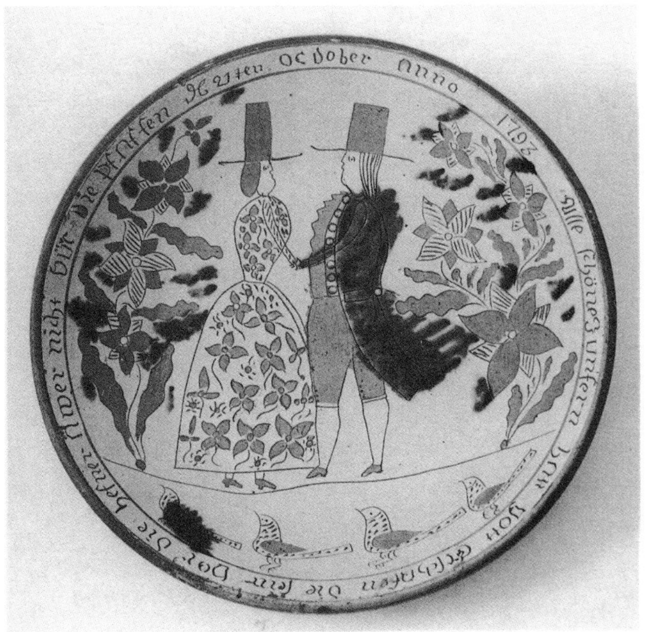

7

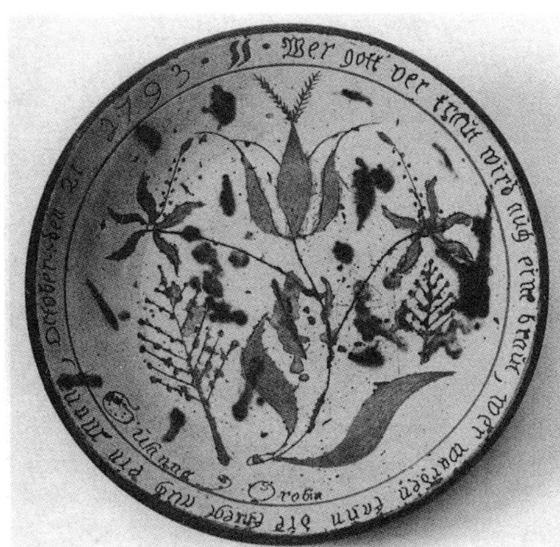

8

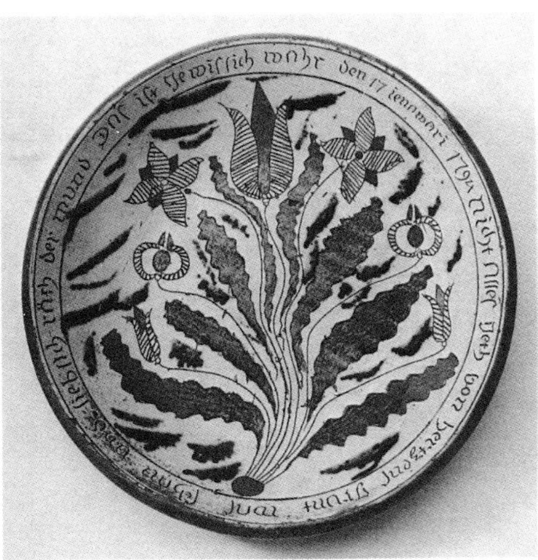

9

7 DISH

Frederick Township, Montgomery County
1793

Inscribed: *Alle schöne Junfern hatt Gott Erschafen Die sein vor die hefner. äwer nicht vür die Pfaffen den 21 ten Ocdober Anno 1793* ("God created all beautiful maidens. They are for the potters but not for the priests. October 21, 1793")

Wheel-thrown redware. Rounded sides, everted edge. Surface covered with white slip daubed with copper oxide (green). Sgraffito decoration and banding. Thin clear yellowish mat lead glaze.

Height 5.7 cm (2¼"), diameter 30.7 cm (12⅛")

Gift of John T. Morris. 00-19

8 DISH

Frederick Township, Montgomery County
1793

Inscribed: *Susanna Grobin   Wer gott ver traut wird auch eine braut, Wer warden kann die kriegt auch ein Mann, Octover den 21, 1793* ("Susanna Grob. She who trusts in God will also become a bride. She who can wait will also get a husband. October 21, 1793")

Wheel-thrown redware. Rounded sides, everted edge. Surface covered with white slip daubed with copper oxide (green). Sgraffito banding and decoration. Thin clear yellowish mat lead glaze.

Height 5.7 cm (2¼"), diameter 30.8 cm (12⅛")

Purchased: Baugh-Barber Fund. 59-41-1

9 DISH

Frederick Township, Montgomery County
1794

Inscribed: *Nicht alles geth von hertzens grunt was schön und lieblich räth der mund das ist gewislich wahr. den 17 ienowari 1794* ("Not everything beautiful and lovely that is said with the mouth comes from the bottom of the heart. And that is true. January 17, 1794")

Wheel-thrown redware. Rounded sides, everted edge. Surface covered with white slip daubed with copper oxide (green). Broad areas of sgraffito decoration. Clear yellowish mat lead glaze. By same hand as nos. 7 and 8.

Height 5.7 cm (2¼"), diameter 30.5 cm (12")

Gift of John T. Morris. 08-219

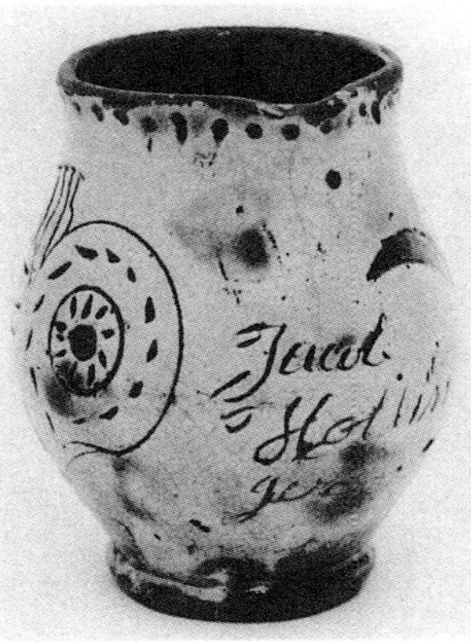

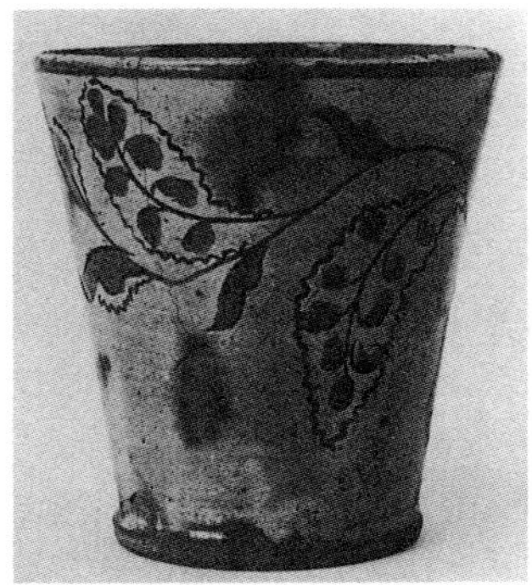

10

12

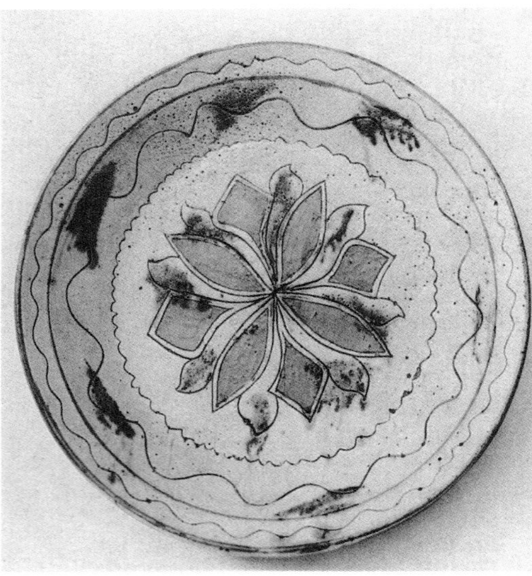

11

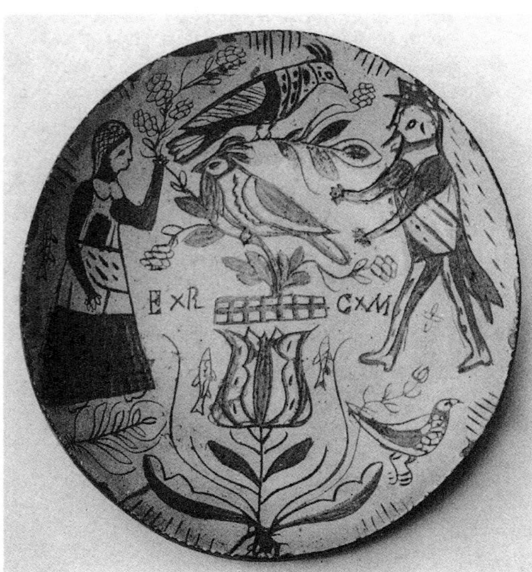

13

10 PITCHER
1800–1820

Inscribed: *Jacob Hollin   Jur.*

Wheel-thrown redware. Applied handle. Surface covered with slip daubed with copper oxide (green). Sgraffito decoration. Clear reddish lead glaze.

8.3 x 9.5 cm (3¼ x 3¾")

Purchased: Baugh-Barber Fund. 38-15-13

11 DISH
Bucks County
1800–1820

Wheel-thrown redware. Rounded sides, square everted edge. Surface covered with white slip daubed with copper oxide (green) and manganese (brown). Sgraffito banding and decoration. Punched dots on petal outlines are probably pattern guide. Slip surface pitted. Clear reddish yellow lead glaze.

Height 5 cm (2"), diameter 31.8 cm (12½")

Purchased: Baugh-Barber Fund. 45-42-6

12 BEAKER
Montgomery County
1800–1820

Wheel-thrown redware. Surface covered with thin white slip daubed with copper oxide (green). Sgraffito decoration. Clear brownish lead glaze inside and out, except bottom.

Height 9.2 cm (3⅝"), diameter 8.8 cm (3⅜")

Purchased: Baugh-Barber Fund. 13-471

13 PLATE
c. 1800–1820

Inscribed: *ExR   CxM*

Molded redware, coggled edge. White slip surface with sgraffito designs. Clear lead glaze.

Height 3.6 cm (1⅜"), diameter 25 cm (9⅞")

Gift of John T. Morris. 00-77

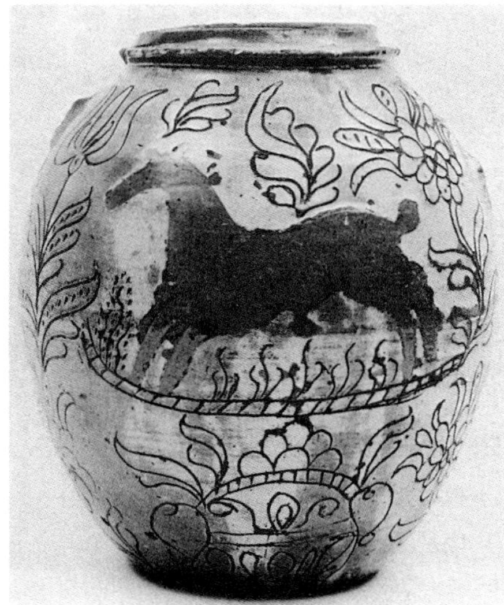

14

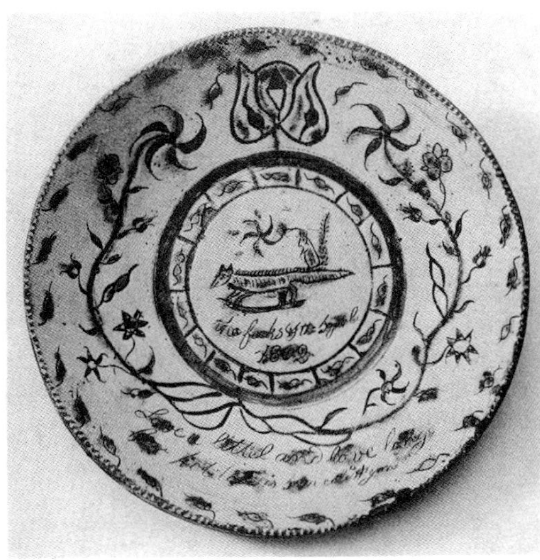

15

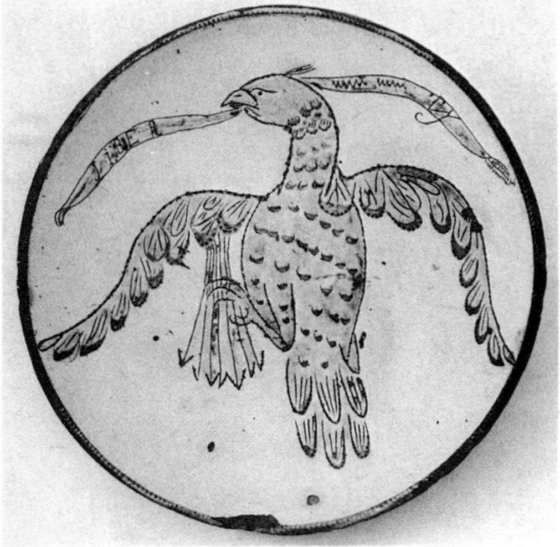

16

14 JAR
1800–1830

Wheel-thrown redware. Raised rim at base. Neck shaped to receive lid (missing). Heavy body. Thin layer of white slip over red body with sgraffito decoration. Design of horse and deer from paper or cloth pattern placed on body before applying slip and removed before glazing. Clear yellowish lead glaze. Applied handles missing.

Height 24 cm (9⅜″), diameter 21.5 cm (8⅜″)

Purchased: Baugh-Barber Fund. 08-343

15 PLATE
Montgomery County
1802

Inscribed: *The focks and the squrl   1802 Love a littel and love longe for hot love is sun cold & gone*

Molded redware, coggled edge. Surface covered with white slip. Sgraffito banding and decoration daubed with copper oxide (green) and manganese (brown). Clear reddish yellow lead glaze. Some pitting in glaze.

Height 5.1 cm (2″), diameter 28 cm (11″)

Gift of John T. Morris. 04-16

16 PLATE
1808–20

Inscribed: *LIBER TY*

Molded redware, coggled edge. Surface covered with white slip. Punched dots outlining bird possibly mark pattern tracing. Sgraffito decoration colored with copper oxide (green), manganese (brown), and oxide of cobalt (blue gray). Clear lead glaze.

Height 4.5 cm (1¾″), diameter 31.5 cm (12⅜″)

Gift of John T. Morris. 03-15

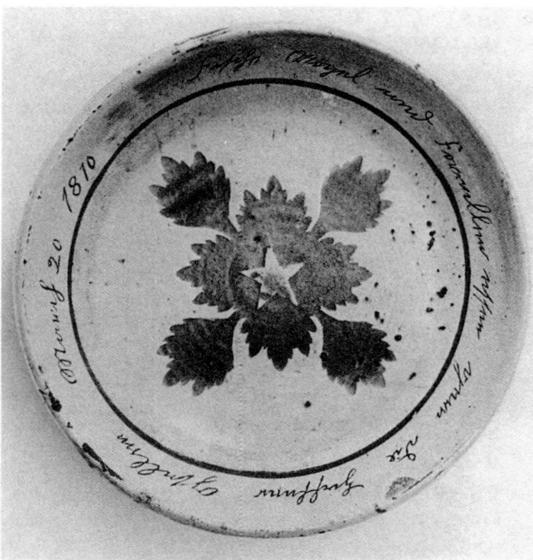

17

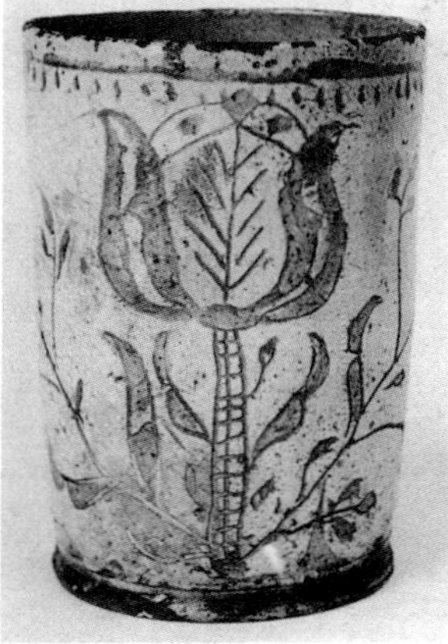

18 obverse   **18** reverse

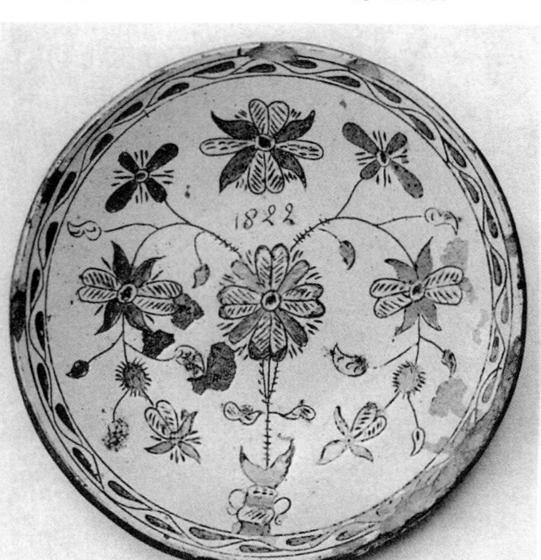

19

17 DISH
Upper Hanover Township, Montgomery
County
1810

Inscribed: *Fische Vögel und Forrellen essen
gern die Haffner Gsellen March 20 1810* ("Fish,
fowl, and trout too are relished by the potter's
crew. March 20, 1810")

Wheel-thrown redware. Straight sides, rolled
everted edge. Sgraffito inscription and
banding. Design from paper pattern placed on
body before coating with slip and removed
before glazing. Thick clear brownish lead
glaze. By same hand as no. 3.

Height 5.1 cm (2″), diameter 28.5 cm (11¼″)

Purchased: Baugh-Barber Fund. 45-42-2

18 MUG
Montgomery County
1816

Inscribed below handle: *1816*

Wheel-thrown redware. Applied strap handle.
Surfaces, except bottom, covered with white
slip touched with copper oxide (green).
Sgraffito decoration. Clear greenish yellow
lead glaze. Impurities in slip and glaze.

Height 16 cm (6¼″), diameter 11 cm (4¼″)

Gift of John T. Morris. 21-46-67

19 PLATE
Frederick Township, Montgomery County
1822

Inscribed: *1822*

Molded redware, plain edge. Heavy body.
Surface covered with white slip daubed with
copper oxide (green). Broad flat sgraffito on
petals and border design. Clear mat lead glaze.
Pitting and losses on surface. Fingerprints in
clay on reverse.

Height 4.2 cm (1⅝″), diameter 23.8 cm (9⅜″)

Purchased: Baugh-Barber Fund. 13-470

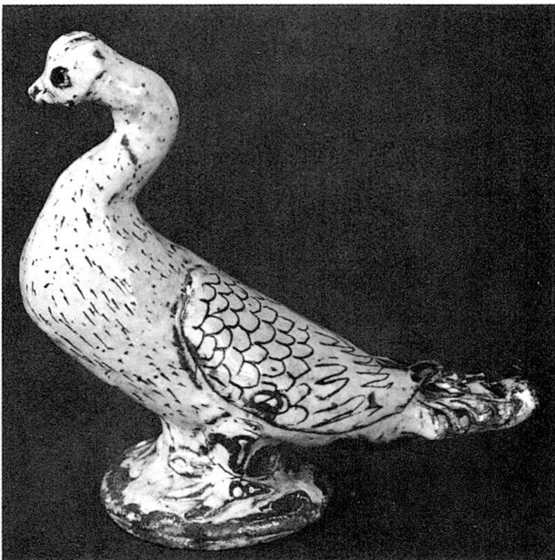

1

1   BIRD WHISTLE
Montgomery County
1800–1810

Modeled redware. Base, feet, and tail feathers attached to hollow body. Two blowing holes in tail. Body covered with white slip daubed with copper oxide (green). Feathers, eyes, and feet delineated with dark brown (manganese) in slip. Clear lead glaze. Similar to forms produced in Switzerland and Alsace.

15.2 x 18.4 cm (6 x 7¼")

Purchased: Baugh-Barber Fund. 30-59-1

2   BIRD WHISTLE
Bucks County
1800–1815

Modeled and wheel-thrown redware. Blowing hole through tail, sounding holes above tail and at neck. Tail, wings, and comb colored with manganese (brown). Clear lead glaze.

8.6 x 9.2 cm (3⅜ x 3⅝")

Purchased: Baugh-Barber Fund. 42-69-2

3   BIRD WHISTLE AND RATTLE
Bucks County
1800–1815

Modeled and wheel-thrown redware. Touches of manganese (black) on hollow red body. Loose piece of clay rattles inside. Clear orange lead glaze.

8.8 x 10.5 cm (3½ x 4⅛")

Purchased: Baugh-Barber Fund. 42-69-1

4   BIRD WHISTLE
1800–1815

Modeled redware. Solid figure; whistle in pipe on back. Feathers incised, four-petal device impressed around base. Daubed with manganese (dark brown). Clear reddish lead glaze.

6.7 x 9.8 cm (2⅝ x 3⅞")

Titus C. Geesey Collection. 69-284-31

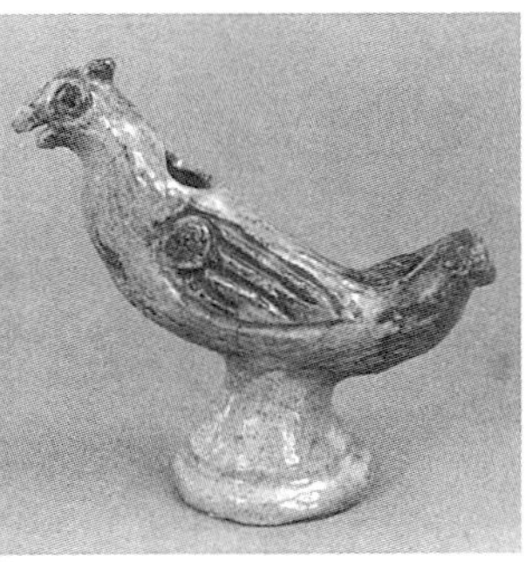

2

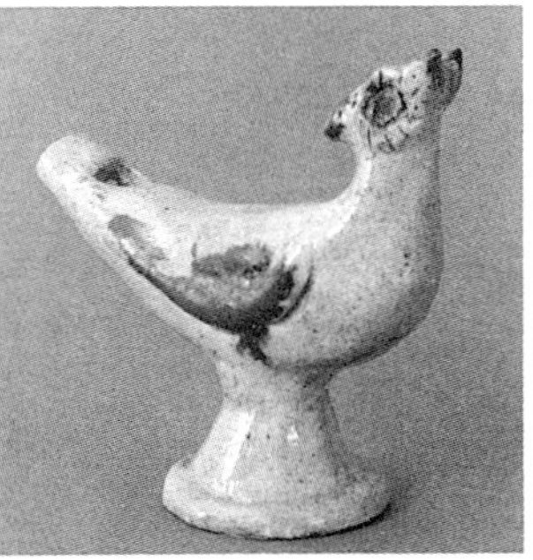

3

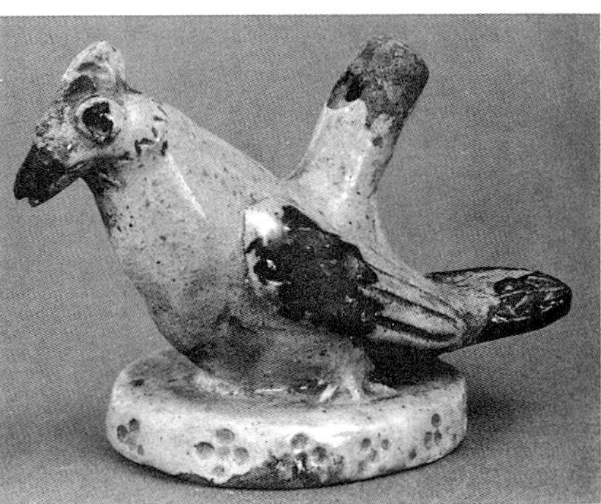

4

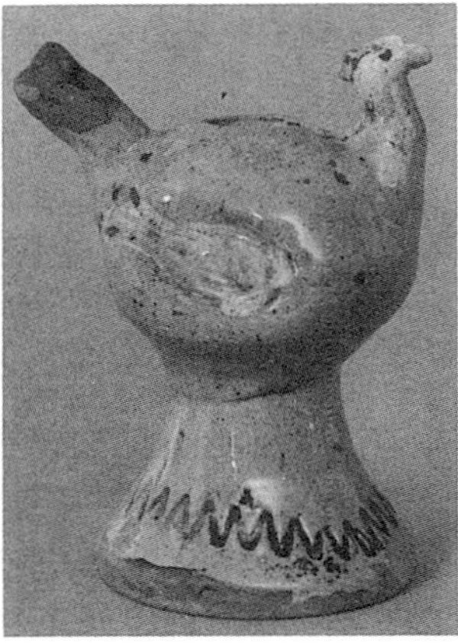

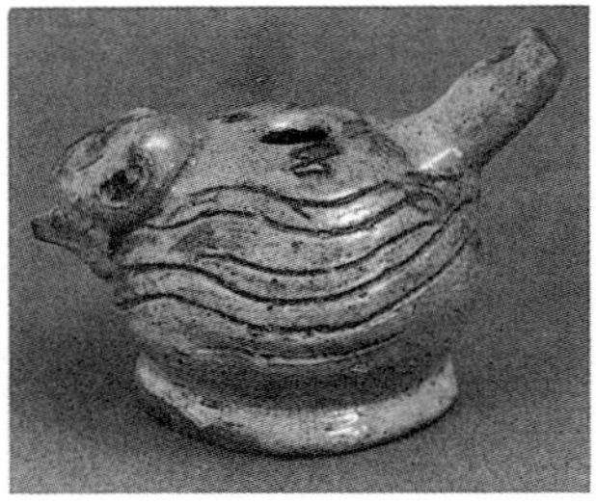

5

7

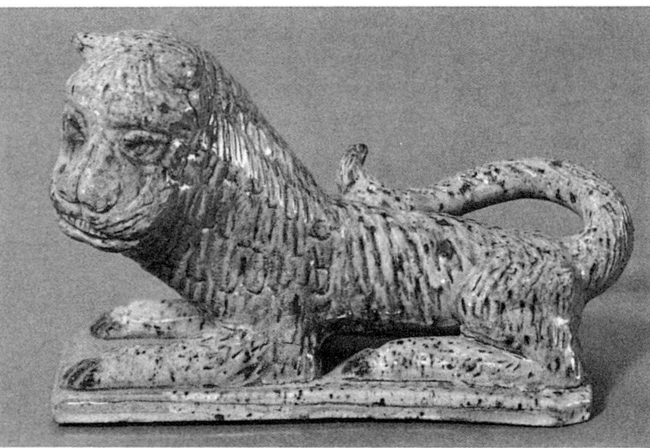

6

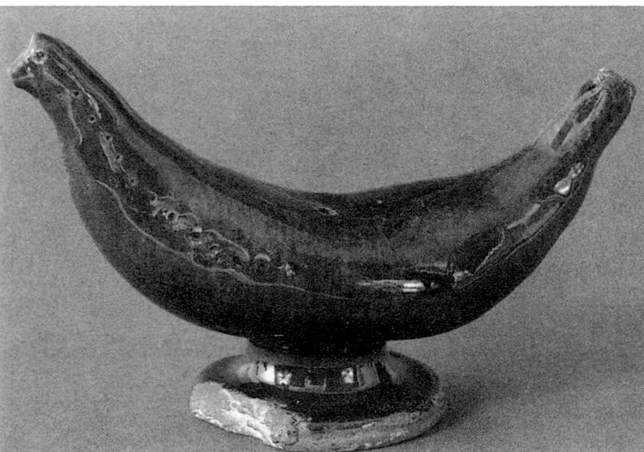

8

5 BIRD WHISTLE
1800–1830

Modeled and wheel-thrown redware. Tail is whistle inserted into hollow body; head is attached. Oval fingerhole in top. Wings are indented and daubed with copper oxide (green) in slip. Hollow pedestal attached to bird. Clear lead glaze.

Height 10.2 cm (4″), diameter 6.4 cm (2½″)

Purchased: Baugh-Barber Fund. 42-69-3

6 LION
Montgomery County
1800–1850

Modeled and slab redware. Platform cut from slab and attached to legs. Body joined at four hocks. Tail attached. Paws daubed and body sprinkled with manganese (brown). Clear lead glaze.

10.5 x 16.5 cm (4⅛ x 6½″)

Purchased: Baugh-Barber Fund. 30-59-13

7 BIRD WHISTLE AND RATTLE
1807

Inscribed: *1807*

Modeled and wheel-thrown redware. Head and tail with blowing hole applied to hollow body. Round piece of unglazed clay rattles inside. Incised lines delineate wings. Daubs of manganese (brown) for eyes. Clear reddish lead glaze.

6 x 9 cm (2⅜ x 3½″)

Titus C. Geesey Collection. 69-284-30

8 BIRD WHISTLE
Bucks County
1812

Marked on bottom: *Juny 1812* [June]

Modeled and wheel-thrown redware. Blowing hole in tail and two sounding holes mid-back. Stippled decoration on neck and head. Opaque manganese (brown) lead glaze.

7.8 x 12.7 cm (3⅛ x 5″)

Purchased: Baugh-Barber Fund. 22-4-6

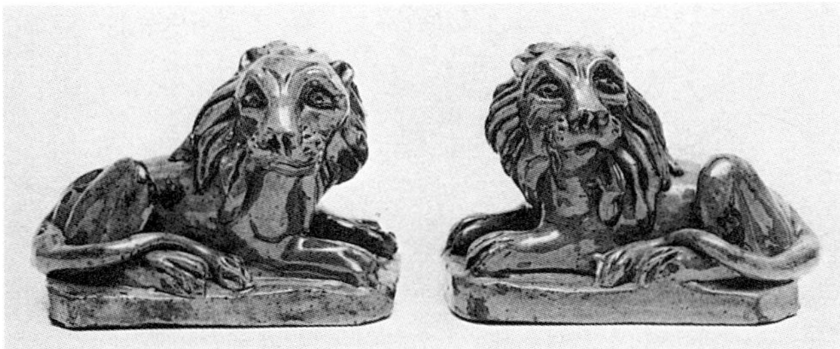

9

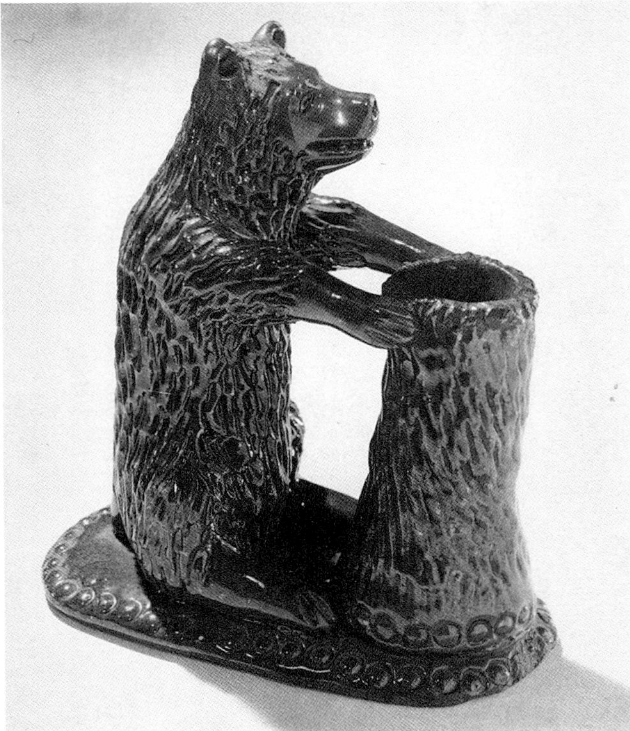

10

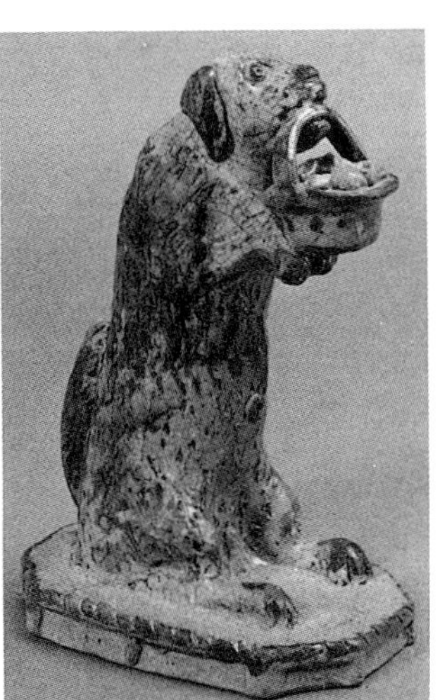

11

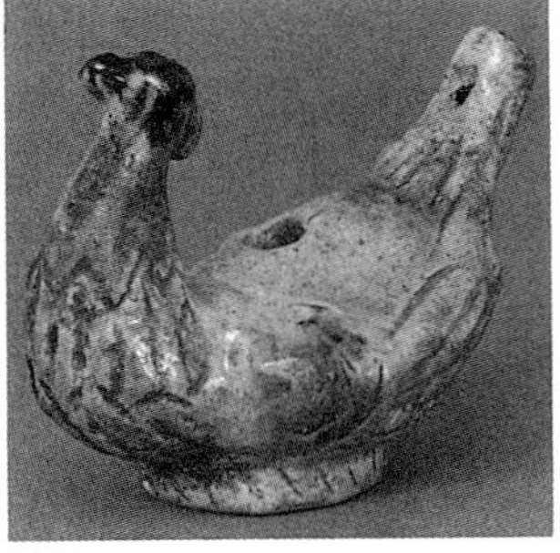

12

9 PAIR OF LIONS
1820–50

Modeled redware. Base and figures partially hollow. Lions' manes carved and applied. Thick clear yellowish lead glaze over deep red body. Used as mantel ornaments.

Left 11.7 x 15.2 cm (4⅝ x 6″)
Right 11.1 x 15.9 cm (4⅜ x 6¼″)

Bequest of Mr. and Mrs. William M. Elkins. 50-92-169a,b

10 VASE
1820–50

Modeled and slab redware. Made in three units: base, tree, and bear. Bear is hollow with rattle inside. Small hole through back. Base decorated with stamped circles. Thick clear brownish lead glaze.

15.5 x 13.2 cm (6⅛ x 5¼″)

Purchased: Baugh-Barber Fund. 30-59-12

11 DOG
Bucks County
1820–50

Modeled redware. Solid figure of dog on platform carrying basket of apples and pears in his mouth. Body delineated with incised lines and daubed with manganese (brown). Clear reddish lead glaze.

18.7 x 13 cm (7⅜ x 5⅛″)

Purchased: Baugh-Barber Fund. 42-10-1

12 BIRD WHISTLE AND RATTLE
1820–50

Modeled redware. Figure of goose sitting on nest. Blow hole in tail and fingerhole in back. Ball of unglazed clay inside. Incised feathers daubed with copper oxide (green) and manganese (black). Clear lead glaze.

6.4 x 9.5 cm (2½ x 3¾″)

Purchased: Baugh-Barber Fund. 42-69-4

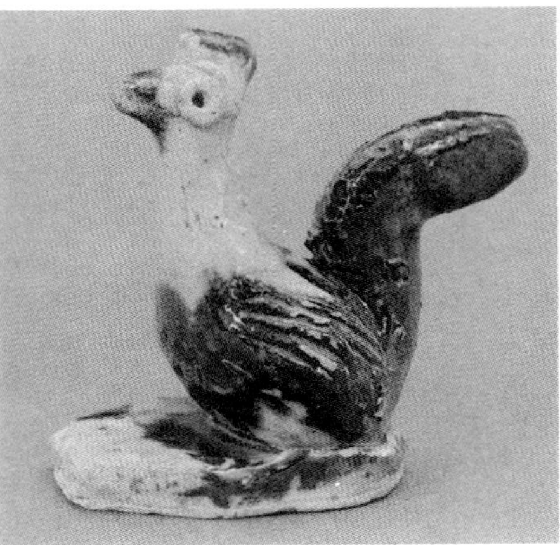

13

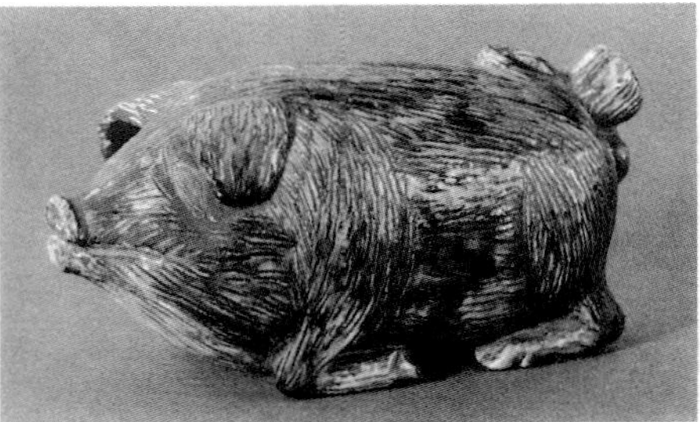

14

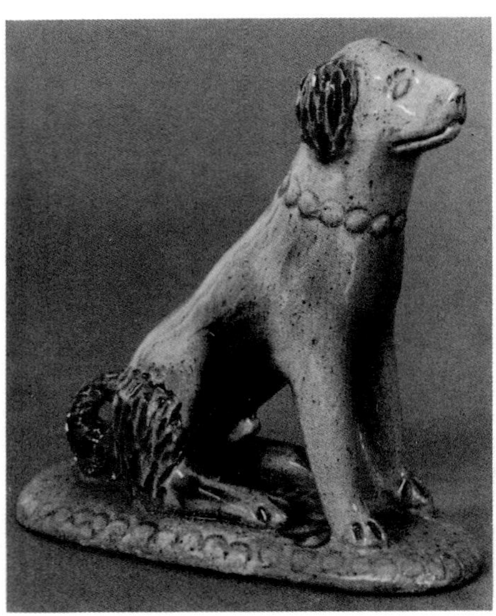

15

13 HEN
1820–60

Modeled redware. Small hole through base in front of figure. Daubed with manganese (brown). Clear lead glaze.

5.7 x 5.7 cm (2¼ x 2¼")

Gift of Joseph H. Himes, in memory of his wife Eilleen C. Himes. 54-62-55

14 FLASK
Shartlesville, Berks County
1820–60

Modeled redware. Bottle opening under tail. Cork missing. Pig's bristles delineated with incised lines. Daubed with manganese (brown). Clear brownish lead glaze.

9.5 x 20.3 cm (3¾ x 8")

Titus C. Geesey Collection. 55-94-16

15 DOG
1830–50

Modeled and slab redware. Slab decorated with stamped circles at edge and foliage under front paws. Daubed with copper oxide (green). Thick clear lead glaze.

9.5 x 8.9 cm (3¾ x 3½")

Purchased: Baugh-Barber Fund. 30-59-7

16 PAIR OF DUCKS
1830–50

Modeled redware. Solid figures have incised eyes and beaks. Border of circles on base. Wings daubed with manganese (brown). Clear reddish lead glaze.

Left 5.8 x 8 cm (2¼ x 3⅛")
Right 5.8 x 7.6 cm (2¼ x 3")

Gift of Joseph H. Himes, in memory of his wife Eilleen C. Himes. 54-62-53,54

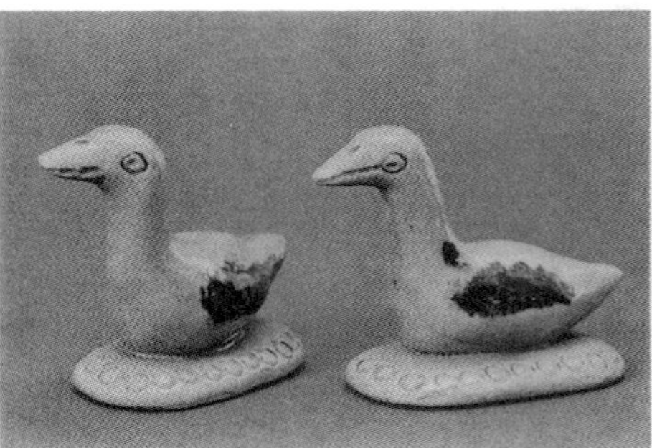

16

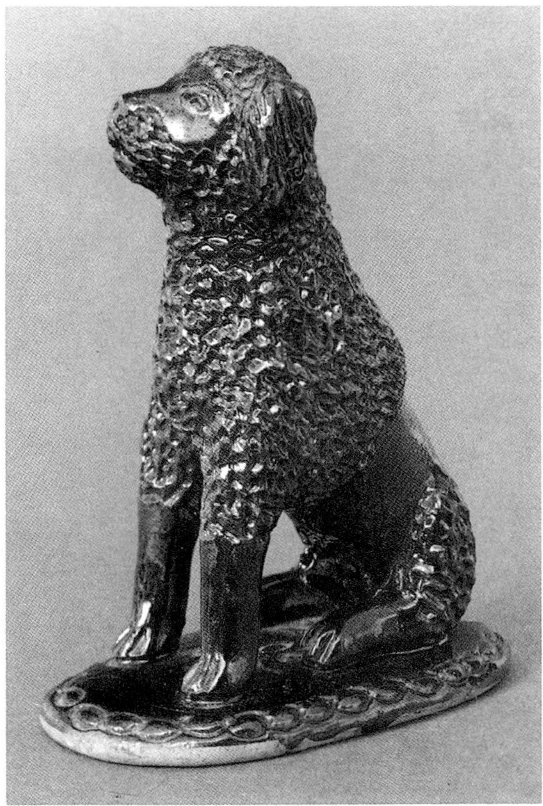

17

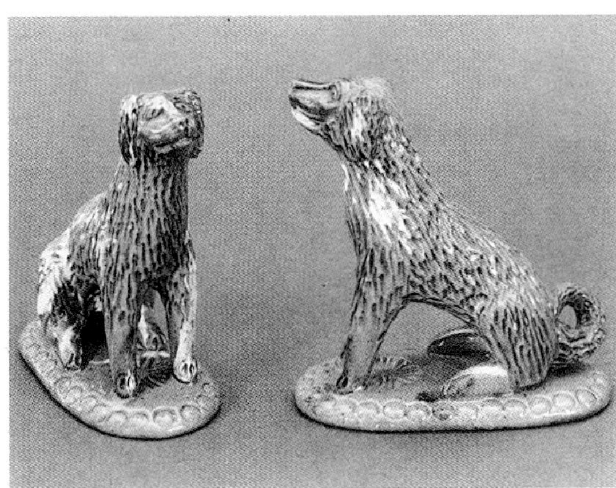

18

17 DOG

1830–50

Incised on bottom: 8

Modeled and slab redware. Incised decoration of linked ovals around base and seven-petaled daisy behind front legs. Manganese (black brown) in thick lead glaze.

10.8 x 8.9 cm (4¼ x 3½")

Gift of Joseph H. Himes, in memory of his wife Eilleen C. Himes. 54-62-52

18 PAIR OF DOGS

1830–50

Incised on bottom of each: 8.C

Modeled and slab redware. Base decorated with impressed circles and star motif between front paws. Dashed with white slip on red body. Clear lead glaze.

Left 10.8 x 9.8 cm (4¼ x 3⅞")
Right 10 x 9.7 cm (3⅞ x 3¾")

Titus C. Geesey Collection. 55-94-18a,b

19 DOG

1840–60

Modeled and slab redware. Slab base decorated with band of impressed round flowers and foliage incised between paws. Surface daubed with white slip and manganese (brown). Thick clear reddish lead glaze.

13.2 x 13.3 cm (5⅛ x 5¼")

Purchased: Baugh-Barber Fund. 30-59-8

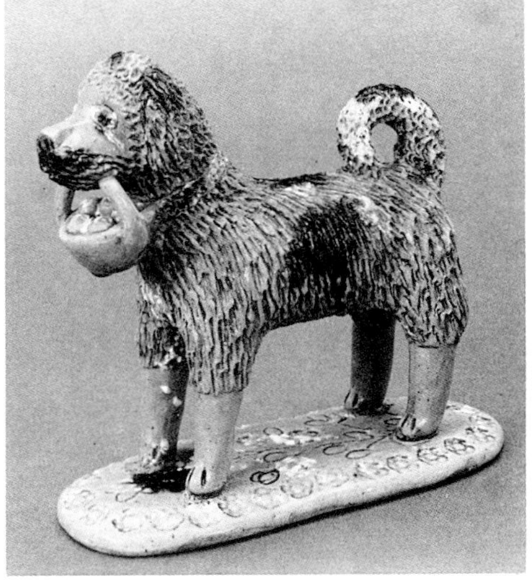

19

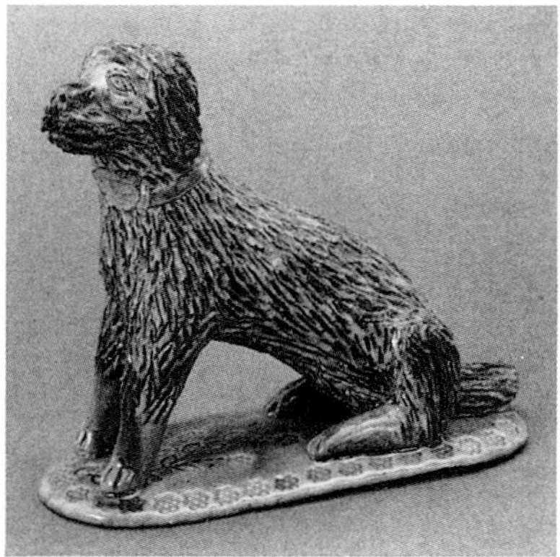

20

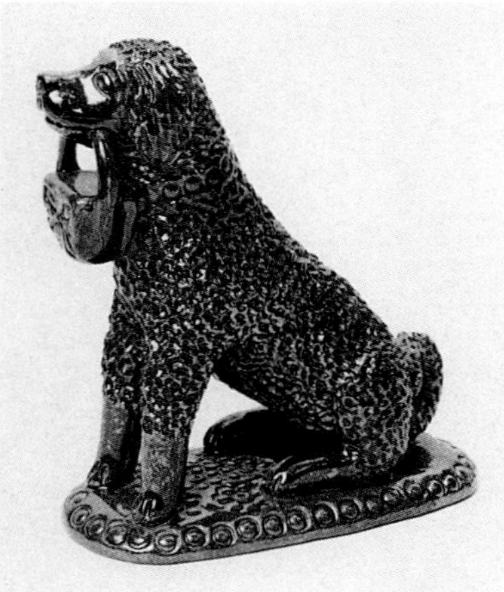

21

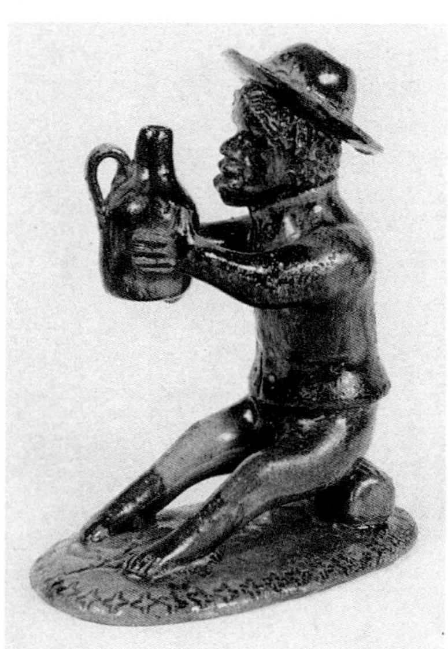

22

20 DOG

1840–60

Modeled and slab redware. Edge of slab decorated with impressed six-petaled daisy. Foliage and daisies incised between paws. Basket suspended from mouth is missing. Splashed with copper oxide (green) and manganese (brown). Clear yellowish lead glaze.

12.4 x 13 cm (4⅞ x 5⅛")

Purchased: Baugh-Barber Fund. 30-59-10

21 DOG RATTLE

1840–60

Modeled redware. Loose clay rattles inside hollow figure. Four-petaled flower motif on front of basket. Semiopaque manganese (brown) lead glaze.

13 x 11.5 cm (5⅛ x 4½")

Gift of Joseph H. Himes, in memory of his wife Eilleen C. Himes. 54-62-50

22 MAN WITH JUG

1840–60

Incised on bottom: 8

Modeled and slab redware. Edge of slab base impressed with banding of four-pointed stars or crosses. Surfaces daubed with manganese (brown). Thick reddish lead glaze.

14.7 x 11.5 cm (5¾ x 4½")

Purchased: Baugh-Barber Fund. 07-247

23 DUCK

1840–60

Modeled redware. Breast feathers and wings delineated with incised lines. Surface covered with white slip daubed with copper oxide (green) and manganese (brown). Single hole in wing feather. Clear lead glaze. Possibly intended as hanging ornament.

3.6 x 4.8 cm (1½ x 1⅞")

Purchased: Baugh-Barber Fund. 30-59-3

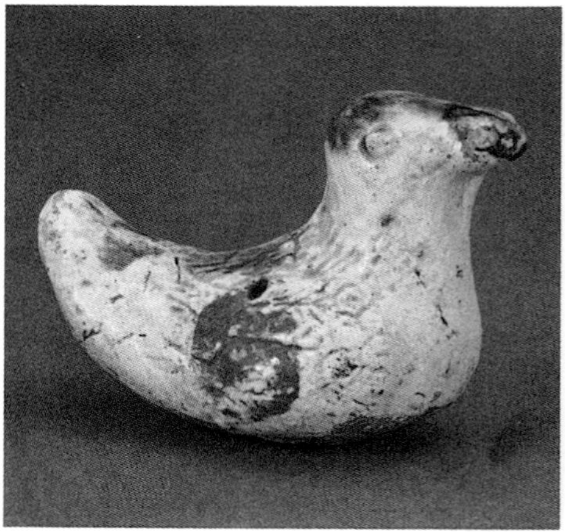

23

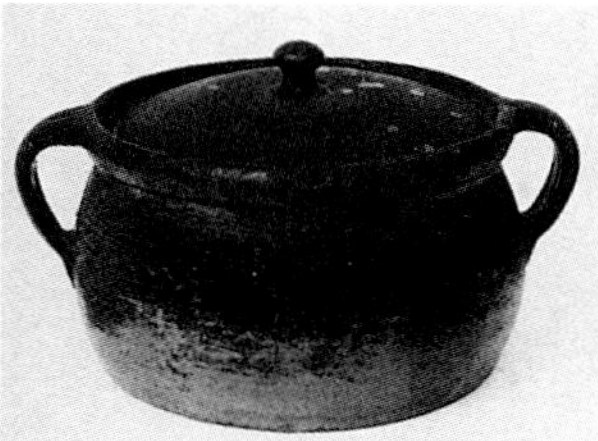

1

1   COVERED POT
Bucks County
1750–1800

Wheel-thrown and molded redware. Applied handles and pouring spout. Lid molded and knop applied. Incised bandings at shoulder. Clear orange brown lead glaze. Blackened from use.

20.3 x 36.8 cm (8 x 14½")

Gift of J. Stogdell Stokes. 28-10-30a,b

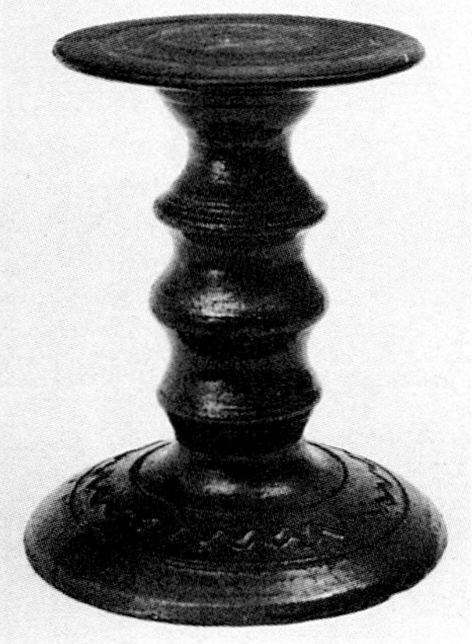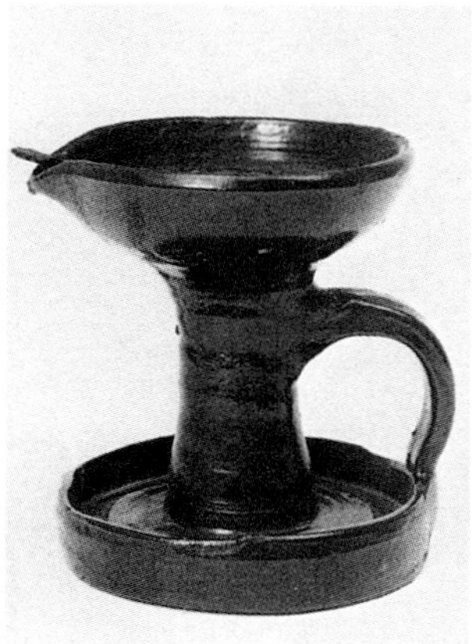

2   **3**

2   LAMPSTAND
Lancaster County
1770–1800

Wheel-thrown redware. Solid base and shaft. Incised banding. Iron oxide (red brown) in clear lead glaze. Same form as one leg of a tile stove.

Height 14 cm (5½"), diameter 12.1 cm (4¾")

Titus C. Geesey Collection. 54-85-5

3   OIL LAMP
1780–1820

Wheel-thrown redware. Applied handle. Thick opaque manganese (brown black) lead glaze.

11.9 x 12.4 cm (4¾ x 4⅞")

Gift of Mrs. William D. Frishmuth. 02-147

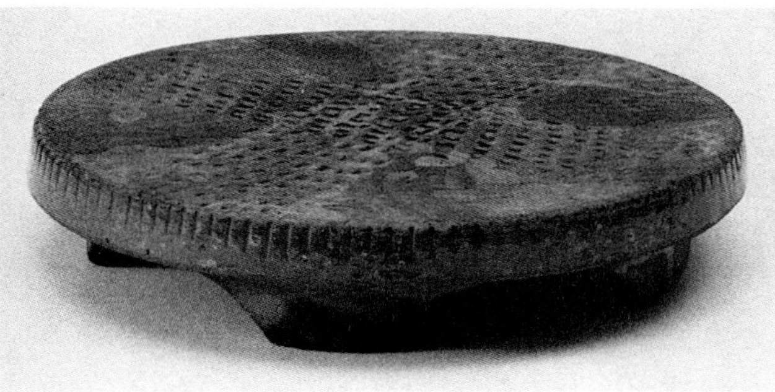

4

4   TRIVET
1780–1840

Wheel-thrown and modeled redware. Five supports cut from raised disk. Coggling on edge and rouletting on top. Four daubs of manganese (brown black) on top. Lead glaze.

Height 3.2 cm (1¼"), diameter 15.9 cm (6¼")

Gift of Joseph H. Himes, in memory of his wife Eilleen C. Himes. 54-62-81

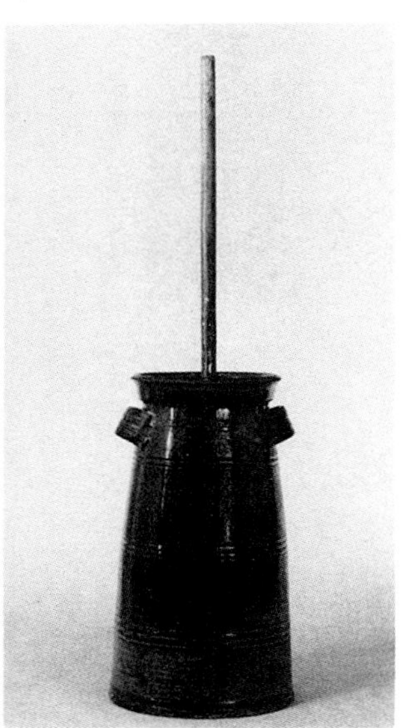

5

5   BUTTER CHURN
Bucks County
1790–1820

Wheel-thrown redware, wood. Applied handles. Flaring neck secures shaped wood top. Dasher handle ends in four shaped blades that are lap-joined and pegged. Opaque lead glaze on interior and exterior, except bottom.

Height 35.4 cm (13⅞"), diameter 20.7 cm (8⅛")

Purchased: Baugh-Barber Fund. 14-24a,b

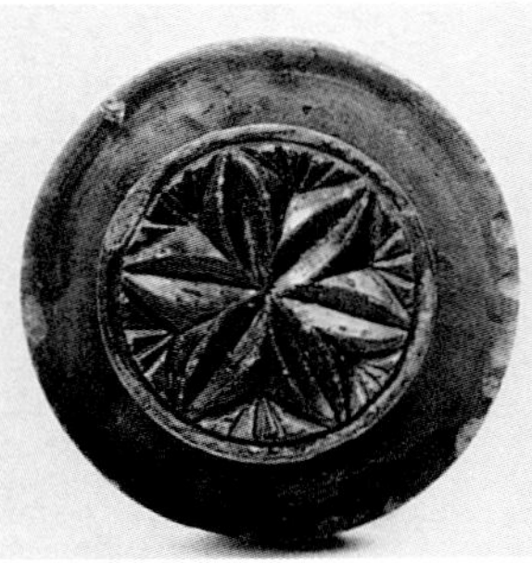

6 reverse

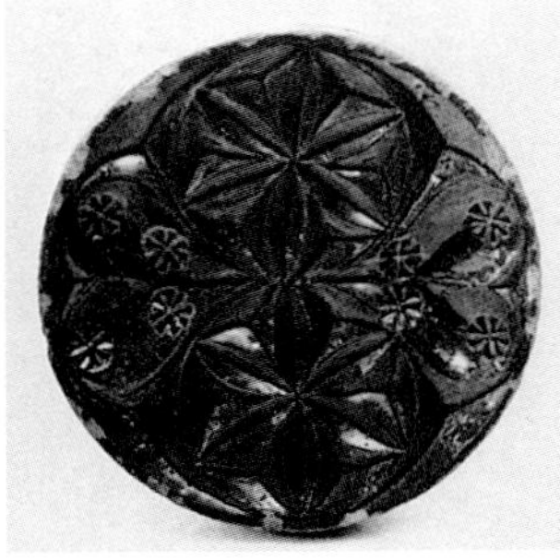

6 obverse

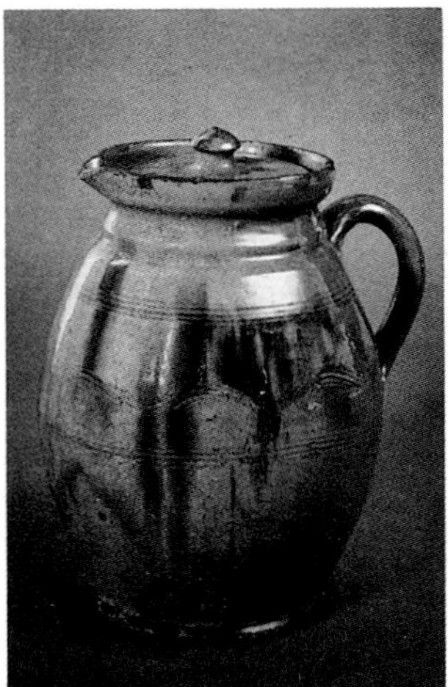

7

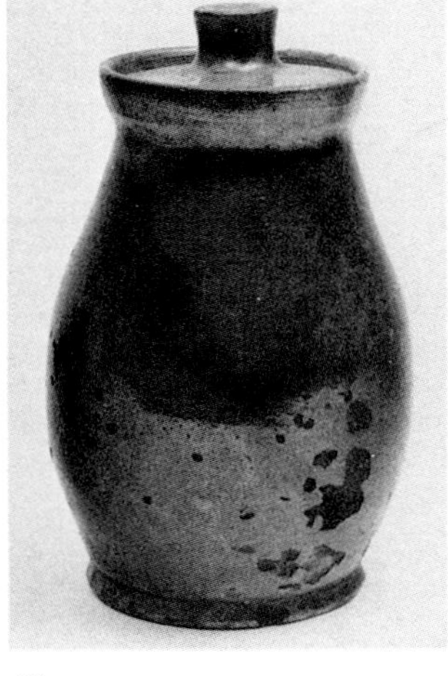

10

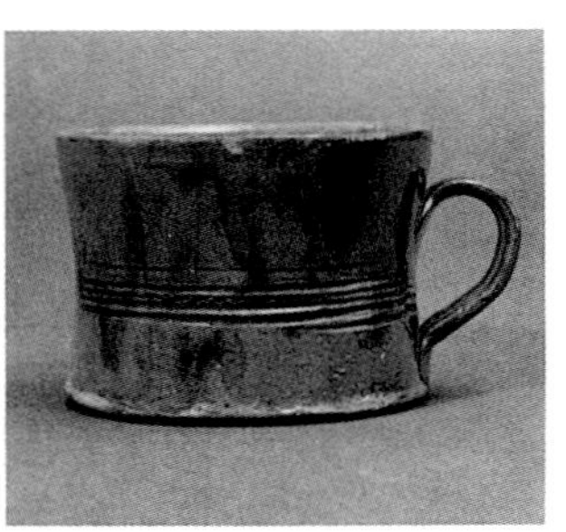

8

9

6   DOUBLE BUTTER PRINT
1800–1820

Wheel-thrown and molded redware. Circles are compass-inscribed; designs are cut and impressed with stamp. Clear brownish lead glaze on mold surfaces.

Height 5.4 cm (2⅛"); diameter obverse 12.2 cm (4¾"), reverse 7.6 cm (3")

Purchased: Baugh-Barber Fund. 57-118-1

7   COVERED PITCHER
Bucks County
1800–1840

Wheel-thrown redware. Applied handle and pouring lip. Lid with raised knop rests on flaring collar. Decorated with incised banding. Clear reddish brown lead glaze daubed with manganese (brown). Similar to ware made in New England and New York.

22.7 x 19.7 cm (8⅞ x 7¾")

Gift of Essex Institute. 25-58-2a,b

8   MUG
Bucks County
1800–1840

Wheel-thrown redware. Applied handle. Surface dappled with manganese (brown). Clear orange lead glaze on interior and exterior.

5.7 x 9.8 cm (2¼ x 3⅞")

Gift of Mrs. Marion Rauch. 59-84-1

9   MUG
Bucks County
1800–1840

Wheel-thrown redware. Applied handle. Thick clear reddish lead glaze with iron speckling on interior and exterior, except bottom.

10.2 x 12.7 cm (4 x 5")

Gift of J. Stogdell Stokes. 28-10-71

10   COVERED JAR
1800–1840

Wheel-thrown redware. Lid with raised knop rests inside neck of jar. Clear reddish brown lead glaze on interior and exterior, except bottom.

Height 21.9 cm (8⅝"), diameter 14.5 cm (5⅝")

Gift of Mrs. William D. Frishmuth. 03-52

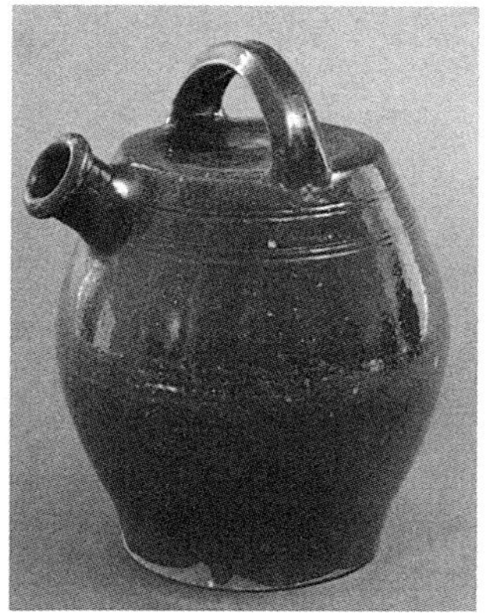

11

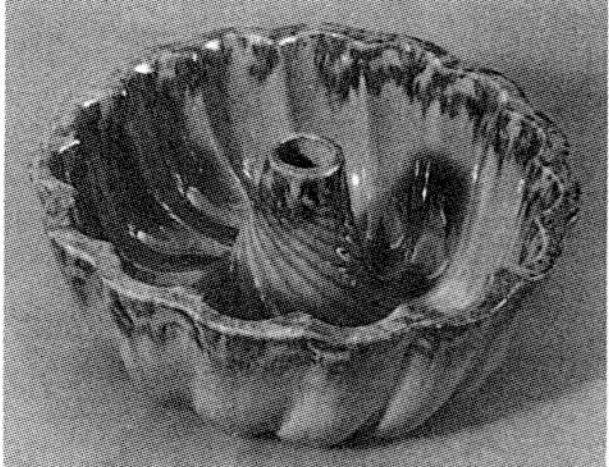

12

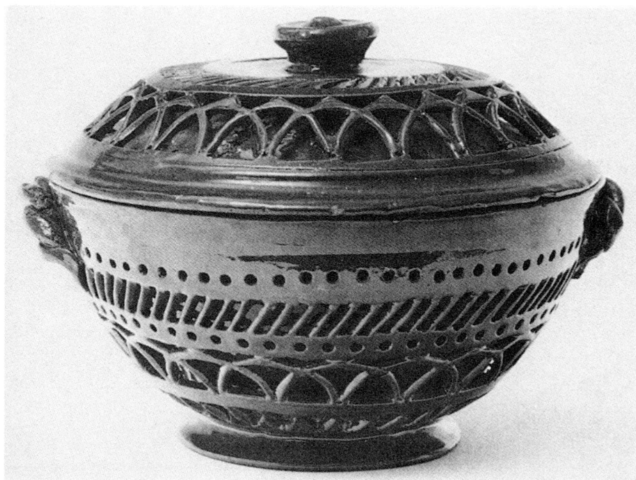

13

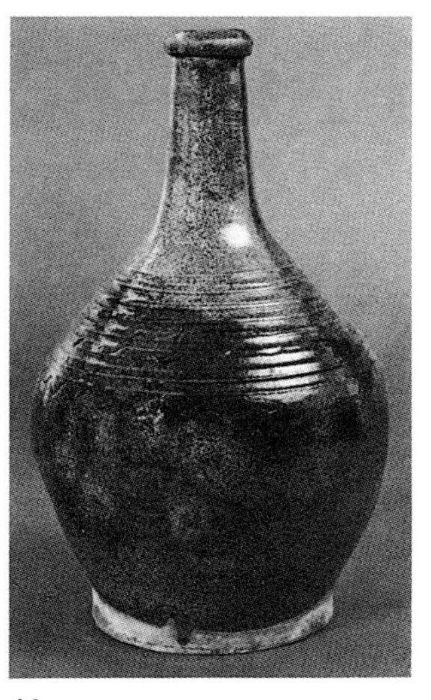

14

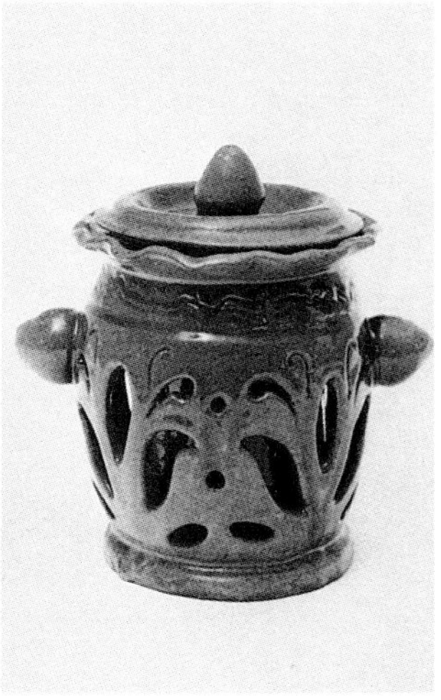

15

11 HARVESTER'S JUG
1800–1840

Wheel-thrown redware. Applied handle and spout. Opaque manganese (brown) lead glaze.

22.8 x 21.6 cm (9 x 8½")

Gift of Joseph H. Himes, in memory of his wife Eilleen C. Himes. 54-62-64

12 CAKE PAN
Bucks County
1800–1840

Incised: *2*

Molded redware. Heavy body. Daubed with manganese (black brown) at rim. Thick clear red lead glaze, pooled inside.

Height 11.5 cm (4½"), diameter 29.5 cm (11⅝")

Gift of Mrs. Annie Hayes. 24-39-1

13 COVERED BOWL
Montgomery County
1800–1840

Wheel-thrown redware. Footed bowl and lid within pierced casing. Applied rope-twist handles and knop. Two layers joined at top rim of bowl and lip of lid and pierced after joining. Manganese (brown) glaze on interior and exterior, except bottom and flange of lid. Three stilt marks on lid and foot.

16 x 22.5 cm (6¼ x 8⅞")

Gift of Joseph H. Himes, in memory of his wife Eilleen C. Himes. 54-62-10a,b

14 BOTTLE
1800–1850

Wheel-thrown redware. Incised with wriggles and scored with concentric bandings. Clear lead glaze with iron (red) and manganese (brown) speckling.

Height 23.5 cm (9¼"), diameter 14.3 cm (5⅝")

Gift of Joseph H. Himes, in memory of his wife Eilleen C. Himes. 54-62-44

15 TOBACCO JAR
Bucks County
1809

Inscribed on front: *J M   1809*

Wheel-thrown redware. Inner jar within pierced outer jar. Applied handles. Knop in one piece with lid. Iron oxide (red) in clear lead glaze. Bottom of jar and lid unglazed.

16.5 x 16.5 cm (6½ x 6½")

Purchased: Baugh-Barber Fund. 43-78-1a,b

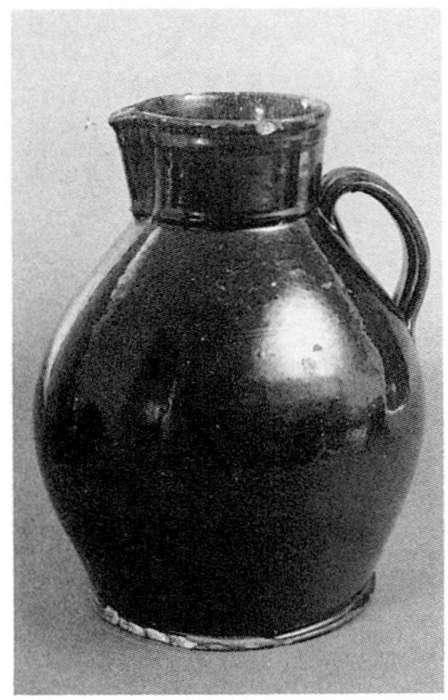

16

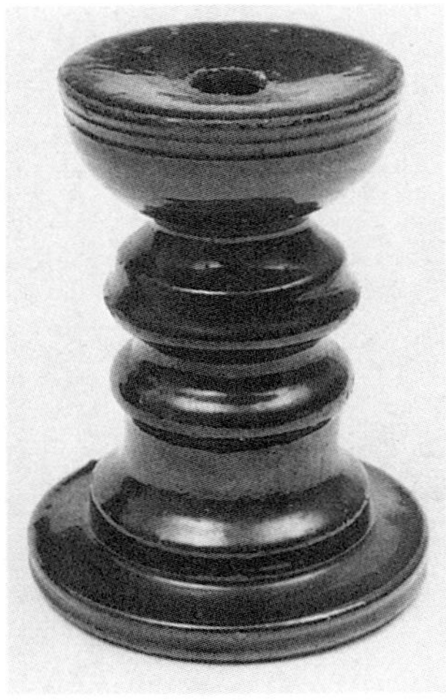

17

16 PITCHER
Montgomery County
1820–40

Wheel-thrown redware. Applied handle.
Incised and raised banding. Thick opaque
manganese (brown) lead glaze inside and out,
except bottom.

30.5 x 25.4 cm (12 x 10″)

Gift of Mrs. William D. Frishmuth. 07-158

17 CANDLESTICK
1820–40

Wheel-thrown redware. Turned shaft with
hollow top. Thick manganese (brown black)
lead glaze.

Height 14.8 cm (5⅞″), diameter 11.5 cm (4½″)

Titus C. Geesey Collection. 54-85-6

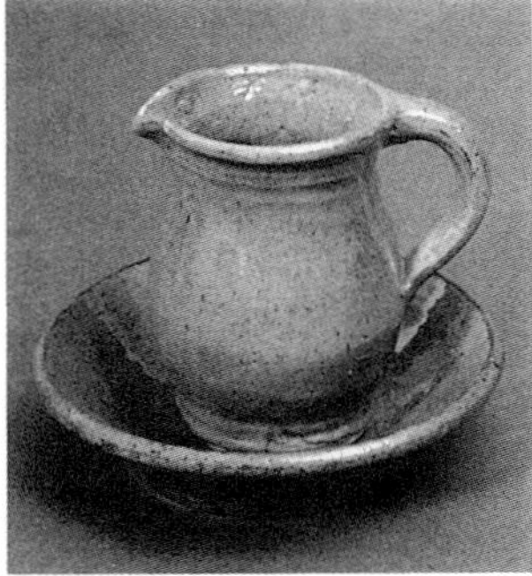

18

18 TOY PITCHER AND BOWL
1820–40

Wheel-thrown redware. Pitcher lead glazed on
interior and exterior, except foot and bottom.
Bowl lead glazed, except bottom.

Pitcher 7.3 x 7.9 cm (2⅞ x 3⅛″), diameter bowl
10.1 cm (4″)

Gift of Joseph H. Himes, in memory of his wife
Eilleen C. Himes. 54-62-37a,b

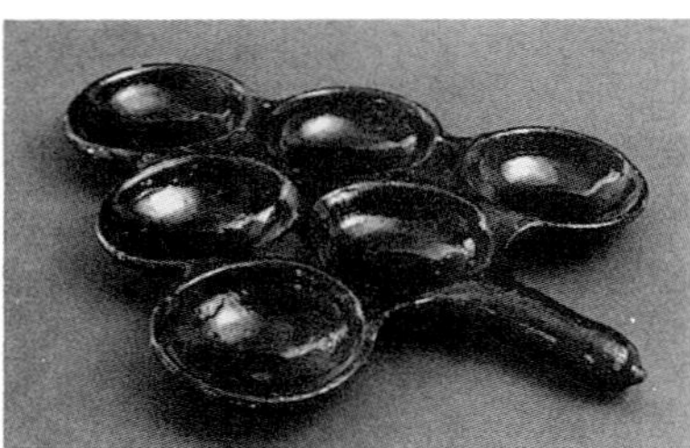

19

19 PANCAKE BAKING PAN
1820–50

Molded and modeled redware. Pans formed
from clay slab pressed over dish molds. Rolled
handle. Reverse reinforced with modeled ribs.
Opaque manganese (brown) lead glaze
obverse and reverse.

2.9 x 33.6 x 27 cm (1⅛ x 13¼ x 10⅝″)

Gift of Joseph H. Himes, in memory of his wife
Eilleen C. Himes. 54-62-66

20 VASE
Bucks County
1820–50

Wheel-thrown redware. Coggled shoulder.
Thick opaque manganese (brown) lead glaze.

Height 24.7 cm (9¾″), diameter 20.3 cm (8″)

Gift of Joseph H. Himes, in memory of his wife
Eilleen C. Himes. 54-62-82

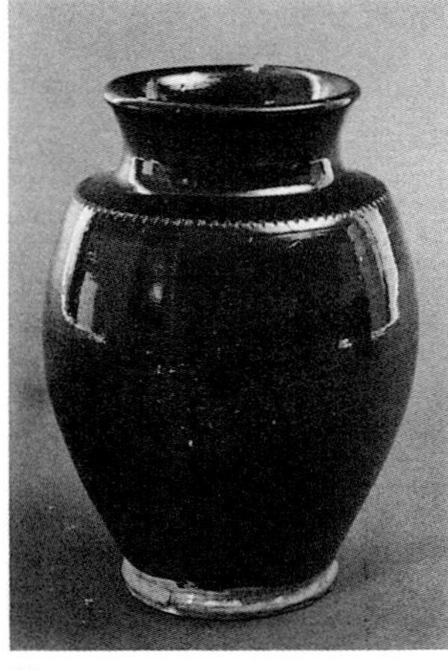

20

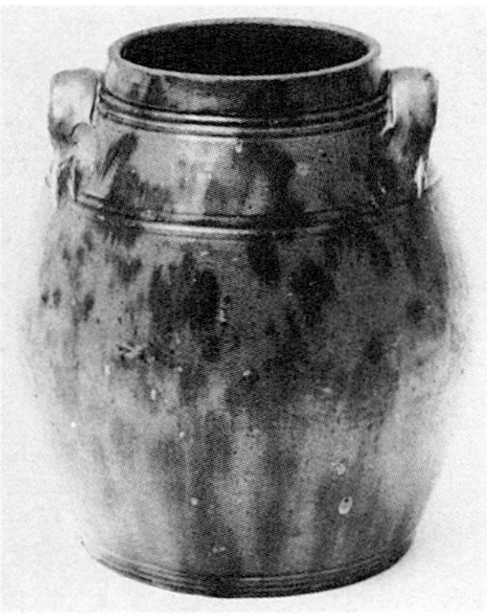

21

21 JAR
1820–50

Incised on bottom: *1715*

Wheel-thrown redware. Applied handles.
Clear brownish lead glaze with manganese
(brown black) mottling.

Height 22.2 cm (8¾″), diameter 20.5 cm (8″)

Purchased: Special Museum Fund. 16-263

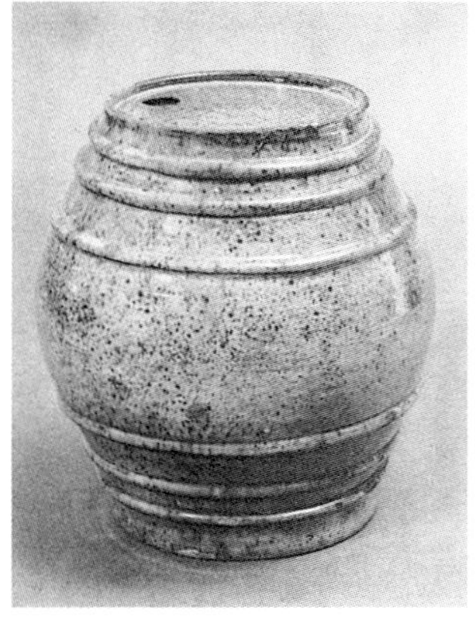

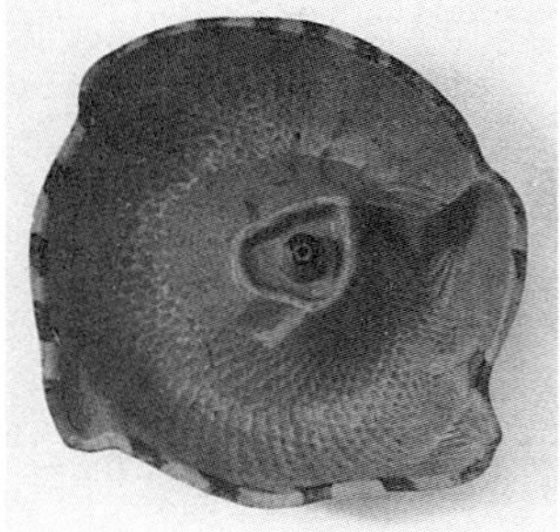

22   **23**

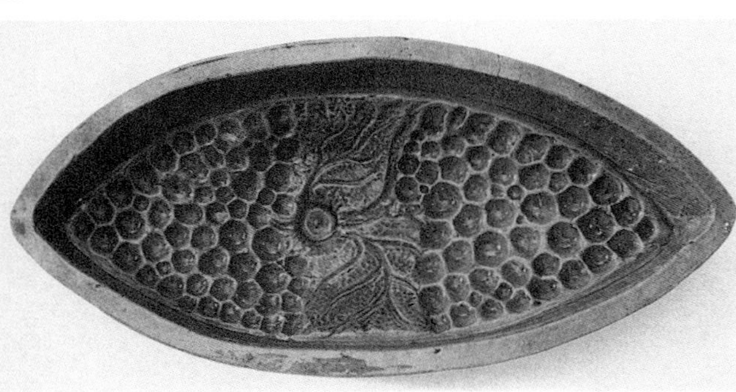

24

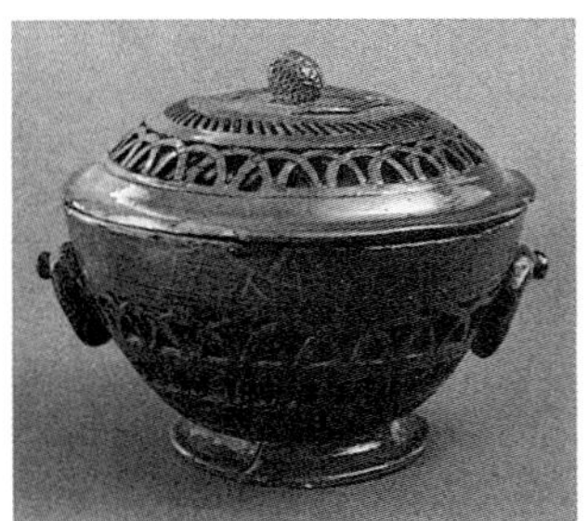

25

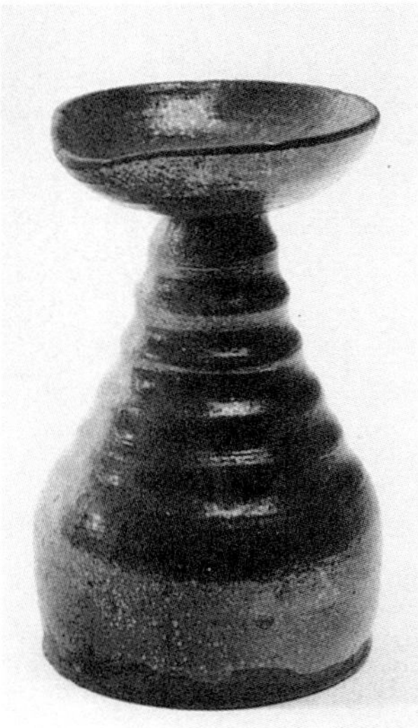

26

22   WHISKY BARREL
1820–50

Wheel-thrown redware. Thick lead glaze colored with copper oxide (green) and speckled with iridescent manganese (brown black) on all surfaces. Cork missing.

Height 19 cm (7½″), diameter 17.8 cm (7″)

Gift of Joseph H. Himes, in memory of his wife Eilleen C. Himes. 54-62-47

23   JELLY MOLD
1830–50

Molded redware. Fish design. Edge daubed with manganese (brown black). Slightly orange lead glaze obverse and reverse.

6 x 29.5 cm (2⅜ x 11⅝″)

Gift of Joseph H. Himes, in memory of his wife Eilleen C. Himes. 54-62-63

24   JELLY MOLD
Bucks County
1840–50

Molded redware. Grape-cluster pattern with central foliage. Thick clear greenish brown lead glaze on obverse.

7.6 x 36.2 cm (3 x 14¼″)

Purchased: Baugh-Barber Fund. 22-24-1

25   COVERED BOWL
1840–60

Wheel-thrown redware. Handles and foot attached. Sprig-molded walnut knop. Outer bowl casing cut in decorative patterns inscribed with compass. Opaque yellowish green lead glaze on all surfaces. Losses and repairs before firing.

20.3 x 27.3 cm (8 x 10¾″)

Gift of Joseph H. Himes, in memory of his wife Eilleen C. Himes. 54-62-11a,b

26   FAT LAMP
Berks County
1841

Incised on bottom: *1841 10*

Wheel-thrown redware. Heavy body. Pan fitted over neck of base. Iron oxide (red) in thick clear lead glaze. Held coiled wick in fat.

Height 16.5 cm (6½″), diameter 10.2 cm (4″)

Purchased: Baugh-Barber Fund. 16-270

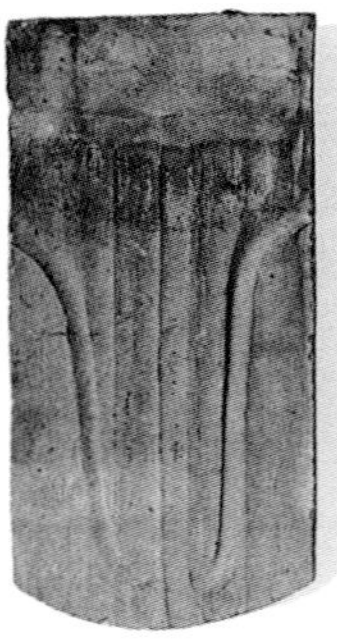

1

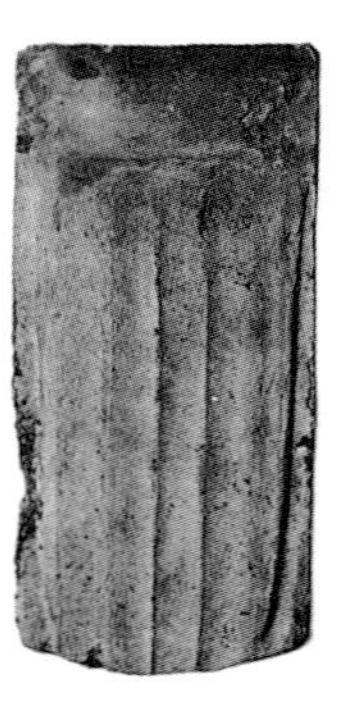
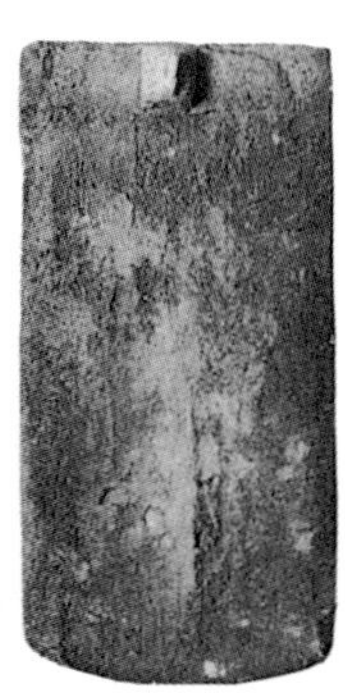

2

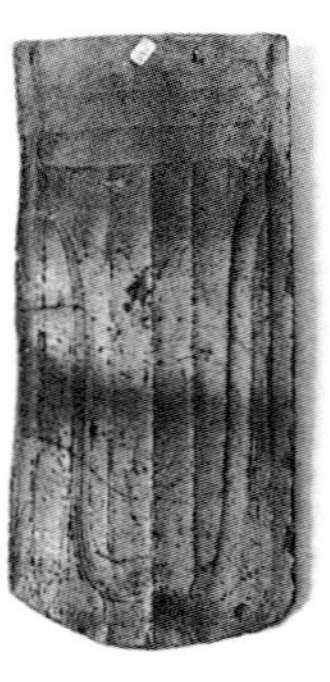
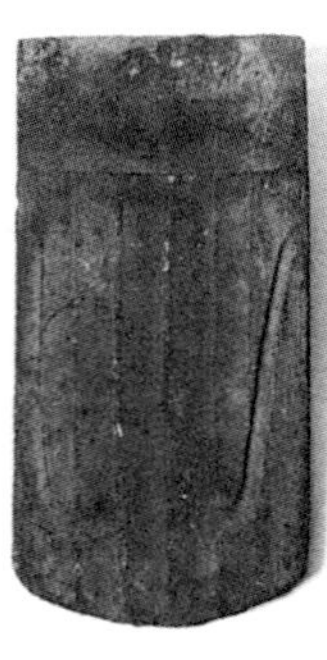

3   **4**

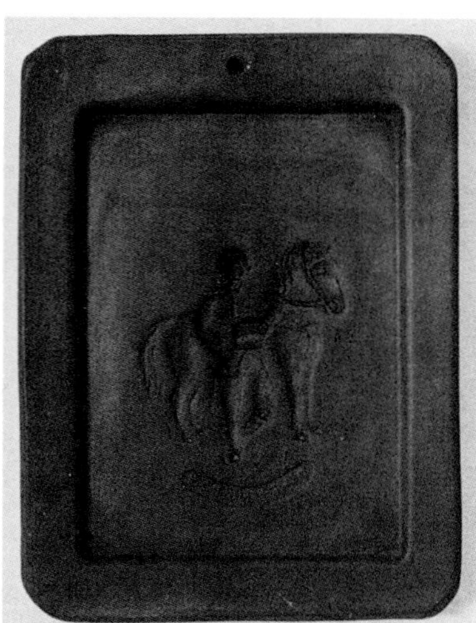

5

1 ROOF TILE
Upper Salford Township, Bucks County
1735–50

Slab redware. Lug applied at top on reverse to hang tile on horizontal roof framing. Obverse fluted with slicking stick; curved lines gouged with fingers. Unglazed red orange body.

32.2 x 17.5 x 1.6 cm (12⅝ x 6⅞ x ⅝")

Gift of Edwin Atlee Barber. 97-687

2 ROOF TILES
1750–1830

Slab redware. Lug applied at top on reverse. Obverse striated with slicking stick in vertical flutes; lines gouged with fingers. Unglazed orange clay body. Common type also made in Ohio.

36.9 x 17.8 x 1.6 cm (14½ x 7 x ⅝")

Gift of Charles Willing. 22-5-1,2

3 ROOF TILE
Bethlehem, Lehigh County
1760–70

Slab redware. Lug applied at top on reverse. Obverse fluted with slicking stick; curved lines gouged with fingers. Random glaze from kiln on body. Common type.

36.8 x 16.8 x 1.6 cm (14½ x 6⅝ x ⅝")

Gift of Edwin Atlee Barber. 97-685

4 ROOF TILE
Bird-in-Hand, Lancaster County
1769–70

Slab redware. Lug applied at top on reverse. Obverse fluted with slicking stick; curved lines gouged with fingers. Unglazed red clay body. Common type.

35.5 x 17.3 x 1.6 cm (14 x 6¾ x ⅝")

Gift of Edwin Atlee Barber. 97-684

5 PLAQUE MOLD
1810–40

Inscribed in reversed lettering:
WASHINGTON

Slab redware. Impression made from iron or clay form. Hanging hole.

21.9 x 16.8 cm (8⅝ x 6⅝")

Purchased: Baugh-Barber Fund. 45-17-1

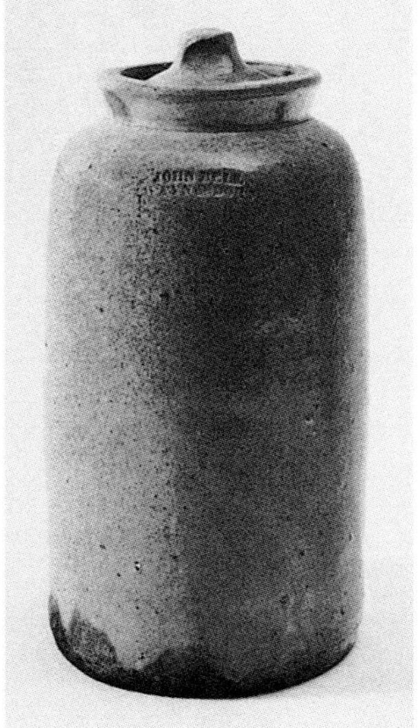

1

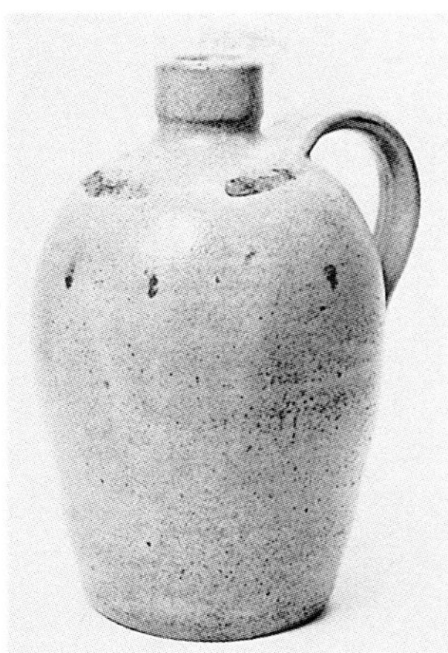

2

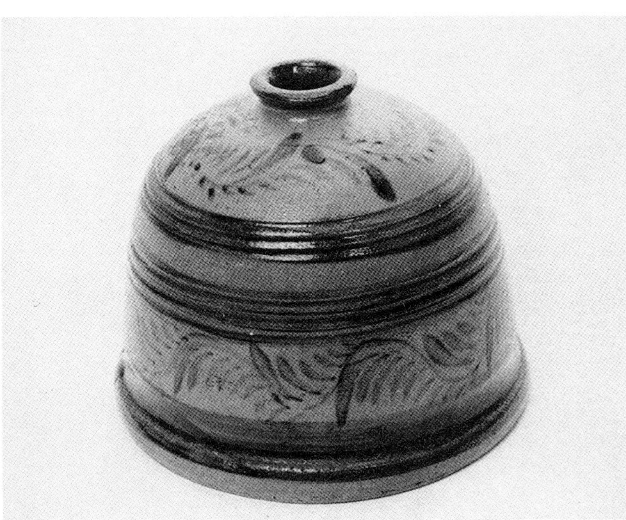

3

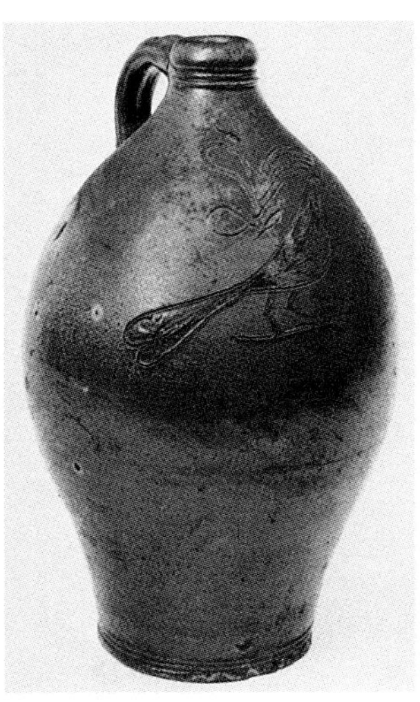

4

1 **JAR**
Waynesboro, Franklin County
1840–50

John Bell

Stamped on shoulder: *JOHN BELL WAYNESBORO*

Wheel-thrown earthenware. Redware lid with pinched knob. Thick opaque grayish green lead glaze on interior and exterior, except bottom.

Height 21.5 cm (8½"), diameter 11.4 cm (4½")

Gift of J. Stogdell Stokes. 28-10-85a,b

---

2 **JUG**
Waynesboro, Franklin County
1840–50

John Bell

Stamped on shoulder: *JOHN BELL WAYNESBORO*

Wheel-thrown stoneware. Applied handle. Blue gray ground with salt glaze on interior and exterior.

Height 23.8 cm (9⅜"), diameter 17.8 cm (7")

Gift of J. Stogdell Stokes. 28-10-87

---

3 **TWINE BOX**
Greensboro, Greene County
1860

A. V. Boughner

Wheel-thrown stoneware. Raised edges at bottom and top and concentric bandings. Cobalt (blue) decoration. Salt glaze.

Height 13.5 cm (5¼"), diameter 17 cm (6¾")

Gift of A. V. Boughner. 03-106

---

4 **JUG**
Philadelphia
1820–60

Attributed to **Henry H. Remmy**

Wheel-thrown buff-colored earthenware. Applied handle. Concentric bandings at base and neck. Incised design of bird on branch colored with cobalt (blue). Thick outlines of cobalt on foliage above bird are not incised. Uneven brownish lead glaze, except on bottom.

Height 39.3 cm (15½"), diameter 24.1 cm (9½")

Gift of J. Stogdell Stokes. 28-83-3

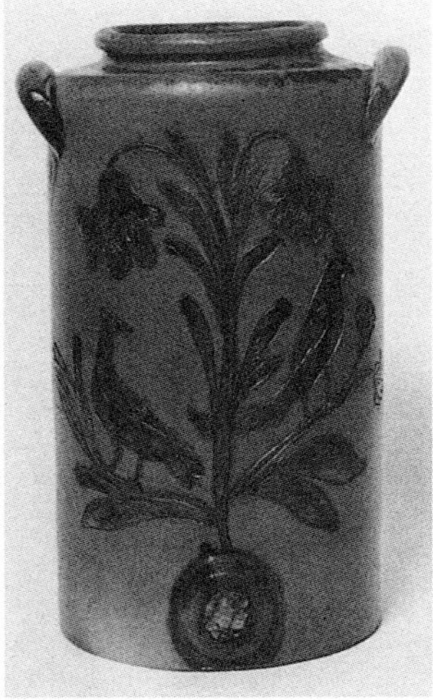

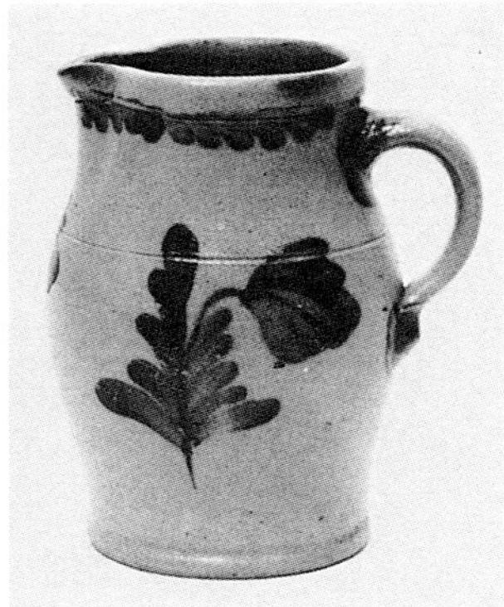

5   **7**

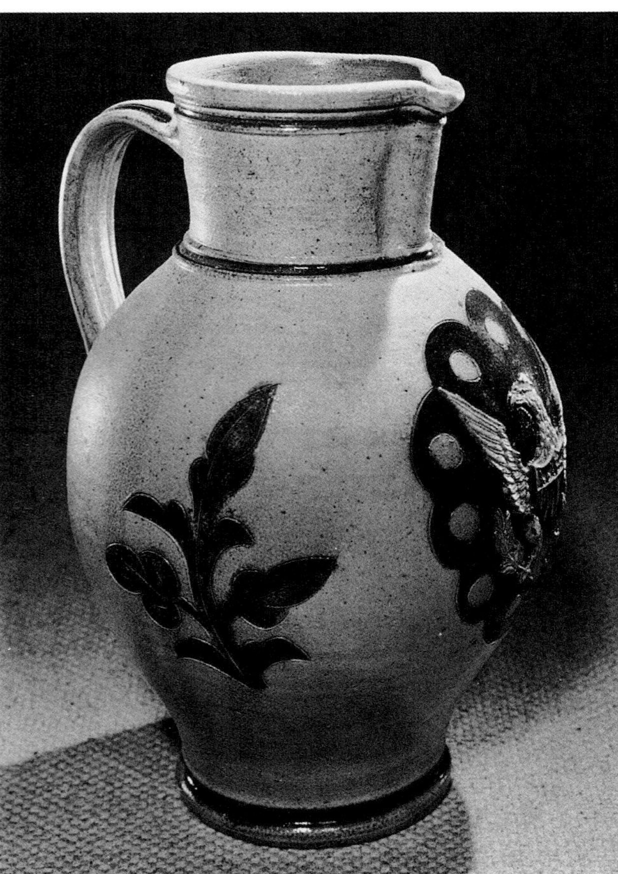

6

5   WATER COOLER
Philadelphia
1830–60

Attributed to **Henry H. Remmy**

Wheel-thrown stoneware. Everted top edge.
Applied handles. Spigot hole. Deeply incised
decoration of two birds perched on branching
lily stalk colored with cobalt (blue). Wreath
of foliage and flowers around shoulder and
between handles. Salt glaze on gray body
inside and out. Similar pieces produced in
Ohio.

Height 41.9 cm (16½″), diameter 29.2 cm (11½″)

Titus C. Geesey Collection. 54-85-27

---

6   PITCHER
Philadelphia
1869–80

Richard C. Remmy

Wheel-thrown stoneware. Applied handle.
Bandings and incised outlines of patterns with
molded eagle motif applied to surface. Cobalt
(blue) decoration on gray ground. Salt glaze.

29.5 x 20.3 cm (11½ x 8″)

Purchased: Special Museum Fund. 15-302

---

7   PITCHER
Philadelphia
1869–80

Attributed to **Richard C. Remmy**

Wheel-thrown stoneware. Applied handle.
Incised banding with cobalt (blue) decoration
on gray ground. Salt glaze with brown glaze
inside.

19 x 15.9 cm (7½ x 6¼″)

Gift of Mrs. Thomas E. Ellis. 74-93-3

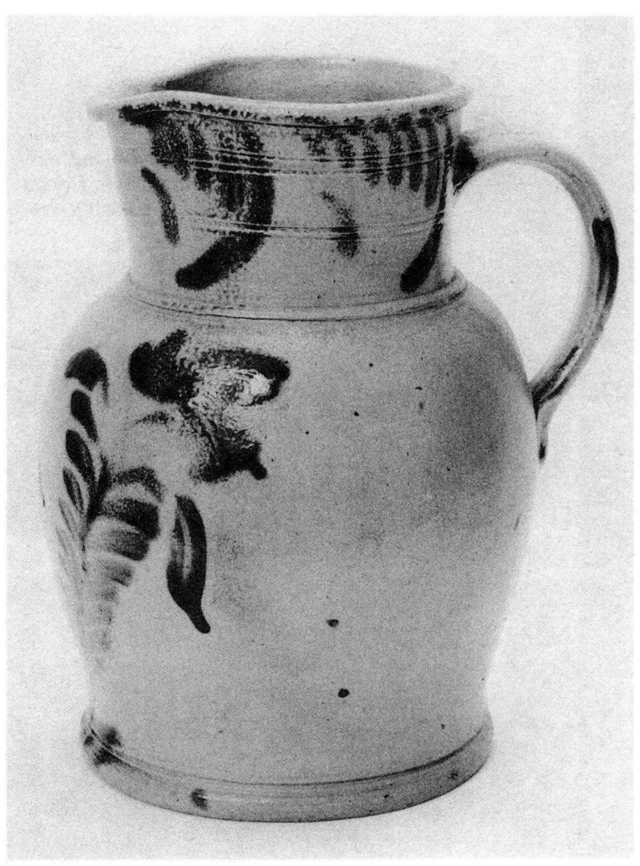

8

8 PITCHER
Philadelphia
1870–80

Attributed to **Richard C. Remmy**

Wheel-thrown stoneware. Applied handle.
Incised bandings and cobalt (blue) decoration
on gray ground. Salt glaze.

27.6 x 23.5 cm (10⅞ x 9¼")

Gift of Mrs. Thomas E. Ellis. 74-93-2

9 MONEY BANK
Philadelphia
1880–84

Attributed to **Richard C. Remmy**

Inscribed: *Anna Jamison*

Wheel-thrown and modeled stoneware. Money
slot. Two-ply twisted handles applied.
Modeled bird finial attached to raised knop.
Cobalt (blue) decoration on gray body. Salt
glaze.

21.2 x 12.7 cm (8⅜ x 5")

Gift of John T. Morris. 92-131

10 MONEY BANK
Philadelphia
1880–84

Attributed to **Richard C. Remmy**

Inscribed: *Clara*

Wheel-thrown and modeled stoneware. Money
slot. Two-ply twisted handles applied.
Modeled bird finial attached to raised knop.
Cobalt (blue) decoration on gray ground. Salt
glaze. Companion to no. 9.

21.6 x 13 cm (8½ x 5⅛")

Gift of Mrs. Thomas E. Ellis. 74-93-1

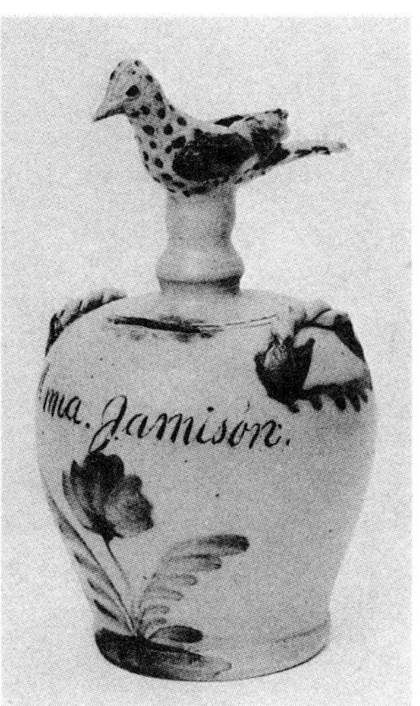

9

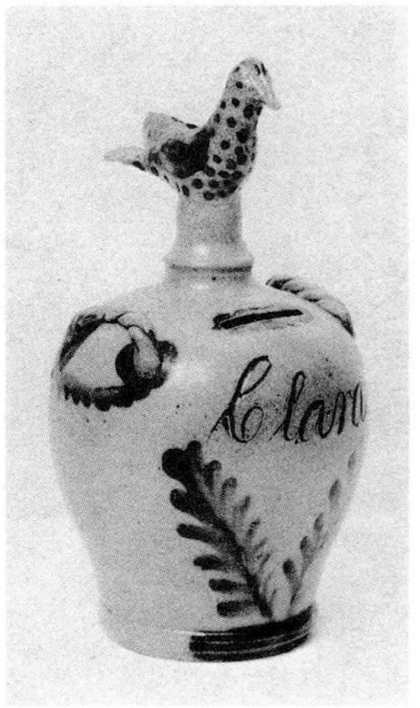

10

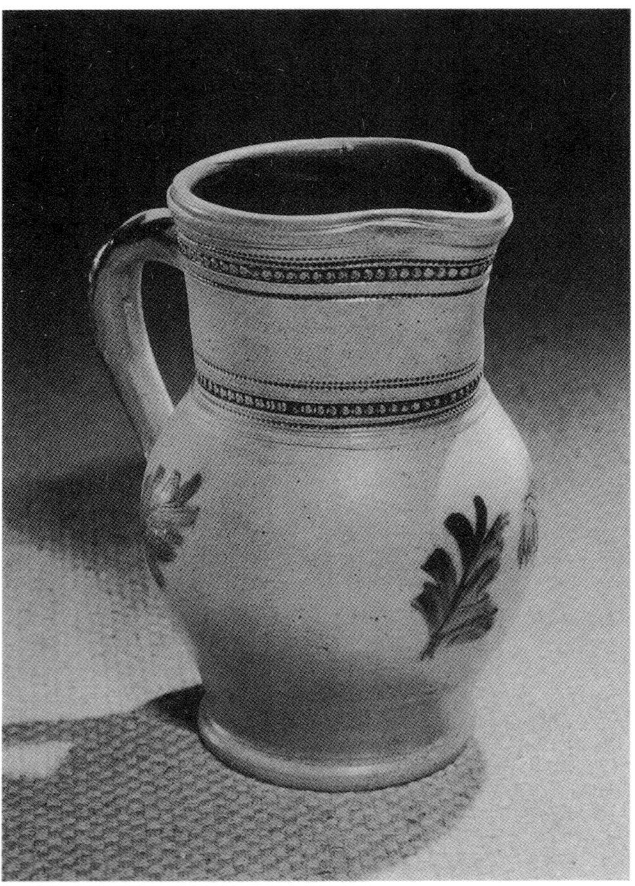

11

11 PITCHER
Philadelphia
1891

Attributed to **Richard C. Remmy**

Incised on bottom: *RCR   Phila   1891*

Wheel-thrown stoneware. Applied handle.
Rouletting and raised bead bandings. Cobalt
(blue) decoration on gray ground. Salt glaze
with brown glaze inside.

15.9 x 13.3 cm (6¼ x 5¼″)

Gift of John T. Morris. 92-133

12 MIXING BOWL
Marion Township, Berks County
1869–80

Attributed to **Daniel P. Shenfelder**

Wheel-thrown earthenware. Everted edge.
Flower design in thin slip colored with cobalt
(blue). Clear brownish lead glaze on interior
and exterior, except bottom.

Height 18.1 cm (7⅛″), diameter 20.6 cm (8⅛″)

Gift of J. Stogdell Stokes. 28-10-77

13 PITCHER
1800–1830

Wheel-thrown stoneware. Applied handle.
Decorated with incised banding at shoulder
and top edge. Brownish gray body with
salt glaze.

37.5 x 27.3 cm (14¾ x 10¾″)

Gift of Mr. and Mrs. J. Stogdell Stokes. 33-70-3

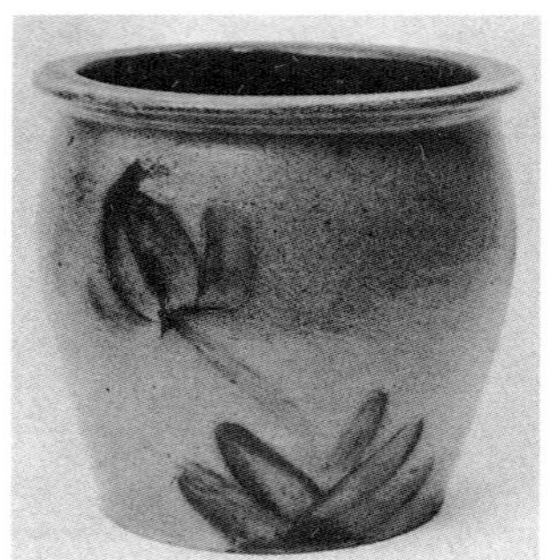

12

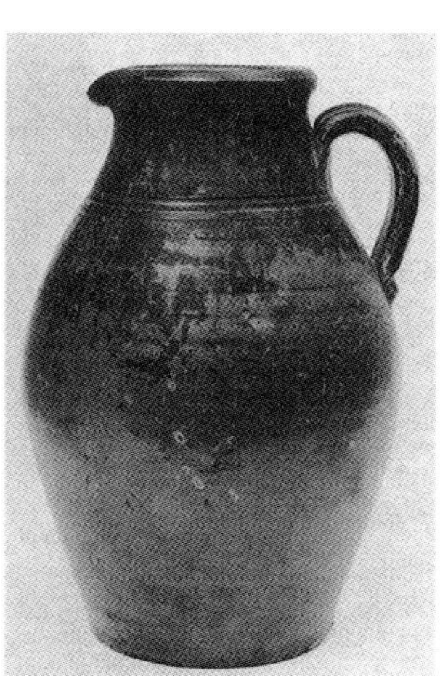

13

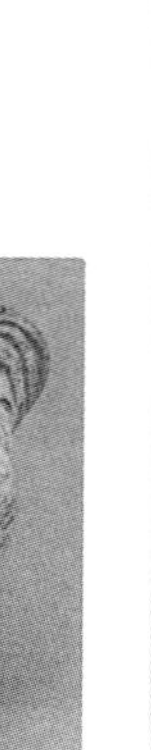

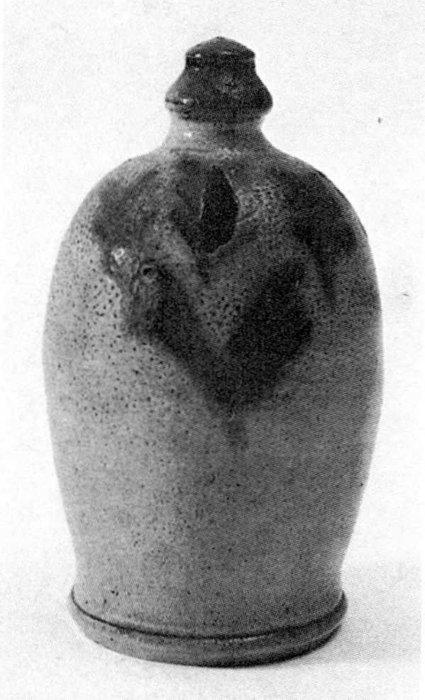

14   **16**

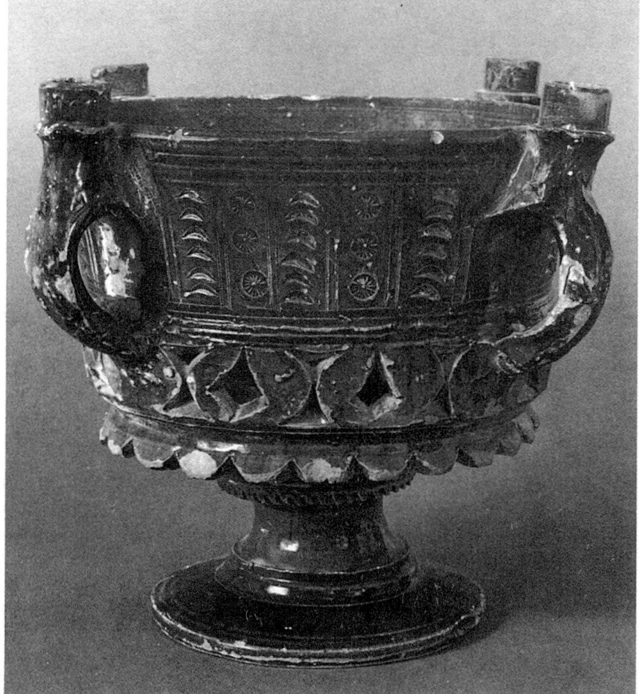

15

14 **MONEY BANK**
1800–1850

Modeled and wheel-thrown buff-colored clay. Neck, head, and tail attached. Iron oxide (red) in slip banding at base with touches on neck, tail, and wing feathers. Clear yellowish lead glaze.

9.5 x 13.3 cm (3¾ x 5¼″)

Titus C. Geesey Collection. 69-284-29

---

15 **COMPOTE BOWL WITH CANDLE SOCKETS**
1820–40

Wheel-thrown and modeled buff-colored clay. Footed bowl within pierced casing joined at line of incised banding. Modeled handles have candle sockets at top. Surfaces decorated with cut edges and stamped daisies alternating with new moon shapes. Thick opaque copper oxide (green) in glaze on all surfaces except rim of foot.

23.5 x 31.1 cm (9¼ x 12¼″)

Titus C. Geesey Collection. 69-284-32

---

16 **MONEY BANK**
1830–60

Wheel-thrown stoneware. Money slot. Cobalt (blue) decoration on gray body. Salt glaze.

Height 17.7 cm (7″), diameter 10.5 cm (4⅛″)

Gift of Mrs. John F. Hudson. 59-15-1

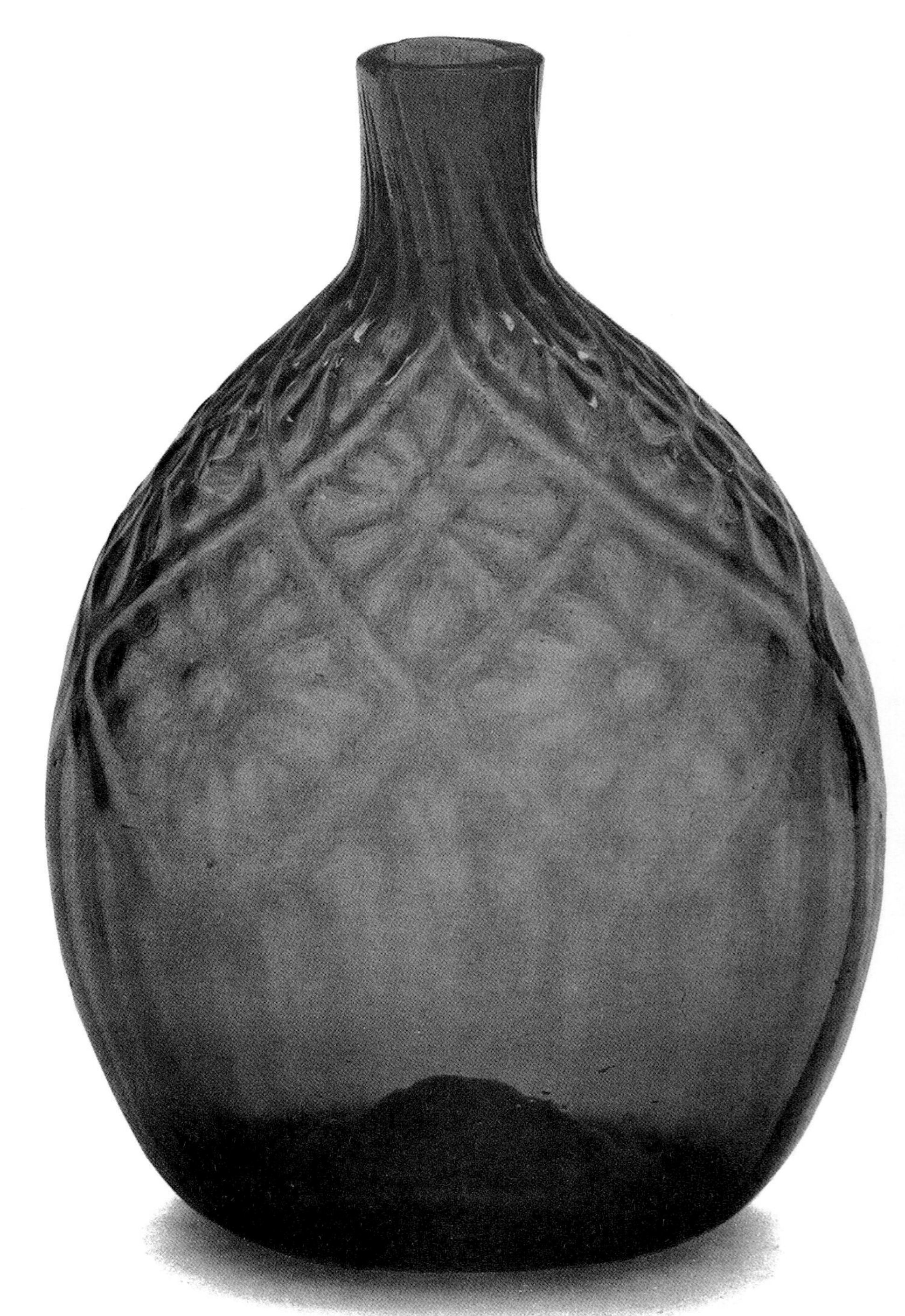

Glass

INTRODUCTION

The entrepreneur Henry William Stiegel, already in the iron business, responded to a market demand created in America by the Nonimportation Agreement by extending his enterprise to glass manufacture, which he investigated in England. Financed by Charles and Alexander Stedman of Philadelphia, Stiegel began manufacturing glass at his factory at Manheim, Lancaster County, in October 1765, and continued until February 1774. His largely European labor source, including skilled glassblowers, arrived, many in Stedman's ships. Stiegel's advertisements for common and flint glass, appearing in Lancaster and Philadelphia newspapers, listed his production of the same variety of forms that had formerly been supplied by English merchants for the American market. Stiegel's European workmen would have been familiar with Continental formulas for glass, similar to common, or non-lead glass. The ingredients for common glass were readily available to Stiegel: white sand from New Jersey, lime or wood ashes, and clinkers from iron forges. Data gathered from spectrographic analyses and fluorescence tests on pieces generally thought to be from the Stiegel factory, the purple bottles in the daisy within diamond pattern, for example, indicate that some Stiegel glass was made without lead, and other pieces with lead, such as the blue sugar bowls and cream jugs with their typically small bases and tightly twisted knops. The pieces included here represent a fraction of the Museum's collection formerly attributed to Stiegel and reflect the current conservative approach to attribution.

BOTTLE
1765–74
See page 240, no. 10

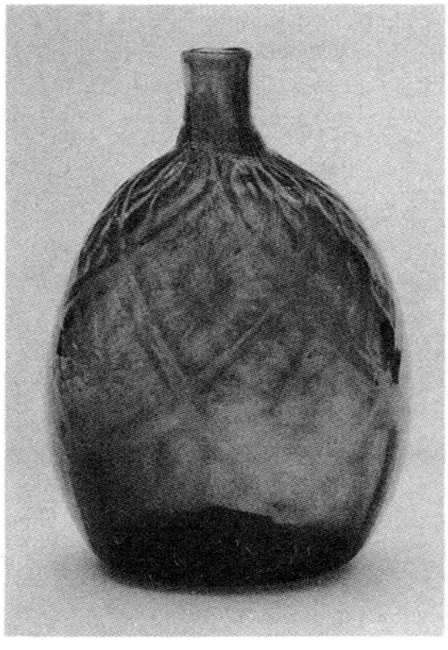

1

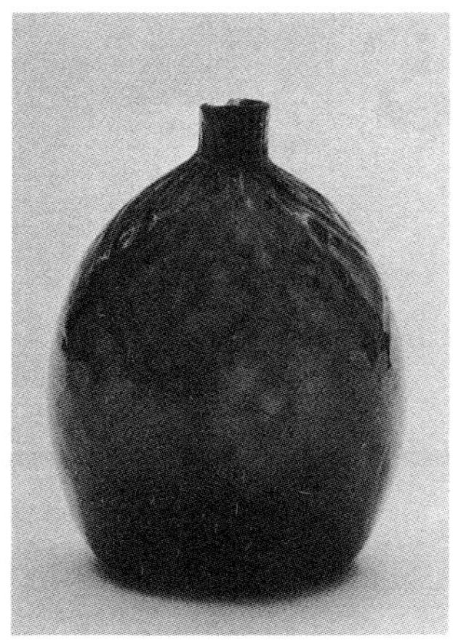

2

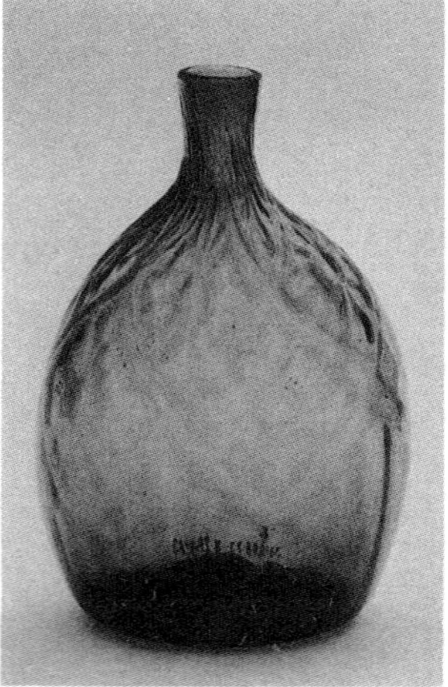

3

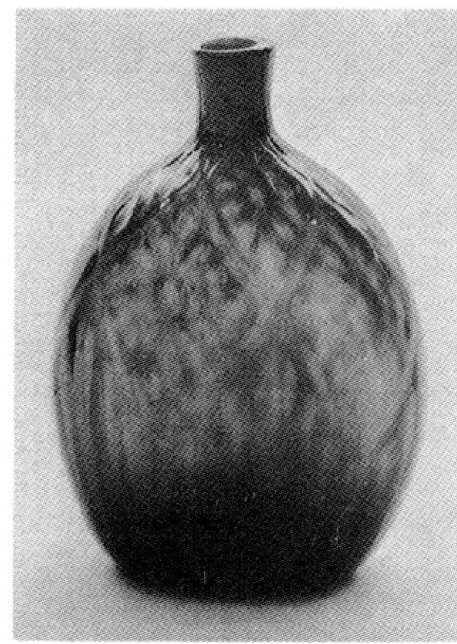

4

1 BOTTLE
Manheim, Lancaster County
1765–74

Attributed to **Henry William Stiegel Glasshouse**

Medium purple non-lead glass. Sides flattened. Pattern-molded and expanded. Three lateral rows of five pattern units (twelve-petal daisy within diamond) over thirty flutes. Flutes extend to pontil mark.

12.7 x 9.2 x 6 cm (5 x 3⅝ x 2¼")

Gift of John Story Jenks. 10-333

2 BOTTLE
Manheim, Lancaster County
1765–74

Attributed to **Henry William Stiegel Glasshouse**

Purple non-lead glass. Sides flattened. Pattern-molded and expanded. Three lateral rows of five pattern units (twelve-petal daisy within diamond) over flutes. Fluting indistinct. Pontil mark. Neck repaired.

11.6 x 9.4 x 7.2 cm (4½ x 3⅝ x 2¾")

Purchased. 23-23-197

3 BOTTLE
Manheim, Lancaster County
1765–74

Attributed to **Henry William Stiegel Glasshouse**

Light purple non-lead glass. Sides flattened. Pattern-molded and expanded. Three lateral rows of five pattern units (twelve-petal daisy within diamond) over thirty flutes. Flutes extend to pontil mark.

13.5 x 9.6 x 7 cm (5¼ x 3¾ x 2¾")

The George H. Lorimer Collection. 38-23-263

4 BOTTLE
Manheim, Lancaster County
1765–74

Attributed to **Henry William Stiegel Glasshouse**

Purple non-lead glass. Sides flattened. Pattern-molded and expanded. Two lateral rows of five pattern units (twelve-petal daisy within diamond) over thirty flutes. Flutes extend to pontil mark.

12.9 x 9.6 x 6.9 cm (5 x 3¾ x 2⅝")

The George H. Lorimer Collection. 53-29-59

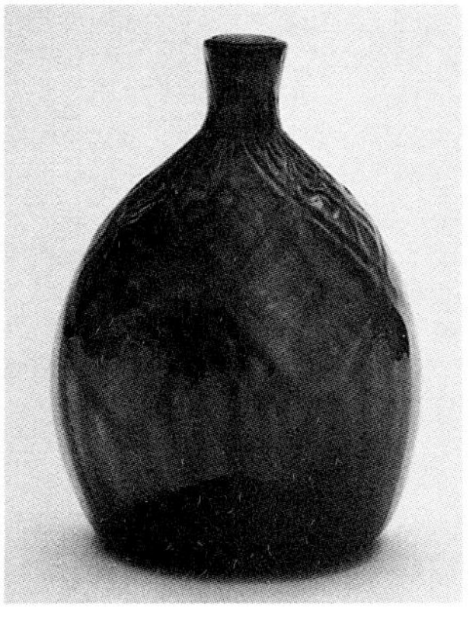

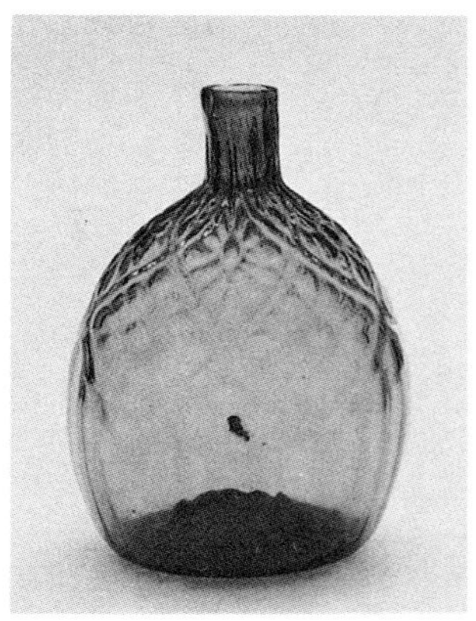

5

6

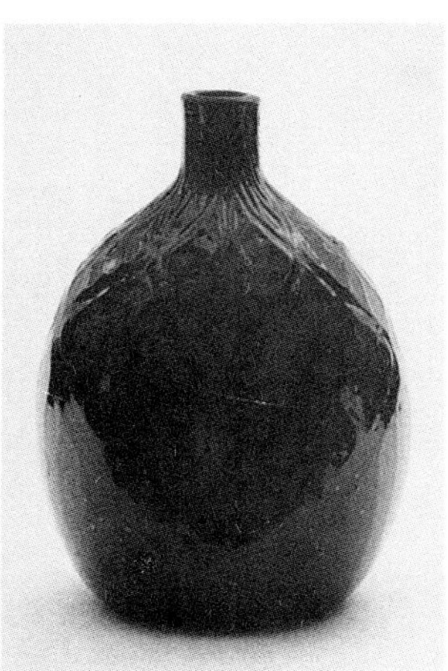

7

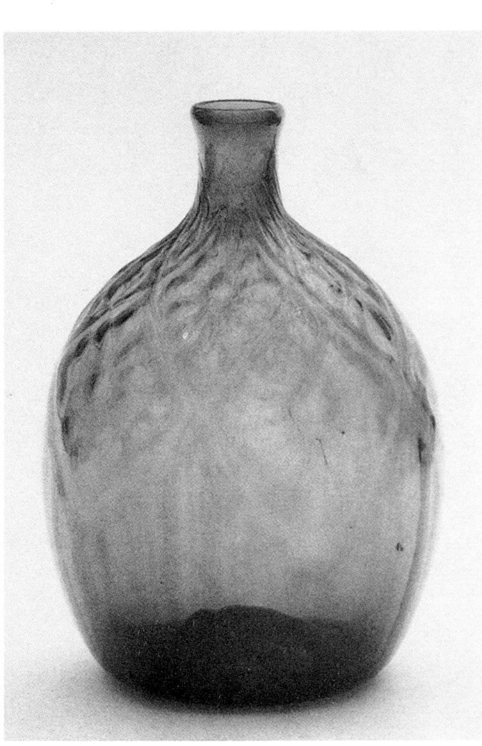

8

5 BOTTLE
Manheim, Lancaster County
1765–74

Attributed to **Henry William Stiegel
Glasshouse**

Purple non-lead glass. Sides flattened.
Pattern-molded and expanded. Three lateral
rows of five pattern units (twelve-petal daisy
within diamond) over thirty flutes. Flutes
extend to pontil mark.

12.1 x 9.2 x 6.9 cm (4¾ x 3⅝ x 2⅝")

The George H. Lorimer Collection. 53-29-60

---

6 BOTTLE
Manheim, Lancaster County
1765–74

Attributed to **Henry William Stiegel
Glasshouse**

Light purple non-lead glass. Sides flattened.
Pattern-molded and expanded. Three lateral
rows of five pattern units (twelve-petal daisy
within diamond) over thirty flutes. Flutes
extend to pontil mark.

11.5 x 8.8 x 7.3 cm (4½ x 3⅜ x 2⅞")

The George H. Lorimer Collection. 53-29-63

---

7 BOTTLE
Manheim, Lancaster County
1765–74

Attributed to **Henry William Stiegel
Glasshouse**

Dark purple non-lead glass. Sides flattened.
Pattern-molded and expanded. Three lateral
rows of five pattern units (twelve-petal daisy
within diamond) over thirty flutes. Flutes
extend to pontil mark.

12.3 x 9.4 x 7 cm (4¾ x 3⅝ x 2¾")

The George H. Lorimer Collection. 53-29-65

---

8 BOTTLE
Manheim, Lancaster County
1765–74

Attributed to **Henry William Stiegel
Glasshouse**

Light purple non-lead glass. Sides flattened.
Pattern-molded and expanded. Three lateral
rows of five pattern units (twelve-petal daisy
within diamond) over thirty flutes. Flutes
extend to pontil mark.

12.9 x 9.4 x 7.3 cm (5 x 3⅝ x 2⅞")

The George H. Lorimer Collection. 53-29-66

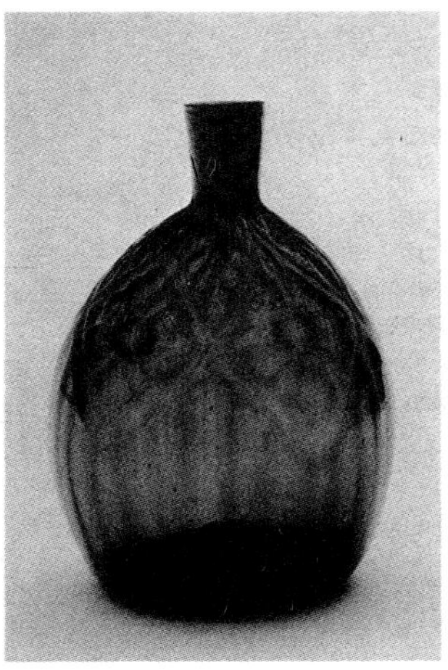

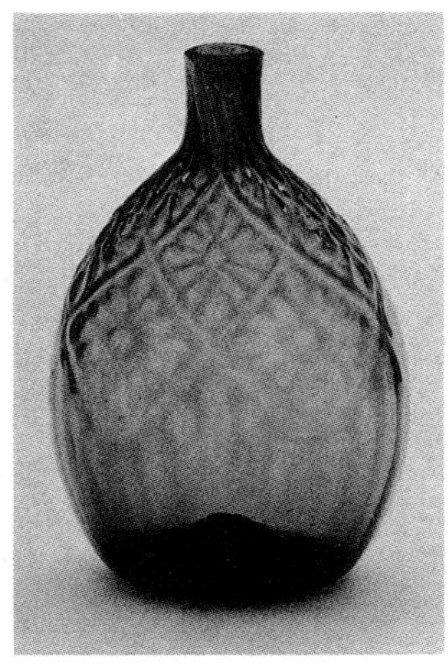

9　　10

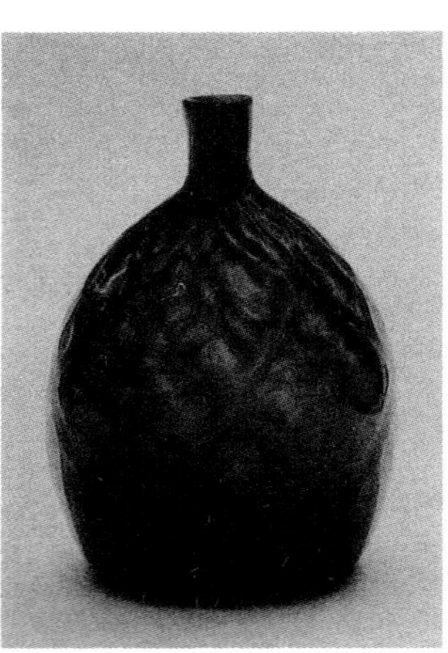

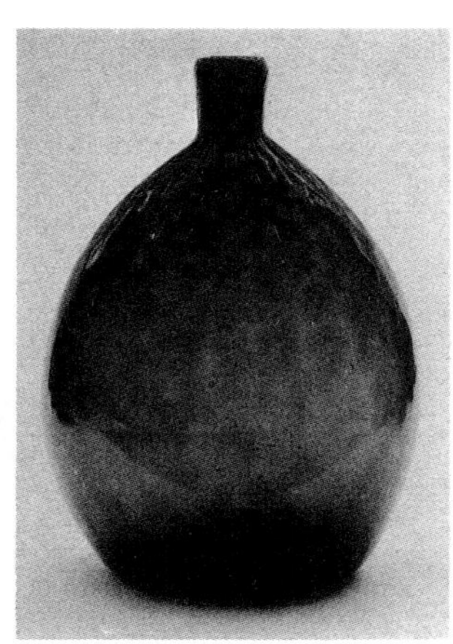

11　　12

9　BOTTLE
Manheim, Lancaster County
1765–74

Attributed to **Henry William Stiegel
Glasshouse**

Purple non-lead glass. Sides flattened.
Pattern-molded and expanded. Two lateral
rows of five pattern units (twelve-petal daisy
within diamond) over thirty flutes. Flutes
extend to pontil mark.

11.8 x 8.8 x 7.2 cm (4⅝ x 3⅜ x 2¾″)

The George H. Lorimer Collection. 53-29-90

10　BOTTLE
Manheim, Lancaster County
1765–74

Attributed to **Henry William Stiegel
Glasshouse**

Light purple non-lead glass. Sides flattened.
Pattern-molded and expanded. Three lateral
rows of five pattern units (twelve-petal daisy
within diamond) over thirty flutes. Flutes
extend to pontil mark.

13 x 9.2 x 6.4 cm (5⅛ x 3⅝ x 2½″)

The George H. Lorimer Collection. 53-29-91

11　BOTTLE
Manheim, Lancaster County
1765–74

Attributed to **Henry William Stiegel
Glasshouse**

Purple non-lead glass. Sides flattened.
Pattern-molded and expanded. Three lateral
rows of five pattern units (twelve-petal daisy
within diamond) over thirty flutes. Flutes
extend to pontil mark.

12.4 x 9.6 x 7.3 cm (4⅞ x 3¾ x 2⅞″)

The George H. Lorimer Collection. 53-29-92

12　BOTTLE
Manheim, Lancaster County
1765–74

Attributed to **Henry William Stiegel
Glasshouse**

Light purple non-lead glass. Sides flattened.
Pattern-molded and expanded. Three lateral
rows of nine pattern units (hexagonal-shaped
eight-petal daisy) over flutes. Fluting
indistinct; extends to pontil mark.

14.1 x 10.6 x 7.8 cm (5½ x 4⅛ x 3⅛″)

The George H. Lorimer Collection. 38-23-266

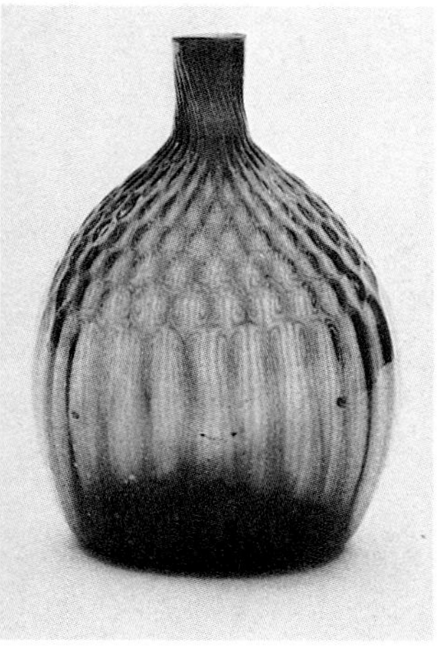
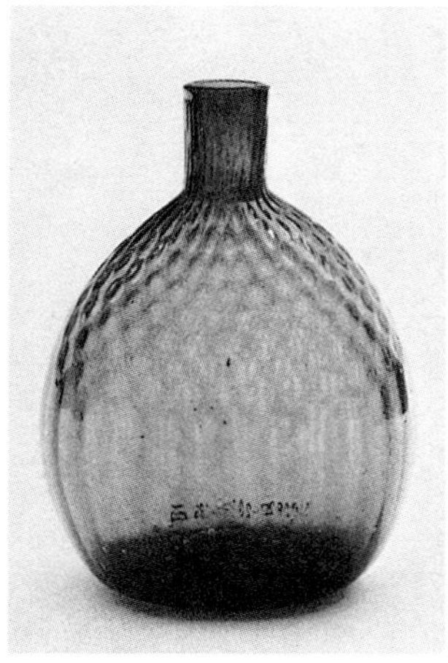

13

14

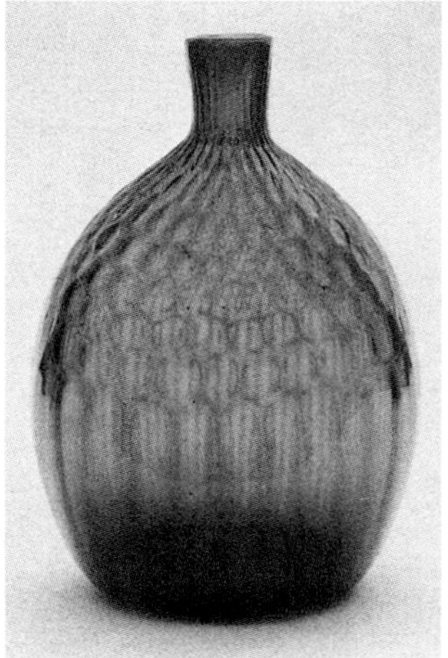

16

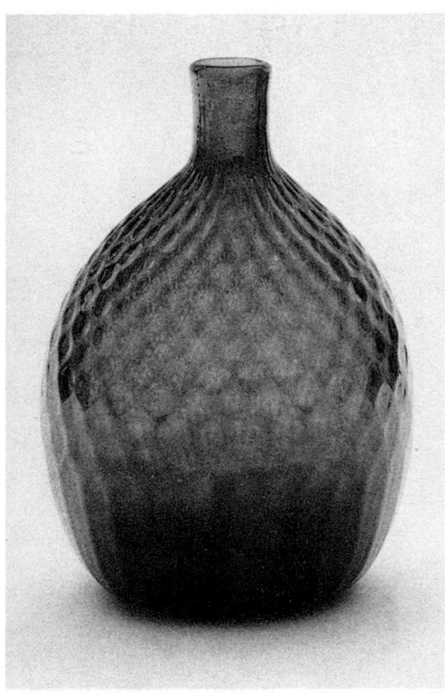

15

---

13 BOTTLE
Manheim, Lancaster County
1765–74

Attributed to **Henry William Stiegel Glasshouse**

Light purple non-lead glass. Sides flattened. Pattern-molded and expanded. Lateral rows of twenty-eight ogivals over twenty-eight flutes. Flutes extend under base. Pontil mark.

12.1 x 9.1 x 6.9 cm (4¾ x 3½ x 2⅝″)

The George H. Lorimer Collection. 38-23-264

---

14 BOTTLE
Manheim, Lancaster County
1765–74

Attributed to **Henry William Stiegel Glasshouse**

Light purple non-lead glass. Sides flattened. Pattern-molded and expanded. Lateral rows of twenty-eight ogivals over twenty-eight flutes. Flutes extend under base. Pontil mark.

11.8 x 9.1 x 6.9 cm (4⅝ x 3½ x 2⅝″)

The George H. Lorimer Collection. 38-23-265

---

15 BOTTLE
Manheim, Lancaster County
1765–74

Attributed to **Henry William Stiegel Glasshouse**

Purple non-lead glass. Sides flattened. Pattern-molded and expanded. Lateral rows of twenty-eight ogivals over twenty-eight flutes. Flutes extend to pontil mark.

12.3 x 8.9 x 7.2 cm (4¾ x 3½ x 2¾″)

The George H. Lorimer Collection. 53-29-61

---

16 BOTTLE
Manheim, Lancaster County
1765–74

Attributed to **Henry William Stiegel Glasshouse**

Purple non-lead glass. Sides flattened. Pattern-molded and expanded. Lateral rows of twenty-eight ogivals over twenty-eight flutes. Flutes extend under base. Pontil mark.

13.3 x 9.8 x 6.9 cm (5¼ x 3¾ x 2⅝″)

The George H. Lorimer Collection. 53-29-62

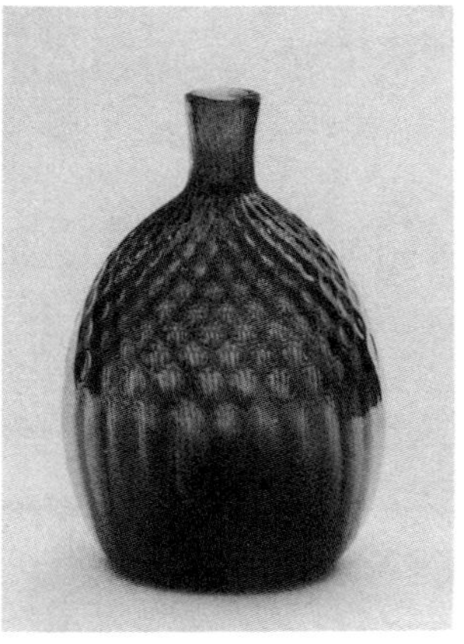

17

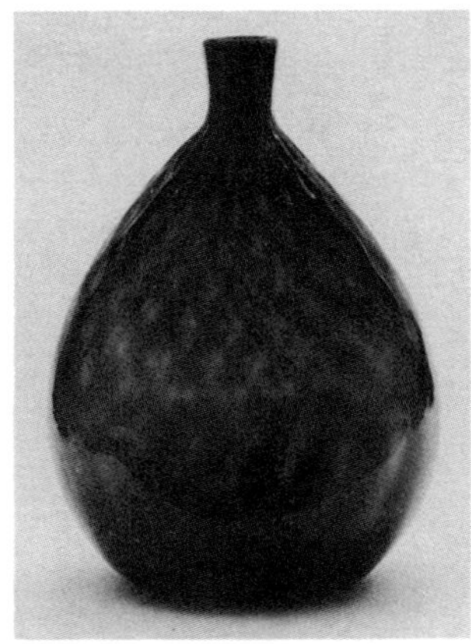

18

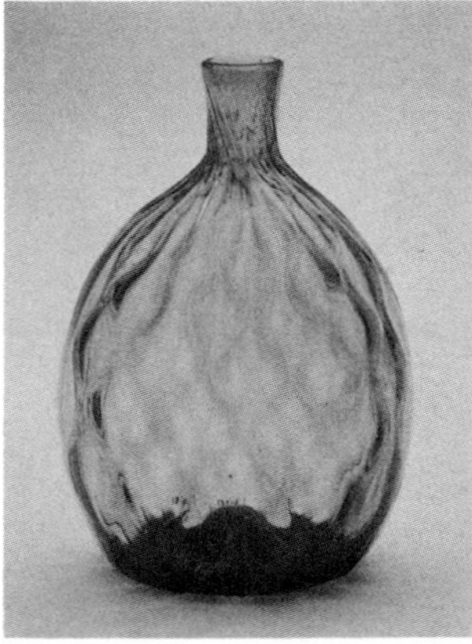

19

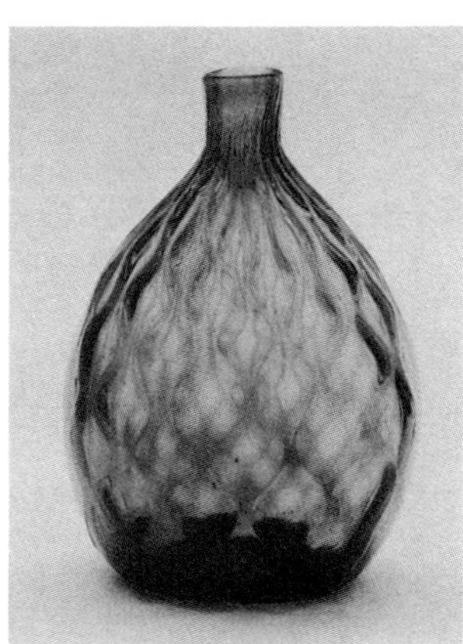

20

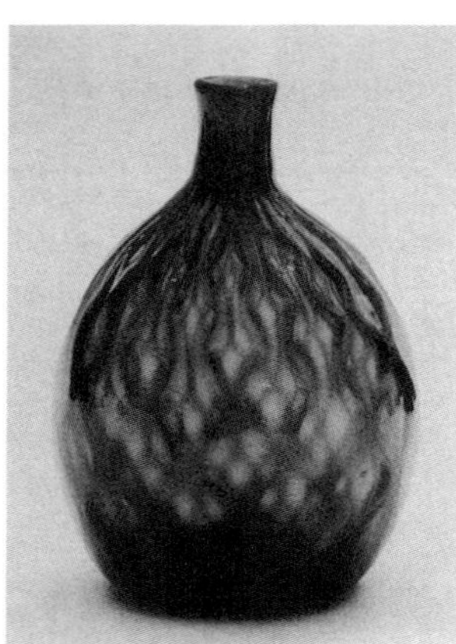

21

17 BOTTLE
Manheim, Lancaster County
1765–74

Attributed to **Henry William Stiegel Glasshouse**

Purple non-lead glass. Sides flattened. Pattern-molded and expanded. Lateral rows of twenty-eight ogivals over twenty-eight flutes. Flutes extend under base. Pontil mark.

12.6 x 9.1 x 7.3 cm (4⅞ x 3½ x 2⅞")

The George H. Lorimer Collection. 53-29-89

18 BOTTLE
Manheim, Lancaster County
1765–74

Probably from **Henry William Stiegel Glasshouse**

Purple non-lead glass. Sides flattened. Pattern-molded and expanded. Lateral rows of twenty ogivals over twenty flutes. Flutes extend to pontil mark.

14.4 x 10.8 x 6.7 cm (5⅝ x 4¼ x 2⅝")

The George H. Lorimer Collection. 53-29-64

19 BOTTLE
Manheim, Lancaster County
1765–74

Attributed to **Henry William Stiegel Glasshouse**

Light purple non-lead glass. Sides flattened. Patterned in six-flute mold, nipped into serpentine diamonds, and expanded. Six-petal device around pontil mark.

13 x 9.4 x 7 cm (5⅛ x 3⅝ x 2¾")

The George H. Lorimer Collection. 38-23-260

20 BOTTLE
Manheim, Lancaster County
1765–74

Attributed to **Henry William Stiegel Glasshouse**

Light purple non-lead glass. Sides flattened. Patterned in six-flute mold, nipped into serpentine diamonds, and expanded. Six-petal device around pontil mark.

13.8 x 10.2 x 7.3 cm (5⅜ x 4 x 2⅞")

The George H. Lorimer Collection. 38-23-261

21 BOTTLE
Manheim, Lancaster County
1765–74

Attributed to **Henry William Stiegel Glasshouse**

Purple non-lead glass. *See* no. 20.

13.3 x 10.2 x 7.5 cm (5¼ x 4 x 2⅞")

The George H. Lorimer Collection. 38-23-262

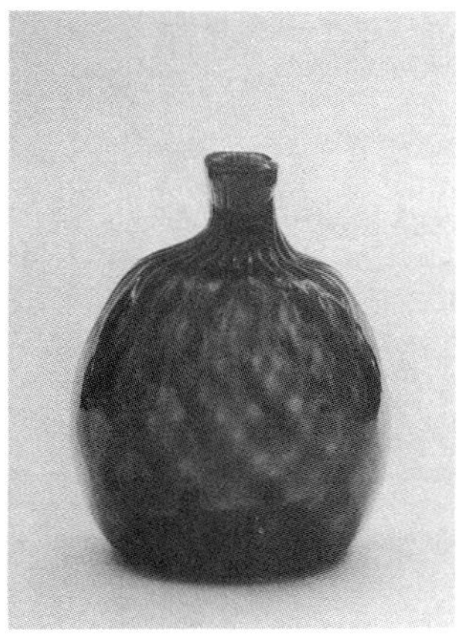
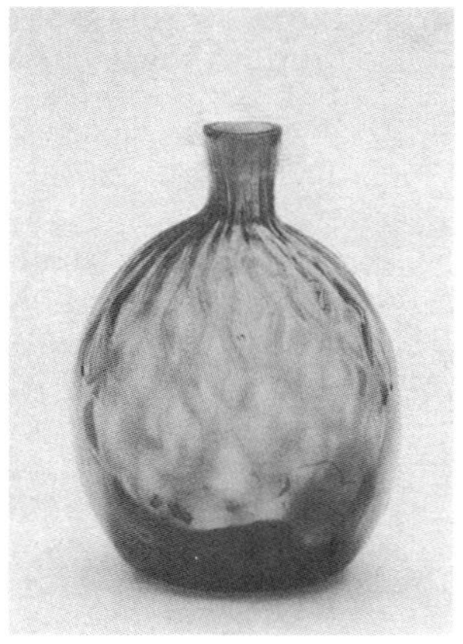

22   **23**

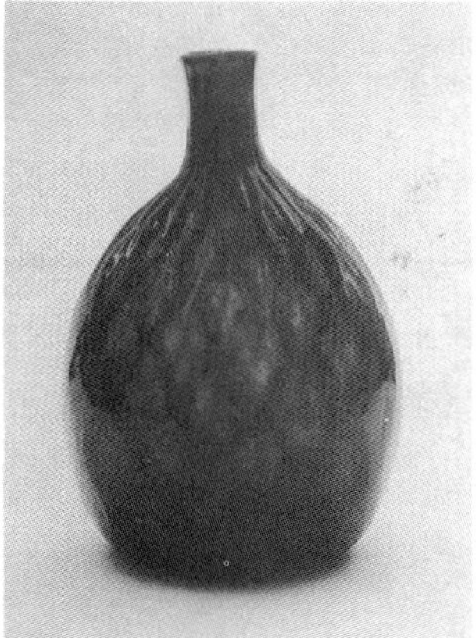

24

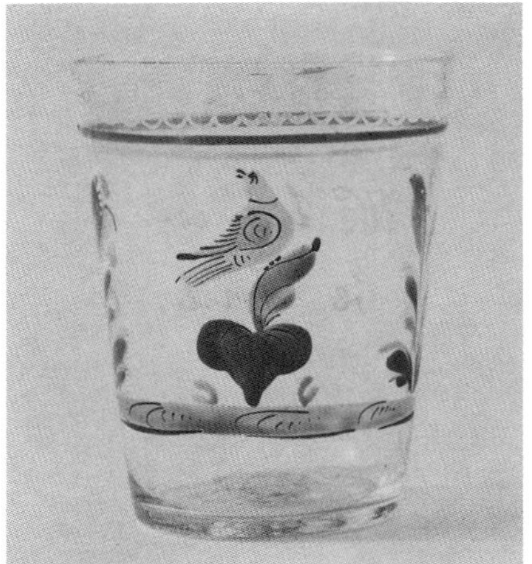

25

22 BOTTLE
Manheim, Lancaster County
1765–74

Attributed to **Henry William Stiegel Glasshouse**

Purple non-lead glass. Sides flattened. Patterned in six-flute mold, nipped into serpentine diamonds, and expanded. Smooth base to pontil mark.

11 x 9.2 x 7 cm (4¼ x 3⅝ x 2¾")

The George H. Lorimer Collection. 53-29-67

---

23 BOTTLE
Manheim, Lancaster County
1765–74

Attributed to **Henry William Stiegel Glasshouse**

Light purple non-lead glass. Sides flattened. Patterned in six-flute mold, nipped into serpentine diamonds, and expanded. Smooth base to pontil mark.

12.1 x 9.4 x 6.5 cm (4¾ x 3⅝ x 2½")

The George H. Lorimer Collection. 53-29-93

---

24 BOTTLE
Manheim, Lancaster County
1765–74

Attributed to **Henry William Stiegel Glasshouse**

Dark purple non-lead glass. Sides flattened. Patterned in six-flute mold, nipped into serpentine diamonds, and expanded. Base impressed with six-petal device around pontil mark.

13.3 x 9.4 x 7.3 cm (5¼ x 3⅝ x 2⅞")

The George H. Lorimer Collection. 53-29-94

---

25 TUMBLER
Manheim, Lancaster County
1772–74

Attributed to **Henry William Stiegel Glasshouse**

Inscribed on reverse: *We two will   be true*

Colorless non-lead glass. Free-blown. Painted decoration of white wavy band above red and yellow bands and bird on heart flanked by floral sprays in red, yellow, blue, green, and white with brown accents.

Height 8.9 cm (3½"), diameter 7.5 cm (2⅞")

Purchased. 23-23-188

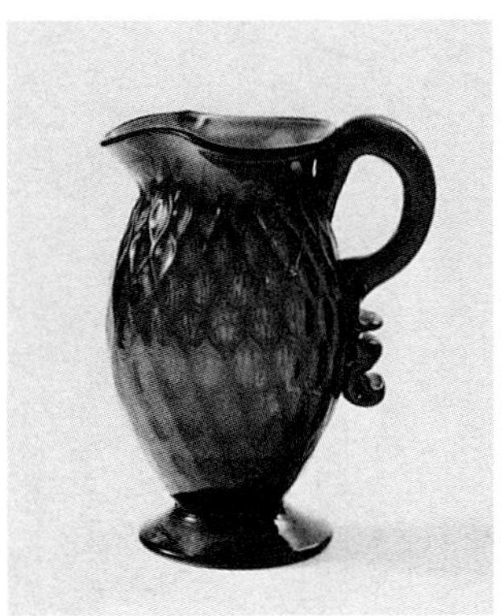

1

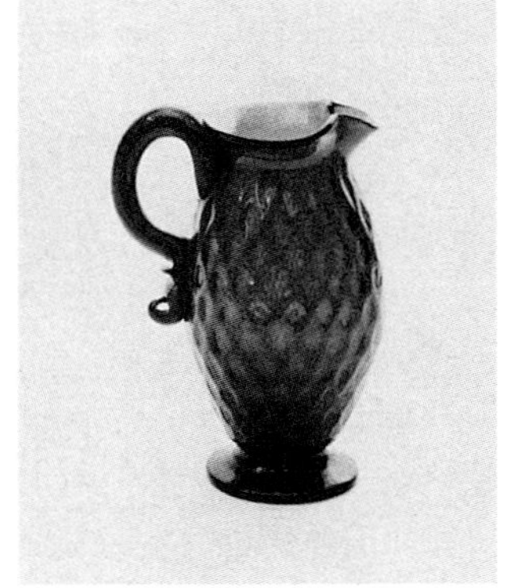

2

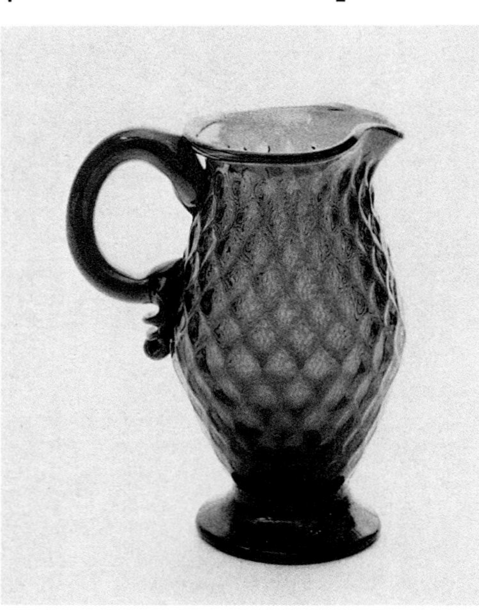

4

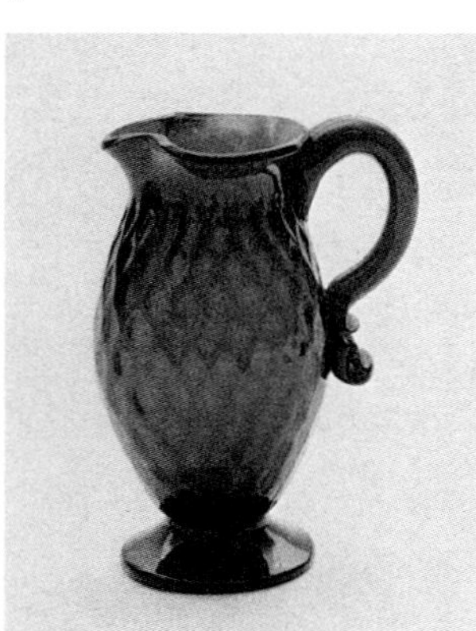

3

1 CREAM JUG
Manheim, Lancaster County
1765–74

Possibly from **Henry William Stiegel Glasshouse**

Blue lead glass. Patterned in fluted mold, nipped into twenty-diamond pattern, and expanded. Applied foot and handle.

Height 9.9 cm (3⅞″), diameter 5.7 cm (2¼″)

R. Wistar Harvey Bequest. 40-16-428

2 CREAM JUG
Manheim, Lancaster County
1765–74

Possibly from **Henry William Stiegel Glasshouse**

Blue lead glass. Patterned in fluted mold, nipped into twenty-diamond pattern, and expanded. Applied foot and handle.

Height 10.2 cm (4″), diameter 6 cm (2⅜″)

The George H. Lorimer Collection. 53-29-70

3 CREAM JUG
Manheim, Lancaster County
1765–74

Possibly from **Henry William Stiegel Glasshouse**

Blue lead glass. Patterned in fluted mold, nipped into twenty-diamond pattern, and expanded. Applied foot and handle.

Height 10.2 cm (4″), diameter 5.7 cm (2¼″)

The George H. Lorimer Collection. 53-29-69

4 CREAM JUG
Manheim, Lancaster County
1765–74

Possibly from **Henry William Stiegel Glasshouse**

Blue lead glass. Patterned in fluted mold, nipped into twenty-diamond pattern, and expanded. Applied foot and handle.

Height 10.2 cm (4″), diameter 6 cm (2⅜″)

The George H. Lorimer Collection. 53-29-68

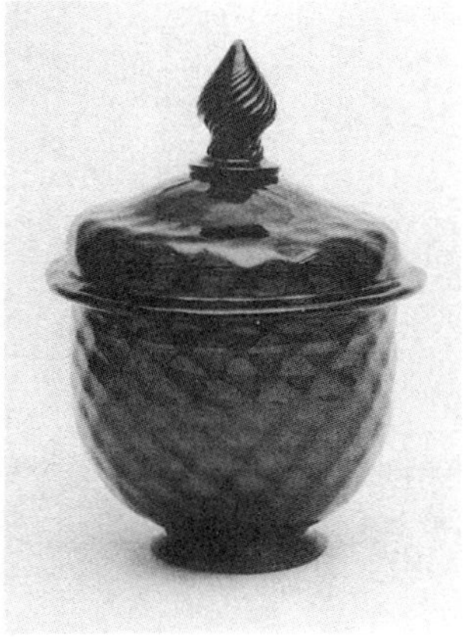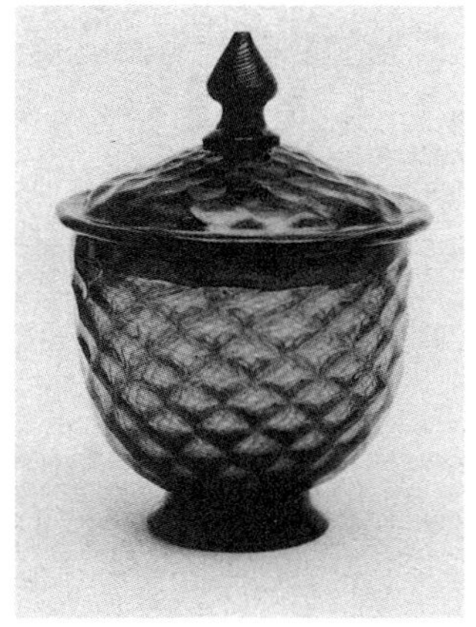

5 6

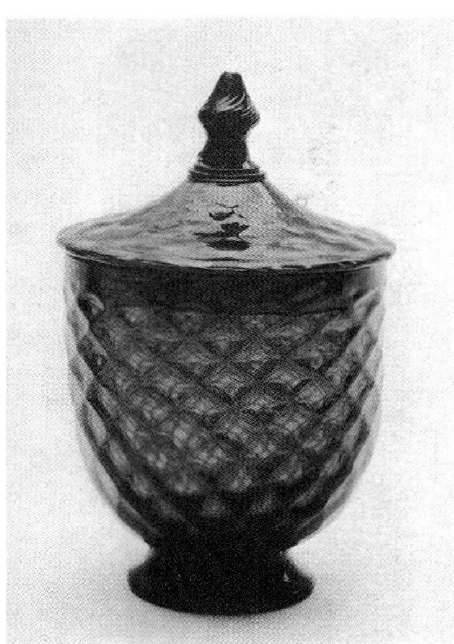

7

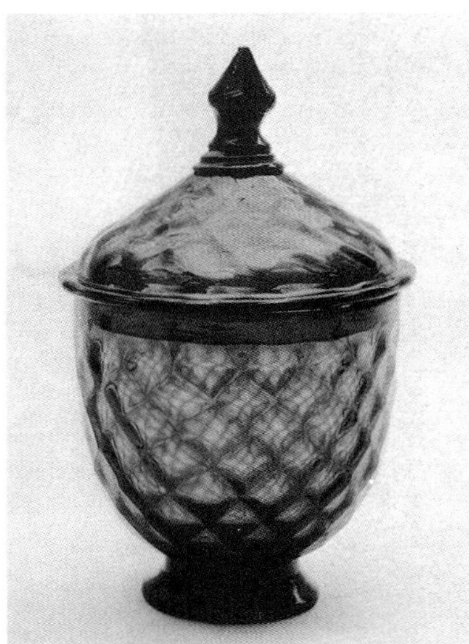

8

5 **SUGAR BOWL**
Manheim, Lancaster County
1765–74

Possibly from **Henry William Stiegel
Glasshouse**

Blue lead glass. Bowl and cover patterned in
twenty-diamond mold and expanded. Flanged
cover has applied finial with swirled ribbing.
Pontil mark inside top. Bowl has applied foot.

Height 15.7 cm (6⅛″), diameter 10.2 cm (4″)

The George H. Lorimer Collection.
53-29-103a,b

---

6 **SUGAR BOWL**
Manheim, Lancaster County
1765–74

Possibly from **Henry William Stiegel
Glasshouse**

Blue lead glass. Bowl and cover patterned in
sixteen-diamond mold and expanded. Flanged
cover has applied finial with swirled ribbing.
Pontil mark inside top.

Height 15.9 cm (6¼″), diameter 11.6 cm (4½″)

The George H. Lorimer Collection.
38-23-334a,b

---

7 **SUGAR BOWL**
Manheim, Lancaster County
1765–74

Possibly from **Henry William Stiegel
Glasshouse**

Blue lead glass. Bowl and cover patterned in
sixteen-diamond mold and expanded. Flanged
cover has applied finial with swirled ribbing.
Pontil mark inside top. Bowl has applied foot.

Height 16.5 cm (6½″), diameter 11.1 cm (4⅜″)

The George H. Lorimer Collection.
38-23-335a,b

---

8 **SUGAR BOWL**
Manheim, Lancaster County
1765–74

Possibly from **Henry William Stiegel
Glasshouse**

Blue lead glass. Bowl and cover patterned in
sixteen-diamond mold and expanded. Flanged
cover has applied finial with swirled ribbing.
Pontil mark inside top. Bowl has applied foot.

Height 16.9 cm (6⅝″), diameter 11 cm (4¼″)

The George H. Lorimer Collection.
38-23-333a,b

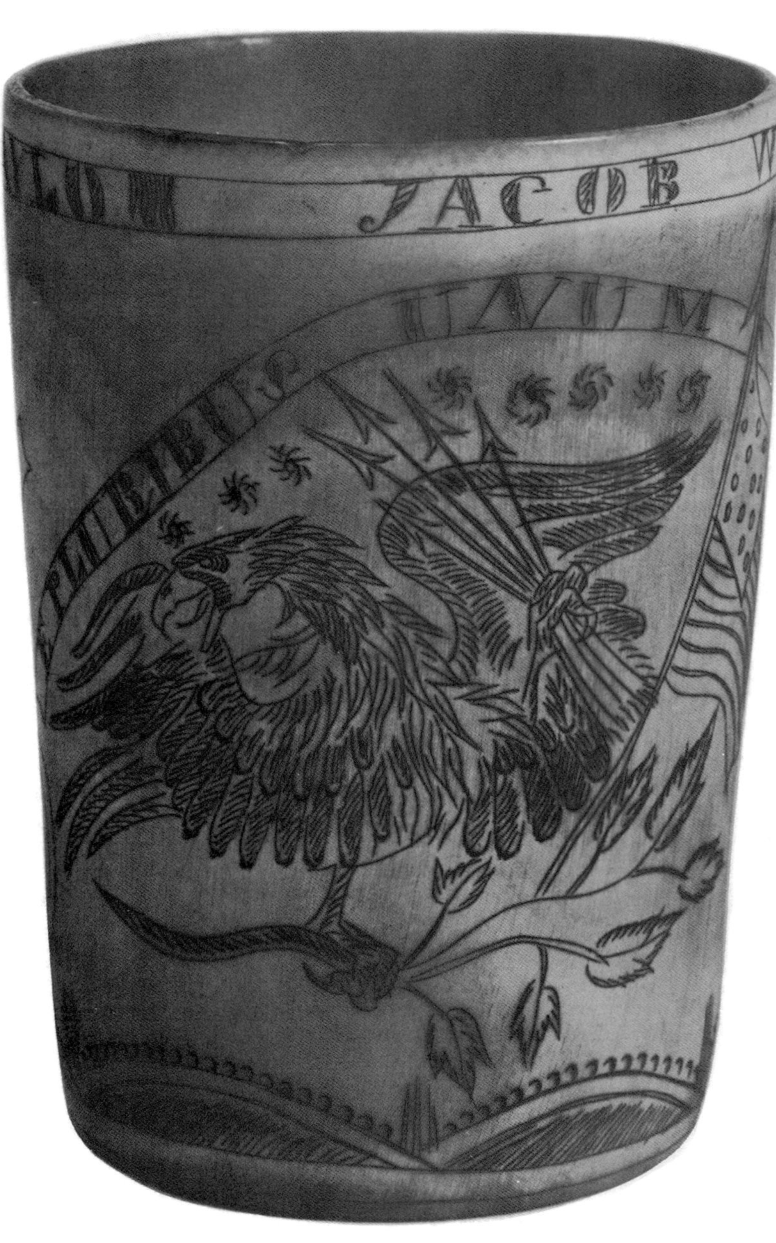

Horn/Eggshell

248 Horn
250 Eggshell

INTRODUCTION

The tradition of the rabbit and the decorated eggs he supposedly hides as an Easter morning surprise for young children is an 18th-century Palatine German contribution to Anglo America. Children made nests of straw or swamp bay to be filled with colorful eggs. Hen, goose, and guinea hen eggs were dyed by wrapping the eggs in red or brown onionskins and simmering in water. Initials, inscriptions, or dates were scratched through the dye coating for special decoration. Bold designs could be achieved with the resist method—coating a design with beeswax or applying a wax-coated paper pattern to the egg before dipping in a dye bath. On Easter morning most eggs were eaten or were exchanged in the custom of "picking eggs"—two children struck their eggs, and the broken egg fell prize to the unbroken one.

Animal products also supplied containers and vessels, such as drinking cups. Animal horns, cow and ox, were tough, waterproof, and, if tightly sealed, floated. They were fashioned into versatile, light containers for men on foot—farmer, hunter, or soldier—who needed to carry gunpowder or whetstones. The horn was cut off at both ends, cleaned and smoothed inside and out, and fitted with a cap and a stopper secured with wooden pins. Decorations were incised, rings for leather thongs carved, walnut juice rubbed in, and the horn polished with vegetable or nut oils.

TUMBLER
1847
See page 249, no. 5

247

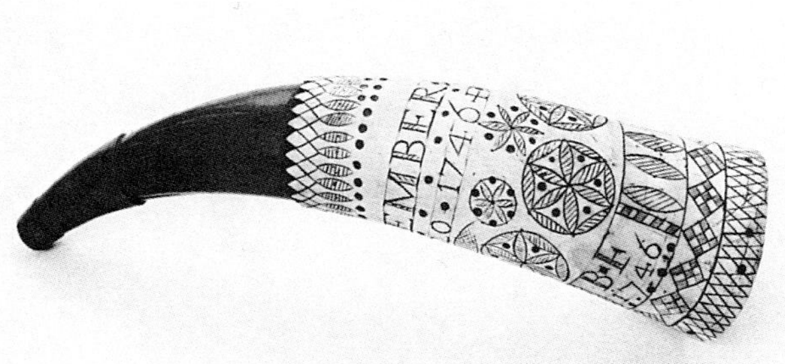

1 obverse

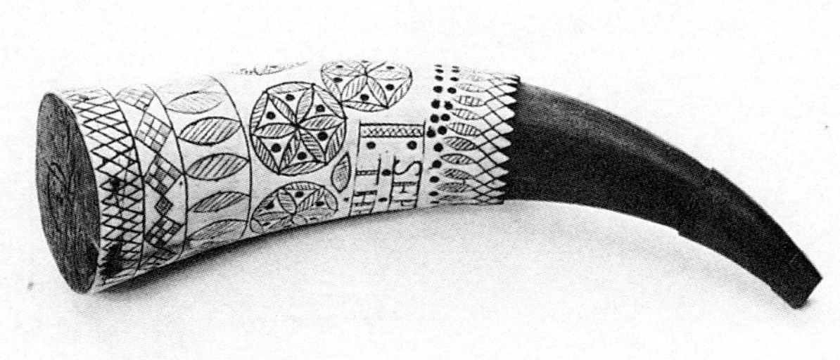

1 reverse

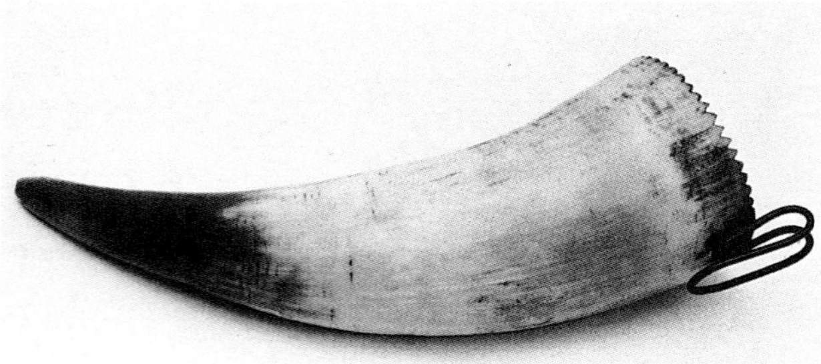

2

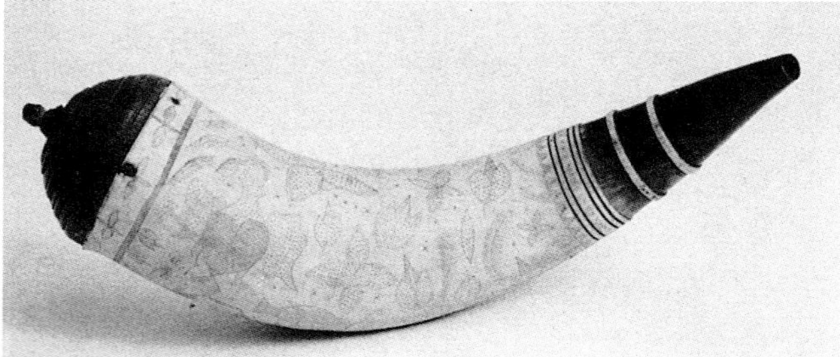

3 obverse

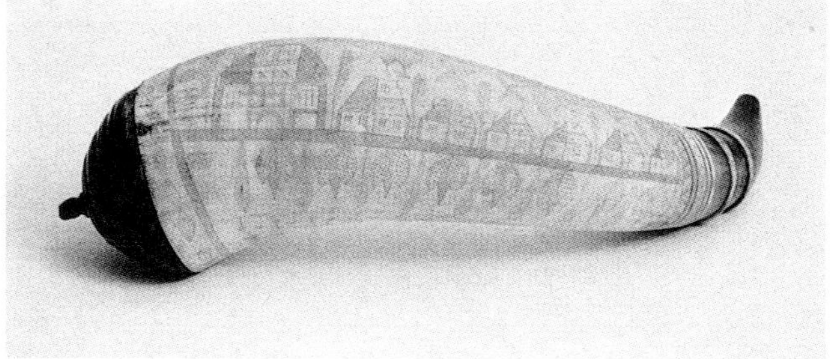

3 reverse

1 POWDER HORN
1746

Inscribed: *B.F 1746 SEPTEMBER the 20. 1746*

Cow horn, pine. Carved and shaped horn with
wood stopper inset and tacked through horn.
Pouring end carved to hold leather thong.
Scrimshaw decoration.

Length 23 cm (9″)

Purchased: Subscription and Museum Fund.
23-23-218

2 WHETSTONE SHEATH
1770–1800

Cow horn, wire. Surface of horn polished with
vegetable oil. Top edge cut in sawtooth pattern
and drilled for bent wire belt hook.

Length 20.2 cm (7⅞″)

Gift of Mrs. William D. Frishmuth. 03-102

3 POWDER HORN
1780–1800

Cow horn, walnut. Carved, domed, wooden
cap with knob finial has flange which fits into
neck of horn and is secured with nails. Pouring
end shaved to leave two raised rings for leather
carrying thong attached to finial. Plug missing
from pouring end. Scrimshaw decoration.

Length 32.3 cm (12⅝″)

Gift of J. Stogdell Stokes. 28-10-45

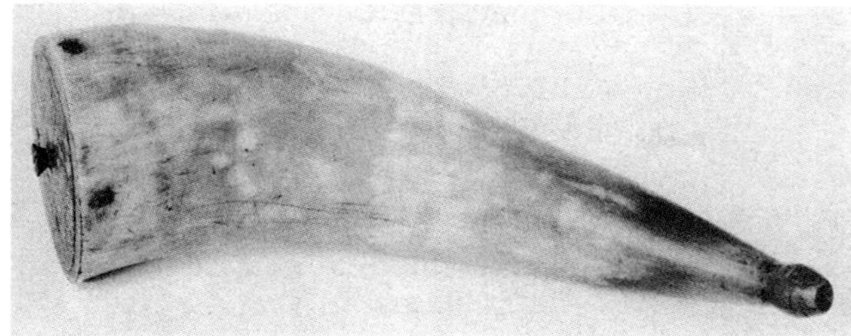

4

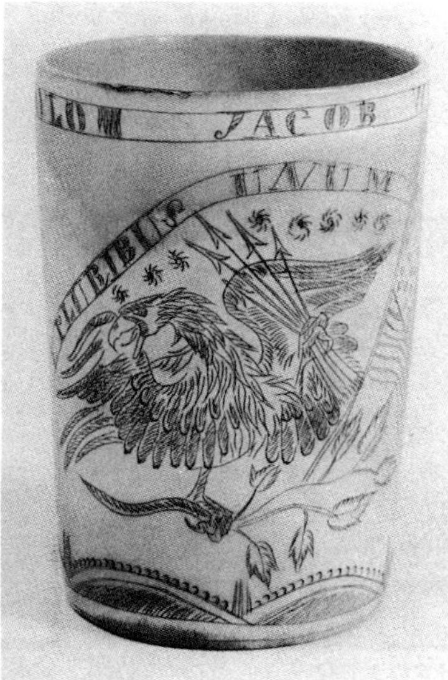

5 obverse

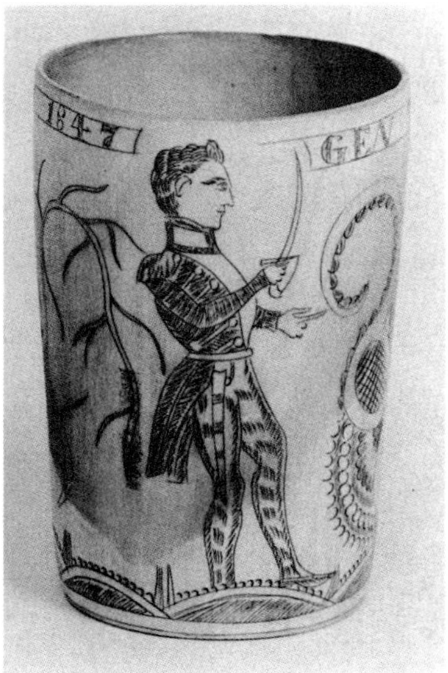

5 reverse

4   **POWDER HORN**
Cocalico Township, Lancaster County
1800–1820

Cow horn, pine, iron. Wide end plugged with
wooden inset and nailed. Screw in center to
hold leather thong.

Length 17.8 cm (7")

Gift of John Jackson. 64-132-1

5   **TUMBLER**
1847

Jacob Wise

Inscribed: *Gen Taylo Jacob Wise 1847*
E Pluribus Unum

Ox horn. Scrimshaw design of uniformed
figure brandishing sword on one side. Eagle
grasping arrows and branch, flag with thirteen
stars, and inscribed banner on other. Stylized
trees and plants on sides.

Height 8.6 cm (3⅜"), diameter 6.4 cm (2½")

Titus C. Geesey Collection. 54-85-113

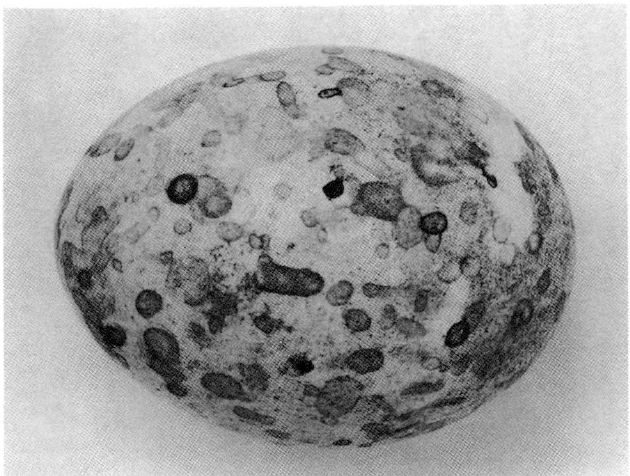

1

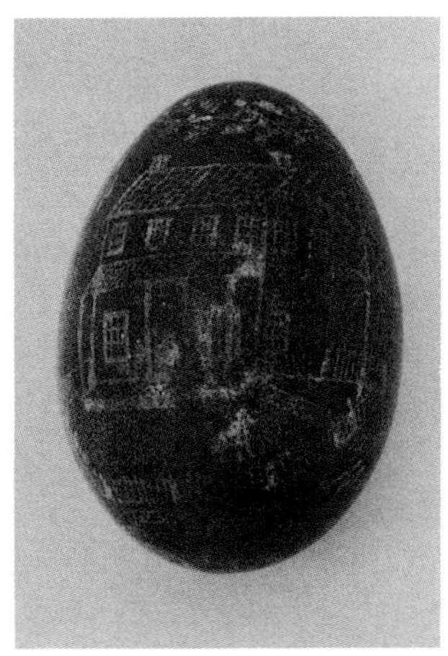

2   3

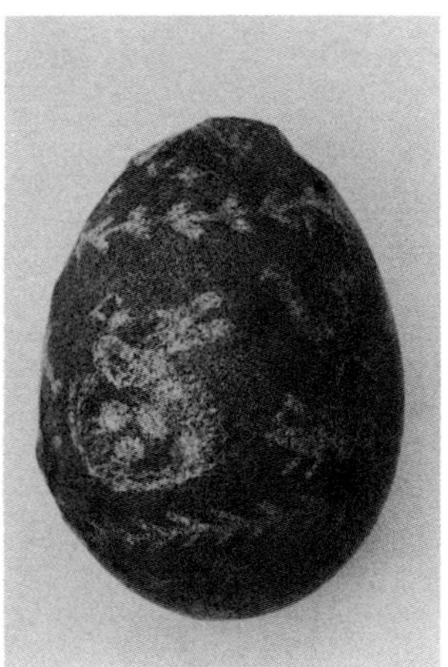

4

1 **DECORATED EGG**
1820–50

Chicken egg. Dappled with tan, brown, red, and black on natural eggshell.

Length 5.4 cm (2⅛″)

Titus C. Geesey Collection. 58-110-21

2 **DECORATED EGG**
1841

Inscribed: *J.S.A. April 10, 1841*

Goose egg. Dyed golden brown with boiled onionskin. Scratched decoration on reverse of a farmhouse and tree.

Length 7.6 cm (3″)

Titus C. Geesey Collection. 58-110-25

3 **DECORATED EGG**
1865

Inscribed: *Mary E. Witmer 1865. Dear Cousin, do not forget me   bg*

Chicken egg. Dyed to deep brown with boiled onionskin. Scratched decoration of barn, farmhouse, fenced yard with flagpole, and returning soldier. Foliage wreath encircles pointed end.

Length 5.4 cm (2⅛″)

Titus C. Geesey Collection. 58-110-22

4 **DECORATED EGG**
1868

Inscribed: *A B 1868*

Chicken egg. Dyed brown with boiled onionskin. Scratched decoration of hen on nest, pig, chicken, hoop-skirted child, eight-pointed star, and tree with wreaths. Eight-pointed stars at each end.

Length 5.4 cm (2⅛″)

Titus C. Geesey Collection. 58-110-27

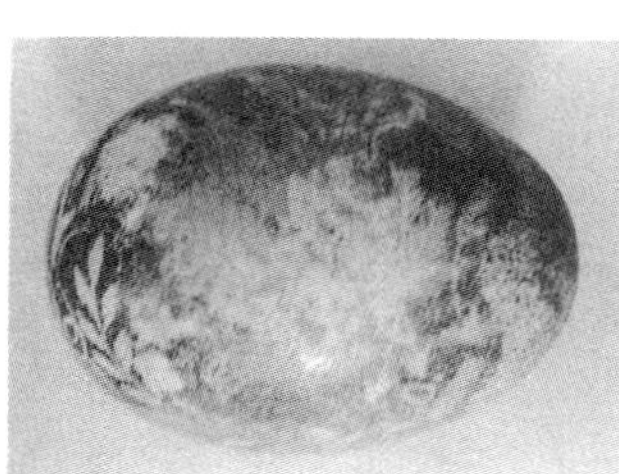
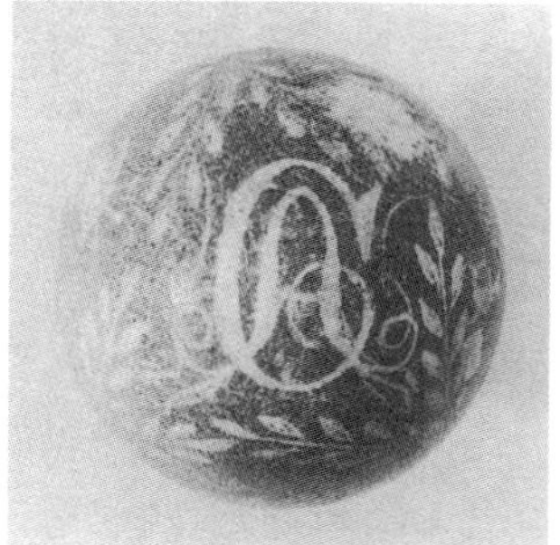

5

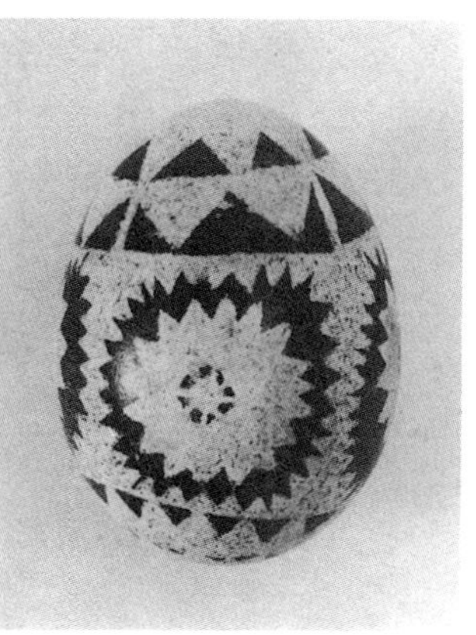
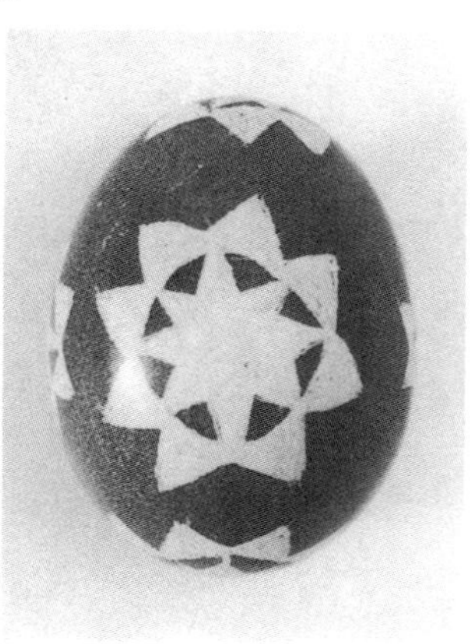

6   **7**

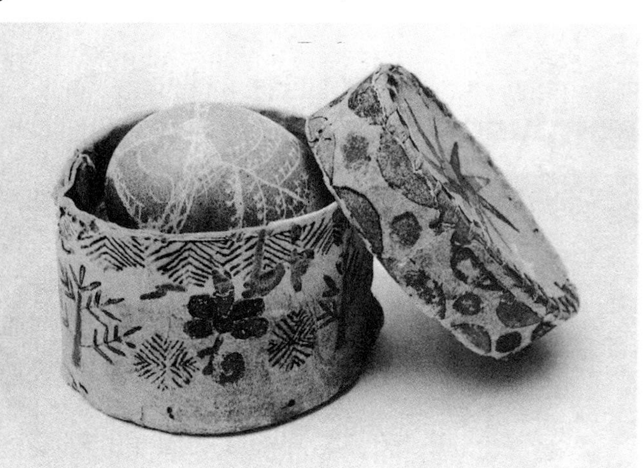

8

5 DECORATED EGG
1881

Inscribed: *W K O April 17 18   81   AC*

Chicken egg. Dyed bluish tan from boiled red onionskin. Scratched decoration of high-buttoned shoe, eagle with arrows, and spray of flowers in floral wreaths. Five-pointed star on pointed end; cypher on blunt end.

Length 5.7 cm (2¼")

Titus C. Geesey Collection. 58-110-29

6 DECORATED EGG
1900–1950

Chicken egg. Resist-dyed brownish red with boiled onionskin on natural eggshell.

Length 5.2 cm (2")

Titus C. Geesey Collection. 58-110-24

7 DECORATED EGG
1900–1950

Chicken egg. Resist-dyed brownish red with boiled onionskin on natural eggshell.

Length 5.2 cm (2")

Titus C. Geesey Collection. 58-110-28

8 EASTER EGG BOX
1800–1850

Inscribed: *S   SS*

Pigments in gum medium, watercolor wash, and ink on laid paper glued to cardboard and sewn with double strand of linen thread. Yellow, red, blue, and green painted decoration. Shown with decorated egg.

5.4 x 7 cm (2⅛ x 2¾")

Titus C. Geesey Collection. 58-110-30b,c

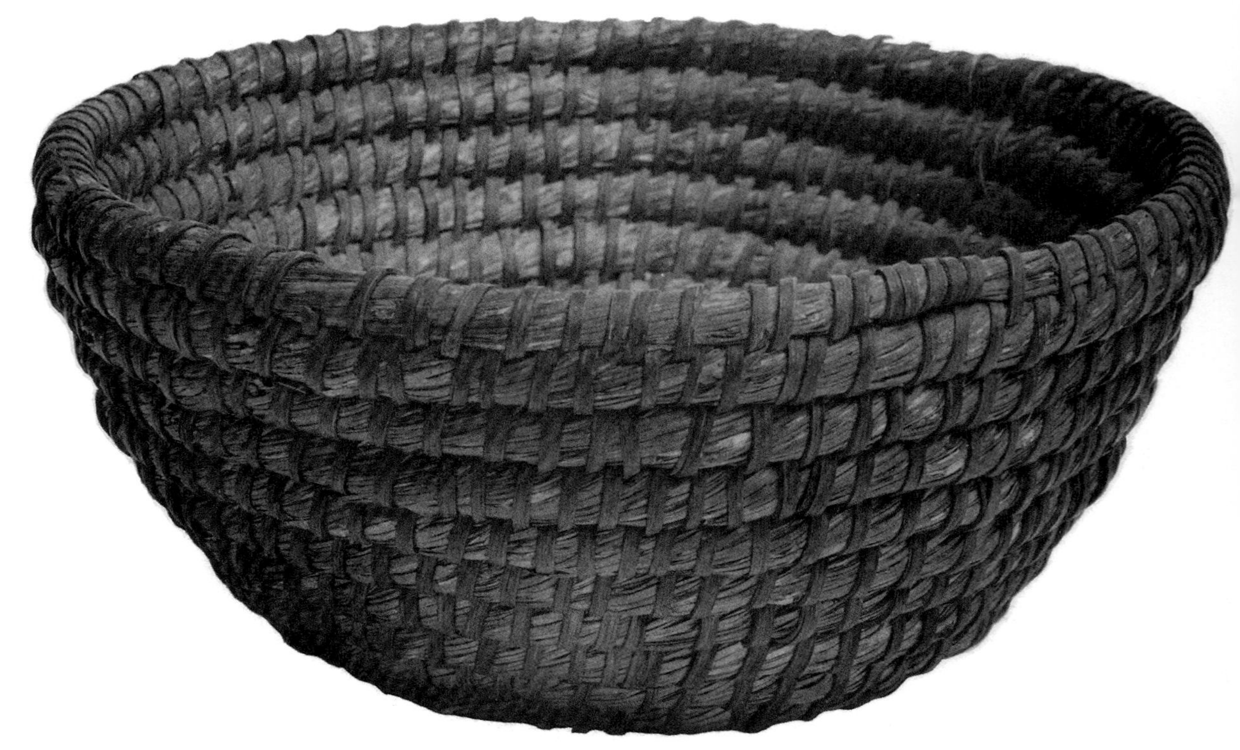

Basketry

INTRODUCTION

The soft, coiled baskets found in most counties in Pennsylvania where the Germans settled were essential house and farm furnishings in the 18th and 19th centuries. Baskets were made easily in traditional forms using traditional methods. Rye straw, common rush, and even wire grass was bundled, coiled, and sewn with strands or splits of hickory or oak. They were strong and supple from residual moisture in the plant fibers, which was renewed with annual washing. The largest baskets were heavy and were designed for storage, not portability. Dried fruits and vegetables were kept in them in barns, sheds, and cold cellars. Sheep's wool was stored in baskets while awaiting washing or carding and seasonal pluckings of goose feathers and down were collected in baskets until a sufficient amount was accumulated for mattresses or pillows. Small, round or oval baskets served many purposes and each household used several, perhaps lined with a linen towel where a wad of well-worked bread dough was placed—under a tree in the summer, near the hearth in the winter—for a slow rise.

Wicker baskets and hamper-type containers woven of oak splits were also produced and were used for harvesting potatoes or apples. These baskets were constructed with ribs and reinforced bottoms, which protected their contents on wagon trips. Domestic manufactories such as potteries packed their fragile products first in straw, then in wicker baskets for safe travel to the marketplace.

BREAD-RAISING BASKET
1800–1850
See page 256, no. 10

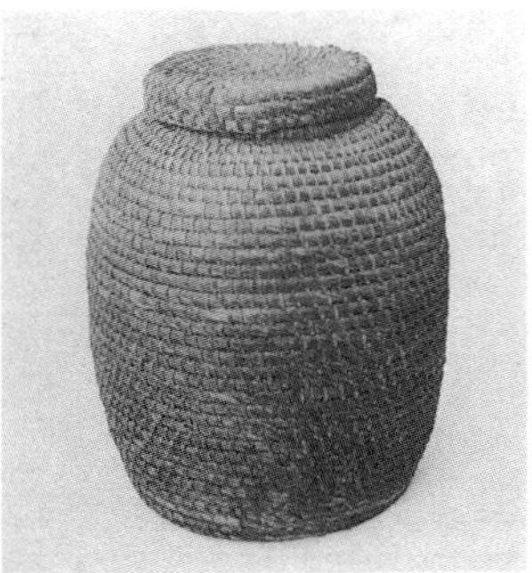

1

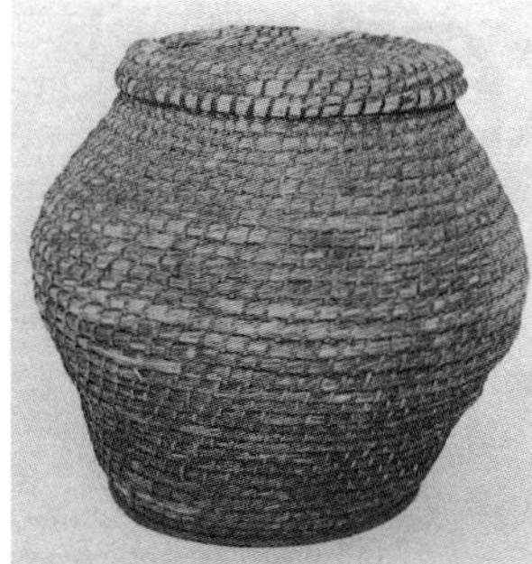

2

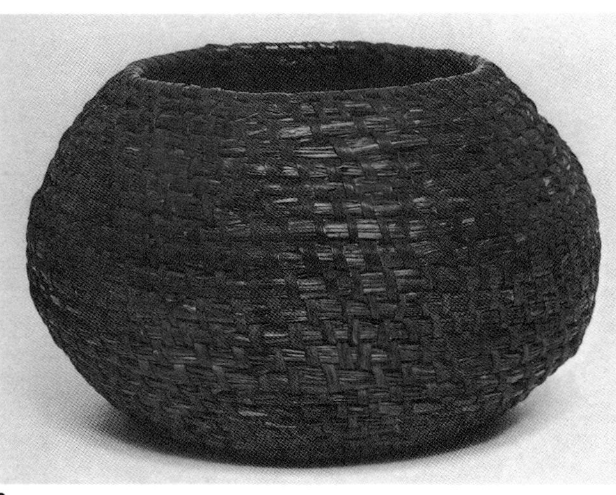

3

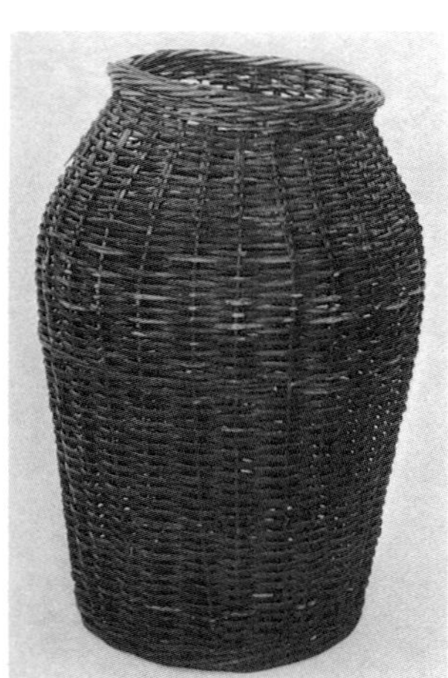

4

1 STORAGE BASKET
1800–1820

Rye straw, oak. Bundled straw twisted into ropes and sewn in single overlay with oak ribbons *(schiene)* in raised coil technique. Lid overlaps. Dried fruits or feathers were stowed in linen bags and placed in basket.

Height 51.7 cm (20⅜″), diameter 46.7 cm (18⅜″)

Gift of Mr. and Mrs. J. Stogdell Stokes. 33-70-2

2 STORAGE BASKET
1800–1820

Rye straw, oak. Bundled straw twisted into ropes and sewn in single overlay with oak ribbons *(schiene)*. Coiled bottom attached. Lid overlaps. Used for storage of dried fruits, vegetables, or feathers.

Height 62 cm (24⅜″), diameter 62 cm (24⅜″)

Gift of J. Stogdell Stokes. 31-48-1a,b

3 STORAGE BASKET
1800–1820

Rye straw, oak. Bundled straw twisted into ropes and sewn in single overlay with oak ribbons *(schiene)* in raised coil technique.

Height 20 cm (7⅞″), diameter 31 cm (12¼″)

Gift of J. Stogdell Stokes. 28-10-105

4 STORAGE BASKET
1800–1820

Oak splits. Oak ribs and ribbons *(schiene)* in single under-and-over weave with rolled border at top. Woven bottom raised in center.

Height 64.8 cm (25½″), diameter 49.7 cm (19½″)

Gift of J. Stogdell Stokes. 28-10-104

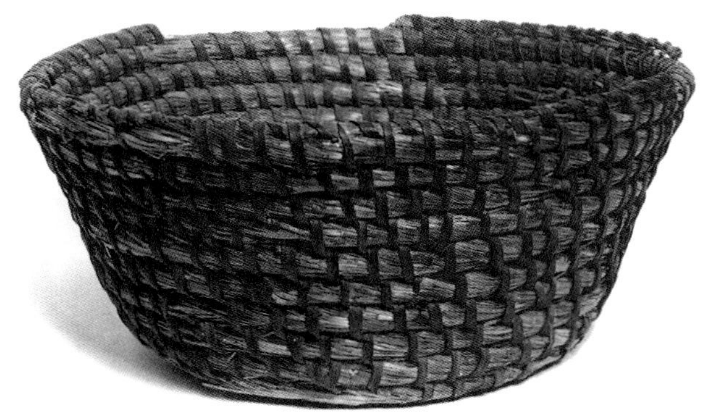

5

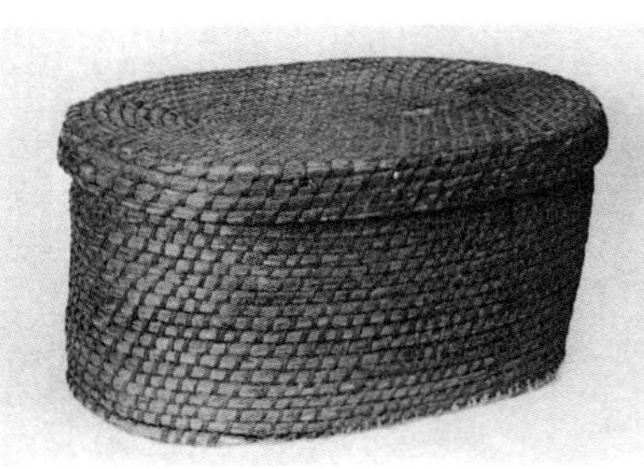

6

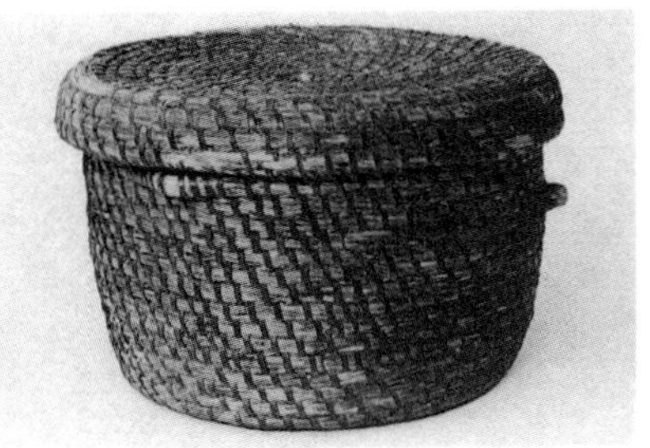

7

8

5 **BREAD-RAISING BASKET**
1800–1820

Rye straw, oak. Bundled straw twisted into ropes and sewn in single overlay with oak ribbons *(schiene)* in raised coil technique. Two handles fashioned from top coil are broken. Dough put in basket to raise.

Height 16.5 cm (6½″), diameter 48.2 cm (19″)

Gift of H. K. Deisher. 14-299

6 **STORAGE BASKET**
1800–1850

Rye straw, oak. Bundled straw twisted into ropes and sewn in single overlay with oak ribbons *(schiene)*. Flat, coiled bottom sewn to sides; lid separate. Stored apples, potatoes, or goose feathers.

Height 63.5 cm (25″), diameter 69.2 cm (27¼″)

Gift of Mrs. William D. Frishmuth. 10-313

7 **STORAGE BASKET**
Kutztown, Berks County
1800–1850

Rye straw, oak. Bundled straw twisted into ropes and sewn with oak ribbons *(schiene)*. Coiled bottom inset and sewn. Lid has overlapping edge.

30.5 x 66 x 40.6 cm (12 x 26 x 16″)

Purchased: Annual Membership Fund. 14-282

8 **STORAGE BASKET**
1800–1850

Rye straw, oak. Bundled straw twisted into ropes and sewn in single overlay with oak ribbons *(schiene)* in raised coil technique. Lid overlaps. Handle fashioned from one coil released from overlay stitch.

Height 32.7 cm (12⅞″), diameter 54.4 cm (21″)

Purchased. 15-231,a

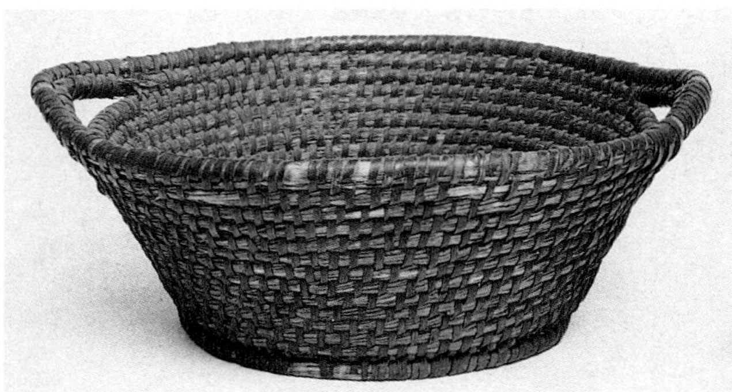

9

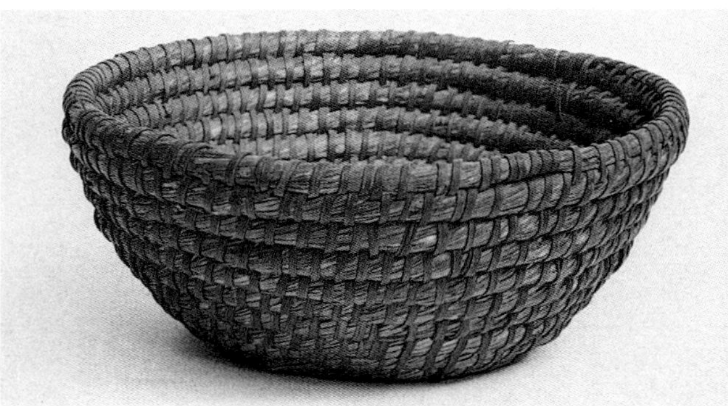

10

11

9 BREAD-RAISING BASKET
1800–1850

Rye straw, oak. Bundled straw twisted into ropes and sewn in single overlay with oak ribbons *(schiene)*. Coiled bottom attached. Handles formed from two coils released from overlay.

Height 19 cm (7½″), diameter 47 cm (18½″)

Gift of Joseph G. Lester. 28-82-1

10 BREAD-RAISING BASKET
1800–1850

Rye straw, oak. Bundled straw twisted into ropes and sewn in single overlay with oak ribbons *(schiene)*. Sides continuous with bottom.

Height 17.3 cm (6¾″), diameter 38.4 cm (15¼″)

Gift of Mrs. William D. Frishmuth. 02-545

11 BEEHIVE
1800–1850

Rye straw, oak. Bundled straw twisted into ropes and sewn in single overlay with oak ribbons *(schiene)*. Domed lid covers four sections. Repaired.

Height 43.4 cm (17″), diameter 38.9 cm (15¼″)

Purchased: Annual Membership Fund. 14-283

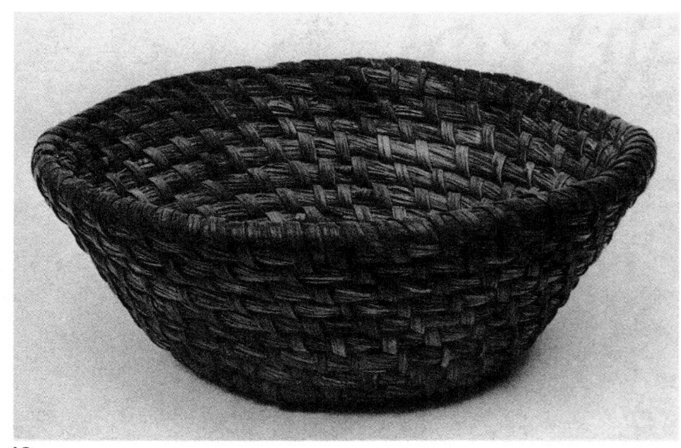

12

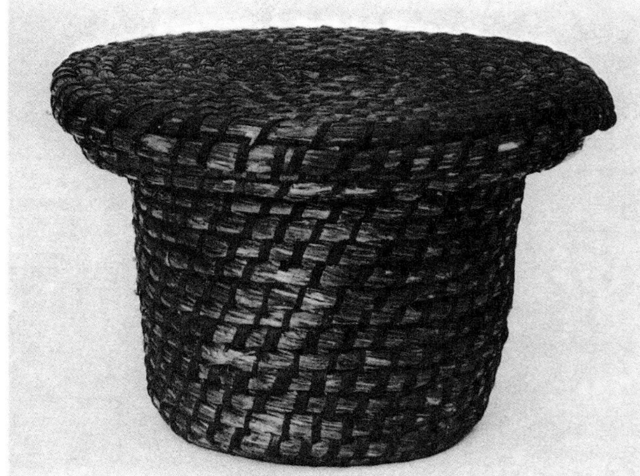

13

12 BREAD-RAISING BASKET
1820–50

Rye straw, oak. Straw ropes twisted and sewn in single overlay with oak ribbons *(schiene)* in raised coil technique.

Height 10 cm (3⅞″), diameter 31 cm (12⅛″)

Gift of Mrs. William D. Frishmuth. 02-544

13 HAT BASKET
1820–50

Rye straw, oak. Bundled straw twisted into ropes and sewn in single overlay with oak ribbons *(schiene)* in raised coil technique. Lid overlaps.

Height 24.1 cm (9½″), diameter 34.9 cm (13¾″)

Gift of Mrs. William D. Frishmuth. 12-170a,b

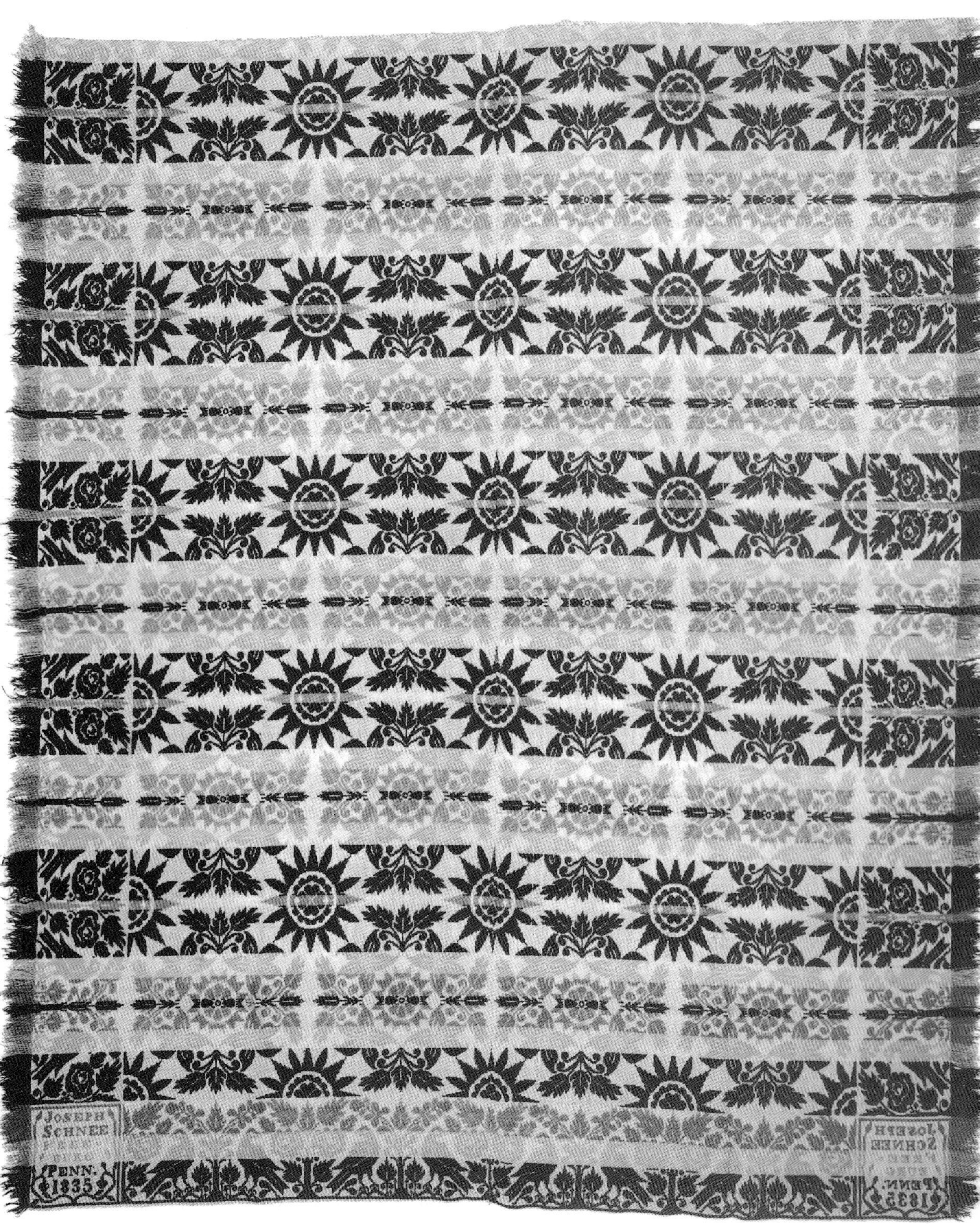

JOSEPH
SCHNEE
FREE-
BURG
PENN.
1835

Textiles

INTRODUCTION

Wool and flax, the staples of 18th-century domestic textiles, grew bountifully in Pennsylvania. The rich, limestone-based, well-watered fields energetically farmed by Pennsylvania Germans allowed their settlements self-sufficiency in producing annually an adequate supply of textile crops for clothing, household, and farm needs.

The production and processing of flax and wool went on year round, with all ages and both sexes participating. The process was seasonal, rhythmic, and dirty. Flax was planted in early April just before the sheep were sheared. It was harvested in July after the wool had been sorted, washed, picked, combed, and readied for spinning. Preparing the flax took the rest of the summer. Pulled up by its roots to get the longest stem fibers, the flax was left to dry. After being threshed in a barn to remove the seeds for the next year's planting, the stalks were soaked for weeks in a still pond to ret out the woody part of the stem. The smells from the retting pond were unpleasant enough to be noted in diaries. The flax was dried again and subjected to the flax brake and the scutching knife to remove the last bit of woody core and shives. The remaining bundle of supple fibers was drawn over and through the hatchel to separate the long, strong fibers from the shorter ones, which were put aside for further processing and then woven into tow cloth or sacking. The long flax

COVERLET
1835
See page 269, no. 11

259

fibers were braided into "tresses" ready for the spinner's distaff or
the flax wheel. A spinning scene of 1841 was described in Dr. W. A.
Helffrich's autobiography: "A farmer's spinning-room in those days
presented a strange sight. The boys sat or lay on the wood-chest
behind the stove. In the center of the room, suspended from the ceiling, hung a wooden contrivance to which was fastened the old-
fashioned fat-lamp, about which the mother, daughters and hired
girls, clad in homespun, home-made tight-fitting dresses, often so
covered with dust as to be unrecognizable, sat at their wheels night
after night, spinning and talking" (translated in *The Pennsylvania-
German*, vol. 9, no. 2, 1908, p. 83).

The regimen of processing wool and flax readied the raw materials for weaving, sometimes for a household weaver, but more often
for a professional craftsman. From the outset of settlement in Pennsylvania, tax records reveal that a large number of weavers were
active. The first German settlement in Pennsylvania, in 1683, largely
linen weavers from Krefeld, Germany, established an important
weaving center in Germantown. Later county tax records, particularly
those available after 1785, indicate a high proportion of weavers in
comparison to other tradesmen, like potters, cordwainers, or blacksmiths, evidence that weavers' services were essential and profitable.
Lancaster County weavers, many of Swiss Mennonite heritage,
were especially active, and the large town of Lancaster was a marketplace for local and more distant western settlements. In 1769-70,
Lancaster weavers produced over 27,000 yards of cloth, and in 1777,
Lancaster County weavers and tailors were pressured to produce
clothing and blankets for the American troops at Valley Forge.

Weavers were necessarily versatile. Inventories, account books,
and diaries describe the varieties of textiles produced by weavers.
They wove tough, utilitarian cloth for grain sacks, ticking for feather
beds and bolsters, as well as fine bed linens in checked patterns, and
coverlets. Damask float weaves, usually bleached white, were commissioned for table covers and fine toweling. Colorfully striped strip
carpets of cotton, wool, linen, or cotton rags in warp-faced weaves
were popular for bedroom and parlor in the mid-19th century.

Weaving was heavy work. Some was done for local sale but
most textiles, especially coverlets, were commissioned. Weavers
often bartered their skills for staples: Daniel Maddin's 1789 account
with Anthony Wayne for potatoes was settled by hours of weaving.
Diaries and other records suggest that many weavers were itinerant,
working in homes on household equipment, while others had permanent shops with several looms to which customers brought
homespun thread.

Closely associated with weaving was dyeing and Pennsylvania
Germans prized colorful textiles. The term "Blew dyer" appears frequently in tax records. The blue dyer specialized in the technique of
resist-dyeing on linen and also dyed loose yarns with indigo. Pennsylvania Germans were active in other textile processes, such as
fulling and calendering, as well as color printing, especially in
the counties where there was an English market.

Coverlet weavers produced some of the most distinctive Pennsylvania textiles up to industrialization, about 1860. The multiharness loom and, after 1825, the jacquard loom, were the coverlet weaver's equipment. Both the free double-cloth and the closely tied single weaves are found in Pennsylvania German weaving. Usually the warps were unbleached or bleached cotton, and the wefts were colored wool. Strong reds, blues, and greens were woven into bold geometric patterns of flowers or stars, with various borders and fringes. Weavers often carried pattern books, like John Landes's (p. 323, no. 3) to show his customers the variety of patterns he could weave. Pattern books also recorded loom drafts and preserved as well as passed on traditional designs. The weaver often supplied the materials, especially the cotton, which was not a local farm product. Because he provided the materials, Jacob Oberholtzer of Bucks County was paid $4.00 for weaving a coverlet in the 1830s, while William Eschbach was paid $1.75 for weaving only. The wool and cotton for weaving coverlets was carefully counted on clock reels, which would click off 300 yards into a skein or cut. Martin Overholt's design of about 1790 in the "Old Snow Bowl Pattern" required twenty-five cuts each of blue wool and white cotton to produce one coverlet.

Young women were taught embroidery skills at home and in school. Embroidered towels, sheets, and samplers show designs adapted from almanac woodcuts, embroidery pattern books, weavers' pattern books, primers, and in some cases from drawings of buildings like the Lancaster Alms House (p. 278, no. 4, p. 279, no. 6). Some of these needleworked pieces reflect the assimilation of English techniques and designs taught in German-settled regions in the "select schools," summer schools taught by Quakers who spoke "pure" English and taught English reading, writing, and sewing.

Show towels, usually made in several pieces joined with bands of embroidery, crochet, or darned net, were placed over a towel that was to be used and hung on a door or side of a cupboard. In contrast, the decorated hand towel, usually embroidered only at the top, was used, with worn or soiled sections easily replaced. These towels were made by and for young women to show the proficiency of their needlework skills to suitors and as marriage dowry or special gifts. Women of all ages gathered together to make quilts. Except for friendship quilts, which were signed by the women who made them, they were rarely signed or dated. Quilt designs were cut from paper or tin, passed down through generations, and carried to different regions and used in various combinations, thus foiling attempts at precise attributions of time, place, or maker.

1

1 BEDCOVER
1820–40

Bleached cotton ground, 40 warps per inch. Two wefts of two-ply cotton every ninth and tenth shot creating ribbing. Candlewick embroidery in two-ply cotton thread. Festoon-with-tassel border, baskets and vases of flowers in corners. Eagle filled with crewelwork in stem stitch and French knots and surrounded by seventeen stars in single-ply cotton thread in center. Loom width 93.3 cm. Hemmed. Knotted cotton fringe applied.

266.7 x 198.1 cm (105 x 78″)

Titus C. Geesey Collection. 55-94-56

2 BEDCOVER
1860–1900

Inscribed: *MDD*

Bleached cotton ground in plain weave, 80 warps per inch. Design in red cotton, green cotton with printed green dots, and gold yellow cotton with printed brown dots. Appliquéd with running stitch.

231.1 x 221 cm (91 x 87″)

Titus C. Geesey Collection. 55-94-54

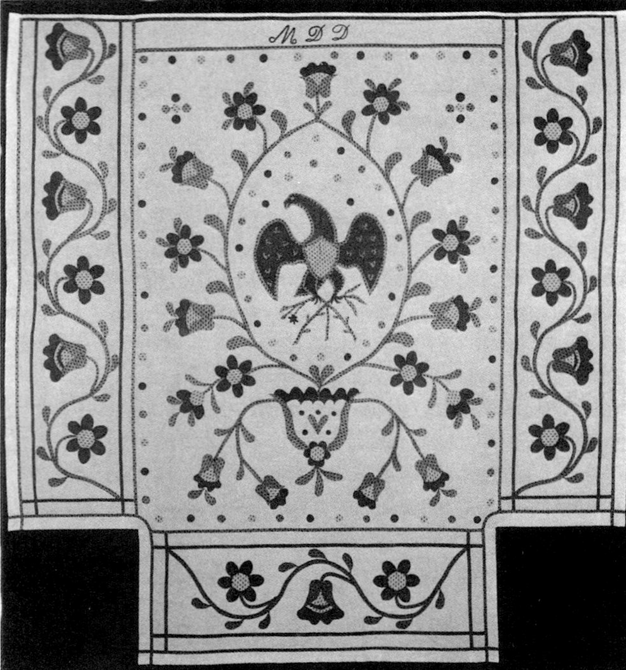

2

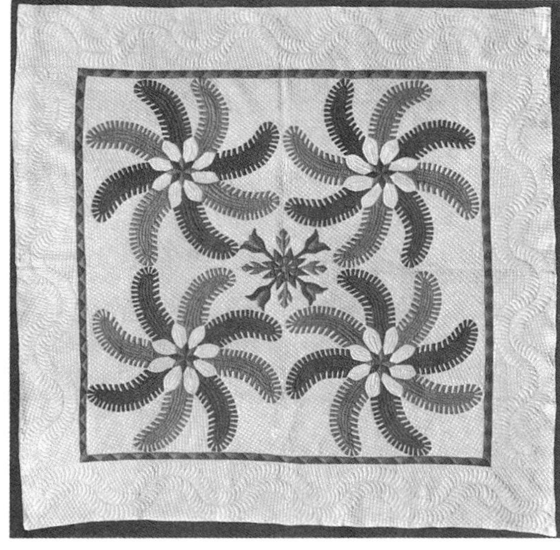

1

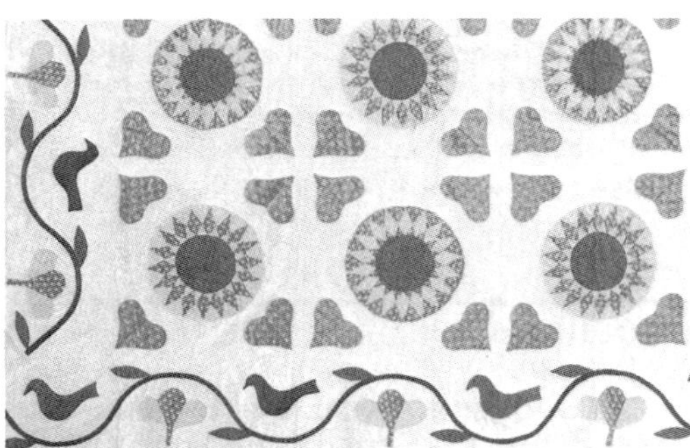

2 quilt detail

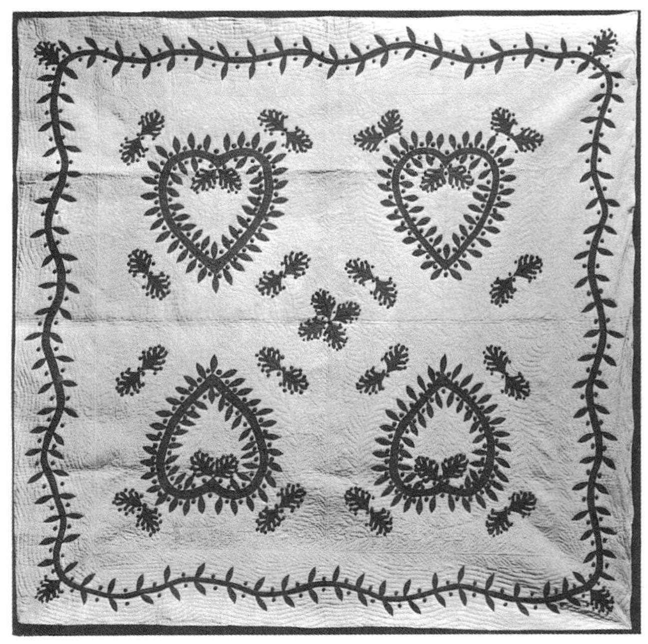

3

1   QUILT
1840–70

Bleached cotton ground in plain weave with printed yellow stripes and dots, 72 warps, 56 wefts per inch. Ground quilted in diamond, crossed-diagonals pattern (1.6 cm per side). Border is quilted in wavy-feather pattern with green and red zigzag banding (3.8 cm wide) and sewn to center unit. Princess-feather appliqué in red and green cotton. Reverse in four pieces of sprig-printed yellow cotton. Cotton batting.

231.4 x 231.4 cm (91⅛ x 91⅛")

Purchased: Edgar V. Seeler Fund. 67-66-1

2   QUILT AND PILLOW SHAMS (2)
1840–80 Quilt
1880–1900 Shams

Bleached cotton ground in plain weave, 64 warps, 64 wefts per inch. Obverse is in thirty sections (each 31.7 x 30.5 cm), with borders 17.1 cm and 16.5 cm wide. Red, green, and yellow printed cotton design, brown vine, and green and brown birds are appliquéd with hem stitch. Quilted tulips and leaves between appliqués. Edges rolled over and sewn to reverse which is in four pieces. Pillow shams have appliqués similar to those of quilt but with different fabrics. Three felled seams and rolled edge on shams.

Quilt 224.8 x 198.1 cm (88½ x 78")
Shams 43.8 x 57.1 cm (17¼ x 22½")

Titus C. Geesey Collection. 55-94-53a,b,c

3   QUILT
1850–80

Bleached cotton ground in plain weave, 80 warps per inch. Obverse in four squares joined to border (26.7 cm wide) with mitered corners. Blue vines and hearts and plumply stuffed red dots appliquéd to ground which is quilted in feather pattern around hearts. Border quilted in wavy lines. Edges rolled over and sewn to reverse which is in three pieces.

221 x 223.5 cm (87 x 88")

Titus C. Geesey Collection. 55-94-55

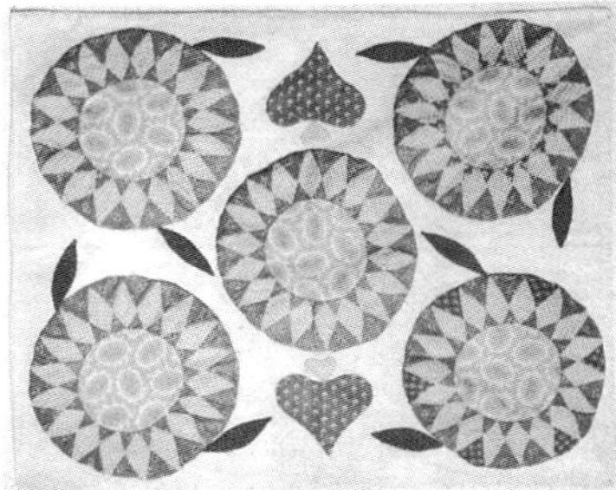

2 sham

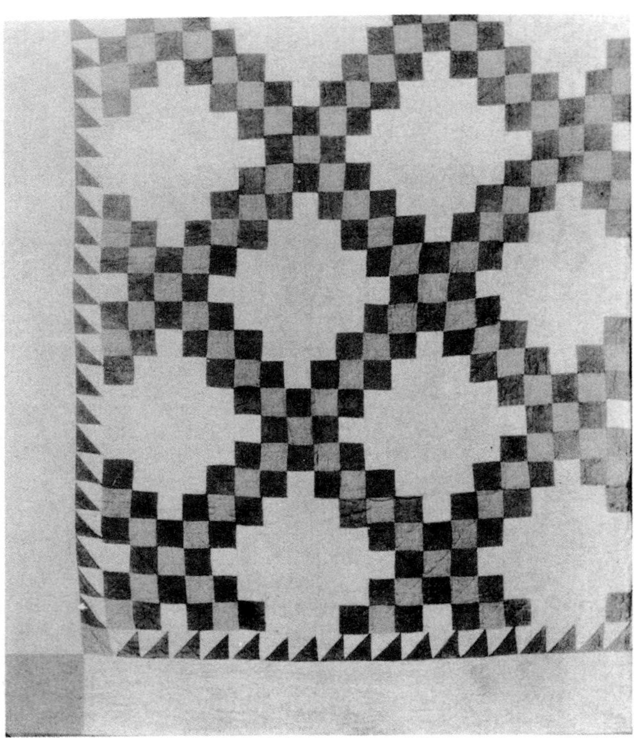

4 detail

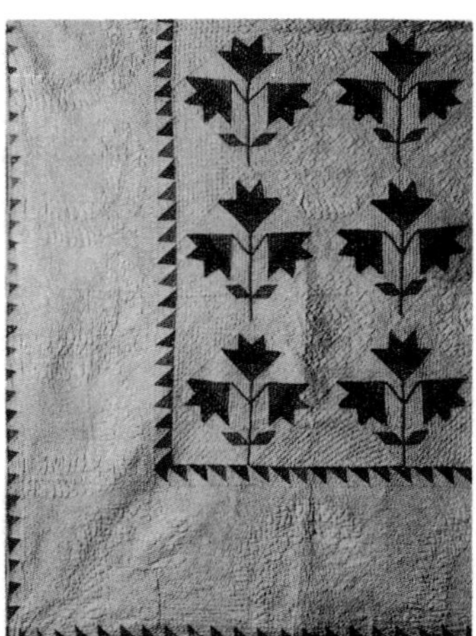

5 detail

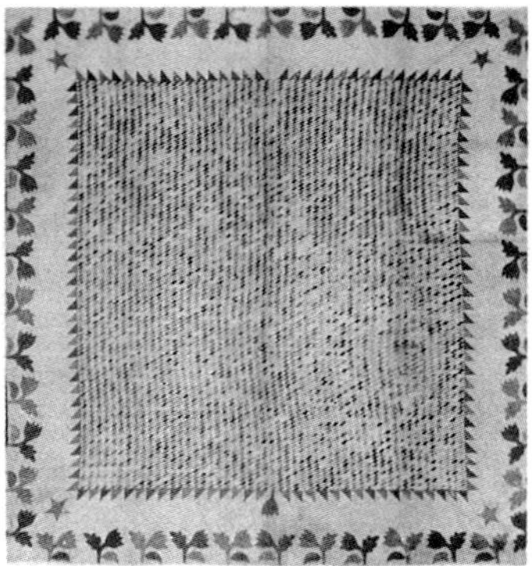

6

4 QUILT
1850–80

Unbleached cotton ground in plain weave, 80 warps per inch. Patches are linen and cotton in plain weave, 72 warps per inch. Triple Irish chain pattern with sawtooth border in red and yellow green patchwork. White centers quilted in pattern of two hearts and open rose on stem with two leaves. Border quilted in running chain pattern. Red corner squares, green edging. Cotton batting.

212.1 x 172.1 cm (83½ x 67¾")

Gift of Mrs. William D. Frishmuth. 02-233

5 QUILT
1850–80

Bleached cotton ground obverse and reverse in plain weave, 80 warps per inch. Patchwork squares (on points) in red and yellow triple-lily pattern. Green stems and leaves appliquéd to squares (on points) which are quilted in rose-of-Sharon pattern. Patchwork sawtooth bandings around border quilted in princess-feather pattern. Edges rolled over and hemstitched to reverse which is in three pieces.

226.1 x 234.3 cm (89 x 92¼")

Gift of Mrs. Edward Browning. 29-50-1

6 QUILT
1850–90

Bleached cotton ground in plain weave, 72 warps per inch. Geometric center pattern in multicolored patchwork quilted to reverse in running stitch in four-petaled flower design. Patchwork sawtooth border and red tulip and green leaf border appliquéd through obverse and reverse. Edging is a rolled hem extension of reverse. Cotton batting.

298.1 x 287 cm (117⅜ x 113")

Gift of Mrs. William D. Frishmuth. 02-234

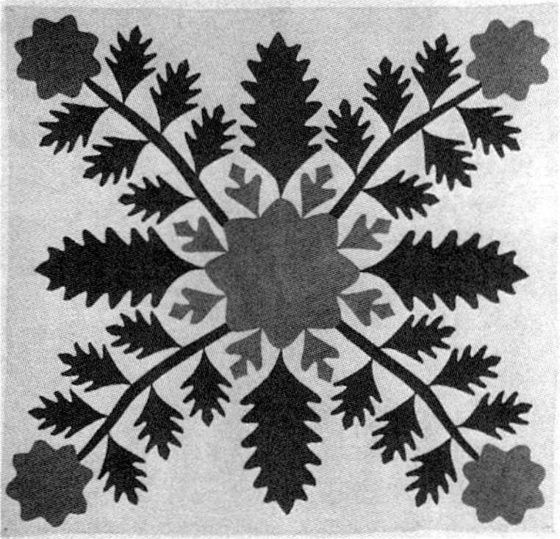

7

8

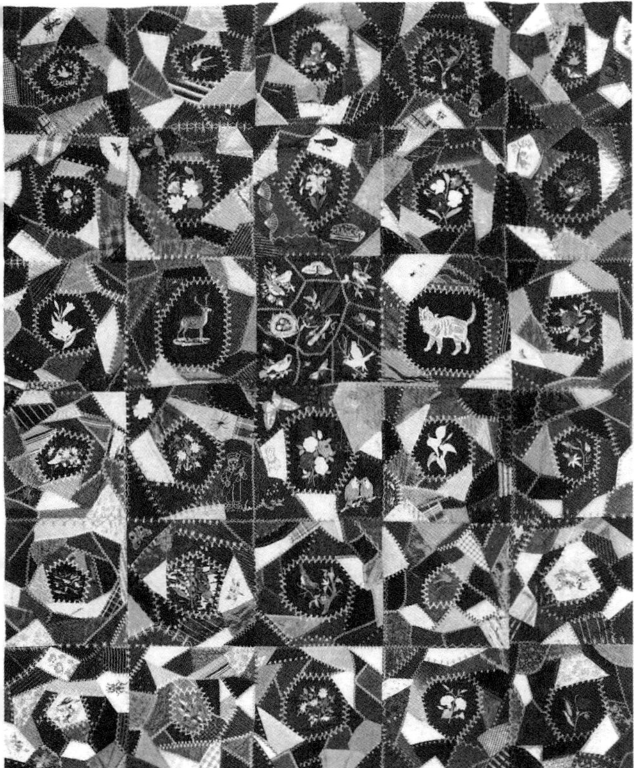

9

7 QUILT SECTION
1850–90

Unbleached cotton ground in plain weave, 72 warps per inch. Rose and oak leaf appliqué in green and red cotton. One selvage.

69.2 x 69.2 cm (27¼ x 27¼")

Gift of Miss Mary Germani. 20-39-4

8 QUILT SECTION
1850–90

Unbleached cotton ground in plain weave, 64 warps per inch. Rose wreath appliqué in red and green cotton. One selvage.

52.7 x 52.7 cm (20¾ x 20¾")

Gift of Miss Mary Germani. 20-39-4a

9 LAP QUILT
Howard, Centre County
1876–80

Lucy Catherine Zeigler Hicks

Obverse: silk, velvet, satin. Reverse: cotton chintz. Crazy patchwork patterns sewn to printed cotton squares. Designs filled with silk thread in satin stitch. Seams oversewn with silk thread in feather, fagoting, knotted insertion, and herringbone stitches. Machine stitching on patchwork and reverse. Made for Amy Josephine Kline Cornwell.

198.1 x 165.1 cm (78 x 65")

Gift of Ralph T. K. Cornwell, in memory of his mother, Amy Josephine Kline Cornwell. 46-8-1

10 QUILT SECTION
1880–1900

Machine-woven calico. Patchwork of rust and yellow baskets alternating with green and black squares.

229.9 x 186 cm (90½ x 73¼")

Gift of Mrs. William D. Frishmuth. 02-235

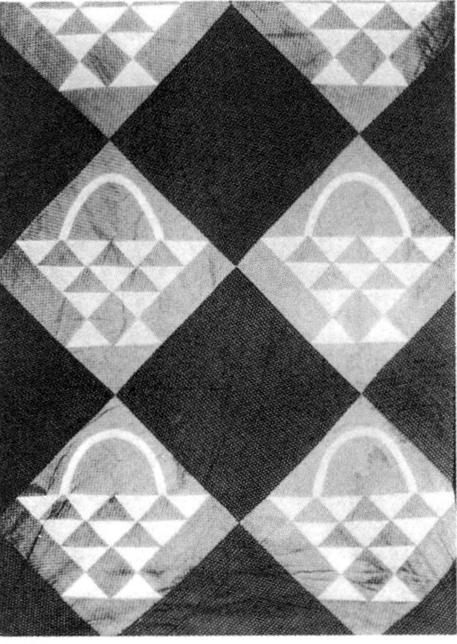

10 detail

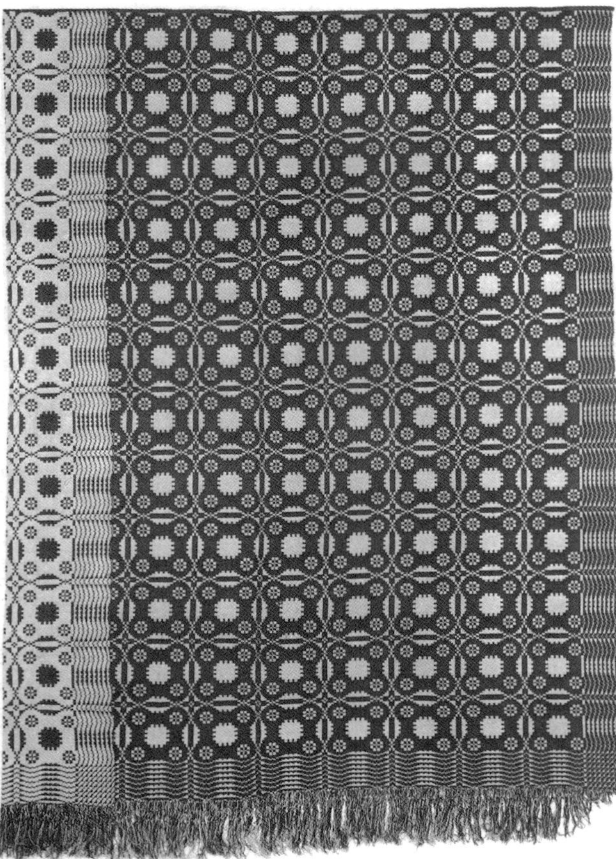

1

1   **COVERLET**
1780–1830

Wool, cotton. Double cloth in balanced plain weave, 24 warps, 24 wefts per inch. Indigo blue wool interwoven with two-ply Z-twist unbleached cotton. Two loom widths, each 99.1 cm, whipped together. Two selvages. Triple-knotted bottom fringe is extension of warp. Top bound with handwoven herringbone twill tape in single-ply blue wool. Shown folded.

232.4 x 198.1 cm (91½ x 78″)

Gift of Mrs. Martha Moore Fogg. 24-11-3

2   **COVERLET**
1800–1830

Wool, cotton. Double cloth in balanced plain weave, 24 warps, 24 wefts per inch. Indigo blue and madder red two-ply Z-twist wool interwoven with two-ply Z-twist unbleached cotton. Reverse: the cotton and red wool are interwoven creating half-tone areas. Two loom widths, each 99.1 cm, whipped together. Two selvages. Single-knotted bottom fringe is extension of warp. Top bound with handwoven herringbone twill tape in single-ply red wool.

236.2 x 198.1 cm (93 x 78″)

Gift of Mrs. William D. Frishmuth. 07-233,a

3   **COVERLET**
1800–1830

Wool, cotton. Double cloth in balanced plain weave, 19 warps, 19 wefts per inch. Indigo blue wool interwoven with two-ply Z-twist unbleached cotton. Two loom widths, each 86.3 cm, whipped together. Two selvages, top hemmed. Bottom fringe is extension of warp. Attributed to ancestor of donor. Shown folded.

219.7 x 172.7 cm (86½ x 68″)

Gift of Miss Marie E. Bucher, in memory of Mrs. William Hipple and Mrs. David H. Bucher. 39-35-1

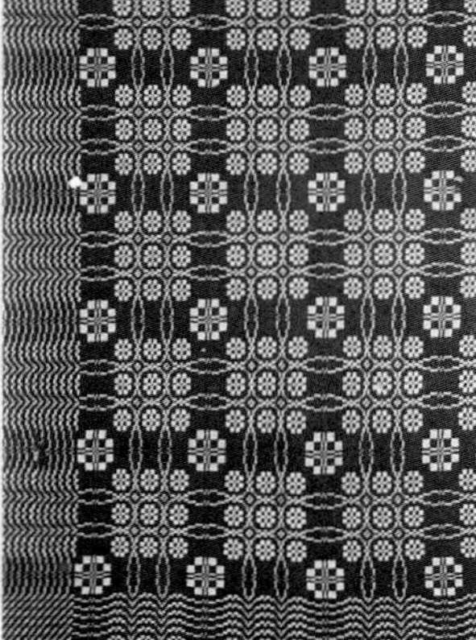

2 detail

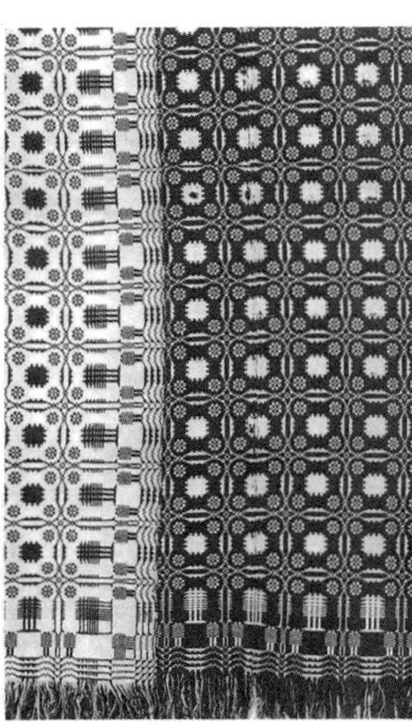

3 detail

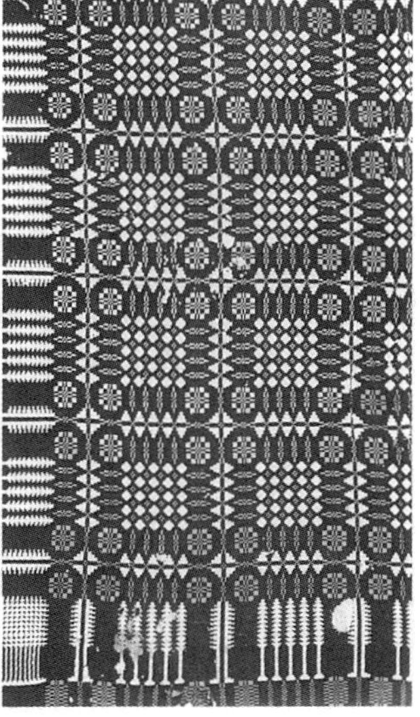

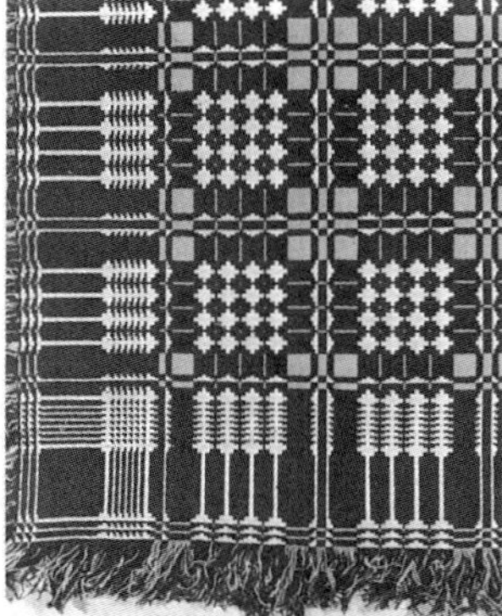

4 detail   **5 detail**

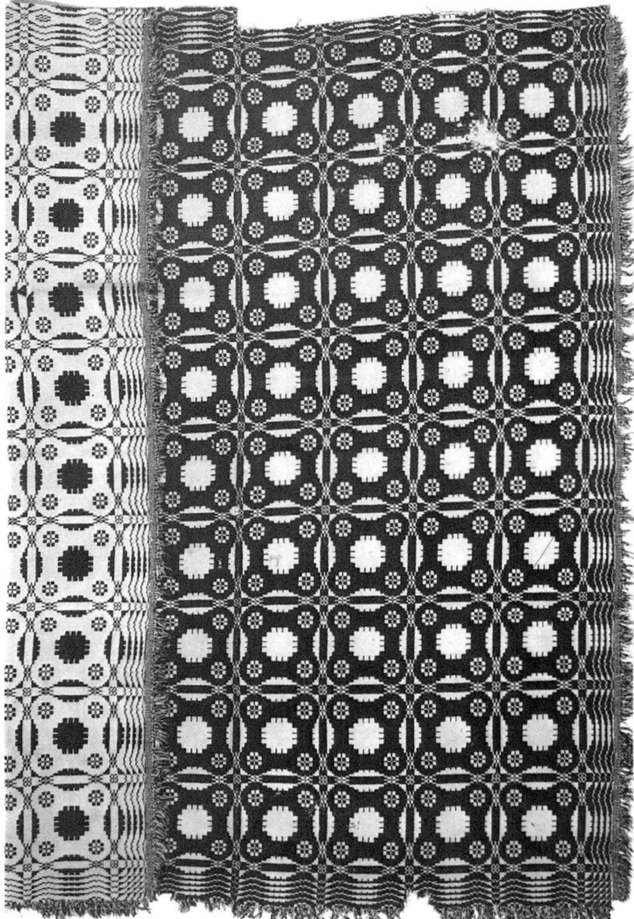

6

4 COVERLET FRAGMENT
1800–1830

Wool, cotton. Double cloth in balanced plain weave, 24 warps, 24 wefts per inch. Indigo blue and madder red two-ply Z-twist wool interwoven with two-ply Z-twist unbleached cotton. Reverse: the cotton and red wool are interwoven creating half-tone areas. Two loom widths, each 90.2 cm, whipped together. Edges cut.

182.9 x 172.7 cm (72 x 68″)

Gift of Mrs. William D. Frishmuth. 07-237

---

5 COVERLET
1800–1840

Wool, cotton. Double cloth in balanced plain weave, 24 warps, 24 wefts per inch. Indigo blue and red two-ply Z-twist wool interwoven with two-ply Z-twist unbleached cotton. Reverse: the cotton and red wool are interwoven creating half-tone areas. Two loom widths, each 92.7 cm, whipped together. Top has rolled hem. Fringe on three sides is extension of warp and weft, no knots.

291.5 x 185.4 cm (114¾ x 73″)

Gift of Mr. and Mrs. George B. Emeny. 68-11-1

---

6 COVERLET
1800–1840

Wool. Double cloth in balanced plain weave, 16 warps, 16 wefts per inch. Two-ply indigo blue wool-twist interwoven with natural wool-twist. Two loom widths, each 96.5 cm, whipped together. Knotted wool fringe with woven heading applied to sides. Knotted bottom fringe is extension of warp. Shown folded.

230.5 x 203.8 cm (90¾ x 80¼″)

Gift of Mrs. William D. Frishmuth. 02-231

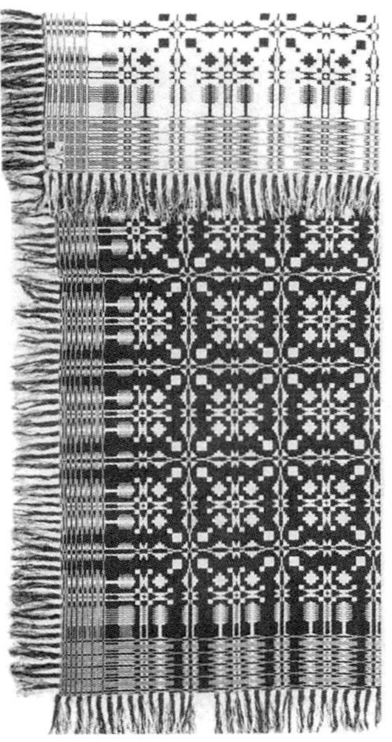

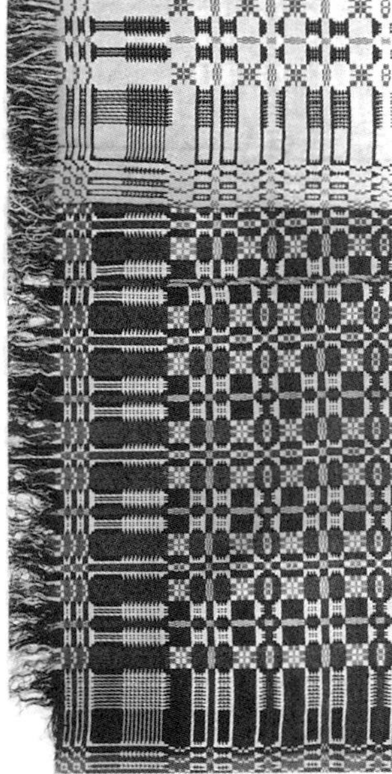

7 detail **9** detail

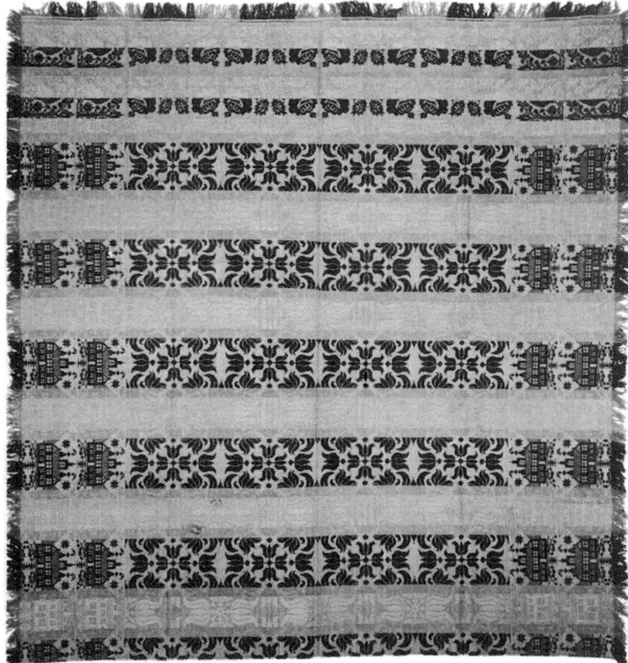

8

7 COVERLET
Lebanon County
1822

Attributed to **C. Reiff**

Inscribed in cross-stitch: *C.R. 1822*

Wool, cotton. Double cloth in balanced plain weave, 32 warps, 32 wefts per inch. Single-ply indigo blue wool-twist interwoven with single-ply unbleached cotton. Two loom widths, each 97.8 cm, whipped together. Top hemmed. Cotton fringe with plain-weave heading applied on three sides. Shown folded.

210.2 x 208.3 cm (82¾ x 82″)

Gift of Mrs. Leona Reiff Norton. 64-135-1

8 COVERLET
Lancaster or Montgomery County
1830–45

Wool, cotton. Single jacquard or tied double cloth. Two single-ply blue cotton ground warps and one single-ply blue cotton tie-down warp interwoven with indigo blue, red, and green two-ply wool-twist pattern wefts. Float lengths of five with one blue cotton ground weft between each pattern weft. 5½ pattern repeats. Two loom widths, each 109.5 cm, whipped together. Side fringe is extension of pattern weft. Applied bottom fringe has plain-weave heading with red, green, and blue wool warps, blue cotton wefts.

241.9 x 219 cm (95¼ x 86¼″)

Titus C. Geesey Collection. 69-284-27

9 COVERLET
1830–50

Wool, cotton. Double cloth in balanced plain weave, 24 warps, 24 wefts per inch. Indigo blue and madder red two-ply Z-twist wool interwoven with two-ply Z-twist unbleached cotton. Reverse: the red and blue wool is interwoven creating half-tone areas in border. Two loom widths, each 106.7 cm, whipped together. Two selvages. Bottom fringe is extension of warp, no knots. Top bound with herringbone tape in single-ply red wool. Shown folded.

235.6 x 213.4 cm (92¾ x 84″)

Bequest of Miss Charlesanna Horner, in the name of her mother, Rosanna Swope Horner. 26-16-1

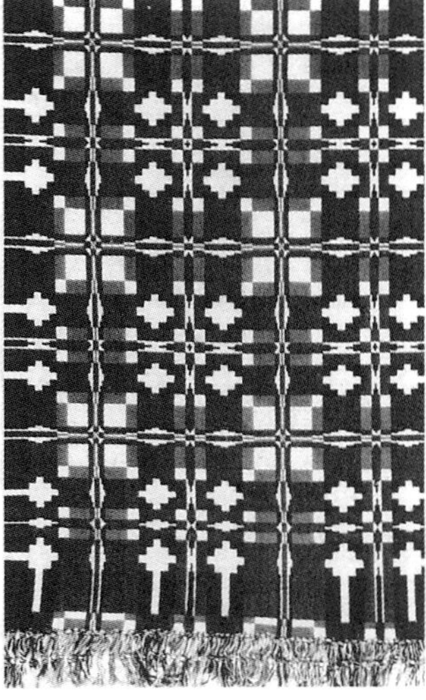

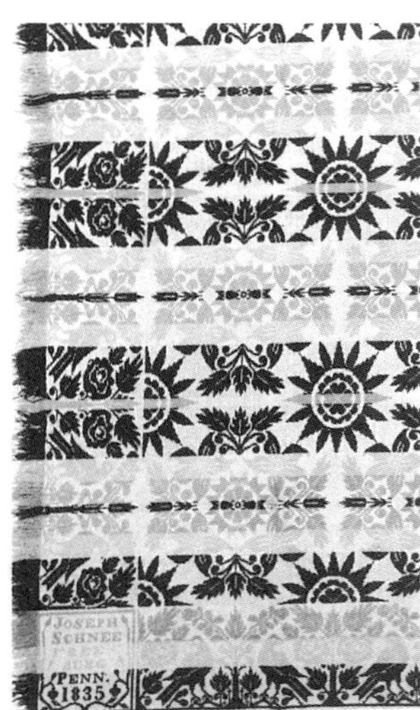

10 detail   **11 detail**

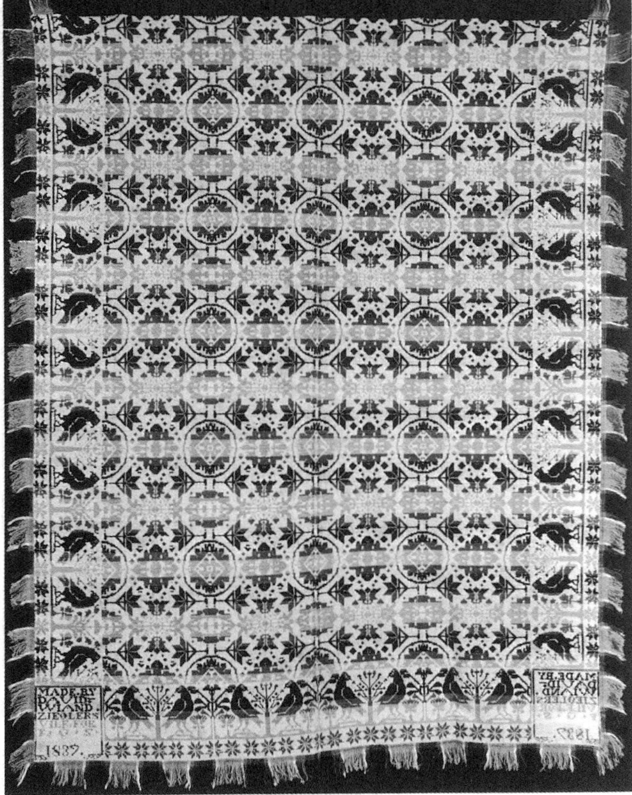

12

10 COVERLET
1830–50

Wool, cotton. Double cloth in balanced plain weave, 24 warps, 24 wefts per inch. Madder red and indigo blue wool interwoven with unbleached cotton. Two loom widths, each 106.3 cm, whipped together. Two selvages, top hemmed. Knotted bottom fringe is extension of warp.

229.9 x 212.6 cm (90½ x 83¾")

Gift of Mrs. John Morton McIlvain, in memory of her husband, Dr. John Morton McIlvain. 29-48-1

11 COVERLET
Freeburg, Snyder County
1835

Joseph Schnee

Inscribed in bottom corners: *JOSEPH SCHNEE FREE- BURG PENN. 1835*

Wool, cotton. Single jacquard or tied double cloth. Two three-ply unbleached cotton ground warps and one single-ply blue cotton tie-down warp interwoven with indigo blue, madder red, and yellow green two-ply wool-twist pattern wefts. Float lengths of five with one unbleached cotton ground weft between each pattern weft. 5⅓ pattern repeats. Two loom widths, each 91.5 cm, whipped together. Side fringe is extension of pattern weft.

238.8 x 182.9 cm (94 x 72")

Gift of Miss Eleanor A. Cantner. 42-95-1

12 COVERLET
Zieglersville, Montgomery County
1837

David Wiand

Inscribed in bottom corners: *MADE. BY DAVID.- WIAND. ZIEGLERS VILF. FOR F.G.S. 1837.*

Wool, cotton. Single jacquard or tied double cloth. Three single-ply bleached cotton ground warps and one bleached cotton tie-down warp interwoven with indigo blue, madder red, and gray green two-ply wool-twist pattern wefts. Float lengths of seven with one bleached cotton ground weft between each pattern weft. Two loom widths, each 97.2 cm, whipped together. Wool and cotton fringe with plain-weave heading applied on three sides.

252.1 x 210.8 cm (99¼ x 83")

Gift of Miss E. Kinsey. 67-10-1

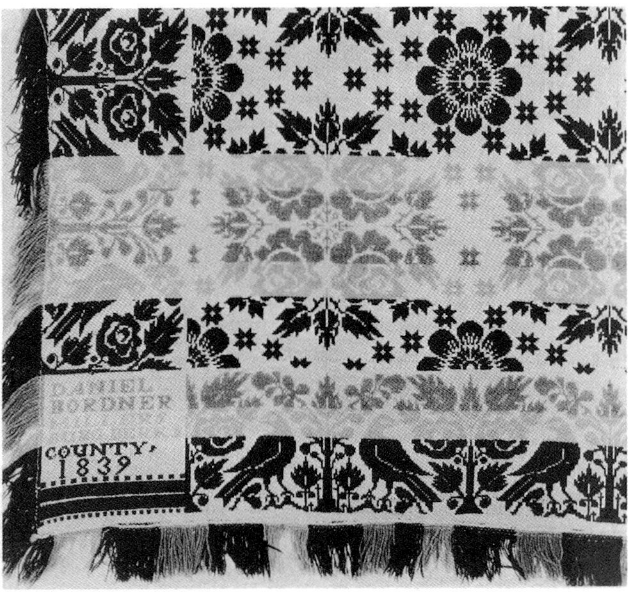

13 detail

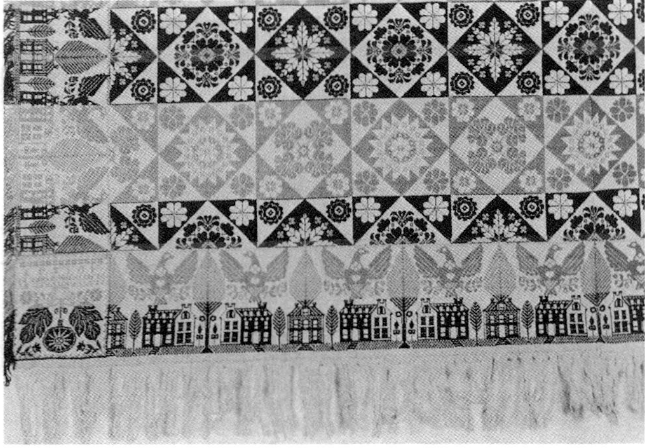

14 detail

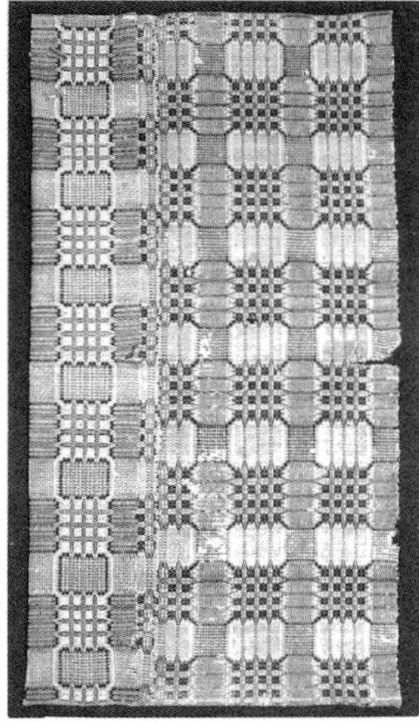

15

13 COVERLET
Millersburg, Berks County
1839

Daniel Bordner

Inscribed in bottom corners: *DANIEL BORDNER MILLERS BURG. BERKS COUNTY, 1839*

Wool, cotton. Single jacquard or tied double cloth. Two three-ply unbleached cotton ground warps and one single-ply blue cotton tie-down warp interwoven with indigo blue, madder red, and green two-ply wool-twist pattern wefts. Float lengths of five with one unbleached cotton ground weft between each pattern weft. 5⅓ pattern repeats. Woven in one piece. Side fringe is extension of pattern weft. Bottom fringe applied.

268 x 213 cm (105½ x 83⅞")

Gift of Mrs. Harry M. Klick. 38-17-1

14 COVERLET
York, York County
1847

Martin Hoke

Inscribed in corners: *MANUFACTURED BY MARTIN HOKE YORK PA A.D. 1847*

Wool, cotton. Single jacquard or tied double cloth. Two three-ply unbleached cotton ground warps and one single-ply blue cotton tie-down warp interwoven with red, indigo blue, and green two-ply wool-twist pattern wefts. Float lengths of five with one unbleached cotton ground weft between each pattern weft. 5⅘ pattern repeats. Two loom widths, each 116.8 cm, whipped together. Side fringe is extension of pattern weft (some uncut). Bottom fringe is extension of ground warp.

250.2 x 233.7 cm (98½ x 92")

Titus C. Geesey Collection. 55-94-57

15 COVERLET
1850–60

Wool, cotton. Four-harness overshot weave. Warps and wefts of indigo blue and pink wool and single-ply unbleached cotton. Two loom widths, each 82.5 cm, whipped together. Two selvages, top and bottom hemmed. Shown folded.

230.5 x 165.1 cm (90¾ x 65")

Purchased: Joseph E. Temple Fund. 22-48-16

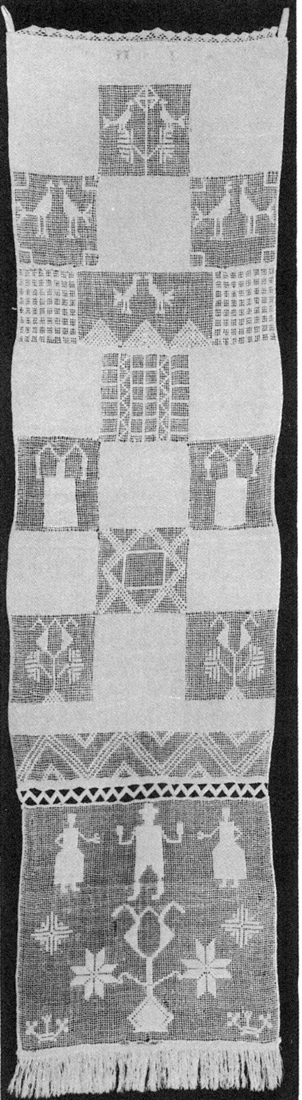

1

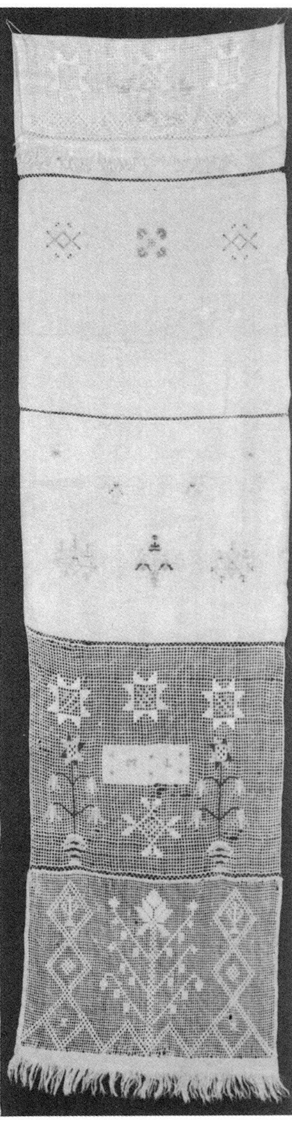

2

1 SHOW TOWEL
1780–1820

Inscribed: *M·L*

Bleached homespun linen ground in plain weave, 48 warps, 48 wefts per inch. Drawnwork and darned net panels of 2 warps, 2 wefts, whipped with linen thread, 9 units per inch; edges whipped with linen thread. Net designs in interlocking and wrapped filling stitches in cotton thread. Inscription in red cotton thread in cross-stitch. Zigzag banding of folded cotton twill tape joins panels. Top border knitted in garter stitch with linen-twist thread. One selvaged, one hemmed side. Unevenly bleached fringe with woven heading applied with overcast stitch. Cotton twill tape hanging loops. Made in two pieces.

146 x 39.4 cm (57½ x 15½")

Titus C. Geesey Collection. 55-94-58

2 SHOW TOWEL
1780–1820

Inscribed: *M L*

Bleached homespun linen ground in plain weave, 48 warps, 48 wefts per inch. Drawnwork and darned net panels: two panels of 4 warps, 4 wefts, loosely whipped with linen thread, 6 units per inch; bottom panel of 3 warps, 3 wefts, tightly whipped with linen thread, 8 units per inch. Net designs in interlocking and wrapped stitches in white, pink, and blue cotton thread; designs in bottom panel in white linen thread. Embroidery in cross-stitch over 2 warps, 2 wefts, in pink cotton, green and white linen thread. Initials in green (faded to brown) linen thread in outline stitch over 3 warps, 3 wefts. Panels joined with twisted fagoting. Sides have rolled hems. Applied fringe top and bottom. Hanging loops of three-strand braided linen thread. Made in six pieces.

157.5 x 41 cm (62 x 16⅛")

Titus C. Geesey Collection. 55-94-61

3 DECORATED HAND TOWEL
Montgomery County
1800–1840

Inscribed: *L M M*

Bleached homespun linen ground in plain weave, 40 warps, 40 wefts per inch. Designs and inscription in red cotton thread in cross-stitch over 2 warps, 2 wefts. Horizontal stripes woven in pink thread. One selvaged, one hemmed side. Top and bottom fringe applied with overcast stitch. Plain-weave linen tape hanging loops. Made in one piece. From Ziegler family in Skippack, Montgomery County.

177.8 x 42.9 cm (70 x 16⅞")

Purchased. 20-35-1

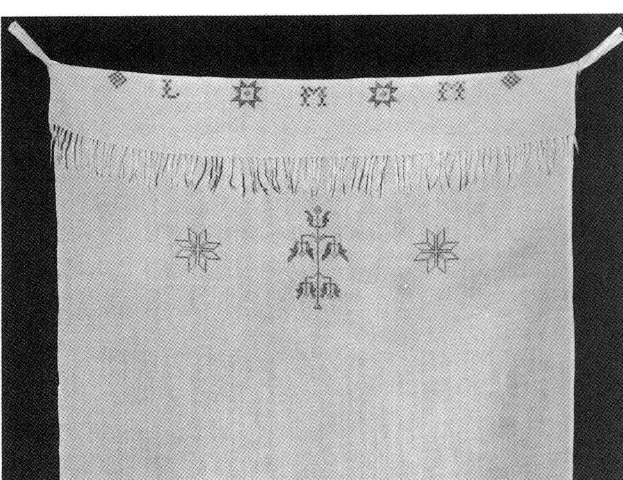

3 detail

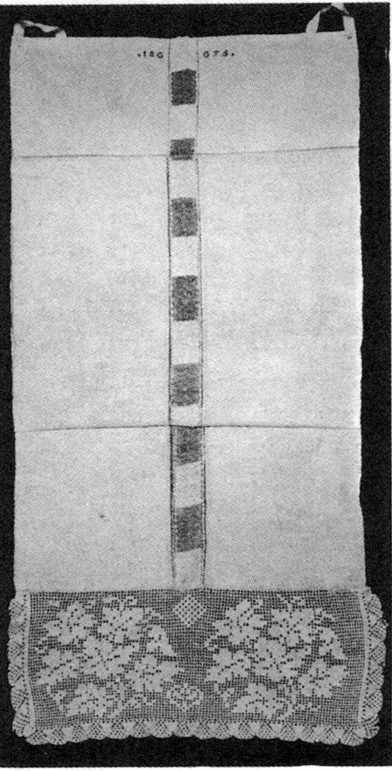

4

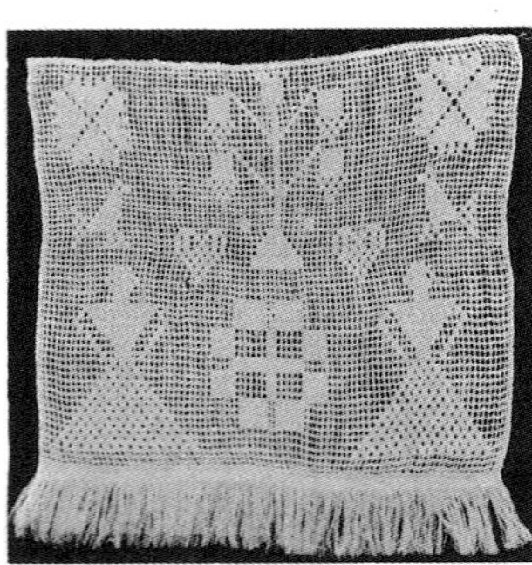

5

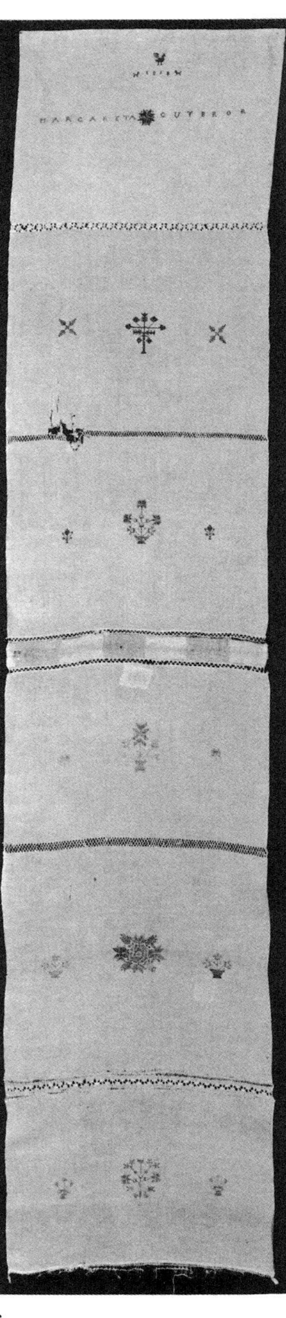

6

4   DECORATED HAND TOWEL
1800–1840

Inscribed: *18G   G75*

Bleached homespun linen ground, 48 warps, 48 wefts per inch. Top panels in plain weave, other panels in pattern of weft-float over 4 warps, alternating with plain weave through 4 warps. Pink and white center band in pattern of face-float weft over linen scrim ground, 24 warps per inch. Crocheted bottom panel whipped to hem, other units joined with herringbone fagoting. Originally a table cover. Plain-weave linen tape hanging loops, inscription in red cotton thread in cross-stitch, and crocheted panel are probably additions. Shown folded.

165.1 x 42 cm (65 x 16½")

Gift of Mrs. William D. Frishmuth. 03-116

5   TOWEL FRAGMENT
1800–1840

Bleached cotton ground, 30 warps, 30 wefts per inch. Drawnwork and darned net of 3 warps, 3 wefts, whipped with linen thread, 7 units per inch. Designs in cotton thread in interlocking woven stitch. Whipped edges. Applied cotton fringe, 40 warps per inch. A decorative panel to be attached to bottom of towel.

40 x 36.2 cm (15¾ x 14¼")

Titus C. Geesey Collection. 55-94-67

6   SHOW TOWEL
1818

Margareta Gutbror

Inscribed: *1818   MARGARETA GUTBROR*

Bleached homespun linen ground in plain weave, 56 warps, 56 wefts per inch. Designs and inscription in red wool thread in cross-stitch over 2 warps, 2 wefts. Drawnwork bandings with wrapped and interlocking stitches in cotton thread. Pink and white middle band in needlework version of huckaback weave, using warp-float face on plain-weave linen, 18 double-thread warps per inch. One selvaged, one hemmed side. Applied fringe.

175.3 x 37.5 cm (69 x 14¾")

Gift of Mrs. William D. Frishmuth. 03-120

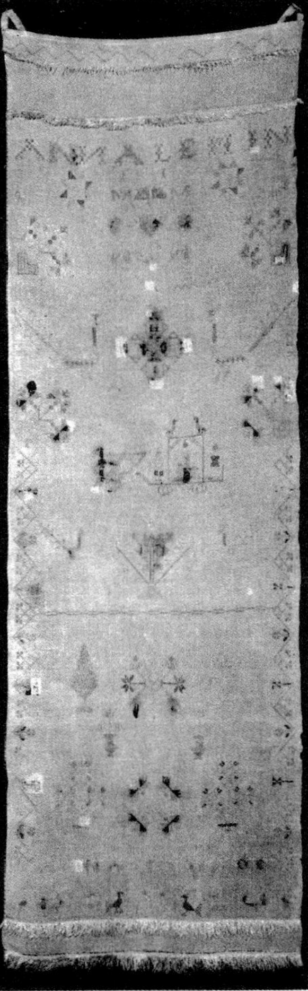

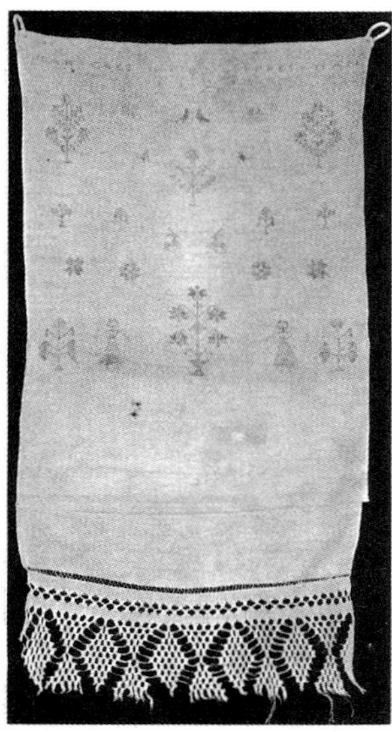

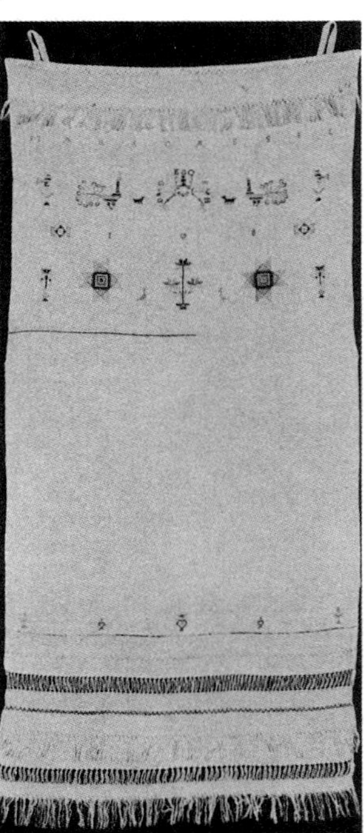

7

7   SHOW TOWEL
1818

Anna Lemin

Inscribed: *ANNA LEMIN 1818 ANNA LEMIEN*

Unbleached homespun linen ground in plain weave, 40 warps, 40 wefts per inch. Designs and inscription in cross-stitch over 3 warps, 3 wefts. Inscription, borders, and large flowers in pink linen thread. Birds and smaller flowers in blue, white, green, and brown silk thread. One selvaged, one hemmed side. Fringed unbleached homespun linen panels, 48 warps per inch, attached top and bottom. Linen twill tape hanging loops. Made in three pieces.

139.1 x 44.1 cm (54¾ x 17⅜")

Gift of J. Stogdell Stokes. 28-16-1

8   DECORATED HAND TOWEL
1827

Margret Kresman

Inscribed: *MAR·GRET·KRES·MAN 1827*

Bleached homespun linen ground in plain weave, 40 warps, 40 wefts per inch. Designs and inscription in single- and two-ply pink cotton thread in cross-stitch over 2 warps, 2 wefts. Bottom panel applied with fagoting in knotted insertion stitch and finished with a band and fringe of drawnwork and needleweaving. Sides hemmed. Cotton cord hanging loops. Made in two pieces. Shown folded.

119.4 x 41.9 cm (47 x 16½")

Titus C. Geesey Collection. 55-94-59

9   DECORATED HAND TOWEL
Norriton, Montgomery County
1828

Mary Cassel

Inscribed: *MARY CASSEL OEHBDDE* [O Edel Herz Bedenk Dein End] *18·28* ("Mary Cassel O noble heart, consider your end 1828")

Bleached homespun linen ground in plain weave, 48 warps, 48 wefts per inch. Black, red, blue, yellow, and tan cotton thread. Designs in cross-stitch over 2 warps, 2 wefts; long-armed cross-stitch over 2 warps, 10 wefts; and hem stitch. Inscription in cross-stitch over 2 warps, 2 wefts. Bandings in cross-stitch, herringbone stitch, and drawnwork. Three cross-stitched bandings unfinished. Bottom panel with drawnwork banding and fringe is applied. One selvaged, one hemmed side. Plain-weave linen tape hanging loops. Made in two pieces. Shown folded.

146 x 42.2 cm (57½ x 16⅝")

Gift of Miss Miriam LeVin. 70-132-3

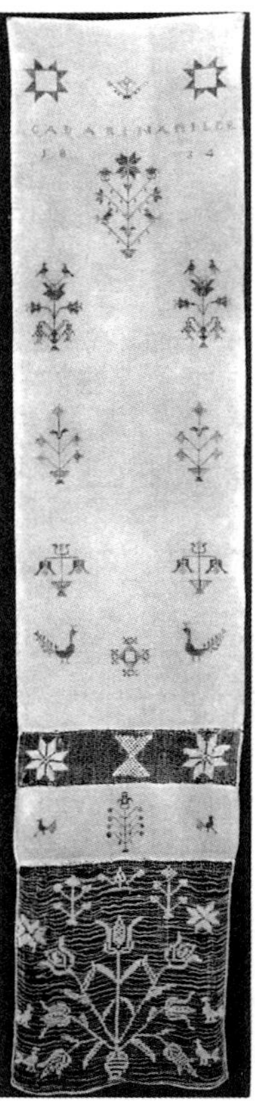

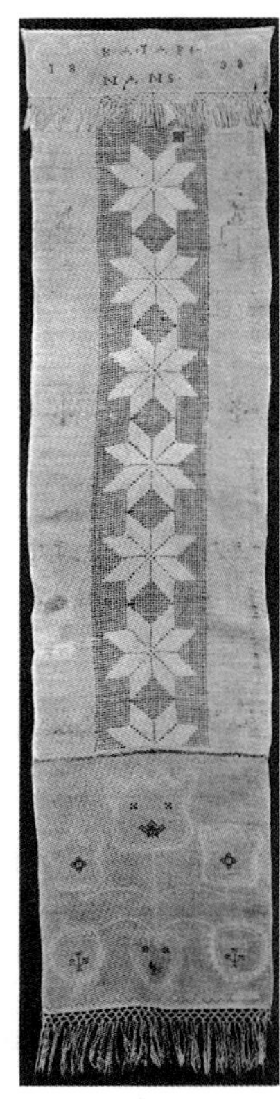

10

11

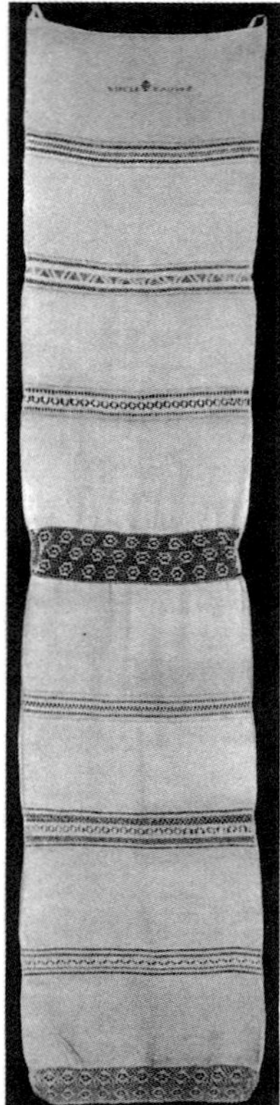

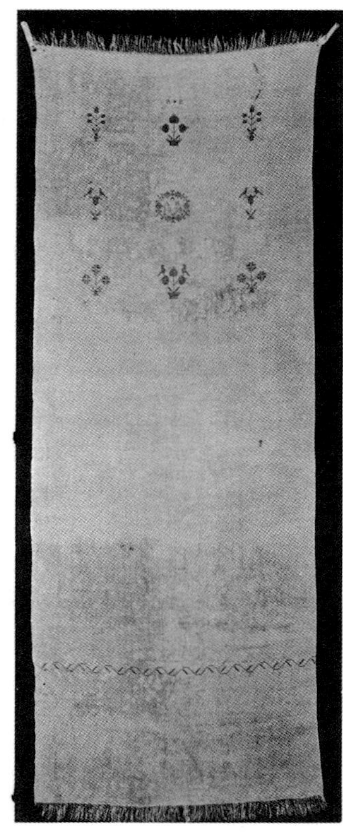

13

12

10 SHOW TOWEL
1834

Cadarina Miler

Inscribed: *CADARINA MILER   1834*

Bleached cotton ground in plain weave, 48 warps, 48 wefts per inch. Designs and inscription in pink cotton thread in cross-stitch over 3 warps, 3 wefts, positioned by a pulled thread. Middle panel of darned net and bottom panel of sewn net have designs in filet darning in two-ply cotton thread. One selvaged side; one side, top hemmed. Made in four pieces.

157.5 x 34.3 cm (62 x 13½")

Titus C. Geesey Collection. 55-94-65

11 SHOW TOWEL
1838

Inscribed: *KA·TA·RI· NA·NS· 1838*

Bleached homespun linen ground in plain weave, 48 warps, 48 wefts per inch in top and bottom panels, 40 warps, 40 wefts per inch in center panel. Drawnwork net of 4 warps, 4 wefts, whipped with linen thread, 8 units per inch. Stars filled in darning stitch; hearts and tulips outlined in buttonhole stitch. Designs and inscription in pink and blue cotton thread in cross-stitch over 3 warps, 3 wefts. Sides hemmed. Knotted cotton fringe applied top and bottom. Made in three pieces.

141.6 x 31.7 cm (55¾ x 12½")

Titus C. Geesey Collection. 55-94-62

12 DECORATED HAND TOWEL
1839

Inscribed: *A·R   AH   1839*

Bleached homespun linen ground in plain weave, 40 warps, 40 wefts per inch. Designs and inscription in red cotton thread in cross-stitch over 2 warps, 2 wefts. One selvaged, one hemmed side. Top and bottom fringe applied with overcast stitch. Plain-weave cotton tape hanging loops. Made in one piece. Stained.

134 x 48.6 cm (52¾ x 19⅛")

Gift of Miss Miriam LeVin. 70-132-2

13 SHOW TOWEL
1840

Inscribed: *18ELI KAU40* [Elizabeth Kauffman]

Bleached homespun linen ground in plain weave, 48 warps, 48 wefts per inch. Drawnwork bandings with wrapped and interlocking stitches. Crocheted lace bandings at center and bottom. Inscription in red cotton thread in cross-stitch over 2 warps, 2 wefts. One selvaged, one hemmed side. Cotton tape hanging loops. Made in three pieces.

163.8 x 37.1 cm (64½ x 14⅝")

Gift of Mrs. William D. Frishmuth. 03-119

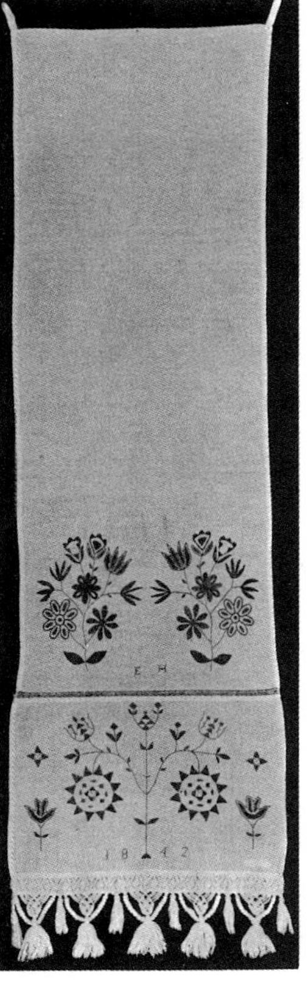

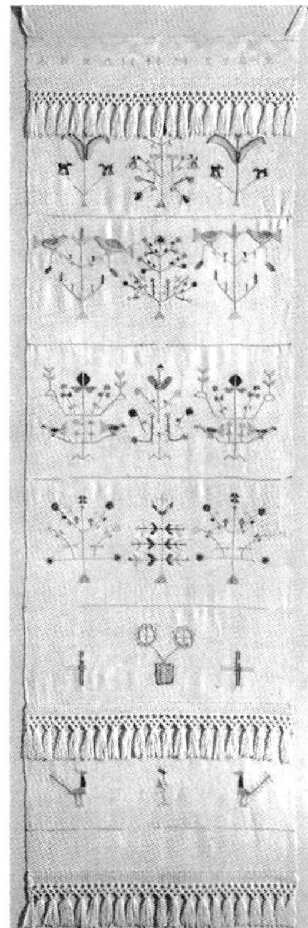

14

15

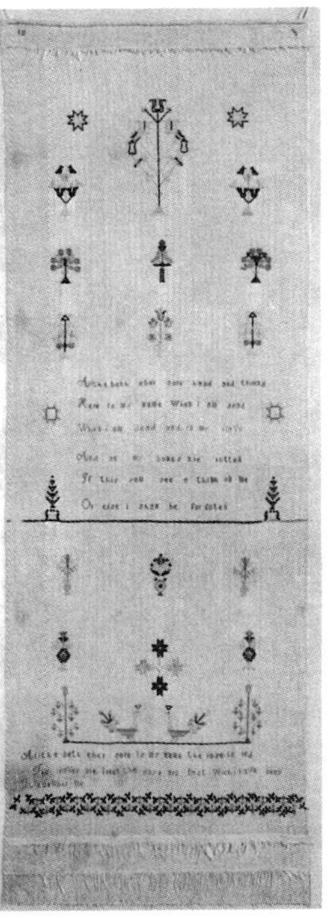

16

14 SHOW TOWEL
Probably Berks County
1842

Inscribed: *EH   1842*

Bleached muslin ground in plain weave, 81 warps, 81 wefts per inch. Designs in red cotton thread outlined in chain stitch, filled with satin stitch; inscription in cross-stitch. Panels joined with needleweaving. Top selvaged, sides hemmed. Knotted cotton fringe on woven tape applied at bottom. Plain-weave cotton tape hanging loops. Made in two pieces.

167.6 x 36.2 cm (66 x 14¼″)

Titus C. Geesey Collection. 55-94-63

15 SHOW TOWEL
1848

Anna Meyer

Inscribed: *ANNA 1848 MEYER*

Bleached homespun linen ground in plain weave, 44 warps, 48 wefts per inch. Peach, yellow, and pink two-ply wool thread. Designs in cross-stitch over 4 warps, 4 wefts, satin stitch, and chain stitch. Inscription in cross-stitch over 4 warps, 4 wefts. Horizontal bands of needleweaving in wool thread through a drawn thread. One selvaged, one hemmed side. Three rows of cotton tape with knotted fringe applied. Herringbone twill cotton tape hanging loops. Made in one piece.

166.4 x 49.5 cm (65½ x 19½″)

Titus C. Geesey Collection. 55-94-66

16 SHOW TOWEL
184[?]

Alithebeth Ebersole

Inscribed: *18 4   Alithebeth ebersole hand and thread   Here is my name When i am dead When i am dead and in my Grave   And all my bones are rotten   If this you see o think on me   Or else i shall be forgoten   Alithebeth ebersole is my name the rose is red   The leaves are Green the days are Past Wich i have seen   Remember me*

Homespun linen ground in plain weave, 40 warps, 32 wefts per inch. Stripes on ground caused by uneven bleaching before weaving. Designs in cross-stitch over 2 warps, 2 wefts, in rust red, blue, yellow, pink, and ivory wool thread. Inscription in two-strand red linen thread in cross-stitch over 2 warps, 2 wefts. Top flap sewn to towel and folded. Two rows of fringe applied at bottom. One selvaged, one hemmed side. Linen tape hanging loops. Made in three pieces.

138.4 x 47.6 cm (54½ x 18¾″)

Titus C. Geesey Collection. 55-94-64

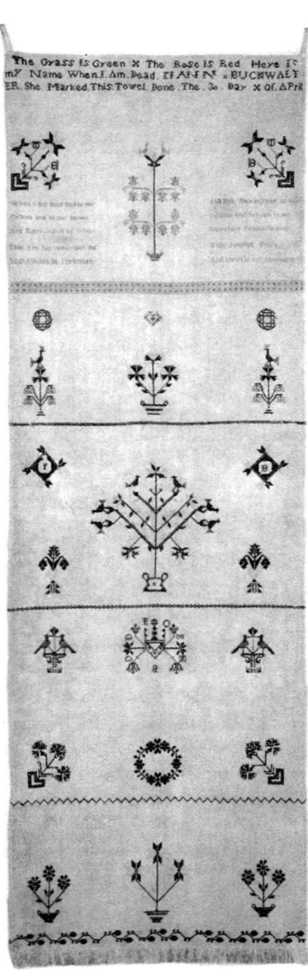

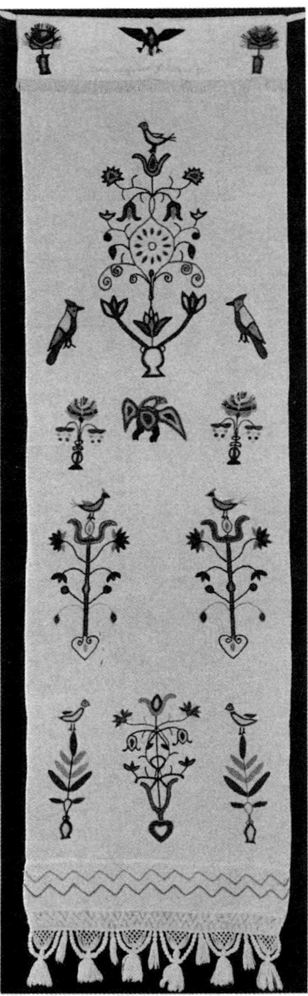

17   18

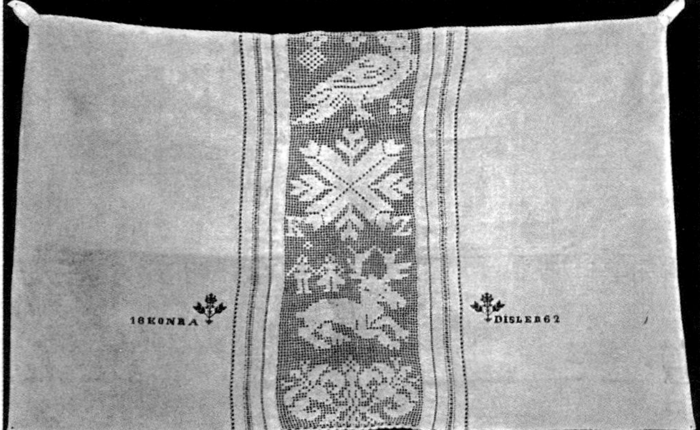

19

17   SHOW TOWEL
1856

Fiann Buckwalter

Inscribed: *The Grass Is Green • The Rose Is Red Here Is   my Name When I Am Dead. FIANN • BUCKWALT   ER. She Marked This Towel Done The 30 Day • Of April   When I am dead and in my   Grave and all my bones Are Rotten AD 1856 When   This you See remember me   Lest I Should Be Forgotten Fiann Buckwalter is my   Name and heaven is my   Salvation Pennsylvania   Is my dwelling Place   And christ is my sustation FB   OEHBDDE* [O Edel Herz Bedenk Dein End] ("O noble heart, consider your end")

Homespun linen ground in plain weave, 48 warps, 48 wefts per inch. Designs and inscription in linen and silk thread in cross-stitch over 2 warps, 2 wefts, and over 3 warps, 3 wefts. Red and green wreath, red birds, blue, yellow, and red flowers. Bottom fringe is whipped extension of warp. Made in one piece.

148.6 x 48.3 cm (58½ x 19")

Gift of J. Stogdell Stokes. 28-10-115

18   SHOW TOWEL
Montgomery County
1860

Sophia Elizabeth G. Witmer

Inscribed: *Sophia Elizabeth G Witmer 1860*

Bleached linen ground in plain weave, 72 warps, 72 wefts per inch. Designs in outline stitch, filled with chain stitch, in red, green, orange, blue, and brown wool thread. Inscription in red cotton thread in running stitch. Top and bottom panels applied with felled seams. One selvaged, one hemmed side. Applied band of cotton net with tied-tassel fringe at bottom. Cotton twill tape hanging loops. Made in three pieces.

161.3 x 43.5 cm (63½ x 17⅛")

Titus C. Geesey Collection. 55-94-60

19   DECORATED HAND TOWEL
1862

Konra Disler

Inscribed: *K Z   18KONRA DISLER62*

Bleached linen ground in plain weave, 48 warps, 48 wefts per inch. Crocheted lace center panel has buttonhole-stitch border. Drawnwork bandings with wrapped and whipped stitches. Inscription in red cotton thread in cross-stitch over 2 warps, 2 wefts. Bottom selvaged, three edges hemmed. Herringbone twill cotton tape hanging loops. Probably originally a table cover.

47 x 77.5 cm (18½ x 30½")

Gift of Mrs. William D. Frishmuth. 03-121

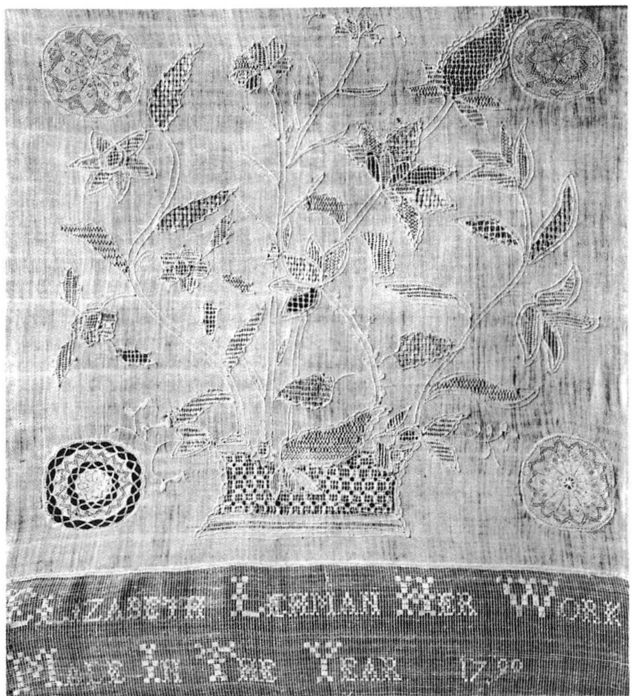

1 detail

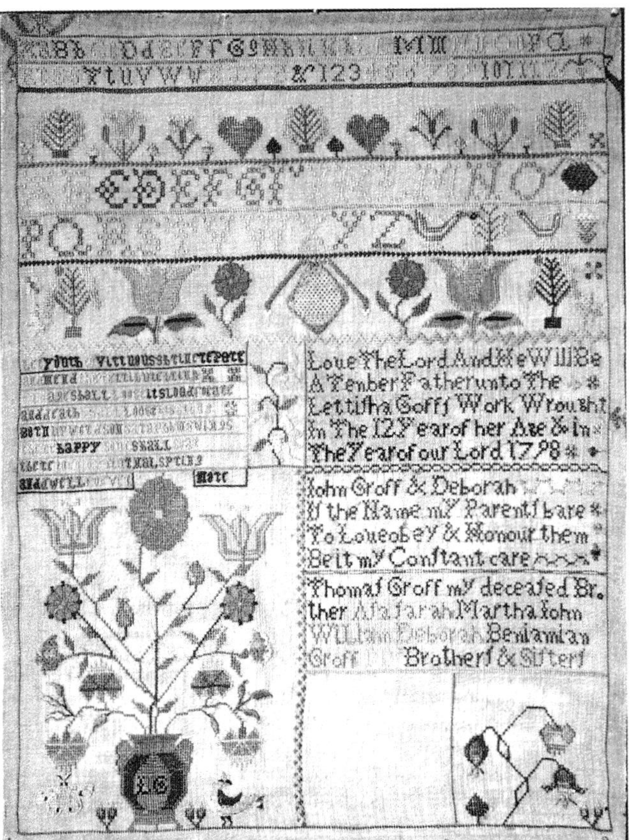

2

1 SAMPLER

1790

Elizabeth Lehman

Inscribed: *Elizabeth Lehman Her Work Made In The Year 1790*

Linen lawn ground, 108 warps, 62 wefts per inch. Designs in deflected element and open white work, outlined in chain stitch. Inscription in filet darning on gauze. Holly-point rondels in corners. Hemmed and sewn to linen band.

50.2 x 45.4 cm (19¾ x 17⅞″)

Gift of Miss Elizabeth Schaffer. 91-13

2 SAMPLER

Lancaster County

1798

Lettisha Groff

Inscribed: *Let youth to virtuous shrine repare   and mend there tribute bring ·· old age shall loose its load forare   and death shall loose its sting · Both upwards on saraphims wings   there happy soul shall soar   there to enjoy eternal spring   and dwell forever more   Love The Lord And He Will Be   A Tenber Father unto Thee · Lettisha Goffs Work Wrought   In The 12 Year of her Age & in · The Year of our Lord 1798 ·· John Groff & Deborah   Is the Name my Parents bare · To Love obey & Honour them · Be it my Constant care · Thomas Groff my deceased Bro   ther Asa Sarah Martha John   Wiliam Deborah Benjamian   Groff My Brothers & Sisters*

Unbleached homespun linen scrim ground, 32 warps, 32 wefts per inch. Gold yellow, blue, red, green, blue green, brown, and ivory silk thread. Lettering in cross-stitch over 2 warps, 2 wefts, and over 1 warp, 1 weft, and eyelet stitch. Bird and some foliage in satin stitch outlined with stem stitch. Flowers in tent, star, and rococo stitches. Bandings in buttonhole insertion and laced herringbone stitches. Unfinished.

52.7 x 40.6 cm (20¾ x 16″)

Titus C. Geesey Collection. 54-85-10

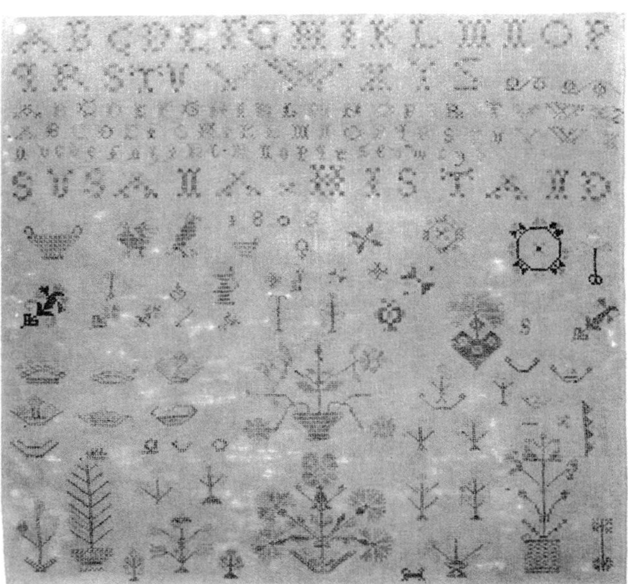

3

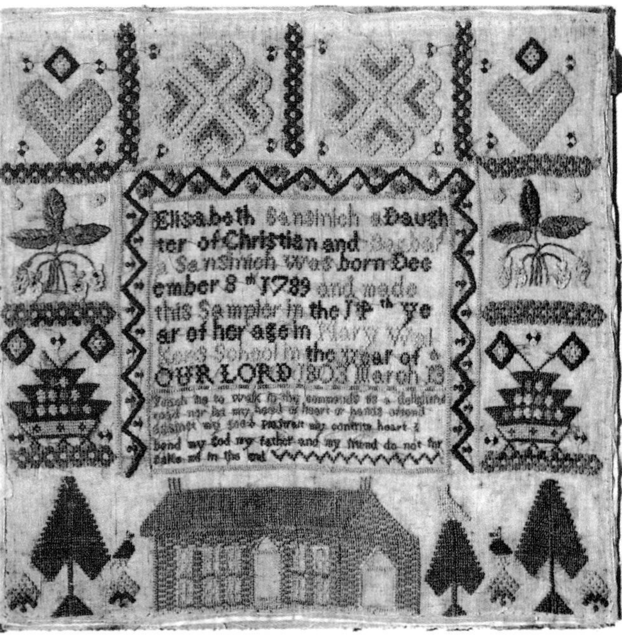

4

3 SAMPLER

1803

Susana Histand

Inscribed: *SUSANA · HISTAND   1803*

Unbleached cotton scrim ground, 32 warps, 32 wefts per inch. Designs and lettering in pink and blue cotton thread in cross-stitch over 2 warps, 2 wefts.

48.6 x 51.7 cm (19⅛ x 20⅜")

The Whitman Sampler Collection. Gift of Pet Incorporated. 69-288-198

4 SAMPLER

Lancaster County

1803

Elisabeth Sansinich

Inscribed: *Elisabeth Sansinich ·Daugh   ter of Christian and Barbar   a Sansinich was born Dec   ember 8ᵗʰ 1789 and made   this Sampler in the 14ᵗʰ ye   ar of her age in Mary Wal   kers School in the year of · OUR LORD 1803 March 13   Teach me to walk in thy commands as a delightful   road nor let my head or heart or hands offend   against my God. prostrait my contrite heart I   bend my God my father and my friend do not for   sake me in the end*

Linen scrim ground, 44 warps, 36 wefts per inch. Silk thread. Blue green trees, brick red building with windows and doors outlined in tan (Lancaster Alms House), and blue, tan, green, and brown inscription in cross-stitch over 2 warps, 2 wefts. Tan banding in cross-stitch over 2 warps, 4 wefts. Rococo stitch on rose and peach, tan and gold hearts; blue and gold, mauve and tan diamond motifs and flags. Green leaves in satin stitch, stems in chain stitch. Made at Mary Walker's school.

32.1 x 32.4 cm (12⅝ x 12¾")

The Whitman Sampler Collection. Gift of Pet Incorporated. 69-288-290

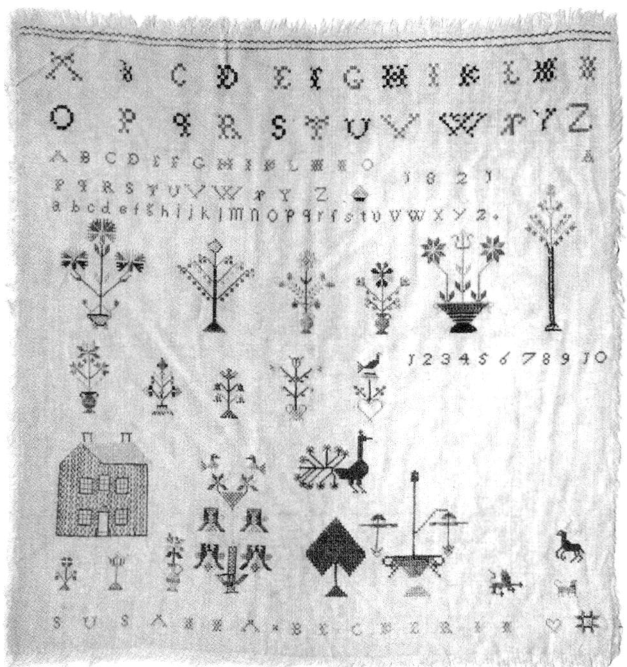

5

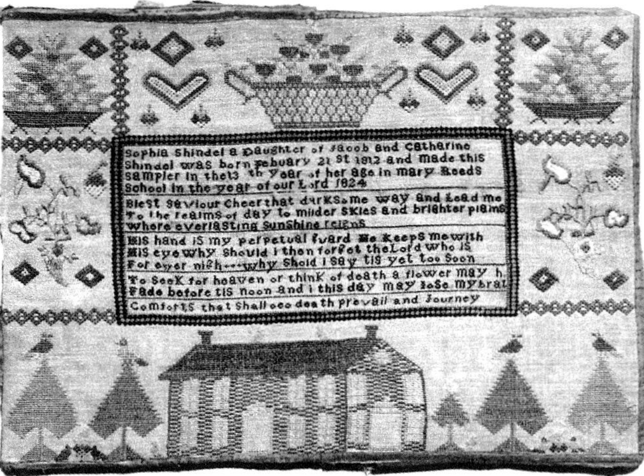

6

5 SAMPLER

1821

Susanna Beckerin

Inscribed: *1821   SUSANNA · BECKERIN*

Bleached homespun linen ground in plain weave, 48 warps, 44 wefts per inch. Two-ply linen and cotton thread. Designs and lettering in cross-stitch over 2 warps, 2 wefts; basket in cross-stitch over 3 warps, 3 wefts. Red and blue banding in long-legged cross-stitch. Blue tree and peacock; red house with blue trim, white roof; red and brown lettering. Flowers and detailing in white, blue green, and yellow silk thread. Unfinished.

43.8 x 39.7 cm (17¼ x 15⅝")

The Whitman Sampler Collection. Gift of Pet Incorporated. 69-288-296

6 SAMPLER

Lancaster County

1824

Sophia Shindel

Inscribed: *Sophia Shindel a Daughter of Jacob and Catharine   Shindel was born Febuary 21st 1812 and made this   sampler in the 13th year of her age in Mary Reeds   School in the year of our Lord 1824   Blest Saviour cheer that darksome way and Lead me   To the realms of day to milder skies and brighter plains   Where everlasting sunshine reigns His hand is my perpetual guard He keeps me with   His eye why should i then forget the Lord who is   For ever nigh · · · why shold i say tis yet too soon   To seek for heaven or think of death a flower may   Fade before tis noon and I this day may lose my brath Comforts that shall · · · death prevail and Journey*

Linen scrim ground, 29 warps, 34 wefts per inch. Silk thread. Green and blue trees, brick red building with doors and windows outlined in blue (Lancaster Alms House), and blue and pink birds and baskets in cross-stitch over 2 warps, 2 wefts. Blue, green, and rose hearts, diamonds, and banding, and black inscription in cross-stitch over 1 warp, 1 weft. Black and pink banding around inscription in rococo stitch. Made at Mary Reed's school.

32.1 x 46 cm (12⅝ x 18⅛")

The Whitman Sampler Collection. Gift of Pet Incorporated. 69-288-301

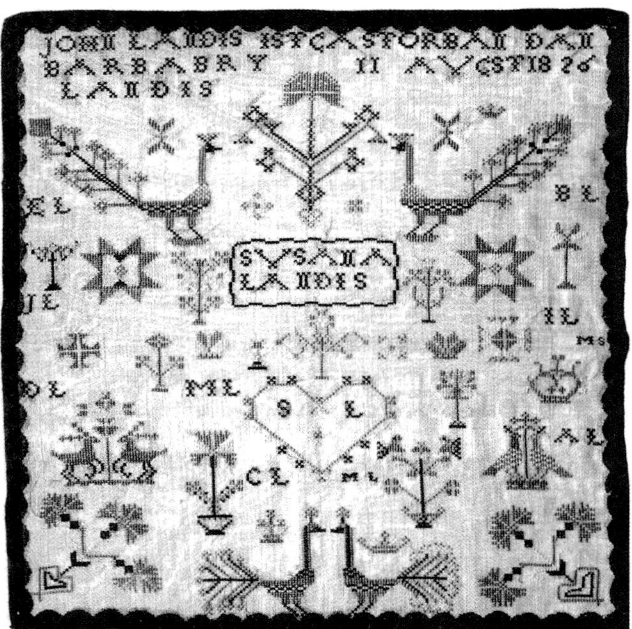

7

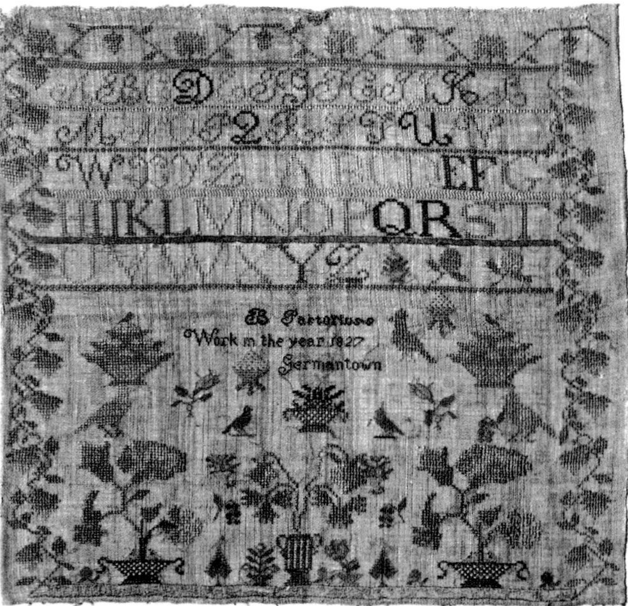

8

7 SAMPLER
Montgomery County
1826–30

Susana Landis

Inscribed: *JOHN LANDIS IST GASTORBAN DAN 11 AUGST 1826   BARBABRY LANDIS   SUSANA LANDIS* ("John Landis is dead on 11 August 1826. Barbara Landis. Susana Landis")

Linen scrim ground, 24 warps, 24 wefts per inch. Designs in red, green, blue, and white silk thread, and lettering in black cotton thread, in cross-stitch over 2 warps, 2 wefts. Scalloped border in satin stitch in black cotton thread. Bound with black satin.

45.7 x 45.7 cm (18 x 18″)

The Whitman Sampler Collection. Gift of Pet Incorporated. 69-288-81

8 SAMPLER
Germantown, Philadelphia County
1827

B. Pastorius

Inscribed: *B Pastoriuss   Work in the year 1827   Germantown*

Unbleached linen scrim ground, 24 warps, 24 wefts per inch. Silk thread. Pink, blue, green, and yellow designs and lettering in cross-stitch over 2 warps, 2 wefts, and over 1 warp, 1 weft, and rococo stitch. Brown inscription in cross-stitch over 2 warps, 2 wefts. Bandings (from top) in long-armed cross-stitch in pink; eyelet stitch in pink; rococo stitch in green; ladder stitch in blue; satin stitch in purple; crosslet stitch in gray; satin stitch in green.

42.2 x 43.8 cm (16⅝ x 17¼″)

The Whitman Sampler Collection. Gift of Pet Incorporated. 69-288-67

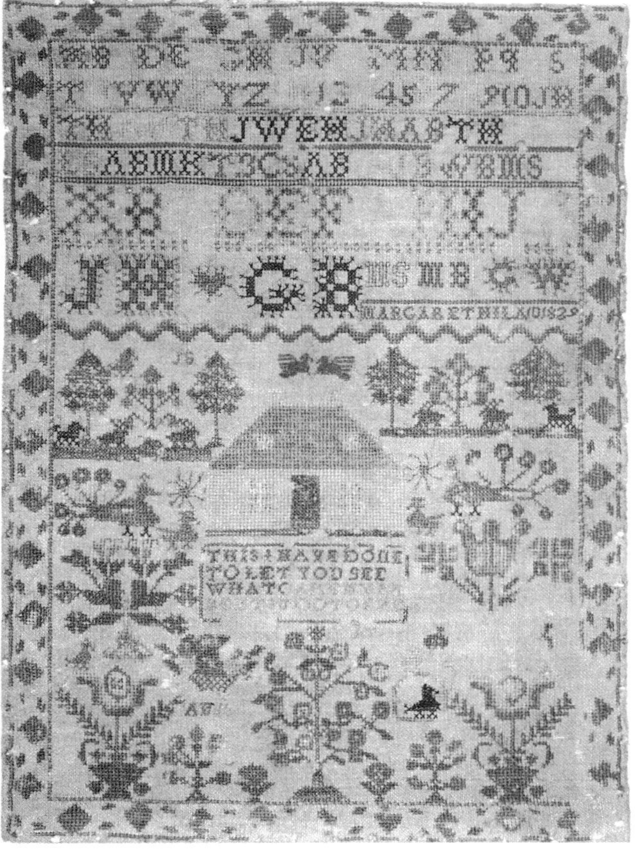

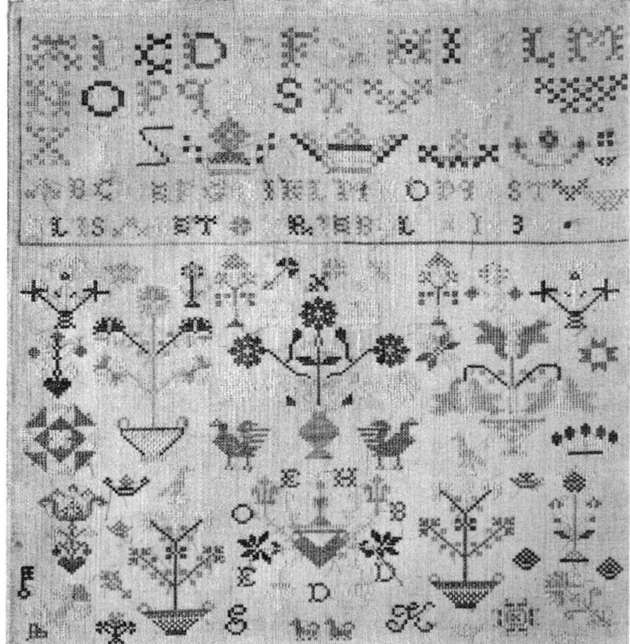

9 SAMPLER

1829

Margaret Hiland

Inscribed: *MARGARET HILAND 1829   THIS I HAVE DONE   TO LET YOU SEE   WHAT CARE MY PA   RENTS TOOT OF ME*

Homespun linen scrim ground, 24 warps, 24 wefts per inch. Designs and lettering in cross-stitch. House in yellow and blue silk thread; foliage and flowers in green and red cotton thread. Some lettering and designs in black wool thread.

43.8 x 32.4 cm (17¼ x 12¾")

The Whitman Sampler Collection. Gift of Pet Incorporated. 69-288-76

10 SAMPLER

Montgomery County

1830

Elisabeth Kriebel

Inscribed: *ELISABET · KRIEBEL · 1830 · OEHBDDE* [O Edel Herz Bedenk Dein End] ("O noble heart, consider your end")

Linen scrim ground, 16 warps, 16 wefts per inch. Designs and lettering in cross-stitch over 2 warps, 2 wefts, in blue, green, red, yellow, black, and brown silk thread.

56.2 x 56.2 cm (22⅛ x 22⅛")

Gift of J. Stogdell Stokes. 28-10-92

11 SAMPLER

Montgomery County

1830–50

Unbleached homespun linen scrim ground, 32 warps, 32 wefts per inch. Designs in cross-stitch in wool thread. Red houses with blue roofs; red, yellow, pink, orange, and lavender flowers; red and yellow baskets. Border vine is green and yellow green with crablike flowers in red, orange, and green. Sewn to finely woven linen, probably for fastening to embroidery frame. Unfinished.

43.5 x 44.5 cm (17⅛ x 17½")

Gift of J. Stogdell Stokes. 28-79-1

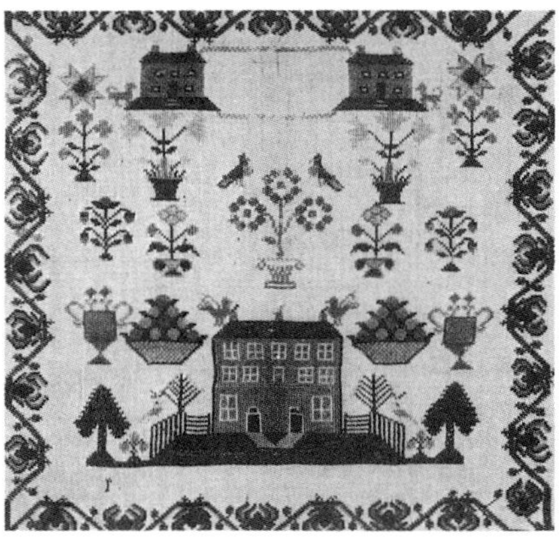

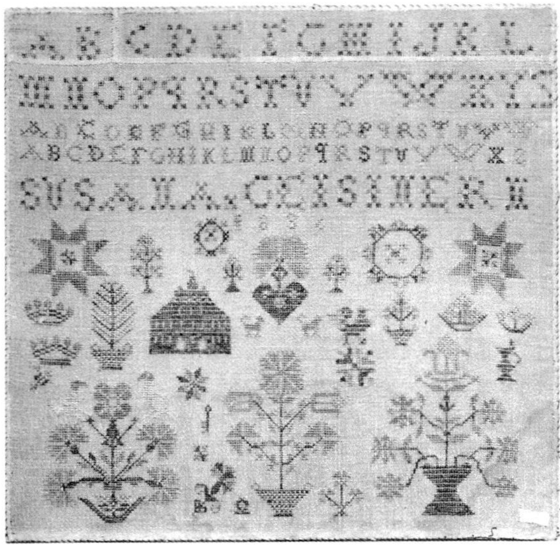

12

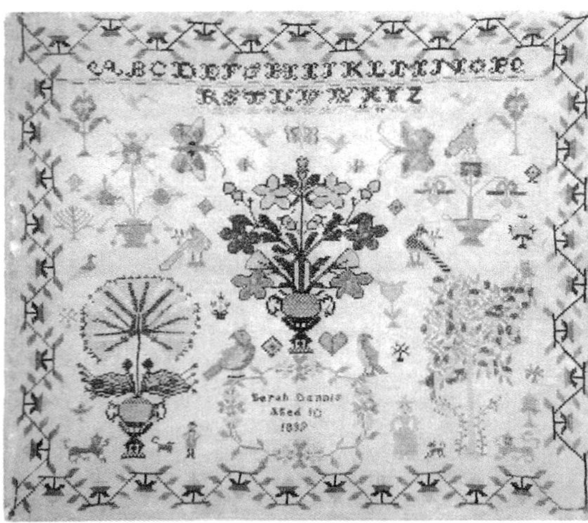

13

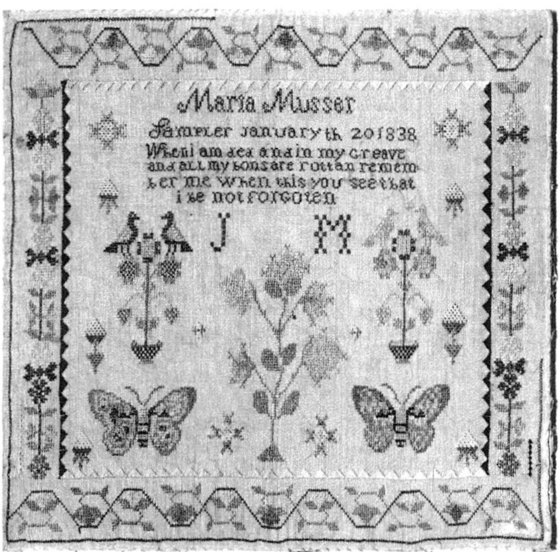

14

12   SAMPLER
1836

Susana Geisiner

Inscribed: *SUSANA · GEISINERN   1836*

Unbleached homespun linen scrim ground, 24 warps, 24 wefts per inch. Designs and lettering in pink red and blue cotton thread in cross-stitch over 2 warps, 2 wefts, and eyelet stitch. Ground pieced at top.

47 x 50.2 cm (18½ x 19¾")

The Whitman Sampler Collection. Gift of Pet Incorporated. 69-288-197

13   SAMPLER
Pennsburg, Montgomery County
1837

Sarah Dennis

Inscribed: *Sarah Dennis   Aged 10   1837*

Loosely woven bleached linen ground in plain weave, 28 warps, 28 wefts per inch. Designs and lettering in cross-stitch in yellow green, blue, pink, gold yellow, and red wool thread.

43.2 x 49.5 cm (17 x 19½")

The Whitman Sampler Collection. Gift of Pet Incorporated. 69-288-82

14   SAMPLER
Lancaster County
1838

Maria Musser

Inscribed: *Maria Musser   Sampler January th 20 1838   When i am ded and in my Greave and all my bons are rottan remem: ber me when this you see that   i be not forgoten J M*

Bleached homespun linen scrim ground, 33 warps, 24 wefts per inch. Designs in cross-stitch over 2 warps, 2 wefts, and rococo stitch, in yellow, blue green, blue, and tan linen and silk thread. Brown inscription in cross-stitch. Sawtooth border in satin stitch in blue and yellow silk thread. Unfinished.

44.5 x 45.4 cm (17½ x 17⅞")

The Whitman Sampler Collection. Gift of Pet Incorporated. 69-288-215

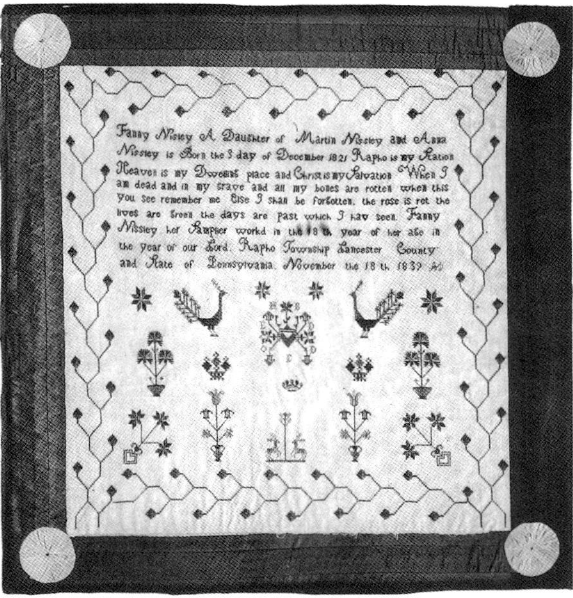

15

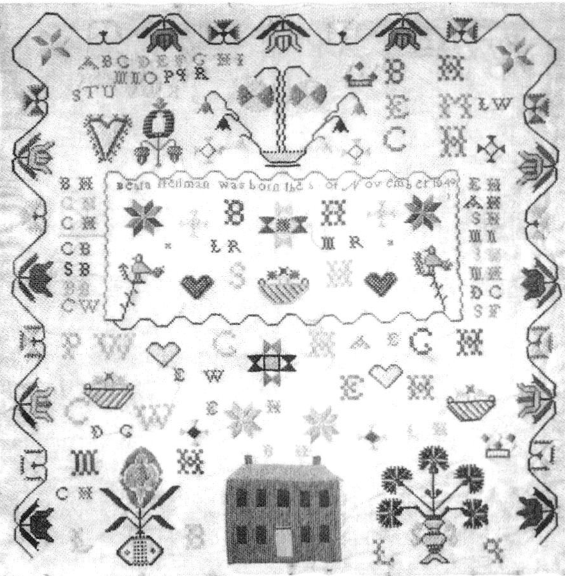

17

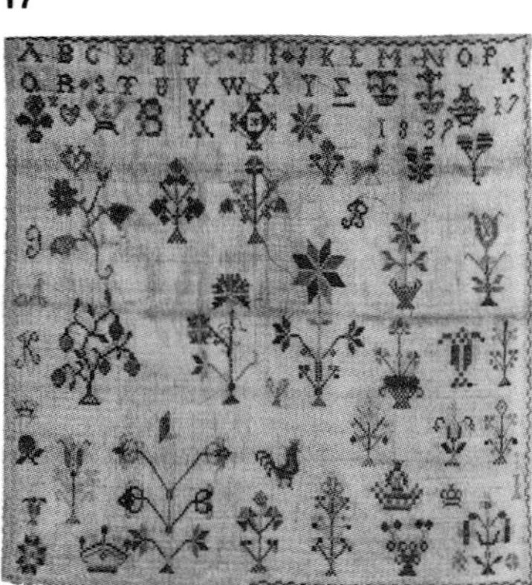

16

15 SAMPLER

Rapho Township, Lancaster County
1839

Fanny Nissley

Inscribed: *Fanny Nisley A Daughter of Martin Nissley and Anna   Nissley is Born the 3 day of December 1821 Rapho is my Station   Heaven is my Dwelling place and Christ is my Salvation When I   am dead and in my grave and all my bones are rotten when this   you see remember me Else I shall be forgotten. the rose is ret the   lives are green the days are past which I hav seen. Fanny   Nissley her Samplier worked in the 18th year of her age in   the year of our Lord. Rapho Township Lancester County   and State of Pennsylvania. November the 18th 1839 AD   OEHBDDE* [O Edel Herz Bedenk Dein End] ("O noble heart, consider your end")

Bleached homespun linen ground in plain weave, 64 warps, 64 wefts per inch. Red and blue designs and green inscription in cotton thread in cross-stitch over 2 warps, 2 wefts. Border of red over green silk ribbons; round pink ruffles in corners.

55.9 x 53.3 cm (22 x 21")

The Whitman Sampler Collection. Gift of Pet Incorporated. 69-288-145

16 SAMPLER

1839

Inscribed: *BK 1839*

Unbleached homespun linen scrim ground, 26 warps, 26 wefts per inch. Designs and lettering in cross-stitch in green, blue, tan, gold yellow, pink, and red two-ply Z-twist linen and silk thread. Unfinished.

45.7 x 46.4 cm (18 x 18¼")

36-16-1

17 SAMPLER

1850–55

Beata Heilman

Inscribed: *Beata Heilman was born the 6 of November 1840*

Double-thread linen (penelope) scrim ground. Designs and lettering in cross-stitch over one unit (2 warps, 2 wefts) in wool thread. Red house with blue roof; red, yellow, and green flowers. Lettering is brown, white, orange, red, yellow, and blue.

64.1 x 64.1 cm (25¼ x 25¼")

The Whitman Sampler Collection. Gift of Pet Incorporated. 69-288-318

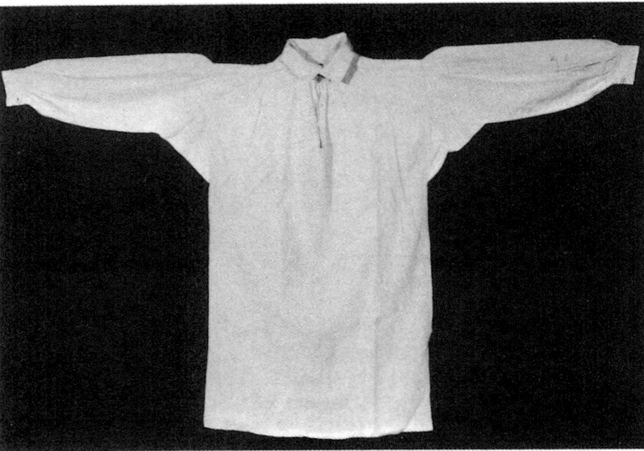

1

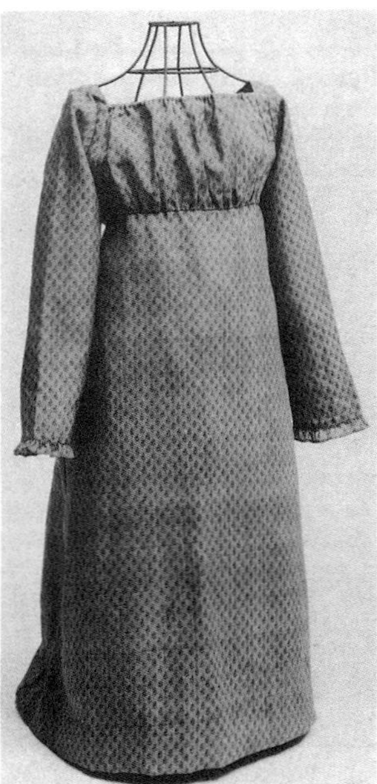

2

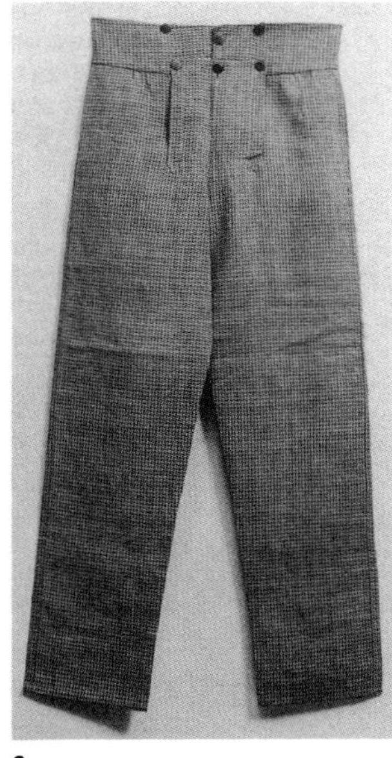

3

1 SHIRT
Germantown, Philadelphia County
1800–1830

Bleached homespun linen in plain weave,
50 warps, 50 wefts per inch. Cuffs have
drawnwork banding and picot ("mice-teeth")
edges. Handmade linen thread buttons at
neck, cuffs, and buttonholes. Front edge of
collar trimmed with knotted running stitch.
Underarm gussets and divided tails at side
seams. Felled seams, rolled hem edges;
bottom is selvage. Worn by Joseph Benner,
Germantown.

Length from back of neck to hem 97.8 cm
(38½″), width at shoulders 54 cm (21¼″)

Gift of Mrs. Eleanor Benner Zall. 62-127-1

2 DRESS
Lancaster County
1820–40

Wool in plain weave, 56 warps, 56 wefts per
inch. Madder red with stamped or printed
black geometric design. Calendered finish.
Loom width 55.9 cm. Selvage has an
unbleached Z-twist linen paired warp. Sleeve
casing and bodice back lined with homespun
linen. Overcast seams, hemmed edges. Plain-
and twill-weave tapes.

Length from shoulder to hem 95.9 cm (37¾″)
Width at shoulders 26 cm (10¼″)

Titus C. Geesey Collection. 55-94-69

3 BROADFALL TROUSERS
1830–40

Four brass buttons marked on reverse: *RICH
GILT COLOR* [with stamped vine and flower
border]; *PLATED* [with abstract leaf design
with concentric circles]; *GILT; WARRANTED
FINE GOLD SURFACE*

Homespun linen in plain weave, 37 warps, 33
wefts per inch. Pattern of four orange tan, four
unbleached warps, repeated in wefts. Felled
seams, whipped raw edges. Buttonholes edged
in buttonhole stitch in unbleached linen
thread. One pewter, eight cast-brass buttons.
Four marked, four unmarked brass buttons.
Pewter button unmarked but has raised mold
line across reverse.

Length 118.7 cm (46¾″), waist 91.4 cm (36″)

Titus C. Geesey Collection. 55-94-68

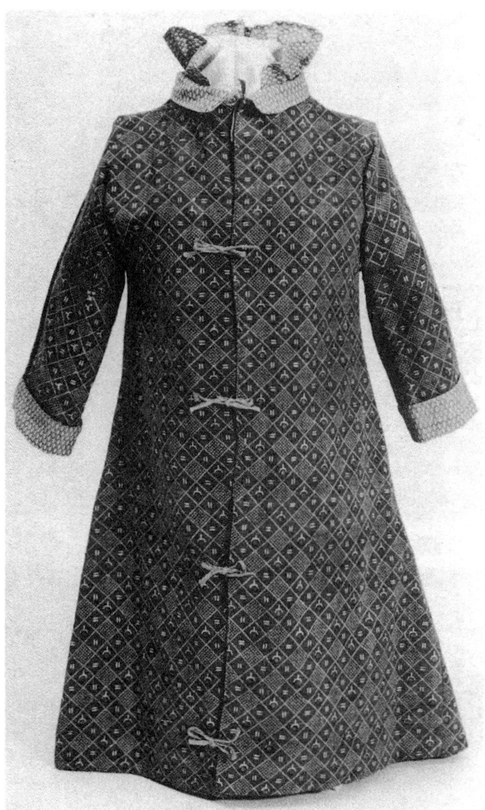

4

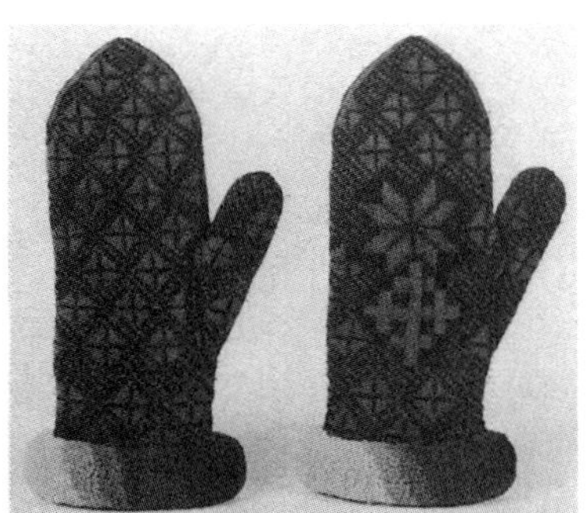

5

4 SMOCK
Lancaster County
1840–80

Reverse (shown): cotton in plain weave, 48 warps, 48 wefts per inch. Resist-dyed blue with stamped red flowers. Obverse: cotton in plain weave, 64 warps, 64 wefts per inch. Roller-printed madder red on unbleached cotton. A girl's reversible garment worn over a dress or jumper. Tied in back. Front fitted by drawing tape set in casing. Handsewn.

Length from back of neck to hem 71.1 cm (28″) Width at shoulders 30.5 cm (12″)

Titus C. Geesey Collection. 55-94-70

5 MITTENS
Low Hill, Lehigh County
1850–70

Wool. Knitted on four needles, 16 stitches, 14 rows per inch. Double thickness. Red and black pattern colors are carried on reverse. Wristband (1.9 cm wide) in garter stitch in red; brown, red, pink, and yellow "plush" cuff is stitched in Turkey work through each row of wristband. Inside of mitten is reinforced with intersecting herringbonelike loops in red wool. Usually worn over gloves.

27.9 x 9.5 cm (11 x 3¾″)

Gift of Dr. John Joseph Stoudt. 64-121-1a,b

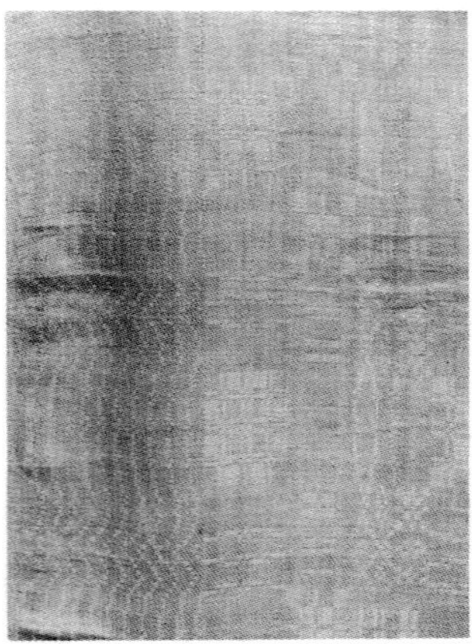

1 detail

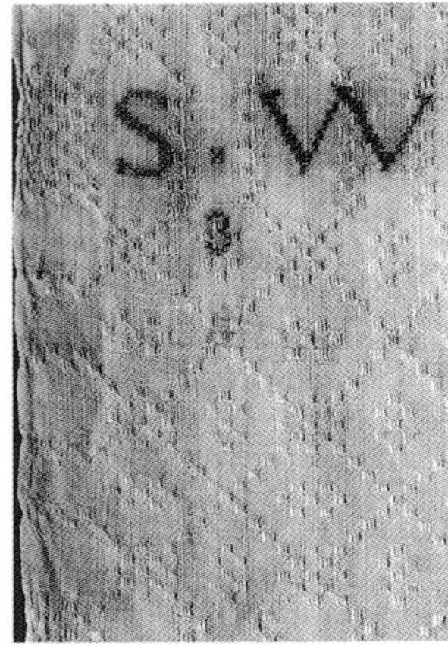

2 detail

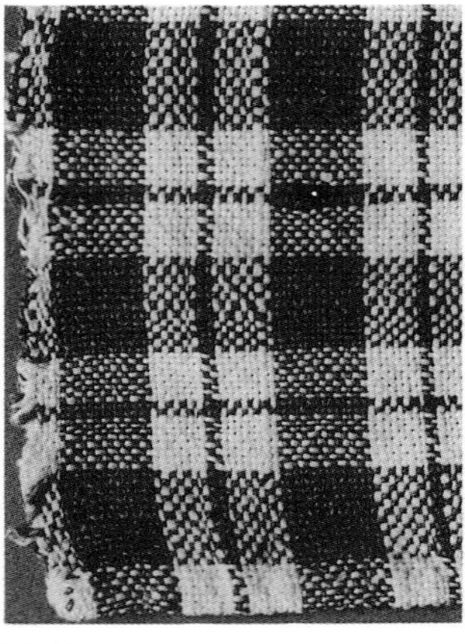

3 detail

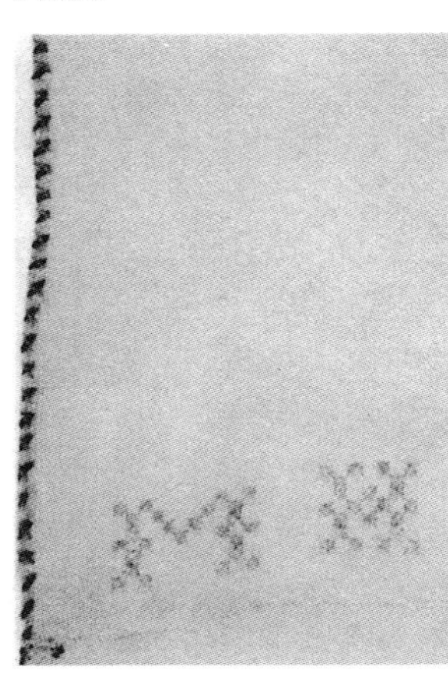

4 detail

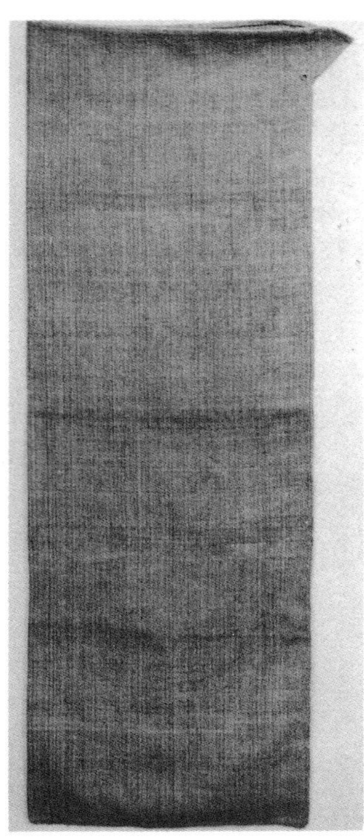

5

1 TABLECLOTH
1780–1820

Linen damask in warp-faced twill weave, 48 warps, 36 wefts per inch. Side border pattern of wavy lines. Center pattern of blocks within intersecting circles. Two loom widths, each 76.2 cm, whipped together.

130.8 x 152.4 cm (51½ x 60″)

Gift of Mr. and Mrs. George B. Emeny. 68-11-4

2 TABLECLOTH
1790–1810

Inscribed: *S · W   3*

Bleached linen in plain weave, 48 warps, 48 wefts per inch. Pattern of warp-float face with 3 warps over 7 wefts in diagonals and blocks. Two loom widths, each 85.1 cm, whipped together. Inscribed in cross-stitch in brown cotton thread.

174.9 x 170.1 cm (68⅞ x 67″)

Gift of Mrs. Rudolph Blankenburg. 19-541

3 SHEET
1800–1850

Homespun linen in plain weave, 40 warps, 40 wefts per inch. Pattern of fourteen blue, eight white, two blue, eight white warps, repeated in wefts. Two loom widths, each 100.3 cm, sewn together.

206.4 x 200 cm (81¼ x 78¾″)

Gift of Mrs. J. Truman Swing. 65-124-2

4 BLANKETS (2)
Berks County
1800–1880

Inscribed: *M H*

Single-ply natural wool in plain weave, 24 warps, 24 wefts per inch. Two loom widths, each 84 cm, whipped together. Top and bottom whipped with blue and pink wool thread in cross-stitch. Inscription in pink wool thread in cross-stitch.

190.5 x 168 cm (75 x 66⅛″) (each)

Gift of Miss Marie E. Bucher, in memory of Mrs. William Hipple and Mrs. David H. Bucher. 39-35-3,4

5 GUNNYSACK
1840–80

Unbleached tow linen and jute in plain weave, 24 tow linen warps, 16 jute wefts per inch. One loom width, 104.1 cm, sewn in felled seams bottom and side. Bias-cut pouring gusset set in at top. Two jute-bound grommets for top closing strings. Probably a grain sack.

139.7 x 51.4 cm (55 x 20¼″)

Gift of Miss Frances Lichten. 60-91-5

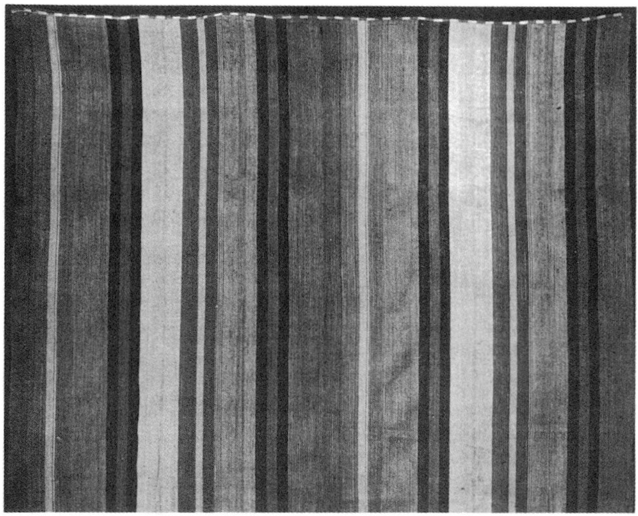

1 detail

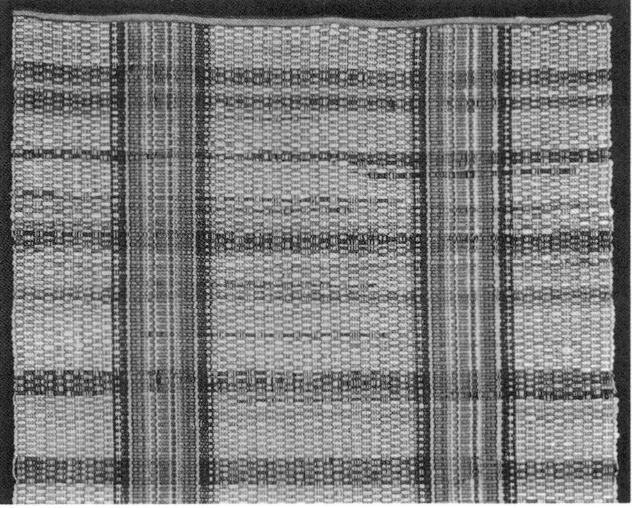

2 detail

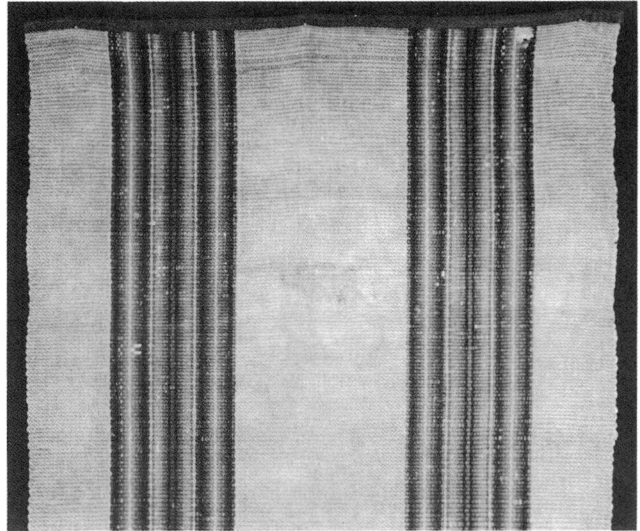

3 detail

1 STRIP CARPETS (2)
Delaware Township, Pike County
1835–50

Abraham B. Decker

Wool in warp-faced weave, 10 warps, 9 wefts per inch. Randomly striped two-ply wool-twist warps in tan, blue green, yellow, indigo blue, and rose; single-ply brown wool wefts. Two selvages, one with a blue warp thread 1.5 cm from edge. Bound top and bottom with piece of same weave. Shown: Two loom widths, each 94.9 cm, whipped together.

495 x 189.9 cm (194⅞ x 74¾")
396.6 x 94.9 cm (156⅛ x 37⅜") (not shown)

Gift of Miss Kate Decker Blair. 36-21-1a,b

2 STRIP CARPET
1850–1900

Wool, cotton, and linen in warp-faced weave, 16 four-ply wool warps, 6 linen and cotton rag wefts per inch. Warp pattern from either selvage: tan alternating with white; gray, white, two tones of green, gold yellow, and magenta to brick red stripes; green and red center stripe. Pattern reverses toward center of carpet. Randomly striped white, red, blue, black, and blue-on-white wefts. Bound with twill tape top and bottom.

496.9 x 91.4 cm (195⅝ x 36")

Purchased. 1976-253-1

3 STRIP CARPET
1850–1900

Wool and cotton in warp-faced weave, 16 cotton and wool warps, 6 rolled cotton rag wefts per inch. Warp pattern from either selvage: unbleached cotton; stripes of gray, red, orange, pink, natural, pink, orange, red, purple, gray, natural, orange, yellow, yellow green, green, and blue green wool; and gray wool center stripe. Pattern reverses toward center of carpet. Rolled rag wefts are unbleached cotton in twill and plain weaves. Bound with twill tape top and bottom.

385.4 x 88.9 cm (151¾ x 35")

Gift of Mrs. John Drayton. 1977-233-1

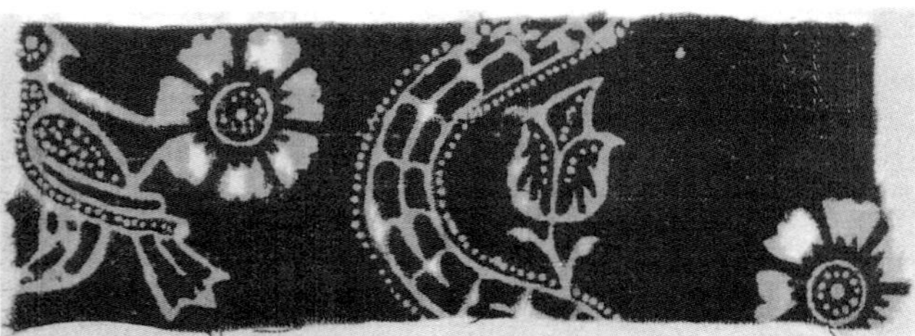

1

1 YARDAGE
Berks County
1780–1800

Unbleached homespun linen in plain weave, 42 warps, 40 wefts per inch. Resist-dyed with indigo (blue). Losses in undyed areas.

8.3 x 24.1 cm (3¼ x 9½")

Gift of I. Heyl Raser. 87-39

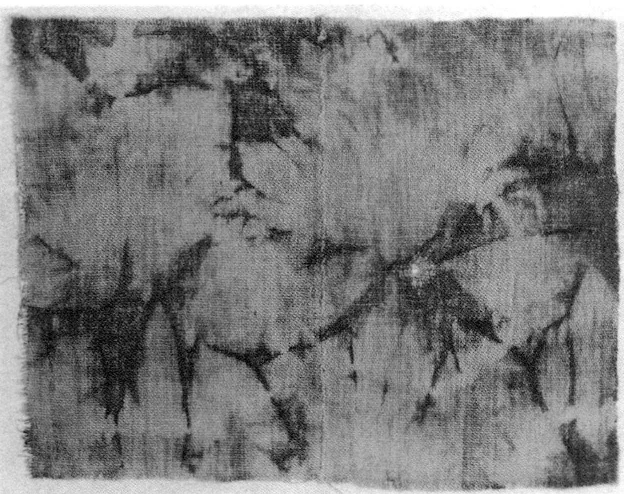

2

2 YARDAGE
Bucks County
1780–1800

Unbleached cotton in plain weave, 40 warps, 32 wefts per inch. Resist-dyed with indigo (blue). Two pieces whipped together.

20.3 x 25.4 cm (8 x 10")

Gift of I. Heyl Raser. 87-40

3 YARDAGE
1800–1850

Homespun linen in plain weave, 40 warps, 40 wefts per inch. Pattern of four blue, eight unbleached warps, repeated in wefts. One selvaged, one hemmed side.

193.7 x 50.2 cm (76¼ x 19¾")

Titus C. Geesey Collection. 58-110-38b

4 YARDAGE (2)
1800–1850

Homespun linen in plain weave, 40 warps, 40 wefts per inch. Square plaid pattern of four indigo blue, eight brown, two white, eight brown, four indigo blue, six white warps, repeated in wefts. Loom width 99 cm.

75.6 x 198.1 cm (29¾ x 78")
173.4 x 47.6 cm (68¼ x 18¾")

Titus C. Geesey Collection. 55-94-71;
69-284-33

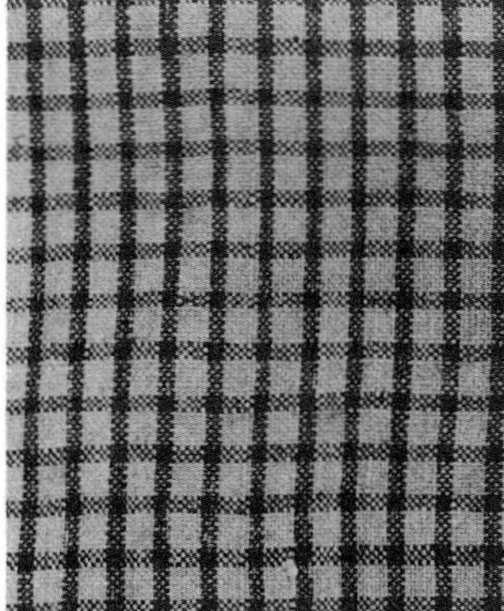

3 detail

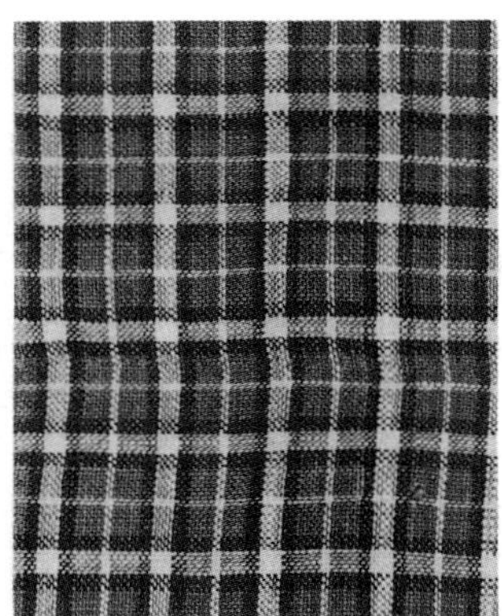

4 detail

5 YARDAGE
1800–1850

Homespun linen in plain weave, 40 warps, 40 wefts per inch. Pattern of four blue, two white, four blue, ten white, two blue, ten white warps, repeated in wefts.

167.6 x 48.9 cm (66 x 19¼")

Titus C. Geesey Collection. 58-110-38d

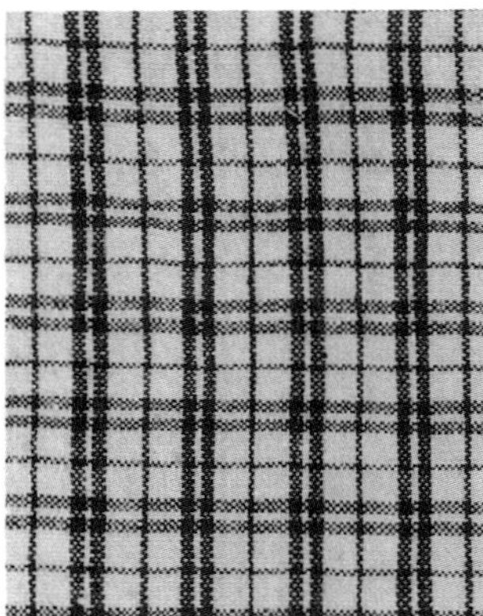

5 detail

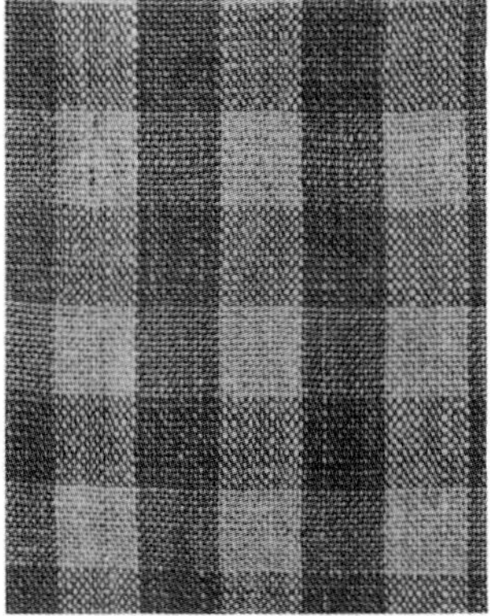

6 detail

6 YARDAGE
1800–1850

Linen in plain weave, 37 warps, 27 wefts per inch. Pattern of 20 brown, 20 unbleached warps, 18 brown, 18 unbleached wefts. Loom width 94 cm. Two selvages.

166.4 x 91.4 cm (65½ x 36")

Titus C. Geesey Collection. 58-110-40

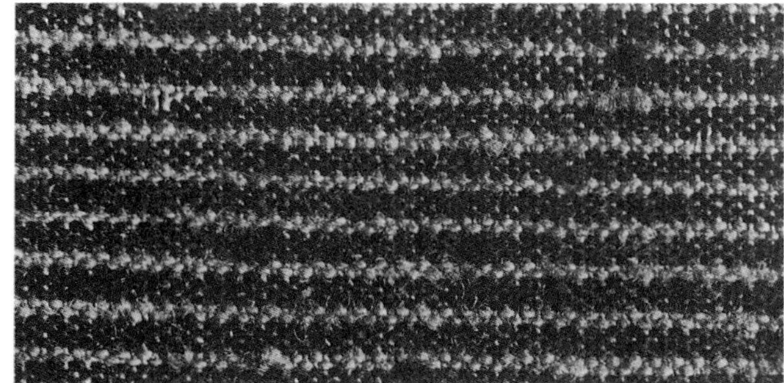

7 detail

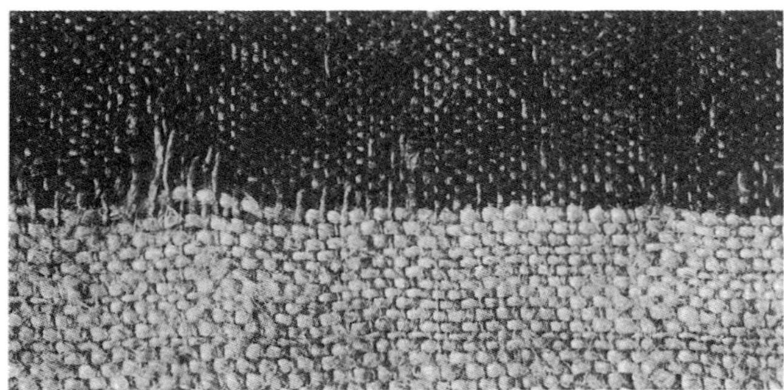

8 detail

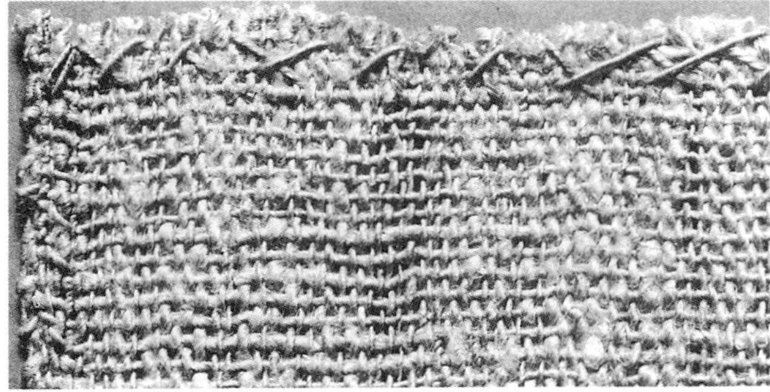

9 detail

10 detail

7   YARDAGE
1800–1850

Linen and wool in plain weave, 15 unbleached linen warps, 20 wool wefts per inch. Stripe pattern of two madder red, four indigo blue wool wefts. One selvage. Linsey-woolsey.

37.8 x 118.1 cm (14⅞ x 46½")

Gift of Mrs. William D. Frishmuth. 33-54-1

8   YARDAGE
1800–1850

Tow linen and wool in plain weave, 15 unbleached tow linen warps, 24 dark blue wool-twist wefts per inch, continuous with the warp end, which has 16 hemp wefts per inch. Two selvages, ends cut.

107 x 159.1 cm (42⅛ x 62⅝")

Gift of Mrs. William D. Frishmuth. 33-54-2

9   SACKING (2)
1850–80

Unbleached tow linen in plain weave, 24 warps, 16 wefts per inch. Random bits of chaff. Loom width 38.7 cm.

165.1 x 38.7 cm (65 x 15¼") (each)

Gift of Mrs. Robert E. Rose, in memory of her husband, Dr. Robert Eustaphiev Rose. 66-214-41,42

10 YARDAGE (2)
1850–1900

Bleached cotton in plain weave, 56 warps, 56 wefts per inch. Resist-dyed with indigo (blue). Two pieces handsewn in felled seam reinforced with buttonhole stitch in blue linen thread.

168.3 x 68.3 cm (66¼ x 26⅞") (each)

Titus C. Geesey Collection. 58-110-41a,b

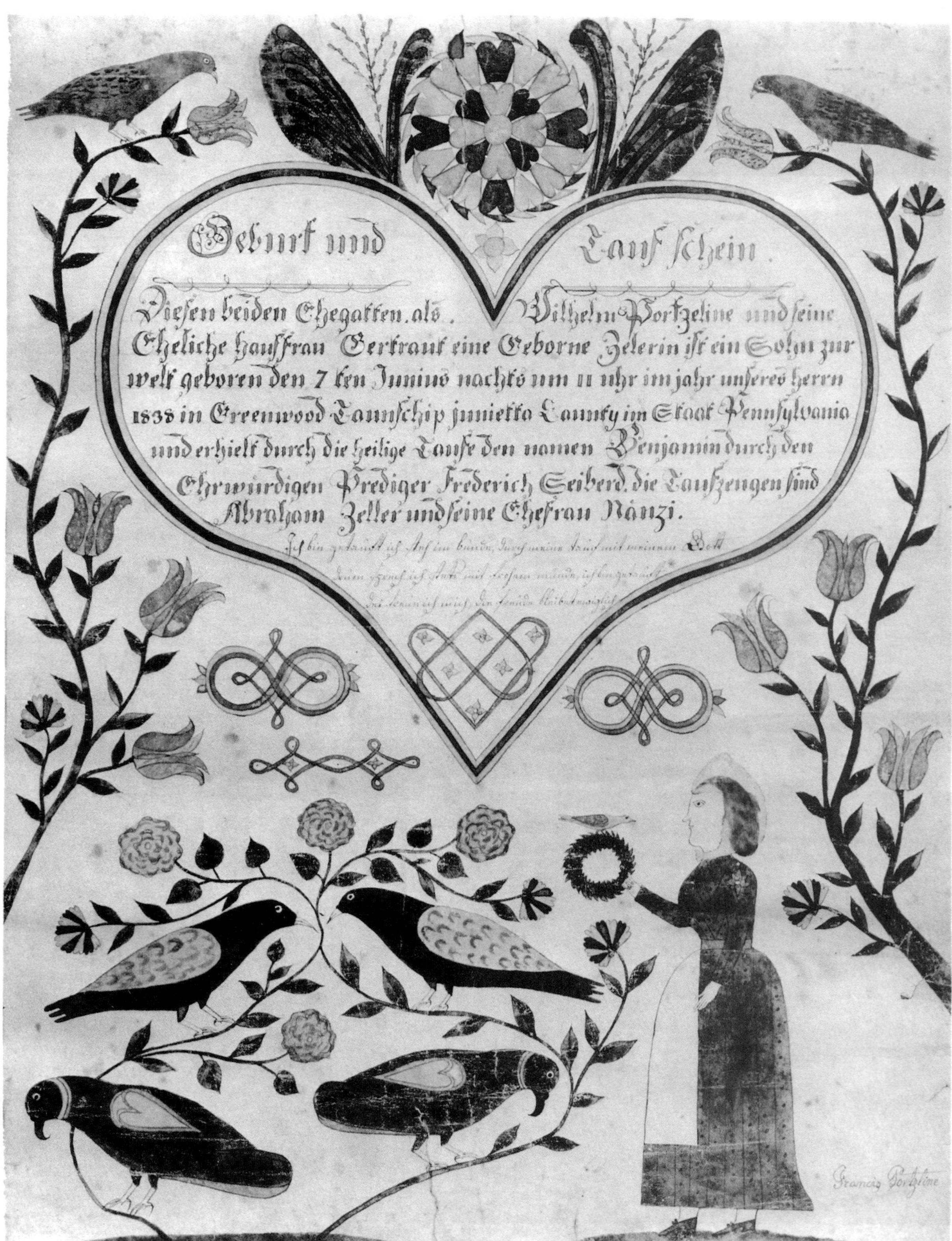

Geburt und Tauf schein
Diesen beiden Ehegatten, als . Wilhelm Portzeline und seine
Eheliche hausfrau Gertraut eine Geborne Zelerin ist ein Sohn zur
welt geboren den 7 ten Junius nachts um 11 uhr im jahr unseres herrn
1838 in Greenwood Taunschip junietta County im Staat Pennsylvania
und erhielt durch die heilige Taufe den namen Benjamin durch den
Ehrwürdigen Prediger Frederich Seibert. die Taufzeugen sind
Abraham Zeller und seine Ehefrau Nänzi.
Ich bin getauft ich steh im bund, durch meinen tauf mit meinem Gott
Francis Portzline

Paper

INTRODUCTION

In addition to printing books and almanacs and illuminating with brilliant colors their fraktur—writing samples, house blessings, birth and baptismal certificates—the Pennsylvania Germans made paper. The natural ingredients of paper were at hand in Germantown, where the first American papermaking enterprise began, in 1690, in a mill founded by William Rittenhouse, who emigrated from Germany. The essential ingredients for laid paper, rags and lint, were the natural by-products of the prosperous weaving industry centered in Germantown. Some sheets of early American paper have a distinctly bluish cast, having been made from old cloth which had been treated by "the blue dyer." The Wissahickon Creek and its tributaries, which tumbled through a rock-lined gorge toward the Schuylkill River, powered numerous mill wheels for grain and lumber, as well as paper, along their courses.

In 1810 there were about 2,500 people employed in America collecting rags for one-hundred eighty-five paper mills, sixty of which were in Pennsylvania. American mills were producing some 50,000 reams of paper for newspapers, 70,000 for books, 333,000 for writing, according to Isaiah Thomas (*The History of Printing in America,* 1810, vol. 2, p. 529). Growth was rapid as regional publishing developed. For example, by 1820, as recorded by the Census of

BIRTH AND BAPTISMAL CERTIFICATE
1840–55
See page 309, no. 44

Manufactures of the United States, the Redstone Mill in Washington Township, Fayette County, used thirty-five tons of rags per year to produce "paper of various kinds."

Expert printing, commencing with the Gutenberg Bible, was another skill that German immigrants brought to Pennsylvania. Colonial presses were busy publishing news, broadsides, and some books, from first settlement, but Christoph Saur's Germantown enterprise was the most prolific before the Revolutionary War. Saur published his great Bible (*see* p. 324, no. 1) in 1743. His German-language newspaper and yearly almanacs were widely distributed in the colonies, North and South, and were influential in spreading opinions and notices of events which, in turn, influenced economic and political concerns. The sheer numbers of German-speaking immigrants in Pennsylvania by 1760 guaranteed a readership. Personal notices of "lost" relatives, advertisements from travelers returning to the Old World willing to carry letters, powers of attorney, and such, put Saur's publishing enterprise at the hub of the German-language communications wheel. Four generations of Saurs ran the presses.

The Pietistic settlement at Ephrata in Lancaster County, founded by Conrad Beissel, made paper by 1743, including some for Christoph Saur's books, and by 1745 had their own press and bindery. The *Martyr's Mirror* (p. 324, no. 2), translated from the Dutch and printed at Ephrata in 1748-49, was the most ambitious publication in America before the Revolutionary War.

By the early 19th century, competent Pennsylvania German printers like the Baumans at Ephrata, Johann Ritter in Reading, and Blumer und Leisenring in Allentown, printed in English and in German, and supplemented their daily business of newspapers and almanacs with general stationary notebooks and custom orders for printed birth and baptismal certificates. Printer's cuts of birds and flowers, motifs probably adapted from English "penny prints," are found on birth and baptismal texts printed for illuminators such as Friederich Sanno, for example, as well as on the covers of commercially sold notebooks used by township collectors. Friedrich Krebs, a prolific illuminator, ordered his blank certificates from several printers. He hand colored and decorated the printed motifs, and added freehand borders to the printed certificates, which he then sold. Unlike the manuscript certificates, which were usually drawn and inscribed by the same hand, the printed certificates were filled in later, sometimes several years after publication. Editions of certificates were printed at various times and were widely circulated, as evidenced by the range of dates and geographical distribution of the owners.

The handsomely colored and hand-drawn family records, writing samples, bookplates, songbooks, hymnals, valentines, and drawings produced by Pennsylvania Germans into the 19th century clearly reflect a European tradition. However, sometimes needlework and textile designs were adapted and added to the decorative and symbolic motifs that had survived from the Old World, medieval tradition. The most obvious examples are the early

Ephrata work, which adapted designs from weaver's notations for decorations in their hymnals, and Schwenkfelder religious texts, decorated with sampler-like motifs, such as work by Maria or Rosina Kriebel (p. 318, no. 9). The woodblocks used on Henrich Otto's printed certificates (p. 296, no. 1) may have been actual textile printing blocks. Fraktur illuminators in Pennsylvania revitalized their inherited tradition.

The materials of the Pennsylvania German artist were varied and several mediums were often combined on one fraktur. Colors were commercially available, as was gold leaf, which the Reverend Henry Young and the Mount Pleasant artist used occasionally. Newspapers advertised verdigris, vermilion, ultramarine, for example, which were sold in apothecaries in most urban centers. Ink was made at home, and the variation in recipes accounts for the intensity and permanence of the black color, which often faded to brown. Christoph Saur printed a recipe for ink in his almanac in 1748 [translation]: "It often happens that if people in our country have something to write they will take gunpowder and water, and make ink . . . if such writing is carried about a bit, it is completely rubbed out so it cannot be read . . . [so] pulverize a piece of cherry-tree gum the size of a bean . . . let it dissolve in as much water as half an egg shell can hold, and add the powder afterward, for then the ink will not wipe out. Whoever takes the gallnuts from oak trees in the late summer when they are ready to fall and are soft, then crushes them and presses the juice into a clean glass or a vessel . . . adds copperas or vitriol the size of a thick hazel nut to a gill of juice, he indeed will have very good ink at that very moment." The relative acidity of such ink concoctions ate through the paper over time. Gum arabic, cherry and peach tree gums, and egg whites were the binding mediums for the colors. Drawings attributed to Samuel Godshall (*see* p. 336, no. 13) show a highly concentrated medium; the surfaces are shiny and brilliant; the reverse paper is raised like a stuffed quilt.

The finest Pennsylvania German illumination was done by schoolmasters and specialists working with a quill pen, ruler, and compass. Their elaborate writing samples included all forms of lettering and script to be copied by students. Most extant writing samples appear to be teachers' examples, but some, as yet unattributed, may be the work of apt pupils.

Most fraktur work was personal—a record, a reward, a greeting, a blessing, a note of ownership. It was not usually framed or hung as house decoration, but depending upon its form, was kept tucked between the leaves of the big family Bible or in a singing book, or pasted inside the lid of a chest. The birth and baptismal certificates of the Lutheran and Reformed Church were important documents, necessary for church membership as a record of the vital statistics of the rites of passage from birth, to confirmation, to marriage. The surrounds of colorful birds, angels, flowers, calligraphic ornaments, and elaborate script suggest the celebratory nature of the events, while the religious texts were central to the spiritual significance.

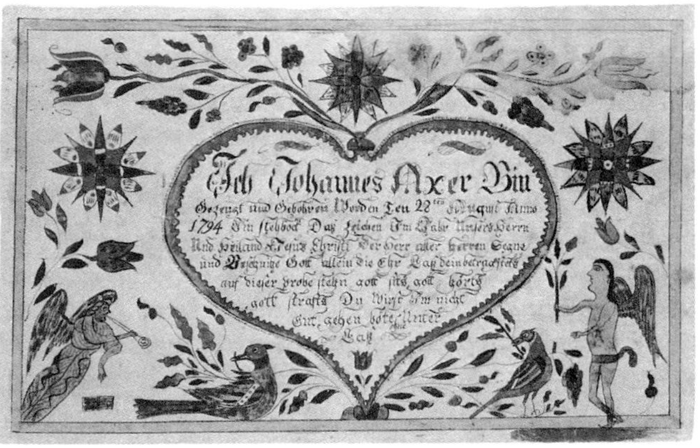

1

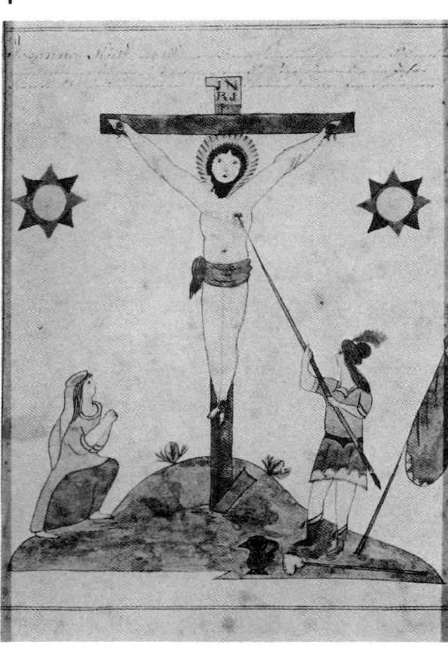

2

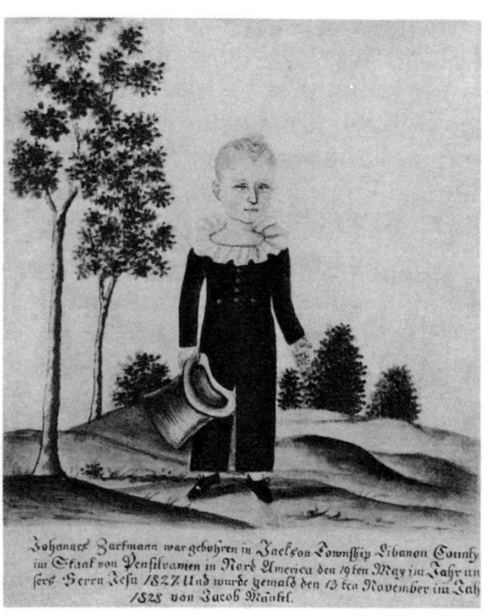

3

1   BIRTH CERTIFICATE
Probably Lancaster County
1794–1800

Inscribed for Johannes Axer, born August 28, 1794

Ink with pigments in gum medium on laid paper. Designs drawn in ink and colored. Red heart, red, brown, and green tulips. Tan angels with red details. Brown foliage, red, brown, blue, and tan berries, red pods. Red brown border.

19.7 x 32.1 cm (7¾ x 12⅝″)

Purchased. 16-290

2   BIRTH CERTIFICATE
Muncy Creek Township, Lycoming County
1825–45

Attributed to the **Reverend Henry Young**

Inscribed for Johannes Kiess, born December 3, 1814, Blooming Grove, Lycoming County

Watercolor wash and ink on wove paper. Designs drawn in ink and colored. Mary Magdalene and soldier in red, blue, and yellow. Christ has a red loincloth. Brown and yellow cross. Red, blue, and yellow stars. Green ground, blue pitcher, red and yellow flag.

32 x 20 cm (12⅝ x 7⅞″)

Titus C. Geesey Collection. 54-85-129

3   BIRTH CERTIFICATE
Lebanon County
November 13, 1828

Jacob Mäntel

Inscribed for Johannes Zartmann, born May 19, 1827, Jackson Township, Lebanon County

Watercolor wash, pigments in medium, and ink on wove paper. Boy in blue suit with brass-colored buttons. Green, blue, and yellow trees with gray and brown trunks.

24.8 x 20.6 cm (9¾ x 8⅛″)

The Collection of Bernice Chrysler and Edgar Garbisch. 67-268-15

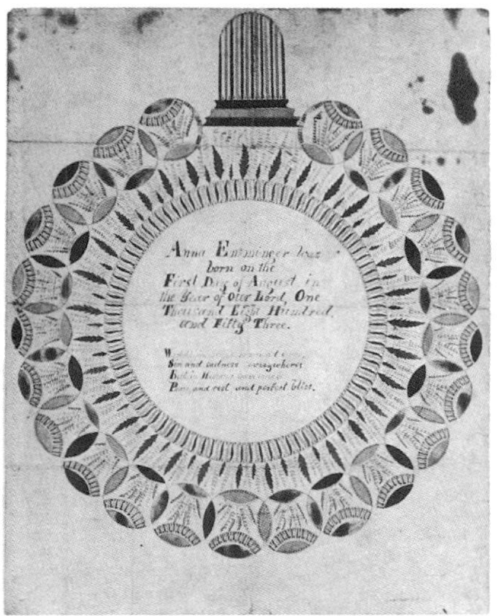

4

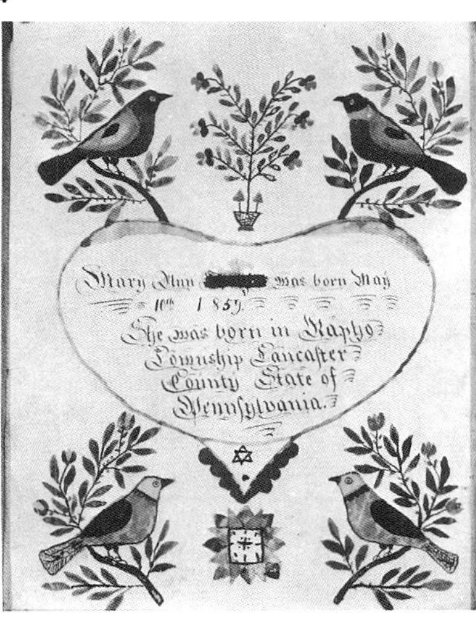

5

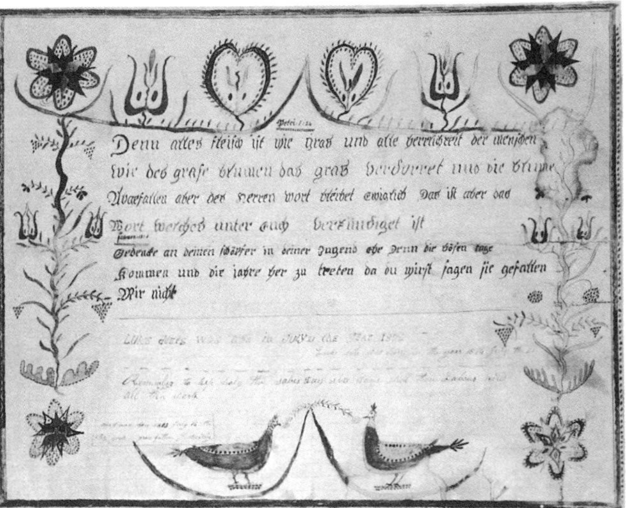

6

4 BIRTH CERTIFICATE

1853–54

Inscribed for Anna Ensminger, born August 1, 1853

Watercolor wash and pencil on wove paper. Designs drawn in pencil between three compass-inscribed concentric circles circumscribed by twenty-three red, yellow, and blue circles. Inner circle green and yellow. Green and red leaves alternate with yellow and red designs. Red, blue, and yellow headstone. Folded, probably around a coin.

24.8 x 19.4 cm (9¾ x 7⅝″)

Bequest of Mr. and Mrs. William M. Elkins. 50-92-241

5 BIRTH CERTIFICATE

Lancaster County

1859

Inscribed for Mary Ann [Fieschler?], born May 10, 1859, Rapho Township, Lancaster County

Ink with pigments in medium on laid paper. Red brown heart, orange, blue, and yellow birds. Green foliage, red and yellow flowers.

26 x 19.7 cm (10¼ x 7¾″)

Bequest of Mr. and Mrs. William M. Elkins. 50-92-239

6 BIRTH CERTIFICATE

Washington Township, Franklin County

July 16, 1883

J. Milly

Inscribed for Luke Deets, born July 21, 1874

Watercolor wash and brown and lavender ink on lined wove paper. Designs drawn in ink and colored. Red tulips, purple grapes. Red birds with green backs and breasts, blue heads. Green, purple, and lavender inscription.

31.8 x 40.3 cm (12½ x 15⅞″)

Bequest of Mr. and Mrs. William M. Elkins. 50-92-254

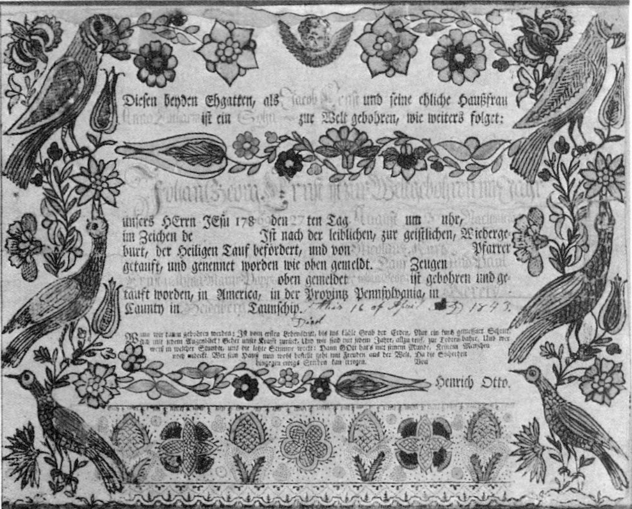

1

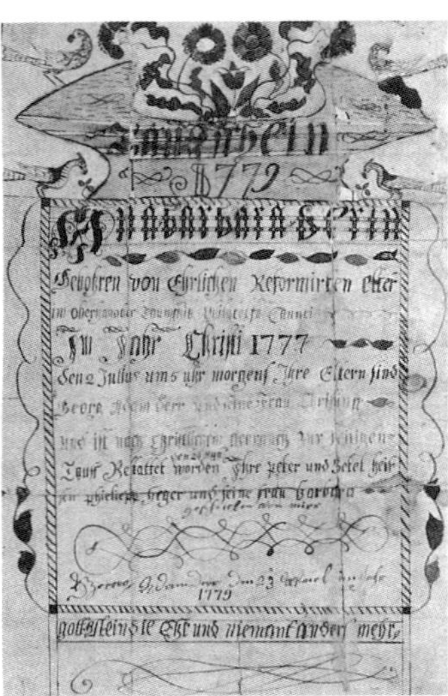

2

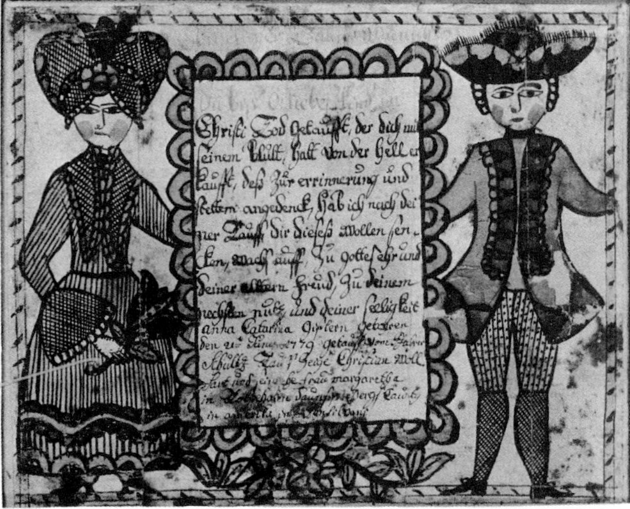

3

1   **BIRTH AND BAPTISMAL CERTIFICATE**
Lancaster County
Printed c. 1770–72

Johan Henrich Otto, printer

Inscribed for Johan Georg Ernst, born August 27, 1769, Heidelberg Township, Berks County

Ink with pigments in medium on laid paper. Relief printed with woodcuts and letterpress; hand colored. Embroidery or textile design at bottom, winged angel head at top, and side borders are printed with woodcuts and hand colored. Green birds with pink red wings, blue buds, green foliage, pink and yellow fuchsias. Orange, green, blue, and yellow bottom band. Horizontal flowers and foliage are drawn in ink and colored red, yellow, blue, and green. For similar designs, *see* nos. 7 and 8.

34.2 x 42.3 cm (13½ x 16⅝")

Titus C. Geesey Collection. 69-284-5

2   **BIRTH AND BAPTISMAL CERTIFICATE**
Montgomery County
April 23, 1779

Georg Adam Derr

Inscribed for Ana Barbara Derr, born July 2, 1777, Upper Hanover Township, Philadelphia [Montgomery] County

Watercolor wash and ink on laid paper. Designs drawn in ink and colored. Red and blue flowers, bandings, and birds. Yellow pediment. Red and blue inscription, last sentence in ink. Edges trimmed.

33.3 x 21.6 cm (13⅛ x 8½")

Bequest of Mr. and Mrs. William M. Elkins. 50-92-250

3   **BIRTH AND BAPTISMAL CERTIFICATE**
Berks County
c. 1780

Attributed to the **Sussel-Washington Artist**

Inscribed for Anna Catarina Gisler, born June 21, 1779, Tulpehocken Township, Berks County

Watercolor wash, watercolor in gum medium, and ink on laid paper. Designs drawn in ink and colored. Green coat and banding on woman's skirt and bodice. Breeches, hat banding (fur), dress, and border are yellow with brown stripes. Cheeks, man's shirt, and flower in woman's headdress are red. Coattails, coat banding, and woman's tulip and skirt ruffle are blue. Green and yellow border around inscription, outlined in brown. Paper folded, probably around a coin.

16.5 x 20.3 cm (6½ x 8")

Titus C. Geesey Collection. 54-85-8

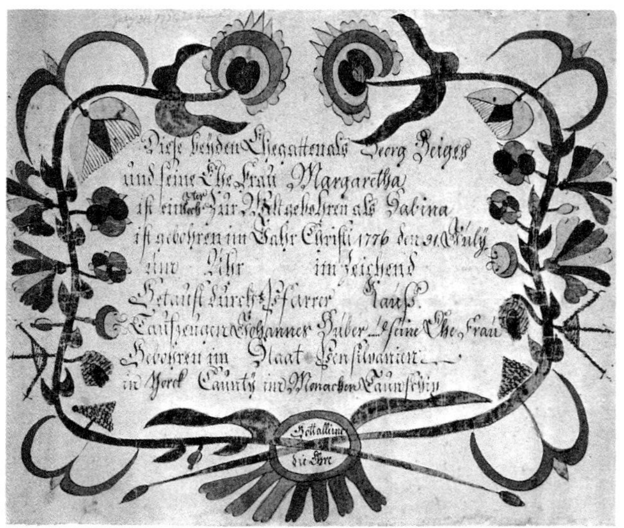

4

4

BIRTH AND BAPTISMAL CERTIFICATE
Lebanon County
Probably 1780–90

Attributed to **Arnold Hoevelmann**

Inscribed for Sabina Heiges, born July 31, 1776, Monaghan Township, York County

Ink with pigments in gum medium on laid paper. Watermark: WC. Designs drawn in ink and colored. Orange red motifs in corners and center bottom. Orange red, yellow, and red brown flowers with green stems and foliage.

34 x 41.3 cm (13⅜ x 16¼")

Gift of J. Stogdell Stokes. 28-10-73

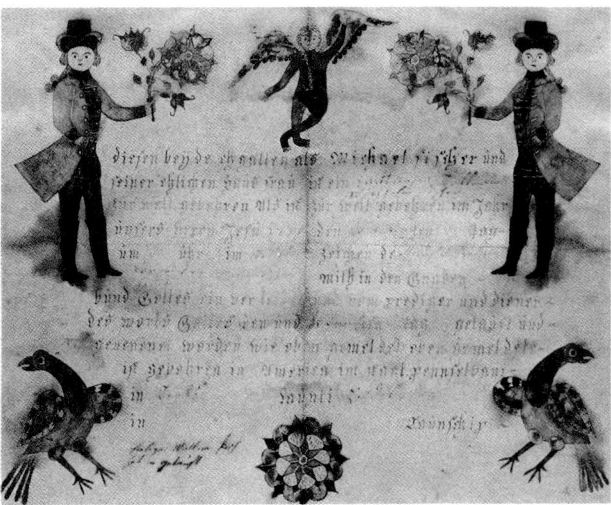

5

5

BIRTH AND BAPTISMAL CERTIFICATE
Berks County
1780–1815

Attributed to the **Cross-Legged Angel Artist**

Inscribed for Willhelm Fischer, born November 30, 1780, Heidelberg Township, Berks County

Red and brown ink with pigments in gum medium on laid paper. Designs drawn in ink and colored. Purple brown angel with green wings and cloth. Men in red coats, green waistcoats, brown breeches, and black boots, hats, and collars. Birds have red breasts, brown necks, yellow and green wings, and green tails.

33.3 x 40.6 cm (13⅛ x 16")

Titus C. Geesey Collection. 69-284-7

6

BIRTH AND BAPTISMAL CERTIFICATE
Lancaster or Berks County
1780–1815

Attributed to the **Cross-Legged Angel Artist**

Inscribed for Cornelius Reichwein, born May 26, 1802, Lancaster County

Red and black ink with pigments in gum medium on laid paper. Designs drawn in ink and colored. Yellow angel with red wings and green cloth. Women in green bodices, red blouses, and red, green, and yellow skirts. Birds have red breasts, brown necks, green tails, and yellow wings with green details.

33 x 40.6 cm (13 x 16")

Titus C. Geesey Collection. 69-284-8

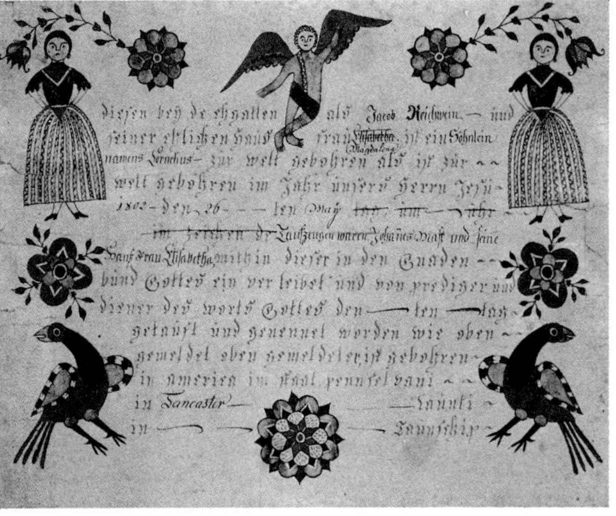

6

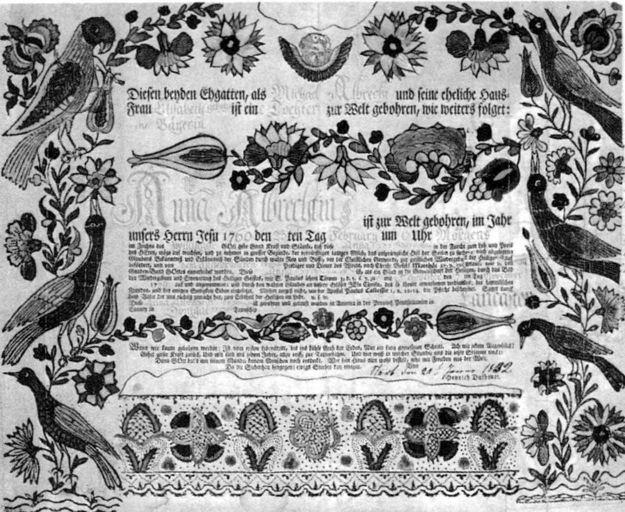

7

7 BIRTH AND BAPTISMAL CERTIFICATE
Lancaster County
Printed c. 1784

Henrich Dulheuer, printer

Inscribed for Anna Albrecht, born February 23, 1760, Donegal Township, Lancaster County

Watercolor wash, pigments in medium, and ink on laid paper. Relief printed with woodcuts and letterpress; hand colored. Embroidery or textile design at bottom, winged angel head at top, and side borders are printed with woodcuts and hand colored. Orange red parrot with yellow and green wings. Green birds with red wings and blue heads. Horizontal flowers and foliage are drawn in ink and colored. Hand-lettering is opaque orange (mixed with white), red, and black. For similar designs, *see* nos. 1 and 8.

34.6 x 42.9 cm (13⅝ x 16⅞")

Titus C. Geesey Collection. 69-284-11

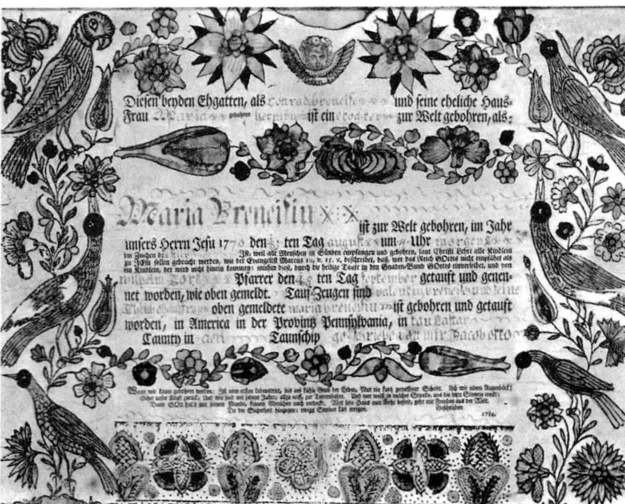

8

8 BIRTH AND BAPTISMAL CERTIFICATE
Lancaster County
Printed 1784

Jacob Otto, artist

Inscribed for Maria Breneise, born August 13, 1770, Earl Township, Lancaster County

Watercolor wash and ink on laid paper. Relief printed with woodcuts and letterpress; hand colored. Embroidery or textile design at bottom, winged angel head at top, and side borders are printed with woodcuts and hand colored. Parrot has a green head, red beak. Green and red birds with blue heads. Red, green, blue, and tan flowers. Horizontal flowers and foliage are drawn in ink and colored. Red hand-lettering. For similar designs, *see* nos. 1 and 7.

34 x 42.2 cm (13⅜ x 16⅝")

Gift of J. Stogdell Stokes. 28-10-91

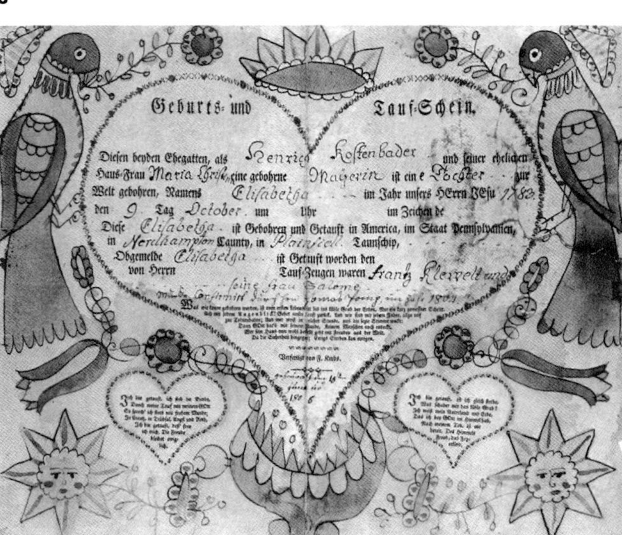

9

9 BIRTH AND BAPTISMAL CERTIFICATE
Dauphin County
Printed 1790–1800

Friedrich Krebs, artist

Inscribed for Elisabetha Kostenbader, born October 9, 1783, Plainfield Township, Northampton County

Watercolor wash and ink on laid paper. Relief printed with letterpress. Designs drawn in ink and colored. Yellow parrots with red heads, red and green wings, and gray green tails. Red and yellow crown and stars.

33 x 40.6 cm (13 x 16")

Bequest of Mr. and Mrs. William M. Elkins. 50-92-243

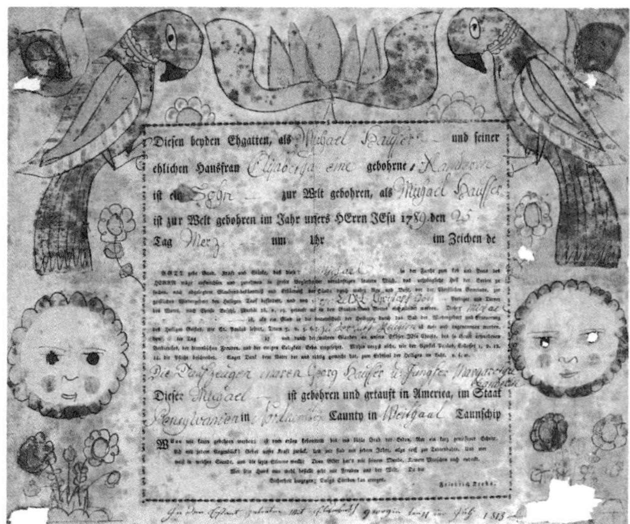

10

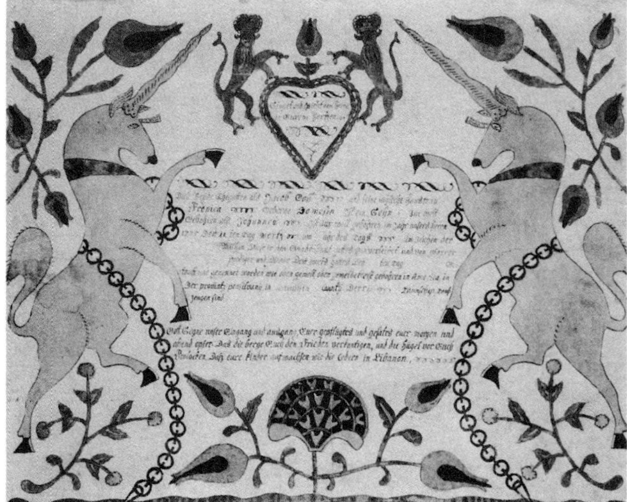

11

10   **BIRTH AND BAPTISMAL CERTIFICATE**
Dauphin County
Printed 1790–1800

Friedrich Krebs, artist

Inscribed for Michael Hausser, born March 25, 1789, Whitehall Township, Northampton [Lehigh] County

Watercolor wash and ink on laid paper. Relief printed with letterpress. Designs drawn in ink and colored. Brown parrots with green and orange wings.

33 x 39.7 cm (13 x 15⅝")

Bequest of Mr. and Mrs. William M. Elkins. 50-92-252

---

11   **BIRTH AND BAPTISMAL CERTIFICATE**
Dauphin County
1790–1800

Attributed to the **C. M. Artist**

Inscribed for Johannes Gass, born March 11, 1775, Derry Township, Dauphin County

Watercolor wash, pigments in medium, ink, and pencil on laid paper. Lettering guidelines in pencil. Designs drawn in ink and colored. Tan unicorns, blue gray lions, red and blue tulips, green foliage.

32.4 x 39.4 cm (12¾ x 15½")

Titus C. Geesey Collection. 69-284-6

---

12   **BIRTH AND BAPTISMAL CERTIFICATE**
Dauphin County
1790–1800

Attributed to the **C. M. Artist**

Inscribed for Eliesabeth Ritzecker, born November 30, 1797, Donegal Township, Lancaster County

Watercolor and ink on laid paper backed with linen. Designs drawn with ink and colored. Peach hearts, green eagles. Blue and yellow bunting under corner hearts. Peach and yellow tulips, green foliage.

30.5 x 36.8 cm (12 x 14½")

Titus C. Geesey Collection. 69-284-2

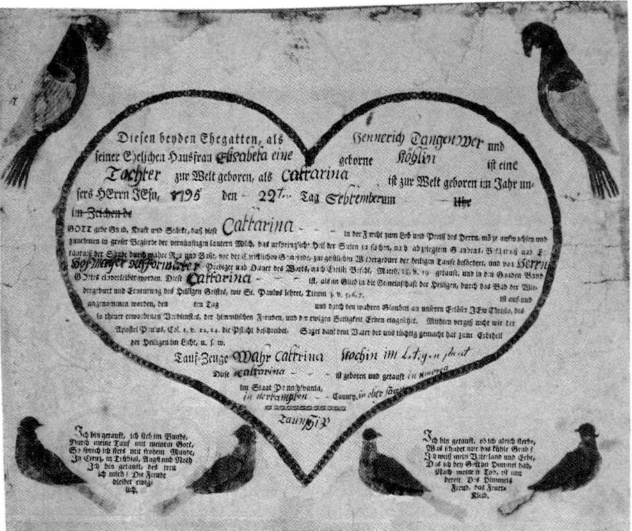

13

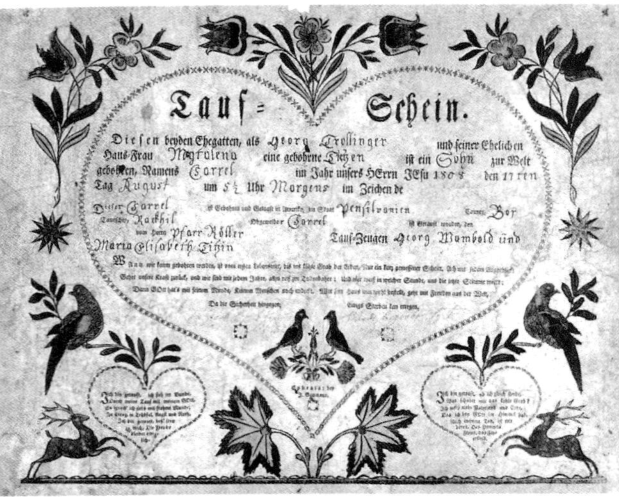

14

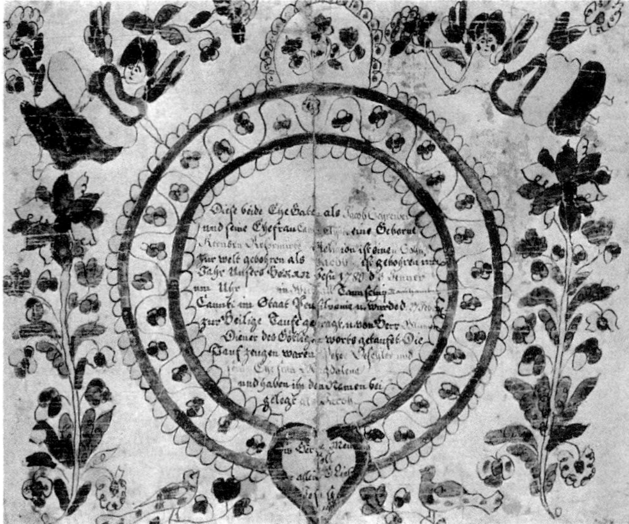

15

13   **BIRTH AND BAPTISMAL CERTIFICATE**
Ephrata, Lancaster County
Printed 1799–1810

Attributed to **J. Baumann**, printer

Inscribed for Cattarina Gangenwer, born September 22, 1795, Upper Saucon Township, Northampton [Lehigh] County

Ink with pigments in gum medium on laid paper. Relief printed with woodcuts and letterpress; hand colored. Outlines of hearts, birds, flowers, and foliage in spandrels printed in peach-colored ink. Green birds with red and yellow wings and tails. Blue heart. Unfinished.

31.8 x 39.4 cm (12½ x 15½")

Bequest of Mr. and Mrs. William M. Elkins.
50-92-248

14   **BIRTH AND BAPTISMAL CERTIFICATE**
Ephrata, Lancaster County
Printed 1799–1810

J. Baumann, printer

Inscribed for Carrel Trollinger, born August 17, 1808, Rockhill Township, Bucks County

Watercolor wash, pigments in gum medium, and ink on laid paper. Relief printed with woodcuts, metal cuts, and letterpress; hand colored. Yellow, green, and red leaves, tulips, and birds. Brown stags.

31.1 x 40.6 cm (12¼ x 16")

Bequest of Mr. and Mrs. William M. Elkins.
50-92-235

15   **BIRTH AND BAPTISMAL CERTIFICATE**
Lehigh County
c. 1800

Attributed to the **Blowsy Angel Artist**

Inscribed for Jacob Schreiber, born January 3, 1780, Whitehall Township, Northampton [Lehigh] County

Ink with pigments in gum medium on laid paper. Designs drawn in ink and colored. Orange circles with yellow ruffles. Yellow and brown angels with orange details. Green foliage and heart.

33 x 40.6 cm (13 x 16")

Bequest of Mr. and Mrs. William M. Elkins.
50-92-249

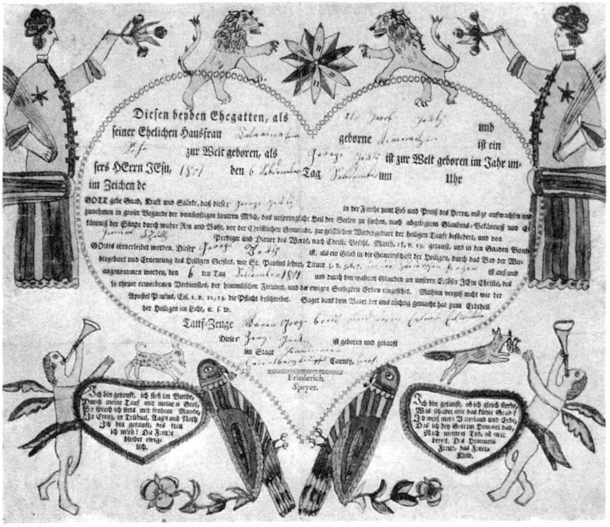

16

16 **BIRTH AND BAPTISMAL CERTIFICATE**
Berks County
Printed c. 1800

Attributed to **Friederich Speyer,** artist

Inscribed for George Yeckly, born September 6, 1801, Heidelberg Township, Berks County

Watercolor wash and ink on laid paper. Relief printed with letterpress. Designs drawn in ink and colored. Yellow lions with red and blue details. Pink angels with red and yellow wings. Red and yellow parrots with green wings and blue and yellow tails. Men in yellow coats.

33.7 x 40.7 cm (13¼ x 16″)

Titus C. Geesey Collection. 69-284-4

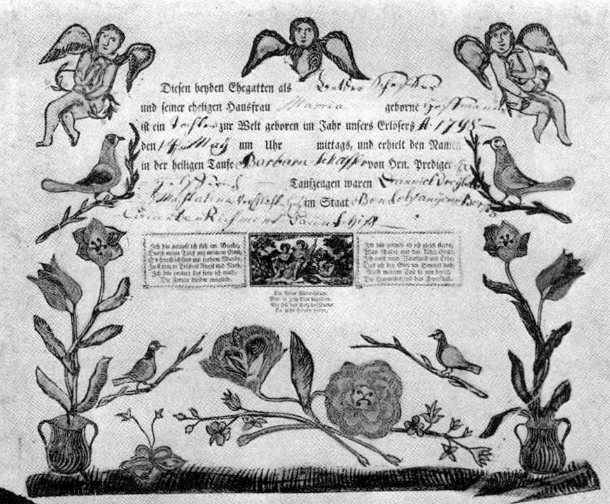

17

17 **BIRTH AND BAPTISMAL CERTIFICATE**
Berks County
Printed c. 1800

Inscribed for Barbara Schaffer, born May 14, 1798, Richmond Township, Berks County

Watercolor wash, pigments in gum medium, and ink on laid paper. Relief printed with woodcuts, metal cuts, and letterpress; hand colored. Red and yellow birds and flowers, blue foliage and grass. Pink angels with yellow wings hold red hearts on yellow vines. Lower-right corner folded before printing.

32.7 x 40.6 cm (12⅞ x 16″)

Bequest of Mr. and Mrs. William M. Elkins. 50-92-253

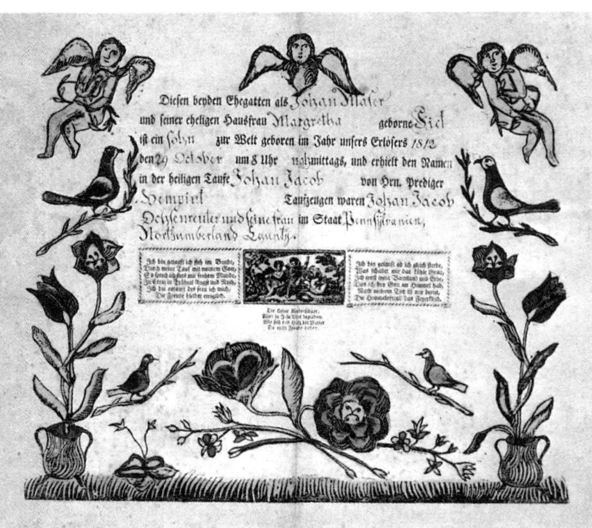

18

18 **BIRTH AND BAPTISMAL CERTIFICATE**
Berks County
Printed c. 1800

Inscribed for Johan Jacob Maser, born October 29, 1812, Northumberland County

Watercolor wash, pigments in gum medium, and ink on laid paper. Relief printed with woodcuts, metal cuts, and letterpress; hand colored. Red birds and flowers with yellow details. Blue foliage and grass.

34.3 x 41.3 cm (13½ x 16¼″)

Titus C. Geesey Collection. 69-284-1

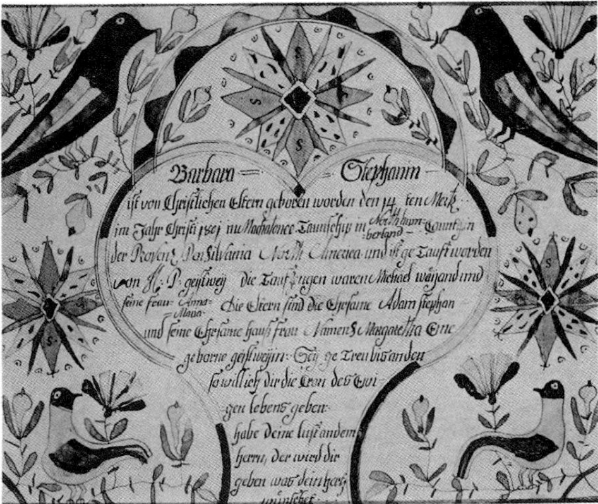

19

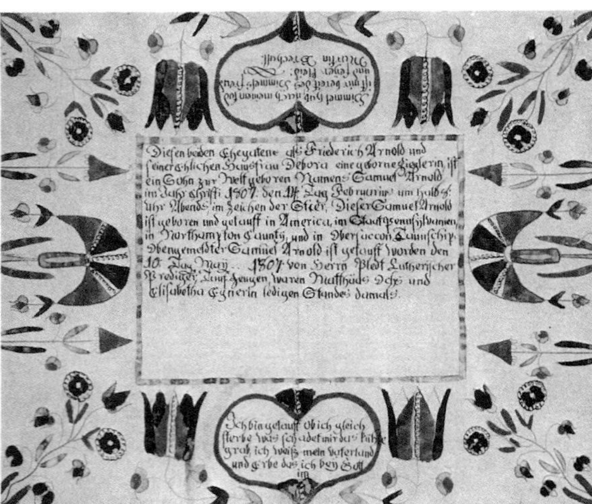

20

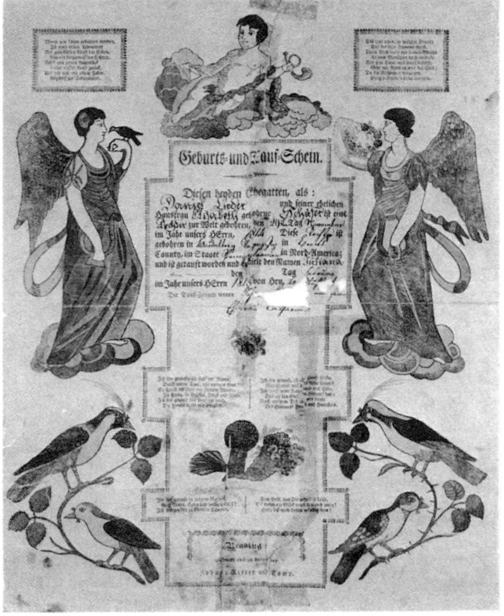

21

19   BIRTH AND BAPTISMAL CERTIFICATE
Northumberland County
1800–1815

Attributed to **Conrad Trevitz**

Inscribed for Barbara Stephan, born March 14, 1801, Mahantango Township, Northumberland County

Watercolor wash, pigment in gum medium, and ink on laid paper. Designs drawn in ink and colored. Green, rust red, tan, and blue compass roses. Small birds tan with blue and brown wings; large birds blue with brown-striped wings. Rust red scalloping above heart. Black and rust red inscription.

32.7 x 40.3 cm (12⅞ x 15⅞")

Bequest of Mr. and Mrs. William M. Elkins. 50-92-245

20   BIRTH AND BAPTISMAL CERTIFICATE
Maxatawny Township, Berks County
1800–1820

Martin Brechall

Inscribed for Samuel Arnold, born February 14, 1807, Upper Saucon Township, Northampton [Lehigh] County

Ink with pigments in gum medium on laid paper. Designs drawn in red ink and colored. Red hearts, blue, green, and red tulips, yellow and red buds. Purple and tan band around inscription.

33 x 40.6 cm (13 x 16")

Bequest of Mr. and Mrs. William M. Elkins. 50-92-255

21   BIRTH AND BAPTISMAL CERTIFICATE
Reading, Berks County
Printed 1802–4

Johann Ritter und Comp., printers

Inscribed for Juliana Lieder, born November 29, 1814, Heidelberg Township, Berks County

Watercolor wash, pigments in gum medium, and ink on wove paper. Relief printed with woodcuts and letterpress; color is probably stamped. Red and yellow angels. Yellow birds with blue and pink wings and orange plumes. Gray clouds, green foliage.

41.9 x 33.3 cm (16½ x 13⅛")

Gift of Warren J. Ellis. 48-78-1

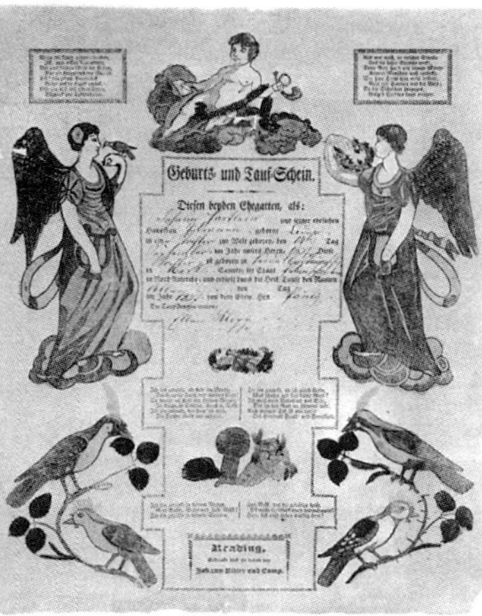

22

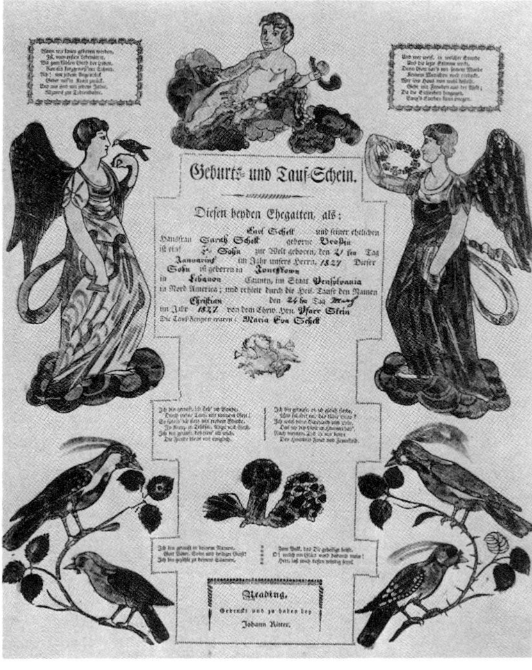

23

22 BIRTH AND BAPTISMAL CERTIFICATE
Reading, Berks County
Printed 1802–4

Johann Ritter und Comp., printers

Inscribed for Ellen Hartlein, born September 14, 1837, Heidelberg Township, Berks County

Watercolor wash, pigments in gum medium, and ink on wove paper. Relief printed; hand colored. Orange and yellow angels. Yellow birds with blue and pink wings, orange details and plumes. Gray clouds, green foliage.

41.3 x 33.7 cm (16¼ x 13¼″)

Gift of Warren J. Ellis. 48-78-2

23 BIRTH AND BAPTISMAL CERTIFICATE
Reading, Berks County
Printed 1805–51

Johann Ritter, printer

Inscribed for Christian Schett, born January 21, 1827, Jonestown, Lebanon County

Ink with pigments in gum medium on laid paper. Relief printed with woodcuts, metal cuts, and letterpress; hand colored. Green and yellow angels with red wings and details. Green, red, and yellow birds.

41.6 x 33.3 cm (16⅜ x 13⅛″)

Gift of Warren J. Ellis. 48-78-3

24 BIRTH AND BAPTISMAL CERTIFICATE
Centre County
1810–20

Attributed to the **Flat Tulip Artist**

Inscribed for Johannes Homan, born September 21, 1814, Haines Township, Centre County

Ink with pigments in gum medium on wove paper. Designs drawn in ink and colored. Orange red cartouche and corner tulips with green and yellow details. Other tulips yellow with orange red and green details.

33 x 40.3 cm (13 x 15⅞″)

Bequest of Mr. and Mrs. William M. Elkins. 50-92-233

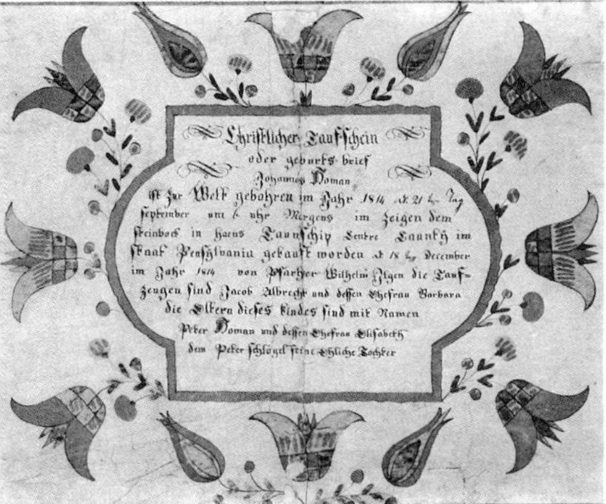

24

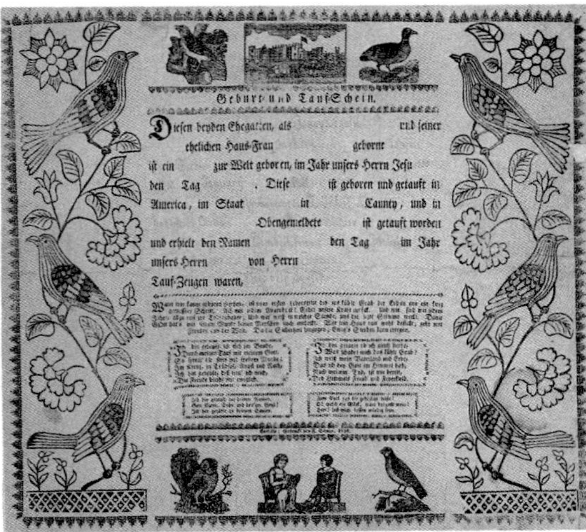

25

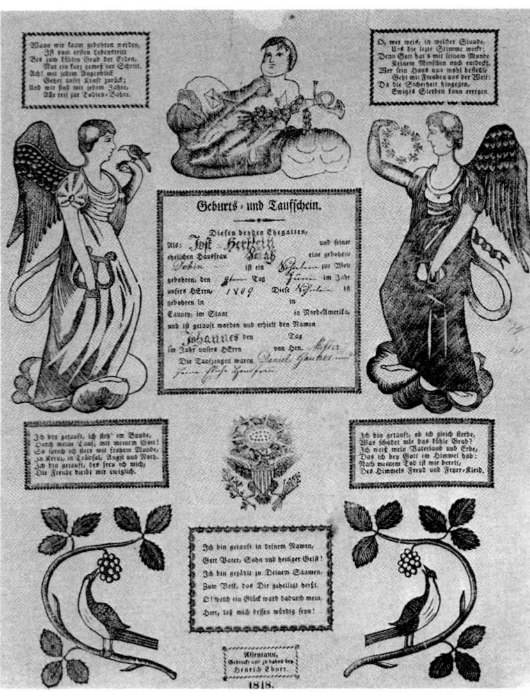

26

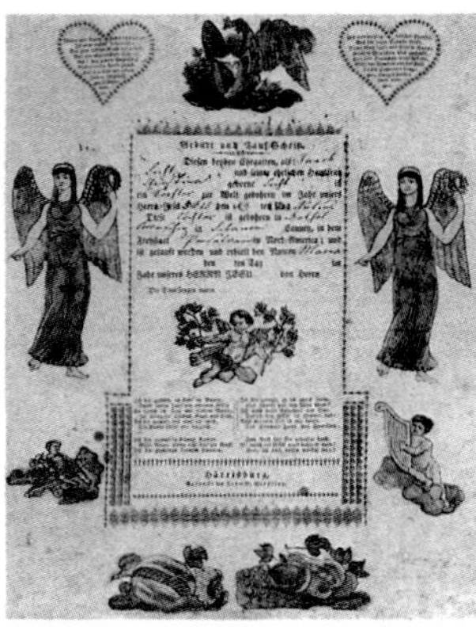

27

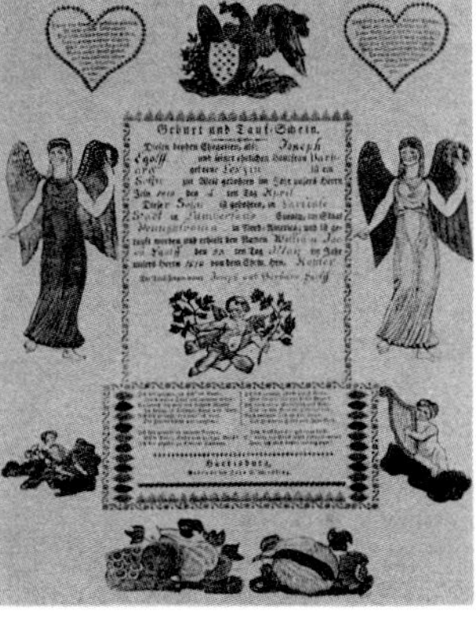

28

25 **BIRTH AND BAPTISMAL CERTIFICATE**
Carlisle, Cumberland County
Printed 1813

Friederich Sanno, printer

Inscribed for Elizabeth Egolff, born January 10, 1813, Carlisle, Cumberland County

Watercolor wash and ink on wove paper mounted on linen. Relief printed with woodcuts, metal cuts, and letterpress. Birds' wings hand-colored red brown.

33.7 x 38.1 cm (13¼ x 15″)

Purchased: Joseph E. Temple Fund. 20-71-8

26 **BIRTH AND BAPTISMAL CERTIFICATE**
Allentown, Lehigh County
Printed 1818

Henrich Ebner, printer

Inscribed for Johannes Hertlein, born June 3, 1809

Ink on laid paper. Relief printed with metal cuts and letterpress. Uncolored.

41 x 33.3 cm (16⅛ x 13⅛″)

Gift of Warren J. Ellis. 48-78-4

27 **BIRTH AND BAPTISMAL CERTIFICATE**
Harrisburg, Dauphin County
Printed 1819–30

John S. Wiestling, printer

Inscribed for Maria Licht, born July 19, 1815, Bethel Township, Lebanon County

Watercolor wash, pigments in gum medium, and ink on laid paper. Watermark: Z. Relief printed with woodcuts and letterpress; hand colored. Angels have red dresses, yellow wings. Putti on lavender clouds. Yellow eagle on blue ground, red shield. Inscription on reverse in Gothic capitals.

40.6 x 33 cm (16 x 13″)

Purchased: Joseph E. Temple Fund. 20-71-4

28 **BIRTH AND BAPTISMAL CERTIFICATE**
Harrisburg, Dauphin County
Printed 1819–30

John S. Wiestling, printer

Inscribed for William Jacob Egolff, born April 4, 1818, Carlisle, Cumberland County

Watercolor wash, pigment in medium, and ink on wove paper. Relief printed with woodcuts, metal cuts, and letterpress; hand colored. Red and yellow angels, yellow eagle on green ground, shield outlined in red. Putti on blue gray clouds. Red, yellow, and green fruit.

38.1 x 30.5 cm (15 x 12″)

Purchased: Joseph E. Temple Fund. 20-71-5

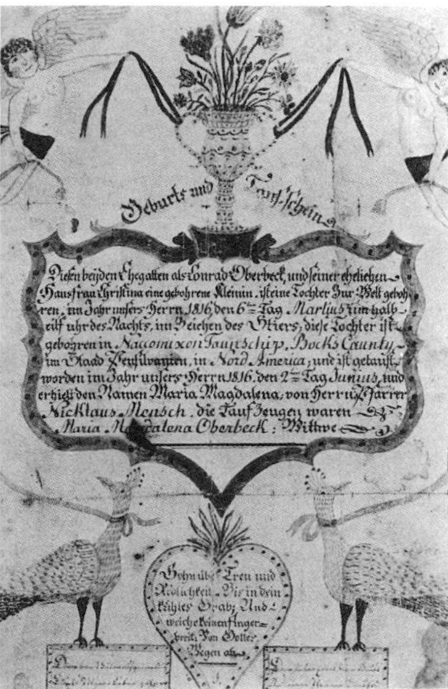

29

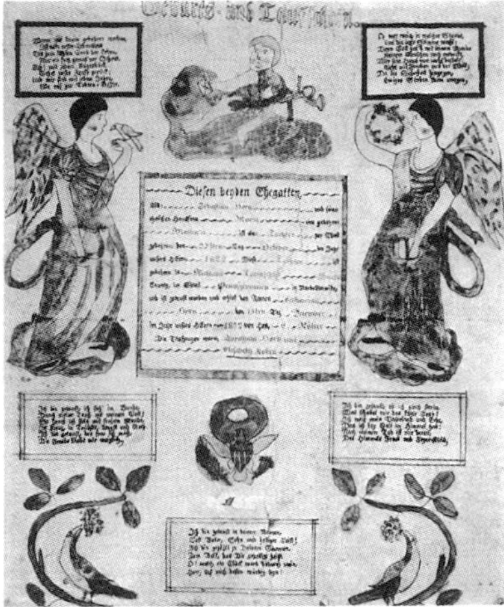

30

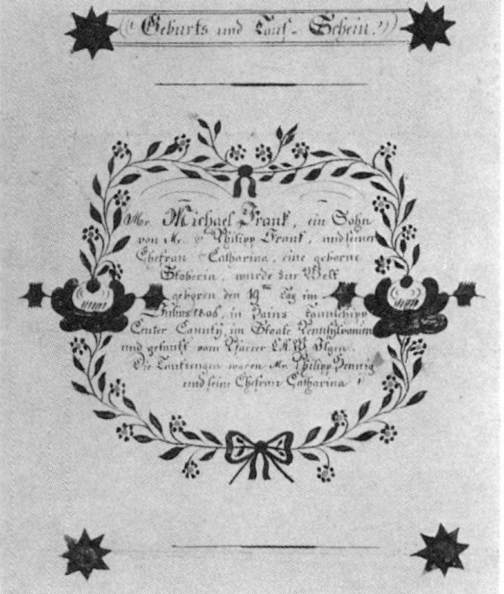

31

29 BIRTH AND BAPTISMAL CERTIFICATE
Virginia
1820–25

Inscribed for Maria Magdalena Oberbeck, born March 6, 1816, Nockamixon Township, Bucks County

Watercolor wash, pencil, and ink on laid paper. Designs drawn in pencil and colored. Orange cartouche with blue details. Yellow and blue urn, yellow, blue, and orange flowers. Angels and peacocks have yellow wings and blue green ribbons and tails. Yellow, orange, and blue heart.

38.4 x 32.1 cm (15⅛ x 12⅝″)

Gift of Mr. and Mrs. Frederick Morris Thayer. 54-8-1

---

30 BIRTH AND BAPTISMAL CERTIFICATE
Possibly Bucks County
1822–24

Inscribed for Catharina Horn, born October 27, 1822, Richland Township, Bucks County

Watercolor wash and ink on wove paper. Designs drawn in ink and colored. Angels in blue skirts, green and brown blouses. Blue, green, and brown birds, flowers, and foliage. Brown and red inscription.

37.8 x 31.1 cm (14⅞ x 12¼″)

Gift of Mrs. William D. Frishmuth. 02-454

---

31 BIRTH AND BAPTISMAL CERTIFICATE
Centre County
1825–45

Attributed to the **Reverend Henry Young**

Inscribed for Michael Frank, born July 19, 1806, Haines Township, Centre County

Watercolor wash, pigments in gum medium, and ink on wove board. Intaglio mark of crown in serrated oval in upper-left corner. Designs drawn in ink and colored. Red and blue stars with centers of iridescent gold in gum medium. Green wreath with blue and yellow forget-me-nots and red roses and ribbons.

29.8 x 18.7 cm (11¾ x 7⅜″)

Bequest of Mr. and Mrs. William M. Elkins. 50-92-240

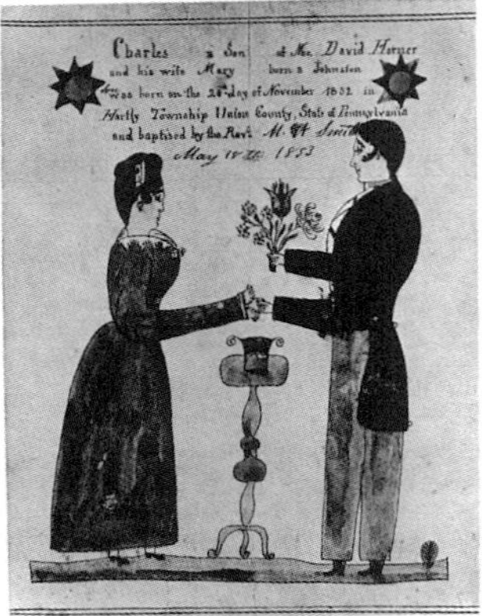

32

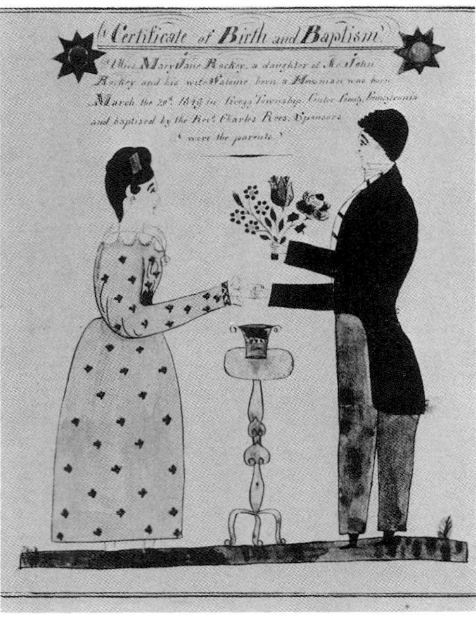

33

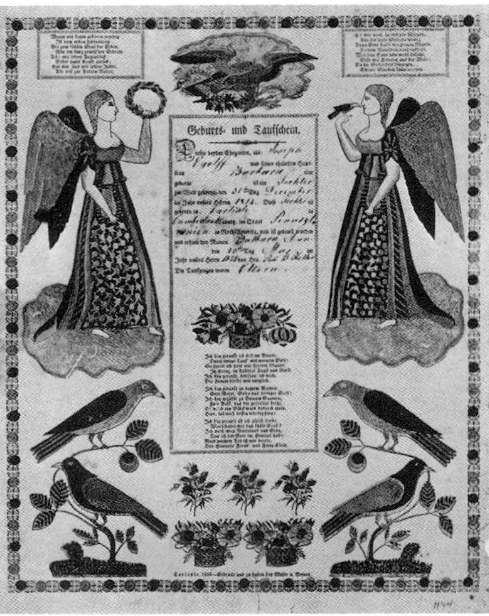

34

32 **BIRTH AND BAPTISMAL CERTIFICATE**
Centre County
1825–45

Attributed to the **Reverend Henry Young**

Inscribed for Charles Horner, born November 20, 1832, Hartley Township, Union County

Watercolor wash, pigments in medium, pencil, and ink on wove paper. Lettering guidelines in pale ink and pencil. Designs drawn in ink and colored. Red orange and blue stars with yellow centers. Woman in orange dress. Man in green pants, black coat, and red-striped vest. Blue gray table with yellow (gilded?) details.

24.4 x 18.7 cm (9⅝ x 7⅜")

The Samuel S. White, 3rd, and Vera White Collection. 67-30-103

33 **BIRTH AND BAPTISMAL CERTIFICATE**
Centre County
1825–45

Attributed to the **Reverend Henry Young**

Inscribed for Mary Jane Rockey, born March 20, 1849, Gregg Township, Centre County

Watercolor wash, gilded pigment in medium, and ink on wove paper. Designs drawn in ink and colored. Woman in yellow dress with green and red sprigs. Green ground, trousers, and foliage. Red and blue stars with gilded centers. Gilded capital letters.

24.1 x 18.7 cm (9½ x 7⅜")

Bequest of Mr. and Mrs. William M. Elkins. 50-92-242

34 **BIRTH AND BAPTISMAL CERTIFICATE**
Carlisle, Cumberland County
Printed 1826

Moser und Peters, printers

Inscribed for Barbara Ann Egolff, born December 31, 1824, Carlisle, Cumberland County

Ink with pigments in medium on wove paper mounted on linen. Relief printed with woodcuts, metal cuts, and letterpress; color is stamped. Orange and yellow designs. Orange stamped over yellow on baskets, dresses, and leaves.

40.6 x 33 cm (16 x 13")

Purchased: Joseph E. Temple Fund. 20-71-6

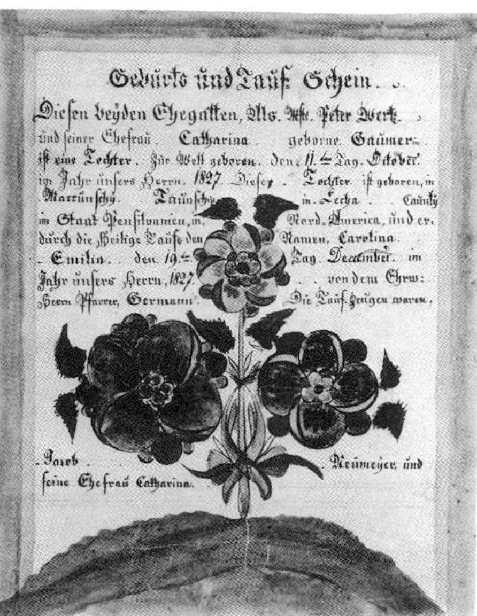

36

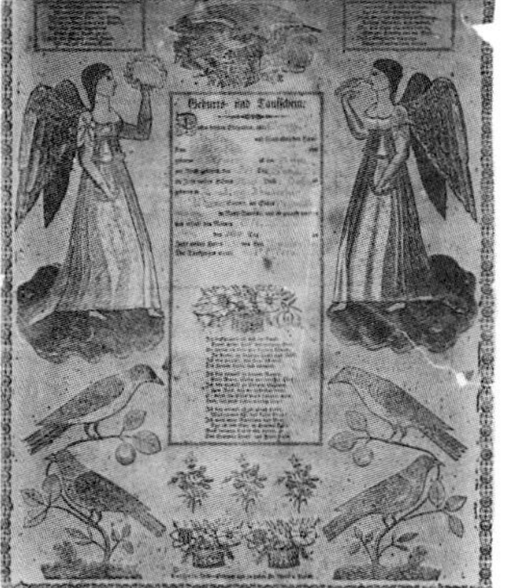

35

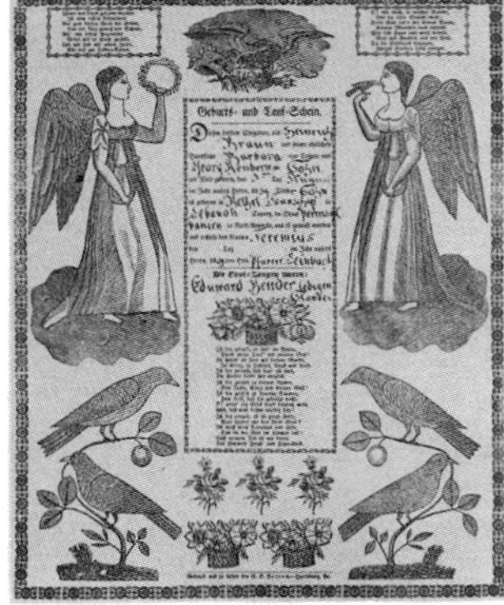

38

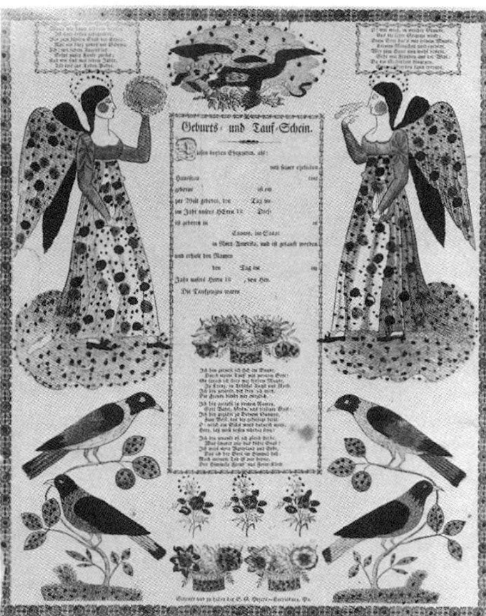

37

35 BIRTH AND BAPTISMAL CERTIFICATE
Carlisle, Cumberland County
Printed 1826

Moser und Peters, printers

Inscribed for Eli Hollinger, born June 20, 1830, Reading Township, Adams County

Ink with pigments in gum medium on wove paper. Relief printed; color is stamped. Orange and yellow designs. Edges trimmed.

40.6 x 31.1 cm (16 x 12¼")

Purchased: Joseph E. Temple Fund. 20-71-1

36 BIRTH AND BAPTISMAL CERTIFICATE
Macungie Township, Lehigh County
1827–28

Inscribed for Carolina Emilia Wertz, born October 11, 1827, Macungie Township, Lehigh County

Watercolor wash, pigment in gum medium, ink, and pencil on wove paper. Lettering guidelines in pencil. Designs drawn in ink and colored. Red, blue, and yellow flowers. Green foliage and "hill." Blue and yellow border.

24.1 x 19 cm (9½ x 7½")

Bequest of Mr. and Mrs. William M. Elkins. 50-92-246

37 BIRTH AND BAPTISMAL CERTIFICATE
Harrisburg, Dauphin County
Printed 1827–47

Gustav Sigismund Peters, printer

Watercolor wash and ink on wove paper. Relief printed with woodcuts, metal cuts, and letterpress; hand colored. Orange and yellow birds with brown wings and tips of tails. Orange red angels with black, red, and yellow dots. Orange border. Blank.

40.3 x 33 cm (15⅞ x 13")

Bequest of Mr. and Mrs. William M. Elkins. 50-92-234

38 BIRTH AND BAPTISMAL CERTIFICATE
Harrisburg, Dauphin County
Printed 1827–47

Gustav Sigismund Peters, printer

Inscribed for Jeremias Braun, born August 3, 1839, Bethel Township, Lebanon County

Ink on wove paper. Relief printed with woodcuts, metal cuts, and letterpress. Uncolored.

41.9 x 33.3 cm (16½ x 13⅛")

Purchased: Joseph E. Temple Fund. 20-71-3

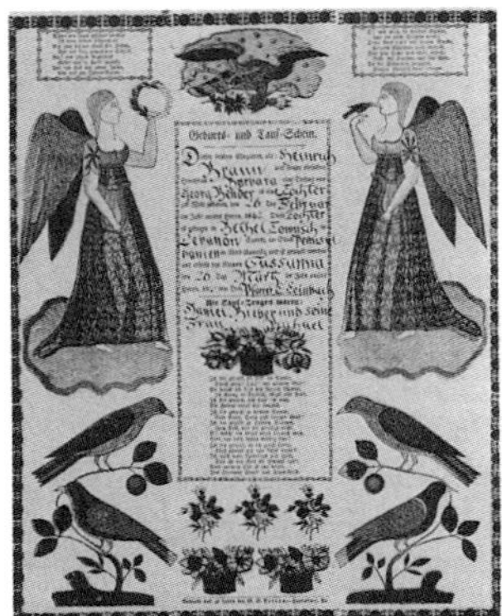

39

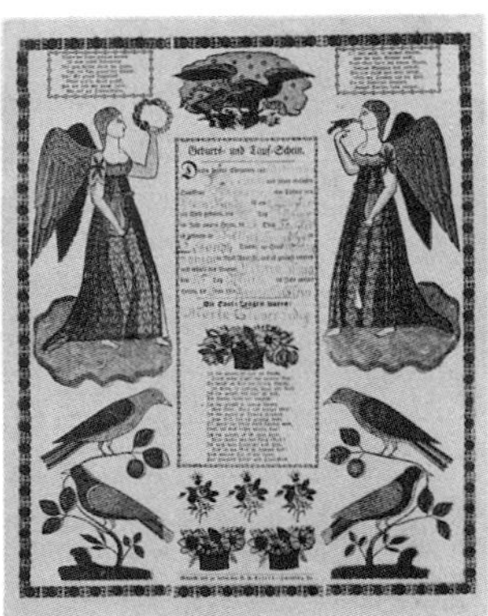

40

39 BIRTH AND BAPTISMAL CERTIFICATE
Harrisburg, Dauphin County
Printed 1827–47

Gustav Sigismund Peters, printer

Inscribed for Sussanna Braun, born February 26, 1842, Bethel Township, Lebanon County

Ink with pigments in medium on wove paper. Relief printed with woodcuts, metal cuts, and letterpress; color is printed. Red and yellow designs. Red over yellow on dresses and leaves.

41.9 x 33.3 cm (16½ x 13⅛″)

Purchased: Joseph E. Temple Fund. 20-71-7

40 BIRTH AND BAPTISMAL CERTIFICATE
Harrisburg, Dauphin County
Printed 1827–47

Gustav Sigismund Peters, printer

Inscribed for Maria Anna Braun, born February 11, 1845, Bethel Township, Lebanon County

Ink with pigments in gum medium on wove paper. Relief printed with woodcuts, metal cuts, and letterpress; color is printed. Gold yellow and red designs.

41 x 32.7 cm (16⅛ x 12⅞″)

Purchased: Joseph E. Temple Fund. 20-71-2

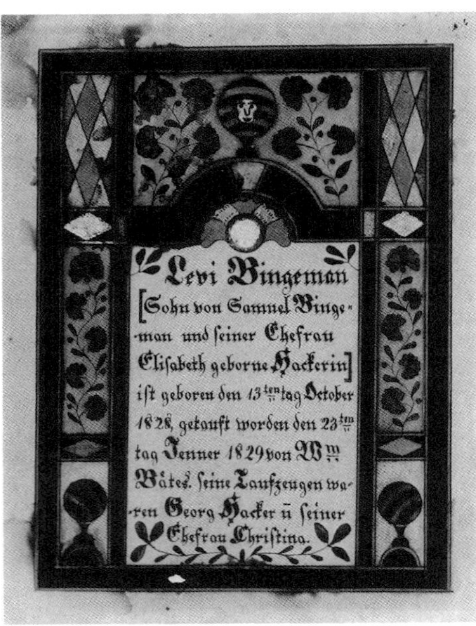

41

41 BIRTH AND BAPTISMAL CERTIFICATE
Lancaster County
1829–30

Attributed to the **Mount Pleasant Artist**

Inscribed for Levi Bingeman, born October 13, 1828

Watercolor wash, gold leaf, and ink on wove paper. Designs drawn in ink and colored. Upper geometric panels in red, tan, and green. Red and brown flowers and foliage on green ground, red and black orbs on tan ground. Black banding and inscription.

25.4 x 19.7 cm (10 x 7¾″)

Gift of J. Stogdell Stokes. 28-10-47

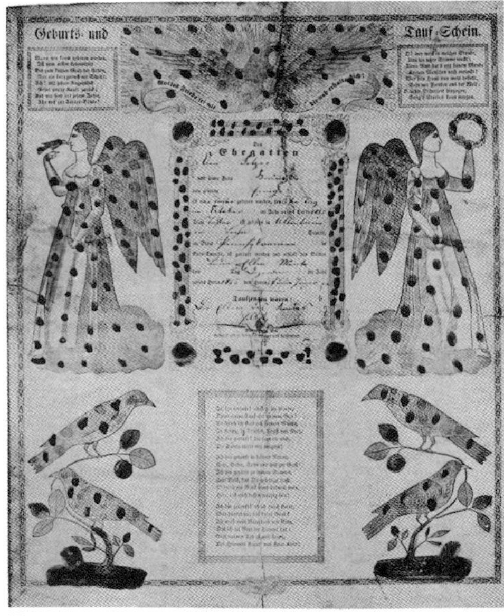

42

42 BIRTH AND BAPTISMAL CERTIFICATE
Allentown, Lehigh County
Printed 1835–42

Blumer und Leisenring, printers

Inscribed for Lidia Ellen Mente Fetzer, born October 3, 1855, Allentown, Lehigh County

Ink with pigments in medium on wove paper. Relief printed with metal cuts and letterpress; hand colored. Red, yellow, and green dots. Green grass and foliage.

43.2 x 34.9 cm (17 x 13¾″)

Gift of Mrs. William D. Frishmuth. 02-455

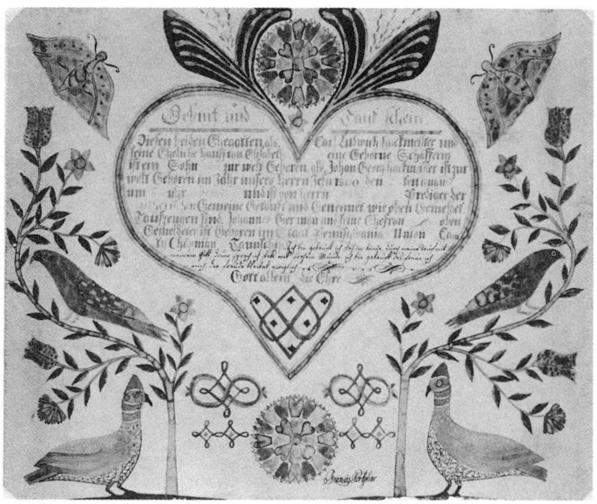

43

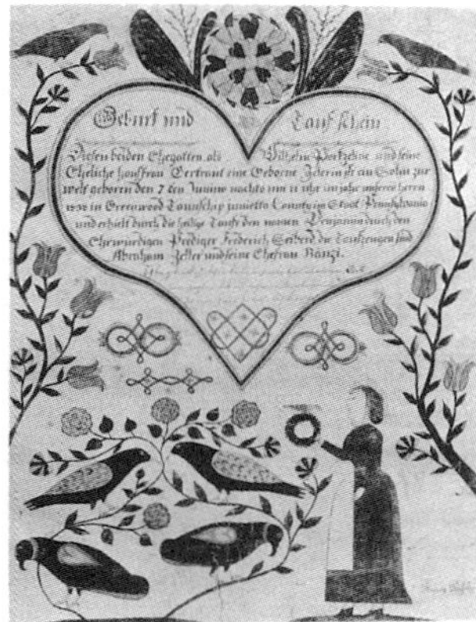

44

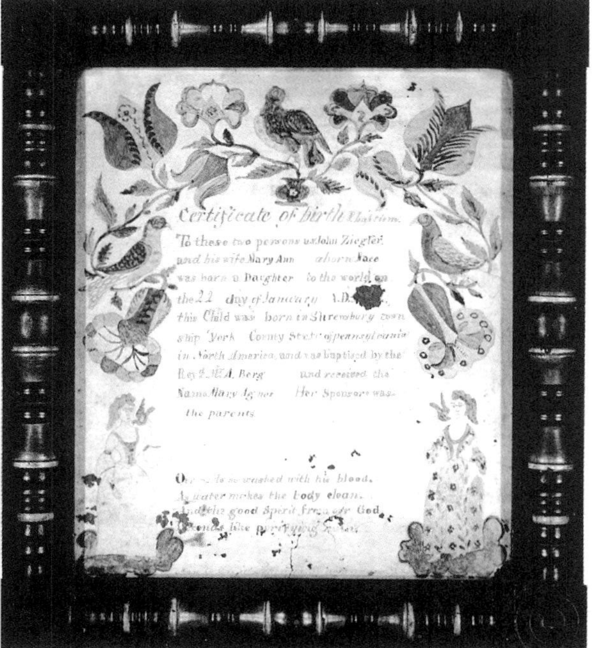

45

43   BIRTH AND BAPTISMAL CERTIFICATE
Union County
1840–55

Francis Portzline

Inscribed for Johan Georg Hackmeister, born August 2, 1800, Chapman Township, Union [Snyder] County

Watercolor wash, pigments in gum medium, and ink on wove paper. Grouse, flowers, and moth (right) are tan with red and blue details. Yellow moth on left. Yellow, red, and purple blue heart rosettes. Red and yellow "pretzels." Perched birds are red with purple blue wing details. Green foliage. Lettering in tan watercolor.

32.7 x 39.4 cm (12⅞ x 15½")

Gift of J. Stogdell Stokes. 28-10-90

44   BIRTH AND BAPTISMAL CERTIFICATE
Juniata County
1840–55

Francis Portzline

Inscribed for Benjamin Portzeline, born June 7, 1838, Greenwood Township, Juniata County

Ink with pigments in gum medium on wove paper. Designs drawn in ink and colored. Upper birds and dress are blue with red details. Red-winged blackbirds, green parrots with red and yellow details. Red and yellow "pretzels." Red, green, and yellow heart rosette, red roses, green foliage.

37.5 x 28.6 cm (14¾ x 11¼")

Gift of J. Stogdell Stokes. 28-10-89

45   BIRTH AND BAPTISMAL CERTIFICATE
Shrewsbury Township, York County
1852–54

Daniel Peterman

Inscribed for Mary Agnes Ziegler, born January 22, ——2, Shrewsbury Township, York County

Watercolor wash, watercolor in gum medium, pencil, and ink on wove paper. Designs drawn in pencil and colored. Women in yellow colonial dresses stand on blue clouds. Red, blue, and yellow tulips and birds. Green center bird and foliage. Red and brown inscription. Lap-joined pine frame is painted black. Split balusters and blocks painted red, yellow, and blue are applied.

35.2 x 30.5 cm (13⅞ x 12") (unframed)

Bequest of Mr. and Mrs. William M. Elkins. 50-92-247

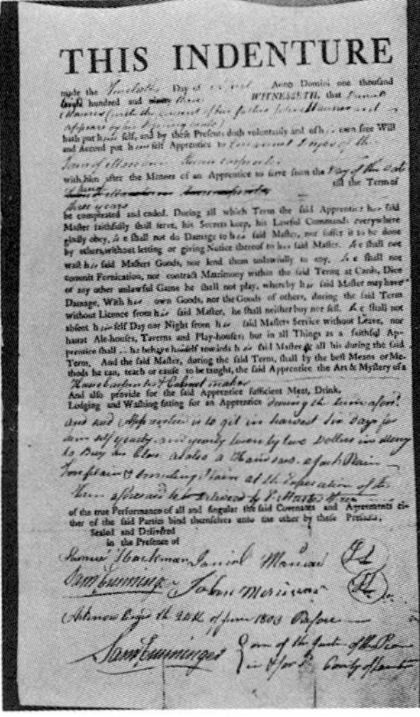

1

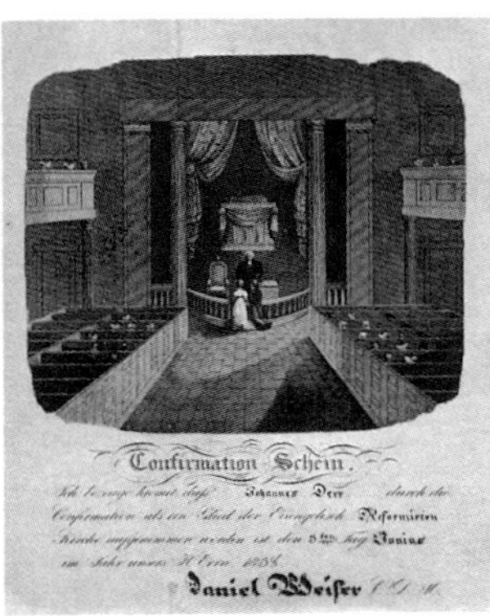

3

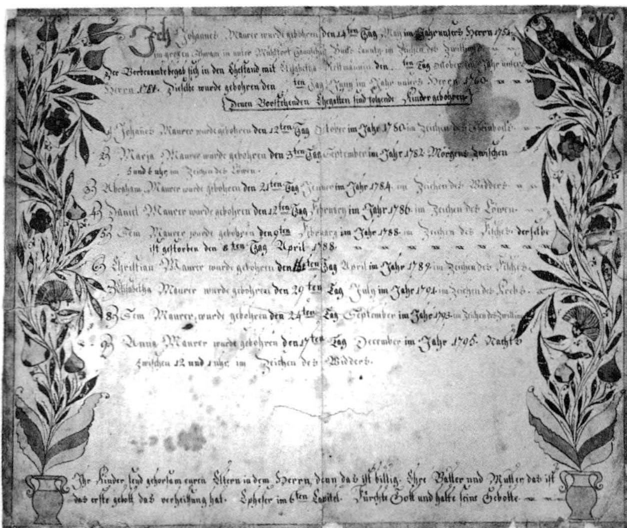

2

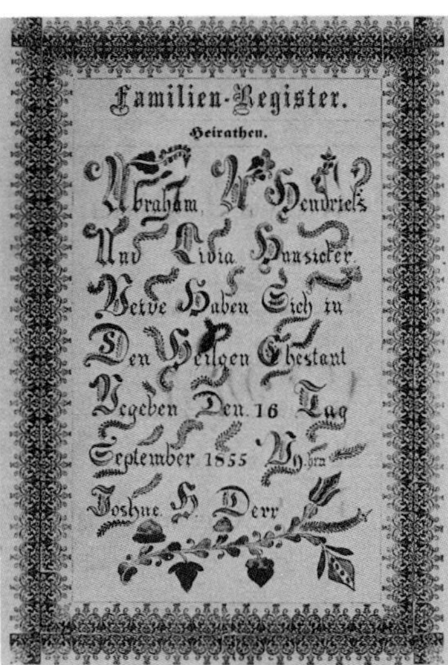

4

1 INDENTURE
Lancaster County
Printed 1790–1800

Ink on wove paper. Relief printed with letterpress. Indenture apprenticing David Maurer, son of John Maurer, to house carpenter Emanuel Dwyer of Manheim, Lancaster County, for three years. Signed June 21, 1803.

32.7 x 18.7 cm (12⅞ x 7⅜″)

Gift of Charles W. Maurer. 17-144

2 FAMILY REGISTER
Hempfield Township, Lancaster County
c. 1795

Attributed to **Christian Strenge**

Inscribed for the Johannes Maurer family

Watercolor wash and ink on laid paper. Designs drawn in ink and colored. Pink and yellow pots, red bird with blue wing and black feathers. Green (faded to brown) foliage. Yellow border with red corners.

32.7 x 39.7 cm (12⅞ x 15⅝″)

Gift of Charles W. Maurer. 17-151

3 CONFIRMATION CERTIFICATE
Inscribed for Johannes Derr, confirmed June 3, 1838

Ink with pigment in medium on wove paper. Engraved. Red signature with black shading.

29.8 x 24.4 cm (11¾ x 9⅝″)

Bequest of Mr. and Mrs. William M. Elkins. 50-92-293

4 FAMILY REGISTER
1855

Inscribed for Abraham A. and Lidia Hunsicker Hendricks

Watercolor wash, ink, and pencil on wove paper. Relief-printed border. Lettering guidelines in pencil. Designs and lettering drawn in ink and colored. Brown ink feathers obverse and reverse. Letters and some feathers on obverse in peach, blue green, gold yellow, and red brown.

21.3 x 14.6 cm (8⅜ x 5¾″)

Bequest of Mr. and Mrs. William M. Elkins. 50-92-238

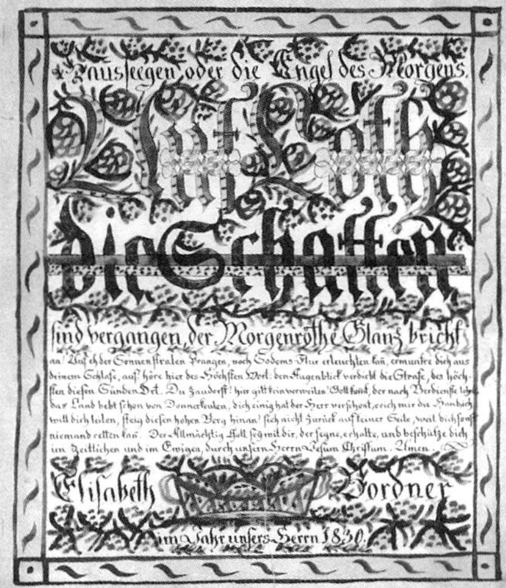

1

1 HOUSE BLESSING
Bethel Township, Berks County
1830

Attributed to **Heinrich Engelhard**

Inscribed for Elisabeth Bordner

Watercolor wash, pigments in gum medium, pencil, and ink on wove paper. Illuminated letters drawn in ink between pencil guidelines and colored; other designs freehand. Red, yellow, blue, and black lettering. Red and green roses. Green vines with red and tan berries. Red and yellow basket. Red border.

32.7 x 27.9 cm (12⅞ x 11″)

Gift of J. Stogdell Stokes. 28-10-88

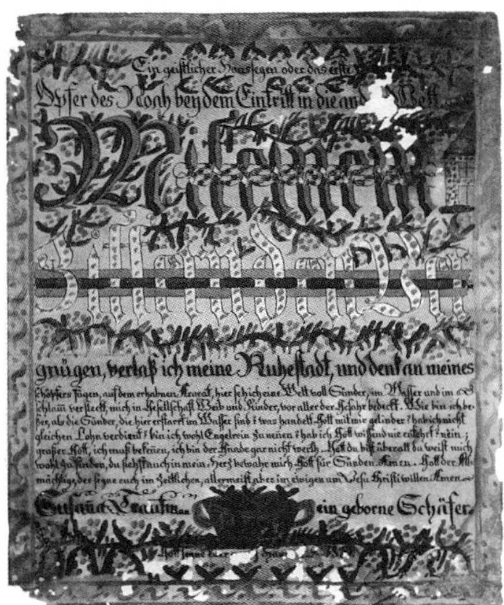

2

2 HOUSE BLESSING
Bethel Township, Berks County
1831

Attributed to **Heinrich Engelhard**

Inscribed for Susanna Trautman

Pigments in gum medium, pencil, and ink on wove paper. Illuminated letters drawn in ink between pencil guidelines and colored; other designs freehand. Red, blue, and yellow lettering. Blue and red basket. Green vines with red berries. Yellow house with red and green dots and blue roof. Red border.

30.5 x 25.4 cm (12 x 10″)

Gift of Mrs. William D. Frishmuth. 08-204

3 HOUSE BLESSING
Lancaster, Lancaster County
Printed c. 1832–34

H. W. Villee, printer

Inscribed for Elisabeth Landes

Ink with pigments in gum medium on wove paper. Relief printed with letterpress. Floral border drawn and colored by hand. Red, yellow, and white flowers. Green foliage.

40 x 31.8 cm (15¾ x 12½″)

Titus C. Geesey Collection. 54-85-130

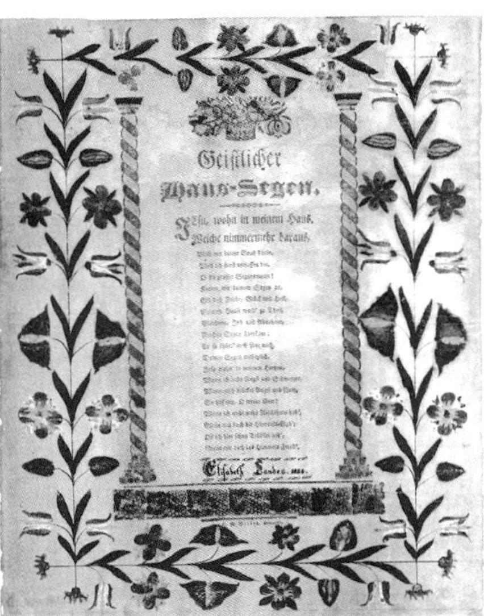

3

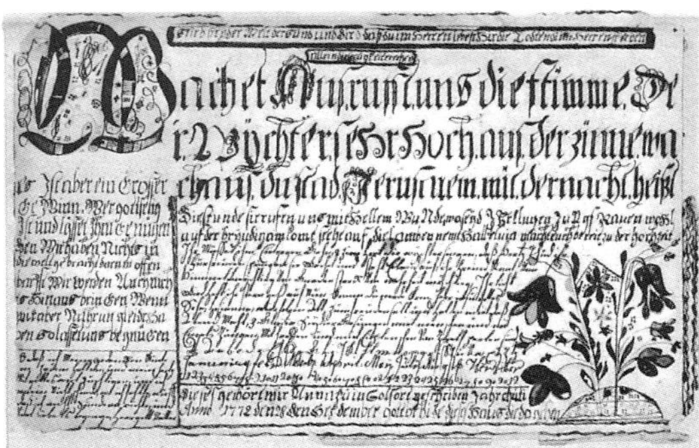

1

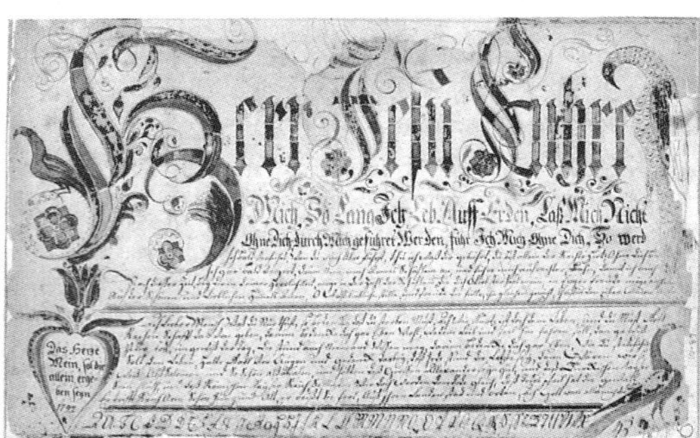

2

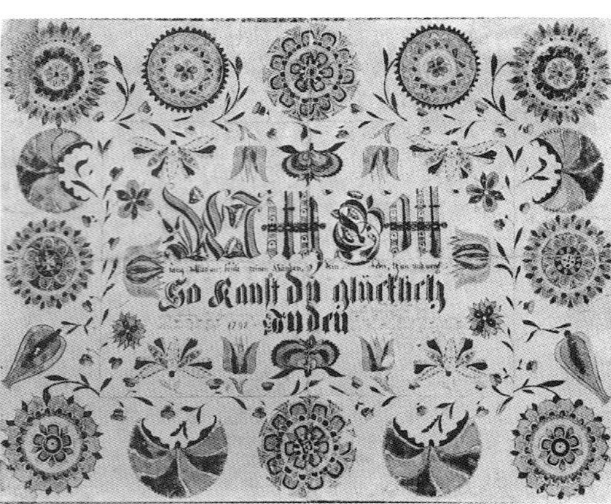

3

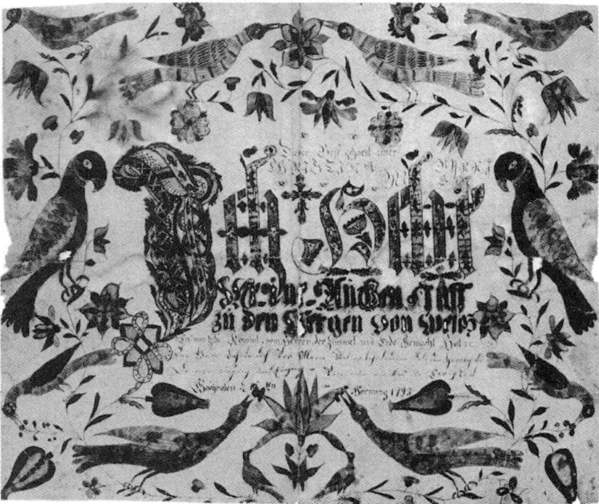

4

1 WRITING SAMPLE
Salford Township, Montgomery County
September 28, 1772

Ink on laid paper. Watermark: Garden of Holland [c. 1770], with addition of bell with clapper under center gate and without lettering below.

20 x 33 cm (7⅞ x 13″)

Gift of the Haas Community Fund. 68-118-61

2 WRITING SAMPLE
Probably Lancaster County
1792

Ink with pigments in gum medium on laid paper. Designs drawn in ink and colored. Red, yellow, and ink illuminated letters. Green bird with red and yellow wings on left. Bird with red breast feathers in upper right; yellow bird with red details in lower right. Ink details.

21 x 34 cm (8¼ x 13⅜″)

Gift of Mrs. William D. Frishmuth. 10-87

3 WRITING SAMPLE
Lancaster County
February 5, 1793

Possibly by the **Huber Artist**

Inscribed for Christina Bearry

Ink with watercolor in gum medium on laid paper. Designs drawn in ink and colored. Red and pink lettering. Red, blue, and yellow flowers, red and yellow border. Ink details.

39.7 x 51.4 cm (15⅝ x 20¼″)

Titus C. Geesey Collection. 55-94-72

4 WRITING SAMPLE
Lancaster County
February 10, 1793

Possibly by the **Huber Artist**

Inscribed for Christina Byrri [Bearry]

Watercolor, pigments in gum medium, and ink on laid paper. Designs drawn in ink and colored. Red, pink, yellow, blue, and brown illuminated letters. Brown parrots with yellow and red wings. Upper corners: red bird with blue details; lower corners: red and brown birds. Upper center: yellow birds with red wings, blue heads; bottom: large birds blue green with red details, small birds red with blue details. Red, blue, and yellow flowers. Ink details. Edges trimmed.

32.1 x 40.3 cm (12⅝ x 15⅞″)

Titus C. Geesey Collection. 55-94-73

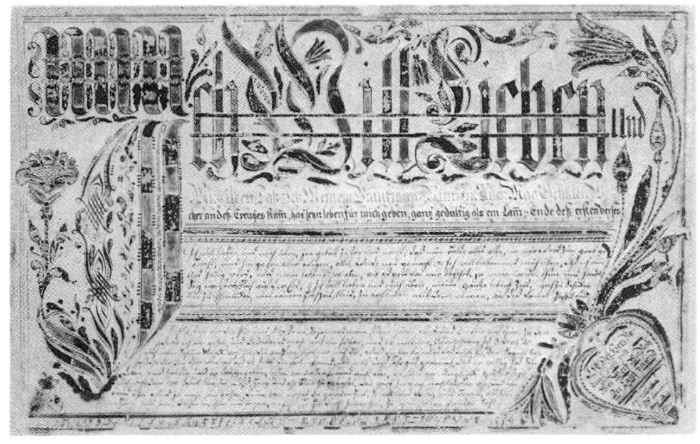

5

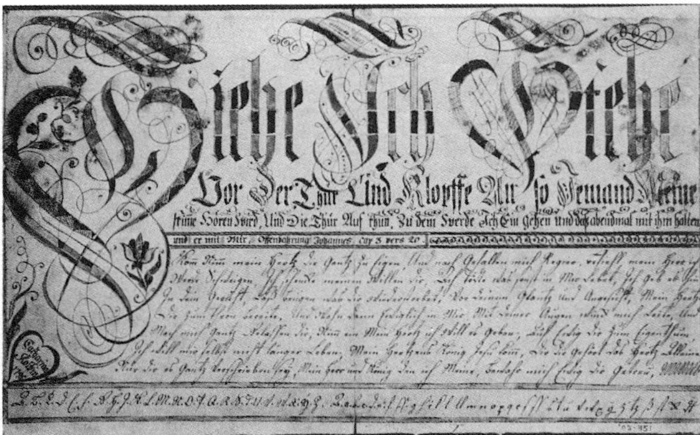

6

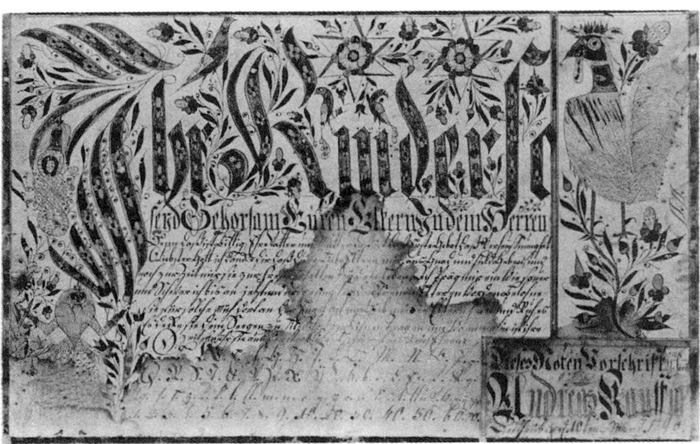

7

5 WRITING SAMPLE
Probably Lancaster County
February 28, 1794

Ink with pigments in gum medium on laid paper. Designs drawn in ink and colored. Orange red, gold yellow, green, and ink illuminated letters. Red orange, yellow, and blue green flowers. Red orange border. Ink details.

21 x 34.5 cm (8¼ x 13⅝")

Titus C. Geesey Collection. 69-284-3

6 WRITING SAMPLE
Montgomery County
1795

Inscribed for Catharina Kolb

Watercolor wash and ink on laid paper. Designs drawn in ink and colored. Red, blue, green, yellow, and ink illuminated letters. Yellow border.

20 x 34.3 cm (7⅞ x 13½")

Gift of Mrs. William D. Frishmuth. 02-451

7 WRITING SAMPLE
Earl Township, Lancaster County
March 10, 1796

Attributed to the **Earl Township Artist**

Inscribed for Andreas Kauffm[an]

Ink with pigments in gum medium on laid paper. Designs drawn in ink and colored. Blue illuminated letters with red details. Red, yellow, and blue flowers with green foliage. Ink details. Paper originally bound in a book or pad.

19.7 x 32.4 cm (7¾ x 12¾")

Purchased. 14-247

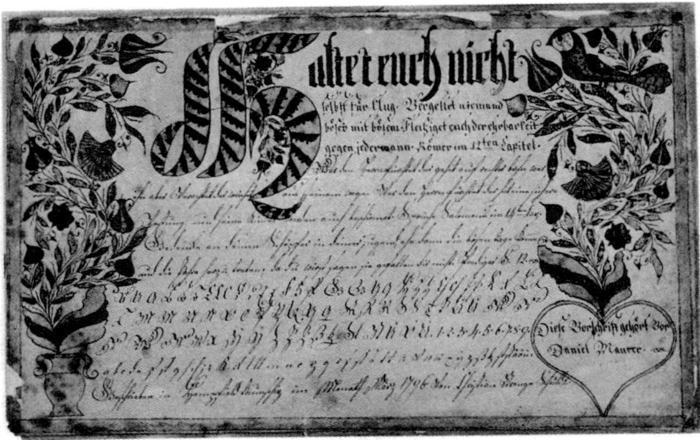

8

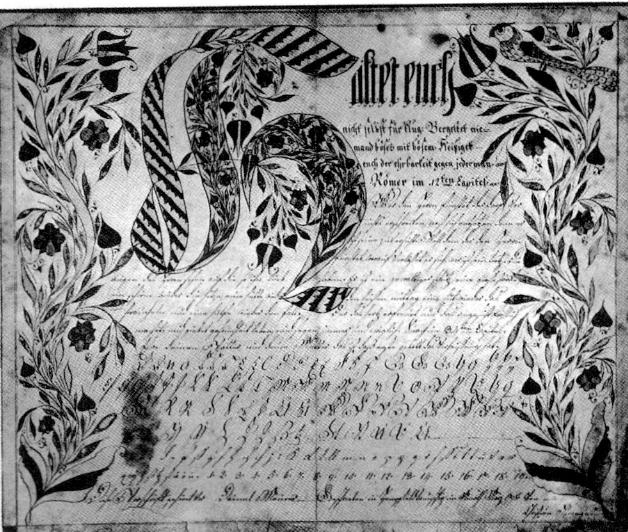

9

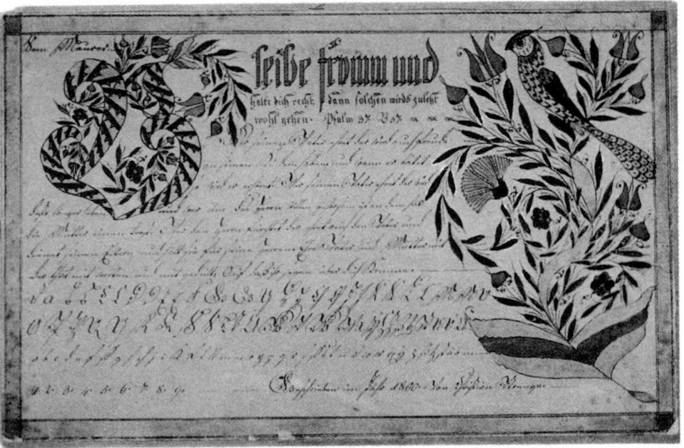

10

8 **WRITING SAMPLE**
Hempfield Township, Lancaster County
March 1796

Christian Strenge

Inscribed for Daniel Maurer

Watercolor wash and ink on laid paper.
Designs drawn in ink and colored. Red and
yellow flowers. Red, yellow, and blue birds.
Yellow illuminated letter with red and ink
stripes. Red and blue Gothic lettering. Yellow
border with red corners. Ink details.

19.4 x 32.7 cm (7⅝ x 12⅞″)

Gift of Charles W. Maurer. 17-146

9 **WRITING SAMPLE**
Hempfield Township, Lancaster County
March 1798

Christian Strenge

Inscribed for Daniel Maurer

Watercolor wash, pigments in gum medium,
and ink on laid paper. Designs drawn in ink
and colored. Yellow illuminated letter with
red, blue, and black details. Red and blue
flowers with green (faded to brown) foliage.
Yellow border with red corners. Ink details.

32.1 x 39.1 cm (12⅝ x 15⅜″)

Gift of Charles W. Maurer. 17-150

10 **WRITING SAMPLE**
Hempfield Township, Lancaster County
1800

Christian Strenge

Inscribed for Sam Maurer

Watercolor wash and ink on laid paper.
Designs drawn in ink and colored. Red and
yellow flowers. Yellow bird with blue and red
details. Yellow illuminated letter with red and
ink stripes. Yellow border with red corners.
Ink details.

19.1 x 31.1 cm (7½ x 12¼″)

Gift of Charles W. Maurer. 17-148

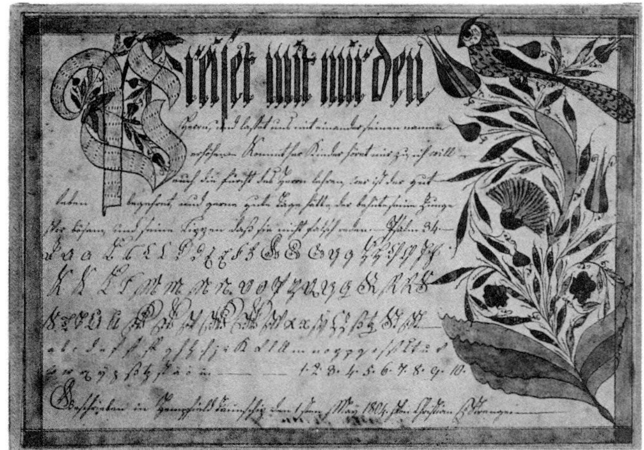

11

11 **WRITING SAMPLE**
Hempfield Township, Lancaster County
May 1, 1804

Christian Strenge

Watercolor wash and ink on laid paper.
Designs drawn in ink and colored. Red,
yellow, and blue flowers. Green foliage with
ink stems. Red-striped illuminated letter.
Yellow, blue, and red bird. Yellow border
with red corners. Ink details.

17.8 x 25.6 cm (7 x 10⅛″)

Gift of Charles W. Maurer. 17-147a

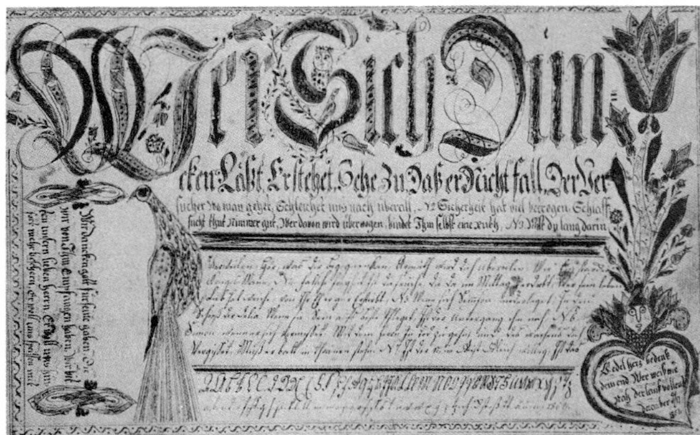

12

12 **WRITING SAMPLE**
Probably Montgomery County
December 17, 1804

Ink with pigments in gum medium on laid
paper. Designs drawn in ink and colored.
Red, blue, and yellow illuminated letters.
Yellow, green, and red bird with yellow and
blue wing. Red, blue, and yellow heart. Ink
details.

20 x 33.3 cm (7⅞ x 13⅛″)

Gift of Edwin Atlee Barber. 97-99

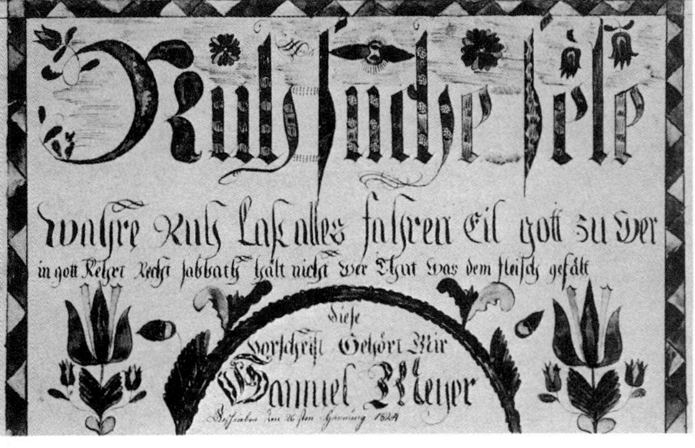

13

13 **WRITING SAMPLE**
Berks or Montgomery County
February 26, 1824

Inscribed for Samuel Meyer

Ink with pigments in gum medium on wove
paper. Designs drawn in ink and colored.
Red, yellow, green, and brown illuminated
letters; part of inscription is red with ink
stripes. Green arch with ink and red details.
Red, green, and yellow border.

20 x 32.4 cm (7⅞ x 12¾″)

Gift of the Haas Community Fund. 68-118-60

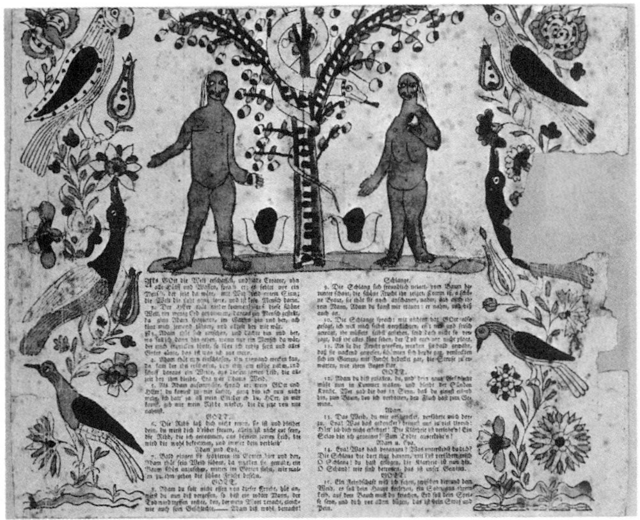

1

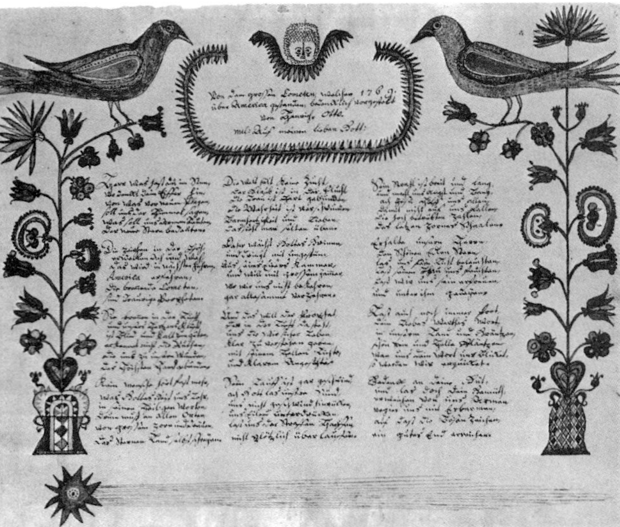

3

1 RELIGIOUS TEXT
Lancaster County
Printed 1785–1800

Watercolor wash and ink on laid paper. Relief printed with woodcuts and letterpress; hand colored. Adam and Eve drawn in ink and colored. Green, tan, and brown design. Edges trimmed.

33 x 40.6 cm (13 x 16″)

Titus C. Geesey Collection. 54-85-11

2 RELIGIOUS TEXT
Lancaster County
February 5, 1794

Probably by **Abraham Maurer**

Watercolor wash and ink on laid paper. Designs drawn in ink and colored red and brown.

19.7 x 15.9 cm (7¾ x 6¼″)

Gift of Charles W. Maurer. 17-149

3 RELIGIOUS TEXT
Montgomery County
1800–1807

Attributed to **Susanna Hubner**

Ink with pigments in gum medium on laid paper. Watermark: FS [Frederick Sheetz, Montgomery County]. Designs drawn in ink and colored. Gold yellow birds with red feathers and green, yellow, and red wings. Red, green, blue, and gold yellow pots. Red comet. Hand-drawn version of Johan Henrich Otto's printed broadside.

33.3 x 40.3 cm (13⅛ x 15⅞″)

Gift of J. Stogdell Stokes. 28-83-1

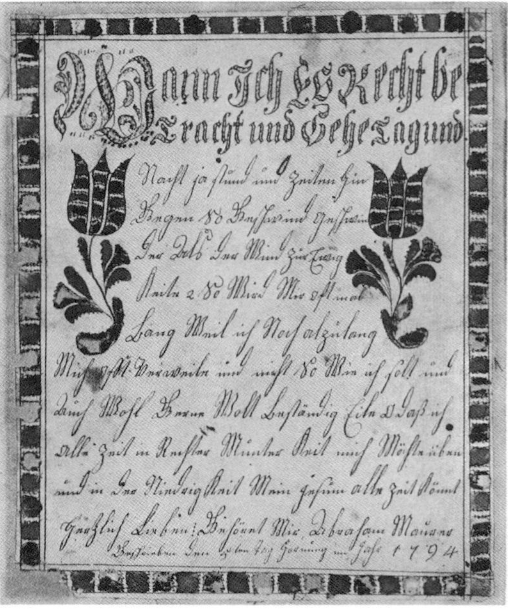

2

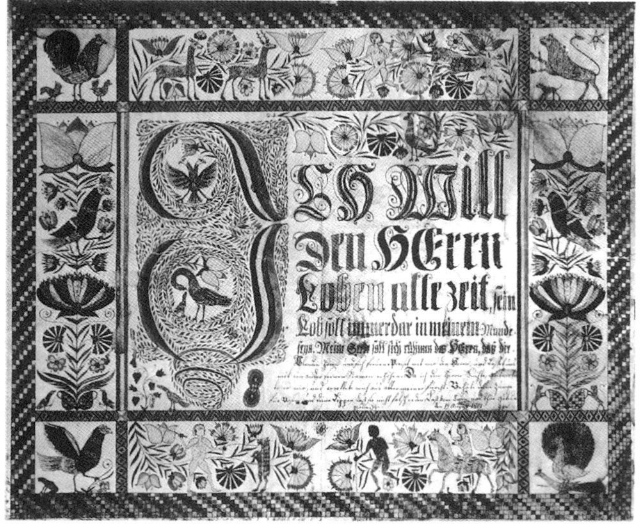

4

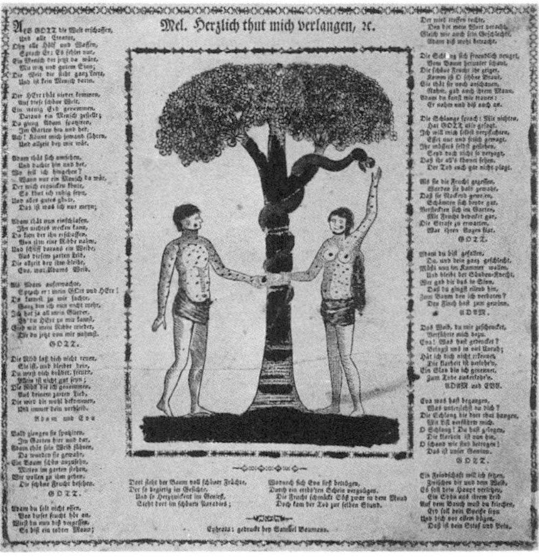

5

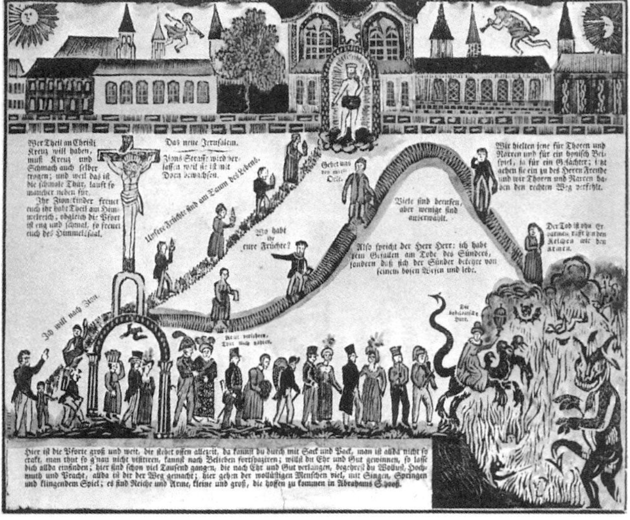

6

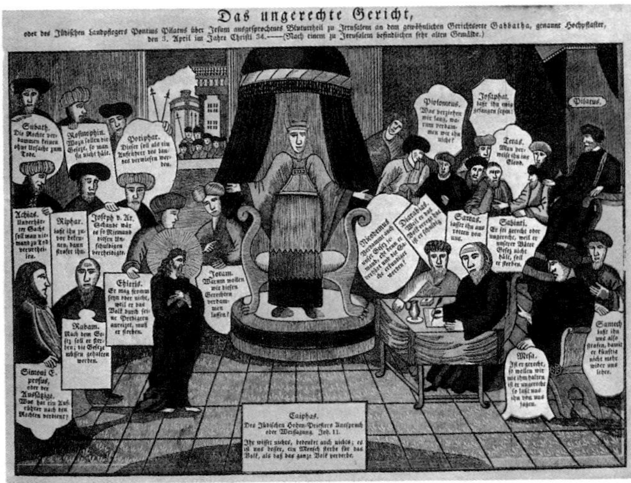

7

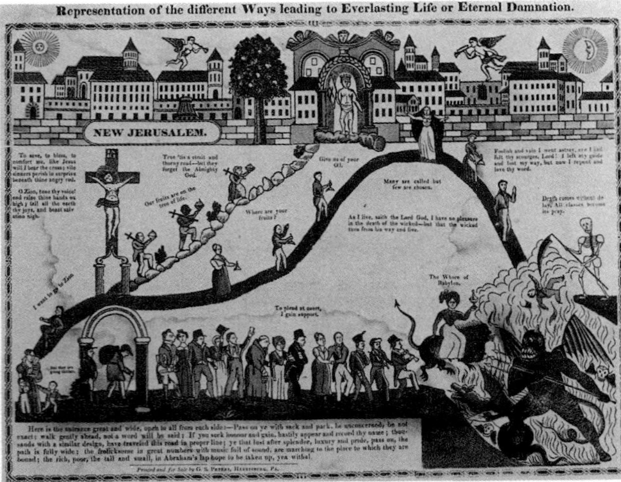

8

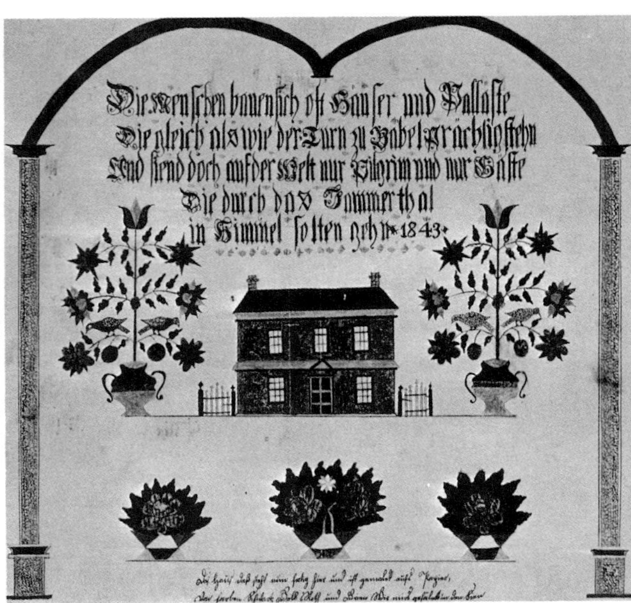

9

7   **RELIGIOUS TEXT**
Harrisburg, Dauphin County
Printed 1827–47

Gustav Sigismund Peters, printer

Watercolor wash and ink on wove paper. Relief printed with letterpress; color is printed. Red brown, yellow, and blue figures. Red brown tent, yellow thrones, blue tablecloth, and yellow green ground. Bottom trimmed.

23.8 x 32.1 cm (9⅜ x 12⅝″)

Gift of John Story Jenks. 13-112

---

8   **RELIGIOUS TEXT**
Harrisburg, Dauphin County
Printed 1827–47

Gustav Sigismund Peters, printer

Watercolor wash and ink on wove paper. Relief printed with letterpress; color is printed. Yellow flames, green ground and trees, red orange dragon and roofs. Central arch blue. Green, yellow, and blue buildings. Yellow, blue, and red orange figures.

30.7 x 38.4 cm (12⅛ x 15⅛″)

Purchased: Joseph E. Temple Fund. 20-71-9

---

9   **RELIGIOUS TEXT**
Montgomery County
1843

Attributed to **Maria** or **Rosina Kriebel**

Pigments in gum medium, pencil, and ink on laid paper. Watermark: Britannia [c. 1790]. Lettering guidelines and designs drawn in pencil and colored. Red arch and house. Green and yellow house trim and roof. Yellow and green vases with red midbands. Red, green, and yellow flowers. Black and red inscription.

31.8 x 34.6 cm (12½ x 13⅝″)

Bequest of Mr. and Mrs. William M. Elkins. 50-92-244

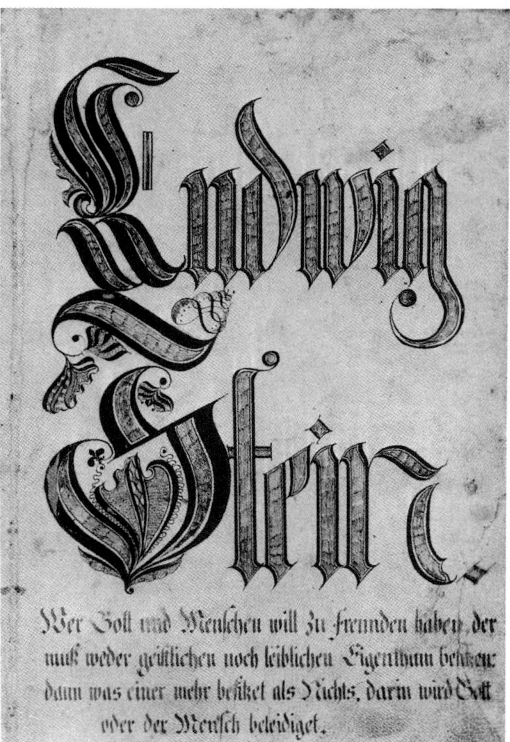

1 **BOOKPLATE**
Ephrata, Lancaster County
1750–60

Inscribed (translation): *Ludwig Stein. Whosoever would have God and man as friends, need have neither spiritual nor material possessions; for whenever one possesses more than nothing, either God or man is thereby offended.*

Ink with pigments in medium on laid paper. Two lettering guidelines at top and two at bottom scored with stylus. Name in black ink, religious text in red. Daubs of red on *L* and *S*. Scored on left; originally bound in a *Martyr's Mirror.*

35.2 x 22 cm (13⅞ x 8⅝″)

Titus C. Geesey Collection. 69-284-12

---

2 **BOOKPLATE**
Bedminster Township, Bucks County
January 2, 1792

Inscribed (translation): *This pretty little booklet belongs to Magdalena Landes. Written the 2nd of January 1792, Bedminster Township, Bucks County. Peace and mercy be upon all who walk by this rule. Galatians 6:16.*

Watercolor wash, pigments in gum medium, and ink on laid paper. Designs drawn in ink and colored red, blue, and green. Brown and red inscription.

13.3 x 7.9 cm (5¼ x 3⅛″)

Gift of Sylvester Krafka. 51-97-1

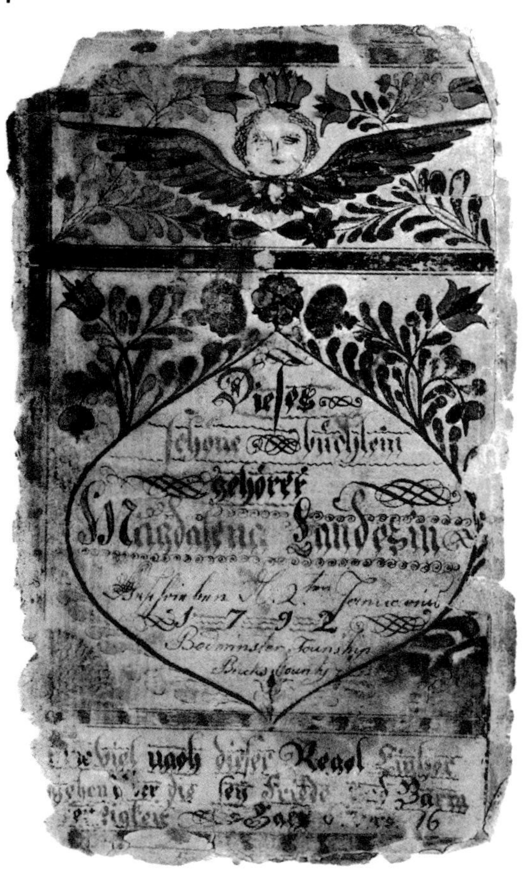

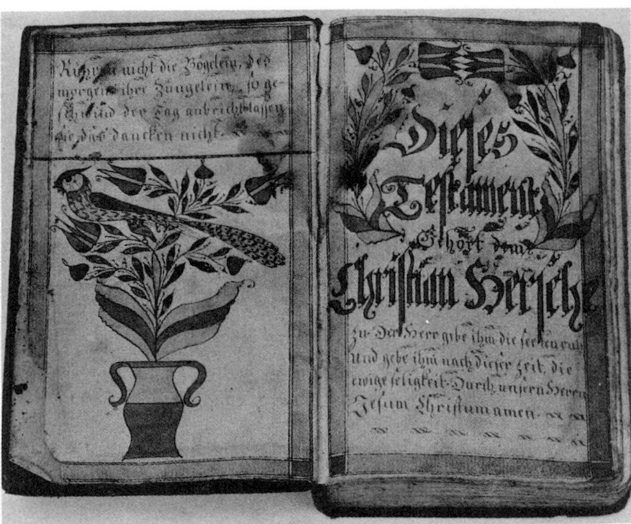

3

3   **BOOKPLATE**
Hempfield Township, Lancaster County
1796–1800

Christian Strenge

Inscribed (translation): *If the little birds do not move their little tongues as soon as day breaks, they do not stop giving thanks.   This Testament belongs to Christian Hersche. The Lord give him peace of mind, and after this time give him eternal salvation. Through our Lord Jesus Christ, Amen.*

Ink with watercolor in medium on endpaper and flyleaf of a New Testament (*see* Paper, Books, Printed, no. 12). Designs drawn in ink and colored. Red, blue, and yellow bird and tulips. Vase and foliage red and yellow. Yellow borders with red corners. Ink details.

16.2 x 10.2 cm (6⅜ x 4″)

Titus C. Geesey Collection. 58-110-34

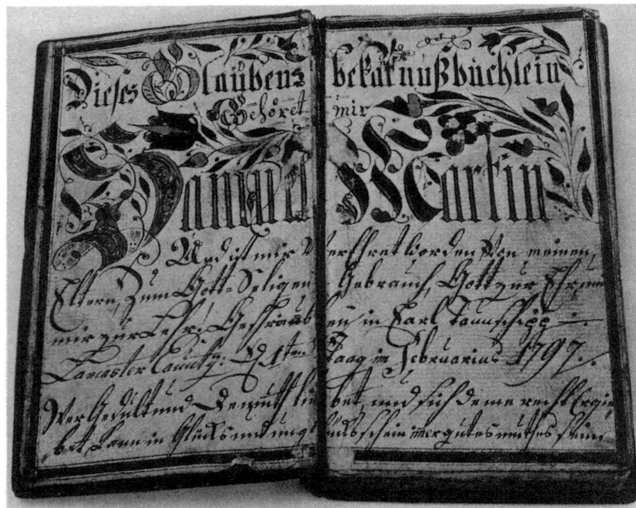

4

4   **BOOKPLATE**
Earl Township, Lancaster County
February 1, 1797

Attributed to the **Earl Township Artist**

Inscribed (translation): *This little catechism belongs to me, Samuel Martin, and was presented to me by my parents for godly use, to the honor of God and as my pattern. Written in Earl Township, Lancaster County, the 1st day of February 1797.   He who loves patience and humility,/And properly yields himself to them,/Can be full of hope,/In the face of fortune and misfortune.*

Watercolor wash, pigments in gum medium, and ink on laid paper. Designs drawn in ink and colored red, blue, and yellow. Pasted to endpaper and flyleaf of a catechism (*see* Paper, Books, Printed, no. 8).

13.7 x 16.2 cm (5⅜ x 6⅜″)

Titus C. Geesey Collection. 58-110-35

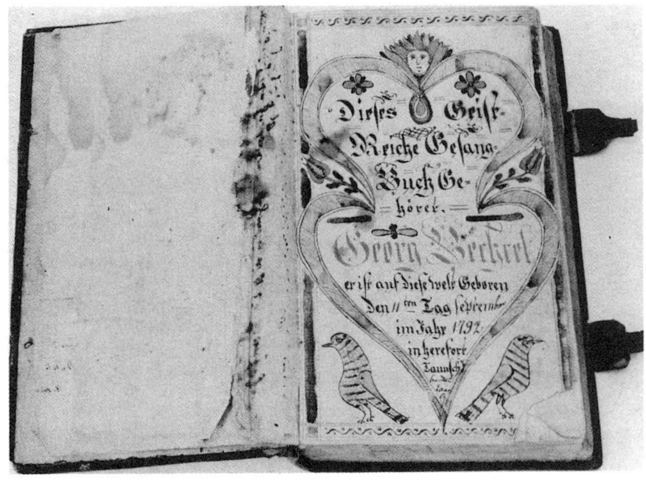

5

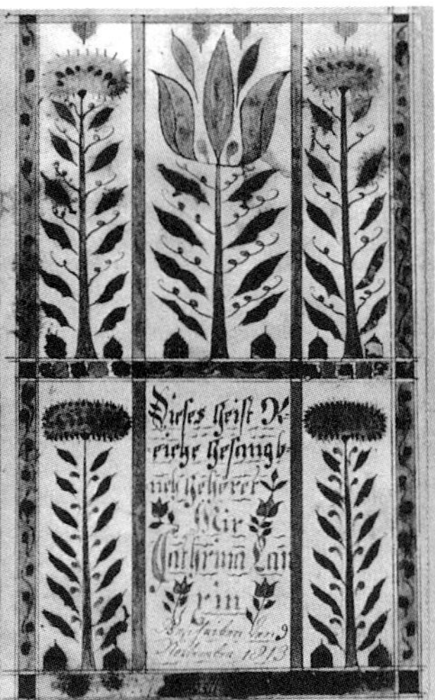

6

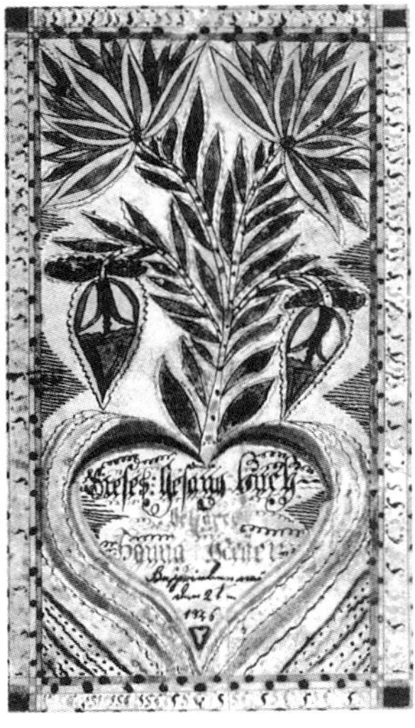

7

5 BOOKPLATE
Hereford Township, Berks County
1803–10

Attributed to the **Hereford Township Artist**

Inscribed (translation): *This spiritual songbook belongs to Georg Bechtel. He was born into this world on the 11th day of September in the year 1792 in Hereford Township, Berks County.*

Ink with pigments in gum medium on laid paper. Designs drawn in ink and colored red and yellow with ink wash details. In a hymnal (*see* Paper, Books, Printed, no. 13).

16.6 x 9.6 cm (6½ x 3¾")

Titus C. Geesey Collection. 58-110-33

6 BOOKPLATE
Bucks County
November 9, 1813

Inscribed (translation): *This spirit-rich songbook belongs to me, Cathrina Laux. Written November 9, 1813.*

Ink with pigments in gum medium on laid paper. Designs drawn in ink and colored. Red and yellow flowers, green stems, gray green foliage. Red and yellow borders with brown ink vine. Red, yellow, and brown ink inscription.

16.2 x 9.8 cm (6⅜ x 3⅞")

Bequest of Mr. and Mrs. William M. Elkins. 50-92-237

7 BOOKPLATE
Bucks County
May 2, 1846

Inscribed (translation): *This songbook belongs to Hanna Meyer. Written the 2nd of May 1846.*

Ink with pigments in gum medium on wove paper. Designs drawn in ink and colored. Red and yellow flowers with green foliage. Blue, red, and yellow heart. Red and yellow borders with blue corners. Binding-thread holes at top.

16 x 9.5 cm (6¼ x 3¾")

Bequest of Mr. and Mrs. William M. Elkins. 50-92-236

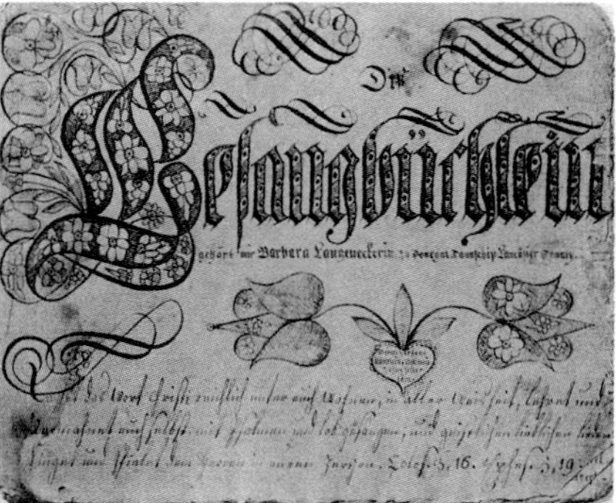

1

1   SONGBOOK
Donegal Township, Lancaster County
1790–1810

Inscribed (translation): *This little songbook belongs to me, Barbara Langenecker, in Donegal Township, Lancaster County. The flower of my heart shall be my Jesus himself. Let the word of Christ dwell richly in you, in all wisdom, teaching and admonishing one another in psalms and hymns and spiritual songs. Singing and making melody in your heart to the Lord. Colossians 3:16. Ephesians 5:19.*

Ink on laid paper. Four sheets folded into sixteen pages. Spine hand sewn with fine twisted twine. Ink drawing and lettering on cover. Fifteen pages of German tunes and verses from Psalms 134, 100, 42, 81, 38, 25, 36, 68, 77, 86, 24, 62, 95, 111.

16.5 x 21 cm (6½ x 8¼″)

Titus C. Geesey Collection. 58-110-32

2   HYMNAL
Hempfield Township, Lancaster County
1796

Attributed to **Christian Strenge**

Inscribed (translation): *The angels sing to God in heaven,/May all praise to him be given,/ The saints and angels sing their praise/To God through everlasting days. Hallelujah./1. Psalm 100. All people that on earth do dwell./2. Blessed Jesus at thy word./3. All praise to thee, eternal Lord./[nos. 4–7 not shown]/8. How brightly beams the morning star./9. The time is surely nigh, that./10. O prepare thou my spirit./11. Follow where God's grace shall lead./[nos. 12–15 not shown]/16. Lord Jesus Christ be present now./17. Lord Jesus, Sun of Grace, true./18. If thou would but suffer God to guide thee./19. Since now the day is ended, and./   This melody book belongs to the industrious pupil, Daniel Maurer. Written in Hempfield Township in the month of January in the year 1796.*

Watercolor wash, pigments in gum medium, and ink on laid paper. Ten pages. Obverse (shown): Five sheets unbound and mounted. Reverse: Two of five sheets have music. Designs drawn in ink and colored. Red, blue, and yellow borders and tulips. Angels have yellow and lavender feathers with ink details. Brown and red inscription. Music in brown ink.

9.5 x 16.2 cm (3¾ x 6⅜″) (page)

Gift of Charles W. Maurer. 17-152

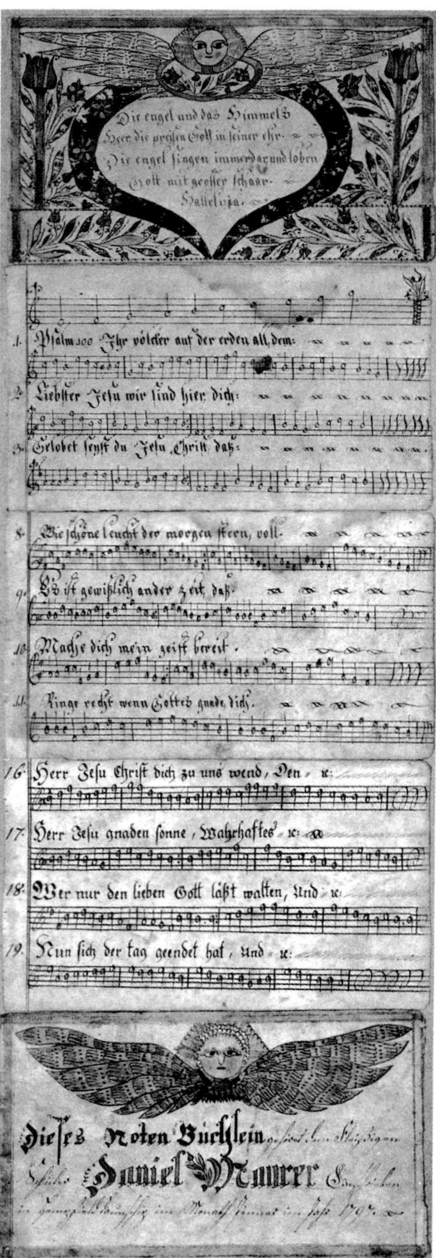

2

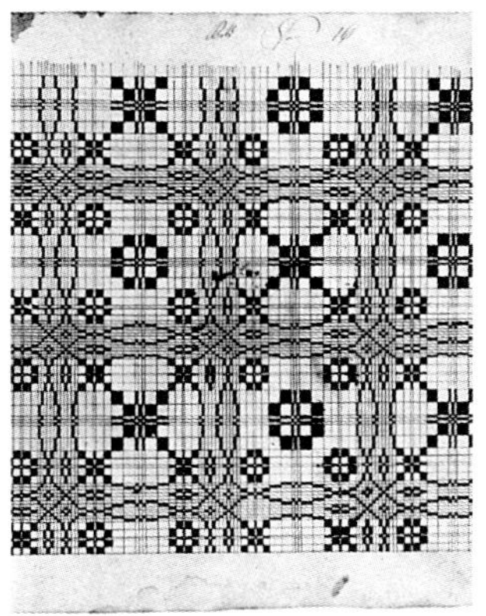

3

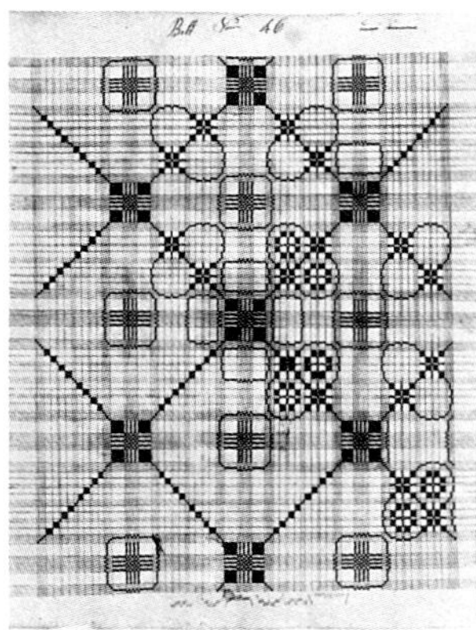

3

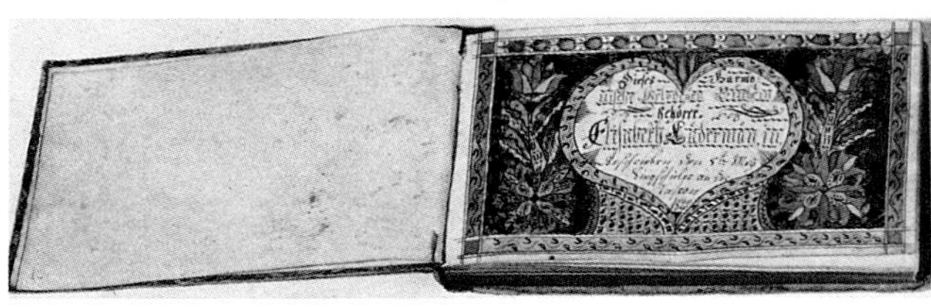

4

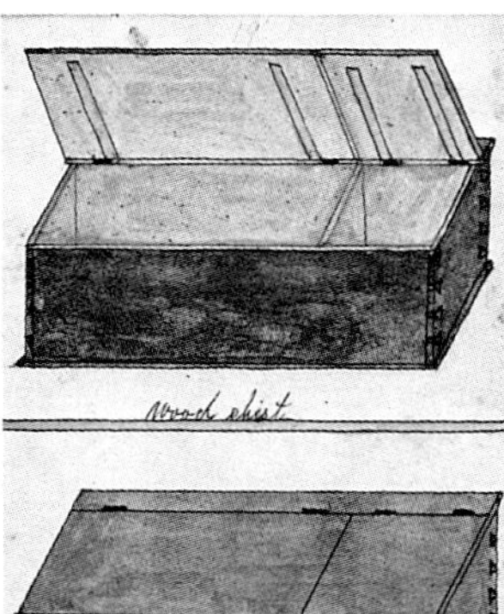

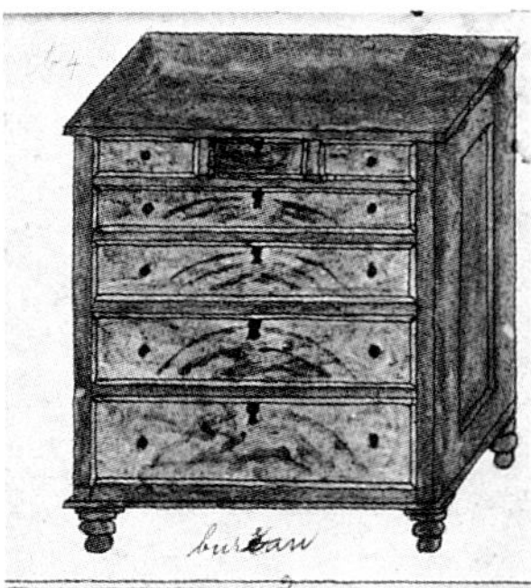

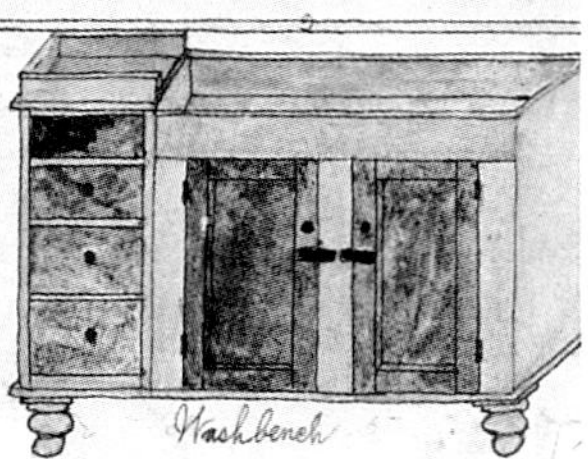

5

5

3 **WEAVING PATTERN BOOK**
Montgomery County
1806–12

Attributed to **John Landes**

Ink with pigments in gum medium on laid paper; leather. Watermarks: AL (Abraham Levan, Jr., Kutztown, Berks County); WL and eagle with dropped wings (William Levis, Upper Darby, Delaware County); SH; JS (John or James Steele, Chester County); ARCH (Adam Rahn and Conrad Herbst, Maidencreek Township, Bucks County); G. Unkley (Berkeley County, Virginia); PRO PATRIA/J.H. LENN. Seventy-seven plates. Brown ink rules filled with patterns in brown, blue, red, and green. Originally bound in leather with 1806 *Pennsylvania Gazette* pasted inside covers.

39.4 x 31.1 cm (15½ x 12¼")

Gift of Mrs. William D. Frishmuth. 07-212

---

4 **SONGBOOK**
Bedminster Township, Bucks County
1823

Inscribed on bookplate (translation): *This little harmonious melody book belongs to Elisabeth Laederman. Singing student in the Deep Run school. Written May 8th 1823.*

Ink with pigments in gum medium on wove paper; leather, cardboard. First twenty-seven pages inscribed with bars, notes, tunes, and titles, four to a page; rest blank. Covers are blue, tan, and black marbleized paper over cardboard. Sewn binding. Leather spine. Bookplate designs drawn in ink and colored. Heart outlined in yellow. Tulips and rosettes red, yellow, and green with black details. Blue green background. Red, green, and yellow borders with red and black details.

10 x 16.9 cm (3⅞ x 6⅝")

Titus C. Geesey Collection. 58-110-36

---

5 **CRAFTSMAN'S HANDBOOK**
Leacock Township, Lancaster County
1890–1900

Henry L. Lapp

Stamped on cover: *HENRY LAPP*

Pigments in gum medium, watercolor wash, ink, and pencil on wove paper. Forty-six pages. Illustrations include furniture, farm implements, games, and counting devices. Facsimile published in 1975 by the Philadelphia Museum of Art.

20.3 x 11.4 cm (8 x 4½")

Titus C. Geesey Collection. 58-110-31

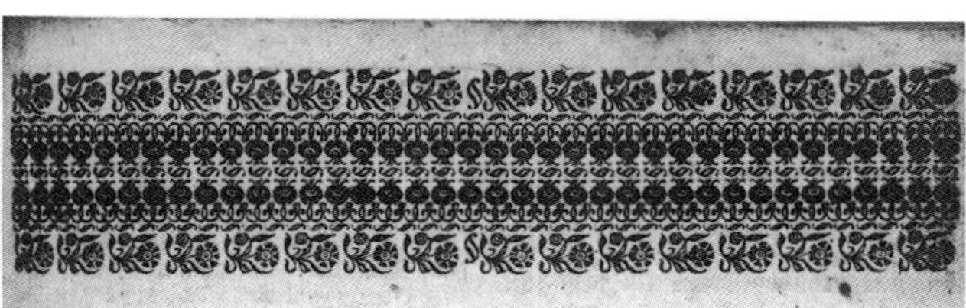

1 tailpiece

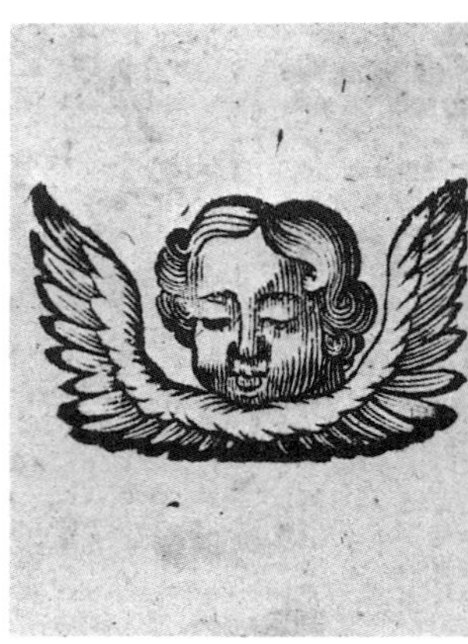

1 headpiece

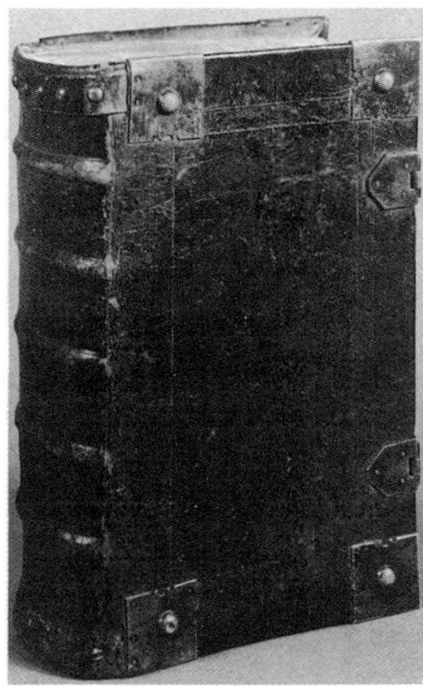

2

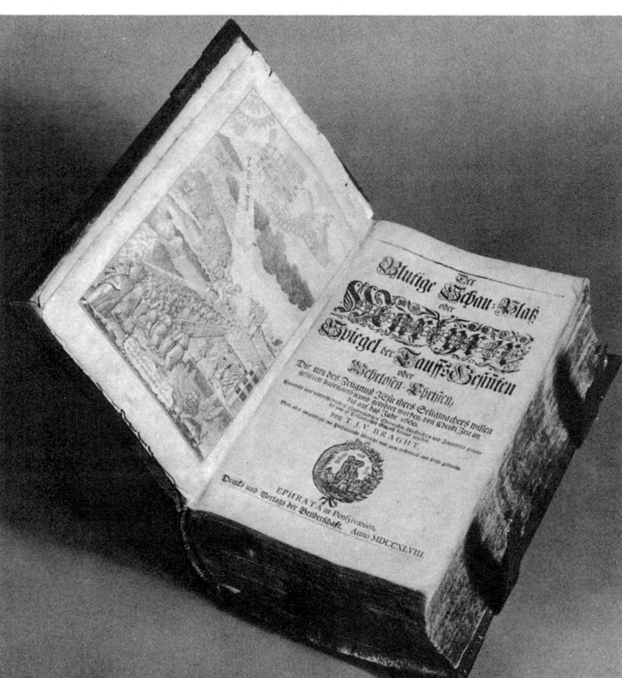

2

1   **NEW TESTAMENT**
Germantown, Philadelphia County
1743

Christoph Saur, printer/publisher

Title: *Das Neue Testament Unsers Herrn und
Henlandes Jesu Christi . . .*

Ink on laid paper; leather, wood, brass, iron.
Relief printed with letterpress. Headpieces;
final tailpiece of winged cherub head. Covers
are leather over beveled wood decorated with
stamped lines. Spine has seven raised sewn
bands. Title stamped on piece of leather and
glued to spine. Leather closing straps inserted
under back leather cover and nailed. Brass
fastening loops with cotter pins are inserted
under front leather cover and nailed. Brass
fastening hooks with decorative cuts are nailed
through leather strap into iron plate.

25.7 x 21 cm (10⅛ x 8¼")

Gift of J. Stogdell Stokes. 36-19-6

2   **BOOK: MARTYR'S MIRROR**
Ephrata, Lancaster County
1748–49

Tieleman Jans Van Braght, author
Ephrata Brüderschaft, printer/publisher

Title: *Der Blutige Schau-Platz oder Märtyrer
Spiegel . . .*

Inscribed on fore pages (translation): *Christian
Hunsicker, born Alsace 1723, died 1795.
Samuel Hunsicker, born May 3, 1753, died
April 30, 1819. Anna Hunsicker, born January
15, 1782, died March 20, 1856. Christian
Hunsicker, born March 26, 1776, died August
5, 1857. Joseph Hunsicker Hamlin.*

Ink on laid paper; leather, wood, brass. Relief
printed. Three pages before frontispiece have
EF and crown watermarks (Ephrata, Lancaster
County). Engraved frontispiece of army of
martyrs marching to heaven has CM watermark
and is mounted on laid paper with EF
watermark. Text is on lighter weight laid paper,
no watermarks.

    Two volumes bound together. Covers
are leather over beveled wood (1.3 cm thick)
with blind-stamped borders of serpentine
vines and three lines. Five sewn bands on
spine outlined with stamped triangles between
two lines which extend and cross irregularly on
covers. Head and foot of spine reinforced with
leather straps which have six brass studs with
clenched fastenings. Brass bosses in four
corners and centers of covers (front center boss
is missing); corner bosses bent over edges and
nailed with brass pins. Lower-left back boss
engraved with 2. Two leather closing straps
fitted with brass hooks.

37.5 x 25.4 cm (14¾ x 10")

37-36-1

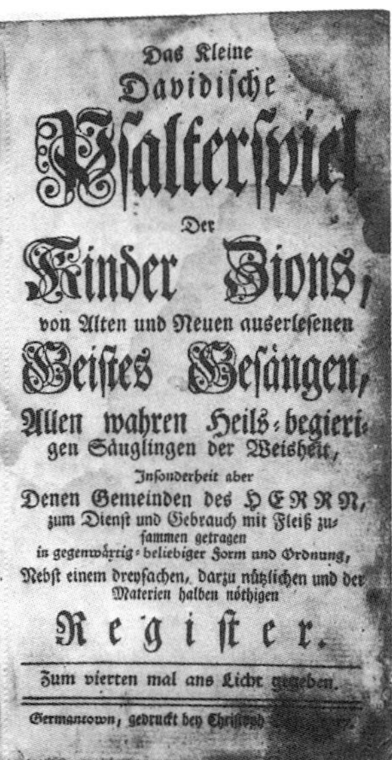

3

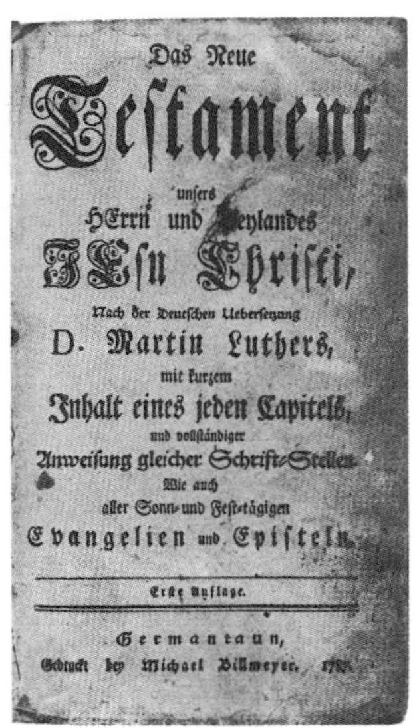

4

5

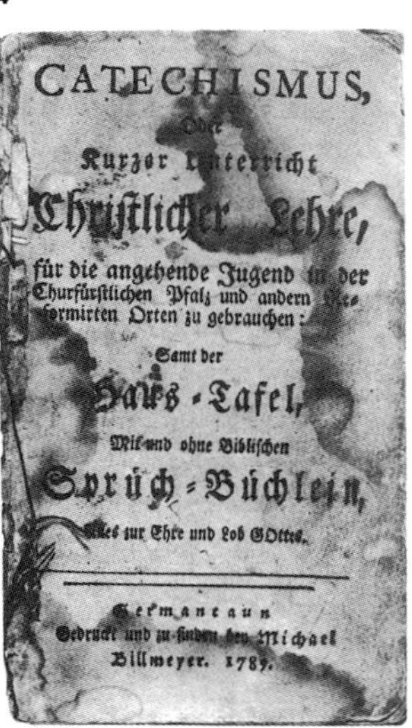

6

3   **HYMNAL (CHURCH OF THE BRETHREN)**
Germantown, Philadelphia County
1777

Christoph Saur, printer/publisher

Title: *Das Kleine Davidische Psalterspiel Der Kinder Zions . . .*

Ink on laid paper; leather, wood. Relief printed with letterpress. 572 pages plus first-line index. Covers are leather over wood. Five raised bands on spine. Two closing straps with brass fastenings (missing).

17.1 x 9.5 cm (6¾ x 3¾")

Gift of Martin Way. 12-148

4   **NEW TESTAMENT**
Germantown, Philadelphia County
1787

Michael Billmeyer, printer/publisher

Title: *Das Neue Testament unsers Herrn und Henlandes Jesu Christi . . .*

Ink on laid paper; leather, wood, brass. Relief printed with letterpress. 537 pages plus index. Headpieces and tailpieces. Covers are leather over wood with a scored line on three sides. Spine sewn with linen thread. Two leather closing straps with brass fastening hooks are riveted to back cover.

17.1 x 10.2 cm (6¾ x 4")

Gift of Mrs. William D. Frishmuth. 03-42

5   **CATECHISM (REFORMED)**
Philadelphia
1788

Carl Cist, printer/publisher

Title: *Catechismus, Oder Kurzer Unterricht Christlicher Lehre . . .*

Ink on laid paper; cardboard, leather. Relief printed with letterpress. 114 pages. Gothic lettering throughout. Covers are black-stippled paper over cardboard. Leather spine.

13.3 x 8.3 cm (5¼ x 3¼")

Gift of Mrs. William D. Frishmuth. 03-45

6   **CATECHISM (REFORMED)**
Germantown, Philadelphia County
1789

Michael Billmeyer, printer/publisher

Title: *Catechismus, Oder Kurzer Unterricht Christlicher Lehre . . .*

Inscribed on flyleaf: *Ann Barbara Loo[?]*

Ink on laid paper; cardboard, leather. Relief printed with letterpress. 118 pages. Covers are paper over cardboard. Leather spine.

14 x 7.9 cm (5½ x 3⅛")

Gift of Mrs. William D. Frishmuth. 03-46

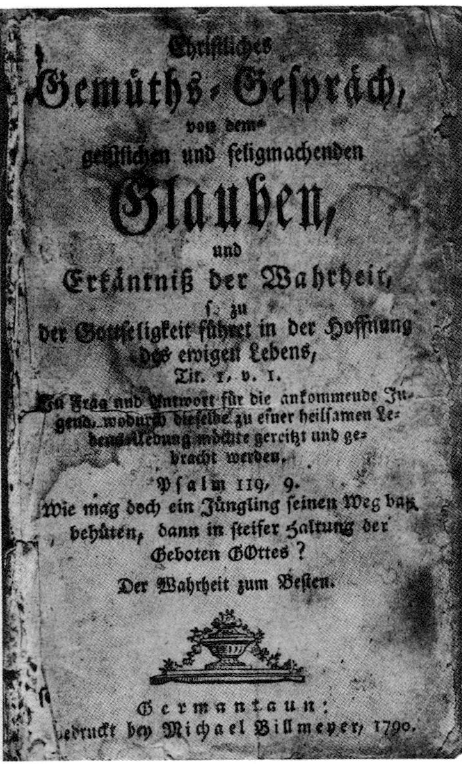

7

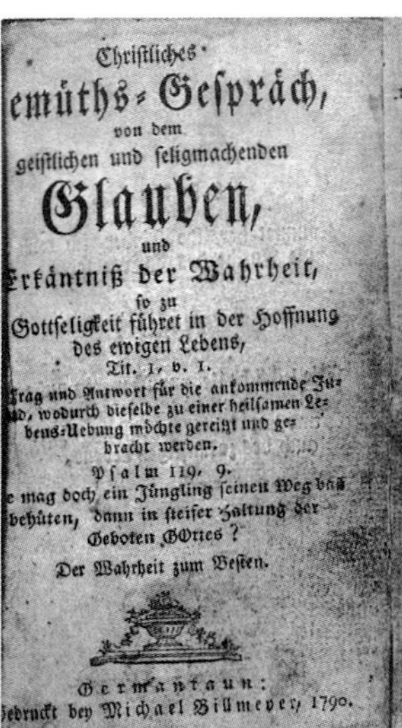

8

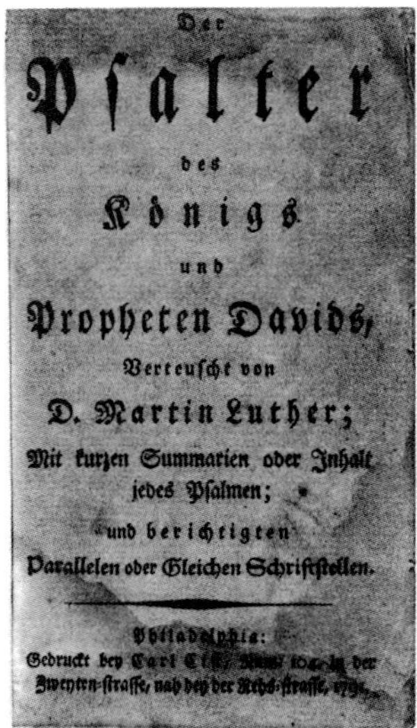

9 and 10

7 CATECHISM (MENNONITE)
Germantown, Philadelphia County
1790

Michael Billmeyer, printer/publisher

Title: *Christliches Gemüths-Gespräch . . .*

Ink on laid paper; leather, wood, brass. Relief printed with letterpress. 241 pages. Covers are leather over wood. Leather closing strap with brass fastening hook is riveted to back cover. Spine repaired.

14 x 8.6 cm (5½ x 3⅜″)

Gift of Mrs. William D. Frishmuth. 03-453

8 CATECHISM (MENNONITE)
Germantown, Philadelphia County
1790

Michael Billmeyer, printer/publisher

Title: *Christliches Gemüths-Gespräch . . .*

Inscribed for Samuel Martin (*see* Paper, Books, Bookplates, no. 4)

Ink on laid paper; leather, wood, iron. Relief printed with letterpress. 241 pages. Headpieces and tailpieces. Covers are leather over wood. One leather closing strap with iron fittings. Spine repaired with stamped linen.

14 x 8.9 cm (5½ x 3½″)

Titus C. Geesey Collection. 58-110-35

9 PSALMBOOK
Philadelphia
1791

Carl Cist, printer/publisher

Title: *Der Psalter des Königs und Propheten Davids . . .*

Ink on laid paper; leather, wood, brass. Relief printed with letterpress. 252 pages. Covers are leather over wood. Leather closing straps with brass fittings.

14 x 7.9 cm (5½ x 3⅛″)

33-30-1

10 PSALMBOOK
Philadelphia
1791

Carl Cist, printer/publisher

Title: *Der Psalter des Königs und Propheten Davids . . .*

Inscribed on flyleaf: *John Roads his book—God Given Gems*

Ink on laid paper; paperboard, leather. Relief printed with letterpress. 210 pages. Blue paperboard covers. Leather spine. Incomplete.

14 x 9.2 cm (5½ x 3⅝″)

Gift of Mrs. William D. Frishmuth. 03-43

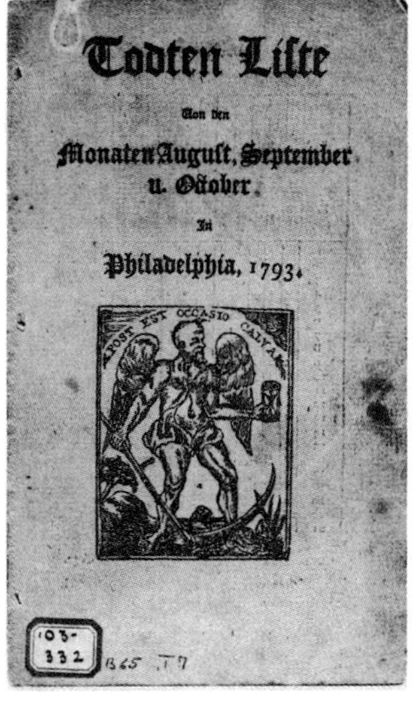

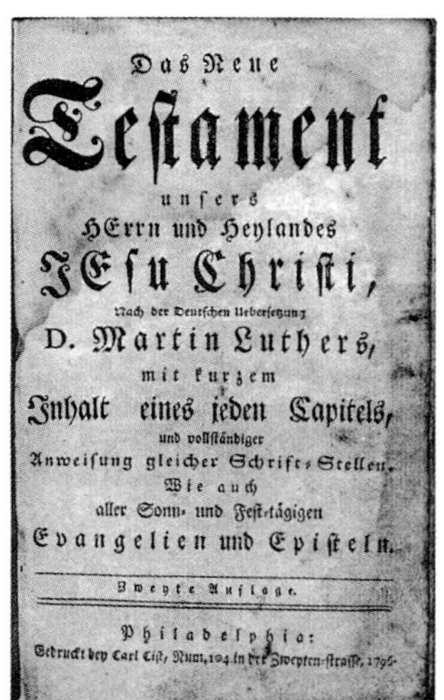

11   **12**

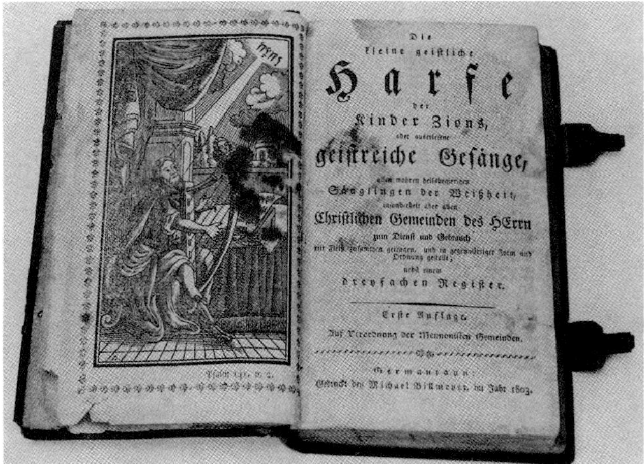

13

11 BOOKLET: DEATH LIST AND WEATHER WATCH
Philadelphia
1793

David Rittenhouse, author/publisher

Title: *Todten Liste Von den Monaten August, September u. October In Philadelphia, 1793;* [not shown] *Wetter Beobach tungen, wie deselben durch David Rittenhouse Esq. In Phila. sund gemacht worden August 1793.*

Ink on laid paper. Relief printed with letterpress; engravings. Sewn without covers. Eleven pages of tables of deaths recorded in Philadelphia churches by day and month. Bound with tables of weather, barometric pressure, and wind direction by time of day, day, and month.

16.2 x 9.5 cm (6⅜ x 3¾")

Gift of Mrs. William D. Frishmuth. 03-331,332

12 NEW TESTAMENT
Philadelphia
1796

Carl Cist, printer/publisher

Title: *Das Neue Testament unsers Herrn und Henlandes Jesu Christi . . .*

Inscribed for Christian Hersche (*see* Paper, Books, Bookplates, no. 3)

Inscribed inside front cover: 7/6

Ink on laid paper; leather, wood, iron. Relief printed with letterpress. 525 pages plus index. Headpieces and tailpieces. Covers are leather over wood with blind-tooled lines front and back. Seven raised sewn bands on spine. Iron fastenings. Closing straps missing.

16.8 x 11.1 cm (6⅝ x 4⅜")

Titus C. Geesey Collection. 58-110-34

13 HYMNAL (MENNONITE)
Germantown, Philadelphia County
1803

Michael Billmeyer, printer/publisher

Title: *Die Kleine geistliche Harfe der Kinder Zions . . .*

Inscribed for Georg Bechtel (*see* Paper, Books, Bookplates, no. 5)

Inscribed on last page: *Georg Bechtel*

Ink on laid paper; leather, wood, brass. Relief printed with woodcuts and letterpress. 412 pages plus first-line index. Headpieces and tailpieces. Frontispiece signed D. Covers are leather over wood with blind-tooled lines around edges, front and back. Five raised bands on spine. Two leather closing straps with brass fittings.

17.1 x 10.8 cm (6¾ x 4¼")

Titus C. Geesey Collection. 58-110-33

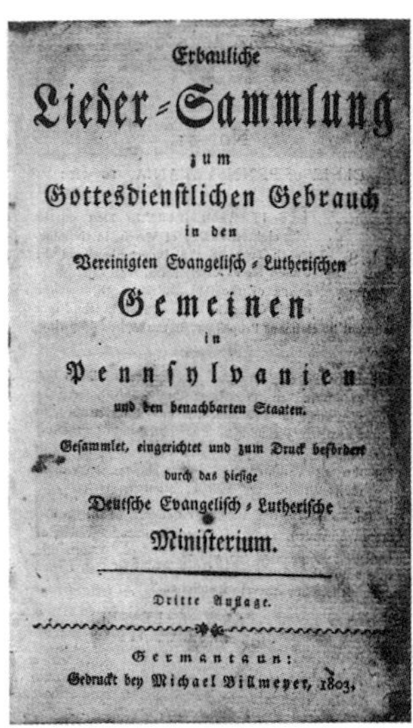

14 hymnal [1803]

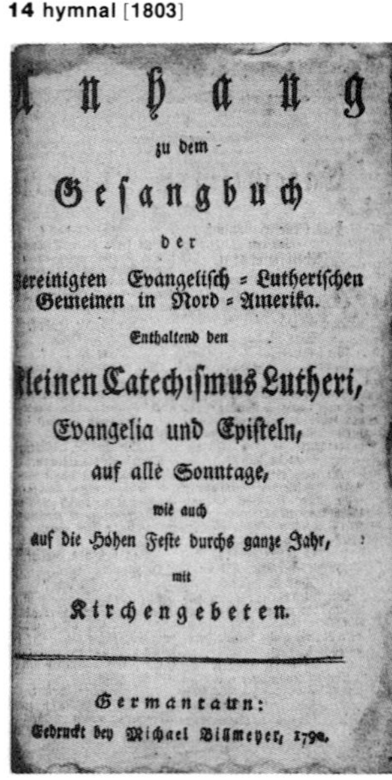

14 hymnal [1790]

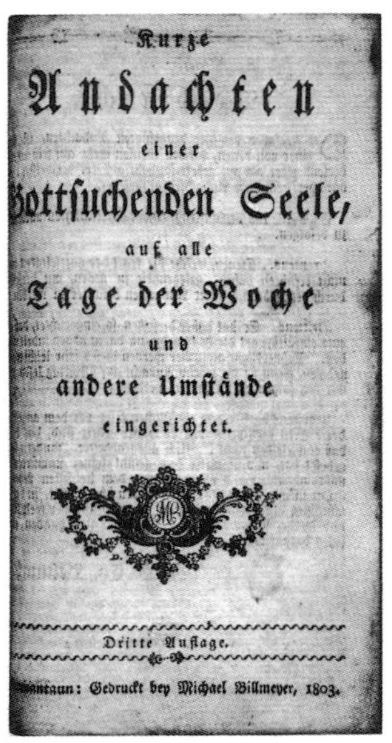

14 devotions

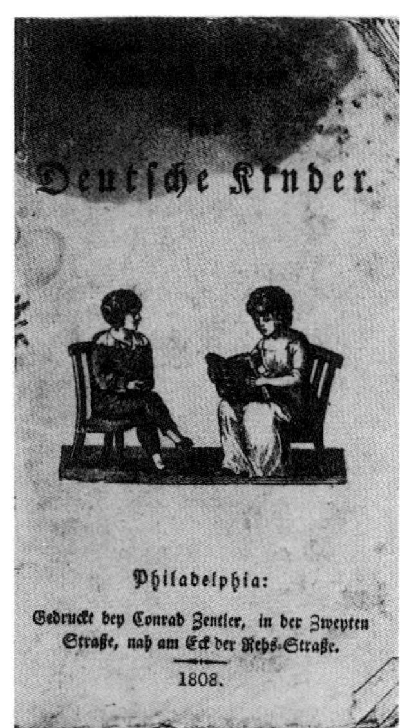

15

**14 HYMNALS AND DAILY DEVOTIONS
(LUTHERAN)**
Germantown, Philadelphia County
1790, hymnal
1803, hymnal and daily devotions

Michael Billmeyer, printer/publisher

Titles: [1790 hymnal] *Anhang zu dem
Gesangbuch der Vereinigten
Evangelisch-Lutherischen Gemeinen in
Nord-Amerika . . . ;* [1803 hymnal] *Erbauliche
Lieder-Sammlung zum Gottesdienstlichen
Gebrauch in den Vereinigten
Evangelisch-Lutherischen Gemeinen . . . ;*
[daily devotions] *Kurze Andachten einer
Gottsuchenden Seele . . .*

Ink on laid paper; leather, wood. Relief
printed with woodcuts and letterpress. Three
books bound as one. Covers are leather over
wood with double-scored lines along spine,
single lines on three sides, front and back.
Five raised bands with stamped lines on
spine. Two leather closing straps (missing).
1790 hymnal: 80 pages. Gospels and epistles.
1803 hymnal: 602 pages plus first-line index.
Frontispiece of Martin Luther signed in plate:
F · Reiche · sc. Daily devotions: 28 pages.
Morning and evening songs. Title page with
rococo cartouche with MB [Michael
Billmeyer] in center.

17.1 x 10.2 cm (6¾ x 4″)

Gift of William M. Simon. 33-30-2

15 READER
Philadelphia
1808

Conrad Zentler, printer/publisher

Title: *Unterhaltungen für Deutsche Kinder.*

Ink on wove paper. Relief printed with cuts,
possibly wood, and letterpress. Thirty-six
pages of short moralistic stories. Paper covers
sponge-painted brown. Introduction signed
Der Berasser, Philadelphia, March 9, 1808.

14 x 8.6 cm (5½ x 3⅜″)

Gift of Mrs. William D. Frishmuth. 03-48

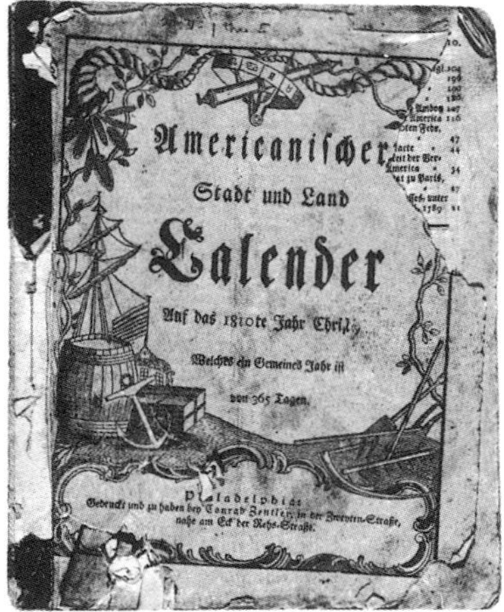

16

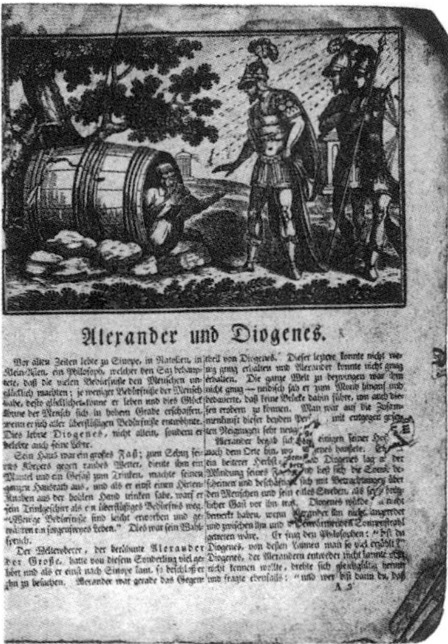

17

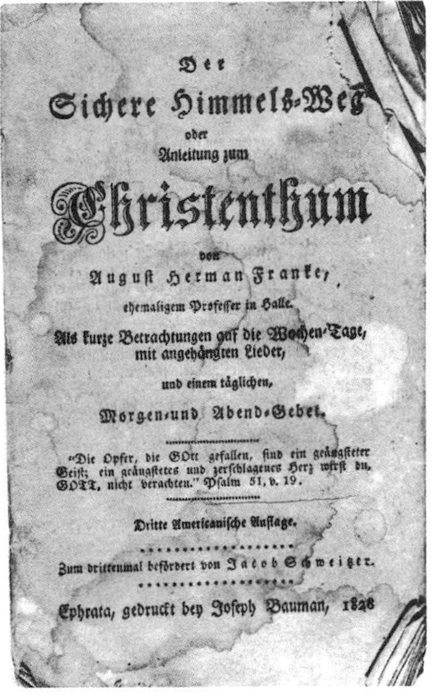

18

16   **ALMANAC**
Philadelphia
1810

Conrad Zentler, printer/publisher

Title: *Americanischer Stadt und Land Calender Auf das 1810te Jahr Christi . . .*

Ink on wove paper. Relief printed with letterpress; engravings. Forty-two pages. Black paper spine sewn with linen thread; hanging loop. Ship, anchor, barrel, rakes, ring dial, telescope, and compass on cover; cartouche at bottom. Included are calendars, moon phases, and court proceedings and sittings.

21.6 x 17.1 cm (8½ x 6¾″)

Gift of Sylvester Krafka. 21-31-1

17   **ALMANAC**
Reading, Berks County
1821

Johann Ritter, printer/publisher

Ink on wove paper. Relief printed with letterpress; engravings. Blue paper spine over three signatures sewn with linen thread. Eagle in sky with *E PLURIBUS UNUM* banner over plowing scene on cover. Included are calendars, perpetual calendars, illustrated stories (shown: Alexander and Diogenes), moon phases, and news of Schuylkill, Beaver, and Armstrong counties.

21 x 17.5 cm (8¼ x 6⅞″)

Gift of Sylvester Krafka. 21-31-3

18   **DAILY DEVOTIONS**
Ephrata, Lancaster County
1828

August Herman Franke, author
Joseph Bauman, printer/publisher

Title: *Der Sichere Himmels-Weg oder Anleitung zum Christenthum . . .*

Ink on wove paper. Relief printed with letterpress. Thirty-five pages. Paper covers and spine sponge-painted brown. Bound with linen thread.

17.1 x 10.8 cm (6¾ x 4¼″)

Gift of Mrs. William D. Frishmuth. 03-47

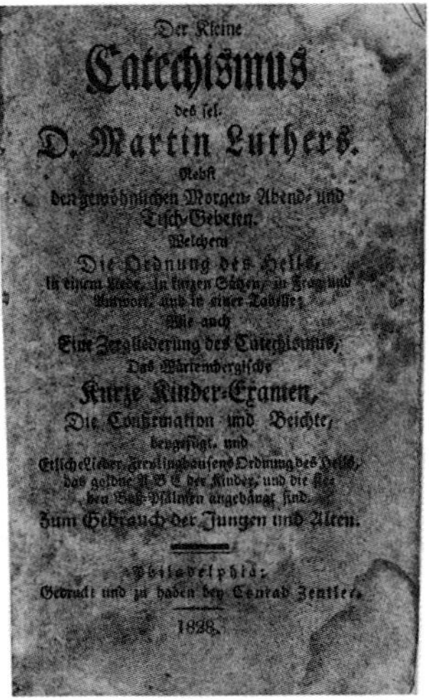

19

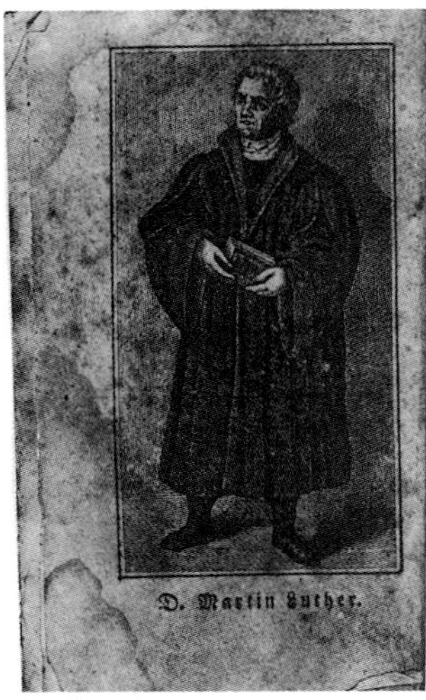

19 frontispiece

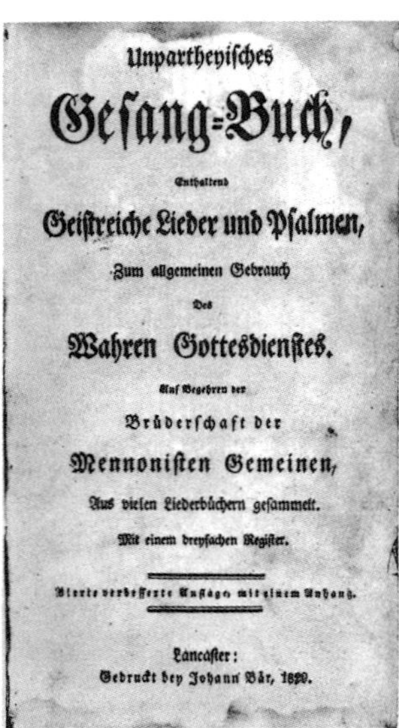

20

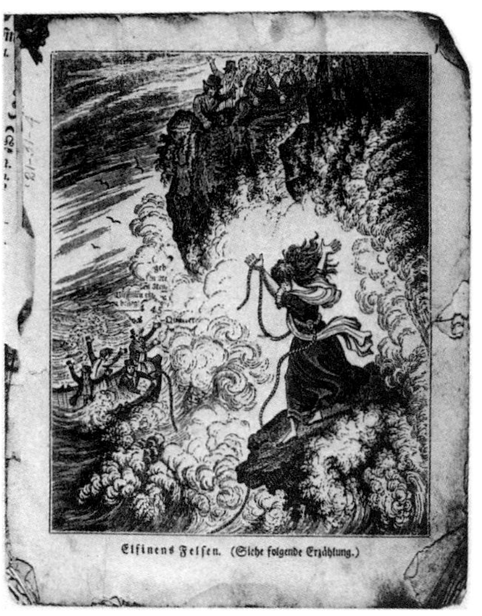

21

19 CATECHISM (LUTHERAN)
Philadelphia
1828

Conrad Zentler, printer/publisher

Title: *Der Kleine Catechismus des sel. D. Martin Luthers . . .*

Ink on wove paper; cardboard, leather. Relief printed with letterpress; engraved frontispiece of Martin Luther. Covers are black paper, overprinted blue, over cardboard. Leather spine.

14.9 x 9.2 cm (5⅞ x 3⅝″)

Gift of Mrs. William D. Frishmuth. 03-44

20 HYMNAL (MENNONITE)
Lancaster, Lancaster County
1829

Johann Bär, printer/publisher

Title: *Unparthenisches Gesang-Buch, Enthaltend Geistreiche Lieder und Psalmen . . .*

Inscribed on flyleaf: *John Bear*

Ink on wove paper; leather, wood, iron. Relief printed with letterpress. 483 pages of music and text, 19 pages of first-line index. Covers are leather over wood. Closing straps (missing) were set into back cover and nailed. Iron fastening hooks set into front cover and nailed.

18.7 x 11.4 cm (7⅜ x 4½″)

Gift of Mrs. William D. Frishmuth. 02-443

21 ALMANAC
Philadelphia
1838

Conrad Zentler, printer/publisher

Title: *Americanischer Stadt und Land Calender Auf das 1838ste Jahr Christi . . .*

Inscribed on back cover: *Property of John Wendel*

Ink on wove paper. Relief printed with letterpress; engravings. Thirty pages. Paper spine sewn with linen thread; hanging loop. Ship, anchor, barrel, rakes, ring dial, telescope, and compass on cover; cartouche at bottom. Included are calendars, moon phases, and court proceedings and sittings.

21.6 x 17.1 cm (8½ x 6¾″)

Gift of Sylvester Krafka. 21-31-4

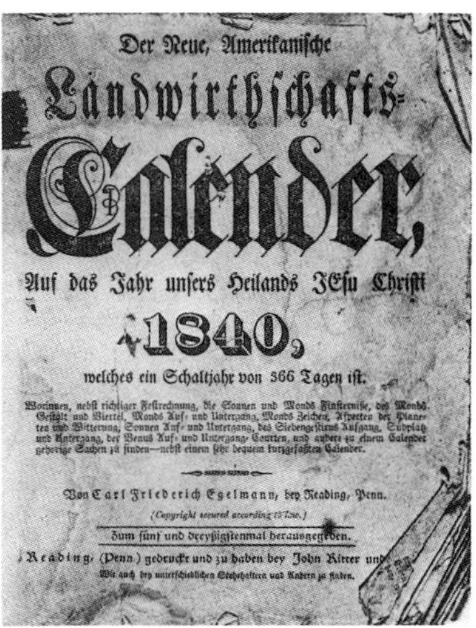

22

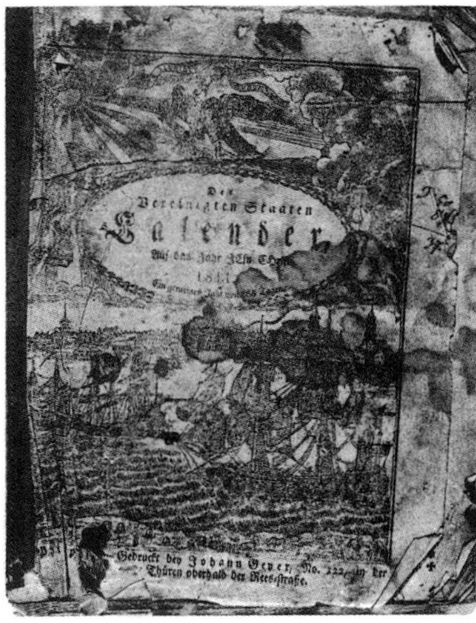

23

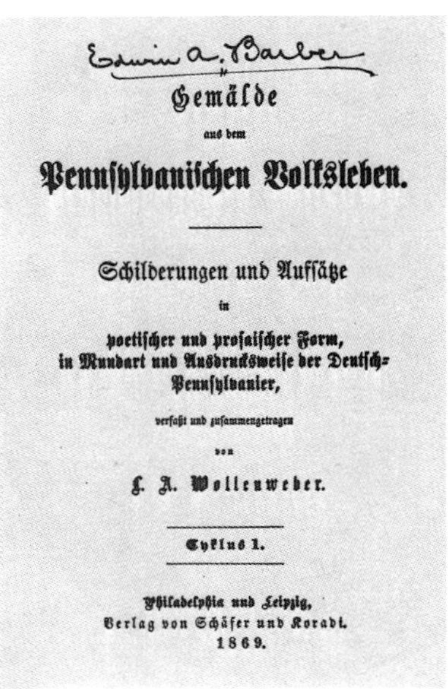

24

22 ALMANAC
Reading, Berks County
1840

Carl Friederich Egelmann, author
John Ritter und Comp., printers/publishers

Title: *Der Neue, Amerikanische Landwirthschafts-Calender, Auf das Jahr unsers Heilands Jesu Christi 1840 . . .*

Ink on wove paper. Relief printed with letterpress. Blue paper spine over three signatures (twelve pages each) sewn with linen twine; hanging loop. Cuts include zodiac signs (fish, ram, bull, and crab).

20.6 x 16.8 cm (8⅛ x 6⅝″)

Gift of Sylvester Krafka. 21-31-5

---

23 ALMANAC
Philadelphia
1844

Johann Geyer, printer/publisher

Title: *Der Vereinigten Staaten Calender, Auf das Jahr Jesu Christi, 1844 . . .*

Ink on wove paper. Relief printed with letterpress; engravings. Some paper is bluish. Blue paper spine sewn with linen thread. Included are calendars, moon phases, news, poems, and zodiac signs. Some manuscript computations.

20.3 x 16.5 cm (8 x 6½″)

Gift of Sylvester Krafka. 21-31-2

---

24 BOOK: PICTURE OF PENNSYLVANIA FOLKLIFE
Philadelphia and Leipzig
1869

L. A. Wollenweber, author
Schäfer und Koradi, printers/publishers

Title: *Gemälde aus dem Pennsylvanischen Volksleben . . .*

Inscribed on title page: *Edwin A. Barber*

Ink on machine-wove paper; paperboard. Relief printed with letterpress. 143 pages. Gothic type throughout. Covers are embossed paper over paperboard. Gold letters on spine.

15.6 x 11.1 cm (6⅛ x 4⅜″)

Gift of Edwin A. Barber. 33-35-2

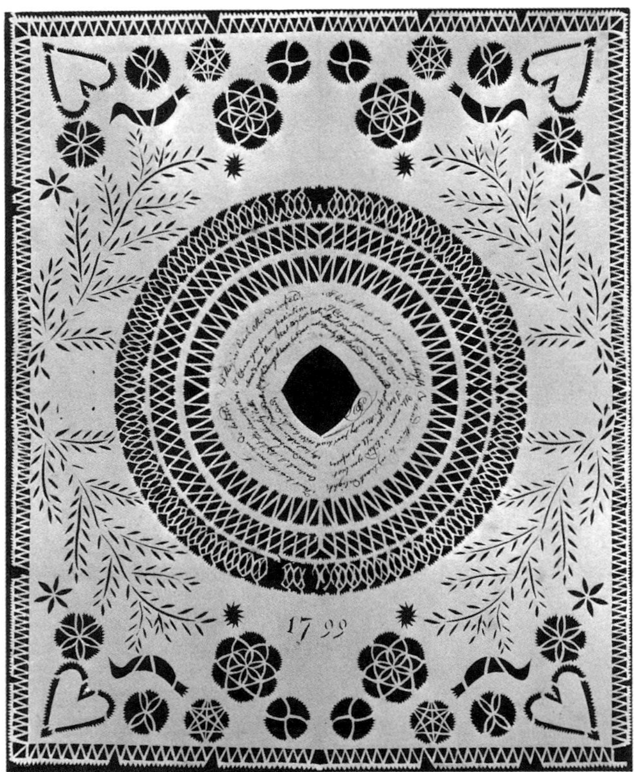

2

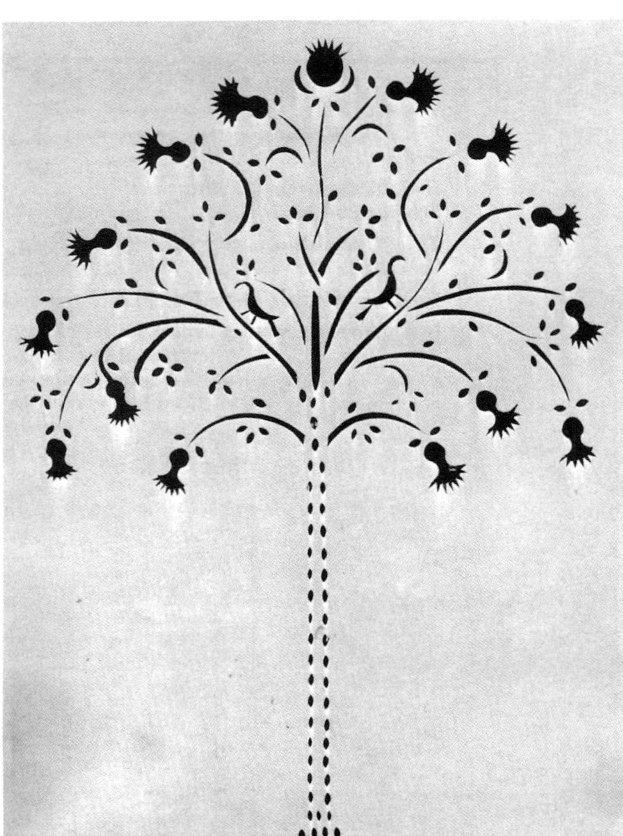

3

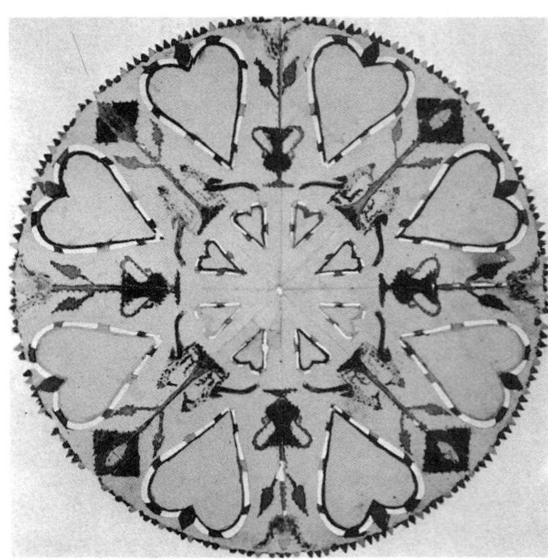

1

1   **VALENTINE**
1780–1820

Watercolor wash and pigments in gum medium on laid paper. Square paper folded three times; design cut out and pinpricked. Blue tulip-vases with red bases. Yellow and red tulips. Red, blue, and green serrate edge.

Diameter 31.8 cm (12½")

Henry M. Phillips Collection. 02-251

2   **VALENTINE**
Paradise Township, Lancaster County
1799

Inscribed: *Four hearts in one you do behold, & they in Each other do infold, I Cut them out on such A Night, & send them to my hearts delight, On such A Night the hour of Nine, I Chuse you for my valintine, I Chuse you out from all the rest, The reson is i liked you best Some draw valentines by lotts, Some draw them that they love not, But I draw you wich I do Chuse, I hope you will not refuse, My heart within my Breast doth Ake, A Tonge I have but dare not speak, If I should speak & should not speed, then my poor heart will break indeed. 1799;* on reverse: *In case your love & sett you free, sleep on my dear and take you rest Wilst my poor hear his bleeding in my breat, O was it you instead of me.*

Ink on wove paper. Cutwork. Folded twice.

46.7 x 38 cm (18⅜ x 15")

Titus C. Geesey Collection. 54-85-9

3   **PICTURE**
1840–50

Wove paper, wool, chintz. Cutwork (*scherenschnitte*) backed with handwoven red wool behind treetop and brown glazed chintz behind tree trunk.

25.4 x 19.1 cm (10 x 7½")

Purchased. 16-258

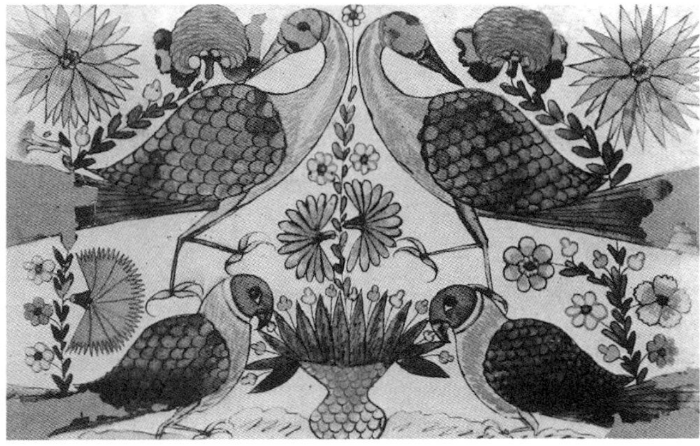

1

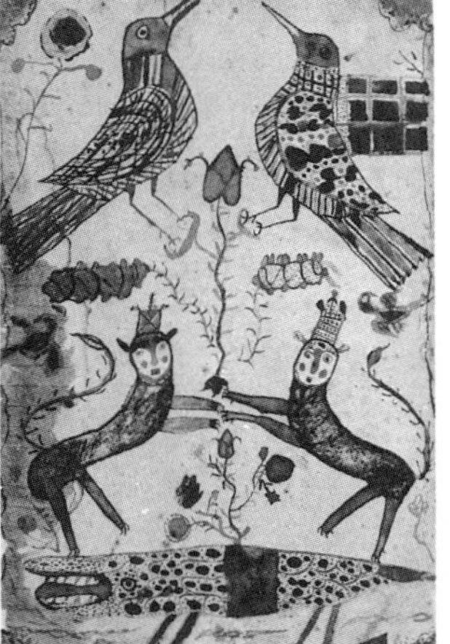

2

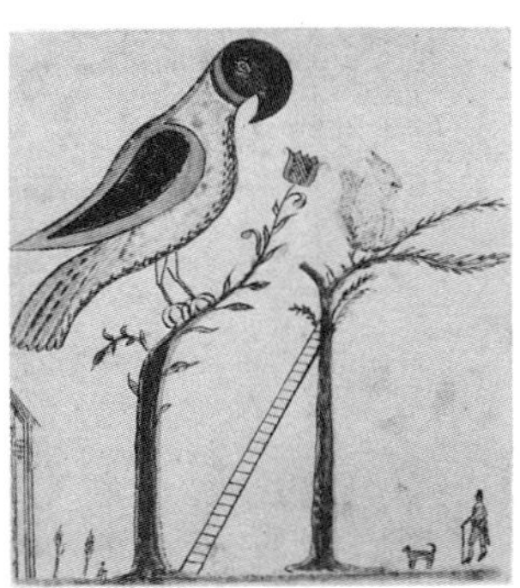

4

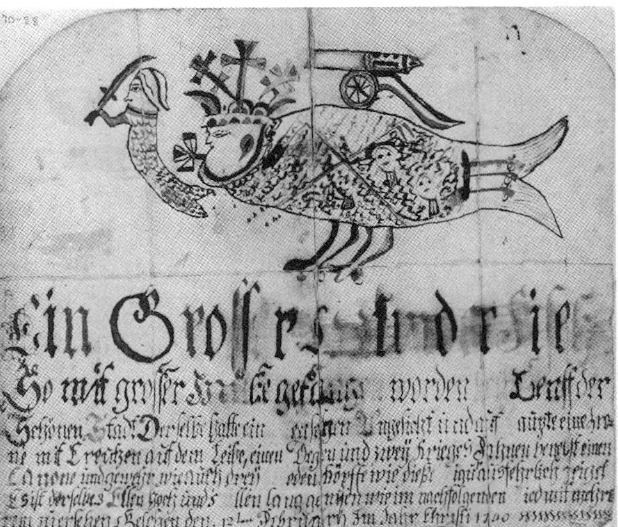

3

1 DRAWING
Lancaster County
1773

Inscribed on reverse in pencil: *made 1773*

Pigments in gum medium, watercolor wash, and ink on laid paper. Designs drawn in paint and ink and colored. Birds have yellow and red necks, green feathers, ink details. Surface losses on tails. Red, blue, and yellow flowers.

19.7 x 32.1 cm (7¾ x 12⅝")

Gift of George H. Lorimer. 25-95-2

2 DRAWING
1780–1820

Ink with pigments in gum medium on laid paper. Designs drawn in paint and ink and colored. Green lions with red legs, tails, and head details. Birds have orange heads and red, orange, and ink bodies. Red and black alligator. Red corner clouds. Ink details.

33 x 21.6 cm (13 x 8½")

Gift of Mrs. William D. Frishmuth. 02-429

3 DRAWING
Probably Montgomery County
1790–1800

Inscribed (translation): *A big wonder fish which was caught with effort near Geneva, the beautiful city. The same had a man's face and on his head a crown with crosses; on his body a dagger, two war flags, a cannon, and three guns as well as three heads. As this drawing shows in detail the same was three ells tall and also five ells long, as is obvious in the following hymn with more. Such a miraculous sign happened on the 11th day of February A.D. 1740.*

Watercolor wash and ink on laid paper, backed with 1791 German-language newspaper. Designs drawn in ink and colored red and tan.

17.1 x 20.6 cm (6¾ x 8⅛")

Gift of Mrs. William D. Frishmuth. 10-88

4 DRAWING
1800–1830

Watercolor wash and ink on wove paper. Bird drawn in pencil and colored tan, red, and blue. Ink details. Tree, man, dog, and squirrel are blue with red details.

19.7 x 17.5 cm (7¾ x 6⅞")

Bequest of Mr. and Mrs. William M. Elkins. 50-92-268

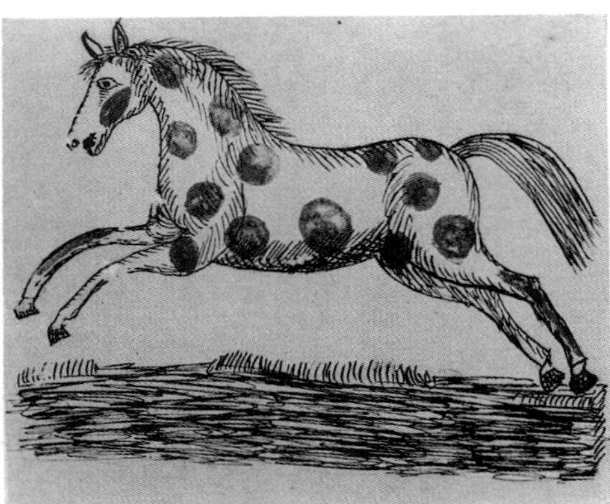

5

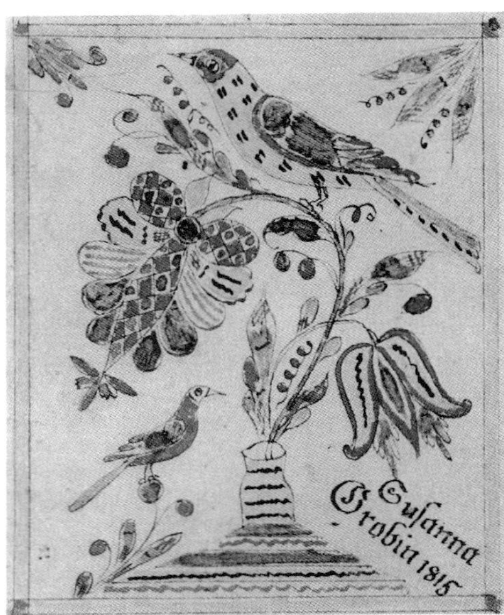

6

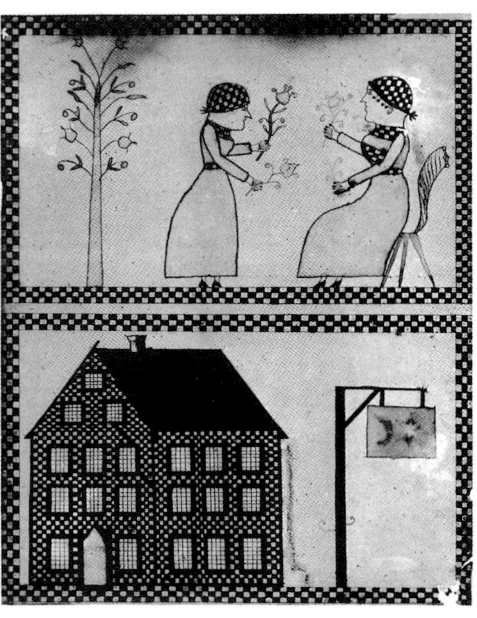

8

5 DRAWING
1800–1850

Ink with pigment in gum medium on blue gray wove paper. Brown ink design with orange dappling on horse.

10.2 x 12.4 cm (4 x 4⅞")

Bequest of Mr. and Mrs. William M. Elkins. 50-92-260

6 DRAWING
Montgomery County
1815

Inscribed: *Susanna Grobin 1815*

Watercolor wash and ink on laid paper. Designs drawn in ink and colored. Yellow vase with ink details. Small bird is red, green blue, and yellow. Large bird has yellow breast, green wing outlined in red, blue and yellow tail. Red, green, blue, yellow, and ink flower. Yellow borders with red corners. Probably a reward of merit.

9.2 x 7.6 cm (3⅝ x 3")

Gift of Mrs. Hattie Grobb Tschabold. 59-41-2

7 DRAWING
Montgomery County
March 27, 1818

David Heebner

Inscribed: *DH;* on reverse: *David Heebner March 27, 1818*

Ink with pigments in gum medium on laid paper. Designs drawn in ink and colored. Yellow tulips with red, blue, yellow, and green details. Red, blue, green, yellow, and crystallized bright aqua blue illuminated letters. Red, yellow, and green border.

7.6 x 20 cm (3 x 7⅞")

Gift of J. Stogdell Stokes. 28-83-2

8 DRAWING
Norriton, Montgomery County
1820–25

Watercolor wash, pencil, and ink on wove paper. Designs drawn in pencil and colored red and green. Ink details. Building is New Moon Tavern, Norriton, Montgomery County. Probably intended as two drawngs to be separated and inscribed.

44.5 x 38.1 cm (17½ x 15")

Gift of Mrs. William D. Frishmuth. 02-434

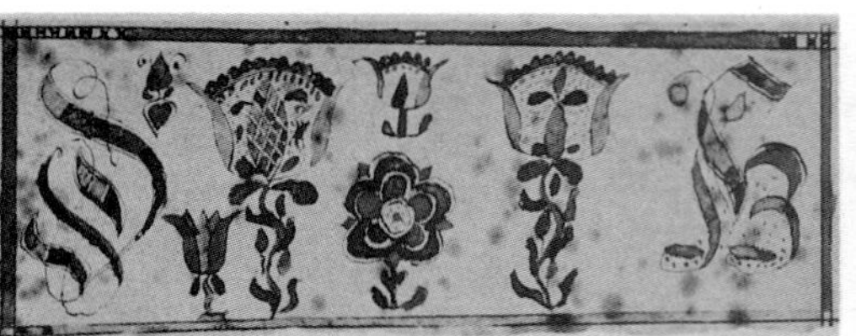

7

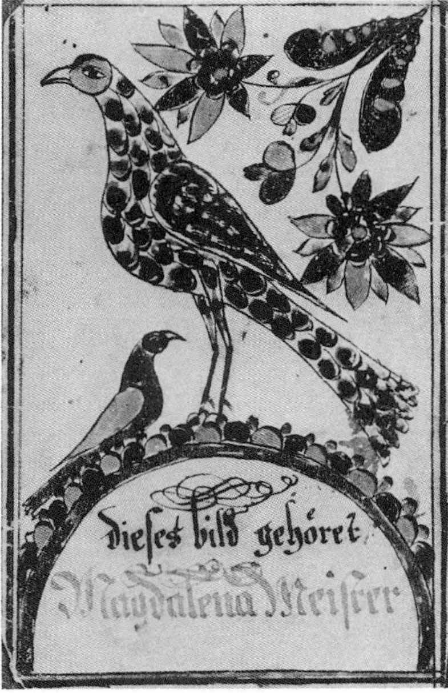

9

9 **DRAWING**
Montgomery County
1820–40

Inscribed (translation): *This drawing belongs to Magdalena Meister*

Watercolor wash, pigments in gum medium, and ink on laid paper. Designs drawn and shaded with ink. Large bird has green yellow breast feathers, gray wing, pink head, and yellow beak. Blue green, pink, and gray flowers and arch. Brown and red inscription. Probably a reward of merit.

10.8 x 7 cm (4¼ x 2¾")

Gift of Mrs. William D. Frishmuth. 07-213

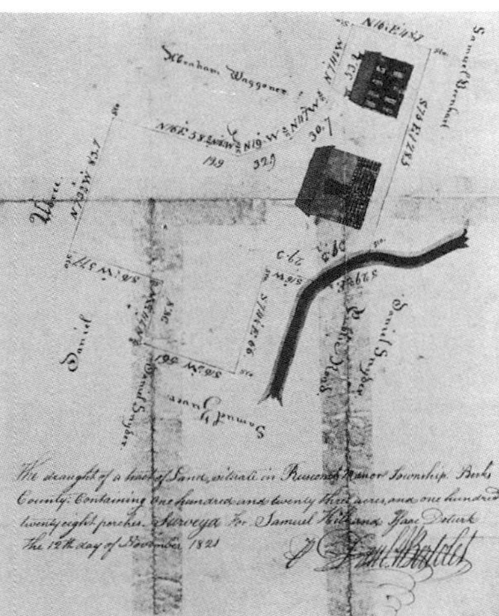

10

10 **SURVEY**
Ruscombmanor Township, Berks County
1821

Daniel A. Bertolet

Inscribed: *The draught of a tract of Land, situate in Ruscomb Manor Township, Berks County: Containing one hundred and twenty three acres, and one hundred twenty eight perches. Surveyd For Samuel Hill and Isaac Deturk the 12th day of November 1821   Danl. A. Bertolet;* on reverse: *Draught for Samuel Hill & Isaac Deturk A P 123: 128*

Watercolor wash and ink on wove paper. Blue house with red roof. Barn is striped brown (logs) with red upper boards and roof.

24.1 x 20 cm (9½ x 7⅞")

Gift of the Haas Community Fund. 68-118-59

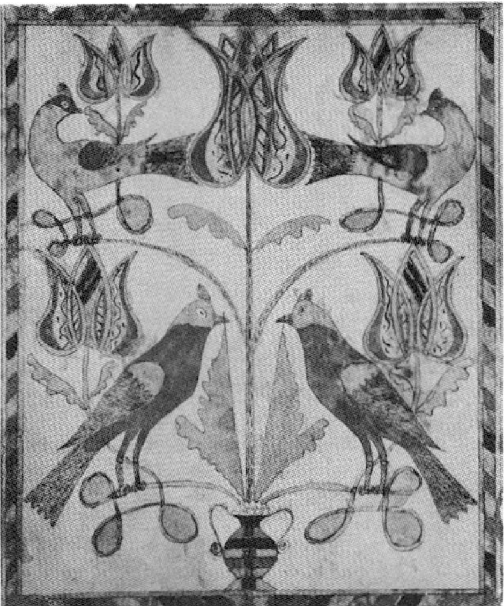

11

11 **DRAWING**
Bucks or Montgomery County
1824

Inscribed: *1824*

Ink with pigments in gum medium on wove paper. Designs drawn in ink and colored. Large birds red with blue green and ink details. Small birds yellow with red and ink details. Red, yellow, and blue green tulips with blue details. Red, yellow, blue, and blue green border. By same hand as no. 12.

30.2 x 25.1 cm (11⅞ x 9⅞")

Gift of Mrs. William D. Frishmuth. 08-203

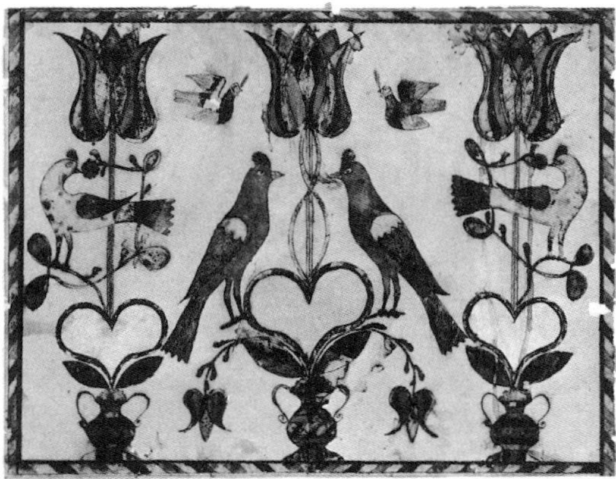

12

12 DRAWING
Bucks or Montgomery County
1825

Inscribed in flowers in center vase: *1825*

Ink with pigments in gum medium on wove
paper. Designs drawn in ink and colored.
Yellow heart. Center birds red with blue,
green, and yellow wings; side birds yellow.
Flying birds blue green with white-tipped
wings, yellow heads. Red, blue, and yellow
border. By same hand as no. 11.

30.5 x 40.3 cm (12 x 15⅞″)

Gift of Mrs. William D. Frishmuth. 08-205

13 DRAWING
Montgomery County
1830–35

Attributed to **Samuel** and/or **Martin Godshall**

Ink with pigments in gum medium on wove
paper. Designs drawn in ink and colored.
Women in red and yellow blouses, yellow and
blue green skirts shaded with red. Blue
ruffled heart with gold yellow scalloping.
Yellow, green, blue, and red birds. Side and
top borders red, bottom border blue. Paint is
brilliant, thick, and crystallized. Reverse is
raised where painted.

31.6 x 19.7 cm (12½ x 7¾″)

Titus C. Geesey Collection. 69-284-9

14 DRAWING
Whitehall Township, Lehigh County
1842

Attributed to **Durs Rudy**

Inscribed (translation): *Freedom, equality,
unity, and fraternity. Anno 1842. General
Washington, commander-in-chief of the
American army.*

Watercolor wash, pigment in gum medium,
and ink on wove paper. Designs drawn in ink
and colored. Red and yellow circles, blue
tents, pink and yellow tulips, green ground
and foliage. Soldiers in blue and yellow coats,
yellow breeches, red vests. Angels' cloths
blue and yellow. Yellow cannon and drum
with red details. Brown cannonballs.

25.1 x 20 cm (9⅞ x 7⅞″)

Titus C. Geesey Collection. 54-85-131

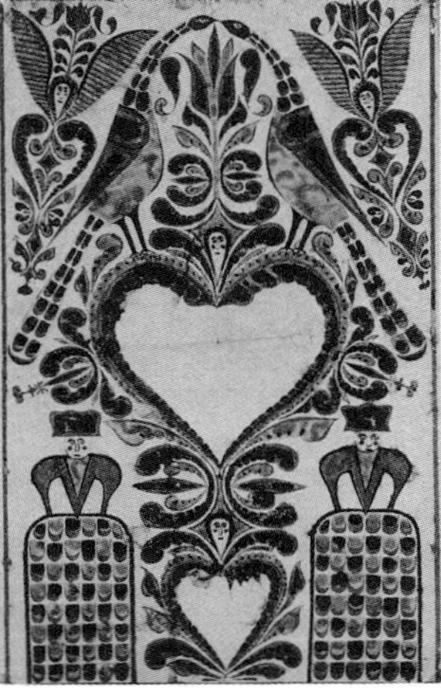

13

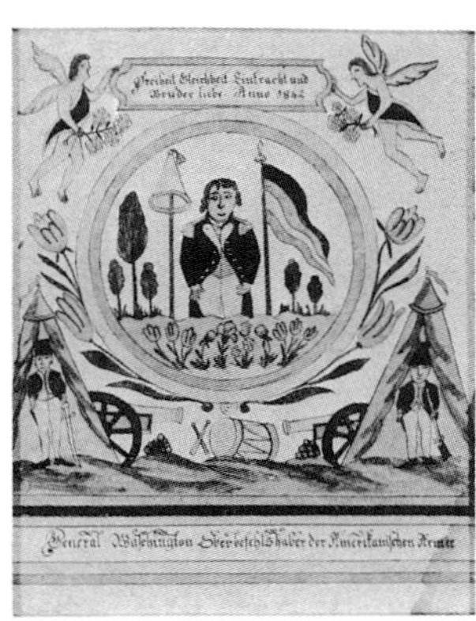

14

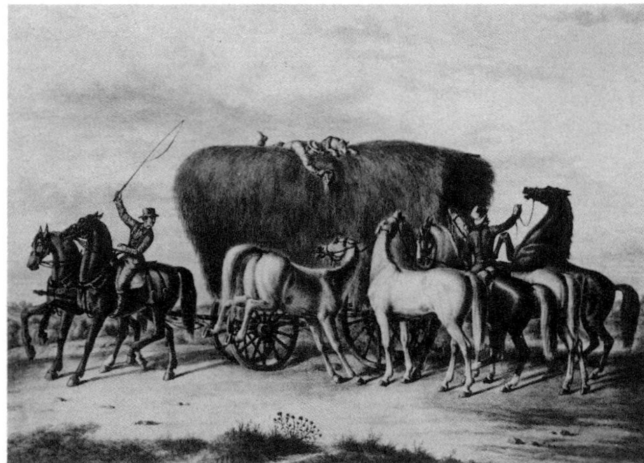

15

15 THE HAY WAGON
Philadelphia
1875–80

Augustus Koellner

Inscribed on reverse: *Harvest Scene in Penna.
by Aug. Kollner of Phila.*

Watercolor on wove paper. Watermark:
J. Whatman Turkey Mill 1875.

40.6 x 59.7 cm (16 x 23½″)

Gift of Seymour Adelman. 46-73-3

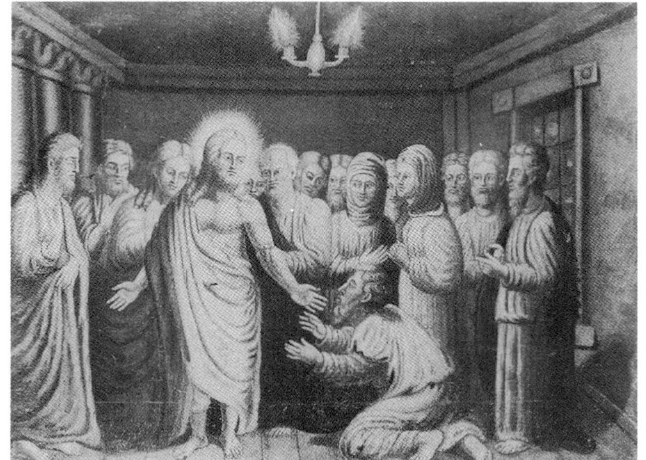

1

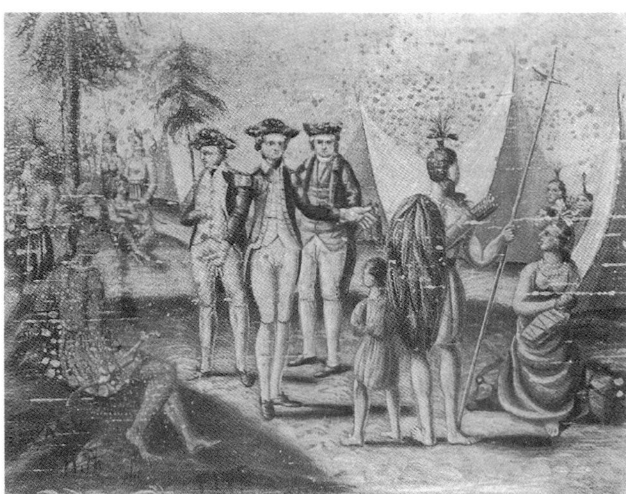

2

1   JESUS IN THE UPPER ROOM
Hummelstown, Dauphin County
1836

John Landis

Inscribed on reverse: *Jno Landis Pinxit 1836*

Oil on canvas. Figures in classical dress in blue, red, and yellow. Classical columns on left; nineteenth-century-style window frame and sash and chandelier. Brown room.

34.6 x 47 cm (13⅝ x 18½")

Titus C. Geesey Collection. 53-125-20

2   TREATY WITH THE FIVE NATIONS
1838

Inscribed: *Treaty With the FIVE NATIONS;* on reverse in pencil: *1738–1820*
Incised on reverse: *1838*

Oil on pine. Central figure (Conrad Weiser, 1696–1760) in blue coat, ivory breeches; figure behind him to right (possibly Governor William Denny, 1709–1765) in gray coat, blue green waistcoat. Indians in red and green with white necklaces. Green ground, gray blue sky. Black inscription. Brown border.

21.6 x 25.1 cm (8½ x 9⅞")

Titus C. Geesey Collection. 69-284-13

Birth Certificates

1   I, Johannes Axer, was conceived and born the 28th of August,
Anno 1794, in the sign of Capricorn in the year of our Lord and
Savior Jesus Christ. The Lord of all lords bless and protect. To
God alone the glory. Let your bearing constantly come under
this test: God sees, God hears, God punishes; you will not
escape him. Pray without ceasing.

2   Johannes Kiess, a son of George Kiess and his wife, Dorothea,
née Allmer, was born on the 3rd day of December in the year
of Christ 1814, in Blooming Grove, Lycoming County,
Pennsylvania.
[On reverse] Married on December 27, 1847, to Maria
Marquand[?]

3   Johannes Zartmann was born in Jackson Township, Lebanon
County, in the state of Pennsylvania in North America, on the
19th of May in the year of our Lord Jesus 1827, and was
painted on the 13th of November in the year 1828 by Jacob
Mäntel.

4   [In English] Anna Ensminger was born on the First Day of
August, in the Year of Our Lord, One Thousand Eight
Hundred, and Fifty Three.

World! in thee is fear and care,
Sin and sadness everywhere;
But in Heaven there ever is
Peace, and rest, and perfect bliss.

5   [In English] Mary Ann [Fieschler?] was born May 10th 1859.
She was born in Rapho Township Lancaster County State of
Pennsylvania.

6   [1] Peter 1:24. For all flesh is like grass and all [the] glory [of
men] like the flower of grass. The grass withers, and the flower
falls, but the Word of the Lord abides forever. That word is
[what] was preached to you.
Ecclesiastes 12:1. Remember also your Creator in the days of
your youth, before the evil days come, and the years draw nigh
when you will say, "I have no pleasure in them."

[In English] Luke deets Was Born in July 21 the Year 1874/
Luke deets was Born in the year 1874 July the 21/Remember
to kep holy the Sabes Day Six Days shal thou Labour and all
thu work/mad and don 1883 July 16 th/By your granfather J
Milly

Birth and Baptismal Certificates

1   To these two married persons, namely Jacob Ernst and his
lawful wife, Anna Catharina, a son was born into the world, as
follows: Johan Georg Ernst was born into the world in the year
of our Lord Jesus 1769 on the 27th day of August at 3 o'clock in
the afternoon in the sign of ———. After the physical, he was
commended to the spiritual rebirth of Holy Baptism and
baptized by Pastor Nicolaus Kurtz and given the name as
indicated above. Baptismal sponsors are Paul Ernst and Anna
Margr[eta] Popp. The aforementioned Johan Georg was born
and baptized in America in the province of Pennsylvania in
Berks County in Heidelberg Township.
[In English in another hand] Died this 16 of April AD 1843.

Scarcely born into the world,
Yet with the first step that is made,
Shortly into death we're hurled,
In measured pace to that dark glade.
In each moment quickly fleeting,
Feeling all our strength retreating,
And with each advancing year,
Grow more ripened for the bier.
And who knows what hour the call
For us to finally wake will come,
God has withheld from all,
The time of our eternal home.

Who has his house in order set,
May leave the world without regret.
When we surety contrive,
Death eternal can deprive.
By Henrich Otto.

2   Baptismal Certificate. 1779. Ana Barbara Derr was born of
honorable Reformed parents in Upper Hanover Township,
Philadelphia County, in the year of Christ 1777 on July 2 at 5
o'clock in the morning. Her parents are Georg Adam Derr and
his wife, Christina. According to the Christian custom, she
was accorded Holy Baptism on August 24. Her godfather and
godmother were Phieliepp Heger and his wife, Barbara.
Written by me, Georg Adam Derr, on April 23 in the year
1779. To God alone the glory and to no one else.

3   Christian Baptismal Wish. O dear child, you have been
baptized into the death of Christ, who with his blood has
ransomed you from hell. As a reminder and constant
remembrance of this, I wish to present you with this after your
baptism. Grow up to the honor of God and the joy of your
parents, to the support of your neighbor, and to your eternal
bliss. Anna Catarina Gisler was born on the 21st of June 1779
and baptized by Pastor Schultz. Baptismal sponsors [were]
Christian Wollfart and his wife, Margaretha, in Tulpehocken
Township in Berks County in America in Pennsylvania.

4   To these two married persons, namely Georg Heiges and his
wife, Margaretha, a daughter named Sabina was born into the
world. She was born in the year of Christ 1776 on July 31 at
——— o'clock in the sign of ———. She was baptized by Pastor
Rauss. Baptismal sponsors [were] Johannes Huber and his
wife. She was born in the state of Pennsylvania in York
County in Monaghan Township. To God alone give glory.

5   To these two married people, namely Michael Fischer and his
legal wife, Cattarina Lollmain, a son named Willhelm Fischer
was born into the world. He was born into the world in the
year of our Lord Jesus 1780 on the 30th day of November at 6
o'clock in the morning in the sign of Aries with baptismal
sponsors Willem Fischer, unmarried. [He was] incorporated
into the gracious covenant of God and baptized by the
preacher and servant of God's Word on the 25th day of
December and given the above name. The above-mentioned
was born in America in the state of Pennsylvania in Berks
County in Heidelberg Township.
[In another hand] Preacher Wiellem Posch[?] baptized him

6   To these two married persons, namely Jacob Reichwein and
his lawful wife, Magdalena, a son named Cornelius was born
into the world. He was born into the world in the year of our
Lord Jesus 1802 on the 26th of May. Baptismal sponsors were
Johannes Mast and his wife, Elisabetha. Thus he was
incorporated into the gracious covenant of God and baptized
on the ——— day of ——— by the preacher and servant of
God's Word and given the above-mentioned name. The
above-mentioned was born in America in the state of
Pennsylvania in Lancaster County in ——— Township.

7   To these two married persons, namely Michael Albrecht and
his lawful wife, Elisabeth, née Bayer, a daughter was born
into the world as continued: Anna Albrecht was born into the
world in the year of our Lord Jesus 1760 on the 23rd day of
February at 6 o'clock in the morning in the sign of Gemini.
May God grant grace, power, and might that this Anna may
grow up in the fear of the Lord, to his honor and praise, and
increase in great yearning for the sincere pure milk and search
for the preexistent salvation of souls, having been enjoined
according to the accepted creed and confession of sins,
through true remorse and repentance before the Christian
congregation, to the spiritual rebirth of Holy Baptism, and
baptized by the designated preacher and servant of the Word,
according to Christ's command in Matthew 28:19, and
incorporated into the covenantal grace of God. This Anna was
received and taken in as a member of the communion of
saints, through the washing of regeneration and the renewal of

the Holy Spirit, as Saint Paul teaches in Titus 3: 5,6,7, along with a sister, on the 7th day of November 1779, and through true faith in our Savior Jesus Christ was made an heir of the reward gained at so great a price—heavenly joy and eternal bliss. Herewith do not forget how the Apostle Paul describes one's obligation (Colossians 1:12–14). Give thanks to the Father, who has qualified us to share in the inheritance of the saints in light, etc. This Anna Albrecht was born and baptized in America in the province of Pennsylvania in Lancaster County in Donegal Township.
Scarcely born into the world, [text repeats as in no. 1]
By Henrich Dulheuer.
[In another hand] Died January 20, 1832.

8   To these two married persons, namely Conrad Breneise and his lawful wife, Maria, née Herman, a daughter named Maria Breneise was born into the world. She was born into the world in the year of our Lord Jesus 1770 on the 13th day of August at 4 o'clock in the morning in the sign of Taurus. She was, since all men are conceived and born in sin, and according to the teaching of Christ all the children are to be brought to Jesus, as the Evangelist Mark describes in chapter 10, verse 15 ff., that whoever does not receive the kingdom of God as a little child shall not enter therein, therefore incorporated into the gracious covenant of God through Holy Baptism and baptized by Pastor Wilhelm Kortz on the 18th day of September and named as above mentioned. Baptismal sponsors were Valentin Breneise and his lawful wife. The above-mentioned Maria Breneise was born and baptized in America in the province of Pennsylvania in Lancaster County in Earl Township. Written by me, Jacob Otto.
Scarcely born into the world, [text repeats as in no. 1]
Written 1784

9   Birth and Baptismal Certificate. To these two married persons, namely Henrich Kostenbader and his lawful wife, Maria Christina, née Mayer, a daughter named Elisabetha was born into the world in the year of our Lord Jesus 1783 on the 9th day of October at ——— o'clock in the sign of ———. This Elisabetha was born and baptized in America in the state of Pennsylvania in Northampton County in Plainfield Township. The above-mentioned Elisabetha was baptized on ——— by Mr. ———. Baptismal sponsors were Frantz Klewelt and his wife, Salome. [She] was confirmed by Mr. Thomas Pomp in the year 1804.
Scarcely born into the world, [text repeats as in no. 1]
Done by F. Krebs.
[In another hand] Married the 15th of June 1806

I am baptized, I stand united,
Through my own baptism, with my God,
And therefore joy my tongue has guided;
Although in fear and pain I've trod,
I am baptized, there's joy in me,
The joy that lasts eternally.

I am baptized! And though I perish,
O grave, where is thy victory?
My patrimony is in heaven,
And it shall never fall from me.
When death arrives, I shall receive,
Far purer joy than those I leave.

10   To these two married persons, namely Michael Hausser and his lawful wife, Elisabetha, née Xander, a son named Michael Hausser was born into the world. He was born into the world in the year of our Lord Jesus 1789 on the 25th day of March at ——— o'clock in the sign of ———. May God grant grace, power, and might that this Michael may grow up [text repeats as in no. 7] and baptized by Mr. Carl Christoph Götz, preacher and servant of the Word, [text repeats as in no. 7]. This Michael was received and taken [text repeats as in no. 7], as Saint Paul teaches in Titus 3: 5,6,7, into the Lutheran religion on the ——— day of ——— 17———, and through true faith [text repeats as in no. 7] of the saints in light, etc. The baptismal sponsors were Georg Hausser and Margaretha Xander, unmarried. This Michael was born and baptized in America in

the state of Pennsylvania in Northampton County in Whitehall Township.
Scarcely born into the world, [text repeats as in no. 1]
Friedrich Krebs
[In another hand] Entered into marriage with Elisabeth George, July 4, 1813

11   Sing and make music to the Lord in your hearts. To these two married persons, namely Jacob Gass and his lawful wife, Fronica, née Domes, a son named Johannes was born into the world. He was born into the world in the year of our Lord 1775 on the 11th day of March at ——— o'clock in the sign of ———. Whereby this child was incorporated into the covenant of grace of God and baptized and named as above mentioned by Pastor ———, preacher and servant of God's Word. The above-mentioned child was born in America in the province of Pennsylvania in Dauphin County, Derry Township. Baptismal sponsors were ———.

God bless our going out and coming in, your plowing and seedtime, your morning and evening sacrifice, that the mountains bring you tidings of peace and the hills dance before you, that your children grow up like the cedars of Lebanon.

12   Sing and make music to the Lord in your hearts. To these two married persons, namely Georg Ritzecker and his lawful wife, Susunna, née Rühm, a daughter named Eliesabeth was born into the world. She was born into the world in the year of our Lord 1797 on the 30th day of November at 5 o'clock in the evening in the sign of Aries[?]. She was incorporated into the covenant of God on the 2nd of December, baptized by Pastor Lup, preacher and servant of God's Word, and given the aforementioned name. The above-mentioned was born in America in the province of Pennsylvania in Lancaster County, Donegal Township. Baptismal sponsors are Catha[rina] [Rüh]m[?].
God bless our going out [text repeats as in no. 11]

13   To these two married persons, namely Hennerich Gangenwer and his lawful wife, Elisabeta, née Köhl, a daughter named Cattarina was born into the world. She was born into the world in the year of our Lord Jesus 1795 on the 22nd day of September at ———. May God grant grace, power, and might that this Cattarina may grow up [text repeats as in no. 7] and baptized by Mr. Hofmayer, Reformed preacher and servant of the Word, [text repeats as in no. 7]. This Cattarina was received and taken in [text repeats as in no. 7] of the saints in light, etc. Baptismal sponsor was Cattrina Koch, unmarried. This Cattarina was born and baptized in America in the state of Pennsylvania in Northampton County in Upper Saucon Township.
I am baptized, I stand united, [text repeats as in no. 9]

14   Baptismal Certificate. To these two married persons, namely Georg Trollinger and his lawful wife, Magtalena, née Tietz, a son named Carrel was born into the world in the year of our Lord Jesus 1808 on the 17th day of August at 5:30 in the morning in the sign of ———. This Carrel was born and baptized in America in the state of Pennsylvania, Bucks County, Rockhill Township. The above-mentioned Carrel was baptized on ——— by the Reverend Pastor Röller. Baptismal sponsors were Georg Wambold and Maria Elisabeth Titz.
Scarcely born into the world, [text repeats as in no. 1]
[In another hand] He died on the 7th of June and was buried the 9th, 1832
Ephrata: by J. Baumann.
I am baptized, I stand united, [text repeats as in no. 9]

15   To these two married persons, namely Jacob Schreiber and his wife, Catahr[ina] Elisabet[h], née Kerner, of the Reformed religion, a son named Jacob was born into the world. He was born in the year of our Lord Jesus 1780 on January 3 at ——— o'clock in Whitehall Township, Northampton County, in the state of Pennsylvania, and was brought to Holy Baptism on February 27 and was baptized by Mr. Blumer, servant of God's Word. The baptismal sponsors were Peter Deschler and

his wife, Magdalena, and gave him the name Jacob.
This heart of mine is naught but thine/O Jesus dear

16   To these two married persons, namely Jacob Yeckly and his lawful wife, Catarina, née Benewitz, a son named George Yeckly was born into the world. He was born into the world in the year of our Lord Jesus 1801 on the 6th day of September at ——— o'clock in the sign of ———. May God grant grace, power, and might that this George Yeckly may grow up [text repeats as in no. 7] and baptized by Imuel [Emmanuel] Schultz, preacher and servant of the Word, [text repeats as in no. 7]. This George Yeckly was received and taken [text repeats as in no. 7], as Saint Paul teaches in Titus 3:5–7, into the Lutheran Church on the 6th day of September 1801, and through true faith [text repeats as in no. 7] of the saints in light, etc. The baptismal sponsors were George Breis and his wife, Elisabeta. This George Yeckly was born and baptized in the state of Pennsylvania, Heidelberg Township, Berks County. Friederich Speyer.
I am baptized, I stand united, [text repeats as in no. 9]

17   To these two married persons, namely Betder [Peter] Schaffer and his lawful wife, Marria, née Hoffmann, a daughter was born into the world in the year of our Savior A[nno] 1798 on May 14 at ——— o'clock and received the name Barbara Schaffer through Holy Baptism by the Reverend Preacher J. Helfferich. Baptismal sponsors were Danniel Dreybelbis and Magdalena Hess, in the state of Pennsylvania, Berks County, Richmond Township.
I am baptized, I stand united, [text repeats as in no. 9]

The host of children dear
Buried in Jesus' blood
Rids mother's heart of fear
And lets joy in it flood.

18   To these two married persons, namely Johan Maser and his lawful wife, Margretha, née Lick, a son was born into the world in the year of our Savior 1812 on October 29 at 8 o'clock in the evening and received the name Johan Jacob through Holy Baptism by the Reverend Preacher Hempink. Baptismal sponsors were Johan Jacob Ochsenreuter and his wife in the state of Pennsylvania, Northumberland County.
I am baptized, I stand united, [text repeats as in no. 9]
The host of children dear [text repeats as in no. 17]

[In English on reverse] Johan Masser born Oct 29 1812, died May 29, 1895, age 82-7-0, text 1 cor 15: 55: 56: 57, Rev Joseph ———, Buried at St. James, Saturday May 31, 1895.

19   Barbara Stephan was born of Christian parents on the 14th of March in the year of Christ 1801 in Mahantango Township in Northumberland County in the province of Pennsylvania, North America, and was baptized by the R[everend] P[reacher] Geistweit. The baptismal sponsors were Michael Weiand and his wife, Anna Maria. The parents are the honorable Adam Stephan and his honorable wife, named Margaretha, née Geistweit. Be thou faithful unto [death] and I will give thee the crown of life. Be joyful in the Lord and he will give thee the desires of thy heart.

20   To these two married persons, namely Friederich Arnold and his lawful wife, Debora, née Ziegler, a son named Samuel Arnold was born into the world in the year of Christ 1807 on the 14th day of February at 7:30 in the evening in the sign of Taurus. This Samuel Arnold was born and baptized in America in the state of Pennsylvania in Northampton County and in Upper Saucon Township. The aforementioned Samuel Arnold was baptized on the 10th day of May 1807 by Mr. Pledt, Lutheran preacher. Baptismal sponsors were Matthaus Ochs and Elisabetha Egner, single at that time.
I am baptized! And though I perish, [text repeats as in no. 9]
Martin Brechall.

21   Birth and Baptismal Certificate. To these two married persons, namely Daniel Lieder and his lawful wife, Elisabeth, née Schäfer, a daughter was born into the world on the 29th day of

November in the year of our Lord 1814. This daughter was born in Heidelberg Township in Berks County in the state of Pennsylvania in North America, and was baptized by Mr. H——— and received the name Juliana on the ——— day of February in the year of our Lord 1815. The baptismal sponsors were ———.
Scarcely born into the world, [text repeats as in no. 1]
I am baptized, I stand united, [text repeats as in no. 9]

Baptized am I, and to thee taken
O God, the Father, Spirit, Son!
And as thy seed am not forsaken
But am with those whose battle's won!
O! What great fortune thus is mine,
Lord! Make me always worthy thine.

Reading: Printed and available at Johann Ritter und Comp.

22   Birth and Baptismal Certificate. To these two married persons, namely Johann Hartlein and his lawful wife, Julianna, née Lider, a daughter was born into the world on the 14th day of September in the year of our Lord 1837. This daughter was born in Heidelberg Township in Berks County in the state of Pennsylvania in North America, and received the name Ellen through Holy Baptism by the Reverend Mr. Pauly on the ——— day of ——— in the year 1837. The baptismal sponsors were Ellen Klopp.
Scarcely born into the world, [text repeats as in no. 1]
I am baptized, I stand united, [text repeats as in no. 9]
Baptized am I, and to thee taken [text repeats as in no. 21]
Reading: Printed and available at Johann Ritter und Comp.

23   Birth and Baptismal Certificate. To these two married persons, namely Carl Schett and his lawful wife, Sarah Schett, née Brossy, a son was born into the world on the 21st day of January in the year of our Lord 1827. This son was born in Jonestown in Lebanon County in the state of Pennsylvania in North America, and received the name Christian through Holy Baptism by the Reverend Pastor Mr. Stein on the 24th day of March in the year 1827. The baptismal sponsors were Maria Eva Schett.
Scarcely born into the world, [text repeats as in no. 1]
I am baptized, I stand united, [text repeats as in no. 9]
Baptized am I, and to thee taken [text repeats as in no. 21]
Reading, Printed and available at Johann Ritter.

24   Christian Baptismal Certificate or Birth Letter. Johannes Homan was born into the world in the year 1814 on the 21st day of September at 6 o'clock in the morning in the sign of Capricorn in Haines Township, Centre County, in the state of Pennsylvania. [He was] baptized on December 18 in the year 1814 by Pastor Wilhelm Ilgen. The baptismal sponsors are Jacob Albrecht and his wife, Barbara. The parents of this child are Peter Homan and his wife, Elisabeth, Peter Schlögel's legitimate daughter, by name.

25   Birth and Baptismal Certificate. To these two married persons, namely Joseph Egolff and his lawful wife, Barbara, née Losz, a daughter was born into the world in the year of our Lord Jesus 1813 on the 10th day of January. This daughter was born and baptized in America in the state of Pennsylvania in Cumberland County and in the city of Carlisle. The above-mentioned daughter was baptized by Mr. Sanno and received the name Elizabeth on the 24th day of February in the year of our Lord 1813. Baptismal sponsors were Elizabeth Losz.
Scarcely born into the world, [text repeats as in no. 1]
I am baptized, I stand united, [text repeats as in no. 9]
Baptized am I, and to thee taken [text repeats as in no. 21]
Carlisle: Printed by F. Sanno, 1813.

26   Birth and Baptismal Certificate. To these two married persons, namely Jost Hertlein and his lawful wife, Sarah, née Deh, a son was born into the world on the 3rd day of June in the year of our Lord 1809. This son was born in ——— County in the state of ——— in North America, and was baptized by Mr. Miller and received the name Johannes on the ——— day of ——— in the year of our Lord ———. The baptismal sponsors were Daniel Gauker and his lawful wife.

Scarcely born into the world, [text repeats as in no. 1]
I am baptized, I stand united, [text repeats as in no. 9]
Baptized am I, and to thee taken [text repeats as in no. 21]
Allentown, Printed and available at Henrich Ebner. 1818.

27 Birth and Baptismal Certificate. To these two married persons, namely Jacob Licht and his lawful wife, Christina, née Licht, a daughter was born into the world in the year of our Lord Jesus 1815 on the 19th day of July. This daughter was born in Bethel Township in Lebanon County in the state of Pennsylvania in North America, and was baptized by Mr. ——— and received the name Maria on the ——— day of ——— in the year of our Lord Jesus ———. The baptismal sponsors were ———.
Scarcely born into the world, [text repeats as in no.1]
I am baptized, I stand united, [text repeats as in no. 9]
Baptized am I, and to thee taken [text repeats as in no. 21]
Harrisburg, Printed by John S. Wiestling.
[In English on reverse] Maria Licht married Wilhelm Turbin October 24, 1841.

28 Birth and Baptismal Certificate. To these two married persons, namely Joseph Egolff and his lawful wife, Barbara, née Losz, a son was born into the world in the year of our Lord Jesus 1818 on the 4th day of April. This son was born in the city of Carlisle in Cumberland County in the state of Pennsylvania in North America, and was baptized by the Reverend Mr. Köhler and received the name William Jacob Egolff on the 23rd day of May in the year of our Lord 1818. The baptismal sponsors were Joseph and Barbara Egolff.
Scarcely born into the world, [text repeats as in no 1]
I am baptized, I stand united, [text repeats as in no. 9]
Baptized am I, and to thee taken [text repeats as in no. 21]
Harrisburg, Printed by John S. Wiestling.

29 Birth and Baptismal Certificate. To these two married persons, namely Conrad Oberbeck and his lawful wife, Christina, née Klein, a daughter was born into the world in the year of our Lord 1816 on the 6th day of March at 10:30 in the evening in the sign of Taurus. This daughter was born in Nockamixon Township, Bucks County, in the state of Pennsylvania in North America, and was baptized by the Reverend Pastor Nicklaus Mensch and received the name Maria Magdalena in the year of our Lord 1816 on the 2nd day of June. The baptismal sponsors were Maria Magdalena Oberbeck, widow.

Son, exercise faithfulness and sincerity, up to the cool grave, and do not step one finger's width off God's way.
Then you may go through this pilgrim life on green meadows, then you may ——— fear and dread ——— stand against death.
Then your grandsons will seek your grave and weep over it, and summer flowers, full of scent, will bloom out of the tears.

30 Birth and Baptismal Certificate. To these two married persons, namely Sebastian Horn and his lawful wife, Maria, née Mollen, a daughter was born into the world on the 27th day of October in the year of our Lord 1822. This daughter was born in Richland Township, Bucks County, in the state of Pennsylvania in North America, and was baptized by Mr. C. Röller and received the name Catharina Horn on the 13th day of December in the year of our Lord 1822. The baptismal sponsors were Abraham Horn and Elisabeth Kob.
Scarcely born into the world, [text repeats as in no. 1]
I am baptized, I stand united, [text repeats as in no. 9]
Baptized am I, and to thee taken [text repeats as in no. 21]

31 Birth and Baptismal Certificate. Mr. Michael Frank, a son of Mr. Philipp Frank and his wife, Catharina, née Stober, was born into the world on the 19th day of July 1806 in Haines Township, Centre County, in the state of Pennsylvania, and baptized by Pastor C.A.W. Ilgen. The baptismal sponsors were Mr. Philipp Hennig and his wife, Catharina.

32 [In English] Charles a Son of Mr. David Horner and his wife Mary born a Johnston son was born on the 20th day of November 1832 in Hartly Township Union County, State of Pennsylvania and baptized by the Revd M. A. Smith May 18th 1853

33 [In English] Certificate of Birth and Baptism. Miss Mary Jane Rockey, a daughter of Mr. John Rockey and his wife Salome, born a Housman, was born March the 20th 1849 in Gregg Township, Center County, Pennsylvania and baptized by the Revd Charles Rees. Sponsors "were the parents."

34 Birth and Baptismal Certificate. To these two married persons, namely Joseph Egolff and his lawful wife, Barbara, née ———, a daughter was born into the world on the 31st day of December in the year of our Lord 1824. This daughter was born in Carlisle in Cumberland County in the state of Pennsylvania in North America, and was baptized by the Reverend Pastor B. Keller and received the name Barbara Ann on the 23rd day of May in the year of our Lord 1825. The baptismal sponsors were the parents.
Scarcely born into the world, [text repeats as in no. 1]
I am baptized, I stand united, [text repeats as in no. 9]
Baptized am I, and to thee taken [text repeats as in no. 21]
Carlisle, 1826—Printed and available at Moser und Peters.

35 Birth and Baptismal Certificate. To these two married persons, namely George Hollinger and his lawful wife, Elisabeth, née Asper, a son was born into the world on the 20th day of June in the year of our Lord 1830. This son was born in Reading Township, Adams County, in the state of Pennsylvania in North America, and was baptized by Mr. Vondersloot and received the name Eli on the ——— day of ——— in the year of our Lord 1830. The baptismal sponsors were the parents.
Scarcely born into the world, [text repeats as in no. 1]
I am baptized, I stand united, [text repeats as in no. 9]
Baptized am I, and to thee taken [text repeats as in no. 21]
Carlisle, 1826—Printed and available at Moser und Peters.

36 Birth and Baptismal Certificate. To these two married persons, namely Peter Wertz and his wife, Catharina, née Gaumer, a daughter was born into the world on the 11th day of October in the year of our Lord 1827. This daughter was born in Macungie Township in Lehigh County in the state of Pennsylvania in North America, and received the name Carolina Emilia through Holy Baptism by the Christian Pastor Germann on the 19th day of December in the year of our Lord 1827. The baptismal sponsors were Jacob Neumeyer and his wife, Catharina.

37 Blank. Printed text nearly identical to that of nos. 38–40.

38 Birth and Baptismal Certificate. To these two married persons, namely Heinrich Braun and his lawful wife, Barbara, a daughter of Georg Bender, a son was born into the world on the 3rd day of August in the year of our Lord 1839. This son was born in Bethel Township in Lebanon County in the state of Pennsylvania in North America, and was baptized by the Reverend Pastor Leinbach and received the name Jeremias on the ——— day of ——— in the year of our Lord 1839. The baptismal sponsors were Eduward Bender, unmarried.
Scarcely born into the world, [text repeats as in no. 1]
I am baptized, I stand united, [text repeats as in no. 9]
Baptized am I, and to thee taken [text repeats as in no. 21]
Printed and available at G. S. Peters,—Harrisburg, Pa.

39 Birth and Baptismal Certificate. To these two married persons, namely Heinrich Braun and his lawful wife, Barbara, a daughter of Georg Bender, a daughter was born into the world on the 26th day of February in the year of our Lord 1842. This daughter was born in Bethel Township in Lebanon County in the state of Pennsylvania in North America, and was baptized by the Reverend Pastor T. Leinbach and received the name Sussanna on the 26th day of March in the year of our Lord 1842. The baptismal sponsors were Daniel Bieber and his wife, Rahael.
Scarcely born into the world, [text repeats as in no. 1]
I am baptized, I stand united, [text repeats as in no. 9]
Baptized am I, and to thee taken [text repeats as in no. 21]
Printed and available at G. S. Peters,—Harrisburg, Pa.

40 Birth and Baptismal Certificate. To these two married persons, namely Heinrich Braun and his lawful wife, Barbara, a

daughter of Georg Bender, a daughter was born into the world on the 11th day of February in the year of our Lord 1845. This daughter was born in Bethel Township in Lebanon County in the state of Pennsylvania in North America, and was baptized by the Reverend Pastor Joh[an] Stein and received the name Maria Anna on the 25th day of March in the year of our Lord 1845. The baptismal sponsors were Maria Stöver, unmarried. Scarcely born into the world, [text repeats as in no. 1] I am baptized, I stand united, [text repeats as in no. 9] Baptized am I, and to thee taken [text repeats as in no. 21] Printed and available at G. S. Peters,—Harrisburg, Pa.

41 Levi Bingeman (son of Samuel Bingeman and his wife, Elisabeth, née Hacker) was born on the 13th day of October 1828, and was baptized by W[illia]m Bätes on the 23rd day of January 1829. The baptismal sponsors were Georg Hacker and his wife, Christina.

42 Birth and Baptismal Certificate. To the married persons O[w]en Fetzer and his wife, Henriette, née Emig, a daughter was born on the 3rd day of October in the year of our Lord 1855. This daughter was born in Allentown in Lehigh County in the state of Pennsylvania in North America. She was baptized by the Reverend Pastor Josua Jäger and received the name Lidia Ellen Mente on the ——— day of December in the year of our Lord 1855. The baptismal sponsors were the parents of the child themselves.
The peace of God be with and preserve you!
Scarcely born into the world, [text repeats as in no. 1] I am baptized, I stand united, [text repeats as in no. 9] Baptized am I, and to thee taken [text repeats as in no. 21] Allentown, Pa. Printed and available at Blumer und Leisenring.

43 Birth and Baptismal Certificate. To these two married persons, namely Carl Ludwich Hackmeister and his lawful wife, Elisabeth, née Schäffer, a son named Johan Georg Hackmeister was born into the world. He was born into the world in the year of our Lord Jesus 1800 on the 2nd of August at 6 o'clock in the evening, and was baptized by Mr. Herbst, preacher of the Lutheran congregation, and given the name indicated above. Baptismal sponsors are Johannes German and his wife. The aforementioned was born in the state of Pennsylvania, Union County, Chapman Township.

I am baptized, I stand united, with my God through my baptism. Therefore I always say with joyful tongue: I am baptized, there's joy in me, the joy that lasts eternally.

To God alone the glory.
Francis Portzline

44 Birth and Baptismal Certificate. To these two married persons, namely Wilhelm Portzeline and his lawful wife, Gertraut, née Zeler, a son was born into the world on the 7th of June at 11 o'clock in the evening in the year of our Lord 1838 in Greenwood Township, Juniata County, in the state of Pennsylvania, and received the name Benjamin through Holy Baptism by the Reverend Preacher Frederich Seiberd. The baptismal sponsors are Abraham Zeller and his wife, Nänzi.
I am baptized, I stand united, [text repeats as in no. 43]
Francis Portzline

45 [In English] Certificate of birth &. baptism. To these two persons as John Ziegler, and his wife Mary Ann aborn Nace was born a Daughter to the world on the 22 day of January A.D. ———2, this Child was born in Shrewsbury town ship York County State of pennsylvania in North America, and was baptised by the Rev^d Mr. A. Berg and received the Name Mary Agnes Her Sponsors was the parents.

Our Souls he washed with his blood,
As water makes the body clean,
And the good Spirit from our God,
Decends like purifying rain.

Made by Daniel Peterman Shrewsbury town. S. Y. C° Pa.

Other

1 [Not transcribed]

2 I, Johannes Maurer, was born on the 14th day of May in the year of our Lord 1751, in Great Swamp in Lower Milford Township, Bucks County, in the sign of Gemini. The aforementioned entered into marriage with Elisabetha Kettmann on ——— day of ——— in the year of our Lord 1781. She was born on the ——— day of June in the year of our Lord 1760.

To the aforementioned married people the following children were born:
1. Johannes Maurer was born on the 12th day of October in the year 1780 in the sign of Capricorn.
2. Maria Maurer was born on the 3rd day of September in the year 1782 between 5 and 6 o'clock in the morning in the sign of Leo.
3. Abraham Maurer was born on the 21st day of January in the year 1784 in the sign of Aries.
4. Daniel Maurer was born on the 12th day of February in the year 1786 in the sign of Leo.
5. Sem Maurer was born on the 9th of February in the year 1788 in the sign of Pisces. He died on the 8th day of April 1788.
6. Christian Maurer was born on the 16th day of April in the year 1789 in the sign of Pisces.
7. Elisabetha Maurer was born on the 29th day of July in the year 1791 in the sign of Cancer.
8. Sem Maurer was born on the 24th day of September in the year 1793 in the sign of Gemini.
9. Anna Maurer was born on the 17th day of December in the year 1795 between 12 and 1 o'clock at night in the sign of Aries.

Children, obey your parents in the Lord, for this is just. Honor father and mother, that is the first commandment with the promise. Ephesians in the 6th chapter. Honor God and keep his commandments.

3 Confirmation Certificate. I hereby certify that Johannes Derr was through confirmation made a member of the Evangelical Reformed Church on the 3rd day of June in the year of our Lord 1838. Daniel Weiser v.d.m.

4 Family Register. Marriages. Abraham A. Hendricks and Lidia Hunsicker. Both [were] entered into Holy Matrimony on the 16th day of September 1855 by Mr. Joshue H. Derr.
[On reverse] Family Register. Births. Abraham A. Hendricks was born on the 20th day of August 1829. Lydia M. Hunsicker was born on the 16th day of November 1838.

House Blessings

1   House Blessing, or the Angels of the Morning. Up, Lot, the shadows are dispersed, the dawning light is breaking! Up, before the rays of sun can pierce and still cast light on Sodom's earth, stir yourself out of sleep, up! Listen to the Word of the Highest here: the punishment of the Highest blots out the moment, this place of sin. You are dumbfounded?! There is no room for delay! God is coming, who metes out just deserts. The land already trembles from the rumblings of thunder; you alone the Lord has spared. Give me your hand, I will lead you, climb up this high mountain! Do not look back in any direction, for otherwise no one can save you. The Almighty God be with you, bless, preserve, and protect you for time and eternity through our Lord Jesus Christ. Amen. Elisabeth Bordner in the year of our Lord 1830.

2   A Spiritual House Blessing, or the First Oblation of Noah upon Entering the New World. With anxious mien I leave my haven and contemplate my maker's deeds upon noble Ararat. Here I, protected from all danger in the company of wife and children, see a world of sinners caught in the water and the slime. How am I better than the sinners helpless here in the water? Why does God deal with me more kindly? Do I not deserve the same? Can I be regarded as angelic? Have I never knowingly dishonored God? No, great God, I must confess, I am not worth such grace. God, you are everywhere, and know where to find me. You look upon my heart, preserve me, God, from sin. Amen. God the Almighty protect you in the temporal, but most of all in the eternal, for the sake of Jesus Christ. Amen. Susanna Trautman, née Schäfer. God bless your [entire] house. [A.] D. 1831.

3   Spiritual House Blessing.
Jesus, in my house abide,
Never from it turn aside,
And therein with thy grace stay,
Otherwise I go astray.
Full of blessings, great art thou!
Come and give thy blessing now,
That health, peace, and felicity,
May this house's portion be.
As Abraham and Job received,
With richest blessings were reprieved.
O! So pour out on me now,
Blessing mild upon my brow.
And abide thou in my heart,
Where fear and pain would tear apart,
When trials sore upon me press,
O help me, God, in my distress!
When wealth no longer mine shall be,
Let me my home in heaven see.
Though I distress must here endure,
Heaven's joys for me are always sure.
Elisabeth Landes, 1834.
H. W. Villee, Lancaster.

Writing Samples

1   Death to the world, to sin and self, so that you may live here in the Lord. Only the dead who die in the Lord will inherit salvation.

Wake, awake, for night is flying,
The watchmen on the heights are crying:
Awake, Jerusalem, at last!
Midnight hears the welcome voices,
And at the thrilling cry rejoices:
Come forth, ye virgins, night is past!
The Bridegroom comes awake,
Your lamps with gladness take; Hallelujah!
And for his marriage feast prepare,
For you must go to meet him there.

Zion hears the watchmen singing,
And all her heart with joy is springing;
She wakes, she rises from her gloom;
For her Lord comes down all glorious,
The strong in grace, in truth victorious,
Her Star is risen, her Light is come!
Ah, come, thou blessed Lord!
O Jesus, Son of God, Hallelujah!
We follow till the halls we see
Where thou hast bid us sup with thee.

Now let all the heavens adore thee,
And men and angels sing before thee,
With harp and cymbal's clearest tone;
Of twelve pearls are [unfinished].

[upper- and lower-case alphabets; list of months; numbers]
This belongs to me, Anna in Salford. Written in the year of Christ 1772, the 28th of September. God bless this house [and] those who go [in and out]. There is great gain in godliness with contentment; for we brought nothing into the world, and we cannot take anything out of the world; but if we have food and clothing, with these we shall be content [1 Timothy 6:6,7,8].
O that I could bridle my thoughts, and discipline my heart with God's Word, and I ——— not shame, ———.

2   Lord Jesus, lead me as long as I live on earth. Let me not be without your guidance. If I direct my ways without you, I am soon undone. But if you lead me, I do what is pleasing to you. You alone are the right shepherd. Without you I soon go astray. Therefore take me, a poor lamb, and lead me on the right path so that after my time here, I may be with you in bliss, so that I may be in the number of sheep, O dear Jesus mine, who look upon you in eternal joy in the beautiful and dear pastures of heaven. O what blessed peace and abundance of joy both are promised by Christ to the victor.

O dear man, whatever you do, take thought that you must die. O how short your life of which you must give account to God. Take thought, therefore, as to where your body and soul will go, for death is certain, but not the day, and the hour no one knows. Take thought, therefore, how you should conduct your life. Keep God before your eyes and remember that each hour could be the last. And were we as wise as Solomon and as comely as Absalom, and had the goods of the great Alexander, and the courage of the Turkish emperor, and the riches of the Roman emperor, yet all of us become the same in death. The sting of death has the power to strike rich, poor, comely, young, and old. He tears them away out of their land, city, and province. O God, when all else forsakes me ———.

This heart of mine is only thine, only to thee given. 1792. [upper-case alphabet]

3   In God all things began,
Commit to him your ways,
The deeds of your life's span,
Thus gladly end your days.

Written the 5th of February in the year 1793.
This writing belongs to me, Christina Bearry. May God give her much blessing and fortune and bring her through these times into everlasting bliss.

4   This letter belongs to me, Christina Byrri [Bearry]. I will lift up my eyes unto the hills from whence my help comes from the Lord who made heaven and earth. The Lord preserve you from all evil, may he preserve your soul. The Lord preserve your going out and your coming in from this time forth and forevermore. Written the 10th of February, 1793.

5   I want to love and strive in all things to please my Bridegroom, who on the Tree of the Cross gave his life for me, totally submissive as a lamb. End of the first verse.

2. I want to love and strive in prayer both day and night to bring all things old in me to the grave, and from now on to have everything in me made new.

3. I want to love and strive to become pure and whole, and conduct my life as God would want it, so that all my doing, ordering, and action may be unblemished on this earth.

4. I want to love and strive throughout my whole lifetime to be comely and adorned in a pure wedding garment, to appear with the pure at the marriage supper of the Lamb.

Behold, I stand at the door and knock; if anyone hears my voice and opens the door, I will come in to him and eat with him and he with me. Revelation chapter 3, verse 20.

O dear pupil, mark well, this saying goes for you and me. What type of friend is this who here says, "Behold I stand at the door." The answer is Jesus, Friend of Souls, who was well intentioned toward us, that he gave up his life willingly unto death for us. If we do not let this friend in, how much could our misfortune be. Woe to him whose heart and ear remain closed when Jesus knocks. He will later knock to get in, but then the door will remain shut. Therefore, while there is still time out of grace, let us willingly and with expectation, as sheep, hear Jesus' voice, open the door, and follow. He leads them through this vale of tears to himself in his halls of joy.

O noble heart, consider your end. Who knows how soon the course is run. Written the 28th of February, Anno 1794. [upper-case alphabets]

6   Behold, I stand at the door and knock; if anyone hears my voice and opens the door, I will come in to him and eat with him and he with me. Revelation chapter 3, verse 20.

Come, take my heart to be your own and at your pleasure direct me. Direct me, Lord, I shall be still, I give my will to you. And put to death in me what comes under your judgment, bend what rebels against you, before your presence and your glory. Prepare my heart as a throne for you, and then live eternally in me. With your eye direct me, and make me perfectly suppliant. Take my heart, I offer it to you, eternally for your possession. I no longer desire to live to myself, king of my heart. O Jesus, come, to you alone my heart belongs, to you alone it can respond. My Lord and King, keep me eternally true to you.

Catharina Kolb 1795
[upper- and lower-case alphabets]

7   Children, obey your parents in the Lord, for this is meet. Honor father and mother, this is the first commandment of promise.

O dear God, I thank you that you have given me such dear parents out of grace and mercy, and have let them live to this time, as a joy to me. Impress on me how much burden and pain it cost my parents to bring me to this point. Reward them for such effort in the heavenly places. Grant my parents peace and rest, let your blessing come over them. Help them to carry their cross and when their time is ended, lead them out of mortality into the kingdom of bliss.

[upper- and lower-case alphabets; numbers]
This note writing belongs to Andreas Kauffm[an]. Written the 10th of March 1796.
[On reverse] AK

8   Be not wise in your own conceits. Repay no man evil for evil. Provide things honest in the sight of all men. Romans in the 12th chapter [verses 16–17].

He that walks in his just way fears the Lord, but he that is perverse in his way despises him. In the fear of the Lord is strong confidence, and his children shall have a place of refuge. Declares Solomon [Proverbs] in the 14th chapter [verses 2, 26].

Remember now your Creator in the days of your youth, before the evil days come, and the years draw nigh, when you will say, "I have no pleasure in them." Ecclesiastes 12:1.

[upper- and lower-case alphabets; numbers]
This writing belongs to Daniel Maurer. Written in Hempfield

Township in the month of March 1796. By Christian Strenge, schoolmaster.
[On reverse] Daniel

9   Be not wise in your own conceits. Repay no man evil for evil. Provide things honest in the sight of all men. Romans in the 12th chapter [verses 16–17].

He who fears the Lord will not be timid, nor play the coward, for he is his hope. Blessed is the soul of the man who fears the Lord! To whom does he look? And who is his support? The eyes of the Lord are upon those who love him, a mighty protection and strong support, a shelter from the hot wind and a shade from the noonday sun, a guard against stumbling and a defense against falling. He lifts up the soul and gives light to the eyes; he grants healing, life, and blessing. Sirach [Ecclesiastes] in the 34th chapter [sic]. Honor thy father and thy mother, that is the first commandment which has a promise.

[upper- and lower-case alphabets; numbers]
This writing belongs to Daniel Maurer. Written in Hempfield Township in the month of March 1798, by Christian Strenge.

10   Sam Maurer. Mark the perfect man, and behold the upright, for the end of that man is peace. Psalm 37:37.

Whoever honors his father will also have joy in his own children and when he prays he will be heard. Whoever honors his father will have a longer life and whoever is obedient for the sake of the Lord, in him his mother takes comfort. Whoever fears the Lord also honors his father and serves his parents and considers them his lords. Honor father and mother in deeds, in words, and in patience, so that their blessing may come upon you.

[upper- and lower-case alphabets; numbers]
Written in the year 1800. By Christian Strenge.
[On reverse] Sam Maurer

11   Praise the Lord with me, and let us exalt his name together. Come, ye children, hearken unto me, I will teach you the fear of the Lord. Who is man that he desireth life and loveth many days. Keep thy tongue from evil and thy lips from speaking deceit. Psalm 34 [verses 3, 11–13].
[upper- and lower-case alphabets; numbers]
Written in Hempfield Township on the 1st of May 1804. By Christian Strenge.
[On reverse] Ann [Maurer]

12   Let he who thinks he stands, take heed lest he falls. The tempter is wherever we go, everywhere he stands waiting.
N.2. Security has deceived many. Sloth can never come to good. Whoever is overcome by it makes himself its slave.
N.3. If you spend much time in that, hear what can overtake you. Poverty will come your way, as a soldier strongly armed.
N.4. False liberty is the plague that wastes at noonday. Whoever loves his life, stay clear of it, before it kills.
N.5. It was when Samson lay down in the lap of Delilah and had his comforts best cared for that his undoing was near.
N.6. It was Simon who missed his chance to go with his Lord to death, and forgot to watch with him, and soon had to stand there in tears.
N.7. If the new spirit is equally willing, if the [unfinished].

[upper- and lower-case alphabets; 1804]
O noble heart, consider your end. Who knows how quickly the course is run. December 17, 1804.
We thank God for his goodness which we have received from him. We pray to our dear Lord that he would ever more provide us, he would have us eat with [unfinished].

13   Seek peace, true peace, seek it, my soul;
Let all else fly, reach God, your goal.
The safe in God keep sabbath true
Nor yield to what the flesh would do.
This writing belongs to me, Samuel Meyer.
Written the 26th of February 1824.

Religious Texts

1   When God created the world and all creatures without any help or compulsion, he said, "Now only a man is lacking who would be there with intelligence and good sense; the world stands empty, no man is there."

2. The Lord came down into the beautiful world, took a little earth and fashioned a man out of it. Adam, walking hither and yon in the garden, said, "If only someone were here to give me direction and be with me constantly."

3. Adam looked around and pondered this and that. "Where shall I go?" said he. "If only there were another person to inspire me, then I would be at peace. Someone to lavish good things, that is what I have in mind."

4. Adam fell into such a sleep that no one could have awakened him. Then came the one who created him, and took a rib from him and created a woman out of it, from this delicate body, to be with him constantly. Eve—that was Adam's wife.

5. When Adam awoke, he said, "My God and my Lord! You came upon me so silently. I am no longer completely whole. I did have all my members until you, Lord, came to me. Give me back my rib which you took from me."

God. 6. "Do not regret the loss of your rib. It is and shall remain yours. You ought to rejoice over it. It is not good to be alone. The rib which I removed from your body shall become you well and will be yours always."

Adam and Eve. 7. Soon they went walking around in the garden, Adam leading his wife. Then they became aware of a tree, lovely to look at, standing in the middle of the garden. "We shall go to it and take a look at the beautiful fruit."

God. 8. "Adam, take heed, you are not to eat of this fruit. If you forget this, you are a dead man. Death will squarely strike he who disregards my word, as well as his offspring. Adam, heed this well!"

Snake. 9. The snake approached in a friendly way and looked down from the tree, pointing out the pretty fruit to her. "Come and eat, O beautiful bride!" She kept on looking, took, and also gave to her husband. "Adam, you can trust me." He took and bit into it, also.

10. The snake said, "For no purpose at all did God say, 'I have made this binding.' Just go ahead and eat, be daring, you have to see for yourselves. Do not be hesitant, so that you may be able to discern everything. Death will not plague you at all."

11. Upon eating the fruit, they suddenly became aware that they were naked. They were both ashamed and hid in the garden, enveloped in fear. They knew well that punishment awaited them.

God. 12. "Adam, you are fallen, you and all your offspring. Now you must be weighted down with care and remain a slave to sin. Who put it into your head to hurry to the tree which I forbade you? The curse is what you have for it."

Adam. 13. "The woman that you gave me seduced me into it. Eve! What did you think would happen? You brought us this unsatisfactory state of affairs. If only I had never known you! All innocence is gone! I am called a slave! A candidate for death!"

Adam and Eve. 14. "Eve! What have you committed? What did you presume to do? The snake hanging there deceitfully seduced me. O snake! You lied, all innocence is gone. O shame! We are deceived, that is our reward."

God. 15. "I will set an enmity between you and your wife. It shall bruise your head, a son from her womb. On your belly you must go, dust shall be your bread, you shall bow low before everything. That is your punishment and pain."

2   When I consider right and see both day and night,
Yes, every hour—so soon doth pass away,
Then comes the judgment day; Lord, give us power.

2. So I must often fear, while I am roaming here,
No good am sowing, not always as I should,
Nor as I wish I could; be constant going.

O that I ever may with earnest every day,
Be onward moving, and in an humble way,
To God unceasing pray, while Jesus loving.

Belongs to me, Abraham Maurer. Written the 5th day of February in the year 1794.
[On reverse] Abraham Maurer   1797   89101112131 U

3   Of the Great Comet, Which Arose over America in 1769, Meditatively Presented by Henrich Otto.
Tune: To My Dear God

Lord, what do you contemplate? With what vigor do you pursue?
Of what new plagues do the skies foreboding tell us,
What can this new star mean for us poor people?

The signs in highest heaven awaken fear and pain,
That America in coming years will experience,
The burning comets are portentous prophets.

They burn there in the sky, and yet the secret places of our hearts
Are blind and loath to good, and do not recognize the rods,
That cause our wounds by the hand of the Almighty.

There is hardly left a man who heeds God's spirit and teaching, in his holy words.
Therefore all places of this star-illumined land
Must cry out at the spectacle of wrath and warning.

No decency in the world, faith now is in decline,
Trust is shackled, and truth evaporated;
Mercy and love are barely seen practiced.

And so God's displeasure grows and presses raging on,
The vigor of his will that shall, if we do not repent,
Destroy us with the greatest woe each and everyone.

And that is the intention of the prophet, standing there in the air,
That he wants to leave with us, living securely,
As his light burns and his countenance flares.

His course is quickly run, O God, do not let our sin
Suddenly run us aground and hasten to submerge us,
Let not the mound of punishment quickly come over us.

His ray is broad and long and brings us fright and fear,
O Jesus, help us all, that on us do not fall,
The last and fearful strokes, the final thunder of wrath.

Preserve to us, O Lord, the beauteous, noble star,
Illumine us with his light, let his doing inspire us,
That we find joy in him and under him prosper.

And let continually, thy dear and precious Word,
Shine brightly in our land and bound with radiance pure,
With thy word shining on us, we once again take heart.

Think upon thy goodness, and let thy countenance spare us,
Poor creatures, rule us with mercy,
So that these ominous signs, may come to good effect.

4   I will bless the Lord at all times; his praise shall continually be in my mouth. My soul makes its boast in the Lord; let the afflicted hear and be glad. O magnify the Lord with me, and let us exalt his name together. I sought the Lord and he answered me, and delivered me from all my fears. Keep your tongue from evil and your lips from speaking deceit. Depart from evil and do good. Psalm 34 [verses 1–4, 13–14]. The 19th of August 1801. G[eorg] G[eist] w[eit]
[Below dancing bear] The bear roars; he's supposed to dance but has not yet learned.
[Inscriptions illegible below black man and above unicorn]

5   Tune: O Sacred Head, Now
[Text repeats as in no. 1, except the stanzas are unnumbered]
There is the tree, full of beautiful fruit, so tempting in the

story and refreshing to the heart in taste, standing there in the beautiful paradise. Through it Eve was deceived by the deadly outward appearance of total satisfaction. The fruit tasted sweet to the mouth, but brought death that very hour. Ephrata: Printed by Samuel Baumann.

6   [Way of Life or Damnation]
Who has his portion in the cross of Christ, must himself bear cross and scorn; and since narrow is the gate, many there be that walk past it.
Children of Zion, rejoice! You have attained your portion in the kingdom of heaven; although the gate is narrow and small, rejoice in the mansions of heaven.
The New Jerusalem.
Zion's street will be deserted, since it is overgrown with thorns.
I want to go to Zion.
Our fruits are on the Tree of Life.
To rightly deal gives me consolation.
Where are your fruits?
Give us of your oil.
Many are called, but few are chosen.
We regarded them as fools and knaves and as a mocking example, indeed as ludicrous; now they enter into the joy of their Lord and we fools and knaves have missed the right way.
Thus saith the Lord: I have no pleasure in the death of the wicked—but that the wicked turn from his way and live.
Death is without mercy, taking to itself rich and poor alike.
The Whore of Babylon.
Here is the entrance great and wide, open to all from each side. Pass on ye with sack and pack, be unconcerned, be not exact. Walk gently ahead, not a word will be said. If you seek honor and gain, hastily appear and record thy name; thousands with a similar design have traveled this road in proper line. Ye that lust after splendor, luxury, and pride, pass on, the path is fully wide. The frolicksome in great music, full of sound, are marching to the place to which they are bound; the rich, poor, the tall and small, in Abraham's lap hope to be taken up, yea withal.

7   The Unjust Judgment, or the Sentence of Blood Spoken over Jesus by the Jewish Procurator Pontius Pilate at the Familiar Place of Judgment, Gabbatha, Named the Pavement, on the 3rd of April in the Year of Christ 34.—(After a very old painting in Jerusalem.)
Subath: The laws condemn no one to death without reason.
Rosinophin: What good are the laws if they are not kept?
Potiphar: This man should be banned as an insurgent in the land.
Piolomeus: Why do we delay? Why not condemn him at once?
Josaphat: Let him be interminably imprisoned!
Pilatus.
Teras: Let him be exiled to misery.
Achias: No one should be sentenced to death on untried facts.
Riphar: Give him a chance to confess, then punish him.
Joseph of Ar[imathea]: It would be a shame if no one came to the defense of this innocent one.
Nicodemus: Does our law sentence anyone without a hearing and a trial of the evidence?
Diarabias: Because he has incited the people, he is guilty.
Sareas: Let him be put away from our midst.
Sabinti: Be he right or wrong, because he has not kept the law of our fathers, he must die.
Simoni Eprosus, or the Leprous One: How can an insurgent deserve justice?
Rabam: According to the law, he must die; the laws must be kept.
Ehieris: Whether he is devout or not, since he incites the people through his preaching, he must die.
Joram: Why do we want to let this righteous one be condemned?
Mesa: If he is right, then we will support him; if he is wrong, then let us drive him out.
Samech: Let us punish him, therefore, so he will not teach against us in the future.
Caiphas: The Jewish high priest's pronouncement or declaration—John 11 [verse 50]: You do not understand that it is expedient for you that one man should die for the people,

and that the whole nation should not perish.
Printed and available at G. S. Peters—Harrisburg

8   [In English] Representation of the different Ways leading to Everlasting Life or Eternal Damnation.
NEW JERUSALEM.
To save, to bless, to comfort me, like Jesus will I bear the cross; vile sinners perish in surprise beneath thine angry rod. O Zion, tune thy voice! and raise thine hands on high; tell all the earth thy joys, and boast salvation nigh.
I want to go to Zion
Our fruits are on the tree of life.
True 'tis a strait and thorny road—but they forget the Almighty God.
Where are your fruits?
Give us of your Oil.
Many are called but few are chosen.
Foolish and vain I went astray, ere I had felt thy scourges, Lord! I left my guide and lost my way, but now I repent and love thy word.
As I live, saith the Lord God, I have no pleasure in the death of the wicked—but that the wicked turn from his way and live.
Death comes without delay, All classes become its pray.
But they are going thither.
To plead at court, I gain support.
The Whore of Babylon.
Here is the entrance great and wide, open to all from each side:—Pass on ye with sack and pack, be unconcerned, be not exact: walk gently ahead, not a word will be said; If you seek honour and gain, hastily appear and record thy name; thousands with a similar design, have traveled this road in proper line; ye that lust after splendor, luxury and pride, pass on, the path is fully wide; the frolicksome in great numbers with music full of sound, are marching to the place to which they are bound; the rich, poor, the tall and small, in Abraham's lap hope to be taken up, yea withal.
Printed and for Sale by G. S. Peters, Harrisburg, Pa.

9   People often build themselves houses and castles grand
That glistening and imposing do as Babel's tower stand.
Although they here upon the earth as guests and pilgrims be
Who through this vale of tears must go, until they heaven see.
1843.

The house now stands completed here,
Painted on this paper clear;
In black and yellow, green and red,
Just as they came into my head.

CHEST OVER DRAWERS
Lehigh or Berks County
1792
Attributed to **John Bieber**
Inscribed on front: *Macht ·da ·le ·na 1792 Lea ·bel ·sper ·ger*
Painted poplar; white pine. Plank construction with wedged
dovetails. Lid and sides made of two boards each, which are joined
with butterflies inset on inside. Lid has two tenons extending
through edge molding in an open joint. Moldings pegged to lid and
case. Bottom of chest meets sides in butt joint, pegged all around.
Drawer fronts overlap case. Drawer bottoms beveled at edges and
let into front, sides, and backboards, which are joined together
with fine, wedged dovetails. Drawer sides extend below bottom
board and act as runners. Top of drawer sides rounded. Columns
and inscription band are black with red outlining and lettering.
Front and end panels painted bluish green, red, brown, and yellow
over white ground. Three painted panels on top with inlaid
figure-eight motif, lover's knot in center.
77.5 x 134.6 x 70 cm (30½ x 53 x 24")
Purchased: Thomas Skelton Harrison Fund, Fiske Kimball Fund,
and Joseph E. Temple Fund. 1982-68-1

WARDROBE
Lancaster County
1760–80
Walnut, poplar. Panel and frame construction with pegged mortise
and tenon joints. Curved rise into fielded panels on doors.
Dovetails not wedged. Deep molded cornice; three drawers in
base unit. Breaks down into eighteen pieces. Ogee bracket feet.
Owned by the Hiestand family, Lancaster County.
226 x 175.3 x 56 cm (89 x 69 x 22")
Gift of Walton Hooker Nason, Jr. 1980-25-1

CHEST OF DRAWERS
Schwaben Creek Valley, Schuylkill County
1838
Inscribed on front and on back: *1838* [twice]
Painted softwoods. Panel and frame construction with pegged
mortise and tenon joints, front rails secured with one peg, side rails
with two pegs. Side panels inset. Back made in two panels. Turned
legs are extensions of corner posts. Four graduated drawers on
poplar runners, which are mortised and tenoned into front rails.
Drawer bottoms beveled and let into sides. Dovetails are wedged.
Painted wood drawer pulls originally secured with dowels, now
with screws. Top painted dark red, edges green with red eight-
petaled rosettes. Drawers green with red borders; corner spandrels
red and yellow; red tree with red and yellow birds; framing red.
Side panels decorated with flaring plant form with red and yellow
buds and tulips in tulip-shaped vase. Corners decorated with red
and yellow spandrels.
100.5 x 101.5 x 49.5 cm (39½ x 40 x 19½")
Gift of Henry P. McIlhenny. 1981-69-1

GOOSE YOKE
1800–1900
Wood. Found tree branch with two prongs fitted through straight
piece extending to each side preventing goose from fitting through
a fence.
35.4 x 23.2 cm (13⅞ x 9⅛")
Gift of Mr. and Mrs. J. Stogdell Stokes. 33-70-12

FLINTLOCK RIFLE
Bucks County
c. 1780
W. Bernhardt
Inlaid in silver on barrel: *W. Bernhardt*
Curly maple, silver, brass. Brass-mounted curly maple stock.
Thirty-eight caliber, octagonal barrel. Engraved flintlock.
Forty-seven silver inlays. Scrolled and chased brass patchbox.
From Woodmansee Collection. (*See* John G. W. Dillon, *The
Kentucky Rifle*, Washington, D.C., 1924, pl. 119, no. 3)
Length 154 cm (60⅝")
Gift of J. Stogdell Stokes. 28-46-24

RIFLE
Philadelphia
1820–50
Jacob Kuntz
Engraved on patchbox: *UTEROA April 9th.1841. TITIAN R.
PEALE. SUA-LEVU July 13th.1840. SALUA-FATA Feby. 25th.1841.*
Iron, walnut, silver, steel. Percussion rifle. Shaped walnut stock
with heel extension ornamented with engraved silver patchbox,
plate, and lid. Carved, checkered wrist. Engraved silver trigger
guard. Engraved steel lockplate, frizzen spring and hammer. Two
steel loops for carrying strap.
Length 128.3 cm (50½")
Gift of Carl Otto von Kienbusch. 59-1-1

RIFLE
Dauphin County
1800–1810
David Glassbrener
Inscribed at the breech: *D. Glassbrener;* engraved on side plate:
No. 110; stamped on flint mechanism: *LONDON Warranted*
Maple, steel, brass, silver. Figured maple stock with brass
furniture, engraved patchbox. Seventeen silver inlays, and
escutcheon. Octagonal, sighted barrel rifled with eight grooves.
Flint mechanism with roller bearings and set trigger. Original
ramrod.
Length barrel 111.8 cm (44")
Bequest of Carl Otto von Kienbusch. 1977-167-858

LADLE
1780–1810
Iron, copper. Long tapering handle ending in hook. Small copper
bowl.
Length 36 cm (14⅛")
Gift of J. Stogdell Stokes. 28-10-40

MEAT FORK
1780–1840
Impressed on handle: *1701*
Wrought iron. Wide shaft ends in hook. Shaft round at end joining
two-pronged fork.
Length 26.7 cm (10½")
Gift of J. Stogdell Stokes. 36-19-3

MEAT FORK
1800–1840
Wrought iron. Long handle flat at top with hanging hook, rounded
handgrip, flat at joint with two-pronged fork.
Length 43.7 cm (17¼")
Gift of H. K. Deisher. 14-292

DISH
Rockhill Township, Bucks County
John Jacob Stoudt
1765–74
Inscribed: *S.S.*
Wheel-thrown redware. Deep dish with narrow foot, flaring sides
with slightly raised rim. Rim has applied reinforcing band. Dish
surface covered with white slip, sgraffito decoration of five flowers
in symmetrical arrangement. Flowers are colored inside sgraffito
lines with orange and green slip applied over base white slip.
Inscribed for the potter's daughter Salome, who married Gabriel
Swartzlander about 1774.
Height 5.7 cm (2¼"), diameter 31.3 cm (12¼")
Purchased: Baugh-Barber Fund. 1980-91-1

COVERED DISH
1800–1840
Wheel-thrown, molded, and cut redware. Elaborately pierced
outer bowl and lid have designs of interlocking semicircles,
triangles, and round holes. Joined to inner bowl and inner lid at
rims. Two attached rope-twist handles, applied knob. Splayed foot.
Manganese-toned (brown), clear lead glaze. Interior glazed in
bottom bowl only.
12.7 x 14.6 cm (5 x 5¾")
Gift of Joseph H. Himes, in memory of his wife Eilleen C. Himes.
54-62-9a,b

PLATE
Rockland Township, Berks County
Johan Drey
1809
Incised on reverse: *Johan Drey 1809*
Molded redware, coggled edge. Surface covered with white slip.
Design cut through the slip in sgraffito technique, daubed with
copper oxide (green). Clear yellowish lead glaze.
Diameter 26 cm (10¼″)
Purchased: Baugh-Barber Fund. 38-15-4

PLATE
Upper Salford Township, Montgomery County
1810–15
Attributed to **John Neis**
Inscribed: *Ein Peifge tuback ist einen so gut As wan man die
daller bei den Metger ver dut* ("A pipe of tobacco does a man as
much good as though he spends his money with the girls.")
Molded redware, coggled edge. Plate covered with white slip.
Sgraffito decoration of horse and rider with flowers and foliage.
Slip coating scraped off within outlines of the horse to brown
underbody. Horse blanket white with incised lines for plaid or
checked pattern. Rider brandishing sword with left hand, right
hand supporting a horn, which he is blowing. Face in profile.
Figure, flowers, and two leaves daubed with copper oxide (green).
Seven short lines incised under front feet of horse. Lead glaze.
Height 4.7 cm (1⅞″), diameter 31.6 cm (12⅜″)
Gift of John T. Morris. 92-53

PLATE
Rockland Township, Berks County
1815–25
Incised on reverse: *Weiss*
Molded redware, crudely coggled edge. Surface covered with slip
colored with copper oxide (green). Sgraffito decoration with white
slip and manganese (black) coloring. Lead glazed.
Height 3.8 cm (1½″), diameter 24.9 cm (9¾″)
Purchased: Baugh-Barber Fund. 38-15-1

DISH
Probably Montgomery County
1816
Inscribed: *ven ech haba ben ech lusteg ven ech keins haba ben ech
dursteg 1816* ("If I have, I am gay. If I have none, I am thirsty.
1816")
Wheel-thrown redware. Impression of a coin on inside of bowl.
Pattern in the shape of a plant with flowers (calla lilies) and
heart-shaped foliage in a flowerpot placed in bottom of bowl, then
white slip applied and pattern shapes lifted, leaving pattern
silhouette on red body of the clay. Wide, flaring flat rim carries
inscription in English-style script letters. Copper oxide (green)
mottling on slip under clear lead glaze. From Jacob Paxson Temple
sale.
Height 5.1 cm (2″), diameter 27.7 cm (10⅞″)
Purchased: Baugh-Barber Fund. 22-4-1

PLATE MOLD
Bucks County
1855
Samuel Harding
Inscribed: *SH*
Wheel-thrown redware. Obverse smooth, reverse hollowed and
inscribed. Beveled edge. Thick body.
Height 3.8 cm (1½″), diameter 13.3 cm (5¼″)
Gift of A.B. Haring. 01-66c

BIRD WHISTLE
Upper Salford Township, Montgomery County
Attributed to **John Neis** Pottery
1810–15
Modeled redware. Manganese (dark brown) lead glaze.
6.9 x 10 cm (2¾ x 3⅞″)
Purchased. 93-181

The following works on paper by **Augustus Koellner**

PHILADELPHIA: LAUREL-HILL CEMETERY, 1848
Inscribed: *Drawn from nature by Aug. Köllner. Lith. by
Deroy—Printed by Cattier*
Colored lithograph, 19 x 28.3 cm (7½ x 11⅛″)
37-39-122

PHILADELPHIA: MERCHANT'S EXCHANGE, 1848
Inscribed: [as above]
Colored lithograph, 19 x 27.6 cm (7½ x 10⅞″)
37-39-123

PHILADELPHIA: GIRARD COLLEGE, 1848
Inscribed: [as above]
Colored lithograph, 18.7 x 27.9 cm (7⅜ x 11″)
37-39-124

BALTIMORE: BATTLE-MONUMENT, 1848
Inscribed: [as above]
Colored lithograph, 19 x 27.9 cm (7½ x 11″)
37-39-125

SARATOGA: SARATOGA LAKE, 1848
Inscribed: [as above]
Colored lithograph, 19 x 27.9 cm (7½ x 11″)
37-39-126

PHILADELPHIA: S.E. VIEW, 1848
Inscribed: [as above]
Colored lithograph, 18.7 x 27.9 cm (7⅜ x 11″)
37-39-135

PART OF SARATOGA, 1848
Colored lithograph, 19 x 27.9 cm (7½ x 11″)
Bequest of Augustus W. Jordan. 46-2-30

SUSPENSION BRIDGE, 1848
Color lithograph, 19 x 27.9 cm (7½ x 11″)
Bequest of Augustus W. Jordan. 46-2-31

MAKING SPORT OF THE BLIND BOY
Inscribed: *A. Kollner Lith.*
Color lithograph, 23.3 x 29.8 cm (9⅛ x 11¾″)
Print Club Permanent Collection. 62-78-2

POINT PLEASANT, BUCKS COUNTY
Inscribed: *A. Köllner fc.*
Etching, 12.4 x 22.5 cm (4⅞ x 8⅞″)
Gift of Dr. Samuel B. Sturgis. 73-268-25

SWAN LAKE, FAIRMOUNT PARK, 1879
Inscribed: *A. Köllner. 1879. Swan Lake, Philada. Fairmont Park*
Pencil and watercolor, 32.8 x 38.8 cm (12⅞ x 15¼″)
Gift of Carl William Gatter. 1976-82-1

The following works on paper by **Augustus Koellner** were given by
Seymour Adelman

AT POINT PLEASANT, BUCKS COUNTY, 1881
Inscribed: *A. Kollner. sketched Aug. 5, 1881*
Watercolor, 30.5 x 33.3 cm (12 x 13⅛″)
46-73-4

FRONT STOOP
Watercolor, 19 x 27.3 cm (7½ x 10¾″)
46-73-5

BACK STOOP
Watercolor, 19 x 27.6 cm (7½ x 10⅞″)
46-73-6

SENATE CHAMBER, WASHINGTON, D.C., 1848
Colored lithograph, 19 x 27.9 cm (7½ x 11″)
46-73-7

TWO HUNTERS TALKING BY FENCE
Etching, 12.7 x 15.2 cm (5 x 6")
46-73-8

MARE AND COLT, 1862
Inscribed: *Phila. Sept. 29th, 1862. Cohocksink Valley near Phila.*
Pencil and watercolor, 20.9 x 29.8 cm (8¼ x 11¾")
46-73-9

MARE AND COLT, 1894
Etching, 22.9 x 30.5 cm (9 x 12")
46-73-10

THREE GOATS
Etching, 12.7 x 15.9 cm (5 x 6¼")
46-73-11

HEAD OF COW
Inscribed: *A. Koellner n.d. Nat. gezeich. & geäzt*
Etching, 11.4 x 8.9 cm (4½ x 3½")
46-73-12

STUDIES OF HORSES AND MULES, 1836
Inscribed: *A. Koellner gez. Febr. 1836*
Pen and ink, 22.2 x 17.1 cm (8¾ x 6¾")
47-73-13

CUPID LEANING ON A COLUMN
Inscribed: *A. Koellner gez. 9 September .33*
Pen and ink, 14.6 x 9.5 cm (5¾ x 3¾")
46-73-14

STUDY OF GOATS, 1836?
Inscribed: *10 Febr.*
Pen and ink, 8.9 x 15.2 cm (3½ x 6")
46-73-15

STUDY OF GOAT AND TWO SHEEP, 1836
Inscribed: *20 Febr. 36*
Pen and ink, 5.1 x 12.1 cm (2 x 4¾")
46-73-16

STUDIES OF HOGS, 1836
Inscribed: *A. Kr. gez Febr. 1836*
Pen and ink, 18.4 x 15.2 cm (7¼ x 6")
46-73-17

STUDY OF GOATS AND SHEEP, 1836
Inscribed: *10. Febr. 36*
Pen and ink, 10.8 x 23.5 cm (4¼ x 9¼")
46-73-18

STUDY OF TWO DONKEYS, 1836
Inscribed: *A. Koellner gez. Febr. 1836*
Pen and ink, 10.2 x 15.2 cm (4 x 6")
46-73-19

STUDIES OF SHEEP, 1836
Inscribed: *K. gez. Febr. 36*
Pen and ink, 21.6 x 14 cm (8½ x 5½")
46-73-20

SHEPHERD PLAYING FLUTE TO SHEPHERDESS, 1836
Inscribed: *A.K. gez. Febr. 1836*
Pen and ink, 12.7 x 15.2 cm (5 x 6")
46-73-21

STUDIES OF DOGS, CAT, SHEEP, 1836
Inscribed: *4 Febr. 36*
Pen and ink, 17.8 x 14.6 cm (7 x 5¾")
46-73-22

STUDIES OF COWS, 1836
Inscribed: *Gez. A.K. Febr. 1836*
Pen and ink, 19.1 x 16.5 cm (7½ x 6½")
46-73-23

STUDY OF CATTLE, 1836
Inscribed: *A. Koellner gez. Febr. 1836*
Pen and ink, 11.4 x 22.9 cm (4½ x 9")
46-73-24

STUDIES OF CATTLE AND A DONKEY, 1836
Inscribed: *A. Koellner gez. Febr. 1836*
Pen and ink, 20.3 x 15.2 cm (8 x 6")
46-73-25

STUDIES OF CATTLE, 1836
Inscribed: *A. Kr. gez. Febr. 1836*
Pen and ink, 20.9 x 15.2 cm (8¼ x 6")
46-73-26

STUDIES OF SHEEP, 1836
Inscribed: *Febr. 1836*
Pen and ink, 16.5 x 11.4 cm (6½ x 4½")
46-73-27

STUDY OF EWE AND LAMB, 1836
Inscribed: *A. Kr. gez. Febr. 1836*
Pen and ink, 6.4 x 12.7 cm (2½ x 5")
46-73-28

CALF
Inscribed: *nach d. Nat. gez. & in Stahl geäzt v. Aug. Koellner*
Etching, 12.7 x 17.1 cm (5 x 6¾")
46-73-29

MAN ON FENCE BETWEEN TWO BULLS
Inscribed: *A. Kollner fect.*
Etching, 15.2 x 19.7 cm (6 x 7¾")
46-73-30

THREE GOATS, 1837
Inscribed: *A. Koellner n.d. Natur gezeich. & radirt*
Etching, 9.5 x 14 cm (3¾ x 5½")
46-73-31

The most useful and comprehensive general bibliography serving as an introduction to Pennsylvania German art can be found in Donald A. Shelley's monograph *The Fraktur-Writings or Illuminated Manuscripts of the Pennsylvania Germans* (The Pennsylvania German Folklore Society, vol. 23, Allentown, Pa., 1961). The most useful bibliography for general research not limited to Pennsylvania, suggesting the wide range of available resources, is Don Yoder's annotated "Folklife Studies Bibliography 1964. Periodicals: Part I," in *Pennsylvania Folklife* (vol. 14, no. 4, Summer 1965, pp. 60–64). Richard S. Dunn's *The Age of Religious Wars 1559–1689* (New York, 1970), a concise work with an efficiently organized bibliography, provides sources for an overview of the European origins of the Pennsylvania Germans and the conditions that provoked their migration to America, especially to Pennsylvania. James T. Lemon's *The Best Poor Man's Country: A Geographical Study of Early Southeastern Pennsylvania* (Baltimore, 1972) provides primary materials in an interpretive context. Using graphs and charts, Lemon documents the patterns of settlement in southeastern Pennsylvania, giving another dimension to an understanding of the dynamics of the agricultural life that absorbed and encouraged regional and seasonal manufacturing. His statistics are important in the consideration of the regional characteristics that are revealed by physical analysis of objects, like the unicorn chests made in Bern Township, Berks County. Lemon's geological surveys are especially useful when combined with other data about communities of artists and makers. For example, examination of township tax records reveals that the concentrations of regional enterprises were based on a ready supply of raw materials. Lemon's cartographical and topographical approach is invaluable in confirming and explaining this phenomenon. Most Pennsylvania German craftsmen pulled their livelihoods from the earth, as stated by the common dish inscription: "From the earth with sense the potter makes everything." Rich clay deposits supported a large number of redware potters in Haycock Township, Bucks County; fields watered by tributaries of the Skippack Creek supported the weavers in Towamencin Township, Montgomery County; and shallow deposits of iron ore throughout Berks and Lancaster counties promoted capital investment in iron manufacturing.

Research on the Pennsylvania German collection of the Philadelphia Museum of Art was drawn from three areas: manuscript and printed primary sources; illustrations from photographic archives, books, and sale and collection catalogues; and observation and analysis of the objects themselves and similar examples in other institutional and private collections. Information thus amassed on each object is filed in a folder, identified by accession number, in the Department of American Art. There was no attempt to compile a definitive bibliography on any single object but simply to determine the time and place of manufacture to facilitate the use of this material for work in art history and other disciplines.

The manuscript materials used are located throughout the state of Pennsylvania, with especially important sources at the Historical Society of Pennsylvania, Philadelphia; as well as The Spruance Library at the Bucks County Historical Society, Doylestown; The Historical Society of Montgomery County, Norristown; The Historical Society of Berks County, Reading; Lancaster County Historical Society, Lancaster; Lancaster Mennonite Historical Society, Lancaster; The Historical Society of York County, York; and the various county courthouses. These institutions provided regional research materials, especially genealogical data, and a treasure trove of receipts, inventories, vendue books, Bible records, diaries, personal notations, recipes, wills, photographs, and other fragments of life, which led to a better understanding of the Pennsylvania Germans and their possessions. Some of these sources have been filmed or transcribed by contributors to the Genealogical Society of Pennsylvania and are deposited at the Historical Society of Pennsylvania, Philadelphia; available there is the systematic, national microfilming project of the Church of Jesus Christ of Latter-Day Saints, providing access to county and township tax records, deeds, wills, church records, and road petitions. Other rich resources at the Historical Society of Pennsylvania, like the diary of John Gehman (1829–1882) of Rockhill Township, Bucks County, and the journal of John Dyer (1760–1806) of Plumstead Township, Bucks County, are readily available on film, providing documents important for understanding the day-to-day work of farming and interaction of commerce. Microfilms of the United States censuses of population and manufacturing, especially the 1820 Census of Manufactures, are useful for statistics of personal data and the size and productivity of regional manufacturing enterprises.

Printed primary sources on Pennsylvania Germans and their art—virtually inseparable subjects—are plentiful. The most recent is the compilation of immigration records in the form of ship lists, edited by Don Yoder, *Pennsylvania German Immigrants, 1709–1786: Lists Consolidated from Yearbooks of the Pennsylvania German Folklore Society* (Baltimore, 1980). Diaries and journals, especially *The Journals of Henry Melchior Muhlenberg*, edited and translated by Theodore G. Tappert and John W. Doberstein (3 vols., Philadelphia, 1942–58), and *The Bethlehem Diary*, vol. 1, *1742–1744*, edited and translated by Kenneth G. Hamilton (Bethlehem, Pa., 1971), as well as craftsmen's records like *The Accounts of Two Pennsylvania German Furniture Makers—Abraham Overholt, Bucks County, 1790–1833, and Peter Ranck, Lebanon County, 1794–1817*, edited and translated by Alan G. Keyser, Larry M. Neff, and Frederick S. Weiser (Sources and Documents of the Pennsylvania Germans, vol. 3, Breinigsville, Pa., 1978), are important for understanding the physical and spiritual distances that existed between various settlements and the influence of one group on another. Publications of county historical societies also are useful, as are county histories. The most useful published materials are the genealogical monographs at the Historical Society of Pennsylvania, the Publications of the Pennsylvania German Society series, and the run of *Pennsylvania Folklife* (Lancaster, Pa.). The latter two publications offer carefully prepared, accurate translations of manuscript materials, many researched in the archives of Europe.

A bibliography of illustrated books consulted would be too cumbersome for this publication. The most useful illustrations are in the most specialized publications, which are listed under the medium headings below. The extensive file of drawings and photographs collected by Frances Lichten is housed at the Philadelphia Museum, and some of these objects were published in her book *Folk Art of Rural Pennsylvania* (New York, 1946).

A number of recently published European books were invaluable in the study of this collection. The text and illustrations in a work introduced by Robert Wildhaber, *Schweizerische Volkskunst* (Zurich, 1968), organized by medium, were extremely helpful. The English edition, *Swiss Folk Art* (Washington, D.C., [1971]), was circulated by the Smithsonian Institution. Other publications deal with national styles or collections: *Volkstümliche Malerei nach alten Motiven*, by Irmgard Gierl (Rosenheim, 1977); *Mobilier Lorrain et Ardennais*, by Lucile Oliver (Paris, n.d.); *Volkskunst in der Schweiz*, by René Creux et al. (Paudex, Switz., 1976); *Alpenlandische Volkskunst*, by Helmut Nemec (Vienna, 1980); *Arts et traditions populaires d'Alsace: La Maison rurale et l'artisanat d'autrefois*, by Georges Klein (Colmar, 1974); *Bauernmöbel aus Süddeutschland, Österreich und der Schweiz*, by Leopold Schmidt (Vienna, 1967); the Berner Heimatbücher series (Bern); and *Deutsche Bauernstuben*, by Margarete Baur-Heinhold (Königstein im Taunus, 1975).

Research in periodicals other than *Pennsylvania Folklife* was by subject index and therefore not comprehensive. Sources consulted include *The Pennsylvania Magazine of History and Biography* (Philadelphia); *Volkskunst* (Munich); *Antiques* (New York); *The Three Forks of Muddy Creek* (Winston-Salem, N.C.); "'S Pennsylvaanisch Deitsch Eck," in *The Morning Call* (Allentown, Pa.); *Bulletin of the National Association of Watch and Clock Collectors, Inc.* (Bryn Mawr, Pa.); and *Der Reggeboge: The Rainbow. Quarterly of the Pennsylvania German Society* (Breinigsville, Pa.).

The third type of research on the collection, the observation and physical analysis of objects, was accomplished as part of a recataloguing and conservation project. Basic structural and technical observations about these objects are included in the handbook entries. An attempt has been made to describe what can be seen, such as wedged dovetails, colored slip over white slip in sgraffito designs, or iron-mold idiosyncrasies, which eventually may help sort out Stiegel factory glass from English models. There is little published information on European construction or craft methods as practiced in America to help in the analysis and attribution of objects in the collection. Differing degrees of restoration are "acceptable," however, obvious, extensive repairs or replacements influenced the amount of effort spent attempting to attribute an object to time and place. Similar pieces in other collections were compared, sometimes by photographs. Objects from collections that appeared in illustrations to have designs similar to those on objects in the Philadelphia Museum often proved to have similar physical characteristics as well upon actual examination.

One book helpful in locating other collections is *Museums, Sites, and Collections of Germanic Culture in North America: An Annotated Directory of German Immigrant Culture in the United States and Canada*, compiled by Margaret Hobbie (Westport, Conn., 1980). The American collections that proved most useful, some for physical analysis, some for comparative exhibits, were the Mercer Museum of the Bucks County Historical Society, Doylestown, Pa.; The Henry Francis du Pont Winterthur Museum, Winterthur, Del.; The Historical Society Museum of Berks County, Reading, Pa.; The Historical Society of York County, York, Pa.; Moravian Historical Society, Nazareth, Pa.; Old Salem, Inc., Winston-Salem, N.C.; Pennsylvania Farm Museum at Landis Valley, Lancaster, Pa.; Ephrata Cloister, Ephrata, Pa.; The Free Library of Philadelphia; and The Barnes Foundation, Merion, Pa.

Two European trips provided useful surveys to help sort out traditional national forms and design. The first—to England, Scotland, Wales, Munich, Mulhouse, Nancy, Colmar, Strasbourg, and Senlis—included stops in between the large collections to see regional exhibitions of the objects of everyday life. The second trip—to Paris, Bois de Boulogne, Basel, Zurich, Bern, Horgen, Thun, and Langnau—was the more productive because it was undertaken with a much broader base of knowledge. The museums in Zurich and Paris, the castle at Thun, the pottery exhibition at Langnau, are treasure chests of prototypes of objects produced in early Pennsylvania. General and specific notes from these trips, in rough and abbreviated form, are recorded in the object research folders in the Department of American Art.

Additional publications consulted are listed below, under medium headings.

Wood

Battison, Edwin A., and Kane, Patricia E. *The American Clock, 1725–1865. The Mabel Brady Garvan and Other Collections at Yale University*. Greenwich, Conn., 1973.

Fabian, Monroe H. *The Pennsylvania-German Decorated Chest*. New York, 1978.

Fabian, Monroe H. "Sulfur Inlay in Pennsylvania German Furniture." *Pennsylvania Folklife*, vol. 27, no. 1 (Fall 1977), pp. 2–9.

Klatt, Erich. *Die Konstruktion alter Möbel: Form und Technik im Wandel der Stilarten*. 3rd ed. Stuttgart, 1977. Details traditional European construction techniques and furniture forms, which were also found in Pennsylvania, such as the wedged dovetail on most case furniture in the collection and the pegged spline joining two planks of a tabletop. Also illustrates the hanging cupboard form and documents Germanic turned and shaped molding profiles similar to Pennsylvania examples like the stair balusters in the Millbach kitchen.

Lawton, Arthur J. "The Pre-Metric Foot and Its Use in Pennsylvania German Architecture." *Pennsylvania Folklife*, vol. 19, no. 1 (Autumn 1969), pp. 37–45.

Snyder, John J., Jr. "The Bachman Attributions: A Reconsideration." *Antiques*, vol. 105, no. 5 (May 1974), pp. 1056–65.

Weiser, Frederick S., and Sullivan, Mary Hammond. "Decorated Furniture of the Schwaben Creek Valley." In Albert F. Buffington et al., *Ebbes fer Alle-Ebber—Ebbes fer Dich: Something for Everyone—Something for You. Essays in Memoriam—Albert Franklin Buffington*, pp. 331–94. Publications of the Pennsylvania German Society, vol. 14. Breinigsville, Pa., 1980.

Metal

Gunnion, Vernon S., and Hopf, Carroll J., eds. *The Blacksmith: Artisan Within the Early Community*. Harrisburg, Pa., 1976.

Kindig, Joe, Jr. *Thoughts on the Kentucky Rifle in Its Golden Age*. York, Pa., 1960. A well-illustrated book emphasizing regional schools or groups of rifle makers.

Lindsay, Merrill. *The Kentucky Rifle*. New York, 1972.

Mercer, Henry C. *The Bible in Iron: Pictured Stoves and Stoveplates of the Pennsylvania Germans*. Edited by Horace M. Mann and Joseph E. Sanford. 3rd ed. Doylestown, Pa., 1961. The standard work identifying most of the cast-iron stove plates and giving sketches of iron furnaces and their masters and owners.

Miller, Frederic K. "The Rise of an Iron Community: An Economic History of Lebanon County, Pennsylvania from 1740–1865." Ph.D. dissertation, University of Pennsylvania, 1948.

Ceramics

Barber, Edwin Atlee. *Tulip Ware of the Pennsylvania-German Potters: An Historical Sketch of the Art of Slip-Decoration in the United States*. Philadelphia, 1903.

Bivins, John, Jr. *The Moravian Potters in North Carolina*. Chapel Hill, N.C., 1972.

Breininger, Lester P., Jr. *Potters of the Tulpehocken*. Myerstown, Pa., 1979.

Conrad, John W. *Ceramic Formulas: The Complete Compendium. A Guide to Clay, Glaze, Enamel, Glass, and Their Colors*. New York, 1973.

Cooper, Ronald G. *English Slipware Dishes 1650–1850*. London, 1968.

Haring, A.B. "Description of the Manufacture of Red Earthenware." Edwin Atlee Barber Papers, Folder 8, Philadelphia Museum of Art Archives.

Jedding, Hermann. *Volkstümliche Keramik aus Deutschsprachiger Ländern*. Hamburg, 1976.

Lasansky, Jeannette. *Central Pennsylvania Redware Pottery: 1780–1904*. Lewisburg, Pa., 1979.

Myers, Susan H. *Handicraft to Industry: Philadelphia Ceramics in the First Half of the Nineteenth Century*. Smithsonian Studies in History and Technology, no. 43. Washington, D.C., 1980.

Nabholz-Kartaschoff, Marie-Louise, ed. *Töpferei in Soufflenheim (Bas-Rhin)*. Basel, 1973. Presents careful profile drawings and design analyses of Alsatian pottery, which were useful in reattributing as European several pieces previously thought to be American.

Strasbourg, Ancienne Douane. *Céramiques populaires alsaciennes*. February 8–April 1, 1973.

Watkins, C. Malcolm. *North Devon Pottery and Its Export to America in the 17th Century*. United States National Museum Bulletin, no. 225. Washington, D.C., 1960. Illustrated with archaeological shards that show marked similarity to the sgraffito designs and the heavy yellow slip on a number of the pieces in the collection.

Wyss, Robert L. *Berner Bauernkeramik*. Berner Heimatbücher, 100/101/102/103. Bern, 1966. The special character of the Langnau potteries is discussed and illustrated.

Glass

Heiges, George L. *Henry William Stiegel and His Associates: A Story of Early American Industry*. Lancaster, Pa., 1948.

Hunter, Frederick William. *Stiegel Glass*. 1914. Reprint. New York, 1950.

Rose, James H. "18th Century Enameled Beakers with English Inscriptions." *Journal of Glass Studies*, vol. 1 (1959), pp. 94–102.

Eggshell/Basketry

Lasansky, Jeannette. *Willow, Oak & Rye: Basket Traditions in Pennsylvania*. Lewisburg, Pa., 1978.

Shoemaker, Alfred L. *Eastertide in Pennsylvania: A Folk Cultural Study*. Kutztown, Pa., 1960.

Textiles

Crosson, Janet Gray. *Let's Get Technical—An Overview of Handwoven Pennsylvania Jacquard Coverlets: 1830–1860*. Lancaster, Pa., 1978. The most important study of Pennsylvania German Jacquard coverlet weaving to date.

Davison, Marguerite Porter. *A Handweaver's Pattern Book*. Rev. ed. Swarthmore, Pa., 1971. Translates weavers' drafts into illustrated woven samples.

Deneke, Bernward. *Volkskunst*. Munich, 1979. Useful for illustrations and text on costume, *beiderwand* weaving, and needlework.

Emery, Irene. *The Primary Structures of Fabrics: An Illustrated Classification*. Washington, D.C., 1966. Contains text, diagrams, and illustrations essential to the technical descriptions of objects.

Gehret, Ellen J. "O Noble Heart. . . . An Examination of a Motif of Design from Pennsylvania German Embroidered Hand Towels." *Der Reggeboge: The Rainbow. Quarterly of the Pennsylvania German Society*, vol. 14, no. 3 (July 1980), pp. 1–14.

Gehret, Ellen J., and Keyser, Alan G. *The Homespun Textile Tradition of the Pennsylvania Germans*. Harrisburg, Pa., 1976.

Heisey, John W., comp.; and Andrews, Gail C., and Walters, Donald R., eds. *A Checklist of American Coverlet Weavers*. Williamsburg, Va., 1978.

Paper

Borneman, Henry S. *Pennsylvania German Illuminated Manuscripts: A Classification of Fraktur-Schriften and an Inquiry into Their History and Art*. New York, 1973.

Gravell, Thomas L., and Miller, George. *A Catalogue of American Watermarks 1690–1835*. Garland Reference Library of the Humanities, vol. 151. New York, 1979.

Rubi, Christian. *Taufe und Taufzettel im Bernerland*. Wabern-Bern, 1968. Colorfully illustrated with baptismal certificates and wishes, the text explains the Swiss custom of sponsors presenting a child with a coin wrapped in an elaborately folded, illuminated baptismal wish.

Sachse, Julius Friederich. *The German Sectarians of Pennsylvania 1708–1800: A Critical and Legendary History of the Ephrata Cloister and the Dunkers*. 2 vols. Philadelphia, 1899–1900. Invaluable for history of the illuminated manuscripts and printing from the Ephrata Cloister.

Shelley, Donald A. *The Fraktur-Writings or Illuminated Manuscripts of the Pennsylvania Germans*. The Pennsylvania German Folklore Society, vol. 23. Allentown, Pa., 1961.

Shoemaker, Alfred L. *Check List of Pennsylvania Dutch Printed Taufscheins*. Lancaster, Pa., 1952.

Weiser, Frederick S. *Fraktur: Pennsylvania German Art*. Ephrata, Pa., 1973. A clear, concise discussion of the categories and significance of Pennsylvania German illuminated manuscripts.

Weiser, Frederick S., and Heaney, Howell J., comps. *The Pennsylvania German Fraktur of the Free Library of Philadelphia*. 2 vols. Publications of the Pennsylvania German Society, vol. 10. Breinigsville, Pa., 1976.

Yoder, Don; Gunnion, Vernon S.; and Hopf, Carroll J. *Pennsylvania German Fraktur and Color Drawings*. Lancaster, Pa., 1969.

A.A. 1780–1800 [29]

A.B. 1868 [250]

A.B.G. c. 1840 [41]

A.C. 1881 [251]

A.H. 1839 [274]

A.H. Probably maker-painter of Bern Twp., Berks Co., chest, 1781 [19]

A.R. 1839 [274]

A.U. *see* Uhler, Andrew [205]

Albrecht [Albrechtin], Anna. b. Feb. 23, 1760, Donegal Twp., Lancaster Co.; d. Jan. 20, 1832. Daughter of Michael and Elisabeth Bayer Albrecht [298, 338]

Albrecht, Barbara. Wife of Jacob Albrecht, Haines Twp., Centre Co., 1814 [340]

Albrecht, Elisabeth Bayer. Daughter of Samuel Byer (d. Sept. 18, 1784). Wife of Michael Albrecht, Donegal Twp., Lancaster Co., 1760 [338]

Albrecht, Jacob. Husband of Barbara Albrecht, Haines Twp., Centre Co., 1814 [340]

Albrecht, Michael. Father or son of Stophel (Christopher) Albrecht. Donegal Twp., Lancaster Co., 1760. Purchased land, Bethel Twp., 1761, with Peter Klob, Philip Marsteller. Owned 150 acres, 2 horses, 3 cows, Donegal Twp., 1771. Owned 200 acres, Donegal Twp., 1773–82. No Albrechts in Donegal Twp., 1790 census [338]

Arnold, Debora Ziegler. Wife of Friederich Arnold, Upper Saucon Twp., Northampton Co., 1807 [340]

Arnold, Friederich. Upper Saucon Twp., Northampton Co., 1807. Schoolteacher at Seider's schoolhouse and at house of John Egner [340]

Arnold, Samuel. b. Feb. 14, 1807, Upper Saucon Twp., Northampton Co.; bap. May 10, 1807. Son of Friederich and Debora Ziegler Arnold [302, 340]

Axer, Johannes. b. Aug. 28, 1794. Possibly son of George (blacksmith) and Elizabeth Kupp Axer, Union or Caernarvon Twp., Berks Co. [294, 338]

B.B. 1789 [214]

B.B. Probably Rockland Twp., Berks Co., c. 1840 [152]

B.F. 1746 [248]

B.G. Possibly cousin of Mary E. Witmer, 1865 [250]

B.K. 1839 [283]

Bacher, Ernest. Potter, 1862–63 [166]

Bachman, Jacob. Carpenter-joiner, Montgomery or Northampton Co., 1780–1800. Possibly descendant of Jacob Bauman (d. 1749), carpenter-joiner, Germantown. Not to be confused with Lancaster family of joiners with the same name [34]

Backhouse, Richard. Owner, Durham Furnace, Durham Twp., Bucks Co., after 1770 [107]

Baecher, Anthony Wise. b. 1824, Falkenberg, Oberpfalz, Bavaria; d. Mar. 31, 1889, Frederick Co., Va. Buried in Catholic cemetery, Winchester, Va. Son of master potter Andreas Bacher (b. 1801), of Falkenberg. Came to Pa. via N.Y., 1848. Employed and resided with farmer-potter David Ditzler, Mount Pleasant Twp., Adams Co., by 1850. Married Anna Margaret Sower (1825–1904) of Adams Co. To Md., c. 1855; established pottery near Winchester, c. 1860 [166]

Bär [Baer, Bear], Johann. b. 1795, Switzerland; d. Lancaster, Pa., 1858. Apprenticed as printer, Columbia, York Co., and Harrisburg. Partner with Samuel Kling, Lancaster, 1817; published *Der Volksfreund*. Sole owner, 1817; published *The People's Friend and Observer*, after 1838. Published agricultural almanac, 1828; German Pennsylvania almanac, 1833; folio German Bible, 1819; and several Mennonite books [330]

Barber, Edwin AtLee. b. Aug. 13, 1851, Baltimore, Md.; d. Dec. 12, 1916. Studied Lafayette College. Work with U.S. Geological and Geographical Survey of the Territories, 1874–75, aroused his interest in pottery. Ph.D., Lafayette, 1893. Honorary Curator of the Department of American Pottery and Porcelain (1892–1901), Curator (1901–6), and Director (1907–16) of the Pennsylvania Museum and School of Industrial Art, now the Philadelphia Museum of Art [197, 331]

Barr, John. Lancaster Co. Fourth partner in Henry William Stiegel's Elizabeth Furnace, Elizabeth Twp., Lancaster Co., 1756 [105]

Bätes [Baetis], William. Minister, Phila., to 1810, when elected pastor of Lutheran church, Brickerville, Lancaster Co., formed c. 1809, when Schaefferstown and Warwick churches united. Served July 1810–Aug. 14, 1836, then retired to Lancaster [342]

Bauman, Joseph. b. Feb. 14, 1790, Ephrata, Lancaster Co.; d. Nov. 27, 1862, Sheperdstown, Cumberland Co. Son of Christian (1755–1815) and Sarah Fahnestock Bauman (1758–1792). Farmer-printer. Married Mary Pitzer (1794–1876). Moved from Lancaster Co. to Allen Twp., Cumberland Co., 1831 [329]

Baumann [Bauman], J[ohn]. b. 1765; d. Nov. 9, 1809. Printer, Ephrata, Lancaster Co. Son of Samuel and Catharine Landes Bauman. Married Margaret Fahnestock (1768–1809) [300, 339]

Baumann [Bauman], Samuel. b. June 25, 1788; d. Apr. 8, 1820, Ephrata, Lancaster Co., of injuries from falling timber. Printer-miller. Son of John and Margaret Fahnestock Baumann. Married Susanna Eckstein Weaver (1788–1875). Succeeded his father at Ephrata Press [317, 346]

Bearry [Byrri], Christina. Possibly daughter of Peter (from Bern, Switzerland) and Margaret Bearry, Heidelberg Twp., Lebanon Co. [312, 343]

Bechtel, Georg. b. Sept. 11, 1792, Hereford Twp., Berks Co. Son of George Bechtel [Becktel], Hereford Twp., by 1757 [321, 327]

Beckerin [Becker], Susanna. 1821. Family name in Adams, Berks, Lancaster, Union, and Lehigh counties [279]

Bell, John. b. Apr. 20, 1800, Hagerstown, Md.; d. 1880, Waynesboro, Franklin Co., Pa. Potter. Eldest son of Peter Bell, Jr. (1775–1847). Active Winchester, Va., 1824; Chambersburg, Pa., 1827–33; Waynesboro, 1833–80. Brother Samuel, potter, Strasburg, Va. Son John W. Bell (d. 1895), potter, active Waynesboro [167, 231]

Bender, Eduward. Bethel Twp., Lebanon Co., 1839 [341]

Bender, Georg. Father of Barbara Bender Braun [341, 342]

Benjamin, William. Master, with George Chambers, Mount Pleasant Furnace, Franklin Co., 1783 [108]

Benner, Joseph. b. 1800, d. 1859. Germantown, Phila. Co., Mennonite. Married Elizabeth Cassel, 1823. Son Joseph C. Benner (1839–1920) married Catherine Detweiler (1844–1917) [284]

Berg, A. Minister, Shrewsbury Twp., York Co., 1842–54 [342]

Bergey, Benjamin. b. Nov. 27, 1797, Franconia Twp., Montgomery Co.; d. Feb. 28, 1854. Buried at Rockhill Mennonite Church, Telford. Son of Jacob Bergey. Married Elizabeth Hendricks (1801–1895). Son John, daughter Esther, and son-in-law Martin Rosenberger, 1854. Owned sawmill and 74 acres, Rockhill Twp., Bucks Co., 1834–43. Rich clay deposits on family farm in Franconia supplied several small, local potteries. Previously nos. 22, 23, p. 211, and no. 24, p. 212 attributed to Bergey [168]

Bergheimer, Susanna. Possibly daughter of John Casper and Elizabeth Catarina Kraeuser Bergheimer, married Oct. 20, 1730, Providence Twp., Montgomery Co. Supposed owner of dish no. 1, p. 206. Edwin A. Barber noted that this dish was a treasured family possession. Physical evidence has failed to confirm its origins; its lightweight body suggests European manufacture and its style is similar to slip-decorated pottery from the vicinity of Hesse, Germany [206]

Bernhardt, W. Probably William Bernhardt, one of two Hessians of that name who settled in Bucks Co. after the Revolutionary War. Son or nephew George A. Bernhardt, active by 1798 (d. 1844), and William Bernhardt (1802–1867) made rifles in Green Twp., Ross Co., Ohio [347]

Bertolet, Daniel A. b. 1781, d. 1868. Descendant of Jean (from Bern, Switzerland) and Susanna Harcourt Bertolet. Married Maria Griesemer, Oley Twp., Berks Co., 1802. Wrote poetry, preached, worked in sawmill, surveyed land. Related to Isaac Deturk [335]

Bieber, Daniel. Husband of Rahael Bieber, Bethel Twp., Lebanon Co., 1842 [341]

Bieber, John. b. 1768, d. 1825. Active Lehigh, Berks counties. Son of Jacob (1731–1798) and Christina Catherine Steinbrenner Bieber. Moved from Oley Twp. to Salisbury Twp., purchased 460 acres from Francis Rhoads for £2,300, by 1786. Taxed as a joiner and known locally as a "dove-tail" carpenter. Married Catherine Holland. Attended church in Oley Twp., Berks Co., 1801. Returned to Salisbury Twp., by 1805. Moved to Ohio, 1812 [347]

Bieber, Rahael. Wife of Daniel Bieber, Bethel Twp., Lebanon Co., 1842 [341]

Billmeyer, Michael. b. Jan 1, 1752; bap. Jan 4, 1752, Christ Evangelical Lutheran Church, York, York Co.; d. Apr./May 1837, Germantown. Son of Jacob (from Zweibrücken, Germany, 1732) and Helena Holtzdorn Billmeyer. Owned house and lot in York, 1780–82. With the First Battalion of York Co., Captain Ephraim Pennington's company, 1784. Probably worked with brother Andrew (1754–1828). Subscriber to the Concord Schoolhouse Fund, Germantown, Apr. 1783. Opened printing shop on west side of Germantown Ave., north of Upsal St., 1784. Petitioned with Peter Liebert for appointment as printers of the minutes and bills of the Pa. General Assembly, Nov. 15, 1785. Married Mary Liebert, daughter of Peter. Purchased Bensall-Deschler house for £750, opposite his father-in-law's house, Feb. 7, 1789. Sons George and Daniel also printers; located 5 N. Fifth St., Phila., 1814 [325–28]

Bingeman, Elisabeth Hacker. Wife of Samuel Bingeman, 1829. Member, Brickerville Lutheran Church, Warwick Twp., Lancaster Co. Resided Elizabeth Twp., Lancaster Co. [342]

Bingeman, Levi. b. Oct. 13, 1828. Son of Samuel and Elisabeth Hacker Bingeman. Member, Brickerville Lutheran Church, Warwick Twp., Lancaster Co. Resided Elizabeth Twp., Lancaster Co. Was a tanner living with William and Lydia Konegmacher and family, Ephrata, Lancaster Co., 1850 [308, 342]

Bingeman, Samuel. Father of Levi Bingeman. Member, Brickerville Lutheran Church, Warwick Twp., Lancaster Co. Resided Elizabeth Twp., Lancaster Co. [342]

Bird, William. d. 1762. Married Bridget Hulings. Miller, ironmaster. Owned forges in Hopewell and Birdsboro; land in Amity, Union, Robeson, and Heidelberg twps., Berks Co. Daughter Mary married George Ross, Jr.; daughter Rachel married

James Wilson, signer of the Declaration of Independence. Estate valued at £12,939, in 1762 [104]

Bixler, Absalom. b. 1802, d. 1884. Grandson of Abraham Bixler (from Bern, Switzerland; d. 1847). Son of Christian Bixler, Earl Twp., Lancaster Co. Married Sarah, before 1824. Farmer, potter, justice of the peace, wood-carver. Made gunstocks during Civil War [168]

Bixler, Sarah. Wife of Absalom Bixler, Earl Twp., Lancaster Co., 1824 [168]

Bladten [Bladt], Margreth. Daughter of Adam Bladt (d. 1819), Bern Twp., Berks Co. Married John Nein. To Montgomery Co., Ohio, by 1822 [24]

Blowsy Angel Artist. Also known as the Flying Angel Artist. Active Northampton (Lehigh) Co., 1800–1810 [300]

Blumer. Probably Pastor Abraham Blumer. b. Dec. 14, 1736, Switzerland; d. Dec. 23, 1822, Whitehall Twp., Northampton Co. Married Susanna Maria Frary (1743–1825), 1770. Reformed minister, Whitehall Twp., from Feb. 1780 [339]

Blumer [Alexander]. b. 1806; d. 1842, Allentown. Proprietor-printer of *Friedensbote*, 1831–42. Son of Jacob (1774–1830), clockmaker and town clerk, and Catharine Rhoads, daughter of Peter. Sister Matilda married Edward D. Leisenring, 1838 [308, 342]

Bordner, Daniel. b. Mar. 23, 1807; d. Dec. 4, 1842. Son of Johannes and Elizabeth Hoffman Bordner. Married Hannah Klahr (b. 1810). Millersburg, Bethel Twp., Berks Co. Coverlet weaver Thomas Bordner, an early settler (c. 1814) of Millersburg. Daniel's son Daniel a tavern keeper. Will probated Apr. 20, 1843 [270]

Bordner, Elisabeth. Bethel Twp., Berks Co., 1830 [311, 343]

Boughner, A. V[ance]. Son of Daniel and [?] Vance Boughner, redware potter, Greensboro, Greene Co., active 1811–18. Took over pottery of Alexander and James Vance and manufactured salt-glazed stoneware, from 1819. Owned 1 kiln, 1860. Sons A.V. and William Boughner worked with him. Pottery still active, 1876 [231]

Branson, William. Arrived Phila., c. 1708; d. 1760. Son of Nathaniel Branson of Berkshire, England. Ironmaster, Redding Furnace, founded c. 1720. Sons-in-law Lynford Lardner, Samuel Flower, and Richard Hockley in iron business [104]

Braun, Barbara Bender. Daughter of Georg Bender. Wife of Heinrich Braun, Bethel Twp., Lebanon Co., by 1839 [341, 342]

Braun, Heinrich. Bethel Twp., Lebanon Co., by 1839 [341, 342]

Braun, Jeremias. b. Aug. 3, 1839, Bethel Twp., Lebanon Co. Son of Heinrich and Barbara Bender Braun [307, 341]

Braun, Maria Anna. b. Feb. 11, 1845, Bethel Twp., Lebanon Co.; bap. Mar. 25, 1845. Daughter of Heinrich and Barbara Bender Braun [308, 342]

Braun, Sussanna. b. Feb. 26, 1842, Bethel Twp., Lebanon Co.; bap. Mar. 26, 1842. Daughter of Heinrich and Barbara Bender Braun [308, 341]

Brechall, Martin. b. c. 1757; d. Feb. 10, 1831, East Penn Twp., Northampton Co. Married Catherine Cunfar (b. 1773), Northampton Co., July 1805. Enlisted near Allentown as private in Congress Regiment, commanded by Capt. Anthony Seeling, 1777; in battles at Short Hills, Brandywine, Monmouth, Newtown, and Yorktown [302, 340]

Breininger, Lester P., Jr. b. 1935. Potter since 1965; Robesonia, Berks Co. Married Barbara Clay [168]

Breis, Elisabeta. Wife of George Breis, Heidelberg Twp., Berks Co., 1801 [340]

Breis, George. Heidelberg Twp., Berks Co., 1801. Husband of
Elisabeta Breis [340]

Breneise, Conrad. d. 1778. Earl Twp., Lancaster Co., 1770.
Husband of Maria Herman. Father of Maria (b. Aug. 13, 1770) [339]

Breneise, Maria. b. Aug. 13, 1770, Earl Twp., Lancaster Co.
Daughter of Conrad (d. 1778) and Maria Herman Breneise.
Married George Jaùs, by Sept. 13, 1789, Earl Twp. Moved to
Harrisburg [298, 339]

Breneise, Maria Herman. Earl Twp., Lancaster Co., 1770. Wife of
Conrad Breneise [339]

Breneise, Valentin. Married, Earl Twp., Lancaster Co., by 1770
[339]

Brinton, John. Ironmaster, Mary Ann Furnace, West Manheim
Twp., York Co., 1780–1800, [107]

Brown [Braun], Michael. b. 1772, d. 1851. Lower Mahantango Twp.,
Schuylkill Co. [31]

Bucher, Heinrich. Long considered to be the maker of a type of
painted bentwood box (*see* p. 11, nos. 6, 7); now known that he was
the owner, not the maker. Other owners' names inscribed on
similar boxes suggest a maker active from 1760 to 1810 near the
border of Berks and Lancaster counties [11]

Buckwalter, Fiann. b. 1843. Probably daughter of David (farmer)
and Mary Buckwalter, Upper Leacock Twp., Lancaster Co. [276]

Buehler, John George. b. June 1812, Schwarzwald Kreis,
Württemberg, Germany; d. May 1887, Leeport, Berks Co. In Pa.,
1842. Itinerant potter, active Bern Twp., Berks Co. Isaac Deturk
and Hollenbach set him up in a log-house pottery. Known for fine
modeling and glazes. Made household wares and roof tiles.
Delivered his pottery to Reading, Pottsville, Shoemakersville,
and Hamburg by wagon [168]

C.C. 1780–85 [160]

C.E. 1780–1800 [125]

C.M. Possibly potter Christian Mench, active Haycock Twp.,
Bucks Co., 1803–6, and Nockamixon Twp., Bucks Co., 1809. Son of
Rev. Nicholas Mench, who owned land adjoining that of Conrad
Mumbouer and John Monday [216]

CM. Probably watermark of a Dutch papermaker [324]

C. M. Artist. Schoolmaster, Mount Joy Twp., Lancaster Co.,
1796 [299]

C.W. *see* Warner, Croasdel, Sr. [205]

C.Y. 1818 [69]

Cassel, Mary. Norriton, Montgomery Co., 1828 [273]

Chambers, George. Partner, with William Benjamin, in Mount
Pleasant Furnace, Franklin Co., organized c. 1783 [108]

Cist, Carl. b. Aug. 15, 1738, St. Petersburg, Russia; d. Dec. 1, 1805,
Bethlehem, Pa. Trained as druggist and apothecary. Arrived Pa.,
1769. Worked as translator for printer Henry Miller. With partner
Melchior Steiner, printed job work on Second St., Phila., at corner
of Coat's Alley, 1775. Published *Philadelphisches Staatsregister*,
July 1779. Married Mary Weiss (1762–1831). Published English-
language monthly *The American Herald*, 1784; *Columbian
Magazine*, 1786. Printer for government under President John
Adams. Printer and bookseller at 104 N. Second St., 1793–1801.
Buried Moravian cemetery, Bethlehem. Widow Mary at 248 High
St., Phila., 1806; she and 5 daughters in Bethlehem, 1823 [325–27]

Clara [Jamison]. *see* Jamison, Clara [233]

Coleman, Robert. b. Nov. 4, 1748, County Donegal, Ireland;
d. Aug. 14, 1825. Clerk for Peter Grubb, assistant to James Old
at Quittopeluille Forge, Lebanon. Rented Elizabeth Furnace,
Elizabeth Twp., Lancaster Co., 1776; owned Elizabeth Furnace,
1784–94. Married Ann Old, Oct. 4, 1773. Prominent citizen,
Lancaster Co. delegate to Constitutional Convention, 1787 [107]

Cope, Michel [Michael]. b. Jan. 1, 1770; d. 1849. Grandson of Yost
Cope (b. c. 1700, Wittenberg, Prussia; d. Nov. 26, 1784) and
Dorothea (b. 1700; d. Oct. 6, 1784), married in Phila., Oct. 2,
1727. Settled on 150 acres, near Souderton, Franconia Twp.,
Montgomery Co. Members, Indian Creek Reformed Church. Son
of John Adam Cope (b. July 2, 1731; d. Dec. 2, 1799) and Margaret
Hartzell (b. Aug. 2, 1743; d. May 7, 1813, daughter of George
Heinrich Hartzell), married Nov. 8, 1762. Owned 350-acre farm,
Hilltown Twp., Bucks Co. Married Margaret Sellers, daughter of
Philip Henry Sellers, Oct. 4, 1801. Hatter, Hilltown Twp., 1799.
Innkeeper, Marlborough Twp., and tax assessor, Upper Hanover
Twp., Montgomery Co., 1816–18. Lived on homestead just south of
Souderton, Franconia Twp. [204]

Cornwell, Amy Josephine Kline. Centre Co., 1876. Daughter of
Lucy Catherine Zeigler Hicks [265]

Cross-Legged Angel Artist. Heidelberg Twp., Berks Co., active
1780–1815 [297]

D.B.G. 1800–1820 [70]

D.M. 1832 [166]

D.R. 1780–1800 [126]

Decker, Abraham B. b. 1801; d. Oct. 8, 1859. Farmer-weaver. Mixed
Twp., Pike Co., 1820; Delaware Twp., Pike Co., 1840. Son Jacob
(1837–1886). Buried Delaware Cemetery, Dingman's Ferry, Pike
Co. [287]

Deets, Luke. b. July 21, 1874. Grandson of J. Milly. Washington
Twp., Franklin Co. [295, 338]

Dennis, Sarah. b. 1827, probably Pennsburg, Montgomery Co.
[282]

Denny, William. b. 1709, d. 1765. Deputy governor of Pa. [337]

Derr, Ana Barbara. b. July 2, 1777, Upper Hanover Twp., Phila.
(Montgomery) Co.; bap. Aug. 24, 1777, Reformed Church.
Daughter of Georg Adam and Christina Derr [296, 338]

Derr, Christina. Wife of Georg Adam Derr, Upper Hanover Twp.,
Phila. (Montgomery) Co., 1777 [338]

Derr, Georg Adam. Fraktur artist, Upper Hanover Twp.,
Montgomery Co., 1777. Took oath of allegiance, Jan. 10, 1777. Son
Johan Georg (b. 1779) [296, 338]

Derr, Johannes. Confirmed June 3, 1838, Evangelical Reformed
Church [310, 342]

Derr, Joshue H. Possibly Oley Twp., Berks Co., 1855 [342]

Derr, Peter. b. 1793, d. 1868. Tulpehocken Twp., Berks Co.
[119, 137, 161]

Deschler, Magdalena. Wife of Peter Deschler, Whitehall Twp.,
Northampton Co., 1780 [339–40]

Deschler, Peter. Whitehall Twp., Northampton Co., 1780 [339]

Deturk, Isaac. Near Friedersburg on Kaufman's Creek, Berks Co.
Son of John (b. 1747) and Elizabeth Bertolet Deturk. Married Miss
Moll [335]

Dirstein, Michael. d. 1841. Son of Michael (b. 1712, Thunerberg
near Bern, Switzerland; d. 1777), weaver, miller, and farmer,

Rockhill Twp., Bucks Co. Inherited family land in Hilltown Twp., Bucks Co. Mennonite farmer, potter, and weaver. Inventory listed weaving and shoemaking equipment [169]

Disler, Konra. Berks or Lancaster Co., 1862 [276]

Dres, Jacob. d. 1841. Mount Joy Twp., Lancaster Co. [23]

Drey, John [Johan]. b. 1780, d. 1870. Son of George (arrived Phila., Sept. 19, 1732) and Catherine Drey. Married Sarah, by 1813. Two sons, Ruben (b. Sept. 18, 1816) and Benjamin (b. Oct. 10, 1819). Members, Christ Lutheran Church, Dryville, Rockland Twp., Berks Co. Potter, Rockland Twp., active 1806–47 [348]

Dreybelbis, Danniel. Richmond Twp., Berks Co., 1798 [340]

Drissell, Elizabeth. Probably Elizabeth Drissell Ruch, sister of John Drissell and daughter of J. Ulrich Drissell (d. 1817), Lower Milford Twp., Bucks Co. [59]

Drissell, John. Probably son of J. Ulrich Drissell (d. 1817), Lower Milford Twp., Bucks Co., who signed township petition in Milford, 1750; listed as carpenter, Allen Twp., 1775. After the Revolutionary War, settled in Milford Twp., 1798, owned two-story house of hewn logs, 34 x 28′. Neighbors David Spinner and John Strawn witnessed his will, 1806. John Drissell, singleman, Milford Twp., 1787. Inherited father's plantation, 1817. Drissell decorated two objects for Mary and Margaret Miller, 1796. Table loom inscribed for his sister Elizabeth Drissell Ruch. A John Drissell living in Tinicum, Bucks Co., 1830 [59]

Dulheuer, Heinrich [Henry]. b. Mark, Westphalia, Germany; d. after 1816. Printer-inventor, Baltimore, 1785. Traveled through N.C., S.C., Muhlenberg Co., Ky. Schoolteacher, Hagers (Elizabethtown), Washington Co., Pa. Printed and distributed handbills in German and English. Known as "The Old Traveler" [298, 339]

Dwyer, Emanuel. House carpenter, Manheim Twp., Lancaster Co., 1803 [310]

E.B. Probably Elizabeth Hendricks Bergey, b. Dec. 17, 1801; d. Sept. 18, 1895. Wife of Benjamin Bergey (1797–1854), miller. Members, Rockhill Mennonite Meeting. Son Benjamin H. Bergey (1835–1900), carpenter, South Perkasie. Daughter Esther Bergey also could have been owner of plate [168]

E.D.F. Lancaster Co., 1790 [28]

E.F. 1800–1820 [65]

EF. Watermark of Ephrata Cloister, by 1748 [324]

E.H. Probably Berks Co., 1842 [275]

E.L. Berks Co., 1825–30 [69]

E.R. Phila., 1764–80 [158]

E.R. Possibly wife-to-be of Christian Mench [216]

E.Y. Waynesboro, Franklin Co., 1835–50 [167]

Earl Township Artist. Active Earl Twp., Lancaster Co., 1790–1800 [313, 320]

Ebersole, Alithebeth. Possibly Harrisburg, Dauphin Co., 1840 [275]

Ebner, Henrich. Allentown, Lehigh Co., active 1817–30. Printer. Ebner & Co., 1821. Published *Oeconomisches Haus-und Kunst-Buch* . . . comp. by John Krauss (Allentown, 1819) and the Moravian yearly textbook, 1823 [304, 340]

Eby, H[enry] R. Probably Lancaster Co. Family name of Swiss Mennonites [132]

Ege, George. b. Holland. Owned land in Berks Co. Founded Reading Furnace, Heidelberg Twp., Berks Co., active 1794–1850 [108]

Egelmann, Carl Friederich. b. May 12, 1782, Neunkirchen, Germany; d. Nov. 30, 1860, Reading, Berks Co. Parents from titled German and Dutch families. Private secretary to Baron Dinklaga, chamberlain of England, in Schulenberg. Arrived Baltimore, 1802; apprenticed to coachmaker; learned copperplate engraving. Made 12 chairs for President James Madison, 1809. Married Anna Maria Schert, 1808; to Chester, Pa., to teach English, 1810. To Heidelberg Twp., Berks Co., where he became organist and choir leader. To Spies Church, Alsace Twp., Berks Co., 1815. Worked for printer John Ritter, doing almanac calculations and engraving, Reading, 1821. Produced scientific books with Ritter, to 1830. Continued to do almanac calculations until his death. Honorary member of the New England Society of Mathematics. Published fraktur blanks, 1810–45. Best known for copybook *Deutsche & Englische Vorschriften*, first published 1821 [331]

Egner, Elisabetha. Probably Upper Saucon Twp., Northampton (Lehigh) Co., 1807 [340]

Egolff, Barbara Ann. b. Dec. 31, 1824, Carlisle, Cumberland Co. Daughter of Joseph and Barbara Losz Egolff [306, 341]

Egolff, Barbara Losz. Carlisle, Cumberland Co., 1813–24. Mother of Elisabeth (b. 1813), William Jacob (b. 1818), and Barbara Ann Egolff (b. 1824) [340–41]

Egolff, Elizabeth. b. Jan 10, 1813, Carlisle, Cumberland Co. Daughter of Joseph and Barbara Losz Egolff [304, 340]

Egolff, Joseph. Carlisle, Cumberland Co., 1813–24. Father of Elizabeth (b. 1813), William Jacob (b. 1818), and Barbara Ann Egolff (b. 1824) [340–41]

Egolff, William Jacob. b. Apr. 4, 1818, Carlisle, Cumberland Co. Son of Joseph and Barbara Losz Egolff [304, 341]

Eisenhauer, Martin. Rockland Twp., Berks Co., 1794–95. Owned 34 acres, 3 horses, 4 cattle [34]

Elisa [Elizabeth Huber Stiegel]. Wife of Henry William Stiegel [105]

Engelhard, Heinrich. Bethel Twp., Berks Co., 1820–30s [311]

Ensminger, Anna. b. Aug. 1, 1853 [295, 338]

Ernst, Anna Catharina. Heidelberg Twp., Berks Co., 1769. Mother of Johan Georg Ernst (b. 1769) [338]

Ernst, Jacob. Heidelberg Twp., Berks Co., 1769. Father of Johan Georg Ernst (b. 1769) [338]

Ernst, Johan Georg. b. Aug. 27, 1769, Heidelberg Twp., Berks Co., d. Apr. 16, 1843. Son of Jacob and Anna Catharina Ernst. Heidelberg Twp., Berks Co., 1769–1820; Hatfield, Montgomery Co., 1830 [296, 338]

Ernst, Paul. Heidelberg Twp., Berks Co., 1769 [338]

Faber, George. d. 1839, Berks Co. Active Sumneytown, Montgomery Co., by 1773. Single man, Reading, Berks Co., 1799, where he may have worked with clockmaker Benjamin Whitman [43, 44]

Fetzer, Henriette Emig. Allentown, Lehigh Co., 1855. Mother of Lidia Ellen Mente Fetzer (b. 1855) [342]

Fetzer, Lidia Ellen Mente. b. Oct. 3, 1855, Allentown, Lehigh Co. Daughter of O[w]en and Henriette Emig Fetzer [308, 342]

Fetzer, O[w]en. Allentown, Lehigh Co., 1855. Father of Lidia Ellen Mente Fetzer (b. 1855) [342]

[Fieschler?], Mary Ann. b. May 10, 1859, Rapho Twp., Lancaster Co. [295, 338]

Fischer, Cattarina Lollmain. Heidelberg Twp., Berks Co., 1780. Mother of Willhelm Fischer (b. 1780) [338]

Fischer, Michael. Heidelberg Twp., Berks Co., 1780. Father of Willhelm Fischer (b. 1780) [338]

Fischer, Willem. Heidelberg Twp., Berks Co., 1780. Unmarried uncle(?) of Willhelm Fischer (b. 1780) [338]

Fischer, Willhelm. b. Nov. 30, 1780, Heidelberg Twp., Berks Co. Son of Michael and Cattarina Lollmain Fischer [297, 338]

Flat Tulip Artist. Centre Co., c. 1810–20 [303]

Flory, John. b. May 3, 1754. Son of Johannes and Anna Danker Flory. Married Susanna, by 1781. Joiner, Manheim Boro., Rapho Twp., Lancaster Co., active 1789–1824 [23]

Flower, Samuel. Active, Redding Furnace, Berks Co., 1743. Married Rebecca Branson, daughter of ironmaster William Branson, 1744. Master, Durham Furnace, Durham Twp., Bucks Co., c. 1756 [104, 106]

Frank, Catharina Stober. Haines Twp., Centre Co., 1806. Mother of Michael Frank (b. 1806) [341]

Frank, Michael. b. July 19, 1806, Haines Twp., Centre Co. Son of Philipp and Catharina Stober Frank [305, 341]

Frank, Philipp. Haines Twp., Centre Co., 1806. Father of Michael Frank (b. 1806) [341]

Franke, August Herman. Author, *Der Sichere Himmels-Weg oder Anleitung zum Christenthum . . .* (Ephrata, Lancaster Co., 1828) [329]

Fretz, Jacob. Family name in Bedminster and Hilltown twps., Bucks Co. No one by that name was identified as a potter in twp. or co. tax records. The name Jacob Fretz inscribed in figure probably identifies owner, not maker. Jacob Fretz (b. Nov. 19, 1798; d. July 31, 1842), wealthy miller, Bedminster Twp. His detailed vendue (Oct. 1, 1843) lists unusual quantity of clothing: "21 shirts, blue coat, pantaloons . . . under jackets . . . great coat, suspenders, hats, gloves, 10 pr. stockings." Inventory (Aug. 16, 1842) includes silver watch ($15), saddle, bridle, and holder ($7) [169]

Funck, Jacob. b. c. 1785; d. 1824, Haycock Twp., Bucks Co. Swiss Mennonite family. Married Anna Switzer (daughter of Anna Switzer of New Britain Twp., Bucks Co., sister of Valentine Switzer), by July 19, 1806. Farmer, turner, potter, active 1805–24. Inventory (Apr. 28, 1824) lists, in part: "turning ley, cross cut saw, turning ley or aul, hand saw, 2 augres, lot board in shop, large rooler, potter molds, glaising mill, all the earthenware, that unburnt, pot blacklead, glaising pot ladles, clay mill." Estate value $979.92 [170]

G.G. [272]

Gangenwer, Cattarina. b. Sept. 22, 1795, Upper Saucon Twp., Northampton Co. Daughter of Hennerich and Elisabeta Köhl Gangenwer [300, 339]

Gangenwer, Elisabeta Köhl. Upper Saucon Twp., Northampton Co., 1795. Mother of Cattarina Gangenwer (b. 1795) [339]

Gangenwer, Hennerich. Upper Saucon Twp., Northampton Co., 1795. Father of Cattarina Gangenwer (b. 1795) [339]

Garrett, W[illiam]. Probably Chester Co., active 1820–30. Probably owner (a baker) of spatula [136]

Gartside, I. Chester or Phila. Co., c. 1830–60 [67]

Gass, Fronica Domes [Thomas]. Derry Twp., Dauphin Co., 1775. Mother of Johannes Gass (b. 1775) [339]

Gass, Jacob. Derry Twp., Dauphin Co., 1775. Father of Johannes Gass (b. 1775) [339]

Gass, Johannes. b. Mar. 11, 1775, Derry Twp., Dauphin Co. Son of Jacob and Fronica Domes Gass [299, 339]

Gast [Gans], Henry. b. Aug. 25, 1806; d. May 30, 1889, Lancaster Co. Married Sophia (1807–1871) [170]

Gauker, Daniel. Lehigh Co.(?), 1809 [340]

Geisiner, Susana. 1836 [282]

Geistweit, Georg. Pastor, St. Peter's Church, Jackson Twp., Northumberland Co., 1794. Schoolmaster, Wolf's Chapel, Centre Co., 1794–1804. On committee that ordained Rev. Frederick Scholl (1787–1865), Indian Creek Reformed Church, Montgomery Co., 1817. Traveling minister, Centre Co. [317, 340, 345]

George, Elisabeth. Married Michael Hausser, July 4, 1813 [339]

Gerber [Graber], R. Family name in Montgomery, Bucks, and York counties. Potter, active 1811–19, working with Andrew Uhler and Heinrich Roth [170]

German, Catarina [Remaly]. b. Feb. 12, 1826, Bucks Co. Married Joseph German (1822–1894) Friedericks Church, Washington Twp., Lehigh Co. [55]

German, Johannes. Chapman Twp., Union (Snyder) Co., 1800. Married [342]

Germann. Pastor, Macungie Twp., Lehigh Co., 1827 [341]

Geyer, Johann [John]. Printer, 122 N. Third St., Phila., active 1805–25. Published a Democratic-Republican weekly newspaper, 1810, and almanacs. Phila. alderman, 1819–25, mayor of Phila., 1814. Press continued to use his name after his retirement [331]

Gibble, John. Manheim Twp., Lancaster Co. Potter, active 1820–56 [170, 171]

Gisler, Anna Catarina. b. June 21, 1779, Tulpehocken Twp., Berks Co. [296, 338]

Glassbrener, David. Riflemaker, Lebanon Twp., Dauphin Co. [347]

Godshall [Gottshall], Martin. b. c. 1785, d. after 1857, Franconia and Salford twps., Montgomery Co. Son of Rev. Jacob (1763–1845) and Barbara Kindig Godshall. Mennonites. One of 11 children. Unmarried. Miller on Perkiomen Creek, Salford Twp., schoolteacher, fraktur illustrator. Gave 2 pieces of ground for local schools [336]

Godshall [Gottshall], Samuel. Salford Twp., Montgomery Co. Schoolteacher. Bachelor brother of Martin Godshall. Fraktur in a freer style than the example no. 13, p. 336, now attributed to Martin [336]

Gorgas, Jacob. b. Aug. 9, 1728, Germantown; d. Mar. 21, 1798, Ephrata, Lancaster Co. Fifth son of John (d. 1741) from Holland and Sophia Rittenhouse Gorgas (d. 1737). Moved to Cocalico Twp., Lancaster Co., c. 1758. Married Christina Mack (1734–1804). Purchased 16 acres and building on W. Main St., Ephrata, 1767, where he and sons Solomon (1764–1838) and Joseph made clocks. After 1799 sons moved west; did cabinetwork. Sergeant, Peter Grubb's battalion, organized Aug. 1776 [42, 43]

Götz, Carl Christoph [Goetz, Charles Christopher]. Pastor, Zion Lutheran Church, Mahanoy Twp., and Himmel's, Washington Twp., Northumberland Co. In Whitehall Twp., Northampton Co., 1789 [339]

Grimin, Mar[ie]chen [Grim, Marie Catherine]. b. c. 1780. Possibly daughter of Valentine Grim, brother of Maria Catherine Grim Kleh (d. 1813). Bern Twp., Berks Co. [23]

Grimm [Grim], Solomon. b. Mar. 8, 1787. Son of Henry (b. May 23, 1756; d. Mar. 2, 1847) and Gertrude Trexler Grim (1764–1845), Maxatawny Twp., Berks Co. Members, Mertz Church. Henry Grim a prosperous miller with 58 acres, 1785, and 300 acres, 1791, adjoining property of his brother Jonathan Grim (b. 1769), tanner, Maxatawny Twp. May have apprenticed with potter John Leisenring, active Maxatawny Twp. by 1786, but worked with [?] Weiss, Rockland Twp., 1815–25 [*see* p. 348]. Brother Daniel Grim (b. Oct. 23, 1802) may have worked with him by 1824. Potter named Grim went to the Shenandoah Valley to work at Jacob J. Eberly's Star Pottery, c. 1870; possibly descendant of the Berks Co. Grims [171]

Grob. 1800–1850 [138]

Grobin [Grob], Susanna. Member of Swiss Mennonite family that settled in Frederick Twp., Montgomery Co., 1717. Daughter of Abraham and Elizabeth Fretz Grob, who migrated to Ontario, c. 1800. Married Michael Law and migrated to Canada, c. 1800. Dish inscribed with her name was recovered in upper New York [215]

Grobin, Susanna. 1815 [334]

Groff, Asa. Brother of Lettisha Groff, Lancaster Co., 1798 [277]

Groff, Benjamian [Benjamin]. Brother of Lettisha Groff, Lancaster Co., 1798 [277]

Groff, Deborah. Sister of Lettisha Groff, Lancaster Co., 1798 [277]

Groff, Deborah. Wife of John Groff. Mother of Lettisha Groff, Lancaster Co., 1798 [277]

Groff, John. Brother of Lettisha Groff, Lancaster Co., 1798 [277]

Groff, John. Father of Lettisha Groff, Lancaster Co., 1798 [277]

Groff, Lettisha. b. 1786. Daughter of John and Deborah Groff. Brothers and sisters Asa, Sarah, Martha, John, Wiliam, Deborah, and Benjamian. Deceased brother, Thomas [277]

Groff, Martha. Sister of Lettisha Groff, Lancaster Co., 1798 [277]

Groff, Sarah. Sister of Lettisha Groff, Lancaster Co., 1798 [277]

Groff, Thomas. d. by 1798. Brother of Lettisha Groff, Lancaster Co. [277]

Groff, Wiliam [William]. Brother of Lettisha Groff, Lancaster Co., 1798 [277]

Grubb, Peter, Jr. Son of Peter Grubb, ironmaster, Cornwall Furnace, active 1765–85. Father and son held interest there until 1798. With partner George Ege built Mount Hope Furnace on Big Chickies Creek, Lancaster Co., 1786 [108]

Gutbror, Margareta. 1818 [272]

H.A.L. c. 1827 [35]

H.R. 1753 [62]

H.S.T. 1796 [130]

H.W. 1772 [58]

Hacker, Christina. Elizabeth Twp., Lancaster Co., 1829. Wife of Georg Hacker [342]

Hacker, Georg. Elizabeth Twp., Lancaster Co., 1829. Husband of Christina Hacker. Brother of Elisabeth Hacker Bingeman [342]

Hackmeister, Carl Ludwich. Chapman Twp., Union Co., 1800. Father of Johan Georg Hackmeister (b. 1800) [342]

Hackmeister, Elisabeth Schäffer. Chapman Twp., Union Co., 1800. Mother of Johan Georg Hackmeister (b. 1800) [342]

Hackmeister, Johan Georg. b. Aug. 2, 1800, Chapman Twp., Union Co. Son of Carl Ludwich and Elisabeth Schäffer Hackmeister. In Chapman Twp., 1840 [309, 342]

Hamlin, Joseph Hunsicker. Lancaster Co. [324]

Harding, Samuel. b. c. 1800, d. 1871. Married Maria States, Nov. 26, 1820, Southampton Twp., Bucks Co. Potter, Haring Pottery, Nockamixon Twp., active 1820–50 [348]

Haring, David. b. Sept. 12, 1801, Haycock Twp., Bucks Co.; d. 1871, Haycock Twp. Son of German-born stonemason. Worked first in Danville, Montour Co., with his father. Returned east to work in his brother John's pottery. Nockamixon Twp. Married Anna Bigley (b. 1804), 1827. Purchased land, log house, and built pottery and kiln. Retired, 1866. Son Israel (b. 1832), a potter. Son Abel (b. 1847) wrote detailed manuscript about their pottery production and methods (Philadelphia Museum of Art) [76, 77, 172, 173]

Haring, Jared R. b. 1832, Nockamixon Twp., Bucks Co. Married Catharine (b. 1838). Listed in 1860 U.S. census as master potter [77, 172]

Haring Pottery. Nockamixon Twp., Bucks Co. [173]

Hartlein, Ellen. b. Sept. 14, 1837, Heidelberg Twp., Berks Co. Daughter of Johann and Julianna Lider Hartlein [303, 340] .

Hartlein, Johann. Heidelberg Twp., Berks Co., 1837. Father of Ellen Hartlein (b. 1837) [340]

Hartlein, Julianna Lider. Heidelberg Twp., Berks Co., 1837. Mother of Ellen Hartlein (b. 1837) [340]

Harwick, Joseph. b. 1788, d. 1866. Son of Samuel Harwick, potter, Haycock Twp., Bucks Co. Married Eve, c. 1816. Bought 6 acres, Nockamixon Twp., Bucks Co., June 1830; paid tax on father's Haycock property until 1825. Left 3 pieces of land to 3 children. Inventory (filed July 21, 1866), in part: "Pot moulds, glazing mill, pot wheel, shaving horse, Dearborn wagon, tongue and shafts, iron pots, stove, clock, desk" [173]

Harwick, Samuel. d. 1842. Potter, Haycock Twp., Bucks Co., active by 1802, when he owned 1 cow and paid tax on pottery operation valued at $320. Owned no land, but pottery valued at $2,060, in 1804. Owned 88 acres, 1 horse, 3 cows, 1806. Inherited or shared the following property with his brother Jacob: 1 two-story stone house, 30 x 20'; 1 pottery shop, 26 x 22'; 1 kiln house, 22 x 18'; 1 log barn, 60 x 20' [173]

Hausser, Elisabetha Xander. Wife of Michael Hausser. Lutheran. Whitehall Twp., Northampton Co., 1789 [339]

Hausser, Georg. Whitehall Twp., Northampton Co., 1789 [339]

Hausser, Michael. b. Mar. 25, 1789, Whitehall Twp., Northampton Co. Son of Michael and Elisabetha Xander Hausser. Lutheran. Married Elisabeth George, July 4, 1813 [299, 339]

Hausser, Michael. Father of Michael (b. Mar. 25, 1789). Lutheran. Whitehall Twp., Northampton Co., 1789 [339]

Haw, H. [Shaw?]. 1800–1850 [75]

Headman, Andrew. d. 1830. Arrived Phila., 1771, with brother Frans Wilhelm, master potter from Friedrichsthal. Formerly member of a Württemberg regiment. Possibly worked with Frans in what became the Headman Pottery on Eighth St., south of Market St., to 1786, when he purchased 7 acres, Richland Twp., Bucks Co. Added 21 acres across the road in Rockhill Twp., 1791. Potters John Herstine, Andrew Headman, Jr., and Michael

Headman worked with him by 1813. His buildings in Richland
Twp. were a one-story house of round logs, 16 x 16'; one-story log
shop, 16 x 16'; a "hew'd" log barn, 38 x 20'; and 5 acres, 1798. Estate
records (filed Jan. 29, 1830) show that he left his most valuable
possession, his clock and case, to son Michael. Sons Andrew, Jr.
(d. 1852), Michael, and John, potters [174]

Headman, Charles. b. Oct. 12, 1826; d. Jan. 12, 1909. Son of Michael
(1789–1876) and Rachel Shellenberger Headman, married Nov. 12,
1815. Potter, active by 1850. Married Mary [174]

Headman, John. b. 1796/97. Son of Andrew (d. 1830). Potter
Rockhill Twp., Bucks Co. Son Peter (b. c. 1825) and journeyman
potter Thomas Walter (b. 1818) lived with him 1850. Peter and
Ferdinand Constantine (b. 1807), journeyman potter from
Hesse-Darmstadt, lived with him, 1860 [175]

Headman, Maria. Wife of Charles Headman (1826–1909) [175]

Headman, Peter. b. c. 1825. Son of John (b. 1796/97) and Hannah
Headman (b. 1806). Potter, Rockhill Twp., Bucks Co. Working with
his father John and journeyman potter Thomas Walter (b. 1818),
1850. Working at family pottery with potter Ferdinand Constantine
(b. 1807, Hesse-Darmstadt), 1860 [76]

Heebner, David. Worcester Twp., Montgomery Co., 1818 [334]

Heger, Barbara. Wife of Phieliepp [Phillip] Heger. Upper Hanover
Twp., Phila. (Montgomery) Co., 1777 [338]

Heger, Phieliepp [Phillip]. Upper Hanover Twp., Phila.
(Montgomery) Co., 1777 [338]

Heiges, Georg. Monaghan Twp., York Co., 1776. Father of Sabina
Heiges (b. 1776) [338]

Heiges, Margaretha. Monaghan Twp., York Co., 1776. Mother of
Sabina Heiges (b. 1776) [338]

Heiges, Sabina. b. July 31, 1776, Monaghan Twp., York Co.
Daughter of Georg and Margaretha Heiges [297, 338]

Heilman, Beata. b. Nov. 6, 1840 [283]

Helbard [Helbert], Maria. Married Peter Kulp of Pottsgrove Twp.,
Montgomery Co. Had 6 children. Owned set of 6 plates by potter
Samuel Paul; one dated Mar. 27, 1798 [193]

Helfferich, J. Probably Reformed minister Rev. John Henry
Helfferich, Berks Co. In U.S. census of 1800, in Weissenburg Twp.,
Northampton Co.; household included 7 children, ages from under
10 to 26 [340]

Hendricks, Abraham A. b. Aug. 20, 1829. Married Lydia M.
Hunsicker, Sept. 16, 1855 [310, 342]

Hendricks, Lydia [Lidia] M. Hunsicker. b. Nov. 16, 1838. Married
Abraham A. Hendricks, Sept. 16, 1855 [310, 342]

Henne, Daniel. Potter, Shartlesville, Bern Twp., Berks Co. Son
Joseph also a potter, between Bernville and Strausstown, Berks
Co., until 1876. Pottery ceased operation, 1880. Edwin A. Barber
noted that some animals with numbers on the bottom were made
in this pottery. Pig-shaped flask (p. 222, no. 14) now attributed to
Henne pottery [222]

Hennig, Catharina. Wife of Philipp Hennig, Haines Twp., Centre
Co., 1806 [341]

Hennig, Philipp. Husband of Catharina Hennig, Haines Twp.,
Centre Co., 1806 [341]

Herbst. Probably Rev. John Herbst, Lancaster Co., 1790 [342]

Herbst, Conrad. d. 1839. Papermaker, with Adam Rahn,
Maidencreek Twp., Berks [not Bucks as in entry] Co., by 1792.
Active to 1809. In District Twp., Berks Co., 1810; Pike Twp., Berks
Co., 1820. Married [323]

Hereford Township Artist. Active Berks Co., c. 1800 [321]

Hersche, Christian. Hempfield and Manheim twps., Lancaster Co.
[320, 327]

Hershey, Adele Hostetter. Daughter of Jacob Henry and Mary
Rebecca Hunsecker Hostetter. Married Hiram F. Hershey [33]

Hertlein, Johannes. b. June 3, 1809. Son of Jost and Sarah Deh
Hertlein, Allentown, Lehigh Co. [304, 340]

Hertlein, Jost. Father of Johannes Hertlein (b. 1809) [340]

Hertlein, Sarah Deh. Mother of Johannes Hertlein (b. 1809) [340]

Hess, Magdalena. 1798 [340]

Hicks, Lucy Catherine Zeigler. Howard, Centre Co., 1875–80 [265]

Hiestand. Family name in Lancaster Co. Wardrobe from S. H.
Hiestand estate, Salunga, Mount Joy–Rapho Twp. area [347]

Hiland, Margaret. 1829. Family name in East Penn Twp.,
Northampton Co. [281]

Hill, Samuel. d. 1831. Cumro Twp., Berks Co. [335]

Himes [Hines], Elizabeth. Probably daughter of John Hines,
Heidelberg Twp., York Co., 1800 [25]

Histand, Susana. 1803 [278]

Hoevelmann, Arnold. b. 1749, d. 1804. To America with Lafayette;
surgeon in Revolutionary War. Lebanon Co., 1790; Cumberland
Co., 1797 [297, 338]

Hoff, George. b. 1733, Hesse-Cassel, Germany; d. 1816, Cocalico
Twp., Lancaster Co. Married Justina Schnertzel, daughter of
George Schnertzel, with whom he apprenticed as a clockmaker in
Germany. To Pa., 1765. Owned house and part of lot on King St.,
Lancaster, where he worked until retirement, 1806. Warden,
Trinity Lutheran Church, assistant to the Lancaster Boro.
burgesses, and member, Friendship Fire Company [42]

Hofmayer. Reformed minister, Upper Saucon Twp., Northampton
Co., 1795 [339]

Hoke, Martin. b. 1802. To Pa. from Baden. Weaver. Dover, York
Co., 1837; York, York Co., 1842–47. Married Mary Elizabeth
Shibbin (widow), c. 1848. Became a medicine healer, and lived on
south side of High St., west of bridge, York, 1852. Brother(?)
Michael, cordwainer, 1860 [270]

Holl, Peter, [III]. d. 1825. Grandson of joiner Peter I (d. 1775), and
Susanna Margaret Holl, who migrated from Switzerland to Augusta
Co., Va., 1741, settling in Manor Twp., Lancaster Co., c. 1765, on
land adjoining that of Christian Kauffman and Abraham Herr. One
of his 4 sons, Peter II, (d. 1784) a turner, married widow Barbara
Smith (d. 1806); no issue. They were neighbors of Christian
Hershey. Another son of Peter I, John or Wendell (both d. by 1773)
or Isaac, was the father of Peter Holl III, turner, joiner, and pump
maker, Manheim and Warwick twps., Lancaster Co. Probably
apprenticed with his uncle Peter Holl II. Purchased 91¾ acres,
Warwick Twp., from Arnold and Barbara Becker, 1789. Son Peter
IV, a miller, Earl Twp., by 1804 [32, 33]

Hollin, Jacob Jur. 1800–1820 [216]

Hollinger, Eli. b. June 20, 1830, Reading Twp., Adams Co. Son of
George and Elisabeth Asper Hollinger [307, 341]

Hollinger, Elisabeth Asper. Reading Twp., Adams Co. Mother of Eli Hollinger (b. 1830) [341]

Hollinger, George. Reading Twp., Adams Co. Father of Eli Hollinger (b. 1830) [341]

Homan, Elisabeth Schlögel. Daughter of Peter Schlögel. Haines Twp., Centre Co. Mother of Johannes Homan (b. 1814) [340]

Homan, Johannes. b. Sept. 21, 1814, Haines Twp., Centre Co. Son of Peter and Elisabeth Schlögel Homan [303, 340]

Homan, Peter. Haines Twp., Centre Co. Father of Johannes Homan (b. 1814) [340]

Horn, Abraham. Richland Twp., Bucks Co., 1820–40. Uncle of Catharina Horn (b. 1822) [341]

Horn, Catharina. b. Oct. 27, 1822, Richland Twp., Bucks Co. Daughter of Sebastian and Maria Mollen Horn [305, 341]

Horn, Maria Mollen. Richland Twp., Bucks Co. Mother of Catharina Horn (b. 1822) [341]

Horn, Sebastian. Richland Twp., Bucks Co. Father of Catharina Horn (b. 1822) [341]

Horner [Hornor], Charles. b. Nov. 20, 1832, Hartley Twp., Union Co. Son of David and Mary Johnston Horner [Hornor] [306, 341]

Horner [Hornor], David. Hartley Twp., Union Co. Father of Charles Horner (b. 1832) [341]

Horner [Hornor], Mary Johnston. Hartley Twp., Union Co. Mother of Charles Horner (b. 1832) [341]

Hostetter, Jacob. b. 1754; d. 1831, New Lisbon, Ohio. Clockmaker, Hanover, York Co. Apprenticed with clockmaker Richard Chester. Member of Congress, 1818–21. To Ohio, 1825 [45]

Hostetter, Mary Rebecca Hunsecker. b. 1851, d. 1822. Daughter of Peter and Lydia Davis Garber Hunsicker, Neffsville, Lancaster Co. Married Jacob Henry Hostetter [33]

Hubener [Hubner], Abraham. Potter, active Northampton and/or Upper Hanover Twp., Montgomery Co. May have been associated with Ludwig Hubener [Huebner], Bethlehem community pottery, and at the same time with George Hubener, potter [175]

Hubener [Huebner], George. b. 1757, d. 1828. Grandson of Hans (1684–1754) from Laubgrund and Maria Scholtz Huebner (d. 1745) from Ober Harpersdorf, Silesia, who settled in Falkner Swamp, Frederick Twp., Montgomery Co., 1734. Son of Hans [John] George (1720–Oct. 1792) and Anna Veronica Dotterer Hubener (1727–1778), who owned a 200-acre farm with stone house and barn in Frederick Twp., on road from Pottstown to Bethlehem (Route 663), Montgomery Co. Nephew of George Hubner (d. 1773), miller, until 1769 in partnership with Henry Antes (d. 1755) in Frederick Twp. Brother of Philip, a weaver, who married Elizabeth Neis, sister of John Neis of Goschenhoppen, Montgomery Co., 1788. Brother of Margaret (b. July 29, 1759; d. Sept. 16, 1823), who married Johannes Neis, the potter. Brother of Captain Frederick, who married Christina Ruschong at Falkner Swamp Reformed Church, 1789. A George Hubener, single man, resided in Lower Saucon Twp., Northampton Co., designated as an innkeeper with 96 acres, an "olymill," 2 horses, 2 cows, 2 sheep, 1782. Married Catherine Hartzel, of Rockhill Twp., 1785. She was the daughter of George (d. 1796) and Catherine Hahn Neis Hartzel [Hartzell] of Franconia Twp. Catherine Hahn Neis Hartzell was also the mother of Johannes Neis. Their children were: Ann (1786–1859), married Henry Stager; John (1788–1870), married Mary Hipple; Susanne (b. 1789); William, married Anna Lehman; Abraham (1797–1868), married Esther; Veronica, married Jacob Renninger, a potter, Upper Hanover Twp., Montgomery Co. Hubener homestead was located near Schwenkfelder settlement at Pennsburg, Upper Hanover Twp., where George may have apprenticed at the Sissholtz pottery, and was close enough to Bethlehem so that he

could have worked with Ludwig Hubener [Huebner], who ran the Bethlehem pottery by 1763. Upper Hanover Twp. tax records list a George Heebner as a potter, taxed for 1 horse, 2 cows, 1787–88. Listed as a tenant, 1788. Attended Falkner Swamp Reformed Church by 1790. Purchased 57¾ acres, Limerick Twp., Montgomery Co., from George Reezer, June 8, 1790. Relocated, still calling himself a potter, to Vincent Twp., Chester Co., by May 28, 1792, selling his Limerick Twp. land to John Craiter for £450. After father died (Oct. 1792), brother John sold family homestead to brother-in-law John Richards, a justice of the peace, for £1,010. Richards retained one tract and conveyed the homestead back to John Hubener, 1794. George Hubeners appear in East Vincent Twp. church records, 1794–97. George and Catherine Hubener bought 186-acre farm and mill, Chester Co., for £1,400 from Charles Albrecht, instrument maker of Phila., 1797, at which time George Hubener was designated on deed as miller instead of potter. Sold Chester Co. property in three units and moved to Manheim Twp., Schuylkill Co., between 1814 and 1815. Two sons and a daughter living with them, 1820 [175, 176]

Huber Artist. Lancaster Co., active 1790–1800 [312]

Huber, Christian. b. 1758; d. Nov. 23, 1820. Brother of George Huber (1758–1784). Listed with his father's household, Manheim Twp., Lancaster Co., 1779. In Warwick Twp., Lancaster Co., listed as a freeman, and probably working with Peter Holl, by 1782. Married 1) Elizabeth (d. after 1792), then 2) Rachel. At his death, owned a brick house and ground in Manheim Twp., adjoining land belonging to John Weaver and John Shriner, a bay horse called Charley, and a gig. Two sons John and George, and a daughter Maria A. Hoober [sic], not yet 21 in 1820. Specified that his sons were to take all personal possessions and that there should not be a public sale. Christian probably received the wardrobe (p. 32, no. 2) from his brother George's estate. Wardrobe passed to his son George (d. 1874) of Manheim Twp. By 1860 George's business was being conducted under a power of attorney issued to Christian Lintner and John N. Eby. Wardrobe passed to his daughter Matilda Eby (Mrs. John N. Eby). Brick house and 71 acres inherited from his father on the Lancaster-Lititz Turnpike Rd., near Neffsville. George Huber's will specified that his possessions were to be sold to satisfy a debt and for his daughter's inheritance. Wardrobe was purchased "near Neffsville" by Lydia Davis Garber Hunsecker (Mrs. Peter, 1813–1903) [32, 33]

Huber, George. b. 1758, d. 1784. Grandson of Gregor Jonas (d. 1741) and Anna Maria Kruetzer Huber, Swiss, settled at Ellerstadt in the Palatinate. Son of Johannes (b. 1704, Ellerstadt) who came to Pa., c. 1742, became a wealthy miller owning property on the Little Conestoga Creek, in Manor and East Hempfield twps., and homestead in Manheim Twp. He married Mary Watson. Brothers of George Huber: Jonas (d. 1792), a joiner and wheelwright in Hempfield Twp.; John, farmer-miller in Manheim and Hempfield twps.; Christian (d. 1820), a joiner and millstone cutter in Manheim and Warwick twps.; and Jacob (b. 1730; d. 1800, Bedford Co.). Married Barbara Oberholtzer (d. 1803), First Reformed Church, Lancaster, 1780. She was the daughter of their neighbors in Hempfield Twp., Magdalena and Christian Oberholtzer (d. 1812), a miller who sold to George's brother John a house, a grist- and sawmill, a plantation and 6 tracts of land in Hempfield and Manheim twps. [32, 33]

Huber, Johannes. York Co., 1776. Married [338]

Hubner, Susanna. b. 1786, d. 1831. Unmarried. Pennsburg, Upper Hanover Twp., Montgomery Co. Schwenkfelder. Sister of Barbara Huber Stauffer [316]

Hunsecker, Lydia Davis Garber. b. 1813, d. 1903. Married Peter Hunsecker of Neffsville, Lancaster Co. [33]

Hunsicker, Anna. b. Jan. 15, 1782, Lancaster Co.; d. Mar. 20, 1856 [324]

Hunsicker, Christian. b. 1723, Alsace; d. 1795, Lancaster Co. [324]

Hunsicker, Christian. b. Mar. 26, 1776, Lancaster Co.; d. Aug. 5, 1857, Dauphin Co. [324]

Hunsicker, Samuel. b. May 3, 1753; d. Apr. 30, 1819, Lancaster Co. [324]

I.A.B. 1832 [166]

I.B.A. 1751 [42]

I.T. *see* Taney, Jacob [202]

Ilgen, Wilhelm. Pastor, Haines Twp., Centre Co., 1806, 1814 [340, 341]

Irion, Ruth Hershey. Daughter of Hiram F. and Adele Hostetter Hershey. Married Louis A. Irion [33]

J.C. 1780–1800 [169]

J.C. [or J.L.] 1800–1840 [131]

J.M. 1809 [227]

J.S.A. 1841 [250]

Jackson, Andrew. b. 1767, Waxhaw, S.C.; d. 1845. Known as "Hero of New Orleans" because of his leadership defending that city from British soldiers, Dec. 1814. Elected 7th president of the U.S., 1828, re-elected, 1832 [35, 205, 211]

Jacob, Albert B. 1880 [9]

Jäger, Josua. Pastor, Allentown, Lehigh Co., 1855 [342]

Jamison, Anna. First cousin of Clara Jamison [233]

Jamison, Clara. b. c. 1881, d. 1973. Doylestown, Pa. Daughter Dorothy Jamison Ley Ellis (Mrs. Thomas E. Ellis, of Sarasota, Fla., in 1973). Remmys [Remmey] were family friends: John A. Remmey's estate sale, Doylestown, 1864, included stoneware pots and birds [233]

Jones. Montgomery Co., 1815 [29]

Jones, Keim & Co. Windsor Furnace, Berks Co. [108]

Jung [Jungin], Mathalena. bap. Oct. 24, 1773, by Rev. Daniel Schumacher, Zion's Church. Daughter of Lorentz and Margretha Jung (1751–1842). Married David Zerby, June 1, 1797, New Goschenhoppen, Pennsburg, Upper Hanover Twp., Montgomery Co. [176]

Jutzae, Jacob. d. Apr. 9, 1799, Bern Twp., Berks Co. Single freeman, Bern Twp., 1779. Married Elizabeth. Children: Elizabeth (married Joseph Joder), Christian, John, Catharine, Molly, Peter, and Michael, 1799 [19]

Kauffman, Andreas. Manor or Manheim Twp., Lancaster Co. [313, 344]

Kauffman, Elizabeth. 1840. Family name in Manor and Mount Joy twps., Lancaster Co. [274]

Kauffman, H. 1800–1850 [61]

Keller, B[enjamin]. Lutheran pastor. Adams Co., 1850 [341]

Keller, Samuel. b. 1800, d. 1851. Haycock Twp., Bucks Co. Son of Christopher Keller (d. 1820). Active potter, 1814–32. Son Samuel (b. 1836) apprenticed to Augustus Smith (b. 1795, Germany), also active Haycock Twp. [177]

Ketterer, J. Berks Co. Tinsmith active 1800–1828. Coffeepot, no. 52, p. 152, may be c. 1810 instead of c. 1840 [152]

Ketterer, John. Rockland Twp., Berks Co. Tinsmith [121]

Kichline [Kaechline, Kechline], John. Probably John Kichline, Jr., son of John Kichline, potter, 334 N. Front St., Phila., 1817. Family

moved to Rockhill Twp., Bucks Co., on 47 acres, 1818. Taxed as potters, Richland Twp., but lived across the county line road, like neighboring Andrew Headman. Homestead of 47 acres had one-story hewn log house, 24 x 18', with barn, 30 x 20', and a smith shop, 12 x 10', built of logs. Associated with the Headman potters, Phila. John, Jr., married Magdalene Rinke, Oct. 28, 1819, Tohickon Reformed Church. Father and son still in Richland Twp., 1822. Father to Phila., 1825, but returned to Richland Twp. homestead, 1834, where he is listed as "gentleman." John, Jr., may have worked at the Headman pottery with Henry Roudebush, 1816, when they inscribed two plates for Sally Steiner, daughter of George Steiner (weaver) neighbors in Richland Twp. [195]

Kiess, Dorothea Allmer. Blooming Grove, Lycoming Co., 1814. Mother of Johannes Kiess (b. 1814) [338]

Kiess, George. Blooming Grove, Lycoming Co., 1814. Father of Johannes Kiess (b. 1814) [338]

Kiess, Johannes. b. Dec. 3, 1814, Blooming Grove, Lycoming Co. Son of George and Dorothea Kiess. Married Maria Marquand, Dec. 27, 1847 [294, 338]

Kiplinger, Henry. Tulpehocken Twp., Berks Co. [112]

Klewelt, Frantz. Plainfield Twp., Northampton Co., 1783. Husband of Salome Klewelt [339]

Klewelt, Salome. Plainfield Twp., Northampton Co., 1783. Wife of Frantz Klewelt [339]

Kline, Michael. Probably Lancaster Co. [116]

Kline, Phillip. d. 1834. Potter active Nockamixon Twp., Bucks Co., by 1806. Worked with John Klein, potter, through 1810 [177]

Klinker, Christian. Active 1773–98. Son of John (d. 1798) and Mary Klinker, Nockamixon Twp., Bucks Co. Married Catherine, after 1788. Sister Madelena married Michael Strebey, "earthen potter," later clockmaker. His sister Catherine married Jacob Stout, Nockamixon Twp. Served as sponsor at Strebey baptisms, Nockamixon Reformed Church, 1793, 1796. Inherited part of family homestead, 1789. Purchased land from John Youngman (blacksmith), 1791. Sold 11 acres to Nicholas Buck (wheelwright), 1793. "Earthen potter" listed on Durham Road, Bucksville. Owned two-story frame house, 28 x 22', one log barn, 50 x 26', Tinicum Twp., Bucks Co., 1798 [177]

Klopp, Ellen. Heidelberg Twp., Berks Co., 1837 [340]

Knisen [Kniss], Amtha [Anna Margaretha]. Probably Northumberland Co. [132]

Kob, Elisabeth. [341]

Koch, Cattrina. Upper Saxon Twp., Northampton Co., 1795 [339]

Koellner [Kollner], Augustus Theodore Frederich Adam. b. 1813, Württemberg, Germany; d. 1906. Studied painting and lithography, Frankfurt. Employed by Carl Ebner (printer), Stuttgart, 1828. Did lithography for Philip Haas, Washington, D.C., 1839. To Phila., by 1840. Worked for P.S. Duval. Married Mary Margaretha Sheck, 1843, German Lutheran Church, Phila. Kollner and Company, 239 Arch St., Phila., 1848. Active through 1870s [336, 348, 349]

Köhler. Cumberland Co., 1818. Reverend [341]

Kolb, Catharina. Probably daughter of John (d. 1804) or Joseph (d. 1815) Kolb, New Hanover Twp., Montgomery Co. [313, 344]

Koradi, [Rudolph]. Publisher, Phila., 1869. In partnership with Christian Schäfer. Consul for Switzerland, 1903, 1907. Residence 1528 Master St., Phila. [331]

Kostenbader, Elisabeth. b. Oct. 9, 1783, Plainfield Twp., Northampton Co. Daughter of Henrich and Maria Christina Kostenbader [298, 339]

Kostenbader, Henrich. Plainfield Twp., Northampton Co., 1783. Father of Elizabeth Kostenbader (b. 1783) [339]

Kostenbader, Maria Christina Mäyer. Plainfield Twp., Northampton Co., 1783. Mother of Elizabeth Kostenbader (b. 1783) [339]

Krebs, Friedrich. d. 1815. Married Anna Maria. Sons Joshua, Frederich Carl (b.c. 1799). Owned property between Harrisburg and Hummelstown, 1796. Schoolmaster, Swatara Twp., 1805. Ordered almost 2,000 fraktur blanks from *Reading Adler* office, 1804. Inventory listed, in part, "a lot papers picterd and papers for birth Dayes." Estate owed John Ritter & Co., $2.67 for printing 500 taufscheins [298, 299, 339]

Kresman, Margret. 1827 [273]

Kriebel, Elisabeth. Upper Hanover Twp., Montgomery Co., 1830. Schwenkfelder [281]

Kriebel, Maria. Montgomery Co., 1843 [318]

Kriebel. Rosina. b. Sept. 24, 1773. Upper Hanover Twp., Montgomery Co. Daughter of Andrew and Susannah Yeakel Kriebel. Married Daniel Diehl, 1818. No issue [318]

Kulp. *see* Maria Helbard (Helbert) [193]

Kuntz, Jacob. b. Sept. 6, 1780, Lehigh Twp., Lehigh Co.; d. Aug. 6, 1876, Phila. Married Barbara (1786–1862), daughter of Jacob and Mary Kohler Newhard, Allentown, 1812. In Kensington, Phila., 1810. Gunsmith; well known for sporting guns and dueling pistols; did fine engraving. Won medal at Franklin Institute, 1833. Rifle no. 8, p. 159, dates to 1820–40, instead of c. 1780 [159, 347]

Kurtz, Nicolaus. Lutheran pastor. Conducted services at Tulpehocken, Berks Co. Christ Church, 1747–70. Second Lutheran Church, Germantown, 1762–64. Son John Daniel Kurtz (1764–1856), also a minister [338]

Kurtz, Wilhelm. b. 1732, d. 1799. Brother of Pastor Nicolaus Kurtz. Assistant to his brother at Tulpehocken, 1759–62. Served Pa. parishes for 40 years [339]

Kutz, Maria [Susanna Scharadin]. b. 1769, d. 1847. Daughter of Jacob and Margaretha Haak Scharadin, from Raumeisen. Married Nicholas Kutz III (b. Feb. 14, 1764; d. 1831). Son Samuel (b. 1800) married Catherine Sell (b. 1797). Samuel inherited his father's homestead and 150 acres, Maxatawny Twp., Berks Co. [21]

L.C. 1800–1850 [61]

L. K. Probably Bucks Co., 1804. The bulb planter, no. 17, p. 210, one of a pair, inscribed for owner, possibly Leonard Keizor, who owned property, 1785, adjoining Wrightstown Pottery run by Jonathan and William Smith [210]

L. M. M. Initialed hand towel, no. 3, p. 271, said to have been made by Ziegler family, Skippack, Montgomery Co. [271]

L.S. 1827 [135]

Lacy [Lacey, Le Cene, Leisse], John. b. c. 1735, Rockhill Twp., Bucks Co.; d. 1811, Hilltown Twp., Bucks Co. Son of John (d. 1738) and Anna Miller Le Cene (b. 1708), who arrived Phila., Sept. 23, 1732, with brother-in-law Michel Miller and brother Paul Le Cene. John Le Cene purchased 200 acres, Rockhill Twp., on Perkiomen Creek, 1735. John Lacey apprenticed with Jacob Stout, potter, who married his widowed mother, 1739. The inscription on the dish no. 134, p.210, the text of a popular reward of merit, written in an English hand, is by Lacey. Jacob Stout bought out John's and his brother Henry's (d. 1815) interest in the Rockhill homestead, 1759. Stout transferred to John Lacey 120 acres, Hilltown Twp., which he had purchased, 1757 [201]

Laederman, Elisabeth. Deep Run school, Hilltown, Bucks Co., May 1823 [323]

Landes, Elisabeth. Probably Lancaster Co., 1834 [311, 343]

Landes, John. b. Feb. 25, 1758; d. Mar. 13, 1821. Weaver, Upper Salford Twp., Montgomery Co. Married Elizabeth Weinberger, daughter of weaver Balthazer Weinberger (d. 1784), Lower Milford Twp., Bucks Co. Purchased 97 acres with buildings (£1,100) from Henry (tailor) and Catherine Roudebush, Providence Twp., Mar. 30, 1803. Called "weaver" of Upper Salford Twp. Son Samuel apprenticed to Balthazer Weinberger, Jr. Son Henry inherited homestead in Milford Twp., Bucks Co., and his son John Landes was a coverlet weaver, 1840 [323]

Landes, Magdalena. Bedminster Twp., Bucks Co., 1792 [319]

Landis, Barbara. Montgomery Co., 1826. Mother of Susana Landis [280]

Landis, John. b. Oct. 15, 1805; d. after 1857. Son of Henry (d. 1824), Hummelstown, Dauphin Co. Lutheran. Studied printing, Harrisburg; active Reading and as itinerant. Studied painting, c. 1830. Traveled in America, England, 1833, and Jerusalem, Palestine, 1845. Exhibited large painting (14 x 22') *Battle of New Orleans* in the Capitol rotunda, Washington, D.C., and in Harrisburg. Did some lithography, wrote poetry, pamphlets. In Lancaster poorhouse, 1857 [337]

Landis, John. d. Aug. 11, 1826, Montgomery Co. Father of Susana Landis [280]

Landis, Susana. Montgomery Co., 1826. Daughter of John (d. 1826) and Barbara Landis. Family name in Montgomery, Lancaster, and Berks counties [280]

Lang, Barbara. Possibly second daughter of Abraham (1743–c. 1800) and Maria Lang, Manheim Twp., Lancaster Co. Several Lang families in Manheim Twp. [20]

Langenecker, Barbara. Donegal Twp., Lancaster Co., 1790 [322]

Lapp, Henry L. b. Aug. 18, 1862, Mascot, Lancaster Co.; d. July 5, 1904, Lancaster Co. Son of Michael K. (1830–1884) and Rebecca Lantz Lapp. Amish. Carpenter and paint dealer, 1890. Cabinetmaker at Bird-in-Hand, Lancaster Co., 1898 [323]

Laux, Cathrina. Hilltown Twp., Bucks Co., 1813 [321]

Leabelsperger, Machtdalena [Magdalena]. b. Nov. 25, 1772; d. Apr. 14, 1844. Grandfather John Georg Leibersperger, from Ilshofen, Württemberg, Germany, came to Pa., 1732. Member, Oley Hill Church, Bechtelsville, Pike Twp., Berks Co.; resided Weisenburg Twp., Northampton (Lehigh) Co.; naturalized, Phila., Sept. 24, 1765. His third child Georg Adam Leibersperger (1726–1799) married Catharina Barbara Kuhntz (1730–1809), Sept. 26, 1749. Farmer, Weisenberg Twp., until after Revolutionary War, when he moved to Maxatawny Twp., Berks Co. Had 11 children. Magdalena was the youngest. Married John Kemmerer (1765–1851), farmer, and lived in Salisbury Twp., near Emmaus. They too had 11 children. Magdalena and husband buried in West Salisbury Church cemetery [347]

Lehman, Elizabeth. Probably Germantown, 1790 [277]

Lehn, Joseph Long. b. Jan. 6, 1798; d. Sept. 16, 1892. Farmer-woodworker, Hammer Creek Valley, Elizabethtown Twp., Lancaster Co., active 1850–90s. Decorated chairs, turned small wood objects. Later examples decorated with decalcomania instead of hand painting [16, 17, 67]

Leidy, John I. b. Mar. 9, 1764; d. Sept. 26, 1846, Durham Twp., Bucks Co. Son of Jacob (b. July 25, 1719, Württemberg, Germany; d. Aug. 18, 1794), tanner, and Barbara Neiss Leidy (b. 1725; d. May 24, 1798). Jacob to Pa. on the *Samuel*, Aug. 17, 1733. Both Leidy and Neis families prominent landowners and trustees of Indian Creek Church, Franconia Twp., Montgomery Co. Jacob divided homestead, with 2 mills, tannery, smithy, and pottery, between sons Jacob and John. John's brother Jacob (1759–1834), tanner, married Veronica Scholl Leidy; their son was John Leidy II, potter (*see* p. 182), and their daughter Elizabeth married Philip Neis, tavernkeeper, and brother of John Neis, potter (*see* pp. 187–91). John married Elizabeth Lerch (b. Aug. 2, 1768; d. Oct. 24, 1833), daughter of Anthony, Jr., and Anna Margaretta Lerch, Hilltown Twp., Bucks Co.; they had 1 son, 2 daughters. Received 10 acres in Hilltown, 1783, from his father and mother "with love" and for £50, which he sold to Henry Shellenberger, 1796, for £200. Took John Hinckle as apprentice for 11 years, 1789, and "to learn him to Read and write a Legable hand when free to give him a good freedom dues besides his other apparrel." Purchased 9½ acres from Christian Wireman, Franconia Twp., 1792. Owned two-story house, 26 x 28', and 111 acres, Lower Saucon Twp., Northampton Co. Journeyman potter John Neiman [Neaman] (d. 1831) worked with him until c. 1798, after which Neaman worked for John Neis, Nockamixon Twp., Bucks Co. To Durham Twp., c. 1832. At his death, owned 62 shares Easton Bank stock, 38 shares Rieglesville Delaware Bridge stock, and land in Ohio [178–81]

Leidy, John II. b. Mar. 9, 1780; d. Sept. 22, 1838, Hilltown Twp., Bucks Co. Nephew of John Leidy I. Son of Jacob (1759–1834), tanner, and Veronica Scholl Leidy (1755–1826), Franconia and Hilltown twps. Married Mary Groff (b. Aug. 27, 1785; d. July 6, 1814), Mar. 3, 1803, Indian Creek Reformed Church, daughter of Jacob (1751–1824), fuller and stonemiller, Upper Salford Twp., and Elizabeth Heebner Groff (b. Apr. 11, 1753; d. 1829), daughter of Melchior and Anna Heebner. Married second wife Elizabeth Singmaster (b. Apr. 23, 1783; d. July 29, 1849), before 1816. Purchased from Isaac Morris a house and 6 acres, Hilltown. Received 75 acres from father and mother for £1,700. Purchased from Christian Weber a house and 37 acres, Whitpain Twp., 1814, which he sold to former brother-in-law Henry Groff (fuller) for £2,100, in 1816. Sister Catherine (b. June 24, 1784) married Jacob Scholl, potter, Apr. 27, 1806. He began potting with his uncle John Leidy I on the Franconia Twp. property; managed that pottery by 1801; employed a neighbor Joseph Cope, by 1804. Burning 11 kilns, 1815. Had 6 kilns active, 1 journeyman, 2 potting wheels, 1 clay and 1 glazing mill in operation, 1820. Lived in Hilltown Twp. and potted in Franconia Twp. At his death, owned several tracts of land in Bucks and Montgomery counties [182]

Leinbach. Pastor, Bethel Twp., Lebanon Co., 1842 [341]

Leisenring, [Edward D.]. b. Sept. 13, 1816; d. Feb. 20, 1882. Son of John Conrad (1759–1824) and Catharine Grob Leisenring (1759–1828). Leisenring family from Silesia. Married Matilda Blumer (1808–1854), 1838, daughter of Jacob (1774–1830), clockmaker, and Catharine Rhoads Blumer, sister of his partner Alexander Blumer. Newspaper publisher, Allentown, for 30 years [308, 342]

Leman, John. b. c. 1800, Switzerland. Itinerant potter trained at Langnau, Switzerland. Worked with Friedrich Hildebrand (1798–1852) near Tylersport, Montgomery Co. [182]

Lemien, Anna. Possibly Northampton Co., 1818 [273]

Lenn, J. H. Papermaker [323]

Lescherin [Lesher], Anna Maria. Family name in Lancaster and Berks counties, 1787 [21]

Levan, Abraham, Jr. Papermaker, Allen Twp., Northampton Co., by 1798, to 1820 [323]

Levis, William. d. 1818. Son of Samuel Levis (d. 1793). Papermaker, Darby Creek, Upper Darby Twp., Delaware Co. Brother Samuel (d. 1813) had a son William, also papermaker [323]

Licht, Christina (née) Licht. Bethel Twp., Lebanon Co., 1815. Wife of Jacob Licht [341]

Licht, Jacob. Bethel Twp., Lebanon Co., 1815. Father of Maria Licht [341]

Licht, Maria. b. July 19, 1815, Bethel Twp., Lebanon Co. Daughter of Jacob and Christina (née Licht) Licht. Married William Turbin, Oct. 24, 1841 [304, 341]

Lieder, Daniel. Heidelberg Twp., Berks Co., 1814. Father of Julianna (b. 1814) [340]

Lieder, Elisabeth Schäfer. Heidelberg Twp., Berks Co., 1814. Mother of Julianna (b. 1814) [340]

Lieder, Julianna. b. Nov. 29, 1814, Heidelberg Twp., Berks Co. Daughter of Daniel and Elisabeth Lieder [302, 340]

Long, Jacob [John]. b. c. 1787. Locksmith, Rapho Twp., Lancaster Co. Worked also in Manheim Twp., Lancaster Co. Produced several distinctive lamps for young women, Rapho Twp., 1840s [119]

Loo[?], Ann Barbara [325]

Losz, Elizabeth. b. Jan. 10, 1813, Carlisle, Cumberland Co. [340]

Lup. Probably Pastor Ludwig Lupp. b. 1733, Marienburg, Prussia; d. 1798, Lebanon, Lebanon Co. Reformed church minister and schoolmaster, Rapho and Mount Joy twps., Lancaster Co., c. 1785–98 [339]

Lynch, Maria. 1856 [137]

M. B. G. [160]

M. D. D. [262]

M.H. c. 1800 [64]

M.H. 1800–1880 [286]

M. L. 1780–1820 [271]

M. L. 1792 [130]

M. S. [161]

Maize, William. b. Union Co. Grandson of Adam Maize, potter. Son of John Maize, potter. Potter, active Millheim Pottery, Centre Co., with his father. Continued pottery with H. H. Weiser after his father's death [183]

Mäntel [Maentel], Jacob. b. 1763, Kassel, Germany. Married Catherine Gutt (from Alsace). Active 1800–1843: in Baltimore, c. 1807; in York Co., 1828; in New Harmony, Ind., by 1841 [294, 338]

Mardes, Barbara. Possibly Franconia or Upper Hanover Twp., Montgomery Co., 1773 [213]

Marquand, Maria. Married Johannes Keiss, Dec. 27, 1847 [338]

Martin, Samuel. Earl Twp., Lancaster Co., 1797, 1830 [320, 326]

Maser, Johan. Northumberland Co., 1812. Father of Johan Jacob Maser (b. Oct. 29, 1812) [340]

Maser, Johan Jacob. b. Oct. 29, 1812, Northumberland Co.; d. May 29, 1895. Son of Johan and Margretha Lick Maser. Family from Württemberg, Germany. First settled Alsace Twp., Berks Co. Resided on father's farm, 128 acres on south side of Line Mountain. Farmer, carpenter, mechanic, township supervisor, deacon and elder of the Reformed church, conducted funeral services. Married Catharine Christ (1816–1890), daughter of Jonathan and Maria Hepler Christ. Had 14 children. Son Jacob (1838–1909), stonemason [35, 301, 340]

Maser, Margretha Lick. Northumberland Co., 1812. Wife of Johan Maser [340]

Mast, Elisabetha. Lancaster Co., 1802. Wife of Johannes Mast [338]

Mast, Johannes. Lancaster Co., 1802. May have resided Berks Co., 1800–1810 [338]

Maurer, Abraham. b. Jan. 21, 1784. Son of John and Elisabetha Kettmann Maurer [316, 342, 345]

Maurer, Anna. b. Dec. 17, 1795 [342,344]

Maurer, Christian. b. Apr. 16, 1789 [342]

Maurer, Daniel. b. Feb. 12, 1786. Apprenticed to house carpenter Emanuel Dwyer, Manheim, Lancaster Co. for 3 years, 1803. Indenture (p. 310, no. 1) incorrectly listed as David instead of Daniel Maurer [310, 314, 322, 342, 344]

Maurer, David. *see* Maurer, Daniel

Maurer, Elisabetha. b. July 29, 1791 [342]

Maurer, Elisabetha Kettmann. b. 1760. Married Johannes Maurer, 1781. Hempfield Twp., Lancaster Co., 1795 [342]

Maurer, Johannes [John]. b. May 14, 1751, Great Swamp, Lower Milford Twp., Bucks Co. Married Elisabetha Kettmann, Great Swamp Reformed Church, Lower Milford Twp., 1791. Had 9 children. Hempfield Twp., Lancaster Co., 1795 [310, 342]

Maurer, Johannes [John]. b. Oct. 12, 1780. Son of Johannes and Elisabetha Kettmann Maurer. Hempfield Twp., Lancaster Co., 1795 [342]

Maurer, Maria. b. Sept. 3, 1782 [342]

Maurer, Sem. b. Feb. 9, 1788; d. Apr. 8, 1788 [342]

Medinger, Jacob. b. 1856, d. 1920. Son of William (1826–1902) of Württemberg, Germany, and Wilhelmina M. Winner Medinger (d. 1916). William traveled in Alsace and Poland before migrating to Pa., July 1854. Settled in Limerick area, Montgomery Co. Samuel Nieffer, potter, hired him as a journeyman potter, 1855, and he worked there for 17 years. Purchased 35 acres, built house and kiln. William and 3 sons, Jacob, Albert, and Wilson, were potters together until 1896. Jacob running pottery alone by 1900. Members, Keeler's Lutheran Church, Obelisk. Pottery had 1 wheel; fired kiln 3 or 4 times per year; employed men and boys to dig clay, used a horse to power the clay mill. Used gasoline engine for grinding clay and pressing apples, 1905. Billhead read "all kinds of earthenware, cider made in season." Annual production between 8,000 and 12,000 pieces of pottery, including plain molded plates, wheel-thrown dishes, with slip, sgraffito, and colored oxides in clear lead glazes. William McAllister (woodcarver) probably did most of the sgraffito work, using stencils of designs from earlier potters such as Hubener, Troxel, and Kline [183]

Meister, Magdalena. Lehigh Twp., Northampton Co. [335]

Mensch, Nicklaus. Pastor, Nockamixon Twp., Bucks Co., 1816. Active Springfield Twp., Bucks Co. Lutheran and Reformed congregations, 1763. Son Christian was a potter [341]

Messner, Samuel. d. 1889. Brecknock Twp., Lancaster Co. [16]

Meyer, Anna. 1848 [275]

Meyer, Hanna. 1846. Probably daughter of Herman Meyer, Milford Twp., Bucks Co. [321]

Meyer, Samuel. Family name in Berks, Montgomery, Lancaster counties [315, 344]

Miler, Cadarina. 1834 [274]

Miller. Probably Peter Miller, schoolmaster and minister, Lehigh Co., 1760–c. 1800; Schuylkill Co., 1806 [340]

Mills, William. d. 1870, Richland Twp., Bucks Co. Son of Henry Mills (d. 1815), Haycock Twp., Bucks Co. Potter. At the time of his death he was a hatter. Brother of Solomon, also a potter. Both may have apprenticed at Mumbouer or Michael Stoneback pottery, c.

1799–1801. Solomon and William rented buildings (1 potter shop, 24 x 18′, 1 log barn, 35 x 22′, 1 log stable, 25 x 22′) from Michael Stoneback, Haycock Twp., 1798 [184]

Milly, J[ohn]. Washington Twp., Franklin Co., 1883. Grandfather of Luke Deets [295, 338]

Mollinger, Friedrich. Clockmaker from Mannheim, Germany. c. 1740 [42]

Monday [Mondau], John [E.]. b. 1809; d. Jan. 1862, Haycock Twp., Bucks Co. Married Phebe Mumbouer (b. 1817), daughter of Conrad and Philippina Mumbouer, Haycock Twp., Bucks Co., c. 1834. Taxed as potter with his father-in-law, Haycock Twp., 1831–39. Listed as Major John Mondau, 1840. Taxed for silver lever watch but no acreage, 1841, and for his silver watch and a gig, 1842. Conrad Mumbouer transferred 211 acres and pottery, Kimbel's Creek at the foot of Haycock Mountain, to Mondau, 1845. Mondau sold adjoining 122 acres, which he had purchased in 1849 from John M. Lands, to heirs of Jacob Detesman for $2,432, in 1850. School director, Haycock Twp., 1854. Mathias Myer, German-born potter, lived with and worked for him, 1850. Charles Moritz, potter (b. Württemberg, Germany), living with and working for him, 1860. Sons Edmund C. (b. 1835) and David (1846–1890) were potters. David served in the Civil War; married Emma Rothrock, 1870, and worked in Kintnersville, Bucks Co. Inventory included horses, heiffers, "appulets and sword," tiles, wagons, cart, and pleasure carriage, bucky sled, log sled and sleigh, 3 old stoves, earthenware, several book accounts due for pottery ware. Died intestate with debts equaling assets. Pottery purchased by Simon Singer for $2,500 [184]

Moser, Gotleib. 1830–40 [191]

Moser, [John B.]. b. June, 1800, Germany; d. Oct. 18, 1874, Allentown. Printer, Carlisle, Pa., 1823–27. To Harrisburg, 1827, in partnership with Gustav S. Peters, to Mar. 19, 1828. To Allentown, where he was an apothecary [306, 307, 341]

Mount Pleasant Artist. Active 1813–35, Warwick Twp., Lancaster Co. Probably first schoolteacher, Evangelical Lutheran Church, Brickerville, Warwick Twp., where William Baetis was minister, 1810–36. Church built new schoolhouse, 1815. Schoolteacher seems to have made bookplates, birth and baptismal certificates for local families. Also active Hellman Twp., York Co., c. 1836 [308]

Mountz, Aaron. b. 1873, d. 1949. Son of William Mountz (d. 1891). Lived on family farm on Conodoguinet Creek, near Carlisle, Cumberland Co. Worked on local bridge constructions, drilled wells. Did woodcarving with Wilhelm Schimmel, to 1890. Farmed, 1929–49 [84]

Muller, George. d. c. 1784. Prosperous miller, Millbach, Lebanon Co., 1752. Built Millbach House, 1750–52. Married Maria Caterina. Left Lebanon Co., 1754, bought farm and mill, N.C. House inherited by son Michael (d. 1814) and wife M. Elizabeth Muller, 1784. House with attached mill privately owned [6]

Muller, M. Elizabeth. Wife of Michael Muller (d. 1814), 1784 [6]

Muller, Maria Caterina. Wife of George Muller, 1752 [6]

Muller, Michael. d. 1814. Son of George and Maria Caterina Muller [6]

Mullin, John. 1856. Possibly of Irish extraction. Family name in Kensington, Phila. Co., Danville, Montour Co., and Phoenixville, Chester Co., c. 1850 [137]

Mumbouer [Mombauer, Mombower, Mumbauer, Mumbower], Conrad. b. June 22, 1761; d. Aug. 2, 1845. Grandson of John Nicholas (b. 1689) and Margaret Mombauer, from Irtzweiler, who arrived on the *Samuel* from Rotterdam, 1739. Son of John, Jr., known as Nicholas (1721–1815) and Magdalene Mombauer (1724–1807). Nicholas in Capt. Frederich Hubner's Company of Associators, Lower Milford Twp., 1775. Brother of John Philip Mumbouer (1749–1834). Married Philippina (Phebe), before 1789;

had 3 daughters and 1 son Nicholas (1789–1828), who predeceased him. Listed in Haycock Twp. tax records with no land, 1794. Worked with Michael and Henry Stoneback, who rented pottery shop, 24 x 18', 1 log barn, 35 x 22', and 1 log stable, 25 x 22', from Joseph Mill. Henry Stoneback died 1793 and Conrad Mombauer individually listed for first time in tax list at Stoneback residence. Owned 99 acres, 2 horses, and 2 cows, 1796. Assessed for 1 old log house, 25 x 10', 1 log barn, 28 x 18', 1 potter shop, 30 x 15', in 1798, which adjoined property where other Stonebacks and Joseph and William Mills were potting. As Capt. Conrad Mombauer, Fourth Regiment, Bucks Co., was exempt from Battalion Day, Mar. 27, 1801. Owned 115 acres, 1811; 105 acres and a dog, 1817. Purchased for $180 a house and 2 tracts of land, Springfield Twp., 1833, from John L. Green (chairmaker), but still worked in Haycock Twp. Transferred pottery and 112 acres "together with the privilege of taking and converting to his [John Mondau's] use all the clay in and upon the lot which David Mumbauer by Dead poll August 21, 1828 did grant and confirm unto Conrad Mombauer . . . " to his son-in-law John Mondau, 1845. Daughter married Joseph Strawn (Strahen). Son Nicholas taxed as a potter, 1812. Conrad Mumbauer's estate worth $3,913. Inventory taken by Peter L. Nicholas, brother of neighboring potters Jacob and Christian Nicholas, included 30-hour clock and case ($8), corner "covert" and contents ($4), 1 stove and pipe ($5) [184–86]

Mumbouer [Mombauer, Mombower, Mumbower], Nicholas. b. 1789, d. 1828. Son of Conrad (1761–1845) and Phebe Mombauer. Worked as a potter with his father. Married Rachel. Farmer and potter. Owned 20 acres, Haycock Twp., 1812; 32 acres and a dog, 1817; 33 acres, 1819; 32 acres with a total property value of $1,540 at his death. Inventory included horses, cows, sow and pigs, buckwheat in the ground, wagons, a sleigh, "2 potter's turning mechene $4.00," glazing mill ($3), stove and pipe in shop ($4), potters' tools in shop (12ᶜ), earthenware in shop ($1.25), lot of ware in kiln ($1.50), lot of barrels, etc. Dishes nos. 61, 62, p. 183, now attributed to Nicholas and/or Philip Mumbouer [183 as PNM]

Mumbouer [Mombower, Mumbauer, Mumbower], Philip. b. c. 1750; d. Jan. 1834, Milford Twp. Son of John, Jr., known as Nicholas (1721–1815) and Magdalene Mombauer (1724–1807). Brother of Conrad, potter. Married 1) Barbara Spinner (sister of David Spinner, potter), Great Swamp Reformed Church, Bucks Co., Feb. 13, 1776. Married 2) Magdalene Leidy (b. Dec. 17, 1763), before 1781. Daughter Magdalene (bap. July 22, 1781). *see* Mumbouer, Nicholas [183 as PNM]

Musser, Maria. Probably Lancaster Co., 1838 [282]

Musser, Nancy. Family name in Rapho Twp., Lancaster Co. [119]

N.J., Phila., 1764–76 [158]

N.S. Probably maker or painter of chest made for Sarah Schupp. Usually numbered his chests [24]

N.S., Katarina. Probably Katarina Nans [274]

Neis, Johannes. b. Mar. 26, 1754; d. Mar. 3, 1826. Son of John (b. 1727; d. before July 11, 1756) and Catherine Hahn Neis (d. 1815) of Franconia Twp., near Indian Creek Church. John purchased land, New Hanover Twp., 1750, 1755. His widow Catherine married George Hartzell, Rockhill Twp., c. 1759, and daughter Catherine married George Hubener, potter. Johannes was brother of Philip (b. 1751), who married Elizabeth Leidy, sister of John Leidy I. Married Catharina Hudt (d. Mar. 1782), daughter of John Hudt, Oct. 22, 1776. Then married Margaret Hubener (b. July 25, 1759; d. Sept. 16, 1823), Goschenhoppen Reformed Church, Nov. 11, 1782. Purchased 150 acres "situate on rich valley creek in Upper Salford Township" from George and Catherine Hartzell (his mother), 1779, and worked as a potter-farmer with Jacob Fillman, until 1791. Sold property to Christian May for £625, and purchased 170 acres and house in Marlborough Twp. Also owned 45 acres of original land grant of his great-grandfather Hans de Neus (d. 1736), Northern Liberties, which he sold to Peter Shoemaker (blacksmith), Abington, 1791. Transferred Marlborough Twp. ground to son-in-law John Miller (cordwainer), June 1811, and to John Heltebeitle, Apr. 8, 1813. Served in the Fourth Company,

FifthBattalion, Phila. County Military Company, 1781, with brothers Abraham (1756–1818) and Philip (1751–1799). He retired from potting in 1791, and from farming c. 1818. Became storekeeper, Marlborough Twp., 1819 [186]

Neis, John. b. 1785, d. 1867. Son of Henry (d. 1819), cordwainer, and Maria Elizabeth Neis, Salford Twp., who owned land, houses, and outbuildings, Rockhill Twp., Bucks Co. Married Barbara Fillman (1784–1842), c. 1808. Probably apprenticed with David Spinner, Milford Twp., and set up as a potter, Upper Salford Twp., on uncle Abraham Neis's 144 acres adjoining the property of another uncle (Johannes Neis), which was sold 1791. Bought and sold small unimproved lots in Marlborough and Bedminister twps., 1805–8. Bought 6 acres, Upper Salford Twp. and owned house, 1812. Administrator of his father's estate sale, 1819–22. Taxed as a potter until 1816; census of 1859 still lists his occupation as potter. Frederick Hildebrand may have been managing pottery, by 1819. His son John Nace, Jr., and probably John Leman, worked at pottery. Listed as "gentleman" with no acres, 1851 [187–91, 348]

Neumeyer, Catharina. Macungie Twp., Lehigh Co., 1827 [341]

Neumeyer, Jacob. Macungie Twp., Lehigh Co., 1827 [341]

Nice [Neis], Abraham. d. after 1856. Son of John and Barbara Fillman Neis, Upper Salford Twp., Montgomery Co. Potter, Upper Salford Twp., Montgomery Co., active 1834–38, with his father and brother. Married Sarah Berndt (b. Sept. 22, 1812; d. Jan. 6, 1853). Members, Indianfield Lutheran Church, Franconia Twp. [191]

Nice, John. d. Sept. 14, 1906. Son of John and Barbara Fillman Neis. Pottery, Upper Salford Twp., Montgomery Co. Owned 64 acres, 2 horses, 3 cows. Pottery attributed to John Nice was produced at the Neis-Nice pottery until the end of the 19th century by owners and journeymen [191–93]

Nissley, Anna. Mother of Fanny Nissley, Rapho Twp., Lancaster Co. Wife of Martin Nissley, by 1821 [283]

Nissley, Fanny. b. Dec. 3, 1821; d. Nov. 11, 1888. Also known as Anna. Daughter of Martin and Anna Nissley, Rapho Twp., Lancaster Co. [283]

Nissley, Martin. Mount Joy, near Donegal Twp., Lancaster Co., Oct. 15, 1771. Husband of Anna Nissley. Father of Fanny Nissley, Rapho Twp., Lancaster Co. [283]

Oberbeck, Christina Klein. Nockamixon Twp., Bucks Co., 1816. Wife of Conrad Oberbeck [341]

Oberbeck, Conrad. Nockamixon Twp., Bucks Co., 1816. Husband of Christina Oberbeck. Father of Maria Magdalena (b. Mar. 1816) [341]

Oberbeck, Maria Magdalena. b. Mar. 6, 1816; bap. June 2, 1816, Nockamixon Twp., Bucks Co. Daughter of Conrad and Christina Klein Oberbeck. Family moved to Va., after 1840 [305, 341]

Oberbeck, Maria Magdalena. Nockamixon Twp., Bucks Co. Widow, 1816 [341]

Ochs, Matthaus. Upper Saucon Twp., Northampton (Lehigh) Co., 1807 [340]

Ochsenreuter, Johan Jacob. Northumberland Co., 1812 [340]

Okle, Lady. Probably Mary Williams Ogle, Bedford Co. Wife of Alexander Ogle (b. Aug. 10, 1766, Frederick Co., Md.; d. Oct. 14, 1832, Somerset Co., Pa.) Son Charles (b. 1798). The subject of a monograph "General Ogle: A Character," by William Elder, in *Periscopics* (New York, 1854), Ogle was a prominent citizen, member of the State House of Representatives (1803, 1804, 1807, 1808, 1811, 1819–23). Mary Ogle was known for her beauty and "christian amiability" [199]

Old, James. Master, Reading Furnace, c. 1772. Active Hopewell Furnace, c. 1788, c. 1793 [107]

Otto, Jacob. Earl Twp., Lancaster Co., 1784 [298, 339]

Otto, Johan Henrich. Active Lancaster Co., 1772. A Johann Henrich Otto was a weaver in Tulpehocken Twp., Berks Co., May 1755. Printed certificates attributed to Otto employ printed textile design as horizontal banding across bottom. Otto may have worked with Frederick Speyer (printer), Berks Co. [296, 316, 338, 345]

P.D.R. Lancaster Co., 1790 [28]

P.N.M. *see* Mumbouer, Philip and Nicholas [183]

Parker and Co. English hardware firm, early 19th century [159]

Pastorius, B. Probably Ann B. Pastorius. Germantown. Great-great-granddaughter of Francis Daniel Pastorius (1651–1719), founder of Germantown, 1683. Daughter of Joseph (1793–1845) and Margaret Brandans Pastorius (d. 1818). Joseph was a lumber and coal merchant at Valley Forge. Ann Pastorius inherited ¼ of her grandfather Daniel's (1749–1831) estate [280]

Paul, Samuel. Potter, active Limerick Twp., Montgomery Co., 1798. Son of Andrew Paul (d. Mar. 1790). Probably working with George Hubener, who owned property, Limerick Twp., 1791, 1792 [193]

Pauly [Pauli]. Probably William (1792–1855) or Charles (1804–1871) Pauli, Reformed ministers [340]

Peale, Titian R. b. 1799, d. 1885. Son of Charles Willson Peale (1741–1827). Married Eliza Laforque, Oct. 10, 1822. Apprenticed near Wilmington to learn cotton spindle-making, until 1814; returned to family home in Germantown. Became interested in natural history by 1816; participated in scientific expeditions sketching and recording specimens. Rifle engraved with his name crucial to outcome of skirmishes with natives on Samoa and the Gilbert Islands, 1838–41, commemorated by Peale when he added engraving to patchbox lid. In his will Peale left his most treasured possessions to his grandson Titian Peale, including "my painting and drawing apparatus and materials, photographic apparatus and materials. My guns, pistols, fishing and sporting apparatus including my rifle with its inscriptions of when and where used and all my books on Natural History" [347]

Peterman, Daniel. b. Dec. 9, 1797; d. Oct. 17, 1871. Son of Daniel and Christina Grubb Peterman. Married Anna Maria Altand, June 22, 1823. Active Shrewsbury Twp., York Co., 1820. Listed in South Co., York, as a laborer with several of his children: William (cooper), Henry and Andrew (shoemakers), and Levi (clerk), 1850 [309, 342]

Peters, Gustav Sigismund. b. 1793, Germany; d. Mar. 22, 1847, Harrisburg, Pa. Printer, Baltimore, Md.; Carlisle, Pa., 1823–27; Harrisburg, 1827–47. Probably introduced color printing to America from Germany [306–8, 317, 318, 341, 342, 346]

Pittnam [Pittman], John. Probably Montgomery Co. Clock repairman, active 1821–26 [44, 46]

Pledt, John. Lutheran minister, active Upper Saucon Twp., Northampton Co., 1807. Present at Brickerville Lutheran Church, Lancaster Co., when cornerstone for new church was laid, Aug. 1806 [340]

Pomp, Thomas. b. Feb. 4, 1773, Skippack Twp., Montgomery Co.; d. 1852. Reformed minister [339]

Popp, Ann Margreta. Heidelberg Twp., Berks Co., 1769 [338]

Portzeline, Benjamin. b. June 7, 1838, Greenwood Twp., Juniata Co. Son of Wilhelm and Gertraut Zeler Portzeline [309, 342]

Portzeline [Portzline], Francis. Emigrated to Pa., 1777. Painted birth and baptismal certificates, Juniata and Union counties, 1838–55 [309, 342]

Portzeline, Gertraut Zeler. Daughter of Benjamin Zeller. Mother of Benjamin Portzeline (b. June 7, 1838). Wife of Wilhelm Portzeline. Perry Twp., Union Co., 1819. Greenwood Twp., Juniata Co., 1838 [342]

Portzeline, Wilhelm. Perry Twp., Union Co., 1819. Greenwood Twp., Juniata Co., 1838. Father of Benjamin Portzeline [342]

Posch, Wiellem. Heidelberg Twp., Berks Co., 1780 [338]

Potts, John. b. 1710, Germantown; d. 1768, Pottstown. Son of Thomas Potts (1680–1752), of Germantown, a Welshman, and Martha Kerlis Potts (d. before 1718). Married Ruth Savage, 1734. Founded Pottstown, 1752. Manager of Warwick and Pottsgrove furnaces, c. 1751 [103, 106]

R.I. Phila., 1764–76 [158]

R.J. Phila., 1764–76 [158]

R.L. 1800–1850 [61]

R.S. 1777 [58]

R.S. 1805 [117, 118]

Raederin, Cadarina. b. 1766. Daughter of Michael (d. 1789) and Catherine Erb Raeder, New Goschenhoppen, Upper Hanover Twp. She or her mother was sponsor at baptism of Catharina Neiss (daughter of Jacob and Maria), 1783 [176]

Rahn, Adam. Papermaker with Conrad Herbst, Maidencreek Twp., Berks Co., 1792–1809 [323]

Rank [Ranck], John. b. 1763, d. 1828. Joiner, active Jonestown, Bethel Twp., Lebanon Co., or his brother John Peter Rank [Ranck] (b. Nov. 3, 1770; d. June 26, 1851). Sons of John Philip, Jr. (d. 1784) and Magdalena Rank (d. 1813), Hanover Twp., Lebanon Co. Chest no. 11, p. 22, now attributed to John or John Peter Rank [Ranck], although chest is unsigned [22]

Rauss, Lucas. b. 1723, Hungary; d. 1788, York, Pa. Active York Co., 1758–88 [338]

Reber, John. b. 1851, d. 1937. Woodcarver in village of Jordan Valley, Lehigh Co., not Tulpehocken Twp., Berks Co., as given in entry. He and his brother Benjamin (both unmarried) did farm work for neighbors [78, 80]

Reed, Mary. Probably Quaker schoolmistress, who held summer sessions to teach English and English-style needlework skills to young women, Lancaster Co., c. 1824 [279]

Rees, Charles. Reverend, Carlisle, Cumberland Co., c. 1824 [341]

Reiche, F[rederick]. Son of Charles Christopher Reiche (b. 1740; d. Dec. 11, 1790), graduate of University of Frankfurt. From Berlin, 1788. Publisher, 1788–90. Frederick worked with his father and made illustrative woodcuts for printers [328]

Reichwein, Cornelius. b. May 26, 1802, Lancaster Co. Son of Jacob and Magdalena Reichwein [297, 338]

Reichwein, Jacob. Lancaster Co., 1802. Listed in 1790 census, Earl Twp., Lancaster Co., with 2 boys under 16 and wife. Not listed in 1800 or 1810 census of Pa. Possibly son of George (d. 1788), Earl Twp., Lancaster Co. [338]

Reichwein, Magdalena. Lancaster Co., 1802. Mother of Cornelius. Wife of Jacob Reichwein [338]

Reiff, C[onrad]. d. 1838. Probably son of Conrad (d. 1785) and Catharina Reiff (d. 1820), Oley Twp., Berks Co. [268]

Reiff, G[eorge]. b. Dec. 23, 1768; d. Nov. 28, 1847. Buried in Lower Skippack Mennonite cemetery. Son of George and Elizabeth Hendricks Reiff. Married Elizabeth Clemens, Feb. 7, 1792. Built large stone house, Skippack Twp., 1799 [14]

Remmy, Henry H[arrison]. b. 1794, New York City; d. Jan. 18, 1878, Phila. Son of John II and Elizabeth Albright Remmy. In Phila. by 1810; established stoneware pottery, Marshall St. near Girard Ave. Married Catherine N.W. Bolgiani (1802–1872), daughter of Francis W. Bolgiani from Baltimore. Managed Baltimore branch of family business, 1818–c. 1835 [231, 232]

Remmy [Remmey], Richard C[linton]. b. Sept. 25, 1835, Phila.; d. 1904, Phila. Son of Henry Harrison (1794–1878) and Catherine N.W. Bolgiani Remmy (1802–1872). Married 1) Agnes Smith (1839–1882), Phila.; 2) Sarah Elizabeth Kaestner (1851–1922). Took over family business manufacturing domestic stoneware, 1859. Company produced industrial wares, fire bricks, connecting pipes, still heads, etc., Cumberland and Commerce sts., Aramingo, Phila., by 1870. Succeeded by son Robert Henry Remmy [232–34]

Rickert, Jacob. Family name in Dauphin, Lancaster and Montgomery counties. Possibly Jacob Rickert, son of Leonard (d. 1811) and Barbara Rickert, Donegal Twp., Lancaster Co. [20]

Rittenhouse, David. b. 1732, Phila. Co.; d. June 26, 1796, Phila. Son of Matthias Rittenhouse. Family moved to Norristown, where David made clocks, 1756–70. Married Eleanor Coulston, 1766. To Seventh and Mulberry sts., Phila., 1770. Clock and scientific-instrument maker. President of the American Philosophical Society after Benjamin Franklin. Most famous for his orreries and his telescope designed to track the transit of Venus across the sun, June 3, 1769 [46, 327]

Ritter, Johann [George]. b. 1779; d. Nov. 24, 1857, Reading, Berks Co. Son of Francis, who owned half interest in *The Reading Adler*, 1797. Partnership with his uncle Jacob Schneider, June 29, 1802–Mar. 27, 1804. Produced newspaper, 1804–23; in partnership with brother-in-law Karl A. Kessler (d. 1823). Married Catharine Frailey, daughter of Peter (sheriff of Berks Co.), 1813. Son Louis (b. Apr. 3, 1813; d. Oct. 16, 1889) worked with father as printer, until 1857. Business advertised as "best equipped Germany printery in The United States," Nov. 13, 1828. Introduced steam-powered presses to newspaper firm, 1852. Nephew Charles Kessler became sole owner, 1857. U.S. congressman, 1840–47 [302, 303, 329, 331, 340]

Ritzecker, Eliesabeth. b. Nov. 30, 1797, Mount Joy Twp., Lancaster Co. Daughter of George and Susanna Ruhm Ritzecker [299, 339]

Ritzecker, George. Mount Joy Twp., Lancaster Co., 1797. Father of Eliesabeth Ritzecker [339]

Ritzecker, Susanna Ruhm. Mount Joy Twp., Lancaster Co., 1797. Mother of Eliesabeth Ritzecker [339]

Roads, John. [326]

Rockey, John. Gregg Twp., Centre Co., 1849. Father of Mary Jane Rockey [341]

Rockey, Mary Jane. b. Mar. 20, 1849, Gregg Twp., Centre Co. Daughter of John and Salome Housman Rockey [306, 341]

Rockey, Salome Housman. Gregg Twp., Centre Co., 1849. Mother of Mary Jane Rockey [341]

Roller. Probably John George Roeller. b. 1775, d. 1840. Lutheran minister. Son of Conrad Roeller (d. 1795). Active Indian Field, Montgomery Co., and Tohickon, Bucks Co., after 1795. Attended cornerstone laying, Hilltown Reformed Church, 1804. Preached at Ridge Valley, Rockhill Twp., 1802 [339]

Roller, C. Probably Conrad Roeller. Lutheran minister. d. 1795, Upper Salford Twp., Montgomery Co. Active New Goschen-hoppen Church, Montgomery Co., and Tohickon, Bucks Co. Succeeded by son John George Roeller [341]

Roth, Heinrich. Son of Jacob (d. before 1785). Probably Whitehall Twp., Northampton Co. Member, Jordan's Lutheran and Reformed church. Married Margaretha. Sister Anna married Johann Heinrich

Ripple [Ribble] (son of Andreas), Egypt Reformed Church, Lehigh Co. [194]

Roudebush, Henry. b. c. 1792. Potter, Upper Hanover Twp., Montgomery Co., by 1818. Married Sophia Troxel, daughter of Henry Troxel. Apprenticed with George Sissholtz, Pennsburg, then worked for Henry Troxel. Witnessed Troxel's will, 1829. Active potter with Troxel, 1814, 1815, 1817–21. Worked with John Kichline, probably Richland Twp., 1816 [194, 195]

Roudenbush, M. Possibly Michael Roudenbush, Upper Hanover, Montgomery Co. (d. 1799). Wealthy farmer whose son Henry was a tailor, New Providence Twp., 1791; another son Michael inherited homestead, 207 acres [11]

Rudy, Durs. b. Dec. 28, 1789, Baden, Germany; d. Feb. 5, 1850, Lehigh Co. Family of Swiss origin. Lutheran. Son of Durs (b. Sept. 7, 1766; d. Aug. 10, 1843) and Maria Magdalena Horner Rudy (b. June 19, 1765; d. Sept. 7, 1855). Brother of Jacob (b. 1787) and Polly (b. 1800). Family to Phila. aboard *Commerce* from Amsterdam, Oct. 9, 1803. Settled first in Reading, Berks Co., then North Whitehall and Heidelberg twps., Lehigh Co. Married Salome Schneider Egner (b. Nov. 15, 1798; d. Oct. 14, 1877), Oct. 29, 1818. Lived in North Whitehall Twp. Had 6 children, by 1827. Owned and ran country store and tavern, Unionville. Played the organ at German Lutheran Church, Unionville. Known in family as an artist who sketched and painted local countryside [336]

Rühm [Ruh], Catharina. Donegal Twp., Lancaster Co., 1797 [339]

Rutter, Thomas. b. 1731; d. 1795, Pottstown. Grandson of Thomas Rutter (d. 1729), of Germantown, founder of Colebrookdale Furnace. Shareholder, Warwick Furnace. Master, Colebrookdale Furnace, Berks Co. [104–6]

S.B. Probably Rockland Twp., Berks Co., c. 1840 [152]

S.H. Mold maker [108]

SH. Papermaker, before 1800 [323]

S.R. 1800–1850 [135]

S.R. c. 1850 [73]

S.S. [Salome Stoudt Swartzlander]. b. c. 1745; d. 1827, Doylestown. Daughter of potter Jacob (1710–1779) and Anna Miller Stoudt (b. 1708), Rockland Twp., Bucks Co. Married 1) Abraham Freed (d. 1773), 1770, New Britain; 2) Gabriel Swartzlander (d. 1814), c. 1774 [347]

S.S.S. [251]

S.W. 1790–1810 [286]

Saleda [Solliday, Salede], Jacob. b. Feb. 2, 1748; d. Apr. 15, 1815. Attended Lutheran Reformed church, Tohickon, Bucks Co. Son of Frederich, from Basel, Switzerland, before 1751. Clockmaker, Bedminster Twp., Bucks Co., and Northampton Co., 1782–1807. Owned 139 acres, 2 horses, 4 cows, 1782. Working with Frederick Salladay, Jr. (joiner), and Henry Saledy (joiner), a single man with no land, 1783. Worked with son Peter, also a clockmaker, until 1807 [44]

Sanno, Friederich. Probably same person as Mr. Sanno, traveling parochial schoolteacher, Bucks Co., c. 1788. Printer of books and fraktur blanks, Carlisle, Cumberland Co., by 1809. May have been practicing minister, Carlisle, where he baptised Elizabeth Egolff and inscribed her record also printed by him [304, 340]

Sansinich, Barbara. Earl Twp., Lancaster Co. Mother of Elizabeth Sansinich, 1803 [278]

Sansinich, Christian. Earl Twp., Lancaster Co. Father of Elizabeth Sansinich, 1803 [278]

Sansinich, Elizabeth. Possibly Elizabeth Sansinich, b. 1789, Ephrata Twp., Lancaster Co., unmarried in 1850. Daughter of Christian and Barbara Sansinich [278]

Saur [Sauer], Christoph[er]. b. 1694, Prussia; d. 1758, Germantown. Married Maria Christina. Only son Christopher, Jr. (b. Sept. 26, 1721, Prussia; d. 1784). Family migrated to Germantown, 1724; to Millbach, Lebanon Co., 1726. Dunker. Close association with Conrad Beisel, Ephrata Cloister; wife entered the Cloister as subprioress, 1730. To Germantown with son; built large (60 x 60') two-story house. Worked as a tailor, clockmaker, optician, and apothecary (served as a doctor for immigrants). Secured printer's equipment and type from Germany and printed first almanac, 1739, and quarto Bible, 1743. Extensive business included papermill, sawmill, type foundry, book bindery, and property on Germantown Rd. and Wissahickon Rd., Roxborough; all confiscated, 1777, and sold, 1779, due to Christopher Saur, Jr.'s Tory sympathies in the Revolution [324, 325]

Schäfer, [Christian F.J.]. d. 1904. Printer/publisher, 314 N. Fourth St., Phila. Married Aurelia F., who survived him. Partnership with Rudolph Koradi [331]

Schaffer, Barbara. b. May 14, 1798, Richmond Twp., Berks Co. Daughter of Peter and Maria Hoffmann Schaffer [301, 340]

Schaffer, Maria Hoffmann. Richmond Twp., Berks Co., 1798. Mother of Barbara Schaffer [340]

Schaffer, Peter. Richmond Twp., Berks Co., 1798. Father of Barbara Schaffer [340]

Schett, Carl. Jonestown, Lebanon Co., 1827. Father of Christian Schett [340]

Schett, Christian. b. Jan. 21, 1827, Jonestown, Labanon Co.; bap. Mar. 24, 1827. Son of Carl and Sarah Brossy Schett [303, 340]

Schett, Maria Eva. Jonestown, Lebanon Co., 1827 [340]

Schett, Sarah Brossy. Jonestown, Lebanon Co., 1827. Mother of Christian Schett [340]

Schimmel, Wilhelm. b. 1817, Hesse-Darmstadt, Germany; d. 1890, Cumberland Co. Almshouse. Itinerant laborer and woodcarver, Conodoquinet Creek Valley, near Carlisle, Cumberland Co. [79, 83, 84, 87]

Schlögel, Peter. Father of Elisabeth Schlögel Homan, Centre Co. [340]

Schnee, Joseph. b. 1792, d. 1838. Weaver. Worked with Benjamin Angstadt (1806–1863), Freeburg, and Mt. Pleasant mills, Snyder (Union) Co. Son William took over mill and worked with Angstadt, Lewisburg, Union Co., 1836–38. Justice of the peace, Washington Twp., 1836 [269]

Scholl, Jacob. b. Apr. 11, 1781; d. Aug. 26, 1851. Grandson of Frederich, who arrived Phila., Sept. 11, 1728. Grandfather member, Reformed church, by 1730, and owned farm, Franconia Twp.; to Hellertown, Northampton Co., 1734; founder of Lower Saucon Reformed Church. Eighth child of Michael (1742–1825) and Margaretta Gerhart Scholl (b. Apr. 4, 1744; d. 1812, daughter of Peter), married Apr. 4, 1763. Father Michael, trustee of Indian Creek Reformed Church, 1764–1825; bought 251 acres, Upper Salford Twp., Montgomery Co., 1774; and served under Capt. Nevel, 1780. Jacob married Catherine Leidy (1784–1838), daughter of Jacob (d. 1834) and Veronica Scholl Leidy (d. 1826), Apr. 26, 1806. Had 9 children. John Leidy II, potter (1780–1838), was his cousin and brother-in-law; John Leidy I, potter (1764–1846), was his uncle-in-law. Trustee, Maiden Reformed Church, 1825–c. 1838. Owned 174 acres, Upper Salford Twp. Owned a "pleasure carriage," 1833. A wealthy farmer, able to loan at least $6,000, in 1840–45; called "independant," 1850 census, when his real estate was valued at $19,000. Primarily a farmer, with a full pottery enterprise on his farm worked by Michael Fillman, son of his aunt Elizabeth (b. 1757), and by John Neis, whose sister Anna Maria

was his aunt-in-law. Fillmans, Scholls, and Nases related through marriage to Gerhardts and Leidys. Wood pastry mold no. 2, p. 68, belonged to Jacob Scholl and the impression he took from it is redware mold no. 109, p. 195 [195–97]

Scholt, I. [138]

Schorb, Josiah. Potter, active near Hanover, York Co., 1850, and Manheim, York Co. Hen no. 13, p. 222, now attributed to Schorb [222]

Schreiber, Catahr[ina] Elisabet[h] Kerner. Whitehall Twp., Northampton Co., 1780 [339]

Schreiber, Jacob. b. Jan.3, 1780, Whitehall Twp., Northampton Co. Son of Jacob and Catahr[ina] Elisabet[h] Kerner Schreiber [300, 339]

Schreiber, Jacob. Whitehall Twp., Northampton Co., 1780. Father of Jacob Schreiber [339]

Schultz, [Christopher]Imuel [Emmanuel]. b. Dec. 25, 1740, Saxony; d. Mar. 11, 1809, Tulpehocken, Berks Co. To Phila., 1765; served as Lutheran minister, 1765–71. In Berks and Lancaster counties, 1771–1809. Married Eve Elizabeth Muhlenberg [338, 340]

Schumacherin [Schumacher], Marg[a]ret. b. 1780; d. 1783. Family name in Bucks, Berks, and Lancaster counties, 1770–1830 [19]

Schuppin [Schupp], Sarah. Family name in Brecknock Twp., Lancaster Co., 1780, and Lower Milford Twp., Bucks Co., 1790s [24]

Schutter, Christian. Potter, active Berks Co., 1840–60 [197]

Seiberd, Frederick. Preacher, Greenwood Twp., Juniata Co., 1838 [342]

Sell, John. Landowner and neighbor of Nicholas Kutz (b. 1764), whose farm was located between Kutztown and Bowers in Berks Co. Kutz's son Samuel Scharadin Kutz (b. 1800) married Catherine Sell (b. 1797), daughter of Johannes and Margaret Sell [21]

Selzer, John. b. Aug. 9, 1774; d. Feb. 1, 1845. Son of Christian Selzer (1749–1831). Brother-in-law of Peter Spycher (clockmaker), Jonestown, Lebanon Co. House carpenter-joiner, Jonestown, Lebanon Co., by 1804 [25]

Shade, P. Probably Upper Swamp Creek, Berks Co. [152]

Sheetz [Schütz], Frederick. Papermaker. Son of Conrad, papermaker (d. 1771), and Catherine Schütz (d. 1786), Lower Merion Twp., Montgomery Co. Owned 1 of 2 family papermills, 1788. Purchased FS mold from Nathan Sellers, 1793. Uncles Henry and Francis Schütz, and his brother Benjamin also papermakers until at least 1821 [316]

Shenfelder, Daniel P. Potter, active Reading, Berks Co., 1869–1900. Stamped pottery "D.P. Shenfelder/Reading, Pa." around an oval with star in center. Possibly the Daniel Shenfelder, b. 1830, son of Joseph (tinsmith), Marion Twp., Berks Co., 1850 [234]

Shindel, Catharine. Lancaster Co., 1812–24. Wife of Jacob Shindel. Mother of Sophia Shindel [279]

Shindel, Jacob. Lancaster Co., 1812–24. Husband of Catharine Shindel. Father of Sophia Shindel [279]

Shindel, Sophia. b. 1812. Daughter of Jacob and Catharine Shindel. Attended Mary Reed's School, Lancaster, 1824. Her design includes Lancaster Almshouse [279]

Singer, Simon. b. 1822, Baden, Germany. Married Rebecca (b. 1829), 1850. Resident potter working with John Bigly, Nockamixon Twp., 1850. Bought the Conrad Mumbouer/John Monday pottery,

Haycock Twp., Bucks Co., at Monday's sheriff sale for $2,500. Pottery continued operation to 1912 [197, 198]

Smith, M.A. Reverend, Union Co., 1853 [341]

Smith Pottery. Wrightstown, Bucks Co. Pottery established before 1770, with close connection to Croasdel Warner's pottery, until it burned down, 1812. Jonathan Smith, potter, with Jacob Neizer, on 39 acres, 1803; Jonathan and William Smith working as potters, 1804. Plates nos. 4 and 5, p. 214, with English inscriptions now attributed to this primarily English Bucks Co. group, based on attributions of other pottery [214]

Smith, Willoughby. b. June 13, 1839, Red Hill, Montgomery Co.; d. Mar. 22, 1905, Womelsdorf, Berks Co. Son of David and Maria Blant Smith. Married Maranda Sophia Feeg (b. Apr. 1, 1846), daughter of Daniel and Rebecca Foltz Feeg, of Heidelberg Twp., Berks Co., in Marion Twp., Berks Co., July 3, 1864. Potter, apprenticed near Pennsburg. Attended Old Goschenhoppen Church, Upper Salford Twp. He and his mother-in-law Rebecca bought two-story log house and pottery owned by Joseph and Maria Feeg, Mar. 30, 1864. Operated as Feeg and Smith, 45–47 E. High St., Womelsdorf, until 1879, when Rebecca Feeg sold her half to Smith. Mail order as well as local business, producing between 75,000 and 100,000 flowerpots per year. Employed 2 journeymen, John Snyder (for 34 years) and Mahlon Fornorman (for 32 years) [198]

Sorman, J. Southern Lancaster Co. [49]

Speyer, Friederich. To Phila. from Germany, Sept. 27, 1752, when he was listed as Georg Friederich Speyer. In German regiment, Berks Co., 1776. Printer, c. 1800. May have worked with or for Henrich Otto [301, 340]

Spinner, David. b. May 16, 1758; d. Nov. 16, 1811. Youngest son of Ulrich Spinner (1717–1769), from Basel, Switzerland, 1739, and Ursula Frick Spinner, also from Basel. Father Ulrich purchased land, Great Swamp, Milford Twp., Bucks Co., Jan. 10, 1739/40 for £12; additional 203 acres, June 1746. Sister Barbara married Philip Mumbouer, 1776. Apprenticed as cordwainer with Henry Neis, Upper Salford Twp., and worked in that profession until 1783. At same time learned potting there with Johannes Neis (1754–1826). Inherited family homestead, Lower Milford Twp., by 1781. Baptismal records of family of sister Susanna Diehl (Mrs. Frederich) record Spinner as sponsor at baptisms, 1779, and Feb. 29, 1781, with his wife or intended wife. Great Swamp Reformed Church records state he married Catharina Kerlacherin (daughter of George), Nov. 26, 1782. Children: Catherine (b. Sept. 29, 1783), Maria (1785–1788), Frederick (b. 1786), David, Jr. (1791–1866). Taxed as potter with 200 acres, 5 horses, 7 cows, and a still, 1782; 203 acres, 4 horses, 6 cows, 1785. Had Negro servant and was tax assessor for Lower Milford Twp., 1789. Purchased 18 acres from Dr. Christian Williams, 1791. Purchased 25 acres with buildings from George and Catherine Sheets, 1793. Purchased 10½ acres from Valentin Bidleman, 1796. Had 329 acres, 1797. The 1798 direct tax listed 1 two-story stone house, 24 x 28′, worth $450, a stone and frame barn, 90 x 30′, a round log barn, 40 x 26′, 2 stables, 17 x 15′, 24 x 10′. Rented a hewn log house (1 story, unfinished), 27 x 22′, to Samuel Huddle. Listed as "Esqr" with taxable property value of $9,711, in 1810. Captain of the First Company of the Last Battalion, May 12, 1783. Justice of the peace and tax collector. Extensive inventory (signed Jan. 1812, filed Aug. 6, 1812), taken by George Sisoll (Sissholz) and Christian Huber showed that his farm enterprise was in full operation. Included in part, 6 horses, 8 hogs, a sow and 9 goats, 13 cattle, and 1 bull, 14 sheep, several wagons, a riding chair and harness, a clay mill, 2 potter's wheels, paint mill, cider mill, still, and 20 acres of grain in the ground. Household furnishings included 7 beds, a clothespress, a case of drawers, a walnut desk and bookcase, clock and case, several iron stoves, pewter plates and dishes, "earthen dishes on dresser; earthen dishes on mantelshelf." Family tradition states nos. 129 and 130, p. 200, were always displayed on Spinner's mantel [198–201]

Steele, James. Partnership with brother John, papermaker, Chester Co., by 1800. Working on his own, 1808–44. Also owned 2 cotton mills, sawmill and gristmill [323]

Steele, John. Printer, Phila., before 1788. Papermaker, Octoraro Creek, West Fallowfield Twp., Chester Co., 1788–1808. Purchased watermark molds from Nathan Sellers. Married Abigail Bailey before 1788. Brother of James [323]

Stein, Johan. Bethel Twp., Lebanon Co., 1827–45 [340, 342]

Stein, Ludwig. b. 1711; d. Aug. 7, 1782. Lancaster Boro., Lancaster Co. Married widow Catharina Heck. Son Frederick (b. Nov. 4, 1734). Owned property on King Street, Lancaster Boro., 1736, which he sold to Andreas Byerly (innkeeper), by 1740. Purchased land, Queen St., 1753, and 1762, and held several mortgages on other properties, 1753–58 [319]

Steiner [Sterner], Sally. b. June 17, 1796. Probably daughter of George (weaver) and Margaret Sterner; members, Tohickon Lutheran congregation; residents, Richland Twp., Bucks Co., 1801–22 [195]

Steinmetz, John. Master, Mary Ann Furnace, West Manheim Twp., York Co. [107]

Stephan, Adam. Mahantango Twp., Northumberland Co., 1801. Father of Barbara Stephan [340]

Stephan, Barbara. b. Mar. 14, 1801, Mahantango Twp., Northumberland Co. Daughter of Adam and Margaretha Geisweit Stephan [302, 340]

Stephan, Margaretha Geistweit. Mahantango Twp., Northumberland Co., 1801. Mother of Barbara Stephan [340]

Stiegel, Henry William. b. May 13, 1729, probably Cologne, Germany; d. probably after 1797, Lancaster Co. Son of John Frederick (d. 1741) and Dorothea Elizabeth Stiegel (1705–1781). Arrived Phila., Aug. 30, 1750, on the *Nancy* (Charles Stedman, master) with widowed mother and brother Anthony. Probably occupied as clerk, using his language skills, for the Stedmans, through whom he made contacts in the Lancaster community. Continued association with the Stedmans in partnerships in iron and glass manufacturing enterprises. Bought Charming Forge, Berks Co., and carried the Stedman's half interest on a mortgage on Charming Forge granted from Isaac Cox, Phila. merchant in 1763. Married 1) Elizabeth Huber (1734–1758), daughter of John Jacob Huber, ironmaster at Elizabeth Furnace, which Stiegel eventually took over; 2) Elizabeth Holtz Wood, Roxborough, 1758. Her sister's children George and Michael Edge [Ege] lived with and apprenticed with Stiegel in iron business. Owned and laid out town of Manheim, Lancaster Co., where his glass manufactory was located and where he built a large house. Glass advertisements for fine tablewares directed toward the Phila., Lancaster, and New York markets. Also supplied glasswares via Lancaster Co. Moravian community, Lititz, to Moravians in N.C. [105, 106, 238–45]

Stofflet, Heinrich. b. 1785. Son of Heinrich (b. 1752, Falkner Swamp, Montgomery Co.; d. 1828) and Abalove Stofflet (1762–1833), Forks Twp., Northampton Co. Potter-farmer, Ruscomb Manor Twp., Berks Co. Owned 43 acres, 1 house, 2 horses, 2 cows, 1832. Married Christiana (b. 1792). Son Jacob (b. 1824), potter living on his father's property, 1850 [201]

Stout [Stoudt], Jacob. b. Oct. 13, 1710, Wolfersweiler, Saarland, in French-occupied Rhineland; d. Apr. 30, 1779, Perkasie, Bucks Co. Trained in Europe as a potter. Arrived Phila., Aug. 30, 1737. Naturalized Apr. 11, 1751. Married widow Anna Miller (Mrs. John) Leisse [Le Cene, Lacy, Lacey] (b. 1708), 1739. Four children: Abraham (1740–1812), Isaac, Catherine, and Salome (1743–1827). Purchased 243 acres, Durham Twp., Bucks Co., for £360 and lived there, 1750. Purchased half interest in 37 acres, house and gristmill, Rockhill Twp., and bought the remaining half, 1754. Listed as a potter, Hilltown. Transferred Hilltown property to stepsons John and Henry Leisse, 1759, and bought out their shares of 200-acre family farm, which their father John had purchased from Thomas Freame, 1735. Stepson John Leisse [Lacy] apprenticed with him as a potter and has been credited with the English-style hand of the inscription on plate no. 134, p. 201, a free rendition of a maxim used frequently in Europe and America [201, 347]

Stout [Stoudt], Salome. b. 1743, d. 1827. Daughter of Jacob Stout [Stoudt]. Married Gabriel Swartzlander, c. 1774 [347]

Stöver, Maria. Bethel Twp., Lebanon Co., 1845 [342]

Strawhen, Thomas. From a family of potters active Haycock and Richland twps., Bucks Co., listed 1796–1825. Owned 55 acres and was a potter, 1796; replaced on tax list by Jacob Tingler, potter, 1797. Thomas, potter, until c. 1832. A Thomas Strawn died in Richland, 1857, leaving widow Jane Foulke Strawn with inventory including cabinet-making tools such as veneering clamps [202]

Strenge, [John] Christian. b. Oct. 15, 1758, Altenhasungen, Hesse-Cassel, Germany; d. Apr. 28, 1828, Lancaster Co. Buried at East Petersburg Mennonite Cemetery, Lancaster Co. Arrived N.Y. with Fifth Royal Grenadier Regiment, 1776. Married 1) Christina (1766–1789), before 1788. Daughter Elizabeth baptised, Trinity Lutheran Church, Lancaster, June 23, 1788. Resided Hempfield Twp., by 1789. Married 2) Mary Eve Miller (b. 1763), 1791, daughter of Michael and Eve Miller, of Lancaster Boro. Daughter Maria Catherine baptised, First Reformed Church, Lancaster, 1796. Bought 6 acres and building, East Petersburg, 1794, and 8 acres, 1810. Worked as schoolmaster and scrivener, justice of the peace [310, 314, 315, 320, 322, 344]

Striepy, Michael. Potter, active Nockamixon Twp., Bucks Co., 1783–91. By 1796, he was "a clockmaker and follows trade" and worked with brother George (single, no acreage, 1796), on 50 acres, Nockamixon Twp. Owned one-story stone house, 30 x 18′, a log barn, 28 x 20′. Also owned unimproved property (no outbuildings), 10 acres, Haycock Twp.; listed as nonresident landowner there, 1798–1802. Served in First Battalion of Bucks Co., commanded by Col. John Hellor, 1783. Married Magdalena Klinker, sister of Christian Klinker (potter, c. 1792) [45]

Sussel-Washington Artist. Traveling minister or schoolmaster, probably Swiss, who served communities in Berks, Lancaster, and Lebanon counties, 1775–1800 [296]

Swope, Benedict. Part owner, Shearwell Furnace, Berks Co., with Dietrich Welker, 1760 [105]

Taney, Jacob. Molded dish no. 136, p. 202, dated 1794, attributed to Jacob Taney (b. 1777), Nockamixon Twp., by Edwin A. Barber; however, Taney's designation as potter does not appear on any records until his son Judah Teaney (b. 1814) became a potter, c. 1827. The Jacob Deany (possibly phonetic spelling of Teaney/ Taney) potting on 15 acres, Nockamixon Twp., 1811–25, was active too late for dish series dated 1794. More likely potter I.T. was Jacob Tingler, active Haycock Twp., Bucks Co. Purchased 55 acres from Thomas Strawhen, 1797. Direct tax, Bucks Co., listed his buildings: 1 stone house, 24 x 15′, 1 kitchen of logs, 18 x 15′, 1 log barn, 35 x 24′, and 1 potter shop, 40 x 20′, 1798. Owned 50 acres, 1800; had no acreage but paid occupation (potter's) tax, 1801. Disappears from Bucks Co. records at that date [202]

Taylo[r], Gen[eral] Zachary. b. 1784, Orange Co., Va.; d. 1850. Defeated Santa Anna at Buena Vista, Feb. 22–23, 1847. Known as "Hero of Buena Vista" and "Old Rough-and-Ready." 12th president of U.S. [249]

Titz [Tietz], Maria Elisabeth. Rockhill Twp., Bucks Co., 1808 [339]

Trautman, Susanna [Schäfer]. Probably Heidelberg Twp., Berks Co., c. 1820 [311, 343]

Trevitz [Trewitz, Treivetts, Triewitz, Trebitz], Conrad. d. 1840, Berks Co. Probably Johann Conrath Triewitz, who with brother Jacob Trewitz (d. 1820) or son Jacob Trewitz (d. 1861, Dauphin Co.) arrived Phila. from Rotterdam on the *Crawford*, Oct. 25, 1773. Fraktur painter, active 1793–1815: Mahanoy Twp., Northumber-land Co., 1800; Fayette Co., 1820; Upper Bern Twp., Berks Co., 1830. Married Eva before 1788. Daughters Catherine (b. 1788) and

Elizabeth (b. 1789) baptised, Summer Hill Church, Schuylkill Co. [302]

Trollinger, Carrel. b. Aug. 17, 1808, Rockhill Twp., Bucks Co.; d. June 7, 1832. Son of Georg and Magtalena Tietz Trollinger [300, 339]

Trollinger, Georg. Rockhill Twp., Bucks Co., 1808. Father of Carrel Trollinger (b. 1808) [339]

Trollinger, Magtalena Tietz. Rockhill Twp., Bucks Co., 1808. Mother of Carrel Trollinger (b. 1808) [339]

Troxel [Troxell], Henry. d. 1829, Upper Hanover Twp., Montgomery Co. Probably worked with George and Philip Sussholtz (d. c. 1826), potters, before becoming active potter on his own, Upper Hanover Twp., Montgomery Co., 1799; listed as having no acreage, 1 horse, 1 cow. Owned 57 acres with horses and cows, 1808–29. Henry Roudebush, who married his daughter Sophia, 1818, was working with Troxell, by 1814. Retired in favor of son Samuel (c. 1803–1870) and devoted himself to farming, c. 1824. Married Sarah (Sophia) Dotterer (b. 1775; d. after 1859). Children: Henry, Samuel, Elizabeth (b. 1800, unmarried, 1850), David (b. 1812; shoemaker), Sophia, Catherine, and Margaret. Called potter in inventory, 1829, listing 34-hour clock and case, 2 bonnet boxes, 2 wool wheels, 6 spinning wheels, and a reel, carpet yarn, a lot of wool in rolls, 6 meal bags, a lot of bread baskets, a potter's clay mill, lead mill and 2 turning benches, potter's tools, etc. [202, 203]

Troxel [Troxell], Samuel. b. c. 1803; d. Nov. 1870, Upper Hanover Twp., Montgomery Co. Son of Henry (d. 1829) and Sarah Dotterer Troxell (b. 1775, d. after 1859). Married Katherina (b. 1818), after 1830. Had 6 children. Potter active 1824–46, on his father's farm, which he inherited. Vice-president of committee organized to create Jackson Co. from parts of Montgomery and Bucks counties, 1840s. Inventory listed clay mill and washed clay, suggesting pottery was still active at his death, although 1850 census does not show a potter as resident on his property and he is listed as a farmer [203–5]

Turbin, Wilhelm. Married Maria Licht (b. 1815), daughter of Jacob and Christina (née Licht) Licht, Oct. 24, 1841 [341]

Uebele, M. Probably Berks Co. [152]

Uhler, Andrew. d. 1859. Son of Andrew (d. 1843) and Elizabeth Rippel Uhler, daughter of neighbor Andreas Rippel (1746–1817), Forks Twp., Northampton Co. Great-uncle Reinerd Ripple [Ribble], potter, East Williams Twp., Northampton Co. John Ribble was his uncle. Owned homestead, 48 acres, on Easton-Wilkesbarre Rd. in common with brother Samuel. Married Anna Malinda Kemmerer. Tax records show his occupation as farmer, suggesting that pottery where this group worked was not on Uhler property. Wood house and ground valued at £200, in 1798 [205]

Unkley, G. Papermaker, active 1802, operating papermill, Lower Saucon Twp., Northampton Co. Purchased watermark molds from Nathan Sellers, 1789–1812 [323]

Van Braght, Tieleman Jans. Dutch complier of German-language *Martyr's Mirror* [324]

Villee, H[erman] W. d. after 1850. Printer, Lancaster Co. Partnership, Baab and Villee, 1826. Published *The Lancaster Eagle*, 1827–30. Published *The Poetical Way to Heaven* (1828), *The German Theology* (1829), and fraktur blanks and broadsides [311, 343]

Vondersloot. Frederick William Von der Sloot, the Younger. d. 1831. Reformed minister, Lower Milford Twp., Bucks Co.; Northampton and Adams counties [341]

W.K.O. 1881 [251]

Walker, Mary. Probably Quaker schoolmistress who taught English and English-style needlework skills to young women, Lancaster Co., c. 1803 [278]

Wambold, Georg. Rockhill Twp., Bucks Co., 1808; Milford Twp., Bucks Co., 1810. Probably son of Abraham and Louisa Wambold, Rockhill Twp. [339]

Warner, Croasdel, Sr. b. Dec. 5, 1729/30; d. c. 1800, Harford Co., Md. Son of Joseph (1701–1746) and Agnes Croasdel Warner (1703–1770). Married Mary Briggs, Middletown Friends Meeting, Wrightstown, Bucks Co. Purchased tract of ground on Durham Rd., Bucks Co., 1756, where he built a "pot house." To Gunpowder, Md., 1770. Pottery burned down, 1812. Sons Amos and Croasdale, and possibly their sister Sarah, returned to Newtown and Wrightstown. Plate no. 146, p. 205, inscribed C. W., now attributed to Croasdel Warner, Sr. [205]

Warner, Polly. Probably b. Jan. 27, 1768. Daughter of John and Elizabeth Warner, Wrightstown, Bucks Co. John was Croasdel Warner, Sr.'s brother [214]

Washington, George. b. 1732, Westmoreland Co., Va.; d. 1799. Plate no. 5, p. 214, dated May 31, 1789, probably commemorates Washington's triumphal passage through Bucks Co., May 1789, in conjunction with his inauguration as 1st U.S. president [214, 230, 336]

Weber, Jacob. b. 1803. Probably son of Jakob Weber (b. 1772; d. Apr. 7, 1865), Lancaster. Shoemaker, Fivepointville, Brecknock Twp., Lancaster Co. Made and decorated small boxes, 1840–50s [16]

Weiand, Anna Maria. Mahantango Twp., Northumberland Co., 1801 [340]

Weiand, Michael. Mahantango Twp., Northumberland Co., 1801 [340]

Weiser, Conrad [Johann]. b. 1696; d. 1760, Berks Co. Arrived Pa., 1728. Important land agent, magistrate, Indian interpreter and peacemaker [337]

Weiser, Daniel. Minister, Goschenhoppen Church, Montgomery Co., 1838–52 [342]

Weiss, C. G. Family name in Lebanon and Lancaster counties. Possibly Christina and George Michael Weise, Cocalico Twp., Lancaster Co., 1767 [69]

Welker, Dietrich [Dieter]. Skippack, Montgomery Co., c. 1745. Married Sara de Haven, Goschenhoppen Church, Montgomery Co., c. 1747. Built Shearwell Furnace, Friedensburg, Berks Co., before 1760. Partnership with Benedict Swope, 1760 [103, 105]

Wendel, John. [330]

Werntz, W. Possibly William Werntz (b. 1826), grandson of John Bitzer (d. 1810), Earl Twp., Lancaster Co. Working as farmer for, and living with, Moses Miller (farmer), Ephrata, Lancaster Co. [134]

Wertz, Carolina Emilia. b. Oct. 11, 1827, Macungie Twp., Lehigh Co.; bap. Dec. 19, 1827. Daughter of Peter and Catharina Gaumer Wertz [307, 341]

Wertz, Catharina Gaumer. Macungie Twp., Lehigh Co., 1827. Mother of Carolina Emilia Wertz (b. 1827) [341]

Wertz, Peter. Macungie Twp., Lehigh Co., 1827. Father of Carolina Emilia Wertz (b. 1827) [341]

Whatman, J. Papermaker, Turkey Mill, 1875 [336]

Whitman, Benjamin. d. after 1844. Clockmaker, Reading, Berks Co., 1799. Worked with George Faber, clockmaker (d. 1839), and William Wittman, listed as painter, in tax records, 1794–1802 [43]

Wiand, David. b. Jan. 3, 1813; d. May 12, 1885. Son of Wendel Weand III (1772–1846) and Catharine Dotterer Weand (1778–1846), Upper Hanover Twp., Montgomery Co. Weaver, Zieglersville, Montgomery Co., 1837 [269]

Wiestling, John S. b. Sept. 18, 1787, Vincent Twp., Montgomery (Chester) Co.; d. Feb. 27, 1842, Columbus, Ohio. Son of Dr. Samuel and Ann Maria Bucher Wiestling. Married Salome Youse, Dec. 24, 1811. Printer and publisher. Partnership with H. W. Peterson, 1814. Published in Harrisburg, 1811–28. To Canton, Ohio, 1837 [304, 341]

Will, William. b. 1742, Neuweid, Germany; d. 1798, Phila. Pewterer. Son of John Will (pewterer), who migrated to N.Y., c. 1752. Married 1) Barbara Colp, Phila., 1764; 2) Anna Clampfer, Phila., 1769. Civic leader, sheriff of city and county of Phila., lieutenant colonel, Pa. militia, representative of the General Assembly. Brothers and son George were also pewterers [157, 158, 160, 161]

Wise, Jacob. Family name in Lancaster and Cumberland counties. Possibly Jacob Wise, "late of the U.S. Army," who married Catherine Young, Lancaster, Feb. 3, 1822 [249]

Witmer, Mary E. 1865 [250]

Witmer, Sophia Elizabeth G. 1860 [276]

Wolf, Henry. Ironworker, active Lancaster Co. 1800–1820 [130]

Wolff, D. Watchmaker and jeweler, 1903 Vine St., Phila. Repaired watches and clocks [45]

Wollenweber, L. A. [331]

Wollfart, Christian. Tulpehocken Twp., Berks Co., 1779. Husband of Margaretha Wollfart [338]

Wollfart, Margaretha. Tulpehocken Twp., Berks Co., 1779. Wife of Christian Wollfart [338]

Xander, Margaretha. Single woman, Whitehall Twp., Northampton Co., 1789 [339]

Yeckly, Catarina Benewitz. Heidelberg Twp., Berks Co., 1801. Wife of Jacob Yeckly. Mother of George Yeckly (b. 1801) [340]

Yeckly, George. b. Nov. 6, 1801, Heidelberg Twp., Berks Co. Possibly George Yeakle, active Germantown, 1851 [301, 340]

Yeckly, Jacob. Heidelberg Twp., Berks Co., 1801. Lutheran. Husband of Catarina Benewitz Yeckly. Father of George Yeckly (b. 1801) [340]

Young, Henry. b. Mar. 12, 1792, Germany; d. Mar. 3, 1861. Arrived Pa., 1819. Taught at a union school, Mifflinburg, West Buffalo Twp., Northumberland (Union) Co. Married Frances Slater, 1820. Minister and fraktur painter, active Centre and Lycoming counties, 1825–47 [294, 305, 306]

Youngk, H. H. Hilltown Twp., Bucks Co. [197]

Zartmann, Johannes. b. May 19, 1827, Jackson Twp., Lebanon Co.; d. 1895. Son of Samuel (1796–1875) and Mary Walborne, married, 1822. Lutheran. Shoemaker and farmer. Married Maria Balsbaugh (d. 1909) [294, 338]

Zeller, Abraham. Greenwood Twp., Juniata Co., 1838 [342]

Zeller, Nänzi. Greenwood Twp., Juniata Co., 1838 [342]

Zentler, Conrad. d. 1848. Printer and publisher, Phila. Office 104 N. 2nd St., 1814–48. Residence 174 N. 5th St.; 233 Lombard St., 1823; 28 N. 2nd St., 1839. Published German weekly, Sept. 9, 1808–Aug. 29, 1811. Published almanacs. George Gilbert did some of his wood engravings [328–30]